CW01667235

THE DICTIONARY OF SECURITIES INSURANCE & FINANCIAL TERMS

English—Japanese Japanese—English

英和 和英 金融・証券・保険〔第3版〕用語辞典

株式会社アイ・エス・エス 編

東京証券取引所 経営企画部審議役
安達精司 監修

編集協力
日本銀行 業務局 安徳久仁理
国際局 原　俊太郎

WAVE出版

第３版刊行の言葉

金融・証券・保険取引の国際化はとどまるところをしらず、また、自由化・多様化・ＩＴ化により多くの新しい商品が生まれ、取引手法も日進月歩で新しくなってきております。

結果として、金融・証券・保険の分野における専門用語は膨大なものとなり、英語・日本語間の用語の確認統一が不可欠の状況となっております。また業界再編の動きが急速に展開すると共に、銀行・信託・証券・生保・損保各業界の相互参入も一気に進み、広範囲にわたる専門用語をコンパクトな一冊にまとめる必要性も増してきております。

1995年に初版を発行した本辞典は、こうした認識のもと、銀行・証券・生損保各業界で働かれる国際ビジネスマンの方々はもちろん、一般企業の財務部、国際部の方々、弁護士、公認会計士、税理士の諸先生方、そして、大学関係者、通訳・翻訳者にとって携帯至便の専門用語辞典を目指し編集した、日本唯一のものです。

本辞典に収録した用語は、編者が永年にわたる通訳・翻訳業務の中で蓄積してきた英和両語の情報をデータベース化し、重要と思われる用語に絞り込んだものです。ただし、新しい用語は日々生まれており、2001年の改訂・新版化を経た後にも、多くの新語情報が集まってきた中で、全面的な改訂・追録作業を行ない、より読者ニーズにかなう内容の第３版にいたしました。膨大な編集作業には万全の注意を払ったとはいえ、遺漏がないとは断言しえず、読者各位のご叱正とご助言を切にお願いする次第です。

最後に、本辞典の第３版化にあたっては、東京証券取引所の経営企画部審議役であられる安達精司氏にご監修を、日本銀行業務局の安徳久仁理氏並びに国際局の原俊太郎氏に編集協力を賜わりました。この場を借りて厚く御礼申し上げたいと存じます。

2004年10月

編　者

目　次

凡　例

I　この辞典は、金融・証券・保険分野において日進月歩で増加していく新しい専門用語に重点をおいて編集した。また、英語についての基礎知識を備えている人が利用することを念頭において編集したので、一般の英語辞典のような品詞や発音記号は省略した。

II　用語の配列については、英和の場合はアルファベット順に配列し、複数を表わすs、またはesは無視した。和英の場合は五十音順で配列し、濁音と半濁音は無視した。

III　同一の用語でも、使用方法が異なる場合は、その二つの訳語を配列した。

ENGLISH-JAPANESE

A

a.p.o.d.b.(accelerated payment of death benefit) 死亡保険金繰上給付支払い
A&H (accident and health) benefit 医療保険給付
A&H (accident and health) insurance 医療保険
A&S (accident and sickness) insurance 医療保険
AA AA 格
AA tranche AA トランシェ
AAA class AAA 格
AAII (American Association of Individual Investors) 米国個人投資家協会
AARP (American Association of Retired Persons) 全米退職者協会
AB Spintab AB スピンタブ
abandon 取下げる
abandonment 廃棄
abandonment clause 委付条項
abandonment of action 訴訟放棄
abandonment of right 権利放棄
abandonment value 廃棄価値
abate 減じる
abatement 減額
abatement claim 減額請求
ABCP (asset-backed commercial paper) 資産担保コマーシャル・ペーパー
abide by 遵守する
abiding sense 固定観念
ability 能力
ability theory of taxation 担税能力説
ability to carry out 遂行能力
ability to exercise a contractual rights 契約上の権利行使能力
ability to generate favorable cash flows 望ましい資金の流れを産み出す能力
ability to make contributions 拠出能力
ability to pay 支払能力
ability to pay basis 支払能力基準
ability to pay dividend 配当能力
ability to pay principle 応能原則
ability to repay the debt 債務返済能力
ABM (activity based management) 活動規準経営管理
abnormal cost 異常原価
abnormal growth model 異常成長モデル
abnormal item 異常項目
abnormal return 異常収益
abnormal settlement of accounts 異常決算
abnormal shrinkage 異常減耗
abode 居住
abolishment of account 口座の廃止
abolishment of system 制度の廃止
abolition 廃止
above market アバブ・マーケット
above par 額面を上回って；平価以上
above unity 1 を上回る
above-normal earnings 超過利益
abridged 簡易の
abridgment 摘要
abrogation 廃止
absconding debtor 失踪債務者
absence 不在
absence of control 支配関係の不存在
absentee 不在者
absentee owner 不在所有者
absentee ownership 不在所有権
absolute 絶対的の
absolute advantage 絶対優位
absolute conveyance 絶対的譲渡
absolute cost 絶対原価
absolute delivery 無条件引渡し
absolute difference 絶対差額
absolute diffusion model 絶対拡散モデル

A

absolute error 絶対誤差
absolute fixed capital 絶対的固定資本
absolute income hypothesis 絶対所得仮説
absolute level 絶対水準
absolute liability 結果責任；無過失責任
absolute percentage 絶対百分率
absolute performance 絶対的パーフォーマンス
absolute probability 絶対確率
absolute profit 純益
absolute rate 絶対的な率
absolute return 絶対的リターン
absolute risk aversion measure 絶対的リスク回避度
absolute sales 無条件売買
absolute terms 絶対的期間
absolute total loss 絶対全損
absolute value 絶対値
absolutism 絶対主義
absorbed bond 完売債券
absorbed burden 配賦済製造間接費
absorbed corporation 吸収された会社
absorbed cost 回収済原価
absorbing state 吸収状態
absorption 完売
absorption account 配賦勘定
absorption and merger 吸収合併
absorption approach アブソープション・アプローチ
absorption cost 全部原価
absorption costing 全部原価計算
absorption of fund 資金吸収
absorption rate 配賦率
abstention 棄権
abstention requirement 節制要件
abstract 要約
abstract of accounts 抜粋計算書
abstract of financial statements 財務諸表摘要書
abstract of title 権利書
absurdity 不合理
abuse 濫用
abuse of rights 権利濫用
abusive 地位濫用の
abusive tax shelter 違法タックス・シェルター
academics 有識者
accelerate 加速する
accelerated benefit 繰上給付
accelerated cash benefit 保険金繰上げ
accelerated cash benefit option 保険金繰上オプション
accelerated cost recovery system 加速償却法
accelerated depreciation 加速減価償却
accelerated depreciation and amortization 加速償却
accelerated depreciation methods 加速償却法
accelerated endowment plan 満期短縮プラン
accelerated land purchase 公共用地先行取得
accelerated method 加速法
accelerated redemption 繰上償還
accelerating dividend 加速的配当
acceleration 期限の利益喪失
acceleration claims 促進クレーム
acceleration clause 期限の利益喪失条項
acceleration coefficient 加速度係数
acceleration demand 期限前返済要求
acceleration of liabilities 債務の期限の利益の喪失
acceleration of registration 登録繰上げ
acceleration principle 加速度原理
accept 受理する
acceptable alternative 選択的な方法
acceptable level 容認できる水準
acceptable trading range 妥当な取引レンジ
acceptance 引受け
acceptance advice 引受通知書
acceptance commission 引受手数料
acceptance credit 引受条件付信用状
acceptance line 引受限度
acceptance notice 引受通知

acceptance of an order 受注
acceptance of bids 応募の受付；入札の受理
acceptance of bill 手形引受け
acceptance of order 受託
acceptance of orders for trading 売買の受託
acceptance of trust assets 信託財産の受入れ
acceptance on security 担保付引受け
acceptance outstanding 手形引受け
acceptance payable 支払手形
acceptance price of net assets 純資産の引受額
acceptance rate 輸入手形決済相場
acceptance receivable 受取手形
acceptance system アクセプタンス方式
acceptances and guarantees 支払承諾
accepting bank 手形引受銀行
accepting rate of exchange 為替引受相場
acceptor 引受人
access card アクセス・カード
access to capital market 金融市場へのアクセス
access to Japan 対日アクセス
accession 権利取得
accessory 補助
accessory contract 付帯契約
accessory equipment 付属設備
accessory product 副産物
accessory to tax evasion 脱税の従犯
accident and health insurance 傷害及び健康保険
accident compensation 災害補償責任
accident death benefit 災害死亡給付
accident death rate 災害死亡率
accident error 偶然誤差
accident insurance 事故保険
accident severity rate 災害強度率
accidental cost 偶発経費
accidental error 偶発誤差
accidental injury 傷害
accommodation 融通
accommodation bill 融通手形
accommodation endorsement 融通裏書
accommodation lands 増価土地
accommodation line 妥協契約
accommodation maker 融通手形の振出人
accommodation note 融通手形
accommodation trades なれあい売買
accommodation works 便益工作物
accommodative monetary policy 金融緩和政策
accompanying document 添付書類
accord 協定
accord and satisfaction 代物弁済
accordant 同意せる
account 勘定；口座；顧客
account analysis 勘定分析
account book 出納簿；帳簿
account chart 勘定科目一覧表
account closing procedure 決算手続
account code 勘定科目コード
account day 会計日
account debtor 売掛債権債務者
account deposit slips 当座勘定入金票
account due from sales on approval 試用販売未収金
account due on consignment-out 委託販売未収入金
account executive アカウント・エグゼクティブ
account for 占める
account form 勘定式
account form income statement 勘定式損益計算書
account form profit and loss statement 勘定式損益計算書
account headings 勘定科目
account in transit 未達勘定
account method 帳簿方式
account number 口座番号
account number plan 勘定科目番号表示法
account of business 営業報告書
account of sales 売上計算書

A

account owed to employees 従業員に対する債務
account paid 支払済み勘定
account payable 買掛債務
account receivable discounted 割引受取勘定
account receivable due from affiliated company 関係会社売掛金
account receivable insurance 売掛保険
account reconcilement 勘定対照表
account rendered 確定勘定
account report service アカウント・レポート・サービス
account rigging 粉飾決算
account stated 確定勘定
account statement 勘定書
account system 勘定システム
account termination 口座解約
account title 勘定科目
account transfer 口座振替
account value 勘定価額
account year basis アカウント・イヤー・ベイシス
account-keeping institution 口座管理機関
accountability 説明責任
accountability unit 責任単位
accountable 責任のある
accountable event 会計事象
accountable officer 会計担当官
accountable person 責任者
accountable receipt 受領証
accountable warrant 会計ワラント
accountancy 会計学
accountancy service 会計監査業務
accountant 会計士
accountant business 経理事務
accountant in bankruptcy 破産清算人
accountant in charge 主任会計士
accountant opinion 監査意見
accountant report 監査人報告書
accountant responsible for the return 申告に対する経理責任者
accountant's liability 会計士責任
accountant's office 会計事務所
accountant's opinion 会計士の意見
accountant's report 会計士の報告書
accountant's responsibility 会計士責任
accounted for as 会計処理される
accounted for as a purchase パーチェス法で会計処理された
accounted for separately 区分処理した
accounted for using equity method 持ち分法で会計処理された
accounting 会計
accounting adjustments 合計修正処理
accounting alternatives 会計上の代替処理
Accounting and Auditing Enforcement Release 会計監査実施通牒
accounting arbitrage 会計上の裁量
accounting audit 会計監査
accounting axiom 会計公理
accounting based on legal requirements 会計法規による規制
accounting beta 会計ベータ
accounting beta value 会計ベータ値
accounting book 会計帳簿
accounting by month 月割計算
Accounting Center 会計センター
accounting changes 会計の変更
accounting concept 会計概念
accounting control 会計管理
accounting convention 会計原則
accounting currency 会計通貨
accounting cycle 会計サイクル；会計循環
accounting data 会計資料
accounting data process 会計事務処理
accounting department 経理課
accounting depreciation 会計上の償却
Accounting Division 会計課
accounting earnings 会計的利益
accounting entity 会計実体
accounting equation 会計等式
accounting error 会計誤差
accounting estimate 会計上の見積り
accounting evidence 会計証拠
accounting firm 会計事務所

accounting for administrative expenses 業務会計
accounting for branch office 支店会計
accounting for business combination 企業結合会計
accounting for changing prices 貨幣価値変動会計
accounting for compensated absences 有給休暇会計
accounting for contingencies 偶発事象会計
accounting for equities 持ち分会計
accounting for external reporting 外部報告会計
accounting for financial instruments 金融商品会計
accounting for foreign currency transaction 外貨建取引の会計処理
accounting for future cost 未来原価計算
accounting for impairment 減損会計
accounting for income tax allocation 税金配布会計
accounting for internal reporting 内部報告会計
accounting for inventories 棚卸資産会計
accounting for ownership equity 資本会計
accounting for price-level change 価格水準変動会計
accounting for property, plan and equipment 有形固定資産の会計処理
accounting for retirement benefit 退職給付会計
accounting for stock option ストック・オプション会計
accounting for tax allocation 税金配分会計
accounting for the cost of pension plans 年金制度上の年金会計
accounting for the government deposits maintained at the Bank 資金経理事務
accounting for valuation differences 評価差額の会計処理
accounting function 会計職能
accounting information system 会計情報システム
accounting interpretations 会計解釈指針
accounting issues 会計上の問題点
accounting machine 会計機
accounting manipulation 会計的操作
accounting manual 会計マニュアル
accounting method 会計処理方法
accounting model 会計モデル
accounting objectives 会計目的
accounting organization 会計組織
accounting period 会計期間
accounting period of merger 合併事業年度
accounting policy 会計方針
accounting postulate 会計公準
accounting practice 会計実務
accounting principles 会計原則
accounting principles for business enterprise 企業会計原則
accounting procedures 会計手続
accounting profession 会計士業
accounting profit 会計上の利益
accounting rate 算定レート
accounting rate of return 会計的利益率
accounting ratio 財務比率
accounting ratio of profits to net worth 会計的自己資本利益率
accounting recognition 会計上の認識
accounting records 会計記録
accounting regulations 経理規程
accounting report 会計報告
Accounting Research Bulletin 会計研究公報
accounting return (ratio) on equity 株主資本利益率
accounting rules 会計通則
Accounting Rules of the Bank 日銀会計規程
accounting sheet of collected amount

A

徴収額計算書
Accounting Standard Board 会計基準審議会
Accounting Standard Division 会計基準部会
accounting standard setting 会計基準設定
accounting standard-setting body 会計基準設定機関
accounting standards 会計基準
Accounting Standards Board of Japan 企業会計基準委員会
accounting standards for business combinations 企業結合に係る会計基準
accounting standards for consolidated financial statements 連結財務諸表原則
accounting standards for financial instruments 金融商品会計基準
accounting standards for foreign currency transactions 外貨建取引会計基準
accounting standards for impairment of fixed assets 固定資産の減損に係る会計基準
accounting standards for reserves for possible loan losses 引当金計上基準
accounting summary 計算サマリー
accounting system 会計制度
Accounting System Committee 会計制度委員会
accounting terminology 会計用語
accounting theory 会計理論
accounting transactions 会計取引
accounting treatment 会計処理
accounting unit 会計単位
accounting valuation 会計的評価
accounting year 会計年度
accounts balance 勘定残高
accounts based on accounting standards 会計基準準拠決算
Accounts Division 会計課
accounts due 未収金
accounts for fiscal year 年度決算
accounts of margin transactions 信用取引勘定
accounts of the Bank of Japan 日本銀行勘定
accounts payable 買掛金；支払勘定；未払金
accounts receivable 受取勘定；受取債権；売掛金
accounts receivable discounted 割引売上債権
accounts receivable financing 売掛金担保融資
accounts receivable turnover (ratio) 売掛金回転率
accounts yet to be settled 未決算勘定
accounts-receivable aging 未収金の経過期間
Accreditation Program 認証制度
accredited buyer 信用状の買い主
accredited investor 適格投資家
accrediting party 信用状開設者
accreted amount 増加金額
accreting swap アクレ・スワップ
accretion 財産の増加
accretion bond アクリーション・ボンド
accrual 発生
accrual accounting 発生主義会計
accrual accounting assumptions 発生主義会計の前提
accrual accounts 発生項目
accrual basis 発生主義
accrual basis accounting 発生主義会計
accrual in equity 資本の増加
accrual item 見越勘定
accrual of benefit 給付の確定
accrual of cause of action 訴訟原因の発生
accrual of discount 割引額期間対応割付
accrual of interest 利息の未払い
accrual period 発生期間
accrual rate 給付確定率；経過金利
accruals 未収支勘定

accrued account 未払勘定
accrued assets 見越資産
accrued benefit 給付額確定済給付額
accrued benefit cost 発生給付費用
accrued benefit method 発生給付方式
accrued benefit method pro-rated on service 勤務の比例配分による発生給付方式
accrued benefit valuation 発生給付評価
accrued benefit valuation method 発生給付評価方式
accrued charge 未払費用
accrued commission 未払手数料
accrued coupons クーポンの既経過分
accrued depreciation 減価償却発生額
accrued dividend 未払配当額
accrued dividend receivable 未収配当金
accrued donation 未払寄付金
accrued expenses payable 未払費用
accrued gains and losses 発生損益
accrued guarantee fee 未収保証料
accrued income 未収利益
accrued income taxes 納税引当金
accrued interest (income) 前受利息
accrued interest computed on a unit-of-trading basis 単位算出経過利子
accrued interest corresponding to the interest accrual period 利子計算期間に対応する利子
accrued interest on loan 貸付未収利息
accrued interest on securities 未収有価証券利息
accrued interest payable 未払利息
accrued interest receivable 未収受取利息
accrued interest subject to non-taxable treatment 非課税扱いの経過利子
accrued interest subject to taxable treatment 課税扱いの経過利子
accrued item 経過項目
accrued liabilities 見越債務
accrued liability 未払債務
accrued market discount 期近物価格上昇
accrued payroll 未払給与
accrued premium 未払保険金
accrued rent 未払家賃
accrued revenue 未収収益
accrued right premium 発生年金権移管金
accrued salaries 未払給料
accrued service 勤続年数
accrued wages 未払工賃
accumulated allowance 累積引当額
accumulated amortization 償却累計額
accumulated amount 累積額
accumulated benefit obligation 累積給付債務
accumulated capital 蓄積
accumulated comprehensive income 包括利益累計額
accumulated debt 累積債務
accumulated deficit 累積赤字
accumulated depreciation 減価償却累計額
accumulated dividend 累積配当
accumulated earning tax 留保収益税
accumulated earnings 利益剰余金
accumulated earnings credit 留保利益控除額
accumulated fund 積立金
accumulated impairment losses 減損損失累計額
accumulated income 累積利益
accumulated income tax prepayment 長期前払い税金
accumulated interest 累積利息
accumulated investment 累積投資
accumulated loss 繰越損失
accumulated plan benefits 年金給付累積額
accumulated preferred stock 累積配当優先株式
accumulated profit 剰余金；留保利益
accumulated profit tax 留保利益税
accumulated surplus 留保剰余金
accumulated value 終価

A

accumulation アキュミュレーション；累積
accumulation area 集積圏
accumulation device 積立手段
accumulation for retirement allowance 退職金積立金
accumulation fund 積立ファンド
accumulation of basic reserve 基本準備金の積立て
accumulation of capital 資本蓄積
accumulation of default compensation reserve 違約損失補償準備金の積立て
accumulation period 積立期間
accumulation plan 積立てプラン
accumulation product 積立型商品
accumulation system アキュミュレーション方式
accumulation trust 収益の元本組入型投資信託
accumulation unit 配当積立ユニット
accumulation value 累積部分
accumulative 累積的
accumulative investment period 累積投資期間
accumulative investment plan 累積投資プラン
accumulative investment unit 累積投資ユニット
accumulative judgment 累積判決
accumulative rate 蓄積利率
accumulative stock 累積配当型株式
accuracy 正確性
accuracy of counting 資産の査定
accuracy of counting in assessment 査定の厳格化
accusation 告発
accusatory part 起訴部分
accused 被告人
accuser 起訴者
ACE (adjusted current earnings) 調整後当期利益
ACE (adjustment for current earnings) 当期利益調整
ACH (automated clearing house) 自動クリアリング・ハウス
achievement 達成
acid ratio 当座比率
acid test ratio 酸性試験比率
acknowledgment 承認
acknowledgment of order 応諾
ACLI (American Council of Life Insurance) アメリカ生命保険協会
acquiescence 黙認
acquired asset 取得資産
acquired company 被買収会社
acquired during the period 期中に取得した
acquired entity 被結合企業
acquired right 既得権
acquired surplus 取得剰余金
acquiree 被取得企業
acquirer アクワイアラー
acquiring bank 取得銀行
acquiring entity 取得企業（結合企業）
acquiring loan claims 貸付債権の譲受
acquiring member 加盟店獲得会員
acquisition 取得
acquisition accounting 買収の会計
acquisition and divesture 取得と売却
acquisition by subsidies 補助金による取得
acquisition cost 取得費用
acquisition cost adjustment 取得原価調整
acquisition cost of assets 資産の取得価額
acquisition cost of depreciable assets 減価償却資産の取得価額
acquisition cost of inventory 棚卸資産の取得価額
acquisition cost of leasehold 借地権の取得価額
acquisition cost of property 資産の取得原価
acquisition cost of securities 有価証券取得価額
acquisition cost price 調達価格
acquisition date 取得日
acquisition difference 取得差額

acquisition for value 有償取得
acquisition multiple method 買収事例方式
acquisition of asset 資産の取得
acquisition of concessions 利権獲得
acquisition of corporate bonds 社債の取得
acquisition of debenture 社債取得
acquisition of membership 加入
acquisition of qualification 資格取得
acquisition of right 権利収得
acquisition of the application right 出願権の取得
acquisition of the qualification 資格の取得
acquisition price 取得価格
acquisition strategy 買収戦略
acquisitive prescription 取得時効
acquit 免訴を言渡す
acquittal of debt 債務免除
acquittance 債務消滅
acreage 地積
across jurisdictions 租税区域全体
across the categories of income 各種利益全体で
across-the-board 全銘柄の
AcSEC (Accounting Standards Executive Committee) 会計基準執行委員会
act of bankruptcy 破産行為
act of God 不可抗力
act of honor 参加引受
act of incorporation 設立法
act of indemnity 免責法
act of insolvency 支払不能行為
act of law 法の行為
act of parliament 国会制定法
act of state 国の行為
act tax 行為税
acting 事務代理
acting of account 計算請求訴訟
acting trading participant 取引代行取引参加者
action 行為
action in damage 損害賠償請求訴訟
action program アクション・プログラム
actionable fraud 詐欺
actionable negligence 訴えうる過失
active account 活勘定
active balance 活動残高
active bond 利息付債券
active buying 買進み
active cardholder 稼動会員
active dealer 積極的ディーラー
active debt 債権
active investment management theory 積極的投資理論
active life fund 現職者基金
active life reserve 健康者責任準備金
active management アクティブ運用
active market 好況市場
active partner アクティブ・パートナー
active portfolio アクティブ・ポートフォリオ
active return アクティブ・リターン
active risk アクティブ・リスク
active risk aversion アクティブ・リスク回避度
active secondary market 活発な流通市場
active stock 人気株
active trust 積極信託
active use 実際の使用
activity accounting 活動会計
activity analysis アクティビティ分析
activity rate 活動率
acts similar to guarantees 保証類似行為
actual absorption costing 実際全部原価計算
actual acquisition cost basis 実際取得原価主義
actual annual percentage rate 実質年利
actual authority 実際権限
actual balance 直物持高
actual basis accounting 実際主義会計
actual benefit 実際給付

A

actual burden rate 実際配賦率
actual cash value 現金換価価値
actual contribution 実際掛金
actual cost 実際原価
actual cost accounting system 実際原価計算制度
actual costing 実際原価計算
actual delivery 現物受渡し
actual delivery of stock sold 現提；現渡し；品渡し
actual demand 実需
actual demand rule 実需原則
actual depreciation 実際償却額
actual exchange rate 直物レート
actual expenses 実費
actual expenses versus budget control 予実管理
actual financial condition 財務の実態
actual foreign exchange position 現物為替持高
actual index price 現実指数
actual insurance coverage 正味補償
actual interest rate 実効金利
actual number of days elapsed 経過実数
actual position 直物持高
actual price 出来値
actual production 生産実績
actual purchase price 実際購入価額
actual rate of growth 現実成長率
actual receipt of stock purchased 現引；品受け
actual reserves 実質引当
actual results of recent stock transactions 株式取引実績
actual results of stock transactions 株式取引の実績
actual return 実際収益
actual return on pension assets 年金資産の実際収益
actual return on plan assets 年金資産実際運用収益
actual state of business 営業状況
actual state of property 財産の状況
actual stock 株の現物
actual surplus 正味剰余金
actual total loss 現実全損
actual trading behavior 実際の取引手口
actual transfer price 実際譲渡価額
actual use 実際使用
actual useful life 実際耐用年数
actual value 実価
actual value assets 実価資産
actual value method 実価法
actual volume 実業操業度
actually expected standard cost 現実的標準原価
actuals 現物
actuarial 保険数理上の
actuarial appraisal 保険数理上の評価
actuarial asset value 保険数理による資産価値
actuarial assumption 保険数理上の仮定
actuarial calculation 数理計算
actuarial calculation factor 保険数理計算要素
actuarial cost method 年金数理費用計算方式
actuarial deficiency 数理上の不足金
actuarial difference 数理計算差異
actuarial experience 保険数理上の実績
actuarial gain 保険数理差益
actuarial gains and losses 保険数理上の損益
actuarial gains or losses 数理的損益
actuarial hours 平均実働時間
actuarial loss 保険数理損
actuarial method 年金利回り法
actuarial present value 保険数理上の現在価値
actuarial rating 数理上の料率設定
actuarial reserve 責任準備金
actuarial risk 保険数理上のリスク
actuarial science 保険数理額
actuarial statistics 数理統計
actuarial technique 保険数理上の技法
actuarial valuation method 保険数理

上の評価方法
actuarial yield 保険数理利回り
actuary 保険計理人
Actuary for Earthquake Insurance 地震保険計理官
Actuary for Mutual Assistance Insurance 共済計理官
actuary's report 保険数理専門家の報告
ACU (**Asian Currency Unit**) アジア通貨単位
acute health care 急患治療
ad hoc 特別な目的に限る
ad hoc adjustment 特別調整
ad hoc arbitration 個別仲裁
ad hoc committee 特別委員会
ad valorem 従価
ad valorem duty 従価税
ad valorem storage 従価保管料
ad valorem tariff 従価税率
ad valorem tax 従価税
ADB (accelerated death benefit) 生前給付
ADB (African Development Bank) アフリカ開発銀行
add-back method 加減法
add-on interest rate アド・オン金利
add-on system アド・オン方式
added float 追加発行
added or deducted 加減した
added value statement 付加価値計算書
addenda 追加文書
adding carry キャリーの向上
adding to holdings 買い増し
adding to USD downside ドル安
addition 付加
addition of scale 規模拡大
addition to reserve 引当金繰入れ
addition to retained earnings 利益剰余金への振替
additional allowance 割増手当
additional amount to a refund of national tax 国税還付加算額
additional amount to refund 還付加算金
additional arrearage charge 延滞加算金
additional benefit 加算給付
additional benefits 追加的給付
additional bond test 追加債券発行限度額基準
additional budget 補正予算
additional capex 設備投資の追加
additional capital 増加資本
additional capital increase 追加出資
additional charge 追加費用
additional charge for deficient return 過少申告加算金
additional collateral 増し担保
additional commission 追加手数料
additional contribution 追加負担金；付加拠出
additional coverage 追加保障
additional debt 追加借入
additional deposit 追加差入れ
additional depreciation 増加償却
additional depreciation deduction 割増償却
additional depreciation on fire-proof buildings 耐火建築物の割増償却
additional depreciation ratio 割増償却率
additional disclosure 追加開示
additional equity 増資
additional establishment 追加設定
additional expenses 追加費用
additional field 追加フィールド
additional freight 割増運賃
additional information 追加情報
additional investment 追加出資
additional lease 追加リース
additional listing 追加上場
additional margin 追証
additional margin deposit 委託証拠金の追加差入れ
additional minimum liability 最低追加債務
additional paid-in capital 資本剰余金；追加払込資本金
additional pension 加給年金
additional pension cost 追加年金費用

A

additional pension liability 追加年金負債
additional provision 特約条項
additional report 追加報告書
additional requirement 追加の規定
additional tax 加算税
additional tax due to failure to file a return 無申告加算税
additional tax due to fraud 重加算税
additional tax due to understatement 過少申告加算税
additional tax for deficient return 過少申告加算税
additional tax on nonpayment 不納付加算税
additional voluntary contribution 追加任意拠出
additions and betterments reserve 増改築積立金
additions and omissions 追加及び省略
additions to plant and equipment 設備新規購入額
additions to reserves 積立金繰入
additions to tax 付帯税
additive subtraction 加法的減算
addressee 名宛人
addressor of letter of credit 信用状発行人
adduce 引証する
ADELA (Atlantic Community Development Group for Latin America) アデラ
adequacy of capital 資本の充実度
adequacy of collateral 担保の適切性
adequacy of coverage リスク・カバー率
adequate 相当な
adequate basis 妥当な基礎
adequate cash value 適正価格
adequate liquidity 適正流動性
adequate profit 適切な利益
adequate protection 十分な保護
adequate substitute for 適切な代替
ADF (Asian Development Fund) アジア開発基金
adjacent 近隣の
adjective law 手続法
adjournment 延期
adjudge 司法的判断を下す
adjudicated bankrupt 破産宣告された
adjudication 判決
adjudication of bankruptcy 破産宣告
adjudication order 破産命令
adjudicator 裁定者
adjunct account 付加勘定
adjust downwards 下方修正する
adjustable basket technique 非対称バスケット方式
Adjustable Life Insurance アジャスタブル保険
adjustable peg アジャスタブル・ペッグ
adjustable peg system 調整可能固定相場
adjustable rate 調整利率
adjustable rate mortgage 変動金利モーゲージ
adjustable rate mortgage loan 調整金利抵当ローン
adjustable rate notes 調整可能利付手形
adjustable rate preferred stock 変動利率優先株
adjusted 調整済
adjusted balance method 修正残高方式
adjusted base 修正基礎額
adjusted basis 調整基準
adjusted beta value 修正ベータ値
adjusted capital gain 調整後譲渡所得
adjusted carrying amount 修正後帳簿価額
adjusted central bank money stock 調整後中央銀行通貨ストック
adjusted cost basis 修正原価主義
adjusted cost of sales 修正後の売上原価
adjusted debit balance of margin transactions 信用取引融資残高
adjusted depreciation cost 修正後の減

価償却費
adjusted dividend increase 調整後配当増加率
adjusted earnings per share 調整済一株当り利益
adjusted EPS increase 調整後ＥＰＳ増加率
adjusted exercise price 修正済行使価格
adjusted gross income 修正総所得
adjusted historical cost 修正取得原価
adjusted income 調整所得金額
adjusted inflation 調整済インフレ
adjusted item 調整済項目
adjusted net income 調整後純利益
adjusted net minimum tax 修正純ミニマム税
adjusted net profit 修正後純利益
adjusted premium 調整保険料
adjusted regression analysis 修正回帰分析
adjusted stockholders' equity 修正株主資本
adjusted surplus 調整剰余金
adjusted trial balance 修正後試算表
adjusting entry 修正記入
adjusting journal entry 修正仕訳
adjustment 調整
adjustment account 照合勘定
adjustment at term-end 期末整理
adjustment entry 整理記入
adjustment factor 調整係数
adjustment for price fluctuations 価格変動修正
adjustment for taxable income 税務調整
adjustment in filing a final tax return 申告調整
adjustment in settling accounts 決算調整
adjustment in the book value 簿価修正額
adjustment inflation 調整インフレ
adjustment item 調整項目
adjustment of accounts 帳簿整理
adjustment of business income 企業利益調整
adjustment of capital 資本修正
adjustment of cost variance 原価差額調整
adjustment of debts 債務調整
adjustment of open positions 建玉の調整
adjustment of organization 体制の構築
adjustment of surplus 剰余金調整
adjustment of the carrying amount 簿価修正
adjustment of the debts of a municipality 地方公共団体の債務の調整
adjustment pressure 調整圧力
adjustment process of balance of payments 国際収支調整過程
adjustment securities 調整証券
adjustments in economic activity 景気調整
adjustments in interest rates 金利調整
adjustments of prior period 前期修正項目
administered price 管理価格
administered-price inflation 管理価格インフレーション
administrated rate liabilities 規制金利負債
administration 事務管理
administration cost 管理コスト
Administration Department 経営企画室
administration estate 遺産管理
administration evaluation 行政評価
administration in bankruptcy 破産管財
administration of construction 工事管理
administration order 管財命令
administrative accounting 管理会計
administrative act 行政行為
administrative action 行政処分
administrative activities 管理活動

administrative and maintenance expenses 維持管理費用
administrative and selling expense 販売管理費
administrative appellate law 行政不服審査法
administrative audit 管理的監査
administrative budget 管理予算
administrative burden 事務負担
administrative cost 管理費
Administrative Counselor 行政相談官
administrative discretion 行政裁量
administrative disposition 行政処分
administrative dispute 行政争訟
administrative expense variance 一般管理費差異
administrative fees 国債事務取扱費
administrative guidance 行政指導
administrative interpretation 行政解釈
administrative law 行政法
administrative legislation 行政立法
administrative litigation 行政訴訟
administrative officer 行政職員
administrative order 行政命令
administrative overhead 管理部門間接費
administrative power 行政権
administrative protest 不服申立て
administrative remedy 行政救済
administrative review 不服審査
administrative vice minister 事務次官
administrator 管財人
administrator in bankruptcy 破産管財人
administrator of bequest 遺産管理人
administrator of tax payment 納税管理人
admissible assets 認容資産
admission 許可
admission fee 加入金；入会金
admission to membership 会員の加入
admitted assets 承認適格資産
admitted company 認可会社
admonition 戒告
adopted concept 借用概念
adoption 採用
adoption of international accounting standards 国際会計基準の採用
adoptive act 任意法
adoptive provisions 任意規定
ADR (American Depository Receipt) 米国預託証券
ADR (asset depreciation range) 資産減価償却範囲
ADS (American Depositary Shares) 米国預託株式
adulterate 原文を改悪する
adulteration 粗悪化
advance 貸付金；上昇
advance account 貸付勘定
advance by customers 得意先前受金
advance collection 繰上徴収
advance corporation tax 前納法人
advance decline ratio 騰落レシオ
advance demand 繰上請求
advance for purchase 仕入代前渡金
advance freight 前払運賃
advance from controlled companies 子会社前受金
advance funded pension 事前積立年金
advance funding method 事前積立方式
advance made on contract 契約前渡金
advance made to salesmen 販売員前渡金
advance money 立替金
advance of salary 給料前払い
advance on a promissory note 手形貸付
advance on account of sellers 仕入前払代金
advance on consignment-in 受託販売立替金
advance on indent 買付委託立替金
advance on subscription 申込証拠金
advance payment 前金
advance payment bond 前払金返還保証証券
advance premium 前納保険料
advance preservative seizure 繰上保全

差押
advance pricing agreement 事前価格確認制度
advance received 前受金
advance received on contract 契約手付
advance received on indents 受託買付前渡金
advance received profit 前受収益
advance refunding 期前借換え
advance repayment 繰上弁済
advance salary 前払給与
advance sale 前売り
advance seizure 繰上差押
advance to subcontractor 下請前払金
advance wages 前払賃金
advance-decline line 騰落線
advance-in-age plan 年増法
advanced accounting 上級会計学
advanced age 高齢
advanced collection on sale contracts 売買契約前受金
advanced countries 先進国
advanced depreciation 圧縮記帳
advanced depreciation deduction 圧縮損
advanced depreciation limit 圧縮限度額
advanced funded pension plan 事前積立年金制度
advanced money 前渡金
advanced processing 川下部門
advanced redemption 繰上償還
advancement 生前贈与分
advantageous placement 有利発行
adventure やま
adversary party 相手方当事者
adverse claim 異議申立
adverse effects 悪影響
adverse element マイナス要因
adverse exchange 逆為替
adverse opinion 否定的意見
adverse physical conditions claims 地下条件クレーム
adverse possession 時効取得
adverse selection 逆選択
advertisement 広告
advertisement for bid 入札公告
advertisement tax 広告税
advertising and general publicity expenses 広告宣伝費
advertising expenses 広告費
advertising media 広告媒体
advertising rate 広告料
advertising regulation 広告規制
advice note 発送通知書
advice of credit 入金通知
advice of debit 引落し通知
advice of subrogation 代位通知書
advice payment 通知払い
advice slip 通知伝票
advise and pay 通知支払い
Adviser to the Minister of Finance 財務省参事
advising bank 通知銀行
advisor 顧問
advisory 助言的
advisory board アドバイザリー・ボード
advisory committee 諮問委員会
advisory opinion 助言的意見
advisory service 投資顧問業
advisory tax board 税務諮問委員会
advocate 弁護士
AED (United Arab Emirates dirham) アラブ首長国連邦ディルハム
AEX (Amsterdam Exchanges) アムステルダム証券取引所
AEX Index AEX 指数
AFA (Afghanistan afghani) アフガニスタン・アフガニ
AFBD (Association of Futures Brokers and Dealers) 先物ブローカー・ディーラー協会
affairs 業務
affect 影響する
affidavit 宣誓供述書
affidavit of claim 給付金支払請求宣誓供述書
affiliate subsidiary 関連子会社

A

affiliated company 関係会社
affiliated credit card 提携カード
affiliated family corporations 同族関係会社
affiliated financial institute 系列金融機関
affiliated group 関連グループ
affiliated loan 提携ローン
affiliated person 特別関係人
affiliation 系列化
affiliation procedure 会員加入手続き
affine term structure model アフィン期間構造モデル
affinity card アフィニティ・カード
affirm 確認する（額を）
affirmation of fact 事実の確認
affirmative covenant 肯定的誓約
affirmed confirmation 承認済コンファメーション
affix 署名を付す
affluence 富
affordability 余裕度
affordability of payment of insurance amount 保険金負担可能性
affordable 負担できる
affranchise 開放する
AFI (Association of Futures Investments) 先物投資協会
AFOF (authorized futures and options funds) 公認先物オプションファンド
Afro-Asian Common Market アジア・アフリカ共同市場
AFTA (ASEAN Free Trade Arrangement) ASEAN 自由貿易地域
after cost 後費用
after effective tax 実効税引き後
after hour trading 立会外取引
after income taxes 法人所得税控除後
after loss アフター・ロス
after market 流通市場
after maturity endorsement 満期後の裏書
after sight 一覧後
after tax 税引き
after tax basis 税引後基準
after tax real rate of return 税引後実質利回り
after tax yield 税引後利回り
after-acquired clause 事後取得資産追加担保条項
after-acquired property 事後取得財産
after-session undertone 引け跡気配
after-tax amount 税引後金額
after-tax gain 税引後の手取り額
after-tax income 税引後利益
after-tax profit rate 税引利益率
after-tax return (ratio) 税引後利益率
after-tax wage 税引給与
aftermarket 新規公開後の売買
afternoon session 後場
afternoon trading session 午後立会い
AFUDC (allowance for funds used during construction) 建設引当金
against all risks 全危険担保
against the above background 以上を踏まえて
against the will 意に反して
age at entry 保険年齢
age at exit 満期年齢
age dependent 年数依存
age distribution 年齢構成
age group 年齢層
age joining limit 加入年齢制限
age last birthday 満年齢
age limit 経過期間の期限；年齢制限
age of discretion 分別年齢
age of eligibility 資格年齢
age of financial statements 財務諸表の日付から経過した期間
age of insured 保険契約年齢
age of loan payments ローン支払済年数
age of policy 保険契約経過年数
age of retirement 退職年齢
age when pension is granted 年金支給開始年齢
age-based premium 年齢別保険料
age-rated system 年齢料率制

aged dependent 老人扶養親族
aged fail エージド・フェール
aged person 老年者
aged population 高齢者人口
aged society 高齢社会
AGEF Index フランスAGEF指数
agency 代理店
agency account 代理店勘定
agency account receivable 代理店貸し
agency agreement 代理店契約書
agency arrangement 取引約定書
agency bookkeeping 代理人簿記
Agency Clearing Participant 他社清算参加者
Agency Clearing Qualification 他社清算資格
agency commission 代理店手数料
agency contract 代理店契約
agency cost 代理店経費
agency fee 代理店手数料
Agency for Cultural Affairs 文化庁
Agency for Natural Resources and Energy 資源エネルギー庁
agency fund 代理人資金
agency ledger 代理店元帳
agency loan 代理貸付
agency margin 取次証拠金
agency market エージェンシー市場
agency mortgage pool 政府系金融機関モーゲージ・プール
agency pool 政府系機関プール
agency relationship 代理関係
agency service 委託の取次
agency subordinated debt 政府系機関劣後債
agency theory エージェンシー理論
agency to receive tax 収納機関
agency transaction 委託取引
agenda 議題
agendum 議事
agent 代理人；取次者
agent bank 幹事行
agent commission 代理手数料
agent development era 外務員開発の時代
agent distribution 募集人販売
agent handling payment of the dividends 配当金の支払を行う機関
agent inspection 代理店検査
agent owned company 代理店出資会社
agent replacement deposit 取次者差換預託
agent system 代理店制度
aggravation 加重事由
aggregate 総計
aggregate active risk 総アクティブ・リスク
aggregate amount 総額
aggregate amount outstanding 未決済総額
aggregate average 総平均
aggregate basis 一括基準
aggregate book value 簿価合計額
aggregate combined ratio 総合合算比率
aggregate corporate profits 全体の企業収益
aggregate cost 総原価
aggregate cost ratio 総合掛金率
aggregate demand 総需要
aggregate demand function 総需要関数
aggregate exercise price 総行使価格
aggregate face amount 額面総額
aggregate fair value 公正価値合計額
aggregate financial information 全体の財務情報
aggregate gross margin 粗利益総計
aggregate investments 投資総額
aggregate limit of liability 総補填限度額
aggregate limits 総額規制
aggregate managed portfolio 総運用ポートフォリオ
aggregate market value 時価総額
aggregate net sales 純売上高総計
aggregate normal portfolio 総ノーマル・ポートフォリオ
aggregate of depreciation deduction 減価償却費累計

A

aggregate proceeds 入金総額
aggregate redemption amount 償還予定額
aggregate social capital 社会総資本
aggregate supply 総供給量
aggregate supply function 総供給関数
aggregate theory 集合理論
aggregate value 総額
aggregated data 合計資料
aggregated information 合計情報
aggregated shipments 一括運送
aggregation 合算；集計
aggregation of assets 資産の集合
aggregation of data データの集計
aggregation of elements 要素の合計
aggregation of income amount 所得金額の合算
aggregation of income from assets 資産所得の合算
aggregation of profit and loss 損益通算
aggregation problem 集計の問題
aggressive growth fund 積極成長ファンド
aggressive growth mutual fund 急成長株ファンド
aggressive investment 攻撃的投資
aggressive portfolio 積極的運用
aggressive securities 攻撃的証券
aggressively held up 高目誘導
aggressiveness アクティブの度合い
aggressor 攻撃者
aggrieved party 被害者
AGI (adjusted gross income) 調整後総所得
AGIC (alternative guaranteed interest contract) 新世代 GIC
aging 経過年数；年齢調べ
aging of the portfolio receivable 債権ポートフォリオの経過期間
aging schedule 売掛金経過明細表
aging valuation 高齢化の評価
agio 発行差金
agrarian laws 土地分配法
agreed benefit 合意給付
agreed cut 合意済みの利下げ
agreed insured value 協定保険価額
agreed interest 約定利息
agreed jurisdiction 合意管轄
agreed order 合意命令
agreed price 協定価格
agreed rate of interest 約定利率
agreed statement of facts 合意事実陳述書
agreed yield to maturity 約定満期利回り
agreed-upon interest rate 約定金利
agreed-upon price 約定値段
agreement 契約；約定
agreement among underwriters 引受業者間契約
agreement for bondholder services 社債管理委託契約
agreement for demerger 分割契約書
agreement for establishment of foreign securities trading account 外国証券取引口座約款
Agreement for Establishment of Futures/Options Trading Account 先物・オプション取引口座設定約諾書
agreement for establishment of margin transactions account 信用取引口座設定約諾書
agreement for exchange of shares 株式交換契約書
agreement for merger 合併契約書
agreement for overdraft 当座貸越約定書
agreement for the account for financial futures transaction 金融先物取引口座設定約諾書
agreement jurisdictional court 合意管轄裁判所
agreement of IMF IMF 協定
agreement of special liquidation 特別清算の同意
Agreement of the International Bank for Reconstruction and Development 国際開発復興銀行協

定
Agreement of the International Monetary Fund 国際通貨基金協定
agreement on commerce 通商協定
agreement to refinance 再融資契約
agreements pertaining to acceptance of orders 受託に関する契約書
Agricultural and Fishery Co-Operative Savings Insurance Corporation 農水産業協同組合貯金保険機構
agricultural bank 農業銀行
agricultural bookkeeping 農業簿記
Agricultural Chemicals Inspection Station 農薬検査所
agricultural credit 農業金融
agricultural economics 農業経済学
agricultural expenditure 農業経営費
agricultural income 農業所得
agricultural insurance 農業保険
agricultural lien 農業先取特権
agricultural production corporation 農業生産法人
agricultural society 農業組合
agricultural tariff 農産物関税
Agriculture and Livestock Industries Corporation 農畜産業振興機構
Agriculture Forestry and Fisheries Finance Corporation 農林漁業金融公庫
Agriculture, Forestry and Fisheries Credit Foundations 農林漁業信用基金
Ahlers model アーラーズ株価モデル
AI (accrued interest) 経過利子
AIA (American Institutes of Accountants) 米国会計士協会
AIBD (Association of International Bond Dealers) 国際債券ディーラー協会
AIBOR (American interbank offered rate) AIBOR
aid and comfort 助力
aid bond 補助公債
aid package 支援策
aid prayer 援助請願
aid recipients 援助を受ける側
aid societies 共済組合
aid with attachment ひも付援助
AIDAS theory アイダス原理
aids 援助金
ailing 業績不振の
air fare 航空料金
air pocket issue 急落銘柄
air transport industry 航空運送業
air transportation industry 空運業
aircraft 航空機
aircraft financing 航空機ファイナンス
aircraft hull insurance 航空機保険
aircraft loan scheme 航空機融資制度
aircraft passenger accident insurance 航空障害保険
airport landing rights 空港発着権
airport revenue bond 空港収入債
airway bill 航空貨物運送状
airway freight 航空運賃
AJE (adjusted journal entry) 修正仕分
aladdin bond アラジン債
alarmist 警告論者
alias 別名
alien 外国人
alien corporation 外国法人
alien insurer 外国保険会社
alien property 外国人財産
alien taxpayer 外国人納税者
alienability 譲渡性
alienable 移転可能な
alienation 譲渡
alimony 扶助
ALL (Albanian lek) アルバニア・レク
all amounts invested in capital 総出資金額
all and singular 例外なしにすべて
all BB rated BB 格全銘柄
all buyers 買い一色
All Enterprises Tankan and Principal Enterprises Tankan (Tankan: Short-Term Economic Survey of Enterprises in Japan) 全国企業短期経済観測調査及び主要企業短期経済観測調査（短観）

A

all gone 売切れ
all in 全経費込み
all in cost オール・イン・コスト
all included directly in capital 全部資本直入
all lines 生損保兼営
all lines insurance 総合保険
all or none(AON) オール・オア・ナン
All Ordinaries Index オーストラリア総合株価指数
all risks coverage 全危険担保
all risks coverage clause 全危険担保約款
all savers certificate 国債利回り連動1年定期
all-inclusive basis 包括基準
all-inclusive income concept 包括主義的利益概念
all-inclusive income statement 包括損益計算書
all-inclusive principle 包括主義
all-issued stocks 発行済株式総数
all-or-none order 一括売買注文
all-pay benefit 全額負担給付
all-purpose balance sheet 万能貸借対照表
all-purpose card 汎用カード
all-purpose financial statements 多目的財務諸表
all-time high 新高値
all-time low 史上最安値
allfinanz 総合金融機関化
alliance 同盟
allied company 同盟会社
allied member 取引所準会員
alligator spread アリゲーター・スプレッド
allocated contract 割当契約
allocated funding instrument 割当積立方式
allocation 配分
allocation and execution of budget 予算の配賦と執行
allocation efficiency 配分効率
allocation model 配分モデル
allocation of cost 取得原価の配分
allocation of new shares to a third party 第三者割当
allocation of resources 資源の分配
allocation over the term 期間配分
allocation ratio 配分率
allot 分割する
allotment 割当
allotment certificate 株式割当証
allotment ledger 割当予算元帳
allotment letter 割当証
allotment of shares 株式割当
allotment system 土地配分制度
allotment to shareholder 株主割当
allotment warden 配分地管理人
allotted amount in constructing public facility 公共施設建設負担額
allow 許容する
allowable for tax purpose 税務上許容される
allowable limit for depreciation amount 償却限度額
allowable maximum amount 許容限度額
allowance 準備金；手当
allowance account 引当金勘定
Allowance Control and Mutual Assistance Insurance Division 給与共済課
allowance for bad loan 貸倒準備金
allowance for dead loans 貸倒引当金
allowance for dependent 扶養控除
allowance for depreciation 減価償却引当金
allowance for doubtful accounts 貸倒引当金
allowance for obsolete inventory 棚卸資産陳腐化引当金
allowance for promotion of employment 就職促進手当
allowance for repairs 修繕引当金
allowance for retirement benefit 退職給付引当金
allowance for uncollectable accounts 貸倒引当金

allowance for undistributed profits 留保控除額
allowance for widow 寡婦控除
allowance in kind 現物支給
allowance method 引当金設定法
allowed alternative treatment 認められる代替処理
allowed amortizable limit 償却限度額
allowed cost 許容原価
allowed depreciation 償却範囲
allowed depreciation limit 償却限度額
allowed limit of accumulation 積立限度額
allowed limit of retirement allowance reserve 退職給与引当金繰入限度額
allowed limit of the bonus payment reserve 賞与引当金繰入限度額
allowed retirement income deduction 退職所得控除
ALM (asset and liability management) 資産負債総合管理
ALM (asset liability management) 資産・負債管理
alongside delivery 自家取り
alpha value アルファ値
alphabet fund アルファベット・ファンド
Alpine bond アルパイン債
ALPS (aircraft lease portfolio securitization) 航空機リース・ポートフォリオ証券化
already-issued bond 既発債
ALSM (asset-liability surplus management) 資産・負債サープラス管理
ALT (automatic liquidity transfer) mechanism 自動流動性移動機構
alteration 変造
alteration demand 変更請求
alteration in listed securities 有価証券の変更上場
alteration of banknotes 変造紙幣
alteration of species 性質の喪失
alteration work 変更工事
alternate care 代替介護
alternate policy 代替契約
alternation 交替
alternative accounting principles 代替会計原則
alternative accounting treatment 代替会計処理
alternative approach 代替的方法
alternative contract 選択契約
alternative costs 代替費用
alternative duties 選択関税
alternative energy 代替エネルギー
alternative estimate 代替見積値
alternative financing choice 代替資金調達手段
alternative funds 代替資金
alternative investment オルタナティブ運用
alternative liquidity 代替流動性
alternative minimum tax 代替ミニマム税
alternative obligation 選択債務
alternative order 択一注文
alternative presentation 代替表示
alternative pricing 選択型価格決定
alternative product 代替製品
alternative production process 代替製造工程
alternative remedy 選択的救済
alternative source of funding 新たな資金調達源
alternative treatment 代替処理
alternative withholding tax on dividends 配当源泉選択課税
altruism 利他主義
aluminum coins (1 yen) アルミニウム貨幣（1 円）
AMA (American Management Association) アメリカ経営者協会
amalgamation 合併
amalgamation procedures 合併手続
amalgamation process 合併過程
amalgamation surplus 合併剰余金
ambiguity 不明瞭
ambit 権限範囲

ambulatory patient 通院患者
AMD (Armenia drum) アルメニア・ドラム
amelioration 改善
amend 修正する
amended budget 修正予算
amended registration statement of a security 訂正有価証券届出書
amended shelf registration statement 修正発行届出書
amended tax return 修正申告
amended usury law 改正貸金業法
amendment 修正
amendments to the articles of incorporation 定款変更
amendments to the by-laws 定款の変更
amerce 罰金を科する
amercement 罰金
American Accounting Association 米国会計学会
American Bankers Association 米国銀行協会
American Bar Association 米国法曹協会
American clause 重複保険における順位主義約款
American College 外務員大学
American depositary share 米国預託株式
American Institute of Accountants アメリカ会計士協会
American Institute of Certified Public Accountants 米国公認会計士協会
American Law Institute 米国法律協会
American Management Association 米国経営者協会
American option アメリカン・オプション
American Society of C.L.U. アメリカ認定生命保険士会
American Stock Exchange アメリカン証券取引所
American type アメリカンタイプ
Americus trust アメリカス信託
Americus Trust Scores アメリカス・トラスト・スコア
Amex Commodity Exchange アメックス商品取引所
AMEX Index アメリカン証券取引所株価指数
AMF (Arab Monetary Fund) アラブ通貨基金
amortization アモチゼーション；債務償還
amortization cost 償却費用
amortization effect アモチゼーション効果
amortization event アモチゼーション事由
amortization fund 減債基金；負債償却準備金
amortization loan 分割返済型貸付
amortization method 償却方法
amortization of bond issuance expenses 債券発行費償却
amortization of bond premium 社債発行差金償却
amortization of deferred assets 繰延資産の償却
amortization of discount 割引額の償却
amortization of discounts on issued bonds 債券発行差金償却
amortization of goodwill 営業権償却
amortization of initial expenses 創業費償却
amortization of intangible assets 無形資産減価償却
amortization of intangible assets and goodwill 無形資産とのれんの償却
amortization of intangibles 無形資産減価償却
amortization of premium プレミアムの償却
amortization of principal 元本の返済
amortization of prior service cost 過去勤務債務の償却額
amortization of start-up expenses 創業費償却
amortization of taxes 税の還元

amortization period 元本償還期間
amortization rate 償却率
amortization schedule 債務償還計画
amortization structure 償還の仕組み
amortize 償還する；償却する
amortized cost 償却原価
amortized cost method 償却原価法
amortized original amount 当初金額の償却後の金額
amortized value 均等利回評価額
amortizing cap アモチ・キャップ
amortizing swap 約定返済付きスワップ
amortizing term loan 分割返済型タームローン
amount 金額
amount added to capital 増資
amount advanced 貸付金額
amount allowable 損金算入限度額
amount already accrued 発生金額
amount appraised 評価額
amount assessed 評価額
amount at maturity 満期金額
amount attributable to goodwill のれんに帰属する金額
amount billed 請求額
amount carried forward 次期繰越高
amount claimed 請求額
amount covered 保険金額
amount credited to capital stock 資本金組入額
amount credited to equity 資本組入額
amount deducted 控除額
amount due 満期支払高
amount equivalent to 相当額
amount financed 貸出額
amount imposed 賦課額
amount in arrears 未払金
amount in hand 有り高
amount initially received 当初受入額
amount invested 出資額
amount issued 発行高
amount issued by types of straight bonds 上場普通債券の種類別発行額
amount listed by types of straight bonds 上場普通債券の種類別上場総額
amount matched within each member 会員社内対当金額
amount of adjustment 修正額
amount of bill 手形金額
amount of capital 資本の額
amount of capital investment 設備投資額
amount of claim 求償額
amount of clearing bill 手形交換高
amount of consumption 消費高
amount of damage 損害額
amount of depreciation 減価償却高
amount of dilution 希薄化の金額
amount of dividends paid 配当金総額
amount of goods purchased 仕入高
amount of income 所得額
amount of income for each taxable year 各事業年度の所得の金額
amount of investment 出資額
amount of loss 欠損額
amount of monthly payment 毎月の返済額
amount of obligations 債務額
amount of proceeds 受取高
amount of profit 利益の額
amount of reinsurance 再保険金額
amount of sales 売上高
amount of savings held per household 一世帯当り貯蓄残高
amount of stock 商品有り高
amount of tax 税額
amount of tax payment 納税額
amount of taxable purchases 課税仕入高
amount of taxable sales 課税売上高
amount of the first payment 初回金
amount of the offset 相殺額
amount of trade receivable 売掛金
amount of trade value 受渡決済代金
amount of transfer credit 移管金額
amount of use 使用量
amount on hand 現在高

amount option 保険金定額受取オプション
amount outstanding 残高
amount outstanding of banknotes issued 銀行券発行残高
amount outstanding of corporate bonds 社債発行残高
amount outstanding of unsettled transactions 未決済残高
amount overbought 買持高
amount oversold 売持高
amount paid 支払高
amount paid per new share 新株一株当りの払込価額
amount paid per new stock 新株一株当り払込価額
amount paid to subcontractors 外注加工費
amount raised 資金調達額
amount raised by stock 株式による資金調達額
amount realized 実現金額
amount receivable 受取金
amount receivable from trade customers 売掛金
amount received 受入金額
amount regarded as dividend 配当額とみなす金額
amount subject 正味危険負担額
amount subscribed 応募金額
amount to be amortized 償却対象額
amount to the outside by distribution of net profit 利益処分による社外流出額
amount weighted 金額加重の
amount withheld 源泉預り
amounts expected to by settled by means of collateral 担保の処分可能見込額
ample liquidity 十分な流動性
AMPS (auction market preferred stock) 入札方式優先株
AMT (alternative minimum tax) 代替ミニマム税
analogy 共通点
analysis 分析
analysis of budget variance 予算差異分析
analysis of cost variances 原価差異分析
analysis of credit 信用分析
analysis of financial statements 財務諸表分析
analysis of income statement 損益計算書分析
analysis of lender's preference 貸手選好分析
analysis of variance 分散分析
analyst アナリスト
analytic approach 分析的アプローチ
analytical accounting 分析的会計
analytical data 分析データ
analytical procedure 分析的手続
analytical reports 分析的報告書
analytical tool 分析ツール
analytics 分析
analyze 分析する
anatomy 詳細な分析
ancestor 被相続人
ancient rent 賃料
ancillary 補助の
ancillary benefit 付随給付
ancillary relief 付随的救済
ancillary services 付随サービス
and interest 経過利子付き
Andean Common Market アンデス共同市場
anecdotal evidence 経緯
ANG (Netherlands Antilles gulden) オランダ領アンティル諸島グルデン
anglers' insurance つり保険
Anguilla (EC (East Caribbean) dollar) アンギラ（EC ドル）
Anhui 安徽省
animal insurance 動物保険
ANNA (Association of National Numbering Agencies) 国際付番機関協会
annex 付属書類
annexation 併合

annexed structure 付属設備
annotation 註釈
announced tax rate 発表税率
announcement 公示
announcement effect 告知効果
announcement of auction 入札の通知
announcement of bids and offers 呼値の周知
announcement of performance results 決算発表
annual accounting 年次決算
annual accounts 年次の決算書
annual audit 年次監査
annual audited financial statement 監査済年次財務報告書
annual basis 年換算
annual business report 事業報告書
annual calculation 年一回の計算
annual capacity 年間生産能力
annual closing 年度締切
annual compensation package 年俸制度
annual compounding 欧州式複利利回り
annual coupon 年払いクーポン
annual dues 年会費
annual earnings 年間所得
annual economic review 経済年報
annual employment 年間雇用率
annual exclusion 年間非課税項目
annual expenditure 歳出
annual fees 年賦課金
annual financial statements 年次財務諸表
annual income 年収
annual increase 年次上昇率
annual installment 年賦
annual interest rate 年利
annual listing fee 上場維持に必要な年間手数料
annual measure 通年の指標
annual meeting 年次総会
annual meeting of shareholders 年次株主総会
annual member 年会員
annual membership fee 年会費
annual payment 年1回後払い
annual pension benefit 年間年金給付額
annual percentage rate 年率のパーセンテージ
annual premium 年間保険料
annual profit disposition amount 年間利益処分額
annual rate of returns 年収益率
annual renewal term insurance 一年毎更新保険
annual report 年次報告書
annual report to stockholders 株主向け年次報告書
annual reporting period 年次報告書期間
annual return 年間リターン
annual revenue 歳入
annual securities statistics 証券統計年報
annual statement 年次計算書
annual value method 年価法
annual yield convention 年一回払いの取決め
annualize 年率換算にする
annualized basis 年率換算
annualized rate 年率
annualized volatility 年率換算したボラティリティ
annualized yield 年利回り
annuitant 年金受給者
annuitization 年金化
annuity 年金保険；年賦金
annuity agreement 年金協約
annuity bond 元利均等払債
annuity certain 確定年金
annuity certain and continuous 確定年金付終身年金
annuity distribution 年金支給額
annuity due 期首払年金
annuity for life 終身年金
annuity fund deposit 年金資金預り金
annuity in perpetuity 永久年金
annuity insurance 年金保険

annuity loan 年金型ローン
annuity payment 年金払い
annuity payout 年金支給額
annuity payout option 年金支払オプション
annuity period 年金期間
annuity policyholder 年金契約者
annuity premium 年金掛金
annuity price 年金価格
annuity product 年金商品
annuity purchase fund 年金購入基金
annuity purchase plan 年金購入方式
annuity purchase rates 年金購入料率
annuity rate 年金給付率
annuity refund 償還式年金
annuity regarded as salaries and wages 給与とみなされる年金
annuity reinsurance 年金再保険
annuity repayment method 元利均等償還方式
annuity rider 年金特約
annuity settlement 年金式分割受取り
annuity starting date 年金保険受給開始日
annuity territory 年金保険領域
annuity unit 年金ユニット
annul 取消す
annulment 無効にすること
annulment of a contract 契約解除
annulment right 取消権
annunciator board 呼び出し板
anomaly 変則
anonymity 匿名性
anonymous 匿名の
anonymous association 匿名組合
ANP/CBS General Index オランダANP-CBS 総合株価指数
antedated check 前日付小切手
antedating 前日付けの
anti-counterfeiting features of banknotes 銀行券の偽造防止策等
anti-dilution 反希薄化
anti-dilution clause 希薄化防止条項
anti-dumping code 反ダンピング法
anti-fraud provision 不正防止条項
anti-inflation インフレ抑止
anti-inflationary credibility インフレ抑止に対する信頼度
anti-monopoly law 独禁法
anti-rebating 割引禁止
anti-social element 反社会勢力
anti-social power 反社会勢力
anti-tie-in 相互販売禁止
anticipated acceptance 満期前引受け
anticipated cost 見込原価
anticipated excess return 予想超過リターン
anticipated holding period 予定保有期間
anticipated loss 予想損失
anticipated proceeds from the collateral 担保の処分見込額
anticipated profit 見込利益
anticipated recovery from the financial guarantee 保証による回収見込額
anticipated transactions 予定取引
anticipation 期限前返済
anticipation of falling market 安値待ち
anticipation of low interest rate 金利先安観
anticipation tax bill 納税準備証券
anticipatory breach of contract 期限前の契約違反
anticipatory hedge 予定ヘッジ
anticompetitive 競争制限的な
antithetic variable 対称変数
antitrust law 反トラスト法
any-and-all bid 全株同一価格買付
AOR (Angola kwanza) アンゴラ・クワンザ
AP (additional premium) 割増保険料
apartment dwellers' comprehensive insurance 団地保険
APB (Accounting Principles Board) 会計原則審議会
APC (Accounting Practices Committee) 監査実務委員会
apparent 明白な

apparent agency 表見代理
apparent authority 表見代理権
apparent danger 明白な危険
apparent rate of interest 表面利率
appeals court 控訴裁判所
appellant 控訴人
appellate court 上訴裁判所
appellee 被控訴人
appendix 添付書類
appetite 興味
appetite for inflation インフレ選好
appetite for yield 高利回商品への投資意欲
appliance 設備
applicable 適用すべき
applicable law 準拠法
applicable standard 適用する基準
applicable statutory useful life 適用しうる法定耐用年数
applicable tax rate 適用税率
applicable useful life 適用しうる耐用年数
applicant 申請人
applicant for initial listing 新規上場申請者
applicant for relocation to other market 上場市場の変更申請者
applicant member 申請会員
application 申請
application agent 申込代理店
application coverage 適用範囲
application date base 申込日基準
application for approval 承認申請
application for delisting 上場廃止申請
application for financial futures transaction account 金融先物取引口座開設申込書
application for listing of a security 有価証券上場申請書
application for membership 会員加入申請
application for obliteration 抹消の申請
application for subscription of corporate bonds 社債応募
application for transfer by customer 顧客による振替の申請
application for withdrawal 脱退申請
application form for change 異動申告書
application form for listing 上場申請書
application form for stock 株式申込書
application hour 申込時間
application money 申込金
application money for stock 株式申込金
application of fund 資金の使途
application of overhead 間接費の割掛け
application procedure for alteration in listed securities 上場有価証券の変更上場申請手続
application procedure for initial listing 新規上場手続
application rate of overhead cost 間接費割賦率
application right 出願権
applications of working capital 運転資金の使徒
applied cost 適用原価
applied factory burden 製造間接費配賦額
applied manufacturing overhead costs account 製造間接費配賦勘定
apply mutatis mutandis 準用する
appointed day 期日
appointed goods 指定商品
appointed representative 指定代理店
appointee 被任命者
appointer 指名権者
appointing authority 仲裁人選定機関
appointment 任命
appointment of depreciation 償却費配賦
appointment sales アポイント商法
appointor 指定権者
apportion 分割
apportionable annuity 端数期間支払年金

A

apportioned tax 配賦税
apportionment 割当
apportionment base 配賦基準
apportionment of a loss 損害の分担
appraisal 評価
appraisal amount 査定額
appraisal fee 鑑定料
appraisal loss 評価損
appraisal method 評価法
appraisal method of securities 有価証券の評価方法
appraisal of assets 資産鑑定
appraisal of dutiable value 課税額評価
appraisal of securities 有価証券評価
appraisal of shares 株式評価
appraisal report 鑑定書
appraisal value 評価額
appraised capital 評価替資本
appraised price 算定価格
appraised value of collateral 担保の評価額
appraisement 評価査定
appraisement method of securities 有価証券評価方法
appraiser 評価人
appreciated market price 時価の上昇
appreciation 騰貴
appreciation duty 増価税
appreciation in value 価値の増加
appreciation surplus 再評価剰余金
appreciation swap アプリシエーション・スワップ
appreciation trend 上昇トレンド
approach 手法
appropriate 割り当てる
appropriate interest rate 適正利率
appropriate portfolio 適切なポートフォリオ
appropriated earned surplus 処分済利益剰余金
appropriated retained earnings 処分済留保金
appropriateness 適切性
appropriation 充当
appropriation bill 歳出法案
appropriation budget 割当型予算
appropriation for the deposit 預託金への繰入れ
appropriation of depreciation 償却費の配賦
appropriation of fiscal resources for redemption 償還財源繰入れ
appropriation of margin 証拠金の充当
appropriation of net income 純利処分
appropriation of profit 利益処分
appropriation of refund 還付金充当
appropriation of retained earnings 利益剰余金の処分
appropriation of surplus 剰余金処分
appropriation surplus 目的積立金
approval 承認
approval of decrease of income tax 所得税減額承認
approval of export license 輸出承認
approval of extension of time to file 申告時間延長承認
approval of filing a blue return 青色申告承認
approval of special liquidation 特別清算承認
approved bidder 指定入札者
approved expenses to be carried over to the following year 繰越明許費
approved list 承認リスト
approved list of investment 投資承認リスト
approved pension funds 適格退職年金基金
approved pension scheme 適格年金制度
approved retirement annuity 適格退職年金
approved retirement annuity contract 適格退職年金契約
approved retirement annuity plan 適格退職年金制度
approved superannuation fund 適格退職年金
approved tender 指定入札
approximate 近似する

approximate amount 概算額
approximate cost 概算原価
approximate factor 近似的ファクター
approximate market price 時価概算額
approximate price 概算価格
approximate value 概算価額
approximation 概算値
appurtenance 財産に付属する権利
APR (annual percentage rate) 年利
APS (auction preferred stock) オークション優先株
apt time 適当な時
APTC (asset pass through certificate) アセット・パススルー証券
APU (Asian Payment Union) アジア支払同盟
AR (all risks) オールリスク担保
AR (autoregressive) 自己回帰
Arab League アラブ連盟
ARB (Accounting Research Bulletin) アジア研究公報
arbitrage 裁定
arbitrage bond 裁定債券
arbitrage business さや取取引
arbitrage data 裁定データ
arbitrage house さや取屋
arbitrage margin 裁定マージン
arbitrage operation さや取売買
arbitrage opportunity 裁定機会
arbitrage position 裁定ポジション
arbitrage possibility 裁定の機会
arbitrage pricing theory 裁定価格決定理論
arbitrage trader さや取業者
arbitrage transaction 裁定取引
arbitrager 裁定取引者
arbitrary 専断的
arbitrary allocation 任意の配分
arbitrary ceiling 裁定的な上限
arbitrary period 裁量期間
arbitrary rule 加入率ルール
arbitrated exchange rate 裁定為替相場
arbitrated rate 裁定相場
arbitration 仲裁
arbitration award 仲裁裁定
arbitration clause 仲裁条項
arbitration in stock サヤ取り
arbitration of exchange 為替裁定
arbitration panel 仲裁委員会
arbitration proceedings 仲裁手続
arbitrator 仲裁人
area coverage 対象分野
area franchise 地域フランチャイズ
area to welcome enterprise 企業誘致地域
arena 立会場
ARIA (American Risk and Insurance Association) ARIA
arithmetic average 単純平均
arithmetic dividend yield average 単純平均利回り
arithmetic mean 算術平均
arithmetic stock price average 単純平均株価
arm's length 独立第三者間取引条件で
arm's length price 独立企業間価格
arm's length principle 独立企業間の原則
arm's length transaction 通常の第三者間取引
ARMA (autoregressive moving average) model 自己回帰移動平均モデル
ARP (adjusted rate preferred stock) 配当率調整優先株
arrangement 債務整理
arranger 斡旋人
arranger fee アレンジャー料
arrear swap アリアー・スワップ
arrearages 延滞
arrears coupon 繰延利札
arrears of local tax 地方税の延滞金
arrival draft 到着後一覧払手形
arrival of shipment 着荷
ARS (Argentine peso) アルゼンチン・ペソ
article 商品
article of the peace 安全保証申立
article on the free list 関税免除品

A

article subject to taxation 課税品
articled clerk 実務修習生
articles in custody 保管品
articles of agreement 契約覚書
articles of association 寄付行為；定款
articles of confederation 連合規約
articles of incorporation 会社定款
Articles of Incorporation of the Tokyo Stock Exchange, Inc. 株式会社東京証券取引所定款
articles of partnership 組合定款
artificial construct 人工的な構成概念
artificial currency 人為的通貨
artificial presumptions 法律的推定
artificial statement 多桁式計算書
artificially 専門的に
as at ・・・日現在
as occasion demands 随時必要に応じて
as per specifications attached 添付明細書通り
as previously reported 修正前の
as spent project cost 実払プロジェクトコスト
ASA (American Standards Association) アメリカ規格協会
ASB (Auditing Standards Board) 監査基準審議会
ASC (All Savers Certificate) ASC
ascending 上昇
ascending curve 上昇カーブ
ascending order 昇順
ascending pattern triangle 上昇トライアングル
ascending tops アセンディング・トップス
ascertain 確かめる
ASD (Accounting Standards Division) 会計部会
ASE (Athens Stock Exchange) アテネ証券取引所
ASEAN (Association of South East Asian Nations) 東南アジア諸国連合会
Asia pacific Economic Cooperation アジア太平洋経済協力会議
Asian Clearing Union アジア清算同盟
Asian Development Bank アジア開発銀行
Asian dollar アジアダラー
Asian dollar bond アジアドル債
Asian dollar market アジアダラー市場
Asian option アジア型オプション
Asian regional currencies アジア通貨
Asian Reserve Bank アジア準備銀行
asked price 売呼値
asked quotation 売り気配；ヤリ気配
asked rate 売値段レート
ASOSAI (Asian Organization of Supreme Audit Institutions) 最高会計検査機関アジア地域機構
aspiration 願望
aspiration level 希求水準
ASR (Accounting Series Release) 会計連続通牒
assault on September's high 9月の高値の突破
assay office 純分検定所
assembly cost 組立費
assembly cost system 組立原価計算
assembly department 組立部門
assembly industry 組立工業
assembly order 組立指図書
assembly order sheet 組立順位表
assembly process 組立工程
assembly production order 組立命令書
assent 受諾
assert claims 抗弁する
assertion 主張
assertory covenants 確認的約束
assess 見積る
assessable income 課税所得
assessable insurance 追徴可能保険
assessable securities 券面外責任付証券
assessed amount 査定額
assessed income 査定所得額
assessed level 評価水準
assessed market value 時価評価額
assessed tax 課税金

assessed valuation 評価価値
assessed value 査定価額
assessee 被査定者
assessing organ 査定機関
assessment 評価
assessment and collection 賦課徴収
assessment and decision 賦課決定
assessment by estimation on the basis of the size of business 外形課税
assessment insurance 賦課保険
assessment of damages 損害賠償額の査定
assessment of economic and financial situation 景況判断
assessment of income tax 申告所得税
assessment of market timing 市場タイミング評価
assessment of the business 事業の評価
assessment of the effectiveness 有効性の評価
assessment plan 評価方式
assessment rate 掛目
assessment rate of collateral 担保掛目
assessment roll 課税原簿
assessor 鑑定人
asset account 資産勘定
asset accounting 資産会計
asset accumulation 資産積立
asset acquisition 資産買取
asset allocation 資産配分
asset allocation mutual fund 資産分配型ミューチュアル・ファンド
asset allocation technique 資産分配法
asset and equities 資産と持分
asset approach アセット・アプローチ
asset assessment 資産査定
asset base swap アセット・ベース・スワップ
asset based commission 資産ベースの手数料
asset basis 資産基準
asset book value 資産簿価
asset bubble 資産のバブル
asset by segment セグメント別資産
asset capitalization 資産計上
asset change 資産の変動
asset class 資産クラス
asset class target アセット・クラス・ターゲット
asset component 資産構成部分
asset coverage 資産担保率
asset deflation 資産デフレ
asset deterioration 資産の悪化
asset devaluation 資産評価切り下げ
asset differentials 資産格差
asset disposition 資産処分
asset distribution 資産分布
asset diversification 資産分散
asset effect 資産効果
asset efficiency 資産効率
asset finance アセット・ファイナンンス
asset for investment purposes 投資目的資産
asset for sale 販売目的資産
asset freeze 資産凍結
asset gap 資産格差
asset given up 引渡資産
asset income 資産所得
asset item 資産項目
asset life 資産耐用年数
asset limit 資産限度
asset management 資産運用
asset management account 資産管理総合口座
asset management policy 資産管理方針
asset mix 資産構成
asset outflow 資産の流出
asset period guidelines 資産耐用年数指針
asset play 含み資産株
asset pool 資産プール
asset pool segment 資産セグメント
asset portfolio 資産構成
asset position 資産状態
asset preference 資産選好
asset price 資産価格
asset pricing model 資産価格評価モデル

A

asset quality 資産内容；資産の質
asset received 受入資産
asset register 資産台帳
asset rental agreement 資産賃貸借契約
asset reserves 資産引当金
asset reshuffling 資産移替
asset return (ratio) 資産収益率
asset revaluation 資産再評価
asset revaluation law 資産再評価法
asset revaluation tax 資産再評価税
asset risk 資産リスク
asset sales 資産売却
asset securitization 資産証券化
asset selection 資産の選択
asset self-assessment criteria 資産自己査定基準
asset settlement 資産決済
asset shift 資産シフト
asset specific rate 資産の特定利率
asset stripper 解体屋
asset stripping 資産解体
asset structure 資産構成
asset swap アセット・スワップ
asset swap transaction アセット・スワップ取引
asset transfer 資産移管
asset turnover ratio 資産回転率
asset utilization 資産活用
asset value 資産価値
asset write down 資産評価減
asset-backed bond 資産担保債券
asset-backed securities 資産担保証券
asset-backed stock 含み資産株
asset-by-asset approach 資産別アプローチ
Asset-Liability Management Office 資金企画室
asset-pass-through certificate アセット・パス・スルー証券
asset-utilization ratios 資産活用率
assets 資産
assets acquired and liabilities assumed 取得した資産及び引受けた負債
assets and equities 資産と持ち分
assets and liabilities 資産と負債
assets attached to business 事業用資産
assets available-for-sale 売却可能資産
assets carried at fair value 公正価値で計上される資産
assets held for disposition 処分目的保有資産
assets money 資産貨幣
assets of choice 投資選択資産
assets of equal value 等価資産
assets off the book 簿外資産
assets pledged as a security 担保として提供されている資産
assets pledged as security 担保差入資産
assets revaluation tax 再評価税
assets subject to lien 担保差入れ資産
assets to be transferred 継承資産
assets under the lease リース資産
assets-backed securities 資産担保型証券
assign 譲渡する
assignable 譲渡可能な
assigned account 担保勘定
assigned accounts receivable 割当債権
assigned amount 担保提供額
assigned risk plan 割当危険分担制度
assigned surplus 特別積立剰余金
assignee 受託者；譲受人
assignment 譲渡
assignment and transfer 譲渡及び移転
assignment at lower-than-proper price 低廉譲渡
assignment charge 譲渡手数料
assignment clause 譲渡条項
assignment expense 割当費用
assignment fee 譲渡手数料
assignment for the benefit of creditors 債権者の利益のための財産権の移転
assignment in blank 白地譲渡
assignment notice 譲渡通知
assignment of accounts receivable 債権譲渡
assignment of business 営業権譲渡
assignment of exercise 権利行使の割当

assignment of listed stocks to sections 上場株券の所属部の指定
assignment of receivables 債権譲渡
assignment of rights 権利譲渡
assignment of sales contract 売買契約の譲渡
assignment of settlement duties 決済の委任
assignment of stock 株式譲渡
assignment order 転付命令
assignment proceeds 譲渡代金
assignor 譲渡者
assimilation 同化
assist 援助する
assistance 援助
assistant certified public accountant 会計士補
Assistant Chief 国税実査官
Assistant Commissioner (Examination and Criminal Investigation) 調査査察部部長
Assistant Commissioner (Planning, Information System Management, Liquor Tax and Industry) 審議官（酒税等担当）
Assistant Commissioner (Revenue Management and Collection) 徴収部部長
Assistant Commissioner (Taxation) 課税部部長
assisted acquisition 救済合併方式
associate アソシエート；関連会社；組合員
associate member アソシエート会員
associated bank 組合銀行
associated company 関連会社
associated fear 関連した懸念
associated probability 関連する確率
associated risk 関連リスク
association 協会
Association Cambiste Internationale 商業会議所
association insurance 団体提供保険
Association of Average Adjusters 海損人協会
Association of Call Loan and Discount Companies 短資協会
Association of Compensation Fund for Consigned Liabilities in Commodity Futures, Inc. 商品取引受託債務補償基金協会
Association of Insurance and Financial Analysts 保険・財務アナリスト協会
Association of International Accountants 国際会計専門家協会
Association of International Bond Dealers 国際債券ディーラー協会
Association of Life Insurance Medicine of Japan 日本保険医学会
Association of South-East Asian Nations 東南アジア諸国連合
associative pension 組合年金
assortment of goods 商品構成
assume 引継ぐ
assumed amount 引受金
assumed bond 保証社債
assumed liability 引継負債
assumed reinsurance 引受再保険
assumed settling day 仮決算日
assuming financial institutions 承継金融機関
assumption of accounting 会計上の仮定
assumption of guarantee 保証の引受け
assumption of liabilities of securities 有価証券債務引受け
assumption of liability 負債の引受け
assumption of risk 危険負担の引受け
assumption reinsurance 総括引受再保険
assumptions 仮定値
assurance 保険
assurance of bill 手形保証
assurance of fairness 公正の確保
assured 被保険者
assured payment mechanism 保証決済方式
assured payment obligation 保証決済債務

assurfinance 保険・金融総合化
ASX (Australia Stock Exchange) オーストラリア証券取引所
asymmetric 非対称の
asymmetry 不均衡
asymmetry of information 情報の非対称性
asynchronous settlement 非同時決済
at a decrease in price 値下がり局面で
at a discount 額面以下
at a premium 額面以上
at an increase in price 値上がり局面で
at arm's length 第三者間取引条件で
at cost 原価で
at four year intervals 四年に一度の割合で
at issue 争点に達した
at loan origination ローン設定時
at low ebb 冷え込む
at maturity buckets 残存期間毎に
at odds with 相容れない
at one's own discretion 任意に
at par 額面通り
at regular intervals 一定期間ごとに
at risk アット・リスク
at sight buying rate 一覧払手形買相場
at sight buying rate with credit 信用状付一覧払手形買相場
at sight rate 一覧払い相場
at the beginning of period 期首で
at the beginning of the year 期首の
at the bounds 上下幅内
at the close of the market 引け際
at the date of issue 公表日
at the end of period 期末で
at the market 成行き
at the money アット・ザ・マネー
at the opening order 寄付値注文
at the time of the extension 延長時
at-closing price transactions 終値取引
at-market アット・マーケット
ATB (Accounting Terminology Bulletin) 会計用語公報
ATM (automated teller machine) 自動預金受払機
atomic power plant construction reserve 原子力発電工事償却準備金
ATP (arbitrage trading program) 裁定取引プログラム
ATS (Austria schilling) オーストリア・シリング
attach 差押える
attachable 差押えできる
attached document 添付書類
attached goods 差押物件
Attached Organizations 特別の機関
attached schedule 付表
attachment 差押え；付属書類
attachment for delinquent tax 滞納処分
attachment of lien 抵当権設定
attachment of the risk リスク・アタッチ
attain 達成する
attainable 達成可能な
attained age 到達年齢
attempt of the 400 mark 400を試す展開
attendance 立会
attendance allowance 介護手当
attendant term 延期賃借権
attest 証明する
attest function 監査証明機能
attest service アテスト業務
attestation 真正の証明
attested copy 認証謄本
attested document 公正証書
attested witness 証明証人
attitude 態度
attorney 弁護士
attorney in fact 代理人
attorney's lien 弁護士リーエン
attractive 妙味のある
attractive trading opportunity 絶好の買い場
attributable cost 帰因する原価
attributable income principle 帰属主義
attributable interest 帰属持ち分

attributable profit 帰属利益
attribute 属性
attribute sampling 属性標本抽出
attributed to 帰属する
attribution analysis 帰因分析
attribution method 配分方法
attribution of benefit 給付の帰属
attribution of income 所得の帰属
attribution of income of business office 事業所所得の帰属
attribution period 帰属期間
auction 競争売買；公募入札
auction clearing yield 落札利回り
auction date 入札日
auction market オークション市場；競売市場
auction methodology 価格競争入札の方法
auction of government bond 国債の入札
auction period 入札期間
auction rate 配当率入札
auction rate preferred stock 配当率入札方式優先株
auction sale 競売
auction stock オークション銘柄
auction system オークション・システム
auctioneer 競売人
auctioning of policies 保険証券の競売
AUD (Australian dollar) オーストラリア・ドル
AUD (Kiribati dollar) キリバス・ドル
audience オーディエンス
audit 監査
audit certificate 監査証明書
audit certification 監査証明
audit committee 監査委員会
audit committee type 監査委員会型
audit corporation 監査法人
audit engagement letter 監査契約書
audit evidence 監査証拠
audit fee 監査報酬
audit file 監査調書
audit firm 監査事務所
audit of banks 銀行監査
audit on bank account 銀行調査
audit on property 財産の調査
audit opinion 監査意見
audit procedure 監査手続
audit report of certified public accountant 公認会計士による監査報告書
audit reporting standards 監査報告基準
audit representation 監査表明
audit risk 監査リスク
audit the books 帳簿を監査する
audit time 監査時期
audit timing 監査のタイミング
audit trail 監査証跡
audit working paper 監査調書
audit year 監査年度
auditability 監査可能性
audited amount 監査済金額
audited financial statements 監査済財務諸表
auditing 会計監査
auditing practice standards 監査実務基準
auditing procedure 監査手続
auditing process 監査処理
auditing theory 監査理論
auditor 監査役；監事
auditor of TSE 東証監事
auditor's independence 監査人の独立性
auditor's liability 監査人の責任
auditor's opinion 監査人の意見
auditors' independence 監査人の独立性
auditors' liability 監査人の責任
augmentation 収入増加
augmentation of earnings 収益増加
Aussie bond 豪ドル債
Aussie dollar 豪ドル
austere budget 緊縮予算
austere fiscal policy 緊縮財政
Austraclear Limited オーストラリア保管振替機構；オーストラクリア

A

Australian Accounting Research Foundation オーストラリア会計研究財団
authentic 真正な
authenticate 認証する
authentication 認証
authenticity 真贋
authorities 当局
authority 権限
authority bond 公社公団債
authority of correction or determination 更正・決定の処分庁
authority to conduct on-site inspections 立入検査権
authority to inquire and inspect 質問検査権
authority to pay 手形授権書
authority to purchase 手形買取授権書
authority to require submission of report and materials 資料提出請求権
authorization 認可
authorization by law 法律の委任
authorization criteria 認証基準
authorization for issue 公表承認
authorization number 認証番号
authorize 権限を授与する
authorized agency 公認機関
authorized agent 指定代理人
authorized bank 公認銀行
authorized bond 授権社債
authorized capital 授権資本
authorized control level 公認規制水準
authorized dealer 公認ディーラー
authorized deferred payment 延納
authorized for publication 公表が認可された
authorized foreign exchange bank 外国為替公認銀行
authorized investment list 投資許可リスト
authorized shares 授権株式
auto sales 自動車販売台数
auto-backed deal 自動車ローン証券
auto-regressive model 自己回帰モデル
autocorrelation 自己相関
autography 自署
automated bond system 自動債券取引システム
automated clearing 自動手形交換
automated order entry system 自動注文入力システム
automated underwriting 自動引受け
automatic account transfer 自動口座振替
automatic adjustment 自動調整
automatic approval system 自動認可方式
automatic benefit increase 自動給付増額
automatic borrower 自動借入
automatic collection service 自動集金サービス
automatic extension 自動延長
automatic fund transfer 自動振替
automatic increase in tax revenue 税収自然増
automatic indexing 自動物価指数連動
automatic investment program 自動投資プログラム
automatic lender pool 自動貸出プール
automatic premium loan 自動振替貸付
automatic provision 自動的な条項
automatic reinstatement 自動復元
automatic reinvestment 自動再投資
automatic renewal 自動更新
automatic renewal time deposit 自動継続定期預金
automatic repo 自動レポ
automatic securities lending 証券の自動貸出
automatic securities lending and borrowing 自動証券貸借
automatic settlement 自動決済
automatic stay 自動停止
automatic transfer service 自動振替サービス
automatic withdrawal 自動引出
automobile accident insurance 自動車

傷害保険
automobile bodily injury liability insurance 対人賠償保険
automobile drivers' liability insurance ドライバー保険
automobile insurance 自動車保険
automobile insurance rating association of Japan 自動車保険料率算定会
automobile liability insurance 自動車損害賠償責任保険
automobile passengers' personal accident insurance 搭乗者傷害保険
automobile physical damage insurance 車両保険
automobile property damage liability insurance 対物賠償保険
automobile receivables 自動車ローン債権
automobile tax 自動車税
automotive acquisition tax 自動車取得税
automotive sales finance 自動車販売金融
automotive tonnage tax 自動車重量税
autonomous agency 独立機関
autonomous investment 独立投資
autonomous item 自発的項目
autonomous recovery 自立回復
autonomous tariff 自主関税
autonomously strong 自律反騰
autonomy 自治
autonomy of the Bank of Japan 日本銀行の自主性
autoregressive conditional heteroskedaticity model 自己回帰条件付不均一分散モデル
auxiliary book 補助簿
auxiliary fund 補助的基金
auxiliary journal 補助帳簿
auxiliary ledger 補助元帳
auxiliary rules 補助規則
AV stocks AV関連株
availability アベイラビリティ
availability clause アベイラビリティ条項
availability of bank 銀行のアベイラビリティ
availability period 資金引出可能機関
availability risk アベイラビリティ・リスク
available assets 利用可能資産
available bond 利用可能債券
available capital 利用可能資本
available evidence 入手可能な証拠
available information 入手可能な情報
available plea 有効な抗弁
available profit 可処分利益
available-for-sale 売却可能
AVC (additional voluntary contribution) 任意付加拠出
average absolute deviation 平均絶対偏差
average actual working hours 平均実働時間
average adjustment 海損清算
average age of inventory 棚卸し資産回転期間
average aggregate amount 平均総額
average balance 平均残高
average balance of acceptances and guarantees 支払承諾平均残高
average balance of loans 貸出金平均残高
average balance of securities held 保有有価証券平均残高
average balance outstanding 平均発行残高
average bond 共同海損盟約書
average career earnings 勤務期間平均給与
average clause 分損担保約款
average collection 平均回収期間
average collection period 売上債権回収期間
average consumer price index 平均消費者物価指数
Average Contracted Interest Rates on Loans and Discounts 国内貸出約

A

定平均金利の推移
average contracted interest rates on loans and discounts of all banks 全国銀行貸出約定平均金利
average contractual interest rate on bank loan 貸出約定平均金利
average cost 平均原価
average cost method 平均原価法
average cost of capital 平均資本コスト
average cost of debt 平均債務コスト
average current cost method 平均時価法
average daily balance 日次平残
average dividend of paying companies 有配会社平均配当金
average dividend paid 平均配当金
average down ナンピン売り
average earnings 平均収益
average earnings throughout service 全勤務期間平均給与
average equity 自己資金平残
average exchange rate 中値
average growth rate 平均伸び率
average income 平均所得
average index monthly earnings 平均標準報酬月額
average interest rate 平均金利
average interest rate cap 平均金利キャップ
average inventory 平均在庫
average issued 平均発行高
average life 平均残存期間
average loan age 平均ローン年数
average margin buying price 信用買い方の平均単価
average maturity of debts 負債平均期間
average method 平均法
average monthly earnings 平均標準月額報酬
average monthly trading volume 月平均売買高
average of daily figures 平均残高
average outstanding 平均残高
average outstanding amount of banknotes issued 銀行券の平均発行高
average over period 期間平均
average period 平均期間
average period of production 平均生産期間
average policy amount 平均保険金額
average premium 平均保険料
average price of competitive auction bidding 募入平均価格
average profit 平均利益
average propensity to consume 平均消費性向
average provision rate 平均引当率
average rate during the period 期中平均レート
average rate of dividend 平均配当率
average remaining service years 平均残存勤務年数
average retail inventory system 小売棚卸平均法
average return 平均利益率
average return on investment 平均投資収益
average salary plan 平均給与方式
average spot rate option 平均スポット・レート・オプション
average stock 平均在庫
average strike price option 平均行使価格オプション
average tax rate 平均税率
average taxation 平均課税
average taxation on fluctuating income 変動所得の平均課税
average term to maturity 平均償還年限
average trading value 平均売買代金
average up ナンピン買い
average value 代金平均
average volatility 平均変動率
average yield 平均利回り
average yield by types of industry 業種別利回り
average yield of listed stocks 上場株式平均利回り
averaged type forward contract アベ

レージタイプ先物為替予約
averaging ナンピン
aversion 回避
aviation fuel tax 航空機燃料税
aviation hull insurance 機体保険
aviation insurance 航空保険
avoidable cost 回避可能原価
avoidable interest 回避可能利息
avoidable risk 排除可能リスク
AVR (asset valuation reserve) 資産評価準備金
away from the market 乖離注文
AWB (air way bill) 航空貨物運送状
AWG (Aruba florin) アルバ・フローリン
axiom 公理
axis 機軸
AZM (Azerbaijan manat) アゼルバイジャン・マナト

B

B

B-piece deal 劣後案件
BA (bank acceptance) 銀行引受手形
BA rate BA レート
baby bond 少額債券
baby fund ベビー・ファンド
back bond 損失補償証書
back dating 後ろの日付にする
back dividend 遡及払い配当金
back door listing 裏口上場
back end benefit 後払給付
back end load 解約手数料
back loaded 手数料後取りの
back money 延滞金
back months 期先物
back office バックオフィス
back pay 遡及的給与
back rent 滞納家賃
back spread 逆ざや
back tax 滞納税
back to back credit バック・ツー・バック信用状
back to back transaction バック・ツー・バック取引
back up 急反転
back-end load charge 後払手数料
back-to-back loan バック・ツー・バック・ローン
back-up facility バックアップ・ファシリティ
back-up line バックアップ・ライン
backdrop 背景
backed up market 急反転市場
background information 背景的事項
background material 背景説明資料
background of conclusions 結論の背景
backing 裏書
backing assets 担保資産
backlog 滞貨
backlog of orders 手持注文
backup withholding 予備源泉徴収
backward countries 後進国
backward difference 後方差分近似値
backward difference approximation 後方差分払人
backward integration 後方統合
backward needs 後向ニーズ
backwardation market 逆ざや相場
backwardation rate 逆日歩
BAD (Bosnia-Herzegovina marka) ボスニア・ヘルツェゴビナ・マルカ
bad debt 貸倒金；不良債権
bad debt account 貸倒勘定
bad debt caused by insolvency 支払不能による貸倒れ
bad debt caused by the legal effect 法律的な消滅による貸倒れ
bad debt expense 貸倒費用
bad debt loss 貸倒損失
bad debt provision 貸倒引当金
bad debt ratio 不良債権率
bad debt recovery 償却済債権回収
bad debt reserve 貸倒引当金
bad debt which runs into the statute of limitation 法律的な消滅になる貸倒れ
bad debt written-off 不良債権償却
bad delivery 不完全受渡し
bad faith 不誠実
bad loan 貸倒れ
bad member 不良会員
bad news 悪材料
bad title 瑕疵権原
baht バーツ
bail-piece 保釈契約書
bailee's liability insurance 受託者賠償責任保険
bailment 寄託
bailor 寄託者
bailout 救済措置
bailout bond 救済債

bailout clause 救済条項
bailout market 救済相場
bailout plan 救済計画
balance 残高
balance account 残高勘定
balance at the bank 銀行預金残高
balance at the beginning of the period 期首残高
balance at the beginning of the year 期首残高
balance at the end of period 期末残高
balance at the end of the term 期末残高
balance billing 差額請求
balance book 残高帳
balance brought forward 繰越残高
balance brought forward from the previous term 前期繰越
balance carried forward to the next term 次期繰越
balance certificate 残高証明書
balance due 不足額
balance form 残高式
balance in hand 手許残高
balance of accounts 勘定尻
balance of clearing 決済尻
balance of current account 経常収支尻
balance of international indebtedness 国際貸借
balance of loans 融資残
balance of monetary movements 金融勘定
balance of nonmonetary transactions 非貨幣性取引収支
Balance of Payments 国際収支統計
Balance of Payments (provisional) 国際収支状況
balance of revenue account 収益残高勘定
balance of stock loans 借株残高
balance of the amount charged to special account 特別勘定残高
balance of the unused credit 融資未実行残高
balance of transfer account 移転収支
balance on ledger 元帳残高
balance order 株金払込命令
balance per bank 銀行残高
balance reconciling type 残高調整式
balance renewal ローンの書換え
balance sheet analysis 貸借対照表分析
balance sheet approach バランスシートアプローチ
balance sheet classification 貸借対照表上の区分
balance sheet date 決算日；貸借対照表日
balance sheet formula 貸借対照表等式
balance sheet items 貸借対照表項目
balance sheet liability method 貸借対照表負債法
balance sheet treatment 貸借対照表の取扱い
balanced budget 均衡予算
balanced budget principle 均衡予算主義
balanced budget theorem 均衡予算定理
balanced form 勘定式
balanced fund バランス・ファンド
balanced fund portfolio バランス・ファンド・ポートフォリオ
balanced growth 均衡成長
balanced manager バランス型マネジャー
balanced public finance 均衡財政
balancing adjustment 平衡控除
balancing figure 差額
baling charges 荷造費
balloon interest バルーン金利
balloon maturity バルーン償還
balloon mortgage バルーン・モーゲージ
balloon payment 満期元本増加支払い
ballot 投票
ban 禁止
BAN (bond anticipation note) 長期債借換予定証券
ban call バンコール
bancassurer 総合金融サービス会社

B

band 変動幅
band and crawl バンド・アンド・クロール
band grading 保険金額帯別等級付け
band wagon effect バンドワゴン効果
bank 銀行
bank acceptance guarantee 銀行手形引受保証
bank account 銀行口座
bank activities 銀行業務
bank affiliated securities firm 銀行系証券会社
bank annuities 永久公債
bank annuity product 銀行年金商品
bank arrangement 銀行約定
bank balance 銀行預金残高
bank basis バンク・ベーシス
bank bill 銀行手形
bank bond 銀行債
bank book 銀行通帳
bank bookkeeping 銀行簿記
bank bookkeeping machine 銀行簿記会計機
bank borrowing 銀行借入
bank capital requirements 銀行自己資本規制
bank card 銀行カード
bank cashier's check 預金小切手
bank caution 銀行の警戒感
bank charges 銀行手数料
bank check 銀行小切手
bank clearing of bill 手形交換決済
bank clerk 銀行出納係
bank credit 銀行信用
bank credit agreement 銀行融資枠
bank credit card 銀行系クレジットカード
bank credit line 銀行与信枠
bank creditor 債権銀行
bank crisis 銀行恐慌
bank dealer 銀行ディーラー
bank debenture 金融債
bank debit card 銀行デビットカード
bank debt 銀行借入
bank deposit 銀行預金
bank deposit balance 銀行預金残高
bank discount 銀行割引料
bank discount basis 銀行割引率
bank discount method 銀行割引方法
bank discount rate 銀行割引率
bank draft 銀行手形
Bank Equity Purchasing Corporation 株式買取機構
bank error 銀行の誤謬
bank examination 銀行検査
Bank Examination and Surveillance Department 考査局
bank examiner 銀行検査官
bank failure 銀行倒産
bank financing 銀行融資
bank for cooperative 協同組合銀行
bank full dealing 銀行フルディーリング
bank fund position 銀行資金ポジション
bank giro 銀行預金振替制度
bank guarantee 銀行保証
Bank Holding Company Act 銀行持株会社法
bank holiday 銀行休業日
bank identification number BIN
bank in insurance 保険業参入銀行
bank insurance fund 銀行保険基金
bank insurance powers 銀行の保険業務の権能
bank interest 銀行利子
bank issuing banknotes 発券銀行
bank lending 銀行貸付
bank letter 銀行経済時評
bank letter of credit 銀行信用状
bank license 銀行免許
bank line バンクライン
bank liquidity 銀行流動性
bank loan 銀行融資
bank loan insurance 銀行貸付保険
bank loan payable 銀行借入金
bank loan secured by mortgage 担保による銀行借入
bank loan-deposit ratio 預貸率
bank mandate 銀行委任書

bank money order 銀行為替
bank of banks 銀行の銀行
Bank of Japan 日本銀行
Bank of Japan Book-Entry Regulations 日本銀行振替決済規程
Bank of Japan Book-Entry System 日本銀行振替決済制度
Bank of Japan credit 日銀信用
Bank of Japan discount rate 公定歩合
Bank of Japan Law 日本銀行法
Bank of Japan Law Enforcement Order 日銀法施行令
Bank of Japan note 日本銀行券
Bank of Japan note issue tax 日本銀行券発行税
Bank of Japan notes and deposits 日本銀行券及び当座預金
Bank of Japan Workshop on Price 物価に関する研究会
Bank of Japan's agent bank 日本銀行代理店
Bank of Spain Circulars スペイン銀行通達
bank of the government 政府の銀行
bank overdraft 銀行当座借越し
bank paper 銀行券
bank placement 銀行預入金
bank point-of-sales 銀行 POS
bank quality 銀行投資適格債
bank rate 銀行利率
bank reconciliation 銀行勘定調整表
bank reference 銀行照会
bank refinancing 銀行借換え
bank remittance 銀行送金
bank remittance bill 送金為替手形
bank reserve 銀行準備
bank senior obligation 銀行の債務
bank sponsored investment contract 銀行投資契約
bank statement 銀行報告書
bank trusted retirement plan 信託型退職年金
bank underwriting insurance 銀行の保険引受
bank usance 銀行ユーザンス
Bank's accounts 日本銀行の会計
bank's automatic accounts transfer system 銀行自動引落システム
bank's standby letter of credit 銀行の信用状
Bank's View of Recent Economic and Financial Developments 経済及び金融の情勢に関する基本的見解
bankable 銀行に担保できる
banker 銀行家
banker's acceptance bill 銀行引受手形
banker's bill 銀行手形
banker's blanket bond 銀行包括保証
banker's credit 銀行信用状
bankers association 銀行協会
bankers syndicate 銀行融資団
banking 銀行事業
banking accounts of all banks 全国銀行銀行勘定
banking business 銀行業務
banking circular 銀行公報
banking day 銀行取引日
banking department 銀行局
banking doctrine 銀行主義
banking facilities 金融機関
Banking Frankfurt バンキング・フランクフルト
banking industry 銀行業界
Banking Law 銀行法
Banking Law and Regulations 銀行法令
banking principle 銀行主義
banking regulation 銀行規制
banking risk 銀行リスク
banking service 銀行サービス
banking syndicate 銀行団
banking transaction contract 銀行取引約定書
banknote custody system 寄託券制度
banknote examination machines 自動鑑査機
banknote supply 銀行券供給
banknotes 発行銀行券
banknotes factor affecting current account balances 日銀当預増減の

B

銀行券要因
bankrupt 破産者
bankrupt entity 破産企業
bankrupt or quasi-bankrupt assets 破産更生債権及びこれらに準ずる債権
bankruptcy 破産
bankruptcy administration 破産の管理
bankruptcy administration cost 管財費用
bankruptcy administrator 破産管財人
bankruptcy and composition 和議
bankruptcy court 破産裁判所
bankruptcy debtor 破産債務者
bankruptcy estate 破産財団
bankruptcy estate equity 破産財団持分
bankruptcy filing 破産申請
bankruptcy law 破産法
bankruptcy notice 破産告知
bankruptcy of enterprise 企業の破綻
bankruptcy petition 破産申立
Bankruptcy Reform Act of 1978 新破産法
bankruptcy remote 倒産隔離
bankruptcy rules 破産規則
Banks Division 1 銀行第１課
Banks Division 2 銀行第２課
banks futures 銀行業先物
bankwire バンクワイヤー
banner 一面の大見出し；一流の
BAPEPAM (Capital Markets Supervisory Board) 資本市場管理庁（インドネシア）
bar 審理
bar chart 棒グラフ
bar code バーコード
barbell portfolio バーベル・ポートフォリオ
barbell portfolio management バーベル型運用
barbell strategy バーベル戦略
bare boat 裸用船の
bare body 裸本文
bare contract 無約因契約
bare trust 裸信託
bare trustee 受動的受託者
bargain 取引
bargain buying 押目買い
bargain counter 本来の価格を下回って売却される証券
bargain for exchange 交換的取引
bargain hunting 押し目買い
bargain purchase 割安な購入
bargain purchase option 割安購入権
bargain renewal option 割安更新オプション
bargain stock 割安株
bargain stock fund 割安株ファンド
bargain unit 交渉単位
bargainee 買受人
bargainer 売主
bargaining power 交渉力
barometer stock 標準株
barrier 障壁
barriers to entry 参入障壁
barter 物々交換
barter trade バーター貿易
base case 基本的見通し
base cost estimate 基礎的費用見積
base currency 基準通貨
base date 基準日
base date for assessment 賦課期日
base date for clearing margin calculation 取引証拠金額算定基準日
base earnings 基礎収益
base earnings per share 希薄化前一株当り利益
base EPS 標準 EPS
base free 制限不動産権
base market value 基準時価総額
base money ベース・マネー
base of taxation 課税標準
base period 基準期間
base premium 基準保険料
base price 基準価格
base rate 基本レート
base reference index 基準日の参照指数

base reference index date 参照指数基準日
base standard cost 基準標準原価
base year 基準年度
base year inventory 基準棚卸資産
base-stock method 基準棚卸法
based on round lots 端株分を含まない
Basel agreement バーゼル合意
Basel Committee バーゼル委員会
Basel Committee on Banking Regulation and Supervision 銀行規制監督に関するバーゼル委員会
baseline budget 基本予算
basic administration policy 運営の基本方針
basic allowance 基礎控除
basic amount 基礎額
basic assumption 基礎想定
basic automobile policy 一般自動車保険
basic balance of account book 基礎口座簿残高
basic balance of payments 基礎収支
basic benefit 基礎給付
basic capital 最低資本
basic convention 基本的公準
basic cost 基本原価
basic deduction 基礎控除
basic deduction for bequest 遺産に係る基礎控除
basic discount rate 基準割引レート
basic dynamics 基本ダイナミクス
basic earnings per share 基本一株当り利益
basic elements 基本的要素
basic exchange rate 基準為替相場
basic financial statements 基本財務諸表
basic industry 素材産業
basic loan rate 基準となる貸付利率
basic lot 単元
basic pension 基礎年金
basic period 基本期間
basic policy 基本方針；基本保険契約
basic precept 基本指針
basic premise 基本的前提
basic principle 基本原則
basic rate 基準相場；基礎率
basic rate of foreign exchange 基本為替レート
basic regulations 基本法規
basic research 基礎研究
basic reserve 基本積立金
basic retirement funds 基礎退職年金基金
basic salary 基本給
basic statistics 基礎統計
basic stockholder 判定の基礎となる株主
basic structure 基本構造
basic tax rate 基本税率
basic taxable year 基準年度
basic thinking 基本的考え方
basic tool 基本ツール
basic value 基本価額
basic wage 基本給
basic year 基本年度
basing consideration 重要なポイント
basing point price 基点価格
basis 基準
basis for calculation 算定基準
basis for conclusions 結論の根拠
basis for recording sales 売上計算基準
basis gap ベーシス・ギャップ
basis market ベーシス・マーケット
basis of accounting 会計処理基準
basis of assessment 課税標準
basis of the calculation 算出基準
basis of the preparation of financial statements 財務諸表作成基準
basis on the amount of salary 給与基準
basis risk ベーシス・リスク
basis swap ベーシス・スワップ
basis to prorate local tax 分割基準
basis trading ベーシス取引
basis transaction ベーシス取引
basket バスケット
basket cross trading バスケット対当取引

B

basket currency バスケット通貨
basket of goods and services 財サービス・バスケット
basket system バスケット方式
basket trading バスケット取引
basket transaction バスケット取引
basket warrant バスケット・ワラント
batch processing 一括処理
batch trading system バッチ取引システム
BB (book-building) formula ブック・ビルディング方式
BB (booking to billing) ratio BB レシオ
BBAISR (British Bankers' Association Interest Settlement Rate) 英国銀行協会金利決済レート
BBB BBB 格
BBD (Barbados dollar) バルバドス・ドル
BC (bills for collection) 代金取立手形
BCBS (Basel Committee on Bank Supervision) バーゼル銀行監督委員会
BD (bank draft) 銀行為替手形
BD form BD 報告書
BDR (bearer depository receipt) 無記名預託証券
BDT (Bangladesh taka) バングラデッシュ・タカ
BE (bill of exchange) 為替手形
be extension of 延長上
be reluctant to sell 売惜しむ
bear 産む
bear bond ベアー・ボンド
bear bull bond ベア・ブル・ボンド
bear call spread ベアー・コール・スプレッド
bear hug ベア・ハッグ
bear index bond ベア・インデックス債
bear interests 弱気筋
bear market 下げ相場；弱気相場
bear out 裏書する
bear raiding 売崩し
bear side 売方
bear spread trading ベア・スプレッド取引
bear squeeze market 踏上げ相場
bear the market 売りたたく
bearer 持参人；無記名の
bearer bond 無記名債券
bearer check 無記名式小切手
bearer common stock 無記名普通株式
bearer debenture 無記名社債
bearer form 無記名式
bearer instrument 持参人払式証券
bearer securities 無記名証券
bearer share 無記名株式
bearer stock 無記名株
bearing date 一定日付のある
bearing duty 消却義務
bearish 先安観；弱気
bearish bet on the growth 成長率について弱気姿勢
bearish channel 弱いチャンネル
bearish consolidation patterns 弱気コンソリデーション・パターン
bearish market 弱気市場
bearish mood 弱気の地合
bearish resistance line 弱気抵抗線
bearish reversal patterns 弱気リバーサル・パターン
bearish sentiment 弱気の地合
bearish support line 弱気支持線
bearish tone 安気配
bearish view 弱気見通し
bears over 売り長
become accommodative 緩和する
become due 期限が来る
BEE (Belgium franc) ベルギー・フラン
beef up 強化する
before due endorsement 満期前の裏書
before fees 手数料差引前
before income tax expense 税引費用前の
before income taxes 法人所得税控除前
before netting 相殺前
before refund of fees 手数料割戻し前
before tax 税引き前

before the deduction of possible loan loss allowance 貸倒引当金控除前
beggar-my-neighbor policy 近隣窮乏化政策
beginning balance 期首残高
beginning day of the taxable year 事業年度開始日
beginning inventory 期首棚卸資産
beginning of the fiscal year 年度初め
behavior ビヘイビア
behavior of financial institution 金融機関の動向
behavior of inflation インフレ動向
behavior of the Nikkei 日経の動き
behavioral adjustment 行動調整
behavioral disease 習慣病
behavioral finance 行動ファイナンス
behavioral framework 行動の枠組み
behavioral theory 行動理論
beige book 地区連銀報告書
Beijing 北京市
being long dollar yen 円でドルをロングにする
BELFOX (Belgian Futures and Options Exchange) ベルギー先物オプション取引所
bellwether bond 指標銘柄
bellwether issue 指標銘柄
belongings 財産
below cost 原価以下で
below market ビロウ・マーケット
below par 額面以下
below par issue 額面割れ銘柄
below the line ビロウ・ザ・ライン
below-investment grade 低格付け
below-market interest rate 市場金利以下の
bench 裁判官
benchmark 標準
benchmark bond 債券指標銘柄
benchmark portfolio ベンチマーク・ポートフォリオ
benchmark rate 基準レート；政策金利
benchmark securities 証券指標銘柄
benchmark yield 指標銘柄利回り
beneficial association 相互扶助団体
beneficial duty 便益関税
beneficial holder 実質所有者
beneficial holders of beneficiary ownership certificates 実質投資主
beneficial holders of preferred equity securities 実質優先出資社員
beneficial investors 実質投資主
beneficial owner 実質所有者
beneficial shareholder 実質株主
beneficiary 受益者
beneficiary certificate 受益証券
beneficiary certificate of investment trust 投資信託の受益証券
beneficiary company 受益企業
beneficiary concealed disbursement 使途秘匿金
beneficiary holders of preferred equity securities 実質優先出資社員
beneficiary interest 受益権
beneficiary interest certificate 受益証券
beneficiary of letter of credit 信用状の名宛人
beneficiary of the retirement annuity 退職年金の受取人
beneficiary ownership 実質所有；投資口
beneficiary ownership certificate 投資証券
beneficiary principle 受益者負担の原則
beneficiary right 受益権
beneficiary right to real estate 不動産信託受益権
beneficiary screening 受益者の審査
beneficiary securities 受益証券
benefit 給付
benefit / years of service method 給付額・勤務年数方式
benefit analysis 便益分析
benefit association 共済団体
benefit check 給付小切手
benefit claim system 給付支払いシステム

B

benefit cost analysis 便益費用分析
benefit credited 確定年金給付額
benefit eligibility 受給資格
benefit entitlement 受給資格付与
benefit formula 年金給付額算定方式
benefit improvement 給付の改善
benefit increase 給付の増加
benefit maximum 給付最高額
benefit obligation 給付債務
benefit of loss 欠損からの便益
benefit of the doubt 善意の解釈
benefit payment 給付支払い
benefit period 給付期間
benefit plan expense 年金費用
benefit policy 給付契約
benefit principle 応益負担の原則
benefit receivable 受取給付額
benefit reduction 給付減額
benefit restriction 給付制限
benefit rider 給付特約
benefit security 給付保証
benefit security ratio 給付保証率
benefit society 共済組合
benefit taxation 扶助料課税
benign 良好な
Benin (CFA (Communauté Financière Africaine) franc) ベニン(CFA フラン)
BEO (Book-Entry-Only) 振替決済のみ
BEP (break even point) 損益分岐点
bequeath 遺贈する
bequest 動産遺贈
bereft of key data release 主要データが発表されていない
Bermudian option バミューダ・オプション
best efforts 委託募集
best efforts basis 最善努力原則
best efforts selling 委託販売
best estimate 最良の見積り
best evidence 最良証拠
best practice 最も望ましい方法
best-efforts issuance 売出発行
beta ベータ
beta adjusted ベータ調整値
beta coefficient ベータ係数
beta service ベータ・サービス
beta value ベータ値
beta value prediction equation ベータの予測方程式
betray the trust 信義に反する
better price 有利な価格
better-than-expected results 予想を上回る業績
betterment 改良
betterment expense 改装費
between the historical extremes 過去最高と最低の間
BGL (Bulgarian lev) ブルガリア・レフ
BHC (bank holding company) 銀行持株会社
BHD (Bahraini dinar) バハレーン・ディナール
bi-weekly mortgage loan 隔週返済住宅ローン
biannual 年二回の
bias バイアス
biased 偏向した
biased to the downside 下落バイアスがかかった
BIBF (Bangkok International Banking Facility) バンコク・オフショア市場
BIC (bank identifier code) 銀行識別コード
bid and ask quotation 気配値段
bid and asked price 呼値
bid and offer 呼値
bid and offer situation 呼値の状況
bid by advertising 競争入札
bid for 買いに出る
bid guarantee insurance 入札保証保険
bid price 買呼値
bid price auction 価格競争入札
bid quotation 買気配
bid wanted 応札募集
bid/offer quotation 一般気配
bid-ask spread 買いと売りの幅
bid-offer spread 呼値スプレッド
bid-to-cover ratio 応札倍率

bidder 入札者
bidding 買唱え；入札
bidding for public offering 公募入札
bidding price 入札価格
bidding up セリ上げ
bids 買呼値
bids on amount 応募額
bids on price 応募価格
biennial 2年に1度の
BIF (Bank Insurance Fund) BIF
BIF (Burundi franc) ブルンジー・フラン
Big Bang ビッグバン
big banks 大手銀行株
Big Board ニューヨーク証券取引所
big push in the downward move 深押し
big uglies 不人気株式
bigger positions ポジション拡大
biggest single day advances and declines 騰落順位
bilateral agreement 二国間協定
bilateral contract 双務契約
bilateral loan 相対ローン
bilateral net credit limit 相対ネット受取限度額
bilateral trade 二国間貿易
bilateral trade agreement 相互貿易協定
bilateralism 双務主義
bilge 船底浸水
bill 請求書；法案
bill accepted 引受済為替手形
bill accepting bank 手形引受銀行
bill accepting house 手形引受商社
Bill and Check Clearing System 手形交換制度
bill and hold shipment 請求済未出荷販売
bill at sight 一覧手形
bill bearer 手形所持人
bill book 手形勘定帳簿
bill bought 買為替
bill broker 手形ブローカー
bill buying and selling rate 手形売買レート
bill buying system 手形買入制度
bill clearance 手形交換
bill clearing 手形交換
bill clearing balance 手形交換尻
bill clearing house 手形交換所
bill collection 手形回収
bill discounted account 割引手形勘定
bill discounting 手形割引
bill drawn for sale 売出手形
bill exchange machine 紙幣両替機
bill for foreclosure 受戻権喪失訴状
bill in domestic currency 邦貨手形
bill in foreign currency 外貨手形
bill market 手形市場
bill obligatory 強制債務証書
bill of credit 信用証券
bill of debt 債務証書
bill of exceptions 抗議趣意書
bill of lading 船荷証券
bill of mortality 死亡記録
bill of others 他行引受
bill of particulars 請求明細書
bill of quantities 数量表
bill of rights 権利章典
bill of sale 譲渡担保証書
bill on demand 参着払手形
bill pass ビル・パス
bill payable at a fixed date 確定日払手形
bill payable to bearer 持参人払手形
bill payable to order 指図人払手形
bill purchasing 手形買入れ
bill purchasing operation 手形買入オペ
bill receivable 取立為替
bill sale ビル・セール
bill sent 仕向送金為替
bill to order 指図証券
billing cycle 請求サイクル
billing practices 請求業務
bills and bonds eligible for market operations 金融調節オペ適格銘柄国債
bills and checks in process of

B

collection 未収手形・小切手
bills and commercial paper purchased 買入手形
bills and notes 手形
bills discounted 割引手形
bills issued for stopgap financing 融通証券
bills market average outstanding 手形売買市場平均残高
bills purchased 買入手形
bills receivable 逆為替
bills sold 売出手形
bimetallism 複本位制
bimonthly 2カ月に1回の
BIN (bank identification number) ビン
binary option バイナリー・オプション
binder 仮契約
binding 拘束力のある
binding agreement 拘束力のある契約
binding clause 拘束条項
binding obligation 拘束力のある義務
binding sale contract 拘束力のある売却契約
binomial distribution 二項分布
binomial lattice 二項格子
binomial model 二項分布モデル
binominal process 二項過程
biological assets 生物資産
BIS (Bank for International Settlements) 国際決済銀行
BIS (Bank for International Settlements) capital ratio 国際統一自己資本比率
BIS standards BIS 基準
black box auction ブラック・ボックス・オークション
black market dealing 闇ディーリング
Black Monday ブラック・マンデー
Black-Scholes formula on option valuation ブラック・ショールズのオプション評価式
Black-Scholes method ブラック・ショールズ方式
Black-Scholes model ブラック・ショールズ・モデル
Black-Scholes option pricing model ブラック・ショールズ・オプション価格決定モデル
Black-Scholes-Merton model ブラック・ショールズ・マートン・モデル
blacklist ブラックリスト
blackout period 停止期間；無給付期間
blank acceptance 白地引受け
blank bill 白地手形
blank book 未記入帳簿
blank check 白地小切手
blank check offering 白紙委任公募
blank endorsement 白地裏書
blank stock 白地株式
blanket bond 包括抵当権付債券
blanket certification form 証券業協会包括誓約書
blanket collateral 根担保
blanket deposit insurance 包括預金保険
blanket guarantee 根保証
blanket hedges 包括ヘッジ
blanket insurance 包括保険
blanket lien 根抵当
blanket mortgage 包括的モーゲージ
blanket order 一括注文
blanket policy 包括保険契約
blanket recommendation すべての会社を対象にした売買推奨
blanket security 根抵当
blanket security interest 根抵当権
blanket system 包括担保設定方式
blazing a trail 新基軸を開く
blended insurance ブレンド型保険
blended rate 混合金利
blind entry 非仕訳記入
blind pool 委任企業連合
blind trust 白紙委任信託
bloc economy ブロック経済
block exemption 集団適用免除
block flow ブロック・フロー
block offer 一括売出
block positioner ブロック・ポジショナー
block sales 大量売買取引

block trader ブロック・トレーダー
block trading 大口売買取引
block transaction 大量玉取引
blockade 封鎖
blockbuster deal 大型債
blocked fund ブロック資金
blood relationship 血縁
Bloomberg ブルームバーグ
blotter 日計表
blotting book 取引日計表
blow-up entity 破綻企業
blowout 即時完売
BLS (Bureau of Labor Statistics) 労働統計局
BLT (build-lease-transfer) 建設・リース・譲渡
blue chip company 一流企業
blue chip equity market 優良銘柄株式市場
blue chip stock 優良株
blue chips 優良銘柄
blue collar ブルーカラー
blue form return 青色申告
Blue Return Association 青色申告会
blue return system 青色申告制度
blue return taxpayer 青色申告者
blue sky law ブルースカイ法
blunder 失策
BMD (Bermuda dollar) バミューダ・ドル
BN (bank note) 銀行券
BND (Brunei dollar) ブルネイ・ドル
board broker ボード・ブローカー
board member 理事会構成員
Board of Audit of Japan 会計検査院
board of directors 取締役会
board of education 教育委員会
Board of Governors 理事会
Board of Governors of the Federal Reserve System 連邦準備制度理事会
Board of Review 課税評価審査委員会
board of supervisors 監理委員会
board of trustees 評議会
board statement 理事会声明
board trading ボード取引
BOB (Bolivian boliviano) ボリビア・ボリビアーノ
BOC (Bank of Canada) カナダ中央銀行
BOC (Bank of China) 中國銀行
bodily injury 身体傷害
bodily injury liability 身体傷害賠償責任
body 本文
body of an instrument 文書の本文
BoE (Bank of England) イングランド銀行
bogey 達成目標
BOGS ギリシャ保管振替機関
bogus dividend タコ配
bogus stock 幽霊株
BOI (Bank of Italy) イタリア銀行
boiler room ボイラールーム
boilerplate 決まり文句
BOJ (Bank of Japan) Short-Term Observation 日銀短観
BOJ (Bank of Japan) Tankan 日銀短観
BOJ account holders 日銀当預取引先
BOJ check 日銀小切手
BOJ current accounts 日銀当預
BOJ lending 日銀貸出
BOJ net 日銀ネット
BOJ-NET (Bank of Japan Financial Network System) 日本銀行金融ネットワークシステム（日銀ネット）
BOJ-NET funds transfer system 日銀ネット（当座預金系）
BOJ-NET JGB services 日銀ネット（国債系）
BOK (Bank of Korea) 韓国銀行
bolsa 証券取引所
BOLTS (bull oil-linked transactions) ブル型原油リンク債
BOM (bill of materials) 材料明細書
Bombay Stock Exchange ボンベイ証券取引所
bona fide contract 善意の契約
bona fide cost 真正の原価
bona fide creditor 善意の債権者
bona fide holder 善意の所持人

B

bonanza 大当り
bond account 債券勘定
bond analyst 債券アナリスト
bond and debenture 債券
bond attribute 債券の属性
bond authorized 社債発行限度
bond broker 債券ブローカー
bond buying operation 債券買いオペ
bond call provision 債券の任意償還条項
bond certificate 社債券
bond classification 債券区分
bond collateral loan 債券担保金融
bond conversion 債券転換
bond conversion option 債券転換オプション
bond convertible into common shares 普通株式に転換可能社債
bond covenant 社債の財務制限条項
bond credit rating 債券格付け
bond creditor 債券権利者
bond cross holding 債券持合
bond dealer 債券ディーラー
bond demand 債券需要
bond discount 債券割引
bond dividend 社債配当
bond equivalent yield 債券換算利回り
bond flotation 起債
bond flotation market 起債市場
bond for public offering 公募債
bond form 保証証券様式
bond fund 債券ファンド
bond futures 債券先物
bond futures option 債券先物オプション
bond futures transaction 債券先物取引
bond gensaki market 債券現先市場
bond held 保有債券
bond holding 債券保有
bond in a pipeline 発行予定債券
bond in portfolio 手持債券
bond in yen issued by nonresidents 非居住者発行円建債
bond index 債券指数
bond index futures 債券指数先物
bond indexed to 連動した社債
bond insurance 保証保険
bond inventory 在庫債券
bond investor 債券投資家
bond issuance 債券発行
bond issuance cost 社債発行費
bond issuance premium 債券発行差金
bond issue 債券銘柄
bond issued 発行済債券
bond issued and purchased by offshore parties 「外－外」外債
bond issued at a discount 債券ディスカウント発行
bond issued at a premium 社債プレミアム発行
bond issued by government related agency 政府系機関債券
bond issues to substitute for government cash payment 繰延債
bond issuing bank 債券発行銀行
bond issuing cost 債券発行費用
bond issuing expense 債券発行費
bond issuing market 起債市場
bond lending 債券貸借
bond lending market カシサイ市場
bond lending transaction 債券貸借取引
bond linked to stock price index 株価指数連動債券
bond loan transaction 債券貸借取引
bond market 債券市場
bond market equilibrium 債券市場均衡
bond mathematics 債券数理学
bond mutual fund 債券ミューチュアル・ファンド
bond of affiliated company 関係会社社債
bond on tap タップ債
bond option 債券オプション
bond option at over-the-counter 債券店頭オプション
bond outstanding 未償還債券
bond payable account 社債勘定

bond portfolio 債券ポートフォリオ
bond premium 社債プレミアム
bond price 債券価格
bond price index 債券価格指標
bond pricing model 債券価格モデル
bond purchase 債券購入
bond quality rating 社債の格付け
bond rally 債券ラリー
bond rating 債券格付け
bond ratio 債券比率
bond refunding 債券借換え
bond register 社債原簿
bond return 債券利回り
bond selection option 債券選択オプション
bond sinking fund 社債減債基金
bond spread 債券スプレッド
bond structure 債券構造
bond subscription 債券応募
bond swap 債券スワップ
bond switching 債券入替取引
bond trader ボンド・トレーダー
bond transaction by investor types 投資家別公社債売買状況
bond transaction with repurchase agreement 債券現先取引
bond transactions with repurchase agreement 公社債現先売買
bond transfer 債券移転
bond trust 公社債投信
bond trust indenture 債券信託証書
bond trustee 債券受託者
bond underwriter 債券引受業者
Bond Underwriters Association 公社債引受協会
bond underwriting 債券引受け
bond unissued 社債未発行高
bond unit trust 単位型債券投資信託
bond weighting 債券投資のウエート
bond with a long maturity 長期社債
bond with common stock warrant 新株引受権付社債
bond with debt warrant デット・ワラント債
bond with stock purchase warrant 株式買取権付社債
bond with subscription warrant 新株引受権付債券
bond with voting right 議決権付社債
bond with warrant ワラント債
bond with warrant attached 新株引受権付社債
bond-stock mixes 債券・株式組合せ
bond's quoted price 債券の取引価格
bonded area 保税地域
bonded debt 債券発行借入金
bonded warehouse 保税倉庫
bonds called by lot 抽選償還当選債券
bonds held to maturity 満期保有債券
bonds issued and outstanding 債券発行高
bonds issued for daily fund raising of the national treasury 融通債
bonds of the International Bank for Reconstruction and Development 世界銀行債
bonds transactions with repurchase agreement 公社債現先売買
bonds used to finance government expenditure 財政支出を賄うための国債
bonds with covered warrant カバード・ワラント債
bonds with detachable warrant 分離型ワラント債
bonds with remaining cash flows 利払いを残している債券
bonds with warrants to new shares 新株引受権付社債券
bonds-cum-warrants 新株引受権付社債券
bonus 賞与
bonus dividend 特別配当
bonus issue 無償交付
bonus method ボーナス方式
bonus paid per employee 一人当りの賞与
bonus payment ボーナス支払い
bonus payment entered into expenses 損金算入賞与

B

bonus plan 賞与制度
bonus stock 無償株
BONY (Bank of New York) ニューヨーク銀行
BOO (build-own-operate) 建設・所有・運営
book account 当座勘定
book audit 帳簿監査
book balance 帳簿残高
book building ブックビルディング
book building method ブックビルディング方式
book closing period 決算期
book credit 売掛金
book entry 帳簿記入
book entry transfer institution 振替決済機関
book inventory 帳簿棚卸資産
book loss 含み損
book money 帳簿貨幣
book of account 勘定帳簿
book of final entry 最終記入簿
book of original entry 原始記入簿
book of regulations 規程集
book premium 表定保険料
book reserve 帳簿準備金
book runner 事務幹事会社
book transfer 口座振替
book value 帳簿価格
book value method 簿価方式
book value of assets 資産の帳簿価額
book value of bond 債券の帳簿価額
book value of properties suffering damage 被害資産の帳簿価額
book value per old stock 旧株一株の帳簿価額
book value per share 一株当り純資産
book value stock purchase plan 簿価株式購入制度
book yield 簿価利回り
book-entry agency 受寄機関
Book-entry JGSs 振決国債
book-entry securities 振替決済証券
book-entry securities transfer service 証券振替決済サービス
book-entry settlement 口座振替決済
book-entry system 振替決済システム
book-entry system for bond 債券保管振替決済制度
book-entry transfer 振替決済
book-entry transfer fee 振替手数料
book-entry transfer of stock certificates 株券の振替
book-entry transfer system 振替決済制度
book-keeping institution 口座を管理する機関
booking 帳簿記入
booking center 記帳場所
bookkeeping 簿記
bookkeeping by double entry 複式記帳法
bookkeeping machine 記帳機
books of account 会計帳簿
boom 好況
boom and bust 大相場
boom town 新興都市
boomer 景気をあおる
boomerang effect ブーメラン効果
booming にわか景気の
boost 景気付け
boost to the sentiment センチメントの改善
boosting 刺激する
BOOT (build-own-operate-transfer) 建設・所有・運営・譲渡
booth ブース
border line risk 境界危険
border tax adjustment 国境税調整
bordereau 再保険報告書
borrowed capital 他人資本
borrowed fund 借入金
borrowed reserves 借入準備
borrowed share 借株式
borrowed stock 借株
borrowed transactions 貸借取引
borrower 借手
borrower category 債務者区分
borrower classification 債務者分類
borrower credit 借手の信用力

borrower demographics 借手の人口構成
borrower migration 借手の移動
borrower's creditworthiness 借手の信用度
borrower's solvency 債務者の支払能力
borrowing 借入金
borrowing account 借入金勘定
borrowing arrangement 借入協定
borrowing at a floating rate 変動金利借入
borrowing cost 借入コスト
borrowing demand 借入需要
borrowing facility 借入枠
borrowing fund 借入資金
borrowing in advance 前借り
borrowing limit 借入限度
borrowing of funds against securities collateral 有価証券担保借入
borrowing of JGBs against cash collateral (JGB repos) 国債借入オペ
borrowing power of securities 有価証券借入能力
borrowing rate 調達金利
borrowing requirement 借入所要額
borrowing short 短期借り
borrowing with collateral 担保付借入
BOS (build-own-sale) 建設・所有・売却
Boston Stock Exchange ボストン証券取引所
BOT (build-operate-transfer) 建設・運営・譲渡
both days included 両端入れ
bottle-neck inflation ボトルネック・インフレーション
bottom 底
bottom fishing 底値買い
bottom line 業績
bottom out 底入れする
bottom price 底値
bottom reversal day ボトム・リバーサル・デー
bottom straddle ボトム・ストラドル
bottom vertical combination ボトム・バーティカル・コンビネーション
bottom-up budget 積上げ予算
bottom-up forecasting ボトム・アップ型予測
bottom-up process ボトムアップ型
bottoming out 底入れ
bought deal 一括買入れ
bought for cash 現金仕入
bought ledger 仕入れ台帳
bounce 不渡返却
bounce from 回復する
bouncing off three month lows 過去3カ月の安値からの反発
boundary 境界線
bounds 境界
bounty 奨励金
bourgeoisie 中産階級
bourse 取引所
bourse tax 取引所税
bourse transaction tax 取引所取引税
boutique 専門証券会社
box 保管箱
box office revenue 興行収入
box spread ボックス・スプレッド
Box-Jenkins method ボックス・ジェンキンス法
BOY (beginning of year) 期首
bp (basis point) ベーシス・ポイント
BP (bill payable) 支払手形
BPC (bearer participation certificate) 無記名参加証券
BPS (book-value per share) 一株当り簿価
BR (bill receivable) 受取手形
bracket creep 料率段階の変更
Brady plan ブレイディ構想
brain drain 頭脳流出
branch 支店
branch account 支店勘定
branch accounting 支店会計
branch banking system 支店銀行制度
branch handling foreign exchange business 外国為替取扱支店
branch ledger 支店元帳

B

branch system 支社制度
brand item ブランド品
brand name 商標
brand-named item 銘柄品
brass coins (5 yen) 黄銅貨幣（5 円）
brass-plate office 表札だけの店
breach 違反
breach of 2001 lows 2001 年の最安値を割込む
breach of close 不法立入
breach of confidence 秘密漏洩
breach of contract 契約違反
breach of covenant 捺印証書契約の違反
breach of duty 義務違反
breach of fiduciary duty 信託義務違反
breach of law 法律違反
breach of privilege 特権濫用
breach of promise 違約
breach of trust 信義違反
breach of warranty 保証違反
breach the required level 基準を下回る
breach the resistance line 下値抵抗線を割込む
breaches of ¥10,000 1 万円の上抜け
breadth 広さ
breadth of the market 市場の深度
break even equation 損益分岐等式
break out 下抜け
break-down 内訳
break-even analysis 損益分岐分析
break-even bond price 損益分岐債券価格
break-even chart 損益分岐図表
break-even line 採算水準
break-even point analysis 損益分岐点分析
break-even price 損益分岐値段
break-even repo rate ブレークイーブン・レポ・レート
break-even time 損益分岐期間
break-even yield 損益分岐利回り
break-up value 清算価値
breakage 破損
breakdown 崩壊
breakdown by industry 業種別内訳
breakdown of revenue and expenditure of general account 一般会計歳入歳出内訳
breed of product 新種商品
Bretton Woods ブレトンウッズ
Bretton Woods Agreement ブレトンウッズ協定
bribery 贈収賄
bridge finance つなぎ融資
bridge loan ブリッジ・ローン
bridge settlement ブリッジ決済
bridging exchange つなぎ為替
bridging pension つなぎ年金
brief 準備書面
brief of title 財産贈与書類
brief rally 一時的反騰
briefing 説明会
bring forward 繰越す
bring over 引渡す
brisk market 活況市場
brisk recovery 順調な回復
British Accounting Association 英国会計協会
British Banker's Association 英国銀行協会
British Export Trade Research Organization 英国貿易振興会
British Pound crisis ポンド危機
BRL (Brazilian real) ブラジル・リアル
broad based stock index 総合株価指数
broad market 大商い
broad market index 広範囲の市場インデックス
broad money ブロードマネー
broad tape 電光情報板
broader employee stock ownership 拡大従業員持株制度
broader portfolio ポートフォリオの分散
broadly-defined liquidity 広義流動性
broken term 特定期間渡し
broker ブローカー
broker agent 株式取引員

broker dealer ブローカー・ディーラー
broker loan ブローカーへの貸付
broker loan rate 証券担保貸付金利
broker market ブローカー市場
broker's broker ブローカーズ・ブローカー
broker's business ブローカー業務
broker's call loan ブローカーのコール・ローン
broker's loan ブローカーズ・ローン
broker's loan interest ブローカーズ・ローン金利
broker's market 業者による投機相場
brokerage ブローカー業務
brokerage agency ブローカー会社
Brokerage Agreement Standards 受託契約準則
brokerage commission 委託手数料
brokerage fee 株式売買手数料
brokerage firm 証券会社
brokerage margin 委託証拠金
brokered CD 証券会社扱 CD
broking 委託売買
broking business 仲介業務
bronze coins (10 yen) 青銅貨幣（10円）
brought forward account 繰越勘定
brought-in capital 持込資本
Brownian motion ブラウン運動
BS (balance sheet) 貸借対照表
BSC (Building Society Commission) ビルディング・ソサイエティ委員会
BSD (Bahamian dollar) バハマ・ドル
BSE (Brussels Stock Exchange) ブリュッセル証券取引所
BTN (Bhutan ngultrum) ブータン・ニュルタム
BTO (build-transfer-operate) 建設・譲渡・運営
BTP イタリア国債
Buba ドイツ連銀金利
bubble economy バブル経済
buck ドル紙幣
bucket shop 場外取引店
bucketeer ノミ屋
budget 予算
budget agreement 予算合意
budget allotment 予算配分
Budget and Management Office 文書局
budget audit 予算監査
budget balance 財政収支
Budget Bureau 主計局
Budget Committee 予算委員会
budget cycle 予算循環
budget deficit 財政赤字
budget deficit reduction 財政赤字削減
budget draft by Ministry of Finance 財務省原案
budget draft by the Ministry of Finance 財務省原案
Budget Examiner 主計官
Budget Information Systems Office 主計事務管理室
Budget Inspector 予算実地監査官
budget outlay 予算支出
budget principle 予算原則
budget surplus 財政黒字
budget system 予算制度
budget variance 予算差異
budgetary account 予算勘定
budgetary appropriation 予算の計上
budgetary control 予算統制
budgetary expenditure 予算支出
budgetary procedure 予算手続き
budgetary process 予算編成
budgeted cost 予算原価
budgeted loss 予算化されている損失
budgeting 予算策定
buffer stock 緩衝在庫
buffer stock financing facility 緩衝在庫融資
builders' risks insurance 船舶建造保険
building account 建築勘定
building and loan association 建築貸付組合
Building and Property Management Office 管理室
building block 構成部分
building expenses 建築費

B

building lease 建築賃借権
building lot 建物用敷地
building lots for sale 分譲地
Building Research Institute 建築研究所
building short positions ショート・ポジションを取る
building society 建築組合
building tax 建築税
building under construction 建設中の建物
buildup 積増し
built-in flexibility ビルトイン・フレキシビリティ
built-in stabilizer 自動安定装置
BULI (three month Treasury bills) 3カ月 TB
bulk buying 生産全量購入
bulk cargo バルクカーゴ
bulk order 一括注文
bulk purchase 一括購入
bull and bear 強気・弱気
bull and bear index 強弱指数
bull bear bond ブル・ベア債
bull buying 強気買い
bull clique 強気筋
bull interests 強気筋
bull market 上げ相場；強気相場
bull position 買持ち
bull speculation 投機買い
bull spread transaction ブル・スプレッド取引
bull the market あおる
bulldog bond ブルドッグ債
bullet 一時払型
bullet bond 満期一括償還債
bullet deal 満期一括償還債
bullet issue 満期一括償還銘柄
bullet loan 一括返済ローン
bullet maturity 満期一括償還
bullet redemption at maturity 満期一括償還
bullet repayment 一括返済
bullet swap ブレット・スワップ
bullish 先高観
bullish channel 強いチャンネル
bullish consolidation patterns 強気コンソリデーション・パターン
bullish factor 強気材料
bullish momentum 強気モメンタム
bullish resistance line 強気抵抗線
bullish reversal patterns 強気リバーサル・パターン
bullish sentiment 強気
bullish support line 強気支持線
bullish tone 強気
bullish view 強気見通し
bunched cost 一括原価
Bund ブンド
Bundesanleihen ブンド
Bundesbank ドイツ連銀
Bundeskassenobligationen ドイツ連邦中期債
Bundesobligationen ドイツ連邦中期特別債
bundled banknotes 帯封された紙幣
buoyant market 活況
burden 負担
burden charge 負担金
Burden Equalization Fund 財政負担均一基金
burden hour 負担時間
burden of paying tax 納税負担
burden of payment of entrance fees 入会金の負担
burden of proof 立証責任
burden of tax 租税負担
burden of tax liability 納税義務の負担
burden rate 配賦率
burden rate of conversion cost 加工費配賦率
burden sharing 責任分担
burdens on enterprises 企業の負担
bureau 局
Bureau of Internal Revenue 内国歳入局
Bureau of Printing and Engraving 印刷証券局
Bureau of the Census 国勢調査局
bureaucrat 官僚

B

burglary insurance 盗難保険
burial insurance 埋葬保険
Burkina Faso (CFA (Communauté Financière Africaine) franc) ブルキナ・ファソ（CFA フラン）
burst 破裂
business 事業
business accountability 企業説明責任
business accounting 企業会計
Business Accounting Council 企業会計審議会
business accounting principles 企業会計原則
business activities 企業活動
business activity 事業活動
business affair 事業事象
business annuity 企業年金
business assets suffering from disaster 被災事業用資産
business barometer 景気指数
business circle 業界
business circumstances 業況
business climate 景気
business closure 事業の閉鎖
business combination 企業結合
business commence expenses 開業費
business community 経済界
business company 事業法人
business concern 企業
business conditions 景気
business conditions index 景気動向指数
business consolidation 企業連結
business continuation insurance 事業継続保険
business continuity 企業の継続性
business continuously carried on 継続的に営まれる事業
business contributing to smooth settlement of funds 資金決済の円滑に資するための業務
business contributing to the maintenance of an orderly financial system 信用秩序の維持に資するための業務
business corporation 事業会社
business cycle 景気循環
business cyclical company 景気循環型企業
business cyclical stock 景気循環株
business day 営業日
business development company 事業開発会社
business diagnosis 企業診断
business economics 企業経済学
business enterprise 営利企業
business entity 企業実体
business entity principle 企業実体の原則
business environment risk index 事業環境リスク指数
business establishment 事業所
business ethics 企業倫理
business event 企業事象
business execution 業務執行
business expansion 事業拡張
business expectation 景況感
business expense deduction 事業支出控除
business expenses 営業費
business finance 事業金融
business finance company 事業金融会社
business finder 事業の発見者
business fixed investments 企業の設備投資
business forecast 景気予測
business form 事業形態
business foundation 事業基盤
business fund 事業資金
business group 企業集団
business health insurance 企業向け医療保険
business hours 営業時間
business income 事業所得
business indicator 景気指標
business information 経済情報
business information service 経済情報サービス
business innovation 事業革新

B

business insurance 事業保険
business integration 事業統合
business interruption 事業停止
business interruption insurance 休業保険
business inventory 企業在庫
business investment 企業投資
business judgment principle 経営判断の原則
business law 事業法
business liability insurance 事業賠償責任保険
business life insurance 事業生命保険
business loan 事業金融
business management 経営管理
business meeting 営業会議
business name 商号
business office 事業所
business office tax 事業所税
business operations audit 業務監査
business opportunity 商機
business outlook 業績見通し
business place 事業所
business plan 事業計画
business portfolio 事業ポートフォリオ
business practice 商習慣
business profit 営業利益
business profit tax 営業収益税
business proprietor 事業主
business reality 事業の実体
business regeneration 事業再生
business regeneration fund 事業再生ファンド
business regeneration investment and loan program 事業再生出融資制度
business regulations 業務規程
business report 業務報告書
business restructuring 事業再構築
business results 業績
business results of the current term 今期業績
business risk 事業リスク
business saving 企業貯蓄
business secret 事業上の秘密
business segment 事業別セグメント
business segment reporting 事業分野報告書
business sentiment 企業の業況感
business statistics 経営統計
business strategy 事業戦略
business succession insurance 事業継承保険
business survey 景気動向調査
business tax 事業税
business terms 取引条件
business tie-up 事業提携
business transaction 企業取引
business trust 事業信託
business unit 事業単位
business with fluctuating profit 利益が変動する事業
business worth 企業価値
business year 事業年度
bust up deal 解体取引
busted 価値のない
busting a trade 取引を白紙にする
but-for income 仮定利益
butterfly spread バタフライ・スプレッド
butterfly spread trading バタフライ・スプレッド取引
buy 4B BB/BB の買い
buy and hold 買い持ち；長期保有
buy and write strategy バイ・アンド・ライト戦略
buy back 買戻す
buy hedge 買いヘッジ
buy high 高く買う
buy minus バイ・マイナス注文
buy on close 引値買い
buy on dip 押目買い
buy on opening 寄付買い
buy on reaction 押目買い
buy on scale きざみ買い
buy out 買収する
buy recommendation 買い推奨
buy sell recommendation 売り・買い推奨
buy side バイ・サイド
buy signal 買いシグナル

buy stop order 逆指値注文
buy term 定期保険を買う
buy-in 処分買い
buy-out arrangement 持株買取協定
buy-write strategy バイ・ライト戦略
buyer 買方
buyer's credit バイヤーズ・クレジット
buyer's guide 購入者手引
buyer's market 買手市場
buyer's over 買い長
buyer's risk 買手負担
buyer's segment 買手のセグメント
buying 買入れ
buying agent 仕入代理店
buying and selling 売買
buying and selling of foreign exchange 外国為替の売買
buying and selling of securities 有価証券売買
buying at top price 天井掴み
buying balance 買い残
buying by institutional investors 機関買い
buying commission 買付手数料
buying cost 仕入原価
buying customer 買付顧客
buying energy 買いエネルギー
buying exchange 買為替
buying offer 買申込み
buying on an yield basis 利回買い
buying on balance 買い越し
buying on commission 委託買付
buying on credit 掛買い
buying on margin 信用買い
buying operation 買いオペレーション
buying opportunity 買い場
buying order 買注文
buying position 買建
buying power 購買力
buying price 買入価格
buying protection プロテクションの買い
buying quotation 買相場
buying rate 買相場
buying rate without credit 信用状なし手形買相場
buying regular member 買付正会員
buying side 買いサイド
buying support 買支え
buying title 権原買入
buying up 買占め
buying USDJPY ドル買い円売り
buying-in and selling-out 競売買
BWP (Botswana pula) ボツワナ・プラ
by business segment 事業別
by class of assets 資産の種類ごとに
by default 契約書に書かれていなくても
by element 要素別の
by fiscal year 年度別
by geographical market 市場地域別
by income layer 収入階層別
by market 市場別の
by measurement 才取り
by mid-year 年の中間までに
by piecemeal 段階的な
by product 副次的結果
by proxy 代理人をもって
by record 記録による
by representation 表示による
by silence 沈黙による
by types of industry 業種別
by types of licenses 免許別
by types of trading 取引種類別
by-laws 細則；定款
By-laws of the Bank of Japan 日本銀行定款
bylaws for the election of officers 役員選挙の細則
bypass trust バイパス信託
BYR (Belarus ruble) ベラルーシ・ルーブル
bystander 傍観者
BZD (Belize dollar) ベリーズ・ドル

C

cabinet approval 閣議了解
cabinet crowd 不活発債券取扱業者
Cabinet decision 閣議決定
Cabinet Legislation Bureau 内閣法制局
Cabinet Office 内閣府
cabinet office ordinance 内閣府令
cabinet order 政令
Cabinet Order and Ordinances 政省令
Cabinet Order and Ordinances of the Securities and Exchange Law 証券取引法政省令
Cabinet Order of the Special Taxation Measures Law 租税特別措置法施行令
Cabinet resolutions 閣議決定
Cabinet Secretariat 内閣官房
cabinet security 不活発証券
cable ポンド対米ドル相場
cable address 宛名略号
cable credit ケーブル・クレジット
cable rise 為替の上昇
cable transfer 電信送金
CAC (Compagnie des Agents de Change) 40 CAC40 指数
CAC 40 index CAC40 種指数
CAC General Index フランス CAC 工業株指数
CAD (Canadian dollar) カナダ・ドル
CAD (Capital Adequacy Directive) 自己資本比率指令
CADE スペイン保管振替機関
CAF (currency adjustment factor) 為替相場調整係数
cafeteria benefit plan カフェテリア制度
CAFR (comprehensive annual financial report) 包括年次財務報告書
cage 出納
CAGR (compound average growth rate) 年平均成長率
calculate 計算する
calculated separately for each category 区分ごとに算定された
calculated tax amount 算出税額
calculating table 速算表
calculation 算定
calculation for division 分かち計算
calculation formula 算出式
calculation of compound interest 複利計算
calculation of theoretical price 理論価格算出
calculation table 計算表
calculator 計算早見表
calendar day 暦日
calendar month 暦月
calendar month delivery 暦月渡
calendar month delivery rate 暦月制先物相場
calendar spread カレンダー・スプレッド
calendar spread transaction 限月間取引
calibration カリブレーション
call コール；召集する
call and bill market コール・手形市場
call bond コール・オプション付き債券
call date 繰上償還日
call feature 繰上償還条項
call loan コール・ローン
call loan dealer 短資会社
call loan market 短資市場
call loan rate コール・ローン・レート
call market コール市場
call market average outstanding コール市場平均残高
call money コール・マネー
call money and discount market コー

ル・手形市場
call money market コール市場；短資市場
call money rate コール・レート
call money transactions コール取引
call on capital 資金需要
call option コール・オプション
call option contract コール・オプション契約
call option premium コール・オプションのオプション料
call option valuation and dividend コール・オプション評価と配当
call premium 任意償還プレミアム
call price 期前償還価格
call protection 償還据置期間
call provision 任意償還条項
call rate コール・レート
call ratio back spread transaction コール・レシオ・バックスプレッド取引
call risk 繰上償還リスク
call spread コール・スプレッド
call swaption コール・スワップション
call trigger コール・トリガー
call warrant コール・ワラント
call-sales merchant 訪問販売業者
callable 繰上償還のできる
callable bond 任意償還債券
callable deal コーラブル債
callable debt 繰上償還可能な債券
callable fixed-income securities コール付債券
callable insurance 解約可能保険
callable loan コーラブル・ローン
callable obligation 任意償還債務
callable preferred stock 償還可能株式
callable securities 任意償還可能証券
callable shares 消却可能株式
callable stock 償還株式
callable swap コーラブル・スワップ
callable swaption コーラブル・スワップション
callable warrant コール・オプション付ワラント
called bond 償還決定債券
calling 償還
CALPERS (California Public Retirement System) カリフォルニア州政府職員退職制度
cambist 為替手形業者
Cameroon (CFA (Communauté Financière Africaine) franc) カメルーン（CFA フラン）
CAMPS (cumulative auction market preferred stock) 入札累積優先株式
Canadian-dollar long-term bond カナダドル長期国債
cancel money 違約金
cancel order 取消し注文
cancelable 解約可能な
cancelable swap キャンセル可能型スワップ
canceled lease リース解約
canceled order 出合注文
canceling date 解約期日
cancellation 解約
cancellation before maturity 中途解約
cancellation before the maturity 期限前解約
cancellation fee 解約手数料
cancellation money 解約金
cancellation of a contract 契約破棄
cancellation of agreement 契約の解約
cancellation of approval for indirect participant 間接参加者の承認の取消
cancellation of approval of filing a blue return 青色申告の承認の取消
cancellation of contract 契約の解除
cancellation of debts of directors 役員の債務免除
cancellation of designation 指定の取消し
cancellation of filing a blue return 青色申告の取消
cancellation of register 登記抹消
cancellation of shares 株式の消却
cancellation of stock by distribution of

C

net profit 利益処分による株式消却
cancellation of treasury stocks 自己株式消却
cancellation of when-issued transaction 発行日取引の解消
cancellation request 解約請求
cancelled check 支払済小切手
candidate for assumption 継続の対象
candlestick chart ろうそく足
cap 上限
CAP (Committee on Accounting Procedure) 会計手続委員会
cap and floor キャップ&フロアー
cap interest rate 上限金利
cap loan キャップローン
cap on interest rate 金利キャップ
capacity cost 能力原価
capacity cost plan 固定費回収計画
capacity to contract 契約能力
capacity utilization rate 設備稼働率
Capex (capital expenditure) 資本的経費
capital 資本
capital account 資本勘定
capital account balance 資本収支
capital accrual 償還差益
capital accumulation 資本の蓄積
capital addition 資本的追加
capital adequacy 資本の充実
capital adequacy ratio 自己資本比率
capital adequacy requirements 自己資本比率規制
capital adequacy requirements against market risk BISマーケット・リスク規制
capital adequacy rule 自己資本比率規制
capital adequacy standards 自己資本基準
capital adjustment 資本の修正
capital and interest 元利
capital and liabilities ratio 資本負債比率
capital appreciation gain 値上益
capital arrangement 固定性配列法
capital asset pricing model 資本資産価格モデル
capital assets 資本資産
capital base 基本金；資本基盤
capital bonus 株式無償発行
capital budget 資本予算
capital budgeting 設備投資計画
capital certainty 元本確実性
capital change 資本の変動
capital coefficient 資本係数
capital commitment 資本支出契約
capital committed 受託資本
capital committee 資本委員会
capital composition 資本構成
capital consolidation 資本連結
capital consumption 資本消費
capital consumption adjustment 資本消費の調整
capital consumption allowance 資本減耗引当て
capital contributed in excess of par (value) 払込剰余金
capital contribution 資本の拠出；出資
capital control 資本統制
capital cost 資本コスト
capital credit 資本信用
capital debenture 劣後債
capital decrease 減資
capital demand curve 資本需要曲線
capital disposition 資本支出
capital distribution 資本配分
capital duty 資本税
capital equipment 資本的設備
capital expenditure 資本支出；設備投資
capital export 資本輸出
capital flight 資本逃避
capital floor 資本最低水準
capital flow キャピタル・フロー
capital forbearance 不足資本の猶予
capital formation 資本形成
capital formation account 資本形成勘定
capital formula 資本等式
capital from stock issuance 株式発行

C

資本
capital fund 資本
capital gain キャピタル・ゲイン
capital gain free of taxation 非課税の譲渡所得
capital gain fund キャピタル・ゲイン・ファンド
capital gain on transfer 譲渡所得
capital gain taxation キャピタル・ゲイン課税
capital gain yield 資本利得率
capital gains from sales of securities 有価証券売却益
capital gearing キャピタル・ギヤリング
capital goods 資本財
capital goods export 資本財輸出
capital guideline 自己資本比率基準
capital immediately after the specified merger 特定合併をした直後の資本
capital import 資本輸入
capital improvement 資本的支出とみられる改良
capital in excess of par or stated value 資本準備金
capital in excess of par value 額面超過資本
capital in real terms 実質資本
capital income 資本所得
capital increase 増資
capital increase by new shares at market price 時価発行増資
capital indexed bonds キャピタル・インデックス債
capital inflow 資本流入
capital inflow back 資金の呼び戻し
capital infusion 資本の注入
capital injection 資本注入
capital intensity 資本集約
capital intensive 資本集約的な
capital interest 資本利子
capital interest tax 資本利子税
capital investment 設備投資
capital investment intention 設備投資意欲
capital investment plan 設備投資計画
capital lease キャピタル・リース
capital leverage 財務レバレッジ
capital levy 資本課税
capital liabilities 資本負債
capital liberalization 資本自由化
capital loan キャピタル・ローン
capital loss キャピタル・ロス；資本損失
capital maintenance 資本維持
capital market 資本市場
capital market line 資本市場線
capital mobilization 資本の出動
capital outflow 資本流出
capital outlay 資本支出
capital paid in excess of par value 額面超過払込資本
capital participation 資本参加
capital position 資本ポジション
capital preservation 資本保全
capital productivity 資本生産性
capital profit 資本利潤
capital provider 資金提供者
capital raising 資本調達
capital receipt 資本的収入
capital recovery 資本回収
capital recovery allowance 資本回収引当金
capital redemption 資金償還
capital redemption insurance 元金償還保険
capital reduction 減資
capital reorganization 資本再編
capital requirements 資金需要
capital reserve 資本準備金
capital resources 資本の源泉
capital risk キャピタル・リスク
capital saving 資本節約的な
capital saving industry 資本節約産業
capital saving technical progress 資本節約的技術進歩
capital securities 資本証券
capital shares 資本株式
capital spending 資本投資
capital stock 資本金

C

capital stock account 資本金勘定
capital stock adjustment 資本ストック調整
capital stock adjustment principle 資本ストック調整原理
capital stock issued 発行済株式
capital stock paid in 払込資本金
capital stock preferred 優先株資本金
capital stock registered 公称資本金
capital stock subscribed 引受済資本金
capital stock tax 資本税
capital stock unpaid 未払込資本額
capital structure 資本構成
capital structure risk 資本構造リスク
capital subscription 出資
capital subscription to an international financial institution 国際金融機関出資
capital sum 一時支給額；資本額
capital sum benefit 支払保険金総額
capital supplier nation 資本供給国
capital surplus 資本剰余金
capital tax 資本税
capital theory 資本理論
capital transaction 資本取引
capital transactions with shareholder 株主との資本取引
capital transfer 資本移転
capital value 資本の価値
capital value method 投資支出分評価法
capital working rate 資本稼働率
capital-intensive merchandise 資本集約的商品
capital-output ratio 資本・産出高比率
capital-reconciliation statement 資本調整表
capital-subordinate company 資本下位会社
capitalism 資本主義
capitalism market economy 資本主義市場経済
capitalist 資本家
capitalist bracket 資本家階級
capitalization 資産化
capitalization criteria 資産化基準
capitalization issue 無償株発行
capitalization of accumulated earnings 利益積立金の資本組入
capitalization of borrowing cost 借入費用の資産化
capitalization of interest 利息の資産化
capitalization of interest cost 借入利息の資産計上
capitalization of loss 損失の資産化
capitalization of reserves 資本組入れ
capitalization of revaluation reserve of joint stock company 株式会社の再評価積立金の資本組入れ
capitalization of revaluation surplus reserve 再評価積立金の資本組入れ
capitalization period 資産計上期間
capitalization rate 還元利回り；資産化率
capitalization ratio 資本化比率
capitalization unit 資産化単位
capitalization weighted 時価総額加重型
capitalization weighted indices 時価総額加重インデックス
capitalize 資本化する
capitalized expense 資産化費用
capitalized health care 産業化医療
capitalized insurer 自己資本を有す保険会社
capitalized interest 資産化利息
capitalized retirement savings policy 資産形成退職貯蓄保険
capitalized surplus 資本金組入剰余金
capitalized value 資本価値
capitalized value of stock 配当還元価額
capitation tax 人頭税
CAPM (capital asset pricing model) 資本資産評価モデル
capped floating rate note キャップ付債
capped loan キャップ付ローン
capped swap キャップ付スワップ

capping キャッピング
CAPS (convertible adjustable preferred stock) 変動利付転換優先株
capsized 転覆
capsule information 詳細情報
capsule shop カプセル店舗
captive agent 専属代理人
captive finance company 金融子会社
captive insurance company 自家保険会社
capture 収集
car accident 自動車事故
car insurance 自動車保険
car tax 自動車税
card counterfeiting カード偽造
card criminal fraud カード犯罪
card discrimination code カード識別コード
card issuer カード会社
card loan カード・ローン
card member カード会員
card merchant カード加盟店
card renewal カード更新
card replacement カード再発行
card shopping カードショッピング
card standardization カードの標準化
card system カードシステム
card system of bookkeeping カード式記帳法
card-holic 多重債務
CARDS (certificates of amortizing revolving debts) クレジットカード証券
care 注意
care and custody 管理責任
care at home 在宅医療
care cost 介護費用
care fee 介護費用
care insurance 介護保険
care of works 工事管理
career agency system 専属外務員制度
career company キャリア・エージェント会社
career sum point plan 職歴総合評価制度
careless business practices 不注意な事務処理
cargo insurance 貨物保険
Carlisle Table カーライル生命表
carriage 運送費
carriage and insurance paid to 運送費・保険料込み
carriage paid to 運送費込み
carried at cost 取得原価で計上される
carried back against taxable profit 課税所得に対し繰戻し控除する
carried interest 繰越持分
carrot equity 追加購入特典付株式
carry キャリー
carry advantage キャリー面での強み
carry at 計上する
carry considerations キャリー・トレードの影響
carry differential キャリー格差
carry dividend 配当を受ける
carry income キャリー・インカム
carry on 経営する
carry out compensation 補填を行う
carry pickup キャリーによる収益
carry premium キャリー面での強み
carry return キャリー・リターン
carry trade キャリー・トレード
carryback 繰戻し
carryback of deficit 欠損金の繰戻し
carryback of loss 損失の繰戻し
carryback of losses 欠損金の繰戻控除
carryback of net loss 欠損金の繰戻し
carryforward of casualty loss 災害損失の繰越
carryforward of net loss 欠損金の繰越
carryforward of net operating loss 純損失の繰越
carryforward to the next term 次期繰越
carrying amount 簿価
carrying broker 顧客勘定を持つブローカー
carrying charge of property 財産保有費用

C

carrying cost 在庫費用
carrying value 繰越価額
carrying-in expenses 搬入費
carryover 繰越
carryover basis 繰越基準
carryover contract 繰延契約
carryover cost 持越費用
carryover of casualty loss 雑損失の繰越
carryover of deficit 欠損金の繰越
carryover of foreign tax credit 外国税額の繰越控除
carryover of foreign tax credit limit 外国税額の控除限度額の繰越
carryover of net loss 純損失の繰越
carryover of tax credit limit 税金控除限度額の繰越
CARS (certificate for automobile receivables) 自動車ローン担保証券
cartage 運賃
carte blanche 白紙委任
cartel カルテル
cartel tariff カルテル関税
Carter bond カーター・ボンド
CASB (Cost Accounting Standards Board) 原価計算基準審議会
cascade tax 累積税
cascade-type turnover tax 累積型取引高税
cascading effect カスケード効果
case 準備書面
case administration 破産の管理
case law 判例法
case law precedent 判例法の先例
case stated 事実記載書
case study ケース・スタディ
cash 現金
cash account 現金勘定
cash accumulation 現金積立
cash advance キャッシング
cash advance and loan 貸出
cash and carry 現金払い
cash and carry system キャッシュ・アンド・キャリー方式
cash and carry trade キャッシュ・アンド・キャリー取引
cash and cash equivalents 現金及び現金等価物
cash and deposits 現預金，預け金
cash and deposits banks accounts 現金預け金勘定
cash and deposits with banks 現金預け金
cash and temporary investments combined 現金投資
cash asset value 現金資産価値
cash assets 現金資産
cash at bank 当座預金
cash audit 現金監査
cash balance 現金残高
cash basis 現金主義
cash basis accounting 現金主義会計
cash basket 現物バスケット
cash before delivery 前金で
cash benefit 現金給付
cash bond 現物債券
cash book 現金出納帳
cash break-even point 収支分岐点
cash budget 現金予算
cash buying rate 現金買相場
cash capital 現金資本
cash card キャッシュカード
cash collateral 金銭担保
cash collateral for government securities borrowed 国債借入担保金
cash collateralized securities lending transactions 現金担保付貸借取引
cash collection 現金回収
cash commitments 現金支払債務
cash commodity 現物商品
cash compensation 現金報奨
cash contribution 資金供与
cash control 現金管理
cash conversion cycle 現金化周期
cash correspondent 現金決済コルレス
cash cow 高収益事業
cash credit 当座貸
cash currency 現金通貨

cash customer 現金顧客
cash cycle 現金循環
cash deficiency 現金不足
cash deficiency undertaking 不足資金負担
cash delivery 即日受渡
cash deposit 現金預金
cash deposit risk 資金預託リスク
cash deposited for payment of interest on corporate bonds 社債利子払資金
cash disbursed 支出
cash disbursement 現金支払
cash disbursement book 支払帳
cash discount 現金割引
cash dispenser 現金支払機
cash dividend 現金配当
cash dividend declared 現金配当決議額
cash down 即金で
cash earnings 現金収益
cash effect 現金への影響
cash equity 現物株
cash equivalent 現金等価物
cash flow キャッシュフロー
cash flow analysis 収支分析
cash flow before extraordinary gain or loss 異常損益項目控除前のキャッシュフロー
cash flow benefit キャッシュフロー上の利点
cash flow break-even point 収支分岐点
cash flow calculation キャッシュフロー計算
cash flow coverage ratio キャッシュフロー負担倍率
cash flow crisis キャッシュフロー危機
cash flow difficulty 困難な資金繰り
cash flow discount キャッシュフロー割引
cash flow effect キャッシュフローへの影響額
cash flow estimate method キャッシュフロー見積法
cash flow forecasts 収支予測
cash flow from financial activities 財務活動からのキャッシュフロー
cash flow from investing activities 投資活動からのキャッシュフロー
cash flow from operating activities 営業活動からのキャッシュフロー
cash flow information キャッシュフロー情報
cash flow interest キャッシュフロー利回り
cash flow ladder analysis キャッシュフロー・ラダー分析
cash flow payment キャッシュフロー支払い
cash flow projection キャッシュフロー予測
cash flow ratio キャッシュフロー・レシオ
cash flow ratio to capital expenditures 設備投資キャッシュフロー率
cash flow ratio to long-term liabilities 長期負債キャッシュフロー率
cash flow return キャッシュフロー・リターン
cash flow risk 資金繰りリスク
cash flow statement 資金収支計算書
cash flow to current liabilities キャッシュフロー対流動負債
cash flow-back 現金回収
cash forecast 資金見込額
cash forward contract キャッシュ・フォワード・コントラクト
cash forward transaction 現物先渡取引
cash generating unit 資金生成単位
cash handling clerk 金銭取扱者
cash in 償還
cash in bank 銀行預金
cash in banks and hand 預金現金
cash in hand 手許現金有高
cash in option 償還選択権
cash in transit 未達現金
cash income 現金収入
cash index 現物指数
cash inflow 現金の流入

C

cash installments 分割払現金
cash issue 現物銘柄
cash items 現金項目
cash journal 現金仕訳帳
cash letter 現金送り状
cash letter of credit 現金信用状
cash liabilities 現金負債
cash loan 現金貸付
cash management 現金管理
cash management bills キャッシュ・マネージメント・ビル
cash management practice 資金管理実務
cash market 現物市場
cash matching 現物対当
cash multiplier 現金乗数
cash on delivery 代金引替渡し
cash on delivery sales 代金引換販売
cash on deposit 預託金
cash on hand 手許現金
cash on shipment 船積払い
cash operations center キャッシュ・オペレーション・センター
cash option 現物オプション
cash or deferred arrangement 401k
cash out 現金引出
cash outgo 現金支出
cash outlay 現金支出
cash over and short 現金過不足
cash over and short account 現金過不足勘定
cash paid to suppliers 仕入代金支払額
cash payment 現金支払
cash payment journal 現金支払帳
cash position 現金持高
cash price 現金価格
cash price equivalent 現金価格相当額
cash proceeds 現金受取額
cash proceeds from issuing shares 株式発行収入
cash purchase 現金買い
cash ratio 現金比率
cash receipt 現金受取り
cash receipt book 現金収納帳
cash received 受入現金
cash received from customers 販売代金回収額
cash records 現金記録
cash redemption 現金償還
cash refund 現金の返還
cash register 現金登録機
cash remittance 現金送金
cash reserve 現金準備高
cash reserve rate 現金準備率
cash reserve ratio 預金支払準備率
cash revenue 資金的収益
cash sale 現金売買
cash sales price 現金販売価格
cash selling rate 現金売相場
cash settled option 現金決済オプション
cash settlement 現物決済
cash settlement amount 現金決済金額
cash settlement option 保険金一括受取選択権
cash slip 現金伝票
cash spread 現物債格付け
cash statement 現金計算書
cash surrender value 解約返戻金
cash tender offer 現金公開買付
cash to be paid or received for settlement 決済のために授受する金銭
cash to current liabilities ratio 現金流動負債比率
cash transaction 現物取引；当日決済取引
cash transaction agency clearing participant 現物他社清算参加者
Cash Transaction Clearing Participant 現物等清算参加者
Cash Transaction Clearing Qualification 現物等清算資格
Cash Transaction Non-Clearing Participant 現物等非清算参加者
cash transferred 移転された現金
cash value 解約価値；時価
cash value buildup 解約返戻金利殖部分
cash value insurance キャッシュ・バ

リュー保険；貯蓄型保険
cash value of coupon 利子の現金支払額
cash value pension 貯蓄型年金
cash-disbursement journal 支払仕訳帳
cash-matching techniques キャッシュ・マッチングの技術
cash-on-cash return キャッシュ・オン・キャッシュ・リターン
cash-out refinancing 資産価値を利用した借換え
cash-receipts journal 収入仕訳帳
cash-secured put 現金預託プット
cash-settled 現金決済の
cash-settled employee benefit 現金決済従業員給付
cash-to-asset ratio 現金・資産比率
cashable goods 換金性商品
cashflow matching swap キャッシュフロー・マッチング・スワップ
cashier 現金出納係
cashier's check 銀行小切手
cashier's department 現金出納課
cashing 現金化
casting vote 決定票
casual expenses 臨時支出
casual loss 偶発損失
casual relation 因果関係
casual work 臨時労働
casualty and surety insurance 損害・保証保険
casualty insurance 災害保険
casualty insurance contract 災害保険契約
casualty insurance premium 損害保険料
casualty loss 災害損失
casualty loss deduction 災害損失控除
casualty losses carried over 繰越災害損失
catalog 営業案内
catalog sales カタログ販売
catastrophe call 災害繰上償還
catastrophic loss reserve 巨大災害損失準備金
catastrophic risk 巨大リスク
catch-up adjustment 遡及修正
catching up lost ground 下落分を埋め合わせる
categories of members 会員の種類
category 範疇
category killer カテゴリーキラー
category of business 業種
category of insurance 保険種類
cats and dogs stock ボロ株
causal analysis 因果分析
causal credit 原因債権
causality 因果関係
cause 原因
cause and effect 因果
cause inducement 動機
cause list 事件目録
cause of action 訴訟原因
cause of bankruptcy 破産原因
cause of default 期限の利益喪失事由
cause of instability 不安定要因
cause proximate 近因主義
cause sine qua non 必要条件
cause this agreement to be executed 契約を締結せしめ
cause-books 事件簿
caution 警戒感
caution money 保証金
cautionary 保証債務の
cautious stance 警戒の姿勢
caveat 手続差止予告
caveat emptor 買手危険負担
caveat subscriptor 売手危険負担
caveat venditor 売手の危険負担
CB (convertible bond) 転換社債
CBD (cash before delivery) 代金先払販売
CBISSO アイルランド保管振替機関
CBO (collateralized bond obligation) 社債担保証券
CCE (current cash equivalent) 現在現金等価物
CCO (chief compliance officer) 最高コンプライアンス責任者
CCP (central counterparty) セントラ

C

ル・カウンターパーティ
CCPC (Cooperative Credit Purchasing Company) 共同債権買取機構
CCU (corporate credit unions) 法人信用組合
CD (certificate of deposit) 譲渡性預金
CD (certificate of deposit) market CD市場
CD annuity CD 年金
CD market CD 市場
CD outstanding CD 発行残高
CDO (collateralized debt obligation) 債務担保証券
CDR (Curacao depository receipt) キュラソー預託証券
CDS (cash deficiency support) キャッシュ・デフィシエンシー・サポート
CEA (Council of Economic Advisers) 経済諮問会議
cease operation 営業を停止する
cease to exist 消滅する
cedant 出再者
ceded premium 出再保険料
cedel セデル
CEDEL (Centrale de Livraison de Baluers Mobilieres) セデル
ceding company 出再会社
ceding insurer 出再保険会社
ceiling 上限
ceiling price 天井相場
ceiling rate 上限金利
ceiling system シーリング方式
cellular approach セルラー・アプローチ
cellular operation 携帯電話事業
censure 譴責
census register 戸籍
census tract 人口調査標準地域
Center for Food Quality Labeling and Consumer Services 農林水産消費技術センター
Central African Republic (CFA (Communauté Financière Africaine) franc) 中央アフリカ共和国（CFA フラン）
Central American Common Market 中米共同市場
central asset accounts 資産管理総合口座
central bank 中央銀行
central bank buying of USDs 中央銀行のドル買い
central bank discount rate 中央銀行割引歩合
central bank intervention 中央銀行の市場介入
central bank money 中央銀行マネー
central bank note 中央銀行券
central comparison system 中央照合システム
Central Cooperative Bank for Agriculture and Forestry 農林中央金庫
Central Council for Financial Services Information 金融公報中央委員会
central counterparty 中央の清算機関
central counterparty services to equities and fixed income products 有価証券債務引受業
central custody and book-entry transfer 保管及び振替
central custody and book-entry transfer services 保管振替事業
Central Customs Laboratory 関税中央分析所
central depository 保管機構
central depository system 保管振替制度
central government 中央政府
central government transfers to local governments 地方交付金
central hub 中継センター
central market 中央市場
central ministries 中央省庁
central parity 中心レート
central payment account 中央決済口座
central rate 中心レート
central securities depository 保管振替機関

central tendency 中心傾向
centralization of capital 資本の集中
centralized economy 集権経済
CEO (chief executive officer) 最高経営責任者
CEPS (convertible exchangeable preferred stock) 転換交換可能優先株
certain assets 確実性資産
certain insurance option 確定年金分割受取選択権
certainty 確実性
certainty equivalence 確実性等価
certainty of redemption 償還確実性
certificate 証明書
certificate holder 証書保有者
certificate number 証書番号
certificate of a seal impression 印鑑証明書
certificate of analysis 分析証明書
certificate of bank deposit balances 銀行預金残高証明書
certificate of completion of tax payment 納税済証書
certificate of deposit 譲渡性定期預金証書
certificate of incorporation 会社設立免許
certificate of incumbency 在職証明
certificate of indebtedness 債務証書
certificate of insurance 保険証明書
certificate of origin 原産地証明
certificate of registry 船舶証明書
certificate of reinsurance 再保険証明書
certificate of seal impression 印鑑証明書
certificate of tax payment 納税証明書
certificate of time deposit 定期預金証書
certificate of title 権原証明書
certificate of weight and measurement 重量容積証明書
certificated financial statement 監査済財務諸表
certificated securities 証書証券
certificated share 株券のある株式
certificateless municipals ペーパーレス地方債
certificates of subscription rights 新株引受権証書
certification 証明
certification of description 記載事項の証明
certification of payment 支払保証
certified abstract 抄本
certified check 支払保証小切手
certified copy 認証謄本
certified copy of commercial registration 商業登記簿謄本
certified copy of company registration 法人登記簿謄本
certified copy of real estate register 不動産登記簿謄本
certified management accountant 公認管理会計士
Certified Public Accountant Law 公認会計士法
Certified Public Accountants and Auditing Oversight Board 公認会計士・監査審査会
certified tax accountant 税理士
certified tax accountant association 税理士会
Certified Tax Accountant Law 税理士法
certifier 証明者
certitude 確認性
cessation 停止
cessation of capitalization 資産化の終了
cession 再保険付保；譲渡
cession by law 法律による譲渡
cession of an obligation 債務譲渡
CF (conversion factor) 変換係数
CFO (chief financial officer) 最高財務責任者
CFP (certified financial planner) 公認フィナンシャル・プランナー
CFTC (Commodity Futures Trading

C

C

Commission) 商品先物取引委員会
CGFS (Committee on Global Financial System) グローバル金融システム委員会
CGT (capital gain tax) キャピタル・ゲイン税
Chad (CFA (Communauté Financière Africaine) franc) チャド（CFA フラン）
chain banking チェーン・バンキング
chairman emeritus 名誉会長
Chairman of the National Public Safety Commission 国家公安委員会委員長
Chairperson of SESC 証券取引等監視委員会委員長
Chakuchi transactions 着地取引
chamber of commerce 商業会議所
chamber of commerce and industry 商工会議所
chance of living 生存率
chance of loss 損害発生率
chance to sell 売場
Chancellor of the Exchequer 英国大蔵大臣
change 変化
change at the time of acquisition 取得時の変動
change claims 変更クレーム
change date 変更日
change in accounting estimate 会計上の見積りの変更
change in depreciation method 償却方法の変更
change in employment 転籍
change in estimate 見積変更
change in foreign exchange rate 外国為替レートの変動
change in growth rate 成長率の変化
change in interest rate 金利の変動
change in law 法律変更
change in par value 額面変更
change in reporting entity 報告主体の変更
change in shareholder's equity 株主持ち分の変動
change in valuation method 評価方法の変更
change of beneficiary 受取人の変更
change of business 事業転換
change of depreciation method 償却方法変更
change of policy 保険種類変更
change of policy contract 保険契約の変更
change of risk 危険の変動
change of tax computation basis 税額計算基準変更
change of taxable year 事業年度の変更
change of the place of tax payment 納税地の変更
change of venue 管轄の移転
change report 変更報告書
changed terms 変更後の条件
changeover 切替
changes in accounting policies 会計方針の変更
changes in accounting principles 会計原則の変更
changes in behavior 行動変化
changes in earnings per share 一株当りの利益の変動
changes in equity interest 持ち分の変動
changes in estimates 見積金額変更
changes in gross margin 粗利益の増減
changes in population 人口の推移
changes in profit 利益の増減
changes in subsidiaries 子会社の変更
changes of owners of the principal 元本所有者異動
changes or correction 変更又は訂正
channel line チャンネル・ライン
channeling back 環流
CHAPS (Clearing House Automated Payment System) CHAPS
characteristic line 特性線
characteristics 特徴
characteristics of banknotes 銀行券の特徴

charge 費用
charge account 売掛金勘定
charge against revenues 損金
charge back チャージバック
charge for call 督促料
charge for collection 取立手数料
charge for collection of bill 手形取立手数料
charge for demand for payment of tax in arrears 滞納督促手数料
charge for development 開発負担金
charge for installment payment 割賦手数料
charge for remittance 為替手数料
charge off 貸倒償却
charge on securities borrowed 有価証券借入料
charge on the declining balance 残債方式
charge plate 登録番号票
charge to provision 引当金計上額
charged against 借方計上する
charged in income statement 損益計算書に費用計上される
charged to a provision 引当金に賦課される
charged to the equity component 資本部分に借方計上される
charges forward 立替払い
charitable contribution 慈善寄付金
charitable donation 慈善寄付
charitable lead trust 生前公益信託
charitable trust 慈善信託
charities and donations 慈善寄附金
chart チャート
chart analysis ケイ線分析
chart of accounts 勘定科目表
chart pattern チャートパターン
chart reading ケイ線分析
charter 基本定款；勅許状
charter contract 用船契約
charter fee チャーター料
charter party B/L チャーターパーティB/L
charter provision 会社設立許可書
charter-land 特許保有地
chartered 公認の
chartered company 勅許会社
chartered financial analyst 公認証券アナリスト
chartered life underwriter 認定生命保険士
chartered public accountant 勅許会計士
chartering broker 甲仲
charterparty 用船契約
chartist チャーティスト
chasing the JPY higher 円を買い上げる
chastity bond チェスティテイ債
chattel 動産
chattel loan 動産貸付
chattel mortgage 動産抵当
chattel paper 動産抵当証券
chattel real 不動産的動産
chatter 二重損
cheap 割安
cheap money 低金利資金
cheap sector 割安なセクター
cheap-jack 行商人
cheapest deliver issue 一番割安な銘柄
cheapest-to-deliver 受渡最割安銘柄
cheapest-to-deliver bond 受渡最割安債券
cheat 詐欺
check act 小切手法
check and balance system 内部管理システム
check and bill clearing 手形交換
check beneficiary 小切手受取人
check drawee 小切手支払人
check drawer 小切手振出人
check guarantee card チェック・ギャランティ・カード
check holder 小切手指図人
check mark 照合済記号
check register 小切手記入帳
check to bearer 持参人払小切手
check to order 指図小切手
check writer チェックライター

check-out counter 勘定口
checkable deposit 当座性預金
checkbook 小切手帳
checkbook stub 小切手帳の控え
C
checking 照合
checking deposit 当座預金
checking inventory 照合棚卸
checking of accuracy 正確性の検証
checking system 小切手制度
chemicals industry 化学業界
chest 金庫
CHF (Liechtenstein franc) リヒテンシュタイン・フラン
CHF (Swiss franc) スイス・フラン
chi-square distribution カイ２乗分布
Chicago Board of Trade シカゴ商品取引所
Chicago Board Options Exchange シカゴ・オプション取引所
Chicago Futures Exchange シカゴ先物取引所
Chicago school シカゴ学派
Chief 係長
chief accountant 会計主任
Chief Budget Inspector 主計監査官
Chief Cabinet Secretary 内閣官房長官
chief examiner 統括国税調査官
Chief Fiscal Loan Inspector 資金監査官
chief insurance regulators 保険規制責任者
Chief Internal Inspector 首席国税庁監察官
chief investigator 統括国税査察官
chief of the tax office 税務署長
Chief Officer for Budget Information Systems 主任主計事務専門官
Chief Personnel Inspector 首席監察官
chief revenue officer 統括国税徴収官
child tax credit 扶養控除
children allowance 児童手当
children's pension 育児年金
Chinese wall チャイニーズ・ウォール
chit 伝票
chit book 送達簿
chit system 伝票払制度
choice and concentration 選択と集中
Chongqing 重慶市
choppy range 荒い展開
chose in action 無体動産
chose in possession 有体動産
chronic 慢性的
chronic absenteeism 慢性的怠業
chronic deflation 慢性的デフレーション
chronic inflation 慢性的インフレーション
chronological 年代順の
chronology 年代順
chumming 仮装売買
churning 過度な売買勧誘；不正乗換勧誘
CHX (Chicago Stock Exchange) シカゴ証券取引所
CI (composite index) 景気総合指数
CIA (certified internal auditor) 公認内部監査人
CICA (Canadian Institute of Chartered Accountants) カナダ勅許会計士協会
CIF (corporate income fund) 会社収益型ファンド
CIF (cost, insurance and freight) CIF
CIF (cost, insurance and freight) price 原価・保険料及び運賃込価格
CIF price 保険料及び運賃込み値段
CIK ベルギー保管振替機関
CIMA (Chartered Institute of Managed Accountants) 管理会計士勅許協会
Cincinnati Stock Exchange シンシナティ証券取引所
CIO (chief information officer) 最高情報責任者
CIO (chief investment officer) 最高投資責任者
CIR (Cox Ingersoll Ross) model CIRモデル
circuit breaker サーキット・ブレーカー
circuit court 巡回裁判所
circuit judge 巡回裁判官

C

circular 回報
circular flow of economic system 経済循環
circular letter 回状
circulating 循環している
circulating assets 循環資産
circulating capital 流通資本
circulating fund 循環資金
circulation 流通
circulation of capital 資本の流通
circulation of cost 原価配賦
circulation of national income 国民所得循環
circulation tax 流通税
circumstances 環境
circumstantial evidence 情況証拠
circumvent 回避する
circus swap サーカス・スワップ
citizen bond 市民債
City シティ
city bank 都市銀行
city planning tax 都市計画税
civic interest 公共性
civil 民事の
civil action 民事訴訟
Civil Aviation College 航空大学校
civil code 民法
civil court 民事裁判所
Civil Engineering Research Institute of Hokkaido 北海道開発土木研究所
civil execution 民事執行
civil fine 民事上の罰金
civil group 市民団体
civil liability 民事責任
civil litigation 民事訴訟
Civil Rehabilitation Law 民事再生法
civil rehabilitation proceedings 民事再生手続
civil remedy 民事上の救済措置
civil service 公務
civil suit 民事訴訟
civilian demand 民需
civilian employed population 民間就労人口
civilian enterprise 民間事業
civilian worker 民間労働者
claim a tax refund 税金の還付請求する
claim agent 保険金支払代理店
claim and delivery 動産回復訴訟
claim cost 保険費用
claim for a refund 還付請求
claim for compensation 求償
claim for correction 更正の請求
claim for damage 損害賠償請求
claim for deduction 控除申請
claim for examination 審査請求
claim for redemption before maturity 期中償還請求権
claim for reduced rent 賃料減額請求権
claim for refund 還付の請求
claim for reimbursement 償還請求
claim for tax refunds 租税還付請求権
claim in bankruptcy 破産債権
claim in foreign currency 外貨建債権
claim management 債権管理
claim notice clause 損害通知条項
claim of payment 支払請求
claim of prepayment of income tax 予定納税額の督促
claim of redemption 償還請求権
claim of the refund of taxes 税金の還付請求
claim paid or payable 保険金
claim payable to a specific person 指名債権
claim payment 保険金支払い
claim period 求償期間
claim processing 保険金支払業務
claim rate 支払請求率
claim receivables 債権
claim similar to account receivable and loan 売掛金・貸付金に準ずる債権
claim the refund 返還を請求する
claim to cash 現金請求
claim under an insurance policy 保険契約による求償
claimant 支払請求者
claimer 権利の主張者
claiming bank 求償銀行

C

claims adjustment 支払請求額査定
claims administrator 給付金支払代行会社
claims equalization reserve 保険金支払平準化準備金
claims on borrowers 債務者に対する債権
claims outstanding 債権残高
claims payable 未払金
claims to cash 現金請求権
clarification 説明
class action 集団訴訟
class action lawsuit 集団代表訴訟
class cost 等級別原価
class of insurance 保険の種類
class of land 地目
class of securities 有価証券の種類
class of security 証券の種類
class of shares 株式の種類
class of the stock 株式の種類
class rate 同一危険群保険料率
class stock 種類株
class-cost system 組別原価計算
class-product production 級別生産物生産
classes of stocks 株式の等級
classification 分類
classification according to holding purpose 保有目的に応じた区分
classification by issuance purpose 発行目的別分類
classification by the form of JGSs 保有形態別
classification by the method of interest payment 利払方式別分類
classification of a taxpayer 納税義務者の区分
classification of accounts 勘定科目一覧表
classification of assets 資産の分類
classification of bad debts 不良債権区分
classification of clearing margin 取引証拠金の区分
classification of debtors 債務者区分
classification of fiscal years 年度区分
classification of item of accounts 勘定科目分類表
classification of securities 有価証券の区分
classification of shares 株式の区分
classification of tax 税の分類
classification process 分類過程
classified income 各種所得
classified income tax 分類所得税
classified risk 別扱い危険
classified stock 分類された株式
classified trial balance 区分式試算表
clause 条項
clause "touch and stay" 寄港滞泊条項
clause as to the binding effect of policy 保険証券の拘束力に関する条項
claused bill of lading 条件付船荷証券
clean bill of lading クリーンB/L
clean credit 無担保信用状
clean float クリーン・フロート
clean letter of credit クリーン信用状
clean loan クリーン・ローン
clean notes 新券
clean opinion 無限定意見
clear band クリア・バンド
clear days 正味日数
clear title 瑕疵の無い権原
clearance and settlement system 清算決済制度
clearance fee 出港手数料
clearance from the board 取締役会の承認
clearance goods 棚卸品
clearance of this level この水準の突破
clearing 清算
clearing account 手形交換勘定
clearing agency 清算機関
clearing agent member 清算会員
clearing agreement 清算協定
clearing balance 交換尻
clearing bank 決済銀行
clearing broker 清算ブローカー
clearing business 決済事務
clearing contract 清算取引

clearing corporation 清算機関
clearing corporation for JGBs (Japanese Government Bonds) 日本国債清算機関
Clearing Entrustment Agreement 清算委託契約
clearing for nonmember 代理交換
clearing function 清算機能
clearing fund 清算基金
clearing house 清算機関
Clearing House Inter-Bank Payment System CHIPS
clearing margin 取引証拠金
clearing margin for customer's account 委託分の取引証拠金
clearing margin for proprietary account 自己分の取引証拠金
clearing member 清算会員
clearing organization 清算機関
clearing participant 清算参加者
clearing price 清算値段
clearing procedure 清算手続
clearing qualification 清算資格
clearing system 集中決済制度；手形交換制度
clearing time 決済時
clearing transaction 清算取引
clearing-entrusted long (short) position 清算受託買（売）建玉
clearing-entrusted transactions 清算受託取引
clearing-house balance 交換残高表
clearinghouse for commodity futures 商品先物取クリアリングハウス
clearinghouse proof 手形交換決算表
clearout of longs ロング・ポジションの手仕舞い
Clearstream ドイツ保管振替機関
CLEO (collateralized lease equipment obligations) CLEO
clerical and administrative service 事務管理サービス
clerical error 誤記
client 得意先
clientele 顧客
clientele effect 顧客効果
Clifford trust クリフォード信託
climbing angle 上昇角
climbing power 上昇力
clique 派閥
CLN (construction loan note) 建設地方債
CLO (collateralized loan obligation) ローン担保証券
CLOB (centralized limit order book) 集中指値注文控帳
clone fund クローン・ファンド
close company insurance 非公開会社事業保険
close down 終値が前日終値と比較して安値である
close market クロース相場
close of the market 引け
close of the session 引け
close one's position 手じまいする
close to resistance level 限界に近づいている
close up 終値が前日終値と比較して高値である
closed account 締切済勘定
closed contract 約款の変更ができない契約
closed corporation 同族会社
closed economy 封鎖経済
closed end 追加設定不可の
closed market 閉鎖市場
closed out 手じまい
closed period クローズド期間
closed-end dual fund クローズド・エンド型デュアル・ファンド
closed-end fund クローズド・エンド型ファンド
closed-end investment company クローズド・エンド投資信託
closed-end mortgage クローズド・エンド型モーゲージ
closed-end mortgage bond クローズド・エンド型モーゲージ債
closed-end trust クローズド・エンド型信託

C

C

closed-end type クローズド・エンド型
closely-held company 非公開会社
closing adjustment 決算整理
closing all accounts in the ledger 元帳の各勘定を締切ること
closing balance 期末残高
closing balance a/c 決算残高勘定
closing contract index price 最終約定指数
closing contract price 立会終了時の約定値段
closing cost 権原移転費用
closing date 締切日
closing entries 決算仕訳
closing foreign exchange rate 決算日の為替レート
closing high 高値引け
closing inventories 期末棚卸高
closing lower 安値引け
closing net liability 期末の負債純額
closing obligation 期末債務
closing of accounts 決算
closing of the ledger 元帳締切
closing of the morning session 前引け
closing of transaction 取引の締結
closing out 手じまい
closing price 引け値段
closing purchase or sale 反対取引
closing quote 最終気配値
closing range 売買価格帯
closing rate 決算日レート
closing retained earnings 期末剰余金
closing session of the year 大納会
closing the ledger 元帳締切
closing the long position 買付の約定についての反対の取引
closing the short position 売付の約定について反対の取引
closing tone 引け味
closing transaction 反対売買
closing trial balance 締切試算表
closing-out cost 手じまいコスト
closure 閉鎖
cloud 疑義
CLP (Chilean peso) チリ・ペソ
CLU (chartered life underwriter) 公認生命保険引受人
club deal クラブ・ディール
club dues 会費
cluster analysis クラスター分析
cluster sampling 集落抽出
CMA (cash management account) 資金総合管理勘定
CMA (cash memorandum account) 資金勘定
CMBS (commercial mortgage-backed securities) 商業モーゲージ担保証券
CME (Chicago Mercantile Exchange) シカゴ商業取引所
CMF (Conseil des Marchés Financiers) 金融市場評議会
CMO (Central Moneymarkets Office) CMO
CMO (chief marketing officer) 最高マーケティング責任者
CMO (collateralized mortgaged obligation) モーゲージ担保証書
CMS (cash management service) キャッシュ・マネージメント・サービス
CMT (constant maturity treasury yield) 米国債理論利回り
CMU (Central Moneymarkets Unit) CMU
CN (credit note) クレジット・ノート
CNS (continuous net settlement) 継続ネット決済
CNY (Chinese yuan) 中国元
co-branded card コ・ブランド・カード
co-defendant 共同被告
co-finance 協調融資
co-heir 共同法定相続人
co-insurance 共同保険
co-lead manager 共同主幹事
co-maker 共同振出人
co-manager 副幹事
co-movement of corporate earnings 企業利益の共変動
co-movement of earnings 利益の共変

動
Co-ordination Division 総務課
Co-ordination Office 調整室
co-owner 共同所有者
co-ownership 共有
co-payment 共同負担
co-sponsor 共同スポンサー
co-trustee 共同管財人
coastwise cargo insurance 内航貨物海上保険
coat tail investment 追随投資
cobweb cycle くもの巣循環
cocktail swap カクテル・スワップ
COCOM (Coordinating Committee for Multilateral Strategic Export Controls) ココム
code 規程
code of conduct 行動規範
code of ethics 倫理規程
code of practice 実務規範
code of procedure 訴訟法典
Code of Procedure for Handling Trade Practice Complain 全米証券業協会紛争処理規則
codification 法典化
Codification of Statements on Auditing Procedures 監査手続概要書
Codification of Statements on Auditing Standards 監査基準概要書
coefficient 係数
coefficient of determination 決定係数
coercive 強制的な
coffers 事業資金源
COFRI (Corporation Finance Research Institute) 企業財務制度研究会
cognitive 認知的な
cognizance 認知
COGS (cost of goods sold) 売上原価
coincidence 一致
coincident indicator 一致指数
coincident series 一致系列
coins reserved for circulation 未流通硬貨
COLA (cost-of-living adjustment) 生計費調整
cold call 電話による取引勧誘
cold cash 手持ちの金
collaboration 提携
collapse 急落；暴落
collapse in oil prices 原油価格の下落
collar カラー
collar option カラーオプション
collared swap カラー付きスワップ
collateral 担保
collateral accumulation projection 担保資産の予想購入額
collateral and guarantee 担保と保証
collateral arrangement 担保の取決め
collateral assignment 担保譲渡
collateral bond 付帯証書
Collateral Center for Short-Term Money Market Transactions 短資取引担保センター
collateral commodity 商品担保
collateral condition 付帯条件
collateral consanguinity 傍系血族
collateral coverage ratio 保全率
collateral deposit 見返預金
collateral deposited in advance 据置担保
collateral export 見返輸出
collateral fact 付随的事実
collateral for defaulter's pay 確保資産
collateral for post-dated payment of postal charges 郵便料金後納担保
collateral import 見返輸入
collateral loan 担保貸付
collateral management 担保管理
collateral manager 担保マネージャー
collateral monitoring system 担保管理システム
collateral note 担保付約束手形
collateral on loans on bills 手形貸付担保
collateral on property 物的担保
collateral optimization 担保の最適化
collateral protection product 担保補償商品
collateral rate 担保付金利
collateral security 担保証券

C

collateral shares 担保株
collateral to be used for loans 貸付に係る担保
collateral trust bond 証券担保信託社債
collateral value 担保価値
collateral value of substitute security 代用証券掛目率
collateralized 有担保の
collateralized bond obligation 債券担保債務証書
collateralized call transactions 有担保コール
collateralized loan 担保付きローン
collateralized loan receivables 債権担保
collateralized mortgage obligations モーゲージ担保債務証書
collateralized overnight 有担保翌日物
collation 照合
collation of seals 捺印の印章照査
collect 徴収する
collectability 回収可能性
collected amount 徴収額
collectible 回収可能な
collectible consideration 回収可能対価
collecting agent 取立業者
collection 回収
collection agency 回収業者
collection and disbursement of funds 出納事務
collection bank 取立銀行
collection basis 回収基準
collection bill 取立手形
collection commission 回収手数料
collection cycle 回収循環
Collection Division 徴収課
collection expenses 取立費用
collection fee 徴収料
collection letter 督促状
collection management technique 回収技術
collection measure 徴収措置
collection of bad debts written off 償却済貸倒金の回収
collection of bill 売掛金回収
collection of claim 債権回収
collection of loan 貸付金の回収
collection of principal 元本の回収
collection of principal and interest 元利回収
collection of rates 租税徴収
collection of securities by purchase 有価証券買集め
collection of taxes 租税徴収
collection of written-off claims 償却債権取立
collection period 回収期間
collection plan 回収計画
collection practices 回収業務
collection rate 回収率
collection record 回収記録
collection society 簡易保険料収集組合
collective bargaining 団体交渉
collective bargaining agreement 団体協約
collective hazard 集団危険
collective insurance 集団扱保険
collective investment fund 合同運用型ファンド
collective investments 合同運用
collective pension 団体年金
collectively renewable 集団扱い更新可能
College Retirement Equities Fund 米国大学教職員退職変額年金基金
collision 衝突
color 表見上の権利
COLTS (continuously offered long-term securities) 継続発行長期証券
column form 外欄形式
columnar format 多欄形式
combination コンビネーション
combination annuity 複合年金保険
combination bond 二重担保公債
combination date 結合日
combination funding plan 年金保険信託併用退職年金
combination of equity interests 持ち分

の結合
combination of securities 有価証券の組合せ
combination order 組合せ注文
combination policy 組合せ保険
combination sale 抱合せ販売
combination strategy コンビネーション戦略
combine 合同
combined 総計の
combined account 合同勘定
combined assets 総資産
combined balance sheet 結合貸借対照表
combined contract 結合契約
combined depreciation 結合償却法
combined employer and employee 会社・従業員折半の
combined entity 結合後企業
combined equity interests 抱合せ株式
combined financial instruments 結合金融商品
combined financial statement 結合財務諸表
combined income statement 合併損益計算書
combined profit and loss statement 結合損益計算書
combined ratio 合算比率
combined results 集計結果
combined single limit 一事故あたりの填補限度額
combined transport document 複合運送書類
combining companies 結合前企業
combining entity 結合当事企業
come to a halt 一服する
come to end 終わりを告げる
come to terms 出合い
comeback from lows 最安値からの回復
comfort language 安心を与える表現
comfort letter コンフォート・レター；念書
comity of nations 国際親交国
commemorative coins 記念貨幣
commemorative dividend 記念配当
Commemorative Organization for the Japan World Exposition '70 日本万国博覧会記念機構
commencement date 開始日
commencement of corporate receivership 会社の整理開始
commencement of reorganization proceedings 更生手続の開始
commendation system 表彰制度
comment letter コメント・レター
commerce and industry 商工業
commerce and industry finance company 商工業金融会社
commerce clause 通商条項
Commerce Department 商務省
commercial accounting 商業会計
commercial and industrial loan 商工ローン
commercial arbitration 商事仲裁
commercial bank 商業銀行
commercial bank credit 民間銀行貸出
commercial bank discount and loan 市中貸出
commercial bank money 市中銀行マネー
commercial banker 商業銀行家
commercial bill 商業手形
commercial bill eligible for rediscounting with the Bank of Japan 日銀再割適格手形
commercial bookkeeping 商業簿記
commercial business 営利事業
Commercial Code 商法
commercial company 営利会社
commercial court 商業裁判所
commercial credit 商業信用
commercial credit insurance 商業信用保険
commercial customs 商習慣
commercial discount 商業割引
commercial effect 商業的効果
commercial enterprise 営利事業
commercial expenses 営業費
commercial finance 商業金融

C

commercial flight 商業フライト
commercial insurer 民間保険会社
commercial invoice 商業送り状
commercial L / C (letter of credit) 商業信用状
commercial lending 商業貸付
commercial liability insurance 事業向け賠償責任保険
commercial line 企業物件保険
commercial loan 商業貸出
commercial mortgage 商業用モーゲージ
commercial mortgage backed securities 商業用モーゲージ担保証券
commercial mortgage loan 商業不動産ローン
commercial mortgage pool 商業用モーゲージ・プール
commercial package policy セット保険
commercial paper コマーシャル・ペーパー
commercial paper outstanding コマーシャル・ペーパー発行残高
commercial pressure 商売上の圧力
commercial production 商業生産
commercial property 商業用不動産
commercial rate of interest 市場金利
commercial rating 商業格付け
commercial real estate loan 商業不動産ローン
commercial register 登記簿
commercial registration 商業登記
commercial risk 事業リスク
commercial statistics 商業統計
commercial success 商業的成功
commercial trader 商業トレーダー
commercial tranche 民間トランシェ
commercial transaction 商行為
Commercial Union Assurance Co. コマーシャル・ユニオン
commercialization 商品化
commercialization of a new product 新製品の企業化
Commerzbank コメルツ銀行株価指数
Commerzbank-Index コメルツ指数
commingled custody 混蔵保管
commingled equity fund 合同運用株式ファンド
commingled investment account 混蔵投資勘定
commingled investment fund 合同運用型ファンド
commingled real estate fund 合同運用不動産ファンド
commission account 手数料勘定
commission advance 手数料前払い
commission agent 委託業者
commission agreement 委託契約
Commission Bancaire 銀行監督委員会
commission broker コミッション・ブローカー
commission del credere 保証付委任
commission disclosure 手数料開示
commission earned 受取手数料
commission for purchase 買入手数料
commission house 証券ブローカー
commission income 手数料収入
commission kickback 不当手数料
commission merchant 仲買人
commission of authority 委託契約書
commission on consignment 委託手数料
commission on sale 販売手数料
commission only policy 手数料のみの保険
commission paid 支払手数料
commission payable 未払手数料
commission rate 手数料料率
commission rebate 手数料割引
commission receivable 未収手数料
commission received 受入手数料
commission sale 手数料販売
commission schedule 手数料明細書
commission splitting 手数料分割
commission structure 手数料構造
commission system 歩合制
commission to consignee 委託販売手数料

Commission's White Paper EC 委員会白書
commissioner 長官
commissioner of insurance 保険局長
Commissioner of SESC (Securities and Exchange Surveillance Commission) 証券取引等監視委員会委員
Commissioner of the Financial Services Agency 金融庁長官
Commissioner of the Financial Supervisory Agency 金融監督庁長官
Commissioner of the National Tax Agency 国税庁長官
Commissioner's Secretariat 長官官房
commissioners for oaths 宣誓管理官
commitment base コミットメント・ベース
commitment fee コミットメント・フィー；約定料
commitment line contract 限度貸付契約
commitment period コミットメント期間
commitment to the provisions of the lease リース条項の確約
commitments 契約債務
committed line of credit 信用供与枠
committed transaction 約定された取引
committee 委員会
committee of inspection 検査委員会
Committee on Accounting Procedure 会計手続き委員会
committee on auditing procedure 監査手続委員会
Committee on Uniform Securities Identification Procedures CUSIP
committee regulations 委員会規則
commodities exchange commission 商品取引所委員会
commodities investment trust 商品投資信託
commoditization 商品性
commodity 商品
commodity account 商品取引口座
commodity backed bond 商品担保債券
commodity based contract コモディティ契約
commodity bloc コモディティ通貨
commodity currency コモディティ通貨
commodity customers agreement 商品顧客契約
commodity demand 商品需要
commodity derivatives 商品デリバティブ
commodity draft 商品代金取立手形
commodity exchange 商品取引所
commodity exchange act 商品取引法
commodity exchange responsibility reserve 商品取引責任準備金
commodity excise 物品税
commodity firms 商品取引企業
commodity flow method コモディティー・フロー法
commodity fund 商品ファンド
commodity futures 商品先物
Commodity Futures Association of Japan 日本商品先物協会
commodity futures contract 商品先物契約
commodity futures index 商品先物指数
commodity futures price 商品先物取引価格
Commodity Futures Trading Commission 米国商品先物取引委員会
commodity index 商品指数
commodity market 商品市場
commodity money 商品貨幣
commodity option 商品オプション
commodity paper 商品証券
commodity pool operator 商品ファンド・オペレーター
commodity price 物価
commodity price index 商品価格指数
commodity security 商品証券

C

commodity space 財空間
commodity statistics 商品統計
commodity swap コモディティー・スワップ
commodity tax 物品税
commodity tax law 物品税法
commodity terms of trade 商品交易条件
commodity trading adviser 商品取引顧問
commodity transaction 商品取引
commodity-linked note 商品連動債
common 入会権
common account 共同勘定
common agriculture policy 共通農業政策
common background 共通の基盤
common carrier 一般通信事業者
common classification 一般的分類
common collateral 共通担保
common concern 共通の懸念
common condition 一般的な条件
common control 共通の支配
common cost 共通原価
common counts 一般項目
common difference 公差
common disaster clause 同時災害条項
common dividend 普通配当
common dollar statements 安定価値に修正した財務諸表
common equity 普通株
common factor risk 共通要因リスク
common financial instruments 普通の金融商品
common gap コモンギャップ
common goods 共通財
common informer 情報提供者
common injunction 普通差止命令
common interest claims 共益債権
common law 普通法
common law action 民事訴訟
common law corporation 普通法株式会社
common law trust 普通法信託
common liquidation 通常解散
common logarithm 常用対数
common market 共同市場
common nuisance 公的不法妨害
common pool 共同プール
common price auction 単一価格入札
common property 共有資産
common risk 共通リスク
common share 普通株式
common shares subscribed 引受普通株式
common stock 普通株式
common stock book value 普通株の帳簿価格
common stock coverage 普通株倍率
common stock equivalents 普通株式相当証券
common stock fund 普通株ファンド
common stock ownership statistics 普通株保有に関する統計
common stock ratio 普通株比率
common stock with par value 額面普通株式
common stock without par value 無額面普通株式
common tariff 共通関税
common trust fund 合同信託基金
common use 慣用
common yield 現在の利回り
common-size balance sheet 百分率貸借対照表
common-size income statement 百分率損益計算書
communication charges 通信費
Communications and Policy Division 政策課
communications control units 通信制御装置
communications industry 通信業界
community コミュニティ
community charge 住民税
community credit コミュニティ・クレジット
community of interests 利害の一致
community reinvestment 地元への再投資

commutation 一時金化
commuted value 一時金換算価格
compact 正式な同意
companies changing the amount of dividend 配当金異動会社
companies previously paying dividend 無配転落企業
companies with employee stock ownership plan 持株制度実施会社
companion bond コンパニオン債
company 会社
company agent 会社指定代理店
company having changed its fiscal year 変則決算会社
company law 会社法
company leverage 企業の負債比率
company limited 株式会社
company limited by guarantee 有限責任保証会社
company matching contribution 企業負担掛金
company organization 会社組織
company representative 会社代理人
company saving 社内預金
company taxation 法人課税
company union 御用組合
company with a committees system 委員会設置会社
company with a corporate auditor system 監査役設置会社
company with reduced capital 減資会社
company's attorney-in-fact 会社の代理人
company's own shares 自己株式
company's own stock 自社株
comparability 比較可能性
comparability of financial statements 財務諸表の比較可能性
comparability over time 期間比較性
comparable information 比較可能な情報
comparable market 比較可能な市場
comparable requirement 相当する要件
comparable returns 比較可能な利益率
comparable securities 類似証券
comparable uncontrolled price method 独立価格比較法
comparative advantage 比較優位
comparative advantage theory 比較優位理論
comparative amount 比較情報の金額
comparative analysis 比較分析
comparative balance sheet 比較貸借対照表
comparative cost 比較原価
comparative cost studies 比較原価調査
comparative financial statements 比較財務諸表
comparative income statement 比較損益計算書
comparative information 比較情報
comparative negligence 過失相殺
comparative profit and loss statement 比較損益計算書
comparative purpose 比較目的
comparative statement 比較計算書
comparative statement of cash flows 比較収支計算書
comparative statistics 比較統計学
comparative year 比較対象年度
comparator 比較対象物
compared to the same period one year earlier 昨年同期比で
compared trade summary 取引サマリー表
comparison 比較
comparison of beta values of funds ファンド・ベータ値の比較
comparison of business transactions 取引事例比較法
comparison slip 照合票
comparison table 比較表
comparison-only member 照合会員
compatible 互換性のある
compelling reason 強制する理由
compensated absence 有給休暇
compensating balance 拘束残高
compensating balance of deposit 補償預金残高

compensating deposit 歩積預金
compensating error 相殺誤差
compensating interest 相殺利子
compensation 補償金；補填
compensation benefit 報奨給付
compensation committee 報酬委員会
compensation duties 相殺関税
compensation expense 報奨費用
compensation for damages 損害賠償
compensation for expense and loss 経費補償金
compensation for expropriation 収用補償金
compensation for fixed costs during the suspension of business 休業期間中の固定費の補償
compensation for injuries and deaths 負傷死亡補償金
compensation for loss 損失補填
compensation for lost revenue 収益補償金
compensation for moving expenses 立退費用の補償
compensation for profit from business 業務上の収益の補償
compensation for residual land 残地補償金
compensation for the failure to settle 決済不履行への弁済
compensation for transfer of property in condemnation 移転補償金
compensation of the damage 損害の弁済
compensation paid to directors 役員報酬
compensation plans based on assets 運用資産額比例報酬方式
compensation principle of taxation 租税の受益者負担原則
compensation structure 報酬体系
compensation trade 求償貿易
compensatory budget policy 補整的予算政策
compensatory contract 有償契約
compensatory deposit 両建預金
compensatory effect 補整効果
compensatory financing facility 補償融資
compensatory fiscal policy 補整的財政政策
compensatory item 補整的項目
compensatory stock option 報酬ストック・オプション
compensatory surplus 補整的余剰
competence 職権
competency 能力
competent 所轄
competent authority 主務官庁
competent department 主管部
competent minister 主務大臣
competent parties 能力のある当事者
competent tax office 所轄税務署
competing assets 競合資産
competing interests 対立する利害
competition among markets 市場間競争
competition pressure 競争圧力
competitive auction bidding 価格競争入札
competitive bid 競争入札
competitive depreciation 競争的平価切下げ
competitive disadvantage 競争上の不利益
competitive edge 競争力
competitive harm 競争上の損害
competitive market maker system 競合マーケット・メーカー・システム
competitive market price 競争市場価格
competitive price 競争価格
competitive rate 競争料率
competitive sale 競争販売
competitive tender 競争入札
competitive yield auction 競争的利回入札
competitiveness 競争力
competitiveness concern 競争力の懸念
competitor 競合企業
compilation 調製

compilation of the budget 予算編成
complainant 原告
complaint procedures 苦情処理手続き
complementary goods 補完財
complementary lending facility 補完的貸付制度
complementary loan 補完ローン
complementary means 補完的手段
complementary pension plan 補完年金制度
complete audit 完全監査
complete set 完全な組
complete specialization 完全特化
complete stripping between interest and principal 元本と金利の完全分離
completed contract method 完成基準
completion bonus 完工ボーナス
completion guarantee 完成保証
completion of physical proportion 物理的完成割合
completion of production method 生産基準
completion of unsettled transactions 未決済取引の整理
complex 複雑な
complex capital structure 複雑な資本構造
complex nature 複合性
complex provisions 複雑な規定
complex records 複雑な記録
compliance コンプライアンス
compliance audit コンプライアンス監査
compliance certificate 適法証明書
compliance deviation コンプライアンス違反
Compliance Inspection Office 証券取引検査官室
compliance test 準拠性テスト
compliance with 準拠
compliance with relevant rules and accuracy in their operational procedures 事務の遵法性と正確性
complicated asset class 仕組資産クラス
complimentary goods for shareholders 株主優待
component accounted for reserve 準備金に計上される部分
component analysis 成分分析
component assets 構成資産
component of cash 現金の構成部分
component percentage analysis 構成比率分析
component percentages 構成比率
components of acquisition cost 取得原価の構成要素
components of cost 原価の構成要素
components of financial statements 財務諸表の構成部分
components of other comprehensive income その他包括利益の構成要素
composite cost of capital 資本コスト
composite depreciation 総合減価償却
composite depreciation assets 総合償却資産
composite index 総合指数
composite insurer 複数保険者
composite price コンポジット・プライス
composite stock price index 総合株価指数
composite stock price tables 総合相場表
composite tape 株式相場表示テープ
composite useful life 総合耐用年数
composition 構成；示談
composition of inventory 棚卸資産の構成
composition of working capital 運転資本構成
composition ratio 構成比
composition requirements 構成要件
compound annual rate 複利年率
compound bonus 複利型保険金増額配当
compound discount 複割引
compound entry 複合記入
compound financial instruments 複合

C

金融商品
compound growth rate 複利成長率
compound interest 複利
compound interest method 複利方式
compound interest yield 複利利回り
compound journal entry 複合仕訳
compound multiplier 複合乗数
compound option 複合オプション
compound survivorship assurance 複合連生死亡保険
compound transaction 複合取引
compounded every six months 6カ月複利
compounding rate 配当算入利率
comprehensive allocation 完全期間配分
comprehensive basis 公準
comprehensive bonded area 総合保税地域
comprehensive budget 包括予算
comprehensive general liability insurance 第三者賠償個別保険
comprehensive general liability insurance coverage part 総合賠償責任保険
comprehensive income 包括利益
comprehensive income taxation 総合課税
comprehensive information 包括的な情報
comprehensive insurance 総合保険
comprehensive medical coverage 総合医療保障
comprehensive medical expense insurance 総合医療費保険
comprehensive opinion 総合意見
comprehensive personal liability policy 個人総合賠償責任保険
comprehensive standards 包括的な基準
comprehensive system model コスモ・モデル
comprehensive trade bill 包括通商法案
compromise 妥協
compromise method 折衷方式
comptroller 監督官
comptroller in bankruptcy 破産監査官
compulsory 強制的
compulsory arbitration 強制的仲裁
compulsory audit 強制監査
compulsory benefit 強制的給付
compulsory cancellation 強制解約
compulsory composition 強制和議
compulsory conversion into money 強制換価
compulsory deposit as a condition for loans 歩積両建預金
compulsory execution 強制執行
compulsory insurance 強制保険
compulsory liquidation 強制的清算
compulsory membership 強制加入
compulsory participation 強制加入
compulsory pension 強制加入年金
compulsory reconciliation 強制和議
compulsory sale by auction 強制競売
compulsory social health insurance 強制加入健康保険
compulsory transfer of assets 資産の強制譲渡
compulsory transfer of property 資産の強制譲渡
compulsory winding-up 強制清算
compulsory withdrawal 強制撤退
computation 算定
computation of business income 事業所得の計算
computation of conversion factor 交換比率の算定
computation of factors for conversion of deliverable grades into standardized instrument 標準物と受渡適格銘柄との交換比率の算定
computation of interest on a per diem basis 利子の日割計算
computation of tax amount 税額の計算
computation of useful life 耐用年数の計算
computation on a per diem basis 日割

り計算
computation period 算定期間
computation procedure 計算手続
computational shortcut 簡易計算
computed price 計算価格
computer assisted execution system 自動ディーリング取引システム
computer audit コンピューター監査
computer center 電算センター
Computer-assisted Order Routine and Execution System CORES
computerization コンピューター化
computerized society コンピュータ社会
con 反対投票
concealment 隠蔽
concentrated investment 集中投資
concentration 集中
concentration effect 集中効果
concentration of assets 資産の集中
concentration of credit risk 信用リスクの集中
concentration of enterprise 企業集中
concentration of resources 資源の集中
concept 概念
concept disclosure コンセプト開示
concept of historical cost 原価主義
concept release コンセプト・リリース
concept stage 構想段階
conceptual basis 概念的な基準
conceptual framework 概念的フレームワーク
conceptual merit 概念上の利点
conceptual reason 概念的な理由
concerned 当該の
concerns interested 関係会社
concerted activities 協調行動
concerted intervention 協調介入
concession 権利；手数料
concession agreement 事業権契約
concession contract コンセション・コントラクト
concession hunter 利権屋
concessionaire 営業権所有者
concise disclosure 簡潔な開示
conclusion 結論
conclusion of a transaction contract 売買契約の締結
conclusive evidence 決定的な証拠
conclusive presumption 決定的推定
concord 和解
concordant 一致する
concurrent adjustment 同時修正
concurrent causes 併存原因
concurrent fire insurance 同時火災保険
concurrent jurisdiction 競合管轄権
concurrent lease 併存賃借権
concurrent liens 同順位先取特権
concurrent negligence 競合過失
concurrent subscription offering 同時募集
concurring opinion 賛成意見
condemn 収用する
condemnation of land 土地の収用
condensed account form 要約勘定式
condensed and classified 要約分類された
condensed balance sheet 要約貸借対照表
condensed cash flow statement 要約式キャッシュフロー計算書
condensed financial information 要約財務情報
condensed financial statements 要約式財務諸表
condensed income statement 要約損益計算書
condensed interim financial information 要約中間財務情報
condensed report form 要約報告式
condition collateral 付帯条件
condition concurrent 同時履行条件
condition of the transfer of the property 譲渡の態様
condition precedent 停止条件
condition subsequent 解除条件
conditional 条件付きの
conditional acceptance 条件付引受け
conditional approval 条件付承認

C

C

conditional assignment 条件付譲渡
conditional call 条件付繰上償還
conditional contract 条件付契約
conditional demand deposit 条件付要求払預金
conditional expectation 条件付期待値
conditional liquidity 条件付流動性
conditional loan ひも付融資
conditional loss 機会損失
conditional or unconditional 条件の有無にかかわらず
conditional regression analysis 条件付回帰分析
conditional sale 条件付売買
conditional subsidy from the national treasury 条件付国庫補助金
conditional transaction 条件付取引
conditions 条件
conditions for payment 支払条件
conditions of issuance 発行条件
conditions of operations 業務の条件
conditions of sale 販売条件
conditions of the national economy 経済事情
conditions precedent to the validity 有効に関する先行条件
condolence money 弔慰金
condor type spread transaction コンドルスプレッド取引
conduit バイカイ機関
conduit theory 導管理論
conference 協議
Conference on International Economic Cooperation 国際経済協力会議
conferment 授与
confidence 信頼
confidence building 信頼構築
confidence coefficient 信頼係数
confidence index 信頼度指数
confidence interval 信頼区間
confidence level 信頼度
confidential operation 隠密オペ
confidential relations 信頼関係
confidentiality 機密性
confidentiality agreement 秘密保持契約
confidentiality of information 守秘義務
confidentiality privilege 守秘義務特権
confined to 限定された
confinement cost 療養費用
confirmation 確認
confirmation document 確認書類
confirmation fee 確認手数料
confirmation for financial futures transaction 金融先物取引に関する確認書
confirmation letter 確認状
confirmation note 確認通知書
confirmation of transaction 取引の確認
confirmation request 確認請求
confirmed credit 確認信用状
confirmed letter of credit 確認済信用状
confirming bank 確認銀行
confirming charge 信用状確認手数料
confirming house コンファーミング・ハウス
confiscation 没収
conflict of interest 利害の衝突
conflict of laws 法律の抵触
conflict of risk 利害対立
conformed copy 同一証明付コピー
conforming loan 担保適格融資
conformity 整合性
confrontation 対立
confusion 混同
conglomerate コングロマリット
Congo Republic (CFA (Communauté Financière Africaine) franc) コンゴ（CFA フラン）
Connie Lee (College Construction Loan Insurance Association) 大学建設融資保険協会
connivance 黙認
consanguinity in the second degree 二親等
consecutive advances 連騰
consecutive data sample 連続データ・

サンプル
consecutive declines 続落
consecutive dividend 安定配当
consecutive dividend increase 連続増配
consecutive quarters 連続四半期
consensual contract 諾成契約
consensus コンセンサス
consensus decision 合意に基づく決定
consensus expectation コンセンサス予測
consensus forecast コンセンサス予測
consensus of opinion 一致した意見
consensus on earnings estimate 収益予測のコンセンサス
consent 同意
consent decree 同意判決
Consent to Instruction for Registration 登録請求承諾書
consequence of the breach 違反の帰結
consequential damages 結果損害
consequential loss 間接損失
conservation commission 保全手数料
conservatism 保守主義
conservative accounting 保守的な会計
conservative management 手堅い経営
conservative view 保守的な見方
conservator 財産保管人
consider using taps 追加発行を考える
considerable investment 巨額の投資
considerable rise 急増
considerably low price 著しく低い価格
consideration 対価；約因
consideration clause 約因条項
consideration received 受領対価
consign 委託する
consigned goods 委託品
consignee 荷受け人
consignment 委託
consignment contract 委託契約
consignment fee 委託手数料
consignment goods 委託品
consignment guarantee money 委託証拠金
consignment invoice 委託品送り状
consignment ledger 委託品元帳
consignment of tax liability 納税委託
consignment of tax payment 納付委託
consignment sale 委託販売
consignment sale and purchase 委託売買
consignment sales contract 委託販売契約
consignor 積送人
consistency 一貫性
consistency principle 継続性の原則
consistent approach 継続性のあるアプローチ
consol market コンソル市場
consolidate 統合する
consolidated 連結の
consolidated account 連結勘定
consolidated accounting 連結会計
consolidated accounts 連結決算
consolidated annuities コンソル公債
consolidated assets 連結資産
consolidated balance sheet 連結貸借対照表
consolidated base 連結ベース
consolidated bond 整理社債
consolidated capital 連結資本
consolidated capital adequacy ratio 連結自己資本比率
consolidated current profit 連結経常利益
consolidated financial statements 連結財務諸表
consolidated financial statistics 連結財務統計
consolidated good will 連結のれん
consolidated group 連結グループ
consolidated income 連結利益
consolidated income statement 連結損益計算表
consolidated income tax 連結所得税
consolidated information 連結情報
consolidated journal entry by elimination 連結消去仕訳
consolidated loan 一本化ローン
consolidated market structure 統合市

C

場構造
consolidated mortgage bond 統合抵当証券
consolidated net capital ratio 連結自己資本比率
C
consolidated net loss 連結純損失
consolidated operating income 連結営業利益
consolidated ordinary income 連結経常利益
consolidated profit and loss statement 連結損益計算書
consolidated quotation service 総合気配表示システム
consolidated quotation system 統合気配値情報システム
consolidated recurring profit 連結経常利益
consolidated retained earnings 連結剰余金
consolidated return 連結納税申告
consolidated sales 連結売上
consolidated schedule 連結付属明細票
consolidated statement of cash flow 連結キャッシュフロー計算書
consolidated statement of retained earnings 連結剰余金計算書
consolidated statement paper 連結精算表
consolidated stock ticker 総合株式ティッカー
consolidated subsidiary 連結子会社
consolidated surplus 連結剰余金
consolidated tape 統合テープ
consolidated tax payment system 連結納税制度
consolidated tax return 連結税務申告書
consolidated tax return system グループ課税
consolidated total assets 連結総資産
consolidated total liabilities 連結総負債
consolidated working capital 連結運転資金
consolidation 元利統合；連結
consolidation activity 合併行為
consolidation date 連結日
consolidation excess 連結超過額
consolidation for trading 銘柄併合
consolidation ledger 連結元帳
consolidation loan コンソリデーション・ローン
consolidation of corporations 会社の新設合併
consolidation of mortgages モーゲージの併合
consolidation of operations 事業の結合
consolidation of public bonds 公債整理
consolidation of shares 株式併合
consolidation pattern 調整パターン
consolidation policy 連結方針
consolidation process 連結手続
consolidation range 調整レンジ
consolidation take-over 吸収合併
Consols コンソル公債
consortium コンソーシアム
consortium bank コンソーシアム・バンク
constant 定数
constant capital 不変資本
constant charge 一定額の費用
constant continuously compounded 一定の連続複利
constant cost 固定費
constant currency 恒常通貨
constant divisor 恒常除数
constant dollar (value) accounting 安定価値会計
constant dollar (value) profit 安定価値利益
constant dollar base 恒常ドル・ベース
constant dollar net income 実質ベースに修正した純利益
constant dollar plan 定額法
constant dollars 恒常ドル
constant elasticity of variance model 定弾性分散モデル

constant expenses 固定費
constant growth dividend discount model 定率成長配当割引モデル
constant growth rate model 定率成長モデル
constant growth rate valuation model 定率成長評価モデル
constant maturity 恒常満期
constant maturity swap コンスタント・マチュリティ・スワップ
constant percentage method 定率法
constant periodic rate of interest 一定の期間利子率
constant periodic rate of return 一定率の期間収益額
constant proportion 一定比率
constant purchasing power 安定購買力
constant purchasing power accounting 安定購買力会計
constant rate of return to maturity 満期までの収益の一定率
constant ratio plan 定率投資法
constant risk tolerance 不変リスク許容度
constant value 安定価値
constant variance 等分散
constant yield method 定率利回り法
constant yield principles 一定利回基準
constituents 構成銘柄
constitution 定款
constrained allocation 限界値範囲内での配分
constraint 制約
construct 構築する
construction 解釈
construction account 建設費勘定
construction bond 建設国債；建設保証
construction claim 建設クレーム
construction contract 建設請負契約
construction contract expense 工事契約費用
construction contract in progress 進行中の工事契約
construction cost 工事原価
construction expenditure 建設支出
construction in progress 未成工事
construction industry 建設業
construction loan 建設ローン
construction of completion 完成工事高
construction overhead 工事間接費
construction revenue 工事収入
construction subsidy 建設助成金
construction work 建設工事
construction work account receivable 工事未収金
construction work revenue 建設工事収入
constructive 擬制の
constructive bonus 認定賞与
constructive delivery 擬制の引渡し
constructive dividend 推定的配当
constructive eviction 擬制の追立
constructive fraud 推定詐欺
constructive obligation 推定債務
constructive ownership みなし所有
constructive receipt 認定収入
constructive sale 擬制売却
constructive service 間接送達
constructive taxable year みなし事業年度
constructive terms 推定的条件
constructive total loss 推定全損
constructive trust 法定信託
construe 解釈する
consular invoice 領事送り状
consulting sales コンサルティング・セールス
consumables 消耗品
consumed cost 費消原価
consumer 消費者
consumer advocate 消費者団体
consumer bank 消費者銀行
consumer confidence 消費者の信頼
consumer credit 消費者信用
consumer credit company 消費者信用会社
consumer credit control law サラ金規制法
consumer credit life insurance 消費者

信用生命保険
consumer credit protection 消費者信用保護
Consumer Credit Protection Act 消費者信用保護法
consumer credit rate 消費者金利
consumer credit report 消費者信用情報
consumer debenture 個人投資家向け債券
consumer demand 消費者需要
consumer durables 耐久消費財
consumer electronics 家電
consumer expenditure 消費者支出
consumer finance 消費者金融
consumer finance company 消費者金融会社
consumer goods 消費財
consumer group 消費者団体
consumer group credit life insurance 消費者団体信用生命保険
consumer installment credit 消費者信用残高
consumer interest rate 消費者ローン金利
consumer leasing 消費者リース
consumer lines insurance 消費者向け保険
consumer loan 消費者金融
consumer protection 消費者保護
consumer research 消費者調査
consumer sector stock 消費者関連株
consumer spending 消費者支出
consumer's behavior 消費者行動
consumer's cooperative society 消費生活協同組合
consumer's credit file 個人信用情報
consumer's union 消費者団体
consummate 完了する
consumption based 消費ベースの
consumption demand 消費需要
consumption entry 消費税申告
consumption function 消費関数
consumption growth 消費の伸び
consumption lag 消費ラグ
consumption level 消費水準
consumption multiplier 消費乗数
consumption of resources 資源の費消
consumption pattern 消費パターン
consumption plan 消費計画
consumption quota 消費割当
consumption tax 消費税
Consumption Tax Law 消費税法
Consumption Tax Office 消費税室
consumption transfer tax 消費譲与税
consumption trend 消費動向
consumption unit 消費単位
contango 株式決済猶予金；日歩
contemplation of bankruptcy 破産予期
contemporaneous indexation タイム・ラグのない指数連動
contemporaneous reserve accounting 同時積立方式
contemporary capitalism 現代資本主義
contender 論争者
content of transactions 取引の内容
content report 報告内容
content-certified mail 内容証明郵便
contention 争い
contentious case 訴訟事件
contents insurance 家財保険
contents rate 家財保険料率
contestable period 可争期間
contestant 異議申立人
continental depositary receipts コンチネンタル預託証書
continental form of closing the ledger 大陸式元帳締切手続
continental law 大陸法
contingency 偶発事象
contingency fund 緊急資金
contingency insurance 未必利益保険
contingency reserve 偶発損失準備金
contingency risk 偶発的危険
contingent 派生的な
contingent annuitant 継続年金受取人
contingent annuity 条件付年金
contingent assets 偶発資産
contingent beneficiary 次順位保険金

受取人
contingent benefit 条件付給付
contingent charge 偶発費用
contingent claim 派生商品
contingent commission 利益手数料
contingent consideration 条件付対価
contingent credit swap 偶発信用スワップ
contingent debt 偶発債務
contingent estate 不確定財産権
contingent fee 条件付手数料
contingent fund 偶発資金
contingent interest 偶発的持ち分；不定利子
contingent lease payments 変動リース料
contingent liability 偶発債務
contingent liability on bill endorsed 裏書義務
contingent life insurance trust 条件付生命保険信託
contingent loss 偶発損失
contingent on 条件となる
contingent on future events 将来の事象を条件にした
contingent order 条件付注文
contingent outlay 臨時費
contingent payment 条件付支払い
contingent profit 偶発利益
contingent reserve 偶発債務積立金
contingent settlement provisions 条件付決済条項
contingent transaction 偶発取引
contingent use 条件付使用
contingent vesting 不確定年金受給権付与
contingent warrant 偶発性ワラント
continuation 継続
continuation clause 継続約款
continuation of coverage 保障継続
continuation of lease リースの継続
continuation pattern 保合いパターン
continuation provision 更新条項
continued deficit 赤字継続
continued expenses 継続費
continued insurance 延長保険
continued no dividend 無配継続
continuing account 継続勘定
continuing auditor 継続監査人
continuing business 継続事業
continuing company 存続企業
continuing contract 継続契約
continuing deflation 長期化するデフレ
continuing expenditure 継続費
continuing guaranty 無期限保証
continuing interest 継続的な利害関係
continuing loss 継続的な損失
continuing operations 継続事業
continuing services 継続役務
continuing significance 継続的重要性
continuing use 継続使用
continuity 連続性
continuous annuity 連続年金
continuous audit 継続会計監査
continuous buying and selling 継続的売買
continuous compound interest rate 連続複利
continuous compounding calculation 連続複利計算
continuous decline じり安
continuous disability 高度障害
continuous disclosure 継続開示
continuous discounting 連続割引
continuous distribution 連続分布
continuous dividend 連続配当
continuous inventory 継続棚卸
continuous market ザラ場
continuous net settlement 継続差額決済
continuous payment 保険料全期払込み
continuous policy 継続保険
continuous premium 終身払込保険料
continuous probability distribution 連続確率分布
continuous reinsurance cover 継続的再保険
continuous session ザラ場
continuous settlement processing 連続決済処理

C

C

continuous spectrum of borrower types 連続する借り手の変化
continuous time 連続時間
continuous trading 連続売買
continuous transaction of securities 株式等の継続的取引
continuous transactions entered into for profit 営利を目的とした継続的行為
continuously disclosing company 継続開示会社
contra account 対照勘定
contra entry 相対記入
contra-cyclical 反循環的な
contraband 禁制品
contraband of export 輸出禁制品
contraband of import 輸入禁制品
contract 契約
contract balance 契約残高
contract bond 契約保証
contract charge 契約手数料
contract conclusion 契約締結
contract curve 契約曲線
contract date 契約締結日
contract deposit received 契約前受金
contract disclosure 契約の開示
contract embodied in 化体表章される契約
contract entered into by mutual consent 諾成契約
contract for current account services 当座勘定取引契約
contract for the rendering of services 役務契約
contract formation 契約締結
contract holder 契約加入者
contract in bulk 一括契約
contract in kind 要物契約
contract index price 約定指数
contract interest rate 約定利子率
contract law 契約法
contract market 契約市場
contract money 契約金
contract month 限月
contract notice 約定通知
contract of adhesion 附合契約
contract of commission 委任契約
contract of guaranty 保証契約
contract of merger 合併契約書
contract position 契約ポジション
contract price 約定値段
contract price of purchase 買付の約定値段
contract price of sale 売付の約定値段
contract rate 契約料率
contract rate system 契約運賃制
contract ratio 契約率
contract size 契約規模
contract slip 売買確認書
contract term 契約期間
contract type 契約型
contract type accumulative investment plan 契約型継続投資プラン
contract type investment trust 契約型投資信託
contract value 契約金額；約定価額
contract work 請負工事
contract work account receivable 請負工事未収金
contract work system 請負制度
contract worker 契約社員
contract works with the condition of deferred payment attached 延払条件付請負
contract year 契約年度
contracted benefit 約定給付金
contracted in arrangement 残留協定
contracted interest rate 約定金利
contracted out 適用除外
contracted price 約定値段
contracted rate 約定利率
contracted-out benefit 適用除外給付
contracted-out personal pension 適用除外個人年金
contracting after the spike 拡大後の縮小
contracting out 脱退
contracting out of the basic pension 基礎年金からの脱退
contracting out rebate 脱退リベート

contracting parties 契約当事者
contraction 収縮
contractors' all risks insurance 建設工事保険
contractual accumulation plan 利益累積型投信
contractual arrangement 契約上の取決め
contractual commitment 確定約定
contractual documents 契約書
contractual guarantee 約款上の保証
contractual liability 契約債務
contractual liability insurance 契約責任保険
contractual maturity date 約定期日
contractual obligation 契約上の債務
contractual period 契約期間
contractual repayment period 契約上の支払期日
contractual repricing date 契約上の価格改定日
contractual right 契約上の権利
contractual savings 契約型貯蓄
contractual terms and conditions 契約条件
contractual wage 協定賃金
contradiction 矛盾
contrarian 逆バリ投資家
contrary argument 逆の議論
contrary opinion 反対意見
contravention 違反
contravention of listing agreement 上場契約違反
contributed capital 拠出資本
contributed stock 拠出資本
contributed surplus 拠出剰余金
contributing worker 掛金拠出労働者
contribution carryover 拠出金の繰越
contribution corresponding to the target level of benefits 水準掛金
contribution deduction 寄付金控除
contribution due 期日の到来した掛金
contribution equivalent premium 拠出相当保険料
contribution exemption 掛金免除
contribution for social insurance 社会保険分担金
contribution for supplementary components 加算掛金
contribution in aid of construction 工事負担金
contribution in kind 現物拠出
contribution level 掛金水準
contribution margin 貢献利益
contribution margin form 貢献利益式
contribution margin variance 貢献利益差異
contribution money 拠出金
contribution payable 支払うべき掛金
contribution payment 掛金支払い
contribution payment period 拠出期間
contribution plan 拠出制度
contribution rate 掛金率；拠出率
contribution revenue 掛金歳入
contribution to equity 資本の増加
contribution to equity capital 払込出資金
contribution to sales 売上への寄与
contribution to the equity capital 会員出資金
contribution to welfare facilities 福利施設負担額
contribution-defined 確定拠出型の
contributions 出損金
contributions paid 掛金額
contributions to affiliated company 関係会社出資金
contributions to unions 組合の出資金
contributor 拠出者
contributory 出資義務者
contributory benefit 拠出制給付
contributory group insurance 拠出制団体保険
contributory infringement 寄与侵害
contributory negligence 寄与過失
contributory plan 拠出制度
contributory retirement plan 拠出型退職年金
contributory shares of estate 寄与分
control 支配

C

control account 統括勘定
control accounting 統制会計
control and subordination 支配従属
control budget 統制予算
control criterion 支配力基準
control limit 管理限界
control market 支配市場
control measure 抑制措置
control mechanism 管理機構
control number 判定用数値
control of inflation インフレ抑制
control risk 統制リスク
control stock 支配株
controllable expenses 管理可能原価
controlled account 被統括勘定
controlled commodities 規制商品
controlled company 被支配会社
controlled currency 管理通貨
controlled discretion 法規裁量
controlled economy 統制経済
controlled mismatching 対応をずらす
controlled price 管理価格
controlled trade 統制貿易
controller 会計検査官
controlling company 支配会社
controlling equity 支配株主持ち分
controlling interest 経営支配権
controlling relationship 支配関係
controlling stake 支配持ち分
controversy 議論
convener 召集権者
convenience 便宜
convenience of tax collection 徴税上の便宜
convening procedure 召集の手続
convention expense 会議費
convention for the avoidance of double taxation 二重課税防止条約
convention report (NAIC) 年次決算書(NAIC)
conventional annuity 定額年金
conventional auction コンベンショナル方式
conventional bonds 通常債券
conventional commodity market 伝統的商品市場
conventional group annuity 従来型団体年金
conventional insurance 在来型保険
conventional loan コンベンショナルローン
conventional method コンベンショナル方式
conventional method of competitive yield auction 利回りコンベンショナル方式
conventional mortgage 一般モーゲージ
conventional mortgage loan 普通モーゲージローン
conventional mortgage pool コンベンショナル・モーゲージ・プール
conventional option コンベンショナル・オプション
conventional retail inventory system 伝統的小売棚卸法
conventional tariff 協定関税
conventionality 慣例
converge 収斂する
convergence 収斂
convergence analysis 収束分析
convergence in probability 確率収束
convergence with GAAP GAAPとの収斂
convergent fluctuation 収斂性の変動
converse preference 逆特恵
conversion 転換
conversion agent 転換代理人
conversion at market price 時価転換
conversion at par 額面転換
conversion clause 転換条項
conversion conditions 転換条件
conversion cost 加工費
conversion credit provision 転換加算条項
conversion date 転換日
conversion discount 転換ディスカウント
conversion feature 転換条項
conversion into cash 換価処分

conversion of a building for productive use 建物の生産的使用への変更
conversion of debt to equity 負債の資本への転換
conversion of items in foreign currencies 外貨建勘定項目の換算
conversion option 転換オプション
conversion parity 転換パリティ
conversion period 転換請求期間
conversion premium 転換プレミアム
conversion price 転換価格
conversion price formula 転換価格方式
conversion price index 換算価格指数
conversion privilege 転換特典
conversion rate 換算率
conversion ratio 転換比率
conversion right 転換権
conversion rights for shares 株式転換権
conversion table 換算表
conversion terms 転換条件
conversion to gold 金兌換
conversion to the "new yen" immediately after World War II 新円切替
conversion to yen 円転
conversion transaction 転換取引
conversion value 転換価値
convertible assets 転換資産
convertible bond index 転換社債利回り
convertible bond with redemption request right 期中償還請求権付転換社債
convertible bond with warrant ワラント付き転換社債
convertible bonds with option オプション付転換社債
convertible contract 中途切替契約
convertible currency 兌換通貨
convertible debt 転換社債
convertible exchangeable preferred stock 交換可能転換優先株
convertible instruments 転換可能金融商品
convertible insurance 転換特典付保険
convertible into cash 現金と交換可能な
convertible loan 株式転換貸付
convertible mortgage 転換モーゲージ
convertible note 兌換紙幣
convertible preference shares 転換優先株式
convertible preferred stock 転換優先株
convertible reserve 兌換準備
convertible securities 転換証券
convertible stock 転換株式
convertible term insurance 転換特典付定期保険
convertible-bond type corporate bonds with new share reservation rights 転換社債型新株予約権付社債券
convex function 凸関数
convex set 凸集合
convexity コンベクシティ
conveyance of estate 財産譲渡
convict 有罪判決を受けた者
conviction 有罪の決定
convincing proof 確信的立証
convocation 召集
convocation of general meetings 総会の召集
COO (chief operating officer) 最高業務責任者
cook 改ざんする
Cook Islands (New Zealand dollar) クック諸島（ニュージーランド・ドル）
cooling time 冷却期間
cooling-off クーリングオフ
cooling-off period クーリングオフ期間
cooperative association 協同組合
cooperative association on indirect taxes 間接税協力団体
cooperative bank 信用組合
cooperative business association 事業協同組合
Cooperative Financial Institutions

C

Office 協同組織金融室
cooperative financing facility 輸出変動補償融資制度
cooperative insurance 共済保険
cooperative marketing 共同販売
cooperative organization type financial institution 協同組織金融機関
cooperative society 協同組合
coordinated cut 協調利下げ
coordinated intervention 協調介入
coordinated plan 調整済計画
Coordination and Inspection Division 総務検査課
coordination of bond issues 起債調整
COP (Colombia peso) コロンビア・ペソ
Copenhagen Stock Exchange コペンハーゲン証券取引所
Copenhagen Stock Exchange Index コペンハーゲン株価指数
copper-nickel coins (500 yen, 100yen, and 50 yen) 白銅貨幣（旧 500 円, 100 円, 50 円）
Copula function コピュラ関数
copyright 著作権
core 中核
core business 中核事業
core business division 主力部門
core capital 基本的資本；中核資本
core competence コア・コンピタンス
core holding 中核的保有
core market 主力市場
core portfolio コア・ポートフォリオ
core standards 核となる基準
core stock コア・ストック
CORES (Computer-assisted Order Routing and Execution System) CORES
corn hog cycle コーン・ホッグ循環
corner lot 角地
cornering 買占め
corporate accounting 会社会計
corporate accounting principles 企業会計原則
corporate action 会社行為
corporate and public bonds 公社債
Corporate and Treasury Association of Japan 企業財務協議会
corporate assets 会社資産
corporate average tax rate 平均法人税率
corporate banking コーポレート・バンキング
corporate bankruptcy 企業倒産
corporate body 法人団体
corporate bond 社債
corporate bond authorized 社債最高発行限度
corporate bond certificate 社債券
corporate bond fund 社債ファンド
corporate bond holder 社債権者
corporate bond issuance market 社債発行市場
corporate bond issuance premium 社債発行プレミアム
corporate bond valuation 社債評価
corporate bonds and other non-JGB bonds 社債等
corporate bonds with new share reservation rights 新株予約権付社債
corporate borrowers 社債発行企業
corporate businesses 法人企業
corporate capital 法人資本
corporate card 法人カード
corporate charter 認可状
corporate culture 企業文化
corporate customer 法人顧客
corporate debenture 社債
corporate debt 企業債務
corporate debt obligations 企業債務
corporate defined contribution pension plan 企業型確定拠出年金制度
corporate deposit 法人預金
corporate equivalent yield 社債相当利回り
corporate executive 会社重役
corporate finance 事業金融

corporate financing 資金調達
corporate franchise 会社特権
corporate governance コーポレート・ガバナンス
corporate group 系列
corporate guarantee 企業保証
corporate health insurance 団体医療保険
corporate identity コーポレート・アイデンティティー
corporate image 企業イメージ
corporate income 法人所得
corporate income tax 法人税
corporate income tax law 法人所得税法
corporate income tax rate 法人所得税率
corporate income taxes expenses 法人所得税費用
corporate information 会社情報
corporate inhabitant tax 法人住民税
corporate insurance 企業保険
corporate investor 法人投資家
corporate juridical person 社団法人
corporate loan 企業貸付
corporate management 企業経営
corporate member 法人会員
corporate membership 会社名義の会員
corporate name 商号
corporate owned life insurance 企業購入生命保険
corporate paid pension 企業負担保険料
corporate pension insurance 企業年金保険
corporate pension plan 企業年金制度
corporate pension plan operated by multi-employers 規約型企業年金
corporate pension rules 企業型年金規約
corporate policy 企業契約
corporate profile 企業プロフィール
corporate profit 企業利益
corporate profitability 企業収益性
corporate quasi-reorganization 会社の準更生
corporate raider 乗取り屋
corporate registration 法人登記簿
corporate rehabilitation proceedings 会社更生手続
corporate reorganization 会社更生
corporate reorganization trustee 会社更生手続管財人
corporate resolution 取締役会決議
corporate restructuring fund 企業再建ファンド
corporate results 企業業績
corporate right 法人権
corporate savings 法人貯蓄
corporate seal 会社印
corporate sector 企業部門
corporate securities 社債
corporate separation 会社分割
corporate service price index 企業向けサービス価格指数
corporate services prices 企業向けサービス価格
corporate settlement 5営業日渡し
corporate shareholder 法人株主
corporate size 企業規模
corporate split 会社分割
corporate strategy 企業戦略
corporate tax loss carryforward 法人税繰越欠損金
corporate taxable bond 課税社債
corporate treasurer 企業財務担当者
corporate trust 法人信託
corporate vitality 企業活力
corporate-type investment trust 会社型投信
corporation 法人
corporation aggregate 集合法人
corporation amalgamated 被合併法人
corporation capitalized at 500 million yen 資本金5億円の会社
corporation carrying on foreign trade 外国取引をしている会社
corporation ceased to exist after merger 合併により消滅する会社

C

corporation filing a blue return 青色申告法人
corporation finance 会社金融
corporation free from taxation 非課税法人
corporation in public interest 公益法人
corporation in reorganization process 更生会社
corporation in the course of liquidation 清算中の法人
corporation law 会社法
corporation lawyer 顧問弁護士
corporation levy 法人税割り
corporation liable to taxation 納税義務のある法人
corporation personnel 団体職員
corporation qualifying for filing a blue return 青色申告の出来る法人
corporation report 会社レポート
corporation settling accounts twice a year 年二回決算の会社
corporation subject to filing a return 申告義務のある法人
corporation subject to taxation 納税義務のある法人
corporation tax 法人税
Corporation Tax and Consumption Tax Policy Division 税制第二課
corporation tax credit 法人税控除
Corporation Tax Law 法人税法
corporation tax rate 法人税率
Corporation Taxation Division 法人課税課
corporation to receive the transfer of assets and liabilities 継承法人
corporation type 会社型
corporation type investment trust 会社型投資信託
corporation under liquidation 清算手続中の法人
corporation which has transferred its assets and liabilities through split-up 分割法人
corporation's equity 企業持ち分
corporation's own stock 自社株
corpus 信託財産
correction 修正
correction by estimate 推計による更正
correction of errors 過誤の訂正
correction of prior periods 前期修正
corrective market 訂正相場
corrective selling 訂正売り
correlation 相関
correlation analysis 相関分析
correlation between returns 収益率の相関関係
correlation coefficient 相関係数
correlation diagram 相関図
correlation of inflation rate インフレ率の相関
correlation ratio 相関比率
correlation table 相関表
correlative adjustment 対応的調整
correlative industry 関連産業
correspondent account コルレス勘定
correspondent arrangement コルレス契約
correspondent bank コルレス先金融機関
correspondent charge コルレス・チャージ
correspondent financial institution 取引金融機関
correspondent in a business 取引先
correspondent relation コルレス関係
corresponding account 見合勘定
corresponding amount 対応額
corresponding date of one year ago 1年前の応当日
corresponding day 応当日
corresponding deposit 見合預金
corresponding figure 対応する数値
corresponding period of the last year 前年同期
corresponding reduction 対応する減少
corridor 回廊
corridor approach 回廊方式
corrigendum 正誤表

corroborate 補強する
corroborating evidence 補強証拠
corruption 汚職
COSA (cost of sales adjustment) 売上原価修正
cost 原価
cost absorption 原価吸収
cost account 原価勘定
cost accounting 原価計算
cost accounting by department 部門別原価計算
cost accounting by product 製品別原価計算
cost accounting standards 原価計算基準
cost accounting system 原価計算制度
cost accumulation 原価集計
cost adjusted for fair value method 原価修正法
cost allocation 原価配分
cost allocation formula 費用配分方法
cost analysis 原価分析
cost and expenses 原価及び費用
cost and freight 運賃込み
cost audit 原価監査
cost basis 原価主義
cost behavior 費用動向
cost benefit 費用便益の
cost benefit analysis 費用便益分析
cost born by future generations 後代負担
cost card 原価計算書
cost certificate 掛金適正証明書
cost classification 費用分類
cost competitiveness コスト競争力
cost consciousness 原価意識
cost consideration 費用節減
cost control 原価管理
cost convention 原価法
cost curve 費用曲線
cost cutting 費用削減
cost data 費用データ
cost depletion 減耗償却
cost depletion method 取得原価残高比例法
cost distribution 原価配分
cost effective コスト効率の良い
cost effectiveness コスト効率
cost effectiveness analysis 費用対効果分析
cost efficiency コスト効率
cost element 原価要素
cost escalation clause 原価修正条項
cost estimate 費用見積り
cost estimation 原価見積り
cost factor 価格要素
cost finding 原価算定
cost flow assumption 棚卸資産の評価方法
cost for contract work in progress 未成工事支出金
cost for judicial proceedings 訴訟手続費用
cost formula 原価算定方式
cost function 費用関数
cost implication コスト上の問題
cost incurred to date 累積発生原価
cost incurrence コストの発生
cost ledger 原価元帳
cost management 原価管理
cost matching income principle 費用収益対応の原則
cost method 原価法
cost method of depletion 減耗償却の原価法
cost minimization コスト最小化
cost model 原価モデル
cost object 原価対象
cost of acquisition 買収原価
cost of assets purchased 資産購入原価
cost of borrowing 調達費用
cost of carry 資産所有費用
cost of completed work 完成工事原価
cost of construction 工事費
cost of disposal 処分費用
cost of entry 参入費用
cost of equity capital 株式資本コスト
cost of equity transaction 資本取引のコスト
cost of finished goods 製品原価

C

C

cost of fund 資金コスト
cost of goods purchased 仕入原価
cost of insurance 保険費用
cost of inventory 棚卸資産の取得原価
cost of issuing stocks 株式発行費用
cost of liability 負債コスト
cost of living clause 生活費スライド条項
cost of living index 生計費指数
cost of living rider 生計費指数特約
cost of manufactured goods 製造原価
cost of pension 年金のコスト
cost of policy 保険原価
cost of production 製造原価
cost of production budget 製造費予算
cost of production of banknotes 銀行券製造原価
cost of products sold 売却原価
cost of purchase 仕入原価
cost of raising funds 資金調達コスト
cost of repairs 修繕費
cost of restructuring リストラ費用
cost of sales 販売原価
cost of sales method 売上原価法
cost of shareholders' equity 株主資本コスト
cost of short - term funds 短期資金調達費用
cost of tax collection 徴税コスト
cost of temporary repair 仮修繕費
cost of the shares 株式の取得費
cost of the transferred receivable 債権の譲渡原価
cost of transferred properties 譲渡資産の取得費
cost of treasury stock 自己株式の取得原価
cost of work performed 出来高原価
cost overrun 予算超過
cost performance コスト・パフォーマンス
cost plus コスト・プラス
cost plus contract 実費精算契約
cost plus fixed fee contract 定額報酬実費支払契約
cost plus method 原価基準法
cost price 仕入値段
cost push inflation コストプッシュ・インフレ
cost rate 原価率
cost record 原価記録
cost recovery 原価の回収
cost reduction コスト削減
cost report 原価報告書
cost saving コスト節減
cost sharing 費用分担
cost sheet 原価計算表
cost standard 原価基準
cost statement 原価計算書
cost structure コスト構造
cost system 原価計算システム
cost to cost 原価対原価
cost unit 原価単位
cost utility 費用効果
cost value 原価価値
cost variance 原価差額
cost variance account 原価差額勘定
cost, insurance and freight 運賃・保険料込み
cost-based 原価を基礎とする
cost-based accounting 原価主義会計
cost-based measure 原価基準の測定値
cost-or-less principle 原価以下主義
cost-push inflation コスト・プッシュ・インフレ
cost-reduction programs 原価低減計画
cost-sharing benefit コスト分担による便益
cost-to-retail ratio 小売原価率
cost-value association 原価・価値の関連
cost-volume-profit analysis 費用・操業度・利益分析
cost-volume-profit relationship 原価・操業度・利益関係
costing 原価計算
costing method 原価算定方法
costing period 原価計算期間
costing sheet 原価計算表
costing unit 原価計算単位

costs of delivery and safekeeping 搬送・保管のコスト
cosureties 共同保証人
cotenancy 不動産の共同保有
council 評議会
council house 公営住宅
council on alcoholic beverages 酒類審議会
Council on Customs, Tariff, Foreign Exchange and Other Transactions 関税・外国為替等審議会
Council on Economic and Fiscal Policy 経済財政諮問会議
Councilor for Policy Evaluation 政策評価官
Councilor of the Minister's Secretariat 審議官（官房担当）
counselor 参与；相談役；法律顧問
Counselor (of the Minister's Secretariat) 参事官
count out 定足数を満さないと認めて流会する
counter cession 見返再保険
counter cyclical 反循環的
counter cyclicals 非景気循環株
counter party failure 取引先の倒産
counter-benefit 反対給付
counter-party カウンターパーティ
counter-purchase 見返り購入；見返輸入
counterbalance 効果を相殺する
countercheck 再照合する
countercyclical policy 反循環政策
counterdeed 反対証書
counterfeit 偽造
counterfeit Bank of Japan note 偽造日銀券
counterfeit card 偽造カード
countermand 取消す
countermeasure 対策
counteroffer カウンター・オファー
counterpart カウンターパート
counterpart fund 見返資金
counterparty カウンターパーティ
counterparty rating カウンターパーティ格付け
counterparty risk カウンターパーティ・リスク
counterparty trading participant 相手方となる取引参加者
counterpoise 平衡力
countersecurity 逆担保
countersign 副署する
countersignature 連署
countervailing duty 相殺関税
countervailing power 対抗力
country exposure カントリー・エクスポージャー
country fund カントリー・ファンド
country having deficit in capital transaction 資本輸出国
country limit カントリー・リミット
country of incorporation 設立国
country rating 国の格付け
country risk カントリー・リスク
county attorney 郡検事
county borough 特別市
county court 郡裁判所
coupled with 相まって
coupon クーポン；利札
coupon amount 利子支払額
coupon attache カム
coupon attribute クーポン属性
coupon bank debenture 利付金融債
coupon bearing bond 利付債
coupon bond 利付債
coupon collection クーポン取立
coupon curve 利付債利回り曲線
coupon date 利払日
coupon equivalent rate クーポン相当利率
coupon equivalent yield 債券相当利回り
coupon frequency 利払回数
coupon fund 利付資金
coupon hike 表面利率の引上げ
coupon income クーポン収入
coupon interest クーポン金利
coupon off 利札落ち
coupon on 利札付き

coupon pass 米国債の買い切りオペ
coupon paying issues 利付債
coupon payment 利払い
coupon payment date 利払い期日
C
coupon payment period クーポン支払い期間
coupon period 利子支払期間
coupon policy 利札付保険
coupon rate クーポン利率；クーポン・レート；表面利率
coupon received 受取利子
coupon redemption クーポン回収
coupon sale クーポン・セール
coupon swap クーポン・スワップ
coupon yield クーポン利率
coupon-bearing government bond 利付国債
coupon-bearing-convertible-bond type corporate bonds with new share reservation rights 利付転換社債型新株予約権付社債券
coupon-only currency swap クーポンだけの通貨スワップ
course of employment 職務執行過程
court 裁判所
court case 訴訟事件
court of domestic relation 家庭裁判所
court of equity 平衡裁判所
Court of Exchequer 財務裁判所
court of record 記録裁判所
covariance 共分散
covariance analysis 共分散分析
covenant 契約条項
covenant for title 権限担保条項
covenant of seisin 権利担保条項
covenant package 制限条項
covenantee 被契約者
cover カバー
cover dealing カバー・ディーリング
cover note 保険契約覚書
cover the loss 損失を埋める
coverage 保障
coverage by security 担保範囲
coverage limit 保険付保範囲
coverage of multiple establishments 一括適用
coverage ratio カバー率
covered call カバード・コール
covered call option カバード・コール・オプション
covered compensation 保証報酬
covered establishment 適用事業所
covered option カバード・オプション
covered position カバード・ポジション
covered straddle カバード・ストラドル
covered warrant カバード・ワラント
covering cost コストの回収
covering short 空売りの買戻し
covert intervention 覆面介入
CP (commercial paper) コマーシャル・ペーパー
CP (commercial paper) market CP 市場
CP (commercial paper) operation CP オペレーション
CP (counter purchase) カウンターパーチェス
CPA (certified public accountant) 公認会計士
CPA Administration Commission 公認会計士管理委員会
CPE (continuing professional education) 継続専門教育
CPF (Central Provident Fund) 中央積立基金
CPI (consumer price index) 消費者物価指数
CPI (consumer price index) release CPI の発表
CPP (constant purchasing power accounting) 購買力変動会計
CPR (conditional repayment rate) 年間期限前償還率
CPR (constant prepayment rate) 定率期限前償還率
CPSS (clearing and payment services system) 支払い・決済サービス・システム

CPSS (Committee on Payment and Settlement Systems) 支払い・決済委員会
CPT (cost per thousand) CPT
CQS (consolidated quotation system) 総合取引情報システム
CR (closing rate) 決算日レート
Cr. 貸方
craft union 同業組合
crawling peg クローリング・ペッグ
crawling peg system 段階的平価変動制
craze for speculation 投機熱
CRB (Commodity Research Bureau) Index CRB 指数
CRC (Costa Rica colon) コスタリカ・コロン
CRE (commercial real estate) 商業用不動産
cream skimming いいとこどり
create lawsuit 訴訟を引き起こす
creation 創立
credentials 信任状
credibility 信用度
credible 信用できる
credit 貸方；控除；信用
credit accident 信用傷害
credit accommodation 信用供与
credit account 貸方勘定
credit against corporation tax 法人税の控除
credit against tax 税額控除
credit among corporations 企業間信用
credit analysis 与信分析
credit and debit to BOJ accounts 日銀当預の入金・引落
credit and suretyship insurance 信用及び保証保険
credit approval 与信承認
credit assessment 信用評価
credit association 信用組合
credit audit 信用監査
credit authorization terminal 信用照会端末
credit availability クレジット・アベイラビリティ
credit balance 貸方残高
credit bill 信用手形
credit blow-up クレジットの悪化
credit bureau 信用情報センター
credit business 与信業務
credit buying rate 期限付手形買相場
credit capability 信用力
credit card クレジット・カード
credit card burglary insurance クレジット・カード盗難保険
credit card business クレジット・カード業務
credit card company クレジット・カード会社
credit card issued by bank or its subsidiary 銀行系カード
credit card receivables クレジットカード債権
credit card theft insurance クレジットカード盗難保険
credit cards issued by the agent 代行カード
credit carryover 控除額の繰越
credit ceiling 信用限度
credit ceiling application system 貸出限度額適用制度
credit check 信用力チェック
credit collection account 回収口座に貸方計上する
credit concern 信用懸念
credit contraction 信用収縮
credit control 与信管理
credit conversion factor クレジット換算係数
credit cooperative 信用協同組合
credit creation 信用創造
credit crisis 信用恐慌
credit crunch 金融逼迫
credit crunch countermeasure 貸し渋り対策
credit curve クレジット・カーブ
credit customer 掛売得意先
credit decision 信用判断
credit decline 信用の低下
credit default options クレジット・デ

フォルト・オプション
credit demand 資金需要
credit derivative transaction クレジット・デリバティブ取引
C
credit derivatives クレジット・デリバティブ；信用派生商品
credit driven 信用力改善による
credit ease 信用緩和
credit enhancement 信用補完
credit event クレジット・イベント
credit exposure 与信リスク
credit exposure management 与信管理
credit extension 信用期間延長
credit facility クレジット・ファシリティ
Credit Federations of Agricultural Cooperatives 信用農業協同組合連合会
Credit Federations of Fishery Cooperatives 信用漁業協同組合連合会
credit for dividend 配当控除
credit for experimental and research expenses 試験研究費の特別控除
credit for handicapped person 障害者控除
credit for income tax 所得税額の控除
credit guarantee 信用保証
credit guarantee company 信用保証会社
Credit Guarantee Corporation 保証協会
credit health insurance 信用医療保険
credit history クレジット・ヒストリー
credit indices 信用指数
credit inquiry 信用照会
credit instruments 信用証券
credit insurance 信用保険
credit investigation 信用調査
credit life insurance 信用生命保険
credit limit 与信限度額
credit line 貸出枠
credit line system クレジット・ライン制度
credit loan 信用貸し
credit loss 貸倒れ
credit margin 信用証拠金
credit market クレジット市場
credit memorandum 貸方メモ
credit money 信用貨幣
credit note 送金付替票
credit on a debt 債務に対する信用
credit opinion 格付見解
credit option クレジット・オプション
credit past due date 期日到来元本
credit policy クレジット・ポリシー
credit price 掛売値段
credit quality 与信の質
credit rate 貸付金利
credit ratings 信用格付け
credit ratio 信用比率
credit rationing 信用制限
credit records 信用情報
credit reference 信用照会
credit reviews 与信監査
credit risk 信用リスク
credit risk allocation クレジット・リスク配分
credit risk analysis 信用リスク分析
credit risk assets 信用リスク・アセット
credit risk management system 信用リスク管理体制
credit risk policy 信用リスク方針
credit risk profile クレジット・リスク・プロファイル
credit risk weight 信用リスク・ウエート
credit sales accounts 売掛勘定
credit scoring クレジット・スコアリング
credit scoring model 信用評価モデル
credit sector 社債セクター
credit side of the transaction 取引の貸方側
credit slip 入金表
credit spread 信用スプレッド
credit squeeze 金融引締め
credit standing 信用状況
credit standing condition 信用状態

credit status 信用状況
credit strength 信用力
credit substitute 信用供与代替
Credit Suisse Index Generals クレディスイス指数
credit support 信用補完
credit swap クレジット・スワップ
credit system 掛売制度
Credit System Division 信用課
Credit System Stabilization Office 信用機構室
credit term 信用期間
credit terms 掛売条件
credit tightening 金融引締め
credit tracking クレジット追跡
credit tranche クレジット・トランシェ
credit transfer 順送金
credit union 信用組合
credit union exchange 信組為替
credit watch クレジット・ウォッチ；信用格付見直し
credit watch system クレジット・ウォッチ・システム
credit-linked note クレジット・リンク債；クレジット・リンク・ノート
creditable amount of foreign taxes 外国税額の控除限度額
credited in income statement 損益計算書に収益計上される
credited rate 付与加算率
credited service 認定勤務年数
credited to equity account 資本勘定に貸方計上される
credited to shareholders' interests 株主持ち分への貸方計上
credited to the BOJ accounts 日銀当預に貸方計上される
crediting rate 予定利率
creditor 債権者
creditor bank 貸方銀行
creditor committee 債権者委員会
creditor country 債権国
creditor group insurance 債権者団体保険
creditor nation 債権国
creditor side 貸方欄
creditor's equity 債権者持ち分
creditor's voluntary liquidation 債権者による任意清算
creditor's voluntary winding-up 債権者による任意清算
creditors' equity interests 債権者持ち分
creditors' meeting 債権者会議
credits 貸方計上額；債権
credits to the government's deposit account 政府預金への入金
creditworthiness 信用度
creditworthiness of the issuers 発行会社の信用状態
creditworthy 信用力のある
creed 信条
creep back upwards じり高傾向にある
creeping deflation クリーピング・デフレーション
creeping inflation クリーピング・インフレーション
creeping nationalization しのびよる国有化
Crest Settlement Account クレスト決済口座
CrestCo クレスト（英国保管振替機関）
criminal action 刑事訴訟
criminal case 刑事事件
Criminal Code 刑法
criminal investigation 強制調査；査察
Criminal Investigation Division 査察課
criminal investigation system 査察制度
Criminal Law 刑法
criminal of tax evasion 脱税犯
criminal proceedings 刑事訴訟手続
criminal suit 刑事訴訟
crisis 恐慌
crisis at maturity 一括返済リスク
crisis in insurance 保険危機
crisis management 危機管理
crisis rate 危機レート

C

criteria 規準
criteria for delisting 上場廃止基準
criteria for examination 審査基準
criteria for listing 上場基準
Criteria for Listing Examination of Stock 株券上場審査基準
criteria for selecting operation 選定基本要領
critical function 批判的機能
critical issue 深刻な問題
critical mass 限界量
critical path accounting クリティカル・パス会計
critical path method クリティカル・パス・メソッド
critical point 限界点
critical success factor 重要な成功要因
critical terms 重要な条件
critical value 臨界値
criticism 批判
crop 出来高
crop basis 収穫基準
cross クロス
cross access 相互アクセス
cross action 反対訴訟
cross arbitration クロス裁定
cross border ボーダーレス
cross border information 国境のない情報
cross border listing 国外での上場
cross border market 国際市場
cross claim 強制訴訟参加
cross currency swap 通貨スワップ
cross debt 相対債務
cross default クロス・デフォルト
cross default clause クロス・デフォルト条項
cross elasticity 交叉弾力性
cross footing 交差突合せ
cross hedge クロス・ヘッジ
cross held shares 持合い株式
cross holding of shares 株式持合い
cross indemnification 相互賠償
cross liability clause 交叉責任条項
cross license contract クロスライセンス契約
cross margin クロス・マージン
cross margining 現物とレポのポジションの相殺
cross market trade 複数市場間トレード
cross membership 相互会員
cross offer 交叉申込
cross order 両建注文
cross over analysis 交差分析
cross purchase 交互購入
cross rate クロス・レート
cross reference 相互参照；対応表
cross referenced to 参照符号の付いた
cross sectional analysis 横断分析；他企業比較
cross sector セクター間の
cross sell 相互販売
cross selling 並売
cross shareholding 株式持合い
cross trading クロス取引
cross-border funding 国際的な資本調達
cross-border settlement risk クロスボーダー決済リスク
cross-border stock exchange listing 国際的な株式上場
cross-currency interest rate swap クロスカレンシー金利スワップ
cross-currency trade 通貨間取引
cross-demand 反対請求
cross-market spread 市場間スプレッド
cross-sectional valuation approach クロス・セクション評価アプローチ
cross-trade クロス売買
crossed check 横線小切手
crossed trade バイカイ
crossing for the purpose of financing 金融クロス
crossing trading 対当取引
crowd 特定グループ
crowd trading クラウド取引
crowding out クラウディング・アウト
crowding out effect クラウディング・アウト効果

crown jewel 重要部門
crude analogy 大雑把な判断
crude oil futures option 原油先物オプション
crunch 逼迫
cryptographic techniques 暗号技術
crystallization of floating charge 浮動担保の結晶
CS (customer satisfaction) 顧客満足度
CSD ギリシャ保管振替機関
CSD (central securities depository) 証券決済機関
CSR (corporate social responsibility) 企業の社会的責任
CTD (cheapest-to-deliver) 最割安銘柄
CTT (capital transfer tax) 贈与税
culpa 過失
culpable 過失する
cum call 払込付
cum coupon 利札付き
cum new 新株付き
cum right 新株引受権付き
cum rights quotation 権利付相場
cum warrant カムワラント
cum-dividend 配当含み
cum-drawing 抽選付き
cum-interest 利子含み
cum-profit distribution 利益分配金含み
cumulative adjustment 累積修正額
cumulative amount of depreciation 減価償却累計額
cumulative change 累積変化
cumulative deficit 累積赤字
cumulative depreciation 償却累計
cumulative dividend 累積配当
cumulative effect 累積的影響額
cumulative effect of accounting change 会計方針変更による累積的影響額
cumulative error 累積誤差
cumulative exchange difference 累積為替差額
cumulative fiscal deficit 国家予算累積赤字
cumulative investment 累積投資
cumulative legacy 累積的遺贈
cumulative limit 累積限度額基準
cumulative limitation 累積的制限
cumulative loss 累損
cumulative maximum amount 累積限度額
cumulative method 累加法
cumulative minimum premium 累積最低保険
cumulative preference 累積優先
cumulative preference dividends 累積優先配当
cumulative preference right 累積的優先権
cumulative preferred shares 累積的優先株
cumulative preferred stock 累積優先株
cumulative retained profit 留保利益合計
cumulative retrospective adjustment 累積的遡及修正額
cumulative surplus 累積黒字
cumulative taxation 累積課税
cumulative total of required reserves 積数
cumulative translation adjustment 累積為替換算調整
cumulative voting 累積投票
CUP (Cuban peso) キューバ・ペソ
Curacao depositary receipts キュラソー預託証書
curator 後見人
curb market 場外市場
cure period 養生期間
curing effect 治癒効果
currency 通貨
currency adjustment 通貨調整
currency adjustment account 為替換算調整勘定
currency alignment 通貨調整
currency and demand deposits 現金及び預金通貨
currency and monetary control 通貨及び金融の調節

C

C

currency appreciation 通貨騰貴
currency area 通貨圏
currency authority 通貨当局
currency basket 通貨バスケット
currency bloc 通貨ブロック
currency board system カレンシー・ボード制
currency clause 通貨条項
currency commodity 通貨商品
currency control 通貨管理
currency conversion bond カレンシー・コンバージョン債
currency convertible in fact 事実上交換可能通貨
currency crisis 通貨危機
currency deflation 通貨デフレ
currency deposit 通貨性預金
currency depreciation 通貨価値下落
currency devaluation 通貨切下げ
currency exchange restriction 通貨交換制限
currency fluctuation 通貨変動
currency futures 通貨先物
currency futures price movement 通貨先物価格動向
currency futures trading 通貨先物取引
currency hedging 為替ヘッジ
currency in circulation 通貨流通高
currency indemnity 通貨補償
currency inflation 通貨インフレ
currency invoicing 貿易決済通貨
Currency Issue Department 発券局
currency movement 為替動向
currency note 政府通貨
currency option trading 通貨オプション取引
currency overlay カレンシー・オーバーレイ
currency principle 通貨主義
currency purchases 通貨買い
currency risk 為替リスク
currency strength 通貨高
currency substitute 代替通貨
currency swap bond 通貨スワップ債
currency system 通貨体系
currency translation 通貨換算
currency translation differences 外貨換算差額
currency unit 通貨単位
currency upvaluation 通貨切上げ
currency value 通貨価値
currency views 為替見通し
current 流動
current account 当座勘定
current account balance 経常収支
current account check 当座小切手
current account deficit 経常赤字；対外収支の赤字
current account service 当座預金サービス
current account surplus 経常黒字；対外収支の黒字
current account transaction 当座預金取引
current accounts at the central bank 中銀当預
current acquisition cost 現在取得価額
current adjustment 経常的な調整
current amount 現在額
current arrangement 流動性配列法
current asking price 現在の売却値段
current asset investment 短期投資
current asset ratio 流動資産比率
current assets 流動資産
current assets turnover (ratio) 流動資産回転率
current assumption whole life insurance 計算基礎変動型終身保険
current balance 経常収支
current bid price 現在の買値
current bond yield equivalent 政府債換算直接利回り
current budget 経常予算
current cost 現在原価
current cost earnings 現在原価利益
current cost financial statements 現在原価財務諸表
current cost insurance 1年定期式団体保険

current cost/constant dollar accounting 時価主義安定価値会計
current cost/nominal dollar accounting 時価主義名目価値会計
current coupon カレント・クーポン；期間指標
current coupon bond カレント・クーポン・ボンド
current credit accounts with agencies 代理店貸し
current deposit 当座預金
current deposit account 当座勘定
current disbursement approach 賦課方式
current discount 現行割引率
current dollar 経常ドル
current employee 現従業員
current exchange rate 実勢為替相場
current exit value 売却時価
current expenditure 経常支出
current expenditure budget 経費の予算
current expenses 経常費用；当期費用
current exposure カレント・エクスポージャ
current fair value 現在公正価値
current fiscal year 現会計年度
current fund 当座資金
current income 当期利益
current interest rate 現行金利
current level 現水準
current level of stock price 現在の株価水準
current liability 流動負債
current liquidity 現在の流動性
current loan classification 現在のローンの分類
current market price 時価
current market yield spread 実勢市場利回りスプレッド
current maturities of long-term debt 長期負債の今期返済額
current maturity 残存期間；当期満期部分
current maturity of long-term debt 長期負債の当期返済額
current money 流通貨幣
current month delivery 当限
current offer price 現在の売値
current operating performance basis 当期業績主義
current operating performance income statement 当期業績主義による損益計算書
current operating profit 当期営業利益
current pay structure カレント・ペイ構造
current payment 経常支払
current pension expense 当期の年金費用
current period 当期
current period amount 当期の金額
current policy 既契約
current portion 当期分；流動部分
current portion of asset 資産の流動部分
current portion of interest bearing liability 有利子負債の１年内返済分
current portion of liabilities 債務の１年以内返済部分
current portion of long-term debt 短期借入金（長期借入で１年内返済分）
current premium 現行プレミアム
current price 時価
current rate 発生時レート
current rate method 決算日レート法
current ratio 流動比率
current report 臨時報告書
current service 当期勤務
current service cost 現在勤務費用
current status 現況
current tax 当期税金
current tax asset 当期税金資産
current tax expense 当期税金費用
current tax liability 当期税金負債
current term 当期
current term net income 当期純益
current term net loss 当期純損失
current term net profit or loss 当期純

損益
current term settlement of accounts 当期決算
current transaction 経常取引
current transfers 経常移転収支
current value 現在価値
current year 当期
current yield 直接利回り
current-asset cycle 流動資産回転期間
current-first order 流動性配列
current-outlay cost 当期支出原価
currently attainable 現在達成可能な
curtail the expense 経費を削減する
curtailed operation 操業短縮
curtailment of burden 負担軽減
curtailment of expenditure 経費削減
curtailment of mortgage モーゲージの部分繰上返済
curtailment or settlement 縮小または決済
curtailments 部分繰上返済
curve 曲線
curve flattening 長短利回り格差縮小
curving trend line 非直線的トレンド・ライン
cushion bond クッション・ボンド
cushion of cash flow キャッシュフローの余力
CUSIP (Committee on Uniform Securities Identification Procedures) CUSIP
cusp 尖点
custodial account 信託管理勘定；未成年者口座
custodian 株式保管人
custodian account 管理人勘定
custodian bank 保管銀行
custodian charge 保管料
custodian fee 保管手数料
custody 保管
custody account カストディ口座
custody and book-entry transfer institution 保管振替機関
custody assets 自己保有部分
custody bank カストディ銀行
custody fee 保管料
custody in commingled form 混蔵保管
custody of securities 証券の保管
custody of stock certificates 株券の保管
custody ratio 保管比率
custom free 税関手数料
custom index カスタム・インデックス
custom tailored 誂えの
Custom-Houses 税関
custom's invoice 税関送り状
customary practice 慣行
customary tenure estates 慣習上の保有権
customer 顧客
customer advance 前受金
customer base 顧客基盤
customer ledger 顧客口
customer loyalty 顧客の忠実性
customer relations カスタマー・リレーション
customer relationship 顧客との関係
customer repo カスタマー・レポ
customer transaction 対顧客取引
customer's account 顧客勘定；顧客口座
customer's agreement and consent 取引約諾書
customer's deposits 得意先受入保証金
customer's ledger 得意先元帳
customer's liabilities for acceptances and guarantees 支払承諾見返金
customer's loan 信用取引貸出
customer's man 証券営業マン
customer's margin 委託証拠金
customer's order 委託注文
customers mobilizing power 顧客動員力
customers' broker 証券外務員
customers' deposits 預り金
customers' ledger 売掛金元帳
customers' liabilities on guaranties 保証債務見返り
customers' securities 保管有価証券
customized 顧客仕様の

customized performance standards カスタム・パフォーマンス・スタンダード
Customs Administration Research Office 税関調査室
customs and exercise 関税と間接税
Customs and Tariff Bureau 関税局
customs autonomy 関税自主権
customs clearance 通関
customs clearance basis 通関ベース
Customs Clearance Division 関税局業務課
customs debenture 戻し税証明書
Customs Dissatisfaction Review Committee 関税等不服審査会
customs duty 関税
customs duty refund system 関税還付制度
customs invoice 通関用送り状
customs law 関税法
customs of merchant 商慣習法
customs procedures 通関手続き
customs tariff law 関税定率法
customs tariff table 関税率表
Customs Training Institute 税関研修所
customs union 関税同盟
cut-off point 境界点
cutback 短縮
cutoff clause 給付期間制限条項
cutoff date 締切日
cuttings 利札
CV (coefficient of variation) 変動係数
CVA (current value accounting) 現在価値会計
CWIP (construction work in progress) 建設仮勘定
CY (calendar year) 暦年
cycle 周期
cycle of on-site examination 考査の周期
cyclical 周期的な
cyclical and secular reasons 循環的要因と趨勢的要因
cyclical component 循環的要因
cyclical depression 循環不況
cyclical fluctuation 循環的変動
cyclical growth 循環的成長
cyclical low サイクルの底打ち
cyclical peak 景気の山
cyclical phenomenon 循環現象
cyclical stock 景気循環株
cyclical trough 景気の谷
cyclical upturn 景気の回復
cyclicals 循環株
cylinder シリンダー
CYP (Cyprus pound) キプロス・ポンド
CZK (Czech Republic koruna) チェコ・コルナ

D

D

DA (documents against acceptance) 引受渡し
DAF (delivery at frontier) 国境渡し条件
Daikoku satsu 大黒札
daily allowance 日当
daily average 一日平均
daily balance 日々残高
daily benefit 日額給付
daily chart 日足チャート
daily interest for arrearage 延滞日歩
Daily Life Security Law 生活保護法
daily price limit 値幅制限
daily rate 日歩
daily stock price index 日別株価指数
daily trading limit 値幅制限
daily trial balance 日計表
daimyo bond 大名債
daisy chain 相場操縦
Dajokan satsu 太政官札
damage 損害
damage insurance 損害保険
damaged or worn banknotes 損傷銀行券
damaged property 被害資産
damages payment 損害賠償額
damping effect 抑制効果
DARPS (dutch auction rate preferred stock) ダッチ・オークション・レート優先株
DASL (disclosed automated securities lending) 開示自動証券貸出
data bank データバンク
data base データベース
data capture データ収集
data communications データ通信
data encryption データの暗号化
data enrichment 情報の付加
data entry データ入力
data input 入力データ
data processing business データ処理業務
date and time of delivery 受渡期限
date of authorization 承認日
date of authorization for issue 公表承認日
date of enforcement 施行日
date of execution 執行期日
date of exhaust 貸付超過日
date of expiry 契約満了日
date of issuance 発行日
date of last payment 最終保険料支払日
date of origin 発生した日
date of policy 保険契約日
date of receipt 領収日
date of record 登録日
date of tax levy 課税告知日
date proved by notary 確定日付
dated date 利息起算日
dating 支払期間延長；支払猶予日数
dating backward 後日付の
dating forward 先日付の
day certain 将来の特定の日
day count basis 日割りベース
day loan 当日返済貸付
day of admission 会員加入の日
day of ex-right for the dividend 配当落ち日
day order 当日のみ有効な注文
day trade デー・トレード
day trader デー・トレーダー
day trading 日計り商い
day-to-day activity 日々の活動
day-to-day management 恒常的運営
day-to-day operation 日常業務
day-to-day trader 目先筋
days after sight 一覧後日払
days in arrears 延滞日数
days of grace 支払猶予期間
days of note 手形の日数

days prior to discount on notes payable 手形の経過日数
days to sell inventory 棚卸資産保有日数
daytime bridge 日中ブリッジ
DBFO (design-build-finance-operate) 設計・建設・ファイナンス・運営
DCF (discounted cash flow) ディスカウント・キャッシュフロー
DCM (direct clearing member) 直接清算会員
DD (demand draft) 送金為替手形
DD (direct dealing) intervention 直接取引介入
DDA(Department of Disarmament Affairs) 軍縮局
DDB (deep discount bond) ディープ・ディスカウント債
DDM (dividend discount model) 配当割引モデル
DDP (delivered duty paid) 持込渡し条件
de facto 事実上
de facto existing company 実質的な存続会社
de facto standard 事実上の標準
de jure 法律上
de-concentrate 集中排除する
dead freight 空荷運賃
dead letter 空文
dead loan 貸倒れ
dead loss 丸損
dead stock 不良在庫
dead weight loss of customs duty 関税の死重損失
deadline 期限
deadline for filing 提出締切日
deadline for repayment 弁済期限
deal between speculators 仕手戦
deal stock 買収関連株
dealer ディーラー
dealer commission ディーラー手数料
dealer loan ディーラーローン
dealer market ディーラー市場
dealer paper ディーラーペーパー
dealer participation ディーラーの参加
dealer's fee ディーラー手数料
dealer's margin 取引マージン
dealer's option ディーラーズ・オプション
dealer's position ディーラーポジション
dealers' market 業者間相場
dealing 自己売買
dealing account 取引勘定
dealing cost 取引費用
dealing in transit 未達取引
dealing market ディーリング相場
dealing risk ディーリングリスク
dear money policy 高金利政策
dearth 不足
death backed bonds 生命保険担保債券
death benefit 死亡給付金
death benefit clause 死亡給付条項
death by cause 死亡原因
death payment 死亡保険金支払い
death protection 死亡保障
death rate 死亡率
death tax 相続税
death-in-service benefit 勤務中死亡給付
debacle 瓦解
debanking 脱銀行化
debenture account 債券勘定
debenture assignment 社債券譲渡
debenture bond 社債券
debenture capital 借入資本
debenture convertible at par 額面転換社債
debenture holder 債券保有者
debenture interest 社債利子
debenture issuing expenses 社債発行費
debenture redemption 社債償還
debenture redemption reserve 減債積立金
debenture stock 無償還社債
debenture trust 社債券信託
debenture with lump-sum interest payment at maturity 利子一括払

利付金融債
debenture with warrant ワラント債
debit 引き落とす
debit account 借方勘定
debit advice 借記通知書
debit authorization 借記授権書；引落承認
debit balance 借方残高
debit cap 信用枠上限；保証額上限
debit card デビット・カード
debit insurance デビット保険
debit memorandum 借方メモ
debit note デビット・ノート
debit policy デビット保険
debit side 借方
debit side of the transaction 取引の借方側
debit slip 支払伝票
debit spread デビット・スプレッド
debit transfer 逆引振替
debited from the BOJ accounts 日銀当預から引落される
debited to 借方計上される
debt 負債
debt account 負債勘定
debt agreement 借入契約
debt amortization fund 負債償却準備金
debt and equity investments 社債と持分への投資
debt asset ratio 負債・資産比率
debt assumption 債務引受
debt balance 債務残高
debt bomb 負債爆弾
debt capital 他人資本
debt capital market 債券市場
debt ceiling 債務限度
debt collection 債権回収
debt collector 債務回収業者
debt covenant 負債条項
debt coverage 債務返済能力
debt cross デット・クロス
debt deferral 債務繰延べ
debt deflation デフレの悪循環
debt dependence ratio 国債依存度
debt discount 負債のディスカウント
debt discount and expenses 社債発行差金
debt dynamics 負債ダイナミクス
debt equity ratio 負債比率
debt equity swap 債務株式化；デット・エクイティ・スワップ
debt expense 社債発行費用
debt exposure 貸出リスク
debt factoring 債権買い取り
debt finance 借入による資金調達
debt for collection 取立債務
debt guarantee 債務保証
debt in foreign currency 外貨建債務
debt in U.S. dollar ドル建て債務
debt instrument 債務手段
debt instruments 債券
debt investment 債券投資
debt leverage 債務レバレッジ
debt limit 負債限度
debt loan 借入金
debt management 債務管理；社債管理
Debt Management Office 国債管理局
debt management policy 公債管理政策
debt maturity 負債期間
debt mix 負債構造
debt obligation 債務証券
debt off the book 簿外借金
debt premium 負債のプレミアム
debt ratio 負債比率
debt reduction 債務消滅
debt relief 債務免除
debt renegotiation 債務再交渉
debt repayment 負債返済
debt restructuring 債務の再編
debt retirement 債務返済
debt securities 債務証券
debt securities market 債務証券市場
debt service 債務の返済
debt service fund 借入返済基金；減債基金
debt service ratio 債務返済比率
debt servicing 元利の支払い
debt servicing cost 債務返済コスト
debt servicing schedule 債務償還計画

debt to bond swap 債務の債券化
debt to equity ratio 負債純資産比率
debt to equity swap 債務の株式化
debt trust 債務信託
debt warrant デット・ワラント債
debt/equity fund 債券・株式ファンド
debt/equity relationship 負債と株式の関係
debt-credit transaction 貸借取引
debt-equity hybrids 債券株式混合証券
debt-equity ratio 負債・資本比率
debt-to-income ratio 対所得負債比率
debtor 債務者
debtor account 借方勘定
debtor and creditor accounts 貸借勘定
debtor and estate 債務者及び破産財団
debtor balance 借方残高
debtor bank 借方銀行
debtor country 債務国
debtor firm 債務企業
debtor in possession 占有債務者
debtor nation 債務国
debtor side 借方欄
debtors' deposit 債務者預金
debts and credits 債権債務
debts in default 期限の利益を喪失している債務
decartelize カルテルを解体する
decelerating trend 減速傾向
deceleration 鈍化
decentralization 分権
decentralization of power 地方分権
decimal trading 少数表示取引
decision 決定
decision maker 意思決定者
decision making 意思決定
decision matrix 決定マトリックス
decision of a general meeting of stockholders 株主総会の決議
decision of a reorganization plan 再建計画の決定
decision of the Board of Directors 取締役会決議
decision of the general meeting 総会の決定
decision on request for reinvestigation 異議決定
decision support system 意思決定支援システム
decision tree 意思決定ツリー
decision-making body 意思決定機関
declaration 申告
declaration against interest 利益に反する供述
declaration date 配当宣言日
declaration form 申告用紙
declaration of bankruptcy 破産宣告
declaration of default デフォルト宣言
declaration of dividend 配当決議
declaration of import 輸入申告
declaration of income 所得申告
declaration of non-payment 支払拒絶宣言
Declaration of Paris パリ宣言
declaration policy 通知保険
declared capital 公示資本
declared income 申告所得
declared profit 計上利益
decline 下落する
decline in demand 需要減
decline in interest rate 金利低下
decline in market value 市場価値の下落
decline in prices of inventories 棚卸資産の価格の低落
declining balance depreciation method 定率減価償却法
declining balance method 定率法
declining business 不振事業
declining growth rate 逓減成長率
declining industry 斜陽産業
declining salary 給与の下落
decomposition 分解分析
decoupling from 異なる展開をする
decrease amount in current term 当期減少額
decrease in book value 帳簿価格の減少
decrease in profit rate 利益率の低下
decrease of income tax 所得税の減額

decreased earnings 減益
decreased receipts 減収
decreasing annuity 逓減年金
decreasing charge 逓減的費用
decreasing rate 低下率
decreasing return 収穫逓減
D
decreasing term insurance 逓減定期保険
decreasing term rider 逓減定期保険特約
decree 判決
decree of distribution 配分判決
decree of insolvency 支払不能判決
decree of nullity 無効判決
decrement 目減り
dedicated bond portfolio 債券のデディケート・ポートフォリオ
dedicated portfolio デディケート・ポートフォリオ
deduct 控除する
deducted 控除された
deducted in determining taxable income 損金算入される
deducted in determining the accounting profit 利益計算上費用に計上される
deductible 控除条件付保険
deductible amount for donation 寄付金の損金算入限度額
deductible clause 控除条項
deductible contribution 課税所得控除可能掛金
deductible expenses 損金
deductible for tax purposes 税務上損金算入される
deductible for the tax purpose 税金上の損金算入となる
deductible liabilities 控除すべき債務
deductible reserve 損金算入できる引当金
deductible temporary difference 将来減算一時差異
deductible timing difference 将来減算一時差異
deduction 控除
deduction against assets 資産の控除項目
deduction for carryforward of deficiency 欠損金の繰越控除
deduction for casualty losses 雑損控除
deduction for damage insurance 損害保険控除
deduction for dependents 扶養控除
deduction for dividends 配当控除
deduction for donation 寄付金控除
deduction for employment income 給与所得控除
deduction for family employees 専従者控除
deduction for foreign taxes 外国税額控除
deduction for insurance proceeds 保険金控除
deduction for life insurance premiums 生命保険料控除
deduction for medical expenses 医療費控除
deduction for old-age person 老年者控除
deduction for physically handicapped person 障害者控除
deduction for retirement income 退職所得控除
deduction for spouse 配偶者控除
deduction for tax purpose 課税所得計算上の損金
deduction for tax reduction 減免税額の控除
deduction for the contribution to small enterprise mutual aid plan 小規模企業共済掛金控除
deduction for widow 寡婦控除
deduction for working student 勤労学生控除
deduction from one's equity 資本項目からの控除項目
deduction from property, plant and equipment 有形固定資産からの控除
deduction from tax for housing savings

住宅貯蓄控除
deduction from the leased asset リース資産からの控除
deduction limit applicable to donation 寄付金損金参入限度額
deduction of entertainment expenses 交際費控除
deduction of estimated expenses 概算経費控除
deduction of foreign corporation tax carried forward 繰越外国税額控除
deduction of interest on borrowed fund 負債利子控除
deduction of liabilities 債務控除
deduction of public pension 公的年金控除
deduction on disposal 処分時の減算
deductions 利益からの控除項目
deductions from income 所得控除
deductions from profit 利益からの控除項目
deductions from working capital 運転資本の減少
deductive method 演繹法
deed of arrangement 債務整理証書
deed of conveyance 譲渡証書
deed of title 権利証書
deemed accounting period みなし事業年度
deemed acquisition date みなし取得日
deemed acquisition price みなし取得価格
deemed approval みなし賛成
deemed bankrupt borrower 破綻懸念先
deemed bounty みなし交付金
deemed corporation みなし法人
deemed deposit みなし預託
deemed dividend みなし配当
deemed donations みなし寄付金
deemed inherited property みなし相続財産
deemed loan loss 貸倒懸念債権
deemed participation みなし加入
deemed request for reconsideration みなし審査請求
deemed stock price みなし株価
deemed tax assessment みなし課税負担
deemed transfer みなし譲渡
deep discount 割引率の大きい
deep market 十分な市場
deep rock doctrine ディープロック主義
deep-rooted inflation 慢性的インフレ
deeper setback 大きな下落
defacement 汚染
default 債務不履行
Default Compensation Fund 違約損失補償基金
Default Compensation Reserve 違約損失積立金
default compensation reserve fund 違約損失補償基金
default correlation デフォルト相関
default curve デフォルト曲線
default free デフォルトリスクのない
default fund デフォルト基金
default loss デフォルト損失
default loss compensation reserve 違約損失補償準備金
default of obligation 債務不履行
default on clearing obligation 決済不履行
default on mortgage obligation モーゲージ債務不履行
default rate デフォルト率
default receivables デフォルト債権
default risk 債務不履行リスク
default risk premium 債務不履行のプレミアム
defaulted bond 無償還債券
defaulter 不履行者
defeasance 権利消滅条件；ディフィーザンス
defeasance clause ディフィーザンス条項
defeasance in substance 実質ディフィーザンス
defeasible 無効にできる

defeasible title 取消されうる権原
defeat 無効にする
defect 瑕疵
defective 不完全な
defective check 不正小切手
defective goods 仕損品
defective random variables 不完全確率変数
defective title 瑕疵のある権原
defend 抗弁する
defend bond 国防債券
defense 抗弁
defense attorney 被告側弁護士
defense expenditure 防衛費
Defense Facilities Administration Agency 防衛施設庁
defensive management ディフェンシブ運用
defensive stock ディフェンシブ銘柄
defer the payment 支払いを遅らせる
deferment 繰延べ
deferment account 繰延勘定
deferment clause 支払猶予条項
deferment of investment 投資繰延べ
deferment of taxation 課税見送
deferral 延期；繰延べ
deferral accounting 繰延会計
deferral amortization method 繰延償却法
deferral method 繰延法
deferral of cost variances 原価差額の繰延べ
deferral of tax 税金の繰延べ
deferral percentage 課税繰延額対給与比率
deferred 据置き
deferred and accrued accounts 経過勘定
deferred annuity 据置型年金
deferred assets 繰延資産
deferred assets on bond issue 債券繰延資産
deferred assurance 据置保険
deferred bond 繰延債
deferred charge 繰延費用
deferred charge account 繰延費用勘定
deferred charge before amortization 償却前繰延資産
deferred compensation arrangement 繰延給与制度
deferred compensation expense 繰延報酬費用
deferred consumption 消費の先送り
deferred coupon 繰延利払い
deferred coupon bond 金利繰延債
deferred credit 繰延貸方項目
deferred debit 繰延借方項目
deferred delivery 延渡し
deferred depreciation 繰延償却
deferred distribution 配当据置支給
deferred expenditure 繰延支出
deferred expenses 繰延費用
deferred export 延払輸出
deferred foreign tax 繰延外国税
deferred foreign tax assets 繰延外国税資産
deferred foreign tax liabilities 繰延外国税負債
deferred gross profit 繰延売上利益
deferred group annuity 団体据置年金
deferred hedge accounting 繰延ヘッジ会計処理
deferred hedge loss 繰延ヘッジ損失
deferred hedging gain 繰延ヘッジ利益
deferred income tax charge 繰延法人税費用
deferred income tax liability 繰延法人税債務
deferred income taxes 繰延税
deferred interest 延払利息
deferred interest account 前受利息勘定
deferred interest bond 利息繰延債券
deferred interest mortgage 利払繰延モーゲージ
deferred item 繰越項目
deferred liabilities 繰延負債
deferred life annuity 据置終身年金
deferred life insurance 据置生命保険
deferred payment 後払い

deferred payment annuity 据置年金保険
deferred payment basis 延払基準
deferred payment credit 後日払信用状
deferred payment of income tax 所得税延納
deferred payment sales 延払条件付販売
deferred pension 繰延年金
deferred perpetuity 据置年金
deferred policy acquisition cost 繰延契約費用
deferred portion 繰延分
deferred premium 繰延保険料
deferred profit or loss on hedges 繰延ヘッジ損益
deferred profit sharing 据置利益分配
deferred rebate system 運賃延戻制
deferred recognition 遅延認識
deferred repairs 繰延修繕費
deferred retirement 定年延長
deferred revenue 繰延収益
deferred savings 据置貯金
deferred settlement 繰延決済
deferred share 劣後株式
deferred stock 後配株
deferred swap ディファード・スワップ
deferred tax account 繰延税勘定
deferred tax accounting 税効果会計
deferred tax assets 繰延税金資産
deferred tax assets valuation allowance 繰延税金資産評価引当金
deferred tax balance 繰延税金残高
deferred tax effect of the provision 引当金の税効果
deferred tax effects 繰延税効果
deferred tax expense 繰延税金費用
deferred tax income 繰延税金収益
deferred tax liabilities 繰延税金負債
deferred tax rule 税効果規則
deferred vesting 受給権繰延付与
deficiency 欠損
deficiency account 欠損勘定
deficiency bill 一時借入手形
deficiency carried-forward 繰越不足金
deficiency guarantee 不足額保証
deficiency in assets 債務超過
deficiency in insurance premium 保険料の欠損
deficiency in retirement allowance fund 退職金積立不足
deficiency letter 不備指摘書
deficiency reserve 不足責任準備金
deficit 赤字
deficit account 欠損金勘定
deficit amount 欠損金額
deficit at the beginning of a period 前期繰越欠損金
deficit budget 赤字予算
deficit busting plan 赤字削減計画
deficit carried forward 繰越決損金
deficit covered by directors 役員により補填された欠損金
deficit covering government bond 歳入補填国債
deficit disposition statement 欠損金処理計算書
deficit finance 赤字財政
deficit for the current term 当期損失金
deficit in aggregate amount 総額の不足額
deficit in cash 現金不足額
deficit net worth 負の純資産
deficit of fiscal balance 財政赤字
deficit on revaluation of investments 投資再評価損
deficit reconciliation statement 不足金処理計算書
deficit reduction 赤字削減
deficit spending 財政赤字；超過支出
deficit statement 欠損金計算書
deficit-covering bond 赤字国債
deficit-covering finance 赤字金融
defined asset fund 確定資産ファンド
defined benefit 確定給付
defined benefit accounting 給付建会計処理

D

D

defined benefit corporate pension plan 確定給付企業年金制度
defined benefit Keogh plan 給付建てキオ・プラン
defined benefit multi-employer plan 給付建複数事業主制度
defined benefit obligation 給付建債務
defined benefit pension plan 確定給付建年金制度
defined benefit plan 確定給付型年金プラン
defined compensation plan 適格補償制度
defined contribution accounting for 掛金建会計処理
defined contribution annuity plan 確定拠出型年金プラン
defined contribution arrangement 掛金建ての取決め
defined contribution Keogh plan 掛金建てキオ・プラン
defined contribution pension 確定拠出年金
defined contribution pension plan 確定拠出年金制度
defined contribution plan 確定拠出制度
defined dollar benefit 確定拠出給付
defined terms 定義された用語
definite change 明確な変動
definite insurance 確定保険
definite insurance policy 確定保険証券
definite matrix 定置行列
definite settlement of accounts 確定決算
definition 定義
definition of characteristic line 特性線の定義
definition of fair value 時価の定義
definitive bond 正式本券
definitive proxy statement 最終委任状勧誘書類
definitive sentence 終局判決
deflate 過少にする
deflation デフレ
deflation caused by yen appreciation 円高デフレ
deflation expectation デフレ期待
deflation floor デフレ・フロアー
deflation gap デフレーション・ギャップ
deflation policy デフレ政策
deflationary effect デフレ効果
deflationary gap デフレ・ギャップ
deflationary period デフレ期間
deflationary pressure デフレ圧力
deflationary spiral デフレ・スパイラル
deflator デフレーター
deflection of tax liability 税金債務の転嫁
defunct company 抹消会社
degradation 悪化
degree 等級
degree of concentration 集中度
degree of concentration of control 支配集中度
degree of consanguinity 親等
degree of dependence 依存度
degree of dependence upon exports 輸出依存度
degree of dependence upon imports 輸入依存度
degree of financial leverage 財務面の増益効果度
degree of impairment 減損の度合い
degree of monopoly 独占度
degree of operating leverage 営業面の増益効果度
degressive cost 逓減原価
degressive tax 逓減課税
del credere agent デル・クレデール・エージェント
del credere commission 支払手数料
delay 延滞
delay claims 遅延クレーム
delay of evacuation 明渡しの遅滞
delayed delivery 特約日受渡し
delayed interest 遅延利息

delayed opening 開始延期
delayed payment 延納
delayed payment terms 延払条件
delayed recognition 認識の延期
delayed retirement 退職延期
delayed retirement credit 退職年金加算
delaying settlement 繰延決済
delegate 委任する
delegated legislation 委任立法
delegation 権限付与
delegation by law 法律の委任
delegation of authority 権限委任
delegation of authority to rules 規則への委任
deletion from ledger 原簿の末梢
deletion of exclusion 免責事項の削除
deletion of registration 登録除却
deliberative council 審議会
deliberative members 審議委員
delinquency 滞納
delinquency amount 延滞金
delinquency in payment 支払いの遅滞
delinquency tax 延滞税
delinquent charge 遅延損害金
delinquent taxpayer 滞納者
delist 上場廃止する
delisting 上場廃止
deliverability 業務遂行確実性
deliverable bills 受渡適格短期証券
deliverable bond 受渡適格債
deliverable grade 受渡適格の
deliverable issue 受渡適格銘柄
deliverable items 決済物件
delivered 引渡済み
delivered at frontier price 国境渡値段
delivered business 証券受渡済契約
delivered duty paid 仕向地持込渡し（関税込）
delivered duty unpaid 仕向地持込渡し（関税抜）
delivered ex quay 埠頭持込渡し
delivered ex ship 本船持込渡し
delivered money due to merger 合併交付金
delivered price 引渡価格
delivered stock due to merger 合併交付株式
delivery 受渡し
delivery against payment 支払渡し
delivery basis 引渡基準
delivery date 受渡決済日
delivery day 受渡日
delivery deadline 受渡時限
delivery expenses 発送費
delivery instruction 引渡指図
delivery month 限月
delivery note 納品書
delivery notice 受渡通知
delivery obligation 交付債務
delivery of agreement 約款の交付
delivery of articles 物品納付
delivery of dividends 配当支払い
delivery of due bill 有価証券引渡票の交付
delivery of long-term contract work 長期工事引渡し
delivery of policy 保険証券の交付
delivery of subsidies 補助金交付
delivery order 荷渡指図書
delivery price 受渡決済値段
delivery schedule 納期
delivery settlement 受渡決済
delivery system by calendar month 暦月渡制
delivery to order 指図人渡し
delivery versus payment DVP
delivery versus payment settlement DVP 決済
delivery-certified mail 配達証明郵便
delivery-versus-payment (DVP) for JGSs 国債 DVP
Delphi forecast デルファイ予測
delta デルタ
delta hedge デルタヘッジ
delta neutral hedge デルタニュートラルヘッジ
delta value デルタ値
delving into the reserves 準備金に充当する

D

DEM (German mark) ドイツ・マルク
demand 需要；請求
demand account 要求払勘定
demand analysis 需要分析
demand and supply 需給
demand bill 一覧払手形
demand curve 需要曲線
demand debt 要求払債務
demand deficiency 需要不足
demand deposit 要求払預金
demand elasticity 需要弾力性
demand for capital 資本需要
demand for conversion 転換請求
demand for investing funds 投資のための資金需要
demand for money 貨幣需要
demand for name registration 名義書換請求
demand for tax payment 納付の督促
demand for withdrawal 交付請求
demand for withdrawal of stock certificates 株券の交付請求
demand forecast 需要予測
demand function 需要関数
demand function for money 貨幣需要関数
demand in reconvention 反訴
demand index 需要指数
demand liability 要求払負債
demand loan 当座貸付
demand note 要求払手形
demand of times 時代の要請
demand pressure 需要圧力
demand prospect 需要見通し
demand side economics 需要サイド経済学
demand to hold securities 証券保有の需要
demand-and-supply balance 需給バランス
demand-pull inflation ディマンドプル・インフレ
demand-to-hold schedule 保有需要曲線
demarcation 区割り
dematerialization 無券面化
dematerialized 証書発行を伴わない
dematerialized securities 証書発行を伴わない証券
demerger 会社の分割
demerit デメリット
demise 死亡
demobilization 動員解除
democratization 民主化
demographic analysis デモグラフィック分析
demographic change 人口構成の変化
demographic data 人員データ
demographic mix 人口構成
demographic ratio 人口統計的比率
demographic scoring デモグラフィック・スコアリング
demographic shift 人口推移
demographic statistics 人口統計
demographic transition 人口推移
demographic variables 人口統計上の変数
demographics 人口統計
demolition expenses 取りこわし費
demonetarization 廃貨
demonstration 立証
demonstration effect デモンストレーション効果
demurrage 停船料
demutualization 株式会社化
demutualizing 非相互化
denationalization 非国営化
denial 否認
denial of opinion 意見差控え
denominated in a foreign currency 外貨建て
denominated in each currency 各国通貨建て
denominated in foreign currency 外貨建ての
denominated in home currency 自国通貨建て
denominated in yen 円建て
denomination 額面金額
denomination of banknotes 紙幣金額

denomination reduction デノミ
denomination related stocks デノミ関連株
denominator 分母
denominator level 基準操業度
dent 落ち込み
dental expense insurance 歯科治療費保険
department audit 部門監査
Department of Commerce 米国商務省
Department of Justice 司法省
Department of State 米国国務省
Department of Trade and Industry 貿易産業省
Department of Treasury 米国財務省
department store sales 百貨店売上高
department variance on overhead 部門間接費差異
departmental burden 部門負担費
departmental charge 部門費
departmental cost 部門原価
departmental cost accounting 部門別原価計算
departmental costing 部門別原価計算
departmental expenses 部門費
departmental expenses budget 部門費予算
departmental overhead 部門間接費
departmental process cost system 工程別総合原価計算
departmental profit 部門別利益
departure 逸脱
dependant 被扶養者
dependence 依存
dependence effect 依存効果
dependence on foreign trade 貿易依存
dependence on public debt 公債依存
dependent allowance 家族手当
dependent family member 扶養家族
dependent variables 従属変数
depleted cost 償却後原価
depletion allowance 減価引当
depletion assets 減耗資産
depletion deduction system 減耗控除制度
depletion of assets 資産の減耗
depletion of natural resources 天然資源減耗償却費
depletive 減耗可能な
deployment 展開
depopulation 人口減
deposit 預託
deposit account 預託勘定
deposit account pension 預金勘定年金
deposit administration 預託管理
deposit administration contract 預託管理契約
deposit administration fund 預託管理基金
deposit as collateral 担保預金
deposit at financial institutions 金融機関預金
deposit at notice 通知預金
deposit book 預金通帳
deposit by the Ministry of Finance 財務省預託金
deposit certificate 預金証書
deposit company 寄託会社
deposit contracts for securities 有価証券の消費寄託契約
deposit currency 預金通貨
deposit diary 預金記入帳
deposit due from bank 銀行預け金
deposit due to bank 銀行預り金
deposit fee 預託手数料
deposit float フロート預金
deposit for public auction 公売保証金
deposit for tax payment 納税準備金
deposit from employees 従業員預り金
deposit fund 預託基金
deposit in current account 当座預金
deposit in transit 未達預け入れ
deposit in trust 信託預金
deposit insurance 預金保険
deposit insurance bailout 預金保険救済
Deposit Insurance Law 預金保険法
deposit insurance system 預金保険制度
deposit law 供託法

deposit ledger 預金元帳
deposit liability 預金債務
deposit loan 預金貸付
deposit market 預金市場
deposit minus checks and bills on hand 実勢預金
D
deposit money 預金通貨
deposit multiplier 預金乗数
deposit of margin 証拠金の預託
deposit of non-debtor 非債務者預金
deposit of public money 公金預金
deposit of securities on contracts 保証差入有価証券
deposit of stock certificates 株券の預託
deposit of the security in lieu of cash 代用差入れ
deposit of title-deeds 権利書寄託
deposit office 供託所
deposit on a net basis 実勢預金
deposit on contract 預り保証金
deposit option 利息受取方法選択権
deposit paid on construction work 工事前渡金
deposit payoff 預金全額支払い
deposit rate 預金金利
deposit received 預り金
deposit received for guarantees 預り保証金
deposit received from employee 社員預り金
deposit received on sale 預り保証金
deposit requiring advance notice for withdrawal 通知預金
deposit reserve ratio 預金準備率
deposit share 預金シェア
deposit slip 預金伝票
deposit system 預金制度
deposit taking business 預金集め
deposit through deduction from monthly pay 天引貯金
deposit to be lent to a third party 導入預金
deposit transfer 預金振替方式
deposit under a fictitious name 架空名義預金
deposit war 預金戦争
deposit window 預金窓口
deposit with depository 保管振替機関への預託
deposit with fixed maturity date 確定期日預金
deposit with landlord 敷金
deposit with other bank 他行預け金
deposit with the central bank 中央銀行への預け金
deposit withdrawal 預金の引出
deposit-to-loan ratio 預金歩留り
depositary agreement 預託契約
depositary bank 預託銀行
depositary organization 預託機関
depositary trust company 証券保管振替機関
deposited article 供託物
deposited money 預託金
deposited securities 預託有価証券
deposited stock certificate 預託株券
deposition 証言記録
depositor 供託者
depositor protection 預金者保護
depository and book-entry transfer system for stocks 株券等に関する保管振替制度
depository assets 預託資産
depository bank 保管銀行；預託銀行
depository correspondent デポジトリー・コルレス
depository institution 預金受入金融機関
depository period 預託期限
Depository Receipts of Singapore シンガポール預託証書
depository shares 預託株式
deposits (excluding those of the government) 預金（政府預金除く）
deposits and guarantees 敷金と保証金
deposits and savings 預貯金
deposits for tax payment 納税準備預金
deposits from other banks 他行からの預金

deposits in the Bank of Japan current accounts 日銀当座預金
deposits of funds of national annuities 国民年金預託金
deposits on long-term leases 長期賃貸契約預り金
deposits paid to trade creditors 仕入前払代金
deposits with agencies 機関預け金
deposits with public utility corporations 公益事業会社預け金
deposits with the Bank of Japan 日銀預け金
deposits with Trust Fund Bureau 資金運用部預託金
Deposits, Loans, and Discounts Outstanding (Amount Outstanding of Deposits by Depositor, Loans and Discounts Outstanding by Industry, and Others) 預貸金調査結果
depreciable 減価償却可能な
depreciable amount 償却額
depreciable and amortizable assets 償却可能資産
depreciable assets 減価償却資産
depreciable cost 減価償却原価
depreciable leased assets 減価償却可能リース資産
depreciable life 償却可能年数
depreciable limit 償却限度額
depreciable property 償却資産
depreciable property for non-business 非営業用償却資産
depreciable property used in business 営業用償却資産
depreciated 減価償却後の
depreciated cost 減価償却後原価
depreciated original cost 減価償却後原始原価
depreciated replacement cost 減価償却後の再調達原価
depreciated value 減価償却後価額
depreciation 減価償却
depreciation account 償却勘定
depreciation accounting 減価償却会計
depreciation adequacy 減価償却妥当性
depreciation and amortization 償却
depreciation and amortization expense 減価償却費
depreciation base 減価償却基礎額
depreciation burden 減価償却負担
depreciation by depreciation rate 減価率による償却
depreciation fund 減価償却基金
depreciation in excess of the limit 超過償却
depreciation insurance 新価保険
depreciation method 減価償却法
depreciation of building 建物減価償却
depreciation of currency 通貨価値の低下
depreciation of currency value 通貨価値の低下
depreciation of deposit by inflation 預金目減り
depreciation of dollar ドル安
depreciation of ship costs 船価償却
depreciation of time value 時間価値の減価
depreciation of yen 円安
depreciation on assets 資産の減価償却
depreciation on obsolete assets 陳腐化資産の償却
depreciation on property 資産の減価償却
depreciation period 減価償却年数
depreciation policy 減価償却方針
depreciation rate 減価償却率；償却率
depreciation reserve 減価償却引当金
depreciation reserve ratio 減価償却引当金比率
depreciation unit 減価償却単位
depressed price 低迷価格
depression 不況
depression cartel 不況カルテル
depression of business 不景気
deprivation 剥奪
depth of market 板寄せ；市場の厚み

D

depth of the market 市場の活発さ
deputy 代理
Deputy Budget Examiner 主計官補佐
Deputy Chief Cabinet Secretary 内閣官房副長官
Deputy Commissioner (International Affairs) 審議官(国際担当)
Deputy Commissioner for International Affairs 国際担当参事官；参事官（国際）；参事官（国際）
Deputy Commissioner of the National Tax Agency 国税庁次長
Deputy Director of 課長補佐
Deputy Director-General 担当審議官
Deputy Director-General of the Budget Bureau 主計局次長
Deputy Director-General of the Customs and Tariff Bureau 審議官(関税局担当)
Deputy Director-General of the Financial Bureau 審議官(理財局担当)；理財局次長
Deputy Director-General of the International Bureau 審議官(国際局担当)
Deputy Director-General of the Planning and Coordination 参事官
Deputy Director-General of the Planning and Coordination Bureau 審議官
Deputy Director-General of the Supervisory Bureau 参事官（監督局）
Deputy Director-General of the Tax Bureau 審議官(主税局担当)
deputy governor 副総裁
Deputy Governor of the Bank of Japan 日銀副総裁
Deputy Secretary-General of Executive Bureau 事務局次長
Deputy Vice Minister 官房長
Deputy Vice Minister for Policy Planning and Co-ordination 総括審議官
derate 税率を軽減する
derecognition 認識の消滅；認識の中止
derecognition criteria 認識の中止基準
derecognize 認識を取消す
deregulated interest rate 自由金利
deregulated interest rate product 自由金利商品
deregulation 規制緩和
deregulation of finance 金融自由化
deregulation of financial and capital market 金融・資本市場の自由化
derivation of revenue 収益を得ること
derivative assets デリバティブ資産
derivative demand 派生需要
derivative deposit 派生的預金
derivative financial instrument デリバティブ金融商品
derivative income 派生的所得
derivative instrument 派生商品
derivative lawsuit 株主代表訴訟
derivative liabilities デリバティブ負債
derivative market 派生商品市場
derivative pass-through securities market 派生パス・スルー証券市場
derivative portfolio 派生商品ポートフォリオ
derivative product 派生商品
derivative securities 派生証券
derivative suit 派生訴訟
derivative transaction 派生取引
derivative type contract デリバティブ型契約
derivatives デリバティブ
derivatives market 金融派生商品市場
derived demand 派生的需要
derived function 導関数
derived income 派生的収入
DES (Data Encryption Standard) DES暗号
DES (debt equity swap) デット・エクイティ・スワップ
DESA(Department of Economic and Social Affairs) 経済社会局
descending 下降

descending curve ディセンディング・カーブ
descending order 降順
descending tops ディセンディング・トップス
descending triangle ディセンディング・トライアングル
descending triangle pattern 下降トライアングル
describable meaning 説明できる意味
description 記載
description of business 営業科目
descriptive data 記述データ
descriptive financial statements 説明付財務諸表
descriptive function 記述的機能
descriptive information 説明情報
descriptive statistics 記述的統計
design 意匠
design fee 意匠料
designated account 指定口座
designated bid 指名入札
designated city 指定都市
designated clearing participant 指定清算参加者
designated currency 指定通貨
designated deposit 指定預金
designated direct participant 指定参加者
designated exchange 指定取引所
designated financial institution 指定金融機関
designated fund 指定基金
designated money in trust 指定金銭信託
designated nominee 指定名義人
designated settlement time of 13:00 交換尻時点（13 時）
designated settlement time of 15:00 3 時時点（15 時）
designated settlement time of 17:00 為決時点（17 時）
designated settlement time of 9:00 朝金時点（9 時）
designated statistics 指定統計
designated stock 指定銘柄
designated trading 指定取引
designated-time settlement 時点決済
designation for transfer 振込指定
designation of business year 事業年度の指定
designation of hedges ヘッジ指定
designation of place for tax payment 納税地指定
designation of security 有価証券の銘柄
desk-top analysis 机上調査
destination 仕向地
destruction 損壊
destruction of asset 資産の破棄
destruction of environment 環境破壊
destructive disposition 破壊処分
detachable 分離型の
detachable warrant 分離型ワラント
detached employees 出向社員
detail 詳細
detailed account form 細目勘定式
detailed analysis 詳細な分析
detailed audit report 長文式監査報告書
detailed check 精査
detailed classification 詳細な分類
detailed enforcement regulations 施行細則
detailed requirement 詳細な規定
detailed statement 内訳書
details of account 勘定明細
details of distribution 分売要領
detection risk 発見リスク
deter 思いとどまらす
deteriorate 落ち込む
deteriorated assets 劣化資産
deterioration 悪化
deterioration of capacity 能力の低下
determinable amount 決定可能額
determinable cash flow 算定可能なキャッシュフロー
determinant 決定要因
determination date convention 更改日決定方法

D

determination of acquisition cost 取得価額の算定
determination of commencement of bankruptcy procedure 破産手続開始決定
determination of composition 和議の決定
determination of dividend 配当の決定
determination of taxable year 事業年度の決定
determination of the necessary adjustments 修正事項の決定
determine auction results 募入の決定
determining factor 決定要因
deterrent 抑止力
detraction 毀損
detriment 損傷
Deutch mark ドイツ・マルク
Deutche Borse AG ドイツ証券取引所
devaluation 切下げ
devaluation of government bonds 国債の評価減
devaluation risk 切下げリスク
devalue 切下げる
develop and import scheme 開発輸入
developed countries 先進国
developed economies 先進諸国
developer 開発業者
developing 発展途上にある
developing countries 発展途上国
developing country 開発途上国
development activities 開発活動
development assistance 開発援助
Development Bank of Japan 日本政策投資銀行
Development Bank of Japan Law 日本政策投資銀行法
development capital 開発資本
development cost 開発費
development cost of residential site 宅地造成費
development expense 開発費用
development finance 開発金融
Development Finance Division 開発金融課
development fund 開発資金
development gap 開発格差
Development Institutions Division 開発機関課
development of a new market 新市場の開拓
development of distribution channel 販路の開拓
development of knowledge 知識の開発
development of resources 資源開発
development of technology 技術振興
development of the market 市場の発展
development of venture business ベンチャー育成
development phase 開発段階
development policy 開発政策
Development Policy Division 開発政策課
development regulation 開発規制
development stage enterprise 開発準備中の企業
developmental stage 発展段階
developments in final demand 最終需要の動向
developments in the financial and capital markets 金融資本市場の動向
deviation 乖離
device 仕掛
devise 遺贈
devitalize 活力を奪う
devotion 専念
DFA (deposit facility agreement) 預金ファシリティ合意
DFLA (deposit facility loan agreement) 預金ファシリティ融資合意
DGACM (Department of General Assembly and Conference Management) 総会・会議管理局
DI (diffusion index) 景気動向指数
DI (diffusion index) of the coincident indicator 景気一致指数
DI (diffusion index) of the lagging indicator 景気遅行指数
DI (diffusion index) of the leading

indicator 景気先行指数
diagonal 主対角線
diagonal spread ダイアゴナル・スプレッド
diagram ダイアグラム
dialogue ダイアログ
diamond formation ダイヤモンド・フォーメーション
diary on securities market 証券経済日誌
DIC (Deposit Insurance Corporation) 預金保険機構
dichotomy 二分法
diff (Eurorate differential) ユーロ金利差先物
difference among issues 銘柄間格差
difference amount 差額
difference by renewal 更新差金
difference from exchange of property 交換差金
difference in yield 利回格差
difference resulting from offsetting futures contracts 先物取引差金
differences 差金
different account 口座相違
different jurisdiction 管轄違い
differential account 差額勘定
differential analysis 差分分析
differential coefficient 微分係数
differential cost 差額原価
differential costing 差額原価計算
differential earnings amount 差額利益額
differential equation 微分方程式
differential gain 差益
differential of return 収益率格差
differential weighting 加重の差別化
differentials 格差
differentiation 差別化
diffusion index 景気動向指標
diffusion of risks 危険分散
diffusion rate 普及率
diggings 採掘料
digital government 電子政府
digitized treasury fund 電子国庫
dilemma ジレンマ
diligence 注意
diluted earnings per share 希薄化後一株当り利益
dilution 希薄化
dilution factor 希薄化率
dilution of earnings per share 一株当り利益の希薄
dilutive 希薄化の
dilutive common stock 潜在的株式
dilutive effect 希薄化の影響
dilutive securities 希薄化証券
dimension 次元
diminished responsibility 責任軽減
diminishing balance depreciation 定率償却
diminishing balance method 逓減原価法
diminishing marginal productivity 生産力の逓減
diminishing return 収穫逓減
diminution 減少
dip 後退
DIP (debtor in possession) 占有継続債務者；DIP
dip down 下落
diplomacy 外交
direct aid 直接援助
direct association 直接的関連
direct attack 直接攻撃
direct banking ダイレクト・バンキング
direct budget transfer 予算繰入れ
direct capital 直接資本
direct capitalization 直接収益還元法
direct cause 直接原因
direct claim of claimant 被害者直接請求
direct consequence 直接的影響
direct cost 直接費
direct costing 直接原価計算
direct currency transaction 直接為替取引
direct deal 直取引
direct debit 口座引落

D

direct debiting 直接借方記入
direct deduction 直接の控除
direct department 直接部門
direct department cost 部門個別費
direct deposit 直接預託
direct disposal 直接処理
direct evidence 直接証拠
direct exchange arbitrage 直接為替裁定
direct exercise 直接行使
direct expense 直接経費
direct finance 直接金融
direct financing lease 直接金融型リース
direct foreign tax credit 外国税額直接控除
direct insurance 元受保険
direct insurer 元受保険会社
direct interest 直接の利害関係
direct intervention 直接介入
direct investment 直接投資
direct inward investment 対内直接投資
direct issuance 直接発行
direct issue paper 直接売りペーパー
direct labor 直接労働
direct labor cost 直接労務費
direct liability 確定負債
direct link 直接リンク
direct loan 直貸し
direct market 元受市場
direct material cost 直接材料費
direct method 直接法
direct method of depreciation 直接償却
direct national tax 直接国税
direct or equity investment 直接投資
direct overhead 直接経費
direct paper ダイレクトペーパー
direct participant 直接参加者
direct participant's account 参加者口座
direct participation program 直接参加方式
direct payment 直接支払い
direct placement 私募
direct premium written 計上元受保険料
direct presentation 直接表示
direct pricing 直接積算法
direct purchase 直接購入
direct reduction 直接減額
direct selling 直販
direct tax 直接税
direct tax credit 税額直接控除
direct test 直接テスト
direct trade 直接貿易
direct transaction 直取引
direct valuation 直接評価
direct write-off 直接償却
direct writing policy 直接募集契約
direct writing premium 元受保険料
direct yield 直接利回り
directed economy 統制経済
directed money trust 指定金銭信託
direction 指図
direction of interest rate 金利の方向
directional index 方向性指数
directional movement 方向性
directive 通達
director 取締役
Director (Analysis and Brewing Technology) 鑑定企画官
Director (International Examination) 国際調査管理官
Director (Liquor Tax and Industry) 酒税企画官
Director (Management and Co-ordination) 国税企画官
Director (Mutual Agreement Procedures) 国際企画官
Director (Property Valuation) 資産評価企画官
Director (Public Relations) 広報広聴官
Director (Research and Planning) 企画官
Director (Taxation) 課税企画官
Director for Corporate Accounting and Disclosure 企業開示参事官
Director for Development Issues 開発

企画官
Director for Fiscal Affairs, Policy Evaluation and Expenditure Review 主計企画官（財政分析，政策評価，予算執行調査）
Director for Fiscal Investment and Loan Appropriation 計画官
Director for Fiscal Investment and Loan Program System 財政投融資企画官
Director for Government Debt Management Policy 国債企画官
Director for Health and Welfare 厚生管理官
Director for Intellectual Property Rights 知的財産専門官
Director for Intelligence 密輸情報専門官
Director for Inter-Division Affairs 主計企画官（調整）
Director for International Co-operation 国際協力専門官
Director for International Issues on Taxation 主税企画官
Director for Legal Affairs 主計企画官（法規）
Director for Property Tax Policy 主税企画官
Director for Public Relations on Taxation 主税企画官
Director for Research and Planning 調査企画官
Director for Research on Customs and Tariff Classification 関税分類調査官
Director for Trade Negotiations 関税企画官
Director for Trade Remedy Affairs 特殊関税専門官
director having duties in an employee's capacity 兼務役員
Director of 課長
Director, Minister's Secretariat 企画官
Director, Office of 室長
director-general 局長
Director-General of the Budget Bureau 主計局局長
Director-General of the Customs and Tariff Bureau 関税局局長
Director-General of the Financial Bureau 理財局局長
Director-General of the Inspection Bureau 検査局長
Director-General of the International Bureau 国際局局長
Director-General of the Planning and Coordination Bureau 総務企画局長
Director-General of the Supervisory Bureau 監督局長
Director-General of the Tax Bureau 主税局局長
director's retirement allowance 役員退職金
director's salaries and remuneration 役員報酬
directors and officers liability insurance 会社役員賠償責任保険
directors' bonus 役員賞与
directors' retirement benefit 役員退職給与
directors' salary 役員給料
directory statute 指示的法律
directory trust 指示信託
Dirichlet boundary condition ディリクレ境界条件
dirty float ダーティ・フロート
dirty money 不正な金
dirty stock 不適格銘柄
disability 行為無能力
disability allowance 障害手当金
disability annuity 障害年金
disability benefit 障害給付；所得補償給付
disability benefit payment 障害年金給付支払い
disability clause 廃疾条項
disability determination 障害認定
disability income insurance 就業不能所得補償保険

disability insurance 所得補償保険
disability pension 障害年金
disability rate 就業不能率
disability retirement benefit 就業不能退職年金
disablement benefit 障害補償
disabling statutes 財産移転禁止法
disaggregate 要素分解する
disaggregation 区分
disagreement 不同意
disappointing 期待外れ
disappointing consensus コンセンサスを裏切る
disappointing export 輸出の不調
disarray 混乱
disaster recovery 災害復興
disaster reinsurance 災害再保険
disaster relief 災害復旧
disaster risk 災害リスク
disbursed loan ローンの実行部分
disbursement 支払い
disbursement cycle 支払循環
disbursement exceeding receipts (net payments) 支払超過
disbursement slip 出金伝票
disbursements insurance 船費保険
discarded equipment 廃残設備
discharge 解任；免責
discharge of bankruptcy 破産者債務免除
discharge of debt 債務免除
discharge of delinquent tax 延滞税免除
discharge of duties 職務の執行
discharge of lien リーエンの解除
discharge of officers 役員の解任
discharge of repayment 償還免除
discharge of responsibility 責任の遂行
discharge rate 解雇率
discharge statement 履行計算書
discharge the obligation 義務を履行する
disciplinary action 懲戒処分
disciplinary committee 懲罰委員会
disciplinary punishment on certified public accountant 公認会計士懲戒
discipline 懲罰
discipline on members 会員の処分
disclaim report 意見差控報告書
disclaimer ディスクレイマー；免責事項
disclaimer clause 発注者免責条項
disclaimer of opinion 意見差控え
disclaims 意見差控え
disclosed capital stock 公表資本金
disclosed loans 開示債権
disclosed reserves as adjusted 修正済開示準備金
disclosed substance 開示内容
disclosing function 公示機能
disclosure 開示
disclosure by netting 相殺表示
disclosure cautioned securities 開示注意銘柄
disclosure matter 開示事項
disclosure of accounting policies 会計方針の開示
disclosure of terms and conditions of loans 貸出条件の明示
disclosure philosophy 開示の原則
disclosure requirement 開示要件
disclosure status 開示状況
disclosure system ディスクロージャー制度
discontinuance of accounts 口座の廃止
discontinuance of business 事業の廃止；廃業
discontinue an operation 事業を廃止する
discontinued business 非継続事業
discontinued operation 廃止事業
discontinued premium 有限払込保険料
discontinued segment 廃止セグメント
discontinued standards 非継続規準
discontinuity 断絶
discontinuous jumps 不連続な急騰
discount 織り込む
discount and premium 割引と割増

discount bank 割引銀行
discount bank debenture 割引金融債
discount basis 割引ベース
discount bond 割引債
discount broker 割引専門ブローカー
discount cash flow analysis 割引キャッシュフロー分析
discount commission 割引手数料
discount days to run 割引日数
discount dividend reinvestment 配当金割引再投資
discount factor 割引係数
discount fee earned 受取割引料
discount function 割引関数
discount government bond 割引国債
discount house 割引商社
discount issuance 割引発行
discount ledger 割引手形元帳
discount lending rate 公定貸付金利
discount market 割引市場
discount on banker's acceptances 銀行引受手形割引
discount on bill 手形割引
discount on bills bought 買入手形割引料
discount on bills sold with repurchase option 買戻条件付売却手形割引
discount on bonds issued 社債発行差金
discount on bonds payable 社債発行差金
discount on note 手形割引料
discount on note receivable 手形割引
discount on notes payable 支払手形割引
discount paper 割引証券
discount policy 割引政策
discount rate 割引率
discount rate cut 公定歩合引下げ
discount rate hike 公定歩合引上げ
discount rate policy 公定歩合操作
discount register 割引手形記入帳
discount securities 割引証券
discount value 割引価値
discount window 割引窓口
discount yield 割引利回り
discounted at 割引後
discounted basis 割引基準
discounted cash flow 割引収益
discounted premium rate 割引保険料
discounted present value 割引現在価値
discounted rate 現価率
discounted value 割引価格
discounter 手数料割引業者
discounting 割引き
discounting claims 保険金の現価への割引
discounting of bills 手形の割引
discounts ディスカウント債
discounts on bills purchased 買入手形割引料
discounts on bonds payable 社債割引発行差金
discounts paid on bills 支払手形割引料
discounts paid on bills sold 売出手形支払割引料
discouraged 嫌気
discourse 論考
discredit 信用しない
discrepancy 差異
discrete distribution 離散分布
discrete time 離散時間型
discrete variable 離散変数型
discretion 自由裁量
discretion of law 法の裁量
discretion of the insured person 被保険者の裁量
discretional act 裁量行為
discretionary account 売買一任勘定
discretionary account trading 売買一任勘定取引
discretionary cost 裁量原価
discretionary expenses 任意の費用
discretionary fiscal policy 自由裁量的財政政策
discretionary income 裁量所得
discretionary leveraged finance portfolio 一任レバレジッドファイナンス・ポートフォリオ

D

discretionary loan 裁量貸出し
discretionary order 一任注文
discretionary trust 一任信託
discriminant 差別要因
discriminant analysis 判別分析
discriminating customs duty 差別関税
discriminating monopolies 差別独占
discrimination 差別
discriminative price 差別価格
discriminative tariff 差別税率
discriminatory handling 差別的扱い
discussion paper 討議資料
diseconomy 不経済
disendowment 基本財産の没収
disentitle 権利を剥奪する
disequilibrium 不均衡
disequilibrium growth 不均衡成長
disfranchise 公権を剥奪する
disguised act 仮装行為
disguised transaction 偽装取引
dishonest conduct 不信な行為
dishonor 引受拒絶
dishonor notice 不渡通知
dishonorable discharge 懲戒免職
dishonored bill 不渡手形
dishonored check 不渡小切手
disincentive 意欲低下
disinflation ディスインフレ
disinherit 相続権を奪う
disintegration 解体
disinterested 利害関係のない
disintermediation ディスインターメディエーション
disintermidiation of bank 銀行離れ
disinvest 投資を引き上げる
disinvestment 投資解除
disjunctive allegation 択一的申立
dismiss 解雇する
dismissal 却下
disparate ratio 乖離率
disparity 不一致
dispatch 派遣する
dispatch money 早出料
dispersion 分散
displaced diffusion model 拡散変換モデル
disposable income 可処分所得
disposable profit 可処分利益
disposal 処分
disposal date 処分日
disposal of fixed assets 固定資産処分
disposal of long-term investment 長期投資の処分
disposal of premises and equipment 動産不動産処分
disposal of surplus 剰余金の処分
disposal price 処分価格
disposal value 処分価値
disposing capacity 財産処分能力
disposition 自由使用権；処分
disposition by foreclosure sale 公売処分
disposition by suspension of bank credit 銀行取引停止処分
disposition by suspension of business 取引停止処分
disposition cost 処分費用
disposition date 処分日
disposition of a member 会員の処置
disposition of assets 資産の処分
disposition of failure to pay income tax in advance 予定納税額滞納処分
disposition of income 所得の使途
disposition of net income 純益処分
dispositioned amount 取崩額
dispositioning by direct write-down 直接減額による取崩し
dispossess 奪う
dispossession 不法占有
dispute 紛争
dispute settlement 紛争解決
disqualified 不適格な
disqualified substance 不適切な内容
disqualify 資格を喪失せしめる
disregard 切り捨てる
disregard of decimal places 小数点以下切り捨て
disregard of tax rule 税法の無視
disruption 中断
disruption claims 阻害クレーム

disruption of financial markets 金融市場の機能不全
disseminate 公表する
dissemination 公表
dissemination of transaction price 約定値段の公表
dissent 反対する
dissenter 反対人
dissenters' shares 反対株主
dissenting opinion 反対意見
dissimilar assets 異種資産
dissimilarity 相違点
dissolution 解散
dissolution and extinction due to merger 合併による解散・消滅
dissolution of corporation 法人の解散
dissolve 解散する
distinct attribute 独自の属性
distort 歪曲
distrain 差押さえる
distress 差押え
distress goods 破産の整理品
distress infinite 無期限差押
distress sale 差押物件売却
distress selling 投売り
distressed company 経営不振企業
distributable income 配分可能利益
distribution 分配；分与
distribution activities 販売活動
distribution channel 流通経路
distribution date 分売執行日
distribution function 分布関数
distribution industry 流通業界
distribution networks 物流ネットワーク
distribution of benefit 給付の分配
distribution of depository shares 預託証券の分布状況
distribution of local allocation tax 地方交付税交付金
distribution of net assets of investment trusts 投資信託の運用状況
distribution of net profit 利益処分
distribution of overhead cost 間接費分配
distribution of ownership of shares 株式の分布状況
distribution of PBR PBR 分布
distribution of principal and interest 元利金の配分
distribution of profits 利益配当
distribution of property 財産分与
distribution of residual assets 残余財産の分与
distribution of residual property 残余財産分配
distribution of shares 株式の分布
distribution of single day advances and declines 対前日変動率分布
distribution of stock prices 株価水準分布
distribution of stocks 株式分布
distribution of surplus 益金処分
distribution of total returns トータル・リターンの分布
distribution period 配当期間
distribution plan 費用分担法
distribution rate of overhead cost 間接費配賦率
distribution revolution 流通革命
distribution structure 流通機構
distribution tax 配付税
distribution to shareholder 株主への分配
district 管轄区
distrust 不信任
distrust of accounting practices 会計不信
disutility 不効用
disvalue 価値否認
DIV (derived investment value) 推定市場価値評価額
diverge from 乖離する
divergence 乖離
divergence indicator 乖離指標
divergence threshold 乖離限度
diverging forces 幾多の要因
diverse 多様な
diverse assets 多様な資産
diverse exercise of voting right 議決権

D

の不統一行使
diversifiable risk 分散可能リスク
diversification 分散化
diversification benefit 分散投資効果
diversification investment 分散化投資
diversification strategy 多角化戦略
diversified banking business models 多様化した銀行業務モデル
diversified business enterprise 多角経営企業
diversified enterprise 多業種企業
diversified investment 分散投資
diversified portfolio 分散したポートフォリオ
diversified portfolio on stock investment 分散株式投資ポートフォリオ
diversified type common stock fund 分散型普通株ファンド
diversified type investment company 分散型投資会社
diversified type portfolio 分散型ポートフォリオ
diversify 分散する
diversion 流用
diversion of funds 資金の転換
diversity and complexity 多様性と複雑性
diversity score 分散スコア
divest 株式を売却する
divestiture 売却
divestiture of assets 資産の売却
divestment of business 事業の分割
divestment of equity into public hands 株式公開
divesture of assts 資産の整理
divesture of businesses by two or more entities to establish a new entity which issues equity interests in exchange for businesses 共同新設分割
divided coverage 分割付保
dividend 配当
dividend account 配当金勘定
dividend accumulation 配当積立
dividend addition 配当による買増し
dividend allocated 割当済配当
dividend capitalization 配当還元
dividend capture 配当取り
dividend compounding rate 配当算入率
dividend credit 配当金控除
dividend crediting rate 配当保証利率
dividend cut 減配
dividend declaration 配当宣言
dividend declaration date 配当決議日
dividend declared 宣言された配当
dividend decrease 減配
dividend deduction from insurance premium 保険料相殺配当
dividend deposit 配当積立
dividend discount 配当割引
dividend discount method 配当還元方式
dividend discount model 配当還元モデル
dividend discount rate 配当割引率
dividend distribution 配当支払い
dividend earned 受取配当金
dividend equalization reserve 配当平準化積立金
dividend equivalents 配当金同等物
dividend excluded from income 受取配当金益金不算入
dividend exclusion 配当不算入
dividend flow 配当フロー
dividend fluctuation reserve 配当変動準備金
dividend for the second half 後期配当
dividend from capital 資本配当
dividend from stocks owned 株式所有にかかる配当
dividend growth rate 増配率
dividend in arrears 延滞配当金
dividend in kind 現物配当
dividend income 配当所得
dividend off 配当落ち
dividend on 配当付き
dividend on common stock 普通株配当金

dividend on dummy stock 名義株配当
dividend on interest 利息配当
dividend on preferred stock 優先株配当金
dividend on stock 株式配当
dividend option 配当受取選択権
dividend paid 支払配当金
dividend payable 未払配当金
dividend paying agent 配当支払機関
dividend paying company 配当会社
dividend paying insurance 配当付保険
dividend payment 配当支払い
dividend payment bank 配当金支払取扱銀行
dividend payment business commission agreement 配当金支払事務委任契約
dividend payment despite deficit 赤字有配
dividend payout 配当支払い
dividend payout ratio 配当性向
dividend per share 一株当り配当金
dividend policy 配当政策
dividend preferred stock 配当優先株式
dividend propensity 配当性向
dividend puzzle 配当パズル
dividend rate 配当率
dividend ratified 決議された配当
dividend receivable 未収配当
dividend received 受取配当金
dividend reinvestment plan 配当金再投資
dividend requirements 配当支払必要額
dividend reserve 配当積立金
dividend right 配当請求権
dividend rollover plan 配当取り
dividend scale 配当水準
dividend schedule 配当予定
dividend stock 配当株
dividend to policyholders 保険契約者配当
dividend to shareholder 株主への配当
dividend withdrawal 配当金引出
dividend year 配当年度
dividend yield 配当利回り
dividend-included stock price indices 配当込株価指数
dividend-included TOPIX 配当込みトピックス
dividend-paid deduction method 配当損金法
dividend-paying stock 有配株
dividends in arrears 繰越配当金；未払配当
dividends of listed companies 上場会社配当状況
divisibility 分割可能性
divisible claim 可分債権
divisible obligation 可分債務
divisible surplus 配当可能剰余金
division 区分；部門
Division Controlling Local Finance Bureaus 地方課
division of accounting 経理区分
Division of Corporate Finance(SEC) 企業財務局(SEC)
Division of Enforcement(SEC) 法律施行局(SEC)
Division of Investment Management(SEC) 投資管理局(SEC)
division of margin 証拠金の区分
Division of Market Regulation(SEC) 市場規制局(SEC)
division of powers 権力の分立
division of securities 有価証券の区分
division of succession 分割相続制
division of trading sessions 売買立会の区分
division results 部門別損益
divisional breakdown of profit and loss 部門別損益
divisional sales 部門売上
divisional sales breakdown 部門別売上内訳
divisions of accounts 口座の区分
DJF (Djibouti franc) ジブチ・フラン
DJIA (Dow Jones Industrial Average) ダウ工業平均

D

DK (Don't Know) DK 取引
DKK (Danish krone) デンマーク・クローネ
DKK (Greenland krone) グリーンランド・クローネ
DKV (Deutscher Kassenverein AG) ドイツ証券保管機構
DM (Department of Management) 管理局
DMA (Days Moving Average) 日足移動平均線
dock 被告人席
dockage ドック使用料
doctrine of discovered peril 発見危険の原則
document 書類
document against acceptance 引受渡し
document of foreclosure 差押書
document of seizure 差押書
document of title 権利証券
document processing 書類処理
documentary bill 荷為替手形
documentary clean credit 荷落信用状
documentary draft 荷為替手形
documentary evidence 証拠書類
documentary letter of credit 荷為替信用状
documentary stamp 証券用収入印紙
documentary stamp tax 印紙税
documentation bank 契約書類作成銀行
documented discount note ドキュメント・ディスカウント・ノート
documents for opening a U.S. dollar account ドル口座開設書類
Dodge Line ドッジ・ライン
Doi Moi ドイモイ
doing business 営業行為
doldrums 不況
dole 失業手当
dollar account ドル勘定
dollar average method ドル平均法
dollar averaging ドル平均
dollar bloc ドル・ブロック
dollar bond ドル債
dollar call option ドル・コール・オプション
dollar convertible bond ドル建転換社債
dollar cost averaging ドル・コスト平均法
dollar crisis ドル危機
dollar decline ドルの下落
dollar defense ドル防衛
dollar denominated ドル建ての
dollar diplomacy ドル外交
dollar exchange standard ドル為替本位
dollar gap ドル不足
dollar overhung 過剰ドル
dollar parity ドル平価
dollar pool ドル・プール
dollar preference ドル選好
dollar price ドル価格
dollar put option ドル・プット・オプション
dollar shift ドルシフト
dollar shortage ドル不足
dollar wise ドルに換算して
dollar-weighted rate of return ドル加重収益率
domain 活動領域
domain of use 地上権
domestic acceptance 国内引受手形
domestic and foreign exchange commissions 支払為替手数料
domestic capital 国内資本
domestic commodity prices 国内物価
domestic corporate goods prices 国内卸売物価
domestic corporation 内国法人
domestic credit 国内信用
domestic currency 自国通貨
domestic demand 国内需要
domestic demand expansion 内需拡大
domestic demand oriented industry 内需産業
domestic demand related stock 内需関連株
domestic demand stimulation 内需振

興
domestic designated deposit account 国内指定預金
domestic driver 国内要因
domestic equilibrium 国内均衡
domestic exchange 内国為替取引
domestic expenditure 国内支出
domestic factor 国内要因
domestic fiat money 自国通貨
Domestic Fund Transfer System 内国為替制度
domestic income 国内所得
domestic index 国内指数
domestic institutional investor 国内機関投資家
domestic insurance 家計保険
domestic investment 国内投資
domestic law 国内法
domestic liabilities 自国通貨建負債
domestic loan system 本邦ローン方式
domestic market 国内市場
domestic operations 国内事業
domestic optimism 国内の楽観的見方
domestic plan 国内の制度
domestic price 国内価格
domestic recession 国内不況
domestic share 内国株式
domestic source 国内源泉
domestic stock 内国株
domestic tax rate 国内税率
domestic warrants 内国新株引受権証書
domicile 本拠地
domicile for payment of bills and notes 手形の支払場所
domiciled bill 支払地指定手形
dominance 支配
dominant estate 要役地
dominant theme 主要なテーマ
dominate the market シェアの大半を占める
domino effect ドミノ効果
donated capital 贈与資本
donated property 贈与財産
donated stock 贈与株
donated surplus 贈与剰余金
donation 寄付金
donation of property 財産贈与
donation tax 贈与税
donation to designated organization 指定寄付金
donator 寄贈者
done 契約成立
donee 受贈者
donor 寄贈者
DOP (Dominican peso) ドミニカ・ペソ
dormant account 休止勘定
dormant accumulated 潜在的に蓄積されていた
dormant assets 休眠資産
dormant balance 休止残高
dormant partner 匿名組合員
double A AA 格
double accident benefit 倍額支払災害給付
double account interests おどり利息
double accounting 複式会計
double attachment 二重差押
double auction system 二重競売制度
double charge 二重の費用
double check 再鑑
double counting 二重計算
double crossover ダブル・クロスオーバー
double dated 二重満期
double declining balance method 倍額定率法
double dip recession 二番底
double distribution 二重分配
double endorsed check 二重裏書小切手
double endowment assurance 倍額支払養老保険
double indemnity 倍額支払い
double indemnity annuity 倍額支払災害年金
double insurance 重複保険
double jeopardy 二重の危険
double leverage ダブル・レバレッジ
double liability 二重負債

D

double name paper 複名手形
double option ダブルオプション
double peak 二番天井
double price 二重価格
double protection insurance 倍額保障保険
double seizure 二重差押
double settlement 3営業日渡し
double tariff 二重関税
double taxation 二重課税
double top ダブルトップ
double-account system 複会計制度
double-digit 二桁の
double-digit recurring profit growth 二桁増益基調
double-entry bookkeeping 複式簿記
double-up ダブル・アップ
doubtful account 不良債権
doubtful assets 危険債権
doubtful loan 不良貸出
doubtful receivables 貸倒懸念債権
Dow Jones 15 Public Utility Average ダウ公共株15種平均
Dow Jones 20 Bond Index ダウ20種債券指数
Dow Jones 20 Transportation Average ダウ輸送株20種平均
Dow Jones Commodity Index ダウ式商品指数
Dow Jones Industrial ダウ工業株
Dow Jones Industrial Average ダウ平均
Dow Theory ダウ理論
down and out call option ダウン・アンド・アウト・コール・オプション
down leg 下落傾向にある
down payment 頭金
down spread 下ザヤ
downfall 下落；失墜
downgrading 格下げ
downgrading carry expectation キャリー面での収益見通しの引下げ
downhill course 下降線
downside potential 値下がり余地
downside risk 下値不安；下振れのリスク
downside semi-variance 下方半分散
downsizing ダウンサイジング
downstairs merger 逆吸収合併
downstream demutualization 川下の株式会社化
downstream merger 逆吸収合併
downstream product 下流製品
downswing phase 下降局面
downtick 下げ局面
downtrend 下落トレンド
downturn 悪化
downward adjustment 下方修正
downward movement 下げ足
downward phase of the business cycle 景気の下降局面
downward pressure 調整圧力
downward redenomination デノミ
downward revaluation 下方再評価
downward revision 下方修正
downward revision on business results 業績見通しの下方修正
downward rigidity 下方硬直性
DP (document against payment) 支払渡し
DPA(Department of Political Affairs) 政治局
DPC (derivative product company) 派生商品会社
DPI(Department of Public Information) 広報局
DPKO(Department of Peacekeeping Operations) 平和維持活動局
DPS (dividend per share) 一株当り配当
DR (depository receipt) 預託証券
draft at sight 一覧払手形
draft bill of exchange 為替手形
draft payable 支払手形
draft receivable 受取手形
draft statement 草案
dragon bond ドラゴン債
draining reserves 金融引締め
dramatic surge 大商い
drastic 大幅な

drastic change 激変
drastic monetary easing 大胆な金融緩和
draw 振出す
draw a distinction 区別する
draw down 資金引出し
draw down date 融資実行日
drawback 関税払戻し；欠点
drawback allowance 戻し税給付
drawdown period 資金引出可能期間
drawee 名宛人
drawer 振出人
drawer of bill 手形振出人
drawing 振出し
drawing account 引出金勘定
drawing bank 振出銀行
drawing of a bill 手形の振出し
drawing of bill 手形振出し
drawing of number 抽選
drawing right 引出し権
drawings from general reserves 準備金取崩額
drawn bill 振出手形
drawn by the Bank of Japan 日銀が振り出した
dread disease benefit 重病給付
dread disease rider 重病給付特約
dressing お化粧買い
drifting mix 漂流ミックス
driver of capital inflow 資本流入の要因
driving force 推進要因
driving growth 景気を牽引
drop below par 額面割れ
drop dead day 最終期限日
drop-lock bond ドロップ・ロック債
dropout option ドロップアウト・オプション
DRS (deferred rate setting) 条件設定遅延方式
DRS (direct registration system) 直接登録システム
dry measure 乾量
dry weight 乾重量
DSCR (debt service coverage ratio) デット・サービス・カバレッジ・レシオ
DSM (demand side management) 需要管理
DSR (debt service ratio) デット・サービス・レシオ
DTA (double taxation agreement) 二重課税防止条約
DTC (depository trust company) 預託信託会社
dual banking system 二重銀行制度
dual capacity デュアル・キャパシティ
dual character of investment 投資の二重性
dual citizenship 二重公民権
dual closed-end fund デュアル・クローズド・エンド型ファンド
dual convertible bonds デュアル転換社債
dual currency bonds デュアル・カレンシー債
dual economy 二重経済
dual effect 二重の効果
dual exchange market 二重為替相場制
dual fund デュアル・ファンド
dual health insurance coverage 重複医療保険保障
dual income tax system 二元的所得税制
dual interest policy 二重金利政策
dual listing 重複上場
dual rate system 二重運賃制
dual structure 二重構造
dual structure of the economy 経済の二重構造
dual tariff 複関税
dual trading 二重勘定取引
dual tranche デュアル・トランシェ
dual-purpose fund デュアル・ファンド
duality 二重性
due and deferred premiums 未収保険料
due bill 有価証券引渡票
due care 正当な注意

D

due consideration 適切な配慮
due date 期日；弁済期日
due date coming basis 回収期限到来基準
due date for payment 支払期限
due date for settlement 決済期限
due date for tax payment 納期限
due date of benefit payment 給付支払期日
due date of bill 手形満期日
due date of filing tax return 申告期限
due date of payment 払込日
due date of property tax payment 固定資産税納期
due date of the tax return 申告期限
due diligence 精査
due for settlement 決済期限が到来する
due for the year 当年中に支払うべき
due from foreign banks (our account) 外国支店預け
due on sale 売却による全額返済
due on sale clause 売却時返済条項
due process of law 適法手続き
due reason 正当事由
due to foreign banks 外国他店預り
dues 料金
duet bond デュエット債
dull 気乗り薄
dumbbell portfolio ダンベル・ポートフォリオ
dummy account ダミー勘定
dummy company ダミー会社
dummy stock 名義株
dump in premium 余剰保険料
dumping ダンピング
dumping petition ダンピング提訴
duplex system 二重契約主義
duplicate 副の
duplicate coverage 重複保障
duplicate tenor 謄本
duplication 重複
durable consumer goods 耐久消費財
durable goods orders 耐久材受注
durable power of attorney 持続委任状
durable years 耐用年数
duration デュレーション
duration gap デュレーション・ギャップ
duration method デュレーション法
duration of an equity 株式のデュレーション
duration of bond 債券のデュレーション
duration of risk 危険期間
duration of risk clause 保険期間条項
duration statistics デュレーション計算
duration-matching デュレーション・マッチ
duration-weighted yield デュレーション加重利回り
Durbin-Watson ratio ダービン・ワトソン比
during the period 期中
Dutch auction ダッチ・オークション
Dutch auction method ダッチ方式
Dutch guilder bond ダッチギルダー債
dutiable goods 有税品
dutiable value 課税価格
duties and powers of executives 役員の職務及び権限
duties of report 報告義務
duty 職務
duty exemption 免税
duty free 免税の
duty free imports 免税輸入品
duty of care 注意義務
duty of disclosure 告知義務
duty of support 扶養義務
duty to sue and labor 損害防止義務
duty-paid 納税済
DVP (delivery versus payment) for corporate bonds 社債等 DVP
DVP (delivery versus payment) settlement DVP 決済
DVP Settlement Price DVP 清算値段
dwelling house 住居
dynamic analysis 動態分析
dynamic credit swap ダイナミック・クレジット・スワップ
dynamic hedge strategy ダイナミック

・ヘッジ戦略
dynamic input-output analysis 動学的産業連関分析
dynamic multiplier 動学乗数
dynamic portfolio ダイナミック・ポートフォリオ
dynamic programming 動的計画法
dynamic risks 動態的リスク
dynamic socioeconomic structure 活力のある社会経済構造
dynamic statistics 動態統計
dynamic strategies ダイナミック戦略
DZD (Algerian dinar) アルジェリア・ディナール

E

e-Japan Strategy e-Japan 戦略
each layer 各階層
each party retaining one 一通ずつを保有する
each series シリーズ別
each way 手数料各自払い；バイカイ手数料
EAP (enlarged access policy) 拡大融資制度
earlier bid 先に行われた買呼値
earlier offer 先に行われた売呼値
earlier years 過年度
early access to insurance benefit 保険給付の生前利用
early amortization 期限前償還
early application 早期適用
early argument 初期の議論
early completion 早期完了
early exercise 早期行使
early extinguishment 早期消滅
early extinguishment of debt securities 債務証券の早期償還
early leaver 早期退職者
early redemption 繰上償還
early redemption of JGSs 国債繰上償還
early redemption option 繰上償還オプション
early redemption risk 期限前償還リスク
early repayment 繰上返済
early retirement 早期退職
early retirement benefit 早期退職給付
early retirement pension 早期退職年金
early settlement option 早期決済オプション
early settlement provision 早期償還条項
early stage 初期段階
early termination 期限前解約
early warning 早期警告
early withdrawal penalty 期限前解約委員会
earmark 資金などを取っておく
earmarked tax 目的税
earmarking 固定化
earned accrued interest 既経過未収利息
earned basis 発生年度基準
earned finance income 稼得金融収益
earned income 稼得所得
earned income allowance 勤労所得控除
earned income credit 勤労所得控除
earned income exemption 勤労控除
earned income tax 勤労所得税
earned premium 既経過保険料
earned profit 稼得利益
earned rate 収益率
earned reserve 利益準備金
earned right 既得権
earned surplus 利益剰余金
earned surplus carried forward to the following term 繰越利益剰余金
earned surplus reserve 利益準備金
earned surplus statement 利益剰余金計算書
earnest money 契約証拠金；手付金
earnest money received 預り手付金
earning assets 収益資産
earning capacity 収益力
earning coverage 収益力カバレッジ
earning growth rate 増益率
earning power 収益力
earning statement 損益計算書
earning tax 収益税
earnings 収益
earnings announcement 利益発表
earnings assets 収益性資産

earnings base 基準所得
earnings before extraordinary items 特別損益前利益
earnings before interest and taxes 金利税引前利益
earnings before tax 税引前利益
earnings cap 所得上限
earnings contribution 利益への寄与
earnings coverage 収益カバレッジ
earnings coverage ratio 負担利益倍率
earnings deterioration 業績悪化
earnings discount value 収益還元価格
earnings forecast 収益見通し
earnings from continuing operations 継続事業部門利益
earnings growth 収益増
earnings growth expectations 予想増益率
earnings growth rate 収益成長率
earnings growth rate per share 一株当り収益成長率
earnings in cash value 解約返戻金利殖部分
earnings income 稼動所得
earnings model 収益モデル
earnings momentum 利益モーメンタム
earnings on equity 自己資本利益率
earnings outlook 収益見通し
earnings per common stock 普通株式一株当り利益
earnings per share 一株当り利益
earnings per share of common stock 普通株式一株当り純利益
earnings per share ratio 株価収益率
earnings performance 業績
earnings potential 潜在的収益力
earnings price ratio 益回り
earnings process 利益稼得過程
earnings ratio 収益指標
earnings reinvested 再投資利益
earnings related pension 所得比例年金
earnings replacement rate 従前所得置換率
earnings report 収益報告書
earnings retention rate 収益留保率
earnings risk 収益リスク
earnings stability 収益の安定性
earnings stabilizer 収益スタビライザー
earnings target 利益目標
earnings test 所得調査
earnings yield 益回り
earnings yield gap 益回りとの格差
earnings-generating capacity 利益稼得能力
earthquake insurance 地震保険
ease 反落する
easement 地役権
easement appurtenant 付属地役権
easement holder 地役権者
easiness of the money market 金融緩和
easing 緩和
easing decision 利下げの実施
easing of conditions 条件緩和
easing of yield 利回り低下
easing risk aversion リスク回避姿勢の軟化
East African Community 東アフリカ共同体
East Asian Insurance Congress 東アジア保険会議
East Caribbean dollar 東カリブ・ドル
easy くつろぎ模様；小安い
easy credit 金融緩和
easy monetary policy 金融緩和政策
easy money あぶく銭
easy payment 分割払い
EAT (earnings after tax) 税引後利益
EB (exchangeable bond) 他社株償還条項付社債
EBIT (earnings before interest and taxes) 支払利息税引前利益
EBITD (earnings before interest, tax and depreciation) 支払利息・税金・減価償却前利益
EBITDA (earnings before interest, taxes, depreciation and amortization) 支払利息・税金・減

E

価償却控除前利益
EBRD (European Bank for Reconstruction Development) 欧州復興開発銀行
EC joint floating system EC 共同フロート
ECA(Economic Commission for Africa) アフリカ経済委員会
ECB (European Central Bank) 欧州中央銀行
ECD (Euro certificate of deposit) ユーロ CD
ECE (Economic Commission for Europe) ヨーロッパ経済委員会
echo effect 反響効果
echo principle 反響原理
ECI (employment cost index) 雇用コスト指数
ECLAC(Economic Commission for Latin America and the Caribbean) ラテンアメリカ・カリブ経済委員会
ECM (emerging company marketplace) 振興企業市場
ECN (electronic communication network) 電子証券取引システム
ECO (Expanded Co-financing Operations) program 拡大強調融資
ECOA (equal credit opportunity act) 消費者信用均等法
econometric analysis 計量経済分析
econometric model 計量経済モデル
econometrics 計量経済学
economic accounting 経済会計
economic activity 経済活動
economic activity stimulating measure 経済活動刺激策
economic aid 経済援助
economic analysis 経済分析
Economic and Development Review Committee 経済開発検討委員会
economic and financial development 金融経済動向
economic and fiscal policy 経済財政政策
economic and monetary conditions 経済及び金融の情勢
economic and social policy 経済社会政策
economic assistance 経済援助
economic barometer 経済指標
economic benefit 経済的便益
economic bloc 経済圏
economic blockade 経済封鎖
economic boom 好景気
economic center 経済センター
economic characteristics 経済的特徴
economic circles 経済界
economic circumstances 経済環境
economic climate 景気
economic conditions 経済状況
economic continuity 経済的連続性
economic cooperation 経済協力
economic correlation 経済的相関関係
economic cost 経済原価
economic crisis 経済恐慌
economic criteria 経済基準
economic cycle 景気循環
economic data 経済統計
economic decision 経済的意思決定
Economic Deliberation Council 経済審議会
economic determinism 経済決定論
economic development 経済の動向
economic diplomacy 経済外交
economic dualism 二重経済構造
economic dynamics 動態経済学
economic earnings 経済的利益
economic earnings beta 経済的利益ベータ値
economic efficiency 経済の効率性
economic engineering 経済性工学
economic entity 経済実体
economic environment 景気
economic ethics 経済倫理
economic event 経済事象
economic exchange 経済交流
economic factor 経済的要因
economic fluctuation 景気変動
economic force 経済力

economic forecast 経済予測
economic friction 経済摩擦
economic funding ratio 経済積立率
economic goods 経済財
economic growth 景気拡大
economic growth differential 経済成長率格差
economic growth model 経済成長モデル
economic growth policy 経済成長政策
economic growth rate 経済成長率
economic index 経済指数
economic indexes 経済指標
economic indicator 経済指標
economic integration 経済統合
economic life 経済生活
economic malaise 経済疾病
economic maturity 経済的成熟
economic model 経済モデル
economic number effect 経済指標効果
economic observational method 経済的観察方法
economic obsolescence 経済的陳腐化
economic order 経済秩序
economic organization 経済組織
economic outlook 経済見通し
economic overlay 経済的観点
economic package 経済対策
economic path 経済経路
economic performance 経済的業績
economic philosophy 経済理念
economic plan 経済計画
Economic Planning Agency 経済企画庁
economic policy 経済政策
economic prediction 経済予測
economic production run size 経済的生産操業規模
economic progress 経済進歩
economic prospect 経済展望
economic rationality 経済的合理性
economic reach 経済圏
economic reality 経済の実体
economic reasons 経済的な理由
economic recession 景気後退
economic recovery 景気回復
economic reform 経済改革
economic regime 経済体制
economic relationship 経済的関係
economic rent 経済的地代
economic resources 経済的資源
economic reversal 景気の転換
economic revitalization 経済活力創造
economic reward 経済的利益
economic rigidity 経済の硬直性
economic risk 経済的リスク
economic sanction 経済制裁
economic security 経済安全保障
economic significance 経済的重要性
economic size 経済規模
economic slump 景気後退
economic stabilization 経済安定
economic statistics 経済統計
economic stimulus package 景気刺激策
Economic Strategy Council 経済戦略会議
economic strength 経済力
economic structural adjustment 経済構造調整
Economic Summit 先進国首脳会議
economic survey 経済調査
economic system 経済体制
economic table 経済表
economic theory 経済理論
economic tide 経済の流れ
economic transaction 経済的取引
economic unit 経済主体
economic useful life 経済的耐用年数
economic value qualifying for investment in kind 現物出資になり得る経済的価値
economic vitality 経済活力
economic war 経済戦争
economic welfare 経済的厚生
economic white paper 経済白書
economics 経済学
economics fraternity 経済学界
economies of scale 規模の経済
economies of scope 多角化の経済性

E

economist エコノミスト
economy and society 経済社会
economy in transition 移行経済
econophysics 経済物理学
ECOSOC(Economic and Social Council) 経済社会理事会
ECP (Euro commercial paper) ユーロ・コマーシャルペーパー
ECS (Ecuador sucre) エクアドル・スクレ
ECSDA (European Central Securities Depositories Association) 欧州証券決済機関協会
ECU bond ECU債
ECU market ECU市場
ED (exposure draft) 公開草案
EDGAR エドガー
EDGAR (electronic data gathering analysis and retrieval) 電子的データ収集・検索システム
Edge Act エッジ法
edge down 小幅下落
edge up 小幅上昇
Edge-Act company エッジ・アクト法人
edges of the band 許容レンジ
EDI (electronic data interchange) 電子データ交換
EDR (European depositary receipt) 欧州預託証券
education expense 教育費
education industry 教育産業
education IRA (individual retirement account) 教育費用個人退職勘定
education loan 教育ローン
educational insurance 学資保険
EEA (exchange equalization account) 為替平衡勘定
EEC (European Economic Community) 欧州経済共同体
EEK (Estonian kroon) エストニア・クローン
EFF (expanded fund facility) 拡大融資制度
effect 効果
effect of borrowing 他人資本への影響額
effect of change 変更の影響
effect of correction 更正等の効力
effect of discount 割引効果
effect of discounting 割引の影響
effect of exchange rate changes 為替換算修正
effect of impairment 減損の影響
effect of limiting risk 危険限定効果
effect of performance 業績の影響
effect of price increase 価格上昇の影響
effect of selection 選択効果
effect of the limit 制限の影響
effect of transaction 取引の影響
effect on equity interests 自己資本への影響額
effective aggregate tax rate 総合効果税率
effective competition 有効競争
effective control 有効的な支配
effective date 発効日
effective debt 実効債務
effective demand 有効需要
effective exchange rate 実効為替相場
effective hedge 効果的なヘッジ
effective income 実質所得
effective income tax rate 実効税率
effective interest method 実効金利法
effective interest rate 実効金利
effective net worth 実質純資産
effective period 有効期間
effective period of order 注文の有効期間
effective price 実効価格
effective rate 実勢レート
effective rate of interest 有効金利
effective rate of protection 実効保護率
effective sale 端株取引基準株価
effective tariff 実効税率
effective utilization 有効活用
effective volatility 実効ボラティリティー
effective yield 実効利回り
effectiveness of a hedge ヘッジ有効性

effectiveness of diversified investment 分散投資の有効性
effectives 実働人員
effects 動産
efficacy 効率性
efficiency audit 能率監査
efficiency variance 能率差異
efficient allocation 効率的配分
efficient cause 主因
efficient frontier 有効フロンティア
efficient frontier analysis 有効フロンティア分析
efficient market 効率的市場
efficient portfolio 効率的ポートフォリオ
efficient spread 実効スプレッド
efficient statistics 有効統計
EFP (exchange for physical) 現物受渡し
EFTA (European Free Trade Association) 欧州自由貿易連合
EFTS (electronic fund transfer system) 電子資金決済システム
EFV (estimated full value) 推定時価評価額
EGP (Egyptian pound) エジプト・ポンド
EIB (European Investment Bank) 欧州投資銀行
eigenfunction 固有関数
eigenvalue 固有値
eight column work sheet 八桁精算表
EIRR (equity internal rate of return) 自己資本内部収益率
EITF (Emerging Issues Task Force) 緊急問題専門委員会
either or order 二者択一注文
either/or facility アイザー・オア・ファシリティ
EL (export license) 輸出免許
elaboration on 詳述
elapse けいか
elapse of the time 期間の経過
elapse of time 期間の経過
elastic demand 弾力的需要
elastic limit system 屈伸制限制度
elastic tariff 弾力関税
elasticity approach 弾力性アプローチ
elasticity clause 弾力条項
elasticity of demand 需要弾性値
elasticity of demand and supply 需給の弾力性
elasticity of substitution 代替の弾力性
elasticity of supply 供給弾性値
elasticity of tax revenue 税収弾性値
elasticity of the balance of payments 国際収支弾力性
elasticity optimism 弾力性オプティミズム
elasticity pessimism 弾力性ペシミズム
elder title 先権原
elderly market シニア市場
elderly population 高齢者人口
election deposits 選挙供託
election of auditors 監査役の選任
election of directors 取締役の選任
electric appliances futures 電気機器先物
electric appliances industry 電気機器業界
electric industry 電気業界
electric power bonds 電力債
Electric Power Development Co., Ltd. 電源開発株式会社
electric power expense 電力費
electricity and gas tax 電気ガス税
electricity tax 電気税
electromagnetic means 電磁的方法
electromagnetic record 電磁的記録
electronic banking エレクトロニック・バンキング
electronic certification function 電子認証機能
electronic certification service 電子認証業務
electronic commerce 電子商取引
electronic data gathering analysis and retrieval system EDGAR（エドガー）システム
electronic distribution 電子販売

electronic engineering 電子工学
electronic filing 電子申告
electronic form 電子的な形式
electronic fund transfer 電子決済
electronic information processing facility 電子情報処理組織
electronic loan 電子貸付
E
electronic market 電子的市場
electronic money (e-money) 電子マネー
Electronic Navigation Research Institute 電子航法研究所
electronic order transfer system 電子注文伝達システム
electronic payment 電子決済；電子納付
electronic payment of taxes 電子納税
electronic signature 電子署名
electronic trading market 電子取引市場
electronic transaction 電子取引
elementary cost accounting 要素別原価計算
elephant 巨大投資家
eleventh-hour 最後の土壇場
eligibility 加入資格；適格性
eligibility age 加入資格年齢
eligibility date 受給資格日
eligibility for syndicate membership シ団参加資格
eligible bill 割引適格手形
eligible business 適格法人
eligible collateral 適格担保
eligible employee 適格従業員
eligible expense 適格費用
eligible for benefits 受給資格のある
eligible group 適格団体
eligible investment 適格投資
eligible paper 再割適格手形
eligible securities 適格有価証券
eligible security 適格担保
eliminating entry 消却仕訳
elimination 消去
elimination of intercompany indebtedness 会社相互間の貸借の消去
elimination of intercompany ownership 会社相互間の持分の消去
elimination of intercompany profits 会社相互間の利益の消去
elimination of intercompany transactions 会社間取引の相殺消去
elimination of receivables and payables 債権債務の相殺消去
elimination period 除外期間
elite card エリートカード
Elliot Wave Theory エリオット・ウェーブ理論
EMA (European Monetary Agreement) 欧州通貨協定
emancipation 解放
embargo 禁輸
embarrassing 困惑する
embedded derivatives 組込デリバティブ
embedded loss 含み損
embedded option 組込オプション
embedded profit 含み益
embellishment 粉飾
embezzlement 横領
embodying 具体化する
EMC (European Currency Unit) 欧州通貨単位
EMCF (European Monetary Cooperation Fund) 欧州通貨協力基金
emergence 出現
emergency 緊急事態
emergency amortization 緊急償却
emergency auction 緊急オークション
emergency clearing margin 緊急取引証拠金
emergency duty 緊急関税
emergency economic package 緊急景気対策
emergency funds 臨時費
emergency import 緊急輸入
emergency legislation 緊急立法

emergency loan 緊急融資
emergency management headquarter 危機管理本部
emergency measures 非常措置
emergency rate relief 緊急融資
emergency tariff 緊急関税
emergent financial disposition 財政上緊急処分
emerging corporations 新興企業
emerging economy 振興経済国
emerging foreign exchange エマージング通貨の外国為替
emerging market エマージング・マーケット
emerging market counterparts 新興市場の他国
emerging markets 新興マーケット
EMH (efficient market hypothesis) 効率的市場仮説
EMI (European Monetary Institute) 欧州通貨機構
eminent domain 土地収用
EMMPS (exchangeable money market preferred stock) 交換可能マネーマーケット優先株
empiric 経験主義の
empirical analysis 実証的分析
empirical approach 経験的アプローチ
empirical experience 実証的経験
empirical rule 経験則
empirical study 実証研究
employee 従業員
employee benefit 従業員給付
employee benefit arrangement 従業員給付の取決め
employee benefit cost 従業員給付コスト
employee benefit fund 従業員給付基金
employee benefit obligations 従業員給付債務
employee benefit plan 従業員給付制度
employee choice 従業員選択
employee contribution 従業員掛金；従業員拠出
employee coverage 従業員保障
employee health care benefit 従業員医療給付
employee household 雇用者世帯
employee insurance 従業員保険
employee mortality 従業員死亡率
employee paid benefit 被用者負担給付
employee pension benefit plan 従業員年金制度
employee pension plan 被雇用者年金プラン
employee profit sharing plan 従業員利益分配制度
employee relocation expense 従業員配置転換費用
employee retirement benefit 従業員退職給付
Employee Retirement Income Security Act of 1974 従業員退職所得保証法
employee savings plan 従業員貯蓄プラン
employee security plan 従業員保障制度
employee share purchase plan 従業員株式購入制度
employee stock option 従業員ストック・オプション
employee turnover (ratio) 従業員退職率
employee welfare benefit plan 従業員福祉給付制度
employee-director 使用人兼務役員
employees pension fund 従業員年金基金積立金
employees retirement allowance 従業員退職給与金
employees salary and allowance 従業員給与手当
employees union 従業員組合
employees' own conveniences 従業員の自己都合
employees' pension 厚生年金
employees' pension fund 厚生年金基金
employees' pension fund contract 厚生年金基金契約
Employees' Pension Fund rules 厚生年

金基金規約
Employees' Pension Insurance 厚生年金保険
employees' relief fund 扶助基金
employees' remuneration 従業員の報奨
employees' retirement allowance 雇用者退職給与金
employer 使用者
employer contribution 事業主掛金
employer financed benefit 雇用者負担型給付
employer group insurance 事業者団体保険
employer matching contribution 雇用者折半拠出金
employer sponsored 事業者提供の
employer's contribution 企業負担
employer's liability insurance 使用者賠償責任保険
employer's obligation 事業主の債務
employment 雇用
employment adjustment 雇用調整
employment based coverage 雇用関連保障
employment contract 雇用契約
employment cost 人件費
employment data 雇用データ
employment growth 雇用の伸び
employment income 給与所得
employment income deduction 給与所得控除
employment income earner 給与所得者
employment index 雇用指数
employment insurance 雇用保険
employment insurance premium 雇用保険料
employment market 雇用市場
employment multiplier 雇用乗数
employment office 職業安定所
employment opportunities 雇用機会
employment prospectus 雇用見通し
employment statistics 雇用統計
employment termination indemnities 退職手当
empowerment エンパワーメント
EMS (European Monetary System) 欧州通貨制度
EMTA (Emerging Markets Traders Association) エマージング市場取引者協会
EMTN (Euro medium-term note) ユーロ中期債
EMU (European Monetary Union) 欧州通貨同盟
EMU (European Monetary Union) enlargement EMU 拡大
emulate 模倣する
en bloc reinsurance 総括引受再保険
enactment 制定
enactment of regulations 規程の制定
encashment 現金化
enclosure 囲い込み
encourage 奨励する
encouragement 奨励
encouragement of private financing 民間金融奨励
encumber 負わせる
encumbered 抵当権のついている
encumbrance 不動産に伴う負担
end day of operations オペのエンド日
end goal 最終目標
end of the fiscal year 年度末
end of the period 期末
end of the year 期末
end result 最終結果
end-of-day finality 最終時点ファイナリティ
end-user エンド・ユーザー
ending inventory 期末棚卸資産
endogenous change 内生変化
endogenous sector 内生部門
endogenous variable 内生変数
endorsed 裏書された
endorsed bill 裏書手形
endorsed bills exchanged between two related parties 回し手形
endorsed bond 裏書債券
endorsed note 裏書手形

endorsee 被裏書人
endorsement 裏書
endorsement for option contract オプション契約の裏書
endorsement for transfer 裏書譲渡
endorsement in blank 白地式裏書
endorsement to order 指図式裏書
endorsement to transfer 譲渡裏書
endorsement without recourse 遡及義務免除裏書
endorser 裏書人
endow 遺贈する
endowment 基金
endowment annuity 年金付保険
endowment insurance 養老保険
endowment mortgage 養老モーゲージ
endowment option 満期繰上選択権
endowment period 養老年金満期までの期間
endowment policy 養老保険証書
energy conservation 省エネ
energy elasticity エネルギー弾性
energy mutual fund エネルギー株ミューチュアル・ファンド
energy risk エネルギー・リスク
energy sector stock エネルギー株
energy security エネルギー安全確保
energy stockpiling エネルギー備蓄
energy tax エネルギー税
enforce 強制する
enforceable 強行力のある
enforceable right 強制権
enforced currency 強制通貨
enforced liquidation 強制売却処分
enforcement 施行
enforcement day 施行日
Enforcement Division 監視課
enforcement regulations 施行規則
Enforcement Regulations of the Bank of Japan Law 日銀法施行規則
enforcement right 実施権
enfranchisement 公権付与
engage in 携わる
Engel's coefficient エンゲル係数
Engel's law エンゲルの法則
engineering insurance 機械保険
English disease 英国病
English form of balance sheet 英国式貸借対照表
English law 英国法
engraving and printing cost of bond certificates 社債券印刷費用
enhance 価値を高める
enhanced disclosure ディスクロージャの充実
enhanced indexing エンハンスト・インデックス運用
enhanced security 充実確保
enhanced welfare 高福祉
enhancement of asset 資産の増価
enhancement of customer loyalty 顧客の囲い込み
enhancement of goodwill のれんの補完
enhancement of recoverable amount 回収可能額の増加
enhancement to assets 資産の価値増進
enjoin 差止める
enlarged EC (European Communities) 拡大ＥＣ
enlarged European Communities 拡大ＥＣ
enlightening activities 啓蒙活動
enrichment 充実
enrolled agent 登録代理人
enrollment 登録
ensuing account 次期勘定
entente 協商
enter 記入する
enterprise 企業
enterprise accounting 企業会計
enterprise approach 企業全体でのリスク評価
enterprise assets 企業資産
enterprise bankruptcy 企業倒産
enterprise concerned 当該企業
enterprise cost 企業原価
enterprise fund 企業基金
enterprise level 全社レベル
enterprise liabilities 企業の負債

E

enterprise management 企業経営者
enterprise mortgage 企業担保権
enterprise mutual aid plan 企業共済
enterprise tax 事業税
enterprise tax on corporation 法人事業税
enterprise-specific 企業固有の
enterprise-wide financial statements 企業全体の財務諸表
enterprise-wise 企業ごとの
enterprise's operation 企業活動
enterprise's owner 企業の所有者
entertainment 娯楽
entertainment and social expenses 交際費
entertainment expenses not qualifying for deduction 損金不算入の交際費
entire agreement clause 完全合意条項
entire day basis computation 満日計算
entire life of obligation 債務の全期間
entire surplus 剰余金全体
entire tenancy 単独保有
entitle 権利を与える
entitled to 権利がある
entitlement 権限
entity 実体
entity accounting 実体会計
entity ceasing to exist 消滅会社
entity theory 法人理論
entrance fee 入会金
entrant 参入者
entrepreneur 起業家
entrepreneurship 起業家精神
entropy エントロピー
entrust 委託する
entrusted asset 受託商品
entrusted business commission 委託業務手数料
entrustment 委託
entrustment of clearing business 決済事務の委任
entrustment of collection 徴収の嘱託
entrustment on when-issued transactions 発行日決済取引の委託
entrustment to trustee 受託者に対する事務委託
entry 記入
entry age 加入年齢
entry age cost method 加入年齢方式
entry cost 参入コスト
entry into a business affiliation 業務上の提携
entry into insurance business 保険業参入
entry of judgment 判決登録
entry system of a candidate 候補者届出制度
enumeration 列挙
environment assessment 環境評価
environment load 環境負荷
environmental accounting 環境会計
environmental assessment 環境アセスメント
environmental audit 環境監査
environmental data 環境データ
environmental degradation countermeasure 環境対策
Environmental Dispute Coordination Commission 公害等調整委員会
environmental fund 環境株ファンド
environmental governance 環境ガバナンス
environmental impairment liability insurance 環境汚染賠償責任保険
environmental policy 環境政策
environmental protection 環境保護
environmental rating 環境格付け
environmental report 環境報告書
environmental tax 環境税
envisaged obligation 予定された責務
EOE (European Options Exchange) ユーロピアン・オプション取引所
EOE (European Options Exchange) Index EOE 指数
EOI (expression of interest) 関心の表明
EOM (end of month) 月末
EOQ (economic order quantity) 経済的発注量

EPC (engineering, procurement and construction) EPC
EPS (earnings per share) 一株当り利益
equal annual payment method 年間定額払法
equal cost curve 等費用曲線
equal credit opportunity 信用享受の機会均等
equal credit opportunity act 信用機会均等法
equal employment opportunities 雇用機会均等
equal footing イコール・フッティング
equal installment repayment method 元本均等払方式
equal market value 同じ市場価格
equal monthly payment 月額均等払い
equal monthly payments with interest 元利均等返済
equal payment method 元利均等払方式
equal weighted portfolio 等金額ポートフォリオ
equal-weighted average 均等加重平均
equaled date of payment 平均支払期日
equalization account 平衡勘定
equalization dividend 平準化配当
equalization of tax burden 税負担の平準化
equalization of tax collection 徴税の公平
equalization of tax payment 納税の公平
equalization reserve 平準化積立金
equalizing divergences 格差均等化
equalizing dividend 均等化配当
equally divided 均分
equate to maturity 満期日に一致する
equation of exchange 交換方程式
Equatorial Guinea (CFA (Communauté Financière Africaine) franc) 赤道ギニア（CFA フラン）
equilibrium analysis 均衡分析
equilibrium basis 適正ベーシス
equilibrium point 均衡点
equilibrium price 均衡価格
equilibrium rate of exchange 均衡為替相場
equilibrium rate of interest 均衡利子率
equilibrium relationship between markets 市場間の均衡関係
equipment fair value 設備適正価額
equipment fund 設備資金
equipment investment 設備投資
equipment leasing partnership 設備リース・パートナーシップ
equipment trust 設備信託
equitable assignment 衡平法上の譲渡
equitable interest in asset 資産の価値に対する権利
equitable lien 衡平法上のリーエン
equitable mortgage 衡平法上のモーゲージ
equitable obligation 衡平法上の債務
equitable owner 衡平法上の所有者
equitable remedy 衡平法上の救済
equitable title 衡平法上の所有権
equities insurance エクイティ保険
equity account 変額投資勘定；持ち分勘定
equity account reconciliation 資本勘定調整
equity accounting 持ち分会計
equity accounting method 持ち分法
equity and liabilities 資本及び負債
equity annuity 変額年金
equity asset holdings 株式資産保有
equity at book value 自己資本簿価
equity at market value 自己資本時価
equity based life insurance エクイティ生命保険
equity based product エクイティ関連商品
equity benefit 持ち分利益
equity boom 株式ブーム
equity buyback 株式の買戻し
equity call option 株券コールオプション

E

equity capital 株式資本；基本金；出資金
equity capital cycle 自己資本サイクル
equity capital ratio 自己資本規制比率
equity capital ratio to fixed assets 固定資産自己資本率
equity capital ratio to long-term capital 長期負債自己資本率
E
equity capital ratio to long-term liabilities 長期負債自己資本比率
equity capital ratio to total assets 総資本自己資本比率
equity capital ratio to total debt 総負債自己資本率
equity capital ratio to total liabilities 総負債自己資本比率
equity commitment note 株式転換確約社債
equity compensation 持ち分報奨
equity compensation benefit 持ち分報奨給付
equity compensation plan 持ち分報奨制度
equity component 資本部分
equity contract note 株式転換契約付社債
equity contribution 出資
equity contribution in cash 金銭出資
equity contribution in kind 現物出資
equity conversion 持ち分転換
equity convertible 転換社債
equity derivatives 株式派生商品
equity dividend cover 配当倍率
equity exposure 自己資金投資
equity finance エクイティ・ファイナンス
equity financial instrument 持ち分金融商品
equity financing 株式による資金調達
equity floatation 株式公開
equity flotation 株式の公開
equity fund 株式ファンド
equity funding エクイティ積立
equity growth rate 自己資本成長率
equity holder 株主
equity in earnings 純利益に対する持ち分
equity in the house 住宅の資産価値
equity income 持ち分利益
equity income of subsidiary 持ち分法による損益
equity index 株価指数
equity index fund 株式インデックス・ファンド
equity index linked annuity 株価指数連動型年金
equity index product 株価指数商品；株価連動商品
equity indexed 株式連動の
equity inflows 株式市場への資金流入
equity instrument 持ち分証券
equity interest 資本持分
equity interest in net profit 純利益に対する持分
equity investment 株式投資
equity investment trust ユニット投資信託
equity investor 株式投資家
equity IRR 株式 IRR
equity linked bond 株式リンク債
equity linked debt 株式連動債
equity linked life insurance 株価連動生命保険
equity linked swap 株式連動スワップ
equity margin エクイティ・マージン
equity market 株式市場
equity market bubble 株式バブル
equity market maker 株式マーケット・メーカー
equity method 持ち分法
equity method affiliates 持ち分法適用関連会社
equity method investee 持ち分法適用会社
equity method investment 持分法投資
equity of redemption 償還権
equity offering 株式公開
equity option contract 株券オプション取引
equity options 株券オプション

equity options clearing qualification 株券オプション清算指数
equity options non-clearing participant 株券オプション非清算参加者
equity options trading 株券オプション取引
equity options trading participant 株券オプション取引参加者
equity outflow 株式資金の流出
equity owner 持ち分所有者
equity participant 出資者
equity participation 資本参加
equity partner 出資者
equity portfolio 株式ポートフォリオ
equity position 出資比率
equity product 変額商品
equity purchase 株式の取得
equity purchases by institutions 機関投資家による買い
equity put option 株券プットオプション
equity ratio 株主資本比率
equity receiver 会社更生手続きの管財人
equity redemption bond 株式償還債
equity REIT (real estate investment trust) 出資型リート
equity repurchase 株式の買戻し
equity return 株式投資収益
equity revaluation 持ち分評価替
equity risk 株式リスク
equity risk premium 株式リスク・プレミアム
equity securities 出資証券
equity securities dealer 株式ディーラー
equity setback 株価の下落
equity share 持ち分株式
equity share capital 普通株式資本
equity stake 株式の持ち分
equity structure 資本構成
equity swap 株式交換
equity theory 持ち分利益
equity trust エクイティ型投資信託
equity turnover 株主資本回転率
equity upside エクイティの上昇
equity warrant エクイティ・ワラント；株式ワラント
equity weighting 株式組入率
equity write-off 株式評価損
equity-settled 株式決済の
equivalence 等価
equivalent adjustment 対応する修正
equivalent bond yield 債券相応利回り
equivalent coefficient 等価係数
equivalent level annual dividend 均等平準年次配当
equivalent pool 対応するプール
equivalent rent 相当の地代
equivalent tax yield 等価課税利回り
equivalent taxable yield 課税債券相当利回り
equivalent yield 等価利回り
ERA (expense reimbursement allowance) 経費支出手当
era of high interest rate 高金利時代
erection insurance 組立保険
ERISA (Employee Retirement Income Security Act) 従業員退職所得保障法（エリサ法）
ERN (Eritrea nakfa) エリトリア・ナクファ
erosion in equity prices 株価の下落
erosion in purchasing power 購買力の侵食
erosion of confidence 信頼性の揺らぎ
erratic fluctuation 乱高下
error 誤謬
error curve 誤差曲線
error in making the estimate 見積誤差
errors and omissions 誤差脱漏
errors and omissions insurance 過失責任保険
errors in calculation 計算違い
errors in posting 転記上の誤り
ERSC (EU Securities Regulators Committee) EU 証券規制機関委員会
ESC (EU Securities Committee) EU 証

E

券委員会
escalating annuity 逓増保険
escalation clause エスカレーション条項
escalator clause エスカレーター条項
ESCAP (Economic and Social Commission for Asia and the Pacific) 国連アジア太平洋経済社会委員会
escapable cost 回避可能原価
escape clause 免責条項
ESCB (European System of Central Banks) 欧州中央銀行制度
escheat 復権財産
escrow 条件付捺印証書
escrow account エスクロウ勘定
escrow agreement エスクロウ契約
escrow and trust agreement エスクロウ信託契約
escrow credit エスクロウ信用状
escrow fund 寄託資金
escrow letter of credit 寄託信用状
escrow receipt 第三者預託証書
ESCWA(Economic and Social Commission for Western Asia) 西アジア経済社会委員会
ESOP (employee stock ownership plan) 従業員持株制度
ESP (Spanish peseta) スペイン・ペセタ
ESPRIT (European Strategic Programme for R&D in Information Technologies 欧州情報技術研究開発戦略計画
essential condition 必須条件
essential purpose bond 公共目的債
essential structure 基本的構造
essentially bankrupt borrower 実質破綻先
established in ranges レンジ内で推移
established practices 確立した慣行
establishing security interest 担保権の設定
establishment expenses 事業所費
establishment of corporation 法人の設立
establishment of customer's account 顧客口座の開設
establishment of direct participant's account 参加者口座の開設
establishment of hypothec 抵当権の設定
establishment of leasehold 借地権の設定
establishment of tax liability 納税義務の確定
establishment of the right of pledge 質権設定
estate agent 不動産業者
estate at sufferance 容認不動産物件
estate at will 任意不動産物件
estate claims 財団債権
estate contract 不動産契約
estate duty 相続税
estate for years 定期不動産権
estate in possession 所有不動産
estate planning 資産計画
estate tax 相続税
estate upon condition 条件付不動産権
estate upon limitation 制限付不動産権
estimate 見積る
estimate cost 見積原価
estimated annual effective income tax rate 見積年次実効税率
estimated appropriation of budget 経費予算
estimated balance sheet 見積貸借対照表
estimated budget request 概算要求
estimated cost 概算原価
estimated cost accounting 見積原価計算
estimated cost accounting system 見積原価計算制度
estimated cost of construction work 見積工事原価
estimated disposal amount 処分見込額
estimated disposal value 処分可能見込額
estimated exit value 見積売却価額

estimated expenses 見積費用
estimated future income taxes 繰延所得課税債務
estimated holding period return 予想保有期間収益率
estimated liabilities 見積債務
estimated loan loss 貸倒見積高
estimated mining period 採掘予定年数
estimated mining quantity 採掘予定数量
estimated profit 見積利益
estimated profit and loss statement 見積損益計算書
estimated selling price 予想売価
estimated tax 見積税額
estimated tax prepayment 予定納税
estimated timing 見積時期
estimated uncollectable amount 取立不能見込額
estimated uncollectible amount 貸倒見積額
estimated usable period 使用可能期間
estimated useful life 見積耐用年数
estimated useful life of used property 中古資産の見積耐用年数
estimated useful life table 見積耐用年数表
estimated value 見積価額
estimated volume 見積操業度
estimating-cost system 見積原価制度
estimation 見積り
estimation error 推定誤差
estimation process 見積過程
estimation sampling 推定サンプリング
estoppel 禁反言
estovers 必要物
ETB (Ethiopian birr) エチオピア・ビル
ETC (electronic trade confirmation) 電子取引照合
ETC (equipment trust certificate) 設備信託証書
ETF (exchange traded fund) 株価指数連動型投信
ethical discipline 服務
ethical fund 倫理ファンド
ethics 倫理
ETR (estimated total return) 推定総収益率
ETT (electronic transfer of title) 権原の電子移転
EUA (European Unit of Account) 欧州計算単位
Euler equation オイラー方程式
EUR (Euro) ユーロ
EURGBP ユーロ / 英ポンド
EURIBOR (Euro Inter-Bank Offered Rate) ユーロ銀行間出し手レート
Euro area ユーロ圏
euro denominated bond ユーロ債
euro entry ユーロ加盟
Euro yield ユーロ債利回り
Euro-money ユーロマネー
Euro-zone ユーロ圏
Euro-zone economy ユーロ圏の経済
Eurobond ユーロ債
Eurobond market ユーロ債市場
Euroclear ユーロクリア
Euroclear France フランス保管振替機関
Eurocommercial paper ユーロコマーシャル・ペーパー
Eurocredit market ユーロ貸付市場
Eurocurrencies market ユーロ資金市場
Eurocurrency ユーロ資金
Eurocurrency banking market ユーロ金融市場
Eurocurrency market ユーロカレンシー市場
Eurocurrency syndicated loan market ユーロカレンシー・シンジケート・ローン市場
Eurodollar ユーロドル
eurodollar bond ユーロドル債
eurodollar CD (certificate of deposit) ユーロドル CD
Eurodollar deposit ユーロドル預金
Eurodollar depositary interest futures ユーロドル預金金利先物

Eurodollar futures option ユーロドル先物オプション
Eurodollar market ユーロドル市場
Eurodollar time deposit ユーロドル定期預金
Euroland ユーロ圏
Euromark futures ユーロマルク先物
Euromarket ユーロ市場
Euromoney ユーロマネー
Euronote 中期ユーロ債
Euronote facility ユーロノート・ファシリティ
European Atomic Energy Community 欧州原子力共同体
European bond market ユーロボンド市場
European Coal and Steel Community 欧州石炭鉄鋼共同体
European Commission 欧州委員会
European Common Market 欧州共同市場
European Community 欧州共同体
European Fund 欧州基金
European Investment Trust 欧州投資信託機関
European Monetary Fund 欧州通貨基金
European option ヨーロピアン・オプション
European Parliament 欧州議会
European Payment Union 欧州支払同盟
European term 欧州方式
European type ヨーロッパ・タイプ
European Union 欧州連合
European unity 欧州統合
Europound bond ユーロポンド債
Eurosecurity ユーロ証券
euroSF (European Securities Forum) 欧州証券フォーラム
Eurosyndicate loan ユーロシンジケート・ローン
Eurotop 100 Index ユーロトップ100指数
Eurotrack ユーロトラック
Euroyen ユーロ円
Euroyen bond ユーロ円債
Euroyen bond for resident 居住者ユーロ円債
Euroyen bond issue ユーロ円債発行
Euroyen floater ユーロ円変動利付債
Euroyen interest rate ユーロ円金利
Euroyen market ユーロ円市場
EURUSD ユーロ／米ドル
EV (enterprise value) 企業買収価値
EVA (economic value added) 経済的付加価値
evade 忌避する
evaluation 評価
Evaluation Division 審査課
evaluation framework 評価の枠組み
evaluation of individual projects 個別案件評価
evaluation of market mechanism 市場機構の評価
evaluation of performance 業績評価
evaluation of solvency 支払能力評価
evaluation perspectives 評価の視点
evaluator 鑑定人
evasion of corporation tax 法人税の脱税
evasion of income tax 所得税の脱税
even lot 単位株
evening session イーブニング・セッション
evening up 手じまい
event 事象
event of default 不履行事由
event risk イベント・リスク
event subsequent to balance sheet date 貸借対照表日後の発生事項
event subsequent to the balance sheet date 後発事象
evergreen credit エバーグリーン・クレジット
eviction 追い立て
eviction order 立退命令
evidence 証拠
evidence of better growth 景気回復の証拠

evidenced document 証憑書類
evidences of indebtedness 債務証書
evidentiary facts 証拠事実
evil practice 悪用
evolution 進化
evolving practices 進化している実務
EWMA (exponentially weighted moving average) 指数加重移動平均
ex-all 全権利落ち
ex-allotment 子株落ち
ex-ante analysis 事前分析
ex-ante evaluation 事前評価
ex-ante test 事前テスト
ex-coupon 裸値；利札落ち
ex-coupon price of bond 債券裸値
ex-dividend date 配当落日
ex-dividend period 配当落期間
ex-facto 行為に基づく
ex-interest 利落ち
ex-interest bond 利落債券
ex-interest for interest-bearing bond 利付債券の裸値
ex-interest period 利落期間
ex-legal 無弁護士意見地方債
ex-new 権利落ち；新株落ち
ex-new quotation 権利落相場
ex-pit transaction 取引所外取引
ex-post 事後の
ex-post alpha value 事後アルファ値
ex-post analysis 事後分析
ex-post approval 事後の承認
ex-post assessment 事後的な評価
ex-post beta 事後ベータ
ex-post characteristic line 事後特性線
ex-post facto 事後の
ex-post investment 事後的投資
ex-post optimum analysis 事後最適分析
ex-post saving 事後的貯蓄
ex-post variance 事後差異
ex-rights 権利落ち
ex-rights fair value 権利落公正価値
ex-rights of capital increase 増資権利落ち
ex-stock-dividends 株式配当落ち
ex-store 店頭渡しで
ex-warrant エクス・ワラント
ex-warrant bond ポンカス債
exact factor model 厳密ファクター・モデル
exact interest 完全金利
exaggerated return 過大申告
examination 審査
Examination and Criminal Investigation Department 調査査察部
examination and decision 審査裁決
examination by reference 照査
examination contracts 考査契約
Examination Division 調査課
examination fee 審査料
examination fee for relocation to other market 上場市場の変更審査料
examination of banknotes 銀行券の鑑査
examination of entrance qualification 入会審査
examination of financial statements 財務諸表監査
examination of loan application 貸出審査
examination of witness 証人尋問
Examination Office 審査室
examined copy 対照した謄本
Examining Circular 検査公報
except for 除いては
excepted perils 免責危険
excepted period 免責期間
excepted risks 除外危険
exception clause 特例条項
exception of proceeds 保険金の支払禁止
exception principle 例外の原則
exception to amortization of deferred charge 繰延資産の償却の例外
exception to depreciation deduction 減価償却の例外
exception to the Commercial Code 商法の特例

E

exceptional items 例外事項
exceptional nature 例外的な性質
exceptional participant 特例参加者
exceptional rates of tax 例外的税率
exceptional tax treatment 税務上の例外
exceptions 例外規定
excess 小損害免責
excess accumulation tax 超過積立税
excess amount 超過額
excess and deficiency 過不足
excess benefit 超過給付
excess burden 超過負担
excess capacity 過剰設備
excess cash 余剰資金
excess condemnation 付帯収用
excess contribution 超過掛金
excess demand 超過需要
excess disbursement 払超
excess earnings power 超過収益力
excess expense 超過経費
excess fund 超過資金
excess gain tax 超過利得税
excess income 超過所得
excess insurance 超過額保険
excess interest 超過利息
excess limit 超過限度額
excess margin 超過証拠金
excess method 超過方式
excess of debt 債務超過
excess of loss 超過損害額
excess of loss reinsurance 超過損害再保険
excess of loss treaty reinsurance 超過損害額特約再保険
excess over par 資本準備金組入額
excess payment 超過支払い
excess profit 超過利潤
excess profit credit 超過利潤控除
excess profitability 超過利潤性
excess receipt over contract price 値増金
excess reinsurance 超過額再保険
excess reserves 過剰準備
excess return 超過リターン
excess revenue generating power 超過収益力
excess spread 超過スプレッド
excess supply 超過供給
excess yield 超過利回り
excessive competition 過当競争
excessive consumption 過剰消費
excessive debt 過剰債務
excessive detail 過度な情報
excessive gain 不当利得
excessive labor input 過剰雇用
excessive lending 過剰貸付
excessive liquidity 過剰流動性
excessive profit 暴利
excessive savings 過剰貯蓄
excessive seizure 超過差押え
excessive service 過剰サービス
excessive trading 過剰取引
exchange acquisition 取引所買付け
exchange arbitrage transaction 為替裁定取引
exchange at night 夜間交換
exchange bank 為替銀行
exchange bill payable 並為替
exchange bought 買為替
exchange broker 為替ブローカー
exchange business 為替業務
exchange cambiste 為替ディーラー
exchange check for money 金銭の引換券
exchange clause 為替文句
exchange clearing 為替清算
exchange clearing agreement 為替清算協定
exchange contract 為替予約
exchange contract with option 選択権付為替予約
exchange control 為替管理
exchange control regulation 為替管理法令
exchange cover カバー取引
exchange cover rate 出合相場
exchange dealer 為替ディーラー
exchange difference 為替差額
exchange distribution 取引所分配

exchange dumping 為替ダンピング
exchange economy 交換経済
exchange equalization capital 為替平衡資金
exchange equalization fund 為替平衡基金
exchange equalization operation 為替平衡操作
exchange fluctuation 為替変動
exchange fluctuation reserve 為替変動準備金
exchange for collection 取立為替
exchange for foreign payment 対外支払いのための為替
exchange for means of foreign payment 対外支払のための為替
exchange forward contract 先物為替予約
exchange fund 取引所取引基金
exchange fund cover 資金調整取引
exchange fund cover operation 為替資金調整操作
exchange fund operation 資金操作
exchange gain 為替差益
exchange gain and loss 為替換算差損益
exchange gain from the yen appreciation 円高差益
exchange gain from yen appreciation 円高差益
exchange gain or loss 為替差損益
exchange law 取引所法
exchange link 外国為替のリンク
exchange loss 為替差損
exchange manipulation 為替操作
exchange market 取引所市場
exchange marriage profit 為替マリー益
exchange marry 為替マリー
exchange member 取引所会員
exchange of assets 資産の交換
exchange of Bank of Japan notes 日本銀行券の引換え
exchange of equity interests 株式交換
exchange of equivalents 等価交換
exchange of machinery and equipment owned by the government 国有機械設備の交換
exchange of money 両替
exchange of notes 交換公文
exchange of property 資産の交換
exchange of shares 株式交換
exchange operation 為替操作
exchange option 交換オプション
exchange parity 為替平価
exchange position 為替持高
exchange premium 為替プレミアム
exchange privilege 乗換特権
exchange quotation 対顧客為替相場
exchange rate 為替レート
exchange rate against dollar 対ドル為替相場
exchange rate at break-even point 損益分岐為替相場
exchange rate at the end of period 期末為替レート
exchange rate band 為替相場圏
exchange rate basket 通貨バスケット
exchange rate developments 為替の動向
exchange rate fluctuation 為替の変動
exchange rate in favor of yen 円高
exchange rate in foreign currency 外貨建相場
exchange rate per dollar ドル換算レート
exchange rate policy 為替政策
exchange reservation 為替予約
exchange risk 為替リスク
exchange risk cover 為替持高調整操作
exchange risk insurance 為替変動保険
exchange settlement 為替決済
exchange sold 売為替
exchange speculation 為替投機
exchange stabilization fund 為替安定基金
exchange tax 取引所税
exchange ticket 注文執行確認書
exchange traded options 取引所取引オプション

exchange traded transaction 取引所取引
exchange transaction 交換取引
exchange value 交換価値
exchange-for-value settlement 価値交換型決済
exchange-traded issues 上場銘柄
exchangeable corporate bonds 交換社債券
exchangeable debt 交換可能債務証書
exchangeable variable note 短期市場金利連動債
Exchequer 英国大蔵省
exchequer bills 英国大蔵証券
excise duty 物品税
Excise Taxes and General National Tax Rules Policy Division 税制第三課
exclude 除外する
excluded risk 免責危険
exclusion 除外
exclusion clause 除外条項
exclusion from capital gain キャピタルゲインからの控除
exclusion from corporate tax expenses 法人税額の損金不算入
exclusion from expenses of corporation tax 法人税額損金不算入
exclusion from gross profit 益金不算入
exclusion from non-taxable expenses 損金不算入
exclusion from taxation 非課税
exclusion of dividend received from taxable income 受取配当等益金不算入
exclusion of dividends from gross revenue 受取配当の益金不算入
exclusion of expenses of entertainment expense from non-taxable income 交際費の損金不算入
exclusion of loss 損失除外
exclusion of profit accrued from valuation profit 評価益の益金不算入
exclusion of received dividends from taxable income 受取配当金の益金不算入
exclusion of refund from gross revenue 還付金の益金不算入
exclusion of remuneration of director from non-taxable expenses 役員報酬の損金不算入
exclusion ratio 免除比率
exclusionary rule 排除の原則
exclusive account for tax payment 納税専用口座
exclusive agent 独占代理店
exclusive dealing 競争品取扱禁止契約
exclusive distributor 独占販売業者
exclusive distributorship 一手販売権
exclusive jurisdiction 専属管轄権
exclusive listing 専属委任契約
exclusive privilege 独占権
exclusive right 独占権
exclusive right to sell listing 独占販売権
exclusive selling agent 一手販売代理店
exclusive use 専用
exclusive use of a new production method 新生産方式の独占使用
exclusive use of assets 資産の専属的利用
exclusive use of property 資産の専属的利用
exclusive-occupation house 専用住宅
exculpate 身のあかしをたてる
excuse 弁明
executed 既履行の
executed contract of sale 完成売買契約
executing broker 執行ブローカー
executing organization 実行機関
execution creditor 執行債権者
execution of a contract 契約締結
execution of business 事業の遂行
execution of contractual terms 契約内容の実行
execution of duties 業務の執行
execution of loan 融資の実行
execution of order 注文の執行
execution organ 実行機関

execution risk 執行リスク
executive agreement 行政協約
Executive Auditor of the Bank of Japan 日銀監事
executive auditors 監事
executive committee 執行委員会
executive compensation option 役員報奨のためのオプション
executive debtor 執行債務者
executive director 執行役取締役；理事
Executive Director of the Bank of Japan 日銀理事
executive measure 執行処分
executive officer 執行役
executive order 執行命令
executive organ 執行機関
executive pension 経営者年金
executive power 執行権
executive proceedings 執行手続
executive salaries 役員報酬
executive summary 概要
executive vice president 副理事長
executory contract 未確定の契約
executory cost 履行費用
executory interest 将来権
exemplar company 模範となる企業
exempt corporation 適用除外法人
exempt gift 非課税贈与
exempt income 非課税所得
exempt private company 免除私会社
exempt property 非課税財産
exempt securities 適用免除証券
exempt stock exchange 登録免除取引所
exempted amount 控除額
exempted securities 適用除外証券
exemption 免除
exemption agreement 免責約款
exemption and deduction from income 所得控除
exemption clause 除外条項
exemption for aged person 老年者控除
exemption for handicapped person 障害者控除
exemption for taxation 非課税
exemption for working student 勤労学生控除
exemption from return of subsidy 補助金返還免除
exemption from the application 適用除外
exemption from withholding tax on interest payments on JGSs 国債利子に対する所得税の源泉徴収不適用の措置
exemption method 外国所得免除方式
exemption of debt 債務免除
exemption of gift tax 贈与税免除
exemption of inheritance tax 相続税免除
exemption of real estate acquisition tax 不動産取得税の非課税
exemption of taxes 租税免除
exemption regime 適用除外範囲
exemptions 差押禁止債権
exercisable 行使可能な
exercise 行使
exercise date 権利行使日
exercise date measurement 行使日測定
exercise general control over board business 会務を総理する
exercise limit 権利行使の認められている取引量
exercise notice 権利行使通知
exercise of an option オプションの権利行使
exercise of claim on clearing margin 証拠金に対する権利の行使
exercise of judgment 判断の行使
exercise of right 権利行使
exercise of security right 担保権の行使
exercise of stock option ストック・オプションの行使
exercise of subscription rights 新株引受権の行使
exercise of voting right 議決権の行使
exercise of voting right by proxy 議決権の代理行使

exercise of warrant ワラントの行使
exercise period 権利行使期間
exercise price 行使価格
exercise price interval 行使価格の刻み値
exercise price per share 一株当り行使価格
exercise volume 権利行使数量
exercised value 権利行使価額
exert downward pressure 下方圧力をかける
exhaustion 消耗
exhaustive 包括的な
exhaustive expenditure 消耗的経費
exhaustive study 包括的調査
exhibit 添付書類；明細表
EXIM (Export-Import) 輸出入
eximbank 輸出入銀行
existing assets 既存資産
existing balance 現存の残高
existing business 存続事業
existing corporation to receive assets 吸収法人
existing debt 既存債務
existing exposure 与信残高
existing issue 既発銘柄
existing longs 既存のロング・ポジション
existing preferential duties 既存特恵
exit bond エグジット・ボンド
exit fee 解約手数料
exit price 売却価格
exit strategy 売却戦略
exit value 売却価額
exodus 流出
exogenous change 外生的変化
exogenous demand 外生需要
exogenous variables 外生変数
exoneration 免責
exorbitant profit 法外な利益
exotic bond エキゾティック・ボンド
exotic currency エキゾティック・カレンシー
exotic derivatives エキゾティック派生商品
exotic option エキゾティック・オプション
expanded lead manager 拡大主幹事
expansion economy 膨張経済
expansion of currency 通貨膨張
expansion path 拡張経路
expansion period 景気拡大期間
expansionary budget 積極予算
expansionary monetary policy 景気刺激型金融政策
expansive economy 拡大経済
expectancy policy 平均余命保険
expectancy right of dividend 配当期待権
expectant heir 期待相続人
expectation gap 期待のギャップ
expectation hypothesis 期待仮説
expectation of life 平均寿命
expectation theory 期待理論
expected annual volume 期待年間操業度
expected benefit payment 予定給付支払額
expected claims 予定保険金支払額
expected dividend 予想配当
expected earnings 期待収益
expected earnings growth rate 期待利益成長率
expected excess 予想超過額
expected future payment 予想支払額
expected growth rate 予測成長率
expected holding-period rate of return 期待保有期間収益率
expected income 予定収入
expected investment return 期待運用収益
expected investment return ratio 期待運用収益率
expected life 見積耐用年数
expected loss 予想損失
expected market demand 市場の需要見込み
expected mortality rate 予定死亡率
expected output 予想能力
Expected Ownership Distribution of

Depositary Securities on or after Listing Application Date 上場申請日以後における預託証券の分布状況に関する予定書
expected pattern 予測パターン
expected rate of return 期待収益率
expected rate of return on insurance premium invested 予定利率
expected rate of return on plan assets 制度資産の期待収益率
expected retirement benefit 退職給付見込額
expected return 期待収益
expected return on pension assets 期待運用収益
expected return ratio of loan trust 貸付信託予想配当率
expected sales 予測売上
Expected Shareownership Distribution on or after Listing Application Date 上場申請日以後における株式分布状況に関する予定書
expected standard 期待水準
expected total rate of return 期待総収益率
expected utility function 期待効用関数
expected value 期待値
expected volatility 予想変動率
expected wealth effect 期待資産効果
expected yield 期待利回り
expected yield-to-maturity 期待満期利回り
expendable fund 支出可能資金
expendable supplies 消耗品
expenditure 支出
expenditure curtailment 支出削減
expenditure for public bond 公債費
expenditure incurred for the restoring to its original state 原状回復のための支出
expenditure on capital accounts 資本勘定支出
expenditure on unemployment insurance 失業保険支出
expenditure ratio 支出率
expenditure tax 支出税
expenditure unaccounted for 使途不明金
expense account 経費勘定
expense account balance 経費勘定残高
expense budget 経費予算
expense by segment セグメント別費用
expense constant 定数付加保険料
expense distribution 費用配賦
expense factor 経費要素
expense for issuing corporate bond 社債発行費用
expense incurred 発生経費
expense item 費目
expense ledger 経費元帳
expense loading 付加保険料
expense ratio 経費率
expense reduction 経費削減
expense report 経費報告
expense reserve 経費準備金
expense under necessity for the active conduct of business 事業の遂行に必要な経費
expenses for education and culture 教養費
expenses incidental to the receipts of income 収入に付随して発生する費用
expenses incurred for having the user remove 移転料
expenses incurred for maintaining household 家事関連費
expenses incurred for opening of business 開業費
expenses incurred from fire 火災により発生した費用
expenses of bringing up children 養育費
expenses of entering port 入港費用
expenses paid in advance 未経過費用
expenses quota 経費割当
experience assumptions 基礎率
experience premium 経験保険料
experience rating 経験料率
experience table 経験表

experience-based adjustment 実績による修正
experienced judgment 経験上の判断
experimental and research expense 試験研究費
experimental and research expense tax credit 試験研究費税額控除
experimental manufacturing cost 試作費
experimentation 実証研究
expert system エキスパート・システム
expert witness 専門家証人
expiration 期限切れ
expiration date 満期日
expiration date of credit card クレジットカード有効期限
expiration date of the credit card カード有効期限
expiration day of the exercise 権利行使日
expiration of carryforward 繰越期限到来
expiration of obligation 債務消滅
expiration of option オプションの消滅
expired card 期限切れカード
expired cost 消滅原価
expiry 期限満了
expiry date 満了日
expiry date of the credit 信用状期限
expiry of derivatives デリバティブの期限満了
explained variables 被説明変数
explanatory leaflet for financial futures transaction 金融先物取引説明書
explanatory material 説明文書
explanatory note 註記
explanatory variables 説明変数
explicit 明示的
explicit clause 明示的条項
explicit contract 明示の契約
explicit cost 明示的費用
explicit model 明示モデル
explicit prohibition 明確な禁止
explicit requirement 明示要件
exploitation 搾取
exploitation of new resources 新資源の開発
exploration for natural resources 天然資源の探鉱
explosive growth 爆発的な伸び
exponential 指数の
exponential curve 指数曲線
exponential distribution 指数分布
exponential martingale 指数マーチンゲール
exponential smoothing 指数平滑法
exponential utility function 指数効用関数
export advance 輸出前貸し
export advance loan 輸出前貸金融
export advanced account 輸出前貸勘定
export and import price index 輸出入物価指数
export and import statistics 外国貿易統計
export bill 輸出手形
export bounty 輸出奨励金
export cartel 輸出カルテル
export competition 輸出競争
export compliance program 輸出管理規定
export credit 輸出信用
export credit guarantee 輸出信用保証
export declaration 輸出申告
export dependence 輸出依存
export drive 輸出ドライブ
export duties 輸出税
export earnings 輸出利益
export exemption 輸出免税
export financing 輸出金融
export function 輸出関数
export growth 輸出の伸び
export import loan 輸出入ローン
export industry 輸出産業
export law 輸出法
export letter of credit 輸出信用状
export license 輸出承認証
export mix 輸出構成

E

export of capital 資本の輸出
export of goods purchased 他から購入した物品の輸出
export on consignment 委託販売輸出
export permission 輸出許可
export price index 輸出物価指数
export proceeds 輸出代金
export profitability 輸出の収益性
export restriction 輸出規制
export sector 輸出セクター
export stocks 輸出関連株
export subsidy 輸出補助金
export supplier credit 輸出業者信用
export tax 輸出税
export to an overseas territory 移出
export usance 輸出ユーザンス
export volume 輸出高
export-dependent 輸出依存の
export-import bank 輸出入銀行
Export-Import Bank of USA 米国輸出入銀行
exporter 輸出者
expose the primary support 主要支持線が試される
exposure profile リスク・プロファイル
exposure to credit risk 信用リスクへのエクスポージャ
exposure to interest rate 金利リスク
exposure to liquidity risk 流動性リスクへのエクスポージャ
exposure to risk リスクの負担
express contract 明示契約
express trust 明示信託
express warranty 明示保証
expressed need 表明されている要望
expropriation 公用徴収
expropriation by government 政府による収用
expropriation loss 接収による損失
expropriation of land 土地収用
expulsion from membership 除名
expunge the mortgage 抵当権を抹消する
EXQ (ex quay) 埠頭渡し
EXS (ex ship) 着船渡し
extel card エクステル・カード
extendable swap エクステンダブル・スワップ
extended benefit 延長給付
extended bill 延長手形
extended coverage 拡張担保；拡張保障
extended fund facility 拡大信用供与制度
extended insurance 延長保険
extendible maturity 延長可能満期
extending credit 与信の提供
extending losses against major currencies 主要通貨に対して安くなる
extensible swap 延長可能型スワップ
extension 外延；債務返済延期承認書
extension effect 期間効果
extension of credit 信用供与
extension of due date 納期限の延長
extension of free credit 無償の信用供与
extension of loan 融資の実行
extension of special loan 特別融資の実行
extension of the maturity 償還延長
extension of time claims 延長クレーム
extension of time for completion 工期の延長
extension of time to file 提出の延期
extensive income statement 全般の損益計算書
extent of disclosure 開示範囲
extenuation 軽減
external account 対外収支
external appraisal 外部鑑定
external assets 対外資産
external audit 外部監査
external auditor 外部監査人
external balance 対外収支
external bond 外債
external capital 外部資本
external consistency 外部整合性
external customer 外部顧客

E

external debt 対外債務
external demand 外需
external diseconomy 外部不経済
external economy 外部経済
external environment 外部環境
external equilibrium 対外均衡
external evaluation 外部評価
external event 外部事象
external financial auditor 会計監査人
external financing 外部金融
external fund 外部資金
external funding 外部積立
external hazard 外部危険
external liabilities 対外負債
external liquidity 外部流動性
external loan 外債
external pressure 外圧
external purchasing power of money 貨幣の対外価値
external purpose 外部目的
external rate of return 外部収益率
external reporting 外部報告
external reserves 外貨準備
external resources 外部資源
external restrictions 外部からの制限
external sales revenue 外部売上収益
external settlement 市場と参加者間決済
external source of financing 外部の資金源
external source of information 外部情報源
external transaction 外部取引
external transactions account 海外取引勘定
external user 社外利用者
extinction 消滅
extinction of hypothec 抵当権の消滅
extinctive prescription 消滅時効
extinguish 消滅する
extinguishment 消滅
extinguishment of assets 資産の滅失
extinguishment of debt 債務の消滅
extinguishment of hypothec 抵当権の消滅
extinguishment of property 資産の滅失
extinguishment of the debt 負債の消滅
extra budget 補正予算
extra charges 付帯費用
extra cost 追加費用
extra coverage 総額補償
extra depreciation 割増償却
extra dividend 特別配当
extra expenditure 臨時費
extra item 異常項目
extra loss 超過損失
extra money 割増金
extra payment 超過支払い
extra premium 追加プレミアム；割増保険料
extra wage 割増賃金
extra work claims 余分工事クレーム
extra-judicial 裁判外の
extramural 区域外の
extraneous risk 付加危険
extraordinary average 非常海損
extraordinary call 臨時繰上償還
extraordinary depreciation 特別償却
extraordinary expenditure 臨時経費支出
extraordinary expenses 臨時費
extraordinary gain 異常利益
extraordinary gain or loss 特別損益
extraordinary general meeting 臨時総会
extraordinary income 臨時所得
extraordinary item 特別損益項目
extraordinary loss 特別損失
extraordinary measures 非常措置
extraordinary profit and loss 特別損益
extraordinary profit and loss item 特別損益項目
extraordinary profit or loss item 異常損益項目
extraordinary rent 臨時賃貸料
extraordinary repairs 臨時修繕費
extraordinary resolution 臨時決議
extraordinary suspension 臨時停止
extrapolate 推定する

extrapolative 外挿的
extraterritorial application 域外適用
extraterritoriality 治外法権
extraterritoriality on tax laws 免税特権
extrinsic evidence 外部証拠
extrinsic value 付帯価値
EXW (ex works) 工場渡し

F

FA (financial adviser) フィナンシャル・アドバイザー
fabless ファブレス
fabricating cost 製造原価
fabrication 捏造
face amount 額面金額
face amount certificate 額面証書
face of financial statements 財務諸表の本体
face of instrument 証書の文面
face value 額面価額
face value of the position 売買額面金額
face-to-face transactions of low value 小口の対面取引
facilities 設備
facility capital 設備資金
facility fee ファシリティ・フィー
facility management 施設管理運営
fact book 要覧
fact finding 事実認定
fact in issue 主要事実
factor 要因
factor analysis 要因分析
factor beta ファクター・ベータ
factor cost 要素原価
factor income 要素所得
factor price 要素価格
factor return 要素収益率
factor risk ファクター・リスク
factor sensitivity ファクター感応度
factor technology 要素技術
factor's holdback 債権買取会社の保留金
factorage ファクタリング手数料
factoral 製造要素の
factored in 織り込まれる
factoring ファクタリング
factors of production 生産要素
factory 工場
factory account 工場勘定
factory accounting 工場会計
factory backlog 製造受注残
factory bookkeeping 工業簿記
factory burden 工場間接費
factory cost 工場原価
factory cost report 製造原価報告書
factory expenses 製造間接費
factory expenses variance 経費差額
factory furniture 工場用什器
factory furniture and fixtures 工場備品
factory ledger 工場元帳
factory ledger account 工場元勘定
factory overhead budget 製造間接費予算
factory overhead costs 製造間接費
factory supplies 工場用消耗品
facultative reinsurance 任意再保険
facultative reinsurance agreement 任意再保険協定
faculty theory of taxation 支払能力課税説
fade-out formula フェイド・アウト方式
fade-out policy of foreign capital ratio 外資比率削減政策
fail position 不履行ポジション
failed financial institution 破綻金融機関
failed transaction フェール
failing company 破綻企業
failing of record 記録不提出
failure 不履行
failure of consideration 約因の滅失
failure to consider dividend policy 配当への配慮の欠如
failure to deliver 受渡不履行
failure to deliver securities 証券決済未了

failure to file a return 無申告
failure to fulfill obligation 債務不履行
failure to pay 支払不能
failure to receive 受取不履行
failure to settle 決済不履行
failure to settle option contracts オプション取引決済不履行
faint action 無力訴訟
fair 公平な
fair and equitable 公正かつ衡平
fair and orderly market 公平で秩序のある市場
fair average quality 平均品質
Fair Debt Collection Practices Act 公平債券回収法
fair judgment 公正な判断
fair leasehold value 借地権の価格
fair market price 公正な市場価格
fair market value 公正市場価額
fair practice rule 公正慣習規則
fair premium 公正な保険料
fair presentation 適正表示
fair price 公正価格
fair price formation 公正な価格形成
fair rate of return 公正収益率
fair trade 公正取引
fair trade act 公正取引法
fair trade bureau 公正取引局
fair valuation 公正価値評価
fair value 公正価値
fair value accounting 公正価値会計
fair value accounting model 公正価値会計モデル
fair value adjustment 公正価値修正
fair value appraisal 時価評価
fair value appraisal of stocks 株式の時価評価
fair value based method 公正価値基準法
fair value hedge 公正価値ヘッジ
fair value measurement 公正価値測定
fair value model 公正価値モデル
fair value of plan assets 制度資産の公正価値
fair value recognition 公正価値認識
fair value revaluation 公正価値再評価
fair wage 適正賃金
Fair, Isaac & Co. フェアー・アイザック社
fair-trade agreement 公正取引協定
fairly and impartially 公平に
fairness 公平性
fairness opinion 公正意見書
faithful representation 公正な表示
fall across the board 全面安
fall back 反落する
fall due 期日が到来する
fall of gold standard 金本位制度崩壊
fall out of bed 株価急落
fall short of 下回る
fall under 該当する
fallen angel 堕天使
falling at the current moderate pace 現状程度の小幅下落
falling in price 価格下落
falling in stock price 株価の下げ
falling interest rate 金利下落
falling into a weaker range across the board 独歩安
falling market 下げ基調の相場
falling off 下放れ
falling yield environment 利回りの下落局面
false declaration 不正申告
false demonstration 誤謬表示
false documents 虚偽の資料
false missing 偽装紛失
false personation 氏名詐欺
false rally あや戻し
false report 虚偽の報告
false representation 虚偽な表示
false return 虚偽の申告
false statement 虚偽の記載
false trade description 虚偽の商品の表示
false verdict 不当評決
faltering economies 景気の冷え込み
family allowance 家族手当
family benefit 家族給付
family bookkeeping 家計簿

family company 同族会社
family credit 家族控除
family deductible 家族控除額
family fund ファミリーファンド
family group life insurance 家族団体生命保険
family income and expenditure survey 家計調査
family income benefit policy 家族年金保険
family income rider 家族年金特約
family insurance 簡易保険
family medical expense policy 家族医療費保険
family partnership 同族組合
family personal accident policy 家族傷害保険
family policy 家族保険
family protection insurance 家族保障年金保険
family relationship 姻戚関係
family saving survey 貯蓄動向調査
family taxation of assets income 資産所得の世帯合算課税
family term insurance 家族定期年金保険
family trust 家族信託
family unit 家族単位
famine prices 飢餓相場
fan line ファンライン
fan theory ファン理論
fancy stocks 値がさ株
Fannie Mae ファニーメイ
FAO (Food and Agriculture Organization of the United Nations) 国連食糧農業機関
far contract month 期先限月取引
fare 運賃
farm accounting 農業会計
farm mortgage loan 農場抵当貸付
farm subsidy 農業補助金
Farmer MAC (Federal Agricultural Mortgage Corporation) 連邦農業金融抵当金庫
farming of taxes 租税取立請負
farther in 期近
farther out 期先
farthest contract month 第三限月取引
FASB (Financial Accounting Standards Board) 財務会計基準審議会
FASB (Financial Accounting Standards Board) pronouncements 財務会計基準審議会基準書
FASF (Financial Accounting Standards Foundation) 財務会計基準機構
fast growth 急成長
fat cat 大物
fatigue factor 疲労因子
fatter tail 厚いテール
fault 過失
favorable 順調
favorable balance 黒字
favorable balance of overall 総合収支の黒字
favorable balance of payments 国際収支の黒字
favorable balance of trade 貿易収支の黒字
favorable balance on current account 経常収支の黒字
favorable carry 有利なキャリー
favorable cash flows 望ましい現金の流れ
favorable change 有利な変化
favorable factor 好材料
favorable leverage effect 正の増益効果
favorable tax treatment 税優遇措置
favorable trade balance 貿易収支黒字
favorable treatment 優遇措置
favorable variance 有利差異
favored stock 人気株
favorite fifty 人気50銘柄
FB (floor broker) 立会場ブローカー
FBs (financing bills) 政府短期証券
FCBA (Fair Credit Billing Act) 公正信用請求法
FCC (Federal Communications Commission) 連邦通信委員会
FCFV (Free cashflow valuation) フリー・キャッシュフロー・バリュエー

ション
FCIA (Foreign Credit Insurance Association) 外国信用保険協会
FCM (futures commission merchant) 先物取引業者
FCRA (Fair Credit Reporting Act) 公正信用報告法
FDIA (Federal Deposit Insurance Act) 連邦預金保険法
FDIC (Federal Deposit Insurance Corporation) 連邦預金保険公社
FDICIA (Federal Deposit Insurance Corporation Improvement Act) 連邦預金保険公社改革法
fear 警戒
feasibility study フィージビリティスタディ
feasible 実行可能な
featherbedding 水増雇用要求
features 特徴
Fed 連邦準備制度理事会
Fed fund rate FF 金利
Fed fund target FF 金利誘導目標
Fed tightening FRB の利上げ
Fed watcher フェドウォッチャー
Fed wire フェッドワイヤー
Federal Advisory Committee 連邦諮問委員会
federal agency 連邦機関
federal agency securities 連邦機関証券
Federal Banking Commission 連邦銀行委員会
Federal Bankruptcy Act 連邦破産法
federal court 連邦裁判所
Federal Credit Union Act of 1934 連邦信用組合法
federal deficit 米国財政赤字
federal deposit insurance 連邦預金保険
federal district court 連邦地方裁判所
federal employee retirement system 連邦職員退職年金制度
Federal Farm Credit Bank 連邦農業信用銀行
Federal Farm Credit System 連邦農業信用制度
federal fund assets 連邦政府年金資産
federal fund market フェデラルファンド市場
federal fund rate フェデラルファンド・レート
federal gift tax 連邦贈与税
federal government 連邦政府
Federal Home Loan Bank Board 連邦住宅貸付銀行理事会
Federal Home Loan Bank System 連邦住宅貸付銀行制度
federal income tax 連邦所得税
federal income tax expense 連邦法人税費用
federal intermediate credit banks 連邦中期信用銀行
federal involvement 連邦政府介入
Federal Land Bank 連邦土地銀行
federal loan guarantee 連邦政府のローン保証
Federal National Mortgage Association 連邦抵当金庫
federal procurement law 連邦調達法
Federal Reserve Act 連邦準備法
Federal Reserve Bank 連邦準備銀行
Federal Reserve Bank of New York ニューヨーク連邦準備銀行
Federal Reserve Board 連邦準備制度理事会
Federal Reserve District 連邦準備地区
Federal Reserve membership of state banks 州法銀行の連邦準備制度加盟
Federal Reserve Notes 連邦準備証書
Federal Reserve Open Market Committee 連銀公開市場委員会
Federal Reserve open market operation 連邦公開市場操作
Federal Reserve Reform Act 連邦準備改革法
Federal Reserve Regulation 連邦準備制度規則
Federal Savings and Loan Insurance

F

Corporation 連邦貯蓄貸付保険会社
Federal spending 連邦政府支出
federal tax 連邦税
Federal Trade Commission 連邦取引委員会
Federation of Bankers Associations of Japan 全国銀行協会連合会
Federation of Credit Guarantee Corporations 保証協会連合会
Federation of Economic Organizations 経済団体連合会
Federation of Tax Accountants 税理士連合会
Fedwire (Federal Reserve's wire transfer system) フェッドワイヤ
fee 手数料；報酬
fee and commission 手数料
fee based 報酬ベースの
fee business フィー・ビジネス
fee for book-entry transfer 振替決済手数料
fee for issuance of securities 証券発行手数料
fee for legal advice 法律相談料
fee for settlement 決済に係る手数料
fee for undertaking off-auction distribution 立会外分売引受料
fee for underwriters 証券引受業者の手数料
fee income 手数料収入
fee on loans 貸出手数料
fee schedule 報酬表
fee simple 単純不動産
fee simple absolute 絶対的不動産保有権
feedback フィードバック
feedback value フィードバック価値
feedstock 原材料
FEER (fundamental equilibrium exchange rate) ファンダメンタル均衡為替レート
fees after listing 上場後の費用
fees and permits 免許料
fees for off-floor distribution 立会外分売取扱料
fees for original listing 新規上場手数料
fees for stock name transfers 名義書換手数料
fees for withdrawals of stock certificates 交付手数料
FEFSA (Foreign Exchange Fund Special Account) 外国為替資金特別会計（外為特会）
fellowship grant 研究補助金
feneration 高利
FERC (Federal Energy Regulatory Committee) 連邦エネルギー規制委員会
Fertilizer and Feed Inspection Services 肥飼料検査所
FESE (Federation of European Securities Exchanges) 欧州証券取引所連合会
FET (federal excise tax) 連邦物品税
feverish market 熱狂相場
FF (federal fund) フェデラル・ファンド
FF interest フェデラル・ファンド金利
FFA (free from alongside) 舷船渡し
FFB (Federal Financing Bank) 連邦金融銀行
FFIEC (Federal Financial Institution Examination Council) 連邦金融機関検査委員会
FFO (funds from operation) オペレーションからの資金
FGI (financial guarantee insurance) 金融保証保険
FHA (Federal Housing Administration) 連邦住宅局
FHFB (Federal Housing Financing Board) 連邦住宅金融理事会
FHLB (Federal Home Loan Bank) 連邦住宅貸付銀行
FHLMC (Federal Home Loan Mortgage Corporation) 連邦住宅金融抵当金庫
FIA (Futures Industry Association) 先

物協会
fiat 制令
fiat money system 管理通貨制度
fiat standard 管理通貨制度
Fibonacci sequence フィボナッチ数列
FICA (Federal Insurance Contributions Act) 連邦保険拠出金法
FICA (Federal Insurance Contributions Act) tax rate 社会保障税率
FICO (Financing Corporation) 連邦調達公社
fictional theory of corporation 法人擬制説
fictitious account 架空口座
fictitious assets 擬制資産
fictitious capital 擬制資本
fictitious coupon みなし利息
fictitious credit 擬制貸方残高
fictitious demand 仮需要
fictitious dividend タコ配当
fictitious price 掛値
fictitious profit 架空利益
fictitious sales slip 架空売上伝票
fictitious transaction 架空取引
fidelity bond 信用保険
fidelity guarantee insurance 身元信用保険
fidelity insurance 誠実保険
fiduciary 受託者
fiduciary accounting 信託会計
fiduciary bond 受託者保証証書
fiduciary business 信託業務
fiduciary capacity 受託者としての資格
fiduciary contract 信託契約
fiduciary duties 受託業務
fiduciary duty 信任義務
fiduciary estate 信託財産
fiduciary fund 信託基金
fiduciary issue 保証発行
fiduciary law 信託法
fiduciary nature 委任の性質
fiduciary power 信託権限
fiduciary requirement 受託者責任
fiduciary responsibility 受託者責任
field audit 実地監査
field examination 臨店検査
field inspection 現場検査
field inspector 現場検査人
field-work audit standards 監査実施基準
FIFO (first-in, first-out) method 先入先出法
Fifth Amendment 米国憲法修正第５条
fifty percent depreciation ２分の１償却法
fifty percent owned company ２分の１所有会社
FII (franked investment income) 課税済投資収益
file 提出する
file and use 届出後使用制
file income tax return 所得額を申告する
filing ファイリング
filing date 提出日
filing of a seal impression 印鑑届
filing of final return of merger 合併確定申告
filing of final return on corporation tax 法人税確定申告書の提出
filing of return 申告書の提出
filing status 申告区分
fill or kill 即時執行
fill-in 補充注文
fill-or-kill order 即時または取消注文
filling of orders 注文の執行
fillip flop bond フィリップ・フロップ債
FILP (Fiscal Investment and Loan Program) 財政投融資計画
FILP (Fiscal Investment and Loan Program) agency 財投機関
FILP (Fiscal Investment and Loan Program) agency bond 財投機関債
FIM (Finland markka) フィンランド・マルカ
FIN (FASB Interpretation) FASB 解釈指針

F

final accounts 最終決算
final audit 期末監査
final balance 期末残
final balance method 最終残高方式
final beneficiary 最終受益者
final bid-asked quotation 最終特別気配値段
final claim 本クレーム
final cut 最終的な
final day of the accounting period 期末日
final demand 最終需要
final depreciable limit 償却可能限度額
final determination 最終決定
final disposal 最終処理
final disposition of bad loans 不良債権の最終処理
final list of shareholders 最終の株主名簿
final long position 最終買建玉
final maturity 最終満期
final obligation 最終債務額
final payment 最終支払い
final phase 最終局面
final price 最終価格
final process 最終過程
final products 最終製品
final prospectus 最終目論見書
final quarter 第４四半期
final rate of return 最終収益率
final return in the case of loss 損失申告書
final return of liquidation 清算確定申告書
final return of loss 確定損失申告書
final return of merger 合併確定申告書
final salary pension plan 退職時給与年金制度
final salary pension scheme 退職時給与による年金制度
final salary plan 退職時給与による制度
final session of a month 納会
final session of a year 大納会
final settlement 最終決済
final settlement day 最終決済期日
final settlement index price 最終清算指数
final settlement of accounts 確定した決算
final short position 最終売建玉
final special quote 最終気配値段
final tax return 確定申告
final transaction date 最終取引日
final value 終価
final yield 最終利回り
final yield on investment 最終投資利回り
finality 決済完了性
finally settled financial statements 最終的に確定した財務諸表
finance act 財政法
finance bill 金融手形
finance charge 金融費用
finance close 融資合意
finance company 金融会社
finance for prepaid installment sales 前払式割賦販売金融
finance lease ファイナンスリース
finance lease liability ファイナンス・リース債務
Finance Ministry Ordinance 財務省令
finance receivable 貸出債権
finance receivables as collateral 債権担保
finance street 金融街
finance tax cut 減税財源を調達する
financed insurance 保険料融資保険
financed premium 借入保険料
financial accommodation 資金融通
financial accounting 財務会計
Financial Accounting Foundation 財務会計財団
financial accounting principles 財務会計原則
Financial Accounting Standards Advisory Council 財務会計基準諮問委員会
financial accounting standards for business enterprise 企業会計原則

financial accounting statements 財務計算書類
financial accounts 金融勘定
financial activities 金融活動
financial advisor 財務顧問
financial affairs 財務
financial agent 財務代理人
financial agreement 金融協定
financial aid 金融援助
financial analysis 財務分析
financial analyst 証券アナリスト
Financial Analysts Federation 全米アナリスト協会連合会
financial and capital markets 金融資本市場
financial and operational highlights 財務及び営業のハイライト
financial arrangement ファイナンスの仲介
financial asset held for trading 短期売買目的金融資産
financial asset value 金融資産価値
financial assets 金融資産
financial assets and liabilities account 金融資産負債残高表
financial assets available-for-sale 売却可能金融資産
financial assets held for trading 売買目的金融資産
financial assets of individuals 個人金融資産
financial assumption 財務上の仮定
financial audit 財務監査
financial balance 財務バランス
financial base 財務基盤
financial benefit 金銭給付
financial budget 財務予算
Financial Bureau 理財局
financial capital 金融資本
financial center 金融中心地
financial claim 金融債権
financial clique 財閥
financial collapse 金融崩壊
financial commitments 金融上の債務
financial community 金融業界
financial conditions 財政状態
financial conditions index 金融条件指数
financial consultant 財務コンサル
financial contribution 資金協力
financial cost 財務コスト
financial covenant 財務制限条項
financial crisis 金融恐慌
Financial Crisis Relation Office 金融危機対応室
financial cushion 財政的保護
financial data 財務データ
financial decision 金融面での決断
financial deficit 資金不足
financial democracy 財政民主主義
financial development 金融面の動き
financial diagnosis 財政診断
financial difficulty 金融難；財政困難
financial disclosure 財務内容の開示
financial disintermediation 金融機関離れ
financial documents 財務書類
financial dynamics 財務力
financial effect 財務上の影響
financial engineering 金融エンジニアリング
financial environment 金融環境
financial evolution 金融革新
Financial Executive Institute 財務担当経営者協会
financial expenses 金融費用
financial exposure 資金負担
financial facilities 金融サービス
financial flow 財務フロー
financial footing 財政基盤
financial forecast 財務予測
financial forward contract 金融先渡契約
Financial Function Early Strengthening Law 金融機能早期健全化法
financial futures 金融先物
financial futures broker 金融先物取引業者
financial futures clearing house 金融

先物清算機関
financial futures contract 金融先物契約
financial futures exchange 金融先物取引所
financial futures instrument 金融先物商品
financial futures market 金融先物市場
financial futures option 金融先物オプション
Financial Futures Trading Law 金融先物取引法
financial futures transaction 金融先物取引
financial gearing 財務レバレッジ
financial globalization 金融のグローバル化
financial guarantee 金融保証
financial guarantee contract 債務保証契約
financial guarantor 信用保証会社
financial guaranty insurance 信用保証保険
financial highlights 経理のハイライト
financial holding company 金融持株会社
financial impact 財務的影響
financial income 金融収益
financial indexes 金融指標
financial indicators 財務指標
financial information 財務情報
financial information exchange protocol 金融情報交換プロトコル
financial innovation 金融革新
Financial Inspection Manual 金融検査マニュアル
financial institution 金融機関
financial institution for agriculture forestry and fisheries 農林漁業金融機関
financial institution for foreign exchange 外国為替金融機関
financial institution's self-assessment of assets 金融機関による資産の自己査定
financial institutions for long-term credit 長期信用金融機関
financial institutions for small business 中小企業金融機関
financial institutions placed under the hands of financial reorganization administrator 被管理金融機関
financial institutions subject to the Bank's on-site examination 考査先
financial institutions that hold current accounts with the Bank 当座取引先
financial instrument 金融商品
financial instruments for which banks are required to maintain reserves 準預対象金融商品
Financial Intelligence Office 特定金融情報室
financial interest 財務上の持ち分
financial intermediaries or brokers 金融仲介機関
financial intermediary 金融仲介機関
financial intermediary function 金融仲介機能
financial intermediation 金融仲介
financial item 金融項目
financial knowledge 金融知識
Financial Law Board 金融法委員会
financial lease 金融リース
financial leverage フィナンシャル・レバレッジ
financial leverage effect 財務面の増益効果
financial leverage ratio 負債比率
financial liability 金融負債
financial liberalization 金融の自由化
Financial Liberalization Fund 金融自由化対策資金
financial liberalization policy 金融自由化政策
financial loss 財務損失
financial management 財務管理
financial margin 利ざや
financial market 金融市場
financial market analysis 金融市場分

析
financial market globalization 金融市場グローバル化
financial market instability 金融市場の不安定性
financial market liberalization 金融市場の自由化
Financial Markets Department 金融市場局
Financial Markets Division 市場課
financial model 金融モデル
financial needs approach 金融ニーズ法
Financial News index option フィナンシャル・ニューズ指数オプション
financial obligation 金融債務
financial operations 金融業
financial option contract 金融オプション契約
financial option market 金融オプション市場
financial options 金融オプション
financial panic 金融恐慌
financial performance 財務業績
financial planner フィナンシャル・プランナー
financial planning 財務計画
financial policy 金融政策
financial position statement 貸借対照表
financial positions of firms 企業の資金繰り
financial product 金融商品
financial profit 金融収益
financial projection 財務予測
financial public relation 財務広報
financial pyramid 金融ピラミッド
financial rating system 財務格付制度
financial ratio 財務比率
financial recession 金融不況
Financial Reconstruction Commission 金融再生委員会
financial regeneration 金融再生
financial regulation 金融規制
financial regulator 金融規制当局
financial reinsurance 金融再保険
financial reorganization administrator 金融整理管財人
financial report 財務報告書
financial reporting 財務報告
financial reporting accounting 財務報告会計
financial reporting standards 財務報告基準
financial reporting year 財務報告年度
financial representation 財務的表明
financial research center 金融研究所
financial resources 財源
financial restructuring 経営再建
financial retrenchment 経費節減
financial return 財務収益
financial revenue 財務収益
financial review 財務概況
Financial Revitalization Law 金融再生法
financial revolution 金融革命
financial risk 財務リスク
financial savings products 金融貯蓄商品
financial sector 金融セクター
financial sector stocks 金融株
financial service 金融サービス
financial service fee 金融手数料
financial service industry 金融サービス業界
financial slack 財務上のスラック
financial solvency 財務流動性
financial sophistication 金融知識
financial soundness 財務健全度
financial soundness of the Bank of Japan 日本銀行の財務の健全性
Financial Stability Organizations Office 機構業務室
financial state valuation method 財務内容評価法
financial statements 財務諸表
financial statements audit 財務諸表監査
financial statements structure 財務諸表構成

financial statistics 金融統計
financial strain and stress 財務上の負担
financial strength 財務力
financial structure 財務構造
financial supermarket 金融スーパーマーケット
Financial Supervisory Agency 金融監督庁
financial support 金融支援
financial surplus 資金余剰
financial surplus or deficit 資金過不足
financial survey 金融調査
financial synergy 財務上の相乗効果
financial system 金融制度
Financial System Council 金融審議会
Financial System Management Council 金融危機対応会議
financial system policy 金融システム政策
Financial System Research Council 金融制度調査会
financial system stability 金融システムの安定
financial table 金融情報欄
financial target 財務目標
Financial Times Index of Industrial Ordinary Shares フィナンシャルタイムズ工業株価指数
Financial Times Index of Sensitive World Commodity Prices フィナンシャルタイムズ商品相場指数
financial underwriting 財務上の査定
financial variables 財務数値
financial year 会計年度
financial year end 会計期末
financier 出資者
financing activities 資金調達活動
financing adjustment law 資金調整法
financing arrangement 資金手当て
financing bank 貸付銀行
financing burden 金融負担
financing business industry 金融業界
financing by public institutions for implementing policies 制度金融
financing capability 資金調達力
financing charge 金融費用
financing conduit 資金調達を行うための企業
financing corporation 金融会社
financing cost 資金調達費用
financing device 財政援助
financing for carrying inventories 滞貨金融
financing for deficit - covering 赤字融資
financing for sales by installment payment 月賦販売金融
financing for stocks 株式資金調達
financing from brokers' own capital 自己融資
financing lease ファイナンス・リース
financing method 資金調達手段
financing need 資金需要
financing policy 資金調達方針
financing profit or loss 金融損益
financing program 資金調達計画
financing regulation 融資準則
financing regulation law 資金規制法
financing tool 資金調達手段
financing transaction 金融取引
financing vehicle 金融商品
financing with new share reservation right 新株予約権付融資
finder 仲介業者
finder's fee 仲介料
findings 事実指摘
fine 過怠金
fine and penalty 罰科金
fine tuning 微調整
finished goods 完成品
finished goods ledger 製品元帳
finished goods on hand 手持製品
finished product ledger 製品元帳
finished products 完成品
finished products account 製品勘定
finished products inventory 製品棚卸額
finished products on hand 製品手持額
finite difference 有限差分

finite-life limited partnership 有期有限パートナーシップ
fire and casualty insurance 火災損害保険
Fire and Disaster Management Agency 消防庁
Fire and Marine Insurance Rating Association of Japan 損害保険料率算定会
fire and other casualty insurance premiums deduction 損害保険控除
fire clause 火災保険約款
fire insurance 火災保険
fire insurance on dwelling houses 住宅火災保険
fire insurance premium 火災保険料金
fire insurance proceeds 火災保険金
fire loss 火災損失
fire loss suspense account 火災損失未決算勘定
fire mutual insurance 火災相互保険
fire policy 火災保険証書
fire sale 投売り
fire wall ファイヤーウォール
fire-insurance for mortgagee interest 債権保全火災保険
firm 底固い
firm banking ファーム・バンキング
firm bid ファーム・ビッド
firm commitment 全額引受け
firm commitment underwriting 買取引受
firm contract 確定契約
firm offer ファーム・オファー
firm order 確定注文
firm price 確定価格
firm purchase commitment 確定購入契約
firm quote 確定呼値
firm sales contract 確定済販売契約
firm tone of the U.S. dollar ドル高基調
firmer 強保合い
firmer performance of stock markets 株式市場の堅調な相場展開
firmer tone 強含み
firms with high credit ratings 高格付企業
firms with high credit risks 信用力の低い企業
FIRST (fixed interest rate short tranche) 固定金利短期トランシェ
FIRST (Fund's Information Relay SysTem) 信託・証券等データ交換システム
First Amendment 米国憲法修正第1条
first application 初度適用
first bottom 一番底
first call date 第一回繰上償還日
first check 初鑑
first class mail 第一種郵便
first cost 仕入原価
first demand bond ファースト・ディマンド・ボンド
first dollar coverage 無控除保障
first exchange 第一券
first generation on-line system 第一次オンライン
first half of the accounting year 会計年度の上半期
first hitting time 到達時刻
first instance 第一審
first lien mortgage 第一順位モーゲージ
first loss subordination ファースト・ロス信用補完
first mortgage 第一抵当
first mortgage bond 第一順位抵当権付社債
first mortgage loan 第一順位モーゲージ・ローン
first oil crisis 第一次オイル・ショック
first papers 第一次書類
first peak 一番天井
first preferred stock 第一優先株式
first priority 最優先
first purchaser 最初の取得者
first refusal 第一拒否権
first refusal right 優先交渉権
first refusal right to repurchase 優先

F

的買戻権
First Section 市場一部
first section market 一部市場
first session of a month 発会
first session of a year 大発会
first surplus treaty 第一次超過額特約
first theorem 第一定理
first year commission 初年度手数料
first-loss insurance 実損填補
FISC (Center for Financial Industry Information Systems) 金融情報システムセンター
fiscal affairs 財政
fiscal agenda 財務政策
fiscal agent 財務代理人
fiscal agent agreement 財務代理人契約
fiscal agent for treasury fund 国庫財務代理人
fiscal aid 財政援助
fiscal and financial system 財政金融制度
fiscal and monetary policy 財政金融政策
fiscal boost 財政刺激
fiscal closing date 決算日
fiscal consolidation 財政引締め
fiscal constraint 財政制約
fiscal deficit 財政赤字
fiscal discipline 財政節度
Fiscal Division 司計課
fiscal drug 財政膨張の歯止め
fiscal expenditure 財政支出
fiscal illusion 財政錯覚
fiscal inflation 財政インフレ
fiscal inflexibility 財政硬直化
fiscal investment 財政投資
fiscal investment and loan 財政投融資
fiscal investment and loan fund 財政融資資金
Fiscal Investment and Loan Management Division 理財局管理課
Fiscal Investment and Loan Program Division 財政投融資総括課
Fiscal Loan Fund Special Account 財政融資資金特別会計
Fiscal Loan Fund Special Account bonds 財政融資特会債
Fiscal Loan Inspector 資金実地監査官
fiscal outlook 財政見通し
fiscal period 会計期間
fiscal policy 財政政策
fiscal policy stimulus 財政政策による刺激策
fiscal position 財政状態
fiscal privileges of diplomat 外交官課税特権
fiscal reform 財政改革
fiscal reserve 財政準備
fiscal resources 財源
fiscal resources for redemption 償還財源
fiscal revenue 歳入
fiscal squeeze 金融引締め
fiscal stabilizer 財政スタビライザー
fiscal stimulus package 財政刺激策
fiscal surplus 財政黒字
Fiscal System Council 財政制度等審議会
fiscal target 財政目標
fiscal tightness 財政の逼迫
fiscal year 会計年度
fiscal year closed 決算期
fiscal year end 会計期末
Fisher effect フィッシャー効果
Fisher equation フィッシャー方程式
Fisheries Agency 水産庁
Fisheries Research Agency 水産総合研究センター
fishery cooperatives 漁業協同組合
fishery, agriculture and forestry industry 農林水産業
Fitch Investors Service, Inc. フィッチ・インベスター・サービス
FITS (Fixed Income Transaction System) 債券取引システム
5-year government bond futures 中期国債先物取引
5-year discount government bonds 5年割引国債

5-year Japanese government bond 中期国債
5-year zero coupon bond 満期５年のゼロ・クーポン債
fixed amount 定額
fixed amount component 定額部分
fixed amount method 定額法
fixed amount minimum payment 最低限支払義務額
fixed amount per period standard 期間定額基準
fixed amount taxation 定額課税
fixed and variable flexible premium 自在変動型の保険料
fixed annuity 定額年金
fixed arrangement 固定性配列法
fixed asset ledger 固定資産台帳
fixed asset ratio 固定資産比率
fixed asset register 固定資産台帳
fixed asset schedule 固定資産明細表
fixed asset tax 固定資産税
fixed asset to net worth ratio 固定比率
fixed asset turnover (ratio) 固定資産回転率
Fixed Asset Valuation Council 固定資産評価審議会
fixed assets 固定資産
fixed assets acquired as contribution in kind to capital 現物出資により取得した固定資産
fixed assets acquired through merger 合併により取得した固定資産
fixed basket 一定バスケット
fixed benefit retirement plan 給付建退職年金制度
fixed benefits 固定給付
fixed budget 固定予算
fixed capital 固定資本
fixed capital investment 固定資本投資
fixed cash flow 固定金利キャッシュ・フロー
fixed cash payment 固定現金支払額
fixed charge 特定担保
fixed charge coverage 金融費用カバレッジ
fixed charge coverage ratio 固定費用負担倍率
fixed charges 固定費
fixed collateral 根抵当
fixed contribution 一定の掛金
fixed cost 固定費
fixed costs and expenses 固定費
fixed coupon bond 確定利付債
fixed date 確定日
fixed date delivery 確定日渡し
fixed debt 固定借入金
fixed deposit 定期預金
fixed difference 確定差額
fixed exchange rate 固定為替相場
fixed exchange rate regime 固定相場制
fixed exchange rate system 固定為替相場制度
fixed expenses 固定費
fixed fee 定額
fixed fee plus out-of-pocket expense contract 定額報酬実費支払契約
fixed gain 確定利益
fixed general tariff 固定税率
fixed immediate annuity 定額即時年金
fixed income analytics 債券分析
fixed income assets 確定利付資産
fixed income benchmark 債券指標銘柄
fixed income debt 債券
fixed income investment 債券投資
fixed income market 債券市場
fixed income portfolio 債券ポートフォリオ
fixed income securities 確定所得証券
fixed income targets 確定利付ターゲット
fixed income warrant デット・ワラント
fixed installment method 定額法
fixed interest 固定金利
fixed interest bearing securities 確定利付証券
fixed interest investment product 確定利付金融商品
fixed investment trust 固定投資信託

F

fixed liabilities 固定負債
fixed lien 特定担保
fixed life insurance 定額生命保険
fixed liquidity reserve requirements 固定的流動比率制度
fixed loan 固定貸付金
fixed maturity 確定期日
fixed maturity pension annuity contract 固定満期償還退職年金保険

F

fixed mortgage 根抵当権
fixed obligations 確定債務
fixed option plan 固定オプション制度
fixed overhead 固定間接費
fixed parity system 固定平価制
fixed payment bond 確定期日償還債
fixed percentage depreciation method 定率減価償却法
fixed percentage method 定率法
fixed percentage on declining balance method 減価定率法
fixed place of business 恒久的施設
fixed premium 定額保険料
fixed premium whole life insurance 定額保険料終身保険
fixed price 一定値段
fixed price commitment 固定価格契約
fixed price contract 固定価格契約
fixed property 不動産
fixed ratio 固定比率
fixed redemption value 確定償還価値
fixed repayment terms 固定償還期限
fixed return 確定収益
fixed return insurance 定額保険
fixed return securities 固定利回証券
fixed salary 固定給
fixed share 固定シェア
fixed sum policy 定額保険
fixed tax rate 一定税率
fixed term policy 定額払保険
fixed term reverse mortgage 期限付逆モーゲージ
fixed unit investment trust 固定単位型投資信託
fixed wages 固定給
fixed weight index 固定ウエート指数
fixed weighted 固定ウエートの
fixed-amount membership fee 定額会費
fixed-income 確定利付きの
fixed-income risk 債券リスク
fixed-rate 定率
fixed-rate annuity 定額年金
fixed-rate assets 固定金利資産
fixed-rate bond 確定利付債
fixed-rate coupon 固定利付クーポン
fixed-rate debt 固定金利負債
fixed-rate investment 固定利付投資
fixed-rate JGB 固定利付国債
fixed-rate loans repayable 固定金利融資
fixed-rate membership fee 定率会費
fixed-rate mortgage 固定金利モーゲージ
fixed-rate payer 固定金利支払人
fixed-rate receiving and floating-rate paying 受取固定支払変動
fixed-rate securities 固定利付証券
fixed-rate swap 固定金利スワップ
fixed-rate tax reduction 定率減税
fixed-rate transfer 定率繰入れ
fixity of tenure 永久保存
fixtures 付帯設備
FJD (Fiji dollar) フィジー・ドル
FKP (Falkland Islands pound) フォークランド諸島ポンド
flag フラッグ
flat 経過利子無し；持高ゼロ
flat amount 均一金額
flat benefit plan 均一給付制度
flat commission 均一手数料
flat curve フラット・カーブ
flat deductible 定額控除
flat exchange contract 直先同レート為替予約
flat fee 一律の手数料
flat growth 同じ伸び率
flat loan フラット・ローン
flat market フラット・マーケット
flat pension 定額年金

flat percentage 一定率
flat percentage plan 給与比例年金方式
flat price 均一料金
flat rate 直先同レート
flat rate tax 均一税率税
flat salary 均一給与
flat salary pension plan 均一給与年金制度
flat sum pension 均一年金
flat tax 均等税
flattening of curve 長短利回格差平坦化
flattening of the yield curve 利回曲線の平板化
flaw 欠点
flea market ノミの市
fleet insured フリート保険契約者
flexibility 機動力
flexible annuity 自在年金
flexible budget 弾力予算
flexible budget variance 変動予算差異
flexible exchange rate 屈伸為替相場
flexible expense 弾力費用
flexible forward contract レンジ・フォワード取引
flexible funding 基金自由積立
flexible mutual fund 分配型ミューチュアル・ファンド
flexible premium 自在保険料
flexible tariff 伸縮税率
flexible term policy 自由設計定期保険
flexible-premium variable life insurance 変額生命保険
flier 騰貴
flight money 逃避資金
flight of capital 資本の逃避
flight to quality 質への逃避
flip flop FRN (floating rate note) フリップ・フロップ債
flip flop securities フリップ・フロップ証券
FLIRB (front loaded interest reduction bond) 前倒金利削減債
float 資金化期間
floatation cost 起債費用
floater 変動利付債
floating basis フローティング・ベーシス
floating capital 浮動資本
floating charge 浮動担保
floating debt 浮動債務
floating exchange rate 変動為替相場
floating exchange rate regime 変動相場制
floating exchange rate system 変動為替相場制
floating insurance policy 浮動保険証券
floating interest rate 変動金利
floating interest rate account with ceiling 変動上限金利付勘定
floating liability 浮動負債
floating prime rate 市場連動型優遇金利
floating property 包括財産
floating securities 浮動証券
floating shareholder 浮動株主
floating shares 浮動株
floating supply 浮動玉
floating swap 変動金利スワップ
floating system 変動相場
floating to fixed interest rate swap 変動から固定への金利スワップ
floating vote 浮動票
floating-rate bond 変動利付債券
floating-rate certificate of deposit 変動金利 CD
floating-rate coupon 変動利付クーポン
floating-rate debt instruments 金利変動負債商品
floating-rate index 変動金利指標
floating-rate instrument 変動利付債
floating-rate JGB 変動利付国債
floating-rate lending 変動金利貸出
floating-rate market 変動利付債市場
floating-rate mortgage 変動利付モーゲージ
floating-rate note 変動利付債
floating-rate payer 変動金利支払人
floating-rate receiving and fixed-rate

F

paying 受取変動支払固定
floating-rate receiving and floating-rate paying 受取変動支払変動
floor 下限
floor broker フロアーブローカー
floor clerk 場立ち
floor issue 立会場銘柄
floor member 立会場会員
floor middleman 立会い場従業員
floor of protection 最低保障
floor offset pension plan オフセット年金制度
Floor Order Routing and Execution System 立会場事務合理化システム
floor plan 最低給付制度
floor price 下限価格
floor rate 下限金利
floor representative 立会代表者
floor ticket 立会場伝票
floor trader フロアトレーダー
floor trading 立会場取引
floored redemption amount フロアー付償還額
floored swap フロア付きスワップ
flooring debt 一時借入金
flotation of external loan 外債募集
flotation of government bond 公債発行
flotation of loan 起債
flotation of securities 証券発行
flotsam 漂流物
flow chart フローチャート
flow diagram フローダイアグラム
flow of fund 資金の流れ
flow of funds accounts 資金循環勘定
flow of funds analysis 資金循環分析
flow through method フロースルー法
flower bond フラワー・ボンド
fluctuate 変動する
fluctuating 波が大きい
fluctuating and extraordinary income 変動所得及び臨時所得
fluctuating income 変動所得
fluctuation analysis 変動分析
fluctuation clause 変動条項
fluctuation in fair value 公正価値変動
fluctuation in value 価値の変動
fluctuation limit 値幅制限
fluctuation of fair value 時価変動
fluctuation of stock prices 株価値動き
fluctuations in prices of raw materials 原料価格変動
flurry 一時的な活況
fly-by-night 信用のおけない
FmHA (Farmers Home Administration) 農業住宅局
FOB (free on board) 本船渡し
FOC (free of charge) 全費用込み
focus 焦点
follow a declining trend 減少傾向をたどる
follow-up selling 追撃売り
FOMC (Federal Open Market Committee) 連邦公開市場委員会
food financing bills 食糧証券
Food Management Special Account 食糧管理特別会計
food stamp 食料切符
foods industry 食料品業界
Foodstuff Control Special Account 食糧管理特別会計
foot up 合計する
footing 計算突合
footnote 脚注
FOP (free of payment) 非 DVP 決済
FOR (free on rail) 鉄道渡し
for accounting purposes 企業会計上
for bill clearing house purposes only 手形交換のため
for credit management purposes 与信管理目的で
for customer's account 委託分の
for each business year 各決算期の
for its own account 自己の計算によるもの
for one's proprietary account 自己分の
for profit enterprise 利益を目的とする企業
for the presentation purpose 表示の目的上

for the purpose of accounting 会計上
for the purpose of tax law 税法上
for the time being 足元の
forbearance 差控え
force majeure 不可抗力
force majeure clause 不可効力条項
forced auction 強制競売
forced choice 二者択一
forced collection 強制徴収
forced conversion 強制的転換
forced exchange 強制的交換
forced liquidation 強制清算
forced merger 強制合併
forced quotation 作り相場
forced sale 投売り
forced saving 強制貯蓄
forced transaction 強制取引
forced-sale value 強制処分価値
forceful intervention 強硬な介入
forcible disposition 強制処分
forcible execution 強制執行
forcible provisions 強行規定
forecast 予測
forecast broad range 予想レンジ
forecast by the econometric model 計量モデル予測
forecast change 予測の修正
forecast for market tendency 相場観
forecast of performance results 業績予想
forecast of sales 予想売上高
forecasted demand 予測需要量
forecasted purchase 予定購入
forecasted sales 予測売上
forecasting model 予測モデル
foreclose 担保権を行使する
foreclosed assets 担保権行使資産
foreclosed property 差押物件
foreclosing party 差押人
foreclosure 担保権執行
foreclosure of corporate hypothecation 企業担保権の実行
foreclosure order 差押命令
foreclosure sale 担保権行使による売却
foregift 権利金
forehand rent 前払地代
foreign affairs 外務
foreign affiliate 外資系
foreign agents accounts 外国代理店勘定
foreign aid 対外援助
foreign assets 海外資産
foreign banks (branches in Japan) 外国銀行支店
foreign banks in Japan 在日外銀
foreign bill 外国手形
foreign bond 外国債券
foreign branch 海外支店
foreign branch account 海外支店勘定
foreign branch-our account 外国支店仕向け勘定
foreign branch-their account 外国支店被仕向け勘定
foreign buying 外国人による買い
foreign capital 外資
foreign capital flow 海外からの資金の流入
foreign capital inducement 外資吸収
foreign capital intake 外資取入れ
foreign claims and debts 対外債権債務
foreign company 外国企業
foreign corporation 外国法人
foreign corporation tax 外国法人税
foreign corporation tax credit 外国法人税額控除
foreign corporation tax credit carried forward 繰越外国税額の控除
Foreign Corrupt Practices Act 海外不正防止法
foreign crowd 外国人クラウド
foreign currency 外貨
foreign currency account 外貨勘定
foreign currency assets 外貨資産
foreign currency bill receivable 外貨取立外国為替
foreign currency bond 外貨債
foreign currency borrowing 外貨借入
foreign currency cash flow 外貨建てキャッシュフロー
foreign currency debt 外貨債務

F

foreign currency denominated 外貨建て
foreign currency denominated fund 外貨建投資信託
foreign currency deposit 外貨預金
foreign currency deposit account 外貨預金勘定
foreign currency deposit with exchange bank 外貨預託
F
foreign currency designated deposit account 外貨指定預金
foreign currency financial statements 外貨表示財務諸表
foreign currency forward 為替先物契約
foreign currency futures 外国通貨先物
foreign currency futures contracts 外国通貨先物契約
foreign currency hedges 外貨ヘッジ
foreign currency holdings 外貨保有高
foreign currency inflow 外貨流入
foreign currency items 外貨建項目
foreign currency liability 外貨建負債
foreign currency products 為替商品
foreign currency rating 外貨建格付け
foreign currency reserve 外貨準備
foreign currency series securities 外貨建証券
foreign currency transaction 外貨取引
foreign currency translation 外貨換算
foreign currency translation adjustment 外貨換算調整額
foreign currency translation gain or loss 為替損益
foreign currency-denominated bond 外貨建債券
foreign debt 対外債務
foreign debt servicing 対外債務返済
foreign demand 外需
foreign direct investment regulation 直接投資規制
foreign enterprise 外国企業
foreign entity 在外事業体
foreign equity investment 対外株式投資
foreign exchange account 外国為替勘定
foreign exchange allocation 外貨資金割当
foreign exchange allocation system 外貨割当制
Foreign Exchange and Foreign Trade Control Law 外国為替管理法
Foreign Exchange and Foreign Trade Law 外国為替及び外国貿易法（外為法）
foreign exchange bank 外国為替銀行
foreign exchange bill 外国為替手形
foreign exchange bills bought 買取外国為替
foreign exchange broker 外国為替ブローカー
foreign exchange budget 外貨予算
foreign exchange cash position 外国為替現金持高
foreign exchange centralization system 外貨集中制度
foreign exchange control 外国為替管理
foreign exchange conversion rate 外国為替換算率
foreign exchange conversion table 外国為替換算表
foreign exchange difference 外国為替差異
foreign exchange earnings 外貨収入
Foreign Exchange Examiner 為替実査官
foreign exchange exposure 為替リスク
foreign exchange forward contract 外国為替予約
foreign exchange fund bill 外国為替資金証券
Foreign Exchange Fund Securities 外国為替資金証券（為券）
Foreign Exchange Fund Special Account 外国為替資金特別会計
Foreign Exchange Fund Special Account Law 外国為替資金特別会計法

foreign exchange futures 外国為替先物
foreign exchange gain 外国為替差益
foreign exchange gain and loss 外国為替差損益
foreign exchange hedging 為替ヘッジ
foreign exchange intervention 為替介入
foreign exchange law 外為法
foreign exchange loss 外国為替差損
foreign exchange market 外国為替市場（外為市場）
foreign exchange market intervention 為替市場介入
foreign exchange market operation 外国為替市場操作
Foreign Exchange Markets Division 為替市場課
foreign exchange operation 外国為替操作
foreign exchange position 為替持高
foreign exchange position sheet 為替持高表
foreign exchange quotation 外国為替相場
foreign exchange rate 外国為替相場（為替相場）
Foreign Exchange Rates 外国為替相場状況
foreign exchange settlement 外為決済
foreign exchange speculation 外国為替投機
foreign exchange trading loss 外国為替売買損
foreign exchange transaction 為替取引
foreign exchange translation difference 外国為替換算差額
foreign financial futures exchange 海外金融先物取引所
foreign financial institutions 外資系金融機関
foreign fund 外国投信
foreign geographic areas 海外地域別
foreign government bonds 外国国債証券
foreign government securities 外国債証券
foreign governmental authority 外国政府当局
foreign holding 外人投資家による保有
foreign income tax 外国所得税
foreign indirect participant 外国間接参加者
foreign institution 外国機関
foreign insurer 外国保険会社
foreign intermediary 外国仲介業者
foreign investment 海外投資
foreign investment in Japanese securities 対内証券投資
Foreign Investment Law 外資法
foreign investment trust 外国投資信託
foreign investor 外人投資家
foreign investors holding ratio 外人持株比率
foreign judgment 外国の判決
foreign juridical person 外国法人
foreign jurisdiction 領土外管轄権
foreign liabilities 対外債務
foreign loan 国外貸出
foreign market 外国市場
foreign marketable securities 外国投資証券
foreign money bill 外貨手形
foreign money order 外国送金為替
foreign operation 海外事業
foreign owned consumer finance company 外資系消費者金融
foreign plan 国外の制度
foreign pressure 外圧
Foreign Section 外国株市場
Foreign Section of the Tokyo Stock Exchange 東京証券取引所外国部
foreign securities 外国証券
foreign securities company 外国証券会社
foreign securities exchange 外国証券取引所
foreign securities investment 外国証券投資

F

foreign service allowance 国外勤務手当
foreign shareholding ratio 外人持株比率
foreign source income 国外源泉所得
foreign sovereign immunity 外国主権免除
foreign stock 外国株券
foreign stock depositary security 外国株預託証券
foreign stock depository receipts 外国株預託証券
foreign stock market 外国株式市場
foreign stocks unlisted 未上場外国株
foreign subscription right to new shares 外国新株引受権証書
foreign subsidiary 在外子会社
foreign subsidiary corporation 外国子会社
foreign system 外国の制度
foreign tax 外国税額
foreign tax credit method 外国税額控除方式
foreign tax credit system 外国税額控除制度
foreign tax deductible as expenses 損金算入外国税
foreign tax exemption method 外国税額免除方式
foreign tax sparing credit system 外国税額のみなし控除
foreign trade credit 貿易信用
foreign trade data 貿易統計
foreign trade deficit 貿易赤字
foreign trade finance 貿易金融
foreign trade multiplier 外国貿易乗数
foreign trade policy 貿易政策
foreign trade statistics 貿易統計
foreign transaction 外国取引
foreign-exchange linked bonds 為替リンク債
foreigner registration certificate 外国人登録証明書
forejudge 権利を剥奪する
forerunner stock 先駆株
foreseeable future 予測可能な期間
foresight 先見性
forest fire insurance 森林火災保険
forest land 山林
Forest Tree Breeding Center 林木育種センター
forestalling the market 市場妨害
Forestry Agency 林野庁
Forestry and Forest Products Research Institute 森林総合研究所
forestry income 山林所得
forestry income deduction 山林所得の控除
foreword 趣意書；序文
forex club フォレックス・クラブ
forex risk 為替リスク
forfeit 失権する
forfeited share 失権株
forfeiture 没収
forfeiture of bail 保釈金喪失
forfeiture of the grace of time 期限の利益の喪失
forged bill 偽造手形
forged card 変造カード
forged check 偽造小切手
forged note 偽造紙幣
forged stock 偽造株券
forgery of documents 文書偽造
forgery of securities 証券偽造
forgivable loan 返済免除条件付融資
forgiveness of debt 債務免除
forgiveness of liabilities 債務免除
forgiveness of repayment 償還免除
forgo 失う
forgone profit 逸失利益
form 形式
form a base against 底固い動きをする
form of action 訴訟方式
form of bid 入札書
form of stock certificate 株券の様式
form of transactions 売買の態様
form required by law 法律の要求する形式
formal 形式的

formal agreement 正式な契約
formal contract 要式契約
formal lawsuits 本訴
formal plan 正式な計画
formal term 正式な条件
formalities of incorporation 設立手続
format 様式
formation expenses 創業費
formation of secondary market 流通市場の形成
forms control 帳票管理
forms of enterprise 企業形態
formula 公式
formula additions 定式繰入額
formula fund フォーミュラ・ファンド
formula investing フォーミュラ投資
formula plan フォーミュラ・プラン
formula timing フォーミュラ・タイミング
formulate 公式化する
forum 裁判所
forward agreement 先渡取引
forward bid rate 先物為替買相場
forward calendar フォワード・カレンダー
forward cash amount フォワード・キャッシュ額
forward commitment 貸付予約
forward contract 先渡契約
forward currency contract margin 為替予約差額
forward date 先渡日
forward delivery 先渡し
forward deposit 先渡預金
forward difference 前方差分
forward discount 先物ディスカウント
forward discount of U.S. dollar ドル先物安
forward exchange 先物為替
forward exchange agreement 為替先渡取引
forward exchange market 先物為替市場
forward exchange rate 先物為替相場
forward exchange transaction 先物為替取引
forward foreign exchange rate 先物為替予約レート
forward integration 先方統合
forward interest rate 将来利子率
forward looking information 将来情報
forward margin 先渡マージン；証拠金
forward market フォワード・マーケット
forward neutral measure フォワード中立測度
forward neutral valuation フォワード中立評価法
forward offer rate 先物為替売相場
forward operation 先渡取引
forward position 先物為替持高
forward premium 先物為替プレミアム
forward price 先渡価格
forward pricing フォワード価格
forward purchase contract 先渡購入契約
forward quotation 先物為替相場
forward rate 先物相場
forward rate agreement 金利先渡取引
forward rate spread 先渡為替スプレッド
forward real accrued フォワード経過利子
forward real yield フォワード実質利回り
forward settlement 先渡決済
forward spread フォワード・スプレッド
forward swap フォワード・スワップ
forward transaction 為替予約
forward yield フォワード・イールド
forward-forward rate 先一先レート
fostering of new business 新規事業育成
FOT (free on truck) 貨車渡し
FOTRA (free of tax residents abroad) 非居住者非課税
foul B/L ファウル B/L
foul bill 故障手形
foul bill of lading 瑕疵付船荷証券

F

foul means 不正な手段
foundation 財団
foundation anniversary of a corporation 会社の創立記念
foundation collateral 財団抵当
foundation committee 創立委員会
founder 創立者
founder's profit 創業者利益
four contract months 4限月取引
four principles of conducting business necessary to maintain financial system stability 特融等に関する4原則
four year high 四年ぶりの新高値
401 (k) plan 401k年金制度
403 (b) plan 403b年金制度
fourth market 機関投資家間市場
FOX (futures and options exchange) 先物・オプション取引所
FPA (free from particular average) 分損不担保
FRA (forward rate agreement) 金利先渡契約
fraction of a day 一日の一部
fraction of an ordinary share 普通株式の端数
fractional currency 少額通貨
fractional discretion order 部分的一任注文
fractional figure 端数
fractional interest 端数利息
fractional lot 端株
fractional order 端株注文
fractional premium 端数保険料
fractional share 単位未満株
fractional sum 端数金額
fractional year 一年に満たない年
fragility of financial system 金融システムの脆弱性
franchise 小損害免責歩合；独占販売権
franchise agreement フランチャイズ契約
franchise clause 免責歩合条項
franchise fee 加盟店手数料；フランチャイズ料
franchise insurance 集団扱保険
franchise outlet フランチャイズ店
franchise right 販売権
franchise store 加盟店
franchise tax 営業税
franchisee フランチャイズ加盟者
franchiser フランチャイズ運営者
franked income 課税免除所得
Frankfurt Stock Exchange フランクフルト証券取引所
Frankfurter Allgemeine Zeitung Index ドイツFAZ指数
fraternal association 共済組合
fraternal life insurance 共済生命保険
fraternal mutual benefit society 共済組合
fraud 不正
fraud prevention データ改ざん防止
fraudulent act 不正行為
fraudulent action 詐欺的行為
fraudulent bankruptcy 詐欺破産
fraudulent card 悪用カード
fraudulent claims 詐欺請求
fraudulent contract 不正契約
fraudulent conveyance 詐欺譲渡
fraudulent creditor 詐欺債権者
fraudulent gains 不正利得
fraudulent misrepresentation 詐欺表示
fraudulent transfer 詐欺的譲渡
Freddie Mac フレッディマック
Freddie Mac (Federal Home Loan Mortgage Corporation) 連邦住宅金融抵当金庫
free alongside ship 船側渡し
free and clean 抵当に入っていない
free article 免税品
free box 払込済証券保管庫
free capital 自由資本
free carrier 運送人渡し
free cash flow フリー・キャッシュフロー
free economy 自由経済
free enterprise 自由企業体制
free financial fund フリー・フィナン

シャル・ファンド
free floating exchange rate system 自由変動相場制
free from capture and seizure clause 捕獲だ捕不担保条項
free from strikes, riots and civil commotion clause ストライキ騒じょう暴動不担保条項
free goods 自由財；免税品
free issue 無償発行
free list 無税品表
free loan フリーローン
free market 自由市場
free market economy 自由市場経済
free market price 市中相場
free money 自由貨幣
free of charge 費用込み
free of insurance premium 保険料免除の
free of tax 非課税
free of taxation 無税
free offer 自由オファー
free payment 任意受渡し
free payment system 自由返済システム
free period フリー期間
free port 自由港
free price 自由価格
free provision 無償の提供
free rate 自由料率
free reserves 自由準備
free ride period 優遇措置期間
free rider フリー・ライダー
free riding フリー・ライディング
free right of exchange 無料譲渡権
free share 無償株
free silver 銀の自由鋳造
free stock 自由株式
free surplus 自由剰余金
free technical advice 無償の技術援助
free trade 自由貿易
free will 自由意志
free world 自由世界
free yen account 自由円勘定
free yen deposit 自由円預金
free zone 自由地帯
freed up 価格拘束解除
freedom from encumbrance 無負担
freehold 自由保有の
freehold property 自由保有財産
freight 貨物
freight and cartage outward 発送運賃
freight collect 着払い運送費
freight earnings 貨物収入
freight insurance 運賃保険
freight inward 仕入運賃
freight out 販売運賃
freight prepaid 運賃前払い
freight rates 貨物運賃
freight receipts 運賃収入
freight revenue 運賃収入
freight tariff 貨物運賃
freight to collect 運賃着払い
freight usance 運賃ユーザンス
FREIT (finite real estate investment trust) 期限付不動産投資信託
French Institute Index パリ総合株価指数
frequency 頻度
frequency distribution 度数分布
frequency of on-site examination 考査の頻度
fresh capital 新規資本
fresh issue 新発債
fresh pursuit 即時追及
fresh start 再出発
fresh water damage 淡水濡れ
fresh-start method フレッシュ・スタート法
FRF (French franc) フランス・フラン
friction 軋轢
frictional unemployment 摩擦的失業
friendly action 友誼的訴訟
friendly society 友愛組合
friendly takeover 友好的買収
fringe banking フリンジ・バンキング
fringe benefit 付加給付
FRN (floating rate notes) 変動金利債
from a neutral viewpoint 中立な立場から

front end benefit 前払給付
front end commission 先取手数料
front end load 販売手数料
front end of market bonds 債券の短期物
front loaded 手数料先取りの；前倒し
front office 営業部門
front running 先駆け
front-end fee フロント・エンド・フィー
front-foot rule 前回規則
frontier delivery 国境渡し
frontier tax 国境税
fronting フロンティング
frozen account 凍結勘定
frozen assets 凍結資産
frozen credit 焦付債権
frozen stock 売れ残り
FRR (Financial Reporting Release) 財務報告通牒
FRS (Federal Reserve System) 連邦準備制度
fruit 成果
frustration 契約目的の達成不能
FSA (Financial Services Act) 金融サービス法
FSA (Financial Services Agency) 金融庁
FSA (Financial Services Authority) 英国金融監督庁
FSEEC (Federation of Stock Exchanges in the European Community) EC 証券取引所連合会
FSLIC (Federal Savings and Loan Insurance Corporation) 連邦貯蓄貸付保険公社
FT Actuaries All-share Index FT 全種指数
FT Industrial Ordinary Stock Index フィナンシャルタイムズ株価指数
FT Stock Exchange 100 Index FT 100 種指数
FT Stock Index FT 株価指数
FT-SE 100 FT-SE 100 種株価指数
FT-SE Actuaries All Share FT-SE アクチュアリーズ総合指数
FTA (free trade agreement) 自由貿易協定
FTC (Fair Trade Commission) 公正取引委員会
FTC (foreign tax credit) 外国税額控除
FTD (fast-to-default) FTD
FTSE All-World Index FTSE 全世界指数
FTZ (free trade zone) 自由交易圏
fuel account 燃料勘定
fuel cost 燃料費
Fujian 福建省
Fukuoka Local Finance Branch Bureau 福岡財務支局
fulfill contra side application 申込みを対当させる
fulfillment 履行
fulfillment of a contract 契約履行
fulfillment of obligation 義務の履行
fulfillment of procedures 手続きの履行
fulfillment of settlement 決済履行
full age 成年
full amortization 完全償却
full banking service フルバンキング・サービス
full benefit 満額給付
full bodied money 完全貨幣
full capacity 完全操業
full capacity output 完全利用産出量
full cash refund 完全即時償還
full compensation 十分な補償
full consolidation 完全連結
full cost 全部原価
full cost principle 全部原価原則
full costing 全部原価計算
full coupon bond フルクーポン債
full disclosure 完全開示
full eligibility date 完全受給資格日
full employment 完全雇用
full employment policy 完全雇用政策
full employment surplus 完全雇用財政余剰
full equilibrium 完全均衡

full equity method 全部持分法
full funding 完全積立
full hedge フルヘッジ
full insurance 完全保険
full legal tender 完全法貨
full payment 全額支払い
full payment of outstanding balance of the loan 融資残高全額支払い
full payoff 一括完済
full pension 満額年金
full proof 完全証明
full repayment before maturity 早期完済
full replacement coverage 再調達保証保険
full service financial institution 総合金融機関
full steam パワー全開
full time 常勤の
full vesting 完全受給権付与
full year 通年
full year business result 本決算
full-faith-and-credit debt 信義・信用債務
full-fledged secondary market 本格的流通市場
full-life beta 満期までのベータ値
full-scale local production 現地一貫生産
full-time statutory auditor 常任監査役
fully covered option 完全なカバード・オプション
fully depreciated 減価償却済み
fully diluted 完全希薄化した
fully distributed 完売
fully invested 完全運用済み
fully owned subsidiary 全額出資の子会社
fully paid 完全払込みの
fully paid-in capital stock 全額払込済株式
fully paid-up 全額払込
fully participating 全部参加型の
fully secured 全額担保により保全されている
fully valued 完全織込済み
fun money 余裕資金
function 機能
function analysis 機能分析
function cost 機能別原価
function of 関係できまる
function of age 経過年数の関数
function of currency 通貨の機能
function of expense method 費用機能法
function of quantities 変数の関数
function to change the degree of credit risk 信用リスク変換の機能
function to change the degree of liquidity of funds 流動性変換の機能
functional accounting 機能別会計
functional currency 機能通貨
functional currency method 機能通貨法
functional depreciation 機能的減価
functional organization 職能組織
functional pay 職務給
functional pricing 機能的価格設定
functional statement 機能別計算書
fund 基金
fund absorption 資金吸収力
fund account 資金勘定
fund accounting 資金会計
fund accumulation 基金積立
fund analysis 資金分析
fund and trust ファントラ
fund assets 基金資産
fund balance sheet 資金貸借対照表
fund budget 資金予算
fund deposit 年金資産預り金
fund equity 資金持ち分
fund flow statement 資金フロー計算書
fund for financial activities 財務活動資金
fund for foreign exchange operation 外国為替運営資金
fund for payments of interest on JGSs 公債利子支払資金
fund for redemption of JGSs 公債償還

F

資金
fund investment policy 資金運用方針
fund loss ファンド損失
fund management 資金運用
fund management method 資金運用手段
fund manager ファンド・マネージャ
fund obligation 基金債務
fund of funds ファンド・オブ・ファンズ
F
fund performance ファンド運用成果
fund position 資金ポジション
fund procurement cost 資金調達費用
fund procurement needs 資金繰り
fund raising 資金調達
fund raising business 資金調達業務
fund raising capacity 資金調達力
fund raising environment 資金調達環境
fund recovery 投資回収
fund settlement 資金決済
fund shortage 財源不足
fund supply 資金供給
fund surplus 資金剰余金
fund swap 資金関連スワップ
fund switching ファンドの乗換え
fund transfer 資金移転
fund transfer service 資金振替サービス
fund trust ファンド・トラスト
fund unit account 基金単位勘定
fund utilization 資金使途
fundamental analysis ファンダメンタル分析
fundamental changes 構造的変更
fundamental character 基本的性質
fundamental directives of income tax 所得税基本通達
fundamental disequilibrium 基礎的不均衡
fundamental factor ファンダメンタル要因
fundamental figures 基礎数値
fundamental financial approach 基礎的金融商品アプローチ
fundamental market 経済の基礎条件を材料に動く相場
fundamental principle 基本原則
fundamental reform 基本的な改革
fundamental rights 基本的権利
fundamental rules 基本的規則
fundamental statistics 景気統計
fundamental tax 基幹税
fundamental theorem 基本定理
fundamental value 基本価値
fundamentalism 原理主義
fundamentalist 経済基礎条件重視派
fundamentals ファンダメンタルズ
fundamentals deterioration ファンダメンタルズの悪化
funded approach 積立方式
funded benefit 積立給付
funded corporate pensions plan 基金型企業年金
funded debt 長期債務
funded defined benefit pension plan 外部積立確定給付型年金制度
funded defined benefit plan 基金を有する給付建制度
funded defined contribution pension plan 外部積立確定拠出型年金制度
funded insurance trust 保険運用信託
funded pension 積立式年金
funded pension plan 外部積立年金制度
funded plan 基金を有する制度
funded social security 積立式社会保障
funding 資金調達
funding agency 年金基金積立機関
funding consideration 積立上の考慮
funding cost 資金調達コスト
funding instrument 年金基金積立契約
funding plans 資金繰計画
funding policy 借換政策
funding position 積立状況
funding ratio 積立率
funding requirements 積立基準
funding risk 資金調達リスク
funding shortfall 資金不足
funding side 資金調達サイド
funding the deficit 赤字を補填する

funding transactions 資金取引
funds for development of venture business ベンチャー育成ファンド
funds for purchase 買入資金
funds lent by members 自己融資
funds procured 調達資金
funds shortage factor and a funds surplus factor 日銀当預の資金不足要因・資金余剰要因
funds statement ファンド・ステートメント
funds transfer 当預振替
funds transfer service 資金決済サービス
funds-only settlement 資金のみ決済
fungibility 代替可能性
fungible 代用できる
fungible account 混蔵保管口座
fungible goods 代替可能物
fungible securities 代替証券
furniture and fixture 家具什器
furniture and household goods 家財道具
further advance 再貸付
further bout of the dollar weakness さらなるドル安
further directions 続行
further interest rate cut 追加利下げ
further maintenance of the action 訴訟続行
further rise 一段高
furthest month 期先
FUTA (Federal Unemployment Tax Act) 連邦失業保険税法
future benefit 将来給付
future buying power 将来の購買力
future cash flow 将来のキャッシュフロー
future change 将来の変化
future contribution 将来の掛金
future conversion date 将来の転換日
future cost 将来原価
future deductible amount 将来控除対象金額
future dividend 将来配当
future event 将来の事象
future generation 後代
future marketplace 将来の市場
future obligation 将来債務
future path 将来の動向
future period 将来の期間
future prospect 将来性
future recovery 将来の回収
future risk 将来のリスク
future salary increase 将来の給与の上昇
future service 将来の勤務
future service benefit 将来勤務給付
future service cost 将来勤務費用
future service liability 将来勤務債務
future specific risk 将来の固有リスク
future taxable amount 将来課税対象金額
future value 将来価値
future value of an annuity 年金終価
future-dated/post-dated transactions 先日付取引
futures 先物
futures agent 先物取次業者
futures and options agency clearing participant 先物・オプション他社清算参加者
futures brokerage business 先物委託売買業務
futures contract 先物契約
futures dealer 先物ディーラー
futures industry 先物業界
Futures Industry Association 米国先物業者協会
futures instrument 先物商品
futures margin 先物マージン
futures market 先物市場
futures option 先物オプション
futures option market 先物オプション市場
futures position 先物のポジション
futures price 先物価格
futures product 先物商品
futures quotation 先物相場
futures rate 先物レート

futures trading 先物取引
futures trading based on stocks 株券先物取引
futures trading based on the stock price index 株価指数先物取引
futures trading of securities price index 有価証券指数先物取引
futures transaction 先物取引
futures valuation 先物評価
futures valuation model 先物評価モデル
Futures/Options Trading Account 先物・オプション取引口座
fuzzy theory ファジー理論
FX (foreign exchange) 外国為替
FX reserves 外貨準備高
FXYCS (Foreign Exchange Yen Clearing System) 外国為替円決済制度
FY (fiscal year) 年度

G

GA (genetic algorithm) 遺伝的アルゴリズム
GAAP ギャップ（一般に認められた会計原則）
GAAP (generally accepted industry practices) 一般に認められた業界の実務
GAB (General Arrangements to Borrow) 一般借入取決
Gabon (CFA (Communauté Financière Africaine) franc) ガボン（CFA フラン）
gain 利得
gain and loss 損益
gain and loss on shares 株式損益
gain contingency 偶発利得
gain from appreciation in value 価値評価による利得
gain from exchange of property 交換差益
gain from forfeiture 解約益
gain from lapsed policies 失効益
gain from stock retirement 減資差益
gain from surrendered policy 解約益
gain on appreciation of securities 有価証券評価益
gain on disposal 処分益
gain on re-measurement 再測定利得
gain on recovery of claims 債権取立益
gain on redemption of discount bond 割引債償還益
gain on sale 売却益
gain on sale of real estate 不動産売却益
gain on sale of securities 有価証券売却益
gain on sale of stocks 株式売却益
gain on the collection of claims written-off 償却債権取立益
gain on the sale of the trust estate 信託財産の売却利益
gain on transfer of securities 有価証券の譲渡所得
gain or loss accruing to the shareholders 株主にとっての損益
gain or loss on discontinuance 廃止に伴う損益
gain or loss on sale of assets 設備売却損益
gaining 強保合い
gains derived from asset transaction 資産取引から生ずる利得
gains derived from dealings in property 資産取引から生ずる利得
gains from forgiveness of debt 債務免除益
gains from revaluation of fixed assets 固定資産評価益
gains from sale of fixed assets 固定資産売却益
gains from the transfer of assets 資産の譲渡益
gains from the transfer of property 資産の譲渡益
gains of sales 売上増加
gains on bond redemption 社債償還差金
gains on insurance claim 保険差益
gains on sale and redemption of government securities 国債売却償還益
gains on sale, purchase, and redemption, and arising from revaluation of foreign currency assets 外国為替売買償還益
gains or losses from sales of fixed asset 固定資産売却損益
galloping inflation ギャロッピング・インフレーション
gambling 賭け

G

game plan ゲーム・プラン
game theory ゲーム理論
gamma ガンマ
gamma distribution ガンマ分布
gamma exposure ガンマ・エクスポージャー
gamma stock ガンマ株式
gamut 全範囲
GAN (grant anticipation note) 贈与見込証券
Gansu 甘粛省
gap 乖離
gap analysis ギャップ分析
gap between supply and demand 需給ギャップ
gap management technology ギャップ法
gapping horizon ギャップ期間
GARCH (generalized autoregressive conditional heteroskedaticity) model 一般化 ARCH モデル
garnishee 第三債務者
garnisher 債権差押人
garnishment 債権差押通告
gas and water expenses ガス水道費
GASB (Government Accounting Standards Board) 政府会計基準審議会
gasoline tax ガソリン油税；揮発油税
gather in the stops 逆指値売り
gather steam 活況
Gaussian distribution ガウス分布
gazette 官報
GBC (German bearer certificate) ドイツ無記名証書
GBC (global bearer certificate) グローバル無記名証書
GBP (British pound) 英国ポンド
GBP (Guernsey pound) グァーンジー・ポンド
GBP (Jersey pound) ジャージー・ポンド
GCM (general clearing member) 総合清算会員
GDE (gross domestic expenditure) 国内総支出
GDP deflator GDP デフレーター
GDP growth rate GDP の伸び率
GDP implicit price deflator GDP インプリシット・プライス・デフレーター
GDR (global depository receipt) グローバル預託証券
GDS (global depository share) グローバル預託株式
GE (grant element) グラント・エレメント
gearing ギアリング
gearing adjustments ギアリング修正
gearing effect ギアリング効果
gearing policy ギアリング方針
gearing ratio ギアリング・レシオ
GEL (Georgian lari) グルジア・ラーリ
GEM (growing equity mortgage) エクイティ逓増モーゲージ
general acceptability 一般受容性
general acceptance 一般引受け
general account 一般会計
general account assets 一般勘定資産
general account expenditure 一般会計歳出
general accounting principles 一般会計原則
general agency system 総代理店制度
general agent 総代理店
General Agreement on Tariffs and Trade 関税と貿易に関する一般協定（GATT）
general and administrative expense budget 一般管理費予算
general and administrative expenses 一般管理費
General Arrangements to Borrow 一般借入取決め
general assembly 総会
general assembly meeting of members 会員総会
general asset account 一般資産勘定
general audit 一般監査
general audit standards 監査基準

general authority 包括的権限
general average 共同海損
general average act 共同海損行為
general average contribution 共同海損分担額
general average expenditure 共同海損費用
general average sacrifice 共同海損犠牲損害
general balance sheet 一般貸借対照表
general bonded-debt fund 一般公債資金
general book-entry DVP 一般振替DVP
general building scheme 一般住宅地分譲計画
general business 一般事業
general business credit 事業税控除額
general cargo 一般貨物
general cash 一般現金
general closing of accounts 通常決算
general consumer goods 一般消費財
general consumption tax 一般消費税
general contingency reserve 一般偶発債務準備金
General Coordination Division 総務課（総務企画局）
general corporate assets 全般資産
general corporate bond 一般事業債
general corporate revenue and expense 一般事業損益
general corporate revenues and expenses 一般損益
general cost 一般費
general cost of living adjustment 一般物価水準修正
general credit ゼネラル・クレジット
general creditor 一般債権者
general crossed check 一般横線小切手
general election 総選挙
general equilibrium 一般均衡
general expenses 一般経費
general factor 一般的要因
general fixed-assets fund 一般固定資産資金
general force 一般要因
general government section 一般政府部門
general grant 一般補助金
general guidance 一般的指針
general guideline 一般的な指針
general index 総合指数
general indirect cost 一般間接費
general insurance 一般保険
general insurance clause 普通保険約款
general insurance expense 一般保険事業費
general insurance fund 損保資金
general insurance law 保険法
general insurer 損保会社
general issue 一般答弁
general journal 普通仕訳帳
general L/C (letter of credit) 買取銀行無指定信用状
general law 一般法律
general ledger 総勘定元帳
general ledger account 総勘定元帳勘定
general lending rate 一般貸出金利
general liability insurance 賠償責任保険
general lien 一般的リーエン
general liquidity 一般流動性
general loan and collateral agreement 包括融資担保契約
General Managers' Meetings 支店長会議
general market 市場全般
general means of payment 一般的支払手段
general meeting 総会
general meeting for establishment 創立総会
general meeting of investors 投資主総会
general meeting of members 社員総代会
general meeting of shareholders 株主総会

general membership 一般会員
general merchandise 雑貨
general mortgage ゼネラル・モーゲージ
general mortgage bond ゼネラル・モーゲージ付社債
general operating expenses 一般営業活動費
general overhead 一般間接費
general partner 無限責任社員
general partnership 無限責任組合
general place of tax payment 原則的納税地
general practice 一般的な実務
general price index 一般物価指数
general price level 一般物価水準
general price-level accounting 一般物価水準会計
general property tax 一般財産税
general provisions 総則
general provisions of the budget 予算総則
general public investment 一般財投
general public offering 一般募集
general public works 一般公共事業
general purchasing power 一般購買力
general purpose 一般目的
general purpose card 汎用カード
general realignment 一般調整
general reinsurance 一般再保険
general requirements 一般的要求事項
general reserve 一般引当金
general revenue 一般歳入
general revenue resource 一般財源
general revenue sharing 使途自由助成金
general rule of price priority 価格優先の原則
general security agreement 一般担保契約
general statute 一般法
general successor 一般継承人
general tax 普通税
general tax not stipulated in Local Tax Law 法定外普通税
general tax reduction 一般減税
general tax revenue 一般税収
general tax stipulated in Local Tax Law 法定普通税
general terms and conditions of a contract 一般条件書
general terms and conditions of trade 一般貿易条件
general trading participant 総合取引参加者
general transfer 一般振替
general usability 汎用性
general weakness of currency 通貨の総じての下落
general words 総括文句
general, administrative and selling expenses 一般管理費及び販売費
general-purpose financial statements 一般目的財務諸表
generally accepted accounting principle 一般に受け入れられている会計基準
generally accepted accounting standards 一般に公正妥当と認められる会計基準
generally accepted auditing standards 一般に受け入れられている監査基準
generation skipping 世代を飛び越えて
generation skipping trust 世代間信託
generational accounting 世代間会計
generator 生成作用素
generic swap ジェネリック・スワップ
generics ノーブランド商品
generous coupon 高い利率のクーポン
Geneva Convention ジュネーブ条約
gensaki 現先取引
geographic control 地域別管理
geographical location 地理的立地
geographical segment 地域別セグメント
geometric average 幾何平均
geometric mean 幾何平均
geopolitical risk 地政学的なリスク
geopolitical uncertainty 地政学的リスク

German Bunds ドイツ国債
getting ashore 売抜け
GFDL (Gun Free Documentation License) GUN フリー文書利用許諾契約書
GFOF (geared futures and options fund) レバレッジ型先物オプション・ファンド
GHC (Ghanaian cedi) ガーナ・セディ
Gibson paradox ギブソンの逆説
GIC (guaranteed investment contract) 保証投資契約
gift 贈与
gift certificate 商品券
gift splitting 分割贈与
gift tax 贈与税
gift tax credit 贈与税控除
gift tickets account 商品券勘定
gift-edged securities 一流証券
gilt auction ギルト債入札
gilt market 英国国債市場
gilt yield ギルト債利回り
gilt-edged bond ギルト・エッジ債
gilt-edged securities 優良証券
Gilts 英国国債
Gini coefficient ジーニ係数
Ginnie Mae (Government National Mortgage Association) ジニー・メイ
GIP (Gibraltar pound) ジブラルタル・ポンド
gist 趣旨；要領
give weight to 重点をおく
given date 任意の日
given sector 所与のセクター
glamour stock 魅力株
glass and ceramics products industry ガラス・土石製品業界
Glass-Steagall Act グラス・スティーガル法
global awareness 世界的な認知度
global bearer certificate グローバル無記名預託証書
global capital 国際資本
global capital market 国際資本市場
global capital movement 国際資本移動
global carry trade グローバル・キャリー・トレード
global certificate グローバル証券
global credit market 国際金融市場
global currencies market グローバル通貨市場
global custodian グローバル・カストディアン
global custody グローバル・カストディ
global economic cycle 世界的な景気循環
global economic outlook 世界経済の見通し
global economy 世界経済
global environmental problems 地球環境問題
global equity グローバル株式
global financial market 国際金融市場
global imbalance グローバルな不均衡
global integration 世界的な統合
global investment グローバル投資
global investor 世界クラスの投資家
global long-term bond グローバル長期債
global market 世界的な市場
global market price 国際市場価格
global marketing グローバルマーケティング
global minimum variance 大域的最小分散
global monetary turmoil 国際通貨不安
global mutual fund グローバル・ミューチュアル・ファンド
global note facilities グローバル・ノート・ファシリティ
global portfolio グローバル・ポートフォリオ
global recovery 世界的な景気回復
global trading グローバル・トレーディング
globalization グローバル化
globalization of economies 経済のグローバル化

GLS (generalized least squares) 一般化最小２乗法
GMC (guaranteed mortgage certificate) 保証モーゲージ証書
GMD (Gambian dalasi) ガンビア・ダラシ
GMT (Greenwich Mean Time) グリニッジ平均時
GNF (Guinea franc) ギニア・フラン
GNMA (Government National Mortgage Association) ジニー・メイ
GNMA certificate 米国政府抵当金庫証券
GNMA pass-through securities ジニー・メイ・パス・スルー証券
gnomes of Zurich チューリッヒの小鬼
GNP deflator GNPデフレーター
GNP gap GNPギャップ
GNP growth rate GNP成長率
GO (general obligation) bond 一般財源債
go long ロングにする
go out of business 市場から退場する
go undersubscribed 入札が未達になる
go-between 仲立人
goal 目標
God's penny 手付金
going ahead 先駆取引
going away 即時転売債券
going concern 継続企業
going concern assumption 継続企業の前提
going concern value 継続企業価値
going down the credit curve 低いセクターも物色する
going forward 今後
going long 思惑買い
going private 非公開企業
going public 株式公開
going rate 現行の料金
going short 思惑売り
going value 営業財産価値
going-concern principle 継続企業の原則
gold accounts 金投資口座
gold and dollar reserve 金ドル準備
gold and foreign exchange reserve 外貨準備高
gold and silver bimetallism 金銀複本位制度
gold and silver bullion 地金銀
gold basis 金本位基準
gold bond 金債券
gold bug 金信奉者
gold bullion 金地金
gold bullion futures contract 金先物契約
gold bullion standard 金地金本位制
gold center ゴールドセンター
gold certificate 金証券
gold clause 金約款
gold coin standard 金貨本位制
gold collateral 金担保
gold convertible securities 金転換証券
gold exchange 金為替
Gold Exchange of Singapore シンガポール金取引所
gold exchange reserve 金為替準備
gold exchange standard 金為替本位制
gold export point 金輸出点
gold fixing 金建値決定
gold futures 金先物
gold futures option 金先物オプション
gold holdings 金保有高
gold import point 金輸入点
gold index 金指数
gold note 金貨兌換紙幣
gold par value 金平価
gold parity 金平価
gold point 金現送点
gold pool 金プール
gold purchase warrant 金購入ワラント
gold reserve 金準備
Gold Reserve Act of 1934 金準備法
gold rush ゴールドラッシュ
gold standard 金本位制
gold sterilization policy 金不胎化政策
gold tranche ゴールド・トランシェ

gold warrant 金ワラント
golden age 黄金時代
golden cross ゴールデン・クロス
golden handshake 高額役員退職手当
golden parachute ゴールデン・パラシュート
golden ratio 黄金分割比率
golden rule 黄金律
golden section 黄金分割
golden share 黄金株
golf membership rights ゴルフ会員権
golfers' insurance ゴルファー保険
good and collectible 回収確実な
good and lawful men 有資格者
good behavior 善行
good consideration 善良約因
good credit status 信用度の高い
good debt 回収確実な債金
good delivery 適格受渡し
good faith 誠実
good faith deposit 手付
good merchantable quality 販売適性品質
good money 当日資金
good news 好材料
good offices of banking facilities 金融機関の斡旋
good proxy 優れた近似値
good results 好成績
good risk 優良危険
good this month order 当月限り有効な注文
good through 期間指定注文
good value 資金化資金
good yield 好利回り
good-till-canceled orders 取消まで有効な注文
good-till-cancelled order GTC 注文
goods 財貨
goods account 商品勘定
goods and products 商品又は製品
goods carried over 持越し品
goods for sale 販売用商品
goods in process 仕掛品
goods in process ledger 仕掛品元帳
goods in stock 有高
goods in transit 未着品
goods left 売残り
goods on approval 試送品
goods on consignment-in 受託品
goods on hands 手許在庫品
goods returned to vendor 戻し品
goods sold on credit 掛で売った商品
goodwill のれん
governed market 管理市場
governing body 支配機関
governing clause 準拠法条項
governing law 準拠法
government account 政府勘定
government accounting 政府会計
government actuary 政府アクチュアリー
government administrative activity 行政活動
government administrative property 行政財産
government agency bond 政府系機関債券
government agency securities 政府機関証券
government appraisal of land price 地価公示制度
government assistance 政府援助
government audit 政府監査
government backed mortgage 政府保証モーゲージ
government bond 国債
government bond administration 国債に関する事務
government bond auction system 国債入札制度
government bond book-entry system 国債振替決済制度
government bond for tax reduction 減税国債
government bond futures 国債先物取引
Government Bond Futures Clearing Qualification 国債先物等清算資格
government bond futures contract 国

G

債証券先物取引
government bond futures market 国債先物市場
Government Bond Futures Non-Clearing Participant 国債先物等非清算参加者
Government Bond Futures Trading Participant 国債先物等取引参加者
government bond in foreign currency 外貨国債
government bond issuance 国債の発行
government bond redemption 国債の償還
government bond supply curve 国債供給量
government bond system 国債制度
government bond yield 国債利回り
government bonds and corporate debentures 公社債
government bonds converted from Honshu-Shikoku Bridge Authority bonds 本州四国連絡橋債券承継国債
government bonds converted from Japan National Oil Bonds 石油債券承継国債
government bonds converted from Japanese National Railways Settlement Corporation bonds and the like 日本国有鉄道清算事業団債券等承継国債
government bonds in domestic currency 邦貨国債
government bonds issued to Deposit Insurance Corporation 預金保険機構特例業務基金等国債
government bonds package-registered 一括登録国債
government bookkeeping 官庁簿記
government broker 政府ブローカー
government compensation bond 交付公債
government consumption 政府消費
government contractual arrangements 政府関連制度
government credit 政府借款
government creditworthiness 政府の信用力
government current deposit 政府当座預金
government current surplus 政府経常余剰
government debt 公債
Government Debt Consolidation Fund 国債整理基金
Government Debt Division 国債課
government debt management 国債管理
government debt management policy 国債管理政策
government debt portfolio 政府債務
government debt redemption cost 債務償還費
government debt-related expenditure 国債費
government deposits 政府預金
government enterprise 政府企業
government expenditure 歳出金；財政支出
government experts 政府関係者
government finance 財政
government financial institutions 公庫
Government Financial Institutions Division 政策金融課
Government Financial Institutions Inspector 国庫等実地監査官
government fiscal balance 財政収支
government fund 政府資金
government fund transactions 国庫収支
government fund transactions with the public 国庫対民間収支
government funding plan 政府資金調達計画
government grant 政府補助金
government guarantee 政府保証
government guaranteed bond 政府保証債
government guaranteed borrowing 政

府保証借入金
government guaranteed debts 政府保証債務
government guaranteed foreign bond 政府保証外債
Government Housing Loan Corporation 住宅金融公庫
government intervention 政府介入
government life insurance 政府管掌生命保険
government managed annuity 政府管掌年金
Government National Mortgage Association 政府抵当金庫
Government National Mortgage Association debenture ジニー・メイ債
government note 政府紙幣
government obligation 政府保証債
government paper 公債
Government Pension Investment Fund 年金資金運用基金
government policy 政策
government procurement 政府調達
government procurement policy 政府の調達政策
government purchases 政府購入
government related deposit 政府関係預り金
government representatives' right to request the Board to postpone a vote 議決延期請求権
government revenues 歳入金
government saving 政府貯蓄
government saving certificate 政府貯蓄証券
government securities borrowed 借入国債
government securities in custody 保管国債
government sponsored 政府所管の
government subscriptions 政府出資金
government subsidy 政府補助金
government subsidy for construction 建設助成金
government to government trade 政府間貿易
government trade 政府貿易
government transaction 政府取引
government transfers 政府移転収支
Government Trust Fund Law 資金運用部資金法
government-guaranteed public corporation bond 政府保証公営企業債券
government-related financial institutions 政府系金融機関
government-run care insurance 政府介護保険
government-underwritten bonds 政府引受債
Government's Special Account for the Allotment of Local Allocation Tax and Local Transfer Tax 政府地方交付税特別勘定
governmental and municipal accounting 官庁会計
governor 総裁
Governor of the Bank of Japan 日銀総裁
GPM (graduated payment mortgage) 元利返済逓増モーゲージ
grace 猶予
grace of payment 支払猶予
grace of repayment 返済猶予
grace period 猶予期間
graded benefit 段階給付
graded commission 等級別手数料
graded premium 逓増保険料
graded tariff 差等税率
gradual devaluation 徐々の切下
graduated 補整後
graduated call writing 行使価格段階的引上コール・オプション売り
graduated lease 料率変動リース
graduated payment mortgage 元利支払漸増モーゲージ
graduated pension 所得比例年金
graduated security 卒業銘柄
graduated taxation 累進課税

G

graduation clause 卒業条項
Graham and Dodd method グラハム・ドッド法
grain exchange market 穀物取引所
Gramm-Rudman-Hollings Law グラム・ラドマン法
grand distress 全部差押
grand total 総計
grandfather clause 祖父条項
grandfather provision 既得権条項
grant 付与；補助金
grant date 付与日
grant date measurement 付与日測定
grant date value 付与日価値
grant element グラント・エレメント
grant in aid 助成金
grant loan 無償ローン
grant of credit 信用供与
grant of trading qualification 取引資格の付与
grant related to assets 資産に関する補助金
grant related to income 収益に関する補助金
grantee 受給者
granting of licenses or registering of entities 免許制・登録制
grantor 譲与者
Granville theory グランビルの法則
gratis 無償
gratuitous bailment 無償寄託
gratuitous contract 無償契約
gratuitous use of property 無償の財産使用
graveyard market 墓場市場
GRD (Greek drachma) ギリシャ・ドラクマ
great depression 大恐慌
greater fool theory 大馬鹿理論
Greek letters 感応度分析
green card 少額貯蓄等利用者カード
green card system グリーンカード制度
green field business 新規参入事業
green goods 偽ドル
Green Seat Market グリーン・シート市場
greenback 米ドル紙幣
greening of the tax system 税制のグリーン化
Gresham's law グレシャムの法則
grid グリッド
grievance committee 苦情処理委員会
GRIT (grantor retained income trust) 譲与者収入留保信託
GRN (grant anticipation note) 補助金見込債
GRN (gross rent multiplier) 総賃料乗数
grocer 雑貨商
gross amount 総額
gross amount due to 債務総額
gross amount principle 総額主義
gross approach 総額アプローチ
gross assets 総資産
gross base 総額ベース
gross book value 総帳簿価格
gross capital 総資本
gross capital stock 粗資本ストック
gross carrying amount 減価償却控除前帳簿価額
gross cash payments 支出総額
gross cash receipts 収入総額
gross cost 総原価；総費用
gross cost of merchandise sold 総売上原価
gross debt 負債総額
gross dividend 総配当
gross domestic capital formation 国内総資本形成
gross domestic investment 国内総投資
gross domestic product 国内総生産
gross error 過失
gross estate 総遺産
gross expenditure 総支出
gross fund position グロス・ファンド・ポジション
gross income 粗利；総所得
gross income multiplier 総収益乗数
gross income of corporation 法人の益金

gross inflow 総流入
gross insurance premium 総保険料
gross investment 総投資
gross investment in lease リース投資未回収総額
gross investment rate 総投資率
gross issuance 総発行額
gross line 保険総引受額
gross loss 総損失
gross loss on sales 売上総損失
gross margin on sales 売上総利益
gross margin rate 粗利益率
gross margin ratio 粗利率
gross merchandise margin 総商品売買差益
gross method 総額法
gross national demand 国民総需要
gross national expenditure 国民総支出
gross national product 国民総生産
gross national supply 国民総供給
gross national wealth 国民総資産
gross negligence 重過失
gross net premium 正味営業保険料
gross obligation 総債務額
gross of 込みの
gross operating income 業務粗利益
gross operating spread 総営業利幅
gross output 総産出
gross per broker 外務員一人当り総手数料
gross premium 営業保険料
gross premium valuation reserve 営業保険料評価準備金
gross presentation 総額表示
gross product 総生産
gross profit 総利益
gross profit analysis 総利益分析
gross profit margin 売上総利益率
gross profit method 総益法
gross profit percentage 総利益率
gross profit rate 売上総利益率
gross profit ratio 総益率
gross profit test 総益テスト
gross purchase amount 仕入総額
gross redemption グロス償還
gross redemption yield 償還総利回り
gross reproduction rate 総再生産率
gross revenue 総収益
gross sales 総売上高
gross savings 総貯蓄
gross settlement price グロス決済価格
gross spread 引受募集手数料
gross trading volume 総取引高
gross transaction 総取引
gross up グロス・アップ；割戻す
gross up clause グロス・アップ条項
gross up method グロス・アップ方式
gross working capital 総運転資本
gross yield 総利回り
ground floor 有利な立場
ground lease 土地の賃貸借契約
ground-making expenses 土地造成費
groundage 停泊料
grounding clause 乗揚げ条項
group accident insurance 団体傷害保険
group administration plan 集団管理制度
group annuity 団体年金
group annuity insurance 団体年金保険
group annuity pension investment contract 団体年金投資契約
group auction 集団競争売買
group care insurance 団体介護保険
group costing system 等級別原価計算
group coverage 団体保障
group credit insurance association 団体信用生命保険組合
group credit life insurance 団体信用生命保険
group deferred annuity contract 団体据置年金契約
group defined benefit plan グループの給付建制度
group deposit administration contract 団体預託管理契約
group depreciation グループ償却
group discounted premium 団体割引保険料
group endowment insurance 団体養老

保険
group enterprises グループ企業
group financial statements 企業集団財務諸表
group gearing 連結負債比率
group health insurance 団体健康保険
group insurance 団体保険
group insurance annuity 団体保険型年金
group life insurance 団体生命保険
group life insurance for credit 団体信用生命保険
group method 組別法
group mortgage insurance 団体モーゲージ補償生命保険
Group of 5 G5
group of assets 資産グループ
group of employees 従業員グループ
group pension 団体年金
group permanent insurance contract 団体長期保険契約
group personal pension 団体個人年金
group policy 団体保険証券
group premium 団体保険料
group relief グループ税額控除
group rotation 業種の循環
group term insurance 団体定期保険
group underwriting 団体保険査定
group variable annuity 団体変額保険
grouping allowance method 総括引当金
growing at a moderate speed 適度に伸びている
growing currency 成長通貨
growing economy 成長経済
growing equity mortgage 持ち分逓増モーゲージ
growing leverage 債務比率の増大
growth and income fund 成長収益ファンド
growth company 成長企業
growth converging 成長率の収斂
growth curve 成長曲線
growth cycle 景気サイクル
growth fund グロース・ファンド
growth indices グロース指数
growth industry 成長産業
growth of industrial structure 産業構造高度化
growth of investment 投資の伸び
growth phase 成長段階
growth potential 成長性
growth prospect 成長見通し
growth rate 成長率
growth rate of the monetary base マネタリー・ベースの伸び率
Growth Section グロース・セクション
growth stock 成長株
growth strategy 成長戦略
growth theory 成長理論
growth to remain subdued 低成長
growth type グロース型
GSE (government sponsored enterprise) 政府後援企業
GSE (government sponsored enterprises) 政府系機関
GSTPA (Global Straight Through Processing Association) GSTPA
GTAA (global tactical asset allocation) グローバル戦略的資産配分
GTC (good-till-cancelled) order 取消まで有効注文
GTQ (Guatemala quetzal) グアテマラ・ケツァル
GTW (good-this-week) order 週有効注文
Guangdong 広東省
Guangxi 広西チワン族自治区
guarantee 保証
guarantee arrangement contracts 債務保証契約
guarantee business 保証業務
guarantee by endorsement 裏書保証
guarantee charge 保証料
guarantee clause 保証文言
guarantee commission 保証料
guarantee deposits 保証金
guarantee deposits such as construction support deposits 建設協力金等の差入預託保証金

guarantee facility 債務保証
guarantee fee received 受入保証料
guarantee fee received in advance 前受保証料
guarantee for cost over-run 不足資金補填保証
guarantee in favor of the primary guarantor 裏保証
guarantee insurance 保証保険
guarantee letter 保証状
guarantee loan 保証ローン
guarantee money 保証金
guarantee money receivable 未収保証金
guarantee money received 受入保証金
guarantee of clearing fulfillment 決済履行の保証
guarantee of indebtedness 債務保証
guarantee of liabilities 債務保証
guarantee of payment 支払保証
guarantee of repayment 借入返済保証
guarantee of settlement 決済の保証
guarantee of signature 署名証明
guarantee of tax payment 納税保証
guarantee of the executives' status 役員の身分の保障
guarantee work 保証作業
guaranteed account 利率保証勘定
guaranteed amount 保証額
guaranteed annual income 年間保証所得
guaranteed annual wage 年間保証賃金
guaranteed annuity 保証年金
guaranteed benefit 保証給付
guaranteed bond 保証社債
guaranteed cash value 保証解約返戻金
guaranteed cost contract 費用保証契約
guaranteed dividend 確定配当
guaranteed endowment 保証生存保険
guaranteed equity product 保証株価指数連動商品
guaranteed exchange 交換保証
guaranteed index fund 利率保証インデックス・ファンド
guaranteed insurability 無診断保険付保
guaranteed interest 保証利率
guaranteed interest contract 利率保証契約
guaranteed life-time employment 終身雇用
guaranteed minimum 最低保証額
guaranteed minimum annuity 最低支払保証年金
guaranteed principal 元本保証
guaranteed renewable 更新保証付き
guaranteed renewable policy 更新保証保険
guaranteed replacement cost coverage insurance 再調達費保証保険
guaranteed residual value 保証残存価値
guaranteed return contract 利回保証契約
guaranteed securities 保証証券
guaranteed stock 保証株
guaranteed value 保証価格
guaranteed warrant 保証付ワラント
guarantees outstanding 保証残高
guarantor 保証人
guarantor bank 保証銀行
guarantor's right of indemnity 求償権
guaranty deposits 差入預託保証金
guaranty deposits received 預り預託保証金
guaranty insurance 損害担保契約
guaranty money deposited 差入保証金
guardian 後見人
guardianship 後見
guidance 指針
guideline ガイドライン
guideline service life ガイドライン耐用年数
guidelines on eligible collateral 適格担保取扱基本要領
guidelines on money market operations 金融市場調節方針
guild 同業組合
guilder bond ギルダー債

Guizhou 貴州省

Gulf Cooperation Council 湾岸協力会議

GULP (group universal life policy) 団体ユニバーサル保険

GUN (grantor underwritten note) GUN

gun jumping 情報公開前の証券取引

GWP (Guinea-Bissau CFA (Communauté Financière Africaine) franc) ギニアビサウ（CFA フラン）

GYD (Guyana dollar) ギアナ・ドル

H

habit persistence hypothesis 慣習仮説
Hainan 海南省
half day holiday 半休日
half life 元本半減期
half yearly premium 半年払保険料
half-day call transactions 半日物
half-finished goods 半製品
half-year report 半期報告書
half-yearly 半期毎の
halt of business 営業停止
halt of business activities 事業の中断
hammering the market 売りあびせ
hand money 手付金
hand-to-mouth buying 当用買い
handling affairs of the government 国の事務の取扱い
handling cost 取扱費
handling expenses 取扱経費
handling of JGBs business 国債に関する業務の取扱い
hands-off investor 経営不参加投資家
hands-on 実践の
hands-on investor 経営参加投資家
Hang Seng China-Affiliated Corporations Index ハンセン中国レッドチップス指数
Hang Seng Index 香港ハンセン指数
harakiri swap ハラキリスワップ
harbor 蔵匿する
harbor dues 入港税
hard commission 現金手数料
hard currency 硬貨
hard dollar ハード・ドル
hard labor 重労働
hard landing ハード・ランディング
hard loan ハード・ローン
hard money ハード・マネー
hard rally 反騰
hard-line 強硬路線
hardship exemption 紙による提出免除条項
hardware market ハードウエア市場
harm 害
harmless error 無害の誤謬
harmless warrant ハームレス・ワラント債
haulage 船舶旅客運送費
hazard 危険
hazard function ハザード関数
hazard model ハザード・モデル
HCA (historical cost accounting) 取得原価主義会計
HCC (home country control) 自国銀行監督
head 主席
head and shoulders 三尊天井
head office 本店
head office account 本社勘定
head office expenses 本社費用
head tax 人頭税
heading 見出し
headline 表題
headnote 頭注
health and medical care 保健医療
health and welfare benefit 医療福利給付
Health and Welfare Division 厚生課
health benefit 医療給付
health benefit product 医療保険商品
health care ヘルスケア
health care benefit 医療給付
health care benefit plan 医療給付制度
health care benefits to retirees 退職者医療給付
health care cost 医療費用
health care obligation 医療給付債務
health care plan 医療保健制度
health coverage 医療保障
health economics 医療経済学
health expenditure 医療費支出

health industry 健康産業
health insurance 健康保険
health insurance benefit 医療保険給付
health insurance premium 健康保険料
health insurance reserve 健康保険準備金
health insurance underwriting 医療保険査定
Health Maintenance Organization 健康維持機構
health payout 医療給付支払額
health plan 医療保険制度
health policy 医療保険証券
health protection 医療保障
health service 保健
health trust fund 医療保険信託基金
healthy demand 堅調な需要
healthy revenue growth 順調な売上の伸び
healthy trend 高水準
hearing 審問
heated up economy 過熱経済
heath fund 健康組合
heavily indebted country 累積債務国
heavy additional charge imposed 重加算金
heavy currency intervention 大規模市場介入
heavy electrical stocks 重電銘柄
heavy market 荷もたれ感相場
heavy penalty tax 重加算税
heavy share 値がさ株
heavy taxation 重税
Hebei 河北省
hedge ヘッジ
hedge account representation letter ヘッジ勘定代行書
hedge accounting ヘッジ会計
hedge accounting standards ヘッジ会計基準
hedge accounting treatment ヘッジ会計処理
hedge bond ヘッジ・ボンド
hedge buying ヘッジ買い
hedge clause ヘッジ条項
hedge effectiveness ヘッジの有効性
hedge fund ヘッジ・ファンド
hedge gains ヘッジ利益
hedge instrument ヘッジ商品
hedge margin ヘッジ証拠金
hedge operation ヘッジ操作
hedge period ヘッジ期間
hedge ratio ヘッジ比率
hedge selling ヘッジ売り
hedge trading ヘッジ取引
hedge transaction ヘッジ取引
hedged bond ヘッジ債
hedged item ヘッジ対象項目
hedged portfolio ヘッジド・ポートフォリオ
hedged position ヘッジ・ポジション
hedged risk ヘッジ対象リスク；ヘッジ・リスク
hedger ヘッジャー
hedging ヘッジ取引
hedging against inflation インフレ・ヘッジ
hedging cost ヘッジコスト
hedging function ヘッジ機能
hedging gain ヘッジ利得
hedging instrument ヘッジ手段
hedging loss ヘッジ損失
hedging on commodity futures 商品先物取引のヘッジング
hedging on option オプションのヘッジング
hedging policy ヘッジ方針
hedging proportion ヘッジ割合
hedging relationship ヘッジ関係
hedging scheme ヘッジ・スキーム
hedging technique ヘッジ手法
hedging vehicle ヘッジ手段
hegemony 覇権
Heilongjiang 黒竜江省
heir apparent 法定相続人
heir at law 法定相続人
heir general 通常相続人
heir presumptive 推定相続人
heir/heiress 相続人
heir-looms 法定相続動産

HEL (home equity loan) ホーム・エクイティ・ローン
held for sale 販売目的保有
held to maturity 償還期限まで保有
held-to-maturity investment 満期保有投資
held-to-maturity securities 満期保有目的の債券
hell or high water clause ヘル・オア・ハイ・ウォーター条項
hemline theory ヘムライン理論
Henan 河南省
hereditaments 相続財産
heredity 相続
hereinafter 以下
Hessian matrix ヘッセ行列
heterogeneous market 異質市場
heyday 好景気の
HFU (Hungarian forint) ハンガリー・フォリント
HIBOR (Hong Kong inter-bank offered rate) HIBOR；香港銀行間出し手金利
hidden assets 含み資産
hidden bad loans 不良債権隠し
hidden cost 目に見えない費用
hidden guarantee of obligation 簿外債務保証
hidden load 隠れ手数料
hidden profit distributions 秘密の利益処分
hidden reserve 隠匿積立金；秘密積立金
hierarchy 階層
hierarchy of responsibilities 責任の序列
HIFO (highest-in, first-out) 最高価格先出
high cap 大型株
high carry ハイ・キャリー
high cost 原価高
high coverage policy 高額医療保険
high credit 最高与信残高
high current income mutual fund 高収益配当ミューチュアル・ファンド
high degree of positive correlation 高度の正の相関関係
high flyer 注目株
high grade investment 有利な投資
high income brackets 多額納税者
high income group 高額所得者層
high interest policy 高利回り保険
high interest rate 高金利
high interest rate policy 高金利政策
high justice 裁判しうる権限
high level of business activity 高水準の景気
high liquidity 高い流動性
high LTV loan 高 LTV ローン
high possibility 高い公算
high powered money ハイパワード・マネー
high premium convertible debenture 高プレミアム転換社債
high price 高値
high quality 高品質の
high quality corporate bond 優良社債
high quality fund 高格付対象ファンド
high return asset 高利回資産
high roller 金遣いの荒い人
high seas 公海
high street bank 市中銀行
high taxpayers 多額納税者
high ticket item 高額商品
high yield bond 高利回り債
high yield bucket ハイ・イールド銘柄組入枠
high yield currency 高利回り通貨
high yielding assets 高利回資産
high-coupon bond ハイ・クーポン債
high-interest-bearing debenture 高利付社債
high-leveraged レバレッジの高い
high-low method 高低法
high-powered money (monetary base) ハイパワードマネー（マネタリーベース）
high-priced stock 値がさ株
high-risk high-return ハイリスク・ハイリターン

H

high-risk investment 危険率の高い投資
high-tech stock ハイテク株式
higher bid 高い値段の買呼値
higher in quotation 上ざや
higher interest rates application system 高率適用制度
higher offer 高い値段の売呼値
higher order goods 高次財
higher quotation 上値
higher quotation at the close 引け高
higher rated tranche 高格付トランシェ
higher yielding 高利回りの
highest-in first-out method 最高価格先出し法
highly geared warrant ギアリングの高いワラント
highly probable 可能性が高い
highly traded stock 出来高集中銘柄
highs 高値銘柄
highs for the week 今週の高値
hike in official rate 政策金利引上げ
hindrance to business 業務の妨げ
HIPC (harmonized index of consumer prices) 統合物価指数
hire purchase ハイヤ・パーチェス
hire purchase contract 買取選択権付賃貸借契約
histogram method ヒストグラム法
historic level 過去の平均値
historical analysis 実績分析
historical average 過去の平均水準
historical basis 過去の基準
historical beta ヒストリカル・ベータ
historical cash flow キャッシュフロー実績
historical cash flow information キャッシュフローの実績情報
historical change 変動実績
historical cost 取得原価
historical cost basis 取得原価基準
historical cost basis of accounting 取得原価主義会計
historical cost convention 取得原価の慣行
historical cost model 取得原価モデル
historical cost of assets 資産の取得原価
historical cost system 取得原価主義
historical cost/constant-dollar accounting 取得原価主義安定価値会計
historical cost/nominal dollar accounting 取得原価主義名目価値会計
historical data 過去のデータ
historical default rate 過去のデフォルト率
historical exchange rate 取得時為替レート
historical factor 歴史的要因
historical financial data 取得原価主義財務データ
historical financial statements 取得原価主義財務諸表
historical growth rate 過去の成長率
historical information 実績情報
historical level 過去の水準
historical loan loss ratio 過去の貸倒実績率
historical peak 過去最高値
historical precedent 長年の先例
historical rate 発生時レート
historical rate of credit losses 貸倒実績率
historical summary 時系列要約
historical trading range 過去の値動き幅
historical volatility ヒストリカル・ボラティリティー
historical yield 実績利回り
history-dependent derivative 経路依存型派生商品
history-dependent derivative securities 経路依存型派生証券
hive off 新会社設立
HKD (Hong Kong dollar) 香港ドル
HKG peg 香港ドルのペッグ制
HLT (highly leveraged transaction) 負

債比率の大きい企業への貸付
HNL (Honduras lempira) ホンジュラス・レンピラ
Hoffmann's law ホフマンの法則
Hokkaido-Tohoku Development Finance Public Corporation 北海道東北開発公庫
hold above ¥10,000 level 1万円台を維持する
hold harmless agreement 賠償責任免除契約
hold off buying 買入れを手控える
hold-to-maturity 満期までの保有
holder 所持人
holder for value 有償保有者
holder in bad faith 悪意の第三者
holder in due course 正当な保有者；善意の第三者
holder in good faith 善意の所持人
holder of government bond 国債の債権者
holder of lien リーエンの保有者
holder of obligation 債務の保有者
holder of option オプションの買手
holder of preferred capital contribution certificates 優先出資者
holder of record 株主名簿上の株主；原簿上の証券保有者
holders of preferred equity securities 優先出資社員
holders of specified equity securities 特定社員
holders of the record 名簿登録株主
holding company 持株会社
holding cost 保有費用
holding gain 保有利得
holding gain or loss 保有損益
holding high 高保合
holding loss 保有損失
holding of assets 資産の保有
holding period return 保有期間収益率
holding period value-relative 保有期間相対価値
holding the market 買支え
holding up to Asia アジアに対し堅調
holding-purpose category 保有目的区分
holdings of Special Drawing Rights 特別引出権保有額
hollowing out 空洞化
home assurance 住宅保険
home banking ホーム・バンキング
home country 本国
home country control 原籍国主義
home currency 自国通貨
home currency bill bought 邦貨買入外国為替
home economics 家政学
home equity 住宅持ち分
home equity conversion mortgage 住宅持ち分転換モーゲージ
home equity loan 住宅担保ローン
home improvement loan 増改築ローン
home made inflation ホームメード・インフレ
home market 母国市場
home mortgage 住宅抵当証券
home mortgage backed securities 住宅用モーゲージ証券
home office account 本店勘定
home office deduction ホームオフィス控除
home ownership 住宅所有
home port 船籍港
home protection policy モーゲージ償還保険
home reversion arrangement 住宅担保年金
home rule 自治
home sales volume 住宅販売量
home service 内地勤務
home service agent 地区外務員
home state 原籍国
homeowner equity account 住宅資産価値を基にした融資口座
homeowner insurance policy 住宅所有者保険
homestead right 家産
homogeneity 同質

H

homogeneous cost 同質原価
homogeneous market 同質的市場
homogeneous security group 同類証券のグループ
homologation 裁可
Hong Kong depositary receipts 香港預託証書
Hong Kong inter-bank offered rate 香港銀行間出し手レート
honor 引受け
honor obligations 債務を履行する
honor outstanding contracts 未履行契約を履行する
honorarium 謝礼金
hook damage かぎ損
hooked 買いぶらさがり
horizon analysis 投資計画期間分析
horizon return 所有期間利回り
horizontal 水平的
horizontal analysis 水平分析
horizontal approach 水平型アプローチ
horizontal audit 水平的監査
horizontal consolidation 水平統合
horizontal divestiture 水平分割
horizontal equity 水平的公平
horizontal integration 水平的統合
horizontal international specialization 水平的国際分業
horizontal M & A 水平的Ｍ＆Ａ
horizontal merger 水平合併
horizontal multiplier 水平乗数
horizontal specialization 水平的分業
horizontal split 水平分断
horizontal spread ホリゾンタル・スプレッド
horizontal trade 水平的貿易
hospital benefit 入院給付
hospital cash cover 入院日額給付保険
hospital confinement benefit 入院給付特約
hospital expense insurance 入院費保険
hospital indemnity 入院補償
hospital indemnity insurance 入院補償保険
hospital liability policy 入院賠償責任保険
hospital rate 病院料金
hospital revenue bond 病院歳入債
hospitalization insurance 入院保険
host country 受入国
hostile acquisition 敵対的買収
hostile possession 自主占有
hostile takeover 敵対的買収
hot issue 注目銘柄
hot money 国際短期浮動資金
hot money market ホット・マネー市場
hot seller ヒット商品
hours worked 稼働時間
hours-of-service method 使用時間比例法
house account 本店扱い口座
house agency ハウス・エージェンシー
house bill ハウス・ビル
house call 証拠金督促
house insurance 住宅総合保険
house maintenance requirement 証券会社証拠金基準
house margin rule 証拠金内部規則
house mortgage 住宅抵当証券
House of Councillors 参議院
house of issue 証券引受会社
House of Representatives 衆議院
house organ 社内報
house ownership plan 持家制度
house purchase 住宅購入
house rent income 貸家料
house rent received 受取家賃
house rules 証券会社社内規則
household 家計
household assets 家計資産
household consumption expenditure 家計消費支出
household debt 家計債務
household expenditure 家計支出
household expenses 家計費
household income 家計収入
household saving 家計貯蓄
household sector 家計部門
household taxation 世帯課税

householders' comprehensive insurance 住宅総合保険
housing 住宅
housing affordability index 住宅購買力指数
housing allowance 住居手当
Housing and Urban Development Corporation 住宅・都市整備公団
housing benefit 住宅手当
housing bond 住宅債券
housing credit 住宅信用
housing expenses 住居費
housing industry statistics 住宅産業統計
housing inflation 住宅価格上昇
housing investment 住宅投資
housing loan 住宅ローン
housing loan claim 住宅ローン債権
housing loan corporation 住宅金融会社
housing loan guarantee 住宅ローン保証
housing market 住宅市場
housing permits 住宅着工許可件数
housing renewal program ころがし方式
housing savings tax credit 住宅貯蓄控除
housing starts 住宅建築着工数
housing stocks 住宅関連株
housing turnover 住替え
housing turnover component 住替え要因
HPR (holding period return) 所有期間利回り
HR (human relations) 人間関係
HRA (human resources accounting) 人的資源会計
HRK (Croatian kuna) クロアチア・クナ
HTG (Haiti gourde) ハイチ・グルデ
Hubei 湖北省
hull insurance 船舶保険
human capital 人的資本
human engineering 人間工学
human life value 人間の生命価値
human resources 人的資源
human resources development 人材開発
Human Resources Management Department 人事局
human resources policies 雇用政策
humped curve ハンプト・カーブ
Hunan 湖南省
hung up 買いぶらさがり
hunkering down 在庫株式の売払い
hunter's license tax 狩猟免許税
hunters' insurance ハンター保険
hurdle 障害
hurdle rate ハードルレート
hurting sentiment 市場心理の悪化
hush-money 口止料
hybrid annuity 混合年金保険
hybrid cap 混合キャップ
hybrid capital 複合資本
hybrid debt-equity instrument 債券株式合成証券
hybrid instrument ハイブリッド商品
hybrid instruments 複合金融商品
hybrid model 混合型
hybrid plans 混合的な制度
hybrid probability ハイブリッド確率
hybrid securities 複合証券
hybrid selection ハイブリッド選定
hybrid stocks 混合株式
hybrid trading system ハイブリッド・トレーディング・システム
hybrid trust ハイブリッド信託
hybrid variable product ハイブリッド変額商品
hyperinflation 超インフレ
hyperinflationary economy 超インフレ経済
hypothec 抵当権
hypothec of enterprise 企業担保
hypothecated assets 担保資産
hypothecation 担保差入
hypothecation agreement 担保差入同意書
hypothesis 仮定

H

hypothesis test 仮定テスト
hypothesis testing 仮説検定
hypothetical assumption 仮説上の想定
hypothetical case 仮定のケース
hypothetical change 理論上の変化
hypothetical market 仮定上の市場
hypothetical transaction cost 想定取引費用

I

I-bonds インフレ連動債
I-S curve IS 曲線
IAA (insured asset allocation) 保証資産配分
IAAC (International Auditing Practices Committee) 国際監査実務委員会
IAEA (International Atomic Energy Agency) 国際原子力機関
IAG (international accounting guidelines) 国際監査ガイドライン
IAS (international accounting standards) 国際会計基準
IASB (International Accounting Standards Board) 国際会計基準審議会
IASC (International Accounting Standards Committee) 国際会計基準委員会
IASCF (International Accounting Standards Committee Foundation) 国際会計基準委員会財団
IATA (International Air Transport Association) 国際航空運送協会
IBF (international banking facility) account 国際銀行業務勘定
IBRD (International Bank for Reconstruction and Development) 国際復興開発銀行
IBRD special law 世銀特措法
IBST (income before securities transactions) 有価証券取引前利益
IC (integrated circuit) card IC カード
ICA (Institute of Chartered Accountants) 勅許会計士協会
ICAO (International Civil Aviation Organization) 国際民間航空機関
ICC (International Chamber of Commerce) 国際商業会議所
ICC (Interstate Commerce Commission) 州際通商委員会
iceberg theory 氷山理論
ICJ(International Court of Justice) 国際司法裁判所
ICM (individual clearing member) 個人清算会員
ICM (integrated collateral management) 統合担保管理
ICRC(International Committee of the Red Cross) 赤十字国際委員会
ICSD (international securities central depository) 国際的な証券保管振替機関
ICSID 国際投資紛争解決センター
IDA (International Development Association) 国際開発協会
IDB (industrial development bond) 産業開発債券
IDB (inter-dealer broker) 業者間ブローカー
ideal standard cost 理想標準原価
idem 同じ書物からの出典
identical amount 同一金額
identical term 同一期間
identical with 同一の
identifiability 識別可能性
identifiable assets 特定可能資産
identifiable assets and liabilities 識別可能資産及び負債
identification 識別
identification card 身分証明書
identification document 本人確認書類
identification of hedged items ヘッジ対象の識別
identified cost method 個別法
identified risk 特定のリスク
identified shares 特定済株式
identity 同一性
idle assets 遊休資産
idle balance アイドル・バランス
idle capacity 不動能力

idle capacity cost 低操業度原価
idle capacity variance 不動能力差異
idle capital 遊休資本
idle cash 余剰の現金
idle cost 不働費
idle equipment 遊休設備
idle facilities 遊休施設
idle money 行き場の定まらない資金
idle plant 遊休工場
idle time 手待時間
IDR (Indonesian rupiah) インドネシア・ルピア
IE (independent engineer) 中立的なエンジニア
IEP (Ireland punt) アイルランド・プント
IET (interest equalization tax) 利子平衡税
if-converted method 転換仮定法
IFAD(International Fund for Agricultural Development) 国際農業開発基金
IFC(International Finance Corporation) 国際金融公社
IFEMA (international foreign exchange master agreement) 国際外国為替標準契約
IFRS (International Financial Reporting Standards) 国際財務報告基準
IFSC (International Financial Service Center) 国際金融サービス・センター
ignore 却下する
IL (import license) 輸入許可証
illegal 不法の
illegal act 違法行為
illegal dividend 違法配当
illegal employment 不法就労
illegal lending 違法貸付
illegality 不法
illegitimating 違法認定
illiquid 非流動的
illiquid assets 非流動資産
illiquid issues 流動性の低い銘柄
illiquidity 流動性不足
illustrative appendix 例示の付録
illustrative example 適用例
illustrative format 様式の例示
illustrative purpose 例示目的
ILO(International Labour Organization) 国際労働機関
ILS (Islaeli shequel) イスラエル・シェケル
imbalance 不均衡
IMF (International Monetary Fund) 国際通貨基金
IMF Board of Directors IMF 理事会
IMF gold tranche IMF ゴールドトランシェ
IMF loan IMF 借款
IMF par value IMF 平価
IMF stand-by IMF スタンバドバイ
IMF subscription IMF 出資
IMI (investment management institution) 投資管理会社
imitation 類以物の作製
immaterial evidence 重要でない証拠
immaterial issue 重要でない争点
immaterial item 重要性のない項目
immature assets 未成熟資産
immediate 目先の
immediate adjustment 即時の修正
immediate annuity 即時年金
immediate cause 直近原因
immediate family 近親者
immediate future 目先
immediate liquidity 当面の流動性
immediate or cancel order 即時執行注文
immediate order 至急注文
immediate participation 即時加入
immediate payment annuity 一括払年金保険
immediate protection 即時保障
immediate vesting 即時受給権付与
immediate write-off 即時償却
immediately available fund 即日利用可能な資金
immediately preceding 直前の

immediately preceding business year 直前事業年度
immobilization 不動化
immoderate 中庸を欠いた
immovable property 不動産
immovables 不動産
immovables account 不動産勘定
immunity 免除
immunization 免疫化
immunization fund イミュニゼーション・ファンド
IMO (International Maritime Organization) 国際海事機関
impact 影響
impact claims 波及効果クレーム
impact loan インパクト・ローン
impact on business 事業への影響
impact on market 市場への影響
impact statement 影響報告書
impact survey インパクト調査
impaired capital 資本の欠損
impaired company 経営危機にある会社
impaired credit 低信用力
impaired loan 不良債権
impaired property, plant and equipment 減損有形固定資産
impairment 減損
impairment accounting rules 減損会計規則
impairment approach 減損アプローチ
impairment calculation 減損の計算
impairment loss 減損損失
impairment of assets 資産の減損
impairment of contract 契約上の権利の侵害
impairment of inventories 棚卸資産の減損
impairment of obligation of contract 契約上の権利侵害
impairment of value 価値の損耗
impairment rider 条件体特約
impairment test 減損テスト
imparity 不釣合い
impartial taxation 課税の公平
impasse 行詰り
Impeachment Committee 裁判官訴追委員会
impediment 障害
imperative statute 命令的法律
imperfect competition 不完全競争
imperfect competition market 不完全競争市場
imperfect hedge 不完全ヘッジ
imperfect market 不完全市場
imperfect obligation 不完全義務
imperfect trust 不完全信託
imperfection 不完全性
Imperial Household Agency 宮内庁
impersonal account 物的勘定
impersonal deduction 物的控除
impersonal exclusion from taxation 物的課税除外
impersonal security 対物担保
impersonal tax 物税
impertinent 無関係の
impetus 刺激
impignoration 質入
impignorative contract 質入契約
implementation 実施
implementation guidance 適用指針
implementation of derivatives デリバティブの執行
implementation of financing 資金調達の実施
implementation phase 実行段階
implementation stage 実行段階
implication 推断
implicit agreement 暗黙の合意
implicit assumption 暗黙の前提
implicit call price 内在的コール価格
implicit cost 潜在的費用
implicit deflator インプリシット・デフレーター
implicit for tangible assets 有形資産に潜在している
implicit interest 内包金利
implicit rate of interest 計算上の利子率
implicit requirement 非明示的要件

implied 暗黙の
implied authority 黙示権限
implied contract 準契約
implied forward rates インプライド先渡金利
implied license 黙示許容
implied nominal rate 名目金利の理論値
implied probability インプライド確率
implied repo rate インプライド・レポ・レート
implied spread インプライド・スプレッド
implied trust 法定信託；黙示信託
implied value 内在価値
implied volatility インプライド・ボラティリティー
implied warranty 黙示保証
implied yield インプライド・イールド
import bill 輸入手形
import cartel 輸入カルテル
import clearance 輸入通関
import control 輸入管理
import country 輸入国
import credit 輸入信用
import duties tariff 輸入税表
import duty 輸入税
import finance 輸入金融
import financing system 輸入資金貸付制度
import for manufacturing 移入
import function 輸入関数
import guarantee money 輸入保証金
import license 輸入承認証
import on consignment 委託販売輸入
import permit 輸入許可
import price 輸入物価
import price index 輸入物価指数
import quota 輸入割当
import ratio 輸入比率
import restriction 輸入規制
import sector 輸入セクター
import settlement bill system 輸入決済手形制度
import substitute 輸入代替
import surcharge 輸入課徴金
import tax 輸入税
import usance 輸入ユーザンス
import volume 輸入量
import-driven inflation 輸入インフレ
important factor 重要な要素
important matters 重要事項
important part of business 重要な業務
important variable 重要な指標
importation of foreign capital 外資輸入
impose 課す
imposition 賦課
imposition of a fine 過怠金の賦課
imposition of income tax 所得税の課税
imposition of tax 課税
impossibility of performance 履行不能
impossible contract 不能な契約
impost 輸入税
impoverishing theory 窮乏化政策
impression 押印
imprest cash 前渡金
imprest cash fund 小口前払準備金
imprest fund 定額前渡資金
imprest system 定額前渡制
improved credit 信用履歴の改善
improvement 改善
improvement cost 改良費
improvement expense 改良経費
improvement of the property 資産の改良
improvement patent 改良特許
improvement report 改善報告書
improvement to assets 資産の改善
improvement trade 加工貿易
impugn 異議を唱える
impulse buying 衝動買い
imputation 帰属
imputation method インピュテーション方式
imputation of interest みなし利息計算
imputation system インピュテーション方式
impute 帰属させる
imputed cost 帰属原価

imputed discount 帰属割引
imputed income 帰属所得
imputed interest 帰属利子
imputed negligence 帰責過失
imputed price 帰属価格
imputed rate of interest みなし利率
imputed value 帰属価値
IMRO (Investment Management Regulatory Organization) 投資管理規制機関
IMRO (Investment Managers Regulatory Organization) 投資顧問規制機関
IMS (International Monetary System) 国際通貨制度
in a lump sum 一時金で
in a pre-emptive fashion 先手を打つ
in a rally 上昇局面では
in a run-up to the meeting 会合の目前に
in absolute terms 絶対値で
in accordance with 準拠して
in all 総計で
in blank 白地で
in bond 保税
in capitalization terms 時価総額において
in consideration of the foregoing 上記を約因として
in dollar terms ドル建て
in good faith 誠実に
in good standing 優良である
in house management 内部運用
in kind 現物で；同種の
in money terms 貨幣ベースで
in number 件数レベルで
in one's own right どちらでも
in person delivery 対面交付
in real terms 実質ベースで
in red ink 赤字の
in return 見返りとして
in session 開廷期間中
in severalty 単独保有で
in specie 特定の
in terms of revenue 収益面で
in the absence of inflation pressure インフレ圧力がない中
in the context of 関連において
in the light of 鑑みて
in the money イン・ザ・マネー
in transit 未達の
in up trend 上昇傾向にある
in violation of 反する
in-and-out trading 日計り商い
in-and-put dealer 目先筋
in-cycle work 機械運転時作業
in-house exchange 行内交換
in-house product 自社製品
in-port duty 港湾税
in-service 現職の
in-substance defeasance 実質的ディフィーザンス
in-substance defeasance trust 実質的ディフィーザンス・トラスト
inactive 閑散
inactive account 不活動勘定
inactive asset 不活発資産
inactive bond 不人気債券
inactive market 閑散市場
inadequate capital 過少資本
inadmissible 許容しえない
inadmissible assets 不承認資産
inalienable rights 不可譲の権利
inappropriate merger 不適当な合併
inappropriate substance 不適当な内容
inaugural meeting 創立総会
inauguration of business 開業
incapacity benefit 就業不能給付
INCDI (individual non-cancelable disability income protection) 解除不能個人所得保険
incentive 奨励
incentive effect 奨励効果
incentive fee 成功報酬
incentive payment 報償金
incentive plan 奨励制度
incentive stock option 自社株低価格購入権
incentive wage 能力給
inception 開始

inception of lease リースの開始
incidence 出来事
incident 付随条件
incidental appeal 付帯訴訟
incidental conditions 付帯条件
incidental cost 付随費用
incidental expenses 付帯費用
incidental gains 付随的収入
incidental increase payment 一部増額返済
incidental suit 付帯訴訟
incidental transaction 付随的取引
incidents of ownership 所有の付帯権利
include 算入する
including tax 税込み
inclusion 算入
inclusion in gross revenue 益金算入
inclusion of interest into principal 利子の元金組入
inclusion ratio 組込比率
inclusivity 一体性
income 利益
income account 損益勘定
income accrued from domestic sources 国内源泉所得
income accrued from foreign sources 外国源泉所得
income after tax audit 税務調査後所得
income analysis 所得分析
income and expenditure equation 収支方程式
income and expenses 損益
income approach 所得接近法
income arising as a result of exemption of debts 債務免除益
income averaging 所得の平均課税
income basis 所得ベース
income before employee bonus 賞与前所得
income before extraordinary items 経常損益
income before income taxes 税引前利益
income benefit rider 定額給付特約
income bond 配当社債
income bracket 所得層
income by coupon reinvestment クーポン再投資収入
income compensation insurance 所得補償保険
income consumption curve 所得消費曲線
income deduction 利益控除項目
income deposit 所得預金
income derived from business 事業から生ずる所得
income distribution 収益分配；所得配分
income divergence 所得格差
income dividend 収益配当
income earned 稼得利益
income effect 所得効果
income effect of exchange adjustments 為替調整の所得効果
income elasticity 所得弾力性
income endowment 年金付保険
income endowment policy 年金付生命保険
income enhancer インカム・エンハンサー
income factor 所得要因
income from affiliated company 関連会社からの利益
income from assets 資産所得
income from collection of securities by purchase 株式の買集めによる所得
income from continuing operations 継続事業部門の利益
income from discharge of indebtedness 債務免除益
income from discontinued operations 廃止部門からの利益
income from fund management 資金運用収益
income from Japanese sources 国内源泉所得
income from life insurance and endowment contract 生命保険及び養老保険契約からの所得

income from real estate 不動産収入
income from transfer of securities 有価証券の譲渡所得
income from trust deposits 金銭信託利益
income from valuation of assets 財産評価益
income fund インカム・ファンド
income gain インカム・ゲイン
income gearing インカム・ギアリング
income generating effect 所得創出効果
income growth 所得の伸び
income in advance 前受収益
income in respect of an ancestor 被相続人にかかる所得
income inflation 所得インフレーション
income investment company 配当重視投資会社
income level 所得水準
income leveling 利益の平準化
income limited partnership 収益配当型リミテッド・パートナーシップ
income manipulation 所得操作
income mutual fund 収益配当型ミューチュアル・ファンド
income note インカム・ノート
income on liquidation 清算所得
income policy 所得政策；年金式支払生命保険
income property 収益不動産
income protection plan 所得補償制度
income realization 利益実現
income received but unearned 繰延収益
income redistribution 所得再分配
income redistribution effect 所得再分配効果
income related benefit 所得比例給付
income replacement insurance 所得補償保険
income resource 所得源
income return 所得申告
income return blank 所得申告用紙
income security 所得保障
income share 採算株
income share note 利益分配債
income smoothing 利益の平準化
income splitting method 所得分割法
income stability 利益の安定化
income statement 損益計算書
income statement account 損益計算書勘定
income statement approach インカム・ステートメント・アプローチ
income statement audit 損益計算書監査
income statement principles 損益計算書原則
income statement ratio 損益計算書比率
income stock 資産株
income tax 所得税
income tax allocations 所得課税の配分
Income Tax and Property Tax Policy Division 税制第一課
income tax credit 所得税控除
income tax deferred 繰延法人税
Income Tax Law 所得税法
income tax on dividends out of profit 利益の配当に課せられた所得税
income tax on interest on corporate bonds 社債利息に課せられた所得税
income tax prepayment system 予定納税制度
income tax rapid calculation table 所得税の速算表
income tax rate 所得税率
income tax rates table 所得税の税率表
income tax return 所得税申告
income tax return form 所得税申告書
income tax self-assessed 申告納税額
income tax withheld at source 源泉控除所得税
income taxes paid 支払法人税
income taxes payable 未払法人税
income terms of trade 所得交易条件
income test 収入審査
income transfer 所得移転

income unit 収益ユニット
income verification 所得確認
income warrant インカム・ワラント
income yield 直接利回り
income-producing asset 収益性資産
incompetency 禁治産
incompetent person 禁治産者；成年被後見人
incomplete transaction 未完了取引
incontestability clause 不可争条項
inconvertible 兌換できない
inconvertible bank note 不換銀行券
inconvertible banknote 不換紙幣
incorporate 会社を設立する
incorporated body 法人
incorporated school 学校法人
incorporation by reference 参照による編入
incorporation of enterprise 法人設立
incorporation procedures 会社設立手続き
incorporator 会社設立者
incorporeal chattel 無体動産
incorporeal property 無体財産
Incoterms (International Commercial Terms) インコタームズ
increase 増加
increase amount in current term 当期増加額
increase and decrease method 増減法
increase and decrease ratio 騰落レシオ
increase in capital stock 増資
increase in dividend 増配
increase in liability 負債増加額
increase in long-term debt 長期債務の増加
increase in PER PER の上昇
increase in reserve 引当金の増加
increase in sales 売上増加
increase in the capital subscription 増資
increase in the need for external demand 外需拡大
increase of revenue 増収
increased earnings 増益
increased income tax 増加所得税
increased retirement payments 割増退職金
increased revenue and profit 増収増益
increased value insurance 増値保険
increasing annuity 逓増年金
increasing benefit 逓増保険金
increasing domestic demand 内需拡大
increasing insurance 保険金増額保険
increasing interest rate 金利上昇
increasing premium 逓増保険料
increasing working capital 増加運転資本
increment card インクレメント・カード
increment value duty 増価税
incremental analysis 増分分析
incremental borrowing rate of interest 追加借入利子率
incremental budget 積み増し予算
incremental cash flow 増加キャッシュ・フロー
incremental cost 増分原価
incremental cost of capital 増加資本コスト
incremental method 増分法
incremental profit 増分利益
incremental rate of return 増分収益率
incremental return 増加収益
incremental shares 増加株式
incremental value 増分価値
incubation fund インキュベーション・ファンド
incumbency 現職
incumbent director 在任の取締役
incurred 既発生の
incurred but not paid 既発生未払い
incurred claim 保険金支払額
incurred cost 発生原価
incurred loss 既発生損害
incurred to earned basis 発生年度方式
incurrence of additional indebtedness 追加債務負担
incurrence of liability 債務負担
indebtedness 債務

indebtedness of affiliates 関係会社債権
indefeasible 無効としえない
indefinite economic life 無限の経済的耐用年数
indefinite life 無限の耐用年数
indefinite lived 耐用年数が確定しない
indemnification 弁償；補償
indemnification arrangement 補償契約
indemnify 免責とする
indemnity 賠償金
indemnity agreement 補償契約
indemnity allowance 損害補償金
indemnity benefit 補償給付
indemnity clause 損害補償条項
indemnity contract 補償契約
indemnity insurance 実損填補保険
indent 買付委託書
indent account 買付委託勘定
indent ledger 買付委託元帳
indenture 契約書
independence rule 独立性の原則
Independence Standards Board 独立性基準審議会
independent accountant 独立会計士
independent administrative institution 独立行政法人
Independent Administrative Institution Evaluation Committee 独立行政法人評価委員会
Independent Administrative Institution National Youth Houses 国立青年の家
independent appraiser 独立した鑑定人
independent audit 独立監査
independent auditor 会計監査人
independent contract 独立契約
independent contractor 請負人
Independent Insurance Agents of Japan 日本損害保険代理業協会
independent intermediary 独立仲介者
independent liability method 独立責任額比例主義
independent marketing organization 独立販売組織
Independent Organs 外局
independent policy 単独保険商品
independent professional assessment 独立した専門家の査定
independent tax 独立税
independent third party 独立した第三者
independent variables 独立変数
index 指数
index adjustment スライド方式
index arbitrage trading 指数裁定取引
index arbitrager 指数裁定取引者
index bond インデックス債券
index from six months prior 6ヵ月前の応当日の指数
index fund インデックス・ファンド
index holding 指数保有
index issuers インデックス銘柄
index linked insurance 指数保険
index linked products 指数リンク債
index number by aggregative method 総和法指数
index number of production 生産指数
index number trend series 傾向指数
index of financial condition 財政力指数
index of net terms of trade 純交易条件指数
index of producers' inventory of finished goods 生産者製品在庫指数
index of producers' shipments 生産者出荷指数
index of productivity 生産性指数
index of terms of trade 交易条件指数
index of trade 貿易指数
index of urban land prices 全国市街地価格指数
index option インデックス・オプション
index participation インデックス・パーティシペーション
index portfolio 指数ポートフォリオ

I

index ratio インデックス・レシオ；指数比率
index risk 指数リスク
index transaction 指数取引
index warrant 指数ワラント
index-linked bond 指数リンク債
index-linked gilt 物価連動英国国債
index-linked obligation 指数連動債務
index-linked securities 指数連動証券
indexation 指数化
indexation factor 指数化ファクター
indexation lag 指数連動ラグ
indexation of inflation インフレの指数化
indexation period 連動期間
indexed 指数化された
indexed annuity 指数連動年金
indexed benefit 物価スライド給付
indexed cost 指数調整された原価
indexed currency option note 為替オプション付債
indexed insurance product 指数保険商品
indexed par 指数調整後の額面
indexed to inflation or deflation インフレやデフレに連動する
indexed to prices 物価に連動した
indexes of price 価格指数
indexing インデックス運用
indicated bid-asked quotations 気配表示
indicated price 気配値段
indication 気配値；兆候
indication at a store counter 店頭表示
indication method インディケーション方式
indication of interest インディケーション・オブ・インタレスト
indication of trust property 信託財産表示
indicative level 参考水準
indicative price 気配値段
indicative pricing 参考価格
indicator 指標
indicators of control 支配の指標
indict 起訴する
indifference curve 無差別曲線
indigenous capital 土着資本
indirect business tax 間接事業税
indirect cause 間接原因
indirect cost 間接費
indirect credit 間接控除
indirect department cost 間接部門費
indirect deposit 間接預金
indirect disposal 間接処理
indirect evidence 間接証拠
indirect exchange arbitrage 間接裁定
indirect expenses 間接経費
indirect financing 間接金融
indirect foreign tax credit 間接外国税額控除
indirect guarantee 間接保証
indirect incidental expenses 間接的付随費用
indirect investment 間接投資
indirect inward investment 対内間接投資
indirect issue 間接発行
indirect labor cost 間接労務費
indirect liability 間接負債
indirect link 間接リンク
indirect material cost 間接材料費
indirect materials 間接材料
indirect method 間接法
indirect method of depreciation 間接償却
indirect participant 間接参加者
indirect placement 間接引受け
indirect presentation 間接表示
indirect production 間接生産
indirect sales 間接売買
indirect securities 間接証券
indirect tax 間接税
indirect trade 間接貿易
indirect wage 間接賃金
indirect yield 間接利回り
indiscretion 機密漏洩
indisputability 不可争
individual account plan 個人別勘定方式

individual accounting 個別会計
individual accounts 個別決算書
individual allowance method 個別引当法
individual annuity 個人年金
individual asset 個別資産
individual auction 個別競争売買
individual basis 個別基準
individual certificate 被保険者証
individual dealing system 個別売買方式
individual depreciation 個別償却
individual enterprise 個別企業
individual exclusion 個人控除
individual financial statements 個別財務諸表
individual franchise policy 個人集団扱保険
individual health insurance 個人健康保険
individual income tax 個人所得税
individual inhabitant tax 個人住民税
individual investor 一般投資家
individual issue 個別銘柄
individual level cost method 個別平準掛金積立方式
individual life insurance 個人生命保険
individual LIFO 個別後入先出法
individual periods of service 各勤務期間
individual policy 個人保険証券
individual policy pension plan 個人保険型年金制度
individual production 個別生産
individual projects 個別案件
individual proprietor 自営業者
individual retirement pension plan 個人退職年金制度
individual savings account 個人貯蓄勘定
individual selection 個別選択
individual stockholder 個人株主
individual tax return 個人納税申告
individual taxation 個別課税
Individual Taxation Division 個人課税課
individual term insurance 個人定期保険
individual useful life 個別耐用年数
individual variable annuity 個人変額年金
individual with regular income 定収入のある個人
indivisible credit 不可分債権
indorsement of address 住所裏書
indorser 裏書人
induced investment 誘発投資
inducement 誘因
inducement to invest 投資誘因
inductive statistics 帰納的統計
industrial accident reserve 産業事故準備金
industrial accounting 工業会計
industrial assurance 簡易保険
industrial bank 興業銀行
industrial banking インダストリアル・バンキング
industrial bill 工業手形
industrial bond 一般事業債
industrial bookkeeping 工業簿記
industrial capital 産業資本
industrial circles 産業界
industrial classification 産業分類
industrial composition 産業構造
industrial cooperation method 産業協力方式
industrial debenture 事業債
industrial dispute 労働争議
industrial engineering 生産工学
industrial factory foundation 工場財団
industrial fire insurance 簡易火災保険
industrial foundation 工業財団
industrial fund 産業資金
industrial injury 労働災害
industrial insurance 簡易保険
Industrial Investment Special Account 産業投資特別会計
Industrial Investment Special Account Fund 産業投資特別会計資金
industrial law 労働法

I

industrial life insurance 産業生命保険
industrial loan 事業貸付
industrial new design 実用新案
Industrial Ordinary Shares Index 工業株価指数
industrial origin of net national product 産業別国民純生産
industrial output 労働生産
industrial policy 産業政策
industrial production 鉱工業生産
industrial production index 鉱工業生産指数
industrial property 工業所有権
industrial rationalization 産業合理化
industrial real estate 工業用不動産
industrial regeneration 産業再生
industrial revenue bond 産業特定財源債
industrial right 工業所有権
industrial sector 産業部門
industrial stock 工業株
industrial structure 産業構造
industrial structure policy 産業構造政策
industrial union 産業別組合
industrialization 工業化
industrialized countries 工業国
industrials 産業銘柄
industry 産業
industry arrangement 業界の取決め
industry associations 業界団体
industry average 業界平均
industry beta value 産業のベータ値
industry concentration 産業集中
industry effect 産業効果
industry factor 産業的要因
industry focus 業界の集中度
industry information 産業情報
industry norms 業界基準
industry practice 業界慣行
industry realignment 業界再編
industry run 業界運営の
industry segment 業種別セグメント
industry specialist 産業スペシャリスト
industry specialized fund 特定産業ファンド
industry standard 業界基準
industry weighting ratio 業種別組入率
industry-wise 産業別
ineffective portion of hedging ヘッジ非有効部分
inefficiency 非効率
inefficient 非効率的な
inelastic 弾性のない
inelastic demand and supply 非弾力的需給
ineligible 不適格な
ineligible bill 不適格債
inequity 不公平
inertia 慣性
inertia effect 慣性効果
inescapable cost 回避不能費用
inevitable accident 不可避的事故
infamous 証人たる能力を失った
inference 推理
inferior assets 劣等資産
inferior court 下位裁判所
inferior goods 劣等財
inflation インフレーション
inflation accounting インフレ会計
inflation accretion インフレによる増加分
inflation adjusted インフレ調整済み
inflation assumption 想定インフレ率
inflation caused by yen depreciation 円安インフレ
inflation credit インフレ増加分に対する税控除
inflation de-indexation 物価スライド制廃止
inflation differential インフレ格差
inflation distribution インフレ分布
inflation escalation obligation インフレにより増加した債務
inflation expectation インフレ期待
inflation exposure インフレ・エクスポージャー
inflation fear インフレ懸念
inflation floor インフレ・フロアー

inflation forecast インフレ予測
inflation gap インフレ・ギャップ
inflation hedge インフレ・ヘッジ
inflation hedge property インフレ・ヘッジ資産
inflation increase in principal インフレによる元本の増加
inflation index インフレ指数
inflation indexation インフレ指数；物価連動
inflation indexed インフレ連動の
inflation indexed bond 物価連動債
inflation indexed debt instrument インフレ連動債
inflation indexed securities インフレ連動証券
inflation indication インフレ指標
inflation insurance インフレに対する保険
inflation linked bond 物価連動債
inflation linked bonds インフレ連動債
inflation linking 物価連動
inflation protected equity products インフレ・プロテクション型エクイティ商品
inflation protection インフレからの保護；インフレ・プロテクション
inflation psychology インフレ心理
inflation rate インフレ率
inflation related index インフレ関連指数
inflation risk premium インフレ・リスク・プレミアム
inflation sensitivity factor インフレ感応度
inflation spiral インフレ・スパイラル
inflation target インフレ目標
inflation tax relief インフレに基づいた税の減免
inflation uncertainty インフレの不確実性
inflation-linked debt instrument 物価連動債券
inflationary demand curve インフレ需要曲線
inflationary expectations 期待インフレ率
inflationary money supply インフレ・マネー・サプライ
inflationary pressure インフレ圧力
inflationary supply and demand curve インフレ需給曲線
inflationary supply curve インフレ供給曲線
inflexible expense 非弾力費用
inflict a loss 損害を与える
inflow 流入
inflow of foreign capital 外資流入
inflow of resources 資源の流入
influence 影響
influential business sector 影響力のある産業部門
influx 流入
influx of foreign capital 外資流入
informal acceptance 内諾
informal organization 非公式組織
informal practice 非公式慣行
informal sector インフォーマル・セクター
information accounting 情報会計
information audit 情報監査
information coefficient 情報係数
information communications technology 情報通信技術
information criteria 情報量基準
information disclosure 情報開示
Information Disclosure Office 情報公開室
information disclosure statement guarantee 情報開示表明保証
information economics 情報経済学
information highway 情報ハイウェー
information industry 情報産業
information leakage 情報漏洩
Information Management Office 事務管理室
information network system 高度情報通信システム
information pollution 情報公害
information processing 情報処理

information ratio インフォメーション・レシオ
information retrieval 情報検索
information risk 情報リスク
information service 情報サービス
information society 情報社会
information source 情報源
information sources on beta value ベータ値の情報源
information statement 通知書類
information supply 情報発信
information system 情報システム
information system business 情報システム事業
Information System Management Division 事務管理課
Information System Services Department システム情報局
information technology 情報技術
information to be disclosed in the financial statements 財務諸表に開示すべき情報
information value 情報価値
information vendors 情報ベンダー
information-motivated trader 情報動機による取引者
information-motivated transaction 情報動機による取引
informative reporting 有益な報告
informed analysis 調査を重ねた分析
informed judgment 情報に基づく判断
informed trader インフォームド・トレーダー
infrastructure インフラストラクチャ（インフラ）
infrastructure cost インフラ費用
infrastructure improvement インフラ整備
infrastructure stock インフラ関連株
infrastructure work インフラ事業
infringe 侵害する
infringement 権利侵害
infringement of copyright 版権侵害
infringement of ownership 所有権侵害
infringement of patent right 特許権侵害
infusion 投入
ingredient 構成要素
inhabitant tax 住民税
inherent difficulty 固有の困難
inherent in the recognition 認識の必須要件となる
inherent risk 固有リスク
inheritance 相続
inheritance income 遺産所得
inheritance of bequest 遺産相続
inheritance tax 相続税
inheritance tax credit 相続税控除
inheritance tax insurance 相続税準備保険
Inheritance Tax Law 相続税法
inheritance tax on undivided bequest 未分割遺産の相続税
inheritance tax paid in kind 相続税の物納
inheritance tax return 相続税申告
inherited property 相続財産
inhomogeneity 異質
initial 期首の
initial accrued liability 初期発生債務
initial action plan 初期行動計画
initial balance 期首残高
initial buyer 初期の購入者
initial capital 当初資本
initial contract price 最初の約定値段
initial cost 原価
initial cost of business 開業費
initial date in reckoning 起算日
initial delivery 当初渡り
initial depreciation 初期償却
initial direct cost 初期直接費用
initial disclosure event 最初に開示を要する事象
initial down payment 内入金
initial establishment 当初設定
initial expenses 創業費
initial fee 当初の手数料
initial franchise fee 初期フランチャイズ料
initial goods in process 期首仕掛品

initial installment 内入金
initial inventories 期首棚卸資産
initial listing 新規上場
initial listing of securities 有価証券の新規上場
initial listing price 株式公開価格
initial margin 基本証拠金
initial margin requirement 当初証拠金率
initial measurements 当初測定
initial net investment 初期投資額
initial operating loss 当初の営業損失
initial par value 第一次平価
initial payment 頭金
initial portfolio 当初のポートフォリオ
initial premium 当初の保険料
initial recognition 当初認識
initial registration 当初登録
initial requirements 事前要件
initial reserve 初回準備金；年初準備金
initial special depreciation 初年度特別償却
initial work in process account 期首仕掛品勘定
initiate the momentum for an economic recovery 景気回復を主導する
initiation fee 入会金
initiative disposition 貸手の指図権
injection of public fund 公的資金の注入
injunction 差止命令
injunction proceedings 差止手続き
injunctive proceedings 差止命令手続
injury 侵害行為
injury to others 他者への傷害
inland bill 国内手形
inland bill of exchange 内国為替手形
inland exchange 内国為替
inland marine insurance インランドマリーン保険
Inland Revenue イギリス内国歳入庁
inland transportation 国内輸送
innage 残留荷量
innocence 無罪
innocent misrepresentation 善意の不実表示
innocent purchaser 善意の買主
innovation 新規性
innovative 革新的な
innovative strength 革新力
input 投入量
input coefficient 投入係数
input cost 投入費用
input-output analysis 投入産出分析
Input-Output Price Indexes of Manufacturing Industry by Sector 製造業部門別投入・産出物価指数
input-output table 投入算出表
inquiry 照会；問合せ
inquiry agency 信用調査機関
inquiry for corporate information 会社情報に係る照会
inquiry for the balances 残高照会
INR (Indian rupee) インド・ルピー
inscribed bond 記名債券
inscribed securities 記名証券
inscribed stock 記名株
inscribed stock certificate 記名株券
insecurity clause 流抵当約款
insertion of cross reference 参照の挿入
inside build-up 責任準備金増加額
inside buildup of cash value 利殖部分
inside information 内部情報
inside market インサイド・マーケット
inside the room 場内
insider インサイダー
insider information インサイダー情報
insider trading インサイダー取引
Insider Trading and Securities Fraud Enforcement Act of 1988 内部者取引・証券詐欺取締法
insight in markets 市場に対する造詣
insignificant movement 僅かな変動
insolvency 支払不能
insolvency clause 支払不能条項
insolvency law 破産法
insolvency of debtors 債務者不履行

insolvency proceedings 破産手続
insolvency protection system 支払不能保障制度
insolvent corporation 支払不能会社
insolvent debtor 破産者
insolvent liquidation 債務不履行による清算
inspection 検査
Inspection Administrator 検査監理官
Inspection Bureau 検査局
inspection certificate 検査証明書
Inspection Coordination Division 総務課（検査局）
Inspection Manual for Depository Financial Institutions 預金等受入金融機関に係る検査マニュアル
inspection of corporate record 会社記録の検査
inspection of documents 文書の閲覧
inspection of financial institutions 金融機関検査
inspection of property 財産の検分
inspection of transfer account book 振替口座簿の閲覧
Inspector for Mutual Assistance Insurance 共済監査官
Inspector of the Custom-Houses 税関考査官
instability index 不安定指数
installation 据付
installation cost 据付費用
installation work 据付工事
installment 割賦
installment accounts receivable 割賦売掛金
installment agreement 分納の合意
installment basis 割賦基準
installment bond 連続償還債
installment contribution years 分割拠出年数
installment credit 割賦債権
installment method 割賦方式
installment payable 割賦未払金
installment payment 分割払い
installment payment of tax 分割納付
installment plan 賦払い
installment premium 分割保険料
installment purchase 賦払購買
installment receivable 割賦販売債権
installment redemption 分割償還
installment repayment 分割償還
installment sales 割賦販売
installment sales floater insurance 分割販売保険
installment savings 定期積金
installment settlement 分割払い
installment time deposit 積立定期預金
installments receivable 割賦未収入金
instance 申立
Instance Court 海事事件裁判所
instantaneous finality 即時ファイナリティ
instantaneous spot rate 瞬間スポット・レート
Institute Cargo Clauses 新協会貨物約款
institute clauses 協会約款
Institute for Monetary and Economic Studies 日本銀行金融研究所
Institute of Chartered Financial Analysts 米国公認証券アナリスト協会
Institute of Internal Auditors アメリカ内部監査人協会
Institute of London Underwriters ロンドン保険業者協会
institute strikes, riots and civil commotion clauses 協会ストライキ騒じょう暴動担保約款
institute theft, pilferage and non-delivery clauses 協会盗難不着担保約款
institute war clauses 協会戦争危険担保約款
institution 機関
institution buying 法人買付け
institution handling savings 貯蓄取扱機関
Institution of Chartered Accountants in English and Wales 英国勅許会

計士協会
institutional 制度上の
institutional accounting 制度会計
institutional approach 制度研究
institutional arbitration 機関仲裁
institutional broker 機関投資家相手の証券会社
institutional capital 機関投資家資金
Institutional Delivery System ID システム
institutional demand 機関投資家の需要
institutional driver 機関投資家
institutional economics 制度学派
institutional factor 制度上の要因
institutional framework for financial system stability 金融システムの安定化に向けた制度上の枠組み
institutional funding 機関投資家の資金調達
institutional investment 機関投資家による投資
institutional investor 機関投資家
institutional investors' index option 機関投資家指数オプション
institutional portfolio 機関投資家の運用資産
institutional postulate 制度的公準
institutional purchase 機関買い
institutional risk 制度上のリスク
institutional school 制度学派
institutional selling 機関売り
INSTRAW(International Research and Training Institute for the Advancement of Women) 国際婦人調査訓練研修所
instruction 指示
Instruction for Registration of Transfer 移転登録請求書
instruction of exercise 権利行使の指示
instruction to bidders 入札者への指示書
instructions at entrustment 委託時の指示事項
instructions for funds transfers 資金移転指示
instrument 商品
instrument payable to bearer 持参人払証券
instruments for buying operation 買入対象債券
instruments outstanding 残高のある金融商品
insufficient evidence 不十分な証拠
insufficient funds 残高不足
insufficient-funds check 残高不足小切手
insurability 保険引受能力
insurable interest 被保険利益
insurable risk 保険可能リスク
insurable value 保険付可能金額
insurance 保険
insurance accounting 保険会計
insurance affiliate 保険提携会社
insurance against death 死亡保険
insurance age 保険年齢
insurance agency 保険代理店
insurance agency commission 保険代理店手数料
insurance amount 保険金額
insurance benefit 保険給付
insurance bond 保険ボンド
insurance broker 保険ブローカー
insurance brokers act 保険ブローカー法
Insurance Brokers Registration Council 保険ブローカー登録評議会
insurance business 保険業
Insurance Business Division 保険課
Insurance Business Law and Regulations 保険業法令
insurance buyer 保険購入者
insurance carrier 保険会社
insurance certificate 保険証
insurance charge 保険料
insurance claim 保険請求
insurance claims receivable 未収保険金
insurance clause 保険約款

I

insurance company 保険会社
insurance consumer 保険消費者
insurance contract 保険契約
insurance contributions 保険拠出金
insurance council 保険審議会
insurance cover 保険保障
insurance cover note 保険引受証
insurance derivatives 保険デリバティブ
insurance directive 保険通達
insurance distribution 保険販売
insurance dividend 保険契約者配当
insurance enterprise 保険会社
insurance examination 保険審査
insurance exchange 保険取引所
insurance exchange rider 保険乗換特約
insurance expense 保険料
insurance for account to whom it may concern 不特定の他人のためにする保険
insurance function 保険機能
insurance fund 保険基金
insurance futures 保険先物
insurance guaranty fund 保険支払保証基金
insurance history 保険加入歴
insurance holding company 保険持株会社
insurance in force 保有保険契約
insurance industry 保険業界
insurance insolvency 保険金支払不能
insurance intermediary 保険仲介人
insurance law 保険監督法
insurance leverage 保険レバレッジ
insurance liabilities 保険会社負債
insurance license 保険免許
insurance management 保険管理
insurance market 保険市場
insurance money 保険金
insurance of medical expenses 医療費用保険
insurance of substandard lives 標準下体保険契約
insurance option 保険オプション
insurance payable at death 死亡保険
insurance plan 保険制度
insurance policy rate 保険料率
Insurance Policy-holders Protection Corporation 保険契約者保護機構
insurance pool 保険プール
insurance population 保険人口
insurance premium 保険料
insurance premium base 保険料基準
insurance premium calculation 保険料計算
insurance premium contribution 保険料負担
insurance premium conversion plan 保険料転換制度
insurance premium cost 保険料コスト
insurance premium credit 保険料払戻し
insurance premium deduction 保険料控除
insurance premium deposit 保険料預託
insurance premium discount 保険料割引
insurance premium due date 保険料払込期日
insurance premium fund 保険料積立金
insurance premium note 保険料手形
insurance premium offset 保険料相殺
insurance premium outlay 保険料支出
insurance premium rate 保険料率
insurance premium rebate 保険料割引
insurance premium refund 保険料返還
insurance premium reserve 保険料積立金
insurance premium structure 保険料構造
insurance premium tax 保険料税
insurance premium tax relief 保険料課税所得控除
insurance principle 保険原理
insurance proceed 保険金収入
insurance product firm 保険商品取扱業者
insurance product portfolio 保険商品

ポートフォリオ
insurance profit 保険引受利益
insurance proposal form 保険契約申込書
insurance protection 保険保障
insurance purchase 保険購入
insurance rating agency 保険格付機関
insurance register 保険記録簿
insurance regulator 保険監督機関
insurance risk rate 危険保険料率
insurance saving 保険貯蓄
insurance scam 保険詐欺
insurance scheme 保険型年金
insurance sector 保険業界
insurance settlement 保険金支払い
insurance statutory accounting 保険法定会計
insurance subrogation 保険代位
insurance tax 保険税
insurance trust 保険信託
insurance type contract 保険型契約
insurance underwriting 保険引受け
insurance value 保険価額
insurance with annuity 年金付保険
insurance with limited premium 保険料有限払込保険
insurance without medical examination 告知書扱い
insurance world 保険界
insurance year 保険年度
insured account 保険付口座
insured amount 保険金額
insured benefit 担保給付；保険付給付
insured bonds 支払保証地方債
insured event 保険事故
insured loss 損害填補額
insured pension plan 保険型年金
insured peril 被保険危険
insured person 被保険者
insured plan 保険が付された制度
insured property 被保険物
insured retirement product 保険退職商品
insured risk 担保危険
insured unemployment 保険受給失業
insuree 被保険者
insurer 保険者
insurmountable difficulty 容易に回復し得ない状態
intaglio printing 凹版印刷
intake 受入れ
intangible assets 無形資産
intangible capital 無形資本
intangible cost 無形費用
intangible depreciable assets 無形減価償却資産
intangible depreciable property 無形償却資産
intangible effects 無形の効果
intangible fixed assets 無形固定資産
intangible property 無形財産
intangible right 無体権
intangible value 無形価値
intangibles 無形固定資産
integer 整数
integral 不可分な
integral multiple 整数倍
integral part 不可欠部分
integral times 整数倍の
integrated economy 統合経済
integrated operations 統合された事業
integrated production 一貫生産
integrated risk management 統合リスク管理
integration 統合
integration cost 統合費用
integration ratio 統合比率
integration test 給付調整審査
integrity 誠実性
intellectual property backed loan 知的所有権担保ローン
intellectual property right 知的所有権
intended impact 意図的な影響
intensification 激化
intensive investment 集中投資
intention 意思
intention to purchase 購入の意思
intentional 故意の
inter vivos trust 生前信託
Inter-American Development Bank 米

州開発銀行
inter-bank 銀行間の
inter-bank deposit 銀行間預金
inter-bank exchange transaction インターバンク為替取引
inter-bank loan インターバンク・ローン
inter-bank market インターバンク市場
inter-bank rate 銀行間相場
inter-bank spot rate インターバンク直物相場
inter-bank transaction インターバンク取引
inter-branch account 支店相互勘定
inter-branch loss 支店相互間損失
inter-branch profit 支店相互間利益
inter-commodity spread 商品間スプレッド
inter-company account 会社間勘定
inter-company elimination 会社間除去
inter-company loss 会社相互間損失
inter-company profit 会社間利益
inter-corporate analysis 企業間分析
inter-dealer market ディーラー間市場
inter-delivery spread 限月間スプレッド
inter-firm analysis 企業間分析
inter-generational transfer 世代間振替
inter-government 政府間の
inter-industry 産業間の
inter-industry analysis 産業連関分析
inter-industry correlation 産業間相関
inter-industry relation 産業連関
inter-industry-relations table 産業連関表
inter-market 市場間
inter-market spread 市場間スプレッド
inter-month spread transaction 限月間スプレッド取引
inter-office account 本支店勘定
inter-office exchange adjustment account 為替尻換算差金
inter-office rate 本支店レート
inter-period allocation method 期間配分法
inter-period tax allocation 年度間税配分
inter-segment pricing セグメント間振替価格決定
inter-segment transfer セグメント間振替
inter-temporal 異時点間の
interaction 相互作用
interbank money market 銀行間市場
Interbolsa ポルトガル保管振替機関
interchange 交流
intercommon 相互入会する
intercompany reconciliation 会社間の調整
intercompany transaction 会社間取引
interconnectivity 相互接続性
interdepartmental 部門間の
interdepartmental account 部門間勘定
interdepartmental profit 内部振替利益
interdependency of settlement 決済の相互依存
interdependent 相互依存する
interest 持ち分
interest accrual period 利子計算期間
interest accrued from deposit in bank 銀行預金利息
interest advance 前払利息
interest after the maturity 期限後利息
interest and amortization 元利返済額
interest and discounts on foreign currency assets 外貨建資産利息・割引料
interest and discounts on government securities 国債利息
interest and dividend received 受入利息及び配当金
interest and dividends on securities 有価証券利息配当金
interest bearing 利付き
interest bearing bank debenture 利付金融債
interest bearing borrowing 有利子借入金
interest bearing issuance 有利発行

interest bearing liability 有利子負債
interest burden 利子負担
interest cap trading 金利キャップ取引
interest capitalization method 元加方式
interest charge 利子費用
interest claims 利息クレーム
interest component 金利部分
interest computation 利息計算
interest cost 利子費用
interest coupon 利札
interest cover 利子負担
interest coverage ratio インタレスト・カバレッジ・レシオ
interest coverage test インタレスト・カバレッジ・テスト
interest credit 利息付与
interest deduction 利息控除
interest differential 利率格差
interest dividend 利益配当
interest due date 利子支払日
interest earned 受取利息
interest earned on loan receivable 貸付金受取利息
interest element 利息部分
interest equalization tax 金利平衡税
interest expense 利息費用
interest exposure 金利リスク
interest factor 利率要因
interest for arrears 遅延利息
interest for delay 延滞利子
interest for delinquency 延滞利子
interest free credit 無利息信用
interest group 圧力団体
interest in arrears 延滞利子
interest in fair value 公正価値の持ち分
interest included 元利合計
interest income 利子所得
interest incurred during construction 建設利息
interest incurred on advance received 前受金支払利息
interest indexed annuity 金利連動年金
interest indicated on the coupon 利札面に記載される利子
interest maintenance reserve 金利変動準備金
interest margin 金利マージン
interest margin charges 利ざや設定
interest method 利息法
interest of shareholder 株主の利害
interest on bank deposit 銀行利子
interest on borrowed 借入金利子
interest on borrowed fund 負債利子
interest on call loans コールローン利息
interest on call money コールマネー利息
interest on corporate bonds 社債利子
interest on deposit 預金金利
interest on external bond 外債利子
interest on foreign currency deposits 外貨預け金利息
interest on funded debt 長期債利息
interest on government bond 国債利子
interest on government securities 政府証券利息
interest on guaranty capital 基金利息
interest on interest rate swap 金利スワップ支払利息
interest on loans 貸付金利息
interest on loans and discounts 貸出金利息
interest on loans on bills 手形貸付利息
interest on loans rebated 貸付金利息割戻し
interest on obligation 債務の利息
interest on overdrafts for export bills 為替当座貸利息
interest on postal savings 郵便貯金の利子
interest on public bond 公債利子
interest on refund 還付加算金
interest on repurchase agreement 売現先利息
interest on resale agreement 買現先利息
interest on savings deposit 貯金金利
interest on securities 有価証券利息

interest on Special Drawing Rights 特別引出権利息
interest only 金利のみ
interest only loan 利子払いのみ融資
interest only mortgage 元金一括返済モーゲージ
interest only strips 利息のみストリップ債
interest option 金利オプション
interest option transaction 金利オプション取引
interest outlay 利払い
interest paid 支払利息
interest parity 金利平価
interest payable 未払利子
interest payment 利払い
interest payment expense 利払費
interest payment method 利払方法
interest payment moratorium 利息の支払猶予
interest payment of JGSs 国債の利払い
interest payments on foreign debt 対外債務利払い
interest per annum 年利
interest per diem 日歩
interest period 金利期間
interest pricing 金利の決定
interest rate 金利；利息
interest rate abroad 海外金利
interest rate adjustment 金利調整
interest rate anticipation 金利予測
interest rate applied 適用金利
interest rate arbitrage 金利裁定
interest rate arbitrage transaction 金利裁定取引
interest rate change 利子率変化
interest rate collar 金利カラー
interest rate control 金利操作
interest rate differential 金利差
interest rate floor 金利フロアー
interest rate fluctuation 金利変動
interest rate futures 金利先物
interest rate futures contracts 金利先物契約
interest rate futures option trading 金利先物オプション取引
interest rate implicit in the lease リース上の計算利子率
interest rate index 金利指数
interest rate level 金利水準
interest rate minded 金利マインド
interest rate movement 金利動向
interest rate novation 金利更改
interest rate on borrowing 借入金金利
interest rate on cash collateral 担保金利率
interest rate on inter-bank deposit 銀行間預金金利
interest rate on loans 貸出金利
interest rate on loans secured by time deposit 定期預金担保貸出金利
interest rate on the Eurocurrency market ユーロ金利
interest rate on time deposit 定期預金金利
interest rate option 金利オプション
interest rate payable by buyer 買い方金利
interest rate policy 金利政策
interest rate raise 利上げ
interest rate receivable by seller 売り方金利
interest rate risk 金利リスク
interest rate sensitive items 金利感応項目
interest rate sensitivity 金利感応度
interest rate sensitivity information 金利感応性情報
interest rate spread 利ざや
interest rate swap 金利スワップ
interest rate swaption 金利スワップション
interest receivable 未収利息
interest receivable on bank deposits 未収銀行預金利息
interest received 受取利息
interest recognized in cost 原価算入利息
interest reserve rate 積立金利率

interest revenue 利息収益
interest sensitive insurance polity 金利敏感保険契約
interest sensitive policy 変額保険
interest sensitive stock 金利敏感株
Interest Sensitive Whole Life 金利感応型終身保険
interest sensitivity of the pension surplus 年金剰余の金利感応度
interest skimming インタレスト・スキミング
interest spread 金利差
interest strips 金利ストリップ債
interest subsidy 利子補給金
interest surplus 金利差益
interest swap bond 金利スワップ債
interest tax 利子税
interest tax on authorized deferred payment of income tax 所得税の延納に伴う利子税
interest tax on delayed payment 延納にかかる利子税
interest volatility risk 金利変動リスク
interest-bearing bond 利付債
interest-bearing debt 利付負債
interest-bearing investment 利付投資
interest-bearing note 利付手形
interest-bearing security 利付証券
interest-rate parity theory 利子平価理論
interest-sensitive products 金利感応型商品
interested party 関係者；利害関係者
interests in joint ventures ジョイント・ベンチャーの持分
interference 干渉
interference with business 業務への干渉
interference with execution of official duty 公務執行妨害
interference with trade 営業の妨害
intergeneration equity 世代間公平
intergenerational altruism 世代間利他主義
intergenerational redistribution 世代間再配分
interim account 中間勘定
interim audit 期中監査
interim certificate 仮証券
interim closing 中間決算
interim contract 暫定契約
interim date 中間日
interim dividend 中間配当
interim examination date 中間監査日
interim figure 中間数値
interim financial information 中間財務情報
interim financial report 中間財務報告書
interim financial reporting 中間財務報告
interim financial statements 中間財務諸表
interim financing つなぎ資金
interim interest payment 中間払利息
interim liquidating dividend 中途清算配当金
interim loan つなぎ融資
interim measure 経過措置
interim operations 中間営業活動
interim period 中間期間
interim period pre-tax income 中間税引前利益
interim plateau 中期的な安定期
interim receipt 仮領収書
interim report 中間報告
interim results 中間決算
interim return form 中間申告書
interim sales 中間売上
interim statement 中間計算書
interim tax return 中間申告
interim term insurance 一年未満定期保険
interlineations 行間記入
interlocking 連動
interlocking directors 兼任重役
interlocking stockholding 株式持合い
intermediary 仲介者；媒介
intermediary agents 仲介機関
intermediary bank 仲介銀行

intermediary trade 三国間貿易
intermediate accounting 中級会計学
intermediate goods 中間財
intermediate improvement trade 仲継加工貿易
intermediate lag 中間ラグ
intermediate loan 中期ローン
intermediate market outlook 中期予想
intermediate party 中間業者
intermediate product 中間製品
intermediate provision 未確定条項
intermediate securities 中期証券
intermediate stage 中間段階
intermediate target 運営目標
intermediate tariff 中間税率
intermediate tranche 中期トランシェ
intermediate value 中間値
intermediate vehicles 中間的金融商品
intermediation 介在
intermediation fee 仲介手数料
intermediation of trading 取引の媒介
intermittent work 断続労働
internal accounting control 内部会計統制
internal analysis 内部分析
internal audit 内部監査
internal audit report 内部監査報告書
internal audit standard 内部監査基準
internal audit system 内部監査制度
internal auditor 内部監査人
Internal Auditors' Office 検査室
internal bond 内国債
internal business analysis 内部経営分析
internal capital 内部資本
internal cash flow 内部キャッシュフロー
internal check 内部牽制
internal check and balance 内部牽制システム
internal check system 内部牽制制度
internal consistency 内部整合性
internal control 内部統制
internal controlling organization 内部統制組織
internal credit enhancement 内部信用補完
internal credit rating system 内部格付制度
internal debt 内債
internal development 内部開発
internal document 内部資料
internal evaluation 内部評価
internal evidence 内部証拠
internal financial budgeting 内部財務予算
internal financial reporting system 内部財務報告制度
internal financing 自己金融；内部金融
internal fund 内部資金
Internal Inspector 国税庁監察官
internal investment management 自家運用
internal labor market 内部労働市場
internal liability 内部負債
internal management information 内部経営情報
internal profit 内部利益
internal rate of interest rate 内部利子率
internal rate of return 内部収益率
internal rating 内部格付け
internal regulations 内部規程
internal reporting 内部報告
internal reporting purpose 内部報告目的
internal reporting system 内部報告制度
internal reserve 内部留保金
Internal Revenue Code 米国内国歳入法
Internal Revenue Service 米国内国歳入庁
internal rule 社内規程
internal sales 内部売上
internal segment 内部セグメント
internal settlement 参加者間決済
internal source of information 内部情報源
internal structure 内部構造

Internal Subdivisions 内部部局
internal tax 内国税
internal trade 内国貿易
internal transaction 内部取引
internal transfer profit 内部振替利益
internal use 自社使用
internalization 内在化
internalized order 内部化注文
internally created goodwill 自家創出のれん
internally generated 内部創出の
internally generated fund 内部創出資金
internally generated goodwill 自己創設のれん
internally reported segment 内部報告セグメント
international accounting 国際会計
international affairs 対外関係
International Affairs and Research Division 関税局調査課
International Affairs Division 国際課
international agencies 国際機関
international agency bond 国際機関債券
international agreed specialization 合意的国際分業
international aid 外国からの援助
international asset management 国際資産運用
international balance of accounts 国際収支
international balance of payments 国際収支
International Bank for Economic Cooperation 国際経済協力銀行
international banking facilities account IBF 勘定（国際銀行業務勘定）
international banking facility 国際銀行業務
international banking operation 国際銀行業務
international bond 国際債券
international bond market 国際債券市場
international bond trading 国際債券トレーディング
international borrowing 対外借り入れ
international broking 国際ブローキング
International Bureau 国際局
international business 国際事業
international capital 国際資本
international capital market 国際資本市場
international capital movement 国際資本移動
international cartel 国際カルテル
international cash management service 国際 CMS
International Centre for Settlement of Investment Disputes 投資紛争解決国際センター
International Clearing Union 国際清算同盟
International Co-operation Office 国際調整室
international commerce 国際取引
international commercial arbitration 国際商事仲裁
international commodity agreement 国際商品協定
international comparables 国際比較
international comparison 国際比較
international competitiveness 国際競争力
international consortium 国際引受団
international contribution 国際貢献
international convention 国際条約
international copyright 国際著作権
international corporation 国際企業
international crisis 国際危機
international currency 国際通貨
international custody 国際保護預り
international custom 国際慣習法
international debt 対外債務
International Department 国際局
international depositary receipts 国際預託証書

international diversified investment 国際分散投資
international division of labor 国際分業
international division of roles 国際分業
international double taxation 国際二重課税
international economics 国際経済学
international economist 国際エコノミスト
international equilibrium 国際均衡
international equity market 国際株式市場
international equity placement 株式海外売出し
international exchange 国際為替
International Federation of Accountants 国際会計士連盟
International Federation of Stock Exchanges 国際証券取引所連合
international finance 国際金融
international financial community 国際金融業界
international financial institution 国際金融機関
international financial market 国際金融市場
international financial system 国際金融制度
international fund 国際資金
international goods 国際財
international interest-spread 内外金利差
international investment 国際投資
international investment bank 国際投資銀行
international investment position 対外資産残高統計
international investment trust 国際投資信託
international law 国際法
international lease 国際リース
international liquidity 国際流動性
international loan portfolio 国際ローン・ポートフォリオ
international long-term capital movement 国際短期資本移動
international managed currency system 国際管理通貨制度
International Maritime Organization 国際海事機関
international market 国際市場
international market index 国際市場インデックス
international market price 国際市場価格
international marketing 国際マーケティング
international marketing research 国際市場調査
international merchandise 国際商品
International Monetary Exchanges 国際金融取引所
International Monetary Market 国際通貨市場
international monetary turmoil 国際通貨不安
international money management 国際的金融管理
international money market 国際金融市場
international movements of funds 国際資金移動
international mutual fund 国際ミューチュアル・ファンド
international normals 国際ノーマル・ポートフォリオ
international offerings 国際公募
international oil plays 国際的石油株
international operation 国際業務
International Organization of Consumer's Unions 国際消費者機構
International Organization of Securities Commissions 国際証券取引委員会機構
international organizations 国際機関
International Organizations Division 国際機構課

international policy 対外政策
international portfolio 国際ポートフォリオ
international portfolio diversification 国際分散投資
international portfolio investment 国際証券投資
international public law 国際公法
international relations 国際関係論
international reserve 外貨準備
International Resources Bank 国際資源銀行
international securities 国際証券
International Securities Clearing Corporation 国際決済機関
international settlement 国際決済
international settlement currency 国際決済通貨
international short-term capital transaction 国際短期資本取引
international short-term money market 国際短期金融市場
International Society of Securities Administration 国際証券管理者協会
international standards 国際基準
international stock 国際株券
International Swap Dealers Association 国際スワップ・ディーラー協会
international syndicate 国際シンジケート
international tax law 国際租税法
International Tax Policy Division 国際租税課
international trade 国際貿易
International Trade Commission 国際貿易委員会
international tranche 国際トランシェ
international transaction currency 国際取引通貨
international underwriting group 国際引受団
International Union of Credit and Investment Insurers 国際輸出信用保険機構
International Union of Marine Insurance 国際海上保険連合
international unit 国際単位
international valuation standards 国際評価基準
internationalization 国際化
internationally active bank 国際業務展開銀行
interoperability 相互運用性
interperiod allocation 期間配分
interperiod income tax allocation 所得課税の期間相互配分
interpolated rate 期間按分利回り
interpositioning 介在
interpret 解釈する
interpretation clause 解釈条項
interpretation guidance 解釈指針書
interpretation of cash flows キャッシュフローの見方
interpretation of special rule 特例取扱い
interpretations 解釈指針
interregional analysis 地域連関分析
interrelate 相互関連する
interrelationship 相互関係
interruption of prescription 時効の中断
intersegment sales セグメント間売上
interstate 各州間の
Interstate Commerce 州際通商
Interstate Commerce Commission 州際通商委員会
interstate compact 州際協定
interunit pricing 部門間振替価格の決定
interunit transfer 部門間振替
interval 刻み値
intervening period 介在期間
intervention 介入
intervention against market 向かい風介入
intervention by a third party 第三者の介入
intervention by selling dollars ドル売

り介入
intervention conducted on behalf of other central banks 逆委託介入
intervention currency 介入通貨
intervention entrusted to foreign central banks 委託介入
intervention fear 介入への警戒
intervention following market 追い風介入
intervention level 介入水準
intervention operation 介入操作
intervention point 介入点
intervention pool 介入のためのプール
intervention price 介入価格
intervention purchase 介入買い
intervention through brokers ブローカー経由介入
intervention to cap the JPY against the USD 円売りドル買い介入
intervention to stop yen from appreciating against the dollar 円売りドル買い介入
intestacy 無遺言死
intestate distribution 無遺言資産分配
INTOSAI (International Organization of Supreme Audit Institutions) 最高会計検査機関国際組織
intra vires 権限内で
intra-company transfer 内部振替
intra-company transfer price 内部振替価格
intra-company transfer variance 内部振替差額
intra-day margin call 日中証拠金請求
intra-group balance 企業グループ内残高
intraday 1日の中で
intraday deviations 当日変動状況
intraday fluctuation margin 当日中の変動幅
intraday fluctuation rate 当日中の変動率
intraday high and low 日中高低値
intraday overdraft 日中当座貸越
intrafirm analysis 企業内分析
intragroup 企業集団内の
intragroup transaction グループ企業間取引
intramarginal intervention 許容変動幅内介入
intramarket 市場内
intraperiod allocation 期間内配分
intraperiod income tax 所得課税の期間内配分
intraregional trade 地域内貿易
intrastate offering 州内売出し
intrinsic deposit 本来的預金
intrinsic value 本源的価値
intrinsic value based method 本源的価値基準法
introduced mortgage business 提携ローンによるモーゲージ条件
introduced stock 公開株
introducing 取次
introducing broker 紹介ブローカー
introducing firm 注文取次業者
introduction 冒頭部
introduction of banking facilities 金融機関の斡旋
introduction of technology 技術の導入
introduction of the retirement benefit accounting 退職給付会計の適用
invalid card 事故カード
invalid coupon 欠缺利札
invariant 正規の
invasion of privacy プライバシーの侵害
inventories acquired by merger 合併により取得した棚卸資産
inventories of merchandise and supplies 貯蔵品
inventory 棚卸資産
inventory accounts 棚卸資産勘定
inventory adjustment 在庫調整
inventory assets 棚卸資産
inventory at the beginning of the period 期首棚卸資産
inventory at the end of period 期末棚卸資産
inventory audit 棚卸資産監査

inventory budget 在庫予算
inventory capital 在庫資本
inventory carrying cost 保管費
inventory certificate 棚卸証明書
inventory change 在庫変動
inventory control 棚卸し
inventory count 実地棚卸
inventory cycles 在庫循環
inventory excess 過剰在庫
inventory financing 在庫金融
inventory fluctuation account 棚卸資産価格変動勘定
inventory indexes 在庫指数
inventory investment 在庫投資
inventory lending 棚卸資産担保貸付
inventory level 手持在庫水準
inventory loss 棚卸損
inventory management 在庫管理
inventory method 棚卸資産計算法
inventory obsolescence 棚卸資産の陳腐化
inventory of items pledged as security 担保目録
inventory of property 財産目録
inventory of work in process at the beginning of period 仕掛品繰越高
inventory pool 棚卸資産プール
inventory profit 棚卸資産利益
inventory quantities 棚卸数量
inventory ratio 在庫率
inventory recession インベントリー・リセッション
inventory relief 棚卸資産税額控除
inventory sheet 棚卸表
inventory shipment ratio 在庫率
inventory tag 棚卸票
inventory taking 棚卸
inventory turnover 棚卸資産回転率
inventory unit 棚卸単位
inventory valuation 棚卸資産評価
inventory valuation adjustment 在庫評価調整
inventory valuation method 棚卸資産の評価方法
inventory valuation-reserves 棚卸資産評価引当金
inventory value 棚卸評価額
inventory variation 棚卸資産増減
inventory write-down 棚卸資産の評価減
inverse floater 逆フローター債
inverse matrix table 逆行列表
inverse yield 逆利回り
inverted market 逆ざや市場
inverted scale 逆利回連続償還債
inverted yield curve 逆イールド
inverted yield curve phenomena 逆イールド現象
investable fund 運用可能資金
invested assets 運用資産
invested capital 投下資本
investee 被投資会社
investee company 被投資企業
Investigation Division 特別調査課
investing activities 投資活動
investing public 大衆投資家
investment 投資
investment abroad 海外投資
investment account 投資勘定部門
investment administration cost 投資管理コスト
investment advisor 投資顧問
Investment Advisor Act of 1940 投資顧問法
investment advisory industry 投資顧問業界
investment advisory service 投資顧問業
investment analysis 投資分析
investment analyst 投資アナリスト
investment and loan 投融資
investment and loan guideline 投融資指針
investment approvals 投資承認額
investment assets 投資資産
investment bank 投資銀行
investment banking business 投資銀行事業
Investment Banking Financing Company 投資銀行金融機関

investment bond 投資債権
investment boom 投資ブーム
investment budget 投資予算
investment business 投資業
investment business association 投資事業組合
investment buying 投資買
investment by foreign investor 外人投資
investment capital 投資資本
investment certificate 投資証書
investment choice 投資先
investment climate 投資環境
investment club 投資クラブ
investment committee 投資委員会
investment company 投資会社
Investment Company Act of 1940 1940年投資会社法
Investment Company Amendments Act of 1970 1970年改正投資会社法
investment contracts 直接投資総額（契約ベース）
investment counsel 投資顧問
investment counselor 投資カウンセラー
investment credit 投資控除
investment criteria 投資尺度
investment currency 投資通貨
investment curve 投資曲線
investment decision 投資判断
investment demand 投資需要
investment dollar 投資ドル
investment earnings 運用益
investment environment 投資環境
investment expenditure 投資支出
investment experience 投資実績
investment flexibility 投資柔軟性
investment fluctuation fund 投資変動準備金
investment friction 投資摩擦
investment function 投資関数
investment function of profit principle type 利潤原理型投資関数
investment fund 投資信託
investment goods 投資財
investment grade 投資適格
investment grade bond 投資適格債券
investment grade corporate 投資対象企業
investment grade loan 投資適格ローン
investment grade rate 投資適格格付け
investment grade securities 投資適格債
investment history 投資実績
investment holding period 投資期間
investment horizon 投資期間
investment in affiliated company 関連会社への投資
investment in affiliates 関係会社出資金
investment in bonds 社債投資
investment in capital 出資金
investment in equity method affiliates 持ち分法適用関連会社投資
investment in kind 現物出資
investment in kind theory of merger 現物出資説
investment in lease リース投資未回収額
investment in long-term financial instruments 長期金融商品への投資
investment in money 現金出資
investment in short-term products 短期運用
investment in subsidiary 子会社への投資
investment income 運用収益
investment information sources 投資情報源
investment instruction 運用指図
investment insurance trust 保険運用信託
investment judgment 投資判断
investment ledger 有価証券元帳
investment letter 投資目的確認書
investment management 投資運用
investment management company 投資顧問会社
investment management cost 投資管理

費用
investment management criteria 運用管理基準
investment manager 機関投資家
investment manager structure 投資マネジャーの構成
investment market 投資市場
investment merit 投資メリット
investment multiplier 投資乗数
investment objectives 投資目標
investment opportunity 投資機会
investment outlet 投資対象
investment outstanding 投資未回収額
investment overseas 海外投資
investment performance 運用実績
investment period 投資期間
investment philosophy 投資哲学
investment policy 投資政策
investment policy of personal investor 個人投資家の投資方針
investment products 投資商品
investment profit 自己勘定売買益
investment profitability 投資採算
investment program 投資計画
investment propensity 投資性向
investment property 投資不動産
investment property owner 投資不動産所有者
investment purchased register 有価証券買入記入帳
investment rate 投資率
investment ratio 出資比率
investment real estate 投資不動産
investment recovery 投資回収
investment reserve 投資損失準備金
investment result 投資成果
investment revaluation reserve 投資再評価積立金
investment risk 投資リスク
investment securities 投資有価証券
investment securities gains 投資有価証券収益
investment securities markets 投資有価証券市場
investment securities portfolio 投資有価証券ポートフォリオ
investment securities transaction 投資有価証券取引
investment security 投資証券
investment selection summary 投資選択の概括
investment software 投資ソフト
investment stock 投資株
investment strategy 投資戦略
investment strategy committee 投資戦略委員会
investment tax 投資税
investment tools 投資物件
investment trust 投資信託
Investment Trust Association of Japan 証券投資信託協会
investment trust beneficiary certificate 投資信託受益証券
investment trust certificate 受益証券
investment trust management company 投資信託委託会社
investment trust on securities 証券投資信託
investment turnover 投資回転率
investment unit 投資単位
investment value 投資価値
investment vehicle 投資子会社
investment year method 投資年度別方式
investments by owners 株主の出資
investor 投資家
investor briefings 投資家向けセミナー
investor buying 投資家の買い
investor in public bond 公債投資者
investor interest 投資家の関心
investor perceptions 投資家の見方
investor protection trust 加入者保護信託
investor tax year 投資家の税務上の会計年度
investor's share 投資家の持ち分
investors relations インベスターズ・リレーションズ
investors' confidence 投資家の信頼
investors' meeting 加入者集会

invisible account 貿易外収支
invisible export 見えざる輸出
invisible hand 見えざる手
invisible import 見えざる輸入
invisible supply 市場外在荷
invisible trade 貿易外取引
invisible trade balance 貿易外収支
invitation 誘引
invitation telex 勧誘テレックス
invoice 請求書
invoice amount 送り状価格
invoice book 仕切帳
invoice method インボイス方式
invoice-book inward 商品仕入帳
invoice-book outward 商品仕送帳
involuntary 自発的でない
involuntary bankruptcy 強制破産
involuntary conversion 強制転換
involuntary exchange of property 交換処分
involuntary insolvency 強制支払不能
involuntary liquidation 強制清算
involuntary loss or gain 非自然的損益
involuntary participation 強制加入
involuntary termination 会社都合退職
involuntary transfer 強制的譲渡
involuntary unemployment 非自発的失業
inward exchange 被仕向け為替
inward investment 対内投資
inward remittance 被仕向け送金
IOM (index and option market) 指数オプション市場
IOSCO (International Organization of Securities Commissions) 証券監督者国際機構
IOU (I owe you) 借用証書
IP (insurance policy) 保険証券
IPE (International Petroleum Exchange) ロンドン国際石油取引所
IPMA (International Primary Market Association) 国際引受業者協会
IPO (initial public offering) 新規株式公開
IPP (independent power producer) 独立系発電事業者
IPS (investment performance standards) 投資パフォーマンス規準
IPT (investor protection trust) 投資家保護信託
IQD (Iraqi dinar) イラク・ディナール
IRA (individual retirement account) 個人退職積立勘定
IRA (individual retirement account) rollover 個人退職勘定移転
IRC (Inland Revenue Commissioners) 内国歳入委員会
IRCJ (Industrial Revitalization Corporation of Japan) 産業再生機構
iron and steel industry 鉄鋼業界
IRR (Iran rial) イラン・リアル
irrational tax 悪税
irrecoverable cost 回収不能原価
irredeemable 無償還の
irredeemable bond 不償還債
irregular installment payment 不均等払い
irregular practices 不正行為
irregularity 不規則性
irrelevant 関連性のない
irrelevant volatility 不適切な不安定性
irreparable injury 回復不能の侵害
irrespective of 関係なく
irretrievable deprivation 見込みのない喪失
irrevocable 撤回しえない
irrevocable choice 取消不能な選択
irrevocable commitment 取消不能のコミットメント
irrevocable L / C (letter of credit) 取消不能信用状
irrevocable license 取消しえざる許可
irrevocable living trust 取消不能生前信託
irrevocable trust 取消不能信託
IRS (Instruction Reconciliation System) インストラクション照合

システム
I-S curve · L-M curve IS曲線·LM曲線
ISDA (International Swap Dealers Association) 国際スワップ・ディーラーズ協会
ISDA (International Swaps and Derivatives Association) 国際スワップ・デリバティブ協会
ISE (Italian Stock Exchange) イタリア証券取引所
ISIN (International Securities Identification Number) 国際証券識別コード
ISIS (Intermarket Surveillance Information System) 市場間監視情報システム
island reversal pattern アイランド・リバーサル・パターン
ISM (Institute of Supply Management) index ISM指数
ISMA (International Securities Markets Association) 国際証券市場協会
ISO (International Organization for Standardization) 国際標準化機構
isolated 隔離されている
isolated event 独立した事象
ISSA (International Securities Services Association) 国際証券サービス協会
issuance at market price 時価発行
issuance criteria 適債基準
issuance guidelines 適債基準
issuance of Bank of Japan notes 日本銀行券の発行
issuance of banknotes 銀行券の発行
issuance of FBs 政府短期証券の発行
issuance of government bond 公債発行
issuance of JGSs 国債の発行
issuance of new debt 新発債の発行
issuance of new stocks 新株の発行
issuance of preferred shares by subsidiary 子会社による優先株の発行
issuance of stock 株式の発行
issuance pattern 発行パターン
issuance price 発行価格
issuance purpose 発行目的
issuance value 発行価額
issuance volume 発行額
issue 論点
issue at face value 額面発行
issue at intermediate price 中間発行
issue at market price 時価発行
issue at par パー発行
issue at par (value) 額面発行
issue by tender 入札発行
issue difference 発行差額
issue market 発行市場
issue of bond 起債
issue of law 法律上の争点
issue of loan capital 借入資本の発行
issue of public bonds 公共債発行
issue of shares at market price 株式時価発行
issue of the wall between banking and security business 銀行証券垣根論争
issue on a tap basis タップ債として発行する
issue tax 発行税
issue terms 発行条件
issue used in the average 平均株価採用銘柄
issue value 発行価額
issued and outstanding 発行済み
issued at a discount 割引発行された
issued at par 額面発行された
issued capital 発行済資本金
issued capital stock 発行済株式資本金
issued share 発行済株式
issuer 発行会社
issuer defaults 発行体の債務不履行
issuer's cost 発行者費用
issuer's own stock repurchase 自己株券買付
issues in play 買収関連銘柄
issues listed on the over-the-counter market 店頭登録銘柄
issues paper 討議報告書

issues summary 論点整理
issues to shareholder 株主割当
issuing bank 発行銀行
issuing corporation 発行会社
issuing environment 発行環境
issuing house 発行商社
issuing yields 発行利回り
IT-related goods IT 関連商品
ITC (investment tax credit) 投資税額控除
ITC(International Trade Centre) 国際貿易センター
item 項目
item depreciation 個別償却
item in transit 未達項目
item of account 勘定項目
item veto 部分拒否権
itemization 内訳
itemized account 明細勘定
itemized bill 内訳勘定書
itemized deduction 項目別控除
items not affecting cash flows キャッシュフローに影響を与えない項目
items of business 営業種目
items of income 収益項目
items of payment 支払項目
items on income statement 損益計算書項目
itinerant merchants 行商人
ITL (Italian lira) イタリア・リラ
ITO (International Trade Organization) 国際貿易機構
Ito's lemma 伊藤のレンマ
ITS (inter-market trading system) 市場間取引システム
ITU(International Telecommunication Union) 国際電気通信連合

I

J

J curve Jカーブ
J curve effect Jカーブ効果
J-NET J-NET 市場
Jacobson & Ponsbach General Index スウェーデン J&P 総合指数
JAMMO (Japan Multi-Payment Network Management Organization 日本マルチペイメント・ネットワーク運営機構
January barometer 一月指標
Japan Aerospace Exploration Agency 宇宙航空研究開発機構
Japan Agricultural Cooperatives 農業協同組合
Japan Arts Council 日本芸術文化振興会
Japan Association for Financial Planners 日本フィナンシャル・プランナーズ協会
Japan Association of Corporate Executives 経済同友会
Japan Bond Research Institute 日本公社債研究所
Japan Business Federation 日本経済団体連合会（日本経団連）
Japan Chamber of Commerce and Industry 日本商工会議所
Japan Coast Guard 海上保安庁
Japan Commercial Arbitration Association 国際商事仲裁協会
Japan Commodities Fund Association 日本商品投資販売業協会
Japan Credit Industry Association 日本クレジット産業協会
Japan Defense Agency 防衛庁
Japan External Trade Organization 日本貿易振興機構
Japan Federation of Certified Tax Accountants' Associations 日本税理士会連合会
Japan Federation of Economic Organizations 経団連
Japan Finance Corporation for Municipal Enterprises 公営企業金融公庫
Japan Finance Corporation for Small and Medium Enterprise 中小企業金融公庫
Japan Foundation 国際交流基金
Japan fund ジャパン・ファンド
Japan Green Resources Agency 緑資源機構
Japan Highway Public Corporation 日本道路公団
Japan Institute for Labour Policy and Training 労働政策研究・研修機構
Japan Institute of Certified Public Accountants 日本公認会計士協会
Japan International Research Center for Agricultural Sciences 国際農林水産業研究センター
Japan Investors Service 日本インベスターズ・サービス
Japan Meteorological Agency 気象庁
Japan Mint 造幣局
Japan money ジャパン・マネー
Japan National Railways Liquidation Corporation 日本国有鉄道清算事業団
Japan National Tourist Organization 国際観光振興機構
Japan Nuclear Energy Safety Organization 原子力安全基盤機構
Japan Offshore Market 東京オフショア市場
Japan Organization for Employment of the Elderly and Persons with Disabilities 高齢・障害者雇用支援機構
Japan Overseas Development

Corporation 海外貿易開発協会
Japan Patent Office 特許庁
Japan Post 日本郵政公社
Japan premium ジャパン・プレミアム
Japan Scholarship Foundation 日本育英会
Japan Science and Technology Agency 科学技術振興機構
Japan Securities Clearing Corporation 株式会社日本証券クリアリング機構
Japan Securities Dealers Association 日本証券業協会
Japan Securities Depository Center 証券保管振替機構
Japan Securities Finance Company 日本証券金融
Japan Securities Research Institute 日本証券経済研究所
Japan Ship Owners Mutual Protection & Indemnity Association 日本船主責任相互保険組合
Japan Society for the Promotion of Science 日本学術振興会
Japan Tax Association 日本税務協会
Japan Tax Jurisprudence Association 日本税法学会
Japan Water Agency 水資源機構
Japanese 401k Plan 日本版 401 k プラン
Japanese Aviation Insurance Pool 日本航空保険プール
Japanese Bankers Association 全国銀行協会
Japanese banks usance 邦銀ユーザンス
Japanese big bang 日本版ビッグバン
Japanese currency 邦貨
Japanese currency market 円建て市場
Japanese Depositary Receipts 日本預託証書
Japanese equity fund 日本株投信
Japanese government bond futures trading 国債証券先物取引
Japanese Government Bonds held by the Bank of Japan 日本銀行が保有する国債の銘柄別残高
Japanese government-guaranteed debt 日本政府保証債
Japanese Hull Insurer's Union 日本船舶保険連盟
Japanese investment in foreign securities 対外証券投資
Japanese management 日本的経営
Japanese Society of Insurance Science 日本保険学会
Japanese trust certificate 日本信託証券
Japanese yen futures option 日本円先物オプション
Japanese yen short-term interest futures 日本円短期金利先物
jargon 専門語
JAS (Japan Agricultural Standard) 日本農林規格
JASDAQ ジャスダック
JASDEC eligible domestic stock 証券保管振替機構取扱内国株券
JASDEC non-eligible convertible-bond type corporate bonds with new share reservation rights 証券保管振替機構非取扱転換社債型新株予約権付社債券
JASDEC non-eligible domestic stock 証券保管振替機構非取扱内国株券
JB Net (Japan Bond Settlement Network Co.) 債券決済ネットワーク
JB-Net JB ネット
JBIC (Japan Bank for International Cooperation) 国際協力銀行
JCFA (Japan Consumer Finance Association) 日本消費者金融協会
JCIF (Japan Center for International Finance) 国際金融情報センター
JCPA (Japan Commercial Paper Association) 日本 CP 協議会
JCR (Japan Credit Rating Agency) 日本格付研究所
jeopardy 危険

JGB (Japanese government bond) 日本国債
JGB (Japanese government bond) registration system 国債登録制度
JGB borrowing fee rate 国債借入利率
JGB Market Special Participant 国債市場特別参加者
JGB Registration Book 国債登録簿
JGB transactions prior to auction 入札前取引
JGB-MAC (JGB Message Authentication Code) 国債 MAC
JGBs for individual investors 個人向け国債
JGBs of each maturity 各年限の国債
JGS (Japanese government securities) agent 国債代理店
JGS (Japanese government securities) certificate 国債証券
JGS (Japanese government securities) holder 国債権者
JGS (Japanese government securities) holders' title 国債保有者の権利
JGS (Japanese government securities) paying agent 国債支払代理店
JGS (Japanese government securities) settlement service 国債決済業務
JGS paying agents 国債元利金支払取扱店
JGSs (Japanese government securities) 国債
JGSs allocated to each syndicate member in a fixed share 固定シェアでの割当
Jiangsu 江蘇省
Jiangxi 江西省
JICA (Japa International Cooperation Agency) 国際協力機構
Jilin 吉林省
JIS (Japanese Industrial Standards) 日本工業規格
JISC (Japanese Industrial Standards Committee) 日本工業標準調査会
JLL (Japanese leveraged lease) 日本型レバレッジド・リース
JMD (Jamaican dollar) ジャマイカ・ドル
job analysis 職務分析
job applications 有効求職者数
job availability 雇用機会
job classification 職種分類
job cost 個別原価
job cost system 個別原価計算
job creation 雇用創出
job evaluation 職務評価
job function 職能
job hunter 求職者
job lot 小口取引
job order 作業指図書
job order cost system 個別原価計算法
job order costing system 個別原価計算法
job security 雇用確保
job slip 作業伝票
job ticket 作業票
jobber ジョバー
jobbing 回転商い
JOD (Jordanian dinar) ヨルダン・ディナール
joint 共同の
joint account 共同勘定
joint account agreement 共同口座契約
joint action 共同訴訟
joint agreement 連合協約
joint and several 連帯
joint and several bond 連帯証書
joint and several guarantee 連帯保証
joint and several guarantor 連帯保証人
joint and several liability for tax payment 連帯納付責任
joint and several obligation 連帯債務
joint and several obligation for tax liability 連帯納税義務
joint and several tax obligation 国税の連帯納付業務
joint and survivor annuity 共同生存者年金
joint annuity 連生年金
joint audit 共同監査

J

joint bond 合同社債
joint bookrunner ジョイント・ブックランナー
joint control 共同支配
joint cost 結合費用
joint currency float 共同変動相場
joint development 共同開発
joint endowment assurance 連生養老保険
joint enterprise cooperative 企業組合
joint entrustment 共同委託
joint financing 共同融資
joint float 共同フロート
joint floating exchange rate 共同変動相場
joint guarantee 共同保証
joint holding company 共同持株会社
joint inspection 合同検査
joint insured 連生被保険者
joint intervention 協調介入
joint investment 合弁
joint lead ジョイント・リード
joint liability 共同責任
joint life insurance 連生保険
joint management 共同管理
joint marketing 共同販売
joint obligation 合有債務
joint ownership 共有
joint partners 共同パートナー
joint policy 連生保険契約
joint product 連産品
joint purchase 共同買付
joint relationship 共同関係
joint return 合算申告
joint right 合有
joint sales 共同販売
joint stock company 株式会社
joint submission of return 申告書の共同提出
joint surety 連帯保証人
joint survivor annuity 連生生存者年金
joint tax return 合算所得税申告
joint tenancy 合有不動産権
joint trust 合同運用信託
joint undertaking 合弁事業
joint underwriting facilities 割当危険分担制度
joint venture 合弁企業
joint will 共同遺言
joint-and-several liability 連帯保証債務
joint-floating market system 共同変動相場
joint-heir 共同相続人
jointly controlled 共同支配の
jointly controlled assets 共同支配の資産
jointly controlled entity 共同支配企業
jointly controlled operations 共同支配の営業活動体
journal book 仕訳帳
journal entry 仕訳記入
journal ledger 仕訳元帳
journal slip 振替伝票
journal voucher 仕訳証憑
journalizing 仕訳
JPY (Japanese yen) 日本円
JPY cross 円クロス
JPYUSD correction 円ドルの調整
JRTT JNR Settlement Headquarters 国鉄清算事業本部
JSCC (Japan Securities Clearing Corporation) 日本証券クリアリング機構
JSE (Johannesburg Stock Exchange) ヨハネスブルク証券取引所
JST (Japan standard time) 日本標準時間
jubilee 記念日
judge 判事
Judge Impeachment Court 裁判官弾劾裁判所
judgment creditor 判決債権者
judgment debtor 判決債務者
judgment of definite liabilities 債務確定の判定
judgment of exclusion on shareholders' rights 株券の除権判決
judgment set-off 判決債権の相殺
judgmental criteria 判定基準

judicial act 法律行為
judicial definition 判例
judicial judgment 司法審査
judicial legislation 裁判による立法
judicial power 司法権
judicial precedent 判例
judicial proceedings 訴訟手続き
judicial sale 司法処分による売却
jumbo certificate 高額証券
jumbo certificate of deposit 大口預金証書
jumbo issue 大型発行
jump diffusion ジャンプ拡散
jump in the uptrend 一段高
jump process ジャンプ過程
jump rate annuity 利率特進年金
junior accountant 会計士補
junior bond 後順位債券
junior claim 劣後請求権
junior creditor 後順位債権者
junior debt 劣後債務
junior encumbrance 土地に対する後順位の権利
junior issue 下位証券
junior lien 後順位担保
junior lien bond 後順位先取特権付き社債
junior mortgage 後順位抵当
junior securities 劣後証券
junior security 後順位担保
junior stock 劣後株
junior subordinated 下位劣後
junior tranche 下位トランシェ；ジュニア・トランシェ
junk bond ジャンク・ボンド
junk issue ジャンク債
juridical days 開廷日
juridical person 法人
juridical personality 法人格
juridical sale 強制売買
jurisdiction 管轄
jurisdiction of the person 人的管轄権
jurisdiction of the res 対物管轄権
jurisdictional defect 管轄違い
jurisdictional strike 管轄権ストライキ
jurisprudence 法律学
juristic act 法律行為
jury of executive opinion 専門家の共同託宣
jury service 出廷
jusen account 住専口座
just after the opening 寄付きばな
just and equitable principles 信義則
just and equitable principles of transactions 取引の信義則
just compensation 正当な補償
just title 明確な権原
justifiable act 正当行為
justifiable reason to apply 適用する正当な理由
justification 正当化
juvenile comprehensive insurance 子供総合保険
juvenile insurance 子供保険

K

kangaroos オーストラリア株
Kansai International Airport Company, Ltd. 関西国際空港
Kansas City Board of Trade カンザスシティー商品取引所
keep-well agreement 健全性維持契約
keep-well-letter キープ・ウエル・レター
keeping of electronic account books 電子帳簿保存
keeping the currency pair stable 為替の安定
keeping yen capped 円高阻止
Keogh Plan キオ・プラン
kerb market 街頭の証券市場
KES (Kenyan shilling) ケニア・シリング
key assumptions 主要な前提
key currency 基軸通貨
key executive insurance 経営者保険
key factor 主要因
key indicator 主要な指標
key industry 基幹産業
key man insurance 企業幹部保険
key management personnel 重要な役職者
key range breakout 主要抵抗線の突破
key rate 政策金利
key rate cut 公定歩合引下げ
key resistance 主要な抵抗線
key reversal day 相場の大転換日
key risks 主なリスク
key statistics 統計総括表
key theme 重要なテーマ
keymoney 権利金
Keynes effect ケインズ効果
Keynesian ケインズ学派
Keynesian economics ケインズ経済学
Keynesian revolution ケインズ革命
keynote 基調
keystone bond funds キーストン債券ファンド
KHR (Cambodia riel) カンボジア・リエル
kick back キックバック
kick in 献金する
kicker 追加条件
killing 大もうけ
kind of income 所得の種類
kinds of transactions 取引の種類
Kingston Regime キングストン体制
kinked demand curve 屈折需要曲線
Kitchin cycles キチン循環
kite bill 融通手形
kiting 株価操作
kiting check 融通小切手
KLSE (Kuala Lumpur Stock Exchange) クアラルンプール証券取引所
KMF (Comoros franc) コモロ・フラン
knock out 談合競買
knock-down price 値切った価格
knock-down product ノックダウン製品
knock-on effect ノックオン効果
knock-out option ノックアウト・オプション
knock-out option trading ノックアウト・オプション取引
know your customer 顧客熟知規則
knowingly 知りつつ
knowledge 知識
knowledge activities ナレッジ活動
knowledge and discernment 見識
knowledge engineering 知識工学
knowledge industry 知識産業
knowledge intensive industry 知識集約産業
Kondratieff wave コンドラチェフの波
KPW (North Korean won) 北朝鮮ウォン

KRW (Korean won) 韓国ウォン
kura ken 蔵券
KWD (Kuwaiti dinar) クエート・ディナール
KYD (Cayman Islands dollar) ケイマン諸島ドル
KZT (Kazakhstan tenge) カザフスタン・テンゲ

L

L/C (letter of credit) 信用状
L/C (letter of credit) beneficiary 信用状受益者
L/C (letter of credit) confirming bank 信用状確認銀行
LAB (local authority bond) 地方債
labeled price 売価
labor & material payment bond 賃金下請代金支払保証証券
labor account 賃金勘定
labor agreement 労働協約
labor audit 労務監査
labor coefficient 労働係数
labor content 労務費用部分
labor cost 労賃
labor credit association 労働金庫
labor dispute 労働争議
labor economics 労働経済学
labor efficiency 作業効率
labor force 労働力
labor income 労働所得
labor input 労働投入量
labor insurance premium 労働保険料
labor intensive 労働集約
labor law 労働法
labor legislation 労働立法
Labor Management Organization for USFJ Employees, Incorporated Administrative Agency 駐留軍等労働者労務管理機構
labor market 労働市場
labor market data 雇用統計
labor negotiation 労使交渉
labor rate standard 賃率標準
labor rate variance 賃率差異
labor regulations 労働法規
labor relations 労使関係
labor saving 省力化の
labor share 労働分配率
labor time variance 作業時間差異
labor trouble 労使紛争
labor turnover 離職率
labor union 労働組合
labor variance 労務費差異
labor-intensive industry 労働集約的産業
Labour Relations Commission for Seafarers 船員労働委員会
lack 欠ける
lack of intervention 市場介入の手控え
lackluster 伸び悩みの
ladder portfolio management ラダー型運用
Laffer curve ラッファー曲線
lag against 下方修正される
lag analysis ラグ分析
lag effect ラグ効果
lag indicator 遅行指数
lagging 出遅れている
lagging profit 利益の足かせ
lagging series 遅行系列
lagging stock 出遅れ株
laid-down cost 到着原価
laissez-faire レッセフェール
LAK (Lao kip) ラオス・キップ
lame duck 除名会員
land 土地
land account 土地勘定
land and building 土地建物
land category 地目
land charges 土地負担
land contract 土地売買契約
land cost 用地費
land development tax 宅地開発税
land expropriation law 土地収用法
land expropriation right 土地収用権
land for residence 住宅用土地
land for sale 販売用土地
land grading cost 土地造成費
land grant 土地供与

land improvement 土地改良
land improvement enterprise 土地改良事業
land improvement expenses 土地改良費
land law 土地法
land leasehold 借地権
land ledger 土地台帳
land lot 土地
land lot without construction 更地
Land office 国有地管理局
land ownership 土地所有
land price 地価
land proprietor 土地所有者
land purchase for specified business 特定事業の用地買収
land quality terms 用地品質条件
land reform 土地改良
land registration 土地登記
land registry office 土地登記所
land required for 用地
land tax 地租
land tax register book 土地課税台帳
land taxation 土地税制
land taxes reform 土地税制改革
land tenant 土地保有者
land tenure 土地保有
land transportation industry 陸運業
land trust 土地信託
land value tax 地価税
Land Value Tax Law 地価税法
landed estate 地所
landing tax 入国税
landowner 土地所有者
languish 低迷する
languishing 活気を失う
lapping たらい廻し（売掛金の）
LAPR (life assurance premium relief) 生命保険料控除
lapse 失効
lapse of insurance policy 保険契約の失効
lapse of the leasehold 借地権の期間経過
lapse rate 失効率
lapsed contract 失効契約
lapsed days 経過日数
lapsed option 失効オプション
lapsed share 失効株
lapsed time 経過時間
lapsing schedule of fixed assets 固定資産増減明細表
large acquisition 大型買収
large amount deposit interest 大口預金金利
large amount time deposit 大口定期
large amount transaction 大口取引
large block trading 大口取引
large cap stock 大型株
large capital stock 大型株
large change 大きな変動
large company 大企業
large credit 高額債権
large debtor 大口債務者
large depreciable property 大規模償却資産
large holding report 大量保有報告書
large inflation premium 高水準のインフレ・プレミアム
large institutional investors 大手機関投資家
large investment bank 大投資銀行
large lot trading 大口取引
large order 大口注文
large positions 大口建玉
large retirement 大量退職
large risks 巨大リスク
large scale bond issue 債券の大量発行
large shareholder 大株主
large stock dividend 高率株式配当
larger-than-expected rate cut 予想以上の金利引下げ
largess 気前のよい援助
Laspeyres formula ラスパイレス方程式
last close price 前日終値
last cost method 最終仕入原価法
last day of trading 最終取引日
last heir 最終相続人
last payment date 払込期日

L

last price 最終値段
last purchase method 最終仕入原価法
last quotation 引値
last resort ラスト・リゾート
last resort lender 最後の貸し手
last sale 直近売り
last sale price 直前の約定値段
last survivor annuity 最終生存者年金
last three months of a bond life 債券の満期日前の３ヵ月
last trading day 取引最終日
last-in first-out basis 後入先出基準
late charge 遅延損害金
late fee 遅延損害金
late payment charge 遅延損害金
late presentation 呈示の遅延
late shipment 船積遅延
latent ambiguity 潜在的意味不明
latent assets 含み資産
latent call option 潜在的コール・オプション
latent demand 潜在需要
latent equity holdings 保有株の含み
latent loss 含み損
latent return 含み収益
latent unemployment 潜在失業
latent warrant 潜在ワラント
later bid 後に行われた買呼値
later offer 後に行われた売呼値
latter half 下半期
latter half of the year 後期
lattice approach 格子法
launch ローンチ
launch date 発行開始日
launch spread ローンチ・スプレッド
launching of bonds 起債
laundered money ローンダード・マネー
law 法律
Law Amending Part of the Commercial Code 商法等の一部を改正する法律
law book 判例集
law breaking act 違法行為
Law Concerning Amalgamation and Conversion of Financial Institutions 金融機関の合併及び転換に関する法律
Law concerning Book-entry Transfer of Corporate and Other Debt Securities 社債等の振替に関する法律
Law Concerning Central Securities Depository and Book-Entry Delivery 株券等の保管及び振替に関する法律（保振法）
Law Concerning Central Securities Depository and Book-Entry Transfer of Stock Certificates and Other Securities 株券等の保管及び振替に関する法律
Law Concerning Government Bonds 国債に関する法律
Law Concerning Preferred Equity Contribution to Cooperative Financial Institution 協同組織金融機関の優先出資に関する法律
Law Concerning Reserve Deposit Requirement System 準備預金制度に関する法律
law concerning restrictions on the acceptance of subscription, deposit and interest rate, etc. 出資の受入れ，預り金及び金利等の取締りに関する法律（出資法）
law concerning restrictions on the maximum interest rate 利息制限法
Law Concerning Securities Investment Trust and Securities Investment Companies 証券投資信託及び証券投資法人に関する法律
Law Concerning Specified Arbitration for Promotion of Reconciliation of Specified Liabilities, etc. 特定債務等の調整の促進のための特定調停に関する法律
Law Concerning the Regulation of Counterfeit Currency and Securities 通貨及証券模造取締法
Law Concerning the Regulation of Manufacturing of Watermarked

Paper すき入紙製造取締法
Law Concerning the Regulation of Securities Resembling Paper Currency 紙幣類似証券取締法
law concerning the regulations on business related to specified receivables 特定債権法
Law Concerning the Unit of Currency and the Issuance of Coins 通貨の単位及び貨幣の発行等に関する法律
law enforced territory 法施行地
law enforcement regime 法律施行体系
Law Establishing the Cabinet Office 内閣設置法
law for foreign securities company 外国証券業法
Law for Registration of Corporate Bonds 社債等登録法（社登法）
law of diminishing marginal utility 限界効用逓減の法則
law of diminishing return 収益逓減の法則
law of equation of reciprocal demand 相互需要均等の法則
law of increasing public expenditures 経費膨張の原則
law of indifference 一物一価の法則
law of large numbers 大数の法則
law of member firms 会員の法
law of nations 国際法
law of nature 自然法
law of obligations 債権法
Law of Procedure in Non-Contentious Cases 非訟事件手続法
law of ship's flag 旗国法
law of substitution 代替法律
law of succession 相続法
law office 法律事務所
law on bills 手形法
Law on Foreign Securities Firms 外国証券会社に関する法律
Law on Securitization of Specified Assets 特定資産の流動化に関する法律
law relating to tax reduction and postponement of collection for disaster victims 災害減免法
law with expiration date 時限立法
lawful 適法の
lawful age 成年
lawful currency 法定通貨
lawful money 法定通貨
laws and regulations 法令
laws of realty 物権法
laws related to banknotes 銀行券に関する法律
lawsuit 訴訟
lawyer 弁護士
lawyer's fee 弁護士料
lawyer's liability 弁護士責任
lawyer's liability insurance 弁護士賠償責任保険
lax business practices 怠慢な事務処理
lay 素人の
lay-days 陸揚期間
layer 階層
layer of management 管理階層
layoff レイオフ
LBO (leveraged buyout) fund LBO ファンド
LBP (Lebanese pound) レバノン・ポンド
L/C margin money 信用状開設保証金
LCE (London Commodity Exchange) ロンドン商品取引所
LCH (London Clearing House) ロンドン・クリアリング・ハウス
LCM (lower of cost or market) 定価法
LDC (less developed country) 発展途上国
lead 見込客リスト
lead analyst 主任アナリスト
lead bank 幹事銀行
lead manager 主幹事
lead managing underwriter 主幹事会社
lead time リード・タイム
lead underwriting securities company 幹事証券会社
leader of long side 買本尊

leader of short side 売本尊
leadership personality 指導力
leading case 指導的判例
leading counsel 主任弁護人
leading domestic demand 内需を引っ張って
leading edge 最先端
leading series 先行系列
leading share 花形株
leading stock 先導銘柄
leads and lags リーズ・アンド・ラグズ
leak of know-how ノウハウ漏洩
leakage 漏損
lean staff 少数精鋭
leap 大幅増
LEAPS (long-term equity anticipation securities) 長期株式期待証券
learning curve 学習曲線
lease リース
lease accounting リース会計
lease accounting standards リース会計基準
lease acquisition cost リース取得費用
lease agreement リース契約
lease back リースバック
lease backed note リース債権担保証券
lease bond 賃貸借保証
lease classification リース分類
lease contract 賃貸契約
lease deposits リース預託金
lease financing リース金融
lease in perpetuity 永代借地権
lease income リース収益
lease liability リース債務
lease obligation bond リース財源債
lease of land 土地賃貸権
lease of property 資産の賃貸
lease payment リース料
lease payment index リース支払額の指数
lease payment receivable リース料受取額
lease payments payable for the period 期間のリース料
lease period リース期間
lease property リース物件
lease provision リース契約条項
lease purchase agreement リース買取契約
lease receivable リース債権
lease tenant right 借地権
lease term リース期間
lease transactions リース取引
lease-up リースアップ
leaseback リースバック
leaseback transaction リースバック取引
leased asset リース資産
leased equipment liability リース設備資産の債務
leased land 賃借地
leased land under a convention 協定借地
leased property リース資産
leasehold deposit 敷金
leasehold estate 賃借不動産
leasehold improvement 賃貸物件の改良
leasehold improvement account 造作勘定
leasehold insurance 賃借保険
leasehold interest 利用権
leaseholder 借地権者
leasing activity リース行為
leasing arrangement リース契約条件
leasing business リース業務
leasing company リース会社
leasing contract リース契約
leasing industry リース産業
least less developed countries 後発発展途上国
least-squares method 最小二乗法
leave order 指値注文預り
leaving method 留置法
leaving rate on hold 金利を据え置く
leaving rate unchanged 金利を据え置く
ledger 元帳
ledger account 元帳勘定

ledger assets 元帳資産
ledger clerk 元帳係
ledger folio 元帳ページ数
ledger of accounts 口座簿
ledger of customer accounts 顧客口座簿
ledger of listed securities 上場有価証券原簿
ledger of participant accounts 参加者口座簿
ledger transfer 元帳振替
left side of the equation 等式の左側
legacy 遺産
legal 適法の
legal ability person 能力者
legal action 訴訟
legal adviser 法律顧問
legal age 法定年齢
legal aid services 法律相談
legal approvals 法的な承認
legal basis 法的根拠
legal benefit 法定給付
legal boundary 法の枠組
legal capacity 行為能力
legal capital 法定資本
legal changes 法律の変更
legal claim 法的請求権
legal community 法曹界
legal compliance 法令遵守
legal contract 適法契約
legal cost 法律費用
legal counsel 顧問弁護士
legal counterparty 法律の定める相手方
legal defeasance リーガル・ディフィーザンス
legal department 法務部
legal dispute 係争案件
Legal Division 法規課
legal document 法律書類
legal documentation 法的書類
legal durable years 法定耐用年数
legal duty 法律上の義務
legal earned surplus reserve 法定利益準備金
legal effect 法的効力
legal entity 人格；法的実体
legal estate 不動産権
legal evidence 法律上の証拠
legal exemption from income tax 基礎控除
legal expense insurance 訴訟費用保険
legal expert 法律専門家
legal factor 法的要因
legal fee 弁護士報酬
legal final maturity 法律上の最終期限
legal form 法的形式
legal form of equity interest 持ち分の法的形式
legal framework 法的枠組
legal fraud 法定詐欺
legal fruits 法定果実
legal guardian 法定後見人
legal heir 家督
legal identity 法人格
legal inefficiency 法律による非効率
legal interest rate 法定利率
legal investment 適法投資
legal jurisdiction 法制度
legal lending limit 法定貸出限度枠
legal liability 法定責任
legal liability insurance 法定賠償責任保険
legal lien 法的リーエン
legal limit 法的制約
legal liquidation 法的整理
legal list 適法投資リスト
legal matter 法律問題
legal merger 法的合併
legal monopoly 法的独占
legal mortgage 普通法上のモーゲージ
legal notice 適法な通知
legal obligation 法的債務
Legal Office 国際局外国為替室
legal office 法律事務所
legal organ 正当な権限を有する機関
legal ownership 法律上の所有
legal person 法人
legal portion of legacy 法定相続分
legal possession 法律上の占有

L

legal precedent 法律上の先例
legal presumption 法律上の推定
legal procedure 裁判手続
legal proceedings 法的手段
legal process 合法的手続
legal rate of interest 法定金利
legal relations 法律関係
legal relationship 法的関係
legal relationship in tax 租税法律関係
legal representation 法律代理人
legal representative 法定代理人
legal reserve 法定準備金
legal reserve for security transactions 証券取引責任準備金
legal reserve insurance 法定準備金積立保険
legal resistance 法的対抗策
legal responsibility 法的責任
legal restrictions 法律上の制限
legal right 法的権利
legal right of set-off 相殺する法的権利
legal risk 法的リスク
legal section 法務部
legal services 法律業務
legal status 法人格；法律上の身分
legal status of issuance 起債根拠法；発行根拠法
legal subrogation 法定代位
legal tax cut 減税
legal tender 法定通貨
legal tender note 強制通用力ある紙幣
legal term 法定期限
legal terminology 法律用語
legal theory 法理論
legal title 普通法上の所有権
legal transfer 法的譲渡
legal valuation 法定評価
legal valuation method of inventory 法定棚卸評価法
legal violation 法律の抵触
legal welfare expense 法定福利費
legally bankrupt borrower 破綻先
legally defined payment instrument that should not be refused by any creditor in satisfaction of any debt 強制通用力
legally protected from 法的に保全されている
legally secured portion 遺留分
legatee 遺産受取人
legend 凡例
legibility 読み易さ
legislation 立法措置
legislative action 法的措置
legislative change 法令による変更
legislative department 立法部
legislative risk 法的リスク
legislature 立法府
LEI (leading economic indicators) 景気先行指標
lemon 運用成績の悪い投資
lender 貸手
lender bank 貸出銀行
lender of last resort 最終の貸し手
lender's preference 貸手の選好
lender's risk 貸手の危険
lending 貸付
lending a street name 名義貸し
lending ability 貸出能力
lending agreement 貸付契約
lending and borrowing contracts for securities 有価証券の消費貸借契約
lending at a premium プレミアム貸付
lending attitude 貸出姿勢
lending criteria 貸出基準
lending of development funds 開発資金貸付
lending of funds against securities collateral 有価証券担保貸付
lending of securities 有価証券の貸付
lending operation 貸出業務
lending or borrowing of securities 有価証券の貸借
lending policy 貸出政策
lending practice 融資慣行
lending rate 貸出金利
lending securities 貸し証券
lending standards 与信基準
lending stock 貸株

L

lending terms 貸出条件
lending window 貸付窓口
length of service 在職期限
Leontief's paradox レオンチェフ逆説
LESOP (leveraged employee stock ownership plan) レバレッジド従業員持株制度
less 控除して
less fees 手数料差し引き後
less-developed country 開発途上国
lessee 賃借人
lesser evil 問題の少ない制度
lessor 賃貸人
let 賃貸
letter bond 非登録債
letter of acceptance 落札決定書
letter of administration 遺産管財状
letter of advice on the drawing of bills 手形振出通知
letter of allotment 割当状
letter of attorney 委任状
letter of award 落札決定書
letter of confirmation of collateral 担保差入証
letter of credit advising bank 信用状通知銀行
letter of indemnity 損害補填契約書
letter of intent 合意確認書
letter of last instructions 最終指示書
letter of license 支払期日延期書面
letter of recommendation 推薦書
letter of undertaking 念書
letter or credit issuing bank 信用状発行銀行
letter securities 非登録私募債
letter stock 売却制限株式
letters denoting credit 信用を表すアルファベット
letters patent 特許証
letters to stockholders 株主へのメッセージ
level 水準
level accident insurance 標準傷害保険
level annual premium method 平準積み立て方式
level annuity 定額年金
level benefit 定額給付
level contribution 平準拠出
level debt service 均等債務返済
level funding cost 平準積立コスト
level income option 収入平準化オプション
level load 定率手数料
level of consumer confidence 消費者信頼度
level of education 教育水準
level of employment 雇用水準
level of living 生活水準
level of precision 精度の水準
level of price 物価水準
level of production 生産水準
level off 横ばいになる
level pay floating rate note 定額支払変動利付債
level payment 元利均等払い
level premium 平準保険料
level premium reserve 平準保険料式積立金
level term insurance 定額定期保険
level unchanged 水準維持
level yield 一定利回り
leveling effect on the gap ギャップの縮小
leverage レバレッジ
leverage change レバレッジ変化
leverage effect レバレッジ効果
leverage factor レバレッジ係数
leverage factor ratio レバレッジ比率
leverage ratio 負債比率
leverage test 負債比率
leveraged buyout レバレッジド・バイアウト
leveraged finance securities レバレッジド・ファイナンス証券
leveraged holding レバレッジド・ホールディング
leveraged investment company レバレッジド投資会社
leveraged lease レバレッジド・リース
leveraged loan レバレッジド・ローン

L

leveraged option レバレッジド・オプション
leveraged position レバレッジド・ポジション
leveraged recap レバレッジド資本再構成
leveraged recapitalization レバレッジド・リキャピタライゼーション
leveraged stock レバレッジド・ストック
leveraged strategic acquisition レバレッジド・ストラテジック・アクイジション
leveraged swap レバレッジド・スワップ
levy 課金；課す
levy in kind 物納税
levy of attachment 財産差押
levy of tax 課税
liabilities account 負債勘定
liabilities and capital 負債及資本
liabilities and capital accounts 負債資本勘定
liabilities and shareholders' equity 負債及び資本の部
liabilities and stockholders' equity 負債及び資本の部
liabilities exceeding assets 債務超過
liabilities for guarantee 保証債務
liabilities for guarantee against repairs 修繕保証引当金
liabilities in substance 実質は負債
liabilities incurred 引き受けた負債
liabilities portfolio 債務ポートフォリオ
liabilities reserve 負債性引当金
liability 負債
liability accounting 負債会計
liability by segment セグメント別負債
liability component 負債部分
liability for damage 責任の所在
liability for endorsement 保証債務
liability for health care benefit 医療給付金債務
liability hedge 負債ヘッジ
liability held for trading 売買目的で保有する負債
liability insurance 責任保険
liability item 負債項目
liability limits 填補限度額
liability management 負債管理
liability method 負債法
liability of estimated amount 見積による債務
liability rate 負債の金利
liability ratio 負債利率
liability reserve 責任準備金
liability reserve valuation 責任準備金評価
liability risk management 債務リスク管理
liability side 負債側
liability structure 負債構造
liability swap 債務スワップ
liability under litigation 訴訟の債務
liability without fault 無過失責任
liaison 駐在員
liaison office 連絡事務所
Liaoning 遼寧省
liberalization of capital transaction 資本取引自由化
liberalization of exchange control 為替自由化
liberalization of interest rate 金利の自由化
liberalization of trade 貿易自由化
liberalization rate 自由化率
liberty 自由
liberty of contract 契約の自由
LIBID (London inter-bank bid rate) ロンドン銀行間取り手金利
Libor ライボー
license agreement ライセンス契約
license expense 免許料
license fee 使用許諾料
license renewal 免許更新
license tax 免許税
licensed tax accountant 税理士
licensing system 免許制
licensor 使用許諾者

lien リーエン
lien holder 抵当権者
lien of partners 組合員先取特権
lien plan 保険金削減支払制度
lien theory 先取特権理論
lienor 留置権者
life 期間
life and annuity 生命保険及び年金
life and general coverage 生損保契約
Life and Health Insurance Guaranty Association 生命・健康保険保証協会
Life and Health Insurance Guaranty Association Model Act 生命・健康保険保証協会モデル法
Life and Health Insurance Guaranty Fund 生命・健康保険保証基金
life annuity certain 保証期間付終身年金
life annuity insurance 終身年金保険
life assurance 生命保険
life beneficiary 生命保険受取人
life consultant ライフ・コンサルタント
life cover 生命保険保障
life cycle ライフ・サイクル
life estate 生涯不動産権
life expectancy 平均余命
life fund 生命保険資金
life income policy 終身年金保険
Life Income Tax Act of 1959 1959年生命保険会社所得税法
life insurance 生命保険
life insurance annuity 年金生命保険
life insurance assets 生命保険資産
Life Insurance Association of Japan 生命保険協会
life insurance company 生命保険会社
life insurance company purchase 生保買い
life insurance company taxation 生命保険会社課税
life insurance contract 生命保険契約
life insurance cost 生命保険コスト
life insurance in force 生命保険契約保有高
life insurance insolvency fund 生命保険保障基金
life insurance market 生命保険市場
life insurance payout 生命保険支払額
life insurance policy 生命保険証券
life insurance premium 生命保険料
life insurance premiums deduction 生命保険料控除
life insurance trust 生命保険信託
life interest 一生間の権利
life of bond 債券の償還までの期間
life of hedge ヘッジの期間
life of option オプション期間
life of policy 保険証券の期間
life protection product 生活保障商品
life stock 生保株
life table 生命表
life tenancy 永代借地人
life underwriter 生命保険募集人
life underwriting 生保契約査定；生命保険販売
life-long education 生涯教育
life-to-call 期前償還までの据置期間
lifestyle infrastructure 生活基盤
lifetime annuity 終身年金
lifetime employment commitment 終身雇用
lifetime insurance 終身保険
lifetime learning credit 生涯教育控除
lifetime monthly benefit 終身保険月額給付
lifetime reverse mortgage 終身リバース・モーゲージ
lifetime wages 生涯賃金
LIFFE (London International Financial Futures and Options Exchange) ロンドン国際金融先物オプション取引所
LIFO (last-in, first-out) method 後入先出法
lifo adaptation of retail method 後入先出売価還元法
LIFO reserve 後入先出法引当金
lifting charge 為替取扱手数料

L

lifting of a leg 取引の一方を解消
lifting of gold embargo 金輸出解禁
lifting of regulatory disposition 処置の解除
lifting of yen 円の買い支え
light and fuel expenses 光熱費
light oil delivery tax 軽油引取税
light vehicle tax 軽自動車税
like goods 同種商品
like transaction 類似する取引
likelihood 尤度
likelihood ratio test 尤度比検定
LIMEAN (London interbank mean rate) ロンドン銀行間仲値金利
limit calculation 指値算定法
limit down ストップ安
limit high ストップ高
limit low ストップ安
limit of a loan 貸付限度
limit of deductible of entertainment expense 交際費の繰入限度額
limit of indemnity 補償限度額
limit of liability 塡補責任限度額
limit of overdrawn account 過振限度
limit of price 値段の限度
limit of risk 最高保険金額
limit of the range of price fluctuation 制限値幅
limit on close order 引値指値注文
limit on recognition 認識上の制限
limit order 指値注文
limit order information system 指値注文情報システム
limit price 指値
limit to provision for bad debt reserve 貸倒引当金勘定繰入限度額
limit up ストップ高
limitation 制限
limitation factor 制限的要因
limitation for claiming payment of dividends 配当金の除斥期間
limitation of actions 出訴期限
limitation of trading on proprietary account 自己計算による取引の制限
limitation on deposit payoff ペイオフ
limitation on dividend 配当制限
limitation on foreign tax credit 外国税額の控除限度額
limitation on interlocking 業務兼業制限
limitation on proprietary right of land 上地
limitation on the deductible amount of donation 寄付金損金参入限度額
limitations on disposal 資産譲渡制限
limited annuity 有期限年金
limited audit 限定監査
limited branching 特定地域支店設置
limited changes 限定的な変更
limited convertibility 制限付転換性
limited discretion 限定的裁量
limited distribution 数量制限付分売
limited exceptions 制限的な例外
limited factor 制限因子
limited form of title 限定された形の権原
limited guarantee 制限的保証
limited income method 所得源泉説
limited legal tender 制限法貨
limited liability 有限責任
limited liability company 有限責任会社
limited life 期限付の
limited life assets 有限耐用年数資産
limited life preferred equity 期限付優先株
limited life preferred stock 期限付優先株
limited obligation bond 特定財源債
limited offering 限定募集
limited opinion 限定意見
limited partnership 合資会社；有限責任組合
limited payment insurance 有限払込保険
limited policy 限定支払保険証書；特定保険
limited purpose trust company 限定目的信託会社

limited recourse 制限付償還請求権
limited recourse finance 限定リコース・ファイナンス
limited recourse loan 制限償還請求権付きローン
limited recourse obligation リミテッド・リコース債務
limited retention 自己保有限度額
limited review 部分的な検討
limited risk 限定リスク
limited tax bond 特定税源債
limited tax liability 制限納税義務
limited tax rate 制限税率
limited to 限定された
limited trading authorization 限定売買取引認可
limited useful life 有限の耐用年数
limited warranty 限定保証
limits of corridor 回廊の制限額
line department ライン部門
line graph 折れ線グラフ
line item 表示項目
line items of income statement 損益計算書表示項目
line of business 営業科目
line of credit 貸出予約枠
line of discount 割引限度
line-by-line reporting 科目ごとの報告
linear accelerator 線型加速度係数
linear bond リニア債
linear correlation 線形相関
linear interpolation 線形補間
linear model 線形モデル
linear programming 線型計画法
linear regression 線型回帰
linear warranty 承継担保
link note リンク債
linked bond リンク債
linked contract 連動契約
linked presentation ひも付表示
linked to the performance of other funds 他ファンド連動型の
linker market インフレ連動債市場
linkers 物価連動債
linking index 連動指数
linking price index 連動物価指数
lion's share 最も大きな比率
liquefied petroleum and gas tax 石油ガス税
liquid assets 流動資産
liquid capital 流動資本
liquid deposit 流動性預金
liquid investment 流動性のある投資
liquid market 流動性のある市場
liquid part 流動部分
liquid reserve 流動性準備金
liquid stock 流通銘柄
liquid-asset hypothesis 流動資産仮説
liquidate 現金化する
liquidate an enterprise 企業を清算する
liquidated account 確定勘定
liquidated company 清算済会社
liquidated corporation 清算した法人
liquidated damages 損害賠償額
liquidated debt 確定債務
liquidating partner 清算人
liquidation 換金；整理
liquidation account 清算勘定
liquidation affairs 清算事務
liquidation and rationalization 整理合理化
liquidation balance sheet 清算貸借対照表
liquidation dividend 清算配当
liquidation event 清算事由
liquidation final return 清算確定申告
liquidation income due to merger 合併による清算所得
liquidation income from dissolution 解散による清算所得
liquidation income tax 清算所得税
liquidation of assets 資産売却
liquidation of claim 債権の弁済
liquidation of clearing margin 取引証拠金の換金
liquidation of duties 関税査定
liquidation of inventory 棚卸資産の取崩し
liquidation of investments 投資の売却

L

liquidation of liabilities 債務の処理
liquidation of mortgage モーゲージの清算
liquidation of seized property 差押財産の換価
liquidation of speculative accounts 玉整理
liquidation office 清算事務所
liquidation preference 清算優先権
liquidation price 清算値
liquidation proceedings 清算手続
liquidation profit and loss 清算損益
liquidation value 清算価値
liquidator 清算人
liquidator in bankruptcy 破産清算人
liquidator of a corporation 会社の精算人
liquidity 流動性
liquidity adjusted 流動性調整済みの
liquidity analysis 流動性分析
liquidity creation 流動性創出
liquidity crisis 流動性危機
liquidity crunch 信用逼迫
liquidity demand 流動性需要
liquidity differential 流動性格差
liquidity dilemma 流動性ジレンマ
liquidity diversification 流動性分散
liquidity effect 流動性効果
liquidity facility 信用供与枠
liquidity in benchmark bonds 指標銘柄の流動性
liquidity in hand 手元流動性
liquidity index 流動指数
liquidity management 資金繰り；流動性管理
liquidity needs 流動性のニーズ
liquidity of the banking system 銀行流動性
liquidity of the market 市場の流動性
liquidity position 流動性ポジション
liquidity preference 流動性選好
liquidity preference hypothesis 流動性選好仮説
liquidity preference theory 流動性選好理論
liquidity premium 流動性プレミアム
liquidity ratio 流動性比率
liquidity risk 流動性リスク
liquidity scarcity 流動性の不足
liquidity scheme 流動性スキーム
liquidity shortage 資金不足
liquidity transfer 資金移動
liquidity trap 流動性のワナ
liquidity-driven issue 流動性相場株
liquidity-driven market 流動性指向相場
liquidity-motivated transactions 流動性動機による売買
Liquor Tax and Industry Division 酒税課
list of assets 財産目録
list of beneficial shareholders 実質株主名簿
list of differences between 対照表
list of holders of fractional shares 端株原簿
list of members 会員名簿
list of property 財産目録
list of shareholders 株主名簿
list quotation 相場表
listed bond market 上場債券市場
listed bonds 上場債券
listed brand 上場銘柄
listed company 上場会社
Listed Comparison System 上場株式照合システム
listed firm 上場企業
listed foreign stocks 上場外国株式
listed futures 上場先物
listed issue 上場銘柄
listed options 上場オプション
listed product 上場商品
listed securities 上場証券
listed stock 上場株
listed stock price index 上場株価指数
listed stocks used in the computation of indices 指数用上場株式
listed warrants 上場新株引受権証券
listing 上場；不動産仲介委託契約
listing agent 上場代理人

L

listing agreement 上場契約
listing application 上場申請
listing broker 不動産仲介業者
listing by application 申請による上場
listing examination 上場審査
listing examination criteria 上場審査基準
listing examination fees 上場審査費
listing fee 新規上場料
listing of new stocks 新株券の上場
listing of stock 株式の上場
listing on Mothers マザーズへの上場
listing on the First Section 一部上場
listing on the Second Section 二部上場
listing regulations 上場規程
listing requirements 上場要件
litigation 訴訟
litigation on personnel 人的訴訟
litigation settlements 訴訟の解決
little guy 小口投資家
livery 占有引渡し
livestock insurance 動物保険
living 生計
living account 活動勘定
living benefit 生前給付
living benefit company 生前給付会社
living benefit policy 生前給付保険
living cost 生計費
living expenses 生活費
living proceeds 生前給付金
living standard 生活水準
living trust 生前信託
LKR (Sri Lanka rupee) スリランカ・ルピー
Lloyd's policy ロイズ証券
LLR (lender of last resort) 最後の貸し手
LME (London Metal Exchange) ロンドン金属取引所
load factor 負荷率
load spread option 手数料配分オプション
loading 付加保険料
loading charges 積込費用
loading surplus 付加益
loan account 貸付勘定
loan age ローンの既払い年数
loan agreement 金銭貸借契約
loan amortization 分割返済
loan amount 融資額
loan application 融資申込み
loan application examination 融資審査
loan arrangement 貸付の取決め
loan asset management 融資資産運用
loan asset quality 貸出資産の質
loan association 金融組合
loan at nil 無利息融資
loan attachment 債権差押え
loan balance ローン残高
loan business on real estate 不動産貸付業
loan business on real property 不動産担保貸付業
loan capital 借入資本
loan claims ローン債権
loan classification 債権区分
loan commitment 融資の約束
loan commitments 貸出コミットメント
loan conditions 融資条件
loan consent 融資承諾
loan exposure 貸出リスク
loan extension 借款供与
loan facilities for financing bond trading 公社債流通金融制度
loan for carrying inventories 滞貨融資
loan for consumption 消費ローン
loan for exchange 交換貸借
loan foreclosure order 債権差押命令
loan from banks 銀行借入
loan fund 貸付資金
loan guarantee fee 貸し出し保証手数料
loan guarantees for defense industry 国防産業に対する融資保証
loan insurance 融資保険
loan interest rate 貸出利率
loan ledger 貸付元帳
loan limit 融資限度

L

loan loss 貸倒れ
loan loss allowance 貸倒引当金
loan loss coverage 債権損失カバレッジ
loan loss provision 貸倒引当金
loan loss provisioning 貸倒引当金の計上
loan loss reserve 貸倒引当金
loan of subscription payment funds 払込融資貸付
loan on bill 手形貸付
loan on bond 債券担保貸付
loan on deeds 証書貸付
loan on mortgage 不動産抵当貸付
loan on personal guarantee 保証貸し
loan on policy 証書貸付
loan on real estate 不動産貸付
loan on real property 不動産貸付
loan on security 担保貸し
loan origination ローン開始時期
loan origination fee 融資組成手数料
L
loan outstanding 借入金残高
loan participation ローンパーティシペーション
loan payable 借入金
loan period 融資期間
loan portfolio ローン・ポートフォリオ
loan position ローン・ポジション
loan rate 貸出金利
loan receivable 貸付金
loan receivable in securities 貸付有価証券
loan received 借款享受
loan redemption 借入金償還
loan repayment 借入の返済
loan restrictions 融資規制
loan risk 融資リスク
loan sales ローン債権売買
loan secured by deposit 預金担保貸付
loan secured by government bonds or corporate debentures 公社債担保貸付
loan secured by intellectual property rights 知的所有権担保融資
loan secured by real estate 不動産抵当貸付金
loan secured by securities 有価証券担保貸付金
loan securities 貸付証券
loan shark 高利貸し
loan size ローンの額
loan society 金融組合
loan spread ローン・スプレッド
loan stock 貸株；長期社債
loan subparticipation 貸出債権分売
loan swap ローン・スワップ
loan term 融資年限
loan to affiliated companies 系列融資
loan to affiliated company 関係会社貸付金
loan to customers account 貸付金勘定
loan to director 役員貸付金
loan to financial institutions 金融機関貸付金
loan to subsidiary 子会社貸付金
loan transaction 貸借取引
loan trust 貸付信託
loan trust for small enterprises 中小企業貸出信託
loan value 貸付価額；貸付限度額
loan with third party's guarantee 保証付貸付
loan without interest 無利子の金銭貸与
loan written off 償却債権
loan-loss provisions and write-offs 貸倒引当・償却
loan-loss ratio 貸倒率
loan-to-value ratio 融資比率
loanable fund 貸付資金
loanable funds theory 貸出資金理論
loanable issue 貸借銘柄
loanable resources 貸出資金
loanable value 掛目
loaned flat 無利息貸付
loaned securities liabilities 担保差入部分
loans and bills discounted 貸出金
loans and bills discounted accounts 貸出金勘定
loans and discounts by industry 業種

別貸出統計
loans and investments 投融資
loans and receivables 貸付金及び債権
loans at risk 危険債権
loans by private financial institutions 民間金融機関貸出
loans by public financial institutions 公的金融機関貸出
loans collateralized by bills, JGSs, or other marketable securities 手形・国債その他の有価証券を担保とする貸付
loans disclosed subject to the Financial Revitalization Law 金融再生法開示債権
loans for which accrued interest is not shown 未収利息不計上貸出金
loans in arrears 延滞債権
loans in bankruptcy and regeneration 破綻更生債権
loans in margin transactions 信用取引貸付金
loans in the pool プール内のローン
loans outstanding per employee 従業員一人当り貸出金残高
loans overdue for three months or longer 3ヶ月以上延滞債権
loans past due three months or more 履行期日到来後3ヶ月以上経過した債権
loans received 貸付受入金
loans requiring attention 要注意先債権
loans to Account for Early Strengthening of Financial Functions 金融機能早期健全化会計貸付
loans to borrowers in legal bankruptcy 破綻先債権
loans to Financial Reconstruction Account 金融再生会計貸付
loans to General Account 一般会計貸付
loans to Special Account 特別会計貸付
loans to substandard borrowers 要管理先債権
loans to the government 国に対する貸付
LOB (lease obligation bond) リース債権債
lobbying 院外運動
lobbying contract 院外契約
LOC (letter-of-credit) backed 信用状を裏付けにした
local allocation taxes 地方交付税
local area network 企業内高速情報通信網
local authorities 地方自治体
local autonomy 地方自治
local bank 地方銀行
local borrowing 現地での借入
Local Branch Offices 地方支分部局
local company 地元企業
local consumption tax 地方消費税
local content ローカル・コンテント
local content ratio 現地調達率
local contents 現地調達
local cost 現地コスト
local credit 国内発行信用状
local currency 現地通貨
local currency rating 自国通貨建格付け
local dealers 地場筋ディーラー
local distribution tax 地方配布税
local economies 地域経済
local expectation hypothesis 局所的期待仮説
local expenditure 地方費
Local Finance Bureaus 財務局
local government 地方自治体
local government bond 地方債
local grant tax 地方交付税
local law 地域法
local martingale 局所マーチンゲール
local names 現地投資家
local production factory 現地生産工場
local public entity 地方自治体
local public finance 地方財政
Local Public Finance Law 地方財政法
local public finance plan 地方財政計画

local public goods 地方公共財
local road tax 地方道路税
local stock exchange 地方証券取引所
local tax 地方税
Local Tax Law 地方税法
local tax payment 地方税納付
local tax rate 地方税率
local time 現地時間
local transfer tax 地方譲与税
locals ローカルズ
location 所在地
location of loss or damage 損失発生地
location of transfer account book 振替口座簿の備付け
location quotient 特化係数
lock in gain 利益の確定
lock-in 確定
lock-in effect ロックイン効果
lock-up ロックアップ
lock-up option ロックアップ・オプション
lock-up period ロック・アップ期間
lockbox ロックボックス
locked in vesting 拘束受給権
locked market ロックド・マーケット
locked-in trade 照合済取引
loco price 現場渡値段
locomotive theory 機関車論
log 記録
log linear 対数線形
logarithmic chart 対数グラフ
logarithmic spiral 対数渦巻線
logarithmic utility function 対数効用関数
logic 論理
logical consistency 論理的整合性
logistic regression ロジスティック回帰
lognormal distribution 対数正規分布
Lombard borrowing ロンバード借入れ
Lombard credit ロンバード貸付
Lombard lending ロンバード貸出
Lombard rate ロンバード・レート
Lombard Street ロンバード街
Lombard-type lending ロンバード型貸付
London acceptance ロンドン・アクセプタンス
London clearing banks ロンドン手形交換所加盟銀行
London Club ロンドン・クラブ
London depositary receipts ロンドン預託証書
London Discount Market Association ロンドン割引市場協会
London gold market ロンドン金市場
London Inter-Bank Offered Rate ロンドン銀行間出し手金利
London interbank bid rate ロンドン銀行間取手金利
London International Financial Futures Exchange ロンドン国際金融先物取引所
London refinance ロンドン・リファイナンス
London school ロンドン学派
long account 買い玉
long and medium-term interest rate 長中期金利
long butterfly spread transaction ロング・バタフライ・スプレッド取引
long calendar spread transaction ロング・カレンダー・スプレッド取引
long call ロング・コール
long cash period 長期現物期間
long condor ロング・コンドル
long coupon ロング・クーポン
long duration securities 長期デュレーション証券
long exchange 長期為替
long hedge 買持ちヘッジ
long hedging 買いつなぎ
long list ロング・リスト
long lived 耐用年数の長い
long position 買建玉；ロング・ポジション
long position risk 買持ちリスク
long put ロングプット
long run average 長期平均
long service allowance 勤続手当

long straddle ロング・ストラドル
long strip ロング・ストリップ
long the swap スワップを買う
long treasury bond 長期米国財務省証券
long waves 長期波動
long-arm jurisdiction 域外適用管轄権
long-care coverage 長期介護保険
long-dated bill 長期手形
long-dated forwards 長期先渡取引
long-dated issue 長期債
long-dated real rate 長期実質金利
long-form audit report 長文式監査報告書
long-form report 長文式報告書
long-lived assets 長期資産
long-run 長期
long-run equilibrium 長期均衡
long-run supply curve 長期供給曲線
long-run trend 長期トレンド
long-run trend rate 長期トレンド水準
long-service leave benefit 長期勤続休暇給付
long-term accounts payable in foreign currency 長期外貨建債務
long-term accounts receivable in foreign currency 長期外貨建債権
long-term asset ratio to equity capital 自己資本長期資産率
long-term assets 長期資産
long-term bill 長期手形
long-term bond 長期債
long-term borrowing 長期借入金
long-term business 長期事業
long-term buy and hold strategy 長期保有戦略
long-term buying 長期買い
long-term capital 長期資本
long-term capital balance 長期資本収支
long-term capital gains 長期譲渡所得
long-term capital transaction 長期資本取引
long-term comprehensive insurance 長期総合保険
long-term contract 長期請負工事
long-term contract work 長期請負
long-term credit 長期信用
long-term credit bank 長期信用銀行
long-term credit market 長期金融市場
long-term debt 長期債務
long-term debt assumed 長期債務増加
long-term debt ratio 長期債務比率
long-term direction 長期戦略
long-term disability benefit 長期障害給付
long-term downward trend 長期下落トレンド
long-term economic growth rate 長期的経済成長率
long-term employee benefit 長期従業員給付
long-term employee benefit obligation 長期従業員給付債務
long-term finance 長期金融
long-term financial performance 長期的財務業績
long-term financing 長期資金調達
long-term foreign currency rating 外貨建長期ソブリン格付け
long-term forward exchange agreement 長期為替予約
long-term fund 長期資金
long-term gain 長期利得
long-term goal 長期目標
long-term government bond 長期国債
long-term income 長期所得
long-term interest rate 長期金利
long-term investment 長期投資
long-term investment property 長期保有の資産
long-term liabilities 長期債務
long-term link 長期的リンク
long-term loan 長期貸付金
long-term loan payable 長期借入金
long-term loan receivable 長期貸付金
long-term loss 長期損失
long-term money market 長期金融市場
long-term national bond of England 英国長期国債

L

long-term operation 長期事業活動
long-term performance 長期の運用成績
long-term planning 長期計画
long-term postponement of credit 債権棚上げ
long-term postponement of debt servicing 債権棚上げ
long-term prepaid rent 長期前払家賃
long-term prime rate 長期プライムレート
long-term rate 長期利率
long-term real yield 長期実質利回り
long-term savings needs 長期的貯蓄ニーズ
long-term securities 長期債
long-term solvency 長期支払能力
long-term suspended claims 長期棚上債権
long-term yield 長期利回り
long-term-lease 長期賃貸借契約
longer bullish stance 長期的な強気
longer dated bonds 長期債
longer-term interest rate より長期タームの金利
longest remaining life bonds 最長期債
look-back call option ルック・バック・コール・オプション
look-back option ルック・バック・オプション
look-back option transaction ルック・バック・オプション取引
look-back put option ルック・バック・プット・オプション
looking toppy 高止まりで
loose leaf book ルーズリーフ式帳簿
looser labor markets 労働需給の緩和
Lorenz curve ローレンツ曲線
losers game 敗者のゲーム
loss 損失
loss account 損失勘定
loss adjuster 損害査定人
loss adjustment expense 損害査定費
loss allocation 損失の配分
loss arising from casualty 災害による損失
loss brought forward from the previous term 前期繰越損失
loss carried forward 繰越欠損金
loss carried forward to the following term 次期繰越欠損金
loss carryback 欠損金の繰戻し
loss cut 損切り
loss disposal statement 損失処理計算書
loss due to disaster 災害損失金
loss due to spoiled work 仕損費
loss for the current term 当期損失金
loss for the current year 当期損失金
loss forwarded 繰越欠損金
loss frequency 損害発生頻度
loss from amalgamation 合併差損
loss from bad debts 貸倒損失
loss from capital reduction 減資差損
loss from damaged business assets 被災事業用資産の損失
loss from difference of price 差損金
loss from dividend income 配当所得損失
loss from fluctuation of foreign exchange rate 為替差損
loss from foreign exchange rate fluctuations 為替相場の変動による損失
loss from liquidation of properties 資産の清算による損失
loss from litigation 訴訟による損失
loss from merger 合併差損
loss from redemption of bond 社債償還差損
loss from revaluation of securities 有価証券評価損
loss from the revaluation of fixed assets 固定資産評価損
loss from the sale of fixed assets 固定資産売却損
loss from valuation of assets 資産の評価損
loss from valuation of property 資産評価損

loss function 損失関数
loss incurred by revaluation of assets 資産評価損
loss leader ロス・リーダー
loss making division 不採算部門
loss making operations 赤字経営
loss not yet recognized 未認識損失
loss of dividend income 配当所得の損失
loss of productivity claims 生産性喪失クレーム
loss of profit insurance 利益保険
loss of property 資産損失
loss of sovereignty 国家主権の喪失
loss of work 作業損失
loss on asset abandoned 資産廃棄損
loss on assets 資産損失
loss on curtailments 縮小による損失
loss on disposal 処分による損
loss on insurance claims 保険金差損
loss on property abandoned 資産廃棄損
loss on property destroyed 資産喪失費
loss on property revaluation 資産評価損
loss on re-measurement 再測定損失
loss on retirement of fixed assets 固定資産除却損失
loss on sale 売却損
loss on sale of assets 資産の売却損
loss on sale of fixed assets 固定資産の売却損
loss on sale of property 資産売却損
loss on sale of real estate 不動産売却損
loss on sale of securities 有価証券売却損
loss on sales returns 返品差損費
loss on settlements 清算による損失
loss on the disposal of problem loans 問題債権処理損失
loss payable clause 第三者払約款
loss per share 一株当り損失
loss prevention 損失防止
loss provision 損失引当金
loss qualifying for necessary expenses 必要経費になる損失
loss ratio 損害率
loss recognition 損失認識
loss recognized in increasing reserve for advanced depreciation 圧縮引当金繰入損
loss recovery ratio 損失回収率
loss resulting from casualty 災害損失
loss share 損失の分担
loss-of-income coverage 所得補償保険
loss-sharing rule 損失分担ルール
losses on redemption of government securities 国債償還損
losses on sale and redemption of government securities 国債売却償還損
losses on sale, purchase, and redemption, and arising from revaluation of foreign currency assets 外国為替売買償還損
losses sustained 被った損失
lost card 紛失カード
lost policy 紛失保険証券
lost-or-not-lost clause 遡及条項
lot bond ロット債
lot money 競売手数料
lot size 取引規模
LOTS (limit order trading system) 指値注文売買システム
lottery 抽選
lotting out 分譲
Louvre Accord ルーブル合意
low against the dollar ドルに対し安値
low balance method 最低残高法
low beta portfolio ベータ値が低いポートフォリオ
low capacity utilization 設備稼働率が低いこと
low capital intensive industry 資本集約性の低い産業
low carry on the dollar ドルの低キャリー
low cost 低コスト
low cost insurance 低保険料保険
low coupon securities 表面利率の低い

L

銘柄
low coupon teasers 低利のティーザー物
low dividend stock 低配株
low earnings 低収益
low growth 低成長
low growth industries 低成長産業
low income countries 低所得国
low income group 低所得者層
low inflation 低インフレ
low interest loan 低金利ローン
low level 低水準
low load fund 低手数料ファンド
low par issue 低額面株式
low price 安値
low price product 低価格商品
low return asset 低利回り資産
low risk stock 安全性の高い株式
low short rate 低い短期金利
low turnover 薄商い
low yielding currency 低金利通貨
low- and moderate-income 低中所得
low-load policy 低い手数料の保険
low-priced imports 低価格輸入品
lower bid 低い値段の買呼値
lower class 下層階級
lower closing quotation 引け安
lower end 下限
lower end of the market 低価格市場
lower hurdle 低い障害
lower in quotation 下ザヤ
lower level 下位レベル
lower level segment 下位セグメント
lower limit 下限
lower limit rate 下限相場
lower management 下級管理
lower of いずれか低い方
lower of cost or market price 原価，時価のいずれか低い方
lower offer 低い値段の売呼値
lower order goods 低次財
lower price 下値
lower quotation 下値
lower quoted real yield 低い実質利回り
lower rated class 低格付クラス
lower risk portfolio 低リスク・ポートフォリオ
lower tax rate 低税率
lower up-front cost 低い頭金
lower volatility asset 低ボラティリティ資産
lower-of-cost-or-market method 低価法
lower-of-cost-or-market value basis 低価主義
lower-priced stock 低位株
lowering of interest rate 金利引下げ
lowest strata 最下層
lowest taxable limit 課税最低限
lows for the week 今週の安値
loyalty rebate 特約リベート
LRD (Liberian dollar) リベリア・ドル
LSE (Lisbon Stock Exchange) リスボン証券取引所
LTFX (long-term foreign exchange) 長期為替
LTIP (long-term incentive plan) 長期報奨制度
LTL (Lithuanian litas) リトアニア・リタス
LTM (leverage transaction merchant) レバレッジ取引マーチャント
LTPR (long-term prime rate) 長プラ
lucrative terms 有利な条件
LUF (Luxembourg franc) ルクセンブルグ・フラン
lump sum 一括
lump sum benefit 一時払給付
lump sum cash payment 一時金支払い
lump sum contract 定額請負契約
lump sum death benefit 死亡一時金
lump sum freight 総括運賃
lump sum money 一時金
lump sum payment 一時払い
lump sum payment of dividends at maturity 収益満期払い
lump sum payment of retirement allowance 退職金の一括支給
lump sum pension 一時恩給

lump sum purchase 一括購入
lump sum repayment 一括完済
lump sum retirement benefit 定年退職一時金給付
Luxembourg Monetary Institute ルクセンブルグ金融協会
luxurious house for rent 高級賃貸住宅
luxury tax 奢侈税
LVL (Latvian lat) ラトビア・ラット
LYD (Libyan dinar) リビア・ディナール
LYON (liquid yield option note) LYON

M

M&A&D (merger, acquisition and divesture) 買収・合併・撤退
M0 growth Mゼロの伸び
M2+CD Statistics M2＋CD 統計
M2's behavior M2 の動き
M3 growth M3 の伸び
MA (moving average) 移動平均
MAC (Message Authentication Code) メッセージ認証コード
Macao マカオ
macaroni defense マカロニ防衛
MACD (moving average convergence and divergence) 移動平均収斂・乖離
MacFadden Act of 1927 マクファデン法
machine bookkeeping 機械簿記
machine tool 機械工具
machine-hour rate 機械時間率
machine-hour rate method 機械時間率配賦法
machinery acquired by small sized entrepreneur 中小企業用の機械
machinery and equipment 機械設備
machinery and tool 機器
machinery credit insurance 機械類信用保険
machinery for rationalization of production 生産合理化用機械設備
machinery industry 機械業界
machinery insurance 機械保険
macro accounting マクロ会計
macro analysis マクロ分析
macro hedge マクロ・ヘッジ
macro hedges マクロ・ヘッジ
macro model マクロ・モデル
macro picture マクロ経済
macro view 大勢観
macro-economy マクロ経済
macro-perspective マクロ的な観点
macroeconomic マクロ経済的
macroeconomic analysis マクロ経済分析
macroeconomic factor マクロ経済要因
macroeconomic indicators 景気指標
macroeconomic model マクロ経済モデル
macroeconomic policy マクロ経済政策
MACRS メイカーズ（修正加速償却法）
MACRS (modified accelerated cost recovery method) 修正加速償却法
MAD (Moroccan dirham) モロッコ・ディルハム
Madrid Stock Exchange マドリッド証券取引所
magnetic tape 磁気テープ
magnify 拡大する
magnitude of economic change 経済変化の大きさ
magnitude of the cycle 景気循環の振幅
mail confirmation メール・コンファメーション
mail credit メール・クレジット
mail credit facility メール・クレジット・ファシリティ
mail days 郵便日数
mail exchange bill 文書為替
mail order 通信販売
mail transfer 普通為替
mail transfer payable 送金為替
mail-order loan メールオーダー・ローン
mailing cost 郵送料
main account 主要勘定
main books 主要帳簿
main budget 本予算
main business 本業
main contract 主契約
main customer 主要取引
main equity instrument 主持ち分金融

商品
main financial instruments 主金融商品
main income earner 主たる所得者
main materials 主要原材料
main office 主たる事務所
Main Organs 本省
main product 主製品
main registration 主登録
mainstream 主流
maintaining the dollar peg ドルとの連動
maintenance 維持
maintenance agency 維持管理機関
maintenance and repairs 修繕費
maintenance bond 瑕疵修補保証証券
maintenance call 追加証拠金
maintenance clause 扶養約款
maintenance department 営繕課
maintenance expenditure 維持費用
maintenance expense 維持費
maintenance fee 管理費
maintenance fund 維持資金
maintenance lease メンテナンス・リース
maintenance margin 維持証拠金
maintenance of an orderly financial system 信用秩序の維持
maintenance of books and records 帳簿書類の整理保存
maintenance of confidence 信頼維持
maintenance of fair trade 公正取引の確保
maintenance of financial capital 貨幣資本維持
maintenance of margin 委託保証金の維持
maintenance of membership 組合員資格の保持
maintenance of physical capital 実際資本維持
maintenance requirement 維持証拠金
maintenance reserve 維持準備金
major 大手
major acquisition 大型買収
major banks 大手銀行
major bottom 大底
major bracket 上位集団
major commodity 主要産品
major component 主要な内訳
major cycles 主循環
major economic power 経済大国
major foreign stock price indexes 外国主要株価指数
major industrial nations 先進国
major industry 主要産業
major investments 大規模な投資
major leagues 先進工業国
major market index メジャー・マーケット指数
major medical expense insurance 高額医療費保険
major medical insurance 高額医療保険
major move メジャー・ムーブ
major nations 主要国
major order 大量受注
major peak 大天井
major product 主製品
major raw materials 主要な原材料
major relationship bank 主力銀行
major stockholders 主要な株主
major trend 大勢
majority 過半数
majority decision 多数決
majority interest 過半数持ち分
majority of stockholders 株主の過半数
majority of voting rights 議決権の多数決
majority shareholders 過半数株主
majority vote of the shareholders present 出席した株主の議決権の過半数
majority-owned subsidiary 過半数所有従属会社
make ends meet 収支を合わせる
make good the loss 損失を補填する
make-ready time 段取り時間
maker's credit 延べ払い輸入
making a trial balance 試算表を作る
making of a price 値付け

making two-sided markets 両方向の値付け
making up for a deficit 赤字補填
making up for loss 損失の補填
Malaysia Commodity Exchange マレーシア商品取引所
maldistribution 偏在
Maloney Act of 1938 マロニー法
malpractice 不当行為
malpractice insurance 業務上過誤保険
man hour rate 工数率
managed account 合同運用勘定
managed assets 管理資産
managed crawling peg 管理クローリング・ペッグ
managed currency 管理通貨
managed float 管理フロート
managed floating rate system 管理フロート制
managed fund 合同運用ファンド
Managed Fund Contract マネージド・ファンド契約
managed issues 管理銘柄
managed liabilities 管理債務
managed price 管理価格
managed trade 管理貿易
management 運用
management accounting 管理会計
management agreement 経営委託契約
management analysis 経営分析
management and collection 管理回収
management base 経営基盤
management business of investment trust 投資信託委託業務
management buyout マネージメント・バイアウト
management by objective 目標管理
management capability 経営能力
management committee 経営委員会
management company 運用会社
management consultant 経営コンサルタント
management contract 管理契約
management cultures 経営体質
management decision 経営意思決定
management discussion and analysis 経営分析及び解説
management engineering 経営工学
management fee 運用手数料；幹事手数料
management group 引受幹事団
management index 経営指標
management information system 経営情報システム
management integration 経営統合
management know-how 経営ノウハウ
management labor relation 労使関係
management of clearing margin 取引証拠金の管理
management of derivatives デリバティブの管理
management of juristic act 法務処理
management of supply 供給管理
management of the default compensation reserve 違約損失補償準備金の運用
management organization 管理組織
management participation 経営参加
management participation right 経営参加権
management personnel 役職者
management plan 経営計画
management purpose 経営目的
management report 運用報告書
management representation 経営者の表明
management responsibility 経営責任
management rights 経営権
management science マネージメント・サイエンス
management service for bill for collection 取立手形管理サービス
management strategy 経営戦略
management structure 経営組織
management style 運用スタイル
Management Supervisor 監督評価官
management support receiving entity 経営支援先
management team 経営陣
management through figures 計数管理

management's discussion and analysis of earnings 経営者の利益に関する討議と分析
management's discussion and analysis of financial condition and operating results 経営者による財務状況と経営成績の討議及び分析
management's stewardship 経営者の責務遂行
manager 幹事
manager evaluation 運用機関による評価
manager-client relations 投資管理者と顧客の関係
manager's contribution マネージャーの寄与度
managerial accounting 管理会計
managerial auditing 経営監査
managerial choices 経営判断
managerial investment trust 管理型投資信託
managerial involvement 管理上の関与
managerial philosophy 経営理念
managerial resources 経営資源
managers 幹事団
managing bank 幹事銀行
managing director 常務取締役
managing governor 常務理事
managing underwriter 幹事証券
mandate 主幹事の指名獲得；マンデート
mandate bid マンデートの入札
mandate letter マンデート・レター
mandate on remission 差戻命令
mandated offer 強制適用
mandated pension plan 強制加入年金制度
mandated surrender value 法定返戻金
mandatory 必須の
mandatory clause 必須条件
mandatory collateral substitution 強制担保差し換え
mandatory control 法的規制
mandatory convertible bond 強制転換社債
mandatory convertible securities 強制転換証券
mandatory convertibles 強制転換社債
mandatory field 必須フィールド
mandatory injunction 命令的差止命令
mandatory line of credit 法定信用枠
mandatory real name transaction 強制実名取引
mandatory recognition 強制的な認識
mandatory redeemable 強制償還の
mandatory redemption 強制償還
mandatory retirement 強制退職
mandatory securities valuation reserve 法定有価証券評価準備金
mandatory sinking fund requirement 強制的減債基金条項
mandatory state insurance 強制加入国営保険
mandatory termination 会社都合退職
manifest 積み荷目録
manifold 多方面の
manipulation 操作
manipulation of account 粉飾
manipulation of the market 価格操作
manner of depreciation 償却方法
manner similar to 準じた方法
manner similar to straight line depreciation method 定額法に準じた方法
manual of accounting instructions 会計執務規定
manual of accounting procedure 会計手続規定
manufacture order 製造指図書
manufactured goods 製品
manufacturer 製造業者
manufacturer's risks 製造者リスク
manufacturer's warranty 製造業者の保証
manufacturing accounting 工業会計
manufacturing bases 生産拠点
manufacturing bookkeeping 工業簿記
manufacturing burden 製造間接費
manufacturing cost 製造原価
manufacturing cost variance 製造原価

差額
manufacturing costing 製造原価計算
manufacturing defect 製造上の欠陥
manufacturing department 製造部門
manufacturing expenses 製造経費
manufacturing headcount 製造業雇用者数
manufacturing industry 製造産業
manufacturing license 製造許可
manufacturing output 製造業生産指数
manufacturing overhead allocation 製造間接費配賦
manufacturing overhead costs 製造間接費
manufacturing overhead costs budget 製造間接費予算
manufacturing overhead costs ledger 製造間接費元帳
manufacturing payroll 製造業雇用者数
manufacturing process 製造工程
manufacturing taxation 製造課税
manufacturing technology 生産技術
map 点描する
mapleleaf coin メイプルリーフ・コイン
MAR (managed account report) マネージド・アカウント・レポート
margin 証拠金
margin account 証拠金勘定；信用取引口座
margin agreement 信用取引契約
margin buying 信用買い
margin call 追加証拠金
margin collateral 信用取引委託保証金
margin cost 証拠金コスト
margin credit 証拠金余剰
margin debit 証拠金不足
margin debt 証拠金負債
margin deficiency 証拠金不足
margin deposit 受入証拠金
margin for borrowed stocks 借証券担保金
margin for stocks lent 信用取引貸証券受入金
margin for transactions 売買証拠金
margin for when-issued transactions 発行日決済取引に係る委託証拠金
margin improvement 利ざやの拡大
margin loan trading regulations 信用取引規程
margin money system 証拠金制度
margin of profit 利益率
margin of safety 安全性マージン；投資安全確保の範囲
margin on commodity futures 商品先物取引の証拠金
margin purchase 信用買い
margin rate 証拠金率
margin ratio 利幅率
margin required method 必要証拠金法
margin requirement 必要証拠金
Margin Rules 証拠金規則
margin securities 信用取引銘柄
margin system 証拠金システム
margin trading 信用取引
margin transaction 証拠金取引
marginable securities 信用取引証券
marginal analysis 限界分析
marginal benefit 限界便益
marginal capital 限界資本
marginal capital coefficient 限界資本係数
marginal capital expenditure 限界資本支出
marginal clauses 欄外約款
marginal condition 限界条件
marginal cost 限界費用
marginal cost curve 限界費用曲線
marginal cost of production 限界生産費
marginal costing 限界原価計算
marginal credit 限界信用
marginal deduction system 限界控除制度
marginal demand 限界需要
marginal efficiency 限界効率
marginal efficiency of capital 資本限界効率
marginal efficiency of investment 投資限界効率

marginal factor 限界要素
marginal firm 限界企業
marginal incentive 限界インセンティブ
marginal income 限界利益
marginal income ratio 限界利益率
marginal income statement 限界損益計算
marginal investor 限界投資家
marginal loan-deposit ratio 限界預貸率
marginal net suitability 限界正味適合度
marginal principle 限界原理
marginal production 限界生産
marginal productivity 限界生産性
marginal profit 限界利益
marginal profit ratio 限界利益率
marginal propensity to consume 限界消費性向
marginal propensity to import 限界輸入性向
marginal propensity to save 限界貯蓄性向
marginal rate of return 限界収益率
marginal rate of substitution 限界代替率
marginal ratio 限界比率
marginal revenue 限界収益
marginal rise 微増
marginal seal 捨て印
marginal tax rate 限界税率
marginal theory 限界理論
marginal unit cost 限界単位原価
marginal utility 限界効用
marginal utility of money 貨幣の限界効用
marginal valuation 限界評価
marginal value 限界価値
marginal value curve 限界価値曲線
margins of solvency 支払余力
Marine Accident Inquiry Agency 海難審判庁
Marine and Fire Insurance Association of Japan 日本損害保険協会
marine and transport insurance 海上及び運送保険
marine bill of landing 海上船荷証券
marine cargo insurance 貨物海上保険
Marine cargo policy 貨物海上保険証券
marine insurance 海上保険
marine insurance account 海上保険勘定
Marine Insurance Act of 1906 イギリス海上保険法
marine perils 海上危険
marine surveyor 海事検査人
Marine Technical College 海技大学校
marine transportation 海運
marine transportation industry 海運業
mariner's lien 海員の先取特権
marital deduction 配偶者控除
maritime 海事の
maritime affairs 海事
maritime belt 領海
maritime bonds 海事債
maritime court 海事裁判所
Maritime Disaster Prevention Center 海上災害防止センター
maritime hypothecation 海事抵当
maritime insurance 海上保険
maritime law 海事法
maritime lien 海事先取特権
maritime mortgage 海事抵当
maritime perils 海上危険
maritime traffic 海運
mark bond マルク債
mark up 利益を乗せる
mark-downs 下口銭
mark-to-market account 値洗い勘定
mark-to-market basis 値洗い基準
mark-to-market date 値洗い日
mark-to-market value 値洗い価値
mark-up 手数料
mark-up rate マークアップ率
mark-ups 上口銭
marked appreciation 大幅な上昇
marked checks 記号小切手
marked down 低い売価がついている

market analysis 市場分析
market annuity price 市場年金価格
market assessment 市場評価
market awareness 市場の認識度
market based information 市場実勢に基づいた情報
market basket contract マーケット・バスケット方式
market basket index マーケット・バスケット指数
market behavior 相場の動き
market beta 市場ベータ
market cap 時価総額
market capitalization 市場時価総額
market competition 市場の競争
market condition 市況状況
market conduct 市場活動
market congestion 起債ラッシュ
market consensus 市場のコンセンサス
market control 市場支配；市場統制
market conventions 市場慣行
market crash 相場の大幅下落
market creating effect 市場創造効果
market cycle 市場周期
market demand 市場需要
market demand curve 市場需要曲線
market directional risk 市場の方向性リスク
market discipline 市場原理
market discount rate 市場割引率
market duration trade マーケット・デュレーション・トレード
market economy 市場経済
market economy model 市場経済モデル
market efficiency 市場の効率性
market environment 市場環境
market equilibrium 市場均衡
market equilibrium curve 市場均衡曲線
market exiting 市場撤退
market expansion effect 市場拡張効果
market extinction 市場消滅
market facilities 市場施設
market failure 市場の失敗
market feasibility 販売可能性
market for start-ups 振興市場
market forecast 市場予測
market hours 立会時間
market in favor of buyer 買手市場
market in favor of sellers 売手市場
market index 市場指数
market information 相場情報
market information center 市況情報センター
market information source 市場の情報源
Market Information System 相場報道システム
market insight 市場の考察
market integrity 市場の完全性
market interest rate 市中金利
market intervention 市場介入
market jitters 市場の不安
market leaders 市場の主導株
market liberalization 市場の規制緩和
market making condition 値付け状況
market making function 値付け機能
market manipulation 相場操縦
market mechanism 市場原理；市場メカニズム
market milking 市場をあやつる
market model 市場モデル
market momentum 市場の勢い
market mood 市場の地合い
market neutral investment management マーケット・ニュートラル運用
market of a stock exchange 証券取引所の市場
market of the exchange 取引所有価証券市場
market on close 引け注文
market opening 市場開放
market opportunity 市場機会
market order 成行注文
market overt 公開の市場
market overview 市場概況
market parlance 市場用語
market penetration 市場への進出

market perception 市場の見方
market performance 市場の成果
market place 市場
market player 市場参加者
market portfolio 市場ポートフォリオ
market practice 市場慣行
market prediction 市場予測
market price 市場価格
market price analysis 時価分析
market price basis 時価主義
market price method 時価方式
market price movement 市場価格の変動
market price of risk リスクの市場価格
market psychology 市場心理
market purchase price 仕入時価
market quotation 相場気配
market rally 相場の上昇
market rate 市場相場；短期金利
market rate of interest 市場利子率
market rate of intervention 市場介入金利
market recovery 市況回復
market reform 市場改革
market regulations 市場の規程
market report 市況報告
market research 市場調査
market return マーケット・リターン
market rhythm 市場の基調
market risk 市場リスク；マーケット・リスク
Market Risk Inspection Office 市場リスク検査室
market risk sensitive 市場リスクに敏感な
market sector 市場セクター
market segmentation 市場細分化
market segmentation hypothesis 市場分断仮説
market sensitivity 市場感応度
market sentiment 市場の地合い
market share 市場占有率
market spread 市場スプレッド
market stabilization operation 市場安定操作
market stabilizing transaction 安定操作取引
market state 市場の実勢
market structure 市場構造
market supervision 売買監理
market survey 市場調査
market theory 市場理論
market timer マーケット・タイマー
market timing 市場のタイミング
market timing assessment 市場タイミングの評価
market tone 市場の気配
market transaction 取引
market transaction price 市場取引価格
market valuation 市場評価
market value 時価；時価総額
market value adjusted annuity 市場価格調整済年金
market value adjustment 市場価格調整
market value analysis 時価分析
market value basis 時価主義
market value method 時価法
market value of inventory 棚卸資産の時価
market value per share 株価
market value weighted index 市場価値加重平均指数
market view 市場の考え
market volatility 市場のボラティリティ
market yield 市場利回り
market yield on government bonds 国債の市場利回り
market-based value 市場における価値
market-determined 市場によって決定される
market-driven 市場に目を向けた
market-if-touched order マーケット・イフ・タッチド・オーダー
market-on-close order マーケット・オン・クローズ・オーダー
market-price based accounting 時価会計

market-related value 市場関連価値
market's adjustment 市場の調整
marketability 市場性
marketable debt 市場性証券
marketable debt securities 市場性債券
marketable order 市場性のある注文
marketable securities 市場性のある有価証券
marketable securities listed on a securities exchange 証券取引所に上場されている有価証券
marketable title 売買可能権原
marketable value 市場価値
marketing budget マーケティング予算
marketing channel 販売経路
marketing expense マーケティング経費
marketing function マーケティング機能
marketing mix マーケティング・ミックス
marketing pull マーケティング・プル
marketing push マーケティング・プッシュ
marketing right 市場販売権
marketout 証券買取停止
marketout clause 証券買取停止条項
marking 値入
marking to market 値洗い
Markov chain マルコフ連鎖
Markov property マルコフ性
Markowitz theory マーコビッツ理論
marry マリー
marrying transaction of securities company 証券マリー
Marshall curve マーシャル曲線
Marshall Islands (US dollar) マーシャル諸島（米国ドル）
Marshall Plan マーシャルプラン
Marshallian demand curve マーシャル的需要曲線
Marshallian K マーシャルのK
martingale process マーチンゲール過程
Maruyu program マル優制度
Maruyu tax-exempt savings system マル優
MAS (medical savings account) 医療貯蓄勘定
MAS (Monetary Agency of Singapore) シンガポール通貨庁
mass communication マス・コミュニケーション
mass consumption society 大衆消費社会
mass production 大量生産
mass production techniques 大量生産技術
mass risks 大衆リスク
mass sales 大量推奨販売
massive potential 巨大な潜在力
master agreement マスター契約
master bill 表紙手形
master contract 基本契約
master L/C 原信用状
master lease マスターリース
master netting arrangement 基本的相殺契約
master plan 基本計画
master policy 基本証券
master trust マスター・トラスト
master trustee 総幹事受託者
master-netting contract マスター・ネッティング契約
match 一致させる
match making 見合い
match plan 折半方式
matched book 売り買いの一致
matched maturities 期間の一致
matched order なれあい売買
matched trade 照合済取引
matching 対当
matching concept 対応の概念
matching cost with revenue 費用収益対応
matching costs and revenues 費用収益の対応
matching funds 見合基金
matching of bids and offers 呼値の付合せ

matching of revenue and expense 収益と費用の対応
matching positions 対等数量
matching principle 対応原則
matching ratio 照会適合率
matching revenue with cost 収益費用対応
matching swap マッチング・スワップ
matching transaction マッチング取引
material allegation 重要な主張
material alternation 重要な変造
material change 重要な変更
material cost 材料費
material cost variance 原材料価格差異
material decrease 重大な減少
material effect 重大な影響
material error 重大な誤謬
material evidence 証拠物件
material exception 重大な例外
material fact 重要事実
material for repair 修理用材料
material impact 重大な影響
material in process 仕掛材料
material misrepresentation 重大なる不実表示
material plan 重要な制度
material price variance 材料価格差異
material quantity variance 材料数量差異
material requisition note 材料出庫請求書
material supplementary information 重要補完情報
material transaction 重要な取引
material usage variance 材料数量差異
material variance 実質的相違
materiality 重要性
materiality principle 重要性原則
materialized securities 証書発行のある証券
materials budget 材料予算
materials department 資材部
materials distribution sheet 材料仕訳帳
materials for investigation 調査資料
materials in storage 貯蔵原材料
materials inventory 材料在庫高
materials ledger 材料元帳
materials on hand 手持資材
materials price standard 材料標準価格
materials purchased 材料仕入高
materials purchased report 原材料仕入報告書
materials received report 原材料受入報告書
materials specification 材料仕様書
materials variance 材料費差額
maternity and paternity leave 出産育児休暇
mathematical description 数学的解説
mathematical economics 数理経済学
mathematical finance 数理ファイナンス
mathematical statistics 数理統計
matrix マトリックス
matrix bookkeeping 行列簿記
matrix multiplier 行列乗数
matrix presentation マトリックス表示
matrix pricing model マトリックス価格決定モデル
matrix trading マトリックス・トレーディング
matter 基礎事実
matter in deed 証書事項
matter in issue 争点事項
matter of record 記録事項
matters to be notified 届出事項
matters to be reported 報告事項
mature 期限が来る
mature assets 成熟資産
mature company 成熟企業
mature economy 成熟経済
mature liabilities 支払期限の到来した債務
mature phase 成熟段階
mature plans 成熟したプラン
matured bill 満期手形
matured bond 満期債券
matured liability 満期債務
matured notes 満期手形

maturing 満期を迎える
maturing bonds 満期到来債
maturing liability 満期間近の債務
maturities of assets 資産の期日
maturity 償還期限；満期
maturity basket 満期バスケット
maturity date 満期日
maturity distribution range 満期分布の差
maturity gap exposure 運用と調達の期間ギャップ
maturity grouping 期日別区分
maturity guarantee 満期保証
maturity list 満期日表
maturity matching 満期対当
maturity mismatch 期間のミスマッチ
maturity of operations オペのエンド日
maturity payment 満期時償還額
maturity proceeds 満期受取金
maturity repayment 満期返戻金
maturity schedule 満期スケジュール
maturity stripping マチュリティ・ストリッピング
maturity structure 満期日構成
maturity swap マチュリティ・スワップ
maturity value 満期価値
maturity-designated time deposit 期日指定定期預金
maverick risk 異端者リスク
max overweight 最大オーバーウエイト
max underweight 最大アンダーウエイト
maximal collateral 根抵当
maxims 法律格言
maximum amount of the overdraft 当座貸越極度額
maximum and minimum tariff system 最高最低税率制
maximum benefit 給付の最高額
maximum capacity 最大生産能力
maximum contribution 拠出限度額
maximum deductible contribution 課税控除掛金限度額
maximum gain 利得上限
maximum inventory 最大在庫量
maximum issuance limit system 最高発行額制限制度
maximum level 最高水準
maximum likelihood 最尤度
maximum likelihood method 最尤法
maximum limit for interest rate 付利最高限度
maximum limit of contracts 約定の制限数量
maximum limit of fluctuation ストップ値
maximum limit of overdraft 貸越極度額
maximum loan value 貸出限度額
maximum loss estimates 最大損失推定値
maximum number of the business days 最大営業日数
maximum operating ratio 最有利操業度
maximum price 最高価格
maximum special depreciation allowance 特別償却限度額
MBA (Bond Market Association) 債券市場協会
MC (marginal cost) 限界コスト
MD&A (management's discussion and analysis) 経営者による討議及び分析
MDB (multilateral development bank) 多国間開発銀行
MDL (Moldovan leu) モルドバ・レウ
mean absolute deviation 平均絶対偏差
mean deviation 平均偏差
mean difference 平均差異
mean reserve 年央準備金
mean return 収益平均値
mean reversion 平均回帰
mean reverting 平均回帰する
mean reverting process 平均回帰過程
mean sample 標本サンプル
mean squared convergence 平均２乗収束
mean squared error 平均２乗誤差

mean value 平均値
mean-per-unit difference method 差額推定法
mean-variance 平均と分散
mean-variance portfolio selection 平均・分散ポートフォリオ選択
meaning of redemption 償還の定義
means for hedging ヘッジ手段
means of foreign payment 対外支払手段
means of payment 支払手段
means of storing value 価値保蔵（貯蓄）機能
means test 資産調査
measure 測定値
measure of investment 投資尺度
measure of return 収益率測度
measure of risk リスク測度
measure of value 価値尺度
measure to mitigate radical changes 激変緩和措置
measurement 測定
measurement base 測定基礎
measurement basis 測定基準
measurement cargo 容積貨物
measurement contract 測定契約
measurement currency 測定通貨
measurement date 測定日
measurement method 測定方法
measurement of cost 原価の測定
measurement of equity 資本の測定
measurement of inventories 棚卸資産の測定
measurement principle 測定原則
measurement requirement 測定要件
Measures for Facilitating Money Market Operations オペの実行手段
measures in case of vacancy 欠員の場合の措置
measuring gap メジャリング・ギャップ
measuring unit 測定単位
mechanical efficiency 機械効率
mechanical trading 機械化取引
mechanism 仕組み
mechanization method 機械化方式
mechanized accounting 機械化会計
media 媒体
media advertising 媒体広告
media commission 媒体手数料
media effect メディア効果
media mix メディア・ミックス
media strategy メディア戦略
median 中位数
mediate descent 間接相続
mediate powers 付随権限
mediation 仲介
mediation regulations 仲介規程
Medicaid メディケイド
medical benefit 医療給付
medical benefit delivery 医療給付の提供
medical benefit utilization 医療給付の利用
medical corporation 医療法人
medical cost 医療費
medical credit 医療費控除
medical examination 医療検査
medical expense insurance 医療費保険
medical expenses 医療費
medical expenses deduction 医療費控除
medical industry 医療産業
medical jurisprudence 法医学
medical liability 医療賠償責任
medical payment insurance 医療費保険
medical service 医療サービス
medical treatment cost 医療コスト
Medicare メディケア
Medicare Economic Index メディケア経済指標
medium gilt 中期ギルト債
medium note auctions 中期債入札
medium of capital transfer 資本移転手段
medium of exchange 決済機能
medium policy 中位の額の契約
medium rating 信用度中

medium term 中期
medium-sized stock 中型株
medium-term bond 中期債
medium-term coupon-bearing government bonds 中期利付国債
medium-term decline 中期的な下落
medium-term financial assets 中期金融資産
medium-term funding 中期資金の調達
medium-term government securities funds 中期国債ファンド
medium-term loan 中期ローン
medium-term note ミディアム・ターム・ノート
medium-term outlook 中期展望
medium-term policy principle 中期政策方針
medium-term target 中期目標
meeting debt maturities 債務返済
meeting of bond holders 社債権者集会
Meeting of Central Bank Governors of the G-10 Countries G10中央銀行総裁会議
meeting of ordinary equity contributors 普通出資者総会
meeting of preferred equity contributors 優先出資者総会
meeting of promoters 発起人会
Meiji Tsuho satsu 明治通宝札
meliorate 改善する
melon cutting 高額配当
member bank 加盟銀行
member banks of the clearing house 手形交換所加盟銀行
member banks of the Federal Reserve System 連邦準備制度加盟銀行
member banks of the Regional Banks Association of Japan (regional banks) 地方銀行協会加盟行
member banks of the Second Association of Regional Banks 第二地銀加盟行
member banks of the Second Association of Regional Banks (regional banks II) 第二地方銀行協会加盟行
member firm 会員会社
member governor 会員理事
member of stock exchange 取引所会員
member organization 会員組織
member representative 会員代表者
member securities company 会員証券会社
member short sale ratio 会員空売比率
member's fee 取引所会費
member's store 加盟店
member's voluntary winding-up 株主による任意清算
membership 加盟権
membership admission 会員加入
membership business 会員ビジネス
membership certificate 会員証書
membership corporation 会員組織の法人
membership equity 会員持ち分
membership fee 会費
membership guarantee deposit 会員信認金
membership in the capacity of a corporation 会社名儀の会員
membership organization 会員制組織
membership rights 会員権
membership subscription fee 会員出資金
memorandum account 備忘勘定
memorandum for offering 募集要項
memorandum of association 基本定款
memorandum of balance sheet audit 貸借対照表監査の覚書
memorandum of protest 拒絶証書
memorandum price 備忘価格
memorandum value 備忘価額
memorandum-check 不呈示特約小切手
memorial dividend 記念配当
menu approach メニュー・アプローチ
mercantile agency 商事代理
mercantile law 商業法
mercantile paper 商業手形
mercantile partnership 商業組合
mercantile risk 商品危険

merchandise (goods) 商品
merchandise account 商品勘定
merchandise book 商品売買帳
merchandise bookkeeping 商業簿記
merchandise cost 商品原価
merchandise in transit 未達商品
merchandise inventory 商品在庫
merchandise inventory account carried over 繰越商品勘定
merchandise ledger 商品元帳
merchandise management 商品管理
merchandise mix 商品構成
merchandise procurement cost 商品調達原価
merchandise resources 仕入先
merchandise turnover ratio 商品回転率
merchant 加盟店
merchant bank マーチャント・バンク
merchant banker 投資銀行家
merchant fee 加盟店手数料
merchant law 商業法
merchant outlet 加盟店店舗
merchantable 市場性のある
merely nominal persons 単なる名義人
merged company 被合併会社；被合併会社
merger 合併
merger accounting 合併会計
merger and acquisition 合併・買収
merger and acquisition business M&Aビジネス
merger and divesture 合併分割
merger for establishing a new entity on an equal basis 対等合併
merger for the creation of a new company 新設合併
merger of a domestic corporation 内国法人の合併
merger of corporation 会社の吸収合併
merger of guaranty 保証契約の混同による消滅
merger procedures 合併手続
merger ratio 合併比率
merger split-up 吸収分割
merger terms 合併条件
merging company 合併会社；合併会社
merit goods 価値財
merit increase 成功報酬
Merton model マートン・モデル
message from president 社長からのメッセージ
metal products industry 金属製品業界
method 手法
method based on the calendar year 暦年基準による方法
method of average price at the close of the preceding month 繰越平均単価払出法
method of comparative analysis 比較分析法
method of historical cost 取得原価法
method of making a resolution 議決方法
method of moments モーメント法
method of offering for subscription 募集方法
method of redemption 償還方法
method of resolution 決議方法
method of settlement 決済方法
method of simple interest 単利法
methodology 方法論
metropolitan inhabitant tax 都民税
Mexican central bank メキシコ中央銀行
Mexican Stock Exchange メキシコ証券取引所
mezzanine bond メザニン債
mezzanine bracket メザニン・ブラケット
mezzanine debt メザニン債
mezzanine finance メザニン・ファイナンス
mezzanine money 転換社債
mezzanine tranche メザニン・トランシェ
MGF (Malagasy franc) マダガスカル・フラン
MICEX (Moscow Interbank Currency Exchange) モスクワ銀行間通貨取

引所
micro accounting ミクロ会計
micro hedge ミクロヘッジ
microanalysis ミクロ分析
microeconomic improvement ミクロ経済の改善
microeconomics ミクロ経済学
microeconomy ミクロ経済
mid cap 中型株
Mid-America Commodity Exchange ミッド・アメリカ商品取引所
mid-market level 中値
mid-market value 仲値
mid-maturities 中期物
mid-point 中間点
mid-range product 中価格品
middle capitalization stock 中型株
middle management 中間管理職
middle of last month 先月半ば
middle range technology 中間技術
middle-size company 中堅企業
middle-sized stock 中堅株
middleman 仲介代理人
Midwest Stock Exchange ミッドウエスト証券取引所
MIGA (Multilateral Investment Guarantee Agency) 多国間投資保証機関
migration 移動
Milan Stock Exchange ミラノ証券取引所
mild recession マイルド・リセッション
milestone 工程目標
milestone date 達成時期
military law 軍事法
military power 軍事大国
milk the market 株式市場を操る
millions of units 百万単位
mimicking 擬似
mine マイン
mineral ore 鉱物
mineral product tax 鉱産税
mini investment ミニ投資
mini max. principle ミニ・マックス原理
mini stock ミニ株式市場
mini tap ミニ・タップ
mini. max. bond ミニ・マックス債
mini-refunding ミニ・リファンディング
minimum access 最低限輸入業務
minimum annual return 最低年間利益
minimum bid 最低入札価格
minimum capital 最低自己資本
minimum capital requirement 最低資本要件
minimum capital system 最低資本金制度
minimum cash balance 最小現金残高
minimum conversion exercise price 最低転換行使価格
minimum cost rule 原価比較法
minimum denomination 最低券面単位
minimum denomination on which interest is calculated 付利単位
minimum disclosure 最低限の開示
minimum elements 最低限の要素
minimum exempt income 最低免税所得
minimum expected rate of return 最低期待収益率
minimum expense for tax collection 最小徴税費
minimum face value 最低額面金額
minimum fluctuation 最小値幅
minimum fluctuation unit 最小変動単位
minimum freight 最低運賃
minimum fund 最低資金
minimum funding requirement 最低積立要件
minimum funding standard 最低積立基準
minimum guarantee 最低保証金
minimum inventory 最低在高
minimum items 最低限の項目
minimum lease payments payable 未払最低リース料総額
minimum lease payments receivable

未収最低リース料総額
minimum lending rate 最低貸出歩合
minimum liability 最小負債
minimum liability requirement 最小負債計上要件
minimum line items 最小限の項目
minimum liquidity ratio 最低流動性比率
minimum lot 最小単位
minimum maintenance 最低証拠金
minimum margin 最低利幅
minimum margin requirement 最低証拠金率
minimum marginal cost 最小限界費用
minimum payment 最低支払額
minimum pension liabilities 最小年金債務
minimum pension liability adjustment 最小年金債務調整額
minimum policy amount 最低保険金
minimum premium 最低保険料
minimum premium rate 最低保険料率
minimum price fluctuation of equity options 株券オプション取引の呼値単位
minimum profit 最小利潤
minimum quantity 最低注文量
minimum rate 最低料率
minimum rate of interest 最低利率
minimum redemption floor 償還時の元本保証
minimum requirements 最低限の要件
minimum reserve requirement 最低積立規準額
minimum sacrifice 最低の犠牲
minimum scheme contribution 最低拠出額
minimum solvency standard 最低支払能力基準
minimum standard 最低基準
minimum stock 最低在高
minimum structure 最小限の構成
minimum surplus 資本最低限度
minimum surrender value 最低返戻金
minimum taxable income 課税最低限
minimum taxation 最低課税
minimum tick 最小ティック
minimum total lease payments 最低リース料総額
minimum total sub-lease payments 最低サブリース料総額
minimum unit of exercise 最小単位の権利行使
minimum value 最小値
minimum value method 最小価値法
minimum variance frontier 最小分散フロンティアー
minimum variance portfolio 最小分散ポートフォリオ
minimum variation of bids and offers 呼値の単位
minimum vesting standard 最低受給権付与基準
minimum wage 最低賃金
mining accounting 鉱業会計
mining and manufacturing 鉱工業
mining area 鉱区
mining concession 採掘権
mining industry 鉱業
mining lease 鉱業賃借権
mining partnership 鉱業組合
mining products 鉱産物
mining property 鉱業資産
mining rights 鉱業権
mining tax 鉱業税
Minister for Financial Services 金融担当大臣
Minister for Public Management, Home Affairs, Posts and Telecommunications 総務大臣
Minister of Agriculture, Forestry and Fisheries 農林水産大臣
Minister of Economy, Trade and Industry 経済産業大臣
Minister of Education, Culture, Sports, Science and Technology 文部科学大臣
Minister of Finance 財務大臣
Minister of Foreign Affairs 外務大臣
Minister of Health, Labour and Welfare

厚生労働大臣
Minister of Justice 法務大臣
Minister of Land, Infrastructure and Transport 国土交通大臣
Minister of State for Administrative Reform and Regulatory Reform 行政改革・規制改革担当大臣
Minister of State for Defense 防衛庁長官
Minister of State for Disaster Management 防災担当大臣
Minister of State for Economic and Fiscal Policy 経済財政担当大臣
Minister of State for Financial Services, Economic and Fiscal Policy 金融担当・経済財政政策担当大臣
Minister of State for Food Safety Commission and Related Matters 食品安全担当大臣
Minister of State for Gender Equality 男女共同参画担当大臣
Minister of State for Industrial Revitalization Corporation 産業再生機構担当大臣
Minister of State for Okinawa and Northern Territories Affairs 沖縄及び北方対策担当大臣
Minister of State for Science and Technology Policy 科学技術政策担当大臣
Minister of State for Special Zones for Structural Reform 構造改革特区担当大臣
Minister of the Environment 環境大臣
Minister's Secretariat 大臣官房
ministerial clearance 当局の許可
ministerial ordinance 省令
ministerial power 事務的権能
Ministry of Agriculture, Forestry and Fisheries 農林水産省
Ministry of Economy, Trade and Industry 経済産業省
Ministry of Education, Culture, Sports, Science and Technology 文部科学省
Ministry of Finance 財務省
Ministry of Foreign Affaires 外務省
Ministry of Health, Labour and Welfare 厚生労働省
Ministry of Justice 法務省
Ministry of Land, Infrastructure and Transport 国土交通省
Ministry of Public Management, Home Affairs, Posts and Telecommunications 総務省
Ministry of the Environment 環境省
Minneapolis Grain Exchange ミネアポリス穀物取引所
minor 未成年者
minor account 未成年者の取引口座
minor cycle 小循環
minor rally 小戻し
minor tax credit 未成年者控除
minority 少数派
minority buy-out 少数株主持ち分の買い取り
minority control 少数支配
minority interest 少数株主持ち分
minority interest amount 少数株主持ち分金額
minority interest holder 少数株主
minority representation 少数代表法
minority shareholders 少数株主
minority shareholders' right 少数株主権
mint par of exchange 法定平価
mint price 鋳造価格
mintage 鋳造貨幣
MINURCA (United Nations Mission in the Central African Republic) 国連中央アフリカ共和国ミッション
MINURSO (United Nations Mission for the Referendum in Western Sahara) 国連西サハラ住民投票ミッション
minus factor マイナス要因
minus growth マイナス成長
minus tick マイナス・ティック
minus-ceiling マイナス・シーリング

minutes 議事要旨
minutes of meeting of the board of directors 取締役会議事録
MIPONUH (United Nations Civilian Police Mission in Haiti) 国連ハイチ文民警察ミッション
mirror swap 反対スワップ
mirrored trade 反対取引
misapplication 使込み
misappropriation 背任
misappropriation of funds 不当支出
misappropriation of goods 物品横領
miscalculation 計算誤り
miscellaneous accounts 雑勘定
miscellaneous accounts payable 諸未払金
miscellaneous accounts receivable 諸未収金
miscellaneous assets 雑資産
miscellaneous expenses 雑費
miscellaneous gains 雑益
miscellaneous income 雑所得
miscellaneous local taxes 雑種税
miscellaneous loss 雑損
miscellaneous provision 雑則
miscellaneous receipts 雑収入
miscellaneous revenue 雑収益
misconduct 違反行為
misery index 貧困指数
misfeasance 不法行為
misfit portfolio 乖離ポートフォリオ
misfit return 乖離リターン
misfit risk 乖離リスク
misinterpretation 解釈の誤り
misjoinder 誤った併合
mismatch between assets and liabilities 資産と負債のミスマッチ
mismatch risk ミスマッチ・リスク
mismatched FRN ミスマッチ変動利付債
mismatching ミスマッチ
misnomer 氏名誤記
mispresentation 不実表示
mispriced security 割高・割安証券
mispricing ミスプライス
missing of the market 取引の失敗
missing the market 市場を失うこと
mission 任務
mission statement 基本規約
misstatement 不実記載
mistake of fact 事実の錯誤
mistake of law 法律の錯誤
misunderstanding 誤解
MIT (market if touched) order 条件付成行注文
MIT (municipal investment trust) 地方債投資信託
mitigate 緩和する
mitigation 軽減
mix 構成比率
mixed 気迷い
mixed account 混合勘定
mixed assets 混合資産
mixed capitalist economy 混合資本主義体制
mixed collateral 混合抵当
mixed company 混合会社
mixed contract 混合契約
mixed economy 混合経済
mixed farming 混合農業
mixed gift 混合贈与
mixed insurance 生死混合保険
mixed inventory 混合棚卸
mixed policy 混合保険
mixed portfolio 混合ポートフォリオ
mixed property 混合財産
mixed question of law and fact 法律と事実との混合問題
mixed reserve 混合準備金
mixed strategy 混合戦略
mixed surplus 混合剰余金
mixed tariff 混合関税
mixed transaction 混合取引
mixed trust ミックス・トラスト
mixed undertaking 公私混合企業
mixed variance 混合差異
mixed views 分かれた見解
mixture 混合
MJDS (multi-jurisdictional disclosure system) 多数国同時開示システム

M

MKD (Macedonian denar) マケドニア・デナール
MLP (minimum lease payment) 最低リース支払額
MLR (minimum lending rate) 最低貸出金利
MM (market maker) マーケット・メーカー
MMK (Myanmar kyat) ミャンマー・キャット
MML (money market loan) 市場金利連動型貸出
MNE (multinational enterprise) 多国籍企業
MNT (Mongolian tugrik) モンゴル・トゥグリク
MOB (municipal over bond) spread 地方債とTBの利回り格差
mobile shop 移動店舗
mobilization 動員
MOC (market on close) order 引注文
mode 最頻値
mode of transportation 輸送方法
mode premium 一回分の保険料
model モデル
model analysis モデル分析
model error モデル誤差
model price モデル価格
model theory モデル理論
moderate recovery 緩やかな回復
moderation 縮小
modern economics 近代経済学
modern market economy 現代市場経済
modern portfolio theory 現代ポートフォリオ理論
modernization of smaller enterprise 中小企業の近代化
modernization program 近代化計画
modest economic expansion 景気の穏やかな回復
modest profit 小さな利益
modest rebound 穏やかな景気回復
modestly-priced 割安な
modification 修正
modified accounts 修正財務諸表
modified accrual basis 修正発生主義
modified all-inclusive theory 修正包括主義
modified auditor's report 修正監査報告書
modified capitalism 修正資本主義
modified cash refund annuity 修正償還年金
modified delivery-date basis 修正受渡日基準
modified duration モディファイド・デュレーション
modified endowment 修正養老保険
modified funding 修正積立
modified historical cost 修正取得原価
modified loan 変更された貸付
modified pass-through 変更型パス・スルー
modified restructuring 修正リストラクチャリング
Modigliani-Miller theory モジリアーニ・ミラーの命題
MoM (month-on-month) 前月比
moment モーメント
moment generating function 積率母関数
momentum はずみ
momentum indicators モーメンタム指標
momentum oscillator モーメンタム・オシレータ
momentum strategy モーメンタム戦略
Monaco (French franc) モナコ（仏フラン）
monadic operation 単項演算
monetarism マネタリズム
monetarist マネタリスト
monetarization of government bonds 国債の貨幣化
monetary accommodation 金融緩和
Monetary Agency of Singapore シンガポール通貨監督庁
monetary aggregate マネー・サプライ
monetary agreement 通貨協定

M

monetary amount 貨幣額
monetary analysis 貨幣分析
monetary and credit control 金融・信用規制
Monetary and Economic Studies 金融研究
monetary and financial policy 通貨・金融政策
monetary approach 貨幣的アプローチ；マネタリー・アプローチ
monetary assets 貨幣性資産
monetary authority 通貨当局
Monetary Base and the Bank of Japan's Transactions マネタリー・ベースと日本銀行の取引
monetary bloc 通貨ブロック
monetary capital 貨幣資本
monetary claims for housing loans 住宅貸付債権
monetary claims purchased 買現先勘定
monetary control 金融調節；通貨管理
monetary control matters 金融調節事項
monetary control purpose 通貨管理目的
monetary crisis 通貨危機
monetary current assets 貨幣性流動資産
monetary current liabilities 貨幣性流動負債
monetary easing 金融緩和；量的緩和
monetary easing measures 金融緩和措置
monetary effect 貨幣効果
monetary excess 過剰流動性
monetary expansion 金融拡大
monetary financial assets 貨幣性金融資産
monetary financial liabilities 貨幣性金融負債
monetary growth 金融拡大
monetary growth model 貨幣成長モデル
monetary illusion 貨幣幻想
monetary indicators 金融指標
monetary instability 通貨不安
monetary interest rate 貨幣利子率
monetary items 金銭項目
monetary management 通貨管理
monetary measurement principle 貨幣的測定の原則
monetary multiplier 貨幣乗数
monetary obligation 金銭債務
monetary policy 金融政策
monetary policy stimulus 金融政策による刺激策
monetary policy tool 金融政策手段
monetary receivables 金銭債権
monetary receivables and payables in foreign currencies 外貨建金銭債権債務
monetary receivables or payables 金銭債権債務
monetary reform 通貨改革
monetary regime 金融体制
monetary reserve 通貨準備
monetary restraint 金融引締め
monetary stability 通貨安定
monetary standard 本位制度
monetary standard policy 本位政策
monetary stringency 金詰り
monetary survey マネタリー・サーベイ
monetary system 貨幣制度
monetary target マネタリー・ターゲット
monetary tightening 金融引締め
monetary transfer 貨幣的トランスファー
monetary trust 金銭信託
monetary union 通貨同盟
monetary unit 通貨単位
monetary valuation 貨幣的評価
monetary working capital 貨幣運転資本
monetization of the debt 債務の貨幣化
money and/or property distributed per stock 一株当りの価額あるいは資産額

M

money appropriated 充当金
money at call コール資金
money back guarantee 保険料返還保証
money bill 金銭法案
money borrowed for short-term 短期借入金
money borrowed to purchase stocks 株式取得の為の借入金
money broker 金融業者
money center bank マネーセンター・バンク
money changer 両替商
money claim 金銭債権
money contribution 金銭出資
money deposited 預け金
money earmarked 充当金
money entrusted 寄託金
money entrusted to the financial agent 財務代理人への信託金
money exchange 外国通貨両替
money flow 資金循環
money flow analysis マネー・フロー分析
money flow table 資金循環表
money game マネーゲーム
money illusion 貨幣的錯覚
money in bank 預金
money in token of sympathy 見舞金
money in trust 金銭信託
money judgment 金銭判決
money laundering マネー・ロンダリング
money lender 金融業者
money lending business 金銭貸付業
money making 営利
money management 資金運用
money manager 資産運用者
money market 短期金融市場
money market account 短期金融勘定；マネー・マーケット・アカウント
money market broker 短資業者
money market certificate 市場金利連動型定期預金
money market conditions index 金融市場情勢指標
money market control 金融市場調節
money market data 金融市場データ
money market dealer 短資会社
money market deposit 資金市場からの預金
money market deposit account 短期金融市場預金勘定
money market differential 金融市場格差
money market fund 短期金融商品ファンド；マネー・マーケット・ファンド
money market index 短期金融市場指数
money market instrument 短期金融商品
money market intervention 金融市場介入
money market loan 市場金利連動型貸出
money market management 金融調節
money market mutual funds 短期証券投資信託
money market note マネー・マーケット・ノート
money market operations 短期金融市場操作
money market placement 資金市場への預け金
money market preferred stock マネー・マーケット優先株
money market rate 市中金利；短期金利
money market securities 金融市場証券
money market unit trust マネー・マーケット・ユニット・トラスト
money market yield マネー・マーケット利回り
money multiplier 通貨乗数
money order 送金為替
money paid in part 内金
money paid temporarily 一時金
money paid under mistake 非債弁済
money purchase plan 定額拠出年金
money rate 金利

money received 入金
money settlement instructions 資金決済指図
money spread マネー・スプレッド
money stock 通貨ストック
Money Stock (preliminary) マネー・サプライ（速報）
money supply マネー・サプライ
money supply control マネー・サプライ管理
money tolerance 決済金額誤差許容範囲
money value 貨幣価値；現金支払額
money veil theory 貨幣ベール観
money-weighted rate of return 金額加重収益率
monitor 監視する
monitored loans 管理債権
monitoring 監視
monitoring cost 監視コスト
monitoring of delivery 受け渡しの監視
monoline insurance company 専門保険会社
monometallic standard 単本位制度
monopolistic competition 独占的競争
monopoly 占有権
monopoly assessment 専売課税
monopoly capital 独占資本
monopoly position 独占地位
monopoly price 独占価格
monopoly profit 専売利益
monopsony 需要独占
monopurpose credit card 単一目的カード
monorate of exchange system 単一為替市場制
Monroe Doctrine モンロー主義
Monte Carlo simulation モンテカルロ・シュミレーション
Montenegro (Yugoslav dinar) モンテネグロ（ユーゴ・ディナール）
month order 月内有効注文
month to which the last trading day pertains 最終取引日の属する月
month-end delivery 月末渡し
month-to-month change 対前月比変化
monthly accounting 月末決算
monthly allotment of depreciable period 減価償却の月割計算
monthly annuity 月払年金
monthly average 月中平均
monthly average method 月次総平均法
monthly balance sheet 月次貸借対照表
monthly change 月次変化
monthly chart 月足チャート
monthly closing average 終値月中平均
monthly compounding of interest 月次複利計算
monthly highs and lows 月間高低
monthly income policy 毎月支払保険
monthly income statement 月次損益計算書
monthly indemnity 月額補償
monthly installment 月賦
monthly installment sales 月賦販売
monthly interest rate 月利
monthly investment plan 月掛投資計画
monthly payment 毎月払い
monthly pension 月額の年金
monthly premium 月額保険料
monthly report 月報
Monthly Report of Recent Economic and Financial Developments 金融経済月報
monthly reversal マンスリー・リバーサル
monthly settlement 月次決済
monthly settlement of accounts 月次決算
monthly spread 月間スプレッド
monthly statement 月次計算書
monthly statement of account 月計表
monthly trial balance 月次試算表
Montreal Exchange モントリオール証券取引所
Montserrat (EC (East Caribbean) dollar) モンテセラト（東カリブ・ドル）
MONUA (United Nations Observer

Mission in Angola) 国連アンゴラ監視団
Moody's ムーディーズ
Moody's investment grade ムーディーズ投資適格
MOP (Macau pataca) マカオ・パタカ
moral consideration 道徳的約因
moral hazard 道義的危険；モラル・ハザード
moral obligation 道徳上の義務
moral obligation bond 道義的支払保証債券
moral risks モラル・リスク
moral suasion 道義的説得
moral turpitude 不道徳行為
moratorium モラトリアム
moratorium period 支払猶予期間
moratory interest 損害賠償利子
more current period より長い中間期
more or less terms 数量過不足容認条件
moribund property 無くなりかけている財産
morning report 早朝レポート
morning session 前場
morning trading session 午前立会い
mortality 廃棄率
mortality profit 死差益
mortality rate 死亡率
mortgage モーゲージ
mortgage agency 抵当機関
mortgage annuity モーゲージ年金
mortgage application モーゲージ申込み
mortgage backed bond モーゲージ担保債券
mortgage backed certificate モーゲージ担保証券
mortgage backed securities 抵当証券；モーゲージ証券
mortgage bank 抵当銀行
mortgage bond 物上担保付社債
mortgage bond coupon モーゲージ社債金利
mortgage business 住宅ローン事業
mortgage by transfer 譲渡担保
mortgage cancellation モーゲージ償還
mortgage clause 抵当権設定約款
mortgage collateral type モーゲージ担保型
mortgage commitments モーゲージ承認件数
mortgage correspondent モーゲージ取次業者
mortgage credit 不動産金融
Mortgage Credit Association 抵当信用組合
mortgage credit bond 抵当信用債
mortgage creditor モーゲージ権者
mortgage debentures 担保付社債券；モーゲージ付社債券
mortgage debentures in trust 担保付社債信託
mortgage debentures trust law 担保付社債信託法
mortgage debt モーゲージ債務
mortgage debtor 抵当権設定者
mortgage delinquency モーゲージ債務不履行
mortgage derivatives モーゲージ派生商品
mortgage documents 抵当証書類
mortgage elasticity モーゲージの価格弾力性
mortgage finance company 抵当金融会社
mortgage fund モーゲージ・ファンド
mortgage guarantee insurance モーゲージ保証保険
mortgage holder モーゲージ利用者
mortgage indebtedness モーゲージ債務
mortgage indemnity policy モーゲージ補償保険
mortgage insurance 抵当保険
mortgage interest deduction 住宅ローン金利控除
mortgage interest payment 住宅ローン金利
mortgage investment trust 担保付投資

M

信託
mortgage lending 不動産担保貸付；モーゲージ貸付
mortgage life insurance モーゲージ生命保険
mortgage loan 抵当ローン
mortgage market モーゲージ市場
mortgage note 抵当証券
mortgage of goods 動産モーゲージ（譲渡抵当）
mortgage of ship 船舶抵当権
mortgage participation certificates モーゲージ参加証券
mortgage pass-through certificate モーゲージ・パス・スルー証書
mortgage payable 抵当借入金
mortgage payment モーゲージ返済額
mortgage payment protection モーゲージ返済保障
mortgage pool モーゲージ・プール
mortgage portfolio モーゲージ・ポートフォリオ
mortgage process モーゲージ設定手続
mortgage rate 住宅ローン金利；モーゲージ・レート
mortgage refinancing モーゲージ借り換え
mortgage REIT (real estate investment trust) モーゲージ不動産投資信託
mortgage rights 抵当権
mortgage securities 抵当証券
mortgage servicing rights モーゲージ・サービシング権
mortgage strips モーゲージ・ストリップ証券
mortgage swap モーゲージ・スワップ
mortgage term モーゲージ期間
mortgage the right 権利を担保に供する
mortgage writing bank モーゲージ発行銀行
mortgageable chattels 抵当となりうる動産
mortgagee モーゲージ（譲渡抵当）権者
mortgages 抵当権付借入；モーゲージ債
mortgages receivable 担保付貸付金
mortgagor 抵当権設定者
most active list 大商銘柄リスト
most deliverable bond 受渡最適債券
most favored nation clause 最恵国条項
most favored nation treatment 最恵国待遇
most recent purchase method 最終仕入原価法
most seriously affected countries 最深刻被影響国
Mothers マザーズ
motion 動議
motion day 申立審理日
motivation 動機
motivation research 動機調査
motor insurance 自動車保険
MOU (memorandum of understanding) 覚書
mounting 据付
mounting concerted efforts 共同歩調を取る
movable and immovable asset account 動産不動産勘定
movable band ムーバブル・バンド
movable property in trust 動産信託
movables 動産
movables comprehensive insurance 動産総合保険
move down 繰り下げる
move into high yield ハイ・イールド債への移行
movement in equity 資本の変動
movement in fair value 公正価値の変動
movement of equity 資本の増減
movement of funds 資金移動
movement of market price 値動き
movements in net liability 負債の純額の変動
moving at around 前後で推移している
moving average convergence 移動平均収束

moving average cost method 移動平均法
moving average deviations 移動平均値
moving average index 移動平均指数
moving average inventory method 移動平均棚卸法
moving average method 移動平均法
moving average model 移動平均モデル
moving downward 下降
moving equilibrium 移動均衡
moving weighted average 移動加重平均
moving weighted average method 移動加重平均法
MPC (Market Performance Committee) 市場動向委員会
MPM (Monetary Policy Meeting) 金融政策決定会合
MRO (Mauritanian ougiya) モーリタニア・オーギヤ
MRR (minimum retail rate) 最低貸出金利
MSE (mean square error) 平均自乗誤差
MSS (Management System Standard) マネージメントシステム企画
MSVR (mandatory securities valuation reserve) 証券評価準備金
MTL (Maltese lira) マルタ・リラ
MTN (medium term note) メディアム・ターム・ノート
MTP (money transfer payable) 普通買為替
MUD (municipal utility district) 地方公共事業体
multi factor 多因子
multi-currency clause 多通貨条項
multi-currency intervention 複数通貨介入
multi-currency MMF 外貨建 MMF
multi-employer plan 多事業主制度
multi-employer welfare agreement 多事業主福祉制度
multi-factor model 複数要因モデル
multi-family house 多世帯住宅
multi-line company 多種目販売会社
multi-market listed company 重複上場企業
multi-national group 多国籍グループ
multi-national insurance pooling 多国間保険共同受託
multi-sectoral analysis 多部門分析
multibank holding company 複数銀行持株会社
multilateral agreement 多国間協定
multilateral clearing agreement 多角的清算協定
multilateral initiative 多国間交渉
Multilateral Investment Guarantee Agency 多数国間投資保証機関
multilateral lending institutions 国際金融機関
multilateral settlement 多角決済
multilateral trade negotiations 多角的貿易交渉
multilevel marketing マルチ商法
multinational bank 多国籍銀行
multiple banking system 複数銀行制度
multiple correlation 多元相関
multiple currency accounting 多通貨会計
multiple equilibriums 複数均衡
multiple evidence 多元的証拠
multiple income 複数所得
multiple institutions 複数機関
multiple life plan 複数生存者連生保険
multiple line agent 生損保併売外務員
multiple listing 同時上場
multiple maturity deposit 複数満期預金
multiple option funding facilities マルティプル・オプション・ファンディング・ファシリティ
multiple payment credit card 割賦カード
multiple peril insurance 複合危険保険
multiple price auction 競争入札オークション；コンベンショナル方式
multiple protection insurance 高倍率保障保険

multiple purpose bank account 総合口座
multiple regression 多重回帰
multiple regression analysis 多重回帰分析
multiple regression model 多重回帰モデル
multiple step 区分式
multiple tariff system 複関税制
multiple tax rate 複数税率
multiple-step form 多段階式
multiple-step income statement 区分損益計算書
multiple-step statement 複数区分計算書
multiplicity of action 訴訟の重複
multiplied effect 波及効果
multiplier 乗数
multiplier analysis 乗数分析
multiplier effect 乗数効果
multiplier theory 乗数理論
multiply listed company 重複上場企業
multivariate analysis 多変量解析
municipal bond 地方債
municipal bond fund 地方公共団体債券ファンド
municipal bond insurance 地方債信用保険
municipal bond interest 地方債利息
municipal bond unit investment trust 単位型地方債投資信託
municipal bylaws 条例
municipal corporation 地方公共団体
municipal finance 都市財政
municipal futures 地方債先物
municipal inhabitants tax 市町村民税
municipal note 地方債
municipal ordinances 地方条例
municipal property tax 市町村固定資産税
municipal revenue bond 地方特定財源債
municipal securities 地方債証券
municipal securities dealer 公共債ディーラー
municipal tax 市町村税
municipal tax free bond 非課税地方債
municipal tobacco excise tax 市町村たばこ税
MUR (Mauritius rupee) モーリシャス・ルピー
mutatis mutandis 準用
mutilated check 毀損小切手
mutilated security 毀損証券
mutilation 損傷
mutilation of documents 文書毀損
mutual account 相互計算
mutual agreement procedure 相互協議
mutual aid 共済
mutual aid association 共済組合
mutual aid association of government offices 官公庁共済組合
mutual aid contract for retirement allowance 退職金共済契約
mutual aid money 共済金
mutual aid organization for specific retirement allowance 特定退職金共済団体
mutual aid premium 共済掛金
mutual aid system 共済金制度
mutual assistance insurance 共済保険
mutual ballot 互選
mutual benefit society 相互福利社団
mutual company 相互会社
mutual condition 相互条件
mutual covenant 相互捺印契約
mutual credits 相互貸借
mutual cross holding of shares 株式相互持合い
mutual debt 相対債務
mutual exclusion doctrine 相互免除理論
mutual fund ミューチュアル・ファンド
mutual fund debit program ミューチュアル・ファンド自動積立プログラム
mutual fund reinvestment program ミューチュアル・ファンド再投資プログラム

M

mutual fund underwriters ミューチュアル・ファンド引受業者
mutual holding company 相互持株会社
mutual insurance 相互保険
mutual interest 相互の利益
mutual life insurance company 生命保険相互会社
mutual life insurance policy 相互生命保険契約
mutual offset system 相互決済制度
mutual premium payment 相互掛金
mutual promise 相互約束
mutual protection association 相互補償組合
mutual savings bank 相互貯蓄銀行
mutual sharing 相互共有
mutual sharing of interests 持ち分の継続
mutual vote 互選
mutual wills 相互遺言
mutual-aid pension 共済年金
mutuality of obligation 債務の相互性
mutuality of remedy 救済の相互性
mutually exclusive event 相互独立的出来事
MVA (market value added) 市場付加価値
MVR (Maldives rufiyaa) モルディブ・ルフィア
MWK (Malawi kwacha) マラウィ・クワチャ
MXN (Mexican peso) メキシコ・ペソ
myopic portfolio 近視眼的ポートフォリオ
MYR (Malaysian ringgit) マレーシア・リンギット
MZM (Mozambique metical) モザンビーク・メティカル

N

N.H.K bond 放送債
NACCS (Nippon Automated Cargo Clearance System) Operations Organization 通関情報処理センター
NACHA (National Automated Clearing House Association) 全米 ACH 協会
NACT 全米企業財務担当者協会
NAD (Namibia dollar) ナミビア・ドル
NAFTA (North America Free Trade Agreement) 北米自由貿易協定
Nagoya Stock Price Index 名証株価指数
NAIC (National Association of Insurance Commissioners) 全米保険監督官協会
naked call ネーキッド・コール
naked contract 無約因契約
naked option ネーキッド・オプション
naked position ネーキッド・ポジション
naked warrant ネーキッド・ワラント
name borrowing 名義借り
name list 人名簿
name of issue 銘柄
name of the JGS holder 登録名義人
name selection 銘柄選別
name share 記名株
name transfer 名義書換
named bill 記名式手形
named fiduciary 指名受託者
named insured 指名被保険者
named peril 特定危険
named perils insurance 特定危険担保保険
nano-second ナノ秒
NAPM (National Association of Purchasing Management) 全米購買部協会
NAR (National Association of Realtors) 全米不動産業協会
narrative form 報告式
narrow 縮小する
narrow based stock index 業種別株価指数
narrow market 閑散市場；売買高の少ない市場
narrow market securities 品薄株
narrow movement 小幅往来
narrow range 小幅；狭いボックス圏
narrow seas 海峡
narrow spread 小ザヤ
narrowing of spread さや寄せ
narrowing rate differentials 金利差の縮小
NASD Form FR-1 NASD 様式 FR-1
NASDAQ ナスダック
NASDAQ (National Association of Securities Dealers Automated Quotation) ナスダック
NASDAQ Composite Index ナスダック総合株価指数
NASDAQ Japan ナスダック・ジャパン
National Accounting Office 主計局
national accounts 国民勘定
National Agency for Automotive Safety and Victims' Aid 自動車事故対策機構
National Agency for the Advancement of Sports and Health 日本スポーツ振興センター
National Agency of Vehicle Inspection 自動車検査独立行政法人
National Agriculture and Bio-oriented Research Organization 農業・生物系特定産業技術研究機構
National Archives of Japan 国立公文書館
national assets 固有財産

National Association of Accountants 米国会計人協会
National Association of Cost Accountants アメリカ原価計算士協会
National Association of Investors Corporation 全米投資家協会
National Association of Securities Dealers 全米証券業協会
National Association of Securities Dealers Automated Quotations 店頭銘柄気配自動通報システム
National Association of Securities Dealers' Automated Quotation 店頭銘柄気配自動通報
national averages 全国平均
national balance sheet 国民貸借対照表
National Bank Act of 1863 国法銀行法
national bank notes 国立銀行紙幣
national burden ratio 国民負担率
national capital 国民資本
national capital account 国民資本勘定
national capital sheet 国民資本表
national care system 公的介護制度
National Center for Industrial Property Information 工業所有権総合情報館
National Center for Seeds and Seedings Independent Administrative Institution 種苗管理センター
National Center for Teachers' Development 教員研修センター
National Center for University Entrance Examinations 大学入試センター
National Conference of Stock Exchanges 全国証券取引所協議会
National Consumer Affairs Center of Japan 国民生活センター
national coverage insurance 国民皆保険
national credit 国家信用
National Credit Union Administration 全国信用組合本部
national custom 国の習慣
national debt 国家債務
national debt service cost 国債費
national debt service expenditure 公債費
national debt service payment 国債費
National Diet Library 国立国会図書館
national disposable income 国民可処分所得
national economic accounting 国民経済計算
national economic activities 国民経済活動
national economic budget 国民経済予算
national economy 国民経済
national expenditure 国民支出
National Farmers Academy 農業者大学校
National Federation of Credit Guarantee Corporations 全国信用保証協会連合会
National Federation of Labor Credit Associations 労働金庫連合会
national finance 国家財政
National Fisheries University 水産大学校
National Food Research Institute 食品総合研究所
National Foundation for Consumer Credit 全米消費者金融財団
national full line firm 総合証券会社
National Futures Association 全米先物協会
national health care cost 国民医療費コスト
national health care plan 国民医療制度
National Health Insurance Program 国民健康保険
national health insurance tax 国民健康保険税
national income accounting 国民所得会計
national income accounts 国民所得勘

定
national income analysis 国民所得分析
national income distributed 分配国民所得
national income statistics 国民所得統計
National Institute for Agro-Environmental Sciences 農業環境技術研究所
National Institute for Environmental Studies 国立環境研究所
National Institute for Japanese Language 国立国語研究所
National Institute for Materials Science 物質・材料研究機構
National Institute for Rural Engineering 農業工学研究所
National Institute for Sea Training 航海訓練所
National Institute of Advanced Industrial Science and Technology 産業技術総合研究所
National Institute of Agrobiological Sciences 農業生物資源研究所
National Institute of Health and Nutrition 国立健康・栄養研究所
National Institute of Industrial Health 産業医学総合研究所
National Institute of Industrial Safety 産業安全研究所
National Institute of Information and Communications Technology 情報通信研究機構
National Institute of Radiological Sciences 放射線医学総合研究所
National Institute of Special Education 国立特殊教育総合研究所
National Institute of Technology and Evaluation 製品評価技術基盤機構
national insurance contribution 国民医療保険料
national insurance rate 国民保険料率
national interest 国益
National Life Finance Corporation 国民生活金融公庫
National Livestock Breeding Center 家畜改良センター
National Maritime Research Institute 海上技術安全研究所
national market exchanges 全米市場取引所
national markets 国内市場
national median 全国中央値
national minimum ナショナル・ミニマム
National Museum of Art 国立美術館
National Mutual Insurance Federation of Agricultural Cooperatives 全国共済農業協同組合連合会
national natural disaster coverage 国民自然災害保険
national output 国民産出高
national pension 国民年金
National Pension Fund 国民年金基金
National Pension Fund Association 国民年金基金連合会
National Pension Insurance 国民年金保険
National Pension Plan 国民年金制度
National Personnel Authority 人事院
National Police Agency 警察庁
national practices 国内慣行
National Printing Bureau 国立印刷局
national property 国有財産
National Property Acquisition and Disposition Division 国有財産業務課
National Property Appraiser 国有財産評価指導官
National Property Examination and Appraisal Division 国有財産審理課
National Property Information Office 国有財産情報室
National property Inspector 国有財産監査指導官
National Property Policy Planning and Legal Division 国有財産企画課
national public employee 国家公務員
National Public Safety Commission 国

N

家公安委員会
National Public Service Law 国家公務員法
National Research Institute for Cultural Properties 文化財研究所
National Research Institute for Science and Disaster Prevention 防災科学技術研究所
National Research Institute of Brewing 酒類総合研究所
National Research Institute of Fire and Disaster 消防研究所
national reserve fund 全国準備基金
national retirement income policy 国民退職所得制度
National Salmon Resources Center さけ・ます資源管理センター
National Science Museum 国立科学博物館
national sector 公共部門
National Securities Clearing Corporation 米国証券取引所決済機関
national social insurance program 国民社会保険制度
national standards 国内基準
National Statistics Center 統計センター
national subsidy 国庫補助金
national tariff 国定税率
national tax 国税
National Tax Agency 国税庁
national tax collection 国税徴収
National Tax Collection Law 国税徴収法
National Tax College 税務大学校
National Tax Council 国税審議会
national tax examiner 国税調査官
national tax investigator 国税査察官
national tax procedure law 国税通則法
National Tax Receipt Fund 国税収納金整理資金
National Tax Tribunal 国税不服審判所
National Tax Violations Control Law 国税犯則取締法
National Traffic Safety and Environment Laboratory 交通安全環境研究所
national treasury 国庫
national treasury spending 国庫支出金
national treatment 内国民待遇
national trust ナショナル・トラスト
national wealth 国富
national wealth statistics 国富統計
National Women's Education Center, Japan 国立女性教育会館
nationalization 国有化
natural attrition 自然減
natural boundary 自然的境界
natural business year 自然営業年度
natural capital 自然資本
natural disaster 天災地変
natural disaster relief loans 天災資金
natural fruits 天然果実
natural increase 自然増
natural insurance premium 自然保険料
natural law 自然法
natural liberty 自然的自由
natural logarithm 自然対数
natural person 自然人
natural presumption 自然的推定
natural rate of interest 自然利子率
natural rate of unemployment 自然失業率
natural resources 天然資源
natural rights 自然権
natural support 自然的支持
natural year 暦年
nature of business 業務の内容
nature of expense 費用の性質
nature of expense method 費用性質法
nature of financial service 金融業の性質
nature of transaction 取引の性質
Nauru (Australian dollar) ナウル（豪ドル）
Naval Court 海事審判所
navigable 航行可能な

NDA (non-disclosure agreement) 守秘義務契約
NDP (net domestic product) 国内純生産
near cash asset 準現金資産
near contract month 期近限月取引
near future 目先
near maturity 期近
near money 準通貨
near term rally 足元での上昇
near the money ニア・ザ・マネー
near time prospect 目先観
near-panic market 恐慌相場
near-term bond 期近債
near-term outlook 短期見通し
near-term reversal 短期的な相場反転
nearby contract 期近物
nearbys 期近物
nearest contract month 直近限月
nearing its all time lows 最安値に近づく
necessaries 生活必需品
necessary documentary evidence 必要な証拠書類
necessary expense 必要経費
necessary expenses in the case of closing business 事業を廃止した場合の必要経費
necessary household furniture 必需家具
necessary matters 所要事項
necessary party 必要当事者
necessary tax procedure 必要な税務手続
Necigef オランダ保管振替機関
neck line ネックライン
negate 無効にする
negative 弱含み
negative amortization ネガティブ・アモチゼーション；負の返済
negative amount 負の金額
negative assets 消極資産
negative assurance 消極的保証
negative averments 消極的主張
negative capital 負債
negative carry ネガティブ・キャリー
negative cash flow 負のキャッシュフロー
negative clause 担保保留条項
negative confirmation 消極的確認
negative correlation 負の相関
negative covenant 否定的誓約
negative covenants ネガティブ・コベナント
negative definite matrix 不定置行列
negative duration 負のデュレーション
negative effect 負の効果；マイナス影響
negative equity 債務超過；マイナスの資産価値
negative evidence 消極的証拠
negative factor マイナス要因
negative goodwill 消極のれん；負ののれん
negative growth マイナス成長
negative impact マイナス影響
negative implication for the dollar ドル相場への圧迫
negative income tax 負の所得税
negative inflation マイナスのインフレ率
negative influence マイナスの影響
negative interest 逆金利
negative interest per diem 逆日歩
negative interest rate margin 逆ざや
negative interest rate spread 逆ざや
negative investment management 消極的投資管理
negative leverage effect 負のレバレッジ効果
negative list ネガティブ・リスト
negative market reaction 市場の反対派の勢い
negative monetary position 金銭債務状態
negative option ネガティブ・オプション
negative option sales 押付商法
negative past service cost 負の過去勤務費用

negative plea 消極的抗弁
negative pledge clause 担保制限条項；ネガティブ・プレッジ条項
negative pledge pari passu clause ネガティブ・プレッジ・パリパス条項
negative prescription 消滅時効
negative property 消極財産
negative statute 禁止的法律
negative territory ネガティブ領域
negative testimony 消極的証言
negative valuation accounts 消極的評価勘定
negative wealth effect 逆資産効果
negative working capital 負の運転資本
negative yield 逆イールド
negative yield curve 右下がり利回曲線
negligence 過失
negligence clause 免責条項
negligent misrepresentation 過失不実表示
negligible amount 無視しうる価額
negligible risk 僅かなリスク
negotiable 譲渡可能
negotiable asset 譲渡可能な資産
negotiable bill 流通手形
negotiable CD (certificate of deposit) 譲渡可能定期預金証書
negotiable document 流通権原証券
negotiable instrument 流通証券
Negotiable Instruments Act 流通証券法
negotiable L/C (letter of credit) 買取可能信用状
negotiable order of withdrawal deposit NOW 預金
negotiable rate mortgage 利率交渉型モーゲージ
negotiable securities submitted in payment of treasury funds 代用納付証券
negotiable time certificates of deposits 譲渡可能定期預金証書
negotiated commission 交渉手数料
negotiated contract 随意契約
negotiated market 相対市場
negotiated paper 譲渡性証書
negotiated rate 交渉料率
negotiated sale 協議発行
negotiated trading 相対取引
negotiated transaction 相対取引
negotiated underwriting 協議引受
negotiating bank 手形買取銀行
negotiation charge 手形買取手数料
negotiation credit 外国為替取組信用状
negotiation of endorsed documentary drafts 荷為替手形の買取
negotiation on terms and conditions 条件交渉
neighborhood benefits 隣地者の受益
neighborhood effect 近隣効果
neighboring countries 近隣諸国
Neimenggu 内蒙古自治区
NEO (non-equity options) 非株式オプション
neo-quantity theory of money 新貨幣数量説
nepotism 縁故採用
nervous market 神経質な市場環境
nervous shock 精神的衝撃
nest egg 蓄え
net aftertax gain 税引後正味キャピタル・ゲイン
net amount 純額
net amount after provision for loss 貸倒引当金控除後の金額
net amount at risk 正味危険金額
net amount expected to be collected 正味回収予定額
net amount presentation 純額表示
net amount principle 純額主義
net approach 純額アプローチ
net asset per share 一株当り純資産
net asset value 純資産価値
net asset value per unit 一ユニット当り純資産価値
net assets 純資産；正味財産
net assets available 利用可能な純資産
net assets per share 一株当り純資産
net assets value 正味資産価額

net avails 正味手取額
net base 純額ベース
net basis 純額基準
net block flow ネット・ブロック・フロー
net bond-related gains and losses 債券純損益
net book value 正味帳簿価額
net borrowed reserves 純借入準備
net budget 予算純計
net business profit 業務純益
net buyer ネット買手
net capital 必要資本金
net capital deficiencies 債務超過
net capital regulation ratio 自己資本規制比率
net capital requirement 純資本要件
net capital rule ネット・キャピタル・ルール
net capital stock 正味資本ストック
net carrying amount 計上純額；帳簿価額純額
net carryover cost 純持越費用
net cash ネット・キャッシュ
net cash balance 純現金収支
net cash flow ネット・キャッシュフロー
net cash from operating activities 営業活動による資金純額
net cash inflow 正味現金流入
net cash used in investing activities 投資活動で使用された資金純額
net change 純増減；前日比変動幅
net changes in each element 科目別純変動額
net collectible amounts 正味回収可能額
net commodity terms of trade 純商品交易条件
net cost 純原価
net creditor country 純債権国
net cumulative 正味累積の
net current assets 正味流動資産
net cycle time 正味運転時間
net debit cap 利用上限額
net debt 純負債；純有利子負債
net debt cap 支払債務額上限
net decrease 純減少額
net deferred hedging loss 繰延ヘッジ損失純額
net deferred tax liability 繰延税金負債純額
net disposal proceeds 正味処分受取金
net earnings 純利益
net earnings ratio to capital 資本利益率
net earnings ratio to total assets 総資産利益率
net employee benefit assets for defined benefit plan 給付建制度の正味資産
net employee benefit liabilities for defined benefit plan 給付建制度の正味負債
net equity assets 正味持ち分資産
net equity interest assets 正味持ち分資産
net estate 正味相続財産
net export 純輸出
net external assets 対外純資産
net external liabilities 対外純負債
net financial income 純金融収入
net fixed assets 正味固定資産
net foreign credit 対外純貸出し
net free reserves 純自由準備
net gain 純利得
net gearing 純負債比率
net income 純益
net income before taxes 税引前当期剰余金
net income for the year 当期純利益
net income per share of common stock 普通株式一株当り純利益
net income ratio 純利益率
net income to net worth ratio 純利益・純資産比率
net income to sales 売上純利益率
net increase 純増
net increase and decrease 純増減
net interest 純利息

net interest cost 純利息費用
net interest payment 正味金利支払い
net investment 純投資
net investment in lease 正味リース投資未回収額
net investment income per share 一株当り運用益
net investment outstanding 正味投資未回収額
net lease ネット・リース
net level premium reserve 平準保険料準備金
net liabilities 純負債
net liability 負債純額
net line 正味保有額
net liquidity balance 純流動性収支
net long positions 買超数量
net loss 純損失
net method 純額法
net monetary asset 正味貨幣資産
net monetary item 正味貨幣項目
net monetary liability 正味貨幣負債
net monetary position 純貨幣ポジション
net national welfare 国民福祉指標
net non-current assets 正味非流動資産
net of 控除後の
net of allowance and provision 引当金控除後の
net of cash acquisition 現金取得控除後
net of commission 手数料差引き後
net of income taxes 所得税を控除して
net of reserves 貸倒引当金控除後受取債権
net of reserves for bad debt 貸倒引当金控除後の
net of tax 税額控除後の純額で
net open position ネット・オープン・ポジション
net operating cycle 正味営業循環日数
net operating earnings 経常純益額
net operating income 業務純益
net operating loss 純営業損失
net operating loss assumed from a transfer of corporation 被合併会社から引き継いだ欠損金
net operating profit 業務純益
net output 純産出
net payment 純額決済
net payment cost index 正味払込保険料指数
net pension plan assets 年金プラン純資産
net position 差引建玉
net premium 純保険料
net present value 純現在価値
net price 裸値段
net price index ネット・プライス・インデックス
net price trading 裸値取引
net proceeds 正味受取代金
net production value 正味生産高
net profit 純益
net profit after depreciation 償却後純利益
net profit appropriation account 利益処分勘定
net profit attributable to common shareholders 普通株主に帰属する純利益
net profit before corporate tax 法人税引前純利益
net profit before corporation tax 法人税控除前純利益
net profit before depreciation 償却前純利益
net profit before tax and extraordinary item 税金及び異常損益項目控除前利益
net profit before the adjustment of tax 税金調整前純利益
net profit for the period 当期純利益
net profit from ordinary activities 経常活動からの利益
net profit margin 売上純利益率
net profit on sales 売上純益
net profit or loss 純損益
net profit or loss account 純損益計算
net profit or loss for the period 期間純損益

net profit or loss section 純損益区分
net profit ratio 純益率
net profit ratio to sales 売上高純利益率
net profit to net worth 自己資本利益率
net purchase 正味仕入高
net quick assets 正味当座資産
net realizable 正味実現可能な
net realizable value 正味実現可能価格
net realized capital gain 正味実現キャピタル・ゲイン
net receipt 揚げ超
net receipts 正味受取額
net receivables 純債権
net results 純損益
net retention 正味保有
net sale proceeds 売却手取額
net sales 正味売上高
net saving 純貯蓄
net seller ネット売手
net selling price 正味売却価格
net settlement 差金決済；純額決済
net settlement information ネット決済情報
net short hedging 純売りつなぎ
net short positions 売超数量
net stock-related gains and losses 株式純損益
net succession 純相続財産
net supply of industrial funds 産業資金供給状況
net surplus 純剰余金
net tangible asset ratio to long-term debt 長期負債正味固定資産
net tangible assets per share 一株当り正味有形資産
net taxable assets 純課税財産
net total 差引合計額
net trading volume 純取引高
net transaction 純取引
net translation difference 純換算差額
net value 正味価額
net working capital 正味運転資本
net worth 自己資本；正味資産
net worth equity 純資産
net worth equity capital 自己資本
net worth gearing ratio 自己資本負債比率
net worth method 資産負債増減法
net worth of collateral 担保余力
net worth ratio 自己資本比率
net write-off 正味貸し倒れ償却
net yield 税引利回り
net-of-tax method 税引後法
netted against 相殺される
netting ネッティング
netting arrangement ネッティング契約
netting by novation 更改によるネッティング
netting ratio ネッティング決済率
netting system member ネッティング会員
Network Systems Management Office 情報管理室
neutral basis 中立的な基準
neutral central bank activities 中央銀行の中立姿勢
neutral equilibrium 中立的均衡
neutral hedge ニュートラル・ヘッジ
neutral money principle 中立貨幣政策
neutral reading 中立
neutral territory 中立領域に
neutrality 中立性
neutrality of taxation 租税の中立性
new account 新規勘定
new banking law 新銀行法
New Basel Capital Accord 新 BIS 規制案
new bond 新発債
new business 新規事業
new business development 新規事業開発
new business premium 新契約保険料
new business ratio 新契約率
New Caledonia (CFP (Comptoirs Francais du Pacifique) franc) ニューカレドニア（CFP フラン）
new capacity 新設備
New Currency Act of 1871 新貨条例

New Deal ニュー・ディール
new description 新規記載
new description or record 新規記載又は記録
new design 新案
new discounts 新規ディスカウント物
new economics 新経済学
new economy ニュー・エコノミー
New Energy and Industrial Technology Development Organization 新エネルギー・産業技術総合開発機構
new face bond 新顔債
new field 新規分野
new financial resource bonds 新規財源債
New Financial Stabilization Fund 新金融安定化基金
new foreign exchange law 新外国為替管理法
new futures 新先物
new high 新高値
new home sales 新規住宅販売
new house for rent 新築賃貸住宅
New Institute Cargo Clauses 新協会貨物約款
new issuance 新規発行
new issue 新規案件
new issue value of outstanding bonds 公社債現存額
new issue volume of outstanding bonds 公社債発行額
new job offer 新規求人
new lending 新規貸出
new listing 新規上場
new loan 新規貸出
new low 新安値
new monetary adjustment system 新金融調節
new money 新規資金
new money interest rate 新規投資金利
new money preferred ニューマネー優先株
new mortgage 新規のモーゲージ
new option grant 新規オプション付与
new order 新規受注
new policy premium 新規保険料
new position 新規のポジション
new premium 新規プレミアム
new record 新規記録
new scheme for monetary control 新金融調節方式
new share 新株
new share issuing expense 新株発行費
new share off 新株落ち
new shares issued through rights-offering 新株落ちに係る増加新株
new shares issued through stock-dividends 株式配当落ちに係る増加新株
new social indicators 国民生活指標
new stock 新株
new stock price indexes 新株価指数
new tax 新税
new trial 再審
new type of gold standard 新型の金本位制
new welfare economics 新厚生経済学
New York acceptance credit ニューヨーク引受信用状
New York Curb Exchange ニューヨーク場外取引所
New York inter-bank offered rate ニューヨーク銀行間出し手金利
New York Mercantile Exchange ニューヨーク商品取引所
New York money market ニューヨーク金融市場
New York Offshore Center ニューヨーク・オフショア市場
New York refinance ニューヨーク・リファイナンス
New Zealand Stock Exchange ニュージーランド証券取引所
newly deficit 赤字転落
newly established corporation with assets and liabilities transferred 新設法人
newly industrialized countries 新工業国群

newly listed company 新規上場会社
newly listed corporation 新規上場企業
newly-issued corporate bond 新規発行社債
next closing of account 次期決算
next day fund 翌日資金化資金
next generation 次世代
next-in first-out method 次入先出法
NGN (Nigerian naira) ナイジェリア・ナイラ
NI (national income) 国民所得
NIC (net interest cost) 発行者支払コスト
niche スキ間
nickel-brass coins (500 yen) ニッケル黄銅貨幣（新500円）
NICS (newly industrialized countries) 新興工業国
NIEO (New International Economic Order) 新国際経済秩序
NIFO (next-in, first-out) 次入先出
nifty fifty 人気50銘柄
Niger (CFA (Communauté Financière Africaine) franc) ニジェール（CFAフラン）
night court 夜間裁判所
night deposit safe 夜間金庫
night session 夜間取引
NII (net interest income) 純受取利息
Nikkei 225 日経平均
Nikkei 225 Futures 日経225先物取引
Nikkei 225 index futures 日経平均株価先物
Nikkei 225 Index option 日経225指数オプション
Nikkei 225 Options 日経225オプション
Nikkei 225 Stock Average 日経平均株価
Nikkei 300 Futures 日経300先物取引
Nikkei 300 Index fund 日経300株価指数連動型上場投資信託
Nikkei 300 Investment Trust 日経300投資信託
Nikkei 300 Options 日経300オプション
Nikkei 300 Stock Price Index 日経300株価指数
Nikkei Average 日経平均
Nikkei Dow-Jones Average 日経ダウ
Nikkei index 日経平均
Nikkei Stock Average 日経平均株価
Ningxia 寧夏回族自治区
NIO (Nicaraguan Cordoba) ニカラグア・コルドバ
NIPA (national income and product account) 国民所得生産勘定
Nippon Export and Investment Insurance 日本貿易保険
Nippon Keidanren 日本経済団体連合会（日本経団連）
NISA (Nuclear and Industrial Safety Agency) 原子力保安・安全院
NLG (Netherlands gulden) オランダ・グルデン
NMS (National Market System) 全米市場システム
NMS (normal market size) 通常市場規模
NNA (national numbering agency) 付番機関
NNE (net national expenditure) 国民純支出
NNP (net national product) 国民純生産
no action letter ノー・アクション・レター
no assignable contract 譲渡禁止契約
no claim discount 無事故割引
no consideration 無約因抗弁
no contest 不抗争
no dividend 無配
no dividend company 無配会社
no effect 無効
no fault 無過失
no fault automobile insurance ノーフォルト自動車保険
no lapse guarantee 無失効保証
no load investments 手数料不要投資商品

no load life policy 手数料不要生命保険
no load mutual fund 手数料不要ミューチュアル・ファンド
no load stock ノー・ロード・ストック
no loss no profit ノーロス・ノープロフィット
no par value 無額面
no protest 拒絶証書不要
no residual value 残存価値ゼロ
no value stock 無額面株式
no-down 頭金無しで
no-par insurance 無配当保険
no-par value stock 無額面株式
no-par-value stock 無額面株式
NOB (notes over bonds) spread NOB スプレッド
node 節点
node method ノード方式
NOE (notice of execution) 執行通知
NOI (net operating income) 純収益
noise あや
NOK (Norwegian krone) ノルウェー・クローネ
NOL (net operating loss) 正味営業損失
NOL (net operation loss) 営業純損失
nominal account 名目勘定
nominal amount 額面金額
nominal arrangement 名目的取決め
nominal assets 名目資産
nominal bond yield 債券名目利回り
nominal bonds 固定利付通常債券
nominal capital 名目資本
nominal compensation 名目賃金
nominal consideration 名目対価
nominal coupon 表面利率
nominal deposit 表面預金
nominal dollars 名目ドル
nominal exercise price 名目行使価格
nominal fixed rate debt 名目固定金利債券
nominal GDP growth 名目 GDP 成長率
nominal gilts 通常英国国債
nominal GNP 名目ＧＮＰ
nominal GNP growth 名目 GNP 成長率
nominal government debt 通常国債
nominal gross deposit 表面預金
nominal income 表面所得；名目収入
nominal instruments 通常利付債券
nominal interest rate 表面金利
nominal liabilities 名目債務
nominal multiplier 名目乗数
nominal national income 名目国民所得
nominal par 名目額面
nominal partner 名目的パートナー
nominal price quotation 呼値
nominal profit 名目利益
nominal proxy 無権代理
nominal quotation 名目相場
nominal quote 名目呼値
nominal rate of discount 名目割引率
nominal rate of interest 名目利率
nominal rate of protection 名目保護率
nominal rate of return 名目収益率
nominal return 名目利回り
nominal share capital 名目株式資本
nominal space 名目の世界
nominal tax rate 表面税率
nominal terms 名目ベース
nominal trading 通常取引
nominal transaction 名目取引
nominal value 額面価額
nominal wage 名目賃金
nominal wealth tax 名目的財産税
nominal world 名目ベースの世界
nominal yield 名目利回り
nominalism 名目主義
nominals 通常債券
nominate 指名する
nominated subcontractor 指定下請業者
nomination buying 指名買い
nomination committee 指名委員会
nominative security 記名式証券
nominee 名義人
non-abandonment undertaking 出資維持保証
non-accredited investor 非適格投資家

N

non-accrual basis 不計上基準
non-accrual of interest 利息計上停止
non-accrual system 益金不算入制度
non-accumulating 非累積の
non-amortizable securities 一時払有価証券
non-amortized past service cost 未償却過去勤務費用
non-annualized 非年換算の
non-assessable 券面外の責任が付いていない
Non-Bank Finance Companies Office 金融会社室（ノンバンク管理室）
non-bank financial institution 非銀行金融機関
non-borrowed reserves 非借入準備
non-business activity 非事業活動
non-business expenses 事業外経費
non-business organization 非営利組織
non-business property 非営業用資産
non-callable bond ノンコーラブル・ボンド
non-callable insurance 解約不能保険
non-callable treasury 満期償還財務省証券
non-cancelable 解約不能な
non-cancelable contract 解約不能契約
non-cancelable guarantee 取消不能保証
non-cancelable operating lease 解約不能オペレーティング・リース
non-cancellable guarantee 取り消し不能保証
non-cash assets 非現金資産
non-cash benefit 非現金給付
non-cash consideration 非現金対価
non-cash expense 非資金的費用
non-cash financial assets 非現金性金融資産
non-cash financing activities キャッシュフローを伴わない財務活動
non-cash investing activities 収支を伴わない投資活動
non-cash investment activities キャッシュフローを伴わない投資活動
non-cash item 非資金的項目
non-cash revenue 非資金的収益
non-cash transaction 非資金的取引
non-claim 請求懈怠
non-classification 非分類
non-clearing member 非清算会員
non-clearing participant 非清算参加者
non-collateralized bond 無担保社債
non-commercial enterprise 非営利会社
non-commercial trader 非商業トレーダー
non-competitive bid 非競争入札
non-competitive facility 非競争枠
non-competitive tender 非競争入札
non-compliance 非準拠
non-compliant operation 法令違反操業
non-consolidated capital adequacy ratio 単体自己資本比率
non-contributory benefit 無拠出給付
non-contributory pension plan 非拠出年金制度
non-contributory plan 非拠出制度
non-controllable cost 管理不能原価
non-controllable risk 管理不能リスク
non-cost items 非原価項目
non-cumulative 非累積的
non-cumulative dividend 非累積型配当
non-cumulative preference stock 非累積優先株
non-cumulative preferred stock 非累積型優先株式
non-current 非流動
non-current assets 非流動資産
non-current liabilities 長期債務
non-current liability 非流動負債
non-current portion 非流動部分
non-current portion of asset 資産の非流動部分
non-dealing securities 売買目的以外の有価証券
non-declarant 未宣言者
non-deductible 非控除の
non-deductible taxes 損金不算入の租税課金

N

non-delivery 受渡不履行
non-depository correspondent ノンデポジトリー・コルレス
non-depreciable assets 非償却資産
non-depreciable property 非償却資産
non-derivative instruments 非デリバティブ商品
non-derivative monetary assets 非デリバティブ貨幣性資産
non-derivative monetary liabilities 非デリバティブ貨幣性負債
non-detachable 非分離型
non-detachable warrant 分離不能ワラント
non-determined period 定めのない期間
non-disclosure 非開示
non-discretionary 自由裁量のない
non-discretionary trust 限定信託
non-diversified investment company 非分散投資型投資会社
non-dividend 無配
non-draft export 無為替輸出
non-draft import 無為替輸入
Non-DVP Settlement 非 DVP 決済
non-endorsable bill 裏書禁止手形
non-equity index futures 非株式指数先物
non-exclusive 非独占的
non-executive 非経営執行者
non-expendable fund 使用不能資金
non-family corporation 非同族会社
non-farm 非農業
non-feasance 義務不履行
non-financial accounts 非金融勘定
non-financial assets 非金融資産
non-financial disclosure 非財務的開示
non-financial market 非金融市場
non-financial transaction 金融外取引
non-first year 次年度以降の
non-fleet insured ノンフリート契約者
non-forfeiture act 不没収法
non-forfeiture benefit 不没収給付
non-forfeiture condition 没収不許可条件
non-fulfillment 不履行
non-fulfillment of a contract 契約不履行
non-fulfillment of settlement 決済不履行
non-fund transactions 収支を伴わない取引
non-fungible account 分別保管口座
non-genuine agreement 裏契約
non-government bond 民間債
non-government market 非政府債市場
non-guaranteed element 非保証要素
non-homogeneity 非同質性
non-inclusion of income tax credit in deductible expenses 所得税控除額の損金不算入
non-installment 非割賦
non-installment credit card 一括払いカード
non-insurable risk 保険不能保険
non-insurance annuity 非保険型年金
non-interest-bearing bond 非利付債
non-interest-bearing liability 無利子負債
non-interest-paying liability 非金利負債
non-interest-sensitive item 金利非感応項目
non-introduced stock 未公開株
non-investment cooperative association 非出資組合
non-investment grade 非投資適格
non-investment income 資産運用外収入
non-joinder 不併合
non-juridical organization 法人格のない社団
non-legal standards 法律になっていない基準
non-life insurance 損害保険
non-life insurance agent 損害保険代理店
non-life insurance company 損害保険会社
Non-Life Insurance Institute of Japan

損害保険事業研究所
non-linear correlation 非線形相関
non-linear model 非線形モデル
non-linear regression 非線形回帰
non-linearity 非線形
non-liquid assets 非流動性資産
non-lump payment 非一時金支給
non-management director 社外取締役
non-marine agency system ノンマリン代理店制度
non-market economy 非市場経済
non-market risk 非市場性リスク
non-market risk sources 非市場性リスクの源泉
non-marketable 市場性のない
non-marketable issue 非市場性証券
non-marketable securities 非市場性証券
non-member firm 非会員証券会社
non-member governor 会員外理事
non-member securities company 非会員会社
non-monetary 非貨幣性
non-monetary asset 非貨幣性資産
non-monetary benefit 非貨幣性給付
non-monetary grant 非貨幣性の補助金
non-monetary indirect security 非貨幣的間接証券
non-monetary items 非金銭項目
non-monetary liability 非貨幣性負債
non-monetary working capital 非貨幣運転資本
non-money trust 金外信託
non-negative definite matrix 非不定値行列
non-negotiable 流通性のない
non-negotiable bill 裏書禁止手形
non-negotiable endorsement 裏書禁止裏書
non-negotiable instrument 非流通証券
non-negotiable safekeeping receipts 譲渡不能保護預り証
non-operating 営業外の
non-operating assets 非運用資産
non-operating expenditure 営業外支出
non-operating expense 営業外費用
non-operating gain and loss 営業外損益
non-operating income 営業外収入
non-operating profit 営業外利益
non-operating profit and loss 営業外損益
non-operating revenue 営業外収益
non-operating section 営業外損益区分
non-opinion report 無限定監査報告書
non-order bill 指図禁止手形
non-participating insurance 無配当保険
non-participating life insurance policy 無配当生命保険証書
non-participating preferred stock 非参加優先株式
non-payment protest 不渡通知
non-payments 未納
non-pensioner 年金未加入者
non-performance 不履行
non-performance of contract 契約不履行
non-performing assets 不稼動資産
non-performing capital 未稼働資本
non-performing claim 不稼動債権
non-performing mortgage 不履行モーゲージ
non-permanent resident 非永住者
non-personal family corporation 非同族の同族会社
non-personnel expenses 物件費
non-production indirect cost 非製造間接費
non-productive loan 非生産的融資
non-profit accounting 非営利会計
non-profit corporation 非営利会社
non-profit enterprise 非営利企業
non-profit entity 非営利団体
non-profit institution 非営利機関
non-profit making business 非営利事業
non-profit-making activity 公益事業
non-profit-making company 非営利会社

non-proportional reinsurance 非比例割合再保険
non-public company 非公開企業
non-public information 非公開情報
non-public issues 非公募債
non-purpose loan 目的自由ローン
non-qualifying annuity 非適格年金保険
non-qualifying pension plan 非適格年金制度
non-rate earnings assets 非金利資産
non-rate-sensitive liability 金利非感応負債
non-rated 無格付債券
non-reciprocal 非相互的
non-reciprocal transfer 一方的譲渡
non-recourse ノン・リコース
non-recourse debt 非求償債務
non-recourse finance 償還請求権のない融資
non-recourse financial liabilities 遡及義務のない金融負債
non-recourse form ノンリコース形式
non-recourse loan ノンリコース・ローン
non-recurring 非経常的な
non-recurring cost 一時費用
non-recurring gain 臨時利得
non-recurring item 臨時損益項目
non-recurring loss 経常外損失
non-recurring profit 経常外利益
non-recurring profit and loss 経常外損益
non-redeemable 非償還の
non-refundable 還付されない
non-refundable guarantee deposit 返還不能な保証金
non-registered 登記未済
non-regular employment 臨時雇用
non-repeating 一時的な
non-resident 非居住者
non-resident foreign currency account 非居住者外貨預金勘定
non-resident foreign currency deposits 非居住者外貨預金
non-resident yen account 非居住者円預金勘定
non-resident yen deposit 非居住者円預金
non-residential assets 非住宅用資産
non-residents and foreign corporations 非居住者及び外国法人
non-risk assets 非危険資産
non-risk interest rate 非危険利子率
non-sampling error 非標本誤差
non-seasonally adjusted 季節調整前の
non-settled 未決済
non-state pension 非公的年金
non-statistical sampling 非統計的サンプル
non-stochastic model 非確率モデル
non-strategic division 非戦略部門
non-suit 訴えの却下
non-surrenderable 解約不能の
non-synchronous trading 非同時取引
non-tariff measures 非関税措置
non-tax exempt bond 非免税債
non-tax payment 税外負担
non-tax qualified pension 非適格年金
non-tax receipts 税外収入
non-taxable account 非課税口
non-taxable corporation 非課税法人
non-taxable document 非課税文書
non-taxable exchanges of properties 収用換地
non-taxable goods 免税品
non-taxable goods for special use 特殊用途免税
non-taxable gross income 非課税益金
non-taxable income 非課税所得
non-taxable interest income 非課税利子所得
non-taxable interest on deposits for tax payment 納税準備預金の利子の非課税
non-taxable property 非課税財産
non-taxable receiving 未納税引取り
non-taxable registration license 非課税登録免許
non-taxable saving account 非課税貯

蓄口
non-taxable savings 非課税貯蓄
non-taxable securities 非課税有価証券
non-taxable transaction 非課税取引
non-tie-up loan 非提携ローン
non-trade payable 非営業債務
non-traditional asset class 非伝統的なアセット・クラス
non-transferability 非譲渡性
non-transferable 非譲渡性の
non-transferable financial instrument 非譲渡性金融商品
non-trustee 非管財人型
non-trustee bankrupt company 非管財人型倒産企業
non-user 不行使
non-vested benefit 未確定給付
non-vesting 権利が確定していない
non-voting stock 無議決権株
non-wage benefit 賃金外給付
nonferrous metals industry 非鉄金属業界
nonresident etc. account 非居住者等口
noon clause 正午条項
Nordic Council 北欧理事会
Nordic Council of Ministers 北欧閣僚会議
Norges Bank ノルウェー中央銀行
Norinchukin Bank 農林中央金庫
normal and average use hours 通常使用時間
normal asset mix ノーマル・アセット・ミックス
normal assets 正常資産
normal auditing procedures 正規の監査手続
normal borrowers 正常先
normal burden rate 正常配賦率
normal capacity 正常生産能力
normal cost 正常原価
normal depreciation 正常償却
normal distribution 正規分布
normal equation 正規方程式
normal goods 正常財
normal investment practice 通常の投資慣行
normal market 順ざや市場
normal operating cycle 正常な営業循環
normal period for delivery 受渡しに係る通常の期間
normal practices in Japan 社会一般情勢
normal price 正常価格
normal probability distribution 正規確率分布
normal procedure 正規の手続き
normal processing 一般処理
normal profit 正常利潤
normal rate of exchange 正常為替相場
normal receivables 一般債権
normal return 正常利益
normal return (ratio) 正常収益率
normal spoilage 正常仕損
normal standard cost 正常標準原価
normal stock level 正常在庫高
normal target allocation ノーマル・ターゲット・アロケーション
normal tax 普通税
normal trading unit 取引単位
normal yield curve 順イールド
normalization 正規化
normalized earnings 標準化収益
normalized EPS 標準 EPS
normalized to 100 in 2000 2000 年を 100 とした
North Atlantic Assembly 北大西洋評議会
North Atlantic Free Trade Area 北大西洋自由貿易地域
North Atlantic Treaty Organization 北大西洋条約機構
North Brent 北海ブレント
north-south problem 南北問題
north-south summit 南北サミット
north-south trade 南北貿易
Northern Ireland (sterling pound) 北アイルランド（イギリス・ポンド）
nostro 当方国
nostro account 当方勘定

not deductible for tax purpose 損金不算入
not otherwise provided 別段の定めがない限り
not rated 無格付け
not-for-profit 非営利法人
notarial charges 公証料
notarized deed 公正証書
notary 公証人
notary fee 公証料
note 中期証券
note at sight 一覧払約束手形
note collection 手形回収
note description 注記事項
note discounted 割引手形
note dishonored 不渡手形
note endorsed 回り手形
Note for Delivery in Registered Bonds 登録債決済確約書
note for payment of tonnage dues トン税納付書
note issuance facilities 債券発行保証枠
note issuance facility 手形発行枠；ノート・イッシュアンス・ファシリティ
note issued by a third party 第三者によって発行された手形
note of payment 支払通知書
note of protest 拒絶覚書
note payable 支払約束手形
note payable register 支払手形記入帳
note purchase agreement 債務買取契約
note receivable discounted 割引手形
note received discounted 割引手形
note register 手形記入帳
noteholders meeting 債券保有者会議
notes and accounts payable 支払債務
notes and accounts receivable 受取債権
notes and bills discounted 割引手形
notes and bills endorsed 裏書手形
notes and bills payable 支払手形
notes and bills receivable 受取手形
notes endorsed for payment 裏書譲渡手形
notes material 注記文書
notes payable book 支払手形記入帳
notes receivable register 受取手形記入帳
notes to the financial statements 財務諸表注記
noteworthy 注目に値する
notice 通知
Notice of a Security 有価証券通知書
notice of abandonment 委付通知
notice of board of directors' meeting 取締役会召集通知
notice of demand to guarantor 納付催告書
notice of determination 決定通知書
notice of increase or decrease and balance of direct participant's account 参加者口座の増減額及び残高の通知
notice of lien 先取特権通知
notice of loss and damage 事故通知
notice of payment 納入告知
notice of redemption 償還通知
notice of sale 販売通知
notice of seizure 差押通知書
Notice of Shelf Registration Having Taken Effect 発行登録効力発生通知書
notice to inform of taking effect 効力発生通知書
notice to inform of taking effect of securities registration statement 有価証券届出効力発生通知書
notice to quit 解約予告
noticeably fluctuating goods 価格変動の著しい物品
notification 催告
notification in writing 文書による通知
notification of the taxable year 事業年度の届出
notification of appropriation of refund 還付金充当通知書
notification of auction results 募入決

定の通知
notification of audit 監査の事前通知
notification of estimated tax prepayment 予定納税額の通知
notification of incorporation 設立届
notification of opening of business 開業届
notification of payment of refund 還付金支払通知書
notification of tax agent 納税管理人の届出
notification of tax payment 納税告知書
Notification of the Ministry of Finance 財務省通達
notification of transfer of place of tax payment 納税地異動の届出
notification procedure 通告処分
notifying bank 通知銀行
notional certificate 擬制証書
notional defined contribution みなし掛金建て
notional income 観念上の所得
notional principal 想定元本
notorious possession 公然の占有
notwithstanding かかわらず
novation 更改
novel feature 新しい特徴
novelty 新案
NOW (negotiable order of withdrawal) account 譲渡可能払戻指図預金勘定（NOW 勘定）
NOW, THEREFORE, in consideration of そこで約因として
NP (normal profit) 正常利益
NPL (non-performing loan) disposal 不良債権処理
NPL (non-performing loan) problem 不良債権問題
NPO (non-profit organization) NPO 法人
NPR (Nepalese rupee) ネパール・ルピー
NRSRO (nationally recognized statistical rating organization) 米国証券市場認知の統計的格付機関
NRV (net realizable value) 正味実現可能価額
NSCC (National Securities Clearing Corporation) 全米証券決済機構
NSCD (national securities central depository) 国の証券振替機関
NSE (National Stock Exchange) インド国立証券取引所
NSO (non-qualifying stock options) 非適格ストック・オプション
NTB (non-tariff barrier) 非関税障壁
NTT bond NTT 債
NTT break up NTT 分割
nuclear energy insurance 原子力保険
nuclear energy liability insurance 原子力損害賠償責任保険
nuclear energy property insurance 原子力財産保険
nudge 注意喚起
nudge ahead of 優勢である
nudge stock 貸株注意喚起銘柄
NUG (non-utility generator) 非公益電気事業者
nuisance 不法妨害
null and void 無効な
nullify 無効にする
nullity 無効
number of contract months 限月取引の数
number of coupon payments 利払回数
number of days' purchases in accounts payable 買掛債権回転日数
number of days' sales in inventories 棚卸し資産回転日数
number of days' sales in receivables 売上債権回転日数
number of directors 取締役の員数
number of floating shares 浮動株式数
number of machines installed 据付台数
number of new stocks issued per old stock 旧株一株につき発行された新株の数

number of payments remaining 残存返済回数
number of publicly offered shares 公開株式数
number of scheduled payments 返済回数
number of settlement transactions 決済口数
number of shareholders 株主数
number of shares authorized 授権株式数
number of shares less than the unit of trading 売買単位未満数量
number of shares making up a basic lot 一単元の株式数
number of shares outstanding 社外流通株式数
number of shares owned by the special few 少数特定者持株数
number of stocks held 持株数
number of stocks issued 発行済株式数
number of trading 売買の回数
number of units of ordinary equity contribution 普通出資の口数
N
number of years elapsed 経過年数
number of years since incorporation 設立後経過年数
numbered accounts 番号口座
numeraire ニューメレール
numerator 分子
numeric target 数値目標
numerical information 数値情報
numerical integration 数値積分法
numerical reconciliation 数字的調整
NY Dow ダウ平均
NYCE (New York Cotton Exchange) ニューヨーク綿花取引所
NYFE (New York Futures Exchange) ニューヨーク先物取引所
NYSE (New York Stock Exchange) ニューヨーク証券取引所
NYSE (New York Stock Exchange) composite index ニューヨーク証券取引所総合指数
NYSE (New York Stock Exchange) Index ニューヨーク証券取引所株価指数
NYSE Composite ニューヨーク総合指数
NYSE Composite Stock Index NYSE総合株価指数
NZD (New Zealand dollar) ニュージーランド・ドル

O

O/D (overdraft) 当座貸越
OAD (option adjusted duration) オプション調整後デュレーション
OAPEC (Organization of Arab Petroleum Exporting Countries) アラブ石油輸出国機構
OAS (option adjusted spread) オプション調整後スプレッド
OASDI (Old Age, Survivors and Disability Insurance) 老齢遺族傷害年金
OASI (Old Age and Survivors Insurance) 老齢遺族年金
oath 宣誓
object cost 要素別原価
object of pledge 質権の目的
object of taxation 課税物件
object tax 目的税
objection in writing 書面による異議
objection to discipline 処分に対する異議
objection to disposition 処置に対する異議
objective defeasance trust 客観的ディフィーザンス・トラスト
objective function 目的関数
objective indicator 客観指標
objective information 客観的情報
objective probability 客観的確率
objective proof 客観的な証拠
objective statement 要素別計算書
objective value 客観的価値
objectivity 客観性
obligating event 債務発生事象
obligation 債務
obligation bond 債務債券
obligation fees 負担費
obligation of bookkeeping 記帳業務
obligation of signature and seal 自署押印の義務
obligation to acquire the approval 承認を得る義務
obligation to file return 申告義務
obligation to make an asset payment 財産支払義務
obligation to pay 支払義務
obligation to transfer a proprietary right 財産移転義務
obligations hereunder 本契約に基づく義務
obligations incurred 発生債務負担
obligations of the failed financial institution 破綻金融機関債務
obligations to compensate 補填義務
obligatory reinsurance 義務再保険
obligee 債権者
obligor 債務者
obligor concentration 債務者集中度
obligor risk 債務者のリスク
obliteration 抹消
obliteration accompanied by redemption 償還に伴う抹消
observation period 観測期間
observations 観測値
observed 観察された
observed depreciation 見積減価償却
obsolescence 陳腐化
obsolescence of inventory 棚卸資産陳腐化
obsolescence reserve 陳腐化引当金
obsolescent depreciable property 陳腐化償却資産
obsolete 陳腐化した
obsolete assets 陳腐化資産
obsolete property 陳腐化資産
obstruction of navigation 航行妨害罪
obtainer of employment income 給与所得者
OBU (off shore banking unit) オフショア・バンキング・ユニット

obviation of need 必要性の否定
OCC (option clearing corporation) オプション清算会社
occasional income 一時所得
occupancy 入居状況
occupant 占有者
occupation tax 営業税
occupational benefit 職域給付
occupational disease 職業病
occupational pension 企業年金
occupational superannuation 職域年金
occupational tax 営業免許税
OCD (other checkable deposit) その他当座性預金
ocean freight contract 海上貨物運送契約
OCHA(Office for the Coordination of Humanitarian Affairs) 人道問題調整部
OCO (one-cancels-others) order OCO注文
OCR (Optical Character Reader) 光学式文字読取装置
ODCCP (United Nations Office for Drug Control and Crime Prevention) 国連薬物統制犯罪防止事務所
odd date 確定日渡し
odd date or broken date delivery 特定期日受渡し
odd lot 端株
odd lot consolidation 端株整理
odd lot dealer 端株業者
odd lot differential 端株売買手数料
odd lot shares 端株
odd results おかしな結果
odd to beginners 初心者には変わった方法にうつる
odd-lot short sale ratio 端株空売比率
odd-lot theory 端株理論
odd-lot transaction 端株取引
ODR (official discount rate) cut 公定歩合引下げ
ODR (official discount rate) operation 公定歩合操作
OECD (Organization for Economic Cooperation and Development) 経済協力開発機構
OECD membership OECD 加盟
OECD model double taxation convention OECD モデル租税条約
OeKB オーストリア保管振替機関
of like grade and quality 同等同質の
off balance オフバランス
off limit 出入禁止
off market オフ・マーケット
off market swap オフ・マーケット・スワップ
off-auction basis transaction 立会外ベーシス取引
off-auction cross transaction 立会外対当取引
off-auction distribution 立会外分売
off-auction trading 立会外取引
off-balance sheet assets 簿外資産
off-balance sheet debt 簿外債務
off-balance sheet financial instruments オフバランス・シート金融商品
off-balance sheet items オフバランス・シート項目
off-balance sheet transaction オフバランス・シート取引
off-balance transaction オフバランス取引
off-balance treatment オフバランス化
off-balance-sheet accounting オフバランス会計
off-balance-sheet event 簿外の事象
off-balance-sheet exposure オフバランス項目
off-balance-sheet financing 簿外資金調達
off-balance-sheet liability 簿外負債
off-balanced trade オフバランス取引
off-board frading 場外取引
off-board market 場外市場
off-board transactions 市場外取引
off-board transactions of listed bonds 上場債券市場外売買高

off-exchange futures transaction 場外先物取引
off-exchange transactions 取引所外取引
off-floor distribution 立会外分売
off-hour trading 時間外売買
off-hours trading 立会外売買取引
off-record lending 浮貸し
off-setting account 相殺勘定
off-site monitoring オフサイト・モニタリング
off-taker 引き取り手
off-the-book assets 含み資産
off-the-run issue 周辺銘柄
off-trading session 立会外
offense 犯罪
offer 売唱え
offer by subscription 予約公募
offer curve オファー曲線
offer in compromise 和解提案
offer price 発行価格；募集価格
offer side オファーサイド
offer the deposit 預託する
offer wanted 売り求む
offered price 売呼値
offered rate 出し手レート
offered to the public 公募された
offeree 買付対象者
offeree company 買付対象会社
offering 募集
offering circular 募集案内書
offering date 公開日
offering for sale 売出し
offering for subscription 公募
offering for subscription to bonds 債券応募
offering for the market 市中発行
offering for the public sector 公的部門発行
offering price 公募価格
offering scale 売出価格帯
offering size 入札総額
offering to shareholders 株主割当
office audit 机上調査
office copy 官製謄本
office equipment 事務所機器
office expense account 営業費勘定
office expenses 事務費
office expenses book 営業内訳帳
Office for Consolidation of Specific National Property 特定国有財産整備室
Office for Promotion of Efficient Use of National Property 国有財産有効利用推進室
office found 国庫帰属認定
office furniture 営業用什器
office grant 強制履行
office hours 営業時間
office manual 事務規程
Office of Administrative Law Judges 行政訴訟審判官室
Office of Administrative Law Judges(SEC) 行政訴訟審判官室(SEC)
Office of Administrative Service(SEC) 行政サービス室(SEC)
Office of Administrative Services 行政サービス室
Office of Applications & Report Service 申請報告サービス室
Office of Balance of Payments and International Capital Markets 国際収支室
Office of Budget and Fiscal Operations 予算・会計管理局
Office of Chief Account 主任調査官室
Office of Chief Accountant(SEC) 主任会計士室(SEC)
Office of Communication and Education Service 報道教育サービス室
Office of Comptroller(SEC) 管理官室(SEC)
Office of Consumer Affairs & Information Service 投資家保護室
Office of Consumer Affairs and Information Service(SEC) 消費者業務・情報サービス室(SEC)
Office of Coordination and

O

Examination 総務試験室
Office of Economic Analysis(SEC) 経済分析室（SEC）
Office of EDGAR management(SEC) エドガー管理室（SEC）
Office of Engineering エンジニアリング室
Office of Executive Director(SEC) 事務局長室（SEC）
Office of Foreign Exchange Examiners 為替実査室
Office of General Counsel(SEC) 法律顧問室（SEC）
Office of Information System Management(SEC) 情報システム管理室（SEC）
Office of Inspection of the Custom-Houses 税関考査管理室
Office of International Operations 国際業務課
Office of Liaison, Inspection and ADP Management of the Local Finance Bureaus 業務調整室
Office of Management and Budget 管理室
Office of Management Supervision 監督評価官室
Office of Monitoring and Inspection 審査検査室
Office of Mutual Agreement Procedures 相互協議室
Office of Opinions and Review(SEC) 意見起草室（SEC）
Office of Personnel(SEC) 人事室（SEC）
Office of Public Affairs(SEC) 公報室（SEC）
Office of Public Utility Regulation(SEC) 公益事業規制室（SEC）
Office of Rulings and Legal Affairs 審理室
Office of Secretary 秘書室（SEC）
Office of the General Counsel 法規顧問室
Office of the Vice Minister of Finance for International Affairs 財務官室
Office of Thrift Supervision 貯蓄金融機関監督局
office or other fixed place of business 事務所もしくは他の一定の事業所
office overhead 事務所諸経費
office regulation 社内規程
officer 役員
officer de jure 法律上の職員
officer's bonus 役員賞与
officer's compensation 役員報酬
officer's salary 役員給料
official approval 許認可
official assessment 賦課課税制度
official check 銀行小切手
official credits 公的債権
official deposit 公金預金
Official Development Assistance 政府開発援助
official discount rate 公定歩合
official exchange market 公定市場
official exchange rate 公定為替相場
official foreign exchange reserves 外貨準備高
official information 公報
official inspection 臨検
official interest rate 政策金利
official intervention 公的介入
official invoice 公用インボイス
official mandate 正式なマンデート
official notice of sale 新規債券発行通知
official original issue date 正式発行日
official power 職権
official price 公定価格
official rate 公定レート
official receiver 管選収益管理人
official reserve transactions balance 公的決済収支
official retain 領置
official statement 公式見解
official statistics 政府統計
official to receive national tax 国税収納官吏
Official, Ministry of Finance 財務事務

O

官
offload 投げ売る
offset 相殺
offset error 相殺誤謬
offset item 相殺項目
offsetting criteria 相殺基準
offsetting effect 相殺効果
offsetting order 反対注文
offsetting position 相殺ポジション
offsetting presentation 相殺表示
offsetting purchase transaction 買戻し
offsetting sale transaction 転売
offshoot 子会社
offshore account オフショア勘定
offshore assets 海外資産
offshore banking center オフショア・バンキングセンター
offshore banking facility オフショア金融市場
offshore banking unit オフショア・バンキングユニット
offshore borrowing オフショア調達
offshore center オフショア・センター
offshore fund オフショア・ファンド
offshore guarantee オフショア保証
offshore investment bond オフショア投資債券
offshore lease オフショア・リース
offshore market オフショア市場
offshore production 海外生産
offshore purchase 域外調達
offshore trade 三国間貿易
OFT (Office of Fair Trading) 公正取引庁
OHCHR (Office of the United Nations High Commissioner for Human Rights) 国連人権高等弁務官事務所
OID (original issue discount) 発行時割引額
oil and coal product industry 石油・石炭製品業界
oil concession 石油採掘権
oil money オイルマネー
oil pollution liability insurance 油濁賠償責任保険
oil refinery 石油精製業
oil stock 石油株
oil-linked bond 石油連動債券
OIOS(Office of Internal Oversight Services) 内部監査部
OIP (original issue premium) 発行時額面超過額
Okinawa Custom-House 沖縄地区税関
Okinawa Development Finance Corporation 沖縄振興開発金融公庫
Okinawa Regional Taxation Office 沖縄国税事務所
OLA(Office of Legal Affairs) 法務部
old account 残存勘定
old age income life insurance 老齢年金付生命保険
old age pension 老齢年金
old bank act 旧銀行法
old bond オールド・ボンド
old economy オールド・エコノミー
old foreign exchange act 旧外国為替管理法
old policy 旧保険契約
old share 発行済株式
old threat 以前の脅威
old-age basic pension 老齢基礎年金
old-aged, survivor and disability insurance 老齢遺族障害者年金
oligarchy 寡頭制
oligopolistic control 寡占的支配
oligopolistic economy 寡占経済
oligopoly 寡占
oligopoly industry 寡占産業
oligopoly price 寡占価格
OLO (Obligation Lineaire Obligaties) ベルギー長期国債
OLS (ordinary least squares) regression 最小二乗法回帰分析
OMB (Office of Management and Budget) 行政管理予算局
Omgeo オムジオ
omission 脱漏
omitted dividend 無配
omnibus account 乗合勘定

omnium 担保差入株式総額
OMR (Omani rial) オマーン・リアル
on a cash earning basis キャッシュフロー倍率で
on a delayed basis 遅延で
on a dilutive basis 希薄化ベースで
on a going concern basis 継続企業の基準で
on a item by item basis 個別品目ごとに
on a line-by-line basis 表示項目ごとに
on a multiple yield competitive basis 様々な利回り帯で
on a nationwide basis 全国ベースで
on a prospective basis 将来の期間について
on a quarterly basis 四半期ごとに
on a rolling basis 循環ベースで
on a simple interest basis 単利ベース
on a straight-line basis 定額法で
on a supplementary basis 補足的に
on a year-to-date basis 年初からの累積で
on an accrual basis 発生主義で
on an enterprise-wide basis 企業全体で
on approval 試用で
on balance オンバランス
on board notation 船積完了証
on call 請求次第
on cost 製造費
on credit 掛けで
on customer's account 委託勘定で
on demand selling rate 参着払売相場
on expiration 期限切れ時点で
on inception 開始時
on margin 信用取引で
on one's own account 自己勘定で
on one's proprietary account 自己勘定で
on or before 期日もしくは期日前に
on our risk 当方負担
on passage 運送中
on the back of 支えられて
on the books 掛売帳で
on the cost basis 原価基準で
on the sideline 様子見
on track 勢いがある
on-balance sheet financial instruments オンバランスシート金融商品
on-balance volume オンバランス・ボリューム
on-balance-sheet exposure オンバランス項目
on-balance-sheet transaction オンバランス取引
on-going involvement 継続した関与
on-going test 事後テスト
on-hours trading 立会内売買取引
on-line banking system オンライン・バンキング・システム
on-shore fund 国内投資信託
on-shore market オンショア市場
on-site examination 考査
on-the-close order 引値注文
on-the-opening order 寄付値段注文
one bank holding company 単一銀行持株会社
one contract 一契約
one day contract 一日契約
one day reversal ワン・デー・リバーサル
one day skipped 二営業日渡し
one factor 単因子
one factor model 単一要因モデル
one hundred percent income statement 百分率損益計算書
one hundredth 百分の一
one man company 一人会社
one month lows against 一ヶ月振りの安値
one name paper 単名手形
one notch 1ノッチ
one payment life policy 一時払生命保険
one premium policy 一時払保険
one share one vote rule 一株一議決権ルール
one share shareholder 一株株主
one shot customer 一見客

one sided hedge 片道ヘッジ
one stop filing ワン・ストップ・ファイリング
one time trading 仕切売買
one way 片道
one year budget principle 予算単年度主義
one year rule 1 年基準
one-off 一回限り
one's own convenience 自己都合
onerous 義務を負う
onerous contract 有償契約
onerous gift 負担付贈与
onerous property 負担資産
ongoing assessment 継続評価
ongoing change 恒常的な変化
ongoing correction 調整局面
ongoing factor 経常的要因
ongoing operation 継続事業
online processing オンライン処理
onshore 自国内
open account 未決算勘定
open air market 青空市場
open and current account 交互計算勘定
open auction 公開競売
open bidding 一般競争入札
open board of broker 公開取引会所
open book オープン・ブック
open buying 新規買い
open certificate オープン保険契約
open check 普通小切手
open contract 建て玉
open court 公開の法廷
open cover オープン・カバー；包括保険
open credit オープン・クレジット
open down 安寄り
open economy 開放経済
open end liability 無制限債務
open ended health plan オープン・エンド医療制度
open group 開放団体
open inflation 開放型インフレーション
open insurance 包括予定保険
open interest 建玉残高
open interest in margin transactions 信用取引残高
open interest on buyer's side 買建玉
open interest on seller's side 売建玉
open investment trust 追加型投資信託
open L/C (letter of credit) 買取銀行無指定信用状
open ledger 未決算元帳
open listing 一般委任契約
open lot 更地
open market オープン市場；公開市場
open market committee 公開市場委員会
open market operations 公開市場オペ；公開市場操作
open market quotation 市中相場
open market rate 市中金利
open market selling operation 売りオペ
open market value 公開市場の価値
open money market 公開短期金融市場
open mortgage 開放担保
open mortgage clause 単純モーゲージ条項
open note 無担保手形
open order オープン注文
open outcry 公開セリ方式
open outcry method 公開セリ売買方式
open policy 包括保険証書
open position 建玉
open price オープン価格
open rate method オープン・レート方式
open repo オープン・レポ
open selling 新規売り
open tendering 一般競争入札
open theft 現行窃盗罪
open-end オープンエンド型
open-end bond investment trust 公社債投資信託
open-end fund オープンエンド型ファンド
open-end investment trust オープン型投資信託

open-end lease オープンエンド型リース
open-end management company オープンエンド投資会社
open-end mortgage オープンエンド型モーゲージ
open-end mortgage bond オープンエンド型モーゲージ債券
open-end mutual fund オープンエンド型ミューチュアル・ファンド
open-end type 追加設定型の
open-ended securities investment trusts 追加型証券投資信託
open-up of money market 金融市場開放
opener 信用状発行依頼人
opener of letter of credit 信用状発行依頼人
opening balance 期首残高
opening balance account 開始残高勘定
opening bank 開設銀行
opening charge 信用状発行手数料
opening charge for letter of credit 信用状発行手数料
opening commission 発行手数料
opening contract price 始めの約定値段
opening entry 繰越記帳
opening inventory 期首棚卸高
opening journal entry 開始仕訳
opening net investment 正味投資額の期首残高
opening net liability 期首の負債純額
opening obligation 期首債務
opening price 寄付値段
opening quotation 寄付値段
opening rate 始値
opening rate closing rate 始値引値
opening retained earnings 期首剰余金
opening session 寄付き
opening session of the year 大発会
opening tone 寄付き気配
operand 演算数
operated days 操業日数
operating account 営業活動勘定
operating activities 営業活動
operating assets 運用資産；営業資産；稼動資産
operating budget 営業予算
operating capacity 営業規模
operating capital 営業資本
operating cash 運転資金
operating cash flow 営業上のキャッシュフロー
operating company 業務運営法人
operating condition 営業状況
operating cost 運転費用
operating cost ratio 営業経費率
operating cycle 営業循環
operating cycle rule 営業循環基準
operating decision 業務上の意思決定
operating division 事業部門
operating earning ratio 経営資本利益率
operating efficiency 経営効率
operating expense 営業経費
operating expenses ratio 営業経費率
operating fund 運転資金
operating income 営業利益
operating income on sales 売上営業利益率
operating income to sales 営業利益率
operating item 営業関連項目
operating lease オペレーティング・リース
operating ledger 営業元帳
operating leverage 営業レバレッジ
operating leverage analysis オペレーティング・レバレッジ分析
operating leverage effect 営業面での増益効果
operating loss 営業損失
operating officer 業務執行者
operating payable 営業債務
operating performance ratios 業績比率
operating policies 経営方針
operating profit 営業利益
operating profit and loss 営業損益
operating profit before changes in

working capital 運転資本増減前の営業利益
operating profit level 営業利益段階
operating profit margin 営業利益率
operating profit ratio on sales 売上高営業利益率
operating ratio 営業比率；稼働率
operating receipt 営業収入
operating receivable 営業債権
operating report 営業報告
operating reserve 営業準備金
operating results 営業成績
operating revenue 営業収益
operating review 業務のレビュー
operating section 営業損失区分
operating segment 営業セグメント
operating standing 営業状態
operating statement 損益計算書
operating surplus 営業余剰金
operating target オペの指標；操作目標
operating variable 操作変数
operation 操業
operation capacity 操業度
operation counterparties オペ対象先
operation efficiency 作業能率
operation expenses 作業費
operation in the secondary market 流通市場操作
operation of law 法の作用
operation of the market 市場の運営
operation ratio 操業率
operation variance 操業度差異
operational efficiency 効率性
operational factor 運営要因
operational issues オペレーション上の事柄
operational risk オペレーショナル・リスク
operations conducted in rotation 輪番オペ
Operations Department 業務局
operations for stabilizing the stock market price 株価安定操作
opinion 意見
opinion expression 意見表明
opinion of auditors 監査意見書
opinion shopping 会計士を探す
OPM (option pricing model) valuation オプション価格決定モデル
opportunity borrower 借手の判断による借入
opportunity cost 機会費用
opportunity for growth 成長性
opportunity gain 機会利益
opportunity loss 機会損失
opposite accounts 反対勘定
opposite effect 反対の結果
opposite party 相手方
oppression 職権濫用罪
optimal asset allocation 最適資産配分
optimal bond portfolio 最適な債券ポートフォリオ
optimal capital structure 最適資本構成
optimal condition 最適条件
optimal growth model 最適成長モデル
optimal hedge instrument 最適ヘッジ手段
optimal operating ratio maximal operating ratio 最適操業度最有利操業度
optimal policy mix 最適ポリシー・ミックス
optimal portfolio 最適ポートフォリオ
optimal response 最適反応
optimal scale 最適規模
optimal stopping problem 最適停止問題
optimal stopping time 最適停止時刻
optimal strategy 最適戦略
optimal threshold return 適性上下限界収益率
optimal threshold return ratio 適正上下限界収益率
optimality criterion 最適性基準
OptiMark market オプティマーク市場
optimistic expectation 楽観的な期待
optimization 最適化
optimization method 最適化法

O

optimization model 最適化モデル
optimize 最適化する
optimum allocation of resources 最適資源配分
optimum balance 最適なバランス
optimum capacity 最適操業度
optimum currency 最適通貨地域
optimum distribution 最適分配
optimum foreign exchange reserves 適正外貨準備高
optimum inventory 最適在庫量
optimum output 最適生産量
optimum rate of growth 最適成長率
optimum rate of interest 最適利子率
opting out of scheme 制度からの脱退
opting-out オプティング・アウト
option 選択肢
Option 25 オプション 25
option account オプション口座
option adjusted オプション調整後の
option adjusted convexity オプション調整後コンベクシティ
option adjusted spread model オプション調整スプレッド・モデル
option adjusted yield オプション調整後利回り
option agreement オプション契約
option bond オプション・ボンド
option buyer オプション・バイヤー
option clearing corporation オプション清算会社
option combination プット・コールを組合せたオプション
option contract オプション契約
option contract on the government bond futures 国債証券先物オプション取引
option delivery オプション渡し
option delta オプション・デルタ
option embedded in swaps オプション組込スワップ
option expiration date オプションの満期日
option forward オプション・フォワード
option gamma オプション・ガンマ
option holder オプション契約者
option holder's interest オプションの保有者の持分
option market オプション市場
option money 特権料
option mutual fund オプション・ミューチュアル・ファンド
option on stock index futures 株価指数先物オプション
option performance index オプション・パフォーマンス指数
option period オプション行使可能期間
option pool オプション・プール
option position オプション・ポジション
option premium オプションの取引代金；オプション・プレミアム
option price オプション価格
option pricing theory オプション価格決定理論
option seller オプションの売り手
option settlement index オプション清算指数
option settlement price オプション清算値段
option spread オプション・スプレッド
option theta オプション・セータ
option to double 倍額減債約款
option to kick in オプションが行使される
option trading based on government securities 国債証券先物オプション
option trading based on the stock price index 株価指数オプション取引
option transaction オプション取引
option warrants オプション・ワラント
option writer オプションの売り手
option's contracted life オプションの契約期間
option's term オプション期間
optional assessment 源泉選択課税
optional cargo 揚地選択貨物

optional consumption 選択的消費
optional dividend 選択配当
optional payment bond 受取通貨選択権付債券
optional redemption 任意償還
optional repayment provision 選択的償還条項
optional reserve 任意準備金
optional rider 選択式特約
optional settlement 支払方法選択権
optionality 選択性
optionee 選択権保有者
options bought 買建オプション
options contract value オプション取引代金
options on stock index futures 株価指数先物オプション
options on stock price index 株価指数オプション
options sold 売建オプション
options trading オプション取引
options trading on Japanese government bond futures 国債証券先物オプション取引
or better 指値以上
oral contract 口頭契約
oral testimony 口頭の証言
order 注文
order amount 受注額
order and disposition 表見的所有
order B/L (bill of lading) 指図人式船荷証券
order backlog 受注残
order book 注文控え
order book official オーダー・ブック・オフィシャル
order book trading 注文簿取引
order by telephone 電話注文
order check 指図人支払小切手
order entry 注文エントリー
order for attachment of property 差押命令
order for collection 取立命令
order for relief 救済命令
order imbalance 注文の不均衡
order increase 受注の増加
order negotiation 注文の相対
order of application 適用の順序
order of credit 債権順位
order of liquidity 流動性配列法
order of one's liquidity 流動性の順序
order of preference 選好順位
order of repayment 弁済の順序
order of the size of shareholdings 所有株式数の多い順
order on a scale 刻み注文
order quantity 発注量
order splitting 分割注文
order stock 手持注文
order ticket 注文伝票
order to outside manufacturer 外注
order to pay 支払命令
order without limit 成行注文
order-filling cost 注文履行費
order-taking hours 注文受付時間
orderly export marketing 秩序ある輸出
orderly financial system 秩序ある金融システム
orderly marketing agreement 市場秩序維持協定
orders in hand 受注残高
ordinance by local government 条例
ordinance from the Ministry of Finance 財務省令
ordinance of competent minister 主務省令
ordinary activities 経常的活動
ordinary agent 生保外務員
ordinary and necessary expenses 通常必要な経費
ordinary and necessary movable property for living 生活に通常必要な動産
ordinary and normal recurring operations 通常の運営
ordinary annual expenditure 経常歳出
ordinary annual revenue 経常歳入
ordinary annuity 普通年金
ordinary bank 普通銀行

ordinary bill 並手形
ordinary budget 経常予算
ordinary care 通常の注意
ordinary charges 通常の費用
ordinary collection 普通徴収
ordinary conveyance 通常譲渡証書
ordinary corporate income 普通所得
ordinary corporation 普通法人
ordinary deposit 普通預金
ordinary depreciation and amortization 普通償却
ordinary dividend 普通配当
ordinary equity contributors 普通出資者
ordinary expenditure 経常費用
ordinary foreign tax credit 通常外国税額控除
ordinary general meeting 通常総会
ordinary income 経常利益
ordinary individual life insurance 普通個人保険
ordinary insurance 普通保険
ordinary interest rate 通常の利子率
ordinary inventory 正常在庫
ordinary life insurance 普通生命保険
ordinary life pension trust 普通生命保険年金信託
ordinary life, permanent life, straight life insurance 終身生命保険
ordinary local grant tax 普通交付税
ordinary losses 経常損失
ordinary operations 通常の運営
ordinary partnership 普通組合
ordinary payment 通常決済
ordinary premium 通常保険料
ordinary private company 通常私会社
ordinary profit 経常利益
ordinary profit and loss 経常損益
ordinary remittance 並為替；普通送金
ordinary share transaction 普通株取引
ordinary shareholder 普通株主
ordinary shareholders' equity 普通株主持ち分
ordinary shares outstanding 発行済普通株式
ordinary tax 経常税
ordinary transaction 普通取引
OREO (other real estate owned) その他保有不動産
organic composition of capital 資本の有機的構成
organization audit 組織監査
organization committee 創立委員
organization cost 設立費
organization expenses 創業費
organization expenses amortized 設立償却費
Organization for European Economic Cooperation 欧州経済協力機構
Organization for Management of Domestic Fund Transfers 内国為替運営機構
Organization for Security and Cooperation in Europe 欧州安保協力機構
Organization for Worker's Retirement Allowance Mutual Aid 勤労者退職金共済機構
organization form 組織形態
organization management 組織運営
Organization of American States 米州機構
Organization of Central American States 中米機構
organization of loan ローンの組成
Organization of Pacific Economic Cooperation 太平洋地域経済協力機構
Organization of Petroleum Exporting Countries 石油輸出国機構
organization office 創立事務所
organization planning 組織計画
organization with valid authority 正当な権限を有する機関
organizational changes 組織改革
organizational component 組織的構成要素
organizational grouping 組織的区分
organizational structure 組織構成
organizational unit 組織単位

organizations of primary commodity producers 一次産品生産国機構
organized exchange market 制度証券市場
organized finance 制度金融
organized financial market 制度金融市場
organized margin transactions 制度信用取引
organized market 組織化された市場
organized securities exchange 制度証券取引所
organizer 創立者
original capital 原始資本
original contract 原契約
original cost 取得原価
original cost method 取得原価法
original cost of asset 当初の取得原価
original credit 原信用状
original creditor 原債権者
original document 原本
original entry 原始記入
original equipment manufacturing agreement OEM
original insurance 元受保険
original insurance policy 原保険証書
original issue discount 割引発行
original issue price 当初発行価格
original jurisdiction 第一審管轄権
original margin 当初証拠金
original maturity 当初満期；発行時満期
original money 本源的貨幣
original obligor 原債務者
original package 原包装
original premium 当初の保険料
original purchaser 当初購入者
original register 原簿
original term 当初の期限
original trading partner 原始相手方
origination 創出
origination fee 組成手数料
origination of loan 貸付の実行
originator 発起人
orphan stock オーファン株
Osaka Mercantile Exchange 大阪商品取引所
Osaka Stock Price Index 大証株価指数
oscillation theory 振動理論
oscillator オシレーター
OSE (Osaka Securities Exchange) 大阪証券取引所
OSG(Office of the Secretary-General) 事務総長室
Oslo Stock Exchange オスロ証券取引所
Oslo Stock Exchange Index オスロ証券取引所指数
OTC (over-the-counter) 店頭
OTC (over-the-counter) option 店頭オプション
OTC (over-the-counter) transaction 店頭取引
OTC bulletin board 店頭取引掲示板
OTC company 店頭登録企業
OTC Comparison System OTC 照合システム
OTC firm 店頭取引銘柄
OTC interest rate option 店頭金利オプション
OTC margin stock 店頭証拠金株式
OTC sales yield of public and corporate bonds 公社債店頭売買利回り
OTC stock quotation exchange system 株式店頭気配発表制度
other accounting 他会計
other comprehensive income その他包括利益
other end of the spectrum 対極
other insurance clause 他保険条項
other reserve 別途積立金
OTM put OTM プット
our account 当方勘定
our side 当方
out of date 期限経過
out of line 割安・割高
out of the money アウト・オブ・ザ・マネー
out town bill 他所払手形

O

out town check 他所払小切手
out town delivery 他所渡り
out-cycle work 機械休止時作業
out-in external bonds 外・内外債
out-in transactions 外・内取引
out-of-court settlement 示談解決
out-of-date check 失効小切手
out-of-favor industry 不人気産業
out-of-pocket cost 現金支払原価
out-of-pocket expense 現金支出費
out-of-state 州外の
out-out loan 外・外ローン
out-out transactions 外・外取引
outbuilding 付属建物
outflow 流出
outgo 支出
outgoing president 退任する社長
outlay 出費
outlay cost 支出原価
outlay expiration 支出費消
outlay for advertisement 広告費
outlay tax 間接税
outline アウト・ライン
outline of business operations 業務概況書
outlook for consumer spending 消費見通し
outlook for economic activity and prices 経済・物価の将来展望
outpace 上回る
outperformance アウトパフォーマンス
output 生産高
output coefficient 産出係数
output reduction 操業短縮
output specification 性能発注仕様書
outright アウトライト
outright auction 新規発行
outright base 無条件オペ
outright buying アウトライトの買い
outright buying and selling 単純売買
outright exchange rate アウトライト為替相場
outright forward delivery with option オプション付順月渡
outright forward fixed date delivery 順月確定日渡し
outright forward rates fixed date 順月確定日相場
outright long 単なるロング
outright ownership 完全な所有
outright prohibition 全面的な禁止
outright purchase 買切り
outright purchases of bills 手形買入オペ
outright purchases of bills collateralized by corporate debt obligations 社債等担保手形買入オペ
outright purchases of JGBs 国債買入オペ
outright purchases of TBs (treasury bills)/FBs (financing bills) 短期国債買入オペ
outright sales 売切り
outright sales of bills drawn by the Bank of Japan 手形売出オペ
outright sales of TBs (treasury bills) /FBs (financing bills) 短期国債売却オペ
outright selling アウトライトの売り
outright short 単なるショート
outright transaction アウトライト取引
outside auditor 外部監査役
outside day アウトサイド・デー
outside dealing 場外取引
outside director 社外取締役
outside environment 外部環境
outside experts 外部専門家
outside interests 外部者
outside jurisdiction 管轄外
outside money 外部貨幣
outside money inside money 外部貨幣内部貨幣
outside party 外部の当事者
outside party with interest 外部利害関係者
outside product 外注製品
outside the control 支配できない
outsider 場違い筋
outsized gain 異例の増加

outsourcing アウトソーシング
outsourcing service expenses 業務委託費
outstanding account 未決済勘定
outstanding amount of CP CP 発行残高
outstanding at year-end 年末残高
outstanding balance of BOJ accounts 日銀当預残高
outstanding balance of current accounts 当座預金残高
outstanding balance of current accounts at the Bank of Japan 日銀当座預金残高
outstanding balance of issue amount 発行残高
outstanding balance of loans extended 融資実行残高
outstanding balance of margin trading 信用残
outstanding balance of receivables 債権残高
outstanding balances of credit 信用残高
outstanding bond 既発債
outstanding business 未成立契約
outstanding capital 発行済み資本
outstanding capital stock 資本金現在高
outstanding check 未取付小切手
outstanding claim 未払保険金
outstanding contract amount 契約残高
outstanding cumulative preferred shares 発行済累積優先株
outstanding debt 借越し；未済借金
outstanding feature 際立った特徴
outstanding insurance premiums 未収保険料
outstanding liabilities 未払負債
outstanding liability 負債残高
outstanding loan balance 融資残高
outstanding loans and discounts of all banks by terms 期限別貸出統計
outstanding mortgage 残存モーゲージ
outstanding purchase contracted value 買付残高
outstanding stock 既発行株式
outstanding title 第三者の権原；反対権原
outstanding warrants 既発ワラント
outward freight 往路運賃
outward investment 対外投資
outward remittance 仕向け送金
outwards reinsurance 出再保険
outweigh 上回る
over a period of time 一定期間に渡って
over funding オーバー・ファンディング；過剰積立
over future periods 将来の期にわたって
over par オーバー・パー
over the credit term 信用期間にわたり
over the varying horizons 様々な保有期間において
over time 時間の経過に伴う
over time price of bond 時間の経過に伴う債券価格
over-absorbed burden 間接費配賦超過額
over-absorbed cost 配賦超過原価
over-absorption 超過配賦
over-allotment option 追加割当オプション
over-and-out option オーバー・アンド・アウト・オプション
over-and-short account 過不足勘定
over-capacity 設備過剰
over-carrying cost 持越し費
over-competition 過当競争
over-depreciation 償却超過
over-exuberant economy 過熱経済
over-hedge 過大ヘッジ
over-indebted person 多額債務者
over-indebtedness 債務過多
over-insurance 超過保険
over-investment 過剰投資
over-issue 限外発行銘柄
over-leveraged 過剰債務の
over-loan 貸出超過

O

over-month loan 翌月物
over-month repurchase 翌月物
over-priced 割高
over-reaction 過剰反応
over-reliance 過度の依存
over-speculation 過当投機
over-subscription オーバー・サブスクリプション
over-the-counter currency option 店頭通貨オプション
over-the-counter managed issues 店頭管理銘柄
over-the-counter market 店頭市場
over-the-counter sale 窓口販売
over-the-counter sales yield 店頭売買利回り
over-the-counter stock 店頭株
over-the-month delivery 翌月受渡し
over-the-top warrant オーバー・ザ・トップ・ワラント
over-transfer 過剰振込
over-used hours 超過使用時間
over-valued stock 割高株
overall balance of foreign exchange 為替持高
overall balance of payment 総合収支
overall charge 費用総額
Overall Co-ordination Division 文書課
overall effect 全体的影響
overall evaluation 総括評価
overall level 全体的な水準
overall market price coverage 時価債務カバレッジ
overall position 総合持高
overall profit 総体的利益
overall trade picture 全体の貿易統計
overbanked 銀行が過剰な状態に
overbooked 応募超過
overbought market 過熱相場
overbought position 買持ちポジション
overbuilding 建設過剰
overcapitalization 過大資本
overconfidence 過信
overdraft 当座貸越し
overdraft account 当座借越勘定
overdraft charges 延滞金利
overdraft economy 貸越経済
overdraft facilities 当座借越契約
overdraft interest 過振利息
overdraft line 当座貸越枠
overdrafts for export bills 為替当座貸
overdrawn 貸越し；過振りの
overdrawn account 貸越勘定
overdressing 過度な粉飾
overdue 遅延している
overdue account 期限経過勘定
overdue bill 期限経過手形
overdue check 期限経過小切手
overdue claims 延滞債権
overdue interest 延滞利子
overdue interest on loan on bills 手形貸付延滞利息
overdue interest per diem 延滞日歩
overdue loan 延滞債権
overdue payment 期日到来債権
overestimation of goods traded in 下取商品の過大評価
overestimation of inherited assets 引継資産の過大評価
overestimation of investment in kind 現物出資の過大評価
overfunded 資金が大きく膨張した
overhang だぶつき
overhauling 修繕
overhead cost 間接費
overhead cost distribution 間接費配賦
overhead distribution basis 間接費配賦基準
overhead distribution sheet 部門費計算表
overhead expenses 経営費
overhead rate 間接費配賦率
overhead variance 間接費差異
overheated economy 過熱経済
overheating of business activity 景気過熱
overhung dollar ドル過剰
overland freight 陸上運送費
overlapping account 重複勘定
overlapping benefit 重複給付

overlapping debt 重複債務
overlapping insurance 重複保険
overlay 上乗せ
overnight オーバーナイト
overnight batch settlement 夜間バッチ決済
overnight bridge 夜間ブリッジ
overnight call 翌日物コール
overnight call rate 翌日物コール・レート
overnight delivery 翌日受渡し
overnight money 翌日物
overnight payment 翌日返済
overnight position オーバーナイト・ポジション
overnight processing 夜間処理
overnight rate オーバーナイト・レート
overnight repo 翌日物レポ
overnight transaction オーバーナイト取引
overpaid 過払の
overpayment 過誤納金
overpayment of corporation tax due to window dressing 粉飾決算による法人税の過大納付
overproduction 生産過剰
overreaching clause 所有権留保条項
override 上乗手数料；覆す；歩合
overriding 優先させる
overriding criteria 優先する規準
overriding goal 最優先の目的
overrun 超過の
overs and shorts 過不足
overseas affiliated company 海外関係会社
overseas business 海外事業
overseas demand related stock 外需関連株
overseas economies 海外経済
overseas establishments 在外公館
overseas finance subsidiary 海外金融子会社
overseas flotation 海外起債分
overseas interest rate 海外金利
overseas interests 海外利権
overseas investment 対外投資
overseas investment loss reserve 海外投資損失準備金
overseas investment report 海外投資報告書
overseas legal reserve 海外法定準備金
overseas liability 海外負債
overseas listing 海外での上場
overseas major market 海外主要市場
overseas market development reserve 海外市場開拓準備金
overseas market rate 海外相場
Overseas Private Investment Corporation 海外民間投資公社
overseas production capacity 海外生産能力
overseas production ratio 海外生産比率
overseas securities financing 海外での証券発行
overseas service employee 国外勤務者
overseas technical service transaction 技術等海外取引
overseas transaction 海外取引
overseas transactions for technique 技術等海外取引
overseas travel accident insurance 海外旅行傷害保険
overseas traveling expense 海外旅行費
overseas undertaking corporation 海外事業法人
overselling 売過ぎ
overshoot 目標突破；行過ぎ
oversold 売られすぎ
oversold position 売持ち
overstate 過大表示する
overstatement 過大表示；誇張
overstock 過剰在庫
oversubscribed 応募超過の
oversupply 過剰供給
overt 公の
overt act 明白な行為
overtime hours 所定外労働時間
overtime payment 残業手当

O

overtrading 過度な取引
overvaluation 過大評価
overvalued 割高
overvalued futures 割高な先物
overview 概要
overview of the business results 業績概要
overwithholding 過大源泉徴収
overwriting 過大売り
owing 支払うべき
owing to bank 銀行借入
own account 自己勘定
own bill 自行引受
own capital 自己資本
own equity instruments 自己の持ち分金融商品
own named cards 自社カード
own trading position 自己の売買ポジション
own usance 自行ユーザンス
owned asset management 所有資産運用
owner control 所有者支配
owner occupied property 自己使用不動産
owner of record 名義上の株主
owner of small business 小企業の事業主
owner's equity 自己資本
owner's equity interest 所有主持ち分
owner's risk 荷主危険持ち
owners capital 株主資本
ownership 所有
ownership certificate 所有権証
ownership interest 所有持ち分
ownership of the leases リース物件の所有権
ownership right 所有権
ownership structure 株主構造

P

p.a. (per annum) 年
P/CF (price/cash flow) multiples 株価キャッシュフロー倍率
P&I (principal and interest) 元利金
PA (particular average) 単独海損
PA (pay on application) 請求払い
Paasche formula パーシェ方式
PAB (Panamanian balboa) パナマ・バルボア
PAC (planned amortization class) bond PAC債
Pac-man defense パックマン・ディフェンス
pace of economic expansion 経済成長率
pace of recovery 回復テンポ
Pacific Economic and Cultural Enclave 太平洋経済文化圏
Pacific Insurance Conference 太平洋保険会議
Pacific Stock Exchange パシフィック証券取引所
package and warrants カムとワラント
package automobile policy 自動車総合保険
package deal contract パッケージ・ディール契約
package lease パッケージ・リース
package mortgage 包括抵当
package policy パッケージ保険
package registration 一括登録
packaged insurance 総合保険
packing and wrapping expenses 荷造費
packing charge 包装費
packing credit パッキング・クレジット
packing list 包装明細書
pact 協約
paid amount 払込金額
paid annual leave 年次有給休暇
paid check 支払済小切手
paid interest 返済利息
paid sick leave 有給疾病休暇
paid-in advances 新株払込金
paid-in capital 払込資本
paid-in capital in excess of par value 株式払込剰余金
paid-in capital increase 有償増資
paid-in outstanding shares 有償発行済株式
paid-in surplus 払込剰余金
paid-up annuity 払込済年金
paid-up capital 払込資本
paid-up insurance 払込済保険
paid-up life insurance 払済保険購入式生命保険
paid-up policy 払込済保険
paid-up stock 払込済株式
paid-up value 払込済価額
painting the tape 価格操作
paired shares 一対株
Palau (US dollar) パラオ（米国ドル）
Pan Pacific Basin 環太平洋地域
pan-European 汎欧州
panic buying 買いあさり
panic market 恐慌市場
panic selling ろうばい売り
paper audit 書面監査
paper company ペーパー・カンパニー
paper credit 紙券使用
paper crisis 紙洪水
paper currency 紙幣
paper loss 含み損
paper profit 架空利益
paper trading 架空取引
paperless 無券面の
paperless trading ペーパーレス・トレーディング
paperwork 書類作り

par bond 額面売買社債
par floor 元本保証
par forward パー・フォワード
par issuance 平価発行
par issue 額面発行
par price 額面価格
par redemption amount 額面償還額
par value 額面価額
par value method 額面法
par value of currency 為替平価
par value of exchange rate 為替平価
par value per share 一株当り額面金額
par value share 額面株式資本金
par value stock 額面株式
par yield パー・イールド
paradox of value 価値のパラドックス
paradoxical view 逆説的な考え方
paragraph 項
parallel clearing 相互決済
parallel import 平行輸入
parallel issue 平行起債
parallel loan パラレル・ローン
parallel market パラレル・マーケット
parallel money market 併行市場
parallel rate shift 金利の平行移動
parallel run 最終テスト
parallel shift 平行移動
parallel standard 並行本位制度
parallel transaction 平行取引
parameter パラメーター
parameters 特性
parametric method パラメトリック法
paramount right 優越する権利
parent and subsidiary relationship 親子関係
parent base 単独ベース
parent company 親会社
parent company guaranteed 親会社保証の
parent of a wholly owned subsidiary 完全親会社
parent sales 単独ベースの売上
parent store 本店
parent undertaking 親企業
parent-basis earning outlook 単独ベースの収益見通し
parent's share 親会社の持ち分
parenthetical notes かっこ内注記
Pareto optimal パレート最適
Pareto's constant パレート定数
pari passu 同順位で
pari passu clause パリパス条項
pari-mutuel betting 競馬式賭ばく
Paris Club パリクラブ
parity 平価
parity account パリティ計算
parity adjustment 平価調整
parity grid パリティ・グリッド
parity index パリティ指数
parity line パリティ直線
parity of official exchange rate 公定平価
parity price パリティ価格
parity quotation 平準相場
parity rate of exchange 為替平価
parity value パリティ価値
parking 避難
parliamentary secretary 大臣政務官
Parliamentary Secretary for Finance 財務大臣政務官
parol contract 口頭契約
part time 非常勤の
part-owners 共有者
partial abandonment 一部委付
partial acceptance 一部引受け
partial amendment 一部改訂
partial assignment 一部譲渡
partial audit 部分監査
partial benefit 部分給付
partial cancellation of securities investment trust 証券投資信託の部分解約
partial competitive auction bidding 部分的競争入札
partial costing 部分原価計算
partial delivery 一部受渡し
partial derivative 偏導関数
partial differential equation 偏微分方程式
partial direct write-off 部分的直接償却

partial draw down 分割引出し
partial elasticity 偏弾力性
partial endorsement 一部裏書き
partial equilibrium 部分均衡
partial equity method 部分持分法
partial fair value method 部分資本直入法
partial guarantee 部分保証
partial legal tender 不完全法貨
partial loss 分損
partial opening 部分開放
partial ownership 区分所有権
partial payment 内払
partial pension 部分年金
partial performance 一部履行
partial prepayment 部分繰上返済
partial reserve system 一部準備制度
partial retirement 部分退職
partial shipment 分割船積み
partial tax transfer to local government 地方分与税
partial vesting 部分給付権付与
partial withdrawal 部分解約；部分撤退
partially covered option 部分的なカバード・オプション
partially finished goods ledger 半製品元帳
participant 参加者
participant bond 信認金
participants' fund 参加者基金
participating annuity 参加配当年金
participating bond 利益参加社債
participating business year 参加事業年度
participating dividend 参加配当
participating employee 加入従業員
participating employer 加入事業主
participating enterprise 加入企業
participating insurance 参加保険
participating interests 参加持ち分
participating investment 利益参加型投資
participating life insurance policy 配当付生命保険証券
participating policy dividend 保険の利益配当
participating policy surplus 配当付保険剰余金
participating preferred stock 参加優先株式
participating premium 配当付保険保険料
participating stock 利益配当株
participating unit investment trust 参加型ユニット投資信託
participating whole life insurance 配当付き終身保険
participation 参加
participation agreement パーティシペーション契約
participation bank 参加銀行
participation certificate 参加証券
participation fee 参加金
participation in foreclosure 参加差押
participation in seizure 参加差押
participation loan 参加融資
participation method 参加方式
participation rate 加入率
participation securities 参加証券
participation standard 加入基準
participation stock 参加株
particular contract 特定契約
particular interest 利害関係
particular lien 特定のリーエン
particular loss 分損
particular order 特定の順序
particular point in time 一定時点
particulars 内訳
particulars of account 勘定明細
particulars of transaction 取引内容
parties to lawsuit 訴訟当事者
partition 共有物分割
partition of the estate 遺産分割
partly finished goods 仕掛品
partly paid bond 一部払込債券
partner パートナー
partnership パートナーシップ
partnership agreement パートナーシップ契約

partnership assets 組合財産
partnership insurance パートナーシップ保険
partnership interest パートナーシップ持ち分
partnership property パートナーシップ財産
parts account 部品勘定
party 当事者
party insuring 保険契約者
party with particular interest 特殊関係者
pass dividend 無配にする
pass on 転嫁する
pass-through パス・スルー
pass-through rate パス・スルー比率
pass-through securities パス・スルー証券
passage 通過
passage of time 時間の経過
passage of title 所有権の移転
passbook 通帳
passbook savings account 通帳貯蓄預金口座
passed dividend 無配当
passenger liability insurance 乗客賠償責任保険
passenger traffic receipts 旅客収入
passengers tax 通行税
passing off 詐称通用
passing on commission 手数料払戻し
passive bond 無利子社債
passive business 受動的事業
passive debt 無利息債務
passive income 受動的利益
passive investment management 消極的投資管理
passive investor 受動的投資家
passive loss 受動的損失；パッシブ損失
passive management パッシブ運用
passive market making パッシブ・マーケット・メーキング
passive partner パッシブ・パートナー
passive portfolio パッシブ運用のポートフォリオ
passive strategy 安全型運用
passive trust 消極信託
past assessment 過去の評価
past cost 過去原価
past due balance method 延滞残高方式
past due bill 期限経過手形；不渡手形
past due charge 延滞加算金
past due interest 延滞利息
past due loan 延滞ローン
past due policy 期日経過保険契約
past event 過去の事象
past expense 過去の費用
past experience 過去の経験
past history 過去の歴史
past performance 過去の実績
past practice 過去の慣行
past service cost 過去勤務費
past service credit 過去勤務受給額
past service funding 過去勤務債務積立
past service liability 過去勤務債務
past transaction 過去の取引
patent 特許
patent account 特許権勘定
patent ambiguities or defects 明らかな曖昧さあるいは誤り
patent ambiguity 明らかな意味不明
patent applied for 特許出願中
patent attorney 特許弁理士
Patent Bureau 特許局
patent dispute 特許紛争
patent fee 特許料
patent law 特許法
patent pending 特許出願中
patent period 特許有効期間
patent right 特許権
patented article 特許品
patentee 特許所有権者
path 経路
path dependency 経路依存
path dependent option 経路依存型オプション
path finder 先導役
path-independency 経路独立性
pattern information processing パターン情報処理

pattern of economic benefits 経済便益パターン
pattern of portfolio return ポートフォリオの収益パターン
pattern recognition パターン認識
pawn 動産質
pawn-shop 質屋
pax Americana パックス・アメリカーナ
pay 賃金
pay according to ability 能力給
pay according to function 職務給
pay after tax 税引給与
pay back method 回収期間法
pay by card カード決済
pay down 一部返済；現金払い
pay level 給与水準
pay off 完済する；リターンをもたらす
pay package 給与体系
pay roll audit 給料監査
pay-as-you-go 現金払い主義
pay-as-you-go basis 現金方式
pay-as-you-go system 賦課方式
pay-freeze 賃金凍結
pay-in-kind bond 現物配当株
pay-off curve 収益カーブ
pay-off diagram ペイオフ・ダイヤグラム
pay-off matrix ペイオフ行列
pay-roll register 賃金給料支払簿
pay-through bond ペイ・スルー債券
pay-up 追加支払
payable 支払期日の到来した
payable at sight 一覧払い
payable on a fixed date 確定日払い
payable on demand 要求払い
payable to bearer 持参人払い
payable to holder 所持人払い
payable to order 指図人払い
payables to sales ratio 売上債務比率
payables under repurchase agreement 売現先債務
payday 給料日
payee 受取人
payee bank 被仕向け銀行
payer 支払人
payer bank 支払銀行；仕向け銀行
payer's swaption ペイヤー・スワップション
paying & warrant agency agreement 支払ワラント代理人契約書
paying agent 支払代理人
paying bank 支払銀行
paying in slip 入金伝票
paying person 払込者
paying tax 納付
paying, collecting and refunding tax 税額の納付，徴収及び還付
paymaster 主計
payment 決済
payment account agreement 支払準備勘定契約
payment against acceptance 引受払い
payment against document 証券引替払い
payment agreement 支払協定
payment and receipt 支払い・受取り
payment and receipt of cash 現金の授受
payment and settlement risk 決済リスク
Payment and Settlement Statistics 決済動向
payment and settlement system 決済システム
payment at regular fixed times 定時払い
payment book 支払記入帳
payment by a lump sum at maturity 満期一括払い
payment by beneficiary 受益者負担金
payment by bill 手形払い
payment by cash 現金払い
payment by rough estimate 概算払い
payment by the results 成果配分
payment certifying bank 支払保証銀行
payment clearance 信用決済
payment clearing and settlement 支払決済
payment conditions 弁済条件

payment confirmation 支払確認
payment credit 支払い信用状
payment date 払込期日
payment day 払込日
payment deemed as dividends みなし配当
payment default 決済不履行
payment for another 代納
payment for newly issued JGSs 国債発行代り金の払込
payment handling bank 払込取扱銀行
payment in a short time 短期払い
payment in advance 前金で
payment in full 全額払込
payment in installments 分割納付
payment in kind 代物弁済
payment in part 内払
payment in subrogation 代位弁済
payment in substitution 代物弁済
payment instruction 支払指図；振替依頼
payment instrument 決済手段；支払手段
payment into court 供託
payment into the National Treasury 国庫納付金
payment legs 支払レッグ
payment message 支払指図
payment mismatches 利払いのミスマッチ
payment moratorium 支払猶予
payment obligation 支払債務
payment of capital contribution 出資金の払込み
payment of corporate bonds 社債償還
payment of factor income 要素所得の支払い
payment of principal and interest on JGSs 国債の元利払い
payment of retirement allowance for termination 退職金の打切支給
payment of tax 税金納付
payment of unrealized profit 計算上の利益の払出し
payment on delivery 先払い
payment on interest and discount rate 利子及割引料
payment order 支払指図
payment period 支払期間
payment provisions 支払条項
payment rate 支払率
payment record 支払調書
payment slip 出金伝票
payment statement 支払明細
payment stop 支払停止
payment supra 参加支払い
payment terms and conditions 支払条件
payment to nonresidents 非居住者の給与所得
payment to nonresidents and foreign corporations 非居住者及び外国法人への支払い
payment to rendered services 役務の提供に対する支払い
payment-in-kind preferred stock ペイメント・イン・カインド 優先株
payments leg 資金サイド
payments made quarterly 四半期ごとの支払い
payments on purchase of securities 有価証券取得による支出
payoff function 利得関数
payoff period 回収期間
payoff structure 収益構造
payout annuity 支払年金
payout percentage 支給率
payout period 支払期間
payroll book 賃金台帳
payroll deduction 給与天引；賃金控除
payroll deduction type investment trust 給与天引型投信
payroll tax 給与税
payroll withholding 給与天引
payrolls number 雇用統計
PBGC (Pension Benefit Guaranty Corporation) 年金給付保証公社
PBIT (profit before interest and taxes) 利子税金控除前利益
PBO (projected benefit obligation) 予

測給付債務
PBOT (Philadelphia Board of Trade) フィラデルフィア商品取引所
PBR (price to book-value ratio) 株価純資産倍率
PC (plus commission) 手数料込み
PCMF (pension cash management fund) 年金給付専用ファンド
PCX (Pacific Exchange) パシフィック取引所
peak load ピーク・ロード
pearl harbor file パールハーバー・ファイル
peculiar benefits 特殊受益
pecuniary considerations 金銭的報酬
pecuniary damage 金銭的損害
pecuniary gain 金銭上の利益
pecuniary legacy 金銭遺贈
pecuniary relation 金銭上の関係
pecuniary transaction 金銭取引
pecuniary value 金銭上の価値
peer 同輩
peer companies 同業他社
peer review ピア・レビュー
pegged exchange 釘付け為替相場
pegged exchange rate system 固定為替相場制度
pegged market 釘付相場
pegged stock 釘付株
pegging 価格の安定化
PEN (Peruvian nuebo sol) ペルー・ヌエボソル
PEN (protected equity note) 保護付エクイティ・ノート
penal 処罰し得る
penal interest 違約利子
penal provision 罰則
penal sum 違約金額
penal tax 追徴税
penalty against employer and employee 両罰規定
penalty bid ペナルティ・ビッド
penalty charge 遅延損害金
penalty clause 罰則条項
penalty heavier than imprisonment 禁固以上の刑
penalty money 違約金
penalty on delayed delivery 延滞補償金
penalty rate 延滞金利
penalty tax 加算税
pending 未決の
pending action 未解決の行為
pending lawsuit 係争中の訴訟
pending litigation 係争中の訴訟
penetration of phones 電話の普及率
penetration of tight money policy 金融引締政策の浸透
penetration price 浸透価格
penetration rate 加入率
pennant ペナント
penny stock 安値株式
pension 年金
pension accrual 年金給付発生分
pension actuary 年金数理人
pension adjustment 年金掛金調整
pension administration 年金管理
pension and life insurance schemes 企業年金・企業保険
pension annuity 退職年金保険
pension assets 年金資産
pension award 年金支給
pension benefits 年金給付
pension buildup 年金積立
pension business 年金業務
pension business lines 年金商品
pension calculation 退職年金計算
pension cap 年金受給額上限
pension certificate 年金証書
pension commitments 年金約定
pension contract 年金契約
pension cost 年金コスト
pension credit 年金給付額
pension eligibility 年金受給資格
pension entitlements 年金受給権
pension equity 年金持ち分
pension expense 年金費用
pension financing 年金財政
pension financing method 年金財政方式

pension fund 年金基金
pension fund assets 年金基金資産
Pension Fund Association 厚生年金基金連合会
pension fund beneficiary 年金基金の受益者
pension fund investment 年金基金の資産運用
pension fund management 年金基金管理
pension fund method 年金積立金算定方式
pension fund spread 年金プランのスプレッド
pension fund surplus 年金基金の剰余
pension fund's mission 年金基金の使命
pension guarantee 年金保証
pension income 年金収入
pension investment fund trust 年金投資基金信託
pension level 年金水準
pension liability 年金負債
pension mobility 年金移管
pension money 年金資金
pension mortgage 年金担保住宅ローン
pension pan funding 年金費用積立
pension parachute 年金パラシュート
pension participation 年金加入
pension payout 年金支給
pension plan 年金制度
pension plan accounting 年金会計
pension plan annuity 年金費用積立年金保険
pension plan assets 年金制度資産
pension plan documents 年金プラン規定書
pension plan insurance 年金給付保証保険
pension plan liability reserve 年金制度責任準備金
pension plan reversion 超過年金資産の回収
pension plan surplus 年金基金剰余金
pension plan trustee 年金受託者
pension point 年金点数
pension point system 年金ポイント制
pension pool 年金プール
pension program 年金制度
pension provider 年金提供者
pension recipiency 年金受給率
pension reform 年金改革
pension reserve 年金積立金
pension reversion 年金返還
pension right 年金権
pension savings 年金貯蓄
pension scheme 年金制度
pension termination 年金の消滅
pension termination insurance 年金消滅保険
pension transfer 年金制度の移管
pension trust 年金信託
pension valuation 年金評価
pension vesting rate 年金受給権付与率
pensionable age 年金支給開始年齢
pensionable earnings 年金受給対象額
pensioner 年金生活者
pensions accounts 年金運用口
pensions legislation 年金法
pensions-in-payment liabilities 年金受給者に対する債務
pent up demand 潜在的需要
penultimate 最後から二番目の
penultimate profit prospect 最後から二番目の利益期待
People's Bank of China 中国人民銀行
People's Insurance Company of China 中国人民保険公司
PEP (personal equity plan) 個人持株制度
peppercorn rent 名義だけの地代
PER (price earnings ratio) 株価収益率
per annum 一年につき
per annum rate 年利
per capita 一人当り
per capita debt 一人当り公債発行残高
per capita gross national product 一人当り国民総生産
per capita income 一人当りの所得
per capita levy 均等割税率

per capita product 一人当りの生産
per capita rate 一人当り税率
per contra account 対照勘定
per contra noted discounted account 割引手形見返り勘定
per diem 一日当り
per diem allowance 日当
per diem benefit 日額給付
per share data 一株当りの数値
per stripes 法定相続
per-diem rate for call loan コール日歩
percent of capacity use 稼働率
percentage 百分率
percentage balance sheet 百分率貸借対照表
percentage change 騰落率
percentage depletion 比率法減耗償却
percentage distribution 構成比
percentage financial statements 百分率財務諸表
percentage grant 定率補助金
percentage income statement 百分率損益計算書
percentage lease パーセンテージリース
percentage method 百分率法
percentage of capital structure 資本構成比率
percentage of completion basis 工事進行基準
percentage of credit losses 貸倒れ率
percentage of debt collection 負債の回収率
percentage of delinquency 延滞率
percentage of each class of assets to total assets 資産構成比率
percentage of labor hours 累計発生労働時間
percentage of payroll cost 給与比例掛金
percentage of profits available on net worth 自己資本利益率
percentage of profits on net worth 自己資本利益率
percentage of shareholding 持株比率
percentage on diminishing value plan 定率償却法
percentage order パーセンテージ注文
percentage participation 比率分担
percentage savings 節約率
percentage table 百分率表
perception 見方
peremptory 専断的
peremptory instruction 決定的説示
peremptory nonsuit 決定的却下
perennial tax 永久税
perennial tenant right 永久小作権
perfect competition 完全競争
perfect hedge 完全ヘッジ
perfect monopoly 完全独占
perfect obligation 完全債務
perfect title 完全権原
perfected security interest 対抗要件を具備した担保権
perfection of the interest 対抗力の具備
perfection standard cost 完全標準原価
perfectly negatively correlated returns 完全負相関の収益率
perfectly positively correlated returns 完全正相関の収益率
performance accounting 業績評価会計
performance appraisal 業績評価
performance attribution パフォーマンス特性
performance audit 業務監査
performance based 成果主義の
performance based fee 成果報酬
performance basis 成果主義
performance bond 履行保証証券
performance bond insurance 履行保証保険
performance budget 業績予算
performance comparison 業績比較
performance conditions 業績条件
performance criteria 業績基準
performance evaluation パフォーマンス評価
performance fund パフォーマンス・ファンド

performance guarantee 履行保証
performance guarantee deposit 履行証拠金
performance indicators 業績指標
performance margin パフォーマンス証拠金
performance measurement パフォーマンスの測定
performance model 業績モデル
performance of bearing duty by Bank of Japan 日本銀行の消却義務
performance of business 事業の遂行
performance of obligation 債務の履行
performance of obligations of guarantee 保証債務の履行
performance of securities 証券の運用成績
performance period 成果期間
performance report 業績報告書
performance reporting 業績報告
performance reporting issue 業績報告の問題
performance result 成果
performance share 成長株式
performance standard 業績水準
performance statement 業績計算書
performance stock 高成長株
performance target 業績目標
performance unit 業績連動証券
performance-based fee system 業績比例報酬体系
performance-based order 性能発注
performing loans 稼動しているローン
peril 危険
peril clause 危険約款
peril point 危険点
perils clause 危険条項
perils insured against 被保険危険
perils of the sea 海固有の危険
period analysis 期間分析
period call market 定期コール市場
period certain annuity 期間限定年金保険
period commencing on but excluding the date of 片端入れ
period cost 期間原価
period of arrears 延滞期間
period of deferment 据置期間
period of depreciation 償却期間
period of digestion 消化期間
period of economic growth 経済の成長期
period of economic stability 経済の安定期
period of request for reconsideration 審査請求期間
period until maturity 残存償還期間
period-end measurement 期末測定
periodic 定期的な
periodic actual inventory 定期実地棚卸
periodic advice 定期的な助言
periodic allocation of cost 原価の期間配分
periodic audit 定期監査
periodic average 期間平均
periodic average method 総平均法
periodic balance sheet 期末貸借対照表
periodic band 期間帯
periodic charge 期間費用
periodic financial statements 期間財務諸表
periodic general meeting 通常総会
periodic income 期間利益
periodic inventory 定期棚卸
periodic loss 期間損失
periodic maintenance 定期的修繕
periodic payment 定期支払い
periodic pension cost 年金の期間原価
periodic physical inventory 定期実地棚卸
periodic purchase deferred contract 定期払込据置年金保険
periodic rate of interest 期間利子率
periodic rate of return 期間利益率
periodic return 定期的なリターン
periodic securities report 有価証券報告書
periodic trial balance 期末試算表
periodical accounting 期間計算

periodical accounting of profit and loss 期間損益計算
periodical calculation 期間計算
periodical return 定期的収益
periodical transaction 定期的取引
periodicals 定期刊行物
periods during which interest is payable 金利支払期間
PERLS (principal exchange rate linked securities) 元本為替連動証券
permanent account 永久勘定
permanent assets 永久資産
permanent auditor 常任監査役
permanent criteria 永久基準
permanent debt 永久公債
permanent difference 永久差異
permanent disability cover 高度障害保険
permanent domicile 本籍
permanent establishment 恒久施設
permanent facility 恒久的施設
permanent financing 永久貸出し
permanent health insurance 終身健康保険
permanent income hypothesis 恒常所得仮説
permanent injunction 終局差止命令
permanent liability 永久負債
permanent loan 永久貸付
permanent preferred stock 永久優先株
permanent tax reduction 恒久減税
permanent trespass 継続的侵害
permanently restricted assets 永久拘束資産
permeation of tight money policy 金融引締めの浸透
permissible error 許容誤差
permissible investment 容認される投資
permutation 並替え
pernor of profits 利益取得者
perpendicular spread 垂直スプレッド
perpetual annuity 終身年金
perpetual bond 永久債
perpetual debt instrument 永久負債証券
perpetual injunction 永久差止命令
perpetual inventory 継続棚卸
perpetual inventory method 継続記録法
perpetual issue 永久債
perpetual lease 永代借地権
perpetual lessee 永代借地人
perpetual subordinated debt 永久劣後債
perpetual warrant 永久ワラント
perpetuating testimony 証言の証拠保全
perquisite 臨時収入
persistence 持続
persistence rate 継続率
persistent 根強い
person adjudged incompetent 禁治産者；成年被後見人
person for handling securities 有価証券取扱責任者
person in charge of handling information 情報取扱責任者
person receiving employment income 給与所得者
personal accident insurance 傷害保険
personal account 人名勘定
personal action 人的訴訟
personal article floater 個人動産包括保険
personal assets 動産
personal average tax rate 平均個人税率
personal bankruptcy 個人破産
personal bias 個人的偏向
personal bill 個人手形
personal check パーソナル・チェック
personal checking account 個人当座勘定
personal consumption expenditure 個人消費
personal contract 動産契約
personal covenant 人的約款
personal credit 個人信用
personal deposit 個人預金

personal disposable income 個人可処分所得
personal distress 動産差押
personal dividend income 個人配当所得
personal estate 動産
personal exclusion from taxation 人的課税除外
personal exemption 基礎控除
personal expenditure 個人支出
personal family corporation 同族株主の同族会社
personal finance パーソナル・ファイナンス
personal financing 個人向金融
personal guarantee 個人保証
personal hereditament 人的相続財産
personal holding company 同族会社
personal identification number 暗証番号
personal immunity 個人の秘密保持権
personal income 個人所得
personal income from property 個人財産所得
personal income tax 個人所得税
personal inflation 個人的インフレ
personal insurance 人保険
personal interest income 個人利子所得
personal judgment 人的判決
personal knowledge 直接の認識
personal ledger 人名元帳
personal liability 個人負債
personal liability insurance 対人賠償責任保険
personal liberty 人身の自由
personal line 個人保険
personal loan 個人ローン
personal member 個人メンバー
personal mortgage 個人住宅ローン
personal opinion 自己の意見
personal pension 個人年金
personal pension insurance 個人年金保険
personal pension scheme 個人年金制度
personal pension term assurance 個人年金定期保険
personal property 個人財産
personal property floater 動産包括保険証券
personal property tax 動産税
personal rental income 個人賃貸料所得
personal representatives 人格代表者
personal saving 個人貯蓄
Personal Secretary to the Minister 大臣秘書官
personal sector 個人部門
personal security 人的担保
personal service 役務
personal tax 対人税
personal taxation 人的課税
personal trust 個人信託
personal trust fund 個人信託ファンド
personal valuation 個人的評価
personalty 人的財産
personification theory 擬人説
personnel audit 人事監査
personnel cost 人件費
Personnel Division 管理課；人事課
personnel expenses 人件費
Personnel Inspector 監察官
personnel management 人事管理
personnel policy 人事方針
personnel reduction 人員削減
persons having a special interest 特別利害関係者
persons in overseas service 国外勤務者
perspective 視点
persuasive comparison 説得力のある比較
persuasive evidence 説得力のある証拠
pertinent elements 関連項目
pertinent information 関連情報
perusal 精読
peseta ペセタ
peso ペソ
pessimistic inflation expectation インフレ警戒

P

pessimistic scenario 悲観的シナリオ
petition 請願；申立
petition filed for arbitration 調停の申立
petition of right 権利請願
petitioner 申立人
petrobond 原油価格連動型社債
petrochemical complex 石油化学コンビナート
petrochemical industry 石油化学産業
petrodollar オイル・ダラー
petroleum act 石油業法
petroleum financing bills 石油証券
petroleum revenue tax 石油収入税
petroleum tax 石油税
Petroleum tax law 石油税法
petty average 小海損
petty cash 小口現金
petty cash account 小口現金勘定
petty cash book 小口現金の出納帳
petty cash fund 小口資金
petty cash payment 少額現金支払い
petty cash system 小口現金制度
petty current deposit 小口現金預金
petty deposits 小口預金
petty expense analysis book 雑費内訳帳
petty expense break down book 雑費内訳帳
petty expenses 雑費
petty imprest 小口前渡金
petty offense 小罪
petty profit and loss 雑損益
petty sum depreciable assets 少額減価償却資産
petty sum depreciable property 少額償却資産
petty sum wasting property 少額減耗資産
PFI (private finance initiative) 民間資金等活用事業
PGK (Papua New Guinea kina) パプアニューギニア・キナ
phantom account 支給時時価払勘定
phantom income 見かけの所得
pharmaceutical industry 医薬品業界
phase of expansion 景気拡大局面
phase of recession 景気後退局面
phase-out period 段階的廃止期間
phased construction 段階的な建設
phases of economic cycle 景気循環の局面
phasing out 撤退
Philadelphia Fed フィラデルフィア連銀
Philadelphia plan フィラデルフィア・プラン
philanthropy 社会貢献
Philippine Stock Exchange フィリピン証券取引所
Phillips curve フィリップス曲線
philosophy of management 経営哲学
PHLX (Philadelphia Stock Exchange) フィラデルフィア証券取引所
PHP (Philippine peso) フィリピン・ペソ
physical access member 立会場で取引できる会員
physical age 物理的耐用年数
physical assets 有形資産
physical capital 実体資本
physical change 物理的変化
physical commodity 実物商品
physical contingency 物理的予備費
physical counting of inventory 実地棚卸数量
physical counts 実地棚卸
physical delivery 現物引渡し
physical depreciation 物理的減価
physical deterioration 物理的な劣化
physical distribution 物的流通
physical evidence 物的証拠
physical inspection 実査
physical inventory 実地棚卸
physical limit 物理的な限度
physical output 実際生産高
physical payment 実際の支払い
physical securities 現物証券
physical substance 実質的実体
physical useful life 物理的耐用年数

physical variables 物理的変数
physical verification 棚卸
physical wear and tear 物理的減耗
physically handicapped person 身体障害者
physically handicapped person allowance 障害者控除
physician's expense insurance 治療費保険
PIBOR (Paris interbank offered rate) PIBOR
PIBS (permanent interest bearing shares) 永久利付証券
pick up 上向く
pick up bond ピックアップ債
pick-up of inflation rate インフレ率の上昇
pick-up of yield 利回りの改善
picker 小口筋
picking up spread スプレッドの獲得
pickup in demand 需要の回復
picture of the business 業務の概要
piece rate plan 出来高給制度
piecemeal sale 段階的売却
PIG (passive income generator) 受動的所得源
piggy backing 便乗
piggyback registration 相乗り登録
PIK (payment-in-kind) securities PIK証券
pilot plant パイロット・プラント
pilot projects 実用化実験
pilot tests 実用化実験
pilot unit 試作機
PIN number PIN 番号
PIRA (participating interest rate agreement) 利益参加型金利契約
pit ピット
pit broker ピット・ブローカー
pit reporter ピット・レポーター
PITI (principal, interest, tax and insurance) 元利・税金・保険込返済
PKR (Pakistan rupee) パキスタン・ルピー
place 新発証券を販売する
place for tax payment 納税地
place of abode 住所
place of delivery 引渡場所
place of fiduciary 受託取扱場所
place of issue 振出地
place of payment 支払地
placement commission 販売手数料
placement fee 斡旋手数料
placement of assets 資産の運用
placement of bond 社債の販売
placement of deposit 預金の預け入れ
placement of unlisted notes 私募債の発行
placement ratio 販売比率
placement with other banks 他行預け
placing memorandum 私募要領
plain deal 標準案件
plain language 普通語
plain vanilla プレーン・バニラ
plain vanilla floater プレーン・バニラの変動利付債
plain vanilla option プレーン・バニラ・オプション
plain vanilla swap プレーン・バニラ・スワップ
plaintiff 原告
plan administration cost 制度管理コスト
plan amendment 制度修正
plan assets 年金資産
plan beneficiaries 年金受益者
plan benefit 制度給付
plan benefit formula 制度給付算定式
plan cost 制度費用
plan design 制度設計
plan document 制度規約
plan for management improvement 経営改善計画
plan management 制度管理
plan member 制度加入者
plan participant 制度加入者
plan participation 制度加入
plan sponsor 制度提供者；年金制度スポンサー

plan termination 制度の打切り
plan termination insurance 年金制度終了保険
plan trustee 制度受託者
plan winding up 制度終了
plan with insured benefit 保険付給付制度
plan's benefit formula 制度の給付算定式
planned economy 計画経済
planned performance 計画した稼動
planned transaction 計画的取引
Planning and Co-ordination Office 企画調整室
Planning and Coordination Bureau 総務企画局
Planning and Legal Division 企画課
Planning Division 企画課
planning stage 企画段階
plant 工場
plant account 工場設備勘定
plant and equipment 工場設備
plant capacity 設備能力
plant fund 設備資金
plant ledger 固定資産元帳
plant outages 操業停止
plants and buildings 建物
plastic money クレジット・カード
play down 軽視する
playing cards tax トランプ税
playright 興行権
Plaza Accord プラザ合意
PLC (public limited company) 株式会社
pledge 質権；動産質
pledge account 質権口座
pledge of claims 債権質
pledge of shares 株式質
pledged accounts 担保債権
pledged assets 担保資産
pledged collateral 差入担保
pledged revenue 返済原資
pledged securities 差入有価証券
pledged securities as collateral 担保差入有価証券
pledged security 質入有価証券
pledgee 質権者
pledgee's lien 動産質権者の留置権
pledging 担保差入れ
pledging of JGSs as collateral 国債による質権の設定
pledgor 質権設定者
plenipotentiary 全権
PLN (Polish zloty) ポーランド・ズロチ
plowing-back 利益の再投資
plum 特別配当
plunge 大幅な下落
plunger 向こうみずの相場師
plus-tick プラス・ティック
PM (project management) プロジェクト管理
PML (probable maximum loss) 予想最大損失率
point and figure ポイント・アンド・フィギュア
point and figure chart ポイント・アンド・フィギュア・チャート
point and figure method ポイント・アンド・フィギュア法
point elasticity 点弾力性
point in time estimate 一時点における見積り
point of sales 販売時点情報管理
point of sales system POSシステム
point-of-sale cost 販売時費用
points 主張の要点
points of consideration 考慮事項
points reserved 保留論点
poison pill defense 毒薬条項防衛
poison pills ポイズン・ピル
Poisson distribution ポアソン分布
Poisson process ポアソン過程
policy amount 保険金額
policy anniversary 契約応当日
policy application 保険申込み
policy asset allocation ポリシー・アセット・アロケーション
policy asset mix ポリシー・アセット・ミックス
policy assignment 政策手段の割当

policy benefit 保険給付
Policy Board 政策委員会
Policy Board member 政策委員
Policy Board of the Bank of Japan 日銀政策委員会
policy buyback 保険買取り
policy cancellation 保険解約
policy characteristics 保険特性
policy charge 保険契約加算金
policy claim 保険金支払請求
Policy Co-ordination for National Property Management Division 国有財産調整課
policy coordination 政策協調
policy cost 保険費用
policy delivery 保険証券交付
policy depreciation 政策的減価償却
policy design 保険設計
policy dividend 契約者配当金
policy duration 保険経過期間
policy duration effect 時間軸効果
policy effectiveness 政策効果
policy evaluation 政策評価
Policy Evaluation Office 政策評価室
policy exchange 保険契約交換
policy exhibit 保険明細書
policy for promoting competition 競争促進政策
policy for restricting competition 競争制限政策
policy form 保険証券書式
policy holder liabilities 保険契約者債務
policy in force 有効な保険証券
policy inquiry 保険契約照会
policy issuance 保険証券発行
policy issues 政策課題
policy limit 給付限度額
policy loan 保険証券貸付
policy maker 政策当局
policy measures 政策措置
policy measures for economic rebirth 経済新生対策
policy misstep 失策
policy mix ポリシー・ミックス
policy objective 最終目標
policy obligation 保険債務
policy owner 保険証券所有者
policy period 保険期間
Policy Planning and Research Division 総合政策課
policy principle 政策方針
policy proceeds 保険受取金
Policy Proof of Interest 利益保険証券
policy purchase 保険購入
policy rate 政策金利
Policy Research Institute, Ministry of Finance 財務総合政策研究所
policy reserve 責任準備金
policy rider 保険特約
policy significance 政策意義
policy state 政策ポジション
policy summary 契約概要
policy switch 保険契約乗換え
policy term 保険期間
policy tools 政策手段
policy transfer 保険の移転
policy trust 保険契約信託
policy underwriting 保険契約査定
policy valuation 保険契約評価
policy value 保険価額
policy year basis 保険引受年度別計算
policy-based finance 政策金融
policy-based finance assessment 政策金融評価
policy-based financial institution 政策金融機関
policy-based interest rate 政策金利
policy-based tax reduction 政策減税
policy-holders' dividend 保険契約者配当金
policyholder 保険契約者
policyholder dividend 契約者配当
policyholder loan bond 保険契約者貸付担保債券
policyholder obligations 保険加入者への債務
policyholder's surplus 保険契約者剰余金
policyholders' meeting 社員総会

Policyholders' Protection Act 保険契約者保護法
political accountability 政治的責任
political corporation 政治団体
political crisis 政治危機
political environment 政治的環境
political force 政治的要因
political risk 政治リスク
political system stability index 政治安定指数
political turmoil 政治的混乱
politics of pensions 年金の政治的側面
poll tax 人頭税
pollution control facilities 公害予防施設
pollution prevention 公害防止
pool agreement プール協定
pool balance プール残高
pool composition プール構成
pool of financial assets 金融資産のプール
pool of financing プール・オブ・ファイナンシング
pool of funds 資金プール
pool of mortgages モーゲージ・プール
pool of new mortgages 新規モーゲージ・プール
pool operation プール操作
pool with prior exposure to refinancing opportunities 過去に借換え機会があったプール
pool-of-fund approach 資金プール法
pooled account 合同運用勘定
pooled collateral 根担保
pooled common stock account 合同普通株勘定
pooled common stock and publicly traded bond account 合同普通株・公募債勘定
pooled first mortgage 共同第一抵当権
pooled fund 合同運用資金
pooled investment 合同運用投資
pooled private placement bond account 合同私募債勘定
pooled publicly traded bond account 合同公募債勘定
pooled real property account 合同不動産勘定
pooling accounting プーリング会計
pooling arrangement 再保険プール；プール協約
pooling contracts 共同計算契約
pooling of interests 持ち分プーリング
pooling of interests method 持ち分プーリング法
poor credit 低い信用状態
poor economy 景気低迷
poor laws 救貧法
poor performer 運用実績の悪い商品
poor securities trading 証券取引の低迷
poorly capitalized 資金力が乏しい
POP (partial operating profit) 部分業務利益
popular action 民衆訴訟
popular stock 人気株
population 母集団
population density 人口密度
population mean 母平均
population mix 人口分布
population of items 母集団の項目
population statistics 人口統計
population variance 母分散
porcupine provision ヤマアラシ条項
Port and Airport Research Institute 港湾空港技術研究所
port charges 港湾料
port dues 入港税
port risks insurance 係船保険
port toll 港税
portable pension 移動継続年金
portfolio analysis ポートフォリオ分析
portfolio approach ポートフォリオ手法
portfolio assets 運用資産
portfolio balance approach ポートフォリオ・バランス・アプローチ
portfolio basis ポートフォリオ基準
portfolio capital 投資資金
portfolio characteristic line ポートフ

ォリオの特性線
portfolio composition ポートフォリオ構成
portfolio credit ポートフォリオ・クレジット
portfolio diversification ポートフォリオの分散投資
portfolio engineers ポートフォリオ・エンジニア
portfolio flows 投資資金の流れ
portfolio gains 資産売却益
portfolio hedging ポートフォリオ・ヘッジ
portfolio income ポートフォリオ・インカム
portfolio insurance ポートフォリオ・インシュアランス；ポートフォリオ・インシュランス
portfolio investment 証券投資
portfolio linkage ポートフォリオの関連付け
portfolio management ポートフォリオ管理
portfolio manager ポートフォリオ・マネージャー
portfolio method 全資産合同方式
portfolio mix ポートフォリオ・ミックス
P
portfolio monitoring ポートフォリオ・モニタリング
portfolio of accounts receivable 債権のポートフォリオ
portfolio of assets 資産のポートフォリオ
portfolio of customers 顧客のポートフォリオ
portfolio of investment trust 投信銘柄
portfolio of loans and advances 貸出金のポートフォリオ
portfolio of receivables 債権ポートフォリオ
portfolio optimization ポートフォリオ最適化
portfolio optimizer ポートフォリオ・オプティマイザー
portfolio premium 未経過再保険料
portfolio pricing methodology ポートフォリオ価格決定法
portfolio rate 運用資産利回り
portfolio restructuring ポートフォリオの再編
portfolio revision ポートフォリオの修正
portfolio risk ポートフォリオ・リスク
portfolio risk model ポートフォリオ・リスク・モデル
portfolio selection 資産選択；ポートフォリオ選択
portfolio stocks 保有株式
portfolio theory ポートフォリオ理論
portfolio trade ポートフォリオ取引
portfolio transfer 保険の包括移転
portfolio value ポートフォリオの価値
portfolio view ポートフォリオの見地
portfolio's yield ポートフォリオの利回り
position 持ち高
position adjustment ポジション調整
position bookkeeping 平衡簿記
position building ポジション積上げ
position delta ポジション・デルタ
position gamma ポジション・ガンマ
position instruction ポジション指導
position limit 持高限度
position risk ポジション・リスク
position sheet 運用帳
position statement report on tender offer 公開買付意見表明報告書
position theta ポジション・セータ
position trader ポジション・トレーダー
position trading ポジション売買
positional goods 特権的財
positioned amount 繰入額
positioning skewed towards に偏している
positions established with index arbitrages 裁定取引に係る現物ポジション
positions on customer's account 顧客の委託に係る建玉

positive adjustment policies 積極的調整政策
positive amount 正の金額
positive carry ポジティブ・キャリー
positive condition 積極条件
positive confirmation 積極的確認
positive correlation 正の相関
positive covariance 正の共分散
positive credit file ポジティブ情報
positive curve 順イールド
positive economics 実証経済学
positive factor 買い材料
positive figure 黒字
positive financial policy 積極財政
positive information ポジティブ情報
positive law 実定法
positive leverage effect 正のレバレッジ効果
positive monetary position 金銭債権の超過状態
positive prescription 取得時効
positive property 積極財産
positive spread 順ざや
positive yield 順イールド
positive yield curve 正の利回り曲線
possession 占有
possession in deed 現実の占有
possession in law 法定の占有
possession of land 土地占有
possession of property 資産の所有
possessory lien 占有的リーエン
possible loss 潜在的損失
post acquisition change 取得後の変動
post April range 四月以降のレンジ
post audit 事後監査
post close account 締後勘定
post delivery 引渡後の
post entry 追加記入
post for delisting 整理ポスト
post for supervision 監理ポスト
post industrial society 脱工業化社会
post Keynesian ポスト・ケイジアン
post retirement death benefit 退職後死亡給付
post retirement pension 退職後年金
post to the ledger 元帳に転記する
post trade processing cost 約定後処理費用
post-ante evaluation 事後評価
post-balance sheet date 決済日後
post-closing entry 締切後記入
post-closing trial balance 締切後試算表
post-employment benefit 退職後給付
post-employment benefit cost 退職後給付費用
post-employment benefit obligation 退職後給付債務
post-employment medical plan 退職後医療制度
Post-Entry Examination and Customs Area Division 調査保税課
post-qualification 事後資格審査
post-retirement life insurance 退職後生命保険
post-retirement medical care 退職後医療給付
post-tax 税引後
post-tax discount rate 税引後割引率
post-tax profit 税引後利益
post-trade and pre-settlement 取引後から決済前
post-trade processing 取引後処理
postage 郵送料
postage paid 郵税支払済み
postage to be paid on delivery 郵税先払い
postal agencies 郵政官署
postal check 郵便小切手
Postal Life Insurance 簡保
Postal Life Insurance and Postal Annuity Fund 簡保積立金
Postal Life Insurance Fund 簡易生命保険資金
Postal Life Insurance Special Account 簡易生命保険特別会計
postal money order 郵便為替
postal savings deposit 郵便貯金
Postal Savings Law 郵便貯金法
Postal Services Agency 郵政事業庁

postal transfer account 振替口座
postdate 先日付にする
postdated bill or note 先日付手形
postdated check 先日付小切手
posted price 公示価格
posterior analysis 事後分析
posting 記帳；転記
posting of contract price 約定値段の公表
posting of special quote 気配表示
postponed income 収入の先送り
postponement of investment 投資延期
postponement of payment 支払猶予
postponement of tax collection 徴収の猶予
postponement of tax payment 税金の延納
postponement of taxation 課税の延期
postretirement benefit cost 退職後給付コスト
postulate of accounting period 会計期間の公準
postulate of auditing 監査公準
postulate of business entity 企業実体の公準
potential benefit 潜在的な便益
potential collateral 担保可能証券
potential customer 見込顧客
potential demand 潜在需要
potential existence 潜在的存在
potential for gain or loss 損益の潜在的可能性
potential growth 潜在成長率
potential investment 潜在的な投資対象
potential obligation 潜在的債務
potential ordinary shares 潜在的普通株式
potential over-supply produced by new issues 増資圧迫
pound bloc ポンド・ブロック
pound sterling commercial paper 英ポンドＣＰ
pound sterling currency futures 英ポンド通貨先物
pound sterling depositary interest futures 英ポンド預金金利先物
pound sterling time deposit 英ポンド定期預金
poverty line 貧困線
poverty rate 貧困率
poverty trap 貧困のわな
power 権限
power expense 電力費
power group 圧力団体
power in gross 独立指名権
power of appointment 指名権
power of attorney 委任状
power of collection 徴収権
power of representation 代理権
power of sale 売却権
power theory of wages 賃金勢力説
PPA (power purchase agreement) 電力供給契約
PPI (producer price index) 生産者物価指数
PPM (product portfolio management) 製品ポートフォリオ管理
PPP (public private partnership) 公共・民間パートナーシップ
PPT (participant protection trust) 参加者投資信託
PQS (percentage quota system) 比例割当制度
PRA (participating rate agreement) 利益参加金利契約
practicable 実務的に可能
practical consequence 実務的帰結
practical difficulty 実務上の困難
practical economy 実践経済
practical guidance 現実的な指針
practical guideline 実務指針
practical issue 実務上の問題
practical reason 実務上の理由
practical reservation 実務上の疑い
practical seminar 実践セミナー
practicality 実用性
practice 実践
practice of settlement on the 5th, 10th, 15th, 20th, 25th, and the last day of

P

each month (go-toubi) 5・10日決済
practice requirement 実務規定
practice standards 業務基準
practices 慣行
practitioner 実務家
practitioners in the financial markets 市場関係者
pragmatic decisions 現実主義的な決定
pragmatic exception 実際的な例外
pragmatic judgment 実際の判断
pragmatic means 実践的な方法
pragmatic reasons 現実的な理由
prayer 請求趣旨申立て
PRB (purchase return book) 戻し品明細書
pre-acquisition 取得前
pre-acquisition retained earnings 取得日以前の留保利益
pre-closing trial balance 決算整理前試算表
pre-compute 金利先取り
pre-date 前日付
pre-deposited stock certificates 預託前株券
pre-emptive right to common shares 新株引受権
pre-funding 事前積立
pre-maturity redemption 繰上償還
pre-merger registration system 事前届出制
pre-preparatory period 事前準備期間
pre-production cost 段取原価
pre-qualification 事前資格審査
pre-requisite 必須条件
pre-sale cost 売上前費用
pre-tax 税引前
pre-tax discount rate 税引前割引率
pre-trade 取引前
preamble 前文
prearranged trading 事前取決取引
preaudit 事前監査
preauthorized payment 事前承認支払い
prebid agreement プレビッド契約
precarious right 不安定の権利
precedence 優位
precedence among market orders 成行呼値相互間の順位
precedence of bids and offers 呼値の順位
precedence of customer's orders 委託注文の順位
precedence rule on tax collection 徴収順位
precedent 先例
preceding article 前条
preceding business year 前事業年度
preceding fiscal year 前年度
preceding month 前月
preceding page 前葉
preceding period 前期
preceding year 前年
precipitous rise 急騰
precise value 正確な価値
precision 精度
precision in presentation 表示単位
precision instruments industry 精密機器業界
precision machinery 精密機械
precision technology 精密技術
precontract 先契約
precursor 先駆的商品
predecessor auditor 前任監査人
predecessor company 被合併会社
predetermined burden rate 予定配賦率
predetermined cost 予定原価
predetermined cost system 予定原価計算
predetermined price あらかじめ設定した値段
predictability 予測可能性
predicted cost 予想原価
prediction error 予測誤差
predictive value 予測価値
predictors of default 債務不履行の予測指標
predominant source 主要な源泉
preemption 優先買取権

preemption entry 先買権の申請
prefabrication 事前加工
prefectural bond 地方債
prefectural government bonds 道府県債
prefectural inhabitants tax 県民税
prefectural location 都道府県分布
prefectural tax 道府県税
preference 選好
preference beneficiary 優先受取人
preference for delay 延期を望む
preference for gold 金選好
preference for interest rate 金利選好
preference item 税制優遇項目
preference of financial assets 金融資産選好
preference of lender 貸手の選好
preference ordering 選好順序
preference risk 偏頗リスク
preference shareholder 優先株主
preference shares 優先株式
preferential 特恵的
preferential benefits to shareholders 株主優待方法
preferential bill 優遇手形
preferential creditor 優先債権者
preferential duty 特恵関税
preferential payment 優先支払い
preferential payment in bankruptcy 破産優先支払い
preferential rate 優遇料率
preferential right 優先権
preferential tariff 特恵関税
preferential tax treatment 優遇税制措置
preferential tax treatment for securities investment 証券投資優遇税制
preferential treatment for the tax law purpose 税法上の優遇措置
preferred bidder 優先入札者
preferred capital contribution certificate 優先出資証券
preferred claims 優先債権
preferred creditor 優先債権者
preferred creditors' right 先取特権
preferred dividend 優先配当
preferred dividend coverage ratio 優先配当負担倍率
preferred equity 優先株
Preferred Equity Contribution Law 優先出資法
preferred equity contribution securities 優先出資証券
preferred equity contribution unit 優先出資口
preferred equity contributors 優先出資者
preferred habitat theory 特定市場選好理論
preferred liability 優先債務
preferred ordinary share 優先的普通株
Preferred Providers Organization 特約医療機構
preferred share 優先株
preferred stock 優先株
preferred stock capital 優先株式資本
preferred stock coverage 優先株倍率
preferred stock ratio 優先株比率
preferred stock with common stock warrant 新株引受権付優先株式
preferred stockholder 優先株株主
preferred treatment 優先処理
prefs 優先株
prejudice 偏見
preliminary 速報
preliminary advice プレ・アド
preliminary announcement of settlement of accounts 決算予備発表
preliminary application 予備申請
preliminary application for listing of a security 有価証券上場予備申請書
preliminary audit 予備監査
preliminary balance sheet 予備貸借対照表
preliminary claim 予備クレーム
preliminary information 予備情報
preliminary injunction 仮処分命令

preliminary notice 事前通知
preliminary prospectus 仮目論見書
preliminary rating 予備格付け
preliminary release for business results 決算短信
preliminary report 速報
preliminary review 予備審査
preliminary statement 予備報告書
premature delivery futures system 早受渡制度
premerger notification 合併事前届出
premier 優良な
premise of a going concern 継続企業を前提に
premises 敷地
premises and equipment 動産・不動産
premium 奨励金；プレミアム
premium and compensation for removal 権利金及び立退料
premium bond プレミアム債
premium cap 保険料の上限
premium condition プレミアム状態
premium credit card 高級カード
premium due 未払保険料
premium earned 経過保険料
premium in addition to the original contract price 請負代金の値増金
premium in arrears 未収保険料
premium income オプション料収入；収入保険料
premium issuance 打歩発行
premium issue プレミアム発行
premium loan 保険料振替貸付
premium on bonds payable 社債割増発行差金
premium on capital stock 株式発行差金
premium on debt 債務証券の発行差金
premium on redemption 償還プレミアム
premium over bond value 対社債プレミアム
premium over conversion value 転換価格を超える額
premium overdue 延滞保険料
premium paid in advance 前納保険料
premium payment for a retirement annuity 退職年金掛金
premium per capita 一人当保険料
premium quotation system プレミアム建値方式
premium reserve 保険料積立金
premium sale 景品付き販売
premium savings bond 割増貯蓄債券
premium securities プレミアム証券
premium surcharge 割増保険料
premium tax 保険料税
preopening expenses 創立準備費
prepaid 前払いの
prepaid asset 前払資産
prepaid card プリペイド・カード
prepaid commission 前払い手数料
prepaid expense 前払費用
prepaid freight 前払運賃
prepaid income 前払利益
prepaid income taxes 前払法人税
prepaid insurance 前払保険料
prepaid insurance premiums 未経過保険料
prepaid interest 前払利息
prepaid pension expense 前払年金費用
prepaid rents on buildings 前受家賃
prepaid salaries and wages 前渡給料賃金
preparation of financial statements 財務諸表の作成
preparatory audit 事前調査
preparer of accounts 決算書の作成者
preparing the financial statements 財務諸表を作成すること
prepay 前払いする
prepayment 期限前償還
prepayment model 期限前償還モデル
prepayment of tax 租税の予納
prepayment of tax on liquidation income 清算所得に対する法人税の予納
prepayment option 期限前償還オプション
prepayment penalty 期限前返済ペナル

ティ；繰上返済違約金
prepayment projection 早期償還予想
prepayment rate 期限前償還率
prepayment rate indicator 期限前償還率指標
prepayment right 期限前返済権
prepayment risk 早期償還リスク
prepayment speed 期限前償還速度
prerefunding 事前借換え
presale order 事前販売
prescribe 規定する
prescribed deadline 時限
prescribed format 統一様式
prescription 時効
prescription extinction 時効の消滅
present contributions 現在の掛金
present cost 現在原価
present data analysis 現状分析
present goods 現在財
present market value 時価
present obligation 現在債務
present price 現在価格
present value 現在価値
present value discounted at compound interest 複利現価
present value factor 現価係数
present value method 現価法
present value of annuity 年金現価
present value of future benefits 給付現価
present value of future cash flow 将来のキャッシュフローの現在価値
present value rate 現価率
present worth 現在価値
presentation currency 表示通貨
presentation for acceptance 引受けのための呈示
presentation for payment 支払呈示
presentation of figures 数値表示
presentation of financial statements 財務諸表の表示
presentation of reimbursements 補填の開示
presentation period for payment 支払呈示期間
presentation requirement 表示要件
presenting bank 呈示銀行
presentment 呈示
presentment of bill of exchange 為替手形の呈示
preservation 没収保全
preservative attachment 債権保全
preservative security 保全担保
preservative seizure 保全差押え
preside over 総理する
president 理事長
president-elect 次期大統領
presold issue 公募前完売債券
press club 記者クラブ
press law 出版法
pressing issue 差し迫った問題
pressure group 圧力団体
pressure on competitive exports 輸出競争力への低下圧力
pressure on pricing 値下げ圧力
pressure on short JPY positions 円のショート・ポジションの解消圧力
pressure the dollar ドルの下落圧力
pressure to cut interest rates 利下げ圧力
presumption 推定
presumption of a real obtainer of income 所得の帰属の推定
presumption of fact 事実上の推定
presumption of rights 権利推定
presumptive evidence 推定証拠
presumptive heir 法定推定相続人
pretax accounting income 税引前会計利益
pretax income to sales 売上税引前利益率
pretax life earnings 生保部門の税引き前利益
pretax profit of the current term 当期税引前利益
pretax rate of return 税引前利益率
prevailing economic conditions 経済状況の実勢
prevailing interest rate 市場の実勢利回り

prevailing market interest rate 実勢市場金利
prevailing mortgage rate 実勢モーゲージ・レート
prevailing price 一般価格
prevailing rate 市場金利
prevailing value 再調達価値
prevailing wage 一般賃金
previous balance method 前月残高ベースの金利計算方法
previous carrying amount 従前の帳簿価額
previous close price 前日終値
previous holder 前所有者
previous indorsements guaranteed 先行裏書の真正証明
previous month 前月
previous term 前期
previous year 前年
price action 値動き
price adjustment 価格調整
price analysis 価格分析
price appreciation 価格の上昇
price auction 価格入札
price auction in USDJPY ドル・円相場
price away from the market 時価から離れた値段で
price before tax 税前価格
price book ratio 株価純資産倍率
price boost 価格上昇
price cartel 価格カルテル
price cash earnings ratio 株価キャッシュフロー倍率
price cashflow ratio キャッシュフロー倍率
price change 値動き
price competition 価格競争
price concession 価格譲歩
price contingency インフレ予備費
price contract 価格契約
price control 価格統制
price cut 値下げ
price deflator 価格デフレーター
price density 価格密度
price determination 価格決定
price development 物価動向
price difference 値幅
price differential 価格差
price differentials between domestic and overseas markets 内外価格差
price discovery 価格の発見
price discrepancies 価格差
price discrimination 価格差別
price divergence 価格の乖離
price earnings multiple 株価収益率
price effect 価格効果
price elasticity 価格弾性値
price elasticity of supply and demand 需給価格弾力性
price factor 変換係数
price filter プライスフィルター
price fixing 値決め
price flexibility 価格の伸縮性
price fluctuation 価格変動
price fluctuation reserve 価格変動準備金
price fluctuation risk 価格変動リスク
price freeze 価格凍結
price hike 値上げ
price including tax 税込価格
price index 物価指数
price index linked 物価指数連動
price index of listed securities 上場有価証券指数
price indication method 価格表示方法
price induced 物価変動による
price information 価格情報
price insurance 価格保険
price interval 価格の刻み
price leader プライス・リーダー
price limit on commodity futures 商品先物取引値幅制限
price line 価格線
price line of futures price 先物価格曲線
price list 価格表
price maker プライス・メーカー
price margin 価格差益
price mechanism 価格メカニズム

price momentum 価格モーメンタム
price movement 価格変動
price movement limit 値幅制限
price movement of stocks 株価の動き
price of corporate bond 社債価格
price of introduced stock 株式公開価格
price of JGB (Japanese government bond) 国債相場
price of new stocks on the day to be paid in 払込期日現在の新株の価格
price of success 成功の代償
price outlook インフレ見通し
price pattern 価格パターン
price policy 価格政策
price policy of agricultural products 農産物価格政策
price priority 価格優先
price protection 価格保護
price quotation 建値
price relatives 相対価格
price revision 価格改正
price rise 値上げ
price risk 価格リスク
price sensitivity 価格感応性
price stability 価格安定
price stabilization policy 物価安定政策
price standards 価格標準
price structure 価格構造
price support 価格維持
price support subsidy 価格維持補助金
price supporting 価格安定操作
price system 価格体系
price theory 価格理論
price trend on stocks 株価トレンド
price variance 価格差異
price variation 物価変動
price volatility 相場の変動
price weighted 平均価格加重
price weighted index 平均価格加重指数
price yield curve 価格・利回り曲線
price-fixing agreement ヤミ価格協定
price-specie-flow mechanism 物価・正貨流出入機構
prices minus tax 税引値段
pricing 価格決定
pricing calculation 価格計算
pricing formula 価格計算式
pricing of policies 保険料設定
pricing policies 価格決定方針
pricing risk 料率設定リスク
pricing strategy 価格決定戦略
pricing supplement 発行条件書
pricing tool 価格決定手段
prima facie 一見したところ
primary account 第一次勘定
primary activity 起債活動
primary advance 第一次的不動産移転行為
primary balance 基本的収支；プライマリー・バランス
primary basis 主要な基礎
primary beneficiary 第一次受取人
primary benefit rule 第一受益者の原則
primary bond market 新発債市場
primary capital 第一次資本
primary carrier 元受保険者
primary CBO (collateralized bond obligation) 募集型 CBO
primary CLO (collateralized loan obligation) 募集型 CLO
primary conditions 主要な条件
primary cost 第一原価
primary currency 第一次貨幣
primary dealer プライマリー・ディーラー
primary demand 基本的需要
primary deposit 本源的預金
primary distributions 第一次分売
primary earnings per share 基本的一株当り利益
primary financial instrument 一次金融商品
primary financial liabilities 一次金融負債
primary financial statements 基本財務諸表
primary format 基本的様式
primary goods 一次産品

primary industry 第一次産業
primary industry product export 第一次産品輸出
primary instruments 基本的金融商品
primary insurance 元受保険
primary issue 主要な論点
primary liability 第一次負債
primary market 発行市場
primary materials 原材料
primary mortgage market モーゲージの新規発行市場
primary objective 最大の目標
primary obligor 第一次債務者
primary offering 第一次募集
primary paper 新発債
primary party 第一当事者
primary proposal 公募型プロポーザル
primary regulation notice 基本通達
primary reserve asset 第一次準備資産
primary securities 本源的証券
primary securities market 証券発行市場
primary user 主たる利用者
primary vehicle 主保険契約
prime bank 有力銀行
prime bankers acceptance 一流銀行引受手形
prime bill 優良手形
prime contract 元契約
prime corporate bond 一流社債
prime cost 素価
prime cost method 素価配賦法
prime factor 主要因
prime interest rate プライム・レート
prime issuer 優良発行体
prime letter of credit 原信用状
Prime Minister 内閣総理大臣
Prime Minister of Japan and His Cabinet 首相官邸
prime name bank 超一流銀行
prime name CD プライム・ネームＣＤ
prime paper 優良手形
prime product 主製品
prime rate 優遇貸出金利
priming 決済口座への入金
primitive securities 原始証券
principal 元本
principal account 主要勘定
principal accounts of financial institution for small-business 中小企業金融機関勘定
principal activity 主要な活動
principal amortization schedule 元本償還方法
principal amount 元金
principal and interest 元利
principal books 主要帳簿
principal clearing participant 自社清算参加者
principal clearing qualification 自社清算資格
principal company 主体会社
principal component 主成分
principal deflation floor デフレ時の元本保証
Principal Figures of Financial Institutions (preliminary) 貸出・資金吸収動向等（速報）
principal issue 主たる論点
principal member プリンシパル会員
principal only 元本のみ
principal only strips 元本のみストリップ債
principal paying 主支払い
principal paying agent 主支払代理人
principal payment 元本支払い
principal payment moratorium 元本の返済猶予
principal payment of JGSs 国債の元本支払い
principal place of business 営業上の本拠
principal portion 元本部分
principal production order 主要製造指図書
principal products 主製品
principal provisions 主要条項
principal repayment 元本返済
principal shareholders 主要株主
principal sum 元本金額

P

principal targets for loans 主な融資対象
principal tax 本税
principal terms and conditions for money market operations 取引基本要領
principal terms and conditions for the Bank's transactions with the government 対政府取引に関する基本要領
Principal Terms and Conditions of Market Operations オペの基本要領
principal transaction 自己取引
principal uncertainty 不確定事象
principal-equal monthly payment 元金均等返済
principal-only securities PO 証券
principle of all-inclusiveness 包括主義の原則
principle of ascertained claim 権利確定主義
principle of balanced budget 健全財政主義
principle of clarity 明瞭性の原理
principle of comparability 比較性の原則
principle of comparative advantage 比較優位の原理
principle of conservatism 保守主義の原則
principle of cost allocation 費用配分の原則
principle of cross liabilities 交差責任主義
principle of disclosure 公開性の原則
principle of double-entry bookkeeping 複式簿記の原則
principle of effective demand 有効需要の原理
principle of equilibrium 貸借平均の原理
principle of equivalence 収支相等の原則
principle of gross budget accounting 総額予算会計
principle of increasing risk 危険逓増の原理
principle of matching 対応の原則
principle of matching costs with revenues 収益費用対応の原則
principle of materiality 重要性の原則
principle of need 必要性原則
principle of orderly system of bookkeeping 正規の簿記の原則
principle of parsimony 節約の原則
principle of perennial tax 永久税主義
principle of priority of national tax claim 国税債権優先の原則
principle of priority to first seizure 差押先着手主義
principle of realization 実現主義の原則
principle of single budget 予算単一主義
principle of surplus section 剰余金区分の原則
principle of taxation on a substantial income earner 実質所得者課税の原則
principle of taxation on actual beneficiary 実質受益者課税の原則
principle of the freedom of contract 契約自由の原則
principle of truth 真実性の原則
principle of unified accounting 会計単一原則
principle that JGBs and TBs should be issued in the market 国債の市中消化の原則
principles of law 法理
printed matter 印刷物
printing and engraving 印刷
Printing Bureau 印刷局
printing with multi-color overlays 多色重ね刷り
prior agreement 事前調整
prior analysis 事前分析
prior approval 事前認可
prior bond 優先権付社債

prior deposit 事前預託
prior interim periods 過去の中間期間
prior items 優先項目
prior lien 先順位留置権
prior lien bond 優先担保権付社債
prior notice 事前の届出
prior period 前期間
prior period profit and loss adjustment 前期損益修正
prior preferred stock 第一優先株
prior redemption 満期前償還
prior service cost 過去勤務費用
prior year 過年度
prior year adjustment items 過年度損益修正項目
priority 優先性
priority area 重点分野
priority between national tax and local tax 国税・地方税間の優劣
priority code 優先コード
priority creditor 優先債権者
priority of attachment 優先差押権
priority of mortgage 抵当の優先権
priority of taxes 租税優先権
priority order of application 充当順位
priority processing 優先処理
private account 内勘定
private accountant 私的会計士
private activity bond 民間事業費
private annuity 自家年金
private assets 個人資産
private automobile policy 自家用自動車保険
private bank 民間銀行
private banking プライベート・バンク事業
private bill 個人手形
private bond 民間債
private business 民間企業
private capital 民間資本
private companies 民間会社
private company 非公開企業
private consumption 民間消費
private contract 随意契約
private convertible bond 私募転換社債
private convertible note 私募転換社債
private corporation 民間会社
private debt 民間債務
private demand 民間需要
private employer pension plan 民間企業年金制度
private enterprise 民間企業
private equity fund プライベート・エクイティ・ファンド
private financial institution 民間金融機関
private fund 自家運用資金
private funding corporation 民間金融会社
private holding company 同族会社
private insurance 自家保険；民間保険
private international law 国際私法
private investment 自家運用
private investment trust 私募投資信託
private investor 民間投資家
private label 非銀行系の
private label card プライベート・ブランド・カード
private ledger 私用元帳
private limited company 有限会社
private loan 民間貸付
private machinery order 民間機械受注高
private market 民間市場
private member 個人会員
private mortgage insurance 民間モーゲージ保険
private note 私募債
private offering 私募
private offering bond 私募債
private passthrough プライベート・パス・スルー
private pension 企業年金保険；個人年金
private pension assets 民間年金資産
private pension fund 民間年金基金
private pension plan 個人年金制度
private placement 私募発行；第三者割当
private placement bond 私募債

P

private placement local bond 縁故地方債
private placement local government bond 私募地方債
private placement municipal bond 縁故地方債
private placement securities 私募証券
private placement special bond 私募特別債
private placement straight bond 私募普通社債
private placement syndicate 私募債シンジケート
private property 私有財産
private purpose bond 非公共目的債
private right 私権
private risk プライベート・リスク
private sale プライベート・セール
private saving 民間貯蓄
private sector 民間部門
private settlement 示談
private spending 民間支出
private subscription 縁故募集
private subscription bond 縁故債
private tender 指名入札
private transaction 民間取引
private trust 私益信託
private undertaking 民間事業
private use 私的使用
Private-Sector Participation Promotion Law 民活法
privately placed bond 非公募債
privately placed note 私募債
privately run 民間の
privatization 民営化
privatization of postal services 郵政民営化
privatization scheme 民営化計画
privileged allocation of issuance to stockholders 株主優先募入
privileged debts 優先支払債務
privileges and immunities 特権及び免除
privity of contract 契約関係
prize of raffle 宝くじの賞金
prize offered for advertisement of the business 事業広告のための賞品
PRO (planned redemption obligation) PRO
pro forma 想定キャッシュフロー；プロフォルマ
pro forma account sales 見積売上勘定書
pro forma adjustment 見積修正
pro forma amount 参考数値
pro forma balance sheet 見積貸借対照表
pro forma bill 見積為替手形
pro forma cash flow statement 見積資金運用表
pro forma comparative information 見積比較可能情報
pro forma data 仮定データ
pro forma draft 見積為替手形
pro forma figure 試算ベース
pro forma financial statements 見積財務諸表
pro forma information 仮定情報
pro forma profit and loss statement 見積損益計算書
pro forma statement of application of funds 見積資金運用表
pro rata 比例配分した
pro rata allocation 比例配分
pro rata payment 按分支払
pro rata premium 按分保険料
pro rata share 比例的な取り分
pro-business 景気重視
pro-cyclical 景気に敏感な
pro-euro member ユーロ加盟賛成派
pro-forma invoice プロフォーマ・インボイス
pro-rata clause プロラタ条項
pro-rated on 比例配分による
pro-trade biased growth 順貿易偏向的成長
probabilistic characteristic lines 確率的特性線
probabilistic forecasting 確率的予測
probability 確率

probability criteria 蓋然性基準
probability curve 確率曲線
probability density function 確率密度関数
probability distributions 確率分布
probability factor 確率要因
probability function 確率関数
probability model 確率モデル
probability of default デフォルト確率
probability of occurrence 発生確率
probability space 確率空間
probability-proportional-to-size 確率比例
probable 推定の
probable cause 相当な理由
probable life 予想耐用年数
probable maximum loss 予想最大損害額
probate 検証する
probation 執行猶予
problem assets 不良資産
problem credit 問題債権
problem loan 問題債権
procedural audit 手続監査
procedure 手続き
procedure of the compulsory conversion into money 強制換価手続
procedures for bond futures trading 債券先物取引制度要綱
procedures for closing the books 決算手続
procedures for the convocation 召集手続き
procedures of auction 入札のプロセス
procedures of closing the books 決算手続
procedures of tax adjustments 税務調査手続
proceed of insurance policy 保険証券の保険金
proceedings 議事
proceeds 受取金
proceeds from allocation 運用収入
proceeds from asset sold 資産売却手取金
proceeds from borrowing 借入による手取金
proceeds from disposal 処分代金
proceeds from disposals 処分受取額
proceeds from disposition of asset 資産の処分による手取金
proceeds from external bond issuance 外債発行代金
proceeds from long-term debt 長期借入からの資金増
proceeds from redemption of securities 有価証券の償還による収入
proceeds from the issuance of shares 株式発行による手取金
proceeds of life insurance 生命保険金
proceeds of loan 貸付けの代わり金
proceeds sale 株式買替
process analysis 工程分析
process control 工程管理
process cost accounting 工程別原価計算
process cost system 総合原価計算
process costing 工程別原価計算
process for the recovery of taxes in arrears 税金滞納処分
process innovation プロセス・イノベーション
process of garnishment 債権差押手続き
process of inspection 検査工程
process of law 法的手続
process of qualification 適格審査
process production 一貫生産
process specification 工程仕様書
processing 加工
processing capabilities 処理能力
processing deal 委託加工貿易
processing deal trade 加工貿易
processing expenses 加工費
processing indicator 処理指示
processing tax 加工税
procurator 代理人
procurement 購買
procurement cost 調達費

producer 生産者
producer price index 生産者物価指数
producer's cartel 生産国カルテル
producer's inventory of finished goods 生産者製品在庫
producer's surplus 生産者余剰
producer's value 生産者価額
producing departments cost 製造部門費
product 製品
product alternatives 代替商品
product analysis 商品分析
product cost 製品原価
product cycle theory プロダクト・サイクル論
product development 商品開発
product driven 製品依存の
product enhancement 製品機能強化
product group 製品群
product innovation era 商品革新の時代
product investment 製品投資
product liability 製造物責任
product liability insurance 製造物責任保険
product life cycle 製品のライフ・サイクル
product market 生産市場
product mix プロダクト・ミックス
product on consignment 委託品
product performance 商品の運用実績
product portfolio management 製品ポートフォリオ・マネージメント
product price 製品価格
product standards 製品基準
product warranties 製品保証
production 生産高
production accord 生産協定
production account 生産勘定
production asset 製造資産
production base 生産拠点
production based activity method 生産比例法
production budget 製造予算
production capacity 生産能力
production capital 生産資本
production card 作業票
production control 生産管理
production cost 製造費用
production department 製造部門
production efficiency variance 製造能率差異
production equipment 製造設備
production expenses 製造経費
production facility 生産設備
production function 生産関数
production goods 生産財
production indexes 生産指数
production labor cost 生産労務費
production level 操業度
production loan プロダクション・ローン
production order 製造指図書
production order cost accounting 個別原価計算
production process 生産工程
production report 生産高報告書
production sharing 生産分配
production statement 製造報告書
production unit 生産単位
production variance 製造差異
production volume budget 製造高予算
production volume variance 操業度差異
productive ability 生産能力
productive life 生産年数
productive wages 直接賃金
productivity 生産性
productivity accounting 生産性会計
productivity analysis 生産性分析
productivity gain 生産性向上
productivity growth 生産性の伸び
productivity improvement 生産性向上
productivity of capital 資本の生産性
productivity ratio 生産性指標
products and completed operation liability insurance 生産物賠償責任保険
products in progress 仕掛品
profession 専門職

professional accountant 職業会計士
professional and academic people 学識経験者
professional auditor 職業監査人
professional discipline 職業上の規範
professional ethics 職業倫理
professional fee 専門家報酬
professional journal 専門誌
professional liability insurance 専門職業人賠償責任保険
professional pronouncements 専門家の意見書
professional's market くろうと相場
professionals くろうと筋
profit 利益
profit account 利益勘定
profit accruing from repayment of bonds and debentures 公社債の償還益
profit after expenses 経費控除後利益
profit and loss 損益
profit and loss account 損益勘定
profit and loss accruals 損益の発生額
profit and loss break-even point 損益分岐点
profit and loss by segment セグメント別損益
profit and loss carried forward 繰越損益
profit and loss equation 損益計算書等式
profit and loss method 損益法
profit and loss on valuation of real estate 不動産評価損益勘定
profit and loss report 損益報告
profit and loss situation 損益状況
profit and loss statement 損益計算書
profit and loss transaction 損益取引
profit announcement 利益の発表
profit appropriation section 利益処分の部
profit available for dividend 配当可能利益
profit center プロフィット・センター
profit commission 利益戻
profit contribution 利益貢献度
profit control 利益管理
profit control chart 利益図表
profit corporation 営利法人
profit curve 利益曲線
profit cycle 収益サイクル
profit debenture 収益社債
profit distribution 分配金
profit for the current term 当期利益金
profit forecast 収益見通し
profit form continuing operations 継続事業利益
profit from amalgamation 合併差益
profit from capital reduction 減資差益
profit from consolidation 連結差益
profit from immovables transactions 不動産売買益
profit from merger 合併差益
profit from operating activities 営業活動からの利益
profit from operations 営業利益
profit from private funds offered 私財提供益
profit from redemption 償還差益
profit from the difference between new and old official prices 価格差益金
profit from trust 信託利益
profit from valuation of assets 資産の評価益
profit growth 利益の伸び
profit growth rate 利益成長率
profit increase 増益
profit inflation 利潤インフレーション
profit insurance 利益保険
profit making business 営利事業
profit making business activities 収益を得るための経済活動
profit management 利益管理
profit margin 利幅
profit margin of interest rate 利ざや
profit on assets sold 財産売却益
profit on redemption of discount bond 割引債の償還益
profit on sale 売却益
profit or loss brought forward from

P

previous business term 前期損益金
profit or loss brought forward from the previous period 前期損益金
profit or loss for the period 期間損益
profit or loss from disposal 処分損益
profit or loss from installment sales 割賦販売損益
profit or loss from operations 操業損益
profit or loss from ordinary activities 経常活動からの損益
profit or loss from retirement of fixed assets 除却損益
profit or loss on foreign exchange 為替換算損益
profit or loss resulting from valuation of assets 資産の評価損益
profit organization 営利法人
profit pickup 収益向上
profit picture 収益拡大
profit potential 潜在的利益
profit prior to consolidation 連結前利益
profit prior to incorporation 会社設立前利益
profit profile 収益構造
profit quota 利益割当
profit rate 利益率
profit rate of paid-up capital 払込資本収益率
profit ratio indices 収益関連指標
profit ratio of capital 資本利益率
profit ratio of net assets 純資産利益率
profit ratio of net worth 資本利益率
profit ratio of operating capital 経営資本利益率
profit resulting from sale of the trust estate 信託財産の処分により生じた売却利益
profit share 利益分配
profit sharing プロフィット・シェアリング
profit sharing arrangement 利益共有契約
profit sharing trust 利潤分配信託
profit slide 利益減
profit taking 利食い
profit taking pullback 利食い売り
profit tax 収益税
profit transferred 振替利益
profit variance 利益差異
profit volume graph 限界利益図表
profit-driven market 業績相場
profit-sharing bond 利益分配社債
profit-sharing plan 利益分配制度
profit-sharing securities 利潤証券
profit-volume ratio 売上高限界利益率
profitability 収益性
profitability and investment analysis ratio 収益性分析
profitability index 収益性指数
profitable line of business 採算ライン
profitable operation 収益性のある営業活動
profiteer 不当利得者
program budgeting プログラム予算
program evaluation プログラム評価
program trade プログラム・トレード
program trading プログラム売買
progress bidding 中間請求
progress expenditure property 製作中の資産
progress payment 出来高払い
progress payments and advances 中間支払額
progressive audit 進行監査
progressive average inventory method 総平均法
progressive cost 逓増費
progressive income tax 累進所得税
progressive ledger 連続元帳
progressive nature 累進制
progressive policy 保険金逓増保険
progressive reserve ratios 超過累進制
progressive tax 累進税
progressive tax rate 累進税率
progressive taxation 累進課税
progressiveness of income tax 所得税の累進度

prohibited period 禁止期間
prohibition against the Bank extending loans to the government 中央銀行による政府与信の禁止
prohibition of deposit transfer 預金の譲渡禁止
prohibition of endorsement 裏書禁止
prohibition of foreclosure on social insurance payment 社会保険給付の差押禁止
prohibition of management official interlocks 管理職員の兼業禁止
prohibition of private monopoly 私的独占の禁止
prohibition of seizure on salaries 給与の差押禁止
prohibition of seizure on social insurance payment 社会保険給付の差押禁止
prohibition of set off for national taxes 国税に関する相殺禁止
prohibition of transfer 譲渡の禁止
prohibitive injunction 禁止的差止命令
prohibitive tax 禁止的税
project 案件
project bond 地方政府機関発行長期債
project evaluation プロジェクト評価
project finance プロジェクト・ファイナンス
project loan プロジェクト・ローン
project note 地方政府機関発行短期債券
project potential プロジェクトの可能性
project risk プロジェクト・リスク
projected balance sheet 見積貸借対照表
projected benefit 予測給付
projected benefit method 予想給付評価方式
projected budget surplus 財政黒字予測
projected cost 予測原価
projected demand 予測需要量
projected dividend 予想配当
projected dividend rate 予測配当率
projected financial statements 見積財務諸表
projected holding-period rate of return 予測保有期間収益率
projected interest rate 予定利率
projected rate 予測率
projected rate of return 予測収益率
projected sales 予想売上高
projected unit credit method 予測単位積増方式
projected useful life 予測耐用年数
projected yield average 予測平均利回り
projection 予測
projection of investment return 投資収益の予測
projects covered 対象事業
prolonged 長期化した
prolonged weakness in the economy 長引く景気の低迷
prominent 卓越した
promise-to-deliver ticket 有価証券引渡票
promisee 受約者
promisor 約諾者
promissory note 約束手形
promissory notes issued by the Japanese government in lieu of subscription fees to international organizations 通貨代用国債
promoter 発起人
promoter's profits 創業者利益
promoter's share 発起人株
promoting mergers tax credit 合併促進税額控除
promotion 昇進
Promotion Committee for the Privatization of the Four Highway-related Public Corporations 道路関係四公団民営化推進委員会
promotion expenses 創業費
promotion of foreign investment in Japan 対内投資促進

prompt corrective action 早期是正措置
prompt payment 即時払い
promulgation 公布
pronounced 明らかな
pronouncement 公表文書
proof of loss 損害の証明
propensity to consume 消費性向
propensity to import 輸入性向
propensity to invest 投資性向
propensity to save 貯蓄性向
propensity to widen 拡大傾向
proper card 自社カード
properties put to use for business 事業の目的に供される資産
property 財産
property abandonment 財産放棄
property accumulation savings 財形貯金
property acquired 取得資産
property acquired by subsidy 補助金によって得た資産
property acquired by the specified investment in kind 特定の現物出資によって取得された資産
property and casualty underwriter 損保会社
property and equipment 固定資産
property and liability insurance 損害保険
property basis applicable to inventories 棚卸資産に適用する資産基準
property casualty insurance 損害保険
property damage 財物損壊
property damage liability 財産損傷賠償責任
property dividend 現物配当
property for advertisement 広告宣伝用資産
property for exchange 交換用資産
property for experimental and research 試験研究用資産
property for residence 居住用財産
property for substitution 代替資産
property for transfer 譲渡資産
property generally prohibited from seizure 一般の差押禁止財産
property in possession 担保権行使不動産
property income 財産所得
property insurance 財産保険
property inventory 不動産一覧
property ledger 財産元帳
property management 財産管理
property market 不動産市場
property not qualifying for capital gain 譲渡所得の基因とされない資産
property not subject to seizure 差押禁止財産
property portfolio 不動産ポートフォリオ
property prices 不動産価格
property put into business 事業の用に供されている資産
property received in the exchange 交換によって取得した資産
property records 資産台帳
property reserved 引当済財産
property right 財産権
property subject to seizure 差押対象財産
property tax 固定資産税
property tax cadaster 固定資産課税台帳
property tax rate 固定資産税の税率
Property Taxation Division 資産課税課
property valuation 財産評価
property ward 財産区
property, plant and equipment 有形固定資産
proportion basis 按分基準
proportional allocation 比例配分
proportional calculation 比例原価計算
proportional cost 比例費
proportional expenses 比例費
proportional method 一括比例配分方式

proportional reinsurance 比例割合再保険
proportional representation 比例代表
proportional reserve method 比例準備法
proportional reserve system 比例準備制度
proportional tax 比例税
proportional taxation 比例課税法
proportionally equal terms 比例的平等条件
proportionally variable cost 比例的可変費用
proportionate change 比例的変化
proportionate consolidation 比例連結
proportionate share 比例的持ち分
proposal 草案
proposal letter プロポーザル・レター
proposal method プロポーザル方式
proposed budget 予算案
propound 定義する
proprietary account 自己勘定
proprietary company 私会社
proprietary information 著作権のある情報
proprietary ledger 自己口
proprietary order 自己分の注文
proprietary product 独自商品
proprietary right 所有権
proprietary trading 自己売買
proprietor 所有者
proprietor deduction 事業主控除
proprietor punishment 業務主処罰制度
proprietors special expense reserve 事業主特別経費準備金
proprietorship 個人事業；所有主持ち分
proprietorship account 所有主勘定
prosecuting attorney 検事
prospective application 将来的な適用
prospective cash receipts 入金予測額
prospective dividend rate 予想配当率
prospective earnings 予想利益
prospective loss 予想損失
prospective pay-off 予想収益水準
prospective PER 予想 PER
prospective profit 期待利益
prospective rating 見込料率算定；予備格付け
prospective reserve 将来準備金
prospective return 予想収益率；予想リターン
prospective risk premium 予想リスク・プレミアム
prospective yield 予想利回り
prospective yield average 予想平均利回り
prospectus 目論見書
prospectus for foundation 設立趣意書
prospectus for securities registration 届出目論見書
prospectus of incorporation 会社設立目論見書
prospectus prepared in connection with shelf registration 発行登録目論見書
prosperous days 好景気時代
protect the collectability of the amount due 債権の回収を担保する
protecting the currency 通貨防衛
protection プロテクション
protection and indemnity risk insurance P＆I保険
protection and indemnity risks P&I 保険
protection conditions against third parties 第三者対抗要件
protection of investors 投資家保護
protection of the full deposited amount 預金の全額保護
protectionist economic regionalism 保護主義的な経済圏
protectionist policies 保護主義政策
protective covenant 保護条項
protective duty 保護関税
protective put プロテクティブ・プット
protective put trading プロテクティブ・プット取引

protective tariff 保護関税
protective trust 保護信託
protectorate 保護領
protest charges 拒絶証書作成手数料
protest waived 拒絶証書不要文言
protestor 拒絶者
protocol 議定書
provable debt 立証できる債権
prove 証明する
proven 確認の
provided that 但し
provider of finance 金融機関
provision 条項
provision account 引当金勘定
provision for bad debts 貸倒引当損
provision for employee bonus 賞与準備金
provision for exchange of information 情報交換規定
provision for general reserves 準備金積立額
provision for income tax 納税引当金
provision for investment loss reserve 投資損失引当金繰入額
provision for loan loss reserve 貸倒引当金繰入額
provision for loss on loans and advances 貸倒引当金
provision for overseas legal reserve 海外法定準備金繰入
provision for possible loan loss reserve 貸倒引当金繰入
provision for repairs 修繕引当金繰入
provision for reserve for overseas investment loss 海外投資損失準備金繰入
provision for reserve for overseas investments 海外投資損失準備金繰入
provision for reserve for price fluctuation 価格変動準備金繰入
provision for site restoration cost 用地修復引当金
provision for surplus 積立金繰入
provision of accounts 口座の提示
provision of ample liquidity 潤沢な流動性供給
provision of an exchange market 取引所の開設
provision of fund 資金供給
provision of funds to the Deposit Insurance Corporation's "Jusen account" 預金保険機構住専勘定拠出金
provision of funds to the New Financial Stabilization Fund 新金融安定化基金拠出金
provision of guarantee 保証の供与
provision of infrastructure インフラの整備
provision of liquidity 流動性の供給
provision of reserve for repairs 修繕引当金繰入れ
provision of social infrastructure 社会的基盤の整備
provisional 仮の
provisional attachment 仮差押え
provisional budget 暫定予算
provisional commission 暫定手数料
provisional disposition 仮処分
provisional execution 仮執行
provisional insurance 予定保険
provisional liquidator 暫定清算人
provisional order 仮命令
provisional policy 予定保険証券
provisional rating 仮格付け
provisional registration 仮登記
provisional residence 仮住所
provisional return 予定申告
provisional seizure 仮差押え
provisional settlement of account 仮決算
provisional sum プロビジョナル・サム
provisional tariff 暫定税率
provisional tax payment system based on the previous year's tax amount 予定納税制度
provisions applied mutatis mutandis 準用規定
proviso 但書

provisory 但書の
provisory clause 但書条項
provocation 挑発
proximate cause 主原因
proximate damage 近接損害
proximity 近似性
proxy 代理
proxy contest 委任状争奪
proxy currency 代用通貨
proxy fight 委任状合戦
proxy for market value 市場価値の代替
proxy material 委任状参考資料
proxy rule 委任状規則
proxy solicitation 委任状勧誘
proxy statement 議決権行使勧誘書類
proxy vote 委任状投票
PRP (profit related pay) 利益連動型給与
PRR (position risk requirement) ポジション・リスク所要額
prudence 注意
prudency audit 経営判断監査
prudent asset structure 堅実な資産構成
prudent basis 慎重主義
prudent man rule 善管注意義務
prudent person rule 受託者責任
PSA (Public Securities Association) 公共債協会
pseudo-random numbers 類似乱数
PSR (price to sales ratio) 株価売上高倍率
psychological effect 心理的効果
psychological line サイコロジカル・ライン
psychological theory of exchange 為替心理説
PTC (participant terminal system) 参加者端末
PTC (pass-through certificate) パス・スルー証書
PTE (Portuguese esucudo) ポルトガル・エスクード
PTS (Proprietary Trading System) 独自取引システム
public accountant 公共会計士
Public Accounting Law 会計法
public acknowledgment 認知
public and corporate bond 公社債
public and corporate bond investment trust 公社債投資信託
public announcement 公告
public announcement of settlement of accounts under ordinary accounting 普通会計決算公告
public annuity 公的年金
public assistance 生活保護
public auction 一般入札；公売
public benefit 公益性
public bidding 公開入札
public body 公共団体
public bond 公債
public bond dealing 公債売買
public capital 公的資金
public capital injection 公的資金注入
public company 公開企業
public compensation bond 交付公債
public confidence 一般の信頼
public confidence in banknotes 銀行券に対する信認
public corporation 公社・公団
public debt 公債；財政赤字
public debt securities 公共債
public document 公開文書
public dues 公課
public economics 公共経済学
public employer retirement plan 公共部門退職年金
public enterprise 公的企業
public expenditure 公共支出
public facilities tax 共同施設税
public facility 公共施設
public finance 国家財政
public finance corporation 公庫
Public Finance Law 財政法
public financial institution 公的金融機関
public fund 公募ファンド
public goods 公共財

public governor 公益代表理事
public hearing 公聴会
public housing authority bond 公営住宅公社債
public impost 公課
public information 公開情報
public inspection 公衆の縦覧
public interest 公益
public interest corporation 公益法人
public investment 公共投資
public investment multiplier 公共投資乗数
public involvement 地域調整
public law 公法
public liability 一般賠償責任
public liability insurance 損害賠償責任保険
public market 公開市場
public measurer 公認検量人
public money 公的資金
public monopoly 専売
public nature 公共性
public notice 公告
public notification 公示催告
public notification of auction 公売広告
public notification of returns 申告書の公示
public offering 公募
public offering auction system 公募入札方式
public offering business 公募業務
public offering issue 公募債
public offering municipal bond 地方債公募
public offering of FBs at a fixed discount rate and underwriting of FBs by the Bank when bids from financial institutions fall short of the amount offered 定率公募・日銀残額引受け
public offering of stock 株式公募
public offering of straight bond 普通社債公募
public offering price 公募価格
public offering share 公募株
public offerings of government bonds 国債の市中消化
public offerings of municipal bonds 公募地方債
public order 公序
public pension 公的年金
public placement 公募
public policy 公共政策；公序
public private partnership 官民協力
public procurement 政府調達
public project 公共プロジェクト
public prosecutor 検察官
Public Prosecutors Office 検察庁
public protection 生活保護
public purpose bond 公共目的債
Public Relations Department 情報サービス局
Public Relations Office 広報室
public sale 公開売却
public sector 公共セクター
public sector corporation 公法人
public sector deficit 財政赤字
public sector enterprise 公的部門事業体
public securities exchange 公開証券市場
public securities markets 公募証券市場
Public Security Investigation Agency 公安調査庁
public selling 売出し
public service 公共事業
public service pension 公的部門年金
public spending 公共支出；財政支出
public subscription 公募
public summons 公示催告
public support system 公的支援制度
public syndicate 公募シンジケート
public telecommunication business 公共通信事業
public tender 公開入札
public trust 公益信託
public use 公共の用
public utilities 公共事業体
public utility 公共事業

public utility accounting 公益事業会計
public utility bond 公益事業債
public utility charges 公共料金
Public Utility Holding Company Act 公益事業持株会社法
public works budget 公共事業予算
public works expenditures 公共事業費
public works outlays 公共工事支出
Public Works Research Institute 土木研究所
public-sector accounting 公共部門会計
publication of market information 相場の公表
publication of performance results 決算公告
publication of transaction price 約定値段の公表
publication of transcripts 議事録の公表
publicly held company 公開会社
publicly held stock 公開株
publicly issued bond 公募債
publicly notified land price 公示地価
publicly offered NTT bonds 公募電電債
publicly offered share 売出株
publicly subscribed share 公募株
publicly traded 公開されている
publicly traded bond 公募債
publicly traded company 公開企業
publish 公表する
published document 公表書類
published financial statements 公表財務諸表
publishing cost 出版費
publishing right 出版権
puffer 競売のサクラ
pull strategy プル戦略
pullback 値下り
pulling-back 後退
pulp and paper industry パルプ・紙業界
pump the market with government bonds 国債を発行する
pump-priming effect 呼び水効果
pump-priming role 呼び水
punishment on penalty tax 追徴処分
punitive damages 懲罰的損害賠償
punitive tariffs 制裁関税
purchase 購買
purchase agent 買入代理人
purchase agreement 買収契約書
purchase allowance 仕入値引
purchase amount 仕入高
purchase and assumption 預金承継方式
purchase and sale statement 売買報告書
purchase book 仕入帳
purchase budget 仕入予算
purchase commission 購入手数料
purchase commitment 売買契約上の債務
purchase consideration 購入対価
purchase contract パーチェス契約
purchase cost 仕入原価
purchase discount 仕入割引
purchase face amount 買収額面金額
purchase fund 買付資金
purchase group 買付グループ
purchase group agreement 引受団契約
purchase investigation 買収の任意調査
purchase ledger 仕入先元帳
purchase loan 購買ローン
purchase method パーチェス法
purchase money 買受代金
purchase money mortgage 土地代金モーゲージ
purchase of CP under repurchase agreement CP 現先
purchase of fractional shares from holders 端株の買取り
purchase of goods and services by government 政府の財貨・サービス購入
purchase of loan 貸付の購入
purchase of net assets 純資産の買入れ
purchase of new issues of public and corporate bonds 公社債消化

P

purchase on credit 掛買い
purchase option 購入選択権
purchase order 購入注文書
purchase payment fund 掛金積立基金
purchase price 購入代金
purchase price prevailing at the date of (physical) inventory taking 棚卸日現在の使用価格
purchase rebate 仕入割戻し
purchase rebate with special payment terms 特約支払条件付仕入割戻
purchase return 仕入返品
purchase right to new shares for capital increase 増資新株買取権
purchase tax 仕入税
purchase transaction 買付
purchase-money obligation 買入代金債務
purchased goodwill 購入のれん
purchased loan 購入した貸付金
purchased parts 買入部品
purchased receivables 購入債権
purchaser 買主
purchases and sales 売買
purchases budget 仕入予算
purchases of FBs (financing bills) under repurchase agreements 政府短期証券買現先オペ
purchases of TBs (treasury bills) /FBs (financing bills) under repurchase agreements 短期国債買現先オペ
purchases of TBs (treasury bills) under repurchase agreements 割引短期国債買現先オペ
purchases rebate 仕入割戻
purchases year 購入年
purchasing expenses 仕入費用
purchasing manager 購買部長
purchasing power 購買力
purchasing power gain or loss 購買力変動損益
purchasing power loss 購買力損失
purchasing power of dollar ドルの購買力
purchasing power of money 貨幣の購買力
purchasing power parity 購買力平価
purchasing power parity theory 購買力平価説
purchasing power risk 購買力リスク
purchasing price 仕入値段
pure asset liability position 純粋資産負債ポジション
pure cap ピュア・キャップ
pure credit risk 純粋クレジット・リスク
pure deferred life annuity 純粋据置終身年金
pure discount bond 純割引債
pure discount securities 純粋割引証券
pure endowment insurance 生存保険
pure exchange 純粋交換
pure expectation hypothesis 純粋期待仮説
pure inflation expectation 純粋インフレ期待
pure monopoly 純粋独占
pure premium 純粋保険料
pure rate of interest 純粋金利
pure risk 純粋リスク
pure securities 純粋証券
pure strategy 純戦略
pure swap 純粋スワップ
pure yield 純粋利回り
purport to 意図する
purpose loan 目的ローン
purpose of finance lease ファイナンス・リースの目的
purpose of financial statements 財務諸表の目的
purpose statement 目的申告書
purposes for using derivatives デリバティブの目的
purview 各号；本文
push down accounting プッシュ・ダウン会計
push pull プッシュ・プル
pushing the dollar down against yen 対円でドルを売り込む
put and call プット・アンド・コール

put bond プット・ボンド
put diagram プット・ダイヤグラム
put guarantee letter プット保証書
put holder プット保持者
put it in pledge 質権の目的とする
put option プット・オプション
put option of shareholder 株式買取請求権
put ratio back spread trading プット・レシオ・バックスプレッド取引
put swaption プット・スワップション
put warrant プット・ワラント
put-call ratio プット・コール比率
put-value line プット価格線
putative 推定上の
puttable 償還請求可能な
puttable bond プッタブル・ボンド
puttable swap プッタブル・スワップ
puttable swaption プッタブル・スワップション
puttable warrant プッタブル・ワラント
putting-out system 前貸制度
PYG (Paraguay guarani) パラグアイ・グァラニ
pyramid management method ピラミッド型管理方式
pyramiding process ピラミッディング過程

P

Q

Q-TIP (qualified terminable interest property) trust Q-TIP 信託
Q1 (first quarter) 第 1 四半期
Q2 (second quarter) 第 2 四半期
Q3 (third quarter) 第 3 四半期
Q4 (fourth quarter) 第 4 四半期
QAR (Qatari rial) カタール・リアル
QE (Quick Estimation) 四半期国民所得統計速報
QFII (Qualified Foreign Institutional Investors) 適格海外機関投資家
Qinghai 青海省
QoQ (quarter-on-quarter) 前期比
quadratic function 二次関数
quadratic programming 二次計画法
quadratic variation 二次変分
qualification 限定条件；適格性
qualification for trading 取引資格
qualification law 資格法
qualification period 認定期間
qualified 適格の
qualified acceptance 条件引受
qualified acceptance of bill 不単純引受
qualified acceptance of inheritance 限定相続
qualified actuary 資格を有する保険数理人
qualified audit opinion 限定監査報告書
qualified auditor's report 限定意見監査報告書
qualified bond 適格債券
qualified business unit クオリファイド・ビジネスユニット
qualified certificate 限定意見証明書
qualified employee 適格従業員
qualified endorsement 限定裏書
qualified foreign intermediary 適格外国仲介業者
qualified institutional investor 適格機関投資家
qualified investment 適格投資額
qualified mortgage 適格モーゲージ
qualified opinion 限定意見
qualified opinion for exclusion 除外事項を記した限定意見
qualified opinion report 条件付監査報告書
qualified pension contract 適格退職年金契約
qualified pension plan 適格退職年金
qualified pension trust fund 適格年金信託基金
qualified plan 適格年金制度
qualified property 制限的財産権
qualified report 限定報告書
qualified retirement annuity 適格退職年金
qualified securities 適格証券
qualified spouse for deduction 控除対象配偶者
qualified tax expert 適格な税務専門家
qualified trust 適格年金信託
qualify as plan asset 制度資産として認められる
qualifying annuity 適格年金
qualifying asset 適格資産
qualifying corporate bond 適格社債
qualifying employee stock option 従業員自社株購入権
qualifying insurance policy 適格保険証券
qualifying lender 適格融資者
qualifying pension funds 適格年金積立金
qualifying reserve 限定準備金
qualifying residential mortgage 適格住宅ローン
qualifying retirement annuity plan 適格退職年金制度

qualifying retirement pension contract 適格退職年金契約
qualifying share 資格株式
qualifying statement 限定意見
qualifying utility 適格公益企業
qualitative analysis 定性分析
qualitative characteristics 質的特徴
qualitative credit control 質的信用規制
qualitative economic policy 質的経済政策
qualitative information 定性情報
qualitative parameters 質的要因
qualitative substantiality test 質的実質性の原則
quality adjustment 質の調整
quality class 高品質クラス
quality control 品質管理
quality cost 品質費用
quality of earnings 利益の質
quality standards 品質基準
quality stock 優良株
quantification 数量化
quantification of risk リスクの定量化
quantified data 数値データ
quantified description 数量表現
quantified guidance 量的な指針
quantify 数量化する
quantitative analysis クオンツ分析；定量分析
quantitative asset allocation 定量アセット・アロケーション
quantitative credit control 量的信用規制
quantitative credit strategy クオンツ・クレジット戦略
quantitative economic policy 量的経済政策
quantitative factor 量的要因
quantitative information 量的情報
quantitative monetary indicator 量的金融指標
quantitative optimization 計量的最適化
quantitative substantiality test 数量的実質性の原則
quantitative threshold 量的基準値
quantitative tool 数量化手段
quantity adjustment 数量調整
quantity discount 数量割引
quantity of output 産出量
quantity of production 生産量
quantity sold 販売数量
quantity standard 数量標準
quantity theory of money 貨幣数量説
quantity variance 数量差異
quantize 通常の通貨以外の通貨で表示する
quanto option クオント・オプション
quantum evaluation 金銭的評価
quarter 四半期
quarter-days 四季支払勘定日
quarter-on-quarter 前期比
quarterly annuity 四半期払年金
quarterly auctions 四半期入札
quarterly earnings 四半期利益
quarterly financial statements 四半期財務諸表
quarterly funding 四半期ごとの資金調達
quarterly income statement 四半期損益計算書
quarterly real growth rate 四半期ベースの実質成長率
quarterly refunding クォータリー・リファンディング
quarterly report 四半期報告書
quash 却下する
quasi 準
quasi co-owner 準共有者
quasi coupon date 仮利払日
quasi easement 準地役権
quasi estoppel 準禁反言
quasi money 準貨幣
quasi-arbitrator 準仲裁人
quasi-contract 準契約
quasi-currency 準通貨
quasi-debt obligations 準債務
quasi-fiduciary relationship 準信認関係

Q

quasi-final return 準確定申告
quasi-government agency 準政府機関
quasi-incompetent person 準禁治産者；被保佐人
quasi-judicial power 準司法的権力
quasi-loan 準借入れ
quasi-loan for consumption 準消費貸借
quasi-member みなし会員
quasi-public corporation 第三セクター
quasi-reorganization 準更生
quasi-share 準株式
quasi-stock 準株式
quest for yield 利回追求
question of fact 争点たる事実
questionnaire アンケート
queuing 待ち行列
quick assets 当座資産
quick assets ratio 当座比率
quick assets to year's cash expenses 年間支出当座比率
quick deposit 当座預金
quick liabilities 短期負債
QUICK-terminal クイック端末
quiet market 保合い相場
quiet period 休眠期間
quiet title 権原確認
quitclaim deed 権利放棄
quitting of business 事業の廃止
quorum 選ばれたグループ；定足数
quorum for a general meeting 総会の定足数
quota 割当量
quota share treaty reinsurance 比例特約再保険
quotation 気配
quotation board 相場掲示板
quotation exchange center 気配交換センター
quotation of over-the-counter issue 店頭気配
quotation on overseas markets 海外相場
quotation price 気配値
quote reporter クオート・レポーター
quoted company 上場会社
quoted driven 呼値主導型
quoted fee 表示した手数料
quoted market price 公表市場価格
quoted price 公表価格；相場
quoted real yield 実勢実質利回り
quoted yield 実勢利回り
quotient 指数
quoting high 高唱え

R

R/D (refer to drawer) 振出人回し
R&I (Rating and Investment Information, Inc.) 格付投資情報センター
RA (reimbursement authorization) 補償授権書
Racketeer Influenced and Corrupt Organization Act 暴力不正腐敗防止法
raider 敵対的買収を考える株式取得者
raiding the market 売崩し
railroad bonds 鉄道債
rainmaker やり手
raising of interest rate 金利引上げ
rally 上昇
rally in the bond market 債券相場の上昇
rally over the last one year 過去一年間に渡る上昇
rallying equities 株価上昇
RAM (reverse annuity mortgage) 逆年金モーゲージ
ramp 加速経路
ramp up 上昇する
rampant inflation 激しいインフレ
ramping 大きく買いを入れる
RAN (revenue anticipation bond) 予定財源債
random default scenario 任意デフォルト・シナリオ
random number 乱数
random price changes 不規則な価格変動
random sample 確率標本；無作法抽出
random variables 確率変数
random walk theory ランダム・ウォーク理論
range 変動幅
range either side of 10.0 10を挟むレンジ
range forward contract レンジ・フォワード取引
range of price fluctuation 値幅
range of prices 価格幅
range trading もみあい
range-bound market ボックス圏の動き
ranking of advances 上昇順位
ranking of declines 下落順位
ranking system ランキング制度
ransom insurance 身代金保険
RAP (regulatory accounting principles) 規制目的会計原則
rapid surge 急増
rare stock 品薄株
rasure 削除
ratable distribution 比例配当
ratable value 課税見積価格
ratchet effect 歯止め効果
rate base 料率の基礎
rate cap 金利キャップ
rate covenant 料金条項
rate cut 利下げ
rate differential 金利スプレッド
rate discrimination 料率の適用差別
rate floor agreement 金利フロア契約
rate hike 利上げ
rate in foreign currency 外国通貨建相場
rate in home currency 自国通貨建相場
rate in overseas market 海外相場
rate issue 格付け
rate of awareness 知名度
rate of change 変化率
rate of charge 徴収率
rate of depreciation to total assets 総資産償却率
rate of earnings on equity 自己資本利益率
rate of economic growth 経済成長率
rate of efficiency of depreciation 減価

償却効率
rate of estimated credit loss 貸倒見込率
rate of estimated expenses 概算経費率
rate of increase 上昇率
rate of interest on deposit 預金利率
rate of involuntary unemployment 完全失業率
rate of listed bond 公社債上場相場
rate of output 操業度
rate of return 収益率
rate of return measurement 収益率測定
rate of return on invested capital 投資利益率
rate of return on investment 投資収益率
rate of return on long-term liabilities plus equity capital 長期資本利益率
rate of return on pension funds 年金基金運用収益率
rate of returned goods unsold 返品率
rate of salary increase 昇給率
rate of sales returns 返品率
rate of special depreciation deduction 特別償却率
rate of stock-turn 商品回転率
rate of technical progress 技術進歩率
rate of turnover 回転率
rate of variable expenses 変動費率
rate of wage increase 賃上率
rate outlook 金利見通し
rate papers 納税告知書
rate regulation 料率規制
rate spread 利ざや
rate structure 料率構造
rated policy 高料率適用契約
ratepayer 租税負担者
rater 格付機関
ratification 批准
rating 格付け
rating agency 格付機関
rating assessment 格付評価
rating change 格付変更
rating limit 格付けの制限
rating of bond 債券の格付け
rating organization tariffs 算定会料率
rating outlook 格付見通し
rating subscriber 格付情報契約者
rating system 格付制度
rating trigger 格付基準
ratio レシオ
ratio analysis 比率分析
ratio call spread transaction レシオ・コール・スプレッド取引
ratio method 比率法
ratio of actual loan losses to the total loans 総貸出貸倒率
ratio of bond issue to total expenditure 公債依存度
ratio of cash to thirty-day debts 現金対一ヶ月負債比率
ratio of compound annual return 年複利収益率
ratio of cost to sales 売上原価率
ratio of current expenses to current income 経常収支率
ratio of current liabilities to net worth 流動負債比率
ratio of direct and indirect taxes 直間比率
ratio of dividends to earnings 利益金対配当比率
ratio of dividends to shareholders' equity 株主資本配当率
ratio of earnings on total capital 総資本純利益率
ratio of expense-to-premium 受取保険料事業費率
ratio of expenses to revenues 収益比率
ratio of fixed assets to long-term capital 固定資産長期資本比率
ratio of fixed assets to net worth 固定資産比率
ratio of fixed liabilities to net worth 固定負債比率
ratio of general expenses to current income 一般経費率
ratio of gross profit to inventory

R

investment 交叉比率
ratio of gross profit to sales 売上総利益率
ratio of individual stock ownership 個人持株比率
ratio of inventory to net working capital 棚卸資産正味運転資本比率
ratio of leasehold to land value 借地権割合
ratio of loans 貸付比率
ratio of merchandise to receivables 商品在高対受取勘定比率
ratio of necessary expenses to gross revenue 経費率
ratio of net profit to gross revenues 純利益対総収益比率
ratio of net worth to debts 資本負債比率
ratio of net worth to fixed capital 資本固定比率
ratio of net worth to total capital 自己資本比率
ratio of net worth to total debt 自己資本対負債比率
ratio of operating income to sales 営業利益率
ratio of operating profit to revenue 営業利益率
ratio of ordinary profits to total capital 総資本経常利益率
ratio of personnel expenses 人件費率
ratio of profit to capital 資本利益率
ratio of profit to net sales 売上高利益率
ratio of profit to net worth 自己資本利益率
ratio of receivable to inventories 受取勘定対棚卸資産比率
ratio of replacement of assets 資産の更新率
ratio of return on total assets 総資産利益率
ratio of return on total capital 総資本収益率
ratio of sales to total assets 総資産売上率
ratio of sales to working capital 運転資本売上率
ratio of saving to disposable income 貯蓄率
ratio of shareholding 持株比率
ratio of total liabilities to net worth 負債比率
ratio of voting rights 議決権比率
ratio writer 原株以上のコール・オプションの売手
rational basis 合理的基準
rational expectation hypothesis 合理的期待仮説
rational structure 合理的な構造
rationale 根拠
rationalization 合理化
rationalization measure 合理化実施
rationalization of production 生産合理化
rationalize 合理化を図る
rationalized 合理的な
rationing 配給制度
raw and processed materials 原材料
raw data 原データ
raw material inventory 原材料在庫
raw materials 材料
RBA (Reserve Bank of Australia) オーストラリア準備銀行
RBC (risk based capital) リスク対応資本
RBNZ (Reserve Bank of New Zealand) ニュージーランド準備銀行
RCC (Resolution and Collection Corporation) 整理回収機構
RCF (retained cash flow) 手許キャッシュフロー
RCH (recognized clearing house) 公認清算機関
RCI (Rank Correlation Index) 順位相関指数
RDF (refuse derived fuel) power generation 固形化燃料発電
re-acquired stock 再取得株式
re-auction 再公売

re-correction 再更正
re-cross-examination 再反対尋問
re-entry 再加入；不動産占有回復
re-estimation 再見積り
re-exchange 戻し為替
re-export 再輸出
re-leasing 再リース
re-named 名称変更された
re-opening リオープン
re-pledge 再担保に入れる
re-recognition 再計上
reach for yield 利回物色
reaching the top price 大天井
reacquisition price 再取得価格
reaction curve 反応曲線
reactionary fall 反落
readjusting entry 再修正記入
readjustment of taxation system 税制整理
ready market 確実な市場
ready money 手許現金
ready reckoner 計算早見表
real account 実在勘定
real accrued interest 実質経過利子
real action 対物訴訟
real amount 現実の金額
real annuity obligation 実質年金債務
real assets 実物資産
real balance effect 実質貨幣残高効果
real capital 実物資本
real cash settlement 最終資金決済
real chattels 物的動産
real commodities 実物商品
real compensation 実質賃金
real contract 対物契約
real cost 実質原価
real cost of borrowing 実質借入コスト
real credit 対物信用
real deposits 実質預金
real disposable income 実質可処分所得
real distress 不動産差押え
real earnings 実質所得
real economic activity 実体経済活動
real economy 実体経済
real entity theory of corporation 法人実在説
real estate 不動産
real estate acquisition tax 不動産取得税
real estate agency 不動産仲介業
real estate agent 不動産業者
real estate appraisal 不動産鑑定
real estate broker 不動産ブローカー
real estate held for sale 販売用土地
real estate in possession 現有不動産物件
real estate in trust 不動産信託
real estate income 不動産所得
real estate industry 不動産業
real estate long-term loan receivable 不動産抵当長期貸付金
real estate market 不動産市場
real estate mortgage 不動産モーゲージ
real estate price 不動産相場
real estate property 不動産
real estate sale 不動産販売
real estate security 不動産担保
real estate stock 不動産株
real estate tax 固定資産税
real estate without encumbrance 無制約の不動産
real estate yield 不動産株投資の利回り
real evidence 物的証拠
real exchange rate 実質為替レート
real flow 実質的なフロー
real GDP 実質 GDP
real GNP growth rate 実質ＧＮＰ成長率
real gross investment 実質総投資
real growth 実質成長
real growth rate 実質成長率
real guarantee 物上保証
real income 実質所得
real income earner 実質所得者
real interest rate 実質金利
real investment 実物投資
real investment return 実質投資収益率
real liabilities 実質債務

R

real money 実質貨幣
real multiplier 実質乗数
real net investment 実質純投資
real obtainer of dividend income 配当所得の帰属者
real obtainer of interest income 利子所得の帰属者
real outgoing 実質出費
real price 実質価格
real price of money 資金の実質価値
real property acquisition tax 不動産取得税
real rate 実質利率
real rate of appreciation 実質価格の上昇率
real rate of exchange 実勢為替相場
real rate of return 実質利回り
real return 実質収益
real return pay-off 実質リターンの収益
real right 物権
real security 物的担保
real space 実質の世界
real term 実質単位
real time リアルタイム
real time communication 瞬時通信
real time processing リアルタイム処理
real time settlement リアル・タイム決済
real transfer 実物的トランスファー
real unit labor cost 実質単位労働コスト
real value 実質価値
real water 真水
real wealth 実質資産
real world 実質価値の世界
real worth 実質価値
real yield 実質金利；実質利回り
real yield calculation 実質利回り計算
real yield differential 実質金利格差
real-bills doctrine 商業手形主義
real-life response 実際の反応
real-time price 現在価格
realignment 再調整
realignment negotiation 再調整交渉
realistic alternative 現実的な代替案
realistic means 現実的な手段
realistic portrayal 現実的表示
reality of market 市場の現実
realizable value 実現可能価額
realization basis 実現主義
realization gain 実現利得
realization of gains 収益の実現
realization of profit and losses 損益の実現
realization of tax liability 納税義務の成立
realization principle 実現主義
realization sales 換金売り
realized appreciation 実現増価額
realized depreciation 実現減価償却
realized gain 実現利得
realized gain and loss 実現損益
realized gross profit on installment sales 割賦売上益
realized income 実現利益
realized loss 実現損失
realized profit 実現利益
realized profit and loss 実現損益
realized return 実現収益
realized revenue 実現収益
realized value 実現価値
realized volatility 実現ボラティィリティー
realized yield 実効利回り
reallocated amount 再割当金
reallocation of income 所得再配分
really rightful person 真実の権利者
realty business 不動産業
reappraisal 評価替え
rear end load 後払手数料
rearrangement of budget item 予算移替
reason for dishonor 不渡事由
reasonable 合理的な
reasonable and probable cause 合理的かつ相当な原因
reasonable approximation 合理的な近似値
reasonable assurance 合理的な保証

R

reasonable certainty 合理的な確実性
reasonable criteria 合理的な基準
reasonable depreciation 相当の償却
reasonable doubt 合理的疑い
reasonable estimate 合理的見積り
reasonable evidence 合理的根拠
reasonable price 値頃
reasonable test 合理性テスト
reasonably calculated value 合理的に算定された価値
reasoning 論証
reassess 再評価する
reassessment 評価替え
reassessment of income tax 所得税の更正決定
reassessment of taxes 課税の更正決定
reassignment of listed stocks to sections 上場株券の所属部の指定替え
reassignment of sections 指定替え
rebalance 見直し
rebalancing 組換え
rebalancing strategies リバランス戦略
rebate 割戻し
rebound 反騰
rebound in profit 利益の回復
rebound in spending 消費の回復
rebuilding demand 建替需要
rebut 対抗する
rebuttable 反証可能な
rebuttable presumption 反証可能な前提
rebutting evidence 反証
recalculate 再計算する
recapitalization 資本再構成
recapitalization of legal reserve 法定準備金資本組入れ
recapture 取戻し
recapture of depreciation 減価償却額の回収
receipt 受領証
receipt and payment bookkeeping 収支簿記
receipt in full 全額領収書
receipt instruction 受取指図
receipt of business 営業の譲受け
receipt of fixed payments 固定額の受取
receipt of floating payments 変動額の受取
receipt of orders 受注
receipt slip 入金伝票
receipt voucher 入金伝票
receipts and payments 収入支出
receipts and payments of treasury funds between the government and the private sector 財政資金対民間収支
receipts exceeding disbursements (net receipts) 受入超過
receipts of dividends 配当収入
receipts of money 入金
receivable and payable contract 債権債務契約
receivable from affiliate 関係会社売掛金
receivables 債権
receivables from customers 立替金
receivables not qualifying for the bad debts reserve 貸倒引当金に繰り入れられない貸金
receivables pool 債権プール
receivables turnover 売上債権回転率
receivables under resale agreement 買現先債権
receive versus payment 現金決済条件
received in arrears 領収未済で
received margin 受入証拠金
receiver 財産管理人
receiver in bankruptcy 破産管財人
receiver's certificate 管財人債務証書
receivership 管財人任命；債権者救済手続
receiving 受取勘定
receiving bank 被仕向銀行
receiving order 財産管理命令
receiving quotation 受取勘定建相場
receiving report 受入報告書
reception stamp 受付印
recess 休会

recession 景気後退
recession period 景気後退期
recession risk 景気後退のリスク
recessionary economic 景気の低迷
recipient 受取人
recipient country 受入国
reciprocal account 対応勘定
reciprocal arrangement 相互協定
reciprocal consignment 相互委託販売
reciprocal contract 双務契約
reciprocal control account 相互統制勘定
reciprocal credit 相殺信用状；抱合せ信用状
reciprocal demand curve 相互需要曲線
reciprocal distribution method 相互配賦法
reciprocal duties 互恵関税
reciprocal relationship 対応関係
reciprocal share holding 株式持合い
reciprocal tax treaty 互恵租税条約
reciprocal transfer of assets 資産の相互交換
reciprocal transfer of property 資産の相互交換
reciprocity 相互主義
recital 証書の説明部
recklessness 無謀
reclaimed land 埋立地
reclaimed materials 再生原材料
reclassification 組替え
reclassification adjustment 再分類調整
reclassification of line items 勘定科目の組替え
reclassify 組替える
recognition 認識
recognition as expense 費用認識
recognition criteria 認識基準
recognition criteria for profit and loss 損益の計上基準
recognition in equity 資本への計上
recognition in the financial statements 財務諸表での認識
recognition lag 認知ラグ
recognition method 認知法
recognition of gain and loss 損益認識
recognition of losses 損失の認識
recognition of sales 売上高の認識
recognition requirement 認識要件
recognition trigger 認識トリガー
recognized in balance sheet 貸借対照表に計上された
recognized in equity 資本に計上された
recognized in equity account 資本勘定に計上される
recognized in financial statements 財務諸表に計上された
recognized in income statement 損益計算書に計上された
recognized in shareholder's equity 株主持ち分に計上された
recognized loss 認識された損失
recognized profit 認識された利益
recognizing as expense 損金経理
recommendation 勧告
recommendation to a member 会員への勧告
recommended stock 推奨株
reconciliation 照合確認；調停
reconciliation account 調整勘定
reconciliation in settling accounts 決算調整
reconciliation item 調整項目
reconciliation of cost variance 原価差額調整
reconciliation of deficit 不足金の処理
reconciliation of surplus 剰余金調整書
reconciliation of the carrying amount 帳簿価額の調整
reconciliation statement for current account 当座照合表
reconstruction expense 改築費
reconstruction of the economy 経済復興
reconstruction works 改築工事
reconversion 再転換
record amount 記録的な額
record date 基準日；記録日

record high 過去最高；既往最高
record keeping 記録保存
record ledger 株主名簿
record low 過去最低；新安値
record of foreclosure 差押調書
record of seizure 差押調書
record on removal 移送申立記録
record price 高値
recorded cost 帳簿原価
recoup 損害を回復する
recoupment 控除権
recourse 遡及償還請求権
recourse agreement リコース契約
recourse debt 求償債務
recourse finance 求償請求権のある融資
recourse form リコース形式
recourse loan リコース・ローン
recourse obligation 遡及債務
recourse right 遡及権
recover high 戻り高値
recoverability 回収可能性
recoverability assessment 回収可能性の評価
recoverability test 回収可能性テスト
recoverable 回収可能な
recoverable amount 回収可能額
recoverable cost 回収可能原価
recoverable expenditure 回収可能支出
recoverable value 回収可能価額
recoveries on loans written off 償却債権の回収
recovering cyclically 循環要因による回復
recovering demand 需要の回復
recovery expectations 景気回復期待
recovery from deficit 黒字転換
recovery in stock prices 株価の回復
recovery of bad debt 貸倒れ回収
recovery of bad debts 貸倒金の回収
recovery of capital 資本の回収
recovery of carrying amount 帳簿価額の回収
recovery of claims written-off 償却債権取立
recovery of credits 債権の回収
recovery of doubtful accounts 貸倒金の回収
recovery of earnings 収益の回復
recovery of investment 投資の回収
recovery of loss 欠損回収
recovery period 原価回収期間
recovery schedule for loans 貸出金回収予定
recovery value 回収可能価値
recruiting expense 募集費
recruitment 社員採用
rectangular distribution 矩形分布
rectification of illegal actions 違法行為の是正
rectification work 調整作業
rectify 救済する；矯正する
recurring audit 連続監査
recurring gain or loss 経常損益
recurring profit 経常利益
recurring profit and loss 経常損益
recurring tax 経常税
recycling 環流
red B/L 赤船荷証券
red clause credit 前貸信用状
red-balance 赤字残額
red-herring prospectus レッドヘリング目論見書
red-ink entry 赤字記入
redeem 償還する
redeem before maturity 繰上げ償還する
redeemable 繰上償還可能な
redeemable bond 償還債券
redeemable for their face value 額面金額による償還
redeemable preference share 償還優先株式
redeemable stock 償還株式
redeemable warrant 償還可能ワラント
redeemed principal 元本償還額
redemption 償還
redemption amount 償還金額
redemption and coupon payments 元利払い

redemption at fixed date 定時償還
redemption at market value 市価償還
redemption at maturity 満期償還
redemption before maturity 期限前償還；繰上償還
redemption by buyback 買入償却
redemption by drawing 抽選償還
redemption by drawing of number くじびき償還
redemption by lottery 抽選償還
redemption by purchase 買入償却
redemption by the number of drawing くじびき償還
redemption by yearly installment 年賦償還
redemption date 償還期日
redemption from tax sale 公売の買戻し
redemption fund 償還基金
redemption gain 償還差益
redemption insurance 償還保険
redemption of bond 債券償還
redemption of corporate bonds 社債の償還
redemption of external loan 外債償還
redemption of foreign loan 外債償還
redemption of government securities 政府証券償還
redemption of JGSs 国債の償還
redemption of pledge 質物受戻し
redemption of principal 元本の償還
redemption price 償還価格
redemption profit 償還益
redemption right 償還請求権
redemption risk 償還リスク
redemption system 減債制度
redemption through secondary market purchase 買入償還
redemption value 償還価額
redemption yield 償還利回り
redeposit 再寄託
rediscount 再割
rediscount policy 再割引政策
rediscount rate 再割引金利
rediscounting 再割引
rediscounting of bills 手形の再割引
rediscounting with the central bank 中央銀行再割引
redistributed cost 再配賦原価
redistribution 再配分
redlining 融資拒否
redress 救済
REDS (refundable escrow deposits) 借換エスクロー預金
reduced access to funds 資金調達力低下
reduced asset price 減資産価格
reduced borrowing costs 調達コストの削減
reduced capital adequacy requirements 自己資本基準の緩和
reduced dividend 減配
reduced duties 関税引下げ
reduced form 誘導形
reduced income tax rate 軽減税率
reduced liquidity 流動性の乏しさ
reduced losses 赤字縮小
reduced paid-up insurance 減額払込保険
reduced pension 減額年金
reduced portion 減少部分
reduced premium rate 減額保険料率
reduced principal 減額後の元本
reduced profit 利益減額
reduced rate 割引料率
reduced rate loan 低利融資
reduced tax rate on dividend paid 配当軽課
reduced tax rate on specified medical corporation 特定医療法人の特別税率
reduced-form method 誘導モデル
reducing or eliminating 減殺
reducing term policy 逓減定期保険
reducing unemployment rate 失業率低減
reduction 減少
reduction and exemption of taxes 減免
reduction in benefit 給付削減
reduction in business activities 事業の

R

縮小
reduction in liability 負債減少額
reduction in price 値引
reduction in tax rate 税率低減
reduction in the amount 減額
reduction in valued amount 評価額の減少
reduction of business 事業規模の縮少
reduction of capital stock 減資
reduction of capital without compensation 無償減資
reduction of expenditures 経費節減
reduction of incidence 負担軽減
reduction of lending ratio 融資比率引下げ
reduction of operation 操業短縮
reduction of par (value) 額面の切下げ
reduction of principal 元本の減少
reduction of regional disparities 地域格差の是正
reduction of the outstanding liability 負債残高の返済部分
reduction of volatility 変動性の減少
reduction or exemption of tax 租税の減免
reduction or forgiveness of interest 金利の減免
reductions in long-term debt 長期借入返済額
redundancy 過剰事項
redundancy plan 余剰人員解雇計画
redundant disclosure 余分な開示
REFCORP (Resolution Funding Corporation) 整理資金調達公社
refer the issue to arbitration 仲裁に委ねる
referable name 要確認先
referee in bankruptcy 破産審理人
referee in case of need 予備支払人
reference 照会
reference asset 対象資産
reference bank 照会先銀行
reference documents 参照書類
reference entity 参照組織
reference index 参照指数
reference obligation 参照債務
reference period 参考期間
reference point 参照点
reference pool 参照プール
reference portfolio 参照ポートフォリオ
reference range 参考相場圏
reference rate 指標金利
reference statistics 参考統計
reference value 参照値
reference yield 参考利回り
reference zone レファレンス・ゾーン
referenced notional 参照額面金額
referenced tranche 参照トランシェ
referral fees 紹介手数料
referred to as 称す
refi index 借換指数
refinance system リファイナンス方式
refinanced loan 借換ローン
refinancing 借換え
refinancing bond 借換債
refinancing cost 借換費用
refinancing elbow 借換エルボー
refinancing incentive 借換インセンティブ
refinancing issue 借換発行
refinancing of instruments 金融商品の再調達
refinancing opportunity 借換機会
refinancing propensity 借換性向
refinancing seasoning 借換えのシーズニング
refinancing wave 借換ブーム
refinement 改良
refix date 更新日
reflation リフレーション
reflation policy リフレーション政策
reflux 還流
reform of economic structure 経済構造改革
reform of financial system 金融制度改革
reform of international monetary system 国際通貨制度改革
reform of securities settlement systems

R

証券決済制度改革
reform of the administrative structure 行政改革
reform of the deposit insurance system 預金保険機構の改革
reform of the medical insurance system 医療保険制度の改革
reformatted version リフォーマット版
refrain from 差し控える
refresher 追加謝金
refund 還付金
refund annuity 掛金償還年金；死亡時払戻金付年金
refund bond 返還保証証券
refund by carrying a loss back to a prior year 繰戻しによる還付
refund by final return 確定申告による還付
refund claim 還付申請書
refund deferred life annuity 償還据置終身年金
refund of clearing margin 取引証拠金の返戻
refund of fees 手数料割戻し
refund of income tax 所得税の還付
refund of overpayment 過誤納金の還付
refund of principal 元本償還
refund of stockholders' equity 株主持ち分償還
refund policy 払戻方針
refund retroactive to the past taxable years 過年度に遡った還付
refund tax 還付税
refunded corporate tax 還付法人税
refunding 払戻
refunding bond 借換債
refunding bonds 借換国債
refunding issue 借換債
refunding of equity 持ち分の払戻し
refunding securities 借替証券
refundment 返戻金
refundment guarantee 前払金返還保証
refundment of stockholders' equity 株主の持分の償還
refurbishment 改装
refusal to accept application 申請の不受理
refusal to deal 取引拒否
refusal to receive 不受理
regeneration 再生
regenerative natural resources 再生可能な天然資源
regional bank 地方銀行
regional bank card 地銀バンクカード
Regional Banks Association of Japan 全国地方銀行協会
regional cartel 地域カルテル
regional development 地域開発
regional economics 地域経済学
regional economy 地域経済
regional exchange 地方取引所
Regional Financial Cooperation Division 地域協力課
regional financial markets 地域金融市場
regional government bond 地方債
regional internationalization 地域国際化
regional office 地方事務所
regional policy 地域政策
regional social capital 地域社会資本
regional social infrastructure 地域社会基盤
regional stock exchange 地方証券取引所
Regional Taxation Bureau 国税局
regional tie-up 地域連携
regionalism 地域主義
regionals 地方業者
register of cancellation of attachment 差押抹消登記
register of participants 参加者名簿
register of settlement of mortgage 抵当権設定登記
registered 登記済み
registered annuity product 登録年金商品
registered bond 記名社債；登録債
registered check 登録小切手

registered common stock 記名式普通株式
registered company 登録会社
registered competitive market maker 登録コンペティティブ・マーケット・メーカー
registered competitive trader 登録コンペティティブ・トレーダー
registered coupon bond 記名クーポン債券
registered financial institution 登録金融機関
registered form 記名式
registered gilts 登録ギルト債
registered government bonds 登録国債
registered head office 本店所在地
registered issues 登録銘柄
registered JGSs 登録国債
registered mail 書留
registered number 登記番号
registered office 本社事務所
registered owner 登録名義人
registered pledgee 登録質権者
registered public accountant 経理士
registered representative 登録証券外務員
registered secondary offering 登録売出し
registered securities 記名証券
registered securities clearing organization 証券取引清算機関
registered share 登録株
registered society 登録組合
registered statistics 届出統計
registered stock 記名株式
registered trade-mark 登録商標
registered trader 登録トレーダー
registrar 登録機関
registrar of companies 会社登記所
registration 届出
registration act for corporate bond 社債登録法
registration agency 登録機関
registration and license tax 登録免許税
Registration and License Tax Law 登録免許税法
registration certificate 権利証
registration fee 登記料
registration formalities 登記手続
registration license 登録免許
registration of a new design 新案登録
registration of a public offering of a security 有価証券の募集に関する届出
registration of a public selling of a security 有価証券の売出しに関する届出
registration of alteration 変更登記
registration of change of land category 地目変換届
registration of claims 債権の届出
registration of copyright 版権登録
registration of depreciation method 償却方法の届出
registration of design 意匠登録
registration of establishment 設立の登記
registration of incorporation 会社の設立登記
registration of lien 抵当権設定登記
registration of physical securities 証券からの登録
registration of signet for financial futures transaction 金融先物取引用印鑑届
registration of the right of pledge 質権登録
registration request 登録請求
registration statement 届出書
registration statement of securities 有価証券届出書
registration statement of securities report 有価証券報告書届出書
registration statement of tender offer 公開買付届出書
registration statement of withdrawal of tender offer 公開買付撤回届出書

R

registration system for corporate bonds and other non-JGB bonds 社債等登録制度
registration tax 登録税
registry office 登記所
regression 回帰
regression analysis 回帰分析
regression analysis method 回帰分析法
regression coefficient 回帰係数
regression equation 回帰方程式
regression model 回帰モデル
regressive expectations 回帰的期待
regressive tax 逆進税
regressive taxation 逆進課税
regular audit 定時監査
regular business 通常業務
regular delivery 通常受渡し
regular dividend 普通配当
regular fee 通常の費用
regular general meeting 定時総会
regular general meeting of shareholders 定時株主総会
regular interest 正規権
regular life insurance 普通生命保険
regular meeting of the Board of Governors 定例理事会
regular member 正会員
regular member handling off-floor distribution 立会外分売取扱正会員
regular members of the Tokyo Stock Exchange 東京証券取引所正会員
regular panel 招集陪審員名簿
regular price 通常の物価
regular purchase 普通の購入
regular settlement 翌営業日渡し
regular wage 基本給
regular way contract 普通契約
regular way of delivery 通常受渡し
regular way transaction 普通取引
regularity 規則性
regulated commodities 統制商品
regulated company 規制対象企業
regulated interest rate 規制金利
regulated investment company 規制投資会社
regulated market 規制市場
regulated prices 規制価格
regulation 規定
regulation of debt collection 回収規制
regulation of lending 融資規制
regulation of stock price 株価規制
Regulation S-X 規則 S-X
Regulation T excess T 規則超過証拠金
regulations according to the labor agreement 労働協約による規定
Regulations and Rules concerning the JGB Book-Entry System 国債振替決済業務規程
regulations for clearing and settlement 清算・決済規程
regulations for retirement allowance 退職金規程
regulations of financial statements 財務諸表規則
Regulations of Procedures of Hearings by the Ministry of Finance 財務省聴聞手続規則
regulations on foreign banks 外国銀行規制
regulations on large-lot loans 大口融資規制
regulator 規制監督当局
regulatory 規制上
regulatory action 行政措置
regulatory agency 規制当局
regulatory approvals 規制当局の承認
regulatory attention 規制当局の注目
regulatory authority 規制当局；行政官庁
regulatory capacity 行政能力
regulatory capital adequacy 自己資本比率規制
regulatory constraint 規制の制約
regulatory disposition 処置
regulatory distortion 規制監督上の歪み
regulatory environment 法規上の環境
regulatory examination 行政検査

regulatory factors 規制要因
regulatory field 規制分野
regulatory measure 規制措置
regulatory reform 行政改革
regulatory sanction 処分
rehabilitation loan 復興ローン
rehabilitation plan 再建計画
rehabilitation tax 再生税
rehabilitator 再建請負人
rehash 繰り返し説明をする
rehearing 再審理
rehypothecation 再担保設定
reimbursable expense 回収される費用
reimbursed expenses 立替経費
reimbursement 弁済
reimbursement authorization 補償支払授権書
reimbursement method 出来高払制
reimbursement obligation 補償債務
reimbursement of cost 原価の補償
reimbursement right 補填の権利
reimbursing bank 補償銀行
REINS (Real Estate Information System) 不動産情報ネットワークシステム
reinstate 復権する
reinstatement 保険契約の復活
reinsurance 再保険
reinsurance accounting 再保険会計
reinsurance agreement 再保険契約
reinsurance broker 再保険ブローカー
reinsurance ceded 出再保険
reinsurance claim 再保険金請求
reinsurance clause 再保険条項
reinsurance commission 再保険手数料
reinsurance contract 再保険契約
reinsurance credit 再保険貸
reinsurance fund 再保険資金
reinsurance leverage 再保険レバレッジ
reinsurance premium 再保険料
reinsurance proceeds 受取再保険金
reinsurance receivables 再保険受取勘定
reinsurance recovery 再保険金
reinsurance transaction 再保険取引
reinsurance treaty 再保険特約
reinvested value 再投資額
reinvestigation organization 異議審理庁
reinvestment 再投資
reinvestment privilege 再投資特権
reinvestment rate 再投資利率
reinvestment risk 再投資リスク
REIT (real estate investment trust) 不動産投資信託
rejected check 支払拒絶小切手
rejection 棄却
rejection certificate 拒絶証書
rejection rate 棄却率
related analysis 関連分析
related company 関係会社
related cost 関連原価
related expense 関連費用
related issue 関連銘柄
related laws 関係法令
related obligations 関連債務
related party 関係者；関連当事者
related party disclosure 関連当事者についての開示
related party transaction 関連当事者間取引
related risk 関連リスク
relational bank リレーショナル銀行
relational database リレーショナル・データベース
relationship bank 取引銀行
relationship lending リレーションシップ貸付
relationship management system 取引先総合管理
relative 相対
relative advantage 比較優位
relative autonomy 相対的な独立性
relative change 相対的変動
relative coupon effect 相対的なクーポン効果
relative credit risk 相対的信用リスク
relative differential 相対的格差
relative error 相対誤差

relative excepted risk 相対的免責危険
relative importance 相対的重要度
relative income 相対所得
relative income hypothesis 相対所得仮説
relative index 相対力指数
relative market value 相対市場価額
relative measures 相対的測度
relative ownership interest 相対的所有持ち分
relative performance 相対的パフォーマンス
relative power index 相対力指数
relative price 相対価格
relative probability 相対的な確率
relative ratio 関連比率
relative revenue 相対収益
relative sales value method 売価按分法
relative share 分配率
relative strength 相対的強弱度
relative valuation 相対評価
relative value 相対的価値
relative value analysis 相対価値分析
relative value anomaly 相対価値アノマリー
relaxation 緩和
relaxation of credit 金融緩和
relaxation of regulations 規制緩和
relaxation of tight money policy 金融緩和政策
release 解除
release clause 解除条項
release from debts 債務免除
release of foreclosure 差押解除
release of lien リーエンの放棄
release of security 担保解除
release of seizure 差押えの解除
release order 荷渡指図書
relegation 左遷
relevance 目的適合性
relevancy 関連性
relevant 関連した
relevant authorities 関係当局
relevant benefit 適格給付
relevant cost 関連原価
relevant information 適切な情報
relevant market 関連する市場
relevant measure 適切な測定値
relevant measurement 適切な測定
relevant range 適合範囲
reliability 信頼性
reliability exception 信頼性の欠如
reliable evidence 信頼できる証拠
reliance on 依拠
reliance on debt 借入依存
relief act 救済法
relief loan 救済融資
relief merger 救済合併
relief method 除却法
relief printing 凸版印刷
religious corporation 宗教法人
reload リロード
reload feature リロード特性
reload option リロード・オプション
relocation 移転；住替え
relocation of listed securities to other market 上場市場の変更
remain pressured against the dollar 対ドルで低下圧力がかかる
remainder 残存
remainder price 残存価格
remainder type 差額式
remainders of financial assets 金融資産の残存部分
remaining amount 残額
remaining asset 残りの資産
remaining carry 残存キャリー
remaining debt 残債
remaining economic age 経済的残存耐用年数
remaining employment period 残存勤務期間
remaining lease term 残存リース期間
remaining life of security 証券残存期間
remaining long ロングの状態にある
remaining monthly balance 未決済月次残高
remaining penalty period 残存ペナル

ティ期間
remaining period 残存期間
remaining period of the lease 賃貸契約の残存期間
remaining term 残存期間
remaining term of the predecessor 前任者の残任期間
remaining transitional amount 変更時差異未処理額
remaining useful life 残存耐用年数
remargin 追証
remarketed account receivables 再販売受取債権
remeasurement 再測定
remedy 救済方法
remedy for violation of private right 権利救済制度
REMIC (real estate mortgage investment conduit) 不動産モーゲージ投資コンディット；REMIC
reminder 督促状
reminder price 備忘価格
remittance abroad 外国送金
remittance advice 送金通知書
remittance check 送金小切手
remittance payable 支払送金
remittance slip 送金伝票
remittee 為替受取人
remitter 権原回復
remitting bank 仕向銀行
remote 可能性が少ない
remote contingency 実現可能性の低い偶発事象
remote possibility 起こりそうもない可能性
removal expenses 除却費用
removed assets 撤去資産
remuneration 報酬
remuneration expense 報酬費用
remuneration for personal services 人的役務の対価
remuneration of officers 役員報酬
render 言い渡す
rendering of service 役務の提供
renegotiated loans 金利減免債権
renegotiation 再交渉
renewable contract 更新可能契約
renewable term life insurance 更新可能定期生命保険
renewal 更新
renewal after the maturity 期限後書替継続
renewal certificate 更新証明書
renewal charge 更新料
renewal commission 継続手数料；更新手数料
renewal date 更新日
renewal expenses 取替費用
renewal fee 更新料
renewal of bills and notes 手形書き換え
renewal or change of the lease 借地契約の更新又は変更
renewal premium 更新保険料
renewal privilege 更新特典
renewed bout of deflation デフレのさらなる進行
renewed strength of yen 円の再びの上昇
renounce 拒絶する
rent arrears 延滞地代
rent charge 地代負担
rent control 家賃統制
rent coverage 賃料負担
rent expense リース料
rent income 賃貸料収入
rent on real estate 不動産賃貸料
rent payable 未払賃貸料
rent reasonably fixed 正当な地代
rent receivable 未収賃貸料
rent revenue 賃料収益
rent roll 地代表
rent service 地代奉仕
rent-free 賃貸料なしの
rental agents' commissions 賃借手数料
rental allowance 家賃手当
rental expense レンタル費用
rental income 賃貸料
rental market value 家賃相場
rental of real property 不動産の賃貸

rental revenue 賃貸収益
rental service 賃貸業
rental starts 賃貸住宅の着工戸数
rental value 賃貸価額
rented house 借家
rented house right 借家権
renter 賃借人
rentier class 不労所得者層
rents and royalties 賃貸料及び使用料収入
rents received 賃貸料収入
reoffering 再募集
reorganization 更生；再編成；組織変更
reorganization and rationalization of special public corporations 特殊法人の整理合理化
reorganization of industrial structure 産業構造調整
reorganization of industry 産業再編成
reorganization plan 更生計画
reorganization proceedings 更生手続き
repackage bond リパッケージ債
repair 修繕
repair and maintenance expense 修繕維持費
repair cost 修繕コスト
repair equalization reserve 修繕平均積立金
repair shop 修繕工場
repairing budget 修繕費予算
repairing expenses 修繕費
repairing risks insurance 船舶修繕保険
reparations 賠償金
repayable on demand 要求払債務
repayment 償還；返済
repayment at one time 一括完済
repayment compensation 弁済補償金
repayment conditions 返済条件
repayment date 返済期日
repayment due date 支払期日
repayment due within one year 一年内返済分
repayment installment 分割返済
repayment money 還付金
repayment moratorium 債務の返済猶予
repayment mortgage 元利返済型モーゲージ
repayment of capital 資本の払戻し
repayment of interest and principal 元利の支払い
repayment of liabilities 債務弁済
repayment of loan 借款返済
repayment period 返済期限
repayment rate 返済率
repayment risk 返済リスク
repayment schedule for borrowed money 借用金返済予定
repayment terms 償還期限
repealed taxes 廃止された税金
repeated calculation 反復計算
repeating audit 反復監査
repercussion effect 波及効果
replaced asset 取替資産
replaced property 買換資産
replaced to become the new book value 評価替えした
replacement 取替え
replacement asset 買換資産
replacement cost 再取得価格；再取得原価
replacement cost accounting 取替原価会計
replacement cost insurance 取替原価保険
replacement cost method 再調達原価法
replacement cost risk 置換コスト・リスク
replacement deposit 差換預託分
replacement expenses 取替費用
replacement financing 再資金調達
replacement income 代替所得
replacement investment 更新投資
replacement method 取替法
replacement of assets 資産の買換え
replacement of business property 事業

用資産の買換え
replacement of collateral 代り担保
replacement of stock certificates 株券の差替え
replacement of trustee 受託者の更迭
replacement option 代替オプション
replacement policy 乗換保険契約
replacement price 取替価格
replacement property by purchase 買換による資産の交換
replacement purchase 買換え
replacement rate 保険乗換率
replacement risk 再取得リスク
replacement swap 代替スワップ
replacement unit 取替単位
replacement value 再調達価額
replacement value insurance 新価保険
repledging 担保再設定
replenishment 補充
replicating portfolio 複製ポートフォリオ
replication 複製
repo market 現先市場；レポ市場
repo member レポ会員
repo rate レポ金利
report date 決算日
report form 報告式
report form balance sheet 報告式貸借対照表
report of independent auditors 監査報告書
report on examination 検査報告書
report on Japanese taxation by the Shoup Mission シャウプ税制報告書
report on profit and loss by segment 事業区分別損益報告
report on results of operations 経営成績の報告
report on state of purchase of treasury stocks 自己株券買付状況報告書
report on the settlement of accounts 決算報告書
reported asset values 公表ベースの資産価値
reported earnings 報告された利益
reported equity 財務報告上の株主資本
reported income tax 報告所得税
reported inflation 公表されたインフレ率
reported period 当期
reported profit 公表利益
reported term 当期の
reporting companies 決算会社
reporting company 報告会社
reporting currency 報告通貨
reporting enterprise 報告企業
reporting form 報告形式
reporting format 報告様式
reporting objective 報告目的
reporting of operating result 経営業績報告
reporting period 報告期間
reporting policy 報告の方針
reporting requirement 報告義務
reporting segment 報告セグメント
reporting system 報告制度
reporting unit 報告単位
repos 現先売買
repossession 商品引揚げ
representation 表明
representation letter 陳述書
representation work 表示作業
representations &warranties 表明と保証
representative consumer 代表的消費者
representative democracy 代表民主制
representative director 代表取締役
representative liquidator 代表清算人
representative money 代表貨幣
representative of corporation 法人の代表者
representative of employees 従業員代表
representative office 駐在員事務所
representative sample 代表的標本
representative suit 代表訴訟
representative trustee 代表受託者
representatives or administrators 代

表者又は管理人
representing issue 代表銘柄
repricing 価格改定
repricing date 金利更改時点
repricing date of interest rate 金利改訂日
repricing interval 金利更改期間
reproduction 再生産
reproduction cost 再生産原価
reproduction on a diminishing scale 縮小再生産
repudiation 拒絶
repurchase agreement 買戻条件付取引
repurchase interest rate レポ金利
repurchase obligation 買戻義務
repurchase price 再取得価格
repurchase rate レポ・レート
repurchase right 買戻請求権
repurchase transaction レポ取引
repurchases of bond 債券解約
reputation 評判
reputed owner 表見的所有者
request 請求
request for correction 更正の請求
request for reconsideration 審査請求
request for reinvestigation 異議申立
request for share distribution 交付要求
request for wage increase 賃上要求
request payment by securities 証券委託納付
requested return 依頼返却
requests for initial registration or initial deposit of issued JGSs 発行国債の当初登録・当初寄託請求
required amount 所要額
required capital coefficient 必要資本係数
required margin 証拠金所要額
required primary disclosures 基本的開示要求事項
required rate of return 要求利益率
required reserve rate 最低支払準備率
required reserve ratio 法定準備率
required return 予定投資収益率
required secondary disclosure 補足的開示要求事項
required success rate 必要成功率
requirements against 対抗要件
requirements for derecognition 認識の消滅要件
requirements for issuing bonds 適債基準
requiring careful management 管理に注意を要する
requisite 必要要件
requisition 依頼書
resale 再販；転売
resale price 再販価格
resale price maintenance 再販価格維持
resale price method 再販売価格基準法
rescheduling リスケジューリング；債務返済計画の変更
rescheduling of debt 債務のリスケジューリング
rescission 解約
rescue bond レスキュー債
rescue package 支援策
research and development 研究開発
research and development cost 研究開発費
research and development expenditures 研究開発費
research and development facilities 研究開発基盤
Research and Development Office 調査研究室
Research and Statistics Department 調査統計局
research cost 研究費
Research Division 調査課
research expenditure 調査費
research findings 研究成果
research institute 研究機関
Research Institute of Economy, Trade and Industry 経済産業研究所
Research Office 調査室
research phase 調査段階
research study 調査研究

resemblance 類似
reservation 難色；留保事項
reservation of ownership 所有権留保
reserve 準備金；引当金
reserve account 準備金勘定；積立金勘定；引当金勘定
reserve accounting 積立金会計
reserve accumulation 外貨準備
reserve adequacy 準備金の妥当性
reserve asset 準備資産
reserve bank 準備銀行
reserve basis 準備金計算基礎
reserve capital 準備資本
reserve cash 現金準備
reserve currency 準備通貨
reserve deposit requirement system 準備預金制度
reserve drawn down 準備金取崩額
reserve for accidents 災害準備金
reserve for additions 増設積立金
reserve for adjustment of sales returns 返品調整引当金
reserve for advanced depreciation 圧縮引当金
reserve for after-care of products 製品保証引当金
reserve for bad debts 貸倒引当金
reserve for bad loan 貸倒準備金
reserve for banknote issuance system 発行保証制度
reserve for bond dealing losses 債券取引損失引当金
reserve for bonus payment 賞与引当金
reserve for compensation for completed works 完成工事補償引当金
reserve for compensation for losses 欠損填補積立金
reserve for construction 新築積立金
reserve for contingencies 危険準備金
reserve for corporate tax 法人税引当金
reserve for depreciation and amortization 償却準備金
reserve for depreciation of real estate 不動産減価償却準備金
reserve for development of overseas market 海外市場開拓準備金
reserve for discount 割引準備金
reserve for dividend 配当積立金
reserve for employee retirement allowance 退職給与引当金
reserve for employees retirement allowance 従業員退職給与引当金
reserve for encumbrance 支出負担準備金
reserve for equalization of dividend 配当平均準備金
reserve for expansion 設備拡張積立金
reserve for extraordinary casualty 異常危険準備金
reserve for foreign exchange fluctuation 外国為替変動準備金
reserve for guarantee for completed work 製品保証等引当金
reserve for improvement of structure of small-and medium-sized enterprise 中小企業構造改善準備金
reserve for intercompany profit 振替利益引当金
reserve for inventory fluctuation 商品価格変動準備金
reserve for investment loss 投資損失引当金
reserve for liability 負債引当金
reserve for liability for commodity transactions 商品取引責任準備金
reserve for loan loss as stipulated in the tax law 個別貸倒引当金
reserve for loss contingency 偶発損失引当金
reserve for loss from fluctuation of foreign exchange rate 為替変動損失準備金
reserve for loss from investment in development of resources 資源開発投資損失準備金
reserve for loss from securities transactions 証券取引損失準備金

reserve for loss on goods unsold 返品調整引当金
reserve for outstanding claims 保険金支払準備金
reserve for overhead 間接費準備金
reserve for pension fund 退職給与積立金
reserve for pensions 恩給引当金
reserve for possible loan losses 貸倒引当金
reserve for possible losses on foreign exchange transactions 外国為替等取引損失引当金
reserve for possible losses on securities transactions 有価証券取引損引当金
reserve for prevention of pollution 公害防止準備金
reserve for price fluctuation 価格変動準備金
reserve for qualifying retirement pension 適格退職年金積立金
reserve for redemption of funds 基金償却積立金
reserve for renewals and replacements 改築積立金
reserve for repairs 修繕引当金
reserve for retirement and severance allowance 退職給与引当金
reserve for retirement annuity 退職年金積立金
reserve for retirement of preferred stock 優先株償還準備金
reserve for revaluation 再評価準備金
reserve for sinking fund 減債基金積立金
reserve for special purpose 特定準備金
reserve for specific purpose 目的積立金
reserve for stock dealing losses 株式取引損失引当金
reserve for tax liability 納税引当金
reserve for tax payment 納税引当金
reserve fund 準備金；積立金
reserve liability 引当金債務
reserve maintenance period 積み期間
reserve period 積立期間
reserve position 準備ポジション
reserve ratio 支払準備率
reserve ratio for credit 信用部分に対する引当率
reserve ratio operation 支払準備率操作
reserve requirement 預金準備率
reserve requirement operation 準備率操作
reserve requirement policy 支払準備率操作
reserve requirement ratio 準備率
reserve requirements of depositary institutions 預金受入機関の所要準備
reserve requirements system 支払準備制度
reserve system 準備制度
reserve tranche リザーブ・トランシェ
reserved profit 留保利益
reserved property 留保資産
reserved surplus 引当剰余金
reset bond リセット債
reset date 金利更改日
reset frequency 更改頻度
resident 居住者
resident alien 居住外国人
resident auditor 駐在監査人
resident card 住民票
resident doctor 研修医
resident foreign corporation 居住外国法人
resident foreign currency deposits 居住者外貨預金
resident registration 住民登録
resident tax 住民税
residential energy credit 住居エネルギー税控除
residential investment 住宅投資
residential mortgage 住宅抵当証券；住宅ローン
residential property 居住用財産

residential property market 住宅用不動産市場
residential rent property 住宅用賃貸物件
residual analysis 残差分析
residual assets 残余財産
residual benefit 残余利益
residual claim 残余請求権
residual class 残余クラス
residual cost 残余原価
residual distribution 残余配分
residual equity 残余持分；潜在株式
residual impact 限定的な影響
residual income 残余利益
residual interest 残余持分
residual interests in the assets 残余財産権
residual market 残余市場
residual maturity 残余期間
residual net income 残余純利益
residual profit 残余利益
residual property 残余財産
residual ratio 残存率
residual return 残差収益率
residual risk 残余リスク
residual share 残余配分
residual standard deviation 残差標準偏差
residual term 残余項
residual valuation 残存評価
residual value 残存価額
residuary estate 残余財産
residuary outlay 残余支出
residue 残余部分
residue of the loan ローンの残存部分
resiliency 速やかな調整
resilient test 弾力性検査
resistance level 関門；抵抗線
resistance line 抵抗線
resistance operation 逆張り
resolution 決議
resolution of court case 訴訟事件の解決
resolution of NPL problem 不良債権問題の解決
resolution of the failed financial institution 破綻金融機関の整理
resource allocation 資源配分
resource distribution 資源配分
resources 資源
respective それぞれの
respite 弁済の猶予
respondent 回答者
response of market 市場の反応
responsibility 責任
responsibility accounting 責任会計
responsibility costing 責任原価計算
responsibility for financial statements 財務諸表に対する責任
responsibility hedge clause 責任回避条項
responsible and recognized dealer 主要ディーラー
rest 一服する
restated 修正後
restated balance 修正再表示残高
restatement 修正再表示
restatement of balance sheet 貸借対照表の修正再表示
restitution 原状回復
restitution costs 損害賠償金
restoration 復権；復興
restoration from disaster 災害復旧
restoration of suspended membership 会員の復権
restoration premium 復元保険料
restraining order 禁止命令
restraint 引締め
restraint measures 引締め政策
restraint of trade 営業制限
restraint of trade agreement 取引制限契約
restraint on alienation 譲渡禁止
restraint on anticipation 未収利益処分禁止
restrict sales 売り惜しみ
restricted account 制限付き勘定
restricted asset 拘束資産
restricted deposit 拘束預金
restricted fund 使途限定資金

restricted L/C (letter of credit) 買取銀行指定信用状
restricted period 制限期間
restricted receipts 特定収入高
restricted resources 規制のある資源
restricted share 制限株式
restricted stock 制限株
restricted surplus 制限付剰余金
restriction of order acceptance 受託制限
restriction of price range 値幅制限
restriction on dividend payment 配当制限
restriction on floatation ratio 起債制限比率
restriction on stock holding 株式の保有制限
restriction on the growth of bank loans 貸出増加額規制
restriction on transfer of shares 株式譲渡制限
restriction on transferability 譲渡制限
restrictions on trading 取引の制限
restrictive condition 制約条件
restrictive covenant 制限条項；不作為約款
restrictive endorsement 制限裏書
restrictive fiscal policy 緊縮財政政策
restrictive injunction 制限的差止命令
restrictive monetary policy 金融引締政策
restrictive practice 制限的慣行
restrictive provision 制限条項
restructured debt 条件変更負債
restructured financial liabilities 再構築された金融負債
restructured loan 貸出条件緩和債権；焦付融資
restructuring capital リストラ資金
restructuring charge リストラ経費
restructuring fund 再生ファンド
restructuring of lending terms 貸出条件緩和
restructuring period リストラの時期
restructuring plan 再建計画
restructuring related stock リストラ関連株
restructuring support 再建支援
resulting adjustment 結果生じる修正
resulting information 結果もたらされる情報
resulting trust 復帰信託
results 実績
results and projections 実績と見込み
results of business 営業実績
Results of Consolidated International Banking Statistics in Japan BIS国際資金取引統計の日本分集計結果
Results of Locational International Banking Statistics in Japan BIS国際与信統計の日本分集計結果
results of operating activities 営業損益
results of ordinary operations 経常損益
Results of Regular Derivatives Market Statistics in Japan (Yoshikuni Statistics) デリバティブ取引に関する定例市場報告（吉国委統計）の日本分集計結果
results of the tax examination 税務調査の結果
resumption of capital inflow 資金流入の再開
resumption of dividend 復配
resumption of intervention operations 市場介入の再開
resumption of suspended trading 取引再開
resumption of trading 取引の再開
resurgence 再燃
retail 小売
retail accounting 小売業会計
retail and consumer spending sector stock 消費支出関連銘柄
retail bank リテール・バンク
retail banking リテール・バンキング
retail broker 小売ブローカー
retail business 小売業
retail cost 小売原価

R

retail credit card 流通系カード
retail excise 小売税
retail industry 小売業界
retail institutions リテール金融機関
retail insurance business 小口保険業
retail inventory method 小売棚卸法
retail investor 最終投資家
retail market 小売市場
retail method 売価還元法
retail payments 小口決済
retail price 小売価格
retail price inflation 小売物価インフレーション
retail sales amount 小売売上高
retail sales tax 小売売上税
retail selling price 小売売価
retail store inventories 小売在庫
retail trade industry 小売業
retained cash flow 手元キャッシュフロー
retained earnings 利益剰余金；留保利益
retained earnings appropriated for bond 減債積立金
retained earnings appropriated for the re-issuance of treasury stock 自己株式再発行積立利益剰余金
retained earnings appropriated for the retirement of bonds 減債積立利益剰余金
retained earnings at the beginning of a period 前期繰越利益金
retained earnings ratio 社内留保率
retained earnings statement 利益剰余金計算書
retained interests 留保持ち分
retained profit 内部留保
retained surplus 利益準備金
retaining fee 弁護士顧問料
retaining lien 弁護士リーエン
retaliatory duties 報復関税
retention 留保
retention money 留保金
retention of earnings 利益留保
retention quotient 正味保険料比率
retention rate 留保率
retention requirement 証拠金維持率
retired employee 退職した従業員
retired equipment 廃残設備
retired from active use 実際の使用が不可能となった
retiree 退職者
retirement 消却
retirement account 退職勘定
retirement accounting 除却会計
retirement accumulation 退職金積立
retirement allowance 退職給与
retirement allowance in a lump sum 退職金の一括支給
retirement allowance plan 退職金制度
retirement allowance regulations 退職給与規程
retirement annuity 退職年金
retirement annuity business 退職年金業務
retirement annuity reserve 退職年金積立金
retirement benefit 退職給付
retirement benefit accumulation 退職給付積立
retirement benefit obligation 退職給付債務
retirement benefit plan 退職給付制度
retirement benefit scheme 退職給付スキーム
retirement benefit trust 退職給付信託
retirement by purchase 買入償却
retirement cost 除却費
retirement coverage 退職保障
retirement date 定年退職日
retirement fund 退職年金基金
retirement income 退職所得
retirement income insurance 退職所得保険
retirement income policy 退職所得付保険
retirement lump-sum grants 退職一時金
retirement method 廃棄法
retirement mutual aid pension 退職共

済年金
retirement of asset 資産の除去
retirement of bond 社債消却
retirement of redeemed preferred stock 償還優先株の償還
retirement of shares 株式消却
retirement of stock 株式の消却
retirement of the asset 資産の廃棄
retirement of treasury stock 自己株式の消却
retirement pay 退職金
retirement pension 退職年金
retirement policy 退職年金保険
retirement price 除却価格
retirement related benefits 退職関連給付
retirement unit 除却単位
retirement vehicle 退職年金
retractable maturity 短縮可能満期
retraining 再研修
retrenchment 切り詰め
retroactive 遡及して
retroactive adjustments 遡及修正
retroactive conversion 遡及転換
retroactive discount 遡及割引率
retroactive levy 遡及徴収
retroactive restatement 遡及修正報告書
retroactively to a date in the past 過去に遡って
retrocession 再々保険
retrogressive accounting 遡求計算
retrospective application 遡及適用
retrospective law 遡及法
retrospective policy 遡及保険
retrospective rate 遡及料率
retrospective restatement 遡及修正再表示
retrust 再信託
return 申告
return (ratio) on capital employed 使用総資本利益率
return (ratio) on sales 売上高利益率
return after due date 期限後申告
return and payment 申告及び納付
return blank 申告用紙
return commission 戻し口銭
return distribution リターン分布
return for no claim 無事故払戻し
return form for insurance premium deduction 保険料控除申告書
return form for retirement income 退職所得申告書
return freight 戻し運賃
return inward 戻り品
return line リターン・ライン
return maximizer リターン極大者
return of insurance premium 保険料返還
return of premium プレミアム還元
return of substitution part 代行部分の返上
return of substitutional part of Employees' Pension Fund 厚生年金基金代行返上
return of the appropriation to the retained earnings 利益剰余金積立の取崩し
return on capital 資本利益率
return on common equity 普通株主資本利益率
return on contributions 掛金額の収益率
return on equity capital 株主資本利益率
return on financial assets 金融資産利益率
return on fixed assets 固定資産に対する収益率
return on invested capital 投下資本利益率
return on investment 投資利益率
return on net worth 株主資本利益率
return on ownership 所有リターン
return on physical capital 物的資本利益率
return on plan assets 制度資産運用益
return on policy 保険契約収益率
return on the capital investment 設備投資の利益率

return premium for cancellation 解約返戻金
return to equilibrium 均衡への回帰
return to shareholder 株主への還元
return volatility リターン変動幅
return without voting 無投票当選
return-of-premium rider 保険料返還特約
returned check 返却小切手
returned goods unsold 返品
returned materials report 原材料返還表
returned non-sufficient-fund check 不渡小切手
revaluation 平価切上げ
revaluation decrease 再評価減少額
revaluation excess 再評価差額
revaluation increase 再評価による増加
revaluation of assets 資産評価換え
revaluation of building 建物再評価
revaluation of stock 株式評価換え
revaluation profit 再評価益
revaluation reserve 再評価積立金
revaluation surplus 再評価剰余金
revaluation surplus reserve 再評価積立金
revaluation surpluses and deficits 再評価損益
revalue 再評価する
revalued amount 再評価額
revalued assets 再評価資産
revalued carrying amount 再評価後の帳簿価額
revealed preference 顕示選好
revenue 売上(非製造業)
revenue abatement method 総支払減額法
revenue account 収入勘定
revenue agent 歳入代理店
revenue and expenditure budget 歳入歳出予算
revenue and expenditure of general account 一般会計歳入歳出
revenue anticipation note 歳入見込証券
revenue bond 歳入債
revenue by segment セグメント別収益
revenue corporate bonds 収益社債
revenue curve 収益曲線
revenue deficit 歳入欠陥
revenue distribution 収益分布
revenue earning activity 収益活動
revenue expenditure 収益支出
revenue from account-opening fees 口座開設金収入
revenue from fund operations 基本財産運用収入
revenue from government enterprise 官業収入
revenue from leases リース収益
revenue from merchandise sale 商品販売による収益
revenue from operations 営業収益
revenue from public bond 公債収入
revenue generating activity 収益稼得活動
revenue generation covering expenditure 収支相償
Revenue Management and Collection Department 徴収部
Revenue Management Division 徴収部管理課
revenue maximization hypothesis 売上高最大化仮説
revenue model 収益モデル
revenue neutral 歳入中立
revenue neutrality 歳入の中立性
revenue officer 収税官
revenue on foreign exchange trading 外国為替売買益
revenue pressures 減収圧力
revenue producing activity 収益活動
revenue projection 収益予測
revenue realization 収益の実現
revenue received in advance 前受収益
revenue recognition 収益の認識
revenue recognition criteria 収益の認識基準
revenue recognizing standard 収益の

R

認識基準
revenue reserve amount 利益積立金額
revenue reserves 利益積立金
revenue securities 歳入債
revenue sharing 歳入交付
revenue sources 歳入源
revenue stamp 収入印紙
revenue sub-agent 歳入復代理店
revenue tax 売上税
reversal 相場の反転
reversal auction 逆入札
reversal cost method 逆算法
reversal criteria 戻入基準
reversal day リバーサル・デー
reversal entry 反対仕訳
reversal in the trend トレンドの転換
reversal of difference 差異の解消
reversal of judgment 判決の破棄
reversal of provision 引当金の戻入
reversal of reserve after revaluation 洗替による取崩し
reversal of reserve for overseas investment loss 海外投資損失準備金戻入れ
reversal of reserve for overseas investments 海外投資損失準備金戻し入れ
reversal of reserve for price fluctuation 価格変動準備金戻し入れ
reversal of special bad debts reserve 債権償却特別勘定の取崩し
reversal of surplus 積立金戻し入れ
reversal of taxation 課税処分取消し
reversal pattern 反転パターン
reversal profit on conversion right for shares 株式転換権戻入益
reverse acquisition 逆取得
reverse conversion 顧客株式による金利稼ぎ
reverse direction 逆方向
reverse dual bond リバース・デュアル債
reverse dual currency bond リバース・デュアル・カレンシー債
reverse dual currency debt 逆デュアル・カレンシー債
reverse floater 逆変動利付債
reverse floating rate note 逆変動利付債
reverse hedge 逆ヘッジ
reverse income tax 逆所得税
reverse leverage 逆レバレッジ
reverse leveraged buyout 逆レバレッジド・バイアウト
reverse mortgage リバース・モーゲージ
reverse offset 逆相殺
reverse operation 逆算
reverse preemption 逆優先権
reverse remittance 逆為替
reverse repo リバース・レポ
reverse repurchase agreement リバース・レポ
reverse share split 逆株式分割
reverse split 逆分割
reverse split of stocks 株式併合
reverse swap リバース・スワップ
reverse takeover 逆買収
reverse telegraphic transfer 電信取立為替
reverse transactions 逆取引
reverse yield gap 利回りの逆乖離
reverse zero coupon swap リバース・ゼロ・クーポン・スワップ
reversed and remanded 破棄差戻
reversed swap 逆スワップ
reversing entry 反対記入
reversing the reserve amount in full to the income in the following period 洗替
reversing trading 反対売買
reversion 復帰財産権
reversionary annuity 復帰年金
reversionary beneficiary 承継保険受取人
reversionary bonus 保険金増額配当
revert to the following day 翌日に繰り下げる
revert to the previous day 前日に繰り

下げる
review 審査
review of financial statements 財務諸表のレビュー
review of the quality of assets 資産査定
revisable trust 修正可能信託
revise downward 下方修正する
revise upward 上方修正する
revised average stock price 修正平均株価
revised budget 修正予算
revised return 修正申告
revised statutes 修正法律
revision 改訂
revision of office regulation 内規の改正
revision of the profit and loss of prior years 過年度損益修正
revision risk 修正リスク
revitalize economic activity 景気を上向かせる
revival of judgment 判決の復活
revival of monetary policy 金融政策の復活
revival of will 遺言の復活
revived quotation 吹き値
revocable L/C (letter of credit) 取消可能信用状
revocable trust 取消可能信託
revocation 撤回；取消
revocation of approval to filing blue return 青色申告承認の取消し
revocation of clearing qualification 清算資格の取消
revocation of probate 検認撤回
revocation of trading qualification 取引資格の取消
revocation of will 遺言の撤回
revocation suit 取消訴訟
revoke 取消す
revolutionary 革新的な
revolving card リボルビング・カード
revolving collateral 根担保
revolving credit リボルビングクレジット
revolving fund 回転資金
revolving guarantee 根保証
revolving L/C (letter of credit) 回転信用状
revolving line of credit 極度貸付枠
revolving loan リボルビング・ローン
revolving trade 回転商い
revolving underwriting facilities リボルビング引受保証枠
reward 報酬
rewinding of the discount 割引の巻戻
rewording 読み替え
rewriting 書換の
RFC (reconstruction finance company) 復興金融会社
RFI (request for information) 情報の要請
RFP (request for proposal) 提案依頼
RIA (registered investment adviser) 登録投資顧問
RIC (registered investment company) 登録投資会社
Ricardo effect リカード効果
rich sector 割高なセクター
rider 特約（保険）；付加条項
rider of redemption by the drawing of lots 抽選償還特約
RIE (recognized investment exchange) 承認証券取引所
RIF (recognized investment exchange) 公認証券取引所
rigged market 相場操縦
right and interest 利権
right in rem 物権
right issue to shareholders 株主に対する割当
right not to pay before due date 期限の利益
right of access アクセス権
right of access to courts 裁判請求権
right of anticipation 期限前返済権
right of avoidance 否認権
right of beneficiary 受益権
right of cancellation 解約権

right of claim 請求権
right of collective bargaining 団体交渉権
right of credit availability クレジット利用権
right of defense 抗弁権
right of design 意匠権
right of eminent domain 土地収用権
right of first refusal 最優先引受権
right of free disposal 自由処分権
right of indemnity 求償権
right of inheritance 相続権
right of lease 賃借権
right of petition 請願権
right of pledge 質権
right of priority 先取権
right of recourse 償還請求権
right of redemption 権利買戻権
right of rescission 契約の解除権
right of resumption 取戻権
right of survivorship 生存者の取得権
right of taxation 課税権
right of trademark 商標権
right offering 株主割当発行
right to assert claims 抗弁権
right to audit 監査権
right to begin 開始権
right to benefit 年金受給権
right to claim refund 返還請求権
right to claim the return of clearing margin 取引証拠金返還請求権
right to claim the return of the clearing fund 清算基金の返還請求権
right to counsel 弁護士の援助を受ける権利
right to obtain foreign money 外貨割当権
right to repurchase 買戻権
right to revoke fraudulent act 詐害行為取消権
right to use 使用権
right to work law 労働権法
rights 権利
rights and liabilities of members 社員権
rights and obligations 権利と義務
rights attached to property 財産に付属する権利
rights attaching to the share 株式に付されている権利
rights existing on real estate 不動産上の権利
rights for profit sharing 共益権
rights issue 株主割当発行増資
rights of beneficiaries 受益者の権利
rights off 権利落ち
rights offering 株主割当
rights on 権利付き
rights receipts 権利預り証
rights-off shares 権利落株式
rigidity 硬直性
rigidity of price 価格硬直性
Riksbank スウェーデン中央銀行
rise across the board 全面高
rise in price 価格上昇
rise in yields 利回り上昇
rise interest rate 金利上昇
rise on stock price 株価上昇
rise-and-fall market 往来相場
rising bottom 上昇トレンドライン
rising phase 上げ局面
rising quotation 上げ相場
rising yield environment 利回りの上昇局面
risk adjustment リスク調整
risk and reward リスクと報酬
risk appetite リスク選好
risk appraisal リスク評価
risk arbitrage リスク・アービトラージ
risk arising from changes in regulations 規制変更リスク
risk arising from changes in tax law 税制変更リスク
risk arising from technology development 技術進歩リスク
risk assessment リスク評価
risk asset ratio リスク・アセット比率
risk assets 危険資産
risk averse attitude リスク回避的態度

risk aversion リスク回避
risk averter リスク回避者
risk based capital standards リスク・ベースの自己資本基準
risk based premium リスク・ベースの保険料
risk bearing capital リスク関連資本
risk capital リスク・キャピタル
risk category リスク・カテゴリー；リスク分類
risk characteristics リスク特性
risk class リスクの種類
risk control リスク管理
risk country control リスク・カントリー・コントロール
risk covered リスクカバー
risk decomposition リスク要素分解
risk differentials リスク格差
risk disclosure statement リスク開示書
risk distribution リスク分散
risk diversification リスク分散
risk estimation リスク見積り
risk evaluation リスク評価
risk exposure リスク・エクスポージャー
risk factor リスク・ファクター
risk free 信用リスクがない
risk free transaction 無リスク取引
risk hedge リスクヘッジ
risk information リスク情報
risk insurance リスク保険
risk insurance product リスク保険商品
risk intermediary function リスク仲介機能
risk lover リスク愛好者
risk management リスク・マネジメント
risk management by financial institutions 金融機関のリスク管理
risk management loan リスク管理債権
risk management policy リスク管理方針
risk management strategy リスク管理戦略
risk management system リスク管理体制
risk neutral attitude リスク・ニュートラル姿勢
risk neutral measure リスク・ニュートラル測度
risk neutral probability リスク・ニュートラル確率
risk of principal 元本リスク
risk parameter リスク要因
risk penalty リスク・ペナルティ
risk perception profile リスク認識プロファイル
risk picture リスク見通し
risk preference リスク選好
risk premium リスク・プレミアム
risk priced in 織り込み済みのリスク
risk profile リスク特性
risk reduction リスク削減
risk reduction measure リスク軽減手段
risk reduction or elimination リスク減殺
risk reduction strategy リスク軽減戦略
risk return preference リスクとリターンの選好
risk sector リスク・セクター
risk securities リスク証券
risk seeking 危険愛好的；リスク負担
risk seeking attitude リスク選好態度
risk selection リスク選択
risk sensitive index リスク感応度指標
risk sharing リスク分散
risk structure リスク構造
risk structure of discount rate 割引率のリスク構造
risk taking リスク負担
risk threshold リスク限度額
risk tolerance リスク許容度
risk transfer リスク移転
risk underwriting リスク査定
risk weight リスク・ウエート
risk-adjusted analysis リスク調整分析

risk-adjusted approach リスク調整法
risk-adjusted assets リスク調整済資産
risk-adjusted capital リスク調整済資本
risk-adjusted discount rate リスク調整後の割引率
risk-adjusted return リスク調整済収益
risk-based capital リスクベース資本金
risk-based capital ratio リスク・ベース自己資本比率
risk-controlled リスク制御
risk-free assets 無リスク資産
risk-free interest rate 無リスク金利
risk-free investment 無リスク投資
risk-free rate 無リスク利率
risk-free real rate of interest 無リスク実質金利
risk-free return 無リスク・リターン
risk-free securities 無リスク証券
risk-managed claims リスク管理債権
risk-monitored loans リスク債権
risk-neutral valuation リスクニュートラル評価法
risk-return group リスク・収益グループ
risk-return relationship リスクと収益の関係
risk-return trade-off リスクと収益率のトレードオフ
riskier assets 高いリスクの資産
riskless arbitrage 無リスク裁定
riskless assets 安全資産
riskless transaction リスクのない取引
risks of loss and theft 紛失・盗難のリスク
risks on transactions 取引に係るリスク
risky リスクの大きい
risky assets リスク資産
risky assets mix リスク資産ミックス
RLT (rehabilitate-lease-transfer) リハビリ・リース譲渡
RMBS (residential mortgage backed securities) 住宅用不動産担保証券
ROA (return on assets) 資産利益率
road show 説明会
robot teller ロボット・テラー
robust 強固な
robust analysis 確実な分析
robust domestic demand 力強い内需
robust earnings 業績好調
robust home sales 好調な住宅販売
rocket scientist ハイテク商品開発者
ROE (return on equity) 株主資本利益率
ROI (return on investment) 投資収益率
ROL (reduction option loan) 金利選択権付ローン
ROL (Romanian leu) ルーマニア・レウ
roll 人名簿
roll down ロール・ダウン
roll forward ロール・フォワード
roll from 10 yrs to WI (when-issued) 10 年物から新発債に乗り換える
roll over 満期書替
rollback ロールバック
rolled into a new loan 新規ローンに含めた
roller coaster swap ローラーコースター・スワップ
rolling down effect ロール・ダウン効果
rolling forward 前倒し
rolling readjustment 波動調整
rolling settlement ローリング決済
rolling yield ローリング・イールド
rolling-forward procedure 先送法
rollover credit 借換え
rollover date 金利更改日
rollover loan ロールオーバー・ローン
rollover of a hedging instrument ヘッジ手段の更新
roly poly CD ローリー・ポーリーＣＤ
Roosa bond ローザ・ボンド
Roosa effect ローザ効果
Roosa plan ローザ構想
root of title 権原の基礎
rotational system 輪番制

R

rough balance sheet 概算貸借対照表
rough cost 概算原価
rough cost book 原価概算表
rough number 概数
round down 切下げる
round lot 最低取引単位；単位株式
round number 概数
round off 四捨五入する
round trip transaction 往復取引
round up 切上げる
round-the-clock market 24時間市場
roundabout production 迂回生産
roundabout trade 迂回貿易
rounding convention 端数桁処理方法
rounding off in calculation 四捨五入
rounding reversal pattern ラウンディング・リバーサル・パターン
route 回送する
routed order ルーティッド・オーダー
routine business 日常業務
routine tasks 単純作業
routine work 経常的な作業
routing 手順
royalties received for use of patents 受入特許権使用料
royalty ロイヤルティ
royalty as to know-how ノウハウ使用料
royalty interest 所有権利権
royalty of patent right 特許権使用料
royalty of the copyright 著作権の使用料
royalty on a book 印税
royalty to be paid every fixed time 定時払使用料
royalty trust ロイヤルティ信託
RP (repurchase agreement) 買戻契約
RP market レポ市場
RPI (retail price index) 小売物価指数
RRSP (registered retirement savings plan) 登録退職金貯蓄制度
RSA (rate sensitive asset) 金利感応資産
RSG (rate sensitive gap) 金利感応ギャップ
RSG (Revenue Support Grant) 政府補助金
RSI (relative strength index) 相対力指数
RSL (rate sensitive liability) 金利感応負債
RTC (Resolution Trust Corporation) 整理信託公社
RTGS (real time gross settlement) 即時グロス決済
RTS (real-time settlement) 即時決済
RUB (Russian ruble) ロシア・ルーブル
rubber product industry ゴム製品業界
RUF (revolving underwriting facility) リボルビング・アンダーライティング・ファシリティ
ruin the reputation 信用を失墜させる
rule absolute 絶対命令
rule against accumulations 永久積立禁止則
rule against perpetuities 永久権禁止の原則
rule day 命令日
rule of law 法の支配
rule of reason 合理の原則
rule off 締め出す
rule out 除外する
rulemaking board 規則制定委員会
rules 規約
rules for action 行為規約
rules for the preparation of financial statements 財務諸表準則
rules of auction 競争売買の原則
rules of thumb 経験則
rules on handling of shares 株式取扱規則
Rules on Margin and Transfer of Unsettled Contracts Pertaining to Futures/Option Contract 先物・オプション取引に係る証拠金及び未決済約定の引継ぎ等に関する規則
rules on pension plan 年金規約
rules on the board of directors 取締役会規則

rules on timely disclosure 適時開示に関する規則
ruling 決定
ruling out 除外
run below 下回る
run upon a bank 取付け
run-down 相場表要約
run-off 契約終了後の残存責任
runaway gap ランナウェイ・ギャップ
running account 当座勘定
running balance ある時点のネット・ポジション
running cost 運転費
running inventory 常時棚卸し
running inventory method 継続棚卸法
running of the market 市況状況
running royalty 継続的使用料
running stock 正常在庫
rush order 注文の殺到
Russell Index ラッセル指数
RWF (Rwanda franc) ルワンダ・フラン
ryo ken 糧券

S

S/O (shipping order) 船積指図書
s-curve S字カーブ
S&L (savings and loan association) 貯蓄貸付組合
S&P 100 spot option S&P100 現物オプション
S&P 500 Stock Price Index S&P500 種株価指数
S&P futures S&P 先物
SA (season adjusted) 季節調整済の
SAAJ (Security Analysts Association of Japan) 日本証券アナリスト協会
sacrifice 犠牲
sacrifice sale 投げ売り
saddle point 鞍点
SAFE (synthetic agreement for forward exchange) 合成為替予約
safe custody 保護預り
safe custody system 保護預り制度
safe deposit box insurance 貸金庫保険
safe harbor セーフハーバー
safe harbor accord セーフハーバー協定
safe harbor lease セーフハーバー・リース
safe-pledge 保釈保証人
safeguard clause セーフガード条項
safeguard provision セーフガード条項
safekeeping deposit 保護預り
safety factor 安全率
safety margin 安全係数
safety margin analysis 安全力分析
safety net セーフティ・ネット
safety reserves 安全準備金
safety stock 安全手持量
safety valve 安全弁
SAFEX (South African Futures Exchange) 南アフリカ先物取引所
sag 軟調
SAIF (Savings Association Insurance Fund) 貯蓄金融機関保険基金
saitori member 才取会員
salaries 給料
salaries and wages 賃金
salary 給与
salary deduction account 給与天引口座
salary deferral 給与繰延べ
salary freeze 給与凍結
salary from secondary source 従たる給与
salary growth 給与の上昇
salary increase 昇給
salary pension plan 給与年金制度
salary projections 給与予測
salary reduction plan 給与天引制度
salary savings 給与天引
salary scale 給与指数
sale 販売
sale amount 売上代金
sale and leaseback transaction セール・アンド・リースバック取引
sale and purchase on credit 掛売買
sale and return 解除条件付き売買
sale by agent 代理販売
sale by brand 銘柄売買
sale by bulk 一括売買
sale by description 表示による売買
sale by grade or type 規格売買
sale by specification 仕様書売買
sale by subscription 予約販売
sale consideration 売却の対価
sale for cash 現金販売
sale in gross 一括売り
sale interchange 売上交換
sale leaseback transaction セール・リースバック取引
sale of goods 財貨の販売
sale of investment 投資の売却
sale on account 掛売り

sale on an underwriting basis 引受売出し
sale on customer's account 顧客の委託に基づく売り付け
sale on standard 標準物売買
sale or return 返還権付売買
sale price 取引価格
sale to arrive 未着品販売
sale transaction 売付
sale value 売却価額
sale with buy-back option 買戻条件付販売
sale with return right 解除条件付売買
sales 売上
sales (volume) budget 売上高予算
sales account 売上勘定
sales accounting 販売会計
sales allowance 売上値引
sales amount 販売金額
sales analysis 売上分析
sales and general administrative expenses 販売管理費
sales and purchases on commission 手数料売買
sales at unreasonably high price 著しく高い価格での販売
sales basis 売上基準
sales book 売上帳
sales budget 販売予算
sales by market segment 市場別売上
sales charge 販売手数料
sales commission 販売手数料；売上歩合
sales contract 売買契約
sales contracts commitments 先物引渡契約
sales cost 売上原価
sales credit 売掛債権
sales department 営業部
sales discount 売上値引
sales earnings 営業収入
sales finance 販売金融
sales finance company 販売金融会社
sales for this term 当期売上高
sales force 販売力
sales forecast 売上予測
sales forecasting 売上高予測
sales growth rate 売上伸び率
sales indicators 売上実績
sales invoice 売上送り状
sales journal 売上仕訳帳
sales ledger 売上元帳
sales literature 販売資料
sales load 販売手数料
sales method 販売方法
sales mix 売上品構成；セールス・ミックス
sales mix variance 売上構成差異
sales network 販路
sales of bond 債券設定
sales of corporate bonds by purchasers 社債消化状況
sales of existing homes 中古住宅販売
sales of FBs (financing bills) under repurchase agreements 政府短期証券売現先オペ
sales of investment trusts 投資信託設定
sales of TBs (treasury bills) /FBs (financing bills) under repurchase agreements 短期国債売現先オペ
sales of TBs (treasury bills) under repurchase agreements 割引短期国債売現先オペ
sales office 営業所
sales on approval 試用販売
sales on consignment 受託販売
sales price 売出価格
sales price variance 販売価格差異
sales proceeds 売上額
sales profit ratio 売上利益率
sales promotion 販売促進
sales promotion expense 販売促進費
sales quota 販売割当
sales rebate 売上割戻し
sales rebate with special payment terms 特別支出条件付売上割引
sales record 販売帳票
sales return 売上の戻り
sales revenue 売上収益

sales slip 売上伝票
sales subsidiary 販売子会社
sales tax 売上税
sales to accounts receivable 売掛債権率
sales to cash 現預金回転率
sales to fixed assets 固定資産売上率
sales to inventories 棚卸資産売上率
sales to receivables 売掛債権回転率
sales to the entity designated by the issuer 親引け
sales type lease 販売型リース
sales under agreement to repurchase 売現先
sales under agreement to resell 買現先
sales value 販売価値
sales volume 売上高
sales year 売却年
sales yield of public and corporate bonds 公社債売買利回り
salient ratio 特殊比率
Sallie Mae 米国奨学資金金庫
Sallie Mae (Student Loan Marketing Association) 米国奨学金融資金庫
Sallie Mae debenture サリー・メイ債
salvage 海難救助
salvage charges 救助料
salvage loss 救助物売得金差引精算
salvage prices 残存価格
salvage value 処分価値
SAM (shared appreciation mortgage) 増価共有モーゲージ
SAM (social accounting matrix) 社会会計マトリックス
SAMA (Saudi Arabia Monetary Agency) サウジアラビア通貨庁
same day effective order 当日有効注文
same day funds 即日資金
same-day substitution 同日代替
same-day value transaction 当日決済取引
sample 商品見本
sample mean 標本平均
sample products 商品見本
sample shipment 見本積送品
samples expense 見本費
sampling 標本抽出
sampling distribution 標本分布
sampling error 標本誤差
sampling survey 標本調査
sampling unit サンプリング単位
samurai bond サムライ債
samurai commercial paper サムライＣＰ
San Paulo Stock Exchange サンパウロ証券取引所
sanction 制裁措置
sandwich generation サンドイッチ世代
sandwich spread サンドイッチ・スプレッド
sans recourse 償還請求に応ぜず
Sao Marino (Italian lira) サンマリノ（イタリア・リラ）
SAP (statement of auditing procedures) 監査手続書
SAPCO (single asset property company) 単一資産会社
SAR (Saudi Arabian riyal) サウジアラビア・リアル
SAR (stock appreciation rights) 株式増価受益権
Sarbanes-Oxley Act 米国企業改革法
SAS (statement on auditing standards) 監査基準書
SAT (structured arbitration transaction) 仕組裁定取引
satellite market 衛星市場
satisfaction of debt 債務の返済
satisfaction of mortgage モーゲージ開放証書
satisfactory 満足すべき
satisfying principle 満足基準
Saturday Night Special サタデー・ナイト・スペシャル
SATURNE System 仏中央銀行国債決済システム
saucer ソーサー
Saudi Arabian Monetary Agency サウジアラビア通貨庁

saving function 貯蓄関数
savings account 貯蓄勘定
savings annuity 貯蓄年金
savings bank 貯蓄銀行
savings bank life insurance 貯蓄銀行生命保険
savings bond 貯蓄債券
savings bond payroll savings plan 貯蓄債券給与天引貯蓄プラン
savings certificate 定額貯蓄商品
savings debenture 貯蓄債券
savings deducted at source 天引貯金
savings deposit 貯蓄預金
savings element 貯蓄部分
savings in preparation for tax payment 納税貯金
savings income 貯蓄収入
savings note 貯蓄債券
savings plan 貯蓄型商品
savings policy 貯蓄保険
savings pool 貯蓄プール
savings product 貯蓄商品
savings rate 貯蓄率
savings share 貯蓄株
savings type insurance 積立保険
savings vehicle 貯蓄手段
savings withdrawal 貯蓄払戻し
savings-for-tax association 納税貯蓄組合
savings-investment theory of income determination 貯蓄・投資の所得決定論
savings-investment theory of interest-rate determination 貯蓄・投資の利子率決定論
SB (straight bond) 普通社債
SBD (Solomon Islands dollar) ソロモン諸島・ドル
SBF120 SBF120 種株価指数
SBIC (small business investment companies) 中小企業投資会社
SBLC (standby letter of credit) スタンバイ信用状
scale analysis 尺度分析
scale merit 規模の利益
scale of central and local public finance 財政規模
scale trading ナンピン売買
scalper スキャルパー
scalping 小ざや稼ぎ
scandal スキャンダル
scarce currency clause 稀少通貨条項
scarce resources 稀少資源
scarce stock 品薄株
scarcity 希少性
scarcity of stock 株不足
scatter chart 散布図表
scatter graph 散布図
scenario analysis シナリオ分析
schedule 明細
schedule form 報告式
schedule of bonds payable 社債明細表
schedule of capital 資本金明細表
schedule of concession 関税譲許表
schedule of depreciation 減価償却費明細表
schedule of financial statements 財務諸表付属明細書
schedule of securities 有価証券明細表
schedule of tangible fixed assets 有形固定資産明細表
schedule of terms and conditions 取引条件書
schedule of the cost of goods manufactured 製造原価明細書
schedule of the marginal efficiency of capital 資本限界効率表
schedule of transactions 取引明細
schedule of vouchers 証憑一覧
schedule payment スケジュール・ペイメント
scheduled amortization 定時減債
scheduled cash flow 予定されているキャッシュフロー
scheduled cost 表示原価
scheduled payment 約定返済
scheduled premium 確定保険料
scheduled redemption 定時償還
scheduled redemption amount 償還予定額

scheduled repayment 定時償還
scheduled territories account 指定地域勘定
scheduler income taxation 分類所得税
schedules of financial statements 財務諸表附属明細書
scheduling technique スケジューリング技法
schema of reproduction 再生産表式
scheme of arrangement 債務整理計画
scheme of operation 事業方法書
schizophrenic premium 二極化プレミアム
school fee savings 教育資金積立
School for Seafarers Training 海員学校
Schuldschein Darlehen 債務証書貸付
scissors-form difference in price 鋏状価格差
SCLV スペイン保管振替機関
scope limitation 範囲の限定
scope of audit 監査範囲
scope of authority 権限範囲
scope of book-entry JGSs 振決国債の範囲
scope of business 事業範囲
scope of exemption of property tax 固定資産税の非課税の範囲
scope of financial instruments 金融商品の範囲
scope of funds 資金の範囲
scope of income subject to withholding income tax 源泉徴収の対象となる所得
scope of money trust funds 金銭信託の範囲
scope of operations 業務の範囲
scope of opinion 意見区分
scope of review レビュー範囲
scope of securities 有価証券の範囲
scope of tax assessment 課税範囲
scope stipulated in the contract 契約の適用範囲
scorched earth defense 焦土作戦
SCORE (special claim on residual equity) 残余持分特別請求権
Scotland (sterling pound) スコットランド（イギリス・ポンド）
SCP (sterling commercial paper) ポンド建てCP
SCR (Seychelles rupee) セイシェル・ルピー
scrap 屑
scrap equipment 廃残設備
scrap value 残存価額
scrapped property 除却資産
scrapping of equipment tax credit 特定設備廃棄税額控除
screening 審査
screening of application for loan 貸出審査
screening of loan application ローン審査
scrip 端株株券
scrip certificate 仮株券；配当証書
scrip dividend 証書配当
scrip issue 株式配当
scrip-less settlement 無券面化決済
script 原文書
scrutiny 審査
SDD (Sudanese dinar) スーダン・ディナール
SDR denominated bond SDR建て債
SDS (same-day settlement) 同日決済
sea brief 中立船証明書
sea law 海事法規
sea letter 中立国船証明書
sea peril 海上危険
seal 検印
seal impression 印鑑
SEAQ (stock exchange automated quotation) for international equities SEAQインターナショナル
season sale 季節売出し
seasonal 季節的な
seasonal adjustment 季節調整
seasonal average 季節平均
seasonal discount 季節割引
seasonal driven inflation 季節要因によ

S

るインフレ
seasonal duties 季節関税
seasonal effects 季節調整
seasonal expenditure 季節的支出
seasonal factor 季節調整要因
seasonal fluctuation 季節変動
seasonal fluctuation adjustment 季節変動調整
seasonal fund 季節資金
seasonal goods 季節商品
seasonal index 季節指数
seasonal merchandise 季節商品
seasonal pattern 季節パターン
seasonal selling pressure 季節的売り圧力
seasonal unemployment 季節的失業
seasonality 季節性
seasonally adjusted 季節変動調整済
seasoned 経験豊かな；年数が経過した
seasoned bond 満期が近づいた債券
seasoned issue 既発銘柄
seasoned loan 経過期間が長いローン
seasoned manager 熟練マネージャー
seasoned mortgage 期間が経過したモーゲージ
seasoning curve シーズニング・カーブ
seasoning period 還流制限期間
seat 会員権
seaworthy 堪航能力のある
SEC accounting SEC 会計
SEC Accounting Releases SEC 会計連続通牒
SEC Docket SEC ドケット
SEC fee SEC 手数料
SEC schedules SEC 付属明細表
SEC standards SEC 基準
secession from a corporation 立退料
Second Association of Regional Banks 第二地銀協会
second decimal place 小数点第 2 位
second deliverance 再引渡
second generation on-line system 第二次オンライン
second half 下期
second half of the year 下半期
second lien mortgage 第二順位モーゲージ
second mortgage 二番抵当
second mortgage bond 二番抵当付き社債
second nearest contract month 第二限月取引
second performance statement 補足的業績報告書
Second Section 市場第二部
second secured 抵当順位第 2 位の
second surplus treaty 第二次超過額特約
second tier 準大手
second-distress 第二差押
second-lien mortgage loan 第二順位モーゲージ・ローン
second-preferred stock 劣後優先株
second-round budgetary negotiation 復活折衝
second-tier pension 上乗年金
second-to-die insurance 遺族保険
secondary activities 付随業務
secondary bond dealing 既発債取引
secondary boycott 第二次ボイコット
secondary capital 補完的自己資本
secondary CDO 流通市場 CDO
secondary claim 後順位の請求権
secondary conveyance 第二次的不動産移転行為
secondary distribution 二次分売
secondary effect 二次的要因
secondary evidence 二次的証拠
secondary format 補足的様式
secondary industry 第二次産業
secondary information 補足的情報
secondary liability 第二次負債
secondary liquidities 第二次流動資産
secondary market 流通市場
secondary market for Japanese government bonds 国債流通市場
secondary market liquidity 流通市場の流動性
secondary mortgage market 抵当証券流通市場；モーゲージ流通市場

secondary obligation 二次的責任
secondary offering 売出し
secondary party 第二当事者
secondary performance report 補完的な業績報告書
secondary qualities 二次的特性
secondary rally 中間戻し
secondary securities 第二次証券
secondary stock 二流株
secondary tax liability 第二次納税義務
secondary trend 二次的トレンド
secrecy agreement 守秘義務契約
secret account 秘密勘定
secret commission 裏口銭
secret language 暗語
secret liability 秘密負債
secret partner 匿名パートナー
secret partnership 匿名組合
secret reserve 秘密積立金
secret service expenses 機密費
secret trust 秘密信託
Secretarial Division 秘書課
secretariat 官房
Secretariat of the Policy Board 政策委員会室
Secretary of State 国務長官
sectional calculation 部門計算
sectional income statement 区分損益計算書
sectional journal 分割仕訳帳
sectional surface rights 区分地上権
sector セクター
sector allocation セクター配分
sector analyst セクター・アナリスト
sector balance sheet 部門別貸借対照表
sector benchmarks セクターの基準値
sector diversification セクター分散
sector specific risk セクター固有リスク
sector-stock price index 業種別株価指数
sectoral approach セクター方式
secular 長期変動要因
secular decline 長期低下
secular pressure 構造的な圧力
secular reason 構造要因
secure proper functioning 適切な機能を確保する
secured account 保証付勘定
secured advance 担保付貸付
secured bond 抵当権付社債
secured call loan 有担保コール
secured claim under reorganization plan 更生担保権
secured corporate bond 有担保社債
secured credit 担保付貸出
secured debenture 担保付債券
secured debt 担保付債務
secured liabilities 担保付負債
secured loan 担保貸し
secured note 担保付約束手形
secured party 担保権者
secured securities 担保付証券
secured transactions 担保付取引
securing completion of transactions 売買の安全をはかる
securing of contract 契約の獲得
securities 有価証券
securities account 有価証券勘定
securities acquired by the specified investment in kind 特定の現物出資によって取得された証券
Securities Act of 1933 1933年証券法
securities activities 証券業務
securities administration 証券行政
securities administration trust 有価証券管理信託
securities analysis 証券分析
securities analyst 証券アナリスト
Securities and Exchange Commission 米国証券取引委員会
Securities and Exchange Law 証券取引法
Securities and Exchange Surveillance Commission 証券取引等監査委員会
securities backed by mortgage loan 抵当ローン担保証券
securities borrowed 借入有価証券
securities broker 証券ブローカー

S

securities business 証券業
Securities Business Division 証券課
securities business tax law 証券取引税法
securities called by lot 抽選償還証券
securities capital 証券資本
securities clearing agency 証券清算機関
securities clearing operation 証券クリアリング業務
securities companies by size of capital 資本金階層別証券会社
securities company 証券会社
securities dealer 証券ディーラー
securities dealers association 証券業協会
securities deposited as collateral 担保差入有価証券
securities deposited from others 保管有価証券
securities eligible for settlement 決済物件
securities exchange 証券取引所
securities exchange clearing house 証券取引清算機関
securities exchange commission 証券取引審議会
securities exchange special tax 取引所特別税
securities finance company 証券金融会社
securities financing 証券金融
securities firm 証券会社
securities for fiduciary issue 保証準備
securities for sale 売却可能証券
securities for which the holding-purpose category has changed 保有目的変更の有価証券
securities futures transactions 証券先物取引
securities given as collateral 担保差入証券
securities handling clerk 有価証券取扱者
securities held by the government 政府保管有価証券
securities held for investment trust 投資信託有価証券
securities held for trading 売買目的有価証券
securities holdings 保有証券
securities house dealer 証券会社ディーラー
securities in lieu of cash 代用有価証券
securities in portfolio 手持証券
securities in trust 有価証券信託
securities income and expense 有価証券損益
securities industry 証券業界
Securities Industry Association 全米証券業者協会
securities inventory 支配玉
securities investment 証券投資
securities investment advisory service 証券投資相談
securities investment by financial institutions 金融機関の有価証券保有
securities investment trust 証券投資信託
securities investment trust sales company 証券投資信託販売会社
Securities Investor Protection Act of 1970 証券投資家保護法
securities investor protection corporation 証券投資家保護会社
securities issuance 証券発行
securities issued by government agency 政府系機関証券
securities ledger 有価証券元帳
securities leg 証券レッグ
securities loan 証券担保ローン
securities loaned 貸付有価証券
securities management 証券管理
securities market 有価証券市場
securities market line 証券市場線
Securities Market Reform Act 証券市場改革法案
Securities Market Stabilization Act 証券市場安定化法案

S

securities of affiliated company 関係会社有価証券
securities offering and listing 証券の発行と上場
securities on property 物的証券
securities on the shelf 一括登録済みの証券
securities option 有価証券オプション
securities option trading 有価証券オプション取引
securities outstanding 発行済証券
securities owned 商品有価証券
securities owned by the government 政府所有有価証券
securities ownership by investment trusts 投資信託の有価証券保有
securities purchase 有価証券買入れ
securities received as collateral 担保有価証券
securities received for guarantee 預り有価証券
securities register 有価証券記入帳
securities regulations 証券規程
securities regulators 証券監督官
securities report for listing 上場のための有価証券報告書
securities report for listing application 上場申請のための有価証券報告書
securities reserve 有価証券準備
securities settlement 証券決済
securities sold register 有価証券売却記入帳
Securities Supervisory Board 証券監督院
securities system 証券システム
securities trading 証券取引
securities transaction 証券取引
securities transaction loss reserve 株式売買損失準備金
securities transaction tax 有価証券取引税
securities transaction tax law 有価証券取引税法
securities transfer tax 有価証券取引税
securities underwriting business law 有価証券引受業法
securities valuation reserve 証券価格変動引当金
securities with fair value 時価のある有価証券
securities with irregularities 事故証券
securities with maturity dates 満期がある有価証券
securities without market value 時価のない有価証券
securities yield 証券利回り
securitization 証券化
securitization by pooling プーリングによる証券化
securitization law 証券化法
securitization market 証券化市場
securitization of bad loans 不良債権の証券化
securitization of leases リース債権の流動化
securitization of real estate 不動産の証券化
securitization products 証券化商品
securitized assets 証券化資産
securitized mortgage 証券化モーゲージ
security 担保
security account 担保勘定
Security Council 安全保障理事会
security credit 証券金融
security credit by banks 銀行による証券金融
security credit by brokers and dealers ブローカー及びディーラーによる証券金融
security deposit for rent 賃貸の保証金
security deposits 担保預り金
security financing by listed companies 上場会社資金調達額
security for costs 訴訟費用の担保
security for tax payment 納税担保
security interest 担保権
security issue 証券の銘柄
security lending 証券貸付
security listing regulations 有価証券上

場規程
security loan 証券担保貸付
security loan transactions with cash collateral 現金担保付債券貸借取引
security management セキュリティ管理
security measures of computer systems コンピュータ・システムの障害対策
security on combined properties 共同担保
security price 証券価格
security priority ranking 担保優先順位
security rating 証券格付け
security right 担保権
security risk curve 証券リスク線
security suretyship 保証人
security trusts 有価証券の信託
security yield curve 証券利回り線
security-specific risk 証券固有のリスク
securtised asset 証券化した資産
seed money 初期投入資金
seeking a market 取引相手探し
segment accounting セグメント会計
segment accounting policy セグメント別会計方針
segment definition セグメント定義
segment disclosure セグメント別開示
segment information セグメント情報
segment of seller 売手のセグメント
segment result セグメント別損益
segmental breakdown 部門別内訳
segmental sales 部門別売上
segmental sales breakdown 部門別売上内訳
segmentation セグメンテーション
segmentation of construction contract 工事契約の分割
segmentation theory 市場分断理論
segregate 区分する
segregate interest and principal 元本と金利を分離する
segregated account 分離勘定
segregation of margin 証拠金の分離
segregation of securities 証券の分別保管
seigniorage 通貨発行益
seized 占有した
seized goods 差押物件
seizor 差押人
seizure 差押え
SEK (Swedish Krona) スウェーデン・クローナ
selected 抜粋の
selected dealer agreement 販売団契約
selected financial data 抜粋財務データ；要約財務データ
selected issue 選定銘柄
selection 選択
selection criteria 選択基準
selection method 選定方法
selection of a necessary appraisal method 必要な評価方法の選択
selection of appraisal method 評価方法の選択
selection of depreciation method 償却方法の選定
selection of risk 危険選択
selection of valuation method 評価方法の選択
selective bid 指名競争入札
selective buying 物色買い
selective credit regulation 選択的信用規制
selective disclosure 選別開示
selective financing 選別融資
selective function 選択的機能
selective lending 選別融資
selective order 択一注文
selective revaluation 選択的な再評価
selective selling 特約販売
selective tendering 指名競争入札
self-accounting system 独立会計制
self-addressed check 自己宛小切手
self-administered 自己管理型
self-amortization mortgage 元利均等返済住宅ローン
self-assessed income tax 申告所得税
self-assessed income tax (final

S

declaration) 申告所得税（確定納付）
self-assessment 自己申告
self-assessment criteria 自己査定基準
self-assessment of credit exposure 与信リスクの自己査定
self-assessment of taxation system 申告納税制度
self-assessment system 自己申告納付制度
self-balancing 独自平均
self-balancing type 増減対照式
self-benefit trust 自益信託
self-collateralization 同時担保
self-consumption 自家消費
self-correction 自己修正
self-defense 正当防衛
self-directed individual retirement account 自主運用型個人退職勘定
self-disserving evidence 自己に不利益な証拠
self-employed 自営の
self-employed deferred annuity 自営業者据置年金
self-employed pension 自営業者年金
self-employed pension plan 自営業者年金制度
self-employed retirement annuity 自営業者退職年金
self-employment 自営
self-employment income 自家営業所得
self-employment tax 個人事業主税
self-enforcement 自力執行権
self-finance 自己金融
self-finance ratio 自己金融比率
self-funding 自己積立
self-insurance 自家保険
self-insurance fund 自家保険基金
self-insurance plan 自家保険制度
self-insurance reserve 自家保険準備金（自家保険積立金）
self-insured 自家保険の
self-investment 自己投資
self-issue cards 自社カード
self-liquidating 自己清算の
self-liquidity 自己流動性
self-management 自営
self-produced fixed assets 自己生産に係る固定資産
self-produced inventories 自己の製造にかかる棚卸資産
self-regarding evidence 自己に関する証拠
self-registration 一括登録制度
self-regulation 自主規制
self-reinsurance 自家再保険
self-reporting 自己申告
self-restraint 自主規制
self-restraint interest 自主規制金利
self-return 自己申告
self-selection 自己選択
self-serving declaration 自己に有利な供述
self-support accounting 独立採算
self-support subsistence 独立生計
self-supporting accounting system 独立採算制
self-supporting debt 特定財源債
self-sustained personal accident insurance 自損事故保険
self-sustaining recovery 自律的な回復
self-tender 自社株買戻し
sell back 売り戻す
sell down セル・ダウン（幹事団以外への販売）
sell low 低く売る
sell on credit 掛売りする
sell on the spot 即売する
sell order 売注文
sell plus order セル・プラス注文
sell side セル・サイド
sell signal 売信号
sell the book 大口株式の成行注文を出す
sell-and-lease agreement 賃借契約
seller 売手
seller financing 売手のファイナンス
seller's monopoly 売手独占
seller's option 売方勝手渡し
seller's option trading セラーズ・オプ

S

ション取引
seller's price 言い値
sellers over 売り長
sellers' market 売手市場
selling agreement 販売契約
selling at a profit 利益確定を目的とした売却
selling charges 販売諸掛り
selling climax セリング・クライマックス
selling commission 売上手数料
selling concession 販売手数料
selling contract 売予約
selling cost 販売費用
selling customer 売付顧客
selling cycle 販売循環
selling dividend 配当を目玉にした販売
selling exchange 売為替
selling expense 販売費
selling expense variance 販売費差異
selling group 販売団
selling group agreement 販売団契約書
selling off 投げ売り
selling offer 売オファー
selling on a consignment basis 委託販売
selling on a rising scale 売り上がり
selling on balance 売り越し
selling on credit 掛売り
selling on rally 戻り売り
selling on spurt 吹き値売り
selling on temporary 戻し売り
selling operation under repurchase agreement 買戻条件付売りオペレーション
selling opportunity 売場
selling out 処分売り
selling overhead 販売間接費
selling position 売建
selling pressure 売り圧力
selling price 売値
selling price inventory method 売価棚卸法
selling price per unit 一品当りの売価
selling profit 売上利益
selling rate 売相場
selling regular member 売付正会員
selling right 売る権利
selling sample 売見本
selling short 空売り
selling side 売りサイド
selling spread オプション料スプレッド取引
selling support 売人気
selling US equities 米国株式の売り
selling, general and administrative expenses 販売一般管理費
semi-annual 半期
semi-annual audit 中間監査
semi-annual audit report 中間監査報告書
semi-annual closing of accounts 中間決算
semi-annual compounding calculation 半年ごとの複利計算
semi-annual coupon payment 半年払いのクーポン
semi-annual market 年二回払いの市場
semi-annual report 半期報告書
semi-annual results 中間決算
semi-annually 半年ごとに
semi-durables 半耐久材
semi-endowment assurance 半額養老保険
semi-finished goods ledger 半製品元帳
semi-fixed cost 準固定費
semi-inflation 準インフレーション
semi-installment 半期賦払い
semi-senior accountant 準上級会計士
semi-tontine 半トンチン
semi-variable charge 準変動費
semi-variable cost 準変動原価
semi-variable expenses 準変動費項目
Semiannual Report on Currency and Monetary Control 通貨及び金融の調節に関する報告書
semiannual summary audit report 中間監査概要書
sender 積送人
sender net debit cap 仕向け超過限度額

Senegal (CFA (Communauté Financière Africaine) franc) セネガル（CFA フラン）
senior accountant 上級会計士
Senior Adviser to the Minister of Finance 財務省参与
senior bond 上位社債
Senior Budget Inspector 上席予算実地監査官
senior claim 上位請求権
senior co-manager 上級副幹事
senior creditor 先順位債権者
senior debt 上位債
Senior Deputy Director-General of the International Bureau 国際局次長
senior employee 幹部従業員
senior executive 経営者
Senior Foreign Exchange Examiner 主任為替実査官
senior issue 上位証券
senior lender 先順位の貸手
senior loan 優先貸付
Senior Loan Officer Opinion Survey on Bank Lending Practices at Large Japanese Banks 主要銀行貸出動向アンケート調査
senior managing director 専務取締役
senior managing governor 専務理事
senior market 高齢者市場
senior mortgage 先順位モーゲージ
senior mortgage bond 先順位担保付社債
senior policyholder 上位保険加入者
senior refunding 長期債への借換え
senior sector 上位債市場
senior securities 優先証券
senior subordinated note 上位劣後社債
senior trader シニア・トレーダー
senior tranche 上位トランシェ
senior unsecured debt 無担保上位債務
senior vice minister 副大臣
Senior Vice Minister for FSA 金融担当副大臣
Senior Vice Minister of Finance 財務副大臣
senior-sub structure 優先劣後構造
seniority based 年功序列の
seniority order wage system 年功序列賃金制度
seniority system 年功制
sensitive market 神経質な市場
sensitivity 感応性
sensitivity adjustment 感応度調整
sensitivity analysis 感応度分析
sensitivity coefficient 感応度係数
sentenced to imprisonment 禁固刑
sentiment 地合い
sentiment index センチメント指標
sentiment indicator 地合指標
SEP (simplified employment plan) 簡易従業員年金
separability 個別分類性
separability criteria 個別分類基準
separable cost 分離可能原価
separate account 個別勘定；分離勘定
separate account assets 分離勘定資産
separate account funding 分離勘定基金積立
separate account policy 分離勘定生命保険
separate acquisition 個別取得
separate and restricted account 別段勘定
separate banking system 分離銀行制度
separate bill 別勘定
separate class 個別の種類
separate classification 個別の分類
separate component 独立の構成部分
separate component of equity 資本持分の個別構成要素
separate customer account 別人格勘定
separate disclosure 個別の開示
separate estate 妻の特有財産
separate financial statements 個別財務諸表；単独財務諸表
separate investment account 分離投資勘定
separate maintenance 別居手当
separate management account 分別管

S

理口
separate property 特有財産
separate return 個別申告書
separate self-assessment taxation 申告分離課税
separate standard 個別の基準
separate tax return 個別納税申告
separate taxation from other income 分離課税
separate withholding taxation 源泉分離課税
separated coupon component 分離利息振決国債
separated principal component 分離元本振決国債
separated taxation 分離課税
separated taxation on dividend income 配当分離課税
separation 元利分離
separation between capital and administration 資本と経営の分離
seqs セクター
sequence of deduction 控除の順序
sequence of tax credits 税額控除の順序
sequential cost system 工程別総合原価計算
sequential processing 逐次処理
sequential terms 前月比で
sequential trading 逐次取引
serial bonds 連続償還債券
serial correlation 系列相関
serial issue 連続発行
serial number 記番号
serial redemption 連続償還債償還
serial securities 連続償還証券
serial zero-coupon bond 連続ゼロ・クーポン債
series シリーズ
Series E Bond シリーズ E 債券
Series EE Bond シリーズ EE 債券
Series HH Bond シリーズ HH 債券
series of option 同一オプション
series of payments 数次の支払い
serve a notice on 通知を送達する
service agreement 業務委託契約
service balance 貿易外収支
service by public notification 公示送達
service contract 役務提供契約
service contribution 役務出資
service cost 勤務費用；補助原価
service credit 勤務期間参入
service economy サービス経済
service fee サービス手数料
service industry サービス業
service life 耐用年数
service life expectancy 継続勤務の期待度
service of process 訴訟手続
service office 営業所
service on a casual basis 不定期な勤務
service potential 用役潜在力
service provision 用役提供
service tax サービス税
service trade サービス貿易
service transaction サービス取引
service unit 用役単位
service-yield basis 生産高比例法
servicer サービサー
services output method 用役生産高法
services related to treasury funds 国庫金に関する業務
servicing 債権回収代行
servicing activity liability 回収サービス業務負債
servicing activity rights 回収サービス権
servicing asset 回収代行資産
servicing burden 債務返済の負担
servicing fee サービシング手数料
servicing fee income サービシング手数料収入
servicing of loan principal and interest 元利金徴収
servicing right 債権回収代行権
servitude 地役権
servitude for use of water 用水地役権
servitude holder 地役権者
SES (Stock Exchange of Singapore) シンガポール証券取引所

SESC (Securities and Exchange Surveillance Commission) 証券取引等監視委員会
SESC (Stock Exchange Executive Council) 証券取引所運営評議会
session 会期
session period 立会時間
SET (Securities Exchange of Thailand) タイ証券取引所
set bill 組手形
set forth 定める
set of accounts 会計帳票
set of exchange 組手形
set up against 対抗する
set-off 相殺
setback 悪目買い；減少
setting 設定
setting body 設定主体
setting mechanism 設定メカニズム
setting up mortgages for the real estate 土地建物に抵当権を設定する
setting up overdraft 貸越設定
settle 決済する
settle accounts 決算を行う
settle net 純額決済する
settled account 清算勘定
settled additional tax due amount 更正決定により確定した追加税額
settlement 決済
settlement account 決済勘定；決済口
settlement agent 決済代行機関
settlement at Japan Securities Clearing Corporation 日証決済状況
settlement bank 決済銀行
settlement by delivery 受渡決済
settlement cycle 決済サイクル
settlement date 決済日
settlement date accounting 決済日基準会計
settlement day 受渡日
settlement day by delivery 受渡決済期日
settlement deadline 決済時限
settlement detail 決済の詳細
settlement discount 決済割引
settlement dividend 消滅時配当
settlement facility 決済機構
settlement failure 決済不履行（フェイル）
settlement finality 支払完了性
settlement for the first half of the year 中間決算
settlement index 清算指数
settlement interval 決済期間
settlement method 決済方式
settlement mode 決済方法
settlement notification 決済通知
settlement of accounts 決算
settlement of accounts for the latter half 下期決算
settlement of balance 帳尻決済
settlement of claim 債権の弁済
settlement of easement 地役権の設定
settlement of JGSs 国債の決済
settlement of leasehold 借地権設定
settlement of liability 負債の決済
settlement of mortgage 抵当権設定
settlement of subsidy 補助金の返済
settlement of superficies 地上権設定
settlement of tax amount 税額の確定
settlement of unsettled transactions 未決済取引の整理
settlement options 保険金受取方法
settlement out of court 示談
settlement period 弁済期限
settlement price 清算値段
settlement statements 決算書類
settlement status 決済状況
settlement time 決済時限
settlement trade 居留地貿易
settlement value 決済価額；決済代金
settlement variation セトルメント・バリエーション
settlement volume 受渡決済数量；決済高
settlements rate 決済比率
settlor 信託設定者
setup time 段取り時間

70% retracement 70%の戻り
sever 分離する
severable contract 可分契約
several contract 分割契約
several covenant 可分条項
several liability 個別責任
several ownership 分割所有権
severally 単独で
severally but not jointly 非連帯保証
severally liable 個別責任の
severance 分離
severance of actions 訴訟の分離
severance of employment 中途退職
severance payment system 退職金制度
SEZ (special economic zone) 経済特区
SFAC (Statement of Financial Accounting Concepts) 財務会計概念基準書
SFAS (Statement of Financial Accounting Standards) 財務会計基準書
SFE (Sydney Futures Exchange) シドニー先物取引所
SG&A (selling, general and administrative) expenses 一般管理販売費
SGD (Singapore dollar) シンガポール・ドル
shadow account 影の勘定
shadow cabinet 影の内閣
shadow price 潜在価格
shadow toll 仮想料金
shakeout 暴落
shaking-out 投げ売り
sham 脱税取引
Shandong 山東省
Shanghai 上海市
Shanxi 山西省；陝西省
share 株式
share account 株式勘定
share allotment certificate 株式割当証書
share allotment letter 株式割当通知
share broker 株式ブローカー
share capital 株式資本
share certificate 株券
share consolidation 株式合併
share deposits 出資預金
share draft account 出資金手形勘定
share drafts シェア・ドラフト
share exchange 株式の交換
share handling 株式取扱い
share holding ratio 株式保有率
share in expense of public service 公共施設の負担額
share incentive 持株奨励
share index 株価指数
share ledger 株式台帳
share of net profit 純利益持分
share of no par value 無額面株式
share of one kind 単一株式
share of ownership interest 所有持ち分の割合
share of profit and loss 損益の持ち分
share of residual property 残余財産の取分
share of the residual property 残余財産の取分
share option ストック・オプション
share option plan ストック・オプション制度
share ownership 株式保有
share premium 株式プレミアム
share price 株価
share price level 株価水準
share price performance 株価値動き
share purchase 株式購入
share purchase warrant 株式購入ワラント
share reinsurance 比例再保険
share repurchase 自社株買い
share repurchase plan 自社株買戻し
share split-down 株式併合
share split-up 株式分割
share transfer agent service office 株式名義書換取扱所
share warrant 新株ワラント
share with par value 額面株式
share-based payment transaction 株式報酬取引

S

shared characteristics 共有する特徴
shared equities 共有持ち分
shared equity mortgage シェアード・エクイティ・モーゲージ
shared risk 共同負担リスク
shareholder 株主
shareholder activism 株主の行動主義
shareholder litigation 株主による訴訟
shareholder of non-family corporation 非同族株主
shareholder service 株式事務
shareholder service agent 株式事務代行機関
shareholder's interest 株主持ち分
shareholder's rights 株主の権利
shareholder's suit 株主訴訟
shareholders ledger 株主元帳
shareholders of record 登録株主
shareholders-oriented management 株主重視の経営
shareholders' account 株主勘定
shareholders' equity 株主資本
shareholders' equity interests 株主持ち分
shareholders' equity section 資本の部
shareholders' interests 自己資本額
shareholders' meeting 株主総会
shareholders' representative suit 株主の代表訴訟
shareholders' resolution 株主決議
shareholders' voluntary liquidation 株主による任意清算
shareholding 株保有
shares held by investment trusts 投信組入株式
shares held in a long position 建て株
shares issued 発行済株式
shares lent by members 自己貸株
shares outstanding 発行済株式
shares qualified for directors 取締役限定株式
shares registered in the name of depository 保管振替機関名義株式
shares reserved for issuance 留保株式
shares sold short 信用売り
sharing costs 経費の分担
shark repellent 鮫よけ
sharp advance market 急騰相場
sharp decline 激減
sharp decline market 急落相場
sharp drop 瓦落
sharp fall 急落
sharp loss 急反落
sharp rally 反騰
sharp rise 急騰
sharp run-up 急騰
sharp sell off in the Nikkei 日経平均の急落
sharp setback 急反落
sharp slowdown 急激な減速
sharp upward revision 大幅上方修正
sharpe ratio シャープ・レシオ
shelf offering 一括募集
shelf registration 発行登録
shelf registration system 発行登録制度
shelf-registration statement 発行届出書
shell branch みせかけの店
shell corporation ペーパー・カンパニー
Shenzhen 深圳
Sherman Anti-trust Act シャーマン反トラスト法
shift in demand 需要変化
shift in interest rate 金利の変動
shift in preference 選好の変化
shift to yen 円シフト
shiftability theory 転嫁性理論
shifting of business center 営業の本拠の移動
shifting of tax burden 租税の転嫁
shinkin bank 信用金庫
Shinkin Central Bank 信金中央金庫
Shinkin Trust Bank しんきん信託銀行
Shinkumi Federation Bank 全国信用協同組合連合会
ship mortgage 船舶モーゲージ
ship order 出荷指図書
ship owner protection and indemnity association 船主責任相互保険組合

ship's bill 船長用船荷証券
ship's husband 船舶管理人
ship's paper 船舶備付書類
shipment 積送品
shipments index 出荷指数
shipped quality terms 船積品質条件
shipper 積送人
shipper's usance シッパーズ・ユーザンス；輸出信用
shipping 海運
shipping articles 船員雇入契約書
shipping charges 船積諸掛かり
shipping commissioners 海事雇用監督官
shipping document 船積書類
shipping expense 発送費
shipping market 海運市場
shipping marks 荷印
shipping receipts 海運収入
shipping tax 船舶税
ships and vessels 船舶
shock absorber ショック・アブゾーバー
shogun bond ショーグン債
shogun convertible bond ショーグンＣＢ
Shoko Chukin Bank 商工組合中央金庫
shop 工場
shop act 商店法
shop cost 工場原価
shop inspection 工場検査
shopbook rule 商品帳簿の法則
shopkeepers' books 帳簿（小売商人の）
shopping around 買い漁り
short ショート
short account 空売り勘定
short against the box 売りつなぎ
short book ショート・ブック
short butterfly ショート・バタフライ
short call ショート・コール
short coupon ショート・クーポン
short covering 買戻決済；空売りの解消
short covering at a loss 踏み
short delivery 納品不足
short drawing ショート・ドローイング
short end 短期債
short EURCHF ユーロ / スイスフランのショート
short fall 短期投資利益
short form 簡易型
short form audit report 短文式監査報告書
short forward position 先物売りポジション
short hedge 売りヘッジ
short interest 空売残高
short lined rally 一時的反騰
short list ショート・リスト
short market 下げ相場
short maturity 短期償還期日
short notice 短期の通知
short period 短期
short position 売持ち
short position risk 売持リスク
short positions 売建玉
short put ショート・プット
short run equilibrium 短期均衡
short run supply curve 短期供給曲線
short sale against the box 売りつなぎ
short sale ratio 空売り比率
short securities transaction 空売り
short selling 空売り
short squeeze ショート・スクイーズ；踏み上げ
short straddle ショート・ストラドル
short strangle ショート・ストラングル
short strap ショート・ストラップ
short strip ショート・ストリップ
short supply 供給不足
short swing profits 短期売買益
short tenure horizon 短期保有目的
short term asset 短期資産
short the swap スワップをショートにする
short title 略称
short-dated bonds 短期債
short-dated securities 残存期間の短い

証券
short-period cost 短期費用
short-tem securities 短期証券
short-term 短期
short-term bond 短期債
short-term bond fund 短期債ファンド
short-term borrowing 短期借入金
short-term capital 短期資本
short-term capital balance 短期資本収支
short-term capital gain 短期譲渡所得
short-term capital transaction 短期資本取引
short-term credit market 短期金融市場
short-term debt 短期負債
short-term debt rating 短期格付け
short-term economic survey of all businesses 全国企業短期経済観測
short-term economic survey of principal enterprises 主要企業短期経済観測
short-term employee benefit 短期従業員給付
short-term facility rate 短期資金レート
short-term finance 短期金融
short-term fluctuations 短期の変動
short-term fund 短期資金
short-term funding requirements 短期資金繰りの調整
short-term gain or loss 短期保有資産売却損益
short-term government bond 短期国債
short-term government bond market 短期国債市場
short-term instrument 短期証券
short-term interest rate 短期金利
short-term investment 短期投資
short-term investment account 短期投資勘定
short-term lending 短期貸付
short-term liabilities 短期負債
short-term link 短期的リンク
short-term liquidity factor 短期流動性要因
short-term loan payable 短期借入金
short-term margin 短期差入保証金
short-term money house 短資業者
short-term note 短期債券
short-term operation 短期事業活動
short-term oriented 短期志向
short-term outlook 短期見通し
short-term prime rate 短期プライムレート
short-term profit taking 短期的な利食い
short-term returns 短期の投資収益
short-term securities borrowed 短期借入有価証券
short-term solvency 短期支払能力
short-term swap 短期スワップ
short-term trading 短期売買の
short-term transaction 短期取引
short-term trending 短期的傾向
short-term yield 短期利回り
shortage 不足額
shortage in deliverable securities 品不足
shortage of funds 資金不足
shortage of special depreciation 特別償却不足額
shortcut procedure 簡便法
shortening of a prearranged period of a construction work 予定工期の短縮
shortening of loan term 融資期間の短縮
shortening of useful life 耐用年数の短縮
shorter dated maturities 満期の近い銘柄
shorter on the curve 短期物
shortest bond on the curve 残存期間の最も短い債券
shortest dated 残存期間が最も短い
shortfall 不足
shortfall in funding for retirement benefit liabilities 退職給付債務積立額不足

S

Shoup's recommendation シャウプ勧告
SHP (St. Helena pound) セントヘレナ・ポンド
shrinkage 在庫減耗
shrinkage variance 減耗差異
SHSE (Shanghai Securities Exchange) 上海証券取引所
shut for dividend 名義書換停止
SIA (Securities Industry Association) 米国証券業協会
SIA (Social Insurance Agency) 社会保険庁
SIAC (Securities Industry Automation Corporation) SIAC
SIB (Securities and Investments Board) 証券投資委員会
SICA (Securities Industry Committee of Arbitration) 証券業仲裁委員会
Sichuan 四川省
sick leave 疾病休業
sick market 閑散市場
sick pay 疾病手当
sickness benefit 疾病給付
sickness insurance 疾病保険
Sicovam (Société Interprofessionelle pour la Compensation des Valeurs Mobilières) フランス証券決済機関
side benefit 副次的効果
side effect 副作用
sideline 兼業
sight bill 一覧払為替手形
sight credit サイト・クレジット
sight draft 一覧払手形
sight L/C (letter of credit) 一覧払信用状
sight note 一覧払約束手形
sight of a bill 手形サイト
sight rate 一覧払為替相場
sight selling rate 一覧払い相場
sight-seeing tax 観光税
sign manual 自署
sign of fragility 脆弱性
sign of impairment 減損の兆候
signature and seal 記名捺印
signature guarantee 署名確認書
signature loan 無担保貸付
signed and sealed 署名捺印
signed check 記名式小切手
signed transfer 記名譲渡
significance level 有意水準
significant accounting policies 重大な会計方針
significant activities 重要な活動
significant amount 重要な金額
significant commitment 多大なコミットメント
significant doubt 重大な疑問
significant effect 重大な影響
significant entity 重要な事業体
significant guarantee paper 多額の保証状
significant improvement 相当の改善
significant influence 重要な影響力
significant movement 多額の変動
significant order 大量注文
significant relationship 重要な関係
significant segment 主要セグメント
significant subsidiaries 重要な子会社
signs 兆候
signs of deterioration 悪化の兆候
signs of rebounding 回復の兆候
silence 沈黙
silent base 裏参加ベース
silent participation 裏参加
silent partner 裏参加者
silver exchange 銀為替
silver standard 銀本位制
SIMEX (Singapore International Monetary Exchange) シンガポール国際金融取引所
similar asset 類似資産
similar financial statements 類似財務諸表
similar goods 類似品
similar investment media 類似の投資媒体
similarity 類似性
simple accounting 単式簿記
simple aggregate 単純総和

simple arbitrage 単純裁定
simple arithmetic average index 単純算術平均指数
simple assault 単純暴行
simple average 単純海損；単純平均
simple average cost method 単純平均法
simple average stock price 単純平均株価
simple average yield 単純平均利回り
simple confession 単純自白
simple contract 単純契約
simple cost accounting 単純総合原価計算
simple discount 単利割引
simple guarantee 単純保証
simple guarantor 単純保証人
simple hypothesis 単純仮説
simple index 単純指数
simple interest 単利
simple IRA (individual retirement account) 単純個人退職勘定
simple journal 単純仕訳帳
simple jump model 単純ジャンプ・モデル
simple listing 簡易上場
simple margin 単利マージン
simple mean value 単純平均値
simple moving average 単純移動平均
simple multiplier 単純乗数
simple obligation 単純債務
simple prediction 単純予測
simple rate of return 単純利益率
simple regression model 単純回帰モデル
simple reproduction 単純再生産
simple reserve method 単純準備法
simple suretyship 単純保証人
simple tariff system 単一税率制
simple trust 単純信託
simplicity 簡素性
simplification 簡素化
simplified bookkeeping system 簡易簿記
simplified calculation 簡便計算
simplified employee pension 簡易従業員退職年金
simplified method 簡便法
simplified method of depreciation 簡便償却
simplified tax system 簡易課税制度
simulated 虚偽の
simulation シミュレーション
simulation of regional vitality 地域活性化
simultaneous book-entry transfer 同時振替決済
simultaneous processing 同時処理
simultaneous tax audit 同時調査
SIN (synthetic interest note) 合成金利ノート
Singapore inter-bank offered rate シンガポール銀行間出し手金利
single A A 格
single accounting system 単会計制度
single balance sheet 単一の貸借対照表
single banking license 単一銀行免許
single bill(bond) 債務負担捺印債務証書
single business year 単年度
single currency 単一通貨
single customer separate account 単一顧客分離勘定
single employer defined benefit pension plan 単一事業主型給付建て年金制度
single employer plan 単一事業主制度
single entry 単式記入
single entry bookkeeping 単式簿記
Single European Act 単一欧州議定書
single exchange rate 単一為替レート
single exempt fund ユニット投信単独運用ファンド
single expression 単式
single extra 一時払特別保険料
single family house 一世帯住居
single financial report 単一財務報告
single group of methods 単一系統の方式
single index model 単一指標モデル

single investment 単一の投資
single life annuity 単生年金
single line item 単一表示項目
single market 市場統合
single maturity deposit 単一満期預金
single name 単一銘柄；単名
single name option 単一銘柄オプション
single name paper 単名手形
single net payment 一回の純額
single option シングル・オプション
single pay life insurance 一時払い生命保険
single payment 一括払い
single payment annuity 一時払い年金
single payment loan 一回払い貸付
single premium 一時払い保険料
single premium annuity 一時払年金
single premium deferred annuities 一時払据置年金
single premium endowment insurance 一時払い養老保険
single premium variable annuity 一時払変額保険
single premium whole life policy 一時払終身保険
single price 一本値
single price auction ダッチ方式
single proprietorship 個人事業主
single purchase annuity 一括購入年金
single purpose 専用の
single regulation 統一規制
single state municipal bond fund 州限定地方債ファンド
single statement 一計算書
single statement approach 単一計算方式
single step 無区分式
single step form 無段階式
single step income statement 単一区分損益計算書
single sum 一時金
single tariff 単一税率
single tax 単一税
single transaction 単一取引
single treatment 単一の処理
single valuation 単一評価
single weighted average discount rate 単一加重平均割引率
single-family detached residence 戸建住宅
single-order term 一定期限払い
single-premium life insurance 一時払生命保険
single-step statement 単一区分計算書
sinker 減債基金債券
sinking 沈没
sinking fund 減債基金
sinking fund account 減債基金勘定
sinking fund arrangement 減債基金契約
sinking fund bonds 減債基金付社債
sinking fund method 償却基金法
sinking fund obligation 減債基金債務
sinking fund payments 減債基金繰り入れ
sinking fund preferred stock 減債基金優先株
sinking fund requirements 減債基金積立額
sinking funds requirements 減債基金積立要件
sinking into a double dip recession 景気の底割れ
SIPC (Securities Investor Protection Corporation) 証券投資家保護公社
sister company 姉妹会社
SIT (Slovenian tolar) スロバニア・トーラル
sit in camera 非公開での開廷
site 所在地
site audit 現場監査
site preparation 整地
site supervisor 現場監督
site survey 実地調査
six column journal 六桁仕訳帳
six month closing of accounts 中間期決算
six months closing of accounts 中間決算

60-year redemption rule 60 年償還ルール
size effect 規模効果
skeleton form T 字型勘定様式
skeleton form account T 字形勘定
skip payment 支払一回飛ばし
skip premium 払込中断保険料
skip-day settlement 翌々日決済
SKK (Slovak koruna) スロバキア・コルナ
skyrocketing 急騰している
skyrocketing price 天井しらずの相場
slackness of money market 金融緩慢
slander 名誉毀損
slaughter sale 投げ売り
sleeping account 休眠口座
sleeping member 休眠会員
sliding cheap じり安
sliding tariff スライド関税
slight negligence 軽過失
slight tightening 小引き締め
slight ups and downs 小浮動
slightly firmer 小じっかり
slightly recover 小戻す
slightly steady 小確り
slightly tightening 小締まる
slimmer profit margins 利益率の低下
slip 伝票
slip bookkeeping 伝票式簿記
slip system 伝票制度
slip system of accounting 伝票式会計法
SLL (Sierra Leone leone) シエラレオーネ・レオーネ
SLMA (Student Loan Marketing Association) サリー・メイ；奨学金融資金庫
SLOB (secured lease obligation bond) 担保付リース債権債
slope of the nominal yield curve 名目イールド・カーブの傾斜
slope risk 傾斜リスク
slow 伸び止まる
slowdown 鈍化
slower growth 低成長
slower growth of domestic demand 内需減速
slowing demand 需要の落込み
slowing economy 景気鈍化
SLR (stock loan return) 証券返却指図
sluggish 緩慢な
sluggish credit 信用供与の鈍化
sluggish level of export 輸出の不調
slumpflation スランプフレーション
SMA (special miscellaneous account) 信用取引特別口座
SMA (Statement of Management Accounting) 管理会計書
small スモール（100 万ドル単位の取引）
small amount transaction 小口取引
small cap 小型株
small capital stock 小型株
small capitalization stock 小型株
small denomination 少額
small dip in profits 小幅減益
small drop 僅かな低下
small enterprise 小企業
small enterprise mutual aid plan 小規模企業共済
small firm effect 小型株効果
small gain 小幅利益
small investor 小口投資家
small issuer 小型の発行体
small loan 小口金融；少額ローン
small lot order 小口注文
small lot trade 小口売買
small margin 小幅
small revaluation 小幅切上げ
small savers certificate 小口預金証券
small scale enterprises 小規模事業者
small sized business proprietor 小規模企業者
small sized stock 小型株
small spread 小ザヤ
small stock dividend 低率株式配当
small sum and important asset 少額重要資産
small sum and important property 少額重要資産

small sum deferred assets 少額繰延資産
small sum deposit 少額預金
small sum properties 少額資産
small sums of deposits and savings 少額預貯金
small sums of dividend income 少額配当所得
small sums of pension paid to old-age persons 少額老齢年金
small sums of savings 少額預金
small trend 小トレンド
small- and medium-sized enterprise modernization activities 中小企業近代化施策
small- and medium-sized enterprises 中小企業
small-savings tax exemption system 少額貯蓄非課税制度
smallest group 最小グループ
smart money 賢い投資家
SME (Small and Medium Enterprise Agency) 中小企業庁
Smithsonian Agreements スミソニアン合意
Smithsonian rate スミソニアン・レート
Smithsonian system スミソニアン体制
smooth absorption 円滑な消化
smooth consumption 順調な消費
smooth settlement of funds 円滑な資金決済
smooth succession 円滑な引き継ぎ
smooth trading operation 円滑な流通
smoothing intervention スムージング介入
smoothing method 平滑法
smoothing operation 安定化介入
smoothing out operation スムージング・アウト・オペレーション
smuggling 密輸
snake in the tunnel トンネルの中のへび
SNB (Swiss National Bank) スイス国立銀行
SNIF (short-term note issuance facility) 短期 NIF
snowballing 雪だるま式の
soar 急騰する
soaring market 高騰市場
SOC (social overhead capital) 社会資本
social accounting 社会会計
social assistance 社会扶助
social assumption 社会的な仮定
social audit 社会監査
social benefit 社会給付
social capital development 社会資本整備
social club 社交クラブ
social consciousness 社会意識
social consequence 社会的影響
social contract 社会契約
social contribution burden 社会保障負担
social cost 社会原価
social development 社会開発
social force 社会的要因
social good 社会有用性
social indicator 社会指標
social indifference curve 社会的無差別曲線
social infrastructure 社会的基盤
social insurance 社会保険
social insurance premium 社会保険料
social insurance premiums deduction 社会保険料控除
social insurance tax 社会保険税
social marginal cost 社会的限界費用
social protection 社会保障
social return 社会還元
social security 社会保障
Social Security Act 連邦社会保障法
social security arrangement 社会保障制度
social security benefit 社会保障給付
social security burden 社会保障負担
social security contribution 社会保障掛金
social security coverage 社会保障範囲

social security disability income insurance 社会保障障害所得補償保険
social security income 公的年金所得
social security number 社会保障番号
social security pension 社会保障年金
social security pension benefit 公的年金給付
social security premiums 社会保険料
social security recipient 社会保障受給者
social security related expenditure 社会保障関係費
social security retirement benefit 社会保障退職給付
social security system 社会保障制度
social security tax 社会保障税
Social Security tax rate 社会保障税率
social security trust fund 社会保障年金信託基金
social welfare function 社会厚生関数
social welfare related facilities 社会福祉関連施設
socialization 社会化
socially conscious mutual fund 社会貢献ミューチュアル・ファンド
socially responsible investment 社会的責任のある投資
society 組合
Society for Worldwide International Financial Telecommunications SWIFT
socioeconomic requirements 社会経済的要請
SOES (small order entry system) 小型注文処理システム
SOFFEX (Swiss Options and Financial Futures Exchange) スイス・オプション金融先物取引所
soft commission 自由競争売買手数料
soft currency 軟貨
soft currency country 軟貨国
soft dollar ソフト・ドル
soft landing ソフト・ランディング
soft loan ソフト・ローン
soft market 弱気相場
soft spot 出遅株
soiled and damaged banknotes 破損銀行券
sola bill 単一手形
solatium 見舞金
sold bill 割引手形
sold book 商品売上帳
sold out 売切れ
sold securities 売付有価証券
sold with recourse 遡及義務ありで売却
sold without recourse 遡及義務なしで売却
sold-out bond 完売債券
sold-out market 品薄相場
sole agency 一手販売
sole agent 一手販売代理店
sole proprietor 個人事業主
sole proprietorship 個人企業
sole right 独占権
solicitation 勧誘
soliciting 募集
soliciting agent 募集機関
solid demand 堅実な需要
solid line 実線
solvency 支払能力
solvency margin ソルベンシー・マージン
solvency margin ratio ソルベンシー・マージン比率
solvency ratio 流動性比率
solvency standards ソルベンシー基準
solvency valuation ソルベンシー評価
solvent 支払能力ある
sooner-than-thought 思っていた以上に早く
SOP (Statement of Position) 参考意見書
sophisticated arrangements 複雑な取引
sophisticated hedging method 高度なヘッジ手法
sophisticated market 高度な市場
SORP (Statement of Recommended

S

Practices) 会計実務勧告書
sorting of receipts and disbursements of treasury funds for government agencies and specific government accounts, calculation of their total amounts, and matching and checking of the figures against those calculated by the government agencies 計算整理事務
SOS (Somali shilling) ソマリア・シリング
sound banking operation 健全な銀行業務
sound buy idea 健全な買いのテーマ
sound capitalization 自己資本の充実
sound management of financial institutions 経営の健全性
soundness 健全性
soundness of corporate management 企業経営の健全性
sour bond 不履行債券
source 出所
source and application of funds 資金の源泉と使途
source and application of funds statement 資金運用表
source of capital 資金源
source of financing 資金源
source of funds 資金源
source of income 所得源泉
source of profit 利源
source of revenue 財源
source of risk リスク源
source of tax 税源
sources in increase in outstanding shares 上場会社発行済株式数増減状況
sources of changes in CABS (current account balances) 日銀当預増減要因
Sources of Changes in Current Account Balances at the Bank of Japan and Market Operations 日銀当座預金増減要因と金融調節
sovereign 主権者
sovereign act 統治行為
sovereign analyst ソブリン・アナリスト
sovereign balance sheet 国のバランスシート
sovereign bank ソブリン銀行
sovereign bond ソブリン債
sovereign ceiling ソブリン・シーリング
sovereign immunity 主権免除
sovereign issuer ソブリン発行体
sovereign loan ソブリン・ローン
sovereign name ソブリン銘柄
sovereign of taxation 課税主体
sovereign power 主権
sovereign rating ソブリン格付け
sovereign recovery value ソブリン発行体回収率
sovereign risk カントリー・リスク；主権リスク；ソブリン・リスク
sovereign state 主権国
sovereignty 主権
SOYD (sum-of-the-years-digits method) 算術級数法
SPA (State Property Agency) 国有財産庁
space arbitrage スペース裁定
SPAN (standard portfolio analysis of risk) 標準ポートフォリオ・リスク分析
span of control 統制範囲
spare plant capacity 遊休設備
SPDC (simultaneous processing of DVP and collateralization) 国債DVP同時担保受払機能
special acceptance 特殊引受け
special account borrowing 特別会計借入金
special account for distribution of local allocation and shared taxes 交付税及び譲与税配付特別会計
Special Account for Foreign Exchange 外国為替特別会計
Special Account for Government Debt

Consolidation Fund 国債整理基金特別会計
Special Account for Health and Welfare Insurance 厚生保険特別会計
special account for inward portfolio investment 証券特別勘定
Special Account for Petroleum and the More Sophisticated Structure of Demand and Supply of Energy Policies 石油及びエネルギー需要構造高度化対策特別会計
Special Account Law of the Government Debt Consolidation Fund 国債整理基金特別会計法
special account of gains on insurance claim 保険差益特別勘定
special account private borrowing 特別会計による民間借入
Special Accounts 特別会計
special addition 特別加算
special administrative region 特別行政区
special admission fee 特別加入金
special advances rate 特別貸出金利
Special Adviser to the Minister of Finance 財務省顧問
special arbitrage account 特別裁定取引勘定
special assessment 特別課徴金
special assessment bond 特別税収債
special assessment fund 特別課税基金
special associated person 特殊関係人
S
special audit 特別監査
special automobile policy 自家用自動車総合保険
special bad debts reserve 債権償却特別勘定
special bank account firm 特別銀行勘定業者
special benefit 特別給付
special benefit theory of taxation 特別便益説
special bid 特別買付け
special bills for installment sales credit マル専手形
special bond 特別債
special bond account 特別債券勘定
special bracket group スペシャル・ブラケット・グループ
special cash account 特別現金勘定
special charges 特別費用
special clause 特別約款
special clearance 特別清算
Special Clearing Charge 特別清算料
special collecting agent 特別徴収義務者
special collection 特別徴収
special collection of inhabitants tax 住民税の特別徴収
special committee 特別委員会
special committee for public and corporate bond 公社債専門委員会
special concession 特権
special condition 特約
special conditions of the contract 特別条件書
special consideration 特別対価
special contribution 特別掛金
special conversion of currency to replace banknotes lost after the Great Kanto earthquake 焼失兌換券の整理
special corporate surtax 法人特別税
special corporate tax 特別法人税
special cost studies 特殊原価調査
special credit 買取銀行指定信用状
special credit for acquisition of dwelling house 住宅取得等特別控除
special credit of corporation tax 法人税額の特別控除
special crossed check 特定線引小切手
special damage 特別損害
special deduction 特別控除
special deduction for blue return 青色申告特別控除
special deduction for capital gains 譲渡所得の特別控除
special deduction for occasional

income 一時所得の特別控除
special deficit financing bond 特例国債
Special Deficit-Financing Bond Law 特例公債法
Special Deficit-Financing Bonds 特例公債
special deposit account 別口預金
Special Deposit for the Default Compensation Fund 違約損失補償基金特別預託金
special deposit scheme 特別預金制度
special deposits 別段預金
special depreciation 特別償却
special depreciation method 特別な償却の方法
special depreciation reserve 特別償却準備金
special dividend 特別配当
Special Drawing Rights 特別引出権
Special Dues 特別負担金
special early retirement 特別早期退職
special economic benefit 特別な経済的利益
special endorsement 記名式裏書；指図式裏書
special equilibrium 特殊均衡
special examiner 特別国税調査官
special exception 特例
special exchange 特別交換
special exemption for spouse 配偶者特別控除
special expenses 特別費
special fund 特別基金
special general meeting 臨時総会
special incentive tax system 促進税制
special income tax 特別所得税
special initial depreciation 特別当初償却
special inspection 特別検査
special interest party 特別利害関係者
special interests 利益集団
special intermediary institution 特別媒介機関
special international transaction accounts 特別国際金融取引勘定
special item 特別項目
special JGSs 特例国債
special journal 特殊仕訳帳
special L/C (letter of credit) 買取銀行指定信用状
special landholding tax 特別土地保有税
special law 特別法
special ledger 特殊元帳
Special Liaison Officer with the Diet 国会連絡調整官
special lien スペシャル・リーエン
special liquidation 特別清算
special loan 特別融資
special loan account interest rate 特別貸付勘定金利
special loan by the Bank of Japan 日銀特融
special local consumption tax 特別地方消費税
special local grant tax 特別地方交付税
special loss 特損
special margin requirement 特別証拠金要件
special margin transaction 特別信用取引
Special Maruyu program 特別マル優制度
special meeting of security holders 臨時株主総会
special meeting of the Board of Governors 臨時理事会
special member 特別会員
special membership fee 特別会費
special merger 特定合併
Special Message 特別教書
special methods of computing depreciation 特別な減価償却方法
special non-taxable treatment on small government bond 特別マル優
special nursing home for the aged 特別養護老人ホーム
special offering 特別売出し
Special Officer for Budget Information

Systems 上席主計事務専門官
Special Officer for Development Finance 開発金融専門官
Special Officer for Efficiency 能率専門官
Special Officer for Information System 電算システム管理官
Special Officer for Information Technology 電算システム専門官
Special Officer for Investigation and Analysis 研究分析官
Special Officer for Lawsuits 訟務専門官
Special Officer for Liaison and Inspection of the Local Finance Bureaus 業務調整官
Special Officer for Official Housing Construction and Maintenance 宿舎技術専門官
Special Officer for Policy Co-ordination for National Property Management 国有財産調整官
Special Officer for Research and Statistics 調査統計官
Special Officer for Research on Accounts 会計調査官
Special Officer for Research on Allowance Control 給与調査官
Special Officer for Research on Budgetary Matters 財政調査官
Special Officer for Research on Customs Area 保税調査官
Special Officer for Research on Finance 理財調査官
Special Officer for Research on Fiscal Investment and Loan Program 財政投融資調査官
Special Officer for Research on Foreign Exchange Fund and Money Markets 資金運用調査官
Special Officer for Research on Government Debt 国債調査官
Special Officer for Research on International Markets 国際市場調査官
Special Officer for Research on Legal Matters 法規調査官
Special Officer for Research on Mutual Assistance 共済調査官
Special Officer for Research on National Property 国有財産調査官
Special Officer for Research on Personnel Management 人事調査官
Special Officer for Research on Tax 主税調査官
Special Officer for Research on Treasury 国庫調査官
Special Officer for Research, Minister's Secretariat 専門調査官
special outlay 別途支出
special participant 特別参加者
special participant deposit 特別参加者預託金
special participant in equity options trading 株券オプション取引特別参加者
special participant in futures trading based on government bonds 国債証券先物取引特別参加者
special participant in stock price index futures trading 株価指数先物取引特別参加者
special participant participation fee 特別参加者参加金
special participants in futures trading and the like 先物取引等特別参加者
special participation right 特別参加権
special payment 特別決済
Special Planning Officer for Public Relations 広報企画専門官
special product firm 専門商品取扱業者
special production order 特定製造指図書
special provisional petroleum surtax 石油臨時特別税
special public institution of the government 特殊法人

special purpose 特定目的
special purpose company 特別目的会社
special purpose entity 特別目的事業体
special purpose financial statements 特定目的財務諸表
special purpose tax 目的税
special quotation 特別気配；特別清算指数
special quote 気配値段
special quote on the bid side 買呼値についての気配表示
special quote on the offer side 売呼値についての気配表示
special rate 特別料率
special regulations 特例
Special Regulations of Business Regulations and Brokerage Agreement Standards Concerning Government Bond Futures Contract 国債証券に係る有価証券先物取引に関する業務規程及び受託契約準則の特例
Special Regulations of Business Regulations and Brokerage Agreement Standards Concerning Government Bond Futures Option Contract 国債証券先物オプション取引に関する業務規程及び受託契約準則の特例
Special Regulations of Business Regulations and Brokerage Agreement Standards Concerning Stock Index Futures Contract 株価指数先物取引に関する業務規程及び受託契約準則の特例
Special Regulations of Business Regulations and Brokerage Agreement Standards Concerning Stock Index Option Contract 株価指数オプション取引に関する業務規程及び受託契約準則の特例
Special Regulations of Business Regulations Concerning Foreign Bonds 外国債券に関する業務規程の特例
Special Regulations of Business Regulations Concerning Government Bonds 国債証券に関する業務規程の特例
Special Regulations of Business Regulations, Margin/Loan Trading Regulations and Brokerage Agreement Standards Concerning ToSTNet Trading ToSTNet 取引に関する業務規程，信用取引・貸借取引規程及び受託契約準則の特例
Special Regulations on Equity Options 株券オプション特例
Special Regulations on Foreign Bonds 外国債券特例
Special Regulations on Government Bond Futures 国債証券先物特例
Special Regulations on Options on Government Bond Futures 国債証券先物オプション特例
Special Regulations on Stock Index Futures 株価指数先物特例
special regulations on stock index futures 株価指数先物取引特例
Special Regulations on ToSTNeT ToSTNet 特例
special repair expenses 特別修繕費
special reserve 特別準備金；特別積立金；特別引当金
special reserve accounts 準備預り金勘定
special reserve fund 別途積立金
special resolution 特別決議
special revenue fund 別途収益基金
special revenue officer 特別国税徴収官
special risks 特別危険
special rule 特例
Special Rule for Brokerage Agreement Standards 受託契約準則の特例
special rule of the business regulations 業務規程特例
special rule of trading of residential assets 居住用資産の売買特例

S

special rule relating to margin 証拠金特例
special settlement dividend 特別決済配当
special settlement index price 特別清算指数
special surplus fund 特別剰余積立金
special surrender value 特別解約返戻金
special tax bond 特別目的税債券
special tax preferences 優遇税制
special tax reduction bond 特別減税国債
special tax treatment for property replacement 買換えの特例
special taxation measures 租税特別措置
Special Taxation Measures Law 租税特別措置法
special tonnage due 特別とん税
special trades trading 過誤訂正立会外取引
special trading accounts 特定取引勘定
special trading income or loss 特定取引損益
special transfer on tax reduction-related special deficit-financing bond 減税特例国債に係る特例繰入れ
special treatment 特別扱い
special valuation method 特別な評価法
special ward 特別区
S
special ward inhabitants tax 特別区民税
special yen 特別円
specialist スペシャリスト
specialist block purchase and sale スペシャリスト大口売買
specialist block purchases 大口買い付け
specialist book スペシャリストブック
specialist insurer 単数保険者
specialization 特化
specialized business 特殊な事業
specialized foreign exchange bank 外国為替専門銀行
specialized fund 特定銘柄投資信託
specialized industry 特別な業種
specialized institution 専門機関
specialized mutual fund 特定銘柄ミューチュアル・ファンド
specialized organization 専門機関
specialty goods 専門品
specie money 正貨
specie points 金の現送点
specie reserve 正貨準備
specific bonds 特殊債
specific category 特定範疇
specific charge 特定担保
specific consumption tax 個別消費税
specific cost 個別原価
specific deadline 具体的な期限
specific duty 従量税
specific identification method 個別法
specific industry 特定業種
specific information 特定情報
specific insurance 特殊保険
specific lien 特定担保
specific mutual aid 特定共済
specific performance 特定履行
specific productive factors 特殊的生産要素理論
specific property tax 個別財産税
specific provisions 具体的規定
specific regional portfolio 特定地域ポートフォリオ
specific reinsurance 個別再保険
specific return 固有のリターン
specific risk 固有のリスク
specific storage 従量保管料
specific tariff 従量税率
specific tax 従量税
specific transitional provisions 具体的な経過規定
specific-order cost system 個別原価計算制度
specification 仕様書
specification cost 仕様書原価
specified assets 特定資産

specified business 特定事業
specified contribution 特定出資
specified corporate bond 特定社債
specified current deposit 特定当座預金
specified day transaction 特約取引
specified disease insurance 特定疾病保障保険
specified disease policy 特定疾病保険
specified donation 特定寄付金
specified equity trust 特定持分信託
specified foreign branch 特定国外営業所
specified interest 特定利子
specified investment corporation 特定投資法人
specified investment in kind 特定現物出資
specified medical corporation 特定医療法人
specified money in trust 特定金銭信託
specified path 特定の動向
specified period 特定の期間
specified pool 特定プール
specified pool trade プール特定取引
specified portion 指定相続分
specified private-sector urban development 特定民間都市開発
specified reallocated amount 特定再割当金
specified stock 特定銘柄
specified transaction accounts 特定取引勘定
specimen of stock certificate 株券見本
specimens of certificates of the security 有価証券の見本
spectral analysis スペクトル分析
spectrum 領域
speculating for difference 差金取引
speculation 投機
speculation for difference 値ざや稼ぎ
speculation for margin 差金取引
speculation in stocks 株式投機
speculation transaction 投機取引
speculative buyers 思惑買筋
speculative buying 思惑買い
speculative dealing 仕手戦
speculative demand 思惑需要
speculative enthusiasm 投機熱
speculative fund 投資資金
speculative gain 投機利潤
speculative grade 投機的格付け
speculative grade bond 投機的債券
speculative import 思惑輸入
speculative market 投機市場
speculative money 投機的資金
speculative motive 投機的動機
speculative name 仕手銘柄
speculative purpose 投機目的
speculative risk 投機的リスク
speculative stock 仕手株
speculative transaction 投機的取引
speculator buying 投機買い
speculators 投機筋
speed resistance line スピード・レジスタンス・ライン
speedy trial 迅速な裁判
spending 支出
spending cut 予算削減
spending increases 支出増大
spending program 財政支出計画
spending spree 散財
spending variance 予算差異
spendthrift 浪費家
spendthrift trust 消費者保護信託
spike 急上昇
spike in risk aversion リスク回避志向の強まり
spike in wealth 資産増加
spillover effect 溢出効果
spin-off 分社
spin-off of ownership 所有権の分配
split スプリット
split acceptance 分割受託
split annuity 分割個人年金
split commission 手数料分配
split dollar life insurance 分担式生命保険
split joint acceptance 分割共同
split ledger account 分割元帳勘定

split offering 分割発行
split order 大口注文の小口執行
split rating 異なった格付け
split sale 分割売り
split taxation 二分二乗法
split-funding 分割拠出
split-up of a company with separated assets transferable to a new entity 新設分割
split-up of a company with shares of a new entity transferable to shareholders of the original entity 人的分割
split-up of a company with shares of a new entity transferable to the original entity 物的分割
splitting a cause of action 請求原因分割
spoilage expenses 仕損品費
spoiled goods 仕損品
spoils of office 役得
sponsor selectivity スポンサーの選択力
sponsor tolerance to risk スポンサーのリスク許容度
sponsor's role スポンサーの役割
sponsored membership account 被保証メンバー口座
sponsored pension 職域年金
sponsored research 委託研究
sponsoring member 幹事会員
sponsoring securities firm 幹事証券会社
spontaneous combustion 自然発火
sporadic buying 散発的な買い
sports gambling スポーツ賭ばく
spot 直物
spot commodity 現物
spot dealing 直物取引
spot delivery 現物渡し
spot delivery month 直近限月
spot exchange 直物為替
spot exchange rate 直物為替相場
spot forward スポット・フォワード
spot fund スポット・ファンド
spot market 直物市場
spot next スポット・ネクスト
spot period スポット期間
spot position 直物持高
spot price 現物価格
spot quotation 直物相場
spot rate スポット・レート
spot sale 即売
spot share 現株
spot spread 現在のスプレッド
spot trading 直物取引
spot transaction 現物取引
spot value 現物価額
spot yield スポット金利
spot-forward spread 直・先スプレッド
spouse 配偶者
spouse exemption on gift tax 贈与税の配偶者控除
spouse tax credit 配偶者控除
spread スプレッド
spread account スプレッド勘定
spread back up スプレッドの拡大
spread banking スプレッド・バンキング
spread between spot rate and futures rate 直物相場と先物相場の価格差
spread bid スプレッド買呼値
spread compression 利回りの圧縮
spread curves スプレッド曲線
spread income スプレッド収入
spread loan スプレッドローン
spread lock agreement スプレッド・ロック契約
spread management スプレッド運用
spread market スプレッド・マーケット
spread of risk リスク分散
spread offer スプレッド売呼値
spread order スプレッド注文
spread position スプレッド・ポジション
spread price スプレッド値段
spread rally スプレッドの縮小
spread risk スプレッド・リスク
spread sheet スプレッド・シート

S

spread tightening スプレッドの縮小
spread trading スプレッド・トレーディング
spread trading between contract months 限月間スプレッド取引
spread transaction スプレッド取引
spread widening スプレッドの拡大
spur economic growth 経済成長を促す
spurt 急増
SPV (special purpose vehicle) 特別目的媒体
SQC (statistical quality control) 統計的品質管理
square スクエア
square matrix 正方行列
square position スクエア・ポジション
squared スクエアの状態にある
squeeze 締め上げ
SRG (Suriname guilder) スリナム・ギルダー
SRI (socially responsible investment) 社会的責任投資
SRO (self regulatory organization) 自主規制機関
SSARS (Statement on Standards for Accounting and Review Services) 会計レビュー業務基準書
SSI (standard settlement information) 決済口座情報
SSI (supplemental security income) 追加的所得補償
SSS (securities settlement system) 証券決済システム
St. Kitts & Nevis (EC (East Caribbean) dollar) セントキッツ＆ネイビス（EC ドル）
St. Lucia (EC (East Caribbean) dollar) セントルシア（EC ドル）
STABEX (stabilization of export earnings) 輸出所得安定化制度
stability 安定性
stability analysis 安定性分析
stability condition 安定条件
stability of the foreign exchange market 為替需給の安定性
stabilization operation 安定操作
stabilization policy 安定化政策
stabilizing 安定促進的
stabilizing transactions 安定操作
stable dividend 安定配当
stable dollar assumption 貨幣価値一定の公準
stable economic growth 安定経済成長
stable money principle 安定貨幣論
stable stock 安定株
stable stockholder 安定株主
stable stockholder operation 株主安定工作
stable value fund 安定価値運用ファンド
stable value portfolio 安定価値ポートフォリオ
stag 短期利益投資家
stage of completion 進捗度
stagflation スタグフレーション
staggered board of directors 取締役任期の分散
staggering maturities 満期の分散
staggering maturity 満期分散
stagnant industry 停滞産業
stagnant market 低迷相場
stagnation 低迷
stake 投資金額（取得額，投資持分）
stake a claim 権利を主張する
stakeholder ステークホルダー
stale B/L (bill of lading) 時期経過船荷証券
stale check 延滞小切手
stalling 弱含みになっている
stamp 印紙
stamp duty law 収入印紙税法
stamp revenue 印紙収入
stand alone investment 単なる投資対象
stand in debt 債務がある
Standard & Poor's スタンダード・アンド・プアーズ
Standard & Poor's 400 Industrial スタンダード・アンド・プアーズ 400 種工業株価指数

S

Standard & Poor's 500 スタンダード・アンド・プアーズ 500 種
Standard & Poor's 500 index スタンダード・プアーズ 500 種株価指数
Standard & Poor's Composite Index スタンダード・アンド・プアーズ総合指数
Standard & Poor's Stock Price Index スタンダード・アンド・プアーズ株価指数
standard agency 標準的な政府系機関
standard amount of clearing margin 取引証拠金基準額
standard annuity mortality table 標準年金死亡表
standard arrangement 標準的な取決め
standard bill of materials 標準材料仕様書
standard burden rate 標準配賦率
standard class 標準体階層
standard clause 標準約款
standard coin 本位貨幣
standard commission 標準手数料
standard correlation 標準相関係数
standard cost 標準原価
standard cost accounting 標準原価計算
standard cost method 標準原価法
standard cross default provision 標準クロス・デフォルト条項
standard currency basket system 標準バスケット方式
standard date 標準日
standard deduction 標準控除
standard default assumption curve 標準デフォルト・モデル・カーブ
standard depletion expenses 標準損料
standard deviation 標準偏差
standard deviation of volatility 変動率の標準偏差
standard disability provisions 標準所得補償約款
standard documentation 標準書式
standard duration 標準的なデュレーション
standard efficient frontier 標準有効フロンティア
standard error 標準誤差
standard error of beta ベータの標準誤差
standard error of estimate 推定値の標準誤差
standard industrial classification 標準産業分類
standard industrial mortality table 標準簡易生命保険表
standard interest rate 標準金利
standard issue 標準銘柄
standard labor cost 標準労務費
standard machine time 標準機械時間
standard manufacturing expense 標準製造間接費
standard materials cost 標準材料費
standard money 本位貨幣
standard money reserve requirement 正貨準備義務
standard money system 本位貨幣制度
standard of performance 標準の性能
standard of price 度量標準
standard of value 価値尺度機能
standard opinion 標準意見
standard option 通常のオプション
standard policy 標準的保険
standard premium 標準保険料
standard price 標準価格
standard price for margin calculation 証拠金基準額
standard profit 標準利益
standard quantity of materials consumed 材料標準消費量
standard rate 標準金利；標準料率
standard rate of charge 徴収標準率
standard ratio for calculating cash collateral 基準担保金率
standard setting 基準設定
standard setting body 基準設定機関
standard silver dollar 標準銀ドル
standard stocks 標準株
standard system 本位制度
standard tax rate 標準税率

S

standard treatment 標準処理
Standard Valuation Law 標準責任準備金評価法
standard value 標準値
standard value for clearing margin rate calculation 取引証拠金率算定基準値
standard wage 基準賃金
standard-cost system 標準原価計算制度
standard-run quantity 標準生産量
standardization 標準化
standardized bonds 標準物
standardized financial statements 標準財務諸表
standardized instrument 標準物
standardized long-term government bonds 長期国債標準物
standardized measurement 標準化された測定方法
standardized mid-term government bonds 中期国債標準物
standardized super long-term government bonds 超長期国債標準物
standardized volatility 標準化ボラティリティー
standards 基準
standards of audit procedures 監査手続基準
standby agreement 残額引受け契約
standby arrangement スタンド・バイ取決め
standby commitment 残額引受け
standby credit スタンドバイ信用状
standby facilities スタンドバイ・ファシリティーズ
standby facility スタンバイ・ファシリティ
standby letters of credit スタンドバイ信用状
standby underwriting 請負募集；残額引受発行
standing auditor 常任監査役
standing body 常設機関
standing charge 恒常費用
standing committee 常設委員会
standing cost 恒常単価
standing expenses 固定費
standing governor 常任理事
standing instruction 自動引落指図
standing order 継続指図書；自動引落依頼
standing production order 継続製造命令書
standing proxy 常任代理人
standing statutory auditor 常勤監査役
standstill スタンドスティル
standstill agreement 弁済の猶予
standstill provision スタンドスティル条項
staple product 主力商品
star system スター・システム
start date 実行日
start day of operations オペのスタート日
start-up 開業
start-up companies 振興企業
start-up cost 開業費用
start-up expenses 創業費
starting-load cost 当初負担原価
state and local government debt 公債
state attorney 州検事
state bank 州法銀行
state bankruptcy 国家破産
state benefit 公的給付
state bond 州債
state branching 州内支店設置
state capital 国家資本
state capitalism 国家資本主義
state controlled bank 国有化銀行
state controlled enterprise 政府管理下企業
state enterprises 国営企業
state franchise tax 州法人税
state government bond 州政府債券
state government debenture 州政府債券
state government securities 州政府証券

state guaranteed debt 政府保証債
state income tax 州所得税
state insurance department 州保険局
state law 州法
state medical care 公的医療給付
state monopoly payment 専売納付金
state of financial standings 経理の状況
state of observance 遵守状況
state of support 支援状況
state of the business operation 業務の状態
state of the union message 一般教書
state pension 公的年金
state plan 公的制度
state price density 状態価格密度
State Redress Law 国家賠償法
state retirement benefit 公的退職給付
state-chartered association 州免許の組織
state-owned company 国有企業
stated amount 券面額
stated capital 表示資本金
stated interest rate 約定利率
stated liabilities 表示負債
stated maturity date 法定償還日
stated par 額面
stated rate of interest 表面金利
stated terms 表示値
stated value 表示価額
stated value no-par stock 記載式無額面株式
statement 計算書
statement classified by account title 勘定科目内訳明細書
statement of account 勘定照合表
statement of accounting policies 会計方針の説明
Statement of Accounting Standard 会計基準書
statement of accounts 決算報告
statement of administrative cost 行政コスト計算書
statement of affairs 財産状態報告書
statement of aggregate recognized gains and losses 総認識利得損失計算書
statement of assets 財産目録
statement of assets and liabilities 資産・負債計算書
statement of borrowings 借入金計算書
statement of capital 資本金計算書
statement of capital surplus 資本剰余金計算書
statement of cash receipts and disbursement 資金繰表
statement of changes 変動計算書
statement of changes in equity 持ち分変動計算書
statement of changes in financial position 財政状態変動表
statement of changes in shareholder's equity 株主持ち分変動計算書
statement of changes in stockholders' equity 資本勘定報告書
statement of comprehensive income 包括利益計算書
statement of declaration 宣誓書
statement of disagreement 不服の申立
statement of disposal and liquidation 処分・清算計算書
statement of earned surplus 利益剰余金計算金
statement of earnings 損益計算書
statement of facts 合意事実記載書
statement of financial condition 財政状態計算書
statement of financial position 貸借対照表
statement of funds 資金計算書
statement of holding period 所有期間明細書
statement of income and expense 収支一覧表
statement of income and retained earnings 剰余金結合計算書
statement of intent 趣意書
statement of investments by and distributions to owners 株主持ち分変動表
statement of items 内訳書

S

statement of legal opinion 法律意見書
statement of liquidation 清算書
statement of loss 損益計算書(純損失の場合)
statement of net assets 純資産計算書
statement of operation earnings 経常利益計算書
statement of operations 事業報告書
statement of opinions 意見書
statement of performance 業績報告書
statement of position 参考意見書
statement of principles 基本方針
statement of production cost 製造原価報告書
statement of receipts and disbursement 収支計算書
statement of reconciliation of bank account 銀行勘定照合表
statement of reserves 引当金計算書
statement of retained earnings 利益余剰金計算書
statement of settlement of accounts 収支決算書
statement of sources and uses of funds 資金運用表
statement of stockholders' equity 株主持ち分計算書
statement of surplus 剰余金計算書
statement of undistributed realized earnings 未分配実現利益計算書
statement of variation of funds 資金移動表
statement of withdrawal 取下届出書
statement of withdrawal of shelf registration 発行登録取下届出書
statement paper 精算表
static analysis 静態分析
static equilibrium 静的均衡
static model 静学モデル
static multiplier 静学乗数
static ratio 静態比率
static return 静態利回り
static risk 静態的リスク
static statistics 静態統計
stating part 主部
stationary state 定常状態
statistical analysis 統計的分析
statistical decision theory 統計的決定理論
statistical error 統計誤差
statistical estimation 統計的見積り
statistical inference 統計的推測
statistical measure 統計的な測度
statistical model 統計モデル
statistical procedure 統計的処理
statistical terminology 統計用語
statistical theory 統計理論
statistics 統計
Statistics Law 統計法
statistics of foreign currency reserves 外貨準備統計
statistics on money supply マネー・サプライ統計
statistics on money supply analysis マネー・サプライ分析統計
status of borrowed money 借用金状況
status of loans 貸出金の状況
status report 現状報告
statute law 制定法
statute of limitation 時効;出訴期限
statute of limitations on collection 徴収権の消滅時効
statute of limitations on refund claim 還付請求権の時効
statutory accounting principle 法定会計原則
statutory assignment 制定法上の譲渡
statutory audit 法定監査
statutory auditors' meeting 監査役会
statutory debt limit 法定発行限度額
statutory depletion method 法定減耗償却法
statutory depreciation 法定償却
statutory depreciation method 法定償却方法
statutory due date of tax payment 法定納期限
statutory due date of tax return 法定申告期限
statutory investment 適法投資

S

statutory merger 強制合併
statutory prospectus 法定目論見書
statutory rate of interest 法定利率
statutory requirements 法律上の要件
statutory reserve 法定準備金
statutory restriction 法令上の制限
statutory security 一般担保
statutory surplus 法定準備金；法定剰余金
statutory tariff 法定税率
statutory useful life 法定耐用年数
statutory valuation method 法定評価方法
statutory valuation method of securities 有価証券の法定評価方法
statutory voting 法定議決権
stay of proceedings 訴訟中止
stay within the current range 現在の取引レンジ内に留まる
staying resilient 底堅い
STD (Sao Tome/Principe dobra) サントメプリンシペ・ドブラ
steady 堅調な
steady at low levels 低水準で安定した
steady market 堅調な市況
steady rise 着実な伸び
steady sales 順調な売上
steepening スティープニング
steeper fall 急落
steering committee 運営委員会
step function 階段関数
step ladder payment method ステップ償還
step rate 段階料率
step-down bond ステップ・ダウン債
step-in right 介入権
step-up bond ステップ・アップ債
step-up coupon ステップ・アップ・クーポン
step-up method 段階方式
step-up swap ステップ・アップ・スワップ
stepped cost 段階式原価
stepped coupon bond 段階的利付債
sterling balance ポンド残高
sterling bonds ポンド建債券
sterling currency futures ポンド通貨先物
sterling exchange standard ポンド為替本位制
sterling floaters ポンド建て変動利付債
sterling securities market 英ポンド建証券市場
sterling swap rate ポンド・スワップ・レート
stewardship 責務遂行
STI (Straits Times Index) ストレイツ・タイムズ指数
sticker price 希望価格
stiffen 締まる
stimulating fiscal policy 景気刺激型財政政策
stimulative fiscal policy 景気刺激型の財政政策
stimulative monetary policy 金融刺激政策
stimulus package 刺激策
stipulated damages 約定損害賠償額
stipulated premium 規定保険料
stipulated price 協定価格
stipulated security 約定担保権
stipulation 条項
stochastic calculus 確率解析
stochastic control 確率制御
stochastic discount factor 確率的割引ファクター
stochastic index ストキャスティック指数
stochastic model 確率モデル
stochastic process 確率過程
stochastic sequence 確率系列
stochastic simulation 確率シミュレーション
stock 株式
stock abbreviation 株式略語
stock account 資本勘定；証券口座
stock acquired by borrowed money 借入金で取得した株式
stock acquired by capital increase 増

資により取得した株式
stock acquired by merger 合併により取得した株式
stock acquired by the investment in kind 現物出資取得株
stock acquired due to merger 合併によって取得した株式
stock acquisition 株式取得
stock adjustment ストック調整
stock ahead 優先取引株式
stock allotted to third party 第三者に割当てられた株式
stock allotted to third persons 第三者割当株
stock arbitrage 株式裁定取引
stock at par 額面株
stock authorized 授権資本
stock bonus 株式ボーナス
stock bonus plan ストック・ボーナス・プラン
stock book 在庫品控帳
stock broker 株式外務員；株式仲買人
stock buyback 株式買戻し
stock capitalization 資本金
stock certificate 株券
stock certificate to bearer 無記名株券
stock collateral loan 株式担保金融
Stock Company Reorganization and Rehabilitation Act 会社更生法
stock compensation plan 株式報償制度
stock consolidation 株式の併合
stock controlling other business 企業支配株式
stock cum rights 増資権利付株式
stock dealing 株式取引
stock dividend 株式配当
stock dividend reinvestment program 株式配当再投資プログラム
stock equity 株式持ち分
stock equity value 株式持分価値
stock exchange 株式取引所
Stock Exchange Automatic Quotation SEAQ
stock exchange clearing house 取引所の清算機関
stock exchange daily official list 株式取引所相場表
stock exchange holiday 株式取引所休日
stock exchange loan 株式取引所貸付
stock exchange panic 株式恐慌
stock exchange seat 株式取引所会員権
stock exchange share 当所株
stock exchange transaction 取引所取引
stock flow ストック・フロー
stock for guarantee 保証株
stock for inflation hedging インフレ・ヘッジ株
stock for margin trading 信用取引銘柄
stock for which listing application is made 上場申請に係る株式
stock funding 株式資金調達
stock future 株先
stock futures transaction 株式先物取引
stock in hand 現在品
stock in the inventory 棚卸品
stock in trade 在庫品
stock index derivatives 株価指数デリバティブ
Stock Index Futures Clearing Participant 株価指数先物等清算参加者
Stock Index Futures Clearing Qualification 株価指数先物等清算資格
Stock Index Futures Non-Clearing Participant 株価指数先物等非清算参加者
stock index futures trading participant 株価指数先物取引参加者
stock inflation ストック・インフレーション
stock insurance company 会社組織保険会社
stock investment 株式投資
stock investment in subsidiary 子会社株式投資
stock investment trust 株式投資信託

stock issuance 株式発行
stock issue at market price 株式の時価発行
stock issuing expenses 株式発行費用
stock ledger 株式台帳
stock lending 証券貸借
stock lending fee 品貸料
stock lending rate 逆日歩
stock level 手持在庫水準
stock linked to subsidiary performance 子会社業績連動株式
stock list 株式上場審査
stock listing agreement 上場契約書
stock loan 株券貸付
stock loan market 貸株市場
stock market 株式市場
stock market crash 株式恐慌
stock market fluctuation 株式市場の変動
stock market valuation 株式市場のバリュエーション
stock market's behavior 株式市場の動き
stock mind ストック・マインド
stock mini-investment 株式ミニ投資
stock name 株式銘柄
stock name transfer expenses 名義書換費
stock of affiliated company 関係会社株式
stock on hand 手持ち株
stock option plan ストック・オプション制度
stock option type warrant ストック・オプション型ワラント
stock portfolio 株式組入状況
stock power 株券譲渡委任状
stock price 株価
stock price analysis 株価分析
stock price average 株価平均
stock price average by size of stocks 規模別株価平均
stock price index 株価指数
stock price index arbitrage transaction 株価指数裁定取引
stock price index by size of stocks 規模別株価指数
stock price index call option 株価指数コール・オプション
stock price index futures 株価指数先物
stock price index futures by industry 業種別株価指数先物取引
stock price index futures contract 株価指数先物契約
stock price index futures non-clearing participant 株価指数先物非清算参加者
stock price index futures trading 株価指数先物取引
stock price index on the market value 時価総額方式の株価指数
stock price index option transaction 株価指数オプション取引
stock price index put option 株価指数プット・オプション
stock price linked bonds 株価リンク債
stock price manipulation 株価操作
stock purchase option 株式買取オプション
stock purchase plan 株式購入制度
stock purchase right 新株引受権
stock purchase warrant 株式買取権証書
stock quotations 株式相場
stock rating 株式の格付け
stock receipt 株券譲渡証
stock record 株式記録
stock redemption 株式償還
stock register 株式元帳
stock related bond 株式関連債
stock repurchase plan 株式買戻し制度
stock right 増資新株買取権
stock risk estimation 株式リスクの推定
stock subscription 株式応募
stock subscription form 株式申込書
stock swap 株式スワップ
stock symbol 株式記号；ストック・シンボル

S

stock taking 実地棚卸
stock trade on credit 株式の信用取引
stock transfer 名義書換え
stock transfer agent 株式代行機関
stock trust 株式投信
stock turnover (ratio) 在庫品回転率
stock used in the average 平均株価採用銘柄
stock valuation 株式評価
stock valuation based on dividend 配当還元株式評価
stock valuation summary 株式評価概要
stock warrants ストック・ワラント
stock without par value 無額面株式
stock yield 株式利回り
stock-based compensation 株式報酬
stock-to-sales ratio 在庫率
stockholder 株主
stockholder of record 株主名簿の株主
stockholder's equity 株主持ち分
stockholder's report 株主報告書
stockholders' equity per share 一株当り株主資本
stockholders' fund 株主資金
stockholders' meeting for merger 合併のための株主総会
stockholders' surplus 株主剰余金
stockholding limit for foreign investors 外人持株制限
Stockholm Stock Exchange ストックホルム証券取引所
stockpile financing 滞貨金融
stolen bill 盗難手形
stolen check 盗難小切手
stop high ストップ高
stop loss 損切り
stop loss buy order 逆指値買注文
stop loss coverage 超過損害保険
stop loss insurance ストップ・ロス保険
stop order 指値注文
stop price 逆指値
stop-and-go policy ストップ・アンド・ゴー政策
stop-limit order 逆指値注文
stop-loss order ストップ・ロス注文；損切り注文
stop-loss trading ストップ・ロス・トレーディング
stop-out price of T-bond T-ボンド入札最安値
stop-payment order 支払停止通知
stoppage of business 営業停止
storage accounts receivable 未収保管料
storage cost 保管費用
storage management 貯蔵品管理
storage of inventories 棚卸資産の保管
store business interruption insurance 店舗休業保険
store of value 価値保蔵手段
stored goods 貯蔵品
storekeepers' comprehensive insurance 店舗総合保険
stores ledger 原材料元帳
stores purchase book 材料仕入帳
STP (straight through processing) STP
straddle ストラドル
straddle position transaction ストラドルポジション取引
straddle trading ストラドル取引
straddling 両建て
straight average cost method 単純平均法
straight B/L (bill of lading) 記名式船荷証券
straight bankruptcy 単純破産
straight bond 社債
straight cash vehicles 現物商品
straight climb 棒上げ
straight corporate bond 普通社債
straight credit ストレート・クレジット
straight currency swap ストレート・カレンシー・スワップ
straight debt 普通借入債務
straight equity 普通株
straight fall 棒下げ

S

straight government bond 普通国債
straight life annuity 終身年金
straight life policy 普通終身保険
straight line amortization 定額償却法
straight line method 定額法
straight term insurance policy 定額保証定期生命保険
straight-line depreciation 定額減価償却法
straight-line interpolation 線形補間法
straightforward 単刀直入の
Straits Times Industrial Index ストレイツ・タイムズ工業株指数
strangle ストラングル
strangle position transaction ストラングル・ポジション取引
strap ストラップ
strategic alliance 戦略的提携
strategic buyout 戦略的買収
strategic decision making 戦略的意思決定
strategic field 戦略分野
strategic industries 戦略産業
strategic investment 戦略投資
strategic partner 戦略的パートナー
strategic risk 戦略リスク
strategy 戦略
stratification 層化
stratified 層別の
stratified sampling 層別標本抽出
stratified society 階層化社会
straw bail 空保証人
straw man 無資力者
stream of cash flows 一連のキャッシュフロー
stream of cash receipts 一連の現金の流入
streamlining of distribution channels 流通合理化
streamlining program 合理化プログラム
street broker 場外仲買人
Street economist 市場エコノミスト
street name 名義
street price 引け後相場
street side 証券会社間
strengthen 強張る
strengthen to the three year highs 3年ぶりの高値となる
strengthening against the dollar 対ドルでの上昇
strengthening of managerial function 管理機能強化
stress test ストレス・テスト
stretched positions 偏ったポジション
strict construction 厳格解釈
strict foreclosure 代物弁済担保物件取得
strict liability 厳格責任
stricter criteria より厳格な基準
strike a balance 妥協点を見出す
strike out 削除する
strike price 権利行使価格
strike rate 行使金利
striking distance of breaking through 超えるのが視野に入る
stringency 厳格性
stringent policy 引締め政策
strip curve ストリップ・カーブ
strip guarantee ストリップ保証
strip player ストリップ・プレイヤー
strip spread ストリップ・スプレッド
strip yield ストリップ利回り
strippable ストリップ適格の
stripped cap ストリップ・キャップ
stripped interest rate cap ストリップ金利キャップ
stripped issue ストリップ銘柄
stripped securities ストリップ証券
stripped zero-coupon ストリップ・ゼロ・クーポン
STRIPS (separate trading of registered interest and principal of securities) ストリップ債
strong against the dollar 対ドルで上昇する
strong and weak 強弱
strong axiom 強公準
strong covenant 強力な制限事項
strong dollar ドル高

strong feeling 強気
strong form ストロング・フォーム
strong form efficiency ストロング型効率性
strong growth 高い伸び
strong incentive 好材料
strong market 強気市況
strong rebound 力強い回復
strong relative to the dollar 対ドルで強い
strong resistance 強い抵抗線
strong yen 円高
stronger half of the band 変動幅の上限
structural 構造的
structural adjustment 構造調整
structural adjustment loan facility 構造調整融資
structural analysis 構造分析
structural change 構造変化
structural choice 構造の選択
structural concern 構造上の懸念
structural equation 構造方程式
structural impediments initiative talks 構造協議
structural inflation 構造的インフレーション
structural liquidity 構造的流動性
structural model 構造モデル
structural outline 構図
structural problem 構造問題
structural reform 構造改革
structural risk 構造リスク
structural unemployment 構造的失業
structurally bearish on 構造的弱気スタンス
structure 構築物
structure of interest rates 金利構造
structure of the government bond futures market 国債先物市場の仕組み
structured bond 仕組債
structured credit product ストラクチャード・クレジット商品
structured equity product 株式仕組商品
structured finance 仕組金融
structured finance market 仕組金融市場
structured financial representation 体系的財務表現
structured note 仕組債
structured securities 仕組証券
structured transaction 仕組取引
struggle against the dollar 対ドルで頭の痛い展開
student comprehensive insurance 学生総合保険
Study Group for the Promotion of the Internationalization of the Yen 円の国際化推進研究会
style analysis スタイル分析
style management スタイル管理
sub-account 下位勘定（サブ・アカウント）
sub-account number サブ口座番号
sub-classification 小分類
sub-custodian サブカストディアン
sub-index サブ指数
sub-letting agreement 転貸契約
sub-LIBOR LIBOR 以下
sub-martingale 劣マーチンゲール
sub-par bond アンダー・パーの債券
sub-subsidiary 孫会社
sub-total 小計
sub-underwriter 下引受会社
subcontract 下請
subcontract factory 下請工場
subcontractor 下請業者
subdivision 内訳区分
subduct 差引く
subdued economic growth 景気低迷
subdued performance 低迷した業績
subgroup 小グループ
subject 科目
subject market サブジェクト・マーケット
subject of futures trading 先物取引の対象
subject premium 基準保険料
subject quote 気配値

subject to condition 条件付で
subject-matter of insurance 保険の目的
subjective basis 主観的基準
subjective judgment 主観的判断
subjective probability 主観的確率
sublease サブリース
sublease payment サブリース料
sublet 転貸し
submission of agreement 約定書の差入れ
submission of collateral 担保の提出
submission of proposals 議案の提出
submit to the exclusive jurisdiction 専属管轄に服する
subordinate debenture 劣後条項付社債
subordinate ledger 補助元帳
subordinate tranche 劣後トランシェ
subordinated 劣後の
subordinated beneficiary rights 劣後受益権
subordinated bond 劣後社債
subordinated capital 劣後資本
subordinated claim 劣後請求権
subordinated creditor 劣後債権者
subordinated debenture 劣後債
subordinated debt 劣後債権
subordinated debt market 劣後債市場
subordinated deposit 劣後預託金
subordinated discount bond 劣後割引債
subordinated funding 劣後資金の調達
subordinated interest 劣後持ち分
subordinated loan 劣後ローン
subordinated payment-in-kind bond 劣後ペイメント・イン・カインド債
subordinated receivables 劣後債権
subordinated securities 劣後証券
subordinated stock 劣後株
subordinated stock with par value 額面劣後株式
subordinated tranche 劣後トランシェ
subordinated unsecured debenture 劣後性無担保社債
subordinates 劣後債
subordination 後順位；従属
subordination clause 劣後条項
subparticipation 裏参加
subprime サブプライム
subrogated performance 代位弁済
subrogated right 代位債権
subrogation 代位；引継ぎ
subrogation arising out of salvage 残存物代位
subrogation payment 代位納付
subrogation receipt 代位領収書
subrogation right 代位権
subrogation right of obligee 債権者代位権
subscribe 出資する
subscribed capital 応募資本
subscribed capital stock 未払込資本
subscriber of shares 株式の引受人
subscriber rate 保険加入者保険料率
subscriber's yield 応募者利回り
subscribing or underwriting 応募又は引受け
subscription 応募
subscription agent 募集代理人
subscription agreement 募集契約
subscription blank 株式申込書
subscription book closed 株式募集締切
subscription book open 株式募集開始
subscription by Bank of Japan 日銀応募
subscription by the Trust Fund Bureau 資金運用部引受
subscription certificate 出資証券
subscription details 募集方法
subscription for shares 株式応募
subscription for stock 株式引受
subscription hour for purchase 買付申込時間
subscription income 予約販売収益
subscription money 申込金
subscription of government bonds in market 市中消化国債
subscription period 募集期間
subscription policy 共同引受保険

subscription price 応募価格
subscription privilege 新株引受特権
subscription ratio 新株引受権比率
subscription right to new shares 新株引受権
subscription rights to new shares 新株引受権証書
subscription warrant 新株引受権証書
subscription warrant to preferred equity contributions 優先出資引受権証書
subscription/contribution bonds 出資・拠出国債
subscription's receivable account 株式引受勘定
subsequent adjustment 事後修正
subsequent change 事後の変動
subsequent depreciation and amortization 以後の償却
subsequent event 後発事象
subsequent event review 後発事象のレビュー
subsequent event which does not require restatement 修正再表示を要しない後発事象
subsequent expenditure 事後の支出
subsequent expenditure on asset purchased 資産取得後の支出
subsequent issue price 再発行価格
subsequent measurements 事後測定
subsequent period 後の期間
subsequent taxable year 次事業年度
subsequent year 次期
subset 小集団
subsidiary 子会社
subsidiary accounts 補助元帳勘定
subsidiary book 補助簿
subsidiary conditions 補足的な条件
subsidiary department 補助部門
subsidiary department charge 補助部門費
subsidiary journal 補助記入帳
subsidiary ledger 補助元帳
subsidiary material cost 補助材料費
subsidiary money 補助貨幣
subsidiary undertaking 子会社
subsidies from the government or local public entities 国又は地方公共団体の補助金
subsidized export 補助金付き輸出
subsidized good 補助付物品
subsidy 補助金
subsidy charged to the special account 特別勘定に算入された補助金
subsidy government bond 交付国債
substance 本質
substance over form 実質優先
substandard 特別条件付きの
substandard loan 回収に問題をもつ貸付
substandard premium 特別条件付保険料
substandard risk 特別条件危険
substantial decline 大幅な減少
substantial evidence 実質的証拠
substantial party 実質的な当事者
substantial performance 実質的履行
substantial shareholding report 大量保有報告書
substantive 実質的な
substantive change 大きな変更
substantive effect 実質的効果
substantive evidence 実質証拠
substantive law 実体法
substantive test 実証性テスト
substitute 代物
substitute assets 代替資産
substitute certificate for government bond 国債代用証書
substitute certificates 代用証書
substitute collateral obligation 代替担保債務
substitute fixed assets 代替固定資産
substitute member representative 臨時会員代表
substitute payee 代理受取人
substitute property 代替資産
substitute representative 代表者代理人
substitute securities 代用有価証券

substituted expenses 代替費用
substitution 入替；代替
substitution account 銘柄入替勘定
substitution account of IMF IMF 代替勘定
substitution asset effect 資産代替効果
substitution benefit 代行給付
substitution effect 代替効果
substitution of land lot 換地処分
substitution swap 代替スワップ
subvention 助成金
subzero growth マイナス成長
success fee 成功報酬
successful bid 落札
successful bidder 落札者
succession 承継
succession of book value in the case of merger 合併の場合の帳簿価額の引継ぎ
succession of endorsement 裏書の連続
succession of liabilities 債務引継ぎ
succession of national tax liability 国税債務の承継
succession of right of taxation 課税権の承継
succession of tax liability 納税義務の継承
succession of tax obligation 納付義務の承継
succession to business 事業継承
successive 次順位の
successive inheritance 相次相続
successor 後継者
S
successor company 承継会社
successor of the deceased 死亡者の相続人
succinct 簡潔な
suction to cash キャッシュへの付着
sue and labor charges 損害防止費用
sue and labor clause 損害防止条項
sue out 申立てて取得する
sufficiency 充足
sufficient liquidity 十分な流動性
suggested resale price 推奨再販価格
suitability rule 適合性規則
suitor 訴訟人
sum 合計額
sum insured left 残存保険金額
sum payable at death 死亡保険金
sum total 合計
sum up 合計する
sum-of-the-units method 生産高比例法
sum-of-the-years-digits method 級数法
summarized financial statements 要約財務諸表
summarized information 要約された情報
summary 要約
summary account 集計勘定；総括勘定
summary audit report 監査概要書
summary budget 総括予算
summary journal 総合仕訳帳
summary measure 集約尺度
summary of earnings 営業成績
summary of significant accounting policies 主要会計方針の要約
summary of statistics 総括表
summary plan 制度概要
summary posting 合計転記
summary procedure 督促手続
summary proceedings 略式手続
summary sheet 集計表
summary statement of business 事業概況説明書
summer time 夏時間
summing-up 証拠の要約
summons 呼出状
sums insured method 保険金額比例主義
sundries 雑費
sundry account 雑勘定
sundry expenses 諸雑費
sundry goods 雑貨
sundry income 雑収入
sundry receipts 雑収入
sundry supplies 消耗品
sunk cost サンク・コスト
sunrise industry 新興産業
sunset provision サンセット条項
sunshine law サンシャイン法；情報公

開法
sunshine trading サンシャイン取引
super 301 Article スーパー 301 条
super floater swap スーパー・フローター・スワップ
super gold tranche スーパー・ゴールド・トランシェ
super long-run 超長期
super long-term 超長期
super majority provision スーパー・マジョリティー条項
super NOW account スーパーNOW勘定
super prime rate スーパー・プライム・レート
super sinker bond スーパーシンカー債
super-long-term government bond 超長期国債
super-national bond 国際機関債
superannuation 恩給
Superannuation Plan 在職死亡保障付退職金積立制度
superannuation reserve 退職金積立金
superannuation scheme 退職年金制度
supercargo 貨物上乗人
superficiary 地上権者
superficies 地上権
superimposed plan 上乗保険
superintendent 監督官
superior courts 上級裁判所
superior obligation 財団債権
superior return 優れた収益
supermajority 絶対過半数
supernational organizations 国際機関
supersede 取って代わる
supertax 付加税
supervision 監理
supervision and order 監督命令
supervisor スーパーバイザー
supervisory 監督的
supervisory analyst 監督資格を有するアナリスト
supervisory authorities 監督当局
Supervisory Bureau 監督局
Supervisory Coordination Division 総務課(監督局)
supplement employee retirement 補足従業員退職給付
supplemental 補足の
supplemental agreement 補完契約
supplemental financial information 補足財務情報
supplemental policies 補完保険
supplemental security income 追加所得補償
supplementary benefit 補足給付
supplementary budget 補正予算
supplementary capital 補完的資本項目
supplementary cost 補足的費用
supplementary disclosure 追加的な開示
supplementary document 追補書類
Supplementary Documents to the Shelf Registration Statement 発行登録追補書類
supplementary financial measure 補足融資
supplementary financial statements 補足財務諸表
supplementary format 補足的様式
supplementary fund 補完ファンド
supplementary income statement information 損益計算書の補足資料
supplementary information 補足情報
supplementary insurance 補足的な保険
supplementary package 景気対策
supplementary pension 加算年金
supplementary plan 補完年金
supplementary proceedings 補充手続
supplementary prospectus 追補目論見書
supplementary provision 付則
supplementary rate 補充率
supplementary registration 付記登録
supplementary schedule 付属明細表
supplementary special deposit scheme 追加特別預金制度
supplementary statement 附属明細書

S

supplier 仕入先
supplier's credit 延払信用
supplies account 消耗品勘定
supplies expenses 消耗品費
supply 支給
supply arrangements 供給契約
supply capacity 供給能力
supply curve 供給曲線
supply function 供給関数
supply of credit 信用供給
supply of subsequent services 以降の役務の提供
supply price 供給価格
supply schedule 供給曲線
supply side 供給サイド
supply side factor 供給側の要因
supply source 供給源
supply-demand balance in macroeconomy マクロ経済の需給バランス
supply-or-pay contract サプライ・オア・ペイ契約
supply-side economics サプライサイドの経済学
support 裏付ける；下支える
support level 下値支持線
support line 下値支持線
support price 維持価格
support ratio 支援比率
support tranche サポート・トランシェ
support trust 扶助信託
supportable assumption 立証可能な想定
supporter 扶養者
supporting documents 付属書類
supporting order 買支え注文
supporting schedule 付属明細書
supporting USD ドルを買い支える
supporting USDJPY ドル・円相場を支える
suppression of deposition 供述録取書（使用の）禁止
suppression of private businesses 民業圧迫
supranational agencies 国際機関
supreme advisor 最高顧問
Supreme Court 最高裁判所
Supreme Court of Japan 最高裁判所
supreme decision making organ 最高意思決定機関
supreme institution 最高機関
supreme law of the land 国の最高法規
surcharge 課徴金
surety 保証
surety bond 保証証券
surety money 保証債務
surety obligation 求償権
surety right 求償権
suretyship 保証
surface right 地上権
surge in demand 需要増
surgical expense insurance 手術費保険
surplus 余剰金
surplus account 剰余金勘定
surplus adjustment 剰余金修正
surplus analysis 剰余金分析
surplus appropriated for redemption fund 債務償還積立金
surplus appropriation statement 剰余金処分計算書
surplus assets 剰余資産
surplus at liquidation 清算剰余金
surplus at the beginning of the period 前期繰越利益余剰金
surplus at the opening of the period 期首剰余金残高
surplus available for dividend 配当可能利益
surplus brought forward from the previous term 前期繰越利益金
surplus capacity 生産余力
surplus charge 剰余金賦課
surplus country 黒字国
surplus credited to equity 資本金組入剰余金
surplus equipment 遊休設備
surplus finance 黒字財政
surplus from capital reduction 減資剰

S

余金
surplus from consolidation 連結剰余金
surplus from merged company 合併差益
surplus funds 剰余資金；余資
surplus insurance 剰余インシュランス
surplus material 余剰材料
surplus on revaluation of properties 固定資産再評価益
surplus profit 剰余益金
surplus profit carried forward to the following term 次期繰越利益金
surplus relief reinsurance 超過額再保険
surplus reserves 剰余積立金
surplus section 剰余金区分
surplus subscription 応募超過
surplus transaction 剰余金取引
surplus treaty reinsurance 超過額特約再保険
surplus value 剰余価値
surprise move 予想外の動き
surprise rate cut 意表をついた利下げ
surprises in earnings 利益の予想外の変動
surrender 権利放棄
surrender of bill 手形引渡し
surrender rate 解約率
surrogate 代替
surrogate measure 代替測定値
surtax 課徴金
surtax on land tax 地租付加税
surtax on national tax 国税付加税
surveillance 監視
survey data 調査データ
survey of households 家計調査
survey on planned capital spending 設備投資計画調査
survey report 鑑定報告書
surveying 測量
surveying fee 鑑定料
surveyor 査定人
survival bond サバイバル・ボンド
survival function サバイバル関数
survival of annuitant 年金受領者の生存
surviving company 存続会社
surviving entity 存続実体
surviving loan 残存ローン
surviving spouse 遺族配偶者
survivor annuity 遺族年金
survivor benefit 遺族給付金
survivor income benefit 遺族年金給付
survivor pension 遺族年金
survivor's pay 破綻メンバー以外による損失負担
survivorship 生存者への権利の帰属
survivorship account 遺族勘定
survivorship bias 存続バイアス
survivorship life insurance 遺族保険
survivorship rider 生存者購入年金
sushi bond スシ・ボンド
suspense account 仮勘定
suspense payment 仮払金
suspense payment account 仮払金勘定
suspense receipts 仮受金
suspense receipts account 仮受金勘定
suspension 停止
suspension from membership 会員権の停止
suspension from transactions 取引停止
suspension of a plan 制度の停止
suspension of acceptance of entrustment of clearing 清算受託の停止
suspension of bank account 銀行取引の停止
suspension of banking transaction 銀行取引停止処分
suspension of business 事業の中止
suspension of business activity 営業活動の停止
suspension of capitalization 資産化の停止
suspension of convertibility 転換停止
suspension of execution 執行停止
suspension of payment 支払停止
suspension of prescription 時効の停止
suspension of qualification for trade

S

取引資格停止
suspension of right 権利停止
suspension of seizure 差押猶予
suspension of statute of limitations 時効の停止
suspension of transactions 立会停止
suspension of transactions in a bill clearing house 手形交換所取引停止処分
suspension of work claims 中断クレーム
suspensive condition 停止条件
suspicion 嫌疑
sustain 維持する
sustainability of rally in equity markets 株価の持続性
sustainable development 持続可能な開発
sustainable equilibrium exchange rate 維持可能な均衡相場
sustainable growth 持続可能な成長
sustainable growth rate 持続可能な経済成長率
sustained economic growth 経済の持続的な成長
sustained equity rally 株式の堅調な上昇
sustenance 生計
SVA (shareholder value added) 株主付加価値
SVC (El Salvador colon) エルサルバドール・コロン
swap スワップ
swap agreement スワップ協定
swap arrangement スワップ協定
swap bid rate スワップ・ビッド・レート
swap bond スワップ債
swap broker スワップ・ブローカー
swap contract スワップ契約
swap cost スワップ・コスト
swap counterparty スワップ・カウンターパーティ
swap coupon スワップ・クーポン
swap deal スワップ取引
swap documentation スワップ契約書
swap margin スワップ・マージン
swap of bond 債券の入替え
swap offer rate スワップ・オファー・レート
swap portfolio スワップ・ポートフォリオ
swap price スワップ価格
swap profit スワップ・プロフィット
swap rate スワップ・レート
swap rate basement スワップ・レートの底値圏
swap spread スワップ・スプレッド
swap spread curve スワップ・スプレッド・カーブ
swap strike スワップ・ストライク
swap trading スワップ取引
swap transaction スワップ取引
swap-in-arrears アリアー・スワップ
swaps clearing system スワップ決済システム
swaption スワップション
sweep account スィープ・アカウント
sweeping 決済口座への払出し
sweetener スィートナー
SWIFT 国際銀行間データ通信システム
SWIFT (Society for Worldwide Inter-Bank Financial Telecommunication) SWIFT
swing スウィング
swing facilities スウィング・ファシリティ（つなぎ融資枠）
swing line つなぎ信用枠
swing loan スウィング・ローン
Swiss Federal Banking Commission スイス銀行監督委員会
Swiss franc note スイス・フラン建債
switch 乗り換え
switch auction 乗換オークション
switch finance スイッチ金融
switch from one retirement benefit plan to another 退職給付制度間の移行
switch from yen to dollars 円ドル・シフト

S

switch from zero coupon bonds ゼロ・クーポン債からの乗換え
switch of bonds 債券入替え
switch order 入替注文
switch reversal 逆入れ替え
switch-back option スイッチ・バック・オプション
sworn statement 宣誓付き供述
Sydney Futures Exchange シドニー先物取引所
symbol system of accounts 勘定記号法
symbolic delivery 象徴的引渡し
symmetric cryptographic algorithm 共通鍵暗号
symmetric key algorithm 共通鍵暗号
symmetrical distribution 対称分布
symmetrical triangle シンメトリカル・トライアングル
symmetrical triangle pattern 対称トライアングル・パターン
symmetrically 対称的に
symmetry with 釣り合う
syndicate 引受団
syndicate composition シ団の構成
syndicate manager シ団幹事
syndicate of guarantor 保証銀行団
syndicate underwriting シ団引受
syndicated credit シンジケート・ローン
syndicated deal シンジケート方式
syndicated loan 協調融資；シンジケート・ローン
syndicated term loan 中長期協調融資
syndication シンジケート団（シ団）
synergy 相乗
synergy committee 共同化委員会
synergy effect 相乗効果
synopsis sheet 概要シート
synthesis 合成
synthesis tax rate 総合税率
synthesize 合成する
synthetic arbitrage シンセティック・アービトラージ
synthetic assets 合成資産
synthetic bond シンセティック・ボンド
synthetic cash arbitrage transaction 合成現物裁定取引
synthetic cash instrument シンセティック・キャッシュ
synthetic CDO シンセティック CDO
synthetic currency 合成通貨
synthetic floating rate 合成変動金利
synthetic index fund 合成指数ファンド
synthetic instruments 合成金融商品
synthetic long シンセティック・ロング
synthetic portfolio 合成ポートフォリオ
synthetic position 合成ポジション
synthetic put シンセティック・プット
synthetic securities 合成証券
synthetic securitization シンセティック・セキュリティゼーション
synthetic short シンセティック・ショート
synthetic swap 合成スワップ
synthetic useful life 総合耐用年数
SYP (Syrian pound) シリア・ポンド
system approach システム・アプローチ
system audit 制度監査
system bid and offer システム呼値
system engineering システム工学
system failure システム障害
system for purchase of foreign exchange bills 外国為替手形買取制度
system for sale of bills drawn by the Bank of Japan 売出手形制度
system issue システム銘柄
system of accounts 会計組織
system of interest rates 利子率体系
System of National Account 国民経済計算体系
system of note issue 発券制度
system related to banknotes 銀行券に関する制度
system related to treasury funds 国庫

S

金に関する制度
system repos システム・レポ
system risk システム・リスク
system value システム価格
systematic allocation 規則的な配分
systematic basis 規則的な基準
systematic sampling 体系的標本抽出
systematic structure 体系的構成
systematic withdrawal plan 定額引出プラン
SZL (Swaziland lilangeni) スワジランド・リランゲニ
SZSE (Shenzhen Stock Exchange) 深圳証券取引所

T

T account T 字型勘定
T contracts 取引日の契約
T form account T 字型勘定
T rate T 料率
T(trade date)+2 settlement 翌々日決済
T(trade day)+1 settlement 翌日決済
T(trade day)+3 settlement 4 営業日目決済
T+0 取引日
T+1 Steering Committee T+1 検討委員会
T+3 4 営業日決済
T+3 settlement T+3 決済
T+7 8 営業日決済
T-account method T 勘定法
T-Bond Futures T-Bond 先物取引
T-bond futures option T-Bond 先物オプション
T-note 財務省中期証券
TA (technical assistance) 外国技術支援
TAA (tactical asset allocation) 戦術的資産配分
table 計算表
table of price factors 換算係数テーブル
table of random numbers 乱数表
table of the present value 現価表
tabular cash book 多桁式現金出納帳
tabular cost 表定コスト
tabular form 表形式
tabular ledger 表式元帳
tabular premium 表定保険料
tabular standard 計表本位
tabulating machine 会計機
tacit 黙示の
tacit contract 黙約
tactical asset allocation 戦術的アセット・アロケーション
tactile mark 識別マーク
Taft-Hartley Act タフト・ハートレー法
tagged borrowers 要注意先
tail テール
tail hedge テール・ヘッジ
tail period テール期間
tailgating 相乗り
tailing テーリング
tailor made 特注の
tailored swap transactions 特殊構造のスワップ
Taiwan 台湾
Taiwan Stock Exchange 台湾証券取引所
take into consideration 織り込む
take out 差額収入
take-and-pay contract テイク・アンド・ペイ契約
take-home pay 税引給与
take-or-pay contract テイク・オア・ペイ契約
takedown 引き出し
takeout loan テークアウト・ローン
takeover 買収
takeover arbitrage 買収による裁定取引
takeover bid 株式公開買付け
takeover boom 買収ブーム
takeover value 買収価値
taking a bath 仕手戦での損
taking a flier 投機を行うこと
taking a post-closing trial balance 繰越試算表作成
talk down 口先介入(下落)
talk up 口先介入(上昇)
talking the JPY down 円安を望む
talking the JPY up 円高を望む
tally 照合
tally man 検数人
tame ken 為券

tandem currencies タンデム通貨
tandem plan 併設プラン
tangible assets 有形資産
tangible cost 有形費用
tangible depreciable property 有形償却資産
tangible fixed assets 有形固定資産
tangible net worth 自己資本
tangible value 有形資産価値
Tankan 短観
tanshi company 短資会社
tap 資金調達する
TAP (trend analysis program) 傾向分析調査
tap bills タップ・ビル
tap issue タップ発行
tap stock タップ債
taper off 下降線をたどる
tapping of resources 資源開発
taps タップス
target assets value 対象資産価額
target company 対象会社
target cost 目標原価
target income 目標利益
target issue ターゲット発行
target level 誘導目標
target liability 対象債務
target payout ratio 目標配当性向
target population 目標母集団
target portfolio ターゲット・ポートフォリオ
target premium 目標保険料
target price 目標価格
target profit 目標利益
target range 目標変動幅
target rating 目標格付け
target return ターゲット・リターン
target risk 巨大危険
target sales 目標売上
target securities 対象証券
target stock 対象株式
target yield 目標利回り
target zone 目標相場圏
target zone of exchange rate 目標為替相場
targets for investment 出資対象
tariff 関税
tariff agreement 料率協定
tariff autonomy 関税自主権
tariff barrier 関税障壁
tariff by agreement 協定料率
tariff commission 税率委員会
tariff cuts 関税引き下げ
tariff escalation 傾斜関税
tariff negotiations 関税交渉
Tariff Policy and Legal Division 関税課
tariff quota 関税割当
tariff quota system 関税割当制度
tariff rate 関税率
tariff schedule 関税表
tariff union 関税同盟
tariff wall 関税障壁
tariff war 関税戦争
task 事業
TAURUS (Transfer and Automated Registration of Uncertificated Stock) TAURUS
TAURUS (Transfer and Automated Registration of Uncertified Stock) 英国証券決済システム
tax 租税
tax absorption タックス・アブソープション
tax absorption credit 源泉課税負担方式
tax account 租税勘定
tax accountant examination 税理士試験
tax accountant fee 税理士報酬
tax accounting 税務会計
tax administration 税政
tax administration system 税務行政組織
tax advantage 税制上の優遇措置
tax advantaged 税制面で優遇されている
tax advantaged vehicle 節税手段
tax advice 税務アドバイス
tax advisor 税務顧問

tax agency 税務代理
tax agent 納税管理人
tax agent of property tax 固定資産税の納税管理人
tax amount 課税額
tax amount settled 調定税額
tax and public charge 公租公課
tax and public dues 公租公課
tax and revenue anticipation 税収歳入見込み
tax and stamp revenues 租税及び印紙収入
tax anticipation bill 租税準備証券
tax anticipation note 税収見返手形
tax anticipation warrant 税収見返りワラント
tax approved defined benefit scheme 税制適格確定給付年金制度
tax arbitrage 税金裁定
tax assessment 租税査定
tax assessment and collection 課税徴収
tax assets 税金資産
tax audit 税務監査
tax authorities 税務当局
tax avoidance 租税回避
tax balance 税金残高
tax base 課税基準；税基盤
tax base of enterprise tax on corporation 法人事業税の課税標準
tax based state pension 税方式公的年金
tax bearer 担税者
tax bearing capacity 担税力
tax benefit for exchange of property 資産交換の税法上の特典
tax benefit rule 税効果規則
tax benefits 税制上の優遇措置
tax bill 課税通知書
tax bracket 税率区分；税率等級
tax burden 租税負担
tax burden ratio 租税負担率
Tax Bureau 主税局
tax cash flow 税金のキャッシュフロー
tax certificate 公売許可書
tax charge 法人税負担
tax claims 租税債権
tax clause 税金条項
tax collected 税金預り金
tax collection 収税；徴税
tax collection by stamp 証紙徴収
tax collection system 徴税機構
tax collector 税務官
Tax Commission 税制調査会
tax computation basis 税額計算基準
tax concession 税制優遇措置
tax consequence 税効果
tax consultation 税務相談
tax convention 租税条約
Tax Counselor 税務相談官
tax court 租税裁判所
tax credit 税額控除
tax credit against the tax payable 納付すべき税金に対する税額控除
tax credit carryback 税務上控除の繰戻し
tax credit carryforward 税務上控除の繰越
tax credit for dividend 配当控除
tax criminal 租税犯
tax cutback 足切計算
tax deductible expenses 税務上の損金
tax deductible in 課税所得計算上損金算入される
tax deductible items 課税控除費目
tax deductible reserve 損金算入できる引当金
tax deduction 税額控除
tax deduction of interest payment 支払利子の課税控除
tax deed 公売証書
tax deferral 課税繰延べ
tax deferred 繰延税
tax deferred annuity 課税繰延年金
tax deferred compensation 課税繰延報酬
tax delinquency 税金の滞納
tax delinquent 税滞納者
tax dispute 税務争訟

tax documents 税務書類
tax dodger 脱税者
tax dodging 脱税
tax due 納税額
tax due date 納税期日
tax due with final return 確定申告による納付
tax effect 税効果
tax effect accounting 税効果会計
tax effect on corporate tax 法人税への税効果
tax efficiency 税効率
tax efficient life policy 節税生命保険
tax equivalent yield 課税換算利回り
tax evader 脱税者
tax evasion 脱税
tax examination 税務調査
tax exclusive price 外税方式
tax exempt 非課税の
tax exempt corporation 非課税法人
tax exempt money market fund 非課税マネー・マーケット・ファンド
tax exempt organization 非課税機関
tax exempt saving 非課税貯蓄
tax exempt security 非課税証券
tax exemption 免税
tax exemption for agricultural income 農業所得の免税
tax exemption for dependents 扶養控除
tax exemption for specific use 特定用途免除
tax exemption limit 免税点
tax expense 税金費用
tax favored benefit 優遇税制給付
tax for default 加算税
tax for transfer of securities 有価証券移転税
tax forms 納税申告用紙
tax free 非課税の
tax free article 非課税品
tax free corporation 非課税法人
tax free exchange 非課税交換
tax free income 免税所得
tax free investment 免税投資
tax free purchase 非課税仕入れ
tax free reserve 非課税引当金
tax free small-sum public bond investment system 少額公債別枠非課税制度
tax free small-sum savings system 少額貯蓄非課税制度
tax function 租税関数
tax gathering season 税収期
tax haven タックス・ヘブン
tax holiday タックス・ホリディ
tax home 課税上の住所
tax in arrears 延滞税
tax in jeopardy 緊急課税
tax in kind 物納税
tax incentive 税制上の優遇措置
tax incidence 租税の帰着
tax inclusive 税込みで
tax inclusive price 内税方式
tax income 税収
tax increase 増税
tax indemnification 税金補償
tax items 税目
tax jurisdiction 税管轄地
tax jurisprudence 税法学
tax law 税法
tax lawyer 納税弁護士
tax lease 税効果リース
tax legislation 税法
tax leverage lease 節税レバレッジ・リース
tax levy on the basis of the size of business 外形標準課税
tax liabilities 租税債務
tax liability 納税義務
tax liability of foreign corporation 外国法人の納税義務
tax lien 租税先取特権
tax loss 税務上の欠損金
tax loss carried back 繰戻税務欠損金
tax loss carryback 課税所得欠損金繰戻し
tax loss carryforward 欠損金繰越
tax manager 納税管理人
tax measures 税制措置

tax obligation 納税義務
tax office 税務署
tax on admission 入場税
tax on bank note system 兌換券発行税
tax on business 企業課税
tax on consumption 消費に対する税
tax on corporate gain 法人利得税
tax on delinquency 滞納税
tax on deposit 預金利子税
tax on dividend 利益配当税
tax on excess issue 制限外発行税
tax on goods and possessions 物税
tax on income 所得に対する税
tax on property 資産税
tax on redemption profit 償還差益課税
tax on the write-up 資産再評価税
tax on transaction 取引に対する税
tax on undistributed profits 留保所得に対する税
tax on unutilized land 未利用地税
tax opinion 税金に関する意見書
tax oriented transaction 節税取引
tax papers 納税告知書
tax paradise タックス・パラダイス
tax payable 未払税金
tax payable account 未払税金勘定
tax paying capacity 担税力
tax payment 納税
tax payment and subrogation by third party 第三者納付及び代位
Tax Payment Association 納税協会
tax payment by securities 証券納付
tax payment by self-assessment 申告納税
tax payment by stamp 印紙納付
tax payment by transfer account 振替納税
tax payment in kind 現物納付
tax payment in money 金銭上納
tax payment slip 納付書
tax penalty 税制上の懲罰
tax period appearing on tax bill 納税通知書上の納税期間
tax planning 節税対策
tax policy 租税政策
tax practitioner 税理士
tax preference item 租税控除項目
tax preferred status 税制優遇措置
tax preparation 納税調整
tax preparation service 納税申告書作成サービス
tax principle 租税原則
tax privilege 租税優遇
tax privileged 優遇税制の
tax procedures 税務上の手続
tax proceeds 税収
tax provision 納税引当額
tax proxy 税務代理
tax qualified pension plan 税制適格年金
tax qualified pension trust 税制適格退職年金信託
tax qualifying policy 税制適格保険契約
tax rate 税率
tax rate applied to upper part of income 上積税率
tax rate higher than standard 超過税率
tax rate of gift tax 贈与税の税率
tax rate schedule 税率表
tax rebate 税金の払戻し
tax receivable 未収税
tax reduction 減税
tax reduction for investment 投資減税
tax reform 税制改革
tax refund 税金還付
tax refund by carryback 繰戻還付制度
tax refund by the carryback of the deficiency 欠損の繰戻還付
tax refund receivable 未収還付税金
tax refunded 還付された租税
tax regulations 税法
tax relief 課税控除；税の減免
tax relief bonds 減税債券
tax relief for non-resident 非居住者に対する減免
tax requisition 課税要件
tax reserve 税金引当金
tax resort タックス・リゾート

tax return 税務申告書
tax return form 納税申告書
tax revenue 税収
tax roll 課税台帳
tax rule 税法規
tax sale 換価処分
tax saving 節税
tax saving leverage lease 節税レバレッジッド・リース
tax schedules 納税申告明細書
tax seal 税印
tax selection 租税選択
tax selling 節税のための売り
tax sharing 税務分担
tax shelter タックス・シェルター
tax spared loan みなし課税対象ローン
tax sparing みなし税額控除
tax sparing loan facility みなし税控除ローン
tax state 租税国家
tax status 課税上の地位
tax status selection 納税申告区分選択
tax structure 税体系
tax suit 税務訴訟
tax surcharge 付加税
tax swap タックス・スワップ
tax system 租税体系
tax system for angel エンジェル税制
tax table 税額表
tax take 税金でとられる金額
tax threshold 課税最低限
tax title 公売に基づく権限
tax transaction 租税取引
tax treatment 税務処理
tax treaty 租税条約
T
tax unpaid 納税未済
tax value 課税価額
tax year 税務上の会計年度
tax yield 税収
tax-exempt paper 免税債
tax-exempt securities 免税証券
taxable 課税しうる
taxable account 課税口
taxable amount 課税金額
taxable bond 課税債
taxable capacity 税負担能力
taxable depreciation 有税償却
taxable document 課税文書
taxable estate 課税遺産
taxable event 課税事象
taxable floor 課税最低限
taxable goods 課税品
taxable income 課税所得
taxable income earned by nonresident 非居住者の課税所得
taxable income entitled to reduced tax rate 軽減税率適用の所得金額
taxable item 課税対象
taxable minimum of property tax 固定資産税の免税点
taxable municipal bond 課税地方債
taxable pension plan 課税年金制度
taxable period 課税期間
taxable pooling 課税プーリング
taxable property 課税財産
taxable purchases 課税仕入れ
taxable sales 課税売上
taxable temporary difference 将来加算一時差異
taxable timing difference 将来加算一時差異
taxable undistributed profits 課税対象留保金額
taxable valuation 課税評価額
taxable value of gift tax 贈与税の課税価格
taxable year 課税年度
taxable year of foreign corporation 外国法人の事業年度
taxable-through-period account 通期課税口
taxation 課税
taxation according to legal portion of legacy 法定相続分課税
taxation allowance for non-life insurance premium 損害保険料控除
taxation at the source 源泉課税
taxation at time of receipt from bonded area 引取課税

taxation by applying upper bracket 上積課税
taxation by estimate 推計課税
Taxation Department 課税部
taxation division 収税課
Taxation Management Division 課税総括課
taxation of income basis 所得割課税
taxation on aggregate income 総合課税
taxation on consent dividend みなし配当税制
taxation on corporation tax basis 法人税割課税
taxation on deemed corporation みなし法人課税
taxation on dividend 配当に対する課税
taxation on enterprise 企業課税
taxation on entertainment and social expenses 交際費課税
taxation on government monopoly 専売課税
taxation on interest or capital gains separately withheld from other income 源泉分離課税
taxation on per capita basis 均等割課税
taxation on retirement annuity 退職年金課税
taxation on retirement pension 退職年金課税
taxation on shipment 移出課税
taxation on small business 小企業課税
taxation regime 租税体系
taxation system 税制
taxation upon the general-public 大衆課税
taxed investors 課税対象となる投資家
taxes 税金
taxes and public charges 租税公課
taxes and rates 国税及び地方税
taxes assessed by taxpayers 申告税
taxes for prior fiscal periods 過年度法人税等
taxflation タックスフレーション
taxi license タクシー免許
taxing power 徴税権
taxpayer 納税者
taxpayer dealing with foreign countries 外国と取引をしている納税者
taxpayer filing a blue return 青色申告者
taxpayer identification number 納税者番号
taxpayer identification number system 納税者番号制度
taxpayer numbering system 納税者番号制度
taxpayer with limited tax liability 制限納税義務者
taxpayer's association 納税組合
taxpayer's option 納税者の選択
taxpayers' suit 納税者訴訟
TB operation TB オペ
TB rate TB 金利
TBA (to be announced) 後日発表
TBD (to be decided) 後日決定
TC (traveler's check) トラベラーズ・チェック
TD (total debt) 債務合計
Teachers' Insurance Annuity Association of America 米国教職員保険・退職年金組合
teaser ARM ティーザー物 ARM
teaser rate 勧誘目的のレート
technical テクニカル要因
technical analysis テクニカル分析
technical analysis indicator テクニカル分析指標
technical assistance 技術協力
technical change あや
technical cooperation 技術提携
technical forecast テクニカル予測
technical graph テクニカル分析用グラフ
technical index テクニカル指標
technical interest rate 評価利率
technical issue 技術的な問題

technical obsolescence 技術的陳腐化
technical official 技官
Technical Official, Ministry 0f Finance 財務技官
technical position 市場内部要因
technical progress 技術進歩
technical provision 保険契約準備金
technical rally あや戻し
technical reaction あや押し
technical rebound 自律反騰
technical standard 技術水準
technical term 専門語
technical theory テクニカル理論
technical trading テクニカル・トレーディング
technically insolvent corporation 技術的に支払い不能な企業
technological advance 技術の進歩
technological changes 技術進歩
technological feasibility 技術的な実現可能性
technological forecasting 技術予測
technological innovation 技術革新
technological support 技術支援
technology export 技術輸出
technology fund ハイテク株ファンド
technology gap 技術格差
technology shares ハイテク株
technology transfer 技術移転
technology transfer agreement 技術移転契約
TED (Treasury bill/Eurodollar) TED
TED (Treasury Eurodollar) spread TEDスプレッド
TED spread trading TEDスプレッド取引
teguchi file 手口ファイル
teigaku deposit 定額貯金
Tel Aviv Stock Exchange テルアビブ証券取引所
Telecommunications Act of 1996 1996年通信法
telecommunications business 電気通信事業
telecommunications carriers 電気通信事業者
telecommunications market 電気通信市場
telegraphic transfer 電信為替
telegraphic transfer bought 買為替
telegraphic transfer buying rate 電信買相場
telegraphic transfer payable 電信送金為替
telegraphic transfer rate TTレート
telegraphic transfer receivable 電信取立為替
telegraphic transfer selling rate 電信売相場
telegraphic transfer sold 売為替
telephone banking テレフォン・バンキング
telephone bill payment 電話料金支払い
telephone booth 電話ブース
telephone loan テレフォン・ローン
telephone market テレフォン・マーケット
telephone rates 電話料金
telephone subscription right 電話加入権
teller テラー
temporal diversification 期間の分散
temporal method テンポラル法
temporary 暫定的
temporary account 仮勘定
temporary advance 一時立替え
temporary annuity 有期年金
temporary bond テンポラリー・ボンド
temporary boom 一時的好況
temporary borrowing 一時借入金
temporary capital 一時的資本
temporary change 臨時変更
temporary demand 仮需要
temporary difference 一時差異
temporary event 一時的な事象
temporary halt 一時中断
temporary holding 臨時挙行
temporary holding of trading session 売買立会の臨時挙行

temporary income 臨時所得
temporary increase 一時的な上昇
temporary injunction 仮差止命令
temporary investment 一時的投資
temporary loan 一時貸付金
temporary loan before bond flotation 起債つなぎ融資
temporary loan on property 資産の一時的貸付
temporary loans to financial institutions 金融機関等に対する一時貸付
Temporary Money Rates Adjustment Law 臨時金利調整法
temporary payment 仮払金
temporary rally 一時的反騰
temporary receipts 仮受金
temporary receipts account 仮受金勘定
temporary repair 仮修繕
temporary residence 居所
temporary seal 仮封
temporary shortage of funds for payment 支払資金の一時的不足
temporary suspension 臨時停止
temporary tariff 暫定関税率
Temporary Tariff Measures Law 関税暫定措置法
temporary tariff rate 暫定税率
temporary tax accountant 臨時税理士
temporary trading halt 売買の一時中断
temporary transfer 一時的な振替
temporary use 一時使用
10 largest shareholders 大株主上位10名
10 line treaty 10ライン特約
ten percent greater or lower than 上下10%
10 year government bond futures 長期国債先物取引
ten years comparative financial summary 10年間の比較財務諸表
10-K report 10-Kレポート
10-Q report 10-Qレポート
10-year coupon bond 満期10年の利付債
10-year coupon-bearing government bonds 10年利付国債
10-year full vesting formula 勤続10年完全受給権付与方式
10-year low 10年振りの低水準
tenancy 不動産権
tenancy at sufferance 容認賃借物件
tenancy at will 任意不動産貸借権
tenancy in common 共有不動産権
tenant 借地人；賃借人
tenant retention テナントの維持
tenant right 借地権
tender 入札引受
tender bill テンダー・ビル
tender bond 入札保証書
tender offer 株式公開買付け
tender offer period 公開買付期間
tender offer report 公開買付報告書
tender offeror 買付申込者
tender operation 入札オペ
tender option テンダー・オプション
tender panel テンダー・パネル
tender period 入札期間
tender price テンダー価格
tenement 保有財産
tenor 満期までの期間
tension 緊張
tentative agreement 暫定合意
tentative auction date 暫定入札日
tentative balance sheet 仮貸借対照表
tentative budget 暫定予算
tentative validity 公定力
tenure 保有権
tenure of office 任期
tenure of the office 在任
term 期間
term addition 定期保険買増し
term asset management 長期資産運用
term bond 単一満期債；中長期債券
term call 期日物
term certain 確定期間
term certificate 定期預金証書
term deposit 定期預金

term fed ターム・フェッド
term fed fund rate ターム・フェド・ファンド・レート
term federal fund ターム・フェデラル・ファンド
term financing 中長期ファイナンス
term financing rate 期間借入れ金利
term for settlement of accounts 決算期
term for which the bonus payment is computed 賞与支給額の計算期間
term instruments ターム物
term insurance 定期保険
term insurance conversion 定期保険転換
term insurance rider 定期保険特約
term life insurance 定期生命保険
term loan ターム・ローン
term mismatch 期間のミスマッチ
term of debt 負債の期限
term of engaging in the business 事業に従事した期間
term of execution 執行期間
term of office 任期
term of payment 支払期限
term of validity 有効期限
term options rider 定期部分買増特約
term payment 定期支払い
term receivable ターム債権
term repo 定期現先
term risk 期間リスク
term RP ターム・レポ
term sheet 条件概要書
term structure 期間構造
term structure model 期間構造モデル
term structure of assets and liabilities 資産と負債の期間構成
term structure of interest rate 金利期間構造
term structure of yield 利回り期間構造
term swap ターム・スワップ
term-end account 期末勘定
term-end outstanding balance 当期末残高
term-end settlement of accounts 期末決算
terminable annuity 有期年金
terminal dividend 消滅時配当
terminal funding 最終積立；年金現価積立方式
terminal funding method 年金現価充足方式
terminal illness benefit 末期症状給付
terminal market 定期市場
terminal pay allowance 退職手当
terminal policy reserve 保険年度末準備金
terminal value 最終価値；終価
termination 満了
termination claim 満期請求額
termination date ターミネーション・デート
termination events 解約事由
termination indemnity 離職補償
termination of a plan 制度の終了
termination of a term 期限満了
termination of employment 解雇
termination provisions 解約条項
termination terms 打ち切り条件
termination trigger 終了事由
terms and conditions 条件
terms and conditions of insurance policy 保険約款
terms and conditions of issuance 発行条件
terms and documentation 条件と契約書
terms of acquisition 買収条件
terms of delivery 受渡条件
terms of forgiveness 返済免除条件
terms of office of auditors 監査役の任期
terms of office of directors 取締役の任期
terms of plan 制度の条件
terms of settlement 決済条件
terms of trade 交易条件
terrier 土地台帳
territorial waters 領海
tertiary industry 第三次産業
TESSA (tax exempt special savings

account) 免税特別貯蓄
test marketing 試験販売
test of internal controls 内部統制のテスト
test statistic 検定統計量
testament 遺言
testamentary trust 遺言信託
testator 遺言者
testify 証言する
testimony 証言
testing 試験
testing audit 試査
testing expenses 試作費
testing new lows 新安値を試す展開
testing times 試す展開
tests for entry 加盟のための条件
textile and apparel industry 繊維製品業界
TFA (tripartite financing agreement) 第三者貸付
TFE (Toronto Futures Exchange) カナダ先物取引所
TFM (transaction flow manager) 取引フロー・マネージャー
THB (Thai baht) タイ・バーツ
their account 先方勘定
thematic apperception test 絵画統覚法
theorem 定理
theoretical 理論的
theoretical 10 year issue 架空 10 年物
theoretical capacity 理論的生産能力
theoretical futures price 理論先物価格
theoretical price 理論価格
theoretical rate of exchange 理論的為替相場
theoretical rates 理論金利
theoretical value 理論値
theoretical value model 理論値モデル
theoretical value of a subscription right 新株引受権理論価値
theory of accounts 勘定理論
theory of approximation 近似値理論
theory of asset preference 資産選好理論
theory of asset valuation 資産評価論
theory of comparative advantage 比較優位説
theory of comparative cost 比較生産費説
theory of credit creation 信用創造論
theory of foreign exchange 為替学説
theory of game ゲームの理論
theory of imputation 帰属理論
theory of interest 利子理論
theory of international indebtedness 国際貸借説
theory of liabilities taxation 租税債務関係説
theory of optimum tariff 最適関税の理論
theory of portfolio selection 資産選択理論
theory of probability 確率論
theory of regulation 規制の理論
theory of tax accounting 税務会計論
thereupon 直ちに
thief 窃盗犯人
thin 閑散
thin capitalization 過少資本
thin capitalization rules 過少資本税制
thin margin 薄い利ざや
thin market 薄商市場
thing in action 債権
things real 不動産
third countries 第三国
third country bill 三国手形
third generation 第三次
third generation on - line system 第三次オンライン
third market 第三市場；店頭取引市場
third mortgage 三番抵当
third party 第三者
third party allocation 第三者割当
third party benefit trust 他益信託
third party check 第三者小切手
third party credit 割賦購入斡旋業
third party credit risk 第三者信用リスク
third party insurance 第三者保険
third party liability cover 第三者賠償

特約保険
third party liability insurance 第三者賠償責任保険
third party sales credit 割賦購入斡旋
third sector corporation 第三セクター
Third World 第三世界
third world countries 第三世界各国
third-party credit support 第三者信用補填
third-party risk 第三者リスク
third-party transfer 付記電文付振替
thousands of units 千単位
threat 脅迫
three digit PER 100 倍台の株価収益率
three factor contribution plan 三要素配当方法
360 day basis 360 日ベース
three line converting method 三線転換法
three surplus factor 三利源
three tier system 三階建制
three year high 3 年ぶりの高値
three-month moving average 三カ月移動平均
threshold 限界
threshold for intervention 介入水準
threshold for recognition 認識の識閾
threshold of materiality 重要性基準値
thrift and savings plans 貯蓄制度
thrift industry 貯蓄金融業界
thrift institution 貯蓄金融機関
thrifts 貯蓄金融機関
thrive below 割込んで上昇する
through B/L (bill of lading) 通し船荷証券
through the decision 決定により
through transportation 一貫輸送
throughout accounting 一貫会計
throughout the target issues 対象銘柄全体の
throughput スループット
throughput contract 生産高保証契約
throw-back rule スローバック原則
thumbnail description 短い説明
thwart 妨げる
Tianjin 天津市
TIBOR (Tokyo Inter-Bank Offered Rate) 東京銀行間取引金利
tick ティック
tick size 呼値単位
tick-test rule ティック・テスト・ルール
ticker 株式相場表示板
ticker symbol 株式略称
ticket 伝票
ticket of leave 仮釈放許可証
ticket sale finance チケット販売金融
tie-in sale 相互販売
tie-up loan 提携ローン
tied aid ひも付援助
tied loan ひも付融資
tied sales 提携販売
tied-agent 専属仲介者
Tier 1 基本的自己資本
Tier 1 capital guideline 基本的項目基準
Tier 2 補完的自己資本
Tier 2 capital 自己資本の補完的項目
tiered rating 段階的料率
tight 窮屈
tight budget 緊縮財政
tight credit 信用逼迫
tight fiscal package 緊縮財成案
tight fiscal policy 財政緊縮政策
tight money policy 金融引締政策
tightened cash flow 資金繰りの悪化
tightened inspection きつい検査
tightened liquidity 資金繰りの悪化
tightening 引締め
tightening bias 引締バイアス
tightening monetary policy 金融引締め
tightening of asset classification 資産区分の厳格化
tightening of liquidity 流動性の逼迫
tightening of risk management リスク管理の厳格化
tightening of short rate 短期金利引上げ
tighter monetary policy 引締色の強い

T

金融政策
tightness of money 金詰り
TIIS (Treasury Inflation-Indexed Securities) TIIS
tilted basket ティルティッド・バスケット
timber delivery tax 木材取引税
timber income 山林所得
time adjusted 時間調整済み
time apportion basis 経過基準
time bargains 定期取引
time based activity method 時間比例法
time bias タイム・バイアス
time bill 期限付手形
time card タイムカード
time cost 時間原価
time decay タイム・ディケイ
time dependent 時間依存の
time deposit 定期預金
time deposit account 定期預金勘定
time deposits available (due) within one year 一年以内の定期預金
time difference theory 時差説
time draft 一覧後定期払為替手形
time effect 時間効果
time expired 期限ながれ
time factor 時間的要素
time filter タイム・フィルター
time for tax payment 納期限
time horizon 取引期間
time lag タイム・ラグ
time limit 期限
time limit of the subscription for new stock 新株の申込期限
time limitation 期間制限
time limited 期日
time loan 定期貸付
time of inclusion in expenses of enterprise tax 事業税の損金算入の時期
time of offer オファー時刻
time of payment 払込時期
time of presentation 呈示期間
time of receipts 収入の時期
time of recognizing gain 収益計上時期
time of recognizing loss 損失計上時期
time option タイム・オプション
time pattern 時間パターン
time payment 定期支払い
time policy 期間保険
time precedence 時間優先
time preference 時間選好
time priority 時間優先の原則
time proportion basis 期間配分基準
time sales 割賦販売
time savings 定期預金
time series analysis 時系列分析
time series behavior 時系列変動
time series behavior of earnings 利益の時系列変動
time series data 時系列データ
time span タイムスパン
time specific price 特定時点の価格
time spread 時間スプレッド
time to expiration 残余期間
time to maturity 残存期間
time transaction 定期取引
time value 時間的価値
time value of money 貨幣の時間的価値
time value of option オプションの時間価値
time variance 時間差異
time weighting factor 期間按分係数
time-dependent parameter 時間依存パラメーター
timeliness 適時性
timely disclosure タイムリー・ディスクロージャー；適時開示
Timely Disclosure Network 適時開示情報伝達システム
times fixed charges 固定債務倍率
times interest earned 利息負担倍率
times interest earned ratio 利息カバレッジ比率
times per year 年間の回転回数
timing 時期
timing difference 期間差異
timing mismatch タイミングのずれ
timing of recognition 認識時点

timing of revenue recognition 収益計上の時期
timing of valuation 評価の時期
timing option タイミング・オプション
timing swap タイミング・スワップ
tipping fee 廃棄物処理委託料
TIPS (Treasury's inflation-protection security) TIPS
title deed 捺印証書；不動産権利書
title document 権利証書
title insurance 権原保険
title insurance company 所有権保険会社
title paramount 優越する権原
title report 権原報告書
title search 権原調査；所有権調査
TJR (Tajiku ruble) タジギスタン・ルーブル
TLC (transferable loan certificate) 譲渡可能貸付証書
TLF (transferable loan facility) 譲渡可能ローン
TLI (transferable loan instrument) 譲渡性証書
TLO (technology licensing organization) 技術移転機関
TLO (total loss only) 全損のみ担保
TMM (Turkmenistan manta) トルクメニスタン・マナト
TND (Tunisian dinar) チュニジア・ディナール
to date 現時点までの
TOB (take-over bid) 公開買付
Tobacco and Salt Industries Office たばこ塩事業室
tobacco consumption tax たばこ消費税
Tobin's Q トービンのＱ
TOF (technical overdraft facility) 当座貸越し
Togo (CFA (Communauté Financière Africaine) franc) トーゴ（CFA フラン）
token 兆し
tokkin 特金
Tokyo Bankers Association 東京銀行協会
Tokyo Clearing House 東京手形交換所
Tokyo Commodity Exchange 東京工業品取引所
Tokyo dollar bond 東京ドル債
Tokyo dollar call market 東京ドル・コール市場
Tokyo foreign exchange market 東京外国為替市場
Tokyo foreign stock market 東京外国株式市場
Tokyo gold market 東京金市場
Tokyo inhabitants tax 都民税
Tokyo International Financial Futures Exchange 東京金融先物取引所
Tokyo loan 本邦ローン
Tokyo market 東京市場
Tokyo offshore center 東京オフショア・センター
Tokyo offshore market 東京オフショア市場
Tokyo Securities Settlement Corporation 東京証券清算株式会社
Tokyo Stock Exchange 東京証券取引所
Tokyo Stock Exchange Price Average 東証平均株価
Tokyo Stock Exchange Second Section Index 東証第二部総合指数
Tokyo Stock Exchange stock price index 東証株価指数
Tokyo Stock Exchange, Inc. 株式会社東京証券取引所
TOL (total overcollateralization level) 超過担保比率
tolerable deviation rate 許容逸税率
tolerable rate 許容率
tolerance 許容差
tolerance level 許容水準
tolerance limit 許容限度
tolerance of the JPY strength 円高容認
tolerance territory 受容領域
toll 通行料

toll charges 通行税
toll gate 道路料金所
toll motorway 有料自動車道
toll revenue bond 料金財源債
toll traverse 私有地通行料
tombstone ad 墓石広告
tomorrow-next トム・ネクスト
tone 気配
tone of the market 気配
tonnage due トン税
tontine annuity トンチン年金
tontine dividend トンチン配当
tools of analysis 分析手法
top 上位
TOP (Tonga pa'anga) トンガ・パアンガ
TOP (total operating profit) 総営業利益
top bidder 最高値の入札者
top end 上限
top heavy 幹部優遇
top line 売上高
top personal tax rate 個人所得税最高税率
top straddle トップ・ストラドル
top tax rate 最高税率
top up 上乗せ
top up holdings 買増す
top vertical combination トップ・バーティカル・コンビネーション
top-down forecasting トップ・ダウン型予測
top-down investment トップ・ダウン型投資
top-reversal day トップ・リバーサル・デー
top-up pension 付加年金
TOPIX トピックス
TOPIX index option TOPIX 指数オプション
TOPIX futures TOPIX 先物取引
TOPIX New Index Series TOPIX ニュー・インデックス・シリーズ
TOPIX option TOPIX オプション
TOPIX trends TOPIX の推移
topless 青天井
topping out 高止まり
topside breakout 高値の突破
Toronto Futures Exchange トロント先物取引所
Toronto Industrial Index トロント工業株指数
Toronto Stock Exchange トロント証券取引所
Torrens System トーレンス式登記法
tort insurance 不法行為責任保険
tort liabilities 不法行為賠償債務
ToSTNeT (Tokyo Stock exchange Trading Network system) trading ToSTNet 取引
total 合計
total amount 総額
total amount of insurance in force 保有契約
total annual earnings 年間の利益総額
total benefit 合計給付額
total book value of assets 総資産の帳簿価額
total buying contract 総買い建玉
total capital 資本金合計
total capital accounts 資本の部合計
total capital profit ratio 総資本収益率
total capitalization 総長期資金
total carrying amount 帳簿価額総額
total cost 全部原価
total cost curve 総費用曲線
total cost of transaction 取引総費用
total costing 全部原価計算
total delta 総デルタ値
total deposit 総預金
total disability 完全疾病
total earnings 総収益
total equity 総持ち分
total equity and liabilities 資本及び負債合計
total external revenue 外部収益合計
total gamma 総ガンマ値
total kappa 総カッパ値
total liabilities 負債合計
total liabilities and capital accounts

T

負債及び資本合計
total liabilities and net worth 総資本
total liabilities and shareholders' equity 負債資本合計
total long-term fund 総長期資金
total loss 全損
total market capitalization 株式時価総額
total market delta 総市場デルタ値
total market value 総市場価額
total maximum liability 責任限度額
total money supply 通貨総供給高
total net income 総所得金額
total net worth 自己資本合計
total operating expenses 営業費用合計
total payment of installments 割賦価格
total production 総生産
total ratio of return 総収益率
total receipts 総収入
total receivables 未収受取勘定合計
total reserve system 全額正貨準備制度
total reserves 総準備
total return 総合利回り
total return swap トータル・リターン・スワップ
total roh 総ロー値
total sales 総売上高
total selling contract 総売り建玉
total shareholders' equity 資本合計
total shares outstanding 総発行済株式数
total starts 着工戸数全体
total stocks issued 総発行済株式数
total sum 総計
total taxable income 課税総所得金額
total theta 総シータ値
total turnover 総出来高
total volume 出来高
totally-held subsidiary 100パーセント子会社
touching the bottom 底入れ
tourist income 観光収入
tourist tax 旅行者税
tout 誇大推奨
town 村
town planning scheme 都市計画
TQC (total quality control) 総合品質管理
TR (trust receipt) 輸入担保荷物保管証
traceable cost 追跡可能原価
track record 過去の記録；業績記録
tracking error 連動誤差
tracking stock 子会社収益連動株式
tracking the rising JPY 円の上昇に追随した
trade 営業；取引
trade acceptance 引受済荷為替手形
trade acceptances payable 引受手形
trade account 営業勘定
trade account payable 買掛金
trade account receivable 売掛金
trade against the trend 逆張り
trade agreement 貿易協定
trade and commerce 通商
trade assets 営業資産
trade associations 証券取引業者協会
trade balance 貿易収支
trade by agreement 協定貿易
trade claim 貿易クレーム
trade comparison 取引照合
trade contractor 職別業者
trade control 貿易統制
trade creation effect 貿易創出効果
trade credit 企業間信用；貿易金融
trade credit terms 取引の与信条件
trade creditor 仕入先
trade date 約定日
trade date accounting 取引日基準会計
trade debtor 売掛先
trade deficit or surplus 貿易赤字・黒字
trade description 商品の記述
trade discount 業者割引
trade ex-coupon 権利落ちで取引される
trade example 取引事例
trade execution 取引の執行
trade expansion act 通商拡大法
trade expenses 営業費

T

trade figure 貿易収支実績
trade friction 貿易摩擦
trade guarantee 決済保証
trade in a weaker range 安値にシフトする
trade liability 営業債務
trade mark 商標
trade mark infringement 商標権侵害
trade matching 取引照合
trade matrix analysis 貿易連関分析
trade name 商号
Trade Negotiations Committee 貿易交渉委員会
trade off トレード・オフ
trade on commission 委託貿易
trade on one's own account 手張り
trade party 取引先
trade payable 営業債務
trade payables 支払債務
trade position 貿易収支
trade receivables 受取債権
trade rights 営業権
trade secret 企業秘密
trade sharing 積取比率
trade statistics 貿易統計
trade surplus amount 貿易収支黒字幅
trade surplus/deficit data 貿易統計
trade tax 営業税
trade terms 定型貿易条件
trade ticket トレード・チケット
trade union 労働組合
trade validation 取引確認
trade weighted basket 貿易加重ベース・バスケット
trade weighted index 貿易加重指数
trade-by-trade basis 取引一件ごと基準
trade-for-trade settlement 取引一件ごとの決済
trade-in 下取り
trade-in articles 下取り品
trade-mark registration law 商標登録法
traded ex-rights 権利落ちする
traded option 取引オプション
traded options contracts at the equity options trading 株券オプション取引の対象
traded policy 上場生命保険証書
traded securities 流通証券
trader トレーダー
trading account 売買勘定
trading account assets 商品勘定資産
trading account securities 売買目的有価証券
trading accounts 投資家；トレーディング対象（アカウント）
trading area 商圏
trading authorization 売買委任
trading collateral 取引担保金
trading conditions 取引条件
trading constraints 取引上の圧迫
trading curve カーブの取引
trading days 立会日数
trading deficit 取引赤字
trading facilities 売買のための施設
trading firm finance 商社金融
trading halt 取引中断；取引の一時停止
trading hour 立会時
trading in trading session 売買立会による売買
trading income or loss 売買等損益
trading know-how 取引ノウハウ
trading limits 航路定限
trading market 流通市場
trading mechanism 売買の仕組み
trading member 取引所会員
trading on equity 自己資本の代用
trading on the OTC (over-the-counter) market 店頭取引
trading opportunity 取引機会
trading outside the floor 立会外取引
trading participant 取引参加者
trading participant acting as lead underwriter 幹事取引参加者
trading participant agreement 取引参加者契約
trading participant fee 取引参加者負担金
trading participant in system trouble

システム障害取引参加者
trading participant regulations 取引参加者規程
trading participant representative 取引参加者代表者
trading participant security deposit 取引参加者保証金の預託
trading participants having a qualification for the settlement 清算資格を有する取引参加者
trading partner 貿易相手国
trading period of contract month 限月取引の期間
trading pit 取引ピット
trading pool トレーディング・プール
trading post 取引ポスト
trading precision 売買の精度
trading profit 証券売買益
trading profit and loss account 売買損益勘定
trading purpose 売買目的
trading range 取引レンジ
trading regulations 取引規則
trading results 営業成績
trading right 取引参加権
trading session 立会
trading stamp トレーディング・スタンプ
trading system 売買システム
trading tax 取引税
trading to correct errors 過誤訂正の取引
trading transaction 商取引
trading unit of the underlying stocks 対象株券の売買単位
trading unit system 取引単位制度
trading value 売買代金
trading variation 最小価格変動単位
trading volume 出来高；取引高
trading volume of over-the-counter bonds 公社債店頭売買高
traditional market 伝統市場
traditional theory 従来の理論
traffic personal accident insurance 交通事故傷害保険
trailing PER 実績基準 PER
trailing PER (price earnings ratio) 実績基準 PER
Training and Professional Development Office 開発研修室
training expenses 訓練費
traitor 信頼を裏切った者
tramper 不定期船
TRAN (tax and revenue anticipation note) 税収歳入見込証券
tranche トランシェ
tranche issue 分割発行方式
tranche trading トランシェ取引
tranche valuation トランシェ評価
tranched トランシェ分けされた
transaction 取引
transaction adjustment payment 差額決済
transaction approach 個別取引毎のリスク評価
transaction chain 取引の流れ
transaction collation 売買照合
transaction contract in futures contract 先物取引の成立
transaction cost 取引コスト
transaction fee 取引手数料
transaction for the account of customer (or agency transaction) 顧客の委託に基づく取引
transaction for the trading participant's own account (or principal transaction) 取引参加者の自己の計算に基づく取引
transaction in assets 資産取引
transaction in foreign currency 外貨建取引
transaction motive 取引動機
transaction of near delivery 期近物取引
transaction on a dealer basis 自己売買
transaction on exchange 取引所取引
transaction restructuring cost 取引再構築コスト
transaction shift 取引シフト
transaction tax 取引税

T

transaction value 取引代金
transaction volume 売買数量
transaction with basis condition ベーシス条件付取引
transaction with delayed settlement 着地取引
transaction with rights receipts 権利預り証付売買
transaction with seller's option 特約日決済取引
transaction with special condition 特約取引
transaction with specified date 特約日取引
transactions between entities under common control 共通支配下の取引
transactions calculated by counting each payment instruction once 片道ベース
transactions effected by member for the accounts of others 受託商い
transactions for customers' accounts 受託取引
transactions in securities 有価証券の売買
transactions on a dealer basis 仕切売買
transactions pertaining to agency-based clearing of securities 有価証券の清算取次
transcript 謄本
transcripts 議事録
Transdniester (ruble) トランス・ドニエストル（ルーブル）
transfer 移転する；譲渡；振替
transfer account 振替勘定
transfer account book 振替口座簿
transfer agent 名義書換代理人
transfer among categories 分類の変更
transfer among subdivisions 内訳区分間の振替
transfer at low price 低額譲渡
transfer books closed 株券名義書換停止
transfer books open 株券名義書換停止解除
transfer contract 譲渡契約
transfer cost 譲渡費用
transfer entry 振替記入
transfer expenditure 移転的経費
transfer expenses 譲渡費用
transfer fee 譲渡手数料
transfer in 移管金受入
transfer in kind 現物移管
transfer income 移転所得
transfer ledger 振替元帳
transfer mechanism トランスファー・メカニズム
transfer number 振替番号
transfer of a budgetary surplus 剰余金繰入れ
transfer of a share-certificate 株券名義書換
transfer of assets 資産譲渡
transfer of book-entry business 振替業の営業譲渡
transfer of business 営業譲渡
transfer of control 支配権の移転
transfer of current account 当座勘定付替え
transfer of development 開発成果の移転
transfer of endorsed note 裏書譲渡
transfer of equity interests 株式移転
transfer of fixed assets given in pledge 担保付固定資産の譲渡
transfer of fund 資金移動
transfer of land tax 地租委譲
transfer of operations 営業譲渡
transfer of ownership 所有権の移転
transfer of ownership of capital 持ち分の譲渡
transfer of positions 建玉の移管
transfer of property 資産譲渡
transfer of property due to the delivery of substitute property 換地処分による譲渡
transfer of real property 不動産の譲渡
transfer of records 契約原票の移管

transfer of rights 利権譲渡
transfer of securities 有価証券の譲渡
transfer of seized goods 差押物件の引継
transfer of shares 株式の譲渡；株式の名義書換
transfer of the business 営業の譲渡
transfer of the entire business 全営業の譲渡
transfer of the place of tax payment 納税地の異動
transfer of the whole business 全営業の譲渡
transfer of title 所有権移転
transfer of transferable credit 信用状の譲渡
transfer of unsettled contracts 未決済約定の引継ぎ
transfer of unsettled transactions 未決済約定の引継ぎ
transfer on books 帳簿上の口座振替
transfer out 移管金支払い
transfer payment 移転支出
transfer premium 移管保険料
transfer price 譲渡価格
transfer pricing 移転価格操作
transfer pricing taxation system 移転価格税制
transfer problem トランスファー問題
transfer profit 振替利益
transfer property 譲渡資産
transfer registration 移転登録
transfer risk 決済リスク
transfer savings account 振替貯金口座
transfer service delegatee 名義書換事務受託者
transfer slip 振替伝票
transfer tax 譲渡税
transfer to legal reserve 法定準備金積立額
transfer to other account 他の口座への振替
transfer to the general loan loss reserve 一般貸倒引当金繰入
transfer transactions 振替取引
transfer voucher 振替伝票
transferability of benefits 給付の通算可能性
transferable account 振替可能勘定
transferable deposits 通貨制預金
transferable financial instrument 譲渡性金融商品
transferable L/C (letter of credit) 譲渡可能信用状
transferable loan 譲渡可能貸出
transferable loan facility 譲渡可能貸付
transferable RUF 譲渡可能ラフ
transferable securities 譲渡性証券
transferee 譲受人
transferee company 譲受会社
transferee corporation 合併法人
transferee of membership equity 会員持ち分の譲受け人
transferor 譲渡人
transferor bank 譲渡銀行
transferor corporation 被合併会社
transferred debt 移管債権
transferred liabilities 債務引渡し
transferred positions 移管された建玉
transferring charge 振替手数料
transferring company 出再会社
transferring out 脱退
transfers between geographic areas 地域間振替
transformation of lump sum payment of retirement allowance to pension plan 退職一時金制度の年金化
transformation of tax transit 税の消転
transgression 侵害
transient 一時的費用
transire 貨物運送免状
transit account 未達勘定
transit clause 運送約款
transit trade 通過貿易
transition benefit 移行給付
transition matrix 推移行列
transition period 移行期間
transition probability 推移確率
transition stage 過渡期
transition years 過渡期の年数

transitional amount resulting from a change in accounting standards 会計基準変更時差異
transitional cost 変更時差異費用
transitional effect 経過規定の影響
transitional liability 経過負債
transitional matters 経過事項
transitional measure 経過措置
transitional option 選択的経過規定
transitional pension 移行時年金
transitional revenue from repealed taxes 旧法による税収入
transitional treatment 経過的処理
transitory income 変動所得
transitory phenomena 一時的な現象
translation adjustments 為替換算調整
translation difference 換算差額
translation gains and losses 為替換算差額
translation method at historical rates 取得時換算法
translation method at the current exchange rate 期末時換算法
translation of foreign currency statements 外貨表示部分の換算
translation of foreign currency transaction 外貨建取引換算
transmission mechanism 波及経路
transmitting bank 取次銀行
transnational corporation 超国籍企業
transparent 透明性のある
transport 輸送
transport insurance 運送保険
transport networks 交通ネットワーク
transportation 運送
transportation bond 交通債
transportation business 運送業
transportation charges 運送料
transportation claim 運送クレーム
transportation company 運送業者
transportation cost 輸送費
transportation equipment 運送設備
transportation equipment futures 輸送用機器先物
transportation equipment industry 輸送用機器業界
transportation in bond 保税運送
transportation insurance 輸送保険
transpose 置き換える
transposed matrix 転置行列
transshipment 積換え
transshipment bill of lading 積換船荷証券
travel advances 前払旅費
traveling audit 巡回監査
traveling benefits 旅費手当
traveling expenses 旅費交通費
traveling expenses for business 出張旅費
traveller's letter of credit 旅行信用状
travelling salesman 巡回販売人
traverse 否認する
treasurer 財務部長
treasuries 米国財務省証券
treasury agent 国庫代理店
treasury auction 国債入札
treasury bill 財務省短期証券
Treasury bill market 財務省短期証券市場
treasury bills 割引短期国債
treasury bond 財務省長期証券
Treasury Bonds Investment Series 財務省投資債券
treasury business 国庫業務
treasury certificate 財務省証書
Treasury Certificate of Indebtedness 財務省債務証書
Treasury debt buyback operations 財務省証券買入消却オペ
treasury deposit 国庫預託金
Treasury Direct トレジャリー・ダイレクト
Treasury Division 国庫課
treasury financing 国債入札
treasury financing bills 財務省証券
treasury fund remittance 国庫金送金
treasury funds 国庫金
treasury funds factor affecting current account balances 日銀当預増減の財政等要因

treasury funds operations 国庫オペレーション
treasury instruments 財務省証券
treasury investments and loans 財政投融資
Treasury issue 米国財務省証券
Treasury market 米国債市場
treasury note 財務省中期証券
treasury product 財務商品
Treasury Savings Bonds 財務省中期貯蓄債券
treasury securities market 財務省証券市場
treasury stock 金庫株；自己株式
Treasury strip 国債ストリップス債
treasury surplus 国庫余裕金
treasury tax and loan account 租税公債勘定
treasury tax and loan note accounts 財務省租税国債証書勘定
Treasury yield 財務省証券利回り；米国債利回り
treating 饗応
treatment 処理
treatment for an impairment of securities 有価証券の減損処理
treatment for components 構成物の処理
treaty 条約
treaty of commerce 通商条約
treaty reinsurance 特約再保険
treaty shopping 条約あさり
treaty wording 再保険特約書
treble tariff 三重関税率
tree model ツリーモデル
tree structure ツリー構造
trend 趨勢
trend analysis 傾向分析
trend channel トレンド・チャンネル
trend follower トレンド・フォロアー
trend GDP growth トレンド GDP 成長率
trend line 傾向線
trend of earnings 収益の傾向
trend pattern 傾向線
trend survey of small businesses 中小企業動向調査
trend towards luxury spending 高級品消費への指向
Trésor フランス財務省
Treuhand bond 信託公社債
trial 試算
trial balance 試算表
trial balance of balances 残高試算表
trial balance of totals 合計試算表
trial balance of totals and balances 合計残高試算表
trial employment period 試用期間
trial jury 公判陪審
trial manufacture 試作
trial period 試用期間
trial product 試作品
trial running expenses 試運転費
trial running of manufacturing equipment 生産設備の試運転
trial sale 試用販売
trial value 試算価値
triangle reversal patterns トライアングル・リバーサル・パターン
triangle trade 三角貿易
tribunal 審判機関
trickle down 通貨浸透説の
trickle through 知れ渡る
trigger トリガー
trigger event 解約事由
trigger for growth 成長の起爆剤
trigger mechanism 清算条項
trigger price トリガー価格
Trilateral Commission 三極委員会
trilemma トリレンマ
TRIM (Trade Related Investment Measures) 貿易関連投資措置
trin 市場強弱測定値
tripartite agreement 三国間協定
triple B BBB 格
triple bottom トリプル・ボトム
triple bottom line 三重の利益
triple crossover method トリプル・クロスオーバー法
triple merit 三重益

T

triple settlement 四営業日渡し
triple tax exempt 三重非課税
triple top トリプル・トップ
triple-DES (Data Encryption Standard) algorithm トリプル DES 暗号
TRL (Turkish lira) トルコ・リラ
TRN (transaction reference number) 取引参照番号
TROR (total return of rate) swap TROR スワップ
troubled government 財政難に苦しむ政府
troubled-loan cleanup 不良債権の処理
truck system 現物給与
true and fair 真実にて公正
true and fair view 真実かつ公正の意見
true assignment 真正譲渡
true DVP (delivery versus payment) 真の DVP
true inflation 真のインフレ率
true interest rate 真利率
true measure 真の値
true payment date 実際の支払日
true reserve 真正準備金
true sale 真正売却
true up 微調整する
TRUF (transferable revolving underwriting facility) 譲渡可能 RUF
truncated 影響の大きい部分を裁断した
truncated to three decimal points 小数第3位で表された
truncation 簡略処理
trust 信託
trust account 信託勘定；信託口
trust accounting 信託会計
trust accounts of all banks 全国銀行信託勘定
Trust Act 信託法
trust administrator 信託管理人
trust agreement 信託契約
trust bank 信託銀行
trust business 信託業
trust by act of law 法定信託
trust company 信託会社
trust contract 信託約款
trust deed 信託証書
trust estate 信託財産
trust execution 信託設定
trust fee 信託報酬
trust for value 有償信託
trust fund 信託基金
trust fund assets 信託財産
Trust Fund Bureau 資金運用部
Trust Fund Bureau Fund 資金運用部資金
Trust Fund Bureau Special Account 資金運用部特別会計
trust fund plan 信託型年金
trust income 信託収入
trust indenture 信託証書
trust instrument 信託証書
trust joint 合同
trust money 委託金
trust obligation participating securities トップス
trust operation 信託業務
trust policy 生命保険信託付契約
trust principal 信託元本
trust property 信託財産
trust receipt トラスト・レシート
trust registration 信託登録
trust saving 信託貯蓄
trust securities 信託証券
trust theory 信託説
trust under agreement 契約信託
trusted pension plan 信託年金制度
trustee 受託者
trustee bank 受託銀行
trustee company 受託会社
trustee for bond issuance 社債発行の受託者
trustee group insurance 受託者団体保険
trustee in bankruptcy 破産管財人
trustee under indenture 信託証書受託者
trustee's report 受託者の報告
trustor 委託者；信託設定者

truth in lending 真実貸付法
truth in lending law 真性貸付法
truth in securities act 証券法の真実
Truth-in-Lending Act 貸付真実法
try-out period 返品期間
TSE 東証
TSE Stock Price Average 東証株価平均
TSLS (two-stage least squares) method 二段階最小自乗法
TTD (Trinidad & Tobago dollar) トリニダード・トバゴ・ドル
TTM (telegraphic transfer middle rate) 仲値
tumbling below 以下に急落する
TUPE (Transfer, Undertaking and Protection of Employment) 公務員再雇用制度
turf war 縄張り争い
turkey 期待外れの投資
Turks & Caicos (US dollar) タークス・カイコス（米ドル）
turn around 反転
turn key system ターン・キー・システム
turn to red figures 赤字転落
turnaround time 所要時間
turndown 落込み
turning point 転換点
turning upward 底離れ
turnkey ターンキー
turnkey contract ターンキー契約
turnover 売上；出来高
turnover (ratio) of capital 資本の回転率
turnover (ratio) of funds 資金回転率
turnover (ratio) of net worth 自己資本回転率
turnover (ratio) of receivables 受取勘定回転率
turnover (ratio) of total liabilities and net worth 総資本回転率
turnover (ratio) of total operating assets 経営資本回転率
turnover increase rate 売上増加率
turnover of commodity 商品回転数
turnover of gross and net working capital 総運転資本及び純運転資本回転率
turnover period 回転期間
turnover rate 回転率
turnover rate of capital 資本回転率
turnover rate on existing houses 既存住宅の買換率
turnover ratio 売買回転率
turnover ratio of commodity 商品回転数
turnover ratio of payables 買入債務回転率
turnover ratio of total liabilities 他人資本回転率
turnover tax 取引高税
turpitude 不正行為
Tuvalu (Australian dollar) ツバル（豪ドル）
TWD (Taiwan dollar) 台湾ドル
24 hours trading 24 時間取引
24 Ore Figure イタリア 24 オーレ総合株価指数
20% depreciation method 5 分の 1 償却法
20 year government bond futures 超長期国債先物
twin deficits 双子の赤字
twin-card ツイン・カード
twisting 乗換募集
2 dollar broker 2 ドルブローカー
two fund monetary separation 2 ファンド現金分離
two layer 2 層の
two nearest contract months 直近の 2 限月取引
two statements 二計算書
two statements approach 分離計算方式
two tier market 二重構造市場
two tier offer 二段階オファー
two way account 相互勘定
two way market ツー・ウェイ・マーケット

two way prices 売値買値同時の価格
two-sided market 双方向市場
two-thirds or more 3分の2以上の
two-tier bid 二重価格買付
TWR (time-weighted rate of return) 時間加重収益率
type of benefit 給付の種類
type of holding 保有形態
type of licenses 免許種類
type of plan 制度の種類
type of treasury funds 国庫金の種類
types of coins by materials 貨幣の種類（材質別）
types of money market operations オペの種類
types of product 商品の種類
TZS (Tanzanian shilling) タンザニア・シリング

U

U.S. dollar short-term interest futures 米ドル短期金利先物
U.S. General Accounting Office 米国会計検査院
U.S. Government General Accounting Office 米国一般会計局
U.S. savings bond 米国貯蓄債
U.S. term アメリカ方式
UAK (Ukraine hryvnia) ウクライナ・グリブナ
uberrima fide 最良誠実
UGX (Uganda shilling) ウガンダ・シリング
UIT (unit investment trust) 単位型投資信託
ultimate cash outflow 最終的な現金流出額
ultimate disposal 最終処分
ultimate inflation hedge 究極のインフレ・ヘッジ
ultimate lender 究極的貸手
ultimate parent company 究極的な親会社
ultimatum 最後のもの
ultra long-term national bond 超長期国債
ultra vires activities 越権行為
ultra-short-term bond fund 超短期債券ファンド
umbrella cover 包括保険
umbrella export credit facility 包括輸出信用方式
umbrella group 傘下企業
umbrella liability policy 企業包括賠償責任保険
umbrella master agreement 包括標準契約書
umbrella personal liability policy 包括個人責任保険
umpire 審判人
UN (United Nations) 国際連合
UN/NGLS (United Nations Non-Governmental Liaison Service) 国連 NGO 連絡サービス
un-certificated securities 非証書証券
un-restated 再表示されない
unabsorbed burden 間接費配賦不足額
unadjusted trial balance 未修正残高試算表
unadmitted assets 非公認資産
UNAFEI (United Nations Asia and Far East Institute For the Prevention of Crime and the Treatment of Offenders) 国連アジア極東犯罪防止研修所
unaffiliated 資本関係のない
unaffiliated stock 非関連会社株
unalienable 渡しえない
unallocated 未配賦の
unallocated benefit 包括給付
unallocated funding instrument 非割当積立方式
unamortized and undepreciated balance 未償却残高
unamortized bond discount 未償却社債割引
unamortized cost 未償却原価
unamortized discount 未償却発行差金
unamortized discount on debenture accounts 債券繰延勘定
unamortized interest during construction 未償却建設利息
unamortized obligation 未償却債務
unamortized premium on bonds 社債発行差益
unamortized premium on investments 未償却投資差金

unanimous 全員一致で
unanticipated disinflation 予期しないディスインフレ
unanticipated inflation 予期しないインフレ
unapplied burden 製造間接費配賦不足額
unappropriated deficit 未処理欠損金
unappropriated earned surplus 未処分利益剰余金
unappropriated earned surplus for current term 当期未処分利益剰余金
unappropriated income 未処分利益
unappropriated losses at the end of the year 当期未処理損失
unappropriated profit 未処分利益
unappropriated profit carried forward 繰越利益
unappropriated retained earnings 未処分剰余金
unappropriated retained earnings at the end of year 次期繰越利益金
unappropriated retained surplus 未処分留保利益
unappropriated surplus at the end of year 期末繰越利益金
unappropriated surplus for the current taxable 当期処分利益余剰金
unassigned surplus 未配分剰余金
unaudited 未監査
unauthorized card 無権カード
unauthorized member 無効会員
unauthorized use 不正使用
unavoidable accident 不可避的事故
unavoidable circumstances やむを得ない事情
unavoidable cost 回避不可能原価
unavoidable dangers 不可避的危険
unavoidable risk by diversified investment 分散投資で排除できないリスク
unbalanced 未決算の
unbalanced budget 赤字予算
unbalanced account 未決算勘定
unbalanced book 未決算帳簿
unbalanced open 未決算
unbiased 偏りのない
unbiased distribution 不偏分布
unbiased estimator 不偏推定量
unbiased test 不偏検定
unbilled 未請求の
unbundled policy アンバンドリングされた保険
unbundling アンバンドル化
unbundling of insurance premium 保険料等分解
uncertain 気迷い
uncertain factor 不透明要因
uncertainty 不透明
unchanged 据え置き
unchanged to slightly higher 強持ち合い
unchanged to slightly lower 弱保合い
UNCHS (United Nations Centre for Human Settlements [Habitat]) 国連人間居住センター（ハビタット）
UNCITRAL (United Nations Commission on International Trade Law) 国際連合国際商取引法委員会
unclaimed 所有者不明の
unclaimed check 未請求小切手
unclaimed dividend 未請求配当金
unclaimed stock 失権株
unclaimed wages 未払賃金
unclassified expenses 雑費
uncollateralized call 無担保コール
uncollateralized overnight call rate 無担保オーバーナイト物金利
uncollectable amount 回収不能額
uncollected balance 未収金
uncollected commission 未収手数料
uncollected funds 未収資金
uncollected income 未収収益
uncollected interest 未収利息
uncollected premium 未収保険料
uncollected rent 未収地代
uncollected revenue 未収収益

uncollectible accounts 貸倒債権
uncollectible loan 焦付き融資
uncollectible loans and advances 回収不能な貸出金
uncommitted facilities 非コミットメント・ファシリティ
uncommitted tranche 非約定トランシェ
uncompleted works 半成工事
unconditional 無条件の
unconditional contract 単純契約
unconditional debt 無条件債務
unconditional drawing right 無条件引出権
unconditional estimate 無条件の推定
unconditional grant 無条件補助金
unconditional liquidity 無条件流動性
unconditional operation 無条件オペレーション
unconditional payables 無条件債務
unconditional receivables 無条件債権
unconditional reserve 別途積立金
unconditional vesting 無条件受給権付与
unconfirmed credit 不確認信用状
unconfirmed L/C 無確認信用状
unconscionable bargain 非良心的契約
unconsolidated affiliates 連結対象外関連会社
unconsolidated net capital ratio 単体の自己資本比率
unconsolidated subsidiary 非連結子会社
unconstitutional 違憲の
uncontrollable expense 管理不能費
uncorrelated return 無相関の収益率
uncovered interest arbitrage アンカバード金利裁定
uncovered option アンカバード・オプション
uncovered position アンカバード・ポジション
UNCRD (United Nations Centre for Regional Development) 国連地域開発センター
uncrossed check 普通小切手
UNCTAD (United Nations Conference on Trade and Development) 国連貿易開発会議
undated bill 無日付手形
undated issue 永久債
UNDCP (United Nations International Drug Control Programme) 国連国際薬物統制計画
undefended 無防禦の
undepreciated wasting property 未償却減耗資産
under absorbed 配賦不足
under development 開発中
under dressing アンダー・ドレッシング
under estimate 過少見積り
under funded 積立金不足の
under hedge 過少ヘッジ
under insurance 一部保険；過少保険
under lease 転貸借
under liquidity 過少流動性
under one currency umbrella 単一通貨の下で
under par 額面割れ
under performing company 業績の悪い会社
under protest 支払拒絶
under repair 修繕中
under reserve 留保条件
under separate cover 別封で
under-absorbed burden 製造間接費配賦不足額
under-banked シ団不成立
under-booked 応募不足
under-depreciation 過少償却
under-margined account 証拠金不足勘定
under-subscribed 引受不調
under-withholding 過少源泉
undercapitalization 過少資本
underdepreciation carried forward 償却不足額の繰越
underemployment 不完全雇用
underemployment equilibrium 過少雇用均衡

U

underemployment multiplier 不完全雇用乗数
underestimation 過少評価
undergoing polarization 二極化する
undergoing prolonged recession 長期不況下
underground economy 地下経済
underground money アングラ・マネー
underinvestment 過少投資
underlying 原資産の
underlying accounting data 基礎的会計データ
underlying assets 原資産
underlying business 発生源となる事業
underlying cause 根本原因
underlying collateral 担保物件
underlying commodities used for consumer price indices 指数採用商品
underlying currency risk 潜在為替リスク
underlying debt 原債務証券
underlying debtor 対象になる債務者
underlying financial condition 基礎になる財務状態
underlying futures contract 原先物契約
underlying index 対象指標
underlying inflation rate 基礎インフレ率
underlying insurance 先順位保険
underlying investment 原投資
underlying market 現物市場
underlying premium 基準保険料
underlying rationale 論理的な根拠
underlying resources 対象となる資源
underlying retention 基本留保；損害保有額
underlying securities 原証券
underlying share 現物株
underlying size 取引単位
underlying stock 原株；対象株券
underlying swap 対象スワップ
underlying trend 基調
underlying value 直物価格
underlying weakness ファンダメンタルの脆弱さ
underpayment 過少納付
underperforming loans 不良債権
underperforming mortgages 不良モーゲージ
understandability 理解可能性
understanding 了解
understate 過少評価する；過少表示する
undertaker 事業者
undertaking 事業
undertakings by borrower 借手の特約
undertone 地合い
undervaluation 過少評価
undervalued 割安
undervalued asset 割安の資産
underweight アンダーウエイト
underwrite 引受ける
underwriter 引受業者
underwriters' allocations 引受行の割当額
underwriting account balance 営業勘定収支残
underwriting agreement 引受契約書；募集引受契約
underwriting business 引受業務
underwriting by the Bank of Japan 日銀引受
underwriting by the Trust Fund Bureau 資金運用部引受
underwriting commission 引受手数料
underwriting commitment 引受額
underwriting company 引受会社
underwriting concession 査定免除
underwriting contract 引受契約
underwriting criteria 保険査定基準
underwriting factor 危険査定要因
underwriting fee 引受手数料
underwriting firm 引受会社
underwriting group 引受団
underwriting limit 引受限度額
underwriting loss 保険引受損失
underwriting market 引受市場
underwriting method 全額引受方式

underwriting of government securities 国債引受
underwriting of new issue securities 新規発行証券の引受
underwriting profit 保険引受利益
underwriting profit and loss 引受損益
underwriting risk 引受リスク
underwriting spread 引受スプレッド
underwriting standards 与信基準
underwriting syndicate 引受シンジケート団；保険引受団
undigested securities 未消化証券
undisbursed loans 未実行貸出
undischargeable claim 罷免責債権
undisclosed accruals 開示されない未払金
undisclosed reserve 非公開準備金
undiscounted amount 割引前の金額
undiscounted basis 割引前基準
undisposed 未処分
undisposed deficit 未処分欠損
undistributed earnings 未分配利益
undistributed profit 未配分利益
undiversifiable risk 分散不能リスク
undivided bequest 未分割遺産
undivided interest 不可分権
undivided profit 未処分利益金
UNDOF (United Nations Disengagement Observer Force) 国連兵力引き離し監視軍
UNDP (United Nations Development Programme) 国連開発計画
undue concentrations 過度の集中
undue influence 不当威圧
undue risks 過大なリスク
unearned 未収
unearned discount 未経過割引料
unearned finance income 未稼得金融収益
unearned income 不労所得
unearned increment 自然増収
unearned insurance premium 未経過保険料
unearned interest 未経過利子
unearned interest and discount 未収利息・割引料
unearned revenue 前受収益
unemployed 失業者
unemployment 失業
unemployment benefit 失業給付
unemployment compensation 失業手当
unemployment insurance 失業保険
unemployment rate 失業率
unemployment tax 失業保険税
unencumbered assets 担保権のつかない資産
UNEP (United Nations Environment Programme) 国連環境計画
UNESCO(United Nations Educational, Scientific and Cultural Organization) 国連教育科学文化機関（ユネスコ）
uneven payment 一定額でない支払い
unexecuted contracts 未履行契約
unexpected event 予想外の事象
unexpected loss 偶発損失
unexpected property loss 臨時資産損失
unexpected return on pension assets 非期待運用収益
unexpired 未経過
unexpired cost 未費消原価
unexpired expenses 未経過費用
unexpired interest 未経過利子
unfair advantage 不正利益
unfair call 不当な履行請求
unfair competition 不正競業
unfair dismissal 不当解雇
unfair labor practice 不当労働行為
unfair method of competition 不公正な競争方法
unfair trade 不当な取引
unfair trade practice 不当営業行為
unfavorable balance 支払超過
unfavorable change 好ましくない変化
unfavorable factor 悪材料
unfavorable leverage effect 負の増益効果
UNFICYP (United Nations

U

Peacekeeping Force in Cyprus) 国連キプロス平和維持軍
unfilled orders 手持注文
unfinished business 残務
unfit for recirculation 再流通に不適格な
unforeseen event 予見されなかった事故
unforeseen liabilities 不測の債務
UNFPA (United Nations Population Fund) 国連人口基金
unfunded 基金のない
unfunded accrued pension cost 未払い年金費用
unfunded actuarial reserve 不足責任準備金
unfunded debt 短期債務
unfunded guaranteed benefit 未積立保証給付
unfunded insurance trust 未積立生命保険信託
unfunded pension 無基金の年金
unfunded pension liability 未積立年金債務
unfunded pension plan 年金賦課方式
unfunded projected benefit obligation 未積立予想給付債務
unguaranteed 無保証の
unguaranteed residual value 無保証残存額
UNHCR (Office of the United Nations High Commissioner for Refugees) 国連難民高等弁務官事務所
unhedge アンヘッジ
unhedged bond ヘッジなしの債券
unhedged risk ヘッジされていないリスク
UNIC (United Nations Information Center) 国連広報センター
UNICEF (United Nations Children's Fund) 国連児童基金（ユニセフ）
UNICRI (United Nations Interregional Crime and Justice Research Institute) 国連地域間犯罪司法研究所
UNIDIR (United Nations Institute for Disarmament Research) 国連軍縮研究所
UNIDO (United Nations Industrial Development Organization) 国連工業開発機関
UNIFEM (United Nations Development Fund for Women) 国連婦人開発基金
unified brand 統一商標
unified clearing organization 統一清算機関
unified credit 譲渡税総合控除
unified operation 統一的な運用
UNIFIL (United Nations Interim Force in Lebanon) 国連レバノン暫定軍
uniform 一律的
uniform accounting policies 統一的な会計方針
uniform accounting regulations 統一会計規則
uniform accounting standards 統一会計基準
uniform accounting system 統一会計制度
Uniform Commercial Code 統一商事法典
uniform cost accounting 統一原価計算
uniform cost accounting system 統一原価計算制度
Uniform Life Insurance Act 統一保険法
Uniform Practice Code 全米証券業協会統一慣習規則
uniform price 単一価格
uniform provisions 統一約款
Uniform Securities Act 統一証券法
uniform series worth factor 年金現価係数
uniform standards 統一基準
uniform yield 単一利回り
uniformed distribution 一様分布
UNIKOM (United Nations Iraq-Kuwait Observation Mission) 国連イラク・クウェート監視団

unilateral contract 片務契約
unilateral record 一方的記録
unilateral transaction 一方的取引
unincorporated company 法人格のない会社
unincorporated joint venture 非会社型合弁事業
uninscribed stock 無記名株式
uninsurable risk 保険引受不可危険
uninsured insurance 無保険者保険
uninsured loss 保険非補填損失
uninsured pension plan 非保険型年金制度
uninsured peril 非担保危険
union label 組合証票
union mortgage clause 標準抵当権者払約款
UNIPOM (United Nations India-Pakistan Observation Mission) 国連インド・パキスタン監視団
unique selling proposition ユニーク・セリング・プロポジション
unique tax treatment 特殊な税務処理
unisex principle 男女同一原則
unissued banknotes 未発行銀行券
unissued capital stock 未発行資本
unissued certificate 予備株券
unissued stock 未発行株式
unit 単位
unit annuity 単位年金
unit banking system 単一銀行制度
unit benefit plan 単位年金購入方式
unit cost 単位原価
unit credit 単位積増し
unit credit cost 単位積増費用
unit credit method 単位年金積み増し方式
unit depreciation 個別償却
unit depreciation method 個別減価償却法
unit grant 単位補助金
unit investment trust company 投信会社
unit linked bond ユニット・リンク保険ボンド
unit linked fund ユニット・リンク・ファンド
unit linked insurance ユニット・リンク保険
Unit Linked Life Insurance ユニット・リンク保険
unit of account 計算単位
unit of account bond ユニット・オブ・アカウント債
unit of amount of book-entry JGSs 振決国債の金額の単位
unit of investment securities 投資口
unit of output 単位出来高
unit of production method 生産高比例法
unit of taxation 課税単位
unit of trading 売買単位
unit posting 個別転記
unit price 単価
unit pricing 単価積算法
unit purchase plan 単位購入方式
unit sales 売上数量
unit shares 単位株
unit trust ユニット・トラスト
unit type 単位型
unit type investment trust 単位型投信；ユニット型投資信託
unit value 規準価格；単位価額
unit-price contract 単価契約
UNITAR (United Nations Institute for Training and Research) 国連訓練調査研修所
unitary exchange rate system 単一為替相場制
unitary tax ユニタリー・タックス
unitary taxation 合算課税
United Nations Capital Development Fund 国連資本開発基金
United Nations Economic Development Administration 国連経済開発局
United States trustee 連邦管財
uniting 結合
units extracted 採掘量
unity bond 統一基金債

U

unity of possession 占有合同
unity of title 権原合同
universal agent 総代理人
universal banking ユニバーサル・バンキング
universal basic pension 国民皆基礎年金
universal coverage 国民皆保険
universal currency 世界通貨
universal legacy 包括遺贈
universal legatee 包括受遺者
universal life insurance ユニバーサル生命保険
universal pension 一律給付年金
universe of securities 同じ性質の証券
unjust enrichment 不当利得
unjustified 不当な
unknown clause 不知約款
unlawful 不法な
unlawful act 不法行為
unlawful assembly 不法集会
unlawful entry 不法占有
unlawfulness 不法
unless otherwise specified 別段の定めがない限り
unlimited facility 無制限ファシリティ
unlimited legal tender 無制限法貨
unlimited liability 無限責任
unlimited liability company 無限責任会社
unlimited marital deduction 無制限配偶者控除
unlimited partnership 合名会社；無限責任組合
unlimited tax bond 無制限税源債
unlimited useful life 無限の耐用年数
unliquidated claim 不確定債権
unlisted assets 簿外資産
unlisted company 未上場会社
unlisted liability 簿外債務
unlisted note 未上場債
unlisted securities 場外証券
unlisted security 未上場証券
unlisted stock 未上場株
unlisted trading 未上場取引
unloading 大量売り
unmargined account 現金取引口座
unmatched 不突合
unmatched book アンマッチド・ブック
unmatched position 対応していない状態
UNMIBH (United Nations Mission in Bosnia and Herzegovina) 国連ボスニア・ヘルツェゴビナ・ミッション
UNMOGIP (United Nations Military Observer Group in India and Pakistan) 国連インド・パキスタン軍事監視団
UNMOP (United Nations Mission of Observers in Prevlaka) 国連プレブラカ監視団
UNMOT(United Nations Mission of Observers in Tajikistan) 国連タジキスタン監視団
unofficial capital flight 非公式資本の流出
UNOMIG (United Nations Observer Mission in Georgia) 国連グルジア監視団
UNOMSIL(United Nations Observer Mission in Sierra Leone) 国連シエラレオネ監視団
UNOPS (United Nations Office for Project Services) 国連プロジェクト・サービス機関
unorganized margin transactions 一般信用取引
unpaid 未払い
unpaid balance of national tax 国税の未払額
unpaid capital 未払資本金
unpaid care 無給介護
unpaid claim 未払保険金
unpaid dividend 未払配当金
unpaid donation 未払寄附金
unpaid interest 経過利息
unpaid principal 未返済元本
unpaid returns 未払返戻金

unpaid tax 未払税金
unperformed part of obligation 債務の未履行分
unprecedented 前例のない
UNPREDEP (United Nations Preventive Deployment Force) 国連予防展開軍
unproductive capital 未稼働資本
unprofitable company 業績の悪い会社
unqualified audit certificate 無限定適正意見の監査証明書
unqualified audit report 無限定監査報告書
unqualified financial statements 未監査財務諸表
unqualified opinion 無限定意見
unqualified opinion report 無条件監査報告書
unqualified report 無制限適正意見
unquoted 公表価格のない
unrated bond 無等級（無格付け）債券
unrated entity 無格付けの法人
unrealised loss 未実現損
unrealised profit 未実現益
unrealizable assets 換価不能資産
unrealized foreign currency gain and loss 未実現為替差損益
unrealized gain 計算上の利益；含み益；未実現利得
unrealized gain and loss 未実現損益
unrealized gain on shares held 株式含み益
unrealized gains in securities 証券含み益
unrealized gross profit on installment sales 割賦売上未実現益
unrealized income 未実現利益
unrealized loss 含み損；未実現損失
unrealized loss on shares held 株式含み損
unrealized profit 未実現利益
unrealized profit and loss 計算上の損益額
unrealized profits and losses 含み損益
unrealized revenue 未実現収入
unreasonable taxation 不当課税
unreasonably 著しく
unrecognized balance 未認識残高
unrecognized financial instruments 未認識金融商品
unrecognized net gain/loss 未認識純損益
unrecognized pension assets 未認識年金資産
unrecognized pension liability 未認識年金債務
unrecognized prior service cost 未認識過去勤務費用
unrecognized transitional obligation 未認識変更時差異債務
unrecovered cost 未回収原価
unregistered 未登記
unregistered debenture 未登録社債
unregistered stock 無登録株
unrelated business income 非関連事業利益
unrelated party 非関連当事者
unreported amount 申告漏れ金額
unreported claim 未報告保険事故
unresolved dispute 未解決の紛争
unrestricted assets 非制限資産
unrestricted power 完全な裁量権
UNRISD (United Nations Research Institute for Social Development) 国連社会開発研究所
UNRWA (United Nations Relief and Works Agency for Palestine Refugees in the Near East) 国連パレスチナ難民救済事業機関
unsalable stock 売残り在庫
UNSCRs (United Nations Security Council Resolutions) 国連安全保障理事会決議
unsealed deposit 開封預り
unseaworthy 堪航能力欠如
unsecured 無担保の
unsecured account 無担保勘定
unsecured bond 無担保社債
unsecured call loan 無担保コール
unsecured credit 無担保信用

U

unsecured creditors 無担保債権者
unsecured debt 無担保債
unsecured liability 無担保負債
unsecured loan 無担保ローン
unsecured mortgage 無担保抵当証券
unsecured obligations 無担保債務
unsecured residual value 無保証残存価値
unsecured trading 無担保取引
unsettled 未決済の
unsettled account 未決済勘定
unsettled contracts 未決済取引
unsettled insurance claims 未決算保険金
unsettled transactions 未決済取引
unsettled transactions on proprietary account 自己の計算による未決済約定
unsettlement of accounts 未決算
unsigned vote 無記名投票
UNSO (United Nations Sudano-Sahelian Office) 国連スーダン・サヘール事務所
unsold 売れ残り
unsolicited rating 勝手格付け
unsubordinated 非劣後
unsubordinated debenture 非劣後無担保社債
unsustainable 持続可能でない
unsystematic risk 非システマティック・リスク
untapped market 未開拓市場
untied loan アンタイド・ローン
untrue 事実に反する
untruncated multiplier 非切断乗数
UNTSO (United Nations Truce Supervision Organization) 国連休戦監視機構
UNU (United Nations University) 国連大学
unused buildings 遊休建物
unused carryforward of tax credit 未使用の繰越税額控除
unused compensated absence 未使用有給休暇
unused credit line 貸出枠残
unused entitlement 未使用付与権利
unused land 遊休土地
unused line of credit 未使用借入限度枠
unused real estate 未使用不動産
unused tax credit 繰越税額控除
unused tax loss carryforward 未使用の税務上の繰越欠損金
unusual casualty reserve 異常危険準備金
unusual gains or losses 臨時的損益
unusual item 異常項目
unusual loss 異常損失
unusual movement 異常な動き
unusual profit and loss 特別損益
unusual profit or loss item 異常損益項目
unusual risks reserve 異常危険準備金
UNV (United Nations Volunteers) 国連ボランティア
unvalued policy 未評価保険
unvested 権利未確定の
unwanted rise 好ましからざる上昇
unwanted takeover 敵対的買収
unwelcome tightening 望ましくない引締め
unwind a trade 取引を手じまう
unwinding 巻戻し
unwritten law 非制定法
up and put option アップ・アンド・プット・オプション
up front 一括前払い
up gap 上放れ
up-down ratio 騰落レシオ
up-front commission 前払手数料
up-front compensation 先払報酬
up-front loading 先取ローディング
up-front payment 契約一時金；前払い
up-front premium 前払いプレミアム
up-pressure 上昇力
up-tick 上向き
update 更新する
upfront cost 初期費用
upgrade in credit 信用力の向上

U

upgrading 改良；格上げ
upkeep cost 維持費
upper earnings limit 報酬額上限
upper end 上限
upper income group 高額所得者層
upper limit 上限
upper limit of a loan 貸し付け限度額
ups and downs 盛衰
upset price 競売寄付値段；最低競売価格
upside 上向き
upside potential 潜在的な上昇余地；値上期待
upstairs market 階上市場
upstream holding company 川上持株会社
upstream product 上流製品
upsurge in long-term interest rates 長期金利の急上昇
upswing 上昇
upswing on business results 業績の上昇
uptrend 上げ足；回復傾向
upturn 好転
upturn in gearing 負債比率上昇
UPU (Universal Postal Union) 万国郵便連合
upward momentum 上げ足
upward pressure 押上圧力；上昇圧力
upward pressure on yield 利回りへの上昇圧力
upward revision 上方修正
upward trend 上昇基調
upwards 上げ基調
urban development 都市開発
Urban Development Corporation 都市基盤整備公団
urban development tax 都市開発税
urban fringe 都市周辺地帯
urban infrastructure 都市基盤
urban remodeling enterprise 都市改良事業
urbanization 都市化
urgent collection 臨時の徴収
Uruguay Round ウルグアイ・ラウンド
US dollar funds settlement 米国ドル資金決済
US equities 米国株式
US government income fund 米国証券収益ファンド
US portfolio assets ドル資産
US Treasury 米国財務省
US treasury benchmark yield 米国債指標利回り
usable period of used property 中古資産の使用可能期間
usable years 使用期間
usance ユーザンス
usance bill 期限付為替手形
usance bill rate 期限付手形相場
usance buying rate 期限付手形買相場
usance granted by foreign bank 外銀ユーザンス
usance L/C (letter of credit) 期限付信用状
usance rate 期限付為替相場
USCP (US commercial paper) 米国コマーシャル・ペーパー
USD (United States of America dollar) 米国ドル
USD fall ドル安
USDJPY down ドルの対円での下落
use and file 使用後届出制
use and file system 使用後届出制度
use benefit 使用便益
use of continuing rights 権利の継続的利用
use of funds 資金の使途
use of market mechanism 市場機能の活用
use tax 使用税
use with care 取扱い注意
used hours 使用時間
used property 中古資産
useful information 有用な情報
useful life 耐用年数
useful life table 耐用年数表
usefulness 利用価値
user cost 使用者原価
user group 利用者グループ

U

user of accounts 決算書の利用者
user of financial statements 財務諸表の利用者
user-owned utility ユーザー所有の公益企業
USGG (US government guaranteed) 米国政府保証付き
usher 廷吏
USIT (unit share investment trust) ユニット・シェア投資信託
USM (unlisted securities market) 未上場証券市場
USTR (United States Trade Representative) 米国通商代表部
usual covenants 通常約款
usual payment term 通常の支払条件
usual policy 標準保険
usurer 高利貸し
usury 高利
UTC (coordinated universal time) 協定世界時
utilities stock 電力・ガス株
utility 有用性
utility and gas industry 電気・ガス業
utility bonds 電力債
utility company 公益企業
utility consumption ユーティリティ消費
utility function 効用関数
utility indicator 効用指標
utility model 実用新案
utility model patent 実用新案権
utility rate 公共料金
utility revenue bond 公共事業財源債
utility theory 効用理論
utilization rate 設備稼働率
utilization ratio 稼働率
utilized cost 利用原価
utmost good faith 最大善意
UTP (unlisted trading privilege) 未上場取引権
UYU (Uruguayan peso) ウルグアイ・ペソ
UZS (Uzbekistan som) ウズベキスタン・スム

V

V formation V 字
VA (Veterans Administration) mortgage 退役軍人住宅ローン
vacancy 欠員
vacancy rate 空室率
vacant building 空屋
vacant land tax 空間地税
vacant lot 空地
vacation 明渡し
vacation pay 休暇手当
vacation with pay 有給休暇
valid 有効な
valid reference point 有効な参照点
validate 正当と認める
validation バリデーション
validity 正当性
valuable consideration 有価約因
valuable feedback loop 貴重な意見
valuable instrument 有価証券
valuable papers 有価証券
valuables 貴重品
valuation 評価
valuation account 評価勘定
valuation actuary 評価アクチュアリー；保険計理人
valuation allowance 評価性引当金
valuation at cost 原価法
valuation basis 評価基準
valuation by lower of cost or market method 低価法による評価
valuation by multiplier 倍率方式による評価
valuation by road rating 路線価方式による評価
valuation characteristics 評価特性
valuation clause 保険評価額条項
valuation cost 評価コスト
valuation criteria for fixed assets 固定資産評価基準
valuation date 評価日
valuation form 積荷価格申告書
valuation gain 評価益
valuation gain or loss 評価損益
valuation gains on securities 有価証券評価差益
valuation item 評価科目
valuation loss 評価損
valuation method 責任準備金評価法
valuation modeling 評価モデル
valuation of assets 資産評価
valuation of bond 公社債の評価
valuation of call option コール・オプションの評価
valuation of common stock 普通株の評価
valuation of company's own stock 自社株の評価
valuation of copyright 著作権の評価
valuation of enterprise 企業評価
valuation of farmland 純農地の評価
valuation of fixed assets 固定資産の評価
valuation of goods 資材評価
valuation of goodwill 営業権の評価
valuation of house 家屋の評価
valuation of inventory 棚卸資産の評価
valuation of leasehold 借地権の評価
valuation of listed stock 上場株式の評価
valuation of loan 貸付金債権の評価
valuation of occupancy right 占用権の評価
valuation of patent right 特許権の評価
valuation of preemptive right 新株引受権の評価
valuation of property 財産の評価
valuation of residential site 宅地の評価
valuation of right of lease 賃借権の評価

valuation of securities 有価証券の評価
valuation of stock without quotation 取引相場のない株式の評価
valuation of work in process 仕掛品の評価
valuation on perfect competitive market 完全競争市場における評価
valuation principle 評価原則
valuation procedures 評価手続き
valuation rate of interest 評価利率
valuation reserve 評価性引当金
valuation standards for securities 有価証券評価基準
valuation technique 評価手法
value 価額
value accounting 価値会計
value added 付加価値
value added analysis 付加価値分析
value added network 付加価値通信網
value added statement 付加価値報告書
value agreement endorsement on dwelling risks 価額協定保険
value appreciation 増価
value approach バリュー・アプローチ
value at-risk バリュー・アット・リスク
value change 価格の変動
value creation 価値上昇
value creation management 価値創造経営
value date 受渡日；決済日
value declared 申告価格
value depletion 価値の低下
value diagram バリュー・ダイヤグラム
value exchange system 価値交換システム
value exercise 価値の認識
value fund バリュー・ファンド
value in use 使用価値
value investor 価値への投資家
value line 情報サービス
value line average バリューライン平均
value line composite index バリューライン総合指数
value line index バリューライン・インデックス
value line investment survey バリューライン投資調査
value line option バリューライン・オプション
value line ranking バリューライン・ランキング
Value Line Stock Index バリューライン株価指数
value next month 翌月渡し
value of assessment 課税価額
value of business 企業価値
value of enterprise 企業価値
value of principal 元本価値
value of shareholder 株主価値
value of the transaction 取引価額
value of transactions settled 決済額
value prevailing at the time of 時点における価値
value productivity 価値生産性
value received 対価受領
value relevant information 価値に関する情報
value stock バリュー株
value today 当日渡し
value tomorrow 翌日渡し
value touchstone 価値基準
value variance 価額差異
value weighted market index 時価総額加重指数
value weighted stock price index 時価総額加重株価指数
value-added product 高付加価値製品
valued at market 時価評価された
valued policy 評価済保険契約
vanilla option バニラ・オプション
vanilla structure 単純な方式
vanilla swaps バニラ・スワップ
vanishing point 消滅時点
vanishing premium 消滅保険料
VaR (value at risk) バリュー・アット・リスク
variability 不安定性
variability factor 変動係数

variability of outcome 結果の変動
variable 変数
variable annuity 変額年金
variable annuity contract 変動年金契約
variable annuity unit 変額年金単位
variable benefit formula 変額給付方式
variable budget 変動予算
variable capital 可変資本
variable cash reserve requirements 可変的現金準備制度
variable charge 変動費
variable constant 可変常数
variable contract 変額契約
variable cost 可変費用
variable cost ratio 変動原価率
variable costs and expenses 変動費
variable expenses 変動費
variable immediate annuity 変額即時年金
variable income computation 変動所得計算
variable indirect cost 変動間接費
variable insurance 変額保険
variable interest bearing 変動利付きの
variable interest entity 変動持ち分
variable interest rate 変動利率
variable investment tax 可変投資税
variable life income 変額終身年金
variable life insurance 変額生命保険
variable marketplace 変額市場
variable option 変動オプション
variable overhead 変動管理費
variable overhead cost 変動間接費
variable payout 変額支払い
variable premium 変額保険料
variable price zone 変動価格圏
variable product 変額商品
variable profit 変動利益
variable rate CD 変動金利 CD
variable rate demand note 変動金利要求払証書
variable rate mortgage loan 変動金利型不動産ローン
variable rate on a swap スワップの変動金利
variable rate preferred stock 変動配当優先株
variable rate premium 変動利率保険料
variable repo 金利入札方式のレポ
variable repurchase interest 金利入札方式のレポ
variable universal life insurance 変額ユニバーサル保険
variable-rate debt 変動金利債務
variable-rate interest 変動金利
variable-rate loan 変動金利ローン
variables sampling 変数サンプリング
variables used in determining prices 価格決定変数
variance 差異
variance accounting 差異分析会計
variance analysis 差異分析
variance decomposition 分散の分解分析
variance of the estimate 評価差額
variance ratio 分散比
variation margin 変動証拠金
variation margin call 変動証拠金支払
various kinds of tax benefits 税法上の特典
VAT (value added tax) 付加価値税
Vatican City (Italian lira) バチカン（イタリア・リラ）
vault 金庫室
vault cash 手許現金
vault system 金庫制度
VBO (vested benefit obligation) 確定給付債務
VE (value engineering) 価値工学
VEB (Venezuelan Bolivar) ベネズエラ・ボリバール
VEBA (Voluntary Employee Beneficiary Association) 任意従業員給付組合
vega ベガ
vega-neutral ベガ・ニュートラル
velocity of circulation 流通速度
velocity of circulation of money 貨幣

の流通速度
vendee 買主
vendor 売主
vendor alliance ベンダー連合
venture 事業
venture business ベンチャー・ビジネス
venture capital ベンチャー・キャピタル
venue 行為地
verbal 口頭の
verdict 評決
verifiability 検証可能性
verification 検証；証明
verification by telephone 電話確認
verification of a seal impression 印鑑照合
verification of authenticity 真偽鑑定
verification purpose 照合目的
versus 対する
versus dollar 対ドル
vertical analysis 垂直分析
vertical divesture 垂直分割
vertical equity 垂直的公平
vertical integration 垂直統合
vertical M&A 垂直的Ｍ＆Ａ
vertical merger 垂直的合併
vertical specialization 垂直的国際分業
vertical spread バーティカル・スプレッド
vertical spread transaction バーティカル・スプレッド取引
vertical system 垂直的構造
vertical territorial customer restrictions 垂直的顧客制限
vertical trade 垂直的貿易
vessel unknown 積載船名未詳
vest 権利を与える
vested 権利の確定した
vested benefit 受給権付与済給付
vested defined contribution plan 受給権確定済みの確定拠出制度
vested in interest 発生確定せる
vested in possession 現有の
vested interest 既得権
vested legacy 確定遺贈
vested liability 確定債務
vested portion 権利確定部分
vested post-employment benefit 権利確定退職後給付
vested remainder 確定残余権
vested renewal commission 据置更新手数料
vested right 既得権
vested share option 権利の確定したストック・オプション
vesting 受給権付与
vesting conditions 権利確定条件
vesting date 権利確定日
vesting date measurement 権利確定日測定
vesting period 権利確定期間
vesting provisions 権利確定条項
vesting requirements 権利確定要件
Veterans Administration 復員軍人局
veto 拒否権
VFM (value for money) バリュー・フォー・マネー
viable 成長しうる
viatical assignment 生命保険証券の譲渡
viatical contract 保険証券買取契約
viatical industry 保険買取業界
viatical provider 保険買取証券提供者
viatical settlement 生命保険証券売却
viator 生命保険原契約者
vibrant market 活気ある市場
vice chairman 副議長
Vice Minister of Finance for International Affairs 財務官
vice president 副総裁
vicinity of the upper limit 天井圏
vicious cycle 悪循環
vicious member merchant 悪質加盟店
views at home and abroad 国内外の見方
vigorous change 力強い変化
vintage of capital 資本の年齢
violation of a contract 契約違反
violation of just and equitable

principles 信義則違反
violation of the conditions of contract 契約条件の違反
violent fluctuation 乱高下
virtually bankrupt borrower 実質破綻先
virtually unchanged 大きな変化のない
virtuous cycle 好循環
vis major 不可抗力
visible supply 発行予定
visual curve-fitting method 作図法
vital statistics 人口動態統計
VND (Vietnamese dong) ベトナム・ドン
vocational training 職業訓練
void 無効な
void agreement 無効な合意
void contract 無効な契約
void transaction 無効取引
voidable 取消可能
voiding of banknotes 銀行券の失効
voiding of small-denomination currency including banknotes 少額通貨整理
volatile fluctuation 不安定な変動
volatile inflation 激しいインフレ
volatile market 価格の変動が著しい市場
volatile movement in fair value 変動の激しい公正価値
volatility ボラティリティ
volatility forecast ボラティリティ予測
volatility of asset prices 資産価格の乱高下
volatility of the return 利益の変動性
volatility ratio ボラティリティ・レシオ
volatility spread ボラティリティ・スプレッド
volatility value ボラティリティ価値
volatility-normalized ボラティリティ標準化
volume accumulation 累積出来高
volume accumulator ボリューム・アキュミュレーター
volume cost 量産原価
volume deleted 取引高削除
volume discount 数量割引
volume efficiency 量産効果
volume indicator 操業度指数
volume of banknotes handled 銀行券取扱高
volume of inventories 在庫量
volume of issuance 発行規模
volume of over-the-counter transaction 店頭売買高
volume of production 生産量
volume of transaction 取引量
volume of transactions settled 決済件数
volume on offer 発行量
volume ratio ボリューム・レシオ
volume rebate 数量リベート
voluntary 任意の
voluntary accumulation plan 任意型継続投資プラン
voluntary additions 任意繰入額
voluntary adjustment 自己否認
voluntary adoption 任意の適用
voluntary arbitration 任意仲裁
voluntary association 任意組合
voluntary audit 任意監査
voluntary bankruptcy 自己破産
voluntary benefit 任意的給付
voluntary cancellation 任意解約
voluntary contribution 任意拠出
voluntary conveyance 無償譲渡
voluntary depreciation 任意償却
voluntary depreciation method 任意償却法
voluntary dissolution 任意解散
voluntary health insurance 任意医療保険
voluntary insurance 任意保険
voluntary liquidation 任意整理
voluntary participation 任意加入
voluntary partnership 任意組合
voluntary pension plan 任意加入年金制度
voluntary place of tax payment 任意納

V

税地
voluntary plan 任意プラン
voluntary redemption 任意償還
voluntary reporting 自主的報告
voluntary reserve 任意準備金
voluntary restraint program 自主規制計画
voluntary restriction of export 輸出自主規制
voluntary retirement 希望退職
voluntary saving 自発的貯蓄
voluntary settlement 無償継承的不動産処分
voluntary tax payment 自主納付
voluntary transactions 自発的な取引
voluntary unemployment 自発的失業
voluntary winding up 任意解散
volunteer 無償取得者
Vostro account 先方勘定
voting 投票
voting bond 議決権付社債
voting common shares 議決権付普通株式
voting company 決議権会社
voting power 議決権
voting right 議決権
voting right of stockholder 株主議決権
voting shares 議決権付株式
voting stock 議決権株式
voting stockholder 議決権保有株主
voting trust 議決権信託
voting trust certificate 議決権信託証書
voucher 伝票
voucher for disbursement 払出証票
voucher payable register 支払伝票記入帳
voucher system 支払伝票制度
vouching 伝票突き合わせ
voyage policy 航海保険
VP デンマーク保管振替機関
VPC スウェーデン保管振替機関
VRA (voluntary restraint agreement) 輸出自主規制協定
VRC (voting right certificate) 議決権証書
VRDO (variable rate demand obligation) 変動金利要求払債
VRM (variable rate mortgage) 変動金利モーゲージ
VRN (variable rate note) VRN
VSE (Vancouver Stock Exchange) バンクーバー証券取引所
VSTE (very short-term financing) facility 超短期ファイナンス制度
VSX (Vienna Stock Exchange) ウィーン証券取引所
vulnerability 脆弱
vulnerable 脆弱な
VUV (Vanuatu vatu) バヌアツ・バツ
VWAP (volume weighted average price) 出来高加重平均株価

V

W

WA (with average) 単独海損担保
WAC (weighted average coupon) 加重平均クーポン
WACC (weighted average cost of capital) 加重平均資本コスト
wage 給与
wage and salary 賃金給料
wage assignment 給料控除
wage ceiling 賃金のシーリング設定
wage contract 賃金協定
wage earner 勤労者
wage freeze 賃金凍結
wage garnishment 給与差押
wage in kind 現物給与
wage income 賃金所得
wage increase 賃上げ
wage index 賃金指数
wage level 賃金水準
wage negotiation 労使交渉
wage rate 賃率
wage related benefit 給与比例給付
wage statistics 賃金統計
wage structure 賃金体系
wage system 賃金体系
wage unit 賃金単位
wage variance 賃金差異
wage-bracket table 簡易税類表
wage-hike drive 賃金闘争
wage-price control 賃金・物価統制
wage-price guideline 賃金物価ガイドライン
wage-push inflation 賃金インフレーション
wager policy 賭博保険（証書）
wages ledger 賃金元帳
wages on job evaluation 職能給
wages payable 未払賃金
wait and see 模様ながめ
wait for reaction 押し目待ち
wait-and-see stance 様子見スタンス
waiting for further development 展開待ち
waiting period 待機期間
waived interest 放棄利息
waiver 放棄する
waiver clause 権利放棄条項
waiver of clearing qualification 清算資格の喪失
waiver of insurance premium 保険料の免除
waiver of lien 先取特権の放棄
waiver of premium 保険料払込免除
waiver of sovereign immunity 主権免除の放棄
waiver of trading qualification 取引資格の喪失
WALA (weighted average loan age) 加重平均ローン経過期間
walk-through test 通査
wall flower 人気の落ちた銘柄
wall paper 価値のない証券
Wall Street ウォール街
Wall Street Journal ウォール・ストリート・ジャーナル
WAM (weighted average maturity) 加重平均満期
wane in inflation pressure インフレ圧力が薄らぐ
waning momentum モメンタムの和らぎ
wanted for cash 現金決済希望
war babies 軍需関連株
war bereaved 戦没者遺族
war brides 軍需関連銘柄
war chest 軍資金
war clause 戦争約款
war pension 戦争年金
war perils 戦争危険
war risk 戦争危険
war risk exclusion clause 戦争危険免

責条項
warehouse charges 倉敷料
warehouse fee 倉庫料
warehouse receipt 倉庫証券
warehousing and carrying charges 保管費
warehousing and harbor transportation service industry 倉庫・運輸関連業
warning against fraud 不正行為に対する警告
warning indicator 警戒指標
warrant 新株引受権証券；ワラント
warrant agent ワラント代理人
warrant agreement ワラント契約書
warrant bond ワラント債
warrant bond redemption ワラント債償還
warrant in bankruptcy 破産者財産差押令状
warrant index ワラント指数
warrant market ワラント市場
warrant of attachment 差押令状
warrant of attorney 委任状
warrant outstanding 発行済みのワラント
warrant parity ワラント・パリティ
warrant purchase price ワラント購入価格
warrant to purchase common shares 普通株式購入権
warrant value ワラント・バリュー
warranted rate of growth 適正成長率
warranty 瑕疵担保責任
warranty claims 保証請求
warranty clause 瑕疵担保条項
warranty cost 保証費用
warranty deed 瑕疵担保証書
warranty obligation 保証債務
warranty provision 保証条項
Warsaw Treaty Organization ワルシャワ条約機構
wash order 回し玉
wash sale 仮装売買
waste 廃棄物
wasting assets 減耗資産
watch and wait 模様ながめ
watch list 格付見直し先；要注意銘柄
watchdog 監視人（監督者，監督機関者）
water acquisition right 水利権
water-bailiff 船舶検査官
watered assets 水増し資産
watered capital 擬制資本
watered stock 架空資本；水増資本
watermark すかし
wave function 波動関数
Wave Theory ウェーブ理論
wave-count structure 波動ストラクチャー
way 通行権
way forward 前進
weak activity 活動の停滞
weak axiom 弱公準
weak dollar 弱いドル
weak form ウィーク・フォーム
weak form efficiency ウィーク型効率性
weak growth 低い成長率
weak market 弱い市場
weak tone 軟調
weaken だれる
weakening 軟化
weakening dollar ドル安
weaker bargaining position 交渉の弱い立場
weaker demand 弱含みな需要
weaker in tandem つれ安
wealth 富
wealth accumulation 資産形成
wealth tax 富裕税
wealth test 富力審査
wear and tear 損耗
weather derivatives 天候デリバティブ
weather insurance 天候保険
wedge ウェッジ
wedge formation ウェッジ・フォーメーション
Wednesday-factor 水曜日要因
week order ウイーク・オーダー

weekend effect 週末効果
weekly accounting 週次決算
weekly chart 週足チャート
weekly payment 一週間払い
weekly premium 週払保険料
weekly reversal ウィークリー・リバーサル
weigh on 足を引っ張る
weight down 圧迫する
weight of evidence 証拠の重さ
weighted 加重
weighted arithmetic average 加重算術平均
weighted average 加重平均
weighted average cost 加重平均コスト
weighted average cost method 加重平均原価法
weighted average discount rate 加重平均割引率
weighted average life 加重平均償還期間
weighted average method 加重平均法
weighted average number of common share outstanding 加重平均普通株数
weighted average of market capitalization 時価総額加重平均値
weighted average probability 加重平均確率
weighted average rate 加重平均金利
weighted average shares 加重平均株数
weighted basis trade 加重平均ベース貿易
weighted index 加重指数
weighted mean method 加重平均法
weighted premium 加重保険料
weighted rebalancing 加重組み換え
weighted risk asset 加重リスク資産
weighted stock price average 加重株価平均
weighting in equity 株式組入比率
weighting ratio 組込み率
welcome enterprise 企業誘致
Welfare and Medical Service 福祉医療機構
welfare benefit 福祉給付
welfare benefit fund 福利厚生基金
welfare economics 厚生経済学
welfare expense 福利厚生費
welfare facilities 福利厚生施設
welfare plan 福利厚生制度
welfare reform 福祉改革
welfare social program 福祉社会制度
welfare state 福祉国家
well-being 健全性
WFP (World Food Programme) 世界食糧計画
what if 仮定に基づく
what-if scenario 仮定のシナリオ
when-distributed transaction 売出条件付取引
when-issued basis 発行日基準
wheregot and wheregone statement 資金源泉運用表
whisper number 非公式業績予測
whisper stock うわさ銘柄
whistle blower 内部告発者
white knight ホワイトナイト
white paper on economic cooperation 経済協力白書
white return 白色申告
White's Tax-Exempt Bond Rating Service ホワイト非課税債格付サービス
whiz kids 若手頭脳集団
WHO (World Health Organization) 世界保健機関
whole life 終身
whole life annuity 終身年金
whole life insurance 終身保険
whole reinsurance 全額再保険
wholesale 卸売
wholesale accounting 卸売会計
wholesale bank ホールセール・バンク
wholesale banking 卸売銀行業務
wholesale business 卸売業
wholesale dealer 卸売商
wholesale establishment 卸売事業
wholesale group insurance 団体扱契約
wholesale insurance 集団扱保険

W

wholesale merchant 問屋
wholesale price 卸売値段
wholesale price index 卸売物価指数
wholesale securities firm ホールセール証券会社
wholesale trade 卸売業
wholesale trade industry 卸売業界
wholesaler 卸売業者
wholesaling 卸売
wholly owned 全株式を所有されている
wholly owned subsidiary 完全子会社
Whoops (Washington Public Power Supply System) ワシントン州公共電力供給システム
WI (when-issued transaction) 発行日取引
wide fluctuation of market 乱高下相場
wide margin 高いマージン
wide opening 大きなスプレッドの立会開始
widely shared view 一般的な見方
widening gap 拡大する格差
wider band ワイダー・バンド
wider margin 拡大相場変動
widespread downturn 全面的な景気後退
widget 架空の商品
widow-and-orphan stock 安定配当株
widow's pension 寡婦年金
width of corridor 回廊の幅
width of currency movements 為替変動幅
wild card option ワイルド・カード・オプション
wild card period ワイルド・カード期間
willful 故意の
willful evasion of the tax 故意の脱税
willful misconduct 故意の不法行為
willfully false 故意の虚偽
Williams Act ウィリアムズ法
willing party 自発的な当事者
willingness to pay 返済意志
Wilshire indices ウイルシャー指数
windfall loss 思いがけない損失
windfall loss or gain 偶発的損益
windfall profit 棚ぼた利益
winding-up 清算
Winding-up Act 解散法
winding-up by the court 強制清算
winding-up of pending affairs 残務整理
winding-up order 清算命令
window 窓口
window dressing 粉飾
window dressing deposit 粉飾預金
window dressing financial statements 粉飾財務諸表
window dressing settlement of accounts 粉飾決算
window guidance 窓口指導
window of opportunity 好機
window plan 早期退職優遇制度
windstorm and flood insurance 風水害保険
WINGS (warrant into negotiable government securities) 国債ワラント
WIPO (World Intellectual Property Organization) 世界知的所有権機関
wire house 大手証券会社
wire room 事務部門
wire transfer 現金振込；電信送金
WISD (weighted implied standard deviation) 加重インプライド標準偏差
with a proviso 条件付
with average 分損担保
with discount 額面以下で
with momentum for recovery 回復基調を維持して
with premium 額面以上で
with recourse 遡及義務あり
with recourse credit 遡及償還義務不免除信用状
with the exception of 除いては
with usage restriction 使用制限のある
with warrants 新株引受権付き
with-profit annuity 配当付年金
with-profit fund 利益配当ファンド

with-profit insurance 配当付保険
withdraw 取崩す
withdraw from 撤退する
withdrawal 撤回；取消
withdrawal benefit 解約払戻金
withdrawal credit 脱退給付金
withdrawal from membership 会員の脱退
withdrawal of banknotes from circulation 銀行券の還収
withdrawal of certificate 証書の交付
withdrawal of deposited margin 証拠金の引出し
withdrawal of membership 脱退
withdrawal of receipt 受理撤回
withdrawal of registration 登録の取消
withdrawal of securities 有価証券の返還
withdrawal of stock certificates 株券の交付
withdrawal of suspension 停止解除
withdrawal plan 引出しプラン
withdrawing member 脱退会員
withdrawn cash to be returned to the government 政府勘定保管金
withholding 天引き
withholding agent 源泉徴収義務者
withholding and payment 源泉徴収と納付
withholding at the source 源泉徴収
withholding income tax 源泉徴収所得税
withholding income tax at source 源泉所得税
withholding of customs appraisement 関税評価差止め
withholding on employment income 給与所得に係る源泉徴収
withholding record of employment income 給与所得の源泉徴収票
withholding tax 源泉課税
withholding tax absorbed loan 源泉課税負担型ローン
withholding tax certificate 源泉徴収票
withholding tax credit 所得税額の控除
withholding tax exempt 非課税扱い
withholding tax exemption 源泉非課税
withholding tax on dividends received 受取配当金源泉税
withholding tax on interest 利子源泉税
withholding tax option 源泉選択
withholding tax rate 源泉徴収税率
withholding tax system 源泉徴収制度
within a tight band 狭いレンジで
within limits on value of call option コール・オプション価値の範囲
within the due date of filing the return 申告書の提出期限内
without any prejudice to 損ねることなく
without credit at sight buying rate 信用状なし一覧払い手形買い相場
without impeachment of man 毀損の責任なしに
without netting 相殺することなしに
without parent company 親抜け
without prejudice 権利を損なわずに
without prejudice to preliminary 既得権を犯さずに
without recourse ウイズアウト・リコース
without recourse credit 遡及償還義務免除信用状
without trial proceedings 裁判によらず
without-profit insurance 無配当保険
WL (whole loan) ホール・ローン
WLS (weighted least squares) 加重最小２乗法
WMA (week moving average) 週足移動平均
WMO (World Meteorological Organization) 世界気象機関
words of limitation 内容表示文言
work 作業
work accident 労働災害
work disease 職業病
work force 従業員
work in process 仕掛品

work in process at the end of period 期末仕掛品
work in process ledger 仕掛品元帳
work order 製造指図書
work performed 実施作業
work related injury 業務上災害
work sheet 精算表
work standard 作業標準
workable competition 有効競争
workers compensation catastrophe cover 労働者災害補償再保険
workers pension 労働者年金
workers union 従業員組合
workers' asset building savings 財形貯蓄
workers' compensation 労働補償
workers'accident comprehensive insurance 労働災害総合保険
working account 活勘定
working age 生産年齢
working assets 運用資産
working balance 運用残高
working budget 実行予算
working capital 運転資金
working capital analysis 運転資本分析
working capital control 運転資金管理
working capital position 運転資本状態
working condition 作業条件
working control 実行支配
working days 労働日数
working generation 勤労世代
Working Group of Financial Markets 金融市場協議会
working hours 作業時間
working interest 賃借権利権
working inventory 運転棚卸資産
working of global economy グローバル経済の作用
working place 事業場
working rules 就業規則
working rules of audit procedures in reporting 監査報告準則
working trial balance 監査試算表
working trial balance sheet 試算表
working years 現役期間
working-capital ratio 運転資本比率
working-hours method 運転時間法
workmen's compensation acts 労働者災害補償法
workmen's compensation insurance 労災保険；労働者災害補償保険
workmen's compensation law 労働者賠償法
workout 問題処理
worksheet method 精算表方式
workshop 作業場
World Bank 世界銀行（世銀）
World Bank bond 世銀債
World Bank group 世銀グループ
world class investor 世界クラスの投資家
world crisis 世界恐慌
world economic outlook 世界経済見通し
world enterprise 世界企業
world index ワールド・インデックス
world market 世界市場
world market portfolio 世界市場ポートフォリオ
world market price 国際市場価格
world marketing 世界マーケティング
world money 世界貨幣
worry free 懸念を解消する
worth and fixed assets ratio 資本固定資産比率
worth to current debt ratio 資本流動負債比率
worth to fixed debt ratio 資本固定負債比率
wrap 元利支払いの保証
wrap account ラップ口座
wraparound 二番譲渡抵当
wraparound annuity 投資対象選択権付年金
wrapper ラップ商品
wrapping-up 結了
write off bad debts 貸倒を償却する
write-down 評価減
write-off 償却
write-off from special bad debts

reserve 債権償却特別勘定の取崩し
write-off of bad loan 不良債権処理
write-off of loans 貸出金償却
write-off of stocks 株式償却
write-offs in current term 当期償却額
write-up 評価増し
writer 売手
writer of the option オプションの売手
writing 売建て
writing company 元受会社
writing naked ネーキッドの売り
written agreement 書面契約
written application 書面申請
written assignment 譲渡証書
written bid and offer 板呼値
written contract 書面契約
written decision 裁決書
written down value 評価減後価格
written examination 筆記試験
written inquiry 書面引合
written law 成文法
written option 売りオプション
written premium 計上保険料
written proxy 代理権を証する書類
written risk management policy リスク管理方針文書
written statement of assurance 確約書
written statement of manners of conducting business 業務方法書
written-off accounts receivable 償却済債権
wrong doing 不正行為
wrongful dismissal 不当解雇
WST (Samoan tala) サモア・タラ
WTI (West Texas Intermediate) WTI
WTO (World Trade Organization) 世界貿易機関

W

X

x-axis 縦軸
XC (ex coupon) 利落ち
XCD (Grenada EC (East Caribbean) dollar) グレナダ(EC ドル)
XD (ex dividend) 配当落ち
Xinjiang 新疆ウイグル自治区
Xizang チベット自治区
XOF (Ivory Coast CFA (Communauté Financière Africaine) franc) コートジボアール (CFA フラン)
XOF (Mali CFA (Communauté Financière Africaine) franc) マリ (CFA フラン)
XR (ex-rights) 株式権利落ち
XW ワラント落ち

Y

y-axis 横軸
Yankee bond ヤンキー・ボンド
Yankee bond market 米国ドル債市場
Yankee-dollar market ヤンキー・ドル市場
year end rally 年末ラリー
year in brief 当年度の概況
year of account 決算年度
year to date 期首から現時点
year to which listing day pertains 上場日が属する年
year-end 年末
year-end adjustment 年末調整
year-end audit 期末監査
year-end balance sheet 期末賃借対照表
year-end closing of accounts 期末決算
year-end demand for fund 年末の資金需要
year-end dividend 期末配当
year-end inventory 期末在庫
year-end market 年末相場
year-end settlement 年末調整
year-end stock 期末在庫
year-to-year changes 経年変動率
year-to-year percentage change 前年比変化率
yearly installment 年賦
yearly net earnings 年間純益
yearly premium 年払保険料
yearly renewal 毎年更新
yearly taxation 年税主義
years certain annuity 保証期間付年金
years elapsed after foundation 設立後経過年数
years for contribution 拠出年数
years of amortization 償却年数
years to maturity 発行年限
years-of-service approach 期間定額規準
yen account specifically for financial futures transaction 金融先物取引専門円口座
yen appreciation 円高
yen bloc 円ブロック
yen bond 円債
yen bull large amount time deposit 円高期待型大口定期預金
yen credit 円借款
yen futures 日本円通貨先物
yen interest rate swap position 円金利スワップ・ポジション
yen loan 円借款
yen rate cap 円金利キャップ
yen rising against the dollar 対ドルでの円高
yen shift 円転換
yen table denominated syndicated loan 円建シンジケート・ローン
yen value 円貨額
yen value per one U.S. dollar 対ドル円貨額
yen vs dollar 対ドルでの円
yen-denominated 円建て
yen-denominated bond 円建債
yen-denominated bonds issued in Japan by foreign institutions 円建外債
yen-denominated export 円建輸出
Yen-Dollar Commission 円・ドル委員会
yen-dollar foreign exchange market ドル・円市場
yen-dollar swap agreement 円ドル・スワップ
yen-quoted 円表示
yen-renminbi swap arrangement 円・人民元スワップ協定
yen's sell off 円の下落
YER (Yemen riyal) イエメン・リアル

yield 利回り
yield adjustments 利息の調整額
yield advantage 利回優位
yield appeal 利回りの魅力
yield auction 利回入札
yield base 利回りベース
yield based on weighted average 加重平均利回り
yield bogeys 利回問題
yield book 利回表
yield by simple interest 単利利回り
yield curve 利回曲線
yield curve differential 利回りの格差
yield curve flattening 利回曲線の平坦化
yield curve inversion 逆イールド
yield curve risk 利回曲線リスク
yield curve swap イールドカーブ・スワップ
yield divergence 利回格差
yield enhancement 利回向上
yield equivalence 利回等価
yield factor 利回要因
yield for holding period 所有期間利回り
yield formula 利回計算
yield improvement switch 利回改善スイッチ
yield measure 利回基準
yield of bond transactions 債券売買利回り
yield on already-issued bond 既発債利回り
yield on bond 債券利回り
yield on funds raised 資金調達利回り
yield on high quality corporate bond 優良社債利回り
yield on investment 運用利回り
yield on loans 貸付金利回り
yield on nominal bond 通常債券の名目利回り
yield on outstanding bond 既発債利回り
yield on public and corporate bond 公社債応募者利回り
yield rate 歩留り
yield rate variance 歩留り差異
yield spread イールド・スプレッド；利回格差
yield standard 利回水準
yield structure 利回構造
yield swap イールド・スワップ
yield to call 繰上償還利回り
yield to maturity 満期利回り
yield to put 買取請求利回り
yield to subscriber 応募者利回り
yielding investment 利回りを生む投資
yields of public and corporate bonds 公社債利回り
yields on long-term bonds 長期国債流通利回り
yo-yo stock ヨーヨー株式
yours ユアーズ（売った時）
YoY (year-on-year) 前年同月比
YTAL (yield to average life) 平均残存期間利回り
YTC (yield to call) コール利回り
YTD (year-to-date) 年初来の
YTM (yield to maturity) 最終利回り
YTP (yield to put) プット利回り
yuan 元
YUM (Yugoslav dinar) ユーゴスラビア・ディナール
Yunnan 雲南省

Z

Z bond Z債券
z rated bond 無等級債券
zai-tech 財テク
zaibatsu 財閥
ZAR (South African rand) 南アフリカ・ランド
ZBB (zero base budgeting) ゼロ・ベース予算
ZECRO (zero cost rate option) ゼロ・コスト・オプション
Zengin System 全銀システム
Zenshinren Bank 全信連
zero coupon perpetual ゼロ・クーポン永久債
zero coupon structure ゼロ・クーポン構造
zero-beta portfolio ゼロ・ベータ・ポートフォリオ
zero-bracket amount ゼロ課税範囲；非課税区分額
zero-cost collar ゼロ・コスト・カラー
zero-cost option ゼロ・コスト・オプション
zero-cost option trading ゼロコスト・オプション取引
zero-coupon bond ゼロ・クーポン債
zero-coupon convertible securities ゼロ・クーポン転換証券
zero-coupon curve ゼロ・クーポン・カーブ
zero-coupon issue ゼロ・クーポン債
zero-coupon securities ゼロ・クーポン証券
zero-coupon T-note ゼロ・クーポンTノート
zero-plus tick ゼロ・プラス・ティック
zero-sum game ゼロ・サム ゲーム
Zhejiang 浙江省
Zillmer deduction チルメル控除
Zillmer quota チルメル歩合
Zillmerized reserve チルメル式責任準備金
ZMK (Zambian kwacha) ザンビア・クワチャ
zone examination 地域別検査
ZRN (Congo Democratic Republic franc) コンゴ民主共和国フラン
ZWD (Zimbabwe dollar) ジンバブエ・ドル

JAPANESE-ENGLISH

ア

アービトラージ arbitrage
アービトラージャー arbitrager
アーラーズ株価モデル Ahlers model
RTGS real time gross settlement
相容れない at odds with
ISM指数 ISM (Institute of Supply Management) index
IS曲線 I-S curve
IS曲線・LM曲線 I-S curve・L-M curve
IMF協定 agreement of IMF
IMFゴールドトランシェ IMF gold tranche
IMF借款 IMF loan
IMF出資 IMF subscription
IMFスタンドバイ IMF stand-by
IMF代替勘定 substitution account of IMF
IMF平価 IMF par value
IMF理事会 IMF Board of Directors
IO interest only
アイザー・オア・ファシリティ either/or facility
ICカード IC (integrated circuit) card
相対記入 contra entry
相対債務 cross debt；mutual debt
相対市場 negotiation market
相対取引 negotiated trading；negotiated transaction
相対ネット受取限度額 bilateral net credit limit
相対ローン bilateral loan
アイダス原理 AIDAS theory
IDシステム Institutional Delivery System
IT関連商品 IT-related goods
安定経済成長 stable economic growth
相 手 方 opposite party
相手方当事者 adversary party
相手方となる取引参加者 counterparty trading participant
アイテマイズ控除 itemized deduction
アイドル・バランス idle balance
相 乗 り tailgating
相乗り登録 piggyback registration
IBF勘定（国際銀行業務勘定） international banking facilities account
相まって coupled with
アイランド・リバーサル・パターン island reversal pattern
アイルランド・プント IEP (Ireland punt)
アイルランド保管振替機関 CBISSO
アウト・オブ・ザ・マネー out of the money
アウトサイド・デー outside day
アウトソーシング outsourcing
アウトパフォーマンス outperformance
アウト・ライト outright
アウトライト為替相場 outright exchange rate
アウトライト取引 outright transaction
アウトライトの売り outright selling
アウトライトの買い outright buying
アウト・ライン outline
青色申告 blue form return
青色申告会 Blue Return Association
青色申告者 blue return taxpayer；taxpayer filing a blue return
青色申告承認 approval of filing a blue return
青色申告承認の取消 revocation of approval of filing a blue return
青色申告制度 blue return system
青色申告特別控除 special deduction for blue return
青色申告の出来る法人 corporation qualifying for filing a blue return
青色申告の取消 cancellation of filing a blue return
青色申告法人 corporation filing a blue return
青空市場 open air market
青 天 井 topless

ア

あ お る bull the market
アカウント・イヤー・ベイシス account year basis
アカウント・エグゼクティブ account executive
アカウント・レポート・サービス account report service
赤　　字 deficit
赤字記入 red-ink entry
赤字金融 deficit-covering finance
赤字経営 loss making operations
赤字継続 continued deficit
赤字国債 deficit-covering bond
赤字財政 deficit finance
赤字削減 deficit reduction
赤字削減計画 deficit busting plan
赤字残額 red-balance
赤字縮小 reduced losses
赤字転落 newly deficit；turn to red figures
赤 字 の in red ink
赤字補填 making up for a deficit
赤字融資 financing for deficit-covering
赤字有配 dividend payment despite deficit
赤字予算 deficit budget；unbalanced budget
赤字を補填する funding the deficit
赤船荷証券 red B/L
空　　地 vacant lot
空　　屋 vacant building
アキュミュレーション accumulation
アキュミュレーション方式 accumulation system
明らかな pronounced
明らかな曖昧さ、あるいは誤り patent ambiguities or defects
明らかな意味不明 patent ambiguity
悪意の第三者 holder in bad faith
悪 影 響 adverse effects
悪 材 料 bad news；unfavorable factor
悪質加盟店 vicious member merchant
悪 循 環 vicious cycle
悪　　税 irrational tax
悪目買い setback
悪　　用 evil practice
悪用カード fraudulent card
アクション・プログラム action program
アクセス・カード access card
アクセス権 right of access
アクセプタンス方式 acceptance system
アクティビティ分析 activity analysis
アクティブ運用 active management
アクティブの度合い aggressiveness
アクティブ・パートナー active partner
アクティブ・ポートフォリオ active portfolio
アクティブ・リスク active risk
アクティブ・リスク回避度 active risk aversion
アクティブ・リターン active return
アクリーション・ボンド accretion bond
アクレ・スワップ accreting swap
アクロニム acronym
アクワイアラー acquirer
アゲインスト・ペイメント against payment
上 げ 足 uptrend；upward momentum
上げ基調 upwards
上げ局面 rising phase
上げ相場 bull market；rising quotation
揚地選択貨物 optional cargo
揚 げ 超 net receipt
明 渡 し vacation
明渡しの遅滞 delay of evacuation
朝金時点（9時） designated settlement time of 9:00
アジア・アフリカ共同市場 Afro-Asian Common Market
アジア開発基金 ADF (Asian Development Fund)
アジア開発銀行 Asian Development Bank
アジア型オプション Asian option
アジア研究公報 ARB (Accounting Research Bulletin)
アジア支払同盟 APU (Asian Payment Union)
アジア準備銀行 Asian Reserve Bank
アジア清算同盟 Asian Clearing Union
アジア太平洋経済協力会議 Asia Pacific

Economic Cooperation
アジア太平洋経済社会委員会 Economic and Social Commission for Asia and the Pacific
アジアダラー Asian dollar
アジアダラー市場 Asian dollar market
アジア通貨 Asian regional currencies
アジア通貨単位 ACU (Asian Currency Unit)
アジアドル債 Asian dollar bond
アジアに対し堅調 holding up to Asia
足切計算 tax cutback
足元での上昇 near term rally
足 元 の for the time being
アジャスタブル・ペッグ adjustable peg
アジャスタブル保険 Adjustable Life Insurance
足を引っ張る weigh on
預 り 金 customers' deposits ; deposit received
預り手付金 earnest money received
預り保証金 deposit on contract ; deposit received for guarantees ; deposit received on sale
預り有価証券 securities received for guarantee
預り預託保証金 guaranty deposits received
預 け 金 money deposited
ASEAN自由貿易地域 AF TA (ASEAN Free Trade Arrangement)
アセット・アプローチ asset approach
アセット・クラス・ターゲット asset class target
アセット・スワップ asset swap
アセット・スワップ取引 asset swap transaction
アセット・パス・スルー証券 APTC (asset pass-through certificate)
アセット・バック・コマーシャルペーパー asset-backed commercial paper
アセット・ファイナンス asset finance
アセット・ベース・スワップ asset base swap
アゼルバイジャン・マナト AZM (Azerbaijan manat)
アセンディング・トップス ascending tops
アソシエート associate
アソシエート会員 associate member
頭　金 down payment ; initial payment
頭金無しで no-down
新しい特徴 novel feature
厚いテール fatter tail
悪　化 degradation ; deterioration ; downturn
悪化の兆候 signs of deterioration
圧縮記帳 advanced depreciation
圧縮限度額 advanced depreciation limit
圧 縮 損 advanced depreciation deduction
圧縮引当金 reserve for advanced depreciation
圧縮引当金繰入損 loss recognized in increasing reserve for advanced depreciation
斡旋手数料 placement fee
斡 旋 人 arranger
アット・ザ・マネー at the money
アット・マーケット at-market
アット・リスク at risk
圧　迫 squeeze
圧迫する weight down
アップ・アンド・プット・オプション up and put option
誂 え の custom tailored
圧力団体 interest group ; power group ; pressure group
軋　轢 friction
アテスト業務 attest service
宛名略号 cable address
アテネ証券取引所 ASE (Athens Stock Exchange)
ア デ ラ ADELA (Atlantic Community Development Group for Latin America)
後入先出基準 last-in first-out basis
後入先出売価還元法 lifo adaptation of retail method
後入先出法 LIFO (last-in, first-out)

method
後入先出法引当金 LIFO reserve
アド・オン金利 add-on interest rate
アド・オン方式 add-on system
後順位担保 junior lien
後に行われた売呼値 later offer
後に行われた買呼値 later bid
後の期間 subsequent period
後 払 い deferred payment
後払給付 back end benefit
後払手数料 back-end load charge ; rear end load
後日付の dating backward
後 費 用 after cost
アドバイザリー・ボード advisory board
アナリスト analyst
アニュイティ・スワップ annuity swap
アニュイティ・ボンド annuity bond
アバブ・ザ・ライン above the line
アバブ・マーケット above market
アファーマティブ・コベナンツ affirmative covenants
アフィニティ・カード affinity card
アフィン期間構造モデル affine term structure model
アフガニスタン・アフガニ AFA (Afghanistan afghani)
あぶく銭 easy money
アブソープション・アプローチ absorption approach
アフター・ロス after loss
アフリカ開発銀行 ADB (African Development Bank)
アフリカ経済委員会 ECA(Economic Commission for Africa)
アプリシエーション・スワップ appreciating swap
アベイラビリティ availability
アベイラビリティ条項 availability clause
アベイラビリティ・リスク availability risk
アベレージタイプ先物為替予約 averaged type forward contract
アポイント商法 appointment sales
アムステルダム証券取引所 AEX (Amsterdam Exchanges)
アメックス商品取引所 Amex Commodity Exchange
アメリカ会計士協会 American Institute of Accountants
アメリカ規格協会 ASA (American Standards Association)
アメリカ経営者協会 AMA (American Management Association)
アメリカ原価計算士協会 National Association of Cost Accountants
アメリカス信託 Americus trust
アメリカス・トラスト・スコア Americus Trust Scores
アメリカ生命保険協会 ACLI (American Council of Life Insurance)
アメリカ内部監査人協会 Institute of Internal Auditors
アメリカ認定生命保険士会 American Society of C.L.U.
アメリカ方式 U.S. term
アメリカン・オプション American option
アメリカン証券取引所 American Stock Exchange
アメリカン証券取引所株価指数 AMEX Index
アメリカンタイプ American type
アモチ・キャップ amortizing cap
アモチ・スワップ amortizing swap
アモチゼーション amortization
アモチゼーション期間 amortisation period
アモチゼーション効果 amortization effect
アモチゼーション事由 amortization event
あ　や noise ; technical change
あや押し technical reaction
あや戻し false rally ; technical rally
誤った併合 misjoinder
洗　替 reversing the reserve amount in full to the income in the following period
洗替による取崩し reversal of reserve after revaluation
荒い展開 choppy range
アラジン債 aladdin bond
争　い contention

新たな資金調達源 alternative source of funding
アラブ首長国連邦ディルハム AED (United Arab Emirates dirham)
アラブ石油輸出国機構 OAPEC (Organization of Arab Petroleum Exporting Countries)
アラブ通貨基金 AMF (Arab Monetary Fund)
アラブ連盟 Arab League
粗　　利 gross income
粗利益総計 aggregate gross margin
粗利益の増減 changes in gross margin
粗利益率 gross margin rate
粗 利 率 gross margin ratio
ARIA ARIA (American Risk and Insurance Association)
アリアー・スワップ arrear swap ; swap-in-arrears
アリゲーター・スプレッド alligator spread
有 り 高 amount in hand ; goods in stock
アルジェリア・ディナール DZD (Algerian dinar)
ある時点のネット・ポジション running balance
アルゼンチン・ペソ ARS (Argentine peso)
アルパイン債 Alpine bond
アルバニア・レク ALL (Albanian lek)
アルバ・フローリン AWG (Aruba florin)
アルファ値 alpha value
アルファベット・ファンド alphabet fund
アルミニウム貨幣（1円） aluminum coins (1 yen)
アルメニア・ドラム AMD (Armenia drum)
アレンジャー料 arranger fee
アンカバード・オプション uncovered option
アンカバード金利裁定 uncovered interest arbitrage
アンカバード・ポジション uncovered position
安 徽 省 Anhui
アンギラ（ECドル） Anguilla (EC (East Caribbean) dollar)
アングラ経済 underground economy
アングラ・マネー underground money
アンケート questionnaire
案　　件 project
暗　　語 secret language
暗号技術 cryptographic techniques
アンゴラ・クワンザ AOR (Angola kwanza)
暗証番号 personal identification number
安心を与える表現 comfort language
安全型運用 passive strategy
安全係数 safety margin
安全資産 riskless assets
安全準備金 safety reserves
安全性の高い株式 low risk stock
安全性マージン margin of safety
安全手持量 safety stock
安 全 弁 safety valve
安全保証申立 article of the peace
安全保障理事会 Security Council
安 全 率 safety factor
安全力分析 safety margin analysis
アンダーウエイト underweight
アンダー・ドレッシング under dressing
アンダー・パーの債券 sub-par bond
アンタイド・ローン untied loan
安定化介入 smoothing operation
安定化政策 stabilization policy
安定価値 constant value
安定価値運用ファンド stable value fund
安定価値会計 constant dollar (value) accounting
安定価値に修正した財務諸表 common dollar statements
安定価値ポートフォリオ stable value portfolio
安定価値利益 constant dollar (value) profit
安 定 株 stable stock
安定株主 stable stockholder
安定貨幣論 stable money principle
安定購買力 constant purchasing power

安定購買力会計 constant purchasing power accounting
安定条件 stability condition
安 定 性 stability
安定性分析 stability analysis
安定操作 stabilization operation ; stabilizing transactions
安定操作取引 market stabilizing transaction
安定促進的 stabilizing
安定配当 consecutive dividend ; stable dividend
安定配当株 widow-and-orphan stock
アンデス共同市場 Andean Common Market
鞍　　点 saddle point
按分基準 proportion basis
按分支払い pro rata payment
按分保険料 pro rata premium
アンバンドリングされた保険 unbundled policy
アンバンドル化 unbundling
アンヘッジ unhedge
アンマッチド・ブック unmatched book
暗黙の合意 implicit agreement
暗黙の前提 implicit assumption

イ

EOE指数 EOE (European Options Exchange) Index
EC共同フロート EC joint floating system
EC証券取引所連合会 FSEEC (Federation of Stock Exchanges in the European Community)
e-Japan戦略 e-Japan Strategy
いいとこどり cream skimming
言 い 値 seller's price
EPC EPC (engineering, procurement and construction)
イーブニング・セッション evening session
EU証券委員会 ESC (EU Securities Committee)
EU証券規制機関委員会 ERSC (EU Securities Regulators Committee)
イールド・カーブ・スワップ yield curve swap
イールド・スプレッド yield spread
イールド・スワップ yield swap
言い渡す render
委 員 会 committee
委員会規則 committee regulations
委員会設置会社 company with a committees system
委員会白書 Commission's White Paper
イエメン・リアル YER (Yemen riyal)
意外の損失 windfall loss
以下に急落する tumbling below
移管金受入 transfer in
移管金額 amount of transfer credit
移管金支払い transfer out
移管債権 transferred debt
移管された建玉 transferred positions
移管保険料 transfer premium
勢いがある on track
域外調達 offshore purchase
域外適用 extraterritorial application
域外適用管轄権 long-arm jurisdiction
異議決定 decision on request for reinvestigation
異議審理庁 reinvestigation organization
異議申立 adverse claim ; request for reinvestigation
異議申立人 contestant
異議を唱える impugn
依　　拠 reliance on
イギリス海上保険法 Marine Insurance Act of 1906
イギリス内国歳入庁 Inland Revenue
育児年金 children's pension
幾多の要因 diverging forces
意　　見 opinion
意見起草室(SEC) Office of Opinions and Review(SEC)
意見区分 scope of opinion
意見差控え denial of opinion ; disclaimer of opinion
意見差控報告書 disclaim report
意 見 書 statement of opinions
意見の差控え disclaimer
意見表明 opinion expression
違 憲 の unconstitutional
移行期間 transition period
移行給付 transition benefit
移行経済 economy in transition
移行時年金 transitional pension
以降の役務の提供 supply of subsequent services
イコール・フッティング equal footing
以後の償却 subsequent depreciation and amortization
遺　　産 legacy
遺産受取人 legatee
遺産管財状 letter of administration
遺産管理 administration estate
遺産管理人 administrator of bequest
遺産所得 inheritance income
遺産相続 inheritance of bequest

遺産に係る基礎控除 basic deduction for bequest
遺産分割 partition of the estate
意　　思 intention
意思決定 decision making
意思決定機関 decision-making body
意思決定支援システム decision support system
意思決定者 decision maker
意思決定ツリー decision tree
維　　持 maintenance
維持価格 support price
維持可能な均衡相場 sustainable equilibrium exchange rate
維持管理機関 maintenance agency
維持管理費用 administrative and maintenance expenses
維持資金 maintenance fund
維持準備金 maintenance reserve
維持証拠金 maintenance margin ; maintenance requirement
維持する sustain
維 持 費 maintenance expense ; upkeep cost
維持費用 maintenance expenditure
異　　質 inhomogeneity
異質市場 heterogeneous market
異時点間の inter-temporal
異種資産 dissimilar assets
移　　出 export to an overseas territory
移出課税 taxation on shipment
意　　匠 design
意 匠 権 right of design
意匠登録 registration of design
意 匠 料 design fee
異常危険準備金 reserve for extraordinary casualty ; unusual casualty reserve ; unusual risks reserve
異常決算 abnormal settlement of accounts
異常原価 abnormal cost
異常減耗 abnormal shrinkage
異常項目 abnormal item ; extra item ; unusual item
異常収益 abnormal return
異常成長モデル abnormal growth model
異常損益項目 extraordinary profit or loss item ; unusual profit or loss item
異常損益項目控除後利益 net profit after extraordinary gain or loss
異常損益項目控除前のキャッシュフロー cash flow before extraordinary gain or loss
異常損失 unusual loss
異常な動き unusual movement
異常利益 extraordinary gain
以上を踏まえて against the above background
イスラエル・シェケル ILS (Islaeli shequel)
いずれか低い方 lower of
以前の脅威 old threat
遺　　贈 devise
遺贈する bequeath ; endow
移送申立記録 record on removal
遺族勘定 survivorship account
遺族給付金 survivor benefit
遺族年金 survivor annuity ; survivor pension
遺族年金給付 survivor income benefit
遺族配偶者 surviving spouse
遺族保険 second-to-die insurance ; survivorship life insurance
依　　存 dependence
依存効果 dependence effect
依 存 度 degree of dependence
委　　託 consignment ; entrustment
委託買付 buying on commission
委託介入 intervention entrusted to foreign central banks
委託加工貿易 processing deal
委託勘定で on customer's account
委託業者 commission agent
委託業務手数料 entrusted business commission
委 託 金 trust money
委託契約 commission agreement ; consignment contract
委託契約書 commission of authority
委託研究 sponsored research

委託時の指示事項 instructions at entrustment
委 託 者 trustor
委託証拠金 brokerage margin；consignment guarantee money；customer's margin
委託証拠金の追加差入れ additional margin deposit
委託する consign；entrust
委託注文 customer's order
委託注文の順位 precedence of customer's orders
委託注文の優先 precedence of customer's order
委託手数料 brokerage commission；commission on consignment；consignment fee
委託取引 agency transaction
委 託 人 consignor
委託の取次 agency service
委託売買 broking；consignment sale and purchase
委託販売 best efforts selling；consignment sale；selling on a consignment basis
委託販売契約 consignment sales contract
委託販売手数料 commission to consignee
委託販売未収入金 account due on consignment-out
委託販売輸出 export on consignment
委託販売輸入 import on consignment
委 託 品 consigned goods；consignment goods；product on consignment
委託品送り状 consignment invoice
委託品元帳 consignment ledger
委託分の for customer's account
委託分の取引証拠金 clearing margin for customer's account
委託貿易 trade on commission
委託募集 best efforts
委託保証金の維持 maintenance of margin
委託保証金率 initial margin requirements
板 寄 せ depth of market
板 呼 値 written bid and offer
イタリア銀行 BOI (Bank of Italy)
イタリア国債 BTP
イタリア証券取引所 ISE (Italian Stock Exchange)
イタリア24オーレ総合株価指数 24 Ore Figure
イタリア・リラ ITL (Italian lira)
異端者リスク maverick risk
1カイ2ヤリ 1 bid, offered 2
一月指標 January barometer
一計算書 single statement
一 契 約 one contract
一 見 客 one shot customer
一時恩給 lump-sum pension
一時貸付金 temporary loan
一時借入手形 deficiency bill
一 時 金 lump-sum money；money paid temporarily；single sum
一時金化 commutation
一時金換算価格 commuted value
一時金支払い lump sum cash payment
一時金で in a lump sum
一時差異 temporary difference
一時支給額 capital sum
一時借入金 flooring debt；temporary borrowing
一時使用 temporary use
一時所得 occasional income
一時所得の特別控除 special deduction for occasional income
一時立替え temporary advance
一時中断 temporary halt
一時的好況 temporary boom
一時的資本 temporary capital
一時的投資 temporary investment
一時的な non-repeating
一時的な活況 flurry
一時的な現象 transitory phenomena
一時的な事象 temporary event
一時的な上昇 temporary increase
一時的な振替 temporary transfer
一時的反騰 brief rally；short lined rally；temporary rally
一時的費用 transient
一時点における見積り point in time estimate

一時投資 temporary investment
一時払い lump-sum payment
一時払型 bullet
一時払給付 lump-sum benefit
一時払込み payment in lump sum
一時払終身保険 single premium whole life policy
一時払据置年金 single premium deferred annuities
一時払生命保険 one payment life policy ; single-premium life insurance
一時払特別保険料 single extra
一時払年金 single payment annuity ; single premium annuity
一時払変額保険 single premium variable annuity
一時払保険 one premium policy
一時払保険料 single premium
一時払有価証券 non-amortizable securities
一時払養老保険 single premium endowment insurance
一時費用 non-recurring cost
一次金融商品 primary financial instrument
一次金融負債 primary financial liabilities
一次産品 primary goods
一次産品生産国機構 organizations of primary commodity producers
一事故あたりの填補限度額 combined single limit
著しく unreasonably
著しく高い価格での販売 sales at unreasonably high price
著しく低い価格 considerably low price
一単元の株式数 number of shares making up a basic lot
一段高 further rise ; jump in the uptrend
一日当り per diem
一日契約 one day contract
一日の一部 fraction of a day
一日の中で intraday
一日平均 daily average
一任信託 discretionary trust
一任注文 discretionary order
一任レバレジッドファイナンス・ポートフォリオ discretionary leveraged finance portfolio
1年以内の定期預金 time deposits available (due) within one year
1年基準 one year rule
1年毎更新保険 annual renewal term insurance
1年定期式団体保険 current cost insurance
1年内返済分 repayment due within one year
1年につき per annum
1年に満たない年 fractional year
1年前の応当日 corresponding date of one year ago
1年未満定期保険 interim term insurance
1ノッチ one notch
一番底 first bottom
一番天井 first peak
一番割安な銘柄 cheapest deliver issue
一部委付 partial abandonment
一部受渡し partial delivery
一部裏書き partial endorsement
一部改訂 partial amendment
一部市場 first section market
一部準備制度 partial reserve system
一部上場 listing on the First Section
一部譲渡 partial assignment
一部増額返済 incidental increase payment
一部入金 partial payment
一部払込債券 partly paid bond
一部引受け partial acceptance
一部返済 pay down
一部保険 under insurance
一部履行 partial performance
一面の大見出し banner
一物一価の法則 law of indifference
一ユニット当り純資産価値 net asset value per unit
一様分布 uniformed distribution
一覧後 after sight
一覧後定期払為替手形 time draft
一覧後日払い days after sight

一覧手形 bill at sight
一覧払い payable at sight
一覧払為替相場 sight rate
一覧払為替手形 sight bill
一覧払信用状 sight L/C (letter of credit)
一覧払相場 at sight rate
一覧払手形 demand bill；draft at sight；sight draft
一覧払手形買相場 at sight buying rate
一覧払約束手形 note at sight；sight note
一律給付年金 universal pension
一律的 uniform
一律の手数料 flat fee
一流企業 blue chip company
一流銀行引受手形 prime bankers acceptance
一流社債 prime corporate bond
一流証券 gift-edged securities
一流の banner
一連のキャッシュフロー stream of cash flows
一連の現金の流入 stream of cash receipts
１を上回る above unity
一回限り one-off
一回の純額 single net payment
一回払貸付 single payment loan
一回分の保険料 mode premium
１カ月振りの安値 one month lows against
一括 lump sum
一括売り sale in gross
一括売出 block offer
一括運送 aggregated shipments
一括買入れ bought deal
一括完済 full payoff；lump sum repayment；repayment at one time
一括基準 aggregate basis
一括契約 contract in bulk
一括原価 bunched cost
一括購入 bulk purchase；lump-sum purchase
一括購入年金 single purchase annuity
一括処理 batch processing
一括注文 blanket order；bulk order
一括適用 coverage of multiple establishments
一括登録 package registration
一括登録国債 government bonds package-registered
一括登録済みの証券 securities on the shelf
一括登録制度 self-registration
一括売買 sale by bulk
一括売買注文 all-or-none order
一括払い lump sum payment；single payment
一括払いカード non-installment card；non-installment credit card
一括払年金保険 immediate payment annuity
一括比例配分方式 proportional method
一括返済 bullet repayment
一括返済リスク crisis at maturity
一括返済ローン bullet loan
一括募集 shelf offering
一括前払い up front
一貫会計 throughout accounting
一貫性 consistency
一貫生産 integrated production；process production
一貫輸送 through transportation
一見したところ prima facie
逸失利益 forgone profit
一週間払い weekly payment
溢出効果 spillover effect
一生間の権利 life interest
一世帯当り貯蓄残高 amount of savings held per household
一世帯住居 single family house
一体性 inclusivity
逸脱 departure
一致 coincidence
一致系列 coincident series
一致させる match
一致指数 coincident indicator
一致した意見 consensus of opinion
一致する concordant
一対株 paired shares
１通ずつを保有する each party retaining one
一定額でない支払い uneven payment

イ

一定額の費用 constant charge
一定期間ごとに at regular intervals
一定期間に渡って over a period of time
一定期限払い single-order term
一定時点 particular point in time
一定税率 fixed tax rate
一定値段 fixed price
一定の掛金 fixed contribution
一定の期間利子率 constant periodic rate of interest
一定の連続複利 constant continuously compounded
一定バスケット fixed basket
一定日付のある bearing date
一定比率 constant proportion
一 定 率 flat percentage
一定率の期間収益額 constant periodic rate of return
一定利回り level yield
一定利回基準 constant yield principles
一手販売 sole agency
一手販売権 exclusive distributorship
一手販売代理店 exclusive selling agent ; sole agent
一般委任契約 open listing
一般営業活動費 general operating expenses
一般横線小切手 general crossed check
一般化ARCHモデル GARCH (generalized autoregressive conditional heteroskedaticity) model
一般会員 general membership
一般会計 general account
一般会計貸付 loans to General Account
一般会計原則 general accounting principles
一般会計歳出 general account expenditure
一般会計歳入歳出 revenue and expenditure of general account
一般会計歳入歳出内訳 breakdown of revenue and expenditure of general account
一般価格 prevailing price
一般化最小2乗法 GLS (generalized least squares)
一般貸倒引当金繰入 transfer to the general loan loss reserve
一般貸出金利 general lending rate
一般貨物 general cargo
一般借入取決め GAB (General Arrangements to Borrow)
一般監査 general audit
一般勘定資産 general account assets
一般間接費 general indirect cost ; general overhead
一般管理販売費 SG&A (selling, general and administrative) expenses
一般管理費 general and administrative expenses
一般管理費及び販売費 general, administrative and selling expenses
一般管理費差異 administrative expense variance
一般管理費予算 general and administrative expense budget
一般教書 state of the union message
一般競争入札 open bidding ; open tendering
一般均衡 general equilibrium
一般偶発債務準備金 general contingency reserve
一般継承人 general successor
一般経費 general expenses
一般経費率 ratio of general expenses to current income
一般気配 bid/offer quotation
一般現金 general cash
一般減税 general tax reduction
一般公共事業 general public works
一般公債資金 general bonded-debt fund
一般購買力 general purchasing power
一般項目 common counts
一般固定資産資金 general fixed-assets fund
一般債権 normal receivables
一般財源 general revenue resource
一般財源債 GO (general obligation) bond
一般債権者 general creditor ; unsecured creditor

一般財産税 general property tax
一般財投 general public investment
一般歳入 general revenue
一般再保険 general reinsurance
一般事業 general business
一般事業債 general corporate bond；industrial bond
一般事業損益 general corporate revenue and expense
一般資産勘定 general asset account
一般自動車保険 basic automobile policy
一般住宅地分譲計画 general building scheme
一般受容性 general acceptability
一般条件書 general terms and conditions of a contract
一般消費財 general consumer goods
一般消費税 general consumption tax
一般処理 normal processing
一般信用取引 unorganized margin transactions
一般税収 general tax revenue
一般政府部門 general government section
一般損益 general corporate revenues and expenses
一般貸借対照表 general balance sheet
一般担保 statutory security
一般担保契約 general security agreement
一般調整 general realignment
一般賃金 prevailing wage
一般通信事業者 common carrier
一般的指針 general guidance
一般的支払手段 general means of payment
一般的な指針 general guideline
一般的な実務 general practice
一般的な条件 common condition
一般的な見方 widely shared view
一般的分類 common classification
一般的要因 general factor
一般的要求事項 general requirements
一般的リーエン general lien
一般投資家 individual investor
一般答弁 general issue
一般に受け入れられている監査基準 generally accepted auditing standards
一般に公正妥当と認められる会計基準 generally accepted accounting standards
一般に認められた会計原則 GAAP (generally accepted accounting principles)
一般に認められた業界の実務 generally accepted industry practices
一般入札 public auction
一般の差押禁止財産 property generally prohibited from seizure
一般の信頼 public confidence
一般賠償責任 public liability
一般費 general cost
一般引当金 general reserve
一般引受け general acceptance
一般物価指数 general price index
一般物価水準 general price level
一般物価水準会計 general price-level accounting
一般物価水準修正 general cost of living adjustment
一般振替 general transfer
一般振替DVP general book-entry DVP
一般法 general statute
一般貿易条件 general terms and conditions of trade
一般法律 general law
一般保険 general insurance
一般保険事業費 general insurance expense
一般募集 general public offering
一般補助金 general grant
一般モーゲージ conventional mortgage
一般目的 general purpose
一般目的財務諸表 general purpose financial statements；general-purpose financial statements
一般要因 general force
一般流動性 general liquidity
一品当りの売価 selling price per unit
一服する come to a halt；rest
一方的記録 unilateral record

一方的譲渡 non-reciprocal transfer
一方的取引 unilateral transaction
一本化ローン consolidated loan
一本値 single price
移転 relocation
移転価格税制 transfer pricing taxation system
移転価格操作 transfer pricing
移転可能な alienable
移転された現金 cash transferred
移転支出 transfer payment
移転収支 balance of transfer account
移転所得 transfer income
移転する transfer
移転的経費 transfer expenditure
移転登記 registration of transfer
移転登録 transfer registration
移転登録請求書 Instruction for Registration of Transfer
移転補償金 compensation for transfer of property in condemnation
移転料 expenses incurred for having the user remove
遺伝的アルゴリズム GA (genetic algorithm)
伊藤のレンマ Ito's lemma
移動 migration
移動加重平均 moving weighted average
移動加重平均法 moving weighted average method
移動均衡 moving equilibrium
移動継続年金 portable pension
移動店舗 mobile shop
移動平均 MA (moving average)
移動平均指数 moving average index
移動平均収束・分散トレーディング法 moving average convergence / divergence trading method
移動平均収斂・乖離 MACD (moving average convergence and divergence)
移動平均棚卸法 moving average inventory method
移動平均値 moving average deviations
移動平均法 moving average cost method ; moving average method
移動平均モデル moving average model
異動申告書 application form for change
意図する purport to
意図的な影響 intended impact
意に反して against the will
移入 import for manufacturing
委任企業連合 blind pool
委任契約 contract of commission
委任状 letter of attorney ; power of attorney ; warrant of attorney
委任状合戦 proxy contest ; proxy fight
委任状勧誘 proxy solicitation
委任状規則 proxy rule
委任状参考資料 proxy material
委任状争奪 proxy contest
委任状争奪戦 proxy fight
委任状投票 proxy vote
委任する delegate
委任の性質 fiduciary nature
委任立法 delegated legislation
違反 breach ; contravention
違反行為 misconduct
違反の帰結 consequence of the breach
意表をついた利下げ surprise rate cut
委付条項 abandonment clause
委付通知 notice of abandonment
イベント・リスク event risk
違法貸付 illegal lending
違法行為 illegal act ; law breaking act
違法行為の是正 rectification of illegal actions
違法タックス・シェルター abusive tax shelter
違法認定 illegitimating
違法配当 illegal dividend
イミーディエイト・オア・キャンセル・オーダー immediate-or-cancel order
イミュニゼーション・ファンド immunization fund
違約 breach of promise
違約金 cancel money ; penalty money
違約金額 penal sum
違約損失積立金 Default Compensation Reserve

違約損失補償基金 default compensation reserve fund
違約損失補償基金特別預託金 special deposit for the default compensation fund
違約損失補償準備金 default loss compensation reserve
違約損失補償準備金の運用 management of the default compensation reserve
違約損失補償準備金の積立て accumulation of default compensation reserve
医薬品業界 pharmaceutical industry
違約利子 penal interest
嫌　　気 discouraged
意欲低下 disincentive
依 頼 書 requisition
依頼返却 requested return
イラク・ディナール IQD (Iraqi dinar)
イラン・リアル IRR (Iran rial)
遺 留 分 legally secured portion
医療給付 health benefit；health care benefit；medical benefit
医療給付金債務 liability for health care benefit
医療給付債務 health care obligation
医療給付支払額 health payout
医療給付制度 health care benefit plan
医療給付の提供 medical benefit delivery
医療給付の利用 medical benefit utilization
医療経済学 health economics
医療コスト medical treatment cost
医療サービス medical service
医療産業 medical industry
医療貯蓄勘定 MAS (medical savings account)
医療賠償責任 medical liability
医 療 費 medical cost；medical expenses
医療費控除 deduction for medical expenses；medical credit；medical expenses deduction
医療費支出 health expenditure
医療費保険 medical expense insurance；medical payment insurance
医療費用 health care cost
医療費用保険 insurance of medical expenses
医療福利給付 health and welfare benefit
医療法人 medical corporation
医療保険 A&H (accident and health) insurance；A&S (accident and sickness) insurance
医療保険給付 A&H (accident and health) benefit；health insurance benefit
医療保険査定 health insurance underwriting
医療保険証券 health policy
医療保険商品 health benefit product
医療保険信託基金 health trust fund
医療保健制度 health care plan
医療保険制度 health plan
医療保険制度の改革 reform of the medical insurance system
医療保障 health coverage；health protection
異例の増加 outsized gain
入　　替 substitution
入替注文 switch order
因　　果 cause and effect
因果関係 casual relation；causality
因果分析 causal analysis
院外運動 lobbying
院外契約 lobbying contract
インカム・エンハンサー income enhancer
インカム・ギアリング income gearing
インカム・ゲイン income gain
インカム・ステートメント・アプローチ income statement approach
インカム・ノート income note
インカム・ファンド income fund
インカム・ワラント income warrant
印　　鑑 seal impression
印鑑照合 verification of a seal impression
印鑑証明 certificate of a seal impression
印鑑証明書 certificate of a seal impression
印 鑑 届 filing of a seal impression
インキュベーション・ファンド incubation

fund
イングランド銀行 BoE (Bank of England)
インクレメント・カード increment card
インコタームズ Incoterms (International Commercial Terms)
インサイダー insider
インサイダー情報 insider information
インサイダー取引 insider trading
インサイド・マーケット inside market
印　　刷 printing and engraving
印 刷 局 Printing Bureau
印刷証券局 Bureau of Printing and Engraving
印 刷 物 printed matter
イン・ザ・マネー in the money
印　　紙 stamp
印紙収入 stamp revenue
印 紙 税 documentary stamp tax
印紙納付 tax payment by stamp
印　　税 royalty on a book
引証する adduce
インストラクション照合システム IRS (Instruction Reconciliation System)
姻戚関係 family relationship
インターナショナル・ポートフォリオ international portfolio
インターバンク為替取引 inter-bank exchange transaction
インターバンク直物相場 inter-bank spot rate
インターバンク市場 inter-bank market
インターバンク取引 inter-bank transaction
インターバンク・ローン inter-bank loan
インターマーケット・スプレッド inter-market spread
インダストリアル・バンキング industrial banking
インタレスト・カバレッジ・テスト interest coverage test
インタレスト・カバレッジ・レシオ interest coverage ratio
インタレスト・スキミング interest skimming
インディケーション・オブ・インタレスト indication of interest
インディケーション方式 indication method
インデックス運用 indexing
インデックス・オプション index option
インデックス債 index linked bond
インデックス債券 index bond
インデックス・パーティシペーション index participation
インデックス・ファンド index fund
インデックス銘柄 index issuers
インデックス・レシオ index ratio
隠匿積立金 hidden reserve
インド国立証券取引所 NSE (National Stock Exchange)
インドネシア・ルピア IDR (Indonesian rupiah)
インド・ルピー INR (Indian rupee)
インパクト調査 impact survey
インパクト・ローン impact loan
インピュテーション方式 imputation method；imputation system
インフォーマル・セクター informal sector
インフォームド・トレーダー informed trader
インフォメーション・レシオ information ratio
インプライド・イールド implied yield
インプライド確率 implied probability
インプライド先渡金利 implied forward rates
インプライド・スプレッド implied spread
インプライド・ボラティリティー implied volatility
インプライド・レポ・レート implied repo rate
インフラ関連株 infrastructure stock
インフラ事業 infrastructure work
インフラ整備 infrastructure improvement
インフラの整備 provision of infrastructure
インフラ費用 infrastructure cost
インプリシット・デフレーター implicit deflator
インフレ圧力 inflationary pressure

インフレ圧力が薄らぐ wane in inflation pressure
インフレ圧力がない中 in the absence of inflation pressure
インフレ・エクスポージャー inflation exposure
インフレーション inflation
インフレ会計 inflation accounting
インフレ格差 inflation differential
インフレからの保護 inflation protection
インフレ感応度 inflation sensitivity factor
インフレ関連指数 inflation related index
インフレ期待 inflation expectation
インフレ・ギャップ inflation gap
インフレ供給曲線 inflationary supply curve
インフレ警戒 pessimistic inflation expectation
インフレ懸念 inflation fear
インフレ指数 inflation index；inflation indexation
インフレ指標 inflation indication
インフレ需給曲線 inflationary supply and demand curve
インフレ需要曲線 inflationary demand curve
インフレ心理 inflation psychology
インフレ・スパイラル inflation spiral
インフレ選好 appetite for inflation
インフレ増加分に対する税控除 inflation credit
インフレ調整済み inflation adjusted
インフレ動向 behavior of inflation
インフレに対する保険 inflation insurance
インフレに基づいた税の減免 inflation tax relief
インフレにより増加した債務 inflation escalation obligation
インフレによる元本の増加 inflation increase in principal
インフレによる増加分 inflation accretion
インフレの指数化 indexation of inflation
インフレの不確実性 inflation uncertainty
インフレ・フロアー inflation floor
インフレ・プロテクション inflation protection
インフレ・プロテクション型エクイティ商品 inflation protected equity products
インフレ分布 inflation distribution
インフレ・ヘッジ hedging against inflation；inflation hedge
インフレ・ヘッジ株 stock for inflation hedging
インフレ・ヘッジ資産 inflation hedge property
インフレ・マネー・サプライ inflationary money supply
インフレ見通し price outlook
インフレ目標 inflation target
インフレやデフレに連動する indexed to inflation or deflation
インフレ抑止 anti-inflation
インフレ抑止に対する信頼度 anti-inflationary credibility
インフレ抑制 control of inflation
インフレ予測 inflation forecast
インフレ予備費 price contingency
インフレ・リスク・プレミアム inflation risk premium
インフレ率 inflation rate
インフレ率の上昇 pick-up of inflation rate
インフレ率の相関 correlation of inflation rate
インフレ連動債 I-bonds；inflation indexed debt instrument；inflation linked bonds
インフレ連動債市場 linker market
インフレ連動証券 inflation indexed securities
インフレ連動の inflation indexed
インベスターズ・リレーションズ investors relations
インベントリー・リセッション inventory recession
インボイス方式 invoice method
インランドマリーン保険 inland marine insurance

ウ

ウィーク・オーダー week order
ウィーク型効率性 weak form efficiency
ウィーク・フォーム weak form
ウィークリー・リバーサル weekly reversal
ウィーン証券取引所 VSX (Vienna Stock Exchange)
ウィズアウト・リコース without recourse
ウィリアムズ法 Williams Act
ウイルシャー指数 Wilshire indices
ウェーブ理論 Wave Theory
ウェッジ wedge
ウェッジ・フォーメーション wedge formation
ウォール街 Wall Street
ウォール・ストリート・ジャーナル Wall Street Journal
迂回生産 roundabout production
迂回貿易 roundabout trade
ウガンダ・シリング UGX (Uganda shilling)
浮 貸 し off-record lending
ウクライナ・グリブナ UAK (Ukraine hryvnia)
受 入 れ intake
受入金額 amount received
受入現金 cash received
受 入 国 host country；recipient country
受入資産 asset received
受入証拠金 margin deposit；received margin
受入超過 receipts exceeding disbursements (net receipts)
受入手数料 commission received
受入特許権使用料 royalties received for use of patents
受入報告書 receiving report
受入保証金 guarantee money received
受入保証料 guarantee fee received
受入利息及び配当金 interest and dividend received
請負工事 contract work
請負工事未収金 contract work account receivable
請負制度 contract work system
請負代金の値増金 premium in addition to the original contract price
請 負 人 independent contractor
請負募集 standby underwriting
受 付 印 reception stamp
受取勘定 accounts receivable
受取勘定回転率 turnover (ratio) of receivables
受取勘定対棚卸資産比率 ratio of receivable to inventories
受取勘定建相場 receiving quotation
受取給付額 benefit receivable
受 取 金 amount receivable；proceeds
受取固定支払変動 fixed-rate receiving and floating-rate paying
受取債権 accounts receivable；notes and accounts receivable；trade receivables
受取再保険金 reinsurance proceeds
受取指図 receipt instruction
受 取 高 amount of proceeds
受取通貨選択権付債券 optional payment bond
受取手形 acceptance receivable；BR (bill receivable)；draft receivable；notes and bills receivable
受取手形記入帳 notes receivable register
受取手数料 commission earned
受 取 人 payee；recipient
受取人の変更 change of beneficiary
受取配当金 dividend earned；dividend received
受取配当金源泉税 withholding tax on dividends received
受取配当金の益金不算入 exclusion of

received dividends from taxable income
受取配当等益金不算入 exclusion of dividend received from taxable income
受取配当の益金不算入 exclusion of dividends from gross revenue
受取不履行 failure to receive
受取変動支払固定 floating-rate receiving and fixed-rate paying
受取変動支払変動 floating-rate receiving and floating-rate paying
受取保険料事業費率 ratio of expense-to-premium
受取家賃 house rent received
受取利子 coupon received
受取利息 interest earned；interest received
受取割引料 discount fee earned
受戻権喪失訴状 bill for foreclosure
受 渡 し delivery
受渡価格 delivery price
受渡期限 date and time of delivery
受渡決済 delivery settlement；settlement by delivery
受渡決済期日 settlement day by delivery
受渡決済数量 settlement volume
受渡決済代金 amount of trade value
受渡決済値段 delivery price
受渡決済日 delivery date
受渡最適債券 most deliverable bond
受渡最割安債券 cheapest-to-deliver bond
受渡最割安銘柄 cheapest-to-deliver
受渡時期 value date
受渡時限 delivery deadline
受渡条件 terms of delivery
受渡通知 delivery notice
受渡適格債 deliverable bond
受渡適格短期証券 deliverable bills
受渡適格の deliverable grade
受渡適格銘柄 deliverable issue
受渡しに係る通常の期間 normal period for delivery
受渡しの監視 monitoring of delivery
受 渡 日 delivery day；settlement day；value date
受渡不履行 failure to deliver；non-delivery
失 う forgo
後ろの日付にする back dating
後向ニーズ backward needs
薄 商 い low turnover
薄商市場 thin market
薄い利ざや thin margin
ウズベキスタン・スム UZS (Uzbekistan som)
内 入 金 initial down payment；initial installment
内 勘 定 private account
内 金 money paid in part
内税方式 tax inclusive price
内 払 partial payment；payment in part
打ち切り条件 termination terms
打歩発行 premium issuance
内蒙古自治区 Neimenggu
宇宙航空研究開発機構 Japan Aerospace Exploration Agency
内 訳 break-down；itemization；particulars
内訳勘定書 itemized bill
内訳区分 subdivision
内訳区分間の振替 transfer among subdivisions
内 訳 書 detailed statement；statement of items
訴えうる過失 actionable negligence
訴えの却下 non-suit
奪 う dispossess
海固有の危険 perils of the sea
産 む bear
埋 立 地 reclaimed land
裏 書 backing；endorsement
裏書義務 contingent liability on bill endorsed
裏書禁止 prohibition of endorsement
裏書禁止裏書 non-negotiable endorsement
裏書禁止手形 non-endorsable bill；non-negotiable bill

ウ

裏書債券 endorsed bond
裏書された endorsed
裏書譲渡 endorsement for transfer ; transfer of endorsed note
裏書譲渡手形 notes endorsed for payment
裏書する bear out
裏書手形 endorsed bill ; endorsed note ; notes and bills endorsed
裏 書 人 endorser ; indorser
裏書の連続 succession of endorsement
裏書保証 guarantee by endorsement
裏口上場 back door listing
裏 口 銭 secret commission
裏 契 約 non-genuine agreement
裏 参 加 silent participation ; subparticipation
裏参加者 silent partner
裏参加ベース silent base
裏付ける support
裏 保 証 guarantee in favor of the primary guarantor
売られすぎ oversold
売り上がり selling on a rising scale
売　　上 net sales ; sales ; turnover
売上(非製造業) revenue
売上営業利益率 operating income on sales
売上送り状 sales invoice
売 上 額 sales proceeds
売上勘定 sales account
売上基準 sales basis
売上計算基準 basis for recording sales
売上計算書 account of sales
売上原価 COGS (cost of goods sold) ; sales cost
売上原価修正 COSA (cost of sales adjustment)
売上原価法 cost of sales method
売上原価率 ratio of cost to sales
売上交換 sale interchange
売上構成差異 sales mix variance
売上債権 trade receivable
売上債権回収期間 average collection period
売上債権回転日数 number of days' sales in receivables
売上債権回転率 receivables turnover
売上債務比率 payables to sales ratio
売上実績 sales indicators
売上収益 sales revenue
売上純益 net profit on sales
売上純利益率 net income to sales ; net profit margin
売上仕訳帳 sales journal
売上数量 unit sales
売 上 税 revenue tax ; sales tax
売上税引前利益率 pretax income to sales
売上増加 gains of sales ; increase in sales
売上増加率 turnover increase rate
売上総損失 gross loss on sales
売上総利益 gross margin on sales
売上総利益率 gross profit margin ; gross profit rate ; ratio of gross profit to sales
売上代金 sale amount
売 上 高 amount of sales ; sales volume ; top line
売上高営業利益率 operating profit ratio on sales
売上高限界利益率 profit-volume ratio
売上高最大化仮説 revenue maximization hypothesis
売上高純利益率 net profit ratio to sales
売上高の認識 recognition of sales
売上高予算 sales (volume) budget
売上高予測 sales forecasting
売上高利益率 ratio of profit to net sales ; return (ratio) on sales
売 上 帳 sales book
売上手数料 selling commission
売上伝票 sales slip
売上値引 sales allowance ; sales discount
売上伸び率 sales growth rate
売上の戻り sales return
売上品構成 sales-mix
売上歩合 sales commission
売上分析 sales analysis
売上への寄与 contribution to sales
売上前費用 pre-sale cost

売上元帳 sales ledger
売上戻り sales returns
売上予測 sales forecast
売上利益 selling profit
売上利益率 sales profit ratio
売上割戻し sales rebate
売り圧力 selling pressure
売りあびせ hammering the market
売り惜しみ restrict sales
売り惜しむ be reluctant to sell
売りオファー selling offer
売りオプション written option
売りオペ open market selling operation
売り・買い推奨 buy sell recommendation
売り買いの一致 matched book
売 掛 け credit sales
売掛勘定 credit sales accounts
売 掛 金 accounts receivable ; amount of trade receivable ; amount receivable from trade customers ; book credit ; trade account receivable
売掛金回収 collection of bill
売掛金回転率 accounts receivable turnover (ratio)
売掛金・貸付金に準ずる債権 claim similar to account receivable and loan
売掛金勘定 charge account
売掛金経過明細表 aging schedule
売掛金担保融資 accounts receivable financing
売掛金元帳 customers' ledger
売掛債権 sales credit
売掛債権回転率 sales to receivables
売掛債権債務者 account debtor
売掛債権率 sales to accounts receivable
売 掛 先 trade debtor
売掛保険 account receivable insurance
売 り 方 bear side ; seller
売り方勝手渡し seller's option
売り方金利 interest rate receivable by seller
売 為 替 exchange sold ; selling exchange ; telegraphic transfer sold
売 切 り outright sales
売 切 れ all gone ; sold out
売 崩 し bear raiding ; raiding the market
売り気配 asked quotation
売 現 先 sales under agreement to repurchase
売現先債務 payables under repurchase agreement
売現先利息 interest on repurchase agreement
売り越し selling on balance
売りサイド selling side
売 信 号 sell signal
売 過 ぎ overselling
売 相 場 selling rate
売 出 し offering for sale ; public selling ; secondary offering
売出価格 issue price ; sales price
売出価格帯 offering scale
売 出 株 publicly offered share
売出条件付取引 when-distributed transaction
売出手形 bill drawn for sale ; bills sold
売出手形支払割引料 discounts paid on bills sold
売出手形制度 system for sale of bills drawn by the Bank of Japan
売出発行 best-efforts issuance
売りたたく bear the market
売　　建 selling position ; writing
売建オプション options sold
売 建 玉 open interest on seller's side ; short positions
売 注 文 sell order
売 り 長 bears over ; sellers over
売超数量 net short positions
売　　付 sale transaction
売付顧客 selling customer
売付正会員 selling regular member
売付の約定について反対の取引 closing the short position
売付の約定値段 contract price of sale
売付有価証券 sold securities
売りつなぎ short against the box ; short sale against the box

ウ

売　　手 seller；writer
売手危険負担 caveat subscriptor
売手市場 market in favor of sellers；sellers' market
売手独占 seller's monopoly
売手の危険負担 caveat venditor
売手のセグメント segment of seller
売手のファイナンス seller financing
売 唱 え offer
売 逃 げ unloading
売 人 気 selling support
売 抜 け getting ashore
売　　主 bargainer；vendor
売　　値 selling price
売値買値同時の価格 two way prices
売値段レート asked rate
売　　場 chance to sell；selling opportunity
売りヘッジ short hedge
売 本 尊 leader of short side
売 見 本 selling sample
売 持 ち oversold position；short position
売持ち高 amount oversold
売持ちリスク short position risk
売り戻す sell back
売り求む offer wanted
売 呼 値 asked price；offered price
売呼値についての気配表示 special quote on the offer side
売 予 約 selling contract
売る権利 selling right
売 残 り frozen stock；goods left
売残り在庫 unsalable stock
ウルグアイ・ペソ UYU (Uruguayan peso)
ウルグアイ・ラウンド Uruguay Round
上 口 銭 mark-ups
うわさ銘柄 whisper stock
上 ざ や higher in quotation
上　　地 limitation on proprietary right of land
上積課税 taxation by applying upper bracket
上積税率 tax rate applied to upper part of income
上　　値 higher quotation
上 乗 せ overlay；top up
上乗手数料 override
上乗年金 second-tier pension
上乗保険 superimposed plan
上 放 れ up gap
上 回 る outpace；outweigh
上 向 き up-tick；upside
上 向 く pick up
運営委員会 steering committee
運営の基本方針 basic administration policy
運営要因 operational factor
運　　送 transportation
運 送 業 transportation business
運送業者 transportation company
運送クレーム transportation claim
運送設備 transportation equipment
運 送 中 on passage
運送人渡し free carrier
運 送 費 carriage
運送費込み carriage paid to
運送費・保険料込み carriage and insurance paid to
運送保険 transport insurance
運送約款 transit clause
運 送 料 transportation charges
運　　賃 cartage；fare
運賃延戻制 deferred rebate system
運賃込み cost and freight
運賃収入 freight receipts；freight revenue
運賃着払い freight to collect
運賃保険 freight insurance
運賃・保険料込み cost, insurance and freight
運賃前払い freight prepaid
運賃ユーザンス freight usance
運転時間法 working-hours method
運転資金 operating cash；operating fund；working capital
運転資金管理 working capital control
運転資金の使途 applications of working capital

運転資本売上率 ratio of sales to working capital
運転資本構成 composition of working capital
運転資本状態 working capital position
運転資本増減前の営業利益 operating profit before changes in working capital
運転資本の減少 deductions from working capital
運転資本比率 working-capital ratio
運転資本分析 working capital analysis
運転棚卸資産 working inventory
運 転 費 running cost
運転費用 operating cost
雲 南 省 Yunnan
運　　用 management
運 用 益 investment earnings
運用会社 management company
運用可能資金 investable fund
運用管理基準 investment management criteria
運用機関による評価 manager evaluation
運用指図 investment instruction
運用残高 working balance
運用資産 invested assets；operating assets；portfolio assets；working assets
運用資産額比例報酬方式 compensation plans based on assets
運用資産利回り portfolio rate
運用実績 investment performance
運用実績の悪い商品 poor performer
運用収益 investment income
運用収入 proceeds from allocation
運用スタイル management style
運用成績の悪い投資 lemon
運 用 帳 position sheet
運用手数料 management fee
運用と調達の期間ギャップ maturity gap exposure
運用報告書 management report
運用利回り yield on investment

エ

AAA格 AAA class
AEX指数 AEX Index
AA格 AA；double A
AAトランシェ AA tranche
ASC ASC (All Savers Certificate)
A格 single A
AB スピンタブ AB Spintab
APB意見書 APB (Accounting Principles Board) Opinion
APBステートメント APB (Accounting Principles Board) Statement
AV関連株 AV stocks
永久貸出 permanent financing
永久勘定 permanent account
永久基準 permanent criteria
永久権禁止の原則 rule against perpetuities
永久公債 bank annuities；permanent debt
永久拘束資産 permanently restricted assets
永久小作権 perennial tenant right
永久差異 permanent difference
永久債 perpetual bond；perpetual issue；undated issue
永久差止命令 perpetual injunction
永久資産 permanent assets
永久税 perennial tax
永久税主義 principle of perennial tax
永久積立禁止則 rule against accumulations
永久年金 annuity in perpetuity
永久負債 permanent liability
永久負債証券 perpetual debt instrument
永久保存 fixity of tenure
永久優先株 permanent preferred stock
永久利付証券 PIBS (permanent interest bearing shares)
永久劣後債 perpetual subordinated debt
永久ワラント perpetual warrant
影響 impact；influence
影響報告書 impact statement
営業案内 catalog
営業内訳帳 office expenses book
営業会議 business meeting
営業外経費 non-operating expenses
営業外支出 non-operating expenditure
営業外収益 non-operating revenue
営業外収入 non-operating income
営業外損益 non-operating gain and loss；non-operating profit and loss
営業外損益区分 non-operating section
営業外の non-operating
営業外費用 non-operating expense
営業外利益 non-operating profit
営業活動 operating activities
営業活動からのキャッシュフロー cash flow from operating activities
営業活動からの利益 profit from operating activities
営業活動勘定 operating account
営業活動による資金純額 net cash from operating activities
営業活動の停止 suspension of business activity
営業科目 description of business；line of business
営業勘定 trade account
営業勘定収支残 underwriting account balance
営業関連項目 operating item
営業規模 operating capacity
営業経費 operating expense
営業経費率 operating cost ratio；operating expenses ratio
営業権 goodwill；trade rights
営業権償却 amortization of goodwill
営業権譲渡 assignment of business
営業権所有者 concessionaire
営業権の評価 valuation of goodwill

営業行為 doing business
営業債権 operating receivable
営業財産価値 going value
営業債務 operating payable ; trade liability ; trade payable
営業時間 business hours ; office hours
営業資産 operating assets ; trade assets
営業実績 results of business
営業資本 operating capital
営業収益 operating revenue ; revenue from operations
営業収益税 business profit tax
営業収入 operating receipt ; sales earnings
営業種目 items of business
営業循環 operating cycle
営業循環基準 operating cycle rule
営業純損失 NOL (net operation loss)
営業準備金 operating reserve
営 業 所 sales office ; service office
営業状況 actual state of business ; operating condition
営業状態 operating standing
営業譲渡 transfer of business ; transfer of operations
営業上のキャッシュフロー operating cash flow
営業上の秘密 trade secret
営業上の本拠 principal place of business
営 業 税 franchise tax ; occupation tax ; trade tax
営業制限 restraint of trade
営業成績 business results ; operating results ; summary of earnings ; trading results
営業セグメント operating segment
営業損益 operating profit and loss ; results of operating activities
営業損失 operating loss
営業損失区分 operating section
営業停止 halt of business ; stoppage of business
営業年度 working year
営業の譲渡 transfer of the business
営業の妨害 interference with trade
営業の本拠の移動 shifting of business center
営業の譲受け receipt of business
営 業 費 business expenses ; commercial expenses ; trade expenses
営 業 日 business day
営業費勘定 office expense account
営業費用合計 total operating expenses
営業比率 operating ratio
営 業 部 sales department
営業部門 front office
営業報告 business report ; operating report
営業報告書 account of business
営業保険料 gross premium
営業保険料評価準備金 gross premium valuation reserve
営業免許税 occupational tax
営業面での増益効果 operating leverage effect
営業面の増益効果度 degree of operating leverage
営業元帳 operating ledger
営業用什器 office furniture
営業用償却資産 depreciable property used in business
営業予算 operating budget
営業余剰金 operating surplus
営業利益 business profit ; operating income ; operating profit ; profit from operations
営業利益段階 operating profit level
営業利益率 operating income to sales ; operating profit margin ; ratio of operating income to sales ; ratio of operating profit to revenue
営業レバレッジ operating leverage
営業を停止する cease operation
英国大蔵省 Exchequer
英国大蔵証券 Exchequer bills
英国大蔵大臣 Chancellor of the Exchequer
英国会計協会 British Accounting Association

エ

英国銀行協会 British Banker's Association
英国銀行協会金利決済レート BBAISR (British Bankers' Association Interest Settlement Rate)
英国金融監督庁 FSA (Financial Services Authority)
英国国債 Gilts
英国国債市場 gilt market
英国式貸借対照表 English form of balance sheet
英国証券決済システム TAURUS (Transfer and Automated Registration of Uncertified Stock)
英国長期国債 long-term national bond of England
英 国 病 English disease
英 国 法 English law
英国貿易振興会 British Export Trade Research Organization
英国ポンド GBP (British pound)
衛星市場 satellite market
営 繕 課 maintenance department
永代借地権 lease in perpetuity；perpetual lease
永代借地人 life tenancy；perpetual lessee
英ポンドＣＰ pound sterling commercial paper
英ポンド建証券市場 sterling securities market
英ポンド通貨先物 pound sterling currency futures
英ポンド定期預金 pound sterling time deposit
英ポンド預金金利先物 pound sterling depositary interest futures
営　　利 money making
営利会社 commercial company
営利企業 business enterprise
営利事業 commercial business；commercial enterprise；profit making business
営利法人 profit corporation；profit organization
営利を目的とした継続的行為 continuous transactions entered into for profit
エージェンシー市場 agency market
エージェンシー理論 agency theory
エージド・フェール aged fail
益金算入 inclusion in gross revenue
益金処分 distribution of surplus
益金不算入 exclusion from gross profit
益金不算入制度 non-accrual system
エキスパート・システム expert system
エキゾティック・オプション exotic option
エキゾティック・カレンシー exotic currency
エキゾティック派生商品 exotic derivatives
エキゾティック・ボンド exotic bond
益 回 り earnings price ratio；earnings yield
益回りとの格差 earnings yield gap
役　　務 personal service
役務契約 contract for the rendering of services
役務出資 service contribution
役務提供契約 service contract
役務の提供 rendering of service
役務の提供に対する支払い payment to rendered services
ECU債 ECU bond
ECU市場 ECU market
益利回り earnings yield
エクアドル・スクレ ECS (Ecuador sucre)
エクイティ型投資信託 equity trust
エクイティ関連商品 equity based product
エクイティ生命保険 equity based life insurance
エクイティ積立 equity funding
エクイティ逓増モーゲージ GEM (growing equity mortgage)
エクイティの上昇 equity upside
エクイティ・ファイナンス equity finance
エクイティ保険 equities insurance
エクイティ・マージン equity margin
エクイティ・ワラント equity warrant
エグジット・ボンド exit bond
エクステンダブル・スワップ extendable

swap
エクス・ワラント ex-warrant
エコノミスト economist
エジプト・ポンド EGP (Egyptian pound)
SIAC SIAC (Securities Industry Automation Corporation)
S&P先物 S&P futures
S&P 100 S&P 100
S&P100現物オプション S&P 100 spot options
S&P500種株価指数 S&P 500 Stock Price Index
SEC会計 SEC accounting
SEC会計連続通牒 SEC Accounting Releases
SEC基準 SEC standards
SEC手数料 SEC fee
SECドケット SEC Docket
SEC付属明細表 SEC schedules
エスカレーション条項 escalation clause
エスカレーター条項 escalator clause
エスクロウ勘定 escrow account
エスクロウ契約 escrow agreement
エスクロウ信託契約 escrow and trust agreement
エスクロウ信用状 escrow credit
S字カーブ s-curve
SDR建て債 SDR denominated bond
STP STP (straight through processing)
エストニア・クローン EEK (Estonian kroon)
SBF120種株価指数 SBF120
エチオピア・ビル ETB (Ethiopian birr)
越権行為 ultra vires activities
エッジ・アクト法人 Edge-Act company
エッジ法 Edge Act
エドガー EDGAR
エドガー管理室(SEC) Office of EDGAR management(SEC)
エドガーシステム electronic data gathering analysis and retrieval system
NTT債 NTT bond
NTT分割 NTT break up
NPO法人 NPO (non-profit organization)
NYSE総合株価指数 NYSE Composite Stock Index
エネルギー安全確保 energy security
エネルギー株 energy sector stock
エネルギー株ミューチュアル・ファンド energy mutual fund
エネルギー税 energy tax
エネルギー弾性 energy elasticity
エネルギー備蓄 energy stockpiling
エネルギー・リスク energy risk
エバーグリーン・クレジット evergreen credit
FRN floating rate note
FRBの利上げ Fed tightening
FF金利 Fed fund rate
FF金利誘導目標 Fed fund target
FT-SEアクチュアリーズ総合指数 FT-SE Actuaries All Shares
FT-SE 100種株価指数 FT-SE 100
FT株価指数 FT Stock Index
FT全種指数 FT Actuaries All-share Index
FT 100種指数 FT Stock Exchange 100 Index
エマージング市場取引者協会 EMTA (Emerging Markets Traders Association)
エマージング通貨の外国為替 emerging foreign exchange
エマージング・マーケット emerging market
EMU拡大 EMU (European Monetary Union) enlargement
M&A ビジネス merger and acquisition business
M3の伸び M3 growth
M0の伸び M0 growth
M2の動き M2's behavior
M2+CD統計 M2+CD Statistics
選ばれたグループ quorum
エリートカード elite card
エリオット・ウェーブ理論 Elliot Wave Theory
エリサ Employee Retirement Income Security Act

エリサ法 ERISA (Employee Retirement Income Security Act)
エリトリア・ナクファ ERN (Eritrea nakfa)
エルサルバドール・コロン SVC (El Salvador colon)
LBOファンド leveraged buyout fund
エレクトロニック・バンキング electronic banking
エレクトロニック・マネー electronic money
円売りドル買い介入 intervention to cap the JPY against the USD；intervention to stop yen from appreciating against the dollar
演 繹 法 deductive method
円 貨 額 yen value
円貨建外国債 yen-denominated foreign bonds
円滑な資金決済 smooth settlement of funds
円滑な消化 smooth absorption
円滑な引き継ぎ smooth succession
円滑な流通 smooth trading operation
延　　期 adjournment；deferral
延期賃借権 attendant term
延期を望む preference for delay
円金利キャップ yen rate cap
円金利スワップ・ポジション yen interest rate swap position
円クロス JPY cross
エンゲル係数 Engel's coefficient
エンゲルの法則 Engel's law
縁 故 債 private subscription bond
縁故採用 nepotism
縁故地方債 private placement local bond；private placement municipal bond
縁故募集 private subscription
円　　債 yen bond
演 算 数 operand
エンジェル税制 tax system for angel
エンジニアリング室 Office of Engineering
円シフト shift to yen
円 借 款 yen credit；yen loan
援　　助 assistance
援 助 金 aids
援助する assist
援助請願者 aid prayer
援助を受ける側 aid recipients
円・人民元スワップ協定 yen-renminbi swap arrangement
延　　滞 arrearages；delay
延滞加算金 additional arrearage charge；past due charge
延滞期間 period of arrears
延 滞 金 back money；delinquency amount
延滞金利 overdraft charges；penalty rate
延滞小切手 stale check
延滞債権 deliquent loan；loans in arrears；overdue claims；overdue loan
延滞残高方式 past due balance method
延 滞 税 delinquency tax；tax in arrears
延滞税免除 discharge of delinquent tax
延滞地代 rent arrears
延滞日数 days in arrears
延滞配当金 dividend in arrears
延滞日歩 daily interest for arrearage；overdue interest per diem
延滞保険料 premium overdue
延滞補償金 penalty on delayed delivery
延滞利子 interest for delay；interest for delinquency；interest in arrears；overdue interest
延滞利息 past due interest
延 滞 率 percentage of delinquency
延滞ローン past due loan
円　　高 exchange rate in favor of yen；strong yen；yen appreciation
円高期待型大口定期預金 yen bull large amount time deposit
円高差益 exchange gain from yen appreciation
円高阻止 keeping yen capped
円高デフレ deflation caused by yen appreciation
円高容認 tolerance of the JPY strength
円高を望む talking the JPY up
円 建 て denominated in yen；

yen-denominated
円建外債 yen-denominated bonds issued in Japan by foreign institutions
円 建 債 yen-denominated bonds
円建市場 Japanese currency market
円建シンジケート・ローン yen table denominated syndicated loan
円建輸出 yen-denominated export
延長可能型スワップ extensible swap
延長可能満期 extendible maturity
延長給付 extended benefit
延長クレーム extension of time claims
延 長 時 at the time of the extension
延 長 上 be extension of
延長手形 extended bill
延長保険 continued insurance ; extended insurance
円でドルをロングにする being long dollar yen
円 転 conversion to yen
円 転 換 yen shift
エンド・ユーザー end-user
円・ドル委員会 Yen-Dollar Commission
円ドル・シフト switch from yen to dollars
円ドル・スワップ yen-dollar swap agreement
円ドルの調整 JPYUSD correction
延 納 authorized deferred payment ; delayed payment
延納にかかる利子税 interest tax on delayed payment
円の買い支え lifting of yen
円の下落 yen's sell off
円の国際化推進研究会 Study Group for the Promotion of the Internationalization of the Yen
円の上昇に追随した tracking the rising JPY
円のショート・ポジションの解消圧力 pressure on short JPY positions
円の再びの上昇 renewed strength of yen
エンパワーメント empowerment
エンハンスト・インデックス運用 enhanced indexing
円 表 示 yen-quoted
円ブロック yen bloc
円 安 depreciation of yen
円安インフレ inflation caused by yen depreciation
円安を望む talking the JPY down
円を買い上げる chasing the JPY higher

オ

追い風介入 intervention following market
追　　証 additional margin；remargin
追い立て eviction
オイラー方程式 Euler equation
オイル・ダラー petrodollar
オイルマネー oil money
押　　印 impression
応益負担の原則 benefit principle
黄 金 株 golden share
黄金時代 golden age
黄金分割 golden section
黄金分割比率 golden ratio
黄 金 律 golden rule
応札倍率 bid-to-cover ratio
応札募集 bid wanted
欧州安保協力機構 Organization for Security and Cooperation in Europe
欧州委員会 European Commission
欧州議会 European Parliament
欧州基金 European Fund
欧州共同市場 European Common Market
欧州共同体 European Community
欧州経済共同体 EEC (European Economic Community)
欧州経済協力機構 Organization for European Economic Cooperation
欧州計算単位 EUA (European Unit of Account)
欧州原子力共同体 European Atomic Energy Community
欧州式複利利回り annual compounding
欧州支払同盟 European Payment Union
欧州自由貿易連合 EFTA (European Free Trade Association)
欧州証券決済機関協会 ECSDA (European Central Securities Depositories Association)
欧州証券取引所連合会 FESE (Federation of European Securities Exchanges)
欧州証券フォーラム euroSF (European Securities Forum)
欧州情報技術研究開発戦略計画 ESPRIT (European Strategic Programme for R&D in Information Technologies)
欧州石炭鉄鋼共同体 European Coal and Steel Community
欧州中央銀行 ECB (European Central Bank)
欧州中央銀行制度 ESCB (European System of Central Banks)
欧州通貨基金 European Monetary Fund
欧州通貨機構 EMI (European Monetary Institute)
欧州通貨協定 EMA (European Monetary Agreement)
欧州通貨協力基金 EMCF (European Monetary Cooperation Fund)
欧州通貨制度 EMS (European Monetary System)
欧州通貨単位 EMC (European Currency Unit)
欧州通貨同盟 EMU (European Monetary Union)
欧州統合 European unity
欧州投資銀行 EIB (European Investment Bank)
欧州投資信託機関 European Investment Trust
欧州復興開発銀行 EBRD (European Bank for Reconstruction Development)
欧州方式 European term
欧州預託証券 EDR (European depositary receipt)
欧州連合 European Union
横線小切手 crossed check
応　　諾 acknowledgment of order
横断分析 cross-sectional analysis
黄銅貨幣（5円） brass coins (5 yen)
応 当 日 corresponding day
応能原則 ability to pay principle

凹版印刷 intaglio printing
往復取引 round trip transaction
応　　募 subscription
応募価格 bids on price；subscription price
応募額 bids on amount
応募金額 amount subscribed
応募資本 subscribed capital
応募者利回り subscriber's yield；yield to subscriber
応募超過 overbooked；surplus subscription
応募超過の oversubscribed
応募の受付 acceptance of bids
応募不足 under-booked
応募又は引受け subscribing or underwriting
往来相場 rise-and-fall market
横　　領 embezzlement
往路運賃 outward freight
大商い broad market；dramatic surge
大商銘柄リスト most active list
大当り bonanza
OEM original equipment manufacturing agreement
OECDモデル租税条約 OECD model double taxation convention
OECD加盟 OECD membership
大型株 high cap；large cap stock；large capital stock
大型債 blockbuster deal
大型買収 large acquisition；major acquisition
大型発行 jumbo issue
大株主 large shareholder
大株主上位10名 10 largest shareholders
大きく買いを入れる ramping
大きな下落 deeper setback
大きなスプレッドの立会開始 wide opening
大きな変更 substantive change
大きな変動 large change
オークション市場 auction market
オークション・システム auction system
オークション銘柄 auction stock
オークション優先株 APS (auction preferred stock)
大口買付け specialist block purchases
大口株式の成行注文を出す sell the book
大口債務者 large debtor
大口建玉 large positions
大口注文 block order；large order
大口注文の小口執行 split order
大口定期 large amount time deposit
大口取引 block trading；large amount transaction；large lot trading
大口融資規制 regulations on large-lot loans
大口預金金利 large amount deposit interest
大口預金証書 jumbo certificate of deposit
大阪証券取引所 Osaka Securities Exchange
大阪商品取引所 Osaka Mercantile Exchange
大雑把な判断 crude analogy
OCO注文 OCO (one-cancels-others) order
オーストラリア会計研究財団 Australian Accounting Research Foundation
オーストラリア株 kangaroos
オーストラリア準備銀行 RBA (Reserve Bank of Australia)
オーストラリア証券取引所 ASX (Australia Stock Exchange)
オーストラリア総合株価指数 All Ordinaries Index
オーストラリア・ドル AUD (Australian dollar)
オーストラリア保管振替機構 Austraclear Limited
オーストリア・シリング ATS (Austria schilling)
オーストリア保管振替機関 OeKB
大相場 boom and bust
大　　底 major bottom
オーダー・ブック・オフィシャル order book official
大　　手 major
OTMプット OTM put

OTC照合システム OTC Comparison System
オーディエンス audience
大手機関投資家 large institutional investors
大手銀行 major banks
大手銀行株 big banks
大手証券会社 wire house
大 天 井 major peak ; reaching the top price
オーナー・トラスト owner trust
オーバー・アンド・アウト・オプション over-and-out option
オーバー・ザ・トップ・ワラント over-the-top warrant
オーバー・サブスクリプション over subscription
オーバーナイト overnight
オーバーナイト取引 overnight transaction
オーバーナイト・ポジション overnight position
オーバーナイト・レート overnight rate
オーバー・パー over par
オーバー・ファンディング over funding
オーバー・ローン over-loan
大馬鹿理論 greater fool theory
大幅上方修正 sharp upward revision
大 幅 増 leap
大 幅 な drastic
大幅な下落 plunge
大幅な減少 substantial decline
大幅な上昇 marked appreciation
オーファン株 orphan stock
オープンエンド医療制度 open ended health plan
オープンエンド型 open-end
オープンエンド型ファンド open-end fund
オープンエンド型モーゲージ債券 open-end mortgage bond
オープンエンド型リース open-end lease
オープンエンド投資会社 open-end management company
オープンエンド・モーゲージ open-end mortgage
オープン価格 open price
オープン型投資信託 open-end investment trust
オープン型ミューチュアル・ファンド open-end mutual fund
オープン・カバー open cover
オープン・クレジット open credit
オープン市場 open market
オープン注文 open order
オープン・ブック open book
オープン保険契約 open certificate
オープン・マネー・マーケット open money market
オープン・レート方式 open rate method
オープン・レポ open repo
大もうけ killing
大　　物 fat cat
オール・イン・コスト all in cost
オールド・エコノミー old economy
オールド・ボンド old bond
オールリスク担保 AR (all risks)
おかしな結果 odd results
置換コスト・リスク replacement cost risk
置き換える transpose
沖縄及び北方対策担当大臣 Minister of State for Okinawa and Northern Territories Affairs
沖縄国税事務所 Okinawa Regional Taxation Office
沖縄振興開発金融公庫 Okinawa Development Finance Corporation
沖縄地区税関 Okinawa Custom-House
遅らせる lag
送り状価格 invoice amount
お化粧買い dressing
起こりそうもない可能性 remote possibility
押上圧力 upward pressure
押付商法 negative option sales
押し目買い bargain buying ; bargain hunting ; buy on dip ; buy on reaction
押し目待ち wait for reaction
汚　　職 corruption
オシレーター oscillator
オスロ証券取引所 Oslo Stock Exchange

オスロ証券取引所指数 Oslo Stock Exchange Index
汚　染 defacement
穏やかな景気回復 modest rebound
落 込 み dent；turndown
オファー曲線 offer curve
おどり利息 double account interests
同じ市場価格 equal market value
同じ書物からの出典 idem
同じ性質の証券 universe of securities
同じ伸び率 flat growth
帯封された紙幣 bundled banknotes
オフ・バランス会計 off-balance-sheet accounting
オフ・バランス取引 off-balanced trade
オファーサイド offer side
オファー時刻 time of offer
オフサイト・モニタリング off-site monitoring
オフショア勘定 offshore account
オフショア金融市場 offshore banking facility
オフショア市場 offshore market
オフショア・センター offshore center
オフショア調達 offshore borrowing
オフショア投資債券 offshore investment bond
オフショア・バンキングセンター offshore banking center
オフショア・バンキング・ユニット OBU (offshore banking unit)
オフショア・ファンド offshore fund
オフショア保証 offshore guarantee
オフショア・リース offshore lease
オプション価格 option price
オプション価格決定モデル OPM (option pricing model) valuation
オプション価格決定理論 option pricing theory
オプションが行使される option to kick in
オプション・ガンマ option gamma
オプション期間 life of option；option's term
オプション組込スワップ option embedded in swaps
オプション・クリアリング・コーポレーション option clearing corporation
オプション契約 option agreement；option contract
オプション契約者 option holder
オプション契約の裏書 endorsement for option contract
オプション口座 option account
オプション行使可能期間 option period
オプション市場 option market
オプション・スプレッド option spread
オプション清算会社 OCC (option clearing corporation)
オプション清算指数 option settlement index
オプション清算値段 option settlement price
オプション・セータ option theta
オプション調整後コンベクシティ option adjusted convexity
オプション調整後スプレッド OAS (option adjusted spread)
オプション調整後デュレーション OAD (option adjusted duration)
オプション調整後の option adjusted
オプション調整後利回り option adjusted yield
オプション調整スプレッド・モデル option adjusted spread model
オプション付順月渡 outright forward delivery with option
オプション付転換社債 convertible bonds with option
オプション・デルタ option delta
オプション取引 options trading
オプション取引決済不履行 failure to settle option contracts
オプション取引代金 options contract value
オプション25 Option 25
オプションの売手 option seller；option writer；writer of the option
オプションの売手の義務 obligation under a option written
オプションの買手 holder of option

オプションの契約期間 option's contracted life
オプションの権利行使 exercise of an option
オプションの時間価値 time value of option
オプションの消滅 expiration of option
オプションの取引代金 option premium
オプションのヘッジング hedging on option
オプションの保有者の持分 option holder's interest
オプションの満期日 option expiration date
オプション・バイヤー option buyer
オプション・パフォーマンス指数 option performance index
オプション・プール option pool
オプション・フォワード option forward
オプション・プレミアム option premium
オプション・ポジション option position
オプション・ボンド option bond
オプション・ミューチュアル・ファンド option mutual fund
オプション料収入 premium income
オプション料スプレッド取引 selling spread
オプション渡し option delivery
オプション・ワラント option warrants
オフセット年金制度 floor offset pension plan
オプティマーク市場 OptiMark market
オプティング・アウト opting-out
オフバランス off-balance
オフバランス化 off-balance treatment
オフバランス会計 off-balance-sheet accounting
オフバランス項目 off-balance-sheet exposure
オフバランス・シート金融商品 off-balance sheet financial instruments
オフバランス・シート項目 off-balance sheet items
オフバランス・シート取引 off-balance sheet transaction
オフバランス取引 off-balance transaction ; off-balanced trade
オフマーケット off-market
オフマーケット・スワップ off-market swap
オペ対象先 operation counterparties
オペのエンド日 end day of operations ; maturity of operations
オペの基本要領 Principal Terms and Conditions of Market Operations
オペの実行手段 Measures for Facilitating Money Market Operations
オペの指標 operating target
オペの種類 types of money market operations
オペのスタート日 start day of operations
オペレーショナル・リスク operational risk
オペレーションからの資金 FFO (funds from operation)
オペレーション上の事柄 operational issues
オペレーティング・リース operating lease
オペレーティング・レバレッジ分析 operating leverage analysis
覚　書 MOU (memorandum of understanding)
オマーン・リアル OMR (Omani rial)
オムジオ Omgeo
思いがけない損失 windfall loss
思いとどまらす deter
思っていた以上に早く sooner-than-thought
主な融資対象 principal targets for loans
主なリスク key risks
思惑売り going short
思惑買い going long ; speculative buying
思惑買筋 speculative buyers
思惑需要 speculative demand
思惑輸入 speculative import
親 会 社 parent company
親会社の持ち分 parent's share
親会社保証の parent company guaranteed
親 企 業 parent undertaking

親子関係 parent and subsidiary relationship
親 抜 け without parent company
親 引 け sales to the entity designated by the issuer
オランダANP-CBS 総合株価指数 ANP/CBS General Index
オランダ・グルデン NLG (Netherlands gulden)
オランダ領アンティル諸島グルデン ANG (Netherlands Antilles gulden)
織り込まれる factored in
織り込み済みのリスク risk priced in
織り込む take into consideration ; digest
オルタナティブ運用 alternative investment
折れ線グラフ line graph
卸 売 wholesale ; wholesaling
卸売会計 wholesale accounting
卸 売 業 wholesale business ; wholesale trade
卸売業界 wholesale trade industry
卸売業者 wholesaler
卸売銀行業務 wholesale banking
卸売事業 wholesale establishment
卸 売 商 wholesale dealer
卸売値段 wholesale price
卸売物価指数 wholesale price index
負わせる encumber
終 値 closing price
終値が前日終値と比較して高値である close up
終値が前日終値と比較して安値である close down
終値月中平均 monthly closing average
終値取引 at-closing price transactions
終わりを告げる come to end
恩 給 superannuation
恩給引当金 reserve for pensions
オンサイトの考査 on-site examination
オンショア市場 on-shore market
オンバランス on balance
オンバランス項目 on-balance sheet exposure
オンバランス・シート金融商品 on-balance sheet financial instruments
オンバランス取引 on-balance sheet transaction
オンバランス・ボリューム on-balance volume
隠密オペ confidential operation
オンライン処理 online processing
オンライン・バンキング・システム on-line banking system

カ

カ

カーター・ボンド Carter bond
カード会員 card member
カード会社 card issuer
カード加盟店 card merchant
カード偽造 card counterfeiting
カード決済 pay by card
カード更新 card renewal
カード再発行 card replacement
カード式記帳法 card system of bookkeeping
カード識別コード card discrimination code
カードシステム card system
カードショッピング card shopping
カードの標準化 card standardization
カード犯罪 card criminal fraud
カード有効期限 expiration date of the credit card
カード・ローン card loan
ガーナ・セディ GHC (Ghanaian cedi)
カーブの取引 trading curve
カーライル生命表 Carlisle Table
外・外取引 out-out transactions
外・外ローン out-out loan
外・内取引 out-in transactions
外　圧 external pressure；foreign pressure
買い漁り panic buying；shopping around
買い一色 all buyers
買入れ buying
買入オペ outright purchases bills collateralized by corporate debt obligations
買入価格 buying price
買入債務 trade payables
買入債務回転率 turnover ratio of payables
買入資金 funds for purchase
買入償還 redemption through secondary market purchase
買入償却 redemption by buyback；redemption by purchase；retirement by purchase
買入代金債務 purchase-money obligation
買入対象債券 instruments for buying operation
買入代理人 purchase agent
買入手形 bills and commercial paper purchased；bills purchased
買入手形割引料 discount on bills bought；discounts on bills purchased
買入手数料 commission for purchase
買入部品 purchased parts
買入れを手控える hold off buying
会員会社 member firm
会員外理事 non-member governor
会員加入 membership admission
会員加入申請 application for membership
会員加入手続 affiliation procedure
会員加入の日 day of admission to membership
会員空売比率 member short sale ratio
会員権 membership rights；seat
会員権の停止 suspension from membership
会員社内対当金額 amount matched within each member
会員出資金 contribution to the equity capital；membership subscription fee
会員証券会社 member securities company
会員証書 membership certificate
会員信認金 membership guarantee deposit
会員制組織 membership organization
会員総会 general assembly meeting of members
会員組織 member organization
会員組織の法人 membership corporation

会員代表者 member representative
会員の加入 admission to membership
会員の種類 categories of members
会員の処置 disposition of a member
会員の処分 discipline on members
会員の脱退 withdrawal from membership
会員の復権 restoration of suspended membership
会員の法 law of member firms
会員ビジネス membership business
会員標識 member's identification mark
会員への勧告 recommendation to a member
会員名簿 list of members
会員持ち分 membership equity
会員持ち分の譲受け人 transferee of membership equity
会員理事 member governor
海員学校 School for Seafarers Training
海員の先取特権 mariner's lien
買受代金 purchase money
買 受 人 bargainee
海　　運 marine transportation；maritime traffic；shipping
海 運 業 marine transportation industry
海運市場 shipping market
海運収入 shipping receipts
買いエネルギー buying energy
買いオペレーション buying operation
外　　延 extension
海外からの資金の流入 foreign capital flow
海外関係会社 overseas affiliated company；overseas affiliated firm
海外起債分 overseas flotation
海外金融子会社 overseas finance subsidiary
海外金融先物取引所 foreign financial futures exchange
海外金利 interest rate abroad；overseas interest rate
海外経済 overseas economies
海外経済協力基金 Overseas Economic Cooperation Fund
海外事業 foreign operation；overseas business
海外事業法人 overseas undertaking corporation
海外資産 foreign assets；offshore assets；overseas asset
海外市場開拓準備金 overseas market development reserve
海外支店 foreign branch
海外支店勘定 foreign branch account
海外主要市場 overseas major market
海外生産 offshore production
海外生産能力 overseas production capacity
海外生産比率 overseas production ratio
海外相場 overseas market rate；quotation on overseas markets；rate in overseas market
海外地域別 foreign geographic areas
海外直接投資 foreign direct investment
海外での証券発行 overseas securities financing
海外での証券発行状況 overseas security financing
海外での上場 overseas listing
海外投資 foreign investment；investment abroad；investment overseas
海外投資損失準備金 overseas investment loss reserve
海外投資損失準備金繰入 provision for reserve for overseas investment loss
海外投資損失準備金戻し入れ reversal of reserve for overseas investment loss
海外投資報告書 overseas investment report
海外取引 overseas transaction
海外取引勘定 external transactions account
海外負債 overseas liability
海外不正防止法 Foreign Corrupt Practices Act
海外貿易開発協会 Japan Overseas Development Corporation
海外法定準備金 overseas legal reserve
海外法定準備金繰入 provision for

カ

overseas legal reserve
海外民間投資公社 Overseas Private Investment Corporation
海外利権 overseas interests
海外旅行傷害保険 overseas travel accident insurance
海外旅行費 overseas traveling expense
外　　貨 foreign currency
外貨預け金利息 interest on foreign currency deposits
外貨借入 foreign currency borrowing
外貨換算 foreign currency translation
外貨換算差額 currency translation differences
外貨換算調整額 foreign currency translation adjustment
外貨勘定 foreign currency account
外貨国債 government bond in foreign currency
外 貨 債 foreign currency bond
外貨債務 foreign currency debt
外貨資金割当 foreign exchange allocation
外貨資産 foreign currency assets
外貨指定預金 foreign currency designated deposit account
外貨集中制度 foreign exchange centralization system
外貨収入 foreign exchange earnings
外貨準備 external reserves；foreign currency reserve；international reserve；reserve accumulation
外貨準備高 FX reserves；gold and foreign exchange reserve；official foreign exchange reserves
外貨準備統計 statistics of foreign currency reserves
外貨証券 foreign currency securities
外貨建て denominated in a foreign currency；foreign currency denominated
外貨建MMF multi-currency MMF
外貨建外国債 foreign currency denominated bond
外貨建格付け foreign currency rating
外貨建勘定項目の換算 conversion of items in foreign currencies
外貨建てキャッシュフロー foreign currency cash flow
外貨建金銭債権債務 monetary receivables and payables in foreign currencies
外貨建項目 foreign currency items
外貨建債券 foreign currency-denominated bond
外貨建債権 claim in foreign currency
外貨建債務 debt in foreign currency
外貨建資産利息・割引料 interest and discounts on foreign currency assets
外貨建証券 foreign currency series securities
外貨建相場 exchange rate in foreign currency
外貨建長期ソブリン格付け long-term foreign currency rating
外貨建投資信託 foreign currency denominated fund
外貨建取引 transaction in foreign currency
外貨建取引会計基準 accounting standards for foreign currency transactions
外貨建取引換算 translation of foreign currency transaction
外貨建取引の会計処理 accounting for foreign currency transactions
外貨建取引の換算 translation of foreign currency transactions
外貨建ての denominated in foreign currency
外貨建負債 foreign currency liability
外貨手形 bill in foreign currency；foreign money bill
外貨取立外国為替 foreign currency bill receivable
外貨取引 foreign currency transaction
外貨表示財務諸表 foreign currency financial statements
外貨表示部分の換算 translation of foreign currency statements
外貨ヘッジ foreign currency hedges
外貨保有高 foreign currency holdings
外貨預金 foreign currency deposit

外貨預金勘定 foreign currency deposit account
外貨予算 foreign exchange budget
外貨預託 foreign currency deposit with exchange bank
外貨流入 foreign currency inflow
外貨割当権 right to obtain foreign money
外貨割当制 foreign exchange allocation system
買 換 え replacement purchase
買換資産 replaced property ; replacement asset
買換えによる資産の交換 replacement property by purchase
買換えの特例 special tax treatment for property replacement
買 掛 金 accounts payable ; trade account payable
買掛債権回転日数 number of days' purchases in accounts payable
買掛債務 account payable
買 い 方 buyer
買い方金利 interest rate payable by buyer
買 為 替 bill bought ; buying exchange ; exchange bought ; telegraphic transfer bought
概　　観 overview
下位勘定（サブ・アカウント） sub-account
会　　期 session
回　　帰 regression
回帰係数 regression coefficient
回帰的期待 regressive expectations
回帰分析 regression analysis
回帰分析法 regression analysis method
回帰方程式 regression equation
回帰モデル regression model
海技大学校 Marine Technical College
会 議 費 convention expense
開　　業 inauguration of business ; start-up
開 業 届 notification of opening of business
開 業 費 business commencement expenses ; expenses incurred for opening of business ; initial cost of business
開業費用 start-up cost
買 い 玉 long account
買 切 り outright purchase
外　　局 Independent Organs
外銀ユーザンス usance granted by foreign bank
会　　計 accounting
会 計 課 Accounting Division ; Accounts Division
会計解釈指針 accounting interpretations
会計概念 accounting concept
会 計 学 accountancy
会計監査 accounting audit
会計監査業務 accountancy service
会計監査実施通牒 Accounting and Auditing Enforcement Release
会計監査人 external financial auditor ; independent auditor
会計管理 accounting control
会 計 機 accounting machine ; tabulating machine
会計期間 accounting period ; fiscal period
会計期間の公準 postulate of accounting period
会計基準 accounting standards
会計基準執行委員会 AcSEC (Accounting Standards Executive Committee)
会計基準準拠決算 accounts based on accounting standards
会計基準書 Statement of Accounting Standards
会計基準審議会 Accounting Standards Board
会計基準設定 accounting standard setting
会計基準設定機関 accounting standard-setting body
会計基準部会 Accounting Standards Division
会計基準変更時差異 transitional amount resulting from a change in accounting standards
会計規程 accounting regulation

カ

会計期末 financial year end；fiscal year end
会計記録 accounting records
会計研究公報 Accounting Research Bulletin
会計検査院 Board of Audit of Japan
会計検査官 controller
会計原則 accounting convention；accounting principles
会計原則審議会 APB (Accounting Principles Board)
会計原則の変更 changes in accounting principles
会計公準 accounting postulate
会計公理 accounting axiom
会計誤差 accounting error
会計サイクル accounting cycle
会 計 士 accountant
会計士業 accounting profession
会計事象 accountable event
会計士責任 accountant's liability；accountant's responsibility
会計実体 accounting entity
会計実務 accounting practice
会計実務勧告書 SORP (Statement of Recommended Practices)
会計執務規定 manual of accounting instructions
会計士の意見 accountant's opinion
会計士の報告書 accountant's report
会計士補 assistant certified public accountant；junior accountant
会計事務所 accountant's office；accounting firm
会計事務処理 accounting data process
会計主任 chief accountant
会計循環 accounting cycle
会 計 上 for the purpose of accounting
会計証拠 accounting evidence
会計上の仮定 assumption of accounting
会計上の裁量 accounting arbitrage
会計上の償却 accounting depreciation
会計上の代替処理 accounting alternatives
会計上の認識 accounting recognition
会計上の見積り accounting estimate
会計上の見積りの変更 change in accounting estimate
会計上の問題点 accounting issues
会計上の利益 accounting profit
会計情報システム accounting information system
会計職能 accounting function
会計処理 accounting treatment
会計処理基準 basis of accounting
会計処理方法 accounting method
会計資料 accounting data
会計士を探す opinion shopping
会計制度 accounting system
会計制度委員会 Accounting System Committee
会計センター Accounting Center
会計組織 accounting organization；system of accounts
会計単位 accounting unit
会計単一原則 principle of unified accounting
会計担当官 accountable officer
会計調査官 Special Officer for Research on Accounts
会計帳票 set of accounts
会計帳簿 accounting book；books of accounts
会計通貨 accounting currency
会計通則 accounting rules
会計的自己資本利益率 accounting ratio of profits to net worth
会計的操作 accounting manipulation
会計的評価 accounting valuation
会計的利益 accounting earnings
会計的利益率 accounting rate of return
会計手続 accounting procedures
会計手続委員会 CAP (Committee on Accounting Procedure)
会計手続規定 manual of accounting procedure
会計等式 accounting equation
会計取引 accounting transactions
会計年度 accounting year；financial year；fiscal year
会計年度の上半期 first half of the

accounting year
会計の変更 accounting changes
会 計 日 account day
会計部会 ASD (Accounting Standards Division)
会計不信 distrust of accounting practices
会計ベータ accounting beta
会計ベータ値 accounting beta value
会 計 法 Public Accounting Law
会計法規による規制 accounting based on legal requirements
会計報告 accounting report
会計方針 accounting policy
会計方針の開示 disclosure of accounting policies
会計方針の説明 statement of accounting policies
会計方針の変更 changes in accounting policies
会計方針変更による累積的影響額 cumulative effect of accounting change
会計マニュアル accounting manual
会計目的 accounting objectives
会計モデル accounting model
会計用語 accounting terminology
会計用語公報 ATB (Accounting Terminology Bulletin)
会計理論 accounting theory
会計レビュー業務基準書 SSARS (Statement on Standards for Accounting and Review Services)
会計連続通牒 ASR (Accounting Series Release)
会計ワラント accountable warrant
外形課税 assessment by estimation on the basis of the size of business
外形標準課税 tax levy on the basis of the size of business
買 気 配 bid quotation
買 現 先 sales under agreement to resell
買現先勘定 monetary claims purchased
買現先債権 receivables under resale agreement
買現先利息 interest on resale agreement
解　　雇 termination of employment
外　　交 diplomacy
外交官課税特権 fiscal privileges of diplomat
会合の目前に in a run-up to the meeting
戒　　告 admonition
外国通貨建相場 rate in foreign currency
外国株券 foreign stock
外国株式市場 foreign stock market
外国株市場 Foreign Section
外国株預託証券 foreign stock depositary security；foreign stock depository receipts
外国からの援助 international aid
外国為替 FX (foreign exchange)
外国為替運営資金 fund for foreign exchange operation
外国為替円決済制度 FXYCS (Foreign Exchange Yen Clearing System)
外国為替及び外国貿易法 Foreign Exchange and Foreign Trade Law
外国為替換算差額 foreign exchange translation difference
外国為替換算表 foreign exchange conversion table
外国為替換算率 foreign exchange conversion rate
外国為替勘定 foreign exchange account
外国為替管理 foreign exchange control
外国為替管理法 Foreign Exchange and Foreign Trade Control Law
外国為替銀行 foreign exchange bank
外国為替金融機関 financial institution for foreign exchange
外国為替現金持高 foreign exchange cash position
外国為替公認銀行 authorized foreign exchange bank
外国為替差異 foreign exchange difference
外国為替差益 foreign exchange gain
外国為替先物 foreign exchange futures
外国為替差損 foreign exchange loss
外国為替差損益 foreign exchange gain and loss

カ

外国為替資金証券 foreign exchange fund bill
外国為替資金特別会計 FEFSA (Foreign Exchange Fund Special Account)
外国為替資金特別会計法 Foreign Exchange Fund Special Account Law
外国為替市場（外為市場） foreign exchange market
外国為替市場操作 foreign exchange market operation
外国為替専門銀行 specialized foreign exchange bank
外国為替操作 foreign exchange operation
外国為替相場 foreign exchange quotation
外国為替相場（為替相場） foreign exchange rate
外国為替相場状況 Foreign Exchange Rates
外国為替手形 foreign exchange bill
外国為替手形買取制度 system for purchase of foreign exchange bills
外国為替投機 foreign exchange speculation
外国為替等取引損失引当金 reserve for possible losses on foreign exchange transactions
外国為替特別会計 Special Account for Foreign Exchange
外国為替取扱支店 branch handling foreign exchange business
外国為替取組信用状 negotiation credit
外国為替の売買 buying and selling of foreign exchange
外国為替のリンク exchange link
外国為替売買益 revenue on foreign exchange trading
外国為替売買償還益 gains on sale, purchase, and redemption, and arising from revaluation of foreign currency assets
外国為替売買償還損 losses on sale, purchase, and redemption, and arising from revaluation of foreign currency assets
外国為替売買損 foreign exchange trading loss
外国為替ブローカー foreign exchange broker
外国為替変動準備金 reserve for foreign exchange fluctuation
外国為替予約 foreign exchange forward contract
外国為替レートの変動 change in foreign exchange rate
外国間接参加者 foreign indirect participant
外国機関 foreign institution
外国企業 foreign company；foreign enterprise
外国技術支援 TA (technical assistance)
外国銀行規制 regulations on foreign banks
外国銀行支店 foreign banks (branches in Japan)
外国源泉所得 income accrued from foreign sources
外国子会社 foreign subsidiary corporation
外国国債証券 foreign government bonds
外国債券 foreign bond
外国債券特例 Special Regulations on Foreign Bonds
外国債券に関する業務規程の特例 Special Regulations of Business Regulations Concerning Foreign Bonds
外国債証券 foreign government securities
外国市場 foreign market
外国支店預け due from foreign banks (our account)
外国支店仕向勘定 foreign branch-our account
外国支店被仕向勘定 foreign branch-their account
外国主権免除 foreign sovereign immunity
外国主要株価指数 major foreign stock price indexes
外国証券 foreign securities
外国証券会社 foreign securities company
外国証券会社に関する法律 Law on

Foreign Securities Firms
外国証券業法 law for foreign securities company
外国証券投資 foreign securities investment
外国証券取引口座約款 agreement for establishment of foreign securities trading account
外国証券取引所 foreign securities exchange
外国所得税 foreign income tax
外国所得免除方式 exemption method
外 国 人 alien
外国新株引受権証書 foreign subscription right to new shares
外国人クラウド foreign crowd
外国人財産 alien property
外国人投資家 foreign investors
外国人登録証明書 foreigner registration certificate
外国人による買い foreign buying
外国人納税者 alien taxpayer
外国信用保険協会 FCIA (Foreign Credit Insurance Association)
外国税額 foreign tax
外国税額控除 deduction for foreign taxes ; FTC (foreign tax credit)
外国税額控除制度 foreign tax credit system
外国税額控除方式 foreign tax credit method
外国税額直接控除 direct foreign tax credit
外国税額の繰越控除 carryover of foreign tax credit
外国税額の控除限度額 creditable amount of foreign taxes ; limitation on foreign tax credit
外国税額の控除限度額の繰越 carryover of foreign tax credit limit
外国税額のみなし控除 foreign tax sparing credit system
外国税額免除方式 foreign tax exemption method
外国政府当局 foreign governmental authority
外国送金 remittance abroad
外国送金為替 foreign money order
外国代理店勘定 foreign agents accounts
外国他店預り due to foreign banks
外国仲介業者 foreign intermediary
外国通貨先物 foreign currency futures
外国通貨先物契約 foreign currency futures contracts
外国通貨両替 money exchange
外国手形 foreign bill
外国投資証券 foreign marketable securities
外国投資信託 foreign investment trust
外国投信 foreign fund
外国と取引をしている納税者 taxpayer dealing with foreign countries
外国取引 foreign transaction
外国取引をしている会社 corporation carrying on foreign trade
外国の制度 foreign system
外国の判決 foreign judgment
外国貿易乗数 foreign trade multiplier
外国貿易統計 export and import statistics
外国法人 alien corporation ; foreign corporation ; foreign juridical person
外国法人税 foreign corporation tax
外国法人税額控除 foreign corporation tax credit
外国法人の事業年度 taxable year of foreign corporation
外国法人の納税義務 tax liability of foreign corporation
外国保険会社 alien insurer ; foreign insurer
買い越し buying on balance
解雇する dismiss
解 雇 率 discharge rate
介護手当 attendance allowance
介護費用 care cost ; care fee
介護保険 care insurance
介　　在 intermediation ; interpositioning
外　　債 external bond ; external loan
外債償還 redemption of external loan ;

redemption of foreign loan
外債発行代金 proceeds from external bond issuance
外債募集 flotation of external loan
外債利子 interest on external bond
介在期間 intervening period
買いサイド buying side
買い材料 positive factor
買支え buying support ; holding the market
買支注文 supporting order
買い残 buying balance
解散 dissolution
下位裁判所 inferior court
概算価格 approximate price
概算価額 approximate value
概算額 approximate amount
概算経費控除 deduction of estimated expenses
概算経費率 rate of estimated expenses
概算原価 approximate cost ; estimated cost ; rough cost
概算貸借対照表 rough balance sheet
概算値 approximation
概算払い payment by rough estimate
概算要求 estimated budget request
解散する dissolve
改ざんする cook
解散による清算所得 liquidation income from dissolution
解散法 Winding-up Act
開始 commencement ; inception
開始延期 delayed opening
開始権 right to begin
開始残高勘定 opening balance account
開始時 on inception
開始仕訳 opening journal entry
開始日 commencement date
海事 maritime affairs
海事検査人 marine surveyor
海事雇用監督官 shipping commissioners
海事債 maritime bonds
海事裁判所 maritime court
海事先取特権 maritime lien
海事事件裁判所 Instance Court
海事審判所 Naval Court
海事抵当 maritime hypothecation ; maritime mortgage
海事の maritime
海事法 maritime law
海事法規 sea law
開示 disclosure
開示債権 disclosed loans
開示されない未払金 undisclosed accruals
開示事項 disclosure matter
開示自動証券貸出 DASL (disclosed automated securities lending)
開示状況 disclosure status
開示注意銘柄 disclosure cautioned securities
開示内容 disclosed substance
開示の原則 disclosure philosophy
開示範囲 extent of disclosure
開示要件 disclosure requirement
外資 foreign capital
外資吸収 foreign capital inducement
外資系 foreign affiliate
外資系金融機関 foreign financial institutions
外資系消費者金融 foreign owned consumer finance company
外資取入れ foreign capital intake
外資比率削減政策 fade-out policy of foreign capital ratio
外資法 Foreign Investment Law
外資輸入 importation of foreign capital
外資流入 inflow of foreign capital ; influx of foreign capital
買いシグナル buy signal
買占め buying up ; cornering
会社 company ; corporation
会社印 corporate seal
会社会計 corporate accounting
会社型 corporation type
会社型投資信託 corporation type investment trust
会社間勘定 inter-company account
会社間除去 inter-company elimination
会社間取引 intercompany transaction
会社間取引の相殺消去 elimination of

intercompany transactions
会社間の調整 intercompany reconciliation
会社間利益 inter-company profit
会社記録の検査 inspection of corporate record
会社金融 corporation finance
会社行為 corporate action
会社更生 corporate reorganization
会社更生手続 corporate rehabilitation proceedings
会社更生手続管財人 corporate reorganization trustee
会社更生手続の管財人 equity receiver
会社更生法 Stock Company Reorganization and Rehabilitation Act
会社資産 corporate assets
会社指定代理店 company agent
会社収益型ファンド CIF (corporate income fund)
会社・従業員折半の combined employer and employee
会社重役 corporate executive
会社情報 corporate information
会社情報に係る照会 inquiry for corporate information
会社清算 winding up
会社整理 arrangement
会社設立許可書 charter provision
会社設立者 incorporator
会社設立手続 incorporation procedures
会社設立前利益 profit prior to incorporation
会社設立免許 certificate of incorporation
会社設立目論見書 prospectus of incorporation
会社相互間損失 inter-company loss
会社相互間の貸借の消去 elimination of intercompany indebtedness
会社相互間の持ち分の消去 elimination of intercompany ownership
会社相互間の利益の消去 elimination of intercompany profits
会社組織 company organization
会社組織保険会社 stock insurance company
会社代理人 company representative
会社都合退職 involuntary termination；mandatory termination
会社定款 articles of incorporation
会社登記所 registrar of companies
会社特権 corporate franchise
会社の吸収合併 merger of corporation
会社の準更生 corporate quasi-reorganization
会社の新設合併 consolidation of corporations
会社の清算人 liquidator of a corporation
会社の整理開始 commencement of corporate receivership
会社の設立登記 registration of incorporation
会社の創立記念 foundation anniversary of a corporation
会社の代理人 company's attorney-in-fact
会社の分割 demerger
会社分割 corporate separation；corporate split
会 社 法 company law；corporation law
会社名義の会員 corporate membership；membership in the capacity of a corporation
会社役員賠償責任保険 directors and officers liability insurance
会社レポート corporation report
会社を設立する incorporate
解　　釈 construction
解釈指針 interpretations
解釈指針書 interpretation guidance
解釈条項 interpretation clause
解釈する construe；interpret
解釈の誤り misinterpretation
外　　需 external demand；foreign demand
回　　収 collection
回収確実な good and collectible
回収確実な貸金 good debt
回収可能価額 recoverable value
回収可能額 recoverable amount

カ

回収可能額の増加 enhancement of recoverable amount
回収可能価値 recovery value
回収可能原価 recoverable cost
回収可能支出 recoverable expenditure
回収可能性 collectability；recoverability
回収可能性テスト recoverability test
回収可能性の評価 recoverability assessment
回収可能対価 collectible consideration
回収可能な collectible；recoverable
回収期間 collection period；payoff period
回収期間法 payback method
回収期限到来基準 due date coming basis
回収技術 collection management technique
回収基準 collection basis
回収規制 regulation of debt collection
回収業者 collection agency
回収業務 collection practices
回収記録 collection record
回収計画 collection plan
回収口座に貸方計上する credit collection account
回収サービス業務負債 servicing activity liability
回収サービス権 servicing activity rights
回収される費用 reimbursable expense
回収循環 collection cycle
回収済原価 absorbed cost
回収代行資産 servicing asset
回収手数料 collection commission
回収に問題をもつ貸付 substandard loan
回収不能額 uncollectable amount
回収不能原価 irrecoverable cost
回収不能な貸出金 uncollectible loans and advances
回 収 率 collection rate
外需拡大 increase in the need for external demand
外需関連株 overseas demand related stock
解　　除 release
解除条件 condition subsequent
解除条件付き売買 sale and return；sale with return right
解除条項 release clause
解除不能個人所得補償保険 INCDI (individual non-cancelable disability income protection)
回　　状 circular letter
海上及び運送保険 marine and transport insurance
海上貨物運送契約 ocean freight contract
海上危険 marine perils；maritime perils；sea peril
海上技術安全研究所 National Maritime Research Institute
海上災害防止センター Maritime Disaster Prevention Center
海上船荷証券 marine bill of lading
海上保安庁 Japan Coast Guard
海上暴行 sea battery
海上保険 marine insurance；maritime insurance
海上保険勘定 marine insurance account
下位証券 junior issue
階上市場 upstairs market
買 信 号 buy signal
買い推奨 buy recommendation
買 進 み active buying
買 相 場 buying quotation；buying rate
買 注 文 buying order
買 い 長 buyer's over
買 い 超 long position
買い超数量 net long positions
買　　付 purchase transaction
買付委託勘定 indent account
買付委託書 indent
買付委託立替金 advance on indent
買付委託元帳 indent ledger
買付グループ purchase group
買付顧客 buying customer
買付残高 outstanding purchase contracted value
買付資金 purchase fund
買付正会員 buying regular member
買付対象会社 offeree company
買付対象者 offeree

買付手数料 buying commission
買付の約定についての反対の取引 closing the long position
買付の約定値段 contract price of purchase
買付申込時間 subscription hour for purchase
買付申込者 tender offeror
買いつなぎ long hedging
買いと売りの幅 bid-ask spread
買 唱 え bidding
買 取 り takeover
買取外国為替 foreign exchange bills bought
買取可能信用状 negotiable L/C (letter of credit)
買取銀行指定信用状 restricted L/C (letter of credit)；special credit；special L/C (letter of credit)
買取銀行無指定信用状 general L/C (letter of credit)；open L/C (letter of credit)
買取請求利回り yield to put
買取選択権付賃貸借契約 hire purchase contract
買取引受 firm commitment underwriting
買取約定 purchase commitments
買いに出る bid for
買　　主 purchaser；vendee
買 い 場 buying opportunity
買いぶらさがり hooked；hung up
買いヘッジ buy hedge
買 本 尊 leader of long side
買い増し adding to holdings
買 増 す top up holdings
買申込み buying offer
買 持 ち bull position；buy and hold
買持ち高 amount overbought
買持ちヘッジ long hedge
買持ちポジション long position；overbought position
買持ちリスク long position risk
買 戻 し offsetting purchase transaction
買戻義務 repurchase obligation
買戻契約 RP (repurchase agreement)
買戻決済 short covering
買 戻 権 right to repurchase
買戻条件付売りオペレーション selling operation under repurchase agreement
買戻条件付取引 repurchase agreement
買戻条件付売却手形割引 discount on bills sold with repurchase option
買戻条件付販売 sale with buy-back option
買戻請求権 repurchase right
買 戻 す buy back
買 呼 値 bid price；bids
買呼値についての気配表示 special quote on the bid side
外人投資 investment by foreign investor
外人投資家 foreign investor
外人投資家による保有 foreign holding
外人持株制限 stockholding limit for foreign investors
外人持株比率 foreign investors holding ratio；foreign shareholding ratio
概　　数 rough number；round number
改正貸金業法 amended usury law
改正投資会社法 Investment Company Amendments Act of 1970
外生需要 exogenous demand
外生的変化 exogenous change
外生変数 exogenous variables
下位セグメント lower level segment
開設銀行 opening bank
改　　善 amelioration；improvement
改善報告書 improvement report
蓋然性基準 probability criteria
改　　装 refurbishment
階　　層 hierarchy；layer
階層化社会 stratified society
回送する route
外 挿 的 extrapolative
改 装 費 betterment expense
海損清算 average adjustment
海損人協会 Association of Average Adjusters
解　　体 disintegration
解体取引 bust up deal

カ

カ

解 体 屋 asset stripper
買　　建 buying position
買建オプション options bought
買 建 玉 long position；open interest on buyer's side
外為決済 foreign exchange settlement
外 為 法 foreign exchange law
階段関数 step function
改築工事 reconstruction works
改築積立金 reserve for renewals and replacements
改 築 費 reconstruction expense
外　　注 order to outside manufacturer
外注加工費 amount paid to subcontractors
外注製品 outside product
改　　訂 revision
開廷期間中 in session
開 廷 日 juridical days
買手危険負担 caveat emptor
買手市場 buyer's market；market in favor of buyer
買手のセグメント buyer's segment
買手負担 buyer's risk
回転商い jobbing；revolving trade
回転期間 turnover period
回転資金 revolving fund
回転信用状 revolving L/C (letter of credit)
回 転 率 rate of turnover；turnover rate
回 答 者 respondent
該当する fall under
街頭の証券市場 kerb market
ガイドライン guideline
ガイドライン耐用年数 guideline service life
下位トランシェ junior tranche
海難救助 salvage
海 南 省 Hainan
海難審判庁 Marine Accident Inquiry Agency
カイ2乗分布 chi-square distribution
介　　入 intervention
介入買い intervention purchase
介入価格 intervention price
介入金利 intervention rate
介 入 権 step-in right
介入水準 intervention level；threshold for intervention
介入操作 intervention operation
介入通貨 intervention currency
介 入 点 intervention point
介入のためのプール intervention pool
介入への警戒 intervention fear
解　　任 discharge
概　　念 concept
概念上の利点 conceptual merit
概念的な基準 conceptual basis
概念的な理由 conceptual reason
概念的フレームワーク conceptual framework
開発援助 development assistance
開発格差 development gap
開発活動 development activities
開発企画官 Director for Development Issues
開発機関課 Development Institutions Division
開発規制 development regulation
開発業者 developer
開発金融 development finance
開発金融課 Development Finance Division
開発金融専門官 Special Officer for Development Finance
開発研修室 Training and Professional Development Office
開発資金 development fund
開発資金貸付 lending of development funds
開発資本 development capital
開発準備中の企業 development stage enterprise
開発成果の移転 transfer of development
開発政策 development policy
開発政策課 Development Policy Division
開発段階 development phase
開 発 中 under development
開発途上国 developing country；less-developed country

開発費用 development cost ; development expense
開発負担金 charge for development
開発輸入 develop and import scheme
会　　費 club dues ; membership fee
回　　避 aversion
回避可能原価 avoidable cost ; escapable cost
回避可能利息 avoidable interest
回避する circumvent
回避不可能原価 unavoidable cost
回避不能費用 inescapable cost
開封預り unsealed deposit
外部売上収益 external sales revenue
外部貨幣 outside money
外部からの制限 external restrictions
外部環境 external environment ; outside environment
外部監査 external audit
外部監査人 external auditor
外部監査役 outside auditor
外部鑑定 external appraisal
外部危険 external hazard
外部金融 external financing
外部経済 external economy
外部顧客 external customer
外部資金 external fund
外部資源 external resources
外部事象 external event
外部資本 external capital
外 部 者 outside interests
外部収益合計 total external revenue
外部収益率 external rate of return
外部証拠 extrinsic evidence
外部情報源 external source of information
外部整合性 external consistency
外部専門家 outside experts
外部積立 external funding
外部積立確定給付型年金制度 funded defined benefit pension plan
外部積立確定拠出型年金制度 funded defined contribution pension plan
外部積立年金制度 funded pension plan
外部取引 external transaction
外部の資金源 external source of financing
外部の当事者 outside party
外部評価 external evaluation
外部不経済 external diseconomy
外部負債 external liabilities
外部報告 external reporting
外部報告会計 accounting for external reporting
外部目的 external purpose
外部利害関係者 outside party with interest
外部流動性 external liquidity
回復基調を維持して with momentum for recovery
回復傾向 uptrend
回復する bounce from
回復テンポ pace of recovery
回復の兆候 signs of rebounding
回復不能の侵害 irreparable injury
解　　放 emancipation
回　　報 circular
開放型インフレーション open inflation
開放経済 open economy
開放式の open-end
開放する affranchise
開放団体 open group
開放担保 open mortgage
外　　務 foreign affairs
外務員一人当り総手数料 gross per broker
外 務 省 Ministry of Foreign Affaires
外務大臣 Minister of Foreign Affairs
会務を総理する exercise general control over board business
解　　約 cancellation ; rescission
解 約 益 gain from forfeiture ; gain from surrendered policy
解約価値 cash value
解約可能な cancelable
解約可能保険 callable insurance
解約期日 canceling date
解 約 金 cancellation money
解 約 権 right of cancellation
解約事由 termination events ; trigger event

カ

解約条項 termination provisions
解約請求 cancellation request
解約手数料 back end load ; cancellation fee ; exit fee
解約払戻金 withdrawal benefit
解約不能オペレーティング・リース non-cancelable operating lease
解約不能契約 non-cancelable contract
解約不能な non-cancelable
解約不能保険 non-callable insurance
解約返戻金 cash surrender value ; return premium for cancellation
解約返戻金利殖部分 cash value buildup ; earnings in cash value
解約予告 notice to quit
解 約 率 surrender rate
概　　要 executive summary ; overview
概要シート synopsis sheet
外欄形式 column form
乖　　離 deviation ; divergence ; gap
乖離限度 divergence threshold
乖離指標 divergence indicator
乖離する diverge from
乖離注文 away from the market
乖離ポートフォリオ misfit portfolio
乖離リスク misfit risk
乖離リターン misfit return
乖 離 率 disparate ratio
改　　良 betterment ; refinement ; upgrading
改良経費 improvement expense
改良特許 improvement patent
改 良 費 improvement cost
下位劣後 junior subordinated
下位レベル lower level
回　　廊 corridor
回廊の制限額 limits of corridor
回廊の幅 width of corridor
回廊方式 corridor approach
確 実 性 certainty
ガウス分布 Gaussian distribution
カウンターオファー counteroffer
カウンター・パーチェス CP (counter purchase)
カウンターパーティ counter-party ; counterparty
カウンターパーティ格付け counterparty rating
カウンターパーティ・リスク counterparty risk
カウンターパート counterpart
家屋の評価 valuation of house
瓦　　解 debacle
価　　額 value
価格・利回り曲線 price yield curve
価格安定 price stability
価格安定操作 price supporting
価格維持 price support
価格維持補助金 price support subsidy
価格改正 price revision
価格改定 repricing
価格カルテル price cartel
価格感応性 price sensitivity
価格競争 price competition
価格競争入札 bid price auction ; competitive auction bidding
価格競争入札の方法 auction methodology
価格協定 price fixing
価格計算 pricing calculation
価格計算式 pricing formula
価格契約 price contract
価格決定 price determination ; pricing
価格決定手段 pricing tool
価格決定戦略 pricing strategy
価格決定変数 variables used in determining prices
価格決定方針 pricing policies
価格下落 falling in price
価格効果 price effect
価格構造 price structure
価格拘束解除 freed up
価格硬直性 rigidity of price
価 格 差 price differential ; price discrepancies
価格差異 price variance
価格差益 price margin
価格差益金 profit from the difference between new and old official prices
価格差別 price discrimination
価格指数 indexes of price

価格上昇 price boost；rise in price
価格上昇の影響 effect of price increase
価格譲歩 price concession
価格情報 price information
価格水準変動会計 accounting for price-level change
価格政策 price policy
価 格 線 price line
価格操作 manipulation of the market；painting the tape
価格体系 price system
価格弾性値 price elasticity
価格調整 price adjustment
価格デフレーター price deflator
価格凍結 price freeze
価格統制 price control
価格入札 price auction
価格の安定化 pegging
価格の乖離 price divergence
価格の刻み price interval
価格の上昇 price appreciation
価格の伸縮性 price flexibility
価格の発見 price discovery
価格の変動 value change
価格の変動が著しい市場 volatile market
価格パターン price pattern
価 格 幅 range of prices
価 格 表 price list
価格表示方法 price indication method
価格標準 price standards
価格分析 price analysis
価格変動 price fluctuation；price movement
価格変動修正 adjustment for price fluctuations
価格変動準備金 price fluctuation reserve；reserve for price fluctuation
価格変動準備金繰入 provision for reserve for price fluctuation
価格変動準備金戻し入れ reversal of reserve for price fluctuation
価格変動の著しい物品 noticeably fluctuating goods
価格変動リスク price fluctuation risk
価格保険 price insurance
価格保護 price protection
価格ボラティリティー price volatility
価格密度 price density
価格メカニズム price mechanism
価格モーメンタム price momentum
価格優先 price priority
価格優先の原則 general rule of price priority
価格要素 cost factor
価格リスク price risk
価格理論 price theory
科学技術振興機構 Japan Science and Technology Agency
科学技術政策担当大臣 Minister of State for Science and Technology Policy
化学業界 chemicals industry
価額協定保険 value agreement endorsement on dwelling risks
価額差異 value variance
係　　長 Chief
書 換 え pyramiding；renewal；rewriting
か ぎ 損 hook damage
書　　留 registered mail
下級管理 lower management
加給年金 additional pension
課　　金 levy
格 quality
格 上 げ upgrading
架　　空 fictitious
架空売上伝票 fictitious sales slip
架空口座 fictitious account
架空資本 watered stock
架空10年物 theoretical 10 year issue
架空取引 fictitious transaction；paper trading
架空の商品 widget
架空名義預金 deposit under a fictitious name
架空利益 fictitious profit；paper profit
各 階 層 each layer
閣議決定 Cabinet decision；Cabinet resolutions
閣議了解 cabinet approval
各勤務期間 individual periods of service

カ

カ

各決算期の for each business year
各　　号 purview
格　　差 differentials
格差均等化 equalizing divergences
格 下 げ downgrading
拡散変換モデル displaced diffusion model
学識経験者 professional and academic people
各事業年度の所得の金額 amount of income for each taxable year
確実性資産 certain assets
確実性等価 certainty equivalence
確実な市場 ready market
確実な分析 robust analysis
学資保険 educational insurance
各州間の interstate
家具什器 furniture and fixture
隔週返済住宅ローン bi-weekly mortgage loan
各種所得 classified income
各種利益全体で across the categories of income
革　　新 innovation
革新的な innovative；revolutionary
革 新 力 innovative strength
確信的立証 convincing proof
学生総合保険 student comprehensive insurance
拡大ＥＣ enlarged EC (European Community)
拡大協調融資 ECO (Expanded Co-financing Operations) program
拡大傾向 propensity to widen
拡大経済 expansive economy
拡大後の縮小 contracting after the spike
拡大従業員持株制度 broader employee stock ownership
拡大主幹事 expanded lead manager
拡大信用供与制度 extended fund facility
拡大する magnify
拡大する格差 widening gap
拡大相場変動 wider margin
拡大融資制度 EAP (enlarged access policy)；EFF (expanded fund facility)
拡　　張 extension
拡張経路 expansion path
拡張担保 extended coverage
拡張保障 extended coverage
格 付 け rating
格付機関 rater；rating agency
格付基準 rating trigger
格付見解 credit opinion
格付情報契約者 rating subscriber
格付制度 rating system
格付投資情報センター R&I (Rating and Investment Information, Inc.)
格付けの制限 rating limit
格付評価 rating assessment
格付変更 rating change
格付見通し rating outlook
格付見直し先 watch list
確　　定 lock-in
確定遺贈 vested legacy
確定価格 firm price
確定勘定 account rendered；account stated；liquidated account
確定期間 term certain
確定期日 fixed maturity
確定期日償還債 fixed payment bond
確定期日預金 deposit with fixed maturity date
確定給付 defined benefit
確定給付型年金プラン defined benefit plan
確定給付企業年金制度 defined benefit corporate pension plan
確定給付債務 VBO (vested benefit obligation)
確定給付建年金制度 defined benefit pension plan
確定拠出型年金プラン defined contribution annuity plan
確定拠出型の contribution-defined
確定拠出給付 defined dollar benefit
確定拠出制度 defined contribution plan
確定拠出年金 defined contribution pension
確定拠出年金制度 defined contribution

pension plan
確定契約 firm contract
確定決算 definite settlement of accounts
確定購入契約 firm purchase commitment
確定債務 fixed obligations ; liquidated debt ; vested liability
確定差額 fixed difference
確定残余権 vested remainder
確定資産ファンド defined asset fund
確定した決算 final settlement of accounts
確定収益 fixed return
確定償還価値 fixed redemption value
確定所得証券 fixed income securities
確定申告 final tax return
確定申告による還付 refund by final return
確定申告による納付 tax due with final return
確定済販売契約 firm sales contract
確定損失申告書 final return of loss
確定注文 firm order
確定年金 annuity certain
確定年金給付額 benefit credited
確定年金付終身年金 annuity certain and continuous
確定年金分割受取選択権 certain insurance option
確定配当 guaranteed dividend
確 定 日 fixed date
確定日付け date proved by notary
確定日払い payable on a fixed date
確定日払手形 bill payable at a fixed date
確定日渡し fixed date delivery ; odd date
確定負債 direct liability
確定保険 definite insurance
確定保険証券 definite insurance policy
確定保険料 scheduled premium
確定約定 contractual commitment
確定呼値 firm quote
確定利益 fixed gain
確定利付き fixed rate
確定利付金融商品 fixed interest investment product
確定利付債 fixed coupon bond ; fixed-rate bond
確定利付資産 fixed income assets
確定利付証券 fixed interest bearing securities
確定利付ターゲット fixed income targets
確定利付きの fixed-income
カクテル・スワップ cocktail swap
稼得利益 income earned
核となる基準 core standards
確　　認 confirmation
確認銀行 confirming bank
確 認 状 confirmation letter
確認書類 confirmation document
確認信用状 confirmed credit
確認済信用状 confirmed letter of credit
確認する affirm
確 認 性 certitude
確認請求 confirmation request
確認通知書 confirmation note
確認的約束 assertory covenants
確認手数料 confirmation fee
確 認 の proven
各年限の国債 JGBs of each maturity
確保資産 collateral for defaulter's pay
額　　面 stated par
額面以下 at a discount ; below par
額面以下で with discount
額面以上 at a premium
額面以上で with premium
額面価格 par price
額面価額 face value ; nominal value ; par value
額 面 株 stock at par
額面株式 par value stock ; share with par value
額面株式資本金 par value share capital
額面金額 denomination ; face amount ; nominal amount
額面金額による償還 redeemable for their face value
額面償還額 par redemption amount
額面証書 face amount certificate
額面総額 aggregate face amount
額面超過資本 capital in excess of par value
額面超過払込資本 capital paid in excess of par value

カ

額面転換 conversion at par
額面転換社債 debenture convertible at par
額面通り at par
額面の切下げ reduction of par (value)
額面売買社債 par bond
額面発行 issue at face value；issue at par (value)；par issue
額面発行された issued at par
額面普通株式 common stock with par value
額面変更 change in par value
額 面 法 par value method
額面劣後株式 subordinated stock with par value
額面割れ drop below par；under par
額面割れ銘柄 below par issue
額面を上回って above par
確　　約 affirmation
確 約 書 written statement of assurance
隔離されている isolated
確立した慣行 established practices
確　　率 probability
確率解析 stochastic calculus
確率過程 stochastic process
確率関数 probability function
確率曲線 probability curve
確率空間 probability space
確率系列 stochastic sequence
確率シミュレーション stochastic simulation
確率収束 convergence in probability
確率制御 stochastic control
確率的特性線 probabilistic characteristic lines
確率的予測 probabilistic forecasting
確率的割引ファクター stochastic discount factor
確率標本 random sample
確率比例 probability-proportional-to-size
確率分布 probability distributions
確率変数 random variables
確率密度関数 probability density function
確率モデル probability model；stochastic model
確率要因 probability factor
確 率 論 theory of probability
隠れ手数料 hidden load
賭　　け gambling
家　　計 household
家計債務 household debt
家計資産 household assets
家計支出 household expenditure
家計収入 household income
家計消費支出 household consumption expenditure
家計調査 family income and expenditure survey；survey of households
家計貯蓄 household saving
家 計 費 household expenses
家計部門 household sector
家 計 簿 family bookkeeping
家計保険 domestic insurance
掛 売 り sale on account；selling on credit
掛売条件 credit terms
掛売りする sell on credit
掛売制度 credit system
掛売帳で on the books
掛売得意先 credit customer
掛売値段 credit price
掛 買 い buying on credit；purchase on credit
掛 金 額 contributions paid
掛金額の収益率 return on contributions
掛金拠出労働者 contributing worker
掛金歳入 contribution revenue
掛金支払い contribution payment
掛金償還年金 refund annuity
掛金水準 contribution level
掛金建会計処理 defined contribution accounting for
掛金建てキオ・プラン defined contribution Keogh plan
掛金建ての取決め defined contribution arrangement
掛金積立基金 purchase payment fund
掛金適正証明書 cost certificate
掛金免除 contribution exemption
掛 金 率 contribution rate

掛　　で　on credit
掛で売った商品　goods sold on credit
掛　　値　fictitious price
掛 売 買　sale and purchase on credit
掛　　目　assessment rate；loanable value
影の勘定　shadow account
欠 け る　lack
下　　限　floor；lower end；lower limit
下限価格　floor price
下限金利　floor rate
下限相場　lower limit rate
加減した　added or deducted
加 減 法　add-back method
囲い込み　enclosure
過去1年間に渡る上昇　rally over the last one year
過去勤務債務　past service liability
過去勤務債務積立　past service funding
過去勤務債務の償却額　amortization of prior service cost
過去勤務受給額　past service credit
過去勤務費　past service cost
過去勤務費用　prior service cost
過去原価　past cost
過去最高　record high
過去最高値　historical peak
過去最高と最低の間　between the historical extremes
過去最低　record low
過去3カ月の安値からの反発　bouncing off three month lows
過去に借換え機会があったプール　pool with prior exposure to refinancing opportunities
過去に遡って　retroactively to a date in the past
過去の貸倒実績率　historical loan loss ratio
過去の慣行　past practice
過去の基準　historical basis
過去の記録　track record
過去の経験　past experience
過去の事象　past event
過去の実績　past performance
過去の水準　historical level
過去の成長率　historical growth rate
過去の中間期間　prior interim periods
過去のデータ　historical data
過去のデフォルト率　historical default rate
過去の取引　past transaction
過去の値動き幅　historical trading range
過去の費用　past expense
過去の評価　past assessment
過去の平均水準　historical average
過去の平均値　historic level
過去の歴史　past history
下　　降　descending；moving downward
下降局面　downswing phase
下 降 線　downhill course
下降線をたどる　taper off
下降トライアングル　descending triangle pattern
加　　工　processing
加 工 税　processing tax
加 工 費　conversion cost；processing expenses
加工費配賦率　burden rate of conversion cost
加工貿易　improvement trade；processing deal trade
過誤訂正立会外取引　special trades trading
過誤訂正の取引　trading to correct errors
過誤納金　overpayment
過誤納金の還付　refund of overpayment
過誤の訂正　correction of errors
火災相互保険　fire mutual insurance
火災損害保険　fire and casualty insurance
火災損失　fire loss
火災損失未決算勘定　fire loss suspense account
火災により発生した費用　expenses incurred from fire
火災保険　fire insurance
火災保険金　fire insurance proceeds
火災保険証書　fire policy
火災保険約款　fire clause
火災保険料金　fire insurance premium
家財道具　furniture and household goods

カ

家財保険 contents insurance
家財保険料率 contents rate
カザフスタン・テンゲ KZT (Kazakhstan tenge)
家　　産 homestead right
加算掛金 contribution for supplementary components
加算給付 additional benefit
加 算 税 additional tax；penalty tax；tax for default
加算年金 supplementary pension
瑕　　疵 defect
瑕疵ある権原 defective title
瑕疵権原 bad title
瑕疵修補保証証券 maintenance bond
瑕疵担保条項 warranty clause
瑕疵担保証書 warranty deed
瑕疵担保責任 warranty
瑕疵付船荷証券 foul bill of lading
瑕疵のある権原 defective title
瑕疵のない権原 clear title
貸　　方 Cr.；credit
貸方勘定 credit account
貸方銀行 creditor bank
貸方計上額 credits
貸方残高 credit balance
貸方メモ credit memorandum
貸 方 欄 creditor side
貸　　株 lending stock；loan stock
貸株市場 stock loan market
貸株注意喚起銘柄 nudge stock
貸金業規制法 law concerning restrictions on money lending business
貸金庫保険 safe deposit box insurance
貸 越 し overdrawn
貸越勘定 overdrawn account
貸越極度額 maximum limit of overdraft
貸越経済 overdraft economy
貸越設定 setting up overdraft
貸し渋り対策 credit crunch countermeasure
貸し証券 lending securities
貸 倒 れ bad loan；credit loss；dead loan；loan loss
貸倒回収 recovery of bad debt
貸倒勘定 bad debt account
貸 倒 金 bad debt
貸倒金の回収 recovery of bad debts；recovery of doubtful accounts
貸倒懸念債権 deemed loan loss；doubtful receivables
貸倒債権 uncollectible accounts
貸倒実績率 historical rate of credit losses
貸倒準備金 allowance for bad loan；reserve for bad loan
貸倒償却 charge off
貸倒損失 bad debt loss；loss from bad debts
貸倒引当金 bad debt reserve；loan loss reserve；provision for loss on loans and advances；reserve for possible loan losses
貸倒引当金勘定繰入限度額 limit to provision for bad debt reserve
貸倒引当金繰入 provision for possible loan loss reserve
貸倒引当金繰入額 provision for loan loss reserve
貸倒引当金控除後受取債権 net of reserves
貸倒引当金控除後の net of reserves for bad debt
貸倒引当金控除後の金額 net amount after provision for loss
貸倒引当金控除前 before the deduction of possible loan loss allowance
貸倒引当金に繰入れられない貸金 receivables not qualifying for the bad debts reserve
貸倒引当金の計上 loan loss provisioning
貸倒引当・償却 loan-loss provisions and write-offs
貸倒引当損 provision for bad debts
貸倒費用 bad debt expense
貸倒見込率 rate of estimated credit loss
貸倒見積額 estimated uncollectible amount
貸倒見積高 estimated loan loss
貸倒れ率 loan-loss ratio；percentage of credit losses
貸倒れを償却する write off bad debts

貸　　出 cash advance and loan
貸 出 額 amount financed
貸出基準 lending criteria
貸出業務 lending operation
貸 出 金 loans and bills discounted
貸出金回収予定 recovery schedule for loans
貸出金勘定 loans and bills discounted accounts
貸出銀行 lender bank
貸出金償却 write-off of loans
貸出金の状況 status of loans
貸出金のポートフォリオ portfolio of loans and advances
貸出金平均残高 average balance of loans
貸出金利 interest rate on loans；lending rate；loan rate
貸出金利息 interest on loans and discounts
貸出限度 loan limit
貸出限度額 maximum loan value
貸出限度額適用制度 credit ceiling application system
貸出コミットメント loan commitments
貸出債権 finance receivable
貸出債権分売 loan subparticipation
貸出資金 loanable resources
貸出・資金吸収動向等（速報） Principal Figures of Financial Institutions (preliminary)
貸出資金理論 loanable funds theory
貸出資産の質 loan asset quality
貸出姿勢 lending attitude
貸出条件 lending terms
貸出条件緩和 restructuring of lending terms
貸出条件緩和債権 restructured loan
貸出条件の明示 disclosure of terms and conditions of loans
貸出審査 examination of loan application；screening of application for loan
貸出政策 lending policy
貸出増加額規制 restriction on the growth of bank loans
貸出超過 over-loan
貸出手数料 fee on loans
貸出能力 lending ability
貸出保証手数料 loan guarantee fee
貸出約定平均金利 average contractual interest rate on bank loan
貸出予約枠 line of credit
貸出リスク debt exposure；loan exposure
貸出利率 loan interest rate
貸 出 枠 credit line
貸出枠残 unused credit line
貸　　付 lending
貸付受入金 loans received
貸付価額 loan value
貸付勘定 advance account；loan account
貸 付 金 advance；loan receivable
貸付金受取利息 interest earned on loan receivable
貸付金及び債権 loans and receivables
貸付金額 amount advanced
貸付金勘定 loan to customers account
貸付銀行 financing bank
貸付金債権の評価 valuation of loan
貸付金の回収 collection of loan
貸付金利 credit rate
貸付金利息 interest on loans
貸付金利息割戻し interest on loans rebated
貸付金利回り yield on loans
貸付契約 lending agreement
貸付限度 limit of a loan
貸付限度額 loan value；upper limit of a loan
貸付債権の譲受 acquiring loan claims
貸付資金 loan fund；loanable fund
貸付証券 loan securities
貸付真実法 Truth-in-Lending Act
貸付信託 loan trust
貸付信託予想配当率 expected return ratio of loan trust
貸付超過日 date of exhaust
貸付投信 loan trust
貸付に係る担保 collateral to be used for loans
貸付の代り金 proceeds of loan

カ

貸付の購入 purchase of loan
貸付の実行 origination of loan
貸付の取決め loan arrangement
貸付比率 ratio of loans
貸付窓口 lending window
貸付未収利息 accrued interest on loan
貸付元帳 loan ledger
貸付有価証券 loan receivable in securities ; securities loaned
貸付予約 forward commitment
家事関連費 expenses incurred for maintaining household
賢い投資家 smart money
カシサイ市場 bond lending market
過　　失 culpa ; fault ; gross error ; negligence
過失する culpable
過失責任保険 errors and omissions insurance
過失相殺 comparative negligence
過失不実表示 negligent misrepresentation
貸　　手 lender
貸手選好分析 analysis of lender's preference
貸手の危険 lender's risk
貸手の指図権 initiative disposition
貸手の選好 lender's preference ; preference of lender
貸 家 料 house rent income
貨車渡し FOT (free on truck)
加　　重 weighted
加重インプライド標準偏差 WISD (weighted implied standard deviation)
加重株価平均 weighted stock price average
加重組換え weighted rebalancing
加重最小2乗法 WLS (weighted least squares)
加重算術平均 weighted arithmetic average
加重指数 weighted index
加重事由 aggravation
加重の差別化 differential weighting
加重平均 weighted average
加重平均確率 weighted average probability
加重平均株数 weighted average shares
加重平均金利 weighted average rate
加重平均クーポン WAC (weighted average coupon)
加重平均原価法 weighted average cost method
加重平均コスト weighted average cost
加重平均資本コスト WACC (weighted average cost of capital)
加重平均償還期間 weighted average life
加重平均普通株数 weighted average number of common share outstanding
加重平均ベース貿易 weighted basis trade
加重平均法 weighted average method ; weighted mean method
加重平均満期 WAM (weighted average maturity)
加重平均利回り yield based on weighted average
加重平均ローン経過期間 WALA (weighted average loan age)
加重平均割引率 weighted average discount rate
加重保険料 weighted premium
加重リスク資産 weighted risk asset
過剰貸付 excessive lending
過剰供給 oversupply
過剰雇用 excessive labor input
過剰サービス excessive service
過剰在庫 inventory excess ; overstock
過剰債務 excessive debt
過剰債務の over-leveraged
過剰事項 redundancy
過剰準備 excess reserves
過剰消費 excessive consumption
過剰設備 excess capacity
過剰貯蓄 excessive savings
過剰積立 over funding
過剰投資 over-investment
過剰取引 excessive trading
過剰ドル dollar overhung
過剰反応 over-reaction

過剰振込 over-transfer
過剰融資 excessive lending
過剰流動性 excessive liquidity；monetary excess
過少源泉 under-withholding
過少雇用 underemployment
過少雇用均衡 underemployment equilibrium
過少資本 inadequate capital；thin capitalization；undercapitalization
過少資本税制 thin capitalization rules
過少償却 under-depreciation
過少申告加算金 additional charge for deficient return
過少申告加算税 additional tax due to understatement；additional tax for deficient return
過少投資 underinvestment
過少にする deflate
過少納付 underpayment
過少評価 underestimation；undervaluation
過少評価する understate
過少表示する understate
過少ヘッジ under hedge
過少保険 under insurance
過少見積り under estimate
過少流動性 under liquidity
可処分所得 disposable income
可処分利益 available profit；disposable profit
過　信 overconfidence
課　す impose；levy
カスケード効果 cascading effect
ガス水道費 gas and water expenses
カスタマー・リレーション customer relations
カスタマー・レポ customer repo
カスタム・インデックス custom index
カスタム・パフォーマンス・スタンダード customized performance standards
カストディ銀行 custody bank
カストディ口座 custody account
課　税 imposition of tax；levy of tax；taxation
課税扱いの経過利子 accrued interest subject to taxable treatment
課税遺産 taxable estate
課税売上 taxable sales
課税売上高 amount of taxable sales
課税価格 dutiable value
課税価額 tax value；value of assessment
課税額評価 appraisal of dutiable value
課 税 額 tax amount
課税換算利回り tax equivalent yield
課税企画官 Director (Taxation)
課税期間 taxable period
課税基準 tax base
課 税 金 assessed tax
課税金額 taxable amount
課 税 口 taxable account
課税繰延べ tax deferral
課税繰延額対給与比率 deferral percentage
課税繰延年金 tax deferred annuity
課税繰延報酬 tax deferred compensation
課 税 権 right of taxation
課税権の承継 succession of right of taxation
課税原簿 assessment roll
課税控除 tax relief
課税控除掛金限度額 maximum deductible contribution
課税控除費目 tax deductible items
課税告知日 date of tax levy
課 税 債 taxable bond
課税債券相当利回り equivalent taxable yield
課税財産 taxable property
課税最低限 lowest taxable limit；minimum taxable income；tax threshold；taxable floor
課税仕入れ taxable purchases
課税仕入高 amount of taxable purchases
課税しうる taxable
課税事象 taxable event
課税社債 corporate taxable bond
課税主体 sovereign of taxation
課税上の住所 tax home
課税上の地位 tax status
課税所得 assessable income；taxable

income
課税所得計算上損金算入される tax deductible in
課税所得計算上の損金 deduction for tax purpose
課税所得欠損金繰戻し tax loss carryback
課税所得控除可能掛金 deductible contribution
課税所得に対し繰戻し控除する carried back against taxable profit
課税処分取消し reversal of taxation
課税済投資収益 FII (franked investment income)
課税総括課 Taxation Management Division
課税総所得金額 total taxable income
課税対象 taxable item
課税対象となる投資家 taxed investors
課税対象留保金額 taxable undistributed profits
課税台帳 tax roll
課税単位 unit of taxation
課税地方債 taxable municipal bond
課税徴収 tax assessment and collection
課税通知書 tax bill
課税年金制度 taxable pension plan
課税年度 taxable year
課税の延期 postponement of taxation
課税の更正決定 reassessment of taxes
課税の公平 impartial taxation
課税範囲 scope of tax assessment
課税評価額 taxable valuation
課税評価審査委員会 Board of Review
課税標準 base of taxation；basis of assessment
課 税 品 article subject to taxation；taxable goods
課 税 部 Taxation Department
課税プーリング taxable pooling
課税物件 object of taxation
課税部部長 Assistant Commissioner (Taxation)
課税文書 taxable document
課税見送 deferment of taxation
課税見積価格 ratable value
課税免除所得 franked income
課税要件 tax requisition
家 政 学 home economics
仮説検定 hypothesis testing
仮説上の想定 hypothetical assumption
寡　　占 oligopoly
寡占価格 oligopoly price
寡占経済 oligopolistic economy
寡占産業 oligopoly industry
寡占的支配 oligopolistic control
下層階級 lower class
可争期間 contestable period
仮装行為 disguised act
仮装売買 chumming；wash sale
仮想料金 shadow toll
家族医療費保険 family medical expense policy
家族給付 family benefit
家族控除 family credit
家族控除額 family deductible
家族傷害保険 family personal accident policy
家族信託 family trust
家族単位 family unit
家族団体生命保険 family group life insurance
家族手当 dependent allowance；family allowance
家族定期年金保険 family term insurance
家族年金特約 family income rider
家族年金保険 family income benefit policy
家族保険 family policy
家族保障年金保険 family protection insurance
加速経路 ramp
加速減価償却 accelerated depreciation
加速償却 accelerated depreciation and amortization
加速償却法 accelerated cost recovery system；accelerated depreciation methods
加速する accelerate
加速的配当 accelerating dividend
加速度係数 acceleration coefficient

加速度原理 acceleration principle
加 速 法 accelerated method
ガソリン油税 gasoline tax
カタール・リアル QAR (Qatari rial)
過 怠 金 fine
過怠金の賦課 imposition of a fine
過大売り overwriting
過大源泉徴収 overwithholding
過大資本 overcapitalization
過大申告 exaggerated return
過大なリスク undue risks
過大評価 overvaluation
過大評価する write up
過大表示 overstatement
過大表示する overstate
過大ヘッジ over-hedge
化体表章される契約 contract embodied in
片端入れ period commencing on but excluding the date of
片　　道 one way
片道ベース transactions calculated by counting each payment instruction once
片道ヘッジ one sided hedge
偏ったポジション stretched positions
偏りのない unbiased
カタログ販売 catalog sales
価値会計 value accounting
価値基準 value touchstone
価値工学 VE (value engineering)
価値交換型決済 exchange-for-value settlement
価値交換システム value exchange system
価 値 財 merit goods
価値尺度 measure of value
価値尺度機能 standard of value
価値上昇 value creation
価値生産性 value productivity
価値創造経営 value creation management
価値に関する情報 value relevant information
価値の増加 appreciation in value
価値の損耗 impairment of value
価値の低下 value depletion
価値のない busted
価値のない証券 wall paper
価値の認識 value exercise
価値のパラドックス paradox of value
価値の変動 fluctuation in value
価値否認 disvalue
価値評価による利得 gain from appreciation in value
価値への投資家 value investor
価値保蔵（貯蓄）機能 means of storing value
価値保蔵手段 store of value
価値を高める enhance
家畜改良センター National Livestock Breeding Center
課　　長 Director of
課長補佐 Deputy Director of
課 徴 金 surcharge；surtax
活 勘 定 active account；working account
活気ある市場 vibrant market
活気を失う languishing
活　　況 buoyant market；gather steam
活況市場 brisk market
学校法人 incorporated school
各国通貨建て denominated in each currency
かっこ内注記 parenthetical notes
合　　算 aggregation
合算課税 unitary taxation
合算所得税申告 joint tax return
合算申告 joint return
合算比率 combined ratio
勝手格付け unsolicited rating；unsolicited rating
活動会計 activity accounting
活動勘定 living account
活動規準経営管理 ABM (activity based management)
活動残高 active balance
活動の停滞 weak activity
活 動 率 activity rate
活動領域 domain
活発な流通市場 active secondary market
割　　賦 installment
割賦売上益 realized gross profit on

installment sales
割賦売上未実現益 unrealized gross profit on installment sales
割賦売掛金 installment accounts receivable

割賦カード multiple payment credit card
割賦価格 total payment of installments
割賦基準 installment basis
割賦購入斡旋 third party sales credit
割賦購入斡旋業 third party credit
割賦債権 installment credit
割賦手数料 charge for installment payment
割賦販売 installment sales ; time sales
割賦販売債権 installment receivable
割賦販売損益 profit or loss from installment sales
割賦方式 installment method
割賦未収入金 installments receivable
割賦未払金 installment payable
合　　併 amalgamation ; merger
合併会計 merger accounting
合併会社 merging company
合併確定申告 filing of final return of merger
合併確定申告書 final return of merger
合併過程 amalgamation process
合併契約書 agreement for merger ; contract of merger
合併行為 consolidation activity
合併交付株式 delivered stock due to merger
合併交付金 delivered money due to merger
合併差益 profit from amalgamation ; profit from merger ; surplus from merged company
合併差損 loss from amalgamation ; loss from merger
合併事業年度 accounting period of merger
合併事前届出 premerger notification
合併条件 merger terms
合併剰余金 amalgamation surplus
合併促進税額控除 promoting mergers tax credit
合併損益計算書 combined income statement
合併手続 amalgamation procedures ; merger procedures
合併により取得した株式 stock acquired due to merger
合併により取得した固定資産 fixed assets acquired through merger
合併により取得した棚卸資産 inventories acquired by merger
合併により消滅する会社 corporation ceased to exist after merger
合併による解散・消滅 dissolution and extinction due to merger
合併による清算所得 liquidation income due to merger
合併のための株主総会 stockholders' meeting for merger
合併の場合の帳簿価額の引継ぎ succession of book value in case of merger
合併・買収 merger and acquisition
合併比率 merger ratio
合併分割 merger and divesture
合併法人 transferee corporation
活力のある社会経済構造 dynamic socioeconomic structure
活力を奪う devitalize
仮　　定 assumptions ; hypothesis
仮定上の市場 hypothetical market
仮定情報 pro forma information
仮 定 値 assumptions
仮定データ pro forma data
仮定テスト hypothesis test
仮定に基づく what if
仮定のケース hypothetical case
仮定のシナリオ what-if scenario
仮定利益 but-for income
家庭裁判所 court of domestic relation
カテゴリーキラー category killer
家　　電 consumer electronics
過当競争 excessive competition ; over-competition
過当投機 over-speculation
寡 頭 制 oligarchy

稼動会員 active cardholder
稼動時間 hours worked
稼動資産 operating assets
稼動しているローン performing loans
稼動所得 earnings income
稼 動 率 operating ratio ; percent of capacity use ; utilization ratio
過 渡 期 transition period ; transition stage
過渡期の年数 transition years
家　　督 legal heir
稼得金融収益 earned finance income
稼得所得 earned income
稼得利益 earned profit
角　　地 corner lot
過度な情報 excessive detail
過度な取引 overtrading
過度な売買勧誘 churning
過度な粉飾 overdressing
過度の依存 over-reliance
過度の集中 undue concentrations
カナダ先物取引所 TFE (Toronto Futures Exchange)
カナダ中央銀行 BOC (Bank of Canada)
カナダ勅許会計士協会 CICA (Canadian Institute of Chartered Accountants)
カナダ・ドル CAD (Canadian dollar)
カナダ・ドル長期国債 Canadian-dollar long-term bond
河 南 省 Henan
加　　入 acquisition of membership
加入企業 participating enterprise
加入基準 participation standard
加 入 金 admission fee
加入資格 eligibility
加入資格年齢 eligibility age
加入事業主 participating employer
加入者集会 investors' meeting
加入者保護信託 investor protection trust
加入従業員 participating employee
加入年齢 entry age
加入年齢制限 age joining limit
加入年齢方式 entry age cost method
加 入 率 participation rate ; penetration rate
加入率ルール arbitrary rule
過熱経済 heated up economy ; over-exuberant economy ; overheated economy
過熱相場 overbought market
金 詰 り monetary stringency ; tightness of money
過 年 度 earlier years ; prior year
過年度損益修正 revision of the profit and loss of prior years
過年度損益修正項目 prior year adjustment items
過年度に遡った還付 refund retroactive to the past taxable years
過年度法人税等 taxes for prior fiscal periods
過　　納 over-payment
可能性が少ない remote
可能性が高い highly probable
カバー・ディーリング cover dealing
カバード・オプション covered option
カバード・コール covered call
カバード・コール・オプション covered call option
カバード・ストラドル covered straddle
カバード・ポジション covered position
カバード・ワラント covered warrant
カバード・ワラント債 bonds with covered warrant
カバー取引 exchange cover
カバー・ノート cover note
カバー率 coverage ratio
過 払 の overpaid
過 半 数 majority
過半数株主 majority shareholders
過半数所有従属会社 majority-owned subsidiary
過半数持ち分 majority interest
カフェテリア制度 cafeteria benefit plan
株　　価 market value per share ; share price ; stock price
株価安定操作 operations for stabilizing the stock market price
株価売上高倍率 PSR (price to sales ratio)
株価規制 regulation of stock price

カ

株価キャッシュフロー倍率 P/CF (price/cash flow) multiples；price cash earnings ratio
株価急落 fall out of bed
株価指数 equity index；share index；stock price index
株価指数オプション options on stock price index
株価指数オプション取引 stock price index option transaction
株価指数オプション取引に関する業務規程及び受託契約準則の特例 Special Regulations of Business Regulations and Brokerage Agreement Standards Concerning Stock Index Option Contract
株価指数コール・オプション stock price index call option
株価指数裁定取引 stock price index arbitrage transaction
株価指数先物 stock price index futures
株価指数先物オプション option on stock index futures；options on stock price index futures
株価指数先物契約 stock price index futures contract
株価指数先物等清算参加者 Stock Index Futures Clearing Participant
株価指数先物等清算資格 Stock Index Futures Clearing Qualification
株価指数先物等非清算参加者 Stock Index Futures Non-Clearing Participant
株価指数先物特例 Special Regulations on Stock Index Futures
株価指数先物取引 futures trading based on the stock price index；stock price index futures trading
株価指数先物取引参加者 stock index futures trading participant
株価指数先物取引特別参加者 special participant in stock price index futures trading
株価指数先物取引特例 special regulations on stock index futures
株価指数先物取引に関する業務規程及び受託契約準則の特例 Special Regulations of Business Regulations and Brokerage Agreement Standards Concerning Stock Index Futures Contract
株価指数先物非清算参加者 stock price index futures non-clearing participant
株価指数商品 equity index product
株価指数デリバティブ stock index derivatives
株価指数プット・オプション stock price index put option
株価指数連動型投信 ETF (exchange traded fund)
株価指数連動型年金 equity index linked annuity
株価指数連動債券 bond linked to stock price index
株価収益率 earnings per share ratio；PER (price earnings ratio)；price earnings multiple
株価純資産倍率 PBR (price to book-value ratio)；price book ratio
株価上昇 rallying equities；rise on stock price
株価水準 share price level
株価水準分布 distribution of stock prices
株価操作 kiting；stock price manipulation
株価トレンド price trend on stocks
株価値動き fluctuation of stock prices；share price performance
株価の動き price movement of stocks
株価の回復 recovery in stock prices
株価の下落 equity setback；erosion in equity prices
株価の下げ falling in stock price
株価の持続性 sustainability of rally in equity markets
株価分析 stock price analysis
株価平均 stock price average
株価リンク債 stock price linked bonds
株価連動商品 equity index product
株価連動生命保険 equity linked life

insurance
株　　券 share certificate ; stock certificate
株券オプション equity options
株券オプション清算指数 equity options clearing qualification
株券オプション特例 Special Regulations on Equity Options
株券オプション取引 equity option contract ; equity options trading
株券オプション取引参加者 equity options trading participant
株券オプション取引特別参加者 special participant in equity options trading
株券オプション取引の対象 traded options contracts at the equity options trading
株券オプション取引の呼値単位 minimum price fluctuation of equity options
株券オプション非清算参加者 equity options non-clearing participant
株券貸付 stock loan
株券コール・オプション equity call option
株券先物取引 futures trading based on stocks
株券上場審査基準 Criteria for Listing Examination of Stock
株券譲渡委任状 stock power
株券譲渡証 stock receipt
株券等に関する保管振替制度 depository and book-entry transfer system for stocks
株券等の保管及び振替に関する法律（保振法） Law Concerning Central Securities Depository and Book-Entry Transfer of Stock Certificates and Other Securities
株券のある株式 certificated share
株券の交付 withdrawal of stock certificates
株券の交付請求 demand for withdrawal of stock certificates
株券の差替え replacement of stock certificates
株券の除権判決 judgment of exclusion on shareholders' rights
株券の振替 book-entry transfer of stock certificates
株券の保管 custody of stock certificates
株券の様式 form of stock certificate
株券の預託 deposit of stock certificates
株券プット・オプション equity put option
株券見本 specimen of stock certificate
株券名義書換 transfer of a share-certificate
株券名義書換停止 transfer books closed
株券名義書換停止解除 transfer books open
寡婦控除 allowance for widow ; deduction for widow
株　　先 stock futures
株　　式 share ; stock
株式IRR equity IRR
株式移転 transfer of equity interests
株式インデックス・ファンド equity index fund
株式応募 stock subscription ; subscription for shares
株式海外売出し international equity placement
株式買替 proceeds sale
株式会社 company limited ; joint stock company ; PLC (public limited company)
株式会社化 demutualization
株式会社東京証券取引所 Tokyo Stock Exchange, Inc.
株式会社東京証券取引所定款 Articles of Incorporation of the Tokyo Stock Exchange, Inc.
株式会社日本証券クリアリング機構 Japan Securities Clearing Corporation
株式会社の再評価積立金の資本組入れ capitalization of revaluation reserve of joint stock company
株式買取オプション stock purchase option
株式買取機構 Bank Equity Purchasing Corporation
株式買取権証書 stock purchase warrant

カ

カ

株式買取権付社債 bond with stock purchase warrant
株式買取請求権 put option of shareholder
株式外務員 stock broker
株式買戻し stock buyback
株式買戻制度 stock repurchase plan
株式額面 par
株式合併 share consolidation
株式勘定 share account
株式関連債 stock related bond
株式記号 stock symbol
株式恐慌 stock exchange panic；stock market crash
株式記録 stock record
株式組入状況 stock portfolio
株式組入比率 weighting in equity
株式組入率 equity weighting
株式決済の equity-settled
株式決済猶予金 contango
株式権利落ち XR (ex-rights)
株式公開 divestment of equity into public hands；equity floatation；equity offering；going public
株式公開買付け takeover bid；tender offer
株式公開価格 initial listing price；price of introduced stock
株式交換 equity swap；exchange of equity interests；exchange of shares
株式交換契約書 agreement for exchange of shares
株式購入 share purchase
株式購入制度 stock purchase plan
株式購入ワラント share purchase warrant
株式公募 public offering of stock
株式裁定取引 stock arbitrage
株式先物取引 stock futures transaction
株式時価総額 total market capitalization
株式時価発行 issue of shares at market price
株式資金調達 financing for stocks；stock funding
株式資金の流出 equity outflow
株式仕組商品 structured equity product
株式資産保有 equity asset holdings
株式市場 equity market；stock market
株式市場の動き stock market's behavior
株式市場の堅調な相場展開 firmer performance of stock markets
株式市場のバリュエーション stock market valuation
株式市場の変動 stock market fluctuation
株式市場への資金流入 equity inflows
株式市場を操る milk the market
株式指数 equity index
株 式 質 pledge of shares
株式資本 equity capital；share capital
株式資本コスト cost of equity capital
株式事務 shareholder service
株式事務代行機関 shareholder service agent
株式取得 stock acquisition
株式取得のための借入金 money borrowed to purchase stocks
株式純損益 net stock-related gains and losses
株式償還 stock redemption
株式償還債 equity redemption bond
株式償却 write-off of stocks
株式消却 retirement of shares
株式上場審査 stock list
株式譲渡 assignment of stock
株式譲渡制限 restriction on transfer of shares
株式所有にかかる配当 dividend from stocks owned
株式スワップ stock swap
株式増価受益権 SAR (stock appreciation rights)
株式相互持合い mutual cross holding of shares
株式相場 stock quotations
株式相場表示テープ composite tape
株式相場表示板 ticker
株式損益 gain and loss on shares
株式代行機関 stock transfer agent
株式台帳 share ledger；stock ledger
株式担保金融 stock collateral loan
株式ディーラー equity securities dealer
株式・手形勘定 share draft account

株式転換確約社債 equity commitment note
株式転換貸付 convertible loan
株式転換契約付社債 equity contract note
株式転換権 conversion rights for shares
株式転換権戻入益 reversal profit on conversion right for shares
株式店頭気配発表制度 OTC stock quotation exchange system
株式投機 speculation in stocks
株式投資 equity investment ; stock investment
株式投資家 equity investor
株式投資収益 equity return
株式投資信託 stock investment trust
株式等の継続的取引 continuous transaction of securities
株式取扱い share handling
株式取扱規則 rules on handling of shares
株式取引 stock dealing
株式取引員 broker agent
株式取引実績 actual results of recent stock transactions
株式取引所 stock exchange
株式取引所会員権 stock exchange seat
株式取引所貸付 stock exchange loan
株式取引所休日 stock exchange holiday
株式取引所相場表 stock exchange daily official list
株式取引損失引当金 reserve for stock dealing losses
株式取引の実績 actual results of stock transactions
株式仲買人 stock broker
株式に付されている権利 rights attaching to the share
株式による資金調達 equity financing
株式による資金調達額 amount raised by stock
株式の買集めによる所得 income from collection of securities by purchase
株式の買戻し equity buyback ; equity repurchase
株式の格付け stock rating
株式の区分 classification of shares
株式の堅調な上昇 sustained equity rally
株式の公開 equity flotation
株式の交換 share exchange
株式の時価発行 stock issue at market price
株式の時価評価 fair value appraisal of stocks
株式の取得 equity purchase
株式の取得費 cost of the shares
株式の種類 class of shares
株式の消却 cancellation of shares ; retirement of stock
株式の上場 listing of stock
株式の譲渡 transfer of shares
株式の信用取引 stock trade on credit
株式のデュレーション duration of an equity
株式の等級 classes of stocks
株式の発行 issuance of stock
株式の引受人 subscriber of shares
株式の分布 distribution of shares
株式の分布状況 distribution of ownership of shares
株式の併合 stock consolidation
株式の保有制限 restriction on stock holding
株式の名義書換 transfer of shares
株式の持ち分 equity stake
株式売却益 gain on sale of stocks
株式配当 dividend on stock ; scrip issue ; stock dividend
株式配当落ち ex-stock-dividends
株式配当落ちに係る増加新株 new shares issued through stock-dividends
株式配当再投資プログラム stock dividend reinvestment program
株式売買損失準備金 securities transaction loss reserve
株式売買手数料 brokerage fee
株式派生商品 equity derivatives
株式発行 stock issuance
株式発行差金 premium on capital stock
株式発行資本 capital from stock issuance
株式発行収入 cash proceeds from issuing shares

カ

株式発行による手取金 proceeds from the issuance of shares
株式発行費用 cost of issuing stocks ; stock issuing expenses
株式バブル equity market bubble
株式払込剰余金 paid-in capital in excess of par value
株式引受け subscription for stock
株式引受勘定 subscription's receivable account
株式評価 appraisal of shares ; stock valuation
株式評価概要 stock valuation summary
株式評価換え revaluation of stock
株式評価損 equity write-off
株式ファンド equity fund
株式ブーム equity boom
株式含み益 unrealized gain on shares held
株式含み損 unrealized loss on shares held
株式プレミアム share premium
株式ブローカー share broker
株式分割 share split-up
株式分布 distribution of stocks
株式併合 consolidation of shares ; reverse split of stocks ; share split-down
株式報酬 stock-based compensation
株式報酬取引 share-based payment transaction
株式報償制度 stock compensation plan
株式ポートフォリオ equity portfolio
株式ボーナス stock bonus
株式保管人 custodian
株式募集開始 subscription book open
株式募集締切 subscription book closed
株式保有 share ownership
株式保有率 share holding ratio
株式マーケット・メーカー equity market maker
株式ミニ投資 stock mini-investment
株式無償発行 capital bonus
株式銘柄 stock name
株式名義書換取扱所 share transfer agent service office
株式申込金 application money for stock
株式申込書 application form for stock ; stock subscription form
株式持合い cross holding of shares ; cross shareholding ; interlocking stockholding ; reciprocal share holding
株式持ち分 stock equity
株式持ち分価値 stock equity value
株式元帳 stock register
株式リスク equity risk
株式リスクの推定 stock risk estimation
株式リスク・プレミアム equity risk premium
株式利回り stock yield
株式略語 stock abbreviation
株式略称 ticker symbol
株式リンク債 equity linked bond
株式連動債 equity linked debt
株式連動スワップ equity linked swap
株式連動の equity indexed
株式ワラント equity warrant
株式割当 allotment of shares
株式割当証 allotment certificate
株式割当証書 share allotment certificate
株式割当通知 share allotment letter
株式を売却する divest
株　　主 equity holder ; shareholder ; stockholder
株主安定工作 stable stockholder operation
株主価値 value of shareholder
株主勘定 shareholders' account
株主議決権 voting right of stockholder
株主決議 shareholders' resolution
株 主 権 shareholder's right
株主構造 ownership structure
株主資金 stockholders' fund
株主資本 owners capital ; shareholders' equity
株主資本回転率 equity turnover
株主資本コスト cost of shareholders' equity
株主資本配当率 ratio of dividends to shareholders' equity

株主資本比率 equity ratio
株主資本利益率 accounting return (ratio) on equity；return on net worth；ROE (return on equity)
株主重視の経営 shareholders-oriented management
株主剰余金 stockholders' surplus
株 主 数 number of shareholders
株主総会 general meeting of shareholders；shareholders' meeting
株主総会の決議 decision of a general meeting of stockholders
株主訴訟 shareholder's suit
株主代表訴訟 derivative lawsuit
株主との資本取引 capital transactions with shareholder
株主に対する割当 right issue to shareholders
株主にとっての損益 gain or loss accruing to the shareholders
株主による訴訟 shareholder litigation
株主による任意清算 shareholders' voluntary liquidation；shareholders' voluntary winding-up
株主の過半数 majority of stockholders
株主の権利 shareholder's rights
株主の行動主義 shareholder activism
株主の出資 investments by owners
株主の代表訴訟 shareholders' representative suit
株主の持ち分の償還 refundment of stockholders' equity
株主の利害 interest of shareholder
株主付加価値 SVA (shareholder value added)
株主への還元 return to shareholder
株主への配当 dividend to shareholder
株主への分配 distribution to shareholder
株主へのメッセージ letters to stockholders
株主報告書 stockholder's report
株主向け年次報告書 annual report to stockholders
株主名簿 list of shareholders；record ledger
株主名簿の株主 stockholder of record
株主持ち分 shareholder's interest；shareholders' equity interests；stockholder's equity
株主持ち分計算書 statement of stockholders' equity
株主持ち分償還 refund of stockholders' equity
株主持ち分に計上された recognized in shareholder's equity
株主持ち分の変動 change in shareholder's equity
株主持ち分への貸方計上 credited to shareholders' interests
株主持ち分変動計算書 statement of changes in shareholder's equity
株主持ち分変動表 statement of investments by and distributions to owners
株主元帳 shareholders ledger
株主優先募入 privileged allocation of issuance to stockholders
株主優待 complimentary goods for shareholders
株主優待方法 preferential benefits to shareholders
株主資本利益率 return on equity capital
株主割当 allotment to shareholder；issues to shareholder；offering to shareholders；rights offering
株主割当発行 right offering
株主割当発行増資 rights issue
株の現物 actual stock
株 不 足 scarcity of stock
株 保 有 shareholding
過 不 足 excess and deficiency；overs and shorts
過不足勘定 over-and-short account
寡婦年金 widow's pension
過振限度 limit of overdrawn account
過振りの overdrawn
過振利息 overdraft interest
可分契約 severable contract
可分債権 divisible claim
可分債務 divisible obligation

カ

カ

可分条項 several covenant
貨幣運転資本 monetary working capital
貨 幣 額 monetary amount
貨幣価値 money value
貨幣価値一定の公準 stable dollar assumption
貨幣価値変動会計 accounting for changing prices
貨幣幻想 monetary illusion
貨幣効果 monetary effect
貨幣錯覚 money illusion
貨幣資本 monetary capital
貨幣資本維持 maintenance of financial capital
貨幣需要 demand for money
貨幣需要関数 demand function for money
貨幣乗数 monetary multiplier
貨幣数量説 quantity theory of money
貨幣性金融資産 monetary financial assets
貨幣性金融負債 monetary financial liabilities
貨幣成長モデル monetary growth model
貨幣制度 monetary system
貨幣性流動資産 monetary current assets
貨幣性流動負債 monetary current liabilities
貨幣的アプローチ monetary approach
貨幣的錯覚 money illusion
貨幣的測定の原則 monetary measurement principle
貨幣的トランスファー monetary transfer
貨幣的評価 monetary valuation
貨幣の限界効用 marginal utility of money
貨幣の購買力 purchasing power of money
貨幣の時間的価値 time value of money
貨幣の種類（材質別） types of coins by materials
貨幣の対外価値 external purchasing power of money
貨幣の流通速度 velocity of circulation of money
貨幣分析 monetary analysis
貨幣ベースで in money terms
貨幣ベール観 money veil theory
貨幣利子率 monetary interest rate
可変資本 variable capital
可変常数 variable constant
可変的現金準備制度 variable cash reserve requirements
可変投資税 variable investment tax
可変費用 variable cost
下方圧力をかける exert downward pressure
下方硬直性 downward rigidity
下方再評価 downward revaluation
下方修正 downward adjustment；downward revision
下方修正する adjust downwards；revise downward
下方半分散 downside semi-variance
加法的減算 additive subtraction
河 北 省 Hebei
ガボン（CFAフラン） Gabon (CFA (Communauté Financière Africaine) franc)
上席主計事務専門官 Special Officer for Budget Information Systems
上席予算実地監査官 Senior Budget Inspector
紙による提出免除条項 hardship exemption
カ ム coupon attache
カムとワラント package and warrants
カム・ワラント cum warrant
加盟銀行 member bank
加 盟 権 membership
加 盟 店 franchise store；member's store；merchant
加盟店獲得会員 acquiring member
加盟店手数料 franchise fee；merchant fee
加盟店店舗 merchant outlet
加盟のための条件 tests for entry
カメルーン（CFAフラン） Cameroon (CFA (Communauté Financière Africaine) franc)
科 目 subject
科目ごとの報告 line-by-line reporting
科目別純変動額 net changes in each

element
貨　物 freight
貨物上乗人 supercargo
貨物運送免状 transire
貨物運賃 freight rate ; freight tariff
貨物海上保険 marine cargo insurance
貨物海上保険証券 marine cargo policy
貨物収入 freight earnings
貨物保険 cargo insurance
カラー collar
カラーオプション collar option
カラー付きスワップ collared swap
空売り selling short ; short securities transaction ; short selling
空売り勘定 short account
空売りされたまま買い戻されてない株式 short interest
空売り残高 short interest
空売りの解消 short covering
空売りの買戻し covering short
空売り比率 short sale ratio
空荷運賃 dead freight
空　文 dead letter
空保証人 straw bail
瓦　落 sharp drop
借入依存 reliance on debt
借入協定 borrowing arrangement
借入金 borrowed fund ; borrowing ; debt loan ; loan payable
借入金勘定 borrowing account
借入金金利 interest rate on borrowing
借入金計算書 statement of borrowings
借入金残高 loan outstanding
借入金償還 loan redemption
借入金で取得した株式 stock acquired by borrowed money
借入金利子 interest on borrowing
借入契約 debt agreement
借入限度 borrowing limit
借入国債 government securities borrowed
借入コスト borrowing cost
借入資金 borrowing fund
借入資本 debenture capital ; loan capital
借入資本の発行 issue of loan capital
借入需要 borrowing demand
借入準備 borrowed reserves
借入所要額 borrowing requirement
借入超過 overborrowing
借入による資金調達 debt finance
借入による手取金 proceeds from borrowing
借入の返済 loan repayment
借入必要額 borrowing requirements
借入費用の資産化 capitalization of borrowing cost
借入返済基金 debt service fund
借入返済保証 guarantee of repayment
借入保険料 financed premium
借入有価証券 securities borrowed
借入利息の資産計上 capitalization of interest cost
借入枠 borrowing facility
借換え refinancing ; rollover credit
借換インセンティブ refinancing incentive
借換エスクロー預金 REDS (refundable escrow deposits)
借換エルボー refinancing elbow
借換機会 refinancing opportunity
借換国債 refunding bonds
借換債 refinancing bond ; refunding bond ; refunding issue
借換指数 refi index
借換証券 refunding securities
借換性向 refinancing propensity
借換えのシーズニング refinancing seasoning
借換発行 refinancing issue
借換費用 refinancing cost
借換ブーム refinancing wave
借換ローン refinanced loan
借　方 debit side
借方勘定 debit account ; debtor account
借方銀行 debtor bank
借方計上される debited to
借方計上する charged against
借方残高 debit balance ; debtor balance
借方メモ debit memorandum
借方欄 debtor side
借　株 borrowed stock

借株残高 balance of stock loans
借 株 式 borrowed share
借 越 し outstanding debt
借証券担保金 margin for borrowed stocks
カ
借　　手 borrower
借手の移動 borrower migration
借手の人口構成 borrower demographics
借手の信用度 borrower's creditworthiness
借手の信用力 borrower credit
借手の特約 undertakings by borrower
借手の判断による借入 opportunity borrower
仮 受 金 suspense receipts ; temporary receipts
仮受金勘定 suspense receipts account ; temporary receipts account
仮格付け provisional rating
仮 株 券 scrip certificate
仮 勘 定 suspense account ; temporary account
仮 契 約 binder
仮 決 算 provisional settlement of accounts
仮決算日 assumed settling day
仮差押え provisional attachment ; provisional seizure
仮差止命令 temporary injunction
仮 執 行 provisional execution
仮釈放許可証 ticket of leave
仮 住 所 provisional residence
仮 修 繕 temporary repair
仮修繕費 cost of temporary repair
仮 需 要 fictitious demand ; temporary demand
仮 証 券 interim certificate
仮 処 分 provisional disposition
仮処分命令 preliminary injunction
仮貸借対照表 tentative balance sheet
仮 登 記 provisional registration
仮　　の provisional
仮 払 金 suspense payment ; temporary payment
仮払金勘定 suspense payment account
仮　　封 temporary seal
仮 命 令 provisional order
仮目論見書 preliminary prospectus
仮利払日 quasi coupon date
仮領収書 interim receipt
カリフォルニア州政府職員退職制度 CALPERS (California Public Retirement System)
下流製品 downstream product
カルテル cartel
カルテル関税 cartel tariff
カルテルを解体する decartelize
カレンシー・オーバーレイ currency overlay
カレンシー・コンバージョン債 currency conversion bond
カレンシー・ボード制 currency board system
カレンダー・スプレッド calendar spread
カレンダー・スプレッド取引 calendar spread transaction
カレント・アサンプション終身保険 current-assumption whole life insurance
カレント・エクスポージャ current exposure
カレント・クーポン current coupon
カレント・クーポン・ボンド current coupon bond
カレント・ペイ構造 current pay structure
川上持株会社 upstream holding company
川下の株式会社化 downstream demutualization
川下部門 advanced processing
為替安定基金 exchange stabilization fund
為替受取人 remittee
為替オプション付債 indexed currency option note
為替介入 foreign exchange intervention
為替学説 theory of foreign exchange
為替換算差額 translation gains and losses
為替換算差損益 exchange gain and loss
為替換算修正 effect of exchange rate changes
為替換算損益 profit or loss on foreign exchange

為替換算調整 translation adjustments
為替換算調整勘定 currency adjustment account
為替管理 exchange control
為替管理法令 exchange control regulation
為替業務 exchange business
為替銀行 exchange bank
為替決済 exchange settlement
為替裁定 arbitration of exchange
為替裁定取引 exchange arbitrage transaction
為替差益 exchange gain
為替差額 exchange difference
為替先物契約 foreign currency forward
為替先渡取引 forward exchange agreement
為替差損 exchange loss ; loss from fluctuation of foreign exchange rate
為替差損益 exchange gain or loss
為替資金調整操作 exchange fund cover operation
為替市場課 Foreign Exchange Markets Division
為替市場介入 foreign exchange market intervention
為替実査官 Foreign Exchange Examiner
為替実査室 Office of Foreign Exchange Examiners
為替自由化 liberalization of exchange control
為替需給の安定性 stability of the foreign exchange market
為替商品 foreign currency products
為替尻換算差金 inter-office exchange adjustment account
為替心理説 psychological theory of exchange
為替政策 exchange rate policy
為替清算 exchange clearing
為替清算協定 exchange clearing agreement
為替操作 exchange manipulation ; exchange operation
為替相場 foreign exchange rate
為替相場圏 exchange rate band
為替相場調整係数 CAF (currency adjustment factor)
為替相場の変動による損失 loss from foreign exchange rate fluctuations
為替損益 foreign currency translation gain or loss
為替ダンピング exchange dumping
為替調整の所得効果 income effect of exchange adjustments
為替ディーラー exchange cambiste ; exchange dealer
為替手形 BE (bill of exchange) ; draft bill of exchange
為替手形業者 cambist
為替手形の呈示 presentment of bill of exchange
為替手数料 charge for remittance
為替投機 exchange speculation
為替動向 currency movement
為替当座貸 overdrafts for export bills
為替当座貸利息 interest on overdrafts for export bills
為替取扱手数料 lifting charge
為替取引 foreign exchange transaction
為替の安定 keeping the currency pair stable
為替の上昇 cable rise
為替の動向 exchange rate developments
為替の変動 exchange rate fluctuation
為替引受相場 accepting rate of exchange
為替プレミアム exchange premium
為替ブローカー exchange broker
為替平価 exchange parity ; par value of currency ; par value of exchange rate ; parity rate of exchange
為替平衡勘定 EEA (exchange equalization account)
為替平衡基金 exchange equalization fund
為替平衡資金 exchange equalization capital
為替平衡操作 exchange equalization operation
為替ヘッジ currency hedging ; foreign exchange hedging
為替変動 exchange fluctuation

カ

為替変動準備金 exchange fluctuation reserve
為替変動損失準備金 reserve for loss from fluctuation of foreign exchange rate
為替変動幅 width of currency movements
為替変動保険 exchange risk insurance
為替マリー exchange marry
為替マリー益 exchange marriage profit
為替見通し currency views
為替持ち高 exchange position；overall balance of foreign exchange
為替持ち高調整操作 exchange risk cover
為替持ち高表 foreign exchange position sheet
為替文句 exchange clause
為替予約 exchange contract；exchange reservation；forward transaction
為替予約差額 forward currency contract margin
為替リスク currency risk；exchange risk；foreign exchange exposure；forex risk
為替リンク債 foreign-exchange linked bonds
為替レート exchange rate
代り担保 replacement of collateral
GUN GUN (grantor underwritten note)
簡易火災保険 industrial fire insurance
簡易課税制度 simplified tax system
簡 易 型 short form
簡易計算 computational shortcut
簡易従業員退職年金 simplified employee pension
簡易従業員年金 SEP (simplified employment plan)
簡易上場 simple listing
簡易生命保険資金 Postal Life Insurance Fund
簡易生命保険特別会計 Postal Life Insurance Special Account
簡易税類表 wage-bracket table
簡 易 の abridged
簡易簿記 simplified bookkeeping system
簡易保険 family insurance；industrial assurance；postal life insurance
簡易保険料収集組合 collection society
換価処分 conversion into cash；tax sale
管　　轄 jurisdiction
管 轄 外 outside jurisdiction
管 轄 区 district
管轄権ストライキ jurisdictional strike
管轄違い different jurisdiction；jurisdictional defect
管轄の移転 change of venue
換価不能資産 unrealizable assets
元加方式 interest capitalization method
環境アセスメント environmental assessment
環境汚染賠償責任保険 environmental impairment liability insurance
環境会計 environmental accounting
環境格付け environmental rating
環境ガバナンス environmental governance
環境株ファンド environmental fund
環境監査 environmental audit
環 境 省 Ministry of the Environment
環 境 税 environmental tax
環境政策 environmental policy
環境対策 environmental degradation countermeasure
環境大臣 Minister of the Environment
環境データ environmental data
環境破壊 destruction of environment
環境評価 environment assessment
環境負荷 environment load
環境報告書 environmental report
環境保護 environmental protection
官業収入 revenue from government enterprise
換　　金 liquidation
換金売り realization sales
換金性商品 cashable goods
元　　金 principal amount
元金一括返済モーゲージ interest only mortgage
元金均等返済 principal-equal monthly payment
元金償還保険 capital redemption insurance

関係会社 affiliated company ; concerns interested ; related company
関係会社売掛金 account receivable due from affiliated company ; receivable from affiliate
関係会社貸付金 loan to affiliated company
関係会社株式 stock of affiliated company
関係会社債権 indebtedness of affiliates
関係会社社債 bond of affiliated company
関係会社出資金 contributions to affiliated company ; investment in affiliates
関係会社有価証券 securities of affiliated company
関 係 者 interested party ; related party
関係当局 relevant authorities
関係なく irrespective of
関係法令 related laws
簡 潔 な succinct
簡潔な開示 concise disclosure
還元利回り capitalization rate
慣　　行 customary practice ; practices
観光収入 tourist income
観 光 税 sight-seeing tax
官公庁共済組合 mutual aid association of government offices
完工ボーナス completion bonus
勧　　告 recommendation
韓国ウォン KRW (Korean won)
韓国銀行 BOK (Bank of Korea)
監　　査 audit
監査委員会 audit committee
監査委員会型 audit committee type
監査意見 accountant opinion ; audit opinion
監査意見書 opinion of auditors
監査概要書 summary audit report
監査可能性 auditability
監査基準 general audit standards
監査基準概要書 Codification of Statements on Auditing Standards
監査基準書 SAS (statement on auditing standards)
監査基準審議会 ASB (Auditing Standards Board)
監査契約書 audit engagement letter
監 査 権 right to audit
監査公準 postulate of auditing
監査時期 audit time
監査試算表 working trial balance
監査実施基準 field-work audit standards
監査実務委員会 APC (Accounting Practices Committee)
監査実務基準 auditing practice standards
監査事務所 audit firm
監査証拠 audit evidence
監査証跡 audit trail
監査証明 audit certification
監査証明機能 attest function
監査処理 auditing process
監査済金額 audited amount
監査済財務諸表 audited financial statements ; certificated financial statement
監査済年次財務報告書 annual audited financial statement
監査調書 audit file ; audit working paper
監査手続 audit procedure ; auditing procedure
監査手続委員会 committee on auditing procedure
監査手続概要書 Codification of Statements on Auditing Procedures
監査手続基準 standards of audit procedures
監査手続書 SAP (statement of auditing procedures)
監査人の意見 auditor's opinion
監査人の責任 auditor's liability
監査人の独立性 auditor's independence
監査人報告書 accountant report
監査年度 audit year
監査の事前通知 notification of audit
監査のタイミング audit timing
監査範囲 scope of audit
監査表明 audit representation
監査報告基準 audit reporting standards
監査報告準則 working rules of audit procedures in reporting
監査報告書 report of independent

auditors
監査報酬 audit fee
監査法人 audit corporation
監 査 役 auditor
監査役会 statutory auditors' meeting
監査役設置会社 company with a corporate auditor system
監査役の選任 election of auditors
監査役の任期 terms of office of auditors
監査リスク audit risk
監査理論 auditing theory
関西国際空港 Kansai International Airport Company, Ltd.
完済する pay off
管 財 人 administrator
管財人債務証書 receiver's certificate
管財人任命 receivership
管財費用 bankruptcy administration cost
管財命令 administration order
観 察 官 Personnel Inspector
観察された observed
換　　算 commutation
換算価格指数 conversion price index
換算係数テーブル table of price factors
換算差額 translation difference
換 算 表 conversion table
換 算 率 conversion rate
閑　　散 inactive；thin
閑散市場 inactive market；narrow market；sick market
監　　視 monitoring；surveillance
監 視 課 Enforcement Division
監視コスト monitoring cost
監視する monitor
監視人（監督者、監督機関者） watchdog
監　　事 auditor；executive auditors
幹　　事 manager
幹事会員 sponsoring member
幹事銀行 lead bank；managing bank
幹 事 行 agent bank
幹事証券会社 sponsoring securities firm；lead underwriting securities company
幹 事 団 managers
幹事手数料 management fee
幹事取引参加者 trading participant acting as lead underwriter
慣習仮説 habit persistence hypothesis
慣習上の保有権 customary tenure estates
乾 重 量 dry weight
甘 粛 省 Gansu
干　　渉 interference
勘　　定 account
勘定価額 account value
勘定科目 account headings；account title
勘定科目一覧表 account chart；classification of accounts
勘定科目内訳明細書 statement classified by account title
勘定科目コード account code
勘定科目の組替え reclassification of line items
勘定科目番号表示法 account number plan
勘定科目表 chart of accounts
勘定科目分類表 classification of item of accounts
勘定記号法 symbol system of accounts
勘 定 口 check-out counter
勘定項目 item of account
勘定残高 accounts balance
勘 定 式 account form；balanced form
勘定式損益計算書 account form income statement；account form profit and loss statement
勘定システム account system
勘 定 書 account statement
勘定照合表 statement of account
勘 定 尻 balance of accounts
勘定対照表 account reconcilement
勘定帳簿 book of accounts
勘定分析 account analysis
勘定明細 details of account；particulars of accounts
勘定理論 theory of accounts
緩衝在庫 buffer stock
緩衝在庫融資 buffer stock financing facility
関心の表明 EOI (expression of interest)
官製謄本 office copy
慣　　性 inertia

慣性効果 inertia effect
完成基準 completed contract method
完成工事原価 cost of completed work
完成工事高 construction of completion
完成工事補償引当金 reserve for compensation for completed works
完成売買契約 executed contract of sale
完 成 品 finished goods ; finished products
完成保証 completion guarantee
関　　税 customs duty ; tariff
関 税 課 Tariff Policy and Legal Division
関税・外国為替等審議会 Council on Customs, Tariff, Foreign Exchange and Other Transactions
関税還付制度 customs duty refund system
関税企画官 Director for Trade Negotiations
関 税 局 Customs and Tariff Bureau
関税局業務課 Customs Clearance Division
関税局局長 Director-General of the Customs and Tariff Bureau
関税局調査課 International Affairs and Research Division
関税交渉 tariff negotiations
関税査定 liquidation of duties
関税暫定措置法 Temporary Tariff Measures Law
関税自主権 customs autonomy ; tariff autonomy
関税譲許表 schedule of concession
関税障壁 tariff barrier ; tariff wall
関税戦争 tariff war
関税中央分析所 Central Customs Laboratory
関税定率法 customs tariff law
関税等不服審査会 Customs Dissatisfaction Review Committee
関税同盟 customs union ; tariff union
関税と間接税 customs and exercise
関税と貿易に関する一般協定（ガット） General Agreement on Tariffs and Trade
関税の死重損失 dead weight loss of customs duty
関税払戻し drawback
関税引下げ reduced duties ; tariff cuts
関 税 表 tariff schedule
関税評価差止め withholding of customs appraisement
関税分類調査官 Director for Research on Customs and Tariff Classification
関 税 法 customs law
関税免除品 article on the free list
関 税 率 tariff rate
関税率表 customs tariff table
関税割当 tariff quota
関税割当制度 tariff quota system
間接外国税額控除 indirect foreign tax credit
間接金融 indirect financing
間接経費 indirect expenses
間接原因 indirect cause
間接控除 indirect credit
間接裁定 indirect exchange arbitrage
間接材料 indirect materials
間接材料費 indirect material cost
間接参加者 indirect participant
間接参加者の承認の取消 cancellation of approval for indirect participant
間接事業税 indirect business tax
間接償却 indirect method of depreciation
間接証券 indirect securities
間接証拠 indirect evidence
間接処理 indirect disposal
間 接 税 indirect tax ; outlay tax
間接税協力団体 cooperative association on indirect taxes
間接生産 indirect production
間接相続 mediate descent
間接送達 constructive service
間接損失 consequential loss
間接賃金 indirect wage
間接的付随費用 indirect incidental expenses
間接投資 indirect investment
間接売買 indirect sales

間接発行 indirect issue
間 接 費 indirect cost；overhead cost
間接引受け indirect placement
間接費差異 overhead variance
間接費準備金 reserve for overhead
間接費の割掛け application of overhead
間接費配賦 overhead cost distribution
間接費配賦基準 overhead distribution basis
間接費配賦超過額 over-absorbed burden
間接費配賦不足額 unabsorbed burden
間接費配賦率 distribution rate of overhead cost；overhead rate
間接費分配 distribution of overhead cost
間接表示 indirect presentation
間接費割賦率 application rate of overhead cost
間接負債 indirect liability
間接部門費 indirect department cost
間 接 法 indirect method
間接貿易 indirect trade
間接保証 indirect guarantee
間接預金 indirect deposit
間接利回り indirect yield
間接リンク indirect link
間接労務費 indirect labor cost
官選収益管理人 official receiver
完全運用済み fully invested
完全親会社 parent of a wholly owned subsidiary
完全織込済み fully valued
完全開示 full disclosure
完全貨幣 full bodied money
完全監査 complete audit
完全期間配分 comprehensive allocation
完全希薄化した fully diluted
完全競争 perfect competition
完全競争市場における評価 valuation on perfect competitive market
完全均衡 full equilibrium
完全金利 exact interest
完全権原 perfect title
完全合意条項 entire agreement clause
完全子会社 wholly owned subsidiary
完全雇用 full employment
完全雇用財政余剰 full employment surplus
完全雇用政策 full employment policy
完全債務 perfect obligation
完全失業率 rate of involuntary unemployment
完全疾病 total disability
完全受給権付与 full vesting
完全受給資格日 full eligibility date
完全償却 full amortization
完全証明 full proof
完全所有子会社 wholly owned subsidiary
完全正相関の収益率 perfectly positively correlated returns
完全操業 full capacity
完全即時償還 full cash refund
完全積立 full funding
完全独占 perfect monopoly
完全特化 complete specialization
完全なカバード・オプション fully covered option
完全な組 complete set
完全な裁量権 unrestricted power
完全な所有 outright ownership
完全なセット complete set
完全年金 full pension
完全払込みの fully paid
完全標準原価 perfection standard cost
完全負相関の収益率 perfectly negatively correlated returns
完全ヘッジ perfect hedge
完全法貨 full legal tender
完全保険 full insurance
完全利用産出量 full capacity output
完全連結 full consolidation
簡 素 化 simplification
簡 素 性 simplicity
観測期間 observation period
観 測 値 observations
環太平洋地域 Pan Pacific Basin
換地処分 substitution of land lot
換地処分による譲渡 transfer of property due to the delivery of substitute property
官庁会計 governmental and municipal

accounting
官庁簿記 government bookkeeping
鑑定企画官 Director (Analysis and Brewing Technology)
鑑 定 書 appraisal report
鑑 定 人 assessor ; evaluator
鑑定報告書 survey report
鑑 定 料 appraisal fee ; surveying fee
監 督 官 comptroller ; management supervisor ; superintendent
監督機関 regulator
監 督 局 Supervisory Bureau
監督局長 Director-General of the Supervisory Bureau
監督資格を有するアナリスト supervisory analyst
監 督 的 supervisory
監督当局 supervisory authorities
監督評価官 Management Supervisor
監督評価官室 Office of Management Supervision
監督命令 supervision and order
カントリー・エクスポージャー country exposure
カントリー・ファンド country fund
カントリー・リスク country risk ; sovereign risk
カントリー・リミット country limit
広 東 省 Guangdong
観念上の所得 notional income
感 応 性 sensitivity
感応度係数 sensitivity coefficient
感応度調整 sensitivity adjustment
感応度分析 Greek letters ; sensitivity analysis
完　売 absorption ; fully distributed
完売債券 absorbed bond ; sold-out bond
ガンビア・ダラシ GMD (Gambian dalasi)
還付加算金 additional amount to refund ; interest on refund
還 付 金 refund ; repayment money
還付金支払通知書 notification of payment of refund
還付金充当 appropriation of refund
還付金充当通知書 notification of appropriation of refund
還付金の益金不算入 exclusion of refund from gross revenue
還付された租税 tax refunded
還付申請書 refund claim
還 付 税 refund tax
還付請求 claim for a refund
還付請求権の時効 statute of limitations on refund claim
還付の請求 claim for refund
還付法人税 refunded corporate tax
幹部従業員 senior employee
幹部優遇 top heavy
GUNフリー文書利用許諾契約書 GFDL (Gun Free Documentation License)
簡便計算 simplified calculation
簡便償却 simplified method of depreciation
簡 便 法 shortcut procedure ; simplified method
簡　保 Postal Life Insurance
官　報 gazette
官　房 secretariat
官 房 長 Deputy Vice Minister
願　望 aspiration
カンボジア・リエル KHR (Cambodia riel)
簡保積立金 Postal Life Insurance and Postal Annuity Fund
元　本 principal
元本確実性 capital certainty
元本価値 value of principal
元本為替連動証券 PERLS (principal exchange rate linked securities)
元本金額 principal sum
元本均等払方式 equal installment repayment method
元本支払い principal payment
元本償還 refund of principal
元本償還額 redeemed principal
元本償還期間 amortization period
元本償還方法 principal amortization schedule
元本所有者異動 changes of owners of the principal

カ

元本と金利の完全分離 complete stripping between interest and principal
元本と金利を分離する segregate interest and principal
元本の回収 collection of principal
元本の減少 reduction of principal
元本の償還 redemption of principal
元本の返済 amortization of principal
元本の返済猶予 principal payment moratorium
元本のみ principal only
元本のみストリップ債 principal only strips
元本半減期 half life
元本部分 principal portion
元本返済 principal repayment
元本保証 guaranteed principal；par floor；principal guaranteed
元本リスク risk of principal
ガンマ gamma
ガンマ・エクスポージャー gamma exposure
ガンマ株式 gamma stock
ガンマ分布 gamma distribution
緩慢な slack；sluggish
官民協力 public private partnership
関門 resistance level
勧誘 solicitation
勧誘テレックス invitation telex
勧誘目的のレート teaser rate
慣用 common use
監理 supervision
監理委員会 board of supervisors
監理ポスト post for supervision
管理課 Personnel Division
管理会計 administrative accounting；management accounting；managerial accounting
管理会計士勅許協会 CIMA (Chartered Institute of Managed Accountants)
管理会計書 SMA (Statement of Management Accounting)
管理回収 management and collection
管理階層 layer of management
管理価格 administered price；controlled price；managed price
管理価格インフレーション administered-price inflation
管理型投資信託 managerial investment trust
管理活動 administrative activities
管理可能原価 controllable expenses
管理官室(SEC) Office of Comptroller(SEC)
管理機構 control mechanism
管理機能強化 strengthening of managerial function
管理局 DM (Department of Management)
管理クローリング・ペッグ managed crawling peg
管理契約 management contract
管理限界 control limit
管理コスト administration cost
管理債権 monitored loans
管理債務 managed liabilities
管理資産 managed assets
管理市場 governed market
管理室 Building and Property Management Office；Office of Management and Budget
管理上の関与 managerial involvement
管理職員の兼業禁止 prohibition of management official interlocks
管理責任 care and custody
管理組織 management organization
管理通貨 controlled currency；managed currency
管理通貨制度 fiat money system；fiat standard
管理的監査 administrative audit
管理人勘定 custodian account
管理費 administrative cost；maintenance fee
管理不能経費 uncontrollable expenses
管理不能原価 non-controllable cost
管理不能費 uncontrollable expense
管理不能リスク non-controllable risk
管理部門間接費 administrative overhead
管理フロート managed float

管理フロート制 managed floating rate system
管理貿易 managed trade
管理銘柄 managed issues
管理予算 administrative budget
元　利 capital and interest；principal and interest
元利回収 collection of principal and interest
元利金 P&I (principal and interest)
元利金徴収 servicing of loan principal and interest
元利均等償還方式 annuity repayment method
元利均等払い level payment
元利均等払債 annuity bond
元利均等払方式 equal payment method
元利均等分割返済 level payment
元利均等返済 equal monthly payments with interest
元利均等返済住宅ローン self-amortization mortgage
元利金の配分 distribution of principal and interest
元利合計 interest included
元利支払漸増モーゲージ graduated payment mortgage
元利支払いの保証 wrap
元利・税金・保険込返済 PITI (principal, interest, tax and insurance)
元利統合 consolidation
元利の支払い debt servicing；repayment of interest and principal
元利払い redemption and coupon payments
元利分離 separation
元利返済額 interest and amortization
元利返済型モーゲージ repayment mortgage
元利返済逓増モーゲージ GPM (graduated payment mortgage)
簡略処理 truncation
環　流 channeling back；recycling
還　流 reflux
還流制限期間 seasoning period
乾　量 dry measure
官　僚 bureaucrat
慣　例 conventionality
関連会社 associate；associated company
関連会社からの利益 income from affiliated company
関連会社への投資 investment in affiliated company
関連グループ affiliated group
関連原価 related cost；relevant cost
関連項目 pertinent elements
関連子会社 affiliate subsidiary
関連債務 related obligations
関連産業 correlative industry
関連した懸念 associated fear
関連情報 pertinent information
関連する確率 associated probability
関連する市場 relevant market
関連性 relevancy
関連当事者 related party
関連当事者間取引 related party transaction
関連当事者についての開示 related party disclosure
関連において in the context of
関連費用 related expense
関連比率 relative ratio
関連分析 related analysis
関連銘柄 related issue
関連リスク associated risk；related risk
緩　和 easing；relaxation
緩和する become accommodative；mitigate

キ

キ

ギアナ・ドル GYD (Guyana dollar)
ギアリング gearing
ギアリング効果 gearing effect
ギアリング修正 gearing adjustments
ギアリングの高いワラント highly geared warrant
ギアリング方針 gearing policy
ギアリング・レシオ gearing ratio
議案の提出 submission of proposals
キーストン債券ファンド keystone bond funds
キープ・ウエル・レター keep-well-letter
帰因する原価 attributable cost
帰因分析 attribution analysis
既往最高 record high
キオ・プラン Keogh Plan
機械運転時作業 in-cycle work
機械化会計 mechanized accounting
機械化取引 mechanical trading
機械化方式 mechanization method
機械休止時作業 out-cycle work
機械業界 machinery industry
機械工具 machine tool
機械効率 mechanical efficiency
機械時間率 machine-hour rate
機械時間率配賦法 machine-hour rate method
機械設備 machinery and equipment
機械簿記 machine bookkeeping
機械保険 engineering insurance；machinery insurance
機械類信用保険 machinery credit insurance
機会損失 conditional loss；opportunity loss
機会費用 opportunity cost
機会利益 opportunity gain
企 画 課 Planning and Legal Division；Planning Division
企 画 官 Director (Research and Planning)；Director, Minister's Secretariat
企画段階 planning stage
企画調整室 Planning and Co-ordination Office
規格売買 sale by grade or type
飢餓相場 famine prices
幾何平均 geometric average；geometric mean
機　　関 institution
機関預け金 deposits with agencies
機関売り institutional selling
機関買い buying by institutional investors；institutional purchase
機関車論 locomotive theory
機関仲裁 institutional arbitration
機関投資家 institutional driver；institutional investor；investment manager
機関投資家相手の証券会社 institutional broker
機関投資家間市場 fourth market
機関投資家資金 institutional capital
機関投資家指数オプション institutional investors' index option
機関投資家による買い equity purchases by institutions
機関投資家による投資 institutional investment
機関投資家の運用資産 institutional portfolio
機関投資家の資金調達 institutional funding
機関投資家の需要 institutional demand
期　　間 life；term
期間按分係数 time weighting factor
期間按分利回り interpolated rate
期間が経過したモーゲージ seasoned mortgage
期間借入金利 term financing rate

期間計算 periodical accounting ; periodical calculation
期間原価 period cost
期間限定年金保険 period certain annuity
期間効果 extension effect
期間構造 term structure
期間構造モデル term structure model
期間差異 timing difference
期間財務諸表 periodic financial statements
期間指定注文 good through
期間指標 current coupon
期間純損益 net profit or loss for the period
期間制限 time limitation
期間損益 profit or loss for the period
期間損益計算 periodical accounting of profit and loss
期間損失 periodic loss
期 間 帯 periodic band
期間定額基準 fixed amount per period standard
期間定額規準 years-of-service approach
期間内配分 intraperiod allocation
期間の一致 matched maturities
期間の経過 elapse of the time ; elapse of time
期間の分散 temporal diversification
期間のミスマッチ maturity mismatch ; term mismatch
期間のリース料 lease payments payable for the period
期間配分 allocation over the term ; interperiod allocation
期間配分基準 time proportion basis
期間配分法 inter-period allocation method
期間比較性 comparability over time
期間費用 periodic charge
期間分析 period analysis
期間平均 average over period ; periodic average
期間保険 time policy
期間利益 periodic income
期間利益率 periodic rate of return
期間利子率 periodic rate of interest
期間リスク term risk
基幹産業 key industry
基 幹 税 fundamental tax
技　　官 technical official
機　　器 machinery and tool
疑　　義 cloud
危機管理 crisis management
危機管理本部 emergency management headquarter
棄　　却 rejection
棄 却 率 rejection rate
希求水準 aspiration level
起 業 家 entrepreneur
起業家精神 entrepreneurship
企　　業 business concern ; enterprise
企業イメージ corporate image
企業会計 business accounting ; enterprise accounting
企業会計基準委員会 Accounting Standards Board of Japan
企業会計原則 accounting principles for business enterprise ; corporate accounting principles
企業会計上 for accounting purposes
企業会計審議会 Business Accounting Council
企業開示参事官 Director for Corporate Accounting and Disclosure
企業貸付 corporate loan
企業課税 tax on business ; taxation on enterprise
企業型確定拠出年金制度 corporate defined contribution pension plan
企業型年金規約 corporate pension rules
企業価値 business worth ; value of business ; value of enterprise
企業活動 business activities ; enterprise's operation
企業活力 corporate vitality
企業間信用 credit among corporations ; trade credits
企業幹部保険 key man insurance
企業間分析 inter-corporate analysis ; inter-firm analysis

キ

企業基金 enterprise fund
企業規模 corporate size
企業共済 enterprise mutual aid plan
企業業績 corporate results
企業組合 joint enterprise cooperative
企業グループ内残高 intra-group balance
企業経営 corporate management
企業経営者 enterprise management
企業経営の健全性 soundness of corporate management
企業経済学 business economics
企業形態 forms of enterprise
企業契約 corporate policy
企業結合 business combination
企業結合会計 accounting for business combination
企業結合に係る会計基準 accounting standards for business combinations
企業結合の会計 accounting for business combinations
企業原価 enterprise cost
企業購入生命保険 corporate owned life insurance
企業ごとの enterprise-wise
企業固有の enterprise-specific
企業再建ファンド corporate restructuring fund
企業在庫 business inventory
企業債務 corporate debt；corporate debt obligations
企業財務協議会 Corporate and Treasury Association of Japan
企業財務局(SEC) Division of Corporate Finance(SEC)
企業財務制度研究会 COFRI (Corporation Finance Research Institute)
企業財務担当者 corporate treasurer
企業資産 enterprise assets
企業事象 business event
企業実体 business entity
企業実体の原則 business entity principle
企業実体の公準 postulate of business entity
企業支配株式 stock controlling other business
企業収益性 corporate profitability
企業集団 business group
企業集団財務諸表 group financial statements
企業集団内の intragroup
企業集中 concentration of enterprise
企業診断 business diagnosis
企業説明責任 business accountability
企業全体で on an enterprise-wide basis
企業全体でのリスク評価 enterprise approach
企業全体の財務諸表 enterprise-wide financial statements
企業戦略 corporate strategy
企業担保 hypothec of enterprise
企業担保権 enterprise mortgage
企業担保権の実行 foreclosure of corporate hypothecation
企業貯蓄 business saving
企業倒産 corporate bankruptcy；enterprise bankruptcy
企業投資 business investment
企業統治 corporate governance
企業取引 business transaction
企業内高速情報通信網 local area network
企業内分析 intrafirm analysis
企業年金 business annuity；occupational pension
企業年金・企業保険 pension and life insurance schemes
企業年金制度 corporate pension plan
企業年金保険 corporate pension insurance；private pension
企業の業況感 business sentiment
企業の継続性 business continuity
企業の資金繰り financial positions of firms
企業の社会的責任 CSR (corporate social responsibility)
企業の所有者 enterprise's owner
企業の設備投資 business fixed investments
企業の破綻 bankruptcy of enterprise
企業の負債 enterprise liabilities
企業の負債比率 company leverage

企業の負担 burdens on enterprises
企業買収価値 EV (enterprise value)
企業秘密 trade secrets
企業評価 valuation of enterprise
企業負担 employer's contribution
企業負担掛金 company matching contribution
企業負担保険料 corporate paid pension
企業物件保険 commercial line
企業部門 corporate sector
企業プロフィール corporate profile
企業文化 corporate culture
企業包括賠償責任保険 umbrella liability policy
企業保険 corporate insurance
企業保証 corporate guarantee
企業向け医療保険 business health insurance
企業向けサービス価格 corporate services prices
企業向けサービス価格指数 corporate service price index
企業持ち分 corporation's equity
企業誘致 invitation of enterprise
企業誘致地域 area to welcome enterprise
企業利益 corporate profit
企業利益調整 adjustment of business income
企業利益の共変動 co-movement of corporate earnings
企業倫理 business ethics
企業連結 business consolidation
企業を清算する liquidate an enterprise
危機レート crisis rate
基　　金 endowment；fund
基金型企業年金 funded corporate pensions plan
基金債務 fund obligation
基金資産 fund assets
基金自由積立 flexible funding
基金償却積立金 reserve for redemption of funds
基金単位勘定 fund unit account
基金積立 fund accumulation
基金のない unfunded
基金利息 interest on guaranty capital
基金を有する給付建制度 funded defined benefit plan
基金を有する制度 funded plan
既経過保険料 earned premium
既経過未収利息 earned accrued interest
既 契 約 current policy
議決延期請求権 government representatives' right to request the Board to postpone a vote
議 決 権 voting power；voting right
議決権株式 voting stock
議決権行使勧誘書類 proxy statement
議決権証書 VRC (voting right certificate)
議決権信託 voting trust
議決権信託証書 voting trust certificate
議決権付株式 voting shares
議決権付社債 bond with voting right；voting bond
議決権付普通株式 voting common shares
議決権の行使 exercise of voting right
議決権の代理行使 exercise of voting right by proxy
議決権の多数決 majority of voting rights
議決権の不統一行使 diverse exercise of voting right
議決権比率 ratio of voting rights
議決権保有株主 voting stockholder
議決方法 method of making a resolution
危　　険 hazard；jeopardy；peril
危険愛好的 risk seeking
危険期間 duration of risk
危険限定効果 effect of limiting risk
危険債権 doubtful assets；loans at risk
危険査定要因 underwriting factor
危険資産 risk assets
危険準備金 reserve for contingencies
危険条項 perils clause
危険選択 selection of risk
危険逓増の原理 principle of increasing risk
危 険 点 peril point
危険の変動 change of risk
危険負担の引受け assumption of risk
危険分散 diffusion of risks

危険保険料率 insurance risk rate
危険約款 peril clause
危険率の高い投資 high-risk investment
棄　　権 abstention
期　　限 deadline；time limit
期限が来る become due；mature
期限切れ expiration
期限切れカード expired card
期限切れ時点で on expiration
期限経過 out of date
期限経過勘定 overdue account
期限経過小切手 overdue check
期限経過手形 overdue bill；past due bill
期限後書替継続 renewal after the maturity
期限後申告 return after due date
期限後利息 interest after the maturity
期限前解約 cancellation before the maturity；early termination
期限前解約委員会 early withdrawal penalty
期限前償還 early amortization；prepayment；redemption before maturity
期限前償還オプション prepayment option
期限前償還速度 prepayment speed
期限前の契約違反 anticipatory breach of contract
期限前返済 anticipation
期限前返済権 right of anticipation
期限前返済ペナルティ prepayment penalty
期限付為替相場 usance rate
期限付為替手形 usance bill
期限付逆モーゲージ fixed term reverse mortgage
期限付信用状 usance L/C (letter of credit)
期限付手形 time bill
期限付手形買相場 credit buying rate；usance buying rate
期限付手形相場 usance bill rate
期限付の limited life
期限付不動産投資信託 FREIT (finite real estate investment trust)
期限付優先株 limited life preferred equity；limited life preferred stock
期限ながれ time expired
期限の利益 right not to pay before due date
期限の利益喪失 acceleration
期限の利益喪失事由 cause of default
期限の利益喪失条項 acceleration clause
期限の利益の喪失 forfeiture of the grace of time
期限の利益を喪失している債務 debts in default
期限別貸出統計 outstanding loans and discounts of all banks by terms
期限前償還モデル prepayment model
期限前償還リスク early redemption risk
期限前償還率 prepayment rate
期限前償還率指標 prepayment rate indicator
期限前返済権 prepayment right
期限前返済要求 acceleration demand
期限満了 expiry；termination of a term
機構業務室 Financial Stability Organizations Office
記号小切手 marked checks
寄港滞泊条項 clause "touch and stay"
旗 国 法 law of ship's flag
記　　載 description
記載式無額面株式 stated value no-par stock
記載事項の証明 certification of description
起　　債 bond flotation；flotation of loan；issue of bond；launching of bonds
起債活動 primary activity
起債根拠法 legal status of issuance
起債市場 bond flotation market；bond issuing market
起債制限比率 restriction on floatation ratio
起債調整 coordination of bond issues
起債つなぎ融資 temporary loan before bond flotation
起債費用 floatation cost
起債ラッシュ market congestion

期　　先 farther out；furthest month
期先限月取引 far contract month
期 先 物 back months
兆　　し token
刻み買い buy on scale
刻み注文 order on a scale
刻 み 値 interval
起 算 日 initial date in reckoning
擬　　似 mimicking
議　　事 agendum；proceedings
機　　軸 axis
基軸通貨 key currency
期　　日 appointed day；due date；time limited
期日が到来する fall due
期日経過保険契約 past due policy
期日指定定期預金 maturity-designated time deposit
期日到来元本 credit past due date
期日到来債権 overdue payment
期日の到来した掛金 contribution due
期 日 物 term call
期日別区分 maturity grouping
期日もしくは期日前に on or before
期　　首 BOY (beginning of year)
期首から現時点 year to date
期首債務 opening obligation
期首残高 balance at the beginning of the period；balance at the beginning of the year；beginning balance；initial balance；opening balance
期首仕掛品 initial goods in process
期首仕掛品勘定 initial work in process account
期首剰余金 opening retained earnings
期首剰余金残高 surplus at the opening of the period
期首棚卸資産 beginning inventory；initial inventories；inventory at the beginning of the period
期首棚卸高 opening inventory
期 首 の at the beginning of the year；initial
期首の負債純額 opening net liability
期首払年金 annuity due
貴 州 省 Guizhou
技術移転 technology transfer
技術移転機関 TLO (technology licensing organization)
技術移転契約 technology transfer agreement
技術格差 technology gap
技術革新 technological innovation
技術協力 technical assistance
技術支援 technological support
技術振興 development of technology
技術進歩 technical progress；technological changes
技術進歩リスク risk arising from technology development
技術進歩率 rate of technical progress
技術水準 technical standard
技術提携 technical cooperation
技術的陳腐化 technical obsolescence
技術的な実現可能性 technological feasibility
技術的な問題 technical issue
技術等海外取引 overseas technical service transaction
技術の進歩 technological advance
技術の導入 introduction of technology
技術輸出 technology export
技術予測 technological forecasting
記述データ descriptive data
記述的機能 descriptive function
記述的統計 descriptive statistics
基　　準 basis；standards
基準外国為替相場 basic rate of foreign exchange
基準価格 base price
基準為替相場 basic exchange rate
基準期間 base period
基準時価総額 base market value
基準所得 earnings base
基準設定 standard setting
基準設定機関 standard setting body
基準操業度 denominator level
基準相場 basic rate
基準棚卸資産 base year inventory
基準棚卸法 base-stock method

キ

基準担保金率 standard ratio for calculating cash collateral
基準賃金 standard wage
基準通貨 base currency
基準となる貸付利率 basic loan rate
基準年度 base year；basic taxable year
基 準 日 base date；record date
基準日の参照指数 base reference index
基準標準原価 base standard cost
基準保険料 base premium；subject premium；underlying premium
基準レート benchmark rate
基準割引レート basic discount rate
基準を下回る breach the required level
規　　準 criteria
規準価格 unit value
議事要旨 minutes
稀少資源 scarce resources
稀少通貨条項 scarce currency clause
希 少 性 scarcity
気 象 庁 Japan Meteorological Agency
机上調査 desk-top analysis；office audit
議 事 録 minutes；transcripts
議事録の公表 publication of transcripts
擬 人 説 personification theory
犠　　牲 sacrifice
規制価格 regulated prices
規制監督上の歪み regulatory distortion
規制監督当局 regulator
規制緩和 deregulation；relaxation of regulations
規制金利 regulated interest rate
規制金利負債 administrated rate liabilities
規制市場 regulated market
規 制 上 regulatory
規制商品 controlled commodities
規制措置 regulatory measure
規制対象企業 regulated company
規制当局 regulatory agency；regulatory authority
規制当局の承認 regulatory approvals
規制当局の注目 regulatory attention
規制投資会社 regulated investment company
規制のある資源 restricted resources
規制の制約 regulatory constraint
規制の理論 theory of regulation
規制分野 regulatory field
規制変更リスク risk arising from changes in regulations
規制目的会計原則 RAP (regulatory accounting principles)
規制要因 regulatory factors
擬制貸方残高 fictitious credit
擬制資産 fictitious assets
擬制資本 fictitious capital；watered capital
擬制証書 notional certificate
擬 制 の constructive
擬制の追立 constructive eviction
擬制の引渡し constructive delivery
擬制売却 constructive sale
帰責過失 imputed negligence
季節売出し season sale
季節関税 seasonal duties
季節資金 seasonal fund
季節指数 seasonal index
季節商品 seasonal goods；seasonal merchandise
季 節 性 seasonality
季節調整 seasonal adjustment；seasonal effects
季節調整済の SA (season adjusted)
季節調整前の non-seasonally adjusted
季節調整要因 seasonal factor
季節的売り圧力 seasonal selling pressure
季節的支出 seasonal expenditure
季節的失業 seasonal unemployment
季節的な seasonal
季節パターン seasonal pattern
季節平均 seasonal average
季節変動 seasonal fluctuation
季節変動調整 seasonal fluctuation adjustment
季節変動調整済 seasonally adjusted
季節要因 seasonal factor
季節要因によるインフレ seasonal driven inflation
季節割引 seasonal discount
期前借換え advance refunding

期前借替え advance refunding
期前償還価格 call price
期前償還までの据置期間 life-to-call
基　礎 basics
基礎インフレ率 underlying inflation rate
基 礎 額 basic amount
基礎給付 basic benefit
基礎研究 basic research
基礎口座簿残高 basic balance of account book
基礎控除 basic allowance；basic deduction；legal exemption from income tax；personal exemption
基礎事実 matter
基礎収益 base earnings
基礎収支 basic balance of payments
基礎数値 fundamental figures
基礎想定 basic assumption
基礎退職年金基金 basic retirement funds
基礎的会計データ underlying accounting data
基礎的金融商品アプローチ fundamental financial approach
基礎的費用見積 base cost estimate
基礎的不均衡 fundamental disequilibrium
基礎統計 basic statistics
基礎になる財務状態 underlying financial condition
基礎年金 basic pension
基礎年金からの脱退 contracting out of the basic pension
基 礎 率 basic rate；experience assumptions
偽　造 counterfeit
偽造カード counterfeit card
偽造株券 forged stock
偽造小切手 forged check
偽造紙幣 forged note
偽造手形 forged bill
偽造日銀券 counterfeit Bank of Japan note
寄 贈 者 donator；donor
偽装取引 disguised transaction
偽装紛失 false missing
規　則 rule
規則S-X Regulation S-X
規 則 性 regularity
規則制定委員会 rulemaking board
規則的な基準 systematic basis
規則的な配分 systematic allocation
規則への委任 delegation of authority to rules
帰　属 imputation
帰属価格 imputed price
帰属価値 imputed value
帰属期間 attribution period
帰属原価 imputed cost
帰属させる impute
帰属主義 attributable income principle
帰属所得 imputed income
帰属する attributed to
帰属持ち分 attributable interest
帰属利益 attributable profit
帰属利子 imputed interest
帰属理論 theory of imputation
帰属割引 imputed discount
起 訴 者 accuser
起訴する indict
起訴部分 accusatory part
毀　損 detraction
毀損小切手 mutilated check
毀損証券 mutilated security
既存債務 existing debt
既存資産 existing assets
既存住宅の買換率 turnover rate on existing houses
既存特恵 existing preferential duties
既存のロング・ポジション existing longs
北アイルランド（イギリス・ポンド） Northern Ireland (sterling pound)
議　題 agenda
期待インフレ率 inflationary expectations
期待運用収益 expected investment return；expected return on pension assets
期待運用収益率 expected investment return ratio
期待仮説 expectation hypothesis
期待効用関数 expected utility function
期待資産効果 expected wealth effect
期待収益 expected earnings；expected

キ

return
期待収益率 expected rate of return
期待水準 expected standard
期待総収益率 expected total rate of return
期待相続人 expectant heir
期 待 値 expected value
期待年間操業度 expected annual volume
期待のギャップ expectation gap
期待外れ disappointing
期待外れの投資 turkey
期待保有期間収益率 expected holding-period rate of return；projected holding-period rate of return
期待満期利回り expected yield-to-maturity
期待利益 prospective profit
期待利益成長率 expected earnings growth rate
期待利回り expected yield
期待理論 expectation theory
機体保険 aviation hull insurance
寄　　託 bailment
寄託会社 deposit company
寄 託 金 money entrusted
寄託券制度 banknote custody system
寄託資金 escrow fund
寄 託 者 bailor
寄託信用状 escrow letter of credit
北大西洋自由貿易地域 North Atlantic Free Trade Area
北大西洋条約機構 NATO (North Atlantic Treaty Organization)
北大西洋評議会 North Atlantic Assembly
北朝鮮ウォン KPW (North Korean won)
期　　近 farther in；near maturity
期近限月取引 near contract month
期 近 債 near-term bond
期 近 物 nearby contract；nearbys
期近物価格上昇 accrued market discount
期近物取引 transaction of near delivery
期　　中 during the period
期中監査 interim audit
期中償還請求権 claim for redemption before maturity
期中償還請求権付転換社債 convertible bond with redemption request right
期中に取得した acquired during the period
期中平均レート average rate during the period
基　　調 keynote；underlying trend
記　　帳 posting
記 帳 機 bookkeeping machine
記帳業務 obligation of bookkeeping
記帳場所 booking center
貴重な意見 valuable feedback loop
貴 重 品 valuables
キチン循環 Kitchin cycles
キックバック kick back
吉 林 省 Jilin
規　　定 regulation
規定する prescribe
規定保険料 stipulated premium
規　　程 code
規 程 集 book of regulations
規程の制定 enactment of regulations
議 定 書 protocol
基点価格 basing point price
機 動 力 flexibility
既 得 権 acquired right；earned right；vested interest；vested right
既得権条項 grandfather provision
既得権を侵さずに without prejudice to preliminary
ギニアビサウ（CFAフラン） GWP (Guinea-Bissau CFA (Communauté Financière Africaine) franc)
ギニア・フラン GNF (Guinea franc)
記　　入 entry
記念貨幣 commemorative coins
記念配当 commemorative dividend；memorial dividend
記 念 日 jubilee
帰納的統計 inductive statistics
機　　能 function
機能通貨 functional currency
機能通貨法 functional currency method
機能的価格設定 functional pricing
機能的減価 functional depreciation

機能分析 function analysis
機能別会計 functional accounting
機能別計算書 functional statement
機能別原価 function cost
気乗り薄 dull
希 薄 化 dilution
希薄化後一株当り利益 diluted earnings per share
希薄化証券 dilutive securities
希薄化の dilutive
希薄化の影響 dilutive effect
希薄化の金額 amount of dilution
希薄化ベースで on a dilutive basis
希薄化防止条項 anti-dilution clause
希薄化前一株当り利益 base earnings per share
希薄化率 dilution factor
既発行株式 outstanding stock
既 発 債 already-issued bond ; outstanding bond
既発債取引 secondary bond dealing
既発債利回り yield on already-issued bond ; yield on outstanding bond
既発生損害 incurred loss
既発生の incurred
既発生未払い incurred but not paid
既発銘柄 existing issue ; seasoned issue
既発ワラント outstanding warrants
揮発油税 gasoline tax
記 番 号 serial number
忌避する evade
寄 付 金 donation
寄付金控除 contribution deduction ; deduction for donation
寄付金損金参入限度額 limitation on the deductible amount of donation
寄付金の損金参入限度額 deduction limit applicable to donation
寄付行為 articles of association
ギブソンの逆説 Gibson paradox
キプロス・ポンド CYP (Cyprus pound)
希望価格 sticker price
希望退職 voluntary retirement
規模拡大 addition of scale
規模効果 size effect
規模の経済 economies of scale
規模の利益 scale merit
規模別株価指数 stock price index by size of stocks
規模別株価平均 stock price average by size of stocks
基本価額 basic value
基本価値 fundamental value
基本為替レート basic rate of foreign exchange
基本期間 basic period
基本規約 mission statement
基 本 給 basic salary ; basic wage ; regular wage
基 本 金 capital base ; equity capital
基本計画 master plan
基本契約 master contract
基本原価 basic cost
基本原則 basic principle ; fundamental principle
基本公準 basic convention
基本構造 basic structure
基本財産 capital assets
基本財産運用収入 revenue from fund operations
基本財産の没収 disendowment
基本財務諸表 basic financial statements ; primary financial statements
基本指針 basic precept
基本準備金の積立て accumulation of basic reserve
基本証券 master policy
基本証拠金 initial margin
基本税率 basic tax rate
基本ダイナミクス basic dynamics
基本通達 primary regulation notice
基本ツール basic tool
基本積立金 basic reserve
基本定款 charter ; memorandum of association
基本定理 fundamental theorem
基本的開示要求事項 required primary disclosures
基本的考え方 basic thinking
基本的規則 fundamental rules

キ

基本的金融商品 primary instruments
基本的権利 fundamental rights
基本的公準 basic convention
基本的構造 essential structure
基本的項目基準 Tier 1 capital guideline
基本的自己資本 Tier 1
基本的資本 core capital
基本的収支 primary balance
基本的需要 primary demand
基本的性質 fundamental character
基本的前提 basic premise
基本的相殺契約 master netting arrangement
基本的な改革 fundamental reform
基本的一株当り利益 primary earnings per share
基本的見通し base case
基本的様式 primary format
基本的要素 basic elements
基本年度 basic year
基本一株当り利益 basic earnings per share
基本法規 basic regulations
基本方針 basic policy ; statement of principles
基本保険契約 basic policy
基本予算 baseline budget
基本留保 underlying retention
基本レート base rate
気前のよい援助 largess
期　末 end of the period ; end of the year
期末の term-end
期末為替レート exchange rate at the end of period
期末監査 final audit ; year-end audit
期末勘定 term-end account
期末繰越利益金 unappropriated surplus at the end of year
期末決算 term-end settlement of accounts ; year-end closing of accounts
期末在庫 year-end inventory ; year-end stock
期末債務 closing obligation
期末残 final balance
期末残高 balance at the end of period ; balance at the end of the term ; closing balance
期末仕掛品 work in process at the end of period
期末時換算法 translation method at the current exchange rate
期末試算表 periodic trial balance
期末剰余金 closing retained earnings
期末整理 adjustment at term-end
期末測定 period-end measurement
期末貸借対照表 periodic balance sheet
期末棚卸資産 ending inventory ; inventory at the end of period
期末棚卸高 closing inventories
期末賃借対照表 year-end balance sheet
期末で at the end of period
期末の負債純額 closing net liability
期末配当 year-end dividend
期末日 final day of the accounting period
気迷い mixed ; uncertain
機密性 confidentiality
機密費 secret service expenses
機密漏洩 indiscretion
義務違反 breach of duty
義務再保険 obligatory reinsurance
義務の履行 fulfillment of obligation
義務不履行 nonfeasance
義務を負う onerous
義務を履行する discharge the obligation
記名株 inscribed stock ; name share
記名株券 inscribed stock certificate
記名株式 registered stock
記名クーポン債券 registered coupon bond
記名債券 inscribed bond
記名式 registered form
記名式裏書 special endorsement
記名式小切手 signed check
記名式証券 nominative security
記名式手形 named bill
記名式普通株式 registered common stock
記名式船荷証券 straight B/L (bill of lading)
記名社債 registered bond

記名証券 inscribed securities；registered securities
記名譲渡 signed transfer
記名捺印 signature and seal
GAAPとの収斂 convergence with GAAP
規　　約 rules
規約型企業年金 corporate pension plan operated by multi-employers
客　　注 customer's order
脚　　注 footnote
逆イールド inverted yield curve；negative yield；yield curve inversion
逆イールド現象 inverted yield curve phenomena
逆委託介入 intervention conducted on behalf of other central banks
逆入替え switch reversal
逆株式分割 reverse share split
逆 為 替 adverse exchange；bills receivable；reverse remittance
逆吸収合併 downstairs merger；downstream merger
逆行列表 inverse matrix table
逆 金 利 negative interest
逆 指 値 stop price
逆指値売り gather in the stops
逆指値買注文 stop loss buy order
逆指値注文 buy stop order；stop-limit order
逆 ざ や back spread；negative interest rate margin；negative interest rate spread
逆ざや市場 inverted market
逆ざや相場 backwardation market
逆　　算 reverse operation
逆 算 法 reversal cost method
逆資産効果 negative wealth effect
逆 取 得 reverse acquisition
逆所得税 negative income tax；reverse income tax
逆進課税 regressive taxation
逆 進 税 regressive tax
逆スワップ reversed swap
逆説的な考え方 paradoxical view
逆 選 択 adverse selection
逆 相 殺 reverse offset
逆 担 保 countersecurity
逆デュアル・カレンシー債 reverse dual currency debt
逆 特 恵 converse preference
逆 取 引 reverse transactions
逆 入 札 reversal auction
逆年金モーゲージ RAM (reverse annuity mortgage)
逆の議論 contrary argument
逆 買 収 reverse takeover
逆 ば り resistance operation；trade against the trend
逆ばり投資家 contrarian
逆引振替 debit transfer
逆 日 歩 backwardation rate；negative interest per diem；stock lending rate
逆フローター債 inverse floater
逆 分 割 reverse split
逆ヘッジ reverse hedge
逆変動利付債 reverse floater；reverse floating rate note
逆 方 向 reverse direction
逆優先権 reverse preemption
逆利回り inverse yield
逆利回連続償還債 inverted scale
逆レバレッジ reverse leverage
逆レバレッジド・バイアウト reverse leveraged buyout
却　　下 dismissal
却下する ignore；quash
客観指標 objective indicator
客 観 性 objectivity
客観的確率 objective probability
客観的価値 objective value
客観的情報 objective information
客観的ディフィーザンス・トラスト objective defeasance trust
客観的な証拠 objective proof
CAC40種指数 CAC 40 index
キャッシュ・マッチングの技術 cash-matching techniques
キャッシュ・アンド・キャリー取引 cash

キ

and carry trade
キャッシュ・アンド・キャリー方式 cash and carry system
キャッシュカード cash card
キャッシュ・デフィシエンシー・サポート CDS (cash deficiency support)
キャッシュ・バリュー保険 cash value insurance
キャッシュフロー cash flow
キャッシュフロー危機 cash flow crisis
キャッシュフロー計算 cash flow calculation
キャッシュフロー実績 historical cash flow
キャッシュフロー支払い cash flow payment
キャッシュフロー上の利点 cash flow benefit
キャッシュフロー情報 cash flow information
キャッシュフロー対流動負債 cash flow to current liabilities
キャッシュフローに影響を与えない項目 items not affecting cash flows
キャッシュフローの実績情報 historical cash flow information
キャッシュフローの見方 interpretation of cash flows
キャッシュフローの余力 cushion of cash flow
キャッシュフロー倍率 price cashflow ratio
キャッシュフロー負担倍率 cash flow coverage ratio
キャッシュフローへの影響額 cash flow effect
キャッシュフロー・マッチング・スワップ cashflow matching swap
キャッシュフロー見積法 cash flow estimate method
キャッシュフロー予測 cash flow projection
キャッシュフロー・ラダー分析 cash flow ladder analysis
キャッシュフロー利回り cash flow interest
キャッシュフロー・レシオ cash flow ratio
キャッシュフロー割引 cash flow discount
キャッシュフローを伴わない財務活動 non-cash financing activities
キャッシュフローを伴わない投資活動 non-cash investment activities
キャッシュへの付着 suction to cash
キャッシュ・マネージメント・サービス CMS (cash management service)
キャッシング cash advance
キャット credit authorization terminal
キャッピング capping
キャップ&フロアー cap and floor
ギャップ期間 gapping horizon
キャップ付債 capped floating rate note
キャップ付スワップ capped swap
キャップ付ローン capped loan
ギャップの縮小 leveling effect on the gap
ギャップ分析 gap analysis
ギャップ法 gap management technology
キャップローン cap loan
キャピタル・インデックス債 capital indexed bonds
キャピタル・ギアリング capital gearing
キャピタル・ゲイン capital gain
キャピタル・ゲイン課税 capital gain taxation
キャピタル・ゲインからの控除 exclusion from capital gain
キャピタル・ゲイン税 CGT (capital gain tax)
キャピタル・フロー capital flow
キャピタル・リース capital lease
キャピタル・リスク capital risk
キャピタル・ローン capital loan
キャピタル・ロス capital loss
キャリア・エージェント会社 career company
キャリー carry
キャリー・インカム carry income
キャリー格差 carry differential
キャリー・トレード carry trade
キャリー・トレードの影響 carry considerations
キャリーによる収益 carry pickup

キャリーの向上 adding carry
キャリー面での強み carry advantage ; carry premium
キャリー面での収益見通しの引下げ downgrading carry expectation
キャリー・リターン carry return
ギャロッピング・インフレーション galloping inflation
ギャロップ・ポール Gallup poll
キャンセル可能型スワップ cancelable swap
休　　会 recess
休暇手当 vacation pay
旧株一株につき発行された新株の数 number of new stocks issued per old stock
旧株一株の帳簿価額 book value per old stock
急患治療 acute health care
休業期間中の固定費の補償 compensation for fixed costs during the suspension of business
休業保険 business interruption insurance
究極的貸し手 ultimate lender
究極的な親会社 ultimate parent company
究極のインフレ・ヘッジ ultimate inflation hedge
窮　　屈 tight
急激な減速 sharp slowdown
救　　済 redress
救済合併 relief merger
救済合併方式 assisted acquisition
救済計画 bailout plan
救 済 債 bailout bond
救済条項 bailout clause
救済相場 bailout market
救済措置 bailout
救済の相互性 mutuality of remedy
救 済 法 relief act
救済方法 remedy
救済命令 order for relief
救済融資 relief loan
休止勘定 dormant account
休止残高 dormant balance
CUSIP Committee on Uniform Securities Identification Procedures ; CUSIP (Committee on Uniform Securities Identification Procedures)
吸収合併 absorption and merger ; consolidation take-over
吸収された会社 absorbed corporation
吸収状態 absorbing state
吸収分割 merger split-up
吸収法人 existing corporation to receive assets
求　　償 claim for compensation
求 償 額 amount of claim
求償期間 claim period
求償銀行 claiming bank
求 償 権 guarantor's right of indemnity ; right of indemnity ; surety right
求償債務 recourse debt
求償請求権のある融資 recourse finance
求償貿易 compensation trade
急 上 昇 spike
求 職 者 job hunter
救助物売得金差引精算 salvage loss
救 助 料 salvage charges
級 数 法 sum-of-the-years-digits method
急 成 長 fast growth
急成長株ファンド aggressive growth mutual fund
急　　増 considerable rise ; rapid surge ; spurt
Q-TIP信託 Q-TIP (qualified terminable interest property) trust
急　　騰 precipitous rise ; sharp rise ; sharp run-up
急騰している skyrocketing
急騰する soar
急騰相場 sharp advance market
キューバ・ペソ CUP (Cuban peso)
急 反 転 back up
急反転市場 backed up market
急 反 落 sharp loss ; sharp setback
救 貧 法 poor laws
給　　付 benefit
給付額確定済給付額 accrued benefit
給付額・勤務年数方式 benefit / years of service method

キ

給付確定率 accrual rate
給付期間 benefit period
給付期間制限条項 cutoff clause
給付金支払請求宣誓供述書 affidavit of claim
給付金支払代行会社 claims administrator
給付契約 benefit policy
給付現価 present value of future benefits
給付減額 benefit reduction
給付限度額 policy limit
給付小切手 benefit check
給付最高額 benefit maximum
給付債務 benefit obligation
給付削減 reduction in benefit
給付支払い benefit payment
給付支払期日 due date of benefit payment
給付支払いシステム benefit claim system
給付受領権 accrued benefit
給付制限 benefit restriction
給付建会計処理 defined benefit accounting
給付建キオ・プラン defined benefit Keogh plan
給付建債務 defined benefit obligation
給付建制度の正味資産 net employee benefit assets for defined benefit plan
給付建制度の正味負債 net employee benefit liabilities for defined benefit plan
給付建退職年金制度 fixed benefit retirement plan
給付建複数事業主制度 defined benefit multi-employer plan
給付調整審査 integration test
給付特約 benefit rider
給付の改善 benefit improvement
給付の確定 accrual of benefit
給付の帰属 attribution of benefit
給付の最高額 maximum benefit
給付の種類 type of benefit
給付の増加 benefit increase
給付の通算可能性 transferability of benefits
給付の分配 distribution of benefit
給付保証 benefit security
給付保証率 benefit security ratio
級別生産物生産 class-product production
窮乏化政策 impoverishing theory
旧法による税収入 transitional revenue from repealed taxes
旧保険契約 old policy
休眠会員 sleeping member
休眠期間 quiet period
休眠口座 sleeping account
休眠資産 dormant assets
給　　与 salary；wage
給与基準 basis on the amount of salary
給与共済課 Allowance Control and Mutual Assistance Insurance Division
給与繰延べ salary deferral
給与差押 wage garnishment
給与指数 salary scale
給与所得 employment income
給与所得控除 deduction for employment income
給与所得者 employment income earner；person receiving employment income
給与所得に係る源泉徴収 withholding on employment income
給与所得の源泉徴収票 withholding record of employment income
給与水準 pay level
給 与 税 payroll tax
給与体系 pay package
給与調査官 Special Officer for Research on Allowance Control
給与天引 payroll deduction；payroll withholding；salary savings
給与天引型投信 payroll deduction type investment trust
給与天引口座 salary deduction account
給与天引制度 salary reduction plan
給与凍結 salary freeze
給与の差押禁止 prohibition of seizure on salaries
給与とみなされる年金 annuity regarded as salaries and wages

給与年金制度 salary pension plan
給与の下落 declining salary
給与の上昇 salary growth
給与比例掛金 percentage of payroll cost
給与比例給付 wage related benefit
給与比例年金方式 flat percentage plan
給与予測 salary projections
急　落 collapse；sharp fall；steeper fall
急落相場 sharp decline market
急落銘柄 air pocket issue
給　料 salaries
給料監査 pay roll audit
給料控除 wage assignment
給料日 payday
給料前払い advance of salary
キュラソー預託証券 CDR (Curacao depository receipt)
キュラソー預託証書 Curacao depositary receipts
教育委員会 board of education
教育産業 education industry
教育資金積立 school fee savings
教育水準 level of education
教育費 education expense
教育費用個人退職勘定 education IRA (individual retirement account)
教育ローン education loan
教員研修センター National Center for Teachers' Development
共益権 rights for profit sharing
共益債権 common interest claims
饗　応 treating
協　会 association
協会ストライキ騒じょう暴動担保約款 institute strikes, riots and civil commotion clauses
協会戦争危険担保約款 institute war clauses
協会盗難不着担保約款 institute theft, pilferage and non-delivery clauses
協会約款 institute clauses
境　界 bounds
境界危険 border line risk
境界線 boundary
境界点 cut-off point
業　界 business circle；industry segments
業界運営の industry run
業界慣行 industry practice
業界基準 industry norms；industry standard
業界再編 industry realignment
業界団体 industry associations
業界の集中度 industry focus
業界の取決め industry arrangement
業界平均 industry average
強化する beef up
行間記入 interlineations
協　議 conference
協議事項 agenda
協議発行 negotiated sale
協議引受 negotiated underwriting
供給価格 supply price
供給過多 oversupply
供給側の要因 supply side factor
供給関数 supply function
供給管理 management of supply
供給曲線 supply curve；supply schedule
供給契約 supply arrangements
供給源 supply source
供給サイド supply side
供給弾性値 elasticity of supply
供給能力 supply capacity
供給不足 short supply
業　況 business circumstances
恐　慌 crisis
恐慌市場 panic market
恐慌相場 near-panic market
競合過失 concurrent negligence
競合管轄権 concurrent jurisdiction
競合企業 competitor
競合資産 competing assets
競合マーケット・メーカー・システム competitive market maker system
強行規定 forcible provisions
強公準 strong axiom
強硬な介入 forceful intervention
強硬路線 hard-line
強固な robust

キ

共　済 mutual aid
共済掛金 mutual aid premium
共済監査官 Inspector for Mutual Assistance Insurance
共 済 金 mutual aid money
共済金制度 mutual aid system
共済組合 aid societies；benefit society；fraternal association；fraternal mutual benefit society；mutual aid association
共済計理官 Actuary for Mutual Assistance Insurance
共済生命保険 fraternal life insurance
共済団体 benefit association
共済調査官 Special Officer for Research on Mutual Assistance
共済年金 mutual-aid pension
共済保険 cooperative insurance；mutual assistance insurance
業者間相場 dealers' market
業者間ブローカー IDB (inter-dealer broker)
業者による投機相場 broker's market
業者割引 trade discount
強　弱 strong and weak
強弱指数 bull and bear index
業　種 category of business
拠出金の繰越 contribution carryover
供述録取書（使用の）禁止 suppression of deposition
業種の循環 group rotation
業 種 別 by types of industry
業種別内訳 breakdown by industry
業種別貸出統計 loans and discounts by industry
業種別株価指数 narrow based stock index；sector-stock price index
業種別株価指数先物取引 stock price index futures by industry
業種別組入率 industry weighting ratio
業種別セグメント industry segment
業種別利回り average yield by types of industry
協　商 entente
鋏状価格差 scissors-form difference in price
行 商 人 cheap-jack；itinerant merchants
行政措置 regulatory action
行政改革 reform of the administrative structure；regulatory reform
行政改革・規制改革担当大臣 Minister of State for Administrative Reform and Regulatory Reform
行政解釈 administrative interpretation
行政活動 government administrative activity
行政官庁 regulatory authority
行政管理予算局 OMB (Office of Management and Budget)
行政救済 administrative remedy
行政協約 executive agreement
行 政 権 administrative power
行政権限 administrative power
行政検査 regulatory examination
行政行為 administrative act
行政コスト計算書 statement of administrative cost
行政サービス室 Office of Administrative Services
行政財産 government administrative property
行政裁量 administrative discretion
行政指導 administrative guidance
行政職員 administrative officer
行政処分 administrative action；administrative disposition
行政相談官 Administrative Counselor
行政訴訟 administrative dispute；administrative litigation
行政訴訟審判官室 Office of Administrative Law Judges
行政能力 regulatory capacity
行政評価 administration evaluation
行政不服審査法 administrative appellate law
行 政 法 administrative law
行政命令 administrative order
行政立法 administrative legislation
強制解約 compulsory cancellation

強制合併 forced merger；statutory merger
強制加入 compulsory membership；compulsory participation；involuntary participation
強制加入健康保険 compulsory social health insurance
強制加入国営保険 mandatory state insurance
強制加入年金 compulsory pension
強制加入年金制度 mandated pension plan
強制換価 compulsory conversion into money
強制換価手続 procedure of the compulsory conversion into money
強制監査 compulsory audit
強制競売 compulsory sale by auction；forced auction
強制権 enforceable right
強制債務証書 bill obligatory
強制執行 compulsory execution；forcible execution
強制実名取引 mandatory real name transaction
強制支払不能 involuntary insolvency
強制償還 mandatory redemption
強制償還の mandatory redeemable
強制処分 forcible disposition
強制処分価値 forced-sale value
強制する enforce
強制する理由 compelling reason
強制清算 compulsory winding-up；forced liquidation；involuntary liquidation
強制訴訟参加 cross claim
強制退職 mandatory retirement
強制担保差換え mandatory collateral substitution
強制調査 criminal investigation
強制徴収 forced collection
強制貯蓄 forced saving
強制通貨 enforced currency
強制通用力 legally defined payment instrument that should not be refused by any creditor in satisfaction of any debt
強制通用力ある紙幣 legal tender note
強制的 compulsory
強制的給付 compulsory benefit
強制的減債基金条項 mandatory sinking fund requirement
強制的交換 forced exchange
強制的譲渡 involuntary transfer
強制的清算 compulsory liquidation
強制的仲裁 compulsory arbitration
強制的転換 forced conversion
強制的な認識 mandatory recognition
強制適用 mandated offer
強制撤退 compulsory withdrawal
強制転換 involuntary conversion
強制転換社債 mandatory convertible bond；mandatory convertibles
強制転換証券 mandatory convertible securities
強制取引 forced transaction
強制売却処分 enforced liquidation
強制売買 juridical sale
強制破産 involuntary bankruptcy
強制保険 compulsory insurance
強制履行 office grant
強制和議 compulsory composition；compulsory reconciliation
矯正する rectify
業績 bottom line；business results；earnings performance
業績悪化 earnings deterioration
業績概要 overview of the business results
業績基準 performance criteria
業績記録 track record
業績計算書 performance statement
業績好調 robust earnings
業績指標 performance indicators
業績条件 performance conditions
業績水準 performance standard
業績相場 profit-driven market
業績の影響 effect of performance
業績の上昇 upswing on business results
業績の悪い会社 under performing company；unprofitable company
業績比較 performance comparison

キ

業績評価 evaluation of performance；performance appraisal
業績評価会計 performance accounting
業績比率 operating performance ratios
業績比例報酬体系 performance-based fee system
業績不振の ailing
業績報告 performance reporting
業績報告書 performance report；statement of performance
業績報告の問題 performance reporting issue
業績見通し business outlook
業績見通しの下方修正 downward revision on business results
業績目標 performance target
業績モデル performance model
業績予算 performance budget
業績予想 forecast of performance results
業績連動証券 performance unit
競争圧力 competition pressure
競争価格 competitive price
競争市場価格 competitive market price
競争上の損害 competitive harm
競争上の不利益 competitive disadvantage
競争制限政策 policy for restricting competition
競争制限的な anticompetitive
競争促進政策 policy for promoting competition
競争的平価切下げ competitive depreciation
競争的利回入札 competitive yield auction
競争入札 bid by advertising；competitive bid；competitive tender
競争入札オークション multiple price auction
競争売買 auction
競争売買の原則 rules of auction
競争販売 competitive sale
競争品取扱禁止契約 exclusive dealing
競争料率 competitive rate
競争力 competitive edge；competitiveness
競争力の懸念 competitiveness concern
供託 payment into court
供託者 depositor
供託所 deposit office
供託物 deposited article
供託法 deposit law
協調介入 concerted intervention；coordinated intervention
協調行動 concerted activities
協調融資 co-finance；syndicated loan
協調利下げ coordinated cut
共通鍵暗号 symmetric cryptographic algorithm；symmetric key algorithm
共通関税 common tariff
共通原価 common cost
共通財 common goods
共通支配下の取引 transactions between entities under common control
共通担保 common collateral
共通点 analogy
共通農業政策 common agriculture policy
共通の基盤 common background
共通の懸念 common concern
共通の支配 common control
共通要因リスク common factor risk
共通リスク common risk
協定 accord
協定価格 agreed price；stipulated price
協定関税 conventional tariff
協定借地 leased land under a convention
協定世界時 UTC (coordinated universal time)
協定賃金 contractual wage
協定貿易 trade by agreement
協定保険価額 agreed insured value
協定料率 tariff by agreement
協同組合 cooperative association；cooperative society
協同組合銀行 bank for cooperative
協同組織金融機関 cooperative organization type financial institution
協同組織金融機関の優先出資に関する法律 Law Concerning Preferred Equity Contribution to Cooperative

Financial Institution
協同組織金融室 Cooperative Financial Institutions Office
共同委託 joint entrustment
共同化委員会 synergy committee
共同海損 general average
共同海損犠牲損害 general average sacrifice
共同海損行為 general average act
共同海損費用 general average expenditure
共同海損分担額 general average contribution
共同海損盟約書 average bond
共同買付 joint purchase
共同開発 joint development
共同関係 joint relationship
共同監査 joint audit
共同管財人 co-trustee
共同勘定 common account；joint account
共同管理 joint management
共同計算契約 pooling contracts
共同口座契約 joint account agreement
共同債権買取機構 CCPC (Cooperative Credit Purchasing Company)
共同市場 common market
共同施設税 public facilities tax
共同支配 joint control
共同支配企業 jointly controlled entity
共同支配の jointly controlled
共同支配の営業活動体 Jointly controlled operations
共同支配の資産 jointly controlled assets
共同主幹事 co-lead manager
共同所有者 co-owner
共同新設分割 divesture of businesses by two or more entities to establish a new entity which issues equity interests in exchange for businesses
共同スポンサー co-sponsor
共同生存者年金 joint and survivor annuity
共同責任 joint liability
共同相続人 joint-heir
共同訴訟 joint action
共同第一抵当権 pooled first mortgage
共同担保 security on combined properties
共 同 の joint
共同パートナー joint partners
共同販売 cooperative marketing；joint marketing；joint sales
共同引受保険 subscription policy
共同被告 co-defendant
共同プール common pool
共同負担 co-payment
共同負担リスク shared risk
共同振出人 co-maker
共同フロート joint float
共同変動相場 joint currency float；joint-floating exchange rate
共同法定相続人 co-heir
共同保険 co-insurance
共同保証 joint guarantee
共同保証人 cosureties
共同歩調を取る mounting concerted efforts
共同持株会社 joint holding company
共同遺言 joint will
共同融資 joint financing
競　　売 auction sale
競売市場 auction market
競売手数料 lot money
競 売 人 auctioneer
競売のサクラ puffer
競 売 買 buying-in and selling-out
競売寄付値段 upset price
脅　　迫 threat
共 分 散 covariance
共分散分析 covariance analysis
興　　味 appetite
業　　務 affairs
業務粗利益 gross operating income
業務委託契約 service agreement
業務委託費 outsourcing service expenses
業務運営法人 operating company
業務概況書 outline of business operations
業務会計 accounting for administrative expenses

キ

業務監査 business operations audit；performance audit
業務基準 practice standards
業務規程 business regulations
業務規程特例 special rule of the business regulations
業 務 局 Operations Department
業務兼業制限 limitation on interlocking
業務執行 business execution
業務執行者 operating officer
業務主処罰制度 proprietor punishment
業務純益 net business profit；net operating income
業務上過誤保険 malpractice insurance
業務上災害 work related injury
業務上の意思決定 operating decision
業務上の事故 on-the-job accident
業務上の収益の補償 compensation for profit from business
業務上の提携 entry into a business affiliation
業務遂行確実性 deliverability
業務調整官 Special Officer for Liaison and Inspection of the Local Finance Bureaus
業務調整室 Office of Liaison, Inspection and ADP Management of the Local Finance Bureaus
業務の概要 picture of the business
業務の妨げ hindrance to business
業務の執行 execution of duties
業務の条件 conditions of operations
業務の状態 state of the business operation
業務の内容 nature of business
業務の範囲 scope of operations
業務のレビュー operating review
業務への干渉 interference with business
業務報告書 business report
業務方法書 written statement of manners of conducting business
協　　約 pact
共　　有 co-ownership；joint ownership
共有資産 common property
共 有 者 co-owners；part-owners
共有する特徴 shared characteristics
共有不動産権 tenancy in common
共有物分割 partition
共有持ち分 shared equities
教 養 費 expenses for education and culture
強力な制限事項 strong covenant
行列乗数 matrix multiplier
行列簿記 matrix bookkeeping
許　　可 admission
巨額の投資 considerable investment
寄与過失 contributory negligence
虚偽な表示 false representation
虚 偽 の simulated
虚偽の記載 false statement
虚偽の商品の表示 false trade description
虚偽の資料 false documents
虚偽の申告 false return
虚偽の報告 false report
漁業協同組合 fishery cooperatives
局 bureau
局所的期待仮説 local expectation hypothesis
局所マーチンゲール local martingale
玉 整 理 liquidation of speculative accounts
曲　　線 curve
局　　長 director-general
極度貸付枠 revolving line of credit
居　　住 abode
居住外国人 resident alien
居住外国法人 resident foreign corporation
居 住 者 resident
居住者外貨預金 resident foreign currency deposits
居住者ユーロ円債 Euroyen bond for resident
居住用財産 property for residence；residential property
居住用資産の売買特例 special rule of trading of residential assets
拠出型退職年金 contributory retirement plan
拠出型の contribution defined
拠出期間 contribution payment period

拠 出 金 contribution money
拠出限度額 maximum contribution
拠出資本 contributed capital；contributed stock
拠 出 者 contributor
拠出剰余金 contributed surplus
拠出制給付 contributory benefit
拠出制団体保険 contributory group insurance
拠出制度 contribution plan；contributory plan
拠出相当保険料 contribution equivalent premium
拠出年数 years for contribution
拠出能力 ability to make contributions
拠 出 率 contribution rate
居　　所 temporary residence
寄与侵害 contributory infringement
拒　　絶 repudiation
拒絶覚書 note of protest
拒 絶 者 protestor
拒絶証書 memorandum of protest；rejection certificate
拒絶証書作成手数料 protest charges
拒絶証書不要 no protest
拒絶証書不要文言 protest waived
拒絶する renounce
巨大危険 target risk
巨大災害損失準備金 catastrophic loss reserve
巨大投資家 elephant
巨大な潜在力 massive potential
巨大リスク catastrophic risk；large risks
許 認 可 official approval
拒 否 権 veto
寄 与 分 contributory shares of estate
許容逸税率 tolerable deviation rate
許容原価 allowed cost
許容限度 tolerance limit
許容限度額 allowable maximum amount
許容誤差 permissible error
許 容 差 tolerance
許容しえない inadmissible
許容水準 tolerance level
許容すべき admissible
許容する allow
許容変動幅内介入 intramarginal intervention
許 容 率 tolerable rate
許容レンジ edges of the band
居留地貿易 settlement trade
切上げる round up
切　　替 changeover
切 下 げ devaluation
切下げリスク devaluation risk
切下げる devalue；round down
切り捨てる disregard
切り詰め retrenchment
既履行の executed
ギリシャ・ドラクマ GRD (Greek drachma)
ギリシャ保管振替機関 BOGS；CSD
キリバス・ドル AUD (Kiribati dollar)
ギルダー債 guilder bond
ギルト・エッジ債 gilt-edged bond
ギルト債入札 gilt auction
ギルト債利回り gilt yield
記　　録 log
記録裁判所 court of record
記録事項 matter of record
記録的な額 record amount
記録による by record
記 録 日 record date
記録不提出 failing to submit a record
記録保存 record keeping
議　　論 controversy
際立った特徴 outstanding feature
均一給付制度 flat benefit plan
均一給与 flat salary
均一給与年金制度 flat salary pension plan
均一金額 flat amount
均一税率税 flat rate tax
均一手数料 flat commission
均一年金 flat sum pension
均一料金 flat price
近因主義 cause proximate
金外信託 non-money trust
金　　額 amount
金額加重収益率 money-weighted rate of return

キ

金額加重の amount weighted
金貨兌換紙幣 gold note
金貨本位制 gold coin standard
銀 為 替 silver exchange
緊急オークション emergency auction
緊急課税 tax in jeopardy
緊急関税 emergency duty ; emergency tariff
緊急景気対策 emergency economic package
緊急資金 contingency fund
緊急事態 emergency
緊急償却 emergency amortization
緊急取引証拠金 emergency clearing margin
緊急問題専門委員会 EITF (Emerging Issues Task Force)
緊急融資 emergency loan ; emergency rate relief
緊急輸入 emergency import
緊急立法 emergency legislation
キングストン体制 Kingston Regime
金　　庫 chest
金 庫 株 treasury stock
金 庫 室 vault
金庫制度 vault system
禁固以上の刑 penalty heavier than imprisonment
禁 固 刑 sentenced to imprisonment
均衡価格 equilibrium price
均衡為替相場 equilibrium rate of exchange
均衡財政 balanced public finance
均衡成長 balanced growth
均 衡 点 equilibrium point
均衡分析 equilibrium analysis
均衡への回帰 return to equilibrium
均衡予算 balanced budget
均衡予算主義 balanced budget principle
均衡予算定理 balanced budget theorem
均衡利子率 equilibrium rate of interest
銀　　行 bank
銀行預り金 deposit due to bank
銀行預入金 bank placement
銀行預け金 deposit due from bank
銀行委任書 bank mandate
銀 行 家 banker
銀行カード bank card
銀行貸付 bank lending
銀行貸付保険 bank loan insurance
銀行借入 bank borrowing ; bank debt ; loan from banks ; owing to bank
銀行借入金 bank loan payable
銀行借換え bank refinancing
銀行為替 bank money order
銀行為替手形 BD (bank draft)
銀行監査 audit of banks
銀行間市場 interbank money market
銀行勘定照合表 statement of reconciliation of bank account
銀行勘定調整表 bank reconciliation
銀行間相場 inter-bank rate
銀行監督委員会 Commission Bancaire
銀行間の inter-bank
銀行間預金 inter-bank deposit
銀行間預金金利 interest rate on inter-bank deposit
銀行規制 banking regulation
銀行規制監督に関するバーゼル委員会 Basel Committee on Banking Regulation and Supervision
銀行休業日 bank holiday
銀行協会 bankers association
銀行業界 banking industry
銀行恐慌 bank crisis
銀行業先物 banks futures
銀行業務 bank activities ; banking business
銀 行 局 banking department
銀行系カード credit card issued by bank or its subsidiary
銀行系クレジット・カード bank credit card
銀行経済時評 bank letter
銀行系証券会社 bank affiliated securities firm
銀 行 券 bank paper ; BN (bank note)
銀行券供給 banknote supply
銀行検査 bank examination
銀行検査官 bank examiner

銀行券製造原価 cost of production of banknotes
銀行券取扱高 volume of banknotes handled
銀行券に関する制度 system related to banknotes
銀行券に関する法律 laws related to banknotes
銀行券に対する信認 public confidence in banknotes
銀行券の鑑査 examination of banknotes
銀行券の還収 withdrawal of banknotes from circulation
銀行券の偽造防止策等 anti-counterfeiting features of banknotes
銀行券の失効 voiding of banknotes
銀行券の特徴 characteristics of banknotes
銀行券の発行 issuance of banknotes
銀行券の平均発行高 average outstanding amount of banknotes issued
銀行券発行残高 amount outstanding of banknotes issued
銀行口座 bank account
銀行公報 banking circular
銀行小切手 bank check；cashier's check ；official check
銀行サービス banking service
銀 行 債 bank bond
銀行残高 balance per bank
銀行識別コード BIC (bank identifier code)
銀行事業 banking
銀行資金ポジション bank fund position
銀行自己資本規制 bank capital requirements
銀行自動引落システム bank's automatic accounts transfer system
銀行主義 banking doctrine；banking principle
銀行準備 bank reserve
銀行照会 bank reference
銀行証券垣根論争 issue of the wall between banking and securities business
銀行信用 bank credit
銀行信用状 bank letter of credit；banker's credit
銀行出納係 bank clerk
銀行送金 bank remittance
銀行第１課 Banks Division 1
銀行第２課 Banks Division 2
銀 行 団 banking syndicate
銀行調査 audit on bank account
銀行通帳 bank book
銀行ディーラー bank dealer
銀行手形 bank bill；bank draft；banker's bill
銀行手形引受保証 bank acceptance guarantee
銀行手数料 bank charges
銀行デビットカード bank debit card
銀行当座借越し bank overdraft
銀行倒産 bank failure
銀行投資契約 bank sponsored investment contract
銀行投資適格債 bank quality
銀行取引停止処分 disposition by suspension of bank credit；suspension of banking transaction
銀行取引の停止 suspension of bank account
銀行取引日 banking day
銀行取引約定書 banking transaction contract
銀行に担保できる bankable
銀行による証券金融 security credit by banks
銀行年金商品 bank annuity product
銀行のアベイラビリティ availability of bank
銀行の銀行 bank of banks
銀行の警戒感 bank caution
銀行の誤謬 bank error
銀行の債務 bank senior obligation
銀行の信用状 bank's standby letter of credit
銀行の保険業務の権能 bank insurance powers
銀行の保険引受 bank underwriting insurance

キ

キ

銀行離れ disintermediation of bank
銀行引受け bank acceptance
銀行引受手形 BA (bank acceptance)；banker's acceptance bill
銀行引受手形割引 discount on banker's acceptances
銀行フルディーリング bank full dealing
銀 行 法 Banking Law
銀行包括保証 banker's blanket bond
銀行報告書 bank statement
銀行法令 Banking Law and Regulations
銀行簿記 bank bookkeeping
銀行簿記会計機 bank bookkeeping machine
銀行保険基金 bank insurance fund
銀行保証 bank guarantee
銀行POS bank point-of-sales
銀行免許 bank license
銀行持株会社 BHC (bank holding company)
銀行持株会社法 Bank Holding Company Act
銀行約定 bank arrangement
銀行ユーザンス bank usance
銀行融資 bank financing；bank loan
銀行融資団 bankers syndicate
銀行融資枠 bank credit agreement
銀行預金 bank deposit；cash in bank
銀行預金残高 balance at the bank；bank balance；bank deposit balance
銀行預金残高証明書 certificate of bank deposit balances
銀行預金振替制度 bank giro
銀行預金利息 interest accrued from deposit in bank
銀行与信枠 bank credit line
銀行利子 bank interest；interest on bank deposit
銀行リスク banking risk
銀行流動性 bank liquidity；liquidity of the banking system
銀行利率 bank rate
銀行割引方法 bank discount method
銀行割引率 bank discount basis；bank discount rate
銀行割引料 bank discount
金 為 替 gold exchange
金為替準備 gold exchange reserve
金為替本位制 gold exchange standard
金銀複本位制度 gold and silver bimetallism
金現送点 gold point
金購入ワラント gold purchase warrant
金 債 券 gold bond
金 先 物 gold futures
金先物オプション gold futures option
金先物契約 gold bullion futures contract
金 地 金 gold bullion
金地金本位制 gold bullion standard
金 指 数 gold index
金 準 備 gold reserve
金準備法 Gold Reserve Act of 1934
金 証 券 gold certificate
金信奉者 gold bug
金 選 好 preference for gold
金 兌 換 conversion to gold
金建値決定 gold pricing
金 担 保 gold collateral
金転換証券 gold convertible securities
金投資口座 gold accounts
金ドル準備 gold and dollar reserve
金の現送点 specie points
金プール gold pool
金不胎化政策 gold sterilization policy
金 平 価 gold par value；gold parity
金保有高 gold holdings
金本位基準 gold basis
金本位制 gold standard
金本位制度崩壊 fall of gold standard
金 約 款 gold clause
金輸出解禁 lifting of gold embargo
金輸出点 gold export point
金輸入点 gold import point
金ワラント gold warrant
禁　　止 ban
禁止期間 prohibited period
禁止的差止命令 prohibitive injunction
禁止的税 prohibitive tax
禁止的法律 negative statute
禁止命令 restraining order

近視眼的ポートフォリオ myopic portfolio
近似する approximate
近似性 proximity
近似値理論 theory of approximation
近似的ファクター approximate factor
緊縮財政 tight budget
緊縮財政案 tight fiscal package
緊縮財政政策 austere fiscal policy；restrictive fiscal policy
緊縮予算 austere budget
近親者 immediate family
禁制品 contraband
近接損害 proximate damage
近接の adjoining
金銭遺贈 pecuniary legacy
金銭貸付業 money lending business
金銭給付 financial benefit
金銭項目 monetary items
金銭債権 monetary receivables；money claim
金銭債権債務 monetary receivables or payables
金銭債権の超過状態 positive monetary position
金銭債務 monetary obligation
金銭債務状態 negative monetary position
金銭出資 equity contribution in cash；money contribution
金銭上納 tax payment in money
金銭上の価値 pecuniary value
金銭上の関係 pecuniary relation
金銭上の利益 pecuniary gain
金銭信託 monetary trust；money in trust
金銭信託の範囲 scope of money trust funds
金銭信託利益 income from trust deposits
金銭貸借契約 loan agreement
金銭担保 cash collateral
金銭的損害 pecuniary damage
金銭的評価 quantum evaluation
金銭的報酬 pecuniary considerations
金銭取扱者 cash handling clerk
金銭取引 pecuniary transaction
金銭の引換券 exchange check for money
金銭判決 money judgment
金銭法案 money bill
勤続10年完全受給権付与方式 10-year full vesting formula
勤続手当 long service allowance
勤続年数 accrued service
金属製品業界 metal products industry
近代化計画 modernization program
近代経済学 modern economics
禁治産 incompetency
禁治産者 incompetent person；person adjudged incompetent
均等加重平均 equal-weighted average
均等化配当 equalizing dividend
均等債務返済 level debt service
均等税 flat tax
均等平準年次配当 equivalent level annual dividend
均等利回評価額 amortized value
均等割課税 taxation on per capita basis
均等割税率 per capita levy
禁反言 estoppel
均分 equally divided
銀の自由鋳造 free silver
銀本位制 silver standard
勤務期間参入 service credit
勤務期間平均給与 average career earnings
勤務中死亡給付 death-in-service benefit
勤務の比例配分による発生給付方式 accrued benefit method pro-rated on service
勤務費用 service cost
禁輸 embargo
金融・信用規制 monetary and credit control
金融エンジニアリング financial engineering
金融援助 financial aid
金融オプション financial options
金融オプション契約 financial option contract
金融オプション市場 financial option market
金融街 finance street
金融会社 finance company；financing corporation

キ

金融会社室（ノンバンク管理室） Non-Bank Finance Companies Office
金融外取引 non-financial transaction
金融革新 financial evolution；financial innovation
金融拡大 monetary expansion；monetary growth
金融革命 financial revolution
金融活動 financial activities
金 融 株 financial sector stocks
金融環境 financial environment
金融勘定 balance of monetary movements；financial accounts
金融監督庁 Financial Supervisory Agency
金融監督庁長官 Commissioner of the Financial Supervisory Agency
金融緩慢 slackness of money market
金融緩和 easiness of the money market；easy credit；monetary accommodation
金融緩和政策 accommodative monetary policy；easy monetary policy；relaxation of tight money policy
金融緩和措置 monetary easing measures
金融機関 banking facilities；financial institution；provider of finance
金融機関貸付金 loan to financial institutions
金融機関検査 inspection of financial institutions
金融機関等に対する一時貸付 temporary loans to financial institutions
金融機関による資産の自己査定 financial institution's self-assessment of assets
金融機関の斡旋 good offices of banking facilities；introduction of banking facilities
金融機関の合併及び転換に関する法律 Law Concerning Amalgamation and Conversion of Financial Institutions
金融機関の動向 behavior of financial institution
金融機関の有価証券保有 securities investment by financial institutions
金融機関のリスク管理 risk management by financial institutions
金融機関離れ financial disintermediation
金融機関預金 deposit at financial institutions
金融危機対応会議 Financial System Management Council
金融危機対応室 Financial Crisis Relation Office
金融規制 financial regulation
金融規制当局 financial regulator
金融機能早期健全化会計貸付 loans to Account for Early Strengthening of Financial Functions
金融機能早期健全化法 Financial Function Early Strengthening Law
金 融 業 financial operations
金融業界 financial community；financing business industry
金融恐慌 financial crisis；financial panic
金融業者 money broker；money lender
金融協定 financial agreement
金融業の性質 nature of financial service
金融組合 loan association；loan society
金融クロス crossing for the purpose of financing
金融経済月報 Monthly Report of Recent Economic and Financial Developments
金融経済動向 economic and financial development
金融研究 Monetary and Economic Studies
金融研究所 financial research center
金融検査マニュアル Financial Inspection Manual
金融公報中央委員会 Central Council for Financial Services Information
金融項目 financial item
金融子会社 captive finance company
金融サービス financial facilities；financial service
金融サービス業界 financial service

industry
金融サービス法 FSA (Financial Services Act)
金 融 債 bank debenture
金融債権 financial claim
金融再生 financial regeneration
金融再生委員会 Financial Reconstruction Commission
金融再生会計貸付 loans to Financial Reconstruction Account
金融再生法 Financial Revitalization Law
金融再生法開示債権 loans disclosed subject to the Financial Revitalization Law
金融再保険 financial reinsurance
金融債務 financial obligation
金融先物 financial futures
金融先物オプション financial futures option
金融先物契約 financial futures contract
金融先物市場 financial futures market
金融先物商品 financial futures instrument
金融先物清算機関 financial futures clearing house
金融先物取引 financial futures transaction
金融先物取引業者 financial futures broker
金融先物取引口座開設申込書 application for financial futures transaction account
金融先物取引口座設定約諾書 agreement for the account for financial futures transaction
金融先物取引所 financial futures exchange
金融先物取引説明書 explanatory leaflet for financial futures transaction
金融先物取引専門円口座 yen account specifically for financial futures transaction
金融先物取引に関する確認書 confirmation for financial futures transaction
金融先物取引法 Financial Futures Trading Law
金融先物取引用印鑑届 registration of signet for financial futures transaction
金融先渡契約 financial forward contract
金融支援 financial support
金融刺激政策 stimulative monetary policy
金融資源 financial resources
金融資産 financial assets
金融資産価値 financial asset value
金融資産選好 preference of financial assets
金融資産の残存部分 remainders of financial assets
金融資産のプール pool of financial assets
金融資産負債残高表 financial assets and liabilities account
金融資産利益率 return on financial assets
金融市場 financial market
金融市場介入 money market intervention
金融市場開放 open-up of money market
金融市場格差 money market differential
金融市場協議会 Working Group of Financial Markets
金融市場局 Financial Markets Department
金融市場グローバル化 financial market globalization
金融市場証券 money market securities
金融市場情勢指標 money market conditions index
金融市場調節 money market control
金融市場調節方針 guidelines on money market operations
金融市場データ money market data
金融市場の機能不全 disruption of financial markets
金融市場の自由化 financial market liberalization
金融市場の不安定性 financial market instability
金融市場評議会 CMF (Conseil des Marchés Financiers)
金融市場分析 financial market analysis
金融市場へのアクセス access to capital market
金融システム政策 financial system policy

キ

キ

金融システムの安定 financial system stability
金融システムの安定化に向けた制度上の枠組み institutional framework for financial system stability
金融システムの脆弱性 fragility of financial system
金融指標 financial indexes；monetary indicators
金融資本 financial capital
金融資本市場 financial and capital markets
金融・資本市場の自由化 deregulation of financial and capital market
金融資本市場の動向 developments in the financial and capital markets
金融収益 financial income；financial profit
金融自由化 deregulation of finance
金融自由化政策 financial liberalization policy
金融自由化対策資金 Financial Liberalization Fund
金融条件指数 financial conditions index
金融上の債務 financial commitments
金融商品 financial instrument；financial product；financing vehicle
金融商品会計 accounting for financial instruments
金融商品会計基準 accounting standards for financial instruments
金融商品の再調達 refinancing of instruments
金融商品の範囲 scope of financial instruments
金融情報交換プロトコル financial information exchange protocol
金融情報システムセンター FISC (Center for Financial Industry Information Systems)
金融情報欄 financial table
金融審議会 Financial System Council
金融スーパーマーケット financial・supermarket
金融政策 financial policy；monetary policy
金融政策決定会合 MPM (Monetary Policy Meeting)
金融政策手段 monetary policy tool
金融政策による刺激策 monetary policy stimulus
金融政策の復活 revival of monetary policy
金融制度 financial system
金融制度改革 reform of financial system
金融制度調査会 Financial System Research Council
金融整理管財人 financial reorganization administrator
金融セクター financial sector
金融損益 financing profit or loss
金融体制 monetary regime
金融担当・経済財政政策担当大臣 Minister of State for Financial Services, Economic and Fiscal Policy
金融担当大臣 Minister for Financial Services
金融知識 financial knowledge；financial sophistication
金融仲介 financial intermediation
金融仲介機関 financial intermediaries or brokers；financial intermediary
金融仲介機能 financial intermediary function
金融中心地 financial center
金 融 庁 FSA (Financial Services Agency)
金融調査 financial survey
金融調節 monetary control；money market management
金融調節オペ適格銘柄国債 bills and bonds eligible for market operations
金融調節事項 monetary control matters
金融庁長官 Commissioner of the Financial Services Agency
金融貯蓄商品 financial savings products
金融手形 finance bill
金融手数料 financial service fee
金融統計 financial statistics
金融取引 financing transaction

金 融 難 financial difficulty
金融ニーズ法 financial needs approach
金融のグローバル化 financial globalization
金融派生商品市場 derivatives market
金融引締め credit squeeze；credit tightening；draining reserves；fiscal squeeze
金融引締政策 restrictive monetary policy；tight monetary policy
金融引締政策の浸透 penetration of tight monetary policy
金融引締めの浸透 permeation of tight money policy
金融逼迫 credit crunch
金融費用 finance charge；financial expenses；financing charge
金融費用カバレッジ fixed charge coverage
金融ピラミッド financial pyramid
金融不況 financial recession
金融負債 financial liability
金融負担 financing burden
金融法委員会 Financial Law Board
金融崩壊 financial collapse
金融保証 financial guarantee
金融保証保険 FGI (financial guarantee insurance)
金融面での決断 financial decision
金融面の動き financial development
金融持株会社 financial holding company
金融モデル financial model
金融リース financial lease
金　　利 interest rate；money rate
金利オプション interest option；interest rate option
金利オプション取引 interest option transaction
金利改訂日 repricing date of interest rate
金利カラー interest rate collar
金利感応型終身保険 interest sensitive whole life
金利感応型商品 interest-sensitive products
金利感応ギャップ RSG (rate sensitive gap)
金利感応項目 interest rate sensitive items
金利感応資産 RSA (rate sensitive asset)
金利感応性情報 interest rate sensitivity information
金利感応度 interest rate sensitivity
金利感応負債 RSL (rate sensitive liability)
金利期間 interest period
金利期間構造 term structure of interest rate
金利キャップ cap on interest rate；rate cap
金利キャップ取引 interest cap trading
金利繰延債 deferred coupon bond
金利下落 falling interest rate
金利減免債権 renegotiated loans
金利更改 interest rate novation
金利更改期間 repricing interval
金利更改時点 repricing date
金利更改日 reset date；rollover date
金利構造 structure of interest rates
金 利 差 interest rate differential；interest spread
金利裁定 interest rate arbitrage
金利裁定取引 interest rate arbitrage transaction
金利差益 interest surplus
金利先取り pre-compute
金利先物 interest rate futures
金利先物オプション取引 interest rate futures options trading
金利先物契約 interest rate futures contracts
金利先安観 anticipation of low interest rate
金利先渡契約 FRA (forward rate agreement)
金利先渡取引 forward rate agreement
金利差の縮小 narrowing rate differentials
金利指数 interest rate index
金利支払期間 periods during which interest is payable
金利上昇 increasing interest rate；interest rate rise

キ

金利水準 interest rate level
金利ストリップ債 interest strips
金利スプレッド rate differential
金利スワップ interest rate swap
金利スワップ債 interest swap bond
金利スワップ支払利息 interest on interest rate swap
金利スワップション interest rate swaption
金利政策 interest rate policy
金利税引前利益 earnings before interest and taxes
金利選好 preference for interest rate
金利選択権付ローン ROL (reduction option loan)
金利操作 interest rate control
金利調整 adjustments in interest rates；interest rate adjustment
金利低下 decline in interest rate
金利動向 interest rate movement
金利入札方式のレポ variable repo；variable repurchase interest
金利の期間構造 term structure of interest rates
金利の決定 interest pricing
金利の減免 reduction or forgiveness of interest
金利の自由化 liberalization of interest rate
金利の平行移動 parallel rate shift
金利の変動 change in interest rate；shift in interest rate
金利の方向 direction of interest rate
金利のみ interest only
金利非感応項目 non-interest-sensitive item
金利非感応負債 non-rate-sensitive liability
金利引上げ raising of interest rate
金利引下げ lowering of interest rate
金利敏感株 interest sensitive stock
金利敏感保険契約 interest sensitive insurance polity
金利部分 interest component
金利フロアー interest rate floor
金利フロアー契約 rate floor agreement
金利平価 interest parity
金利平衡税 interest equalization tax
金利変動 interest rate fluctuation
金利変動準備金 interest maintenance reserve
金利変動負債商品 floating rate debt instruments
金利変動リスク interest volatility risk
金利マージン interest margin
金利マインド interest rate minded
金利見通し rate outlook
金利予測 interest rate anticipation
金利リスク exposure to interest rate；interest exposure；interest rate risk
金利連動年金 interest indexed annuity
金利を据え置く leaving rate on hold；leaving rate unchanged
近隣窮乏化政策 beggar-my-neighbor policy
近隣効果 neighborhood effect
近隣諸国 neighboring countries
勤労学生控除 deduction for working student；exemption for working student
勤労控除 earned income exemption
勤 労 者 wage earner
勤労者退職金共済機構 Organization for Worker's Retirement Allowance Mutual Aid
勤労所得控除 earned income allowance；earned income credit
勤労所得税 earned income tax

ク

グァーンジー・ポンド GBP (Guernsey pound)
グアテマラ・ケツァル GTQ (Guatemala quetzal)
クアラルンプール証券取引所 KLSE (Kuala Lumpur Stock Exchange)
クイック端末 QUICK-terminal
空運業 air transportation industry
空間地税 vacant land tax
空港収入債 airport revenue bond
空港発着権 airport landing rights
空室率 vacancy rate
偶然誤差 accident error
空洞化 hollowing out
偶発経費 accidental cost
偶発誤差 accidental error
偶発債務 contingent debt；contingent liability
偶発債務積立金 contingent reserve
偶発資金 contingent fund
偶発資産 contingent assets
偶発事象 contingency
偶発事象会計 accounting for contingencies
偶発受益者 contingent beneficiary
偶発信用スワップ contingent credit swap
偶発性ワラント contingent warrant
偶発損失 casual loss；contingent loss；unexpected loss
偶発損失準備金 contingency reserve
偶発損失引当金 reserve for loss contingency
偶発的危険 contingency risk
偶発的損益 windfall loss or gain
偶発的持ち分 contingent interest
偶発取引 contingent transaction
偶発費用 contingent charge
偶発利益 contingent profit
偶発利得 gain contingency
クーポン coupon
クーポン回収 coupon redemption
クーポン金利 coupon interest
クーポン再投資収入 income by coupon reinvestment
クーポン支払期間 coupon payment period
クーポン収入 coupon income
クーポン・スワップ coupon swap
クーポン・セール coupon sale
クーポン相当利率 coupon equivalent rate
クーポン属性 coupon attribute
クーポンだけの通貨スワップ coupon-only currency swap
クーポン取立 coupon collection
クーポンの既経過分 accrued coupons
クーポン・パス coupon pass
クーポン利率 coupon rate；coupon yield
クーポン・レート coupon rate
クーリングオフ cooling-off
クーリングオフ期間 cooling-off period
クエート・ディナール KWD (Kuwaiti dinar)
クォータリー・リファンディング quarterly refunding
クオート・レポーター quote reporter
クオリファイド・ビジネスユニット qualified business unit
クオンツ・クレジット戦略 quantitative credit strategy
クオンツ分析 quantitative analysis
クオント・オプション quanto option
釘付株 pegged stock
釘付為替相場 pegged exchange
釘付相場 pegged market
矩形分布 rectangular distribution
くじびき償還 redemption by drawing of number
苦情処理委員会 grievance committee
苦情処理手続き complaint procedures
屑 scrap
具体化する embodying

具体的規定 specific provisions
具体的な期限 specific deadline
具体的な経過規定 specific transitional provisions
口先介入(下落) talk down
口先介入(上昇) talk up
口 止 料 hush-money
覆　　す override
クック諸島（ニュージーランド・ドル） Cook Islands (New Zealand dollar)
クッション・ボンド cushion bond
屈伸為替相場 flexible exchange rate
屈伸制限制度 elastic limit system
屈折需要曲線 kinked demand curve
くつろぎ模様 easy
宮 内 庁 Imperial Household Agency
国に対する貸付 loans to the government
国の格付け country rating
国の行為 act of state
国の最高法規 supreme law of the land
国の事務の取扱い handling affairs of the government
国の習慣 national custom
国の証券振替機関 NSCD (national securities central depository)
国のバランスシート sovereign balance sheet
国または地方公共団体の補助金 subsidies from the government or local public entities
区　　分 disaggregation；division
区分ごとに算定された calculated separately for each category
区 分 式 multiple step
区分式試算表 classified trial balance
区分所有権 partial ownership
区分処理した accounted for separately
区分する segregate
区分損益計算書 multiple-step income statement；sectional income statement
区分地上権 sectional surface rights
区別する draw a distinction
組　　合 society
組 合 員 associate
組合員資格の保持 maintenance of membership
組合員先取特権 lien of partners
組合銀行 associated bank
組合財産 partnership assets
組合証票 union label
組合定款 articles of partnership
組合年金 associative pension
組合の出資金 contributions to unions
組合せ注文 combination order
組合せ保険 combination policy
組 替 え rebalancing；reclassification
組替える reclassify
組込オプション embedded option
組込デリバティブ embedded derivatives
組込比率 inclusion ratio
組 込 率 weighting ratio
組立原価計算 assembly cost system
組立工業 assembly industry
組立工程 assembly process
組立指図書 assembly order
組立順位表 assembly order sheet
組 立 費 assembly cost
組立部門 assembly department
組立保険 erection insurance
組立命令書 assembly production order
組 手 形 set bill；set of exchange
組別原価計算 class-cost system
組 別 法 group method
くもの巣循環 cobweb cycle
クラウディング・アウト crowding out
クラウディング・アウト効果 crowding out effect
クラウド取引 crowd trading
蔵　　券 kura ken
倉 敷 料 warehouse charges
グラス・スティーガル法 Glass-Steagall Act
クラスター分析 cluster analysis
グラハム・ドッド法 Graham and Dodd method
クラブ・ディール club deal
グラム・ラドマン法 Gramm-Rudman-Hollings Law
グラント・エレメント GE (grant element)

グランビルの法則 Granville theory
繰上給付 accelerated benefit
繰上差押 advance seizure
繰上償還 accelerated redemption ; advanced redemption ; prematurity redemption ; redemption before maturity
繰上償還オプション early redemption option
繰上償還可能な redeemable
繰上償還可能な債券 callable debt
繰上償還条項 call feature
繰上償還する redeem before maturity
繰上償還日 call date
繰上償還リスク call risk
繰上償還利回り yield to call
繰上請求 advance demand
繰上徴収 advance collection
繰上返済 early repayment
繰上返済違約金 prepayment penalty
繰上弁済 advance repayment
繰上保全差押 advance preservative seizure
クリア・バンド clear band
クリアリング・ファンド clearing fund
クリーピング・インフレーション creeping inflation
クリーピング・デフレ creeping deflation
繰入額 positioned amount
グリーンカード制度 green card system
グリーン・シート市場 Green Seat Market
クリーン信用状 clean letter of credit
クリーンB/L clean bill of lading
クリーン・フロート clean float
グリーンメール green mail
グリーンランド・クローネ DKK (Greenland krone)
クリーン・ローン clean loan
繰越 carryover
繰越外国税額控除 deduction of foreign corporation tax carried forward
繰越外国税額の控除 foreign corporation tax credit carried forward
繰越価額 carrying value
繰越勘定 brought forward account
繰越期限到来 expiration of carryforward
繰越基準 carryover basis
繰越記帳 opening entry
繰越計算表 post-closing trial balance
繰越欠損金 loss carried forward ; loss forwarded
繰越項目 deferred item
繰越災害損失 casualty losses carried over
繰越残高 balance brought forward
繰越試算表作成 taking a post-closing trial balance
繰越商品勘定 merchandise inventory account carried over
繰越税額控除 unused tax credit
繰越損益 profit and loss carried forward
繰越損失 accumulated loss
繰越配当金 dividends in arrears
繰越不足金 deficiency carried-forward
繰越平均単価払出法 method of average price at the close of the preceding month
繰越明許費 approved expenses to be carried over to the following year
繰越持ち分 carried interest
繰越利益 unappropriated profit carried forward
繰越利益剰余金 earned surplus carried forward to the following term
繰越す bring forward ; carry forward
繰り下げる move down
グリッド grid
クリティカル・パス会計 critical path accounting
クリティカル・パス・メソッド critical path method
グリニッジ平均時 GMT (Greenwich Mean Time)
繰延べ deferment ; deferral
繰延売上利益 deferred gross profit
繰延会計 deferral accounting
繰延外国税 deferred foreign tax
繰延外国税資産 deferred foreign tax assets
繰延外国税負債 deferred foreign tax liabilities

ク

ク

繰延貸方項目 deferred credit
繰延借方項目 deferred debit
繰延勘定 deferment account
繰延給与制度 deferred compensation arrangement
繰延契約 carryover contract
繰延契約費用 deferred policy acquisition cost
繰延決済 deferred settlement；delaying settlement
繰 延 債 bond issues to substitute for government cash payment；deferred bond
繰延資産 deferred assets
繰延資産償却 amortization of deferred assets
繰延資産の償却 amortization of deferred charge
繰延資産の償却の例外 exception to amortization of deferred charge
繰延支出 deferred expenditure
繰延収益 deferred revenue；income received but unearned
繰延修繕費 deferred repairs
繰延償却 deferred depreciation
繰延償却法 deferral amortization method
繰延所得課税債務 estimated future income taxes
繰 延 税 deferred income taxes；tax deferred
繰延税勘定 deferred tax account
繰延税金残高 deferred tax balance
繰延税金資産 deferred tax assets
繰延税金資産評価引当金 deferred tax assets valuation allowance
繰延税金収益 deferred tax income
繰延税金費用 deferred tax expense
繰延税金負債 deferred tax liabilities
繰延税金負債純額 net deferred tax liability
繰延税効果 deferred tax effects
繰延年金 deferred pension
繰延費用 deferred charge；deferred expenses
繰延費用勘定 deferred charge account
繰延負債 deferred liabilities
繰 延 分 deferred portion
繰延ヘッジ会計処理 deferred hedge accounting
繰延ヘッジ損益 deferred profit or loss on hedges
繰延ヘッジ損失 deferred hedge loss
繰延ヘッジ損失純額 net deferred hedging loss
繰延ヘッジ利益 deferred hedging gain
繰 延 法 deferral method
繰延報酬費用 deferred compensation expense
繰延法人税 income tax deferred
繰延法人税債務 deferred income tax liability
繰延法人税費用 deferred income tax charge
繰延保険料 deferred premium
繰延利払い deferred coupon
繰延利札 arrears coupon
クリフォード信託 Clifford trust
繰 戻 し carry back
繰戻還付制度 tax refund by carryback
繰戻税務欠損金 tax loss carried back
繰戻しによる還付 refund by carrying a loss back to a prior year
グループ課税 consolidated tax return system
グループ企業 group enterprises
グループ企業間取引 intragroup transaction
グループ償却 group depreciation
グループ税額控除 group tax relief
グループの給付建制度 group defined benefit plan
グルジア・ラーリ GEL (Georgian lari)
グレーマーケット gray market
CLEO CLEO (collateralized lease equipment obligations)
クレジット・アベイラビリティ credit availability
クレジット・イベント credit event
クレジット・ウォッチ credit watch
クレジット・ウォッチ・システム credit

watch system
クレジット・オプション credit option
クレジット・カード credit card ; plastic money
クレジット・カード会社 credit card company
クレジット・カード業務 credit card business
クレジット・カード債権 credit card receivables
クレジット・カード証券 CARDS (certificates of amortizing revolving debts)
クレジット・カード盗難保険 credit card burglary insurance ; credit card theft insurance
クレジット・カード有効期限 expiration date of credit card
クレジット・カーブ credit curve
クレジット換算係数 credit conversion factor
クレジット市場 credit market
クレジット・スコアリング credit scoring
クレジット・スワップ credit swap
クレジット追跡 credit tracking
クレジット・デフォルト・オプション credit default options
クレジット・デフォルト・スワップ credit default swap
クレジット・デリバティブ credit derivatives
クレジット・デリバティブ取引 credit derivative transaction
クレジット・トランシェ credit tranche
クレジットの悪化 credit blow-up
クレジット・ノート CN (credit note)
クレジット・ヒストリー credit history
クレジット・ファシリティ credit facility
クレジット・ポリシー credit policy
クレジット・ライン制度 credit line system
クレジット・リスク配分 credit risk allocation
クレジット・リスク・プロファイル credit risk profile
クレジット利用権 right of credit availability
クレジット・リンク債 credit-linked note
クレジット・リンク・ノート credit-linked note
グレシャムの法則 Gresham's law
クレスト（英国保管振替機関） CrestCo
クレスト決済口座 Crest Settlement Account
クレディスイス指数 Credit Suisse Index Generals
グレナダ(ECドル) XCD (Grenada EC (East Caribbean) dollar)
クロアチア・クナ HRK (Croatian kuna)
くろうと筋 professionals
くろうと相場 professional's market
グロース型 growth type
グロース指数 growth indices
グロース・セクション Growth Section
クロース相場 close market
クローズド・エンド型 closed-end type
クローズド・エンド型信託 closed-end trust
クローズド・エンド型デュアル・ファンド closed-end dual fund
クローズド・エンド型ファンド closed-end fund
クローズド・エンド型モーゲージ closed-end mortgage
クローズド・エンド型モーゲージ債 closed-end mortgage bond
クローズド・エンド投資信託 closed-end investment company
クローズド期間 closed period
グロース・ファンド growth fund
グローバル化 globalization
グローバル・カストディ global custody
グローバル・カストディアン global custodian
グローバル株式 global equity
グローバル・キャリー・トレード global carry trade
グローバル金融システム委員会 CGFS (Committee on Global Financial System)

ク

グローバル経済 global economy
グローバル経済の作用 working of global economy
グローバル証券 global certificate
グローバル戦略的資産配分 GTAA (global tactical asset allocation)
グローバル長期債 global long-term bond
グローバル通貨市場 global currencies market
グローバル投資 global investment
グローバル・トレーディング global trading
グローバルな不均衡 global imbalance
グローバル・ノート・ファシリティ global note facilities
グローバル・ポートフォリオ global portfolio
グローバル・マーケティング global marketing
グローバル・ミューチュアル・ファンド global mutual fund
グローバル無記名証書 GBC (global bearer certificate)
グローバル無記名預託証書 global bearer certificate
グローバル預託株式 GDS (global depository share)
グローバル預託証券 GDR (global depository receipt)
クローリング・ペッグ crawling peg
クローン・ファンド clone fund
黒　字 favorable balance；positive figure
黒字国 surplus country
黒字財政 surplus finance
黒字転換 recovery from deficit
クロス cross
クロス・カレンシー金利スワップ cross-currency interest rate swap
クロス・カレンシー・スワップ cross currency swap
クロス裁定 cross arbitration
クロス・セクション評価アプローチ cross-sectional valuation approach
クロス・デフォルト cross default
クロス・デフォルト条項 cross default clause
クロス取引 cross trading
クロス売買 cross-trade
クロス・ヘッジ cross hedge
クロスボーダー決済リスク cross-border settlement risk
クロス・ボーダーでの cross border
クロス・マージン cross margin
クロスライセンス契約 cross license contract
クロス・レート cross rate
グロス・アップ gross up
グロス・アップ条項 gross up clause
グロス・アップ方式 gross up method
グロス決済価格 gross settlement price
グロス償還 gross redemption
グロス・スプレッド gross spread
グロス取引高 gross trading volume
グロス・ファンド・ポジション gross fund position
区割り demarcation
郡検事 county attorney
郡裁判所 county court
軍資金 war chest
軍事法 military law
軍需関連株 war babies
軍需関連銘柄 war brides
軍縮局 DDA(Department of Disarmament Affairs)
訓練費 training expenses

ケ

経　緯 anecdotal evidence
経営委員会 management committee
経営意思決定 management decision
経営委託契約 management agreement
経営改善計画 plan for management improvement
経営監査 managerial auditing
経営管理 business management
経営企画室 Administration Department
経営危機にある会社 impaired company
経営基盤 management base
経営業績報告 reporting of operating result
経営計画 management plan
経 営 権 management rights
経営工学 management engineering
経営効率 operating efficiency
経営コンサルタント management consultant
経営再建 financial restructuring
経営参加 management participation
経営参加権 management participation right
経営参加投資家 hands-on investor
経営支援先 management support receiving entity
経営資源 managerial resources
経営支配権 controlling interest
経営指標 management index
経営資本回転率 turnover (ratio) of total operating assets
経営資本利益率 operating earning ratio ; profit ratio of operating capital
経営者による財務状況と経営成績の討議及び分析 management's discussion and analysis of financial condition and operating results
経営者による討議及び分析 MD&A (management's discussion and analysis)
経営者年金 executive pension
経営者の責務遂行 management's stewardship
経営者の表明 management representation
経営者の利益に関する討議と分析 management's discussion and analysis of earnings
経営者保険 key executive insurance
経営情報システム management information system
経 営 陣 management team
経営する carry on
経営成績 operating results
経営成績の報告 report on results of operations
経営責任 management responsibility
経営戦略 management strategy
経営組織 management structure
経営体質 management cultures
経営哲学 philosophy of management
経営統計 business statistics
経営統合 management integration
経営ノウハウ management know-how
経営能力 management capability
経営の健全性 sound management of financial institutions
経営判断 managerial choices
経営判断監査 prudency audit
経営判断の原則 business judgment principle
経 営 費 overhead expenses
経営不参加投資家 hands-off investor
経営不振企業 distressed company
経営分析 management analysis
経営分析及び解説 management discussion and analysis
経営方針 operating policies
経営目的 management purpose
経営理念 managerial philosophy
警　戒 fear

ケ

警 戒 感 caution
警戒指標 warning indicator
警戒の姿勢 cautious stance
経過勘定 deferred and accrued accounts
経過期間が長いローン seasoned loan
経過期間の期限 age limit
経過基準 time apportion basis
経過規定の影響 transitional effect
経過金利 accrual rate
経過項目 accrued item
経過時間 lapsed time
経過事項 transitional matters
経過実数 actual number of days elapsed
経過措置 interim measure；transitional measure
経過的処理 transitional treatment
経過日数 lapsed days
経過年数 aging；number of years elapsed
経過年数の関数 function of age
経過負債 transitional liability
経過保険料 premium earned
経過利子 AI (accrued interest)
経過利子付き and interest
経過利子なし flat
経過利息 unpaid interest
計 画 官 Director for Fiscal Investment and Loan Appropriation
計画経済 planned economy
計画した稼動 planned performance
計画的取引 planned transaction
軽 過 失 slight negligence
景　　気 business climate；business conditions；economic climate
景気一致指数 DI (diffusion index) of the coincident indicator
景気回復 economic recovery
景気回復期待 recovery expectations
景気回復の証拠 evidence of better growth
景気回復を主導する initiate the momentum for an economic recovery
景気拡大 economic growth
景気拡大期間 expansion period
景気拡大局面 phase of expansion
景気過熱 overheating of business activity
景気後退 economic recession；economic slump；recession
景気後退期 recession period
景気後退局面 phase of recession
景気後退のリスク recession risk
景気サイクル growth cycle
景気刺激型金融政策 expansionary monetary policy
景気刺激型財政政策 stimulating fiscal policy
景気刺激型の財政政策 stimulative fiscal policy
景気刺激策 economic stimulus package
景気指数 business barometer
景気指標 business indicator；macroeconomic indicators
景気重視 pro-business
景気循環 business cycle；economic cycle
景気循環型企業 business cyclical company
景気循環株 business cyclical stock；cyclical stock
景気循環の局面 phases of economic cycle
景気循環の振幅 magnitude of the cycle
景気先行指数 DI (diffusion index) of the leading indicator
景気先行指標 LEI (leading economic indicators)
景気総合指数 CI (composite index)
景気対策 supplementary package
景気遅行指数 DI (diffusion index) of the lagging indicator
景気調整 adjustments in economic activity
景気付け boost
景気低迷 poor economy；subdued economic growth
景気統計 fundamental statistics
景気動向指数 business conditions index；DI (diffusion index)
景気動向指標 diffusion index
景気動向調査 business survey
景気鈍化 slowing economy

景気に敏感な pro-cyclical
景気の穏やかな回復 modest economic expansion
景気の回復 cyclical upturn
景気の下降局面 downward phase of the business cycle
景気の底割れ sinking into a double dip recession
景気の谷 cyclical trough
景気の低迷 recessionary economic
景気の転換 economic reversal
景気の冷込み faltering economies
景気の山 cyclical peak
景気変動 economic fluctuation
景気予測 business forecast
景気をあおる boomer
景気を上向かせる revitalize economic activity
景気を牽引 driving growth
景 況 感 business expectation
景況判断 assessment of economic and financial situation
軽　　減 extenuation；mitigation
軽減税率 reduced income tax rate
軽減税率適用の所得金額 taxable income entitled to reduced tax rate
経験主義の empiric
経験上の判断 experienced judgment
経 験 則 empirical rule；rules of thumb
経験的アプローチ empirical approach
経 験 表 experience table
経験保険料 experience premium
経験豊かな seasoned
経験料率 experience rating
傾向指数 index number trend series
傾 向 線 trend line；trend pattern
傾向分析 trend analysis
傾向分析調査 TAP (trend analysis program)
警告論者 alarmist
経済安全保障 economic security
経済安定 economic stabilization
経済援助 economic aid；economic assistance
経済及び金融の情勢 economic and monetary conditions
経済及び金融の情勢に関する基本的見解 Bank's View of Recent Economic and Financial Developments
経 済 界 business community；economic circles
経済改革 economic reform
経済会計 economic accounting
経済外交 economic diplomacy
経済開発検討委員会 Economic and Development Review Committee
経 済 学 economics
経済学界 economics fraternity
経済活動 economic activity
経済活動刺激策 economic activity stimulating measure
経済活力 economic vitality
経済活力創造 economic revitalization
経済環境 economic circumstances
経済企画庁 Economic Planning Agency
経済基準 economic criteria
経済基礎条件 fundamentals
経済基礎条件重視派 fundamentalist
経済規模 economic size
経済恐慌 economic crisis
経済協力 economic cooperation
経済協力開発機構 OECD (Organization for Economic Cooperation and Development)
経済協力白書 white paper on economic cooperation
経済計画 economic plan
経済経路 economic path
経済決定論 economic determinism
経 済 圏 economic bloc；economic reach
経済原価 economic cost
経済構造改革 reform of economic structure
経済構造調整 economic structural adjustment
経済交流 economic exchange
経 済 財 economic goods
経済財政諮問会議 Council on Economic and Fiscal Policy

ケ

ケ

経済財政政策 economic and fiscal policy
経済財政担当大臣 Minister of State for Economic and Fiscal Policy
経済産業研究所 Research Institute of Economy, Trade and Industry
経済産業省 Ministry of Economy, Trade and Industry
経済産業大臣 Minister of Economy, Trade and Industry
経済事象 economic event
経済事情 conditions of the national economy
経済指数 economic index
経済実体 economic entity
経済疾病 economic malaise
経済指標 economic barometer；economic indexes；economic indicator
経済指標効果 economic number effect
経済諮問会議 CEA (Council of Economic Advisers)
経済社会 economy and society
経済社会局 DESA(Department of Economic and Social Affairs)
経済社会政策 economic and social policy
経済社会理事会 ECOSOC(Economic and Social Council)
経済主体 economic unit
経済循環 circular flow of economic system
経済状況 economic conditions
経済状況の実勢 prevailing economic conditions
経済情報 business information
経済情報サービス business information service
経済審議会 Economic Deliberation Council
経済新生対策 policy measures for economic rebirth
経済進歩 economic progress
経済生活 economic life
経済性工学 economic engineering
経済制裁 economic sanction
経済政策 economic policy
経済成長 economic growth
経済成長政策 economic growth policy
経済成長モデル economic growth model
経済成長率 economic growth rate；pace of economic expansion
経済成長率格差 economic growth differential
経済成長を促す spur economic growth
経済戦争 economic war
経済センター economic center
経済戦略会議 Economic Strategy Council
経済組織 economic organization
経済大国 major economic power
経済対策 economic package
経済体制 economic regime；economic system
経済団体連合会 Federation of Economic Organizations
経済秩序 economic order
経済調査 economic survey
経済積立率 economic funding ratio
経済的意思決定 economic decision
経済的関係 economic relationship
経済的観察方法 economic observational method
経済的観点 economic overlay
経済的業績 economic performance
経済的厚生 economic welfare
経済的合理性 economic rationality
経済的残存耐用年数 remaining economic age
経済的資源 economic resources
経済的重要性 economic significance
経済的生産操業規模 economic production run size
経済的成熟 economic maturity
経済的相関関係 economic correlation
経済的耐用年数 economic useful life
経済的地代 economic rent
経済的陳腐化 economic obsolescence
経済的特徴 economic characteristics
経済的取引 economic transaction
経済的な理由 economic reasons
経済的発注量 EOQ (economic order quantity)

経済的付加価値 EVA (economic value added)
経済的便益 economic benefit
経済的要因 economic factor
経済的利益 economic earnings; economic reward
経済的利益ベータ値 economic earnings beta
経済的リスク economic risk
経済的連続性 economic continuity
経済展望 economic prospect
経済統計 economic data; economic statistics
経済統合 economic integration
経済同友会 Japan Committee for Economic Development
経済特区 SEZ (special economic zone)
経済年報 annual economic review
経済の安定期 period of economic stability
経済の基礎条件を材料に動く相場 fundamental market
経済のグローバル化 globalization of economies
経済の硬直性 economic rigidity
経済の効率性 economic efficiency
経済の持続的な成長 sustained economic growth
経済の実体 economic reality
経済の成長期 period of economic growth
経済の動向 economic development
経済の流れ economic tide
経済の二重構造 dual structure of the economy
経済白書 economic white paper
経 済 表 economic table
経済封鎖 economic blockade
経済・物価の将来展望 outlook for economic activity and prices
経済復興 reconstruction of the economy
経済物理学 econophysics
経済分析 economic analysis
経済分析室(SEC) Office of Economic Analysis(SEC)
経済便益パターン pattern of economic benefits
経済変化の大きさ magnitude of economic change
経済摩擦 economic friction
経済見通し economic outlook
経済モデル economic model
経済予測 economic forecast; economic prediction
経済理念 economic philosophy
経 済 力 economic force; economic strength
経済理論 economic theory
経済倫理 economic ethics
警 察 庁 National Police Agency
計算誤り miscalculation
計算価格 computed price
計算基礎変動型終身保険 current assumption whole life insurance
計算サマリー accounting summary
計 算 書 statement
計算上の損益額 unrealized profit and loss
計算上の利益 unrealized gain
計算上の利益の払出し payment of unrealized profit
計算上の利子率 implicit rate of interest
計算書類 financial documents
計算する calculate
計算請求訴訟 action of account
計算整理事務 sorting of receipts and disbursements of treasury funds for government agencies and specific government accounts, calculation of their total amounts, and matching and checking of the figures against those calculated by the government agencies
計算単位 unit of account
計算違い errors in calculation
計算突合 footing
計算手続 computation procedure
計算早見表 calculator; ready reckoner
計 算 表 calculation table
形　　式 form
形 式 的 formal
刑事事件 criminal case

ケ

刑事訴訟 criminal action
刑事訴訟手続 criminal proceedings
軽視する play down
軽自動車税 light vehicle tax
傾斜関税 tariff escalation
傾斜リスク slope risk
形　　状 shape
経常赤字 current account deficit
経常移転 current transfer
経常移転収支 current transfers
経常外損益 non-recurring profit and loss
経常外損失 non-recurring loss
経常外費用 nonrecurring cost
経常外利益 non-recurring profit
経常黒字 current account surplus
経常歳出 ordinary annual expenditure
経常歳入 ordinary annual revenue
経常支出 current expenditure
経常支払 current payment
経常収支 current account balance；current balance
経常収支尻 balance of current account
経常収支の黒字 favorable balance on current account
経常収支率 ratio of current expenses to current income
経常純益額 net operating earnings
経 常 税 ordinary tax；recurring tax
経常損益 income before extraordinary items；recurring profit and loss；results of ordinary operations
経常損失 ordinary losses
経常的活動 ordinary activities
経常的活動からの損益 profit or loss from ordinary activities
経常的活動からの利益 net profit from ordinary activities
経常的な作業 routine work
経常的な調整 current adjustment
経常的要因 ongoing factor
経常取引 current transaction
経常ドル current dollar
経常費用 current expenses；ordinary expenditure
経常予算 current budget；ordinary budget
経常利益 ordinary income；ordinary profit；recurring profit
経常利益計算書 statement of operation earnings
計上純額 net carrying amount
計上する carry at；include；recognize
計上保険料 written premium
計上元受保険料 direct premium written
計上利益 declared profit
継承法人 corporation to receive the transfer of assets and liabilities
継承資産 assets to be transferred
係　　数 coefficient
計数管理 management through figures
ケイ線分析 chart analysis；chart reading
係船保険 port risks insurance
係争案件 legal dispute
係争中の訴訟 pending lawsuit；pending litigation
継　　続 continuation
継続役務 continuing services
継続会計監査 continuous audit
継続開示 continuous disclosure
継続開示会社 continuously disclosing company
継続開示企業 reporting company
継続監査人 continuing auditor
継続勘定 continuing account
継続企業 going concern
継続企業価値 going concern value
継続企業の基準で on a going concern basis
継続企業の原則 going-concern principle
継続企業の前提 going concern assumption
継続記録法 perpetual inventory method
継続勤務の期待度 service life expectancy
継続契約 continuing contract
継続差額決済 continuous net settlement
継続指図書 standing order
継続事業 continuing business；continuing operations；ongoing operation
継続事業部門利益 earnings from

continuing operations；income from continuing operations
継続事業利益 profit form continuing operations
継続した関与 on-going involvement
継続使用 continuing use
継続製造命令書 standing production order
継続性のあるアプローチ consistent approach
継続性の原則 consistency principle
継続専門教育 CPE (continuing professional education)
継続棚卸 continuous inventory；perpetual inventory
継続棚卸法 running inventory method
継続的再保険 continuous reinsurance cover
継続的重要性 continuing significance
継続的使用料 running royalty
継続的侵害 permanent trespass
継続的な損失 continuing loss
継続的な利害関係 continuing interest
継続的に営まれる事業 business continuously carried on
継続的売買 continuous buying and selling
継続手数料 renewal commission
継続ネット決済 CNS (continuous net settlement)
継続年金受取人 contingent annuitant
継続の対象 candidate for assumption
継続発行長期証券 COLTS (continuously offered long-term securities)
継続費 continued expenses；continuing expenditure
継続評価 ongoing assessment
継続保険 continuous policy
継続約款 continuation clause
継続率 persistence rate
携帯電話事業 cellular operation
経団連 Japan Federation of Economic Organizations
経年変動率 year-to-year changes
経費勘定 expense account
経費勘定残高 expense account balance
経費控除後利益 profit after expenses
経費差額 factory expenses variance
経費削減 curtailment of expenditure；expense reduction
経費支出手当 ERA (expense reimbursement allowance)
経費準備金 expense reserve
経費節減 financial retrenchment；reduction of expenditures
経費の分担 sharing costs
経費の予算 current expenditure budget
経費報告 expense report
経費膨張の原則 law of increasing public expenditures
経費補償金 compensation for expense and loss
経費元帳 expense ledger
経費要素 expense factor
経費予算 estimated appropriation of budget；expense budget
経費率 expense ratio；ratio of necessary expenses to gross revenue
経費割当 expenses quota
経費を削減する curtail the expense
計表本位 tabular standard
景品付販売 premium sale
刑法 Criminal Law
ケイマン諸島ドル KYD (Cayman Islands dollar)
啓蒙活動 enlightening activities
契約 agreement；contract
契約一時金 up-front payment
契約違反 breach of a contract；contravention of a contract
契約運賃制 contract rate system
契約応当日 policy anniversary
契約覚書 articles of agreement
契約解除 annulment of a contract
契約概要 policy summary
契約価格 contract price
契約型 contract type
契約型継続投資プラン contract type accumulative investment plan
契約型貯蓄 contractual savings
契約型投資信託 contract type investment

trust

契約加入者 contract holder

契約関係 privity of contract

契約期間 contract term；contractual period

契約規模 contract size

契約曲線 contract curve

契 約 金 contract money

契約金額 contract value

契約原票の移管 transfer of records

契約債務 commitments；contractual liability

契約残高 contract balance；outstanding contract amount

契約市場 contract market

契約社員 contract worker

契約者配当 policyholder dividend

契約自由の原則 principle of the freedom of contract

契約終了後の残存責任 run-off

契 約 書 contractual documents；indenture

契約条件 contractual terms and conditions

契約条件の違反 violation of the conditions of contract

契約条項 covenant

契約証拠金 earnest money

契約上の価格改定日 contractual repricing date

契約上の権利 contractual right

契約上の権利行使能力 ability to exercise a contractual rights

契約上の権利侵害 impairment of obligation of contract

契約上の権利の侵害 impairment of contract

契約上の債務 contractual obligation

契約上の支払期日 contractual repayment period

契約上の取決め contractual arrangement

契約書に書かれていなくても by default

契約書類作成銀行 documentation bank

契約信託 trust under agreement

契約責任保険 contractual liability insurance

契約締結 contract conclusion；contract formation；execution of a contract

契約締結日 contract date

契約手数料 contract charge

契約手付 advance received on contract

契約当事者 contracting parties

契約内容の実行 execution of contractual terms

契約年度 contract year

契約年齢 age at entry

契約能力 capacity to contract

契約の開示 contract disclosure

契約の解除 cancellation of contract

契約の解除権 right of rescission

契約の解約 cancellation of agreement

契約の獲得 securing of contract

契約の自由 liberty of contract

契約の適用範囲 scope stipulated in the contract

契約配当金 policy dividend

契約破棄 cancellation of a contract

契約不履行 non-fulfillment of a contract；nonperformance of a contract

契 約 法 contract law

契約ポジション contract position

契約保証 contract bond

契約前受金 contract deposit received

契約前渡金 advance made on contract

契約満了日 date of expiry

契約目的の達成不能 frustration of a contract objective

契約履行 fulfillment of a contract

契 約 率 contract ratio

契約料率 contract rate

軽油引取税 light oil delivery tax

経 理 課 accounting department

経理規程 accounting regulations

経理区分 division of accounting

経 理 士 registered public accountant

経理事務 accountant business

経理の状況 state of financial standings

経理のハイライト financial highlights

計量経済学 econometrics

計量経済分析 econometric analysis

計量経済モデル econometric model
計量的最適化 quantitative optimization
計量モデル予測 forecast by the econometric model
系　　列 corporate group
系 列 化 affiliation
系列金融機関 affiliated financial institute
系列相関 serial correlation
系列融資 loan to affiliated companies
経　　路 path
経路依存 path dependency
経路依存型オプション path-dependent option
経路依存型派生証券 history-dependent derivative securities
経路依存型派生商品 history-dependent derivative
経路独立性 path-independency
ケインズ学派 Keynesian
ケインズ革命 Keynesian revolution
ケインズ経済学 Keynesian economics
ケインズ効果 Keynes effect
ケーブル・クレジット cable credit
ゲームの理論 theory of game
ゲーム・プラン game plan
激　　化 intensification
激　　減 sharp decline
激　　変 drastic change
激変緩和措置 measure to mitigate radical changes
欠　　員 vacancy
欠員の場合の措置 measures in case of vacancy
血　　縁 blood relationship
月額均等払い equal monthly payment
月額の年金 monthly pension
月額保険料 monthly premium
月額補償 monthly indemnity
結果生じる修正 resulting adjustment
結果責任 absolute liability
結果損害 consequential damages
結果の変動 variability of outcome
結果もたらされる情報 resulting information
月間高低 monthly highs and lows
月間スプレッド monthly spread
決　　議 resolution
決議権会社 voting company
決議された配当 dividend ratified
決議方法 method of resolution
月 計 表 monthly statement of account
欠缺利札 invalid coupon
結　　合 uniting
結合金融商品 combined financial instruments
結合契約 combined contract
結合後企業 combined entity
結合財務諸表 combined financial statement
結合償却法 combined depreciation
結合損益計算書 combined profit and loss statement
結合貸借対照表 combined balance sheet
結合当事企業 combining entity
結 合 日 combination date
結合費用 joint cost
結合前企業 combining companies
決　　済 payment ; settlement
決済価額 settlement value
決 済 額 value of transactions settled
決済株数 settlement volume
決済勘定 settlement account
決済完了性 finality
決済期間 settlement interval
決済期限 due date for settlement
決済期限が到来する due for settlement
決済機構 settlement facility
決済機能 medium of exchange
決済金額誤差許容範囲 money tolerance
決済銀行 clearing bank ; settlement bank
決 済 口 settlement account
決済口数 number of settlement transactions
決済件数 volume of transactions settled
決済口座情報 SSI (standard settlement information)
決済口座への入金 priming
決済口座への払出し sweeping
決済サイクル settlement cycle
決 済 時 clearing time

ケ

決済時限 settlement deadline ; settlement time
決済システム payment and settlement system
決済事務 clearing business
決済事務の委任 entrustment of clearing business
決済手段 payment instrument
決済状況 settlement status
決済条件 terms of settlement
決 済 尻 balance of clearing
決済する settle
決済代金 settlement value
決済代行機関 settlement agent
決 済 高 settlement volume
決済通知 settlement notification
決済動向 Payment and Settlement Statistics
決済に係る手数料 fee for settlement
決済の委任 assignment of settlement duties
決済の詳細 settlement detail
決済の相互依存 interdependency of settlement
決済のために授受する金銭 cash to be paid or received for settlement
決済の保証 guarantee of settlement
決 済 日 settlement date ; value date
決済日基準会計 settlement date accounting
決済日後 post-balance sheet date
決済比率 settlements rate
決済物件 deliverable items ; securities eligible for settlement
決済不履行 default on clearing obligation ; failure to settle
決済不履行（フェイル） settlement failure
決済不履行への弁済 compensation for the failure to settle
決済方式 settlement method
決済方法 method of settlement ; settlement mode
決済保証 trade guarantee
決済履行 fulfillment of settlement
決済履行の保証 guarantee of clearing fulfillment
決済リスク payment and settlement risk ; transfer risk
決済割引 settlement discount
決 算 closing of accounts ; settlement of accounts
決算会社 reporting companies
決 算 期 book closing period ; fiscal year closed ; term for settlement of accounts
決算公告 publication of performance results
決算残高勘定 closing balance account
決算書の作成者 preparer of accounts
決算書の利用者 user of accounts
決算書類 settlement statements
決算仕訳 closing entries
決算整理 closing adjustment
決算整理前試算表 pre-closing trial balance
決算短信 preliminary release for business results
決算調整 adjustment in settling accounts ; reconciliation in settling accounts
決算手続 account closing procedure ; procedures for closing the books
決算年度 year of account
決算発表 announcement of performance results
決 算 日 balance sheet date ; fiscal closing date ; report date
決算日の為替レート closing foreign exchange rate
決算日レート CR (closing rate)
決算日レート法 current rate method
決算報告 statement of accounts
決算報告書 report on the settlement of accounts
決算予備発表 preliminary announcement of settlement of accounts
決算を行う settle accounts
月次計算書 monthly statement
月次決済 monthly settlement
月次決算 monthly settlement of accounts
月次試算表 monthly trial balance

月次総平均法 monthly average method
月次損益計算書 monthly income statement
月次貸借対照表 monthly balance sheet
月次複利計算 monthly compounding of interest
月次変化 monthly change
月足チャート monthly chart
欠　　損 deficiency
欠損回収 recovery of loss
欠 損 額 amount of loss
欠損からの便益 benefit of loss
欠損勘定 deficiency account
欠損金額 deficit amount
欠損金勘定 deficit account
欠損金繰越 tax loss carry-forward
欠損金繰戻し tax loss carry-back
欠損金計算書 deficit statement
欠損金処理計算書 deficit disposition statement
欠損金の繰越 carry-over of deficit；carryforward of net loss
欠損金の繰越控除 deduction for carryforward of deficiency
欠損金の繰戻し carryback of deficit；carryback of net loss
欠損金の繰戻控除 carry-back of losses
欠損填補積立金 reserve for compensation for losses
欠損の繰戻還付 tax refund by the carryback of the deficiency
月中平均 monthly average
決　　定 decision；ruling
決定可能額 determinable amount
決定係数 coefficient of determination
決定通知書 notice of determination
決定的却下 peremptory nonsuit
決定的推定 conclusive presumption
決定的説示 peremptory instruction
決定的な証拠 conclusive evidence
決定により through the decision
決 定 票 casting vote
決定マトリックス decision matrix
決定要因 determinant；determining factor
欠　　点 drawback；flaw
月内有効注文 month order
月　　賦 monthly installment
月賦販売 monthly installment sales
月賦販売金融 financing for sales by installment payment
月　　報 monthly report
月　　末 EOM (end of month)
月末決算 monthly accounting
月末渡し month-end delivery
月　　利 monthly interest rate
結　　了 wrapping-up
結　　論 conclusion
結論の根拠 basis for conclusions
結論の背景 background of conclusions
ケニア・シリング KES (Kenyan shilling)
懸念を解消する worry free
気　　配 quotation；tone；tone of the market
気配交換センター quotation exchange center
気 配 値 indication；quotation price；subject quote；indicative price
気配値段 bid and ask quotation；indicated price；special quote
気配表示 indicated bid-asked quotations；posting of special quote
下　　落 dip down；downfall
下落傾向にある down leg
下落順位 ranking of declines
下落する decline
下落トレンド downtrend
検　　印 seal
原　　因 cause
原因債権 causal credit
減　　益 decreased earnings
現役期間 working years
限　　界 threshold
限界インセンティブ marginal incentive
限界価値 marginal value
限界価値曲線 marginal value curve
限界企業 marginal firm
限界原価計算 marginal costing
限界原理 marginal principle
限界控除制度 marginal deduction system

ケ

限界効用 marginal utility
限界効用逓減の法則 law of diminishing marginal utility
限界効率 marginal efficiency
限界コスト MC (marginal cost)
限界資本 marginal capital
限界資本係数 marginal capital coefficient
限界資本支出 marginal capital expenditure
限界収益 marginal revenue
限界収益率 marginal rate of return
限界収入 marginal revenue
限界需要 marginal demand
限界条件 marginal condition
限界消費性向 marginal propensity to consume
限界正味適合度 marginal net suitability
限界信用 marginal credit
限界生産 marginal production
限界生産性 marginal productivity
限界生産費 marginal cost of production
限界税率 marginal tax rate
限界損益計算 marginal income statement
限界代替率 marginal rate of substitution
限界単位原価 marginal unit cost
限界値範囲内での配分 constrained allocation
限界貯蓄性向 marginal propensity to save
限 界 点 critical point
限界投資家 marginal investor
限界費用 marginal cost
限界評価 marginal valuation
限界費用曲線 marginal cost curve
限界比率 marginal ratio
限界分析 marginal analysis
限界便益 marginal benefit
限界輸入性向 marginal propensity to import
限界要素 marginal factor
限界預貸率 marginal loan-deposit ratio
限界利益 marginal income；marginal profit
限界利益図表 profit volume graph
限界利益率 marginal income ratio；marginal profit ratio
限 界 量 critical mass
限界理論 marginal theory
現会計年度 current fiscal year
限外発行銘柄 over-issue
減　　額 abatement；reduction in the amount
減額後の元本 reduced principal
減額請求 abatement claim
減額年金 reduced pension
減額払込保険 reduced paid-up insurance
減額保険料率 reduced premium rate
厳格解釈 strict construction
厳 格 性 stringency
厳格責任 strict liability
減価償却 depreciation
減価償却会計 depreciation accounting
減価償却額の回収 recapture of depreciation
減価償却可能な depreciable
減価償却可能リース資産 depreciable leased assets
減価償却基金 depreciation fund
減価償却基礎額 depreciation base
減価償却原価 depreciable cost
減価償却控除前帳簿価額 gross carrying amount
減価償却効率 rate of efficiency of depreciation
減価償却後価額 depreciated value
減価償却後原価 depreciated cost
減価償却後原始原価 depreciated original cost
減価償却後の depreciated
減価償却後の再調達原価 depreciated replacement cost
減価償却資産 depreciable assets
減価償却資産の取得価額 acquisition cost of depreciable assets
減価償却済み fully depreciated
減価償却高 amount of depreciation
減価償却妥当性 depreciation adequacy
減価償却単位 depreciation unit
減価償却年数 depreciation period
減価償却の月割計算 monthly allotment of depreciable period

減価償却の例外 exception to depreciation deduction
減価償却発生額 accrued depreciation
減価償却費 depreciation and amortization expense
減価償却引当金 allowance for depreciation；depreciation reserve
減価償却引当金比率 depreciation reserve ratio
減価償却費明細表 schedule of depreciation
減価償却費累計 aggregate of depreciation deduction
減価償却負担 depreciation burden
減価償却法 depreciation method
減価償却方針 depreciation policy
減価償却率 depreciation rate
減価償却累計額 accumulated depreciation；cumulative amount of depreciation
原　　価 cost；initial cost
原価以下主義 cost-or-less principle
原価以下で below cost
原価意識 cost consciousness
原価及び費用 cost and expenses
原価概算表 rough cost book
原価回収期間 recovery period
原価価値 cost value
原価・価値の関連 cost-value association
原価監査 cost audit
原価勘定 cost account
原価管理 cost control；cost management
原価基準 cost standard
原価基準で on the cost basis
原価基準の測定値 cost-based measure
原価基準法 cost plus method
原価吸収 cost absorption
原価記録 cost record
原価計算 cost accounting；costing
原価計算期間 costing period
原価計算基準 cost accounting standards
原価計算基準審議会 CASB (Cost Accounting Standards Board)
原価計算システム costing system
原価計算書 cost card；cost statement
原価計算制度 cost accounting system
原価計算単位 costing unit
原価計算表 cost sheet；costing sheet
原価差異分析 analysis of cost variances
原価差額 cost variance
原価差額勘定 cost variance account
原価差額調整 adjustment of cost variance；reconciliation of cost variance
原価差額の繰延べ deferral of cost variances
原価算定 cost finding
原価算定方式 cost formula
原価算定方法 costing method
原価算入利息 interest recognized in cost
原価、時価のいずれか低い方 lower of cost or market price
原価集計 cost accumulation
原価修正条項 cost escalation clause
原価修正法 cost adjusted for fair value method
原価主義 concept of historical cost；cost basis
原価主義会計 cost-based accounting
原価・操業度・利益関係 cost-volume-profit relationship
原価対原価 cost to cost
原価対象 cost object
原 価 高 high cost
原価単位 cost unit
原 価 で at cost
原価低減計画 cost-reduction programs
原価の回収 cost recovery
原価の期間配分 periodic allocation of cost
原価の構成要素 components of cost
原価の削減 cost savings
原価の測定 measurement of cost
原価の補償 reimbursement of cost
原価配賦 circulation of cost
原価配分 cost allocation；cost distribution
原価比較法 minimum cost rule
原価分析 cost analysis
原 価 法 cost convention；cost method；valuation at cost

ケ

ケ

原価報告書 cost report
原価・保険料及び運賃込価格 CIF (cost, insurance and freight) price
原価見積り cost estimation
原価モデル cost model
原価元帳 cost ledger
原価要素 cost element
原 価 率 cost rate
原価を基礎とする cost-based
減価定率法 fixed percentage on declining balance method
減価引当 depletion allowance
減価率による償却 depreciation by depreciation rate
現価係数 present value factor
現 価 表 table of the present value
現 価 法 present value method
現 価 率 discounted rate；present value rate
現　　株 spot share
原　　株 underlying stock
原株以上のコール・オプションの売手 ratio writer
嫌　　疑 suspicion
研究開発 research and development
研究開発基盤 research and development facilities
研究開発費 research and development cost；research and development expenditures
研究機関 research institute
研究成果 research findings
研 究 費 research cost
研究分析官 Special Officer for Investigation and Analysis
研究補助金 fellowship grant
兼　　業 sideline
現　　況 current status
献金する kick in
現　　金 cash
現金預け金 cash and deposits with banks
現金預け金勘定 cash and deposit account
現金受取り cash receipt
現金受取額 cash proceeds
現金売相場 cash selling rate
現金送り状 cash letter
現金及び現金等価物 cash and cash equivalents
現金及び預金通貨 currency and demand deposits
現 金 化 cashing；encashment
現金買い cash purchase
現金回収 cash collection；cash flow-back
現金買相場 cash buying rate
現金価格 cash price
現金価格相当額 cash price equivalent
現金貸付 cash loan
現金化周期 cash conversion cycle
現金化する liquidate
現金過不足 cash over and short
現金過不足勘定 cash over and short account
現金換価価値 actual cash value
現金監査 cash audit
現金勘定 cash account
現金管理 cash control；cash management
現金給付 cash benefit
現金記録 cash records
現金計算書 cash statement
現金決済 cash settlement
現金決済オプション cash settled option
現金決済希望 wanted for cash
現金決済金額 cash settlement amount
現金決済コルレス cash correspondent
現金決済従業員給付 cash-settled employee benefit
現金決済条件 receive versus payment
現金決済の cash-settled
現金公開買付 cash tender offer
現金項目 cash items
現金顧客 cash customer
現金残高 cash balance
現金仕入 bought for cash
現金資産 cash assets
現金資産価値 cash asset value
現金・資産比率 cash-to-asset ratio
現金支出 cash outgo；cash outlay
現金支出費 out-of-pocket expense

現金支払い cash disbursement；cash payment
現金支払額 money value
現金支払機 cash dispenser
現金支払原価 out-of-pocket cost
現金支払債務 cash commitments
現金支払帳 cash payment journal
現金資本 cash capital
現金収益 cash earnings
現金収入 cash income
現金収納帳 cash receipt book
現金主義 cash basis
現金主義会計 cash basis accounting
現金出資 investment in money
現金取得控除後 net of cash acquisition
現金循環 cash cycle
現金準備 reserve cash
現金準備高 cash reserve
現金準備率 cash reserve rate
現金償還 cash redemption
現金乗数 cash multiplier
現金仕訳帳 cash journal
現金信用状 cash letter of credit
現金出納課 cashier's department
現金出納係 cashier
現金出納帳 cash book
現金請求 claim to cash
現金請求権 claims to cash
現金送金 cash remittance
現金対1カ月負債比率 ratio of cash to thirty-day debts
現金担保付債券貸借取引 security loan transactions with cash collateral
現金担保付貸借取引 cash collateralized securities lending transactions
現金通貨 cash currency
現金積立 cash accumulation
現金手数料 hard commission
現金伝票 cash slip
現金等価物 cash equivalent
現金投資 cash and temporary investments combined
現金登録機 cash register
現金と交換可能な convertible into cash
現金取引 spot transaction
現金取引口座 unmargined account
現金の構成部分 component of cash
現金の授受 payment and receipt of cash
現金の返還 cash refund
現金の流入 cash inflow
現金配当 cash dividend
現金配当決議額 cash dividend declared
現金売買 cash sale
現金払い cash and carry；pay down；payment by cash
現金払主義 pay-as-you-go
現金販売 sale for cash
現金販売価格 cash sales price
現金引出 cash out
現金比率 cash ratio
現金負債 cash liabilities
現金不足 cash deficiency
現金不足額 deficit in cash
現金振込 wire transfer
現金への影響 cash effect
現金方式 pay-as-you-go basis
現金報奨 cash compensation
現金持ち高 cash position
現金預金 cash deposit
現金予算 cash budget
現金預託プット cash-secured put
現金流動負債比率 cash to current liabilities ratio
現金割引 cash discount
原 契 約 original contract
限　　月 contract month；delivery month
限月間スプレッド inter-delivery spread
限月間スプレッド取引 calendar spread trading；inter-month spread transaction；spread trading between contract months
限月取引の数 number of contract months
限月取引の期間 trading period of contract month
権　　限 authority；entitlement；power
権原移転費用 closing cost
権原買入 buying title
権原回復 remitter
権原確認 quiet title

ケ

ケ

権原合同 unity of title
権原証明書 certificate of title
権原調査 title search
権原の基礎 root of title
権原の電子移転 ETT (electronic transfer of title)
権原報告書 title report
権原保険 title insurance
権限委任 delegation of authority
権限担保条項 covenant for title
権限内で intra vires
権限範囲 ambit ; scope of authority
権限付与 delegation
権限を授与する authorize
現行金利 current interest rate
現行窃盗罪 open theft
現行の料金 going rate
現行プレミアム current premium
現行割引率 current discount
健康維持機構 Health Maintenance Organization
健康組合 heath fund
健康産業 health industry
健康者責任準備金 active life reserve
健康保険 health insurance
健康保険準備金 health insurance reserve
健康保険料 health insurance premium
原　　告 complainant ; plaintiff
検　　査 inspection
検査委員会 committee of inspection
検査監理官 Inspection Administrator
検 査 局 Inspection Bureau
検査局長 Director-General of the Inspection Bureau
検査工程 process of inspection
検査公報 Examining Circular
検 査 室 Internal Auditors' Office
検査証明書 inspection certificate
検査報告書 report on examination
減　　殺 reducing or eliminating
現在価格 present price ; real-time price
現 在 額 current amount
現在価値 current value ; present value ; present worth
現在価値会計 CVA (current value accounting)
現在勤務費用 current service cost
現在原価 current cost ; present cost
現在原価財務諸表 current cost financial statements
現在原価利益 current cost earnings
現在現金等価物 CCE (current cash equivalent)
現在公正価値 current fair value
現 在 財 present goods
現在債務 present obligation
現在取得価額 current acquisition cost
現 在 高 amount on hand
現在達成可能な currently attainable
現在の売値 current offer price
現在の買値 current bid price
現在の掛金 present contributions
現在の株価水準 current level of stock price
現在の時価総額 current market value
現在のスプレッド spot spread
現在の取引レンジ内に留まる stay within the current range
現在の売却値段 current asking price
現在の利回り common yield
現在の流動性 current liquidity
現在のローンの分類 current loan classification
現 在 品 stock in hand
減債基金 amortization fund ; debt service fund ; sinking fund
減債基金勘定 sinking fund account
減債基金繰入れ sinking fund payments
減債基金契約 sinking fund arrangement
減債基金債券 sinker
減債基金債務 sinking fund obligation
減債基金付社債 sinking fund bonds
減債基金積立額 sinking fund requirements
減債基金積立金 reserve for sinking fund
減債基金積立要件 sinking funds requirements
減債基金優先株 sinking fund preferred stock
減債制度 redemption system

減債積立金 debenture redemption reserve ; retained earnings appropriated for bond
減債積立利益剰余金 retained earnings appropriated for the retirement of bonds
原債権者 original creditor
原債務者 original obligor
原債務証券 underlying debt
原 材 料 feedstock ; primary materials ; raw and processed materials
原材料受入報告書 materials received report
原材料価格差異 material cost variance
原材料在庫 raw material inventory
原材料仕入報告書 materials purchased report
原材料返還表 returned materials report
原材料元帳 stores ledger
現先取引 gensaki
現先売買 repos
原先物契約 underlying futures contract
検 察 官 public prosecutor
検 察 庁 Public Prosecutors Office
原産地証明 certificate of origin
検　　事 prosecuting attorney
減　　資 capital decrease ; capital reduction ; reduction of capital stock
減資会社 company with reduced capital
減資差益 gain from stock retirement ; profit from capital reduction
減資差損 loss from capital reduction
減資産価格 reduced asset price
減資剰余金 surplus from capital reduction
原始相手方 original trading partner
原始記入 original entry
原始記入簿 book of original entry
原始資本 original capital
原始証券 primitive securities
原 資 産 underlying assets
原資産の underlying
顕示選好 revealed preference
現実指数 actual index price
現実主義的な決定 pragmatic decisions
現実成長率 actual rate of growth
現実全損 actual total loss
現実的な指針 practical guidance
現実的な手段 realistic means
現実的な代替案 realistic alternative
現実的な理由 pragmatic reasons
現実的表示 realistic portrayal
現実的標準原価 actually expected standard cost
現 実 の actual
現実の金額 real amount
現実の占有 possession in deed
堅実な資産構成 prudent asset structure
堅実な需要 solid demand
現時点までの to date
減　　収 decreased receipts
減収圧力 revenue pressures
研 修 医 resident doctor
現従業員 current employee
検　　証 verification
検証可能性 verifiability
検証する probate
減　　少 diminution ; reduction ; setback
減少傾向をたどる follow a declining trend
減少部分 reduced portion
原状回復 restitution
原状回復のための支出 expenditure incurred for the restoring to its original state
現場監査 site audit
原 証 券 underlying securities
現状程度の小幅下落 falling at the current moderate pace
現状分析 present data analysis
現状報告 status report
現　　職 incumbency
現職者基金 active life fund
現 職 の in-service
原子力安全基盤機構 Japan Nuclear Energy Safety Organization
原子力財産保険 nuclear energy property insurance

ケ

ケ

原子力損害賠償責任保険 nuclear energy liability insurance
原子力発電工事償却準備金 atomic power plant construction reserve
原子力保安・安全院 NISA (Nuclear and Industrial Safety Agency)
原子力保険 nuclear energy insurance
減じる abate
原信用状 master L/C ; original credit ; prime letter of credit
現水準 current level
検数人 tally man
件数レベルで in number
減税 legal tax cut
減税国債 government bond for tax reduction
減税債券 tax relief bonds
減税財源を調達する finance tax cut
減税特例国債に係る特例繰入れ special transfer on tax reduction-related special deficit-financing bond
譴責 censure
原籍国 home state
原籍国主義 home country control
建設請負契約 construction contract
建設・運営・譲渡 BOT (build-operate-transfer)
建設過剰 overbuilding
建設仮勘定 CWIP (construction work in progress)
建設業 construction industry
建設協力金等の差入預託保証金 guarantee deposits such as construction support deposits
建設クレーム construction claim
建設工事 construction work
建設工事収入 construction work revenue
建設工事保険 contractors' all risks insurance
建設国債 construction bond
建設支出 construction expenditure
建設・譲渡・運営 BTO (build-transfer-operate)
建設助成金 construction subsidy ; government subsidy for construction
建設・所有・運営 BOO (build-own-operate)
建設・所有・運営・譲渡 BOOT (build-own-operate-transfer)
建設・所有・売却 BOS (build-own-sale)
建設地方債 CLN (construction loan note)
建設中の建物 building under construction
建設費勘定 construction account
建設引当金 AFUDC (allowance for funds used during construction)
建設保証 construction bond
建設・リース・譲渡 BLT (build-lease-transfer)
建設利息 interest incurred during construction
建設ローン construction loan
健全財政主義 principle of balanced budget
健全性 soundness ; well-being
健全性維持契約 keep-well agreement
健全な買いのテーマ sound buy idea
健全な銀行業務 sound banking operation
源泉預り amount withheld
源泉及び使途計算書 source and disposition statement
源泉課税 taxation at the source ; withholding tax
源泉課税負担型ローン withholding tax absorbed loan
源泉課税負担方式 tax absorption credit
源泉控除所得税 income tax withheld at the source
源泉所得税 withholding income tax at source
源泉選択 withholding tax option
源泉選択課税 optional assessment
源泉徴収 withholding at the source
源泉徴収義務者 withholding agent
源泉徴収所得税 withholding income tax
源泉徴収制度 withholding tax system
源泉徴収税率 withholding tax rate
源泉徴収と納付 withholding and payment
源泉徴収の対象となる所得 scope of income subject to withholding income tax

源泉徴収票 withholding tax certificate
源泉非課税 withholding tax exemption
源泉分離課税 separate withholding taxation ; taxation on interest or capital gains separately withheld from other income
現先市場 repo market
舷船渡し FFA (free from alongside)
減速傾向 decelerating trend
原則的納税地 general place of tax payment
減　損 impairment
減損アプローチ impairment approach
減損会計 accounting for impairment
減損会計規則 impairment accounting rules
減損損失 impairment loss
減損損失累計額 accumulated impairment losses
減損テスト impairment test
減損の影響 effect of impairment
減損の計算 impairment calculation
減損の兆候 sign of impairment
減損の度合い degree of impairment
減損有形固定資産 impaired property, plant and equipment
現存の残高 existing balance
現代市場経済 modern market economy
現代資本主義 contemporary capitalism
現代ポートフォリオ理論 modern portfolio theory
現地一貫生産 full-scale local production
建築貸付組合 building and loan association
建築勘定 building account
建築組合 building society
建築研究所 Building Research Institute
建 築 税 building tax
建築賃借権 building lease
建 築 費 building expenses
現地コスト local cost
現地時間 local time
現地生産工場 local production factory
現地調達 local contents
現地調達率 local content ratio
現地通貨 local currency
現地での借入 local borrowing
現地投資家 local names
堅 調 な steady
堅調な市況 steady market
堅調な需要 healthy demand
現　提 actual delivery of stock sold
限定意見 limited opinion ; qualified opinion ; qualifying statement
限定意見監査報告書 qualified auditor's report
限定意見証明書 qualified certificate
限定裏書 qualified endorsement
限定監査 limited audit
限定監査報告書 qualified audit opinion
限定された confined to ; limited to
限定された形の権原 limited form of title
限定支払保険証書 limited policy
限定準備金 qualifying reserve
限定条件 qualification
限定信託 non-discretionary trust
限定相続 qualified acceptance of inheritance
限定的裁量 limited discretion
限定的な影響 residual impact
限定的な変更 limited changes
限定売買取引認可 limited trading authorization
限定報告書 qualified report
限定募集 limited offering
限定保証 limited warranty
限定目的信託会社 limited purpose trust company
限定リコース・ファイナンス limited recourse finance
限定リスク limited risk
検定統計量 test statistics
原データ raw data
原 投 資 underlying investment
限度貸付契約 commitment line contract
兼任重役 interlocking directors
検認撤回 revocation of probate
減　配 dividend cut ; dividend decrease ; reduced dividend
現場監督 site supervisor

ケ

現場検査 field inspection
現場検査人 field inspector
現場渡値段 loco price
現引き actual receipt of stock purchased
現物 actuals；spot commodity
現物移管 transfer in kind
現物受渡し actual delivery；EFP (exchange for physical)
現物オプション cash option
現物価格 spot price
現物価額 spot value
現物株 cash equity
現物為替持ち高 actual foreign exchange position；actual position
現物給与 truck system；wage in kind
現物拠出 contribution in kind
現物決済 cash settlement
現物債格付け cash spread
現物債券 cash bond
現物先渡取引 cash forward transaction
現物支給 allowance in kind
現物市場 cash market；underlying market
現物指数 cash index
現物出資 equity contribution in kind；investment in kind
現物出資取得株 stock acquired by the investment in kind
現物出資説 investment-in-kind theory of merger
現物出資になり得る経済的価値 economic value qualified for investment in-kind
現物出資により取得した固定資産 fixed assets acquired as contribution in-kind to capital
現物出資の過大評価 overestimation of investment in kind
現物証券 physical securities
現物商品 cash commodity；straight cash vehicles
現物対当 cash matching
現物他社清算参加者 cash transaction agency clearing participant
現物で in-kind
現物等清算参加者 Cash Transaction Clearing Participant
現物等清算資格 Cash Transaction Clearing Qualification
現物等非清算参加者 Cash Transaction Non-Clearing Participant
現物取引 cash transaction；spot transaction
現物とレポのポジションの相殺 cross margining
現物納付 tax payment in-kind
現物配当 dividend in-kind；property dividend
現物配当株 pay-in-kind bond
現物バスケット cash basket
現物引渡し physical delivery
現物銘柄 cash issue
現物渡し spot delivery
原文書 script
原文を改悪する adulterate
原簿 original register
原簿上の証券保有者 holder of record
原簿の末梢 deletion from ledger
原包装 original package
原保険証書 original insurance policy
原本 original document
厳密ファクター・モデル exact factor model
県民税 prefectural inhabitants tax
兼務役員 director having duties in an employee's capacity
券面外責任付証券 assessable securities
券面額 par value；stated amount
減免 reduction and exemption of taxes
減免税額の控除 deduction for tax reduction
減耗可能な depletive
減耗控除制度 depletion deduction system
減耗差異 shrinkage variance
減耗資産 depletion assets；wasting assets
減耗償却 cost depletion
減耗償却の原価法 cost method of

depletion
現 有 の vested in possession
現有不動産物件 real estate in possession
原油価格の下落 collapse in oil prices
原油価格連動型社債 petrobond
原油先物オプション crude oil futures option
現預金・預け金 cash and deposits
現預金回転率 sales to cash
権　　利 concession；rights
権利預り証 rights receipts
権利預り証付売買 transaction with rights receipts
権利落ち ex-new；ex-rights；rights off
権利落株式 rights-off shares
権利落公正価値 ex-rights fair value
権利落ちする traded ex-rights
権利落相場 ex new quotation
権利落ちで取引される trade ex-coupon
権利がある entitled to
権利買戻権 right of redemption
権利が確定していない non-vesting
権利確定期間 vesting period
権利確定主義 principle of ascertained claim
権利確定条件 vesting conditions
権利確定条項 vesting provisions
権利確定退職後給付 vested post-employment benefit
権利確定日 vesting date
権利確定日測定 vesting date measurement
権利確定部分 vested portion
権利確定要件 vesting requirements
権利救済制度 remedy for violation of private right
権 利 金 foregift；keymoney
権利金及び立退料 premium and compensation for removal
権利行使 exercise of right
権利行使価格 strike price
権利行使価額 exercised value
権利行使期間 exercise period
権利行使数量 exercise volume
権利行使通知 exercise notice
権利行使の指示 instruction of exercise
権利行使の認められている取引量 exercise limit
権利行使の割当 assignment of exercise
権利行使日 exercise date；expiration day of the exercise
権利収得 acquisition of right
権利取得 accession
権 利 書 abstract of title
権 利 証 registration certificate
権利証券 document of title
権利証書 deed of title；title document
権利章典 bill of rights
権利譲渡 assignment of rights
権利消滅条件 defeasance
権利書寄託 deposit of title-deeds
権利侵害 infringement of rights
権利推定 presumption of rights
権利請願 petition of right
権利担保条項 covenant of seisin
権利付き rights on
権利付相場 cum rights quotation
権利停止 suspension of right
権利と義務 rights and obligations
権利の確定した vested
権利の確定したストック・オプション vested share option
権利の継続的利用 use of continuing rights
権利の主張者 claimer
権利放棄 abandonment of right；quitclaim deed；surrender
権利放棄条項 waiver clause
権利未確定の unvested
権利濫用 abuse of rights
権利を与える entitle；vest
権利を主張する stake a claim
権利を損なわずに without prejudice
権利を担保に供する mortgage the right
権利を剥奪する disentitle；forejudge
原理主義 fundamentalism
原料価格変動 fluctuations in prices of raw materials
権力の分立 division of powers
現 渡 し actual delivery of stock sold

コ

CORES CORES (Computer-assisted Order Routing and Execution System)
コア・コンピタンス core competence
コア・ストック core stock
コア・ポートフォリオ core portfolio
コア・ホールディング core holding
故 意 の intentional ; willful
故意の虚偽 willfully false
故意の脱税 willful evasion of the tax
故意の不法行為 willful misconduct
項 paragraph
公安調査庁 Public Security Investigation Agency
行　　為 action ; teasance
行為規約 rules for action
行 為 税 act tax
行 為 地 venue
行為に基づく ex facto
行為能力 legal capacity
行為無能力 disability
合意確認書 letter of intent
合意管轄 agreed jurisdiction
合意管轄裁判所 agreement jurisdictional court
合意給付 agreed benefit
合意事実記載書 statement of facts
合意事実陳述書 agreed statement of facts
合意済みの利下げ agreed cut
合意的国際分業 international agreed specialization
合意に基づく決定 consensus decision
合意命令 agreed order
公営企業金融公庫 Japan Finance Corporation for Municipal Enterprises
公営住宅 council house
公営住宅公社債 public housing authority bond
公　　益 public interest
公益企業 utility company
公益事業 nonprofit-making activity
公益事業会計 public utility accounting
公益事業会社預け金 deposits with public utility corporations
公益事業規制室(SEC) Office of Public Utility Regulation(SEC)
公益事業債 public utility bond
公益事業持株会社法 Public Utility Holding Company Act
公益信託 charitable trust ; public trust
公 益 性 public benefit
公益代表理事 public governor
公益法人 corporation in public interest
交易条件 terms of trade
交易条件指数 index of terms of trade
高LTVローン high LTV loan
公　　課 public dues ; public impost
効　　果 effect
硬　　貨 hard currency
公　　海 high seas
公開会社 publicly held company
公開買付 TOB (take-over bid)
公開買付意見表明報告書 position statement report on tender offer
公開買付期間 tender offer period
公開買付撤回届出書 registration statement of withdrawal the tender offer
公開買付届出書 registration statement of the tender offer
公開買付報告書 tender offer report
公開価格 offering price
公 開 株 introduced stock ; publicly held stock
公開株式数 number of publicly offered shares
公開企業 public company ; publicly traded company
公開競売 open auction
公開市場 open market ; public market

公開市場委員会 open market committee
公開市場操作 open market operations
公開市場の価値 open market value
公開証券市場 public securities exchange
公開情報 public information
公開性の原則 principle of disclosure
公開セリ売買方式 open outcry method
公開セリ方式 open outcry
公開草案 ED (exposure draft)
公開短期金融市場 open money market
公開取引会所 open board of broker
公開入札 public bidding ; public tender
公開の市場 market overt
公開の法廷 open court
公開売却 public sale
公 開 日 offering date
公開文書 public document
更　　改 novation
更改によるネッティング netting by novation
更改日決定方法 determination date convention
更改頻度 reset frequency
公害等調整委員会 Environmental Dispute Coordination Commission
公害防止 pollution prevention
公害防止準備金 reserve for prevention of pollution
公害予防施設 pollution control facilities
航海訓練所 National Institute for Sea Training
航海保険 voyage policy
光学式文字読取装置 OCR (Optical Character Reader)
高額医療費保険 major medical expense insurance
高額医療保険 high coverage policy ; major medical insurance
高額債権 large credit
高額証券 jumbo certificate
高額商品 high ticket item
高額所得者層 high income group ; upper income group
高額配当 melon cutting
高額役員退職手当 golden handshake
高格付企業 firms with high credit ratings
高格付対象ファンド high quality fund
高格付トランシェ higher rated tranche
効果的なヘッジ effective hedge
効果を相殺する counterbalance
交換オプション exchange option
交換価値 exchange value
交換可能債務証書 exchangeable debt
交換可能転換優先株 convertible exchangeable preferred stock
交換可能マネーマーケット優先株 EMMPS (exchangeable money market preferred stock)
交換経済 exchange economy
交換公文 exchange of notes
交換差益 gain from exchange of property
交換差金 difference from exchange of property
交換残高表 clearing-house balance
交換社債権 exchangeable bond
交換処分 involuntary exchange of property
交 換 尻 clearing balance
交換尻時点（13時） designated settlement time of 13:00
交換貸借 loan for exchange
交換的取引 bargain for exchange
交換取引 exchange transaction
交換によって取得した資産 property received in the exchange
交換比率 conversion factor
交換比率の算定 computation of conversion factor
交換方程式 equation of exchange
交換保証 guaranteed exchange
交換用資産 property for exchange
好　　機 window of opportunity
後　　期 latter half of the year
後期配当 dividend for the second half
抗議趣意書 bill of exceptions
工期の延長 extension of time for completion
高級カード premium credit card
高級賃貸住宅 luxurious house for rent
高級品消費への指向 trend towards luxury

spending
恒久減税 permanent tax reduction
恒久施設 permanent establishment
恒久的施設 fixed place of business；permanent facility
好　　況 boom
好況市場 active market
公共会計士 public accountant
公共企業 public corporation
公共経済学 public economics
公共工事支出 public works outlays
公 共 債 public debt securities
公 共 財 public goods
公共債協会 PSA (Public Securities Association)
公共債ディーラー municipal securities dealer
公共債発行 issue of public bonds
公共事業 public service；public utility；public work
公共事業財源債 utility revenue bond
公共事業体 public utilities
公共事業費 public works expenditures
公共事業予算 public works budget
公共支出 public expenditure；public spending
公共施設 public facility
公共施設建設負担額 allotted amount in constructing public facility
公共施設の負担額 share in expense of public service facility
公 共 性 civic interest；public nature
公共政策 public policy
公共セクター public sector
公共団体 public body
公共通信事業 public telecommunications business
公共投資 public investment
公共投資乗数 public investment multiplier
公共の用 public use
公共部門 national sector
公共部門会計 public-sector accounting
公共部門退職年金 public employer retirement plan
公共プロジェクト public project
公共法人 public corporation
公共・民間パートナーシップ PPP (public private partnership)
公共目的債 essential purpose bond；public purpose bond
公共用地先行取得 accelerated land purchase
公共料金 public utility charges；utility rate
工 業 化 industrialization
工業会計 industrial accounting；manufacturing accounting
工 業 株 industrial stock
工業株価指数 Industrial Ordinary Shares Index
工 業 国 industrialized countries
工業財団 industrial foundation
工業所有権 industrial property；industrial right
工業所有権総合情報館 National Center for Industrial Property Information
工業生産 industrial production
工業手形 industrial bill
工業簿記 factory bookkeeping；industrial bookkeeping；manufacturing bookkeeping
工業用不動産 industrial real estate
鉱　　業 mining industry
鉱業会計 mining accounting
鉱業組合 mining partnership
鉱 業 権 mining rights
鉱業資産 mining property
鉱 業 税 mining tax
鉱業賃借権 mining lease
興業銀行 industrial bank
興 行 権 playright
興行収入 box office revenue
広義流動性 broadly-defined liquidity
公金預金 deposit of public money；official deposit
高 金 利 high interest rate
高金利時代 era of high interest rate
高金利政策 dear money policy；high interest rate policy

鉱　区 mining area
航空運送業 air transport industry
航空運賃 airway freight
航空貨物運送状 AWB (air way bill)
航空機 aircraft
航空機燃料税 aviation fuel tax
航空機ファイナンス aircraft financing
航空機保険 aircraft hull insurance
航空機融資制度 aircraft loan scheme
航空機リース・ポートフォリオ証券化 ALPS (aircraft lease portfolio securitization)
航空障害保険 aircraft passenger accident insurance
航空大学校 Civil Aviation College
航空保険 aviation insurance
航空料金 air fare
航空路 airway
合　計 sum total；total
合計額 sum
合計給付額 total benefit
合計残高試算表 trial balance of totals and balances
合計試算表 trial balance of totals
合計修正処理 accounting adjustments
合計情報 aggregated information
合計資料 aggregated data
合計する foot up；sum up
合計転記 summary posting
好景気 economic boom
好景気時代 prosperous days
好景気の heyday
後継者 successor
攻撃者 aggressor
攻撃的証券 aggressive securities
攻撃的投資 aggressive investment
後　見 guardianship
後見人 conservator；curator；guardian
公権付与 enfranchisement
公権を剥奪する disfranchise
貢献利益 contribution margin
貢献利益差異 contribution margin variance
貢献利益式 contribution margin form
公　庫 government financial institutions；public finance corporation
航行可能な navigable
航行妨害罪 obstruction of navigation
鉱工業 mining and manufacturing
鉱工業生産 industrial production
鉱工業生産指数 industrial production index
公　告 public announcement；public notice
広　告 advertisement
広告規制 advertising regulation
広告税 advertisement tax
広告宣伝費 advertising and general publicity expenses
広告宣伝用資産 property for advertisement
広告媒体 advertising media
広告費 advertising expenses；outlay for advertisement
広告料 advertising rate
交互計算勘定 open and current account
交互購入 cross purchase
公　差 common difference
考　査 on-site examination
口　座 account
口座開設金収入 revenue from account-opening fees
口座解約 account termination
口座管理機関 account-keeping institution
口座相違 different account
口座の区分 divisions of accounts
口座の提示 provision of accounts
口座の廃止 abolishment of account；discontinuance of accounts
口座番号 account number
口座引落し direct debit
口座振替 account transfer；book transfer
口座振替決済 book-entry settlement
口座簿 ledger of accounts
口座を管理する機関 book-keeping institution
公　債 government debt；government paper；public bond；public debt；

コ

コ

state and local government debt
公債依存 dependence on public debt
公債依存度 ratio of bond issue to total expenditure
公債管理政策 debt management policy
公債収入 revenue from public bond
公債償還資金 fund for redemption of JGSs
公債整理 consolidation of public bonds
公債投資者 investor in public bond
公債売買 public bond dealing
公債発行 flotation of government bond；issuance of government bond
公 債 費 expenditure for public bond；national debt service expenditure
公債利子 interest on public bond
公債利子支払資金 fund for payments of interest on JGSs
交 際 費 entertainment and social expenses
交際費課税 taxation on entertainment and social expenses
交際費控除 deduction of entertainment expenses
交際費の繰入限度額 limit of deductibles of entertainment expense
交際費の損金不算入 exclusion of expenses of entertainment expense from non-taxable income
好 材 料 favorable factor；good news；strong incentive
考 査 局 Bank Examination and Surveillance Department
考査契約 examination contracts
考 査 先 financial institutions subject to the Bank's on-site examination
考査の周期 cycle of on-site examination
考査の頻度 frequency of on-site examination
交差責任主義 principle of cross liabilities
交差突合せ cross footing
交差分析 cross over analysis
交叉責任条項 cross liability clause
交叉弾力性 cross elasticity
交叉比率 ratio of gross profit to inventory investment
交叉申込 cross offer
鉱 産 税 mineral product tax
鉱 産 物 mining products
行　　使 exercise
行使価格 strike price
行使価格段階的引上コール・オプション売り graduated call writing
行使価格の刻み値 exercise price interval
行使可能な exercisable
行使金利 strike rate
行使日測定 exercise date measurement
公　　示 announcement
公示価格 posted price
公示機能 disclosing function
公示催告 public notification；public summons
公示資本 declared capital
公示送達 service by public notification
公示地価 publicly notified land price
工　　事 job
工事間接費 construction overhead
工事管理 administration of construction；care of works
工事契約の分割 segmentation of construction contract
工事契約費用 construction contract expense
工事原価 construction cost
工事収入 construction revenue
工事進行基準 percentage of completion basis
工 事 費 cost of construction
工事負担金 contribution in aid of construction
工事前渡金 deposit paid on construction work
工事未収金 construction work account receivable
公　　式 formula
公式化する formulate
公式見解 official statement
合資会社 limited partnership
公私混合企業 mixed undertaking
高 次 財 higher order goods

格 子 法 lattice approach
公社・公団 public corporation
公社・公団債 authority bond
公 社 債 corporate and public bonds；government bonds and corporate debentures；public and corporate bond
公社債応募者利回り yield on public and corporate bond
公社債現先売買 bond transactions with repurchase agreement
公社債現存額 new issue value of outstanding bonds
公社債消化 purchase of new issues of public and corporate bonds
公社債上場相場 rate of listed bond
公社債専門委員会 special committee for public and corporate bond
公社債担保貸付 loan secured by government bonds or corporate debentures
公社債店頭売買高 trading volume of over-the-counter bonds
公社債店頭売買利回り OTC sales yield of public and corporate bonds
公社債投資信託 open-end bond investment trust；public and corporate bond investment trust
公社債の償還益 profit accruing from repayment of bonds and debentures
公社債の評価 valuation of bond
公社債売買利回り sales yield of public and corporate bonds
公社債発行額 new issue volume of outstanding bonds
公社債引受協会 Bond Underwriters Association
公社債利回り yields of public and corporate bonds
公社債流通金融制度 loan facilities for financing bond trading
高収益事業 cash cow
高収益配当ミューチュアル・ファンド high current income mutual fund
公衆の縦覧 public inspection
公 準 comprehensive basis
降 順 descending order
後 順 位 subordination
後順位債券 junior bond
後順位債権者 junior creditor
後順位先取特権付き社債 junior lien bond
後順位担保 junior security
後順位抵当 junior mortgage
後順位の請求権 secondary claim
好 循 環 virtuous cycle
控 除 credit；deduction
控除額の繰越 credit carryover
控 除 額 amount deducted；exempted amount
控 除 権 recoupment
控除条件付保険 insurance with deductibles
控除条項 deductible clause
控除申請 claim for deduction
控除すべき債務 deductible liabilities
控除対象配偶者 qualified spouse for deduction
控除の順序 sequence of deduction
工 場 factory；plant；shop
工場会計 factory accounting
工場勘定 factory account
工場間接費 factory burden
工場原価 factory cost；shop cost
工場検査 shop inspection
工場財団 industrial factory foundation
工場設備 plant and equipment
工場設備勘定 plant account
工場備品 factory furniture and fixtures
工場元勘定 factory ledger account
工場元帳 factory ledger
工場用什器 factory furniture
工場用消耗品 factory supplies
工場渡し EXW (ex works)
恒常除数 constant divisor
恒常所得仮説 permanent income hypothesis
恒常単価 standing cost
恒常通貨 constant currency
恒常的運営 day-to-day management
恒常的な変化 ongoing change

コ

恒常ドル constant dollars
恒常ドル・ベース constant dollar base
恒常費用 standing charge
恒常満期 constant maturity
公称資本金 capital stock registered
交渉手数料 negotiated commission
交渉単位 bargain unit
交渉の弱い立場 weaker bargaining position
交渉料率 negotiated rate
交渉力 bargaining power
公証人 notary
公証料 notarial charges；notary fee
更新 renewal
更新可能契約 renewable contract
更新可能定期生命保険 renewable term life insurance
更新差金 difference by renewal
更新条項 continuation provision
更新証明書 renewal certificate
更新する update
更新手数料 renewal commission
更新投資 replacement investment
更新特典 renewal privilege
更新日 refix date；renewal date
更新保険料 renewal premium
更新保証付き guaranteed renewable
更新保証保険 guaranteed renewable policy
更新料 renewal charge；renewal fee
後進国 backward countries
構図 structural outline
高水準 healthy trend
高水準のインフレ・プレミアム large inflation premium
高水準の景気 high level of business activity
工数率 man hour rate
更生 reorganization
更生会社 corporation in reorganization process
更生計画 reorganization plan
更生担保権 secured claim under reorganization plan
更生手続 reorganization proceedings
更生手続の開始 commencement of reorganization proceedings
更正・決定により確定した追加税額 settled additional tax due amount
更正・決定の処分庁 authority of correction or determination
更正等の効力 effect of correction
更正の請求 claim for correction；request for correction
構成 composition
構成資産 component assets
構成比 composition ratio；percentage distribution
構成比率 component percentages；mix
構成比率分析 component percentage analysis
構成物の処理 treatment for components
構成部分 building block
構成銘柄 constituents
構成要件 composition requirements
構成要素 ingredient
合成 synthesis
合成アセット synthetic asset
合成為替予約 SAFE (synthetic agreement for forward exchange)
合成金融商品 synthetic instruments
合成金利ノート SIN (synthetic interest note)
合成現物裁定取引 synthetic cash arbitrage transaction
合成資産 synthetic assets
合成指数ファンド synthetic index fund
合成証券 synthetic securities
合成スワップ synthetic swap
合成通貨 synthetic currency
合成変動金利 synthetic floating rate
合成ポートフォリオ synthetic portfolio
合成ポジション synthetic position
公正意見書 fairness opinion
公正価格 fair price
公正価値 fair value
公正価値会計 fair value accounting
公正価値会計モデル fair value accounting model
公正価値基準法 fair value based method

公正価値合計額 aggregate fair value
公正価値再評価 fair value revaluation
公正価値修正 fair value adjustment
公正価値測定 fair value measurement
公正価値で計上される資産 assets carried at fair value
公正価値認識 fair value recognition
公正価値の変動 movement in fair value
公正価値の持ち分 interest in fair value
公正価値評価 fair valuation
公正価値ヘッジ fair value hedge
公正価値変動 fluctuation in fair value
公正価値モデル fair value model
公正かつ衡平 fair and equitable
公正慣習規則 fair practice rule
公正市場価額 fair market value
公正収益率 fair rate of return
公正証書 attested document；notarized deed
公正信用請求法 FCBA (Fair Credit Billing Act)
公正信用報告法 FCRA (Fair Credit Reporting Act)
公正取引 fair trade
公正取引委員会 FTC (Fair Trade Commission)
公正取引協定 fair-trade agreement
公正取引局 fair trade bureau
公正取引庁 OFT (Office of Fair Trading)
公正取引の確保 maintenance of fair trade
公正取引法 fair trade act
公正な価格形成 fair price formation
公正な市場価格 fair market price
公正な判断 fair judgment
公正な表示 faithful representation
公正な保険料 fair premium
公正の確保 assurance of fairness
厚 生 課 Health and Welfare Division
厚生管理官 Director for Health and Welfare
厚生経済学 welfare economics
江 西 省 Jiangxi
好 成 績 good results
高成長株 performance stock
広西チワン族自治区 Guangxi
厚生年金 employees' pension
厚生年金基金 employees' pension fund
厚生年金基金規約 Employees' Pension Fund rules
厚生年金基金契約 employees' pension fund contract
厚生年金基金代行返上 return of substitutional part of Employees' Pension Fund
厚生年金基金連合会 Pension Fund Association
厚生年金保険 Employees' Pension Insurance
厚生保険特別会計 Special Account for Health and Welfare Insurance
厚生労働省 Ministry of Health, Labour and Welfare
厚生労働大臣 Minister of Health, Labour and Welfare
公然の占有 notorious possession
構造改革 structural reform
構造改革特区担当大臣 Minister of State for Special Zones for Structural Reform
構造協議 structural impediments initiative talks
構造上の懸念 structural concern
構造調整 structural adjustment
構造調整融資 structural adjustment loan facility
構 造 的 structural
構造的インフレーション structural inflation
構造的失業 structural unemployment
構造的な圧力 secular pressure
構造的変更 fundamental changes
構造的弱気スタンス structurally bearish on
構造的流動性 structural liquidity
構造の選択 structural choice
構造分析 structural analysis
構造変化 structural change
構造方程式 structural equation
構造モデル structural model
構造問題 structural problem

構造要因 secular reason
構造リスク structural risk
構想段階 concept stage
拘束残高 compensating balance
拘束資産 restricted asset
拘束受給権 locked in vesting
拘束条項 binding clause
拘束預金 restricted deposit
拘束力のある binding
拘束力のある義務 binding obligation
拘束力のある契約 binding agreement
拘束力のある売却契約 binding sale contract
公租公課 tax and public charge ; tax and public dues
控訴裁判所 appeals court
控 訴 人 appellant
江 蘇 省 Jiangsu
後　退 dip ; pulling-back
交　替 alternation
交　代 change over
後　代 future generation
公団公庫債 public corporation bonds
構 築 物 structure
公 聴 会 public hearing
好調な住宅販売 robust home sales
硬 直 性 rigidity
交通安全環境研究所 National Traffic Safety and Environment Laboratory
交 通 債 transportation bond
交通事故傷害保険 traffic personal accident insurance
交通ネットワーク transport networks
公定価格 official price
公定貸付金利 discount lending rate
公定為替相場 official exchange rate
公定市場 official exchange market
公定歩合 Bank of Japan discount rate ; official discount rate
公定歩合操作 discount rate policy ; ODR (official discount rate) operation
公定歩合引上げ discount rate hike
公定歩合引下げ discount rate cut ; key rate cut ; ODR (official discount rate) cut
公定平価 parity of official exchange rate
公 定 力 tentative validity
公定レート official rate
工程管理 process control
工程仕様書 process specification
工程分析 process analysis
工程別原価計算 process cost accounting ; process costing
工程別総合原価計算 departmental process cost system ; sequential cost system
工程目標 milestone
肯定的誓約 affirmative covenant
高 低 法 high-low method
公的医療給付 state medical care
公的介護制度 national care system
公的介入 official intervention
公的企業 public enterprise
公的給付 state benefit
公的金融機関 public financial institution
公的金融機関貸出 loans by public financial institutions
公的決済収支 official reserve transactions balance
公的債権 official credits
公的支援制度 public support system
公的資金 public capital ; public fund ; public money
公的資金注入 public capital injection
公的資金の注入 injection of public fund
公的制度 state plan
公的退職給付 state retirement benefit
公的年金 public annuity ; public pension ; state pension
公的年金給付 social security pension benefit
公的年金控除 deduction of public pension
公的年金所得 social security income
公的不法妨害 common nuisance
公的部門事業体 public sector enterprise
公的部門年金 public service pension
公的部門発行 offering for the public sector
好　転 upturn
合　同 combine ; trust joint
合同運用 collective investments

合同運用型ファンド collective investment fund；commingled investment fund
合同運用株式ファンド commingled equity fund
合同運用勘定 managed account；pooled account
合同運用資金 pooled fund
合同運用信託 joint trust
合同運用投資 pooled investment
合同運用ファンド managed fund
合同運用不動産ファンド commingled real estate fund
合同勘定 combined account
合同検査 joint inspection
合同公募債勘定 pooled publicly traded bond account
合同私募債勘定 pooled private placement bond account
合同社債 joint bond
合同信託基金 common trust fund
合同普通株・公募債勘定 pooled common stock and publicly traded bond account
合同普通株勘定 pooled common stock account
合同不動産勘定 pooled real property account
行動規範 code of conduct
行動調整 behavioral adjustment
行動の枠組み behavioral framework
行動ファイナンス behavioral finance
行動変化 changes in behavior
行動理論 behavioral theory
口頭契約 oral contract；parol contract
口頭の証言 oral testimony
高騰市場 soaring market
高度障害 continuous disability
高度障害保険 permanent disability cover
高度情報通信システム information network system
高度な市場 sophisticated market
高度なヘッジ手法 sophisticated hedging method
高度の正の相関関係 high degree of positive correlation
豪ドル Aussie dollar
豪ドル債 Aussie bond
行内交換 in-house exchange
甲仲 chartering broker
購入債権 purchased receivables
購入した貸付金 purchased loan
購入選択権 purchase option
購入対価 purchase consideration
購入代金 purchase price
購入注文書 purchase order
購入手数料 purchase commission
購入年 purchases year
購入の意思 intention to purchase
購入のれん purchased goodwill
購入者手引 buyer’s guide
公認会計士 CPA (certified public accountant)
公認会計士・監査審査会 Certified Public Accountants and Auditing Oversight Board
公認会計士管理委員会 CPA Administration Commission
公認会計士懲戒 disciplinary punishment on certified public accountant
公認会計士による監査報告書 audit report of certified public accountant
公認会計士法 Certified Public Accountant Law
公認管理会計士 certified management accountant
公認機関 authorized agency
公認規制水準 authorized control level
公認銀行 authorized bank
公認検量人 public measurer
公認先物オプション・ファンド AFOF (authorized futures and options funds)
公認証券アナリスト chartered financial analyst
公認証券取引所 RIF (recognized investment exchange)
公認清算機関 RCH (recognized clearing house)
公認生命保険引受人 CLU (chartered life underwriter)

公認ディーラー authorized dealer
公認内部監査人 CIA (certified internal auditor)
公認フィナンシャル・プランナー CFP (certified financial planner)
光 熱 費 light and fuel expenses
公　　売 public auction
公売許可書 tax certificate
公売広告 public notification of auction
公売証書 tax deed
公売処分 disposition by foreclosure sale
公売に基づく権限 tax title
公売の買戻し redemption from tax sale
公売保証金 deposit for public auction
後 配 株 deferred stock
高倍率保障保険 multiple protection insurance
購　　買 procurement；purchase
購買部長 purchasing manager
購 買 力 buying power；purchasing power
購買力損失 purchasing power loss
購買力の侵食 erosion in purchasing power
購買力平価 purchasing power parity
購買力平価説 purchasing power parity theory
購買力変動会計 CPP (constant purchasing power accounting)
購買力変動損益 purchasing power gain or loss
購買力リスク purchasing power risk
購買ローン purchase loan
後発事象 event subsequent to the balance sheet date；subsequent event
後発事象のレビュー subsequent event review
後発発展途上国 least less developed countries
広範囲の市場インデックス broad market index
公判陪審 trial jury
公　　表 dissemination
公表価格 quoted price
公表価格のない unquoted
公表が認可された authorized for publication
公表財務諸表 published financial statements
公表されたインフレ率 reported inflation
公表市場価格 quoted market price
公表資本金 disclosed capital stock
公表承認 authorization for issue
公表承認日 date of authorization for issue
公表書類 published document
公表する publish
公 表 日 at the date of issue
公表文書 pronouncement
公表ベースの資産価値 reported asset values
公表利益 reported profit
高品質クラス quality class
高品質の high quality
公　　布 promulgation
高付加価値製品 value-added product
高 福 祉 enhanced welfare
交付公債 government compensation bond；public compensation bond
交付国債 subsidy government bond
交付債務 delivery obligation
交付税及び譲与税配付特別会計 special account for distribution of local allocation and shared taxes
交付請求 demand for withdrawal
交付手数料 fees for withdrawals of stock certificates
鉱　　物 mineral ore
高プレミアム転換社債 high premium convertible debenture
公平債券回収法 Fair Debt Collection Practices Act
公 平 性 fairness
公平で秩序のある市場 fair and orderly market
衡平法上の救済 equitable remedy
衡平法上の債務 equitable obligation
衡平法上の譲渡 equitable assignment
衡平法上の所有権 equitable title
衡平法上の所有者 equitable owner
衡平法上のモーゲージ equitable mortgage

衡平法上のリーエン equitable lien
抗　　弁 defense
抗弁する assert claims
抗 弁 権 right of defense ; right to assert claims
合　　弁 joint investment
合弁企業 joint venture
合弁事業 joint undertaking
公　　報 official information
公　　法 public law
公 法 人 public sector corporation
広報企画専門官 Special Planning Officer for Public Relations
広 報 局 DPI(Department of Public Information)
広報広聴官 Director (Public Relations)
広 報 室 Public Relations Office
合法的手続 legal process
後方差分近似値 backward difference approximation
後方差分払人 backward difference payer
後方統合 backward integration
候補者届出制度 entry system of a candidate
公　　募 offering for subscription ; public offering ; public placement ; public subscription
公募価格 offering price ; public offering price
公募型プロポーザル primary proposal
公 募 株 public offering share ; publicly subscribed share
公募業務 public offering business
公 募 債 bond for public offering ; public offering issue ; publicly issued bond ; publicly traded bond
公募証券市場 public securities markets
公募シンジケート public syndicate
公募地方債 public offerings of municipal bonds
公募電電債 publicly offered NTT bonds
公募入札 auction ; bidding for public offering
公募入札方式 public offering auction system
公募ファンド public fund
公募前完売債券 presold issue
公　　務 civil service
公務員再雇用制度 TUPE (Transfer, Undertaking and Protection of Employment)
公務執行妨害 interference with execution of official duty
被った損失 losses sustained
合名会社 unlimited partnership
項　　目 item
項目別控除 itemized deduction
合　　有 joint right
合有債務 joint obligation
公用徴収 expropriation
合有不動産権 joint tenancy
公用インボイス official invoice
効用関数 utility function
効用指標 utility indicator
効用理論 utility theory
公　　理 axiom
高　　利 feneration ; usury
高利貸し loan shark ; usurer
高利付社債 high-interest-bearing debenture
高利回債 high yield bond
高利回資産 high return asset ; high yielding assets
高利回商品への投資意欲 appetite for yield
高利回通貨 high yield currency
高利回保険 high interest policy
小　　売 retail
小売売上税 retail sales tax
小売売上高 retail sales amount
小売価格 retail price
小 売 業 retail business ; retail trade industry
小売業界 retail industry
小売業会計 retail accounting
小売原価 retail cost
小売原価率 cost-to-retail ratio
小売在庫 retail store inventories
小売市場 retail market
小 売 税 retail excise
小売棚卸平均法 average retail inventory

system
小売棚卸法 retail inventory method
小売売価 retail selling price
小売物価インフレーション retail price inflation
小売物価指数 RPI (retail price index)
小売ブローカー retail broker
効 率 性 efficacy ; operational efficiency
効率的市場 efficient market
効率的市場仮説 EMH (efficient market hypothesis)
効率的配分 efficient allocation
効率的ポートフォリオ efficient portfolio
高率株式配当 large stock dividend
高率適用制度 higher interest rates application system
合 理 化 rationalization
合理化実施 rationalization measure
合理化プログラム streamlining program
合理化を図る rationalize
合理性テスト reasonable test
合理的疑い reasonable doubt
合理的かつ相当な原因 reasonable and probable cause
合理的基準 rational basis
合理的期待仮説 rational expectation hypothesis
合理的根拠 reasonable evidence
合理的な rationalized ; reasonable
合理的な確実性 reasonable certainty
合理的な基準 reasonable criteria
合理的な近似値 reasonable approximation
合理的な構造 rational structure
合理的な保証 reasonable assurance
合理的に算定された価値 reasonably calculated value
合理的見積り reasonable estimate
合理の原則 rule of reason
好利回り good yield
交　　流 interchange
高料率適用契約 rated policy
効力発生通知書 notice to inform of taking effect
考慮事項 poins of consideration
高　　齢 advanced age
高齢化の評価 aging valuation
高齢社会 aged society
高齢者市場 senior market
高齢者人口 aged population ; elderly population
高齢・障害者雇用支援機構 Japan Organization for Employment of the Elderly and Persons with Disabilities
航路定限 trading limits
港湾空港技術研究所 Port and Airport Research Institute
港 湾 税 in-port duty
港 湾 料 port charges
超えるのが視野に入る striking distance of breaking through
ゴーゴー・ファンド go-go fund
コートジボアール（CFAフラン） XOF (Ivory Coast CFA (Communauté Financière Africaine) franc)
コーポレート・アイデンティティー corporate identity
コーポレート・イメージ corporate image
コーポレート・ガバナンス corporate governance
コーポレート・バンキング corporate banking
コーラブル債 callable deal
コーラブル・スワップ callable swap
コーラブル・スワップション callable swaption
コーラブル・ローン callable loan
コ ー ル call
コール・オプション call option
コール・オプション価値の範囲 within limits on value of call option
コール・オプション契約 call option contract
コール・オプション付債券 call bond
コール・オプション付ワラント callable warrant
コール・オプションのオプション料 call option premium

コール・オプションの評価 valuation of call option
コール・オプション評価と配当 call option valuation and dividend
コール資金 money at call
コール市場 call market；call money market
コール市場平均残高 call market average outstanding
コール・スプレッド call spread
コール・スワップション call swaption
コール付債券 callable fixed-income securities
コール・手形市場 call and bill market；call money and discount market
ゴールデン・クロス golden cross
ゴールデン・パラシュート golden parachute
ゴールデン・ハンドカフ golden hand cuffs
ゴールド・センター gold center
ゴールド・トランシェ gold tranche
ゴールド・ラッシュ gold rush
コール・トリガー call trigger
コール取引 call money transactions
コール日歩 per-diem rate for call loan
コール・マネー call money
コール・マネー利息 interest on call money
コール利回り YTC (yield to call)
コール・レート call money rate；call rate
コール・レシオ・バックスプレッド取引 call ratio back spread transaction
コール・ローン call loan
コール・ローン利息 interest on call loans
コール・ローン・レート call loan rate
コール・ワラント call warrant
コーン・ホッグ循環 corn hog cycle
子 会 社 offshoot；subsidiary；subsidiary undertaking
子会社貸付金 loan to subsidiary
子会社株式投資 stock investment in subsidiary
子会社業績連動株式 stock linked to subsidiary performance
子会社収益連動株式 tracking stock
子会社による優先株の発行 issuance of preferred shares by subsidiary
子会社の変更 changes in subsidiaries
子会社への投資 investment in subsidiary
子会社前受金 advance from controlled companies
小 型 株 small cap；small capital stock；small capitalization stock；small-sized stock
小型株効果 small firm effect
小型注文処理システム SOES (small order entry system)
小型の発行体 small issuer
子株落ち ex-allotment
互換性のある compatible
誤　　記 clerical error
小切手受取人 check beneficiary
小切手記入帳 check register
小切手指図人 check holder
小切手支払人 check drawee
小切手制度 checking system
小切手帳 checkbook
小切手帳の控え checkbook stub
小切手振出人 check drawer
小切手法 check act
顧　　客 account；clientele；customer
顧客株式による金利稼ぎ reverse conversion
顧客勘定 customer's account
顧客勘定を持つブローカー carrying broker
顧客基盤 customer base
顧 客 口 customer ledger
顧客効果 clientele effect
顧客口座 customer's account
顧客口座の開設 establishment of customer's account
顧客口座簿 ledger of customer accounts
顧客熟知規則 know your customer
顧客仕様の customized
顧客動員力 customers mobilizing power
顧客との関係 customer relationship
顧客による振替の申請 application for

transfer by customer
顧客の委託に係る建玉 positions on customer's account
顧客の委託に基づく売付け sale on customer's account
顧客の委託に基づく取引 transaction for the account of customer (or agency transaction)
顧客の囲い込み enhancement of customer loyalty
顧客の忠実性 customer loyalty
顧客のポートフォリオ portfolio of customers
顧客満足度 CS (customer satisfaction)
国営企業 state enterprises
国　　益 national interest
国外貸出 foreign loan
国外勤務者 overseas service employee；persons in overseas service
国外勤務手当 foreign service allowance
国外源泉所得 foreign source income
国外での上場 cross border listing
国外の制度 foreign plan
国　　債 government bond；JGSs (Japanese government securities)
国債依存度 debt dependence ratio
国債MAC JGB-MAC (JGB Message Authentication Code)
国 債 課 Government Debt Division
国債借入オペ borrowing of JGBs against cash collateral (JGB repos)
国債買入オペ outright purchases of JGBs
国債借入担保金 cash collateral for government securities borrowed
国債借入利率 JGB borrowing fee rate
国債管理 government debt management
国債管理局 Debt Management Office
国債元利金支払取扱店 JGS paying agents
国債管理政策 government debt management policy
国債企画官 Director for Government Debt Management Policy
国債供給量 government bond supply curve
国債繰上償還 early redemption of JGSs
国債決済業務 JGS (Japanese government securities) settlement service
国債権者 JGS (Japanese government securities) holder
国債先物市場 government bond futures market
国債先物市場の仕組み structure of the government bond futures market
国債先物等清算資格 Government Bond Futures Clearing Qualification
国債先物等取引参加者 Government Bond Futures Trading Participant
国債先物等非清算参加者 Government Bond Futures Non-Clearing Participant
国債先物取引 government bond futures
国債市場特別参加者 JGB Market Special Participant
国債支払代理店 JGS (Japanese government securities) paying agent
国債事務取扱費 administrative fees
国債償還損 losses on redemption of government securities
国債証券 JGS (Japanese government securities) certificate
国債証券先物オプション特例 Special Regulations on Options on Government Bond Futures
国債証券先物オプション取引 options trading on Japanese government bond futures
国債証券先物オプション取引に関する業務規程及び受託契約準則の特例 Special Regulations of Business Regulations and Brokerage Agreement Standards Concerning Government Bond Futures Option Contract
国債証券先物取引特別参加者 special participant in futures trading based on government bonds
国債証券先物特例 Special Regulations on Government Bond Futures
国債証券先物取引 government bond futures contract；Japanese government bond futures trading

国債証券に係る有価証券先物取引に関する業務規程及び受託契約準則の特例 Special Regulations of Business Regulations and Brokerage Agreement Standards Concerning Government Bond Futures Contract
国債証券に関する業務規程の特例 Special Regulations of Business Regulations Concerning Government Bonds
国債ストリップス債 Treasury strip
国債制度 government bond system
国債整理基金 Government Debt Consolidation Fund
国債整理基金特別会計 Special Account for Government Debt Consolidation Fund
国債整理基金特別会計法 Special Account Law of the Government Debt Consolidation Fund
国債相場 price of JGB (Japanese government bond)
国債代用証書 substitute certificate for government bond
国債代理店 JGS (Japanese government securities) agent
国債調査官 Special Officer for Research on Government Debt
国債DVP delivery-versus-payment (DVP) for JGSs
国債DVP同時担保受払機能 SPDC (simultaneous processing of DVP and collateralization)
国債登録制度 JGB (Japanese government bond) registration system
国債登録簿 JGB Registration Book
国債に関する業務の取扱い handling of JGBs business
国債に関する事務 government bond administration
国債に関する法律 Law Concerning Government Bonds
国債入札 treasury auction；treasury financing
国債入札制度 government bond auction system
国債による質権の設定 pledging of JGSs as collateral
国債の貨幣化 monetarization of government bonds
国債の元本支払い principal payment of JGSs
国債の元利払い payment of principal and interest on JGSs
国債の決済 settlement of JGSs
国債の債権者 holder of government bond
国債の市場利回り market yield on government bonds
国債の市中消化 public offerings of government bonds
国債の市中消化の原則 principle that JGBs and TBs should be issued in the market
国債の償還 government bond redemption；redemption of JGSs
国債の発行 government bond issuance；issuance of JGSs
国債の評価減 devaluation of government bonds
国債の利払い interest payment of JGSs
国債売却償還益 gains on sale and redemption of government securities
国債売却償還損 losses on sale and redemption of government securities
国債発行代り金の払込 payment for newly issued JGSs
国　債　費 government debt-related expenditure；national debt service cost；national debt service payment
国債引受 underwriting of government securities
国債振替決済業務規程 Regulations and Rules concerning the JGB Book-Entry System
国債振替決済制度 government bond book-entry system
国債保有者の権利 JGS (Japanese government securities) holders' title
国債利子 interest on government bond
国債利子に対する所得税の源泉徴収不適用の措置 exemption from withholding

tax on interest payments on JGSs
国債利息 interest and discounts on government securities
国債利回り government bond yield
国債利回り連動１年定期 all savers certificate
国債流通市場 secondary market for Japanese government bonds
国債ワラント WINGS (warrant into negotiable government securities)
国債を発行する pump the market with government bonds
国際エコノミスト international economist
国 際 化 internationalization
国 際 課 International Affairs Division
国際会計 international accounting
国際会計基準 IAS (international accounting standards)
国際会計基準委員会 IASC (International Accounting Standards Committee)
国際会計基準委員会財団 IASCF (International Accounting Standards Committee Foundation)
国際会計基準審議会 IASB (International Accounting Standards Board)
国際会計基準の採用 adoption of international accounting standards
国際会計士連盟 International Federation of Accountants
国際会計専門家協会 Association of International Accountants
国際外国為替標準契約 IFEMA (international foreign exchange master agreement)
国際海事機関 IMO (International Maritime Organization)
国際海上保険連合 International Union of Marine Insurance
国際開発協会 IDA (International Development Association)
国際開発復興銀行協定 Agreement of the International Bank for Reconstruction and Development
国際株券 international stock
国際株式市場 international equity market
国際カルテル international cartel
国際為替 international exchange
国際関係論 international relations
国際観光振興機構 Japan National Tourist Organization
国際監査ガイドライン IAG (international accounting guidelines)
国際監査実務委員会 IAPC (International Auditing Practices Committee)
国際慣習法 international custom
国際管理通貨制度 international managed currency system
国際企画官 Director (Mutual Agreement Procedures)
国際機関 international agencies；international organizations
国際機関債 super-national bond
国際機関債券 international agency bond
国際危機 international crisis
国際企業 international corporation
国際機構課 International Organizations Division
国際基準 international standards
国際競争力 international competitiveness
国際業務 international operation
国際業務課 Office of International Operations
国際業務展開銀行 internationally active bank
国際協力機構 JICA (Japa International Cooperation Agency)
国際協力銀行 JBIC (Japan Bank for International Cooperation)
国際協力専門官 Director for International Co-operation
国 際 局 International Bureau；International Department
国際局外国為替室 Legal Office
国際局局長 Director-General of the International Bureau
国際局次長 Senior Deputy Director-General of the International Bureau
国際均衡 international equilibrium
国際銀行間データ通信システム SWIFT

国際銀行業務 international banking facility；international banking operation
国際銀行業務勘定 IBF (international banking facility) account
国際銀行法 International Banking Act
国際金融 international finance
国際金融機関 international financial institution；multilateral lending institutions
国際金融機関出資 capital subscription to an international financial institution
国際金融業界 international financial community
国際金融公社 IFC(International Finance Corporation)
国際金融サービス・センター IFSC (International Financial Service Center)
国際金融市場 global credit market；global financial market；international financial market
国際金融情報センター JCIF (Japan Center for International Finance)
国際金融制度 international financial system
国際金融取引所 international monetary exchanges
国際経済学 international economics
国際経済協力会議 Conference on International Economic Cooperation
国際経済協力銀行 International Bank for Economic Cooperation
国際決済 international settlement
国際決済機関 International Securities Clearing Corporation
国際決済銀行 BIS (Bank for International Settlements)
国際決済通貨 international settlement currency
国際原子力機関 IAEA (International Atomic Energy Agency)
国際航空運送協会 IATA (International Air Transport Association)
国際貢献 international contribution
国際公募 international offerings
国際公法 international public law
国際交流基金 Japan Foundation
国 際 財 international goods
国際債券 international bond
国際債券市場 international bond market
国際債券ディーラー協会 AIBD (Association of International Bond Dealers)
国際債券トレーディング international bond trading
国際財務報告基準 IFRS (International Financial Reporting Standards)
国際CMS international cash management service
国際事業 international business
国際資金 international fund
国際資金移動 international movements of funds
国際資源銀行 International Resources Bank
国際資産運用 international asset management
国際市場 cross border market；international market
国際市場インデックス international market index
国際市場価格 global market price；international market price；world market price
国際市場調査 international marketing research
国際市場調査官 Special Officer for Research on International Markets
国際私法 international private law
国際司法裁判所 ICJ(International Court of Justice)
国際資本 global capital；international capital
国際資本移動 global capital movement；international capital movement
国際資本市場 global capital market；international capital market
国際収支 international balance of accounts；international balance of

コ

payments
国際収支室 Office of Balance of Payments and International Capital Markets
国際収支状況 Balance of Payments (provisional)
国際収支弾力性 elasticity of the balance of payments
国際収支調整過程 adjustment process of balance of payments
国際収支統計 Balance of Payments
国際収支の黒字 favorable balance of payments
国際商業会議所 ICC (International Chamber of Commerce)
国際証券 international securities
国際証券管理者協会 International Society of Securities Administration
国際証券サービス協会 ISSA (International Securities Services Association)
国際証券識別コード ISIN (International Securities Identification Number)
国際証券市場協会 ISMA (International Securities Markets Association)
国際証券投資 international portfolio investment
国際証券取引委員会機構 International Organization of Securities Commissions
国際証券取引所連合 International Federation of Stock Exchanges
国際商事仲裁 international commercial arbitration
国際商事仲裁協会 Japan Commercial Arbitration Association
国際消費者機構 International Organization of Consumer's Unions
国際商品 international merchandise
国際商品協定 international commodity agreement
国際条約 international convention
国際親交国 comity of nations
国際シンジケート international syndicate
国際スワップ・ディーラーズ協会 ISDA (International Swap Dealers Association)
国際スワップ・デリバティブ協会 ISDA (International Swaps and Derivatives Association)
国際清算同盟 International Clearing Union
国際租税課 International Tax Policy Division
国際租税法 international tax law
国際貸借 balance of international indebtedness
国際貸借説 theory of international indebtedness
国際単位 international unit
国際短期金融市場 international short-term money market
国際短期資本移動 international long-term capital movement
国際短期資本取引 international short-term capital transaction
国際短期浮動資金 hot money
国際担当参事官 Deputy Commissioner for International Affairs
国際調査管理官 Director (International Examination)
国際調整室 International Co-operation Office
国際著作権 international copyright
国際通貨 international currency
国際通貨基金 IMF (International Monetary Fund)
国際通貨基金協定 Agreement of the International Monetary Fund
国際通貨市場 international monetary market
国際通貨制度 IMS (International Monetary System)
国際通貨制度改革 reform of international monetary system
国際通貨不安 global monetary turmoil；international monetary turmoil
国際的金融管理 international money management
国際的石油株 international oil plays

国際的な株式上場 cross-border stock exchange listing
国際的な資本調達 cross-border funding
国際的な証券保管振替機関 ISCD (international securities central depository)
国際電気通信連合 ITU(International Telecommunication Union)
国際統一自己資本比率 BIS (Bank for International Settlements) capital ratio
国際投資 international investment
国際投資銀行 international investment bank
国際投資信託 international investment trust
国際投資紛争解決センター ICSID
国際トランシェ international tranche
国際取引 international commerce
国際取引通貨 international transaction currency
国際二重課税 international double taxation
国際農業開発基金 IFAD(International Fund for Agricultural Development)
国際農林水産業研究センター Japan International Research Center for Agricultural Sciences
国際ノーマル・ポートフォリオ international normals
国際比較 international comparables；international comparison
国際引受業者協会 IPMA (International Primary Market Association)
国際引受団 international consortium；international underwriting group
国際評価基準 international valuation standards
国際標準化機構 ISO (International Organization for Standardization)
国際婦人調査訓練研修所 INSTRAW(International Research and Training Institute for the Advancement of Women)
国際復興開発銀行 IBRD (International Bank for Reconstruction and Development)
国際付番機関協会 ANNA (Association of National Numbering Agencies)
国際ブローキング international broking
国際分業 international division of labor；international division of roles
国際分散投資 international diversified investment；international portfolio diversification
国 際 法 international law；law of nations
国際貿易 international trade
国際貿易委員会 International Trade Commission
国際貿易機構 ITO (International Trade Organization)
国際貿易センター ITC(International Trade Centre)
国際保護預り international custody
国際マーケティング international marketing
国際ミューチュアル・ファンド international mutual fund
国際民間航空機関 ICAO (International Civil Aviation Organization)
国際輸出信用保険機構 International Union of Credit and Investment Insurers
国際預託証書 international depositary receipts
国際リース international lease
国際流動性 international liquidity
国際連合 UN (United Nations)
国際労働機関 ILO(International Labour Organization)
国際ローン・ポートフォリオ international loan portfolio
国勢調査局 Bureau of the Census
国　　税 national tax
国税・地方税間の優劣 priority between national tax and local tax
国税及び地方税 taxes and rates
国税還付加算額 additional amount to the refund of national tax

コ

コ

国税企画官 Director (Management and Co-ordination)
国 税 局 Regional Taxation Bureau
国税債権優先の原則 principle of priority of national tax claim
国税債務の承継 succession of national tax liability
国税査察官 national tax investigator
国税実査官 Assistant Chief
国税収納官吏 official to receive national tax
国税収納金整理資金 National Tax Receipt Fund
国税審議会 National Tax Council
国税審査会 National Tax Council
国 税 庁 National Tax Agency
国税庁監察官 Internal Inspector
国税調査官 national tax examiner
国税庁次長 Deputy Commissioner of the National Tax Agency
国税徴収 national tax collection
国税徴収法 National Tax Collection Law
国税庁長官 Commissioner of the National Tax Agency
国税通則法 national tax procedure law
国税に関する相殺禁止 prohibition of setoff for national taxes
国税の未払額 unpaid balance of national tax
国税の連帯納付業務 joint and several tax obligation
国税犯則取締法 National Tax Violations Control Law
国税付加税 surtax on national tax
国税不服審判所 National Tax Tribunal
告知義務 duty of disclosure
告知効果 announcement effect
告知書扱い insurance without medical examination
小口金融 small loan
小口決済 retail payments
小口現金 petty cash
小口現金勘定 petty cash account
小口現金制度 petty cash system
小口現金の出納帳 petty cash book
小口現金預金 petty current deposit
小口資金 petty cash fund
小 口 筋 picker
小口注文 small lot order
小口投資家 little guy ; small investor
小口取引 job lot ; small amount transaction
小口の対面取引 face-to-face transactions of low value
小口売買 small lot trade
小口保険業 retail insurance business
小口前払準備金 imprest cash fund
小口前渡金 petty imprest
小口預金 petty deposits
小口預金証券 small savers certificate
国定税率 national tariff
国鉄清算事業本部 JRTT JNR Settlement Headquarters
国土交通省 Ministry of Land, Infrastructure and Transport
国土交通大臣 Minister of Land, Infrastructure and Transport
国内卸売物価 domestic corporate goods prices
国内外の見方 views at home and abroad
国内価格 domestic price
国内貸出約定平均金利の推移 Average Contracted Interest Rates on Loans and Discounts
国内慣行 national practices
国内機関投資家 domestic institutional investor
国内基準 national standards
国内均衡 domestic equilibrium
国内源泉 domestic source
国内源泉所得 income accrued from domestic sources ; income from Japanese sources
国内事業 domestic operations
国内支出 domestic expenditure
国内市場 domestic market ; national markets
国内指数 domestic index
国内指定預金 domestic designated deposit account

国内資本 domestic capital
国内需要 domestic demand
国内純生産 NDP (net domestic product)
国内所得 domestic income
国内信用 domestic credit
国内税率 domestic tax rate
国内総支出 GDE (gross domestic expenditure)
国内総資本形成 gross domestic capital formation
国内総生産 gross domestic product
国内総投資 gross domestic investment
国内手形 inland bill
国内投資 domestic investment
国内投資信託 on-shore fund
国内の制度 domestic plan
国内の楽観的見方 domestic optimism
国内発行信用状 local credit
国内引受手形 domestic acceptance
国内不況 domestic recession
国内物価 domestic commodity prices
国 内 法 domestic law
国内輸送 inland transportation
国内要因 domestic driver ; domestic factor
告　　発 accusation
国　　富 national wealth
国富統計 national wealth statistics
国法銀行法 National Bank Act of 1863
国防債券 defend bond
国防産業に対する融資保証 loan guarantees for defense industry
国民医療制度 national health care plan
国民医療費コスト national health care cost
国民医療保険料 national insurance contribution
国民皆基礎年金 universal basic pension
国民皆保険 national coverage insurance ; universal coverage
国民可処分所得 national disposable income
国民勘定 national accounts
国民経済 national economy
国民経済活動 national economic activities
国民経済計算 national economic accounting
国民経済計算体系 System of National Account
国民経済予算 national economic budget
国民健康保険 National Health Insurance Program
国民健康保険税 national health insurance tax
国民産出高 national output
国民支出 national expenditure
国民自然災害保険 national natural disaster coverage
国民資本 national capital
国民資本勘定 national capital account
国民資本表 national capital sheet
国民社会保険制度 national social insurance program
国民純支出 NNE (net national expenditure)
国民純生産 NNP (net national product)
国民所得 NI (national income)
国民所得会計 national income accounting
国民所得勘定 national income accounts
国民所得循環 circulation of national income
国民所得生産勘定 NIPA (national income and product account)
国民所得統計 national income statistics
国民所得分析 national income analysis
国民生活金融公庫 National Life Finance Corporation
国民生活指標 new social indicators
国民生活センター National Consumer Affairs Center of Japan
国民総供給 gross national supply
国民総資産 gross national wealth
国民総支出 gross national expenditure
国民総需要 gross national demand
国民総生産 gross national product
国民貸借対照表 national balance sheet
国民退職所得制度 national retirement income policy
国民年金 national pension

国民年金基金 National Pension Fund
国民年金基金連合会 National Pension Fund Association
国民年金制度 National Pension Plan
国民年金保険 National Pension Insurance
国民年金預託金 deposits of funds of national annuities
国民福祉指標 net national welfare
国民負担率 national burden ratio
国民保険料率 national insurance rate
国務長官 Secretary of State
穀物取引所 grain exchange market
国 有 化 nationalization
国有化銀行 state controlled bank
国有機械設備の交換 exchange of machinery and equipment owned by the government
国有企業 state-owned company
国有財産 national property
国有財産監査指導官 National property Inspector
国有財産企画課 National Property Policy Planning and Legal Division
国有財産業務課 National Property Acquisition and Disposition Division
国有財産情報室 National Property Information Office
国有財産審理課 National Property Examination and Appraisal Division
国有財産庁 SPA (State Property Agency)
国有財産調査官 Special Officer for Research on National Property
国有財産調整課 Policy Co-ordination for National Property Management Division
国有財産調整官 Special Officer for Policy Co-ordination for National Property Management
国有財産評価指導官 National Property Appraiser
国有財産有効利用推進室 Office for Promotion of Efficient Use of National Property
国有地管理局 Land office
国立印刷局 National Printing Bureau
国立科学博物館 National Science Museum
国立環境研究所 National Institute for Environmental Studies
国立銀行紙幣 national bank notes
国立健康・栄養研究所 National Institute of Health and Nutrition
国立公文書館 National Archives of Japan
国立国語研究所 National Institute for Japanese Language
国立国会図書館 National Diet Library
国立特殊教育総合研究所 National Institute of Special Education
国立美術館 National Museum of Art
黒竜江省 Heilongjiang
国連アジア極東犯罪防止研修所 UNAFEI (United Nations Asia and Far East Institute For the Prevention of Crime and the Treatment of Offenders)
国連アジア太平洋経済社会委員会 ESCAP (Economic and Social Commission for Asia and the Pacific)
国連アンゴラ監視団 MONUA (United Nations Observer Mission in Angola)
国連安全保障理事会決議 UNSCRs (United Nations Security Council Resolutions)
国連イラク・クウェート監視団 UNIKOM (United Nations Iraq-Kuwait Observation Mission)
国連インド・パキスタン監視団 UNIPOM (United Nations India-Pakistan Observation Mission)
国連NGO連絡サービス UN/NGLS (United Nations Non-Governmental Liaison Service)
国連開発計画 UNDP (United Nations Development Programme)
国連環境計画 UNEP (United Nations Environment Programme)
国連キプロス平和維持軍 UNFICYP (United Nations Peacekeeping Force in Cyprus)

国連休戦監視機構 UNTSO (United Nations Truce Supervision Organization)
国連教育科学文化機関（ユネスコ） UNESCO(United Nations Educational, Scientific and Cultural Organization)
国連グルジア監視団 UNOMIG (United Nations Observer Mission in Georgia)
国連軍縮研究所 UNIDIR (United Nations Institute for Disarmament Research)
国連訓練調査研修所 UNITAR (United Nations Institute for Training and Research)
国連経済開発局 United Nations Economic Development Administration
国連工業開発機関 UNIDO (United Nations Industrial Development Organization)
国連広報センター UNIC (United Nations Information Center)
国連国際商取引法委員会 UNCITRAL (United Nations Commission on International Trade Law)
国連国際薬物統制計画 UNDCP (United Nations International Drug Control Programme)
国連シエラレオネ監視団 UNOMSIL(United Nations Observer Mission in Sierra Leone)
国連児童基金（ユニセフ） UNICEF (United Nations Children's Fund)
国連資本開発基金 United Nations Capital Development Fund
国連社会開発研究所 UNRISD (United Nations Research Institute for Social Development)
国連食糧農業機関 FAO (Food and Agriculture Organization of the United Nations)
国連人権高等弁務官事務所 OHCHR (Office of the United Nations High Commissioner for Human Rights)
国連人口基金 UNFPA (United Nations Population Fund)
国連スーダン・サヘール事務所 UNSO (United Nations Sudano-Sahelian Office)
国連大学 UNU (United Nations University)
国連タジキスタン監視団 UNMOT(United Nations Mission of Observers in Tajikistan)
国連地域開発センター UNCRD (United Nations Centre for Regional Development)
国連地域間犯罪司法研究所 UNICRI (United Nations Interregional Crime and Justice Research Institute)
国連中央アフリカ共和国ミッション MINURCA (United Nations Mission in the Central African Republic)
国連難民高等弁務官事務所 UNHCR (Office of the United Nations High Commissioner for Refugees)
国連西サハラ住民投票ミッション MINURSO (United Nations Mission for the Referendum in Western Sahara)
国連人間居住センター（ハビタット） UNCHS (United Nations Centre for Human Settlements [Habitat])
国連ハイチ文民警察ミッション MIPONUH (United Nations Civilian Police Mission in Haiti)
国連パレスチナ難民救済事業機関 UNRWA (United Nations Relief and Works Agency for Palestine Refugees in the Near East)
国連婦人開発基金 UNIFEM (United Nations Development Fund for Women)
国連プレブラカ監視団 UNMOP (United Nations Mission of Observers in Prevlaka)
国連プロジェクト・サービス機関 UNOPS (United Nations Office for Project

Services)
国連兵力引き離し監視軍 UNDOF (United Nations Disengagement Observer Force)
国連貿易開発会議 UNCTAD (United Nations Conference on Trade and Development)
国連ボスニア・ヘルツェゴビナ・ミッション UNMIBH (United Nations Mission in Bosnia and Herzegovina)
国連ボランティア UNV (United Nations Volunteers)
国連薬物統制犯罪防止事務所 ODCCP (United Nations Office for Drug Control and Crime Prevention)
国連予防展開軍 UNPREDEP (United Nations Preventive Deployment Force)
国連レバノン暫定軍 UNIFIL (United Nations Interim Force in Lebanon)
固形化燃料発電 RDF (refuse derived fuel) power generation
互恵関税 reciprocal duties
互恵租税条約 reciprocal tax treaty
焦付債権 frozen credit
焦付融資 restructured loan；uncollectible loan
午後立会 afternoon trading session
コ コ ム COCOM (Coordinating Committee for Multilateral Strategic Export Controls)
誤差曲線 error curve
誤差脱漏 errors and omissions
小 ざ や narrow spread；small spread
小ざや稼ぎ scalping
小じっかり slightly firmer；slightly steady
後日決定 TBD (to be decided)
後日発表 TBA (to be announced)
後日払信用状 deferred payment credit
小締まる slightly tightening
故障手形 foul bill
個人会員 private member
個人可処分所得 personal disposable income
個人課税課 Individual Taxation Division
個人株主 individual stockholder
個人企業 sole proprietorship
個人客相手の証券会社 wire houses
個人金融資産 financial assets of individuals
個人健康保険 individual health insurance
個人控除 individual exclusion
個人財産 personal property
個人財産所得 personal income from property
個人事業 proprietorship
個人事業主 single proprietorship；sole proprietor
個人事業主税 self-employment tax
個人資産 private assets
個人支出 personal expenditure
個人住宅ローン personal mortgage
個人集団扱保険 individual franchise policy
個人住民税 individual inhabitant tax
個人消費 personal consumption expenditure
個人所得 personal income
個人所得税 individual income tax；personal income tax
個人所得税最高税率 top personal tax rate
個人信託 personal trust
個人信託ファンド personal trust fund
個人信用 personal credit
個人信用情報 consumer's credit file
個人清算会員 ICM (individual clearing member)
個人生命保険 individual life insurance
個人総合賠償責任保険 comprehensive personal liability policy
個人退職勘定移転 IRA (individual retirement account) rollover
個人退職所得勘定 individual retirement account
個人退職積立勘定 IRA (individual retirement account)
個人退職年金制度 individual retirement pension plan
個人貯蓄 personal saving

個人貯蓄勘定 individual savings account
個人賃貸料所得 personal rental income
個人定期保険 individual term insurance
個人手形 personal bill ; private bill
個人的インフレ personal inflation
個人的評価 personal valuation
個人的偏向 personal bias
個人当座勘定 personal checking account
個人動産包括保険 personal article floater
個人投資家の投資方針 investment policy of personal investor
個人投資家向債券 consumer debenture
個人年金 individual annuity ; personal pension ; private pension
個人年金制度 personal pension scheme ; private pension plan
個人年金定期保険 personal pension term assurance
個人年金保険 personal pension insurance
個人納税申告 individual tax return
個人の秘密保持権 personal immunity
個人賠償責任保険 personal liability insurance
個人配当所得 personal dividend income
個人破産 personal bankruptcy
個人負債 personal liability
個人部門 personal sector
個人別勘定方式 individual account plan
個人変額年金 individual variable annuity
個人保険 personal line
個人保険型年金制度 individual policy pension plan
個人保険証券 individual policy
個人保証 personal guarantee
個人向金融 personal financing
個人向国債 JGBs for individual investors
個人メンバー personal member
個人持株制度 PEP (personal equity plan)
個人持株比率 ratio of individual stock ownership
個人預金 personal deposit
個人利子所得 personal interest income
個人ローン personal loan
コスタリカ・コロン CRC (Costa Rica colon)
コスト競争力 cost competitiveness
コスト構造 cost structure
コスト効率 cost effectiveness ; cost efficiency
コスト効率の良い cost effective
コスト最小化 cost minimization
コスト削減 cost reduction
コスト上の問題 cost implication
コスト節減 cost saving
コストの回収 covering cost
コストの発生 cost incurrence
コスト・パフォーマンス cost performance
コスト・プッシュ・インフレ cost-push inflation ; cost push inflation
コスト・プラス cost plus
コスト分担による便益 cost-sharing benefit
コスモ・モデル comprehensive system model
戸　籍 census register
互　選 mutual ballot ; mutual vote
午前立会 morning trading session
誇大推奨 tout
後代負担 cost born by future generations
戸建住宅 single-family detached residence
誇　張 overstatement
国会制定法 act of parliament
国会連絡調整官 Special Liaison Officer with the Diet
国家公安委員会 National Public Safety Commission
国家公安委員会委員長 Chairman of the National Public Safety Commission
国家公務員 national public employee
国家公務員法 National Public Service Law
国家財政 national finance ; public finance
国家債務 national debt
国家資本 state capital
国家資本主義 state capitalism
国家主権の喪失 loss of sovereignty
国家信用 national credit
国家賠償法 State Redress Law

国家破産 state bankruptcy
国家予算累積赤字 cumulative fiscal deficit
国 境 税 frontier tax
国境税調整 border tax adjustment
国境のない情報 cross border information
国境渡し frontier delivery
国境渡条件 DAF (delivery at frontier)
国境渡値段 delivered at frontier price
国　　庫 national treasury
国庫オペレーション treasury funds operations
国 庫 課 Treasury Division
国庫帰属認定 office found
国庫業務 treasury business
国 庫 金 treasury funds
国庫金送金 treasury fund remittance
国庫金に関する業務 services related to treasury funds
国庫金に関する制度 system related to treasury funds
国庫金の種類 type of treasury funds
国庫債券 treasury notes
国庫財務代理人 fiscal agent for treasury fund
国庫支出金 national treasury spending
国庫収支 government fund transactions
国庫対民間収支 government fund transactions with the public
国庫代理店 treasury agent
国庫調査官 Special Officer for Research on Treasury
国庫等実地監査官 Government Financial Institutions Inspector
国庫納付金 payment into the National Treasury
国庫補助金 national subsidy
国庫預託金 treasury deposit
国庫余裕金 treasury surplus
固定ウエート指数 fixed weight index
固定オプション制度 fixed option plan
固 定 化 earmarking
固定価格契約 fixed price commitment ; fixed price contract
固定額の受取 receipt of fixed payments
固定貸付金 fixed loan
固定借入金 fixed debt
固定為替相場 fixed exchange rate
固定為替相場制度 fixed exchange rate system ; pegged exchange rate system
固定間接費 fixed overhead
固定観念 abiding sense
固 定 給 fixed salary ; fixed wages
固定給付 fixed benefits
固定金利 fixed interest
固定金利キャッシュフロー fixed cash flow
固定金利資産 fixed-rate assets
固定金利支払人 fixed-rate payer
固定金利スワップ fixed rate swap
固定金利短期トランシェ FIRST (fixed interest rate short tranche)
固定金利負債 fixed-rate debt
固定金利モーゲージ fixed-rate mortgage
固定金利融資 fixed-rate loans repayable
固定現金支払額 fixed cash payment
固定債務倍率 times fixed charges
固定シェア fixed share
固定シェアでの割当 JGSs allocated to each syndicate member in a fixed share
固定資産 fixed assets ; property and equipment
固定資産売上率 sales to fixed assets
固定資産回転率 fixed asset turnover (ratio)
固定資産課税台帳 property tax cadaster
固定資産再評価益 surplus on revaluation of properties
固定資産自己資本率 equity capital ratio to fixed assets
固定資産除却損失 loss on retirement of fixed assets
固定資産処分 disposal of fixed assets
固定資産税 fixed asset tax ; property tax ; real estate tax
固定資産税納期 due date of property tax payment
固定資産税の税率 property tax rate
固定資産税の納税管理人 tax agent of

property tax
固定資産税の非課税の範囲 scope of exemption of property tax
固定資産税の免税点 taxable minimum of property tax
固定資産増減明細表 lapsing schedule of fixed assets
固定資産台帳 fixed asset ledger；fixed asset register
固定資産長期資本比率 ratio of fixed assets to long-term capital
固定資産に対する収益率 return on fixed assets
固定資産の減損に係る会計基準 accounting standards for impairment of fixed assets
固定資産の売却損 loss on sale of fixed assets
固定資産の評価 valuation of fixed assets
固定資産の評価損益 profit or loss from the revaluation of fixed asset
固定資産売却益 gains from the sale of fixed assets
固定資産売却損 loss from the sale of fixed assets
固定資産売却損益 gains or losses from the sales of fixed asset
固定資産評価益 gains from the revaluation of fixed assets
固定資産評価基準 valuation criteria for fixed assets
固定資産評価審議会 Fixed Asset Valuation Council
固定資産評価損 loss from the revaluation of fixed assets
固定資産比率 fixed asset ratio；ratio of fixed assets to net worth
固定資産明細表 fixed asset schedule
固定資産元帳 plant ledger
固定資本 fixed capital
固定資本投資 fixed capital investment
固定収入 fixed income
固定償還期限 fixed repayment terms
固定性配列法 fixed arrangement
固定税率 fixed general tariff
固定相場制 fixed exchange rate regime
固定単位型投資信託 fixed unit investment trust
固定的流動比率制度 fixed liquidity reserve requirements
固定投資信託 fixed investment trust
固 定 費 constant cost；constant expenses；fixed charges；fixed cost；fixed costs and expenses；fixed expenses；standing expenses
固定費回収計画 capacity cost plan
固定費用負担倍率 fixed charge coverage ratio
固定比率 fixed asset to net worth ratio；fixed ratio
固定負債 fixed liabilities
固定負債比率 ratio of fixed liabilities to net worth
固定平価制 fixed parity system
固定満期償還退職年金保険 fixed maturity pension annuity contract
固定予算 fixed budget
固定利付クーポン fixed-rate coupon
固定利付国債 fixed-rate JGB
固定利付証券 fixed-rate securities
固定利付通常債券 nominal bonds
固定利付投資 fixed-rate investment
固定利回証券 fixed return securities
5・10日決済 practice of settlement on the 5th, 10th, 15th, 20th, 25th, and the last day of each month (go-toubi)
異なった格付け split rating
こども総合保険 juvenile comprehensive insurance
子供保険 juvenile insurance
湖 南 省 Hunan
5年割引国債 5-year discount government bonds
この水準の突破 clearance of this level
好ましからざる上昇 unwanted rise
好ましくない変化 unfavorable change
後　　場 afternoon session
小　　幅 narrow range；small margin
小幅往来 narrow movement
小幅切上げ small revaluation

コ

小幅下落 edge down
小幅減益 small dip in profits
小幅下げ edge down
小幅上昇 edge up
小幅利益 small gain
小引締め slight tightening
誤　謬 error
誤謬表示 false demonstration
コピュラ関数 Copula function
小 浮 動 slight ups and downs
コ・ブランド・カード co-branded card
5分の1償却法 20％ depreciation method
個別後入先出法 individual LIFO
個別案件 individual projects
個別案件評価 evaluation of individual projects
個別会計 individual accounting
個別貸倒引当金 reserve for loan loss as stipulated in the tax law
個別課税 individual taxation
個別企業 individual enterprise
個別企業に特有の company-specific
個別基準 individual basis
個別競争売買 individual auction
個別決算書 individual accounts
個別原価 job cost；specific cost
個別原価計算 job cost system；production order cost accounting
個別原価計算制度 specific-order cost system
個別原価計算法 job order cost system；job order costing system
個別減価償却法 unit depreciation method
個別財産税 specific property tax
個別再保険 specific reinsurance
個別財務諸表 individual financial statements；separate financial statements
個別資産 individual asset
個別取得 separate acquisition
個別償却 individual depreciation；item depreciation；unit depreciation
個別消費税 specific consumption tax
個別申告書 separate return
個別生産 individual production
個別責任 several liability
個別選択 individual selection
個別耐用年数 individual useful life
個別仲裁 ad hoc arbitration
個別転記 unit posting
個別取引毎のリスク評価 transaction approach
個別納税申告 separate tax return
個別の開示 separate disclosure
個別の基準 separate standard
個別の種類 separate class
個別の分類 separate classification
個別売買方式 individual dealing system
個別引当法 individual allowance method
個別分類基準 separability criteria
個別分類性 separability
個別平準掛金積立方式 individual level cost method
個 別 法 identified cost method；specific identification method
個別銘柄 individual issue
個別目的財務諸表 special purpose financial statements
コペンハーゲン株価指数 Copenhagen Stock Exchange Index
コペンハーゲン証券取引所 Copenhagen Stock Exchange
湖 北 省 Hubei
コマーシャル・ペーパー CP (commercial paper)
コマーシャル・ペーパー発行残高 commercial paper outstanding
コミッション・ブローカー commission broker
コミットメント期間 commitment period
コミットメント・フィー commitment fee
コミットメント・ベース commitment base
コミュニティ community
コミュニティ・クレジット community credit
コメルツ銀行株価指数 Commerzbank Stock Price Index
コメルツ指数 Commerzbank-Index

コメント・レター comment letter
コモディティー・スワップ commodity swap
コモディティー・プール commodity pool
コモディティー・フロー法 commodity flow method
コモディテイー契約 commodity based contract
コモディティー通貨 commodity bloc；commodity currency
小戻し minor rally
コモロ・フラン KMF (Comoros franc)
顧問 advisor
顧問弁護士 corporation lawyer；legal counsel
コモン・ギャップ common gap
小安い easy
固有関数 eigenfunction
固有財産 national assets
固有値 eigenvalue
固有の困難 inherent difficulty
固有のリターン specific return
固有リスク inherent risk；specific risk
雇用 employment
雇用確保 job security
雇用関連保障 employment based coverage
雇用機会 employment opportunities；job availability
雇用機会均等 equal employment opportunities
雇用契約 employment contract
雇用コスト指数 ECI (employment cost index)
雇用市場 employment market
雇用指数 employment index
雇用者世帯 employee household
雇用者折半拠出金 employer matching contribution
雇用者退職給与金 employees' retirement allowance
雇用者負担型給付 employer financed benefit
雇用乗数 employment multiplier
雇用水準 level of employment
雇用政策 human resources policies
雇用創出 job creation
雇用調整 employment adjustment
雇用データ employment data
雇用統計 employment statistics；labor market data；payrolls number
雇用の伸び employment growth
雇用保険 employment insurance
雇用保険料 employment insurance premium
雇用見通し employment prospectus
御用組合 company union
娯楽 entertainment
ゴルファー保険 golfers' insurance
ゴルフ会員権 golf membership rights
コルレス関係 correspondent relation
コルレス勘定 correspondent account
コルレス銀行 correspondent bank
コルレス契約 correspondent arrangement
コルレス先金融機関 correspondent bank
コルレス・チャージ correspondent charge
ころがし方式 housing renewal program
コロンビア・ペソ COP (Colombia peso)
今期業績 business results of the current term
根拠 rationale
コングロマリット conglomerate
今後 going forward
混合 hybrid；mixture
混合会社 mixed company
混合型 hybrid model
混合株式 hybrid stocks
混合勘定 mixed account
混合関税 mixed tariff
混合キャップ hybrid cap
混合金利 blended rate
混合経済 mixed economy
混合契約 mixed contract
混合差異 mixed variance
混合財産 mixed property
混合資産 mixed assets
混合資本主義体制 mixed capitalist economy
混合準備金 mixed reserve
混合剰余金 mixed surplus

コ

混合戦略 mixed strategy
混合贈与 mixed gift
混合棚卸 mixed inventory
混合抵当 mixed collateral
混合的な制度 hybrid plans
混合取引 mixed transaction
混合年金保険 hybrid annuity
混合農業 mixed farming
混合ポートフォリオ mixed portfolio
混合保険 mixed policy
コンゴ（CFAフラン） Congo Republic (CFA (Communauté Financière Africaine) franc)
コンゴ民主共和国フラン ZRN (Congo Democratic Republic franc)
コンサルティング・セールス consulting sales
今週の高値 highs for the week
今週の安値 lows for the week
コンスタント・マチュリティ・スワップ constant maturity swap
コンセション・コントラクト concession contract
コンセプト開示 concept disclosure
コンセプト・リリース concept release
コンセンサス consensus
コンセンサス予測 consensus expectation；consensus forecast
混蔵投資勘定 commingled investment account
混蔵保管 commingled custody；custody in commingled form
混蔵保管口座 fungible account
コンソーシアム consortium
コンソーシアム・バンク consortium bank
コンソリデーション・ローン consolidation loan
コンソル公債 consolidated annuities；Consols
コンソル市場 consol market
コンチネンタル預託証書 continental depositary receipts
コンドラチェフの波 Kondratieff wave
コンドルスプレッド取引 condor type spread transaction
コントローラー controller
困難な資金繰り cash flow difficulty
コンパニオン債 companion bond
コンビネーション combination
コンビネーション戦略 combination strategy
コンピュータ化 computerization
コンピュータ監査 computer audit
コンピュータ・システムの障害対策 security measures of computer systems
コンピュータ社会 computerized society
コンファーミング・ハウス confirming house
コンフォート・レター comfort letter
コンプライアンス compliance
コンプライアンス違反 compliance deviation
コンプライアンス監査 compliance audit
コンベクシティ convexity
コンベンショナル・オプション conventional option
コンベンショナル方式 conventional auction；conventional method；multiple-price auction
コンベンショナル・モーゲージ・プール conventional mortgage pool
コンベンショナル・ローン conventional loan
コンポジット・プライス composite price
根本原因 underlying cause
混　乱 disarray

サ

サーカス・スワップ circus swap
サーキット・ブレーカー circuit breaker
サービサー servicer
サービシング手数料 servicing fee
サービシング手数料収入 servicing fee income
サービス業 service industry
サービス経済 service economy
サービス税 service tax
サービス手数料 service fee
サービス取引 service transaction
サービス貿易 service trade
差　　異 difference ; discrepancy ; variance
裁　　可 homologation
財　　貨 goods
財貨の販売 sale of goods
災害強度率 accident severity rate
災害繰上償還 catastrophe call
災害減免法 law relating to tax reduction and postponement of collection for disaster victims
災害再保険 disaster reinsurance
災害死亡給付 accident death benefit
災害死亡率 accident death rate
災害準備金 reserve for accidents
災害損失 casualty loss ; loss resulting from casualty
災害損失金 loss due to disaster
災害損失控除 casualty loss deduction
災害損失の繰越 carryforward of casualty loss
災害復旧 disaster relief ; restoration from disaster
災害復興 disaster recovery
災害保険 casualty insurance
災害保険契約 casualty insurance contract
災害補償責任 accident compensation
災害リスク disaster risk
在外公館 overseas establishments
在外子会社 foreign subsidiary
在外事業体 foreign entity
再 貸 付 further advance
最 下 層 lowest strata
再 加 入 re-entry
再　　鑑 double check
再 寄 託 redeposit
最近の水準 recent standards
財 空 間 commodity space
採 掘 権 mining concession
採掘予定数量 estimated mining quantity
採掘予定年数 estimated mining period
採 掘 料 diggings
採 掘 量 units extracted
サイクルの底打ち cyclical low
最恵国条項 most favored nation clause
最恵国待遇 most favored nation treatment
再計算する recalculate
再 計 上 re-recognition
財形貯金 property accumulation savings
財形貯蓄 workers' asset building savings
裁 決 書 written decision
債　　権 active debt ; claim receivables ; credits ; receivables
債権回収 collection of claim ; debt collection
債権回収代行 servicing
債権回収代行権 servicing right
債権買取り debt factoring
債権買取会社の保留金 factor's holdback
債権管理 claim management
債権銀行 bank creditor
債権区分 loan classification
債 権 国 creditor country ; creditor nation
債権債務 debts and credits
債権債務契約 receivable and payable contract
債権債務の相殺消去 elimination of

receivables and payables
債権差押え loan attachment
債権差押通告 notice of garnishment
債権差押手続 process of garnishment
債権差押人 garnisher
債権差押命令 loan foreclosure order
債権残高 claims outstanding ; outstanding balance of receivables
債 権 質 pledge of claims
債 権 者 creditor ; obligee
債権者委員会 creditor committee
債権者会議 creditors' meeting
債権者救済手続 receivership
債権者代位権 subrogation right of obligee
債権者団体保険 creditor group insurance
債権者による任意清算 creditor's voluntary liquidation ; creditor's voluntary winding-up
債権者の利益のための財産権の移転 assignment for the benefit of creditors
債権者持ち分 creditor's equity ; creditors' equity interests
債権順位 order of credit
債権償却特別勘定 special bad debts reserve
債権償却特別勘定の取崩し reversal of special bad debts reserve ; write-off from special bad debts reserve
債権譲渡 assignment of accounts receivable ; assignment of receivables
債権損失カバレッジ loan loss coverage
債権棚上げ long-term postponement of credit ; long-term postponement of debt servicing
債権担保 collateralized loan receivables ; finance receivables as collateral
債権取立益 gain on recovery of claims
債権の回収 recovery of credits
債権の回収を担保する protect the collectability of the amount due
債権の譲渡原価 cost of the transferred receivable
債権の届出 registration of claims
債権の弁済 liquidation of claim ; settlement of claim
債権のポートフォリオ portfolio of accounts receivable
債権プール receivables pool
債 権 法 law of obligations
債権ポートフォリオ portfolio of receivables
債権ポートフォリオの経過期間 aging of the portfolio receivable
債権保全 preservative attachment
債権保全火災保険 fire-insurance for mortgagee interest
債　　券 bond and debenture ; debt instruments ; fixed income debt
債券アナリスト bond analyst
債券移転 bond transfer
債券入替 switch of bonds
債券入替取引 bond switching
債券応募 bond subscription ; offering for subscription to bonds
債券オプション bond option
債券買いオペ bond buying operation
債券解約 repurchases of bond
債券価格 bond price
債券価格指標 bond price index
債券価格モデル bond pricing model
債券格付け bond credit rating ; bond rating ; debt rating
債券・株式組合せ bond-stock mixes
債券株式合成証券 hybrid debt-equity instrument
債券株式混合証券 debt-equity hybrids
債券・株式ファンド debt/equity fund
債券借換え bond refunding
債券換算利回り bond equivalent yield
債券勘定 bond account ; debenture account
債券区分 bond classification
債券繰延勘定 unamortized discount on debenture accounts
債券繰延資産 deferred assets on bond issue
債券決済ネットワーク JB Net (Japan Bond Settlement Network Co.)

サ

債券現先市場 bond gensaki market
債券現先取引 bond transaction with repurchase agreement
債券権利者 bond creditor
債券構造 bond structure
債券購入 bond purchase
債券先物 bond futures
債券先物オプション bond futures option
債券先物取引 bond futures transaction
債券先物取引制度要綱 procedures for bond futures trading
債券市場 bond market ; debt capital market ; debt market ; debt securities market
債券市場協会 MBA (Bond Market Association)
債券市場均衡 bond market equilibrium
債券指数 bond index
債券指数先物 bond index futures
債券指標銘柄 benchmark bond ; fixed income benchmark
債券受託者 bond trustee
債券需要 bond demand
債券純損益 net bond-related gains and losses
債券償還 redemption of bond
債券信託証書 bond trust indenture
債券数理学 bond mathematics
債券スプレッド bond spread
債券スワップ bond swap
債券設定 sales of bond
債券選択オプション bond selection option
債券相応利回り equivalent bond yield
債券相当利回り coupon equivalent yield
債券相場の上昇 rally in the bond market
債券貸借 bond lending
債券貸借取引 bond lending transaction ; bond loan transaction
債券担保貸付 loan on bond
債券担保金融 bond collateral loan
債券担保債務証書 collateralized bond obligation
債券ディーラー bond dealer
債券ディスカウント発行 bond issued at a discount
債券転換 bond conversion
債券転換オプション bond conversion option
債券店頭オプション bond option at over-the-counter
債券投資 debt investment ; fixed income investment
債券投資家 bond investor
債券投資のウエート bond weighting
債券取引システム FITS (Fixed Income Transaction System)
債券取引損失引当金 reserve for bond dealing losses
債券の入替え swap of bond
債券の格付け rating of bond
債券の償還までの期間 life of bond
債券の属性 bond attribute
債券の大量発行 large scale bond issue
債券の帳簿価額 book value of bond
債券のデディケート・ポートフォリオ dedicated bond portfolio
債券のデュレーション duration of bond
債券の取引価格 bond's quoted price
債券の任意償還条項 bond call provision
債券の満期日前の3カ月 last three months of a bond life
債券売買利回り yield of bond transactions
債券裸値 ex-coupon price of bond
債券発行 bond issuance
債券発行借入金 bonded debt
債券発行銀行 bond issuing bank
債券発行差金 bond issuance premium
債券発行差金償却 amortization of discounts on issued bonds
債券発行高 bonds issued and outstanding
債券発行費 bond issuing expense
債券発行費償却 amortization of bond issuance expenses
債券発行費用 bond issuing cost
債券発行保証枠 note issuance facilities
債券引受け bond underwriting
債券引受業者 bond underwriter
債券比率 bond ratio
債券ファンド bond fund

債券ブローカー bond broker
債券分析 fixed income analytics
債券ポートフォリオ bond portfolio；fixed income portfolio
債券保管振替決済制度 book-entry system for bond
債券保有 bond holding
債券保有者 debenture holder
債券保有者会議 noteholders meeting
債券ミューチュアル・ファンド bond mutual fund
債券銘柄 bond issue
債券名目利回り nominal bond yield
債券持合い bond cross holding
債券ラリー bond rally
債券リスク fixed-income risk
債券利回り bond return；yield on bond
債券割引 bond discount
再建請負人 rehabilitator
再建計画 rehabilitation plan；restructuring plan
再建計画の決定 decision of a reorganization plan
再建支援 restructuring support
再研修 retraining
財源 financial resources；fiscal resources；source of revenue
財源不足 fund shortage
最高意思決定機関 supreme decision making organ
最高会計検査機関アジア地域機構 ASOSAI (Asian Organization of Supreme Audit Institutions)
最高会計検査機関国際組織 INTOSAI (International Organization of Supreme Audit Institutions)
最高価格 maximum price
最高価格先出 HIFO (highest-in, first-out)
最高価格先出法 highest-in first-out method
最高機関 supreme institution
最高業務責任者 COO (chief operating officer)
最高経営責任者 CEO (chief executive officer)
最高顧問 supreme advisor
最高コンプライアンス責任者 CCO (chief compliance officer)
最高最低税率制 maximum and minimum tariff system
最高裁判所 Supreme Court of Japan
最高財務責任者 CFO (chief financial officer)
最高情報責任者 CIO (chief information officer)
最高水準 maximum level
最高税率 top tax rate
最高投資責任者 CIO (chief investment officer)
最高値の入札者 top bidder
最高発行額制限制度 maximum issuance limit system
最高保険金額 limit of risk
最高マーケティング責任者 CMO (chief marketing officer)
最高与信残高 high credit
再交渉 renegotiation
再更正 re-correction
再構築された金融負債 restructured financial liabilities
再公売 re-auction
最後から二番目の利益期待 penultimate profit prospect
最後の貸し手 LLR (lender of last resort)
最後の土壇場 eleventh-hour
在庫株式の売払い hunkering down
在庫管理 inventory management
在庫金融 inventory financing
在庫減耗 shrinkage
在庫債券 bond inventory
在庫指数 inventory indexes
在庫資本 inventory capital
在庫循環 inventory cycles
在庫調整 inventory adjustment
在庫投資 inventory investment
在庫費用 carrying cost
在庫評価調整 inventory valuation adjustment
在庫品 stock in trade
在庫品回転率 stock turnover (ratio)

在庫品控帳 stock book
在庫変動 inventory change
在庫予算 inventory budget
在 庫 率 inventory ratio；inventory shipment ratio；stock-to-sales ratio
在 庫 量 volume of inventories
催　　告 notification
サイコロジカル・ライン psychological line
財サービス・バスケット basket of goods and services
再々保険 retrocession
財　　産 belongings；property
財産移転義務 obligation to transfer a proprietary right
財産移転禁止法 disabling statutes
財産管理 property management；receivership
財産管理人 receiver
財産管理命令 receiving order
財 産 区 property ward
財 産 権 property right
財産差押 levy of attachment；seizure of property
財産支払義務 obligation to make an asset payment
財産状態報告書 statement of affairs
財産譲渡 conveyance of estate
財産所得 property income
財産処分能力 disposing capacity
財産贈与 donation of property
財産贈与書類 brief of title
財産損傷賠償責任 property damage liability
財産に付属する権利 appurtenance；rights attached to property
財産の検分 inspection of property
財産の状況 actual state of property
財産の増加 accretion of property
財産の調査 audit on property
財産の評価 valuation of property
財産売却益 profit on assets sold
財産評価 property valuation
財産評価益 income from valuation of assets
財産分与 distribution of property
財産放棄 property abandonment
財産保管人 conservator
財産保険 property insurance
財産保有費用 carrying charge of property
財産目録 inventory of property；list of assets；list of property；statement of assets
財産元帳 property ledger
採 算 株 income share
採算水準 break-even line
採算ライン profitable line of business
再資金調達 replacement financing
最終委任状勧誘書類 definitive proxy statement
最終売建玉 final short position
最終買建玉 final long position
最終価格 final price
最終価値 terminal value
最終過程 final process
最終期限日 drop dead day
最終記入簿 book of final entry
最終局面 final phase
最終結果 end result
最終決済 final settlement
最終決済期日 final settlement day
最終決算 final accounts
最終決定 final determination
最終気配値 closing quote
最終気配値段 final special quote
最終債務額 final obligation
最終残高方式 final balance method
最終仕入原価法 last cost method；last purchase method；most recent purchase method
最終資金決済 real cash settlement
最終指示書 letter of last instructions
最終時点ファイナリティ end-of-day finality
最終支払い final payment
最終収益率 final rate of return
最終受益者 final beneficiary
最終需要 final demand
最終需要の動向 developments in final demand

サ

最終処分 ultimate disposal
最終処理 final disposal
最終清算指数 final settlement index price
最終生存者年金 last survivor annuity
最終製品 final products
最終相続人 last heir
最終積立 terminal funding
最終的な final cut
最終的な現金流出額 ultimate cash outflow
最終的に確定した財務諸表 finally settled financial statements
最終テスト parallel run
最終投資家 retail investor
最終投資利回り final yield on investment
最終特別気配値段 final bid-asked quotation
最終取引日 final transaction date；last day of trading
最終取引日の属する月 month to which the last trading day pertains
最終値段 last price
最終の貸し手 lender of last resort
最終の株主名簿 final list of shareholders
最終保険料支払日 date of last payment
最終満期 final maturity
最終目標 end goal；policy objective
最終目論見書 final prospectus
最終約定指数 closing contract index price
最終利回り final yield；YTM (yield to maturity)
再修正記入 readjusting entry
歳　　出 annual expenditure；government expenditure
歳 出 金 government expenditures
歳出法案 appropriation bill
再取得価格 reacquisition price；replacement cost；repurchase price
再取得株式 re-acquired stock
再取得原価 replacement cost
再取得リスク replacement risk
再 出 発 fresh start
最小価格変動単位 trading variation
最小価値法 minimum value method
最小グループ smallest group
最小限界費用 minimum marginal cost
最小現金残高 minimum cash balance
最小限の構成 minimum structure
最小限の項目 minimum line items
再照合する countercheck
最小単位 minimum lot
最小単位の権利行使 minimum unit of exercise
最 小 値 minimum value
最小徴税費 minimum expense for tax collection
最小ティック minimum tick
最小二乗法 least-squares method
最小二乗法回帰分析 OLS (ordinary least squares) regression
最小値幅 minimum fluctuation
最小年金債務 minimum pension liabilities
最小年金債務調整額 minimum pension liability adjustment
最小負債 minimum liability
最小負債計上要件 minimum liability requirement
最小分散フロンティアー minimum variance frontier
最小分散ポートフォリオ minimum variance portfolio
最小変動単位 minimum fluctuation unit
最小利潤 minimum profit
在職期限 length of service；term of office
在職死亡保障付退職金積立制度 Superannuation Plan
在職証明 certificate of incumbency
最初に開示を要する事象 initial disclosure event
最初の取得者 first purchaser
最初の約定値段 initial contract price
再　　審 new trial
再 信 託 retrust
再 審 理 rehearing
再　　生 regeneration
再生可能な天然資源 regenerative natural resources
再生原材料 reclaimed materials
再 生 産 reproduction

再生産原価 reproduction cost
再生産表式 schema of reproduction
再 生 税 rehabilitation tax
再生ファンド restructuring fund
財　　政 fiscal affairs；government finance
財政赤字 budget deficit；deficit of fiscal balance；deficit spending；fiscal deficit
財政赤字削減 budget deficit reduction
財政インフレ fiscal inflation
財政援助 financing device；fiscal aid
財政改革 fiscal reform
財政基盤 financial footing
財政規模 scale of central and local public finance
財政緊縮政策 tight fiscal policy
財政金融政策 fiscal and monetary policy
財政金融制度 fiscal and financial system
財政黒字 budget surplus；fiscal surplus
財政黒字予測 projected budget surplus
財政硬直化 fiscal inflexibility
財政困難 financial difficulty
財政錯覚 fiscal illusion
財政資金対民間収支 receipts and payments of treasury funds between the government and the private sector
財政刺激 fiscal boost
財政刺激策 fiscal stimulus package
財政支出 fiscal expenditure；government expenditure；public spending
財政支出を賄うための国債 bonds used to finance government expenditure
財政支出計画 spending program
財政収支 budget balance；government fiscal balance
財政準備 fiscal reserve
財政上緊急処分 emergent financial disposition
財政状態 financial conditions；fiscal position
財政状態計算書 statement of financial condition
財政状態変動表 statement of changes in financial position
財政診断 financial diagnosis
財政スタビライザー fiscal stabilizer
財政政策 fiscal policy
財政政策による刺激策 fiscal policy stimulus
財政制度等審議会 Fiscal System Council
財政制約 fiscal constraint
財政節度 fiscal discipline
財政調査官 Special Officer for Research on Budgetary Matters
財政的保護 financial cushion
財政投資 fiscal investment
財政投融資 fiscal investment and loan；treasury investments and loans
財政投融資企画官 Director for Fiscal Investment and Loan Program System
財政投融資計画 FILP (Fiscal Investment and Loan Program)
財政投融資総括課 Fiscal Investment and Loan Program Division
財政投融資調査官 Special Officer for Research on Fiscal Investment and Loan Program
財政難に苦しむ政府 troubled government
財政の逼迫 fiscal tightness
財政引締め fiscal consolidation
財政負担均一基金 Burden Equalization Fund
財 政 法 finance act；Public Finance Law
財政膨張の歯止め fiscal drug
財政見通し fiscal outlook
財政民主主義 financial democracy
財政目標 fiscal target
財政融資資金 fiscal investment and loan fund
財政融資資金特別会計 Fiscal Loan Fund Special Account
財政融資特会債 Fiscal Loan Fund Special Account bonds
財政力指数 index of financial condition
最 先 端 leading edge

サ

最善努力原則 best efforts basis
細　　則 by-laws
再 測 定 remeasurement
再測定損失 loss on re-measurement
再測定利得 gain on re-measurement
最大アンダーウエイト max underweight
最大営業日数 maximum number of the business days
最大オーバーウエイト max overweight
最大在庫量 maximum inventory
最大生産能力 maximum capacity
最大善意 utmost good faith
最大損失推定値 maximum loss estimates
最大の目標 primary objective
在宅医療 care at home
財　　団 foundation
財団債権 estate claims ; superior obligation
財団抵当 foundation collateral
再担保設定 rehypothecation
最長期債 longest remaining life bonds
再 調 整 realignment
再調整交渉 realignment negotiation
再調達価額 replacement value
再調達価値 prevailing value
再調達原価法 replacement cost method
再調達費保証保険 guaranteed replacement cost coverage insurance
再調達保証保険 full replacement coverage
裁　　定 arbitrage
裁定価格決定理論 arbitrage pricing theory
裁定為替相場 arbitrated exchange rate
裁定機会 arbitrage opportunity
裁定債券 arbitrage bond
裁 定 者 adjudicator
裁定相場 arbitrated rate
裁定データ arbitrage data
裁定的な上限 arbitrary ceiling
裁定取引 arbitrage transaction
裁定取引者 arbitrageur
裁定取引に係る現物ポジション positions established with index arbitrages
裁定取引プログラム ATP (arbitrage trading program)
裁定の機会 arbitrage possibility
裁定ポジション arbitrage position
裁定マージン arbitrage margin
最低在高 minimum inventory ; minimum stock
最低運賃 minimum freight
最低額面金額 minimum face value
最低貸出金利 MLR (minimum lending rate) ; MRR (minimum retail rate)
最低貸出歩合 minimum lending rate
最低課税 minimum taxation
最低基準 minimum standard
最低期待収益率 minimum expected rate of return
最低給付制度 floor plan
最低競売価格 upset price
最低拠出額 minimum scheme contribution
最低限支払義務額 fixed amount minimum payment
最低限の開示 minimum disclosure
最低限の項目 minimum items
最低限の要件 minimum requirements
最低限の要素 minimum elements
最低券面単位 minimum denomination
最低限輸入業務 minimum access
最低サブリース料総額 minimum total sub-lease payments
最低残高法 low balance method
最低資金 minimum fund
最低自己資本 minimum capital
最低支払額 minimum payment
最低支払準備率 required reserve rate
最低支払能力基準 minimum solvency standard
最低支払保証年金 guaranteed minimum annuity
最低資本 basic capital
最低資本金 minimum capital requirements
最低資本金制度 minimum capital system
最低資本要件 minimum capital requirement
最低受給権付与基準 minimum vesting standard

最低証拠金 minimum maintenance
最低証拠金率 minimum margin requirement
最低注文量 minimum quantity
最低賃金 minimum wage
最低追加債務 additional minimum liability
最低積立基準 minimum funding standard
最低積立規準額 minimum reserve requirement
最低積立要件 minimum funding requirement
最低転換行使価格 minimum conversion exercise price
最低取引単位 round lot
最低入札価格 minimum bid
最低年間利益 minimum annual return
最低の犠牲 minimum sacrifice
最低返戻金 minimum surrender value
最低保険金 minimum policy amount
最低保険料 minimum premium
最低保険料率 minimum premium rate
最低保障 floor of protection
最低保証額 guaranteed minimum
最低保証金 minimum guarantee
最低免税所得 minimum exempt income
最低リース支払額 MLP (minimum lease payment)
最低リース料総額 minimum total lease payments
最低利幅 minimum margin
最低流動性比率 minimum liquidity ratio
最低料率 minimum rate
最 適 化 optimization
最適化法 optimization method
最適化モデル optimization model
最適関税の理論 theory of optimum tariff
最適規模 optimal scale
最適在庫量 optimum inventory
最適最有利操業度 optimal operating ratio
最適資源配分 optimum allocation of resources
最適資産配分 optimal asset allocation
最適資本構成 optimal capital structure
最適条件 optimal condition
最適性基準 optimality criterion
最適生産量 optimum output
最適成長モデル optimal growth model
最適成長率 optimum rate of growth
最適戦略 optimal strategy
最適操業度 optimum capacity
最適通貨地域 optimum currency area
最適停止時刻 optimal stopping time
最適停止問題 optimal stopping problem
最適な債券ポートフォリオ optimal bond portfolio
最適なバランス optimum balance
最適反応 optimal response
最適分配 optimum distribution
最適ヘッジ手段 optimal hedge instrument
最適ポートフォリオ optimal portfolio
最適ポリシー・ミックス optimal policy mix
最適利子率 optimum rate of interest
財 テ ク zai-tech
再 転 換 reconversion
財投機関 FILP (Fiscal Investment and Loan Program) agency
財投機関債 FILP (Fiscal Investment and Loan Program) agency bond
再 投 資 reinvestment
再投資額 reinvested value
再投資特権 reinvestment privilege
再投資利益 earnings reinvested
再投資リスク reinvestment risk
再投資利率 reinvestment rate
サイト・クレジット sight credit
才取会員 saitori member
在日外銀 foreign banks in Japan
歳 入 annual revenue；fiscal revenue
歳 入 金 government revenues
歳入欠陥 revenue deficit
歳 入 源 revenue sources
歳入交付 revenue sharing
歳 入 債 revenue bond；revenue securities
歳入歳出予算 revenue and expenditure budget
歳入代理店 revenue agent
歳入中立 revenue neutral

歳入の中立性 revenue neutrality
歳入復代理店 revenue sub-agent
歳入補填国債 deficit covering government bond
歳入見込証券 revenue anticipation note
在　　任 tenure of the office
在任の取締役 incumbent director
再　　燃 resurgence
差異の解消 reversal of difference
再配賦原価 redistributed cost
再 配 分 redistribution
財　　閥 financial clique；zaibatsu
再発行価格 subsequent issue price
再　　販 resale
再販価格 resale price
再販価格維持 resale price maintenance
再販売受取債権 remarketed account receivables
再販売価格基準法 resale price method
裁判外の extra-judicial
裁 判 官 bench
裁判官訴追委員会 Impeachment Committee
裁判官弾劾裁判所 Judge Impeachment Court
裁判しうる権限 high justice
裁 判 所 court；forum
裁判請求権 right of access to courts
裁判手続 legal procedure
裁判による立法 judicial legislation
再反対尋問 re-cross-examination
再評価益 revaluation profit
再評価額 revalued amount
再評価減少額 revaluation decrease
再評価後の帳簿価額 revalued carrying amount
再評価差額 revaluation excess
再評価資産 revalued assets
再評価準備金 reserve for revaluation
再評価剰余金 appreciation surplus；revaluation surplus
再評価する reassess；revalue
再評価税 assets revaluation tax
再評価損益 revaluation surpluses and deficits
再評価積立金 revaluation reserve；revaluation surplus reserve
再評価積立金の資本組入れ capitalization of revaluation surplus reserve
再評価による増加 revaluation increase
最 頻 値 mode
財物損壊 property damage
差異分析 variance analysis
差異分析会計 variance accounting
再分類調整 reclassification adjustment
再 編 成 reorganization
再 保 険 reinsurance
再保険受取勘定 reinsurance receivables
再保険会計 reinsurance accounting
再保険貸 reinsurance credit
再保険金 reinsurance recovery
再保険金額 amount of reinsurance
再保険金請求 reinsurance claim
再保険契約 reinsurance agreement；reinsurance contract
再保険資金 reinsurance fund
再保険条項 reinsurance clause
再保険証明書 certificate of reinsurance
再保険手数料 reinsurance commission
再保険特約 reinsurance treaty
再保険特約書 treaty wording
再保険取引 reinsurance transaction
再保険プール pooling arrangement
再保険付保 cession
再保険ブローカー reinsurance broker
再保険報告書 bordereau
再保険料 ceded premium；reinsurance premium
再保険レバレッジ reinsurance leverage
再 募 集 reoffering
再見積り re-estimation
債　　務 indebtedness；obligation
債務がある stand in debt
債務回収業者 debt collector
債務買取契約 note purchase agreement
債 務 額 amount of obligations
債務確定の判定 judgment of definite liabilities
債務過多 over-indebtedness
債務株式化 debt-equity swap

債務管理 debt management
債務企業 debtor firm
債務繰延べ debt deferral
債務限度 debt ceiling
債務合計 TD (total debt)
債務控除 deduction of liabilities
債 務 国 debtor country；debtor nation
債務債券 obligation bond
債務再交渉 debt renegotiation
債務残高 debt balance
債 務 者 debtor；obligor
債務者区分 borrower category；classification of debtors
債務者集中度 obligor concentration
債務者に対する債権 claims on borrowers
債務者の支払能力 borrower's solvency
債務者のリスク obligor risk
債務者不履行 insolvency of debtors
債務者分類 borrower classification
債務者預金 debtors' deposit
債務手段 debt instrument
債務償還 amortization
債務償還計画 amortization schedule；debt servicing schedule
債務償還積立金 surplus appropriated for redemption fund
債務証券 debt obligation；debt securities
債務証券の早期償還 early extinguishment of debt securities
債務証券の発行差金 premium on debt
債務証書 bill of debt；certificate of indebtedness；evidences of indebtedness
債務証書貸付 Schuldschein Darlehen
債務譲渡 cession of an obligation
債務消滅 acquittance；debt reduction；expiration of obligation
債務信託 debt trust
債務スワップ liability swap
債務整理 arrangement
債務整理計画 scheme of arrangement
債務整理証書 deed of arrangement
債務総額 gross amount due to
債務担保証券 CDO (collateralized debt obligation)
債務超過 deficiency in assets；excess of debt；liabilities exceeding assets；negative equity
債務調整 adjustment of debts
債務に対する信用 credit on a debt
債務の1年以内返済部分 current portion of liabilities
債務の株式化 debt to equity swap
債務の貨幣化 monetization of the debt
債務の期限の利益の喪失 acceleration of liabilities
債務の債券化 debt to bond swap
債務の再編 debt restructuring
債務の消滅 extinguishment of debt
債務の処理 liquidation of liabilities
債務の全期間 entire life of obligation
債務の相互性 mutuality of obligation
債務の返済 debt service；satisfaction of debt
債務の返済猶予 repayment moratorium
債務の保有者 holder of obligation
債務の未履行分 unperformed part of obligation
債務の履行 performance of obligation
債務のリスケジューリング rescheduling of debt
債務の利息 interest on obligation
債務発生事象 obligating event
債務引受け debt assumption
債務引継ぎ succession of liabilities
債務引渡し transferred liabilities
債務比率の増大 growing leverage
債務負担 incurrence of liability
債務負担捺印債務証書 single bill(bond)
債務不履行 default；default of obligation；failure to fulfill obligation
債務不履行による清算 insolvent liquidation
債務不履行のプレミアム default risk premium
債務不履行の予測指標 predictors of default
債務不履行リスク default risk
債務返済 debt retirement；meeting debt maturities

サ

サ

債務弁済 fulfillment of obligations；repayment of liabilities
債務返済延期承認書 extension
債務返済コスト debt servicing cost
債務返済能力 ability to repay the debt；debt coverage
債務返済の負担 servicing burden
債務返済比率 debt service ratio
債務ポートフォリオ liabilities portfolio
債務保証 debt guarantee；guarantee facility；guarantee of indebtedness
債務保証契約 financial guarantee contract；guarantee arrangement contracts
債務免除 acquittal of debt；debt relief；discharge of debt
債務免除益 gains from forgiveness of debt；income from discharge of indebtedness
債務リスク管理 liability risk management
債務レバレッジ debt leverage
財　　務 financial affairs
財務及び営業のハイライト financial and operational highlights
財務概況 financial review
財務会計 financial accounting
財務会計概念基準書 SFAC (Statement of Financial Accounting Concepts)
財務会計基準機構 FASF (Financial Accounting Standards Foundation)
財務会計基準諮問委員会 Financial Accounting Standards Advisory Council
財務会計基準書 SFAS (Statement of Financial Accounting Standards)
財務会計基準審議会 FASB (Financial Accounting Standards Board)
財務会計基準審議会基準書 FASB (Financial Accounting Standards Board) pronouncements
財務会計原則 financial accounting principles
財務会計財団 Financial Accounting Foundation
財務格付制度 financial rating system
財務活動 financing activities
財務活動からのキャッシュフロー cash flow from financial activities
財務活動資金 fund for financial activities
財 務 官 Vice Minister of Finance for International Affairs
財務監査 financial audit
財務官室 Office of the Vice Minister of Finance for International Affairs
財務管理 financial management
財務技官 Technical Official, Ministry of Finance
財務基盤 financial base
財務業績 financial performance
財 務 局 Local Finance Bureaus
財務計画 financial planning
財務計算書類 financial accounting statements
財務健全度 financial soundness
財務構造 financial structure
財務広報 financial public relation
財務コスト financial cost
財務顧問 financial advisor
財務コンサル financial consultant
財務裁判所 Court of Exchequer
財務指標 financial indicators；financial variables
財務事務官 Official, Ministry of Finance
財務収益 financial return；financial revenue
財 務 省 Ministry of Finance
財務省原案 budget draft by the Ministry of Finance
財務省顧問 Special Adviser to the Minister of Finance
財務省債務証書 Treasury Certificate of Indebtedness
財務省参事 Adviser to the Minister of Finance
財務省参与 Senior Adviser to the Minister of Finance
財務省証券 treasury bonds；treasury instruments；treasury financing bills
財務省証券買入消却オペ Treasury debt buyback operations

財務省証券市場 treasury securities market
財務省証券利回り Treasury yield
財務省証書 treasury certificate
財務省租税国債証書勘定 treasury tax and loan note accounts
財務省短期証券 treasury bill
財務省短期証券市場 treasury bill market
財務省中期証券 T-note；treasury note
財務省中期貯蓄債券 Treasury Savings Bonds
財務省長期証券 treasury bond
財務省聴聞手続規則 Regulations of Procedures of Hearing by the Ministry of Finance
財務省通達 Notification of the Ministry of Finance
財務省投資債券 Treasury Bonds Investment Series
財務省預託金 deposit by the Ministry of Finance
財務省令 Finance Ministry Ordinance
財務上の影響 financial effect
財務上の仮定 financial assumption
財務上の査定 financial underwriting
財務上のスラック financial slack
財務上の相乗効果 financial synergy
財務上の負担 financial strain and stress
財務上の持ち分 financial interest
財務商品 treasury product
財務情報 financial information
財務省令 ordinance from the Ministry of Finance
財務諸表 financial statements
財務諸表監査 examination of financial statements；financial statements audit
財務諸表規則 regulations of financial statements
財務諸表脚注 notes to the financial statements
財務諸表構成 financial statements structure
財務諸表作成基準 basis of the preparation of financial statements
財務諸表準則 rules for the preparation of financial statements
財務諸表注記 notes to the financial statements
財務諸表摘要書 abstract of financial statements
財務諸表での認識 recognition in the financial statements
財務諸表に開示すべき情報 information to be disclosed in the financial statements
財務諸表に計上された recognized in financial statements
財務諸表に対する責任 responsibility for financial statements
財務諸表の構成部分 components of financial statements
財務諸表の作成 preparation of financial statements
財務諸表の比較可能性 comparability of financial statements
財務諸表の日付から経過した期間 age of financial statements
財務諸表の表示 presentation of financial statements
財務諸表の本体 face of financial statements
財務諸表の目的 purpose of financial statements
財務諸表の利用者 user of financial statements
財務諸表のレビュー review of financial statements
財務諸表付属明細書 schedule of financial statements
財務諸表分析 analysis of financial statements
財務書類 financial documents
財務数値 financial variables
財務制限条項 financial covenant
財務政策 fiscal agenda
財務総合政策研究所 Policy Research Institute；Ministry of Finance
財務損失 financial loss
財務体質 financial structure
財務大臣 Minister of Finance

サ

サ

財務大臣政務官 Parliamentary Secretary for Finance
財務代理人 financial agent；fiscal agent
財務代理人契約 fiscal agent agreement
財務代理人への信託金 money entrusted to the financial agent
財務担当経営者協会 Financial Executive Institute
財務データ financial data
財務的影響 financial impact
財務的表明 financial representation
財務内容 financial condition
財務内容の開示 financial disclosure
財務内容評価法 financial state valuation method
財務年度 financial year
財務の実態 actual financial condition
財務バランス financial balance
財務比率 accounting ratio；financial ratio
財務部長 treasurer
財務フロー financial flow
財務分析 financial analysis
財務報告 financial reporting
財務報告会計 financial reporting accounting
財務報告基準 financial reporting standards
財務報告書 financial report
財務報告上の株主資本 reported equity
財務報告通牒 FRR (Financial Reporting Release)
財務報告年度 financial reporting year
財務面の増益効果 financial leverage effect
財務面の増益効果度 degree of financial leverage
財務目標 financial target
財務予算 financial budget
財務予測 financial forecast；financial projection
財務リスク financial risk
財務流動性 financial solvency
財 務 力 financial dynamics；financial strength
財務レバレッジ capital leverage；financial gearing
細目勘定式 detailed account form
最安値からの回復 comeback from lows
再融資契約 agreement to refinance
最 優 先 first priority
最優先の目的 overriding goal
最優先引受権 right of first refusal
最 尤 度 maximum likelihood
最 尤 法 maximum likelihood method
最有利操業度 maximum operating ratio
再 輸 出 re-export
採　　用 adoption
在来型保険 conventional insurance
再リース re-leasing
裁量貸出 discretionary loan
裁量期間 arbitrary period
裁量原価 discretionary cost
裁量行為 discretional act
裁量所得 discretionary income
最良証拠 best evidence
最良誠実 uberrima fide
最良の見積り best estimate
材　　料 raw materials
材料価格差異 material price variance
材料在庫高 materials inventory
材料仕入高 materials purchased
材料仕入帳 stores purchase book
材料出庫請求書 material requisition note
材料仕様書 materials specification
材料仕訳帳 materials distribution sheet
材料数量差異 material quantity variance；material usage variance
材 料 費 material cost
材料費差額 materials variance
材料標準価格 materials price standard
材料標準消費量 standard quantity of materials consumed
材料明細書 BOM (bill of materials)
材料元帳 materials ledger
材料予算 materials budget
再　　割 rediscount
再割当金 reallocated amount
再割適格手形 eligible paper
再 割 引 rediscounting

再割引金利 rediscount rate
再割引政策 rediscount policy
最割安銘柄 CTD (cheapest-to-deliver)
サウジアラビア通貨庁 SAMA (Saudi Arabia Monetary Agency)
サウジアラビア・リアル SAR (Saudi Arabian riyal)
差　益 differential gain
詐害行為取消権 right to revoke fraudulent act
差　額 balance；balancing figure；difference amount
差額勘定 differential account
差額決済 transaction adjustment payment
差額原価 differential cost
差額原価計算 differential costing
差額式 remainder type
差額収入 take out
差額推定法 mean-per-unit difference method
差額請求 balance billing
差額利益額 differential earnings amount
詐　欺 actionable fraud；cheat
詐欺債権者 fraudulent creditor
詐欺譲渡 fraudulent conveyance
詐欺請求 fraudulent claims
詐欺的行為 fraudulent action
詐欺的譲渡 fraudulent transfer
詐欺破産 fraudulent bankruptcy
詐欺表示 fraudulent misrepresentation
先入先出法 FIFO (first-in, first-out) method
先送法 rolling-forward procedure
先駆け front running
先駆的商品 precursor
先駆取引 going ahead
先一先レート forward-forward rate
先高観 bullish
先取権 right of priority
先取手数料 front end commission
先取特権 preferred creditors' right
先取特権通知 notice of lien
先取特権の放棄 waiver of lien
先取特権理論 lien theory
先取ローディング up-front loading
先に行われた売呼値 earlier offer
先に行われた買呼値 earlier bid
先払い payment on delivery
先払報酬 up-front compensation
先日付小切手 postdated check
先日付手形 postdated bill or note
先日付取引 future-dated/post-dated transactions
先日付の dating forward
先　物 futures
先物委託売買業務 futures brokerage business
先物売りポジション short forward position
先物オプション futures option
先物オプション市場 futures option market
先物オプション他社清算参加者 futures and options agency clearing participant
先物オプション取引口座 Futures/Options Trading Account
先物オプション取引口座設定約諾書 Agreement for Establishment of Futures/Options Trading Account
先物オプション取引所 FOX (futures and options exchange)
先物オプション取引に係る証拠金及び未決済約定の引継ぎ等に関する規則 Rules on Margin and Transfer of Unsettled Contracts Pertaining to Futures/Option Contract
先物価格 futures price
先物価格曲線 price line of futures price
先物為替 forward exchange
先物為替売相場 forward offer rate
先物為替買相場 forward bid rate
先物為替市場 forward exchange market
先物為替相場 forward exchange rate；forward quotation
先物為替取引 forward exchange transaction
先物為替プレミアム forward premium
先物為替持高 forward position
先物為替予約 exchange forward contract
先物為替予約レート forward foreign exchange rate

サ

先物協会　FIA (Futures Industry Association)
先物業界　futures industry
先物契約　futures contract
先物市場　futures market
先物商品　futures instrument；futures product
先物ディーラー　futures dealer
先物ディスカウント　forward discount
先物投資協会　AFI (Association of Futures Investments)
先物取次業者　futures agent
先物取引　futures trading；futures transaction
先物取引業者　FCM (futures commission merchant)
先物取引差金　difference resulting from offsetting futures contracts
先物取引等特別参加者　special participants in futures trading and the like
先物取引の成立　transaction contract in futures contract
先物取引の対象　subject of futures trading
先物のポジション　futures position
先物引渡契約　sales contracts commitments
先物評価　futures valuation
先物評価モデル　futures valuation model
先物ブローカー・ディーラー協会　AFBD (Association of Futures Brokers and Dealers)
先物マージン　futures margin
先物レート　forward rate；futures quotation；futures rate
先安観　bearish
作業　work
作業効率　labor efficiency
作業指図書　job order
作業時間　working hours
作業時間差異　labor time variance
作業条件　working condition
作業損失　loss of work
作業伝票　job slip
作業日数　working days
作業能率　operation efficiency
作業場　workshop
作業費　operation expenses
作業票　job ticket；production card
作業標準　work standard
先渡し　forward delivery
先渡価格　forward price
先渡為替スプレッド　forward rate spread
先渡契約　forward contract
先渡決済　forward settlement
先渡購入契約　forward purchase contract
先渡取引　forward agreement；forward operation
先渡日　forward date
先渡マージン　forward margin
先渡預金　forward deposit
差金　differences
差金決済　net settlement
差金取引　speculating for difference；speculation for margin
搾取　exploitation
削除　rasure
作図法　visual curve-fitting method
錯綜相場　crossed market
昨年同期比で　compared to the same period one year earlier
下げ足　downward movement
下げ基調の相場　falling market
下げ局面　downtick
下げ相場　bear market；short market
さけ・ます資源管理センター　National Salmon Resources Center
査察　criminal investigation
査察課　Criminal Investigation Division
査察制度　criminal investigation system
差入担保　pledged collateral
差入保証金　guaranty money deposited
差入有価証券　pledged securities
差入預託保証金　guaranty deposits
差押え　attachment；distress；seizure
差押解除　release of foreclosure
差押禁止債権　exemptions from attachment
差押禁止財産　property not subject to seizure
差押財産の換価　liquidation of seized

property
差押先着手主義 principle of priority to first seizure
差押書 document of foreclosure ; document of seizure
差押対象財産 property subject to seizure
差押調書 record of foreclosure ; record of seizure
差押通知書 notice of seizure
差押人 foreclosing party ; seizor
差押えの解除 release of seizure
差押物件 attached goods ; foreclosed property ; seized goods
差押物件の引継 transfer of seized goods
差押物件売却 distress sale
差押抹消登記 register of cancellation of attachment
差押命令 foreclosure order ; order for attachment of property
差押猶予 suspension of seizure
差押さえる attach ; distrain
差押令状 warrant of attachment
差換預託分 replacement deposit
指図 direction
指図禁止手形 non-order bill
指図小切手 check to order
指図式裏書 endorsement to order ; special endorsement
指図証券 bill to order
指図人式船荷証券 order B/L (bill of lading)
指図人支払小切手 order check
指図人払い payable to order
指図人払手形 bill payable to order
指図人渡し delivery to order
差し迫った問題 pressing issue
差止手続 injunction proceedings
差止命令 injunction
差止命令手続 injunctive proceedings
指値 limit price
指値以上 or better
指値算定法 limit calculation
指値注文 limit order ; stop order
指値注文預り leave order
指値注文情報システム limit order information system
指値注文売買システム LOTS (limit order trading system)
差控え forbearance
差引合計額 net total
差引建玉 net position
差戻命令 mandate on remission
詐称通用 passing off
左遷 relegation
差損金 loss from difference of price
サタデー・ナイト・スペシャル Saturday Night Special
定めのない期間 non-determined period
雑益 miscellaneous gains
雑貨 general merchandise ; sundry goods
雑貨商 grocer
雑勘定 miscellaneous accounts ; sundry account
雑資産 miscellaneous assets
雑収益 miscellaneous revenue
雑収入 miscellaneous receipts ; sundry income ; sundry receipts
雑種税 miscellaneous local taxes
雑所得 miscellaneous income
雑則 miscellaneous provision
雑損 miscellaneous loss
雑損益 petty profit and loss
雑損控除 deduction for casualty losses
雑損失の繰越 carryover of casualty loss
雑損失の繰越控除 carry over of casualty loss
雑費 miscellaneous expenses ; petty expenses ; sundries ; unclassified expenses
雑費内訳帳 petty expense analysis book ; petty expense break down book
査定価額 assessed value
査定額 appraisal amount ; assessed amount
査定機関 assessing organ
査定所得額 assessed income
査定人 surveyor
査定の厳格化 accuracy of counting in assessment

サ

査定免除 underwriting concession
差等税率 graded tariff
サバイバル関数 survival function
サバイバル・ボンド survival bond
サブカストディアン sub-custodian
サブ口座番号 sub-account number
サブジェクト・マーケット subject market
サブ指数 sub-index
サブプライム sub-prime；subprime
サプライ・オア・ペイ契約 supply-or-pay contract
サプライサイドの経済学 supply-side economics
サブリース sublease
サブリース料 sublease payment
差分分析 differential analysis
差　別 discrimination
差別化 differentiation
差別価格 discriminative price
差別関税 discriminating customs duty
差別税率 discriminative tariff
差別的扱い discriminatory handling
差別独占 discriminating monopolies
差別要因 discriminant
サポート・トランシェ support tranche
サボタージュ sabotage
サムライ債 samurai bond
サムライＣＰ samurai commercial paper
鮫よけ shark repellent
サモア・タラ WST (Samoan tala)
さや取り arbitration in stock
さや取業者 arbitrage trader
さや取取引 arbitrage business
さや取売買 arbitrage operation
さや取屋 arbitrage house
さや寄せ narrowing of spread
サラ金規制法 consumer credit control law
更　地 land lot without construction；open lot
ザラ場 continuous market；continuous session
サリー・メイ SLMA (Student Loan Marketing Association)
サリー・メイ債 Sallie Mae debenture
3営業日渡し double settlement
参　加 participation
参加型ユニット投資信託 participating unit investment trust
参加金 participation fee
参加銀行 participation bank
参加差押え participation in foreclosure；participation in seizure
参加事業年度 participating business year
参加支払い payment supra
参加者 participant
参加者間決済 internal settlement
参加者基金 participants' fund
参加者口座 direct participant's account
参加者口座の開設 establishment of direct participant's account
参加者口座の増減額及び残高の通知 notice of increase or decrease and balance of direct participant's account
参加者口座簿 ledger of participant accounts
参加者端末 PTC (participant terminal system)
参加者投資信託 PPT (participant protection trust)
参加者名簿 register of participants
参加証券 participation certificate；participation securities
参加配当 participating dividend
参加配当年金 participating annuity
参加引受 act of honor
参加方式 participation method
参加保険 participating insurance
参加持ち分 participating interests
参加融資 participation loan
参加株 participation stock
参加優先株式 participating preferred stock
三階建制 three tier system
傘下企業 umbrella group
残　額 remaining amount
残額引受け standby commitment
残額引受契約 standby agreement
残額引受発行 stand-by underwriting
三角貿易 triangle trade

3カ月以上延滞債権 loans overdue for three months or longer
3カ月移動平均 three-month moving average
3カ月TB BULI (three month Treasury bills)
参 議 院 House of Councillors
産　　業 industry
産業安全研究所 National Institute of Industrial Safety
産業医学総合研究所 National Institute of Industrial Health
産 業 界 industrial circles
産業開発債券 IDB (industrial development bond)
産業化医療 capitalized health care
産業間相関 inter-industry correlation
産業間の inter-industry
産業技術総合研究所 National Institute of Advanced Industrial Science and Technology
産業協力方式 industrial cooperation method
産業効果 industry effect
産業構造 industrial composition ; industrial structure
産業構造高度化 growth of industrial structure
産業構造政策 industrial structure policy
産業構造調整 reorganization of industrial structure
産業合理化 industrial rationalization
産業再生 industrial regeneration
産業再生機構 IRCJ (Industrial Revitalization Corporation of Japan)
産業再生機構担当大臣 Minister of State for Industrial Revitalization Corporation
産業再編成 reorganization of industry
産業資金 industrial fund
産業資金供給状況 net supply of industrial funds
産業事故準備金 industrial accident reserve
産業資本 industrial capital
産業集中 industry concentration
産業情報 industry information
産業スペシャリスト industry specialist
産業政策 industrial policy
産業生命保険 industrial life insurance
産業的要因 industry factor
産業投資特別会計 Industrial Investment Special Account
産業投資特別会計資金 Industrial Investment Special Account Fund
産業特定財源債 industrial revenue bond
産業のベータ値 industry beta value
産業部門 industrial sector
産業分類 industrial classification
産 業 別 industry-wise
産業別組合 industrial union
産業別国民純生産 industrial origin of net national product
産業銘柄 industrials
産業連関 inter-industry relation
産業連関表 inter-industry-relations table
産業連関分析 inter-industry analysis
残　　業 overtime duties
残業手当 overtime allowance ; overtime payment
三極委員会 Trilateral Commission
サンク・コスト sunk cost
参考意見書 SOP (Statement of Position)
参考価格 indicative pricing
参考期間 reference period
参考水準 indicative level
参考数値 pro forma amount
参考相場圏 reference range
参考統計 reference statistics
参考利回り reference yield
三国間協定 tripartite agreement
三国間貿易 intermediary trade
三国手形 third country bill
散　　財 spending spree
残　　債 remaining debt
残債方式 charge on the declining balance
残差収益率 residual return
残差標準偏差 residual standard deviation
残差分析 residual analysis
参 事 官 Counselor (of the Minister's

Secretariat)；Deputy Director-General of the Planning and Coordination
参事官（監督局） Deputy Director-General of the Supervisory Bureau
参事官（国際） Deputy Commissioner for International Affairs
3時時点（15時） designated settlement time of 15:00
サンシャイン取引 sunshine trading
サンシャイン法 sunshine law
三重益 triple merit
三重関税率 treble tariff
三重の利益 triple bottom line
三重非課税 triple tax exempt
算出基準 basis of the calculation
算出式 calculation formula
算出税額 calculated tax amount
算術級数法 SOYD (sum-of-the-years-digits method)
算術平均 arithmetic average；arithmetic mean
産出係数 output coefficient
産出量 quantity of output
参照額面金額 referenced notional
参照債務 reference obligation
参照指数 reference index
参照指数基準日 base reference index date
参照書類 reference documents
参照組織 reference entity
参照値 reference value
参照点 reference point
参照トランシェ referenced tranche
参照による編入 incorporation by reference
参照の挿入 insertion of cross reference
参照プール reference pool
参照符号のついた cross referenced to
参照ポートフォリオ reference portfolio
賛成意見 concurring opinion
酸性試験比率 acid test ratio
山西省 Shanxi
サンセット条項 sunset provision
三線転換法 three line converting method
残存 remainder
残存価格 remainder price；salvage prices
残存価額 residual value；scrap value
残存価値ゼロ no residual value
残存勘定 old account
残存期間 current maturity；remaining period；remaining term；time to maturity
残存期間が最も短い shortest dated
残存期間の短い証券 short-dated securities
残存期間の最も短い債券 shortest bond on the curve
残存キャリー remaining carry
残存勤務期間 remaining employment period
残存償還期間 period until maturity
残存耐用年数 remaining useful life
残存評価 residual valuation
残存物代位 subrogation arising out of salvage
残存ペナルティ期間 remaining penalty period
残存返済回数 number of payments remaining
残存保険金額 sum insured left
残存モーゲージ outstanding mortgage
残存リース期間 remaining lease term
残存率 residual ratio
残存ローン surviving loan
三尊天井 head and shoulders
残高 amount outstanding；balance
残高勘定 balance account
残高式 balance form
残高試算表 trial balance of balances
残高照会 inquiry for the balances
残高証明書 balance certificate
残高帳 balance book
残高調整式 balance reconciling type
残高のある金融商品 instruments outstanding
残高表 balance sheet
残高不足 insufficient funds
残高不足小切手 insufficient-funds check
残地補償金 compensation for residual

land
参着払売相場 on demand selling rate
参着払手形 bill on demand
算　　定 calculation；computation
算定会料率 rating organization tariffs
算定価格 appraised price
算定可能なキャッシュフロー determinable cash flow
算定期間 computation period
算定基準 basis for calculation
算定レート accounting rate
暫定関税率 temporary tariff
暫定契約 interim contract
暫定合意 tentative agreement
暫定清算人 provisional liquidator
暫定税率 provisional tariff；temporary tariff rate
暫 定 的 temporary
暫定手数料 provisional commission
暫定入札日 tentative auction date
暫定予算 provisional budget；tentative budget
サンドイッチ・スプレッド sandwich spread
サンドイッチ世代 sandwich generation
山 東 省 Shandong
サントメプリンシペ・ドブラ STD (Sao Tome/Principe dobra)
算　　入 inclusion
参入コスト entry cost
参 入 者 entrant
参入障壁 barriers to entry
参入費用 cost of entry
サンパウロ証券取引所 San Paulo Stock Exchange
散発的な買い sporadic buying
三番抵当 third mortgage
ザンビア・クワチャ ZMK (Zambian kwacha)
360日ベース 360 day basis
散 布 図 scatter graph
散布図表 scatter chart
サンプリング単位 sampling unit
3分の2以上の two-thirds or more
サンマリノ（イタリア・リラ） Sao Marino (Italian lira)
残　　務 unfinished business
残務整理 winding-up of pending affairs
参　　与 counselor
三要素配当方法 three factor contribution plan
残余期間 residual maturity；time to expiration
残余クラス residual class
残余原価 residual cost
残 余 項 residual term
残余財産 residual assets；residual property；residuary estate
残余財産権 residual interests in the assets
残余財産の取分 share of residual property
残余財産の分与 distribution of residual assets
残余財産分配 distribution of residual property
残余支出 residuary outlay
残余市場 residual market
残余純利益 residual net income
残余請求権 residual claim
残余配分 residual distribution；residual share
残余部分 residue
残余持ち分 residual equity；residual interest
残余持ち分特別請求権 SCORE (special claim on residual equity)
残余利益 residual benefit；residual income；residual profit
残余リスク residual risk
三 利 源 three surplus factor
残留荷量 innage
残留協定 contracted in arrangement
山　　林 forest land
山林所得 forestry income；timber income
山林所得の控除 forestry income deduction

シ

シ

地 合 い sentiment；undertone
地合指標 sentiment indicator
CRB指数 CRB (Commodity Research Bureau) Index
CIRモデル CIR (Cox Ingersoll Ross) model
CAC40指数 CAC (Compagnie des Agents de Change) 40
GSTPA GSTPA (Global Straight Through Processing Association)
GNPギャップ GNP gap
GNP成長率 GNP growth rate
GNPデフレーター GNP deflator
CMO CMO (Central Moneymarkets Office)
CMU CMU (Central Moneymarkets Unit)
シーズニング・カーブ seasoning curve
GTC注文 good-till-cancelled order
CD市場 CD (certificate of deposit) market
CD年金 CD annuity
CD発行残高 CD outstanding
GDPインプリシット・プライス・デフレーター GDP implicit price deflator
GDPデフレーター GDP deflator
GDPの伸び率 GDP growth rate
G10中央銀行総裁会議 Meeting of Central Bank Governors of the G-10 Countries
ジーニ係数 Gini coefficient
CPIの発表 CPI (consumer price index) release
CPオペレーション CP (commercial paper) operation
CP現先 purchase of CP under repurchase agreement
CP市場 CP (commercial paper) market
CPT CPT (cost per thousand)
CP発行残高 outstanding amount of CP
G5 Group of 5
シーリング方式 ceiling system
仕入運賃 freight inward
仕入原価 buying cost；cost of goods purchased；cost of purchase；first cost；purchase cost
仕 入 先 merchandise resources；supplier；trade creditor
仕入先元帳 purchase ledger
仕入時価 market purchase price
仕 入 税 purchase tax
仕入総額 gross purchase amount
仕入代金支払額 cash paid to suppliers
仕入台帳 bought ledger
仕入代前渡金 advance for purchase
仕入代理店 buying agent
仕 入 高 amount of goods purchased；purchase amount
仕 入 帳 purchase book
仕入値段 cost price；purchasing price
仕入値引 purchase allowance
仕入費用 purchasing expenses
仕入返品 purchase return
仕入前払代金 advance on account of sellers；deposits paid to trade creditors
仕入予算 purchase budget；purchases budget
仕入割引 purchase discount
仕入割戻し purchase rebate
試運転費 trial running expenses
シェアード・エクイティ・モーゲージ shared equity mortgage
シェア・ドラフト share drafts
自　　営 self-employment；self-management
自営業者 individual proprietor
自営業者据置年金 self-employed deferred annuity
自営業者退職年金 self-employed

retirement annuity
自営業者年金 self-employed pension
自営業者年金制度 self-employed pension plan
自営者退職年金 self-employed retirement annuity
Jカーブ J curve
Jカーブ効果 J curve effect
JBネット JB-Net
J-NET市場 J-NET
私益信託 private trust
自益信託 self-benefit trust
ジェネリック・スワップ generic swap
シエラレオーネ・レオーネ SLL (Sierra Leone leone)
支 援 策 aid package ; rescue package
支援状況 state of support
支援比率 support ratio
時　　価 cash value ; current market price ; current price ; present market value
時価会計 market-price based accounting
時価概算額 approximate market price
時価から離れた値段で price away from the market
時価債務カバレッジ overall market price coverage
時価主義 market price basis ; market value basis
時価主義安定価値会計 current cost/constant dollar accounting
時価主義名目価値会計 current cost/nominal dollar accounting
時価総額 aggregate market value ; market cap ; market capitalization ; market value
時価総額加重インデックス capitalization weighted indices
時価総額加重型 capitalization weighted
時価総額加重株価指数 value weighted stock price index
時価総額加重指数 value weighted market index
時価総額加重平均値 weighted average of the market capitalization
時価総額において in capitalization terms
時価総額方式の株価指数 stock price index on the market value
時価転換 conversion at market price
時価のある有価証券 securities with fair value
時価の上昇 appreciated market price
時価の定義 definition of fair value
時価のない有価証券 securities without market value
時価発行 issuance at market price ; issue at market price
時価発行増資 capital increase by new shares at market price
時価評価 fair value appraisal
時価評価額 assessed market value
時価分析 market price analysis ; market value analysis
時価変動 fluctuation of fair value
時 価 法 market value method
時価方式 market price method
自家運用 internal investment management ; private investment
自家運用資金 private fund
自家営業所得 self-employment income
自家再保険 self-reinsurance
自家消費 self-consumption
自家創出のれん internally created goodwill
自家取り alongside delivery
自家年金 private annuity
自家保険 private insurance ; self-insurance
自家保険会社 captive insurance company
自家保険基金 self-insurance fund
自家保険準備金 self-insurance reserve
自家保険制度 self-insurance plan
自家用自動車総合保険 special automobile policy
自家用自動車保険 private automobile policy
私 会 社 proprietary company
資格株式 qualifying share
資格取得 acquisition of qualification
資格年齢 age of eligibility

資 格 法 qualification law
資格を喪失せしめる disqualify
資格を有する保険数理人 qualified actuary
仕　　掛 device
仕掛材料 material in process
仕 掛 品 goods in process；partly finished goods；products in progress；work in process
仕掛品繰越高 inventory of work in process at the beginning of period
仕掛品の評価 valuation of work in process
仕掛品元帳 goods in process ledger；work in process ledger
シカゴ・オプション取引所 Chicago Board Options Exchange
シカゴ学派 Chicago school
シカゴ先物取引所 Chicago Futures Exchange
シカゴ商業取引所 CME (Chicago Mercantile Exchange)
シカゴ証券取引所 CHX (Chicago Stock Exchange)
シカゴ商品取引所 Chicago Board of Trade
市価償還 redemption at market value
歯科治療費保険 dental expense insurance
直 取 引 direct deal；direct transaction
時間依存の time dependent
時間依存パラメーター time-dependent parameter
時間外売買 off-hour trading
時間加重収益率 TWR (time-weighted rate of return)
時間価値の減価 depreciation of time value
時間原価 time cost
時間効果 time effect
時間差異 time variance
時間軸効果 policy duration effect
時間スプレッド time spread
時間選好 time preference
時間調整済み time adjusted
時間的価値 time value
時間的要素 time factor
時間の経過 passage of time
時間の経過に伴う債券価格 over time price of bond
時間パターン time pattern
時間比例法 time based activity method
時間優先 time precedence
時間優先の原則 time priority
時　　期 timing
時期経過船荷証券 stale B/L (bill of lading)
次　　期 subsequent year
次期勘定 ensuing account
次期繰越 balance carried forward to the next term；carryforward to the next term
次期繰越欠損金 loss carried forward to the following term
次期繰越高 amount carried forward
次期繰越利益金 surplus profit carried forward to the following term；unappropriated retained earnings at the end of year
次期決算 next closing of account
次期大統領 president-elect
直 貸 し direct loan
敷　　金 deposit with landlord；leasehold deposit
敷金と保証金 deposits and guarantees
直先同レート flat rate
直先同レート為替予約 flat exchange contract
四季支払勘定日 quarter-days
敷　　地 premises
磁気テープ magnetic tape
識　　別 identification
識別可能資産及び負債 identifiable assets and liabilities
識別可能性 identifiability
識別マーク tactile mark
直　　物 spot
直物価格 underlying value
直物為替 spot exchange
直物為替相場 spot exchange rate
直物市場 spot market
直物相場 spot quotation

直物相場と先物相場の価格差 spread between spot rate and futures rate
直物取引 spot dealing；spot trading
直物持高 actual balance；actual position；spot position
直物レート actual exchange rate
支　給 supply
支給時時価払勘定 phantom account
支給率 payout percentage
至急注文 immediate order
事　業 business；task；undertaking；venture
事業概況説明書 summary statement of business
事業外経費 non-business expenses
事業会社 business corporation
事業開発会社 business development company
事業革新 business innovation
事業拡張 business expansion
事業貸付 industrial loan
事業活動 business activity
事業から生ずる所得 income derived from business
事業環境リスク指数 business environment risk index
事業基盤 business foundation
事業規模の縮小 reduction of business
事業協同組合 cooperative business association
事業金融 business finance；business loan；corporate finance
事業金融会社 business finance company
事業区分別損益報告 report on profit and loss by segment
事業計画 business plan
事業継承 succession to business
事業継承保険 business succession insurance
事業継続保険 business continuation insurance
事業形態 business form
事業権契約 concession agreement
事業広告のための賞品 prize offered for advertisement of the business
事業債 industrial debenture
事業再構築 business restructuring
事業再生 business regeneration
事業再生出融資制度 business regeneration investment and loan program
事業再生ファンド business regeneration fund
事業資金 business fund
事業資金源 coffers
事業支出控除 business expense deduction
事業事象 business affair
事業者 undertaker
事業者団体保険 employer group insurance
事業者提供の employer sponsored
事業所 business establishment；business office；business place
事業上の通常の危険 ordinary risks of business
事業上の秘密 business secret
事業所所得の帰属 attribution of income of business office
事業所税 business office tax
事業所得 business income
事業所得の計算 computation of business income
事業所費 establishment expenses
事業信託 business trust
事業税 business tax；enterprise tax
事業税控除額 general business credit
事業税の損金算入の時期 time of inclusion in expenses of enterprise tax
事業生命保険 business life insurance
事業戦略 business strategy
事業単位 business unit
事業提携 business tie-up
事業停止 business interruption
事業転換 change of business
事業統合 business integration
事業に従事した期間 term of engaging in the business
事業主 business proprietor
事業主掛金 employer contribution
事業主控除 proprietor deduction
事業主特別経費準備金 proprietors special

expense reserve
事業主の債務 employer's obligation
事業年度 business year
事業年度開始日 beginning day of the taxable year
事業年度の決定 determination of taxable year
事業年度の指定 designation of business year
事業年度の届出 notification of the taxable year
事業年度の変更 change of taxable year
事業の結合 combination of operations
事業の実体 business reality
事業の縮小 reduction in business activities
事業の遂行 execution of business ; performance of business
事業の遂行に必要な経費 expense under necessity for the active conduct of business
事業の中止 suspension of business
事業の中断 halt of business activities
事業の廃止 discontinuance of business ; quitting of business
事業の発見者 business finder
事業の評価 assessment of the business
事業の分割 divestment of business
事業の閉鎖 business closure
事業の目的に供される資産 properties put to use for business
事業の用に供されている資産 property put into business
事業の連結 consolidation of operations
事 業 場 working place
事業賠償責任保険 business liability insurance
事業範囲 scope of business
事 業 費 business expenses
事業部門 operating division
事業分野報告書 business segment reporting
事 業 別 by business segment
事業別セグメント business segment
事業への影響 impact on business
事 業 法 business law
事業報告書 annual business report ; statement of operations
事業法人 business company ; corporation
事業方法書 scheme of operation
事業ポートフォリオ business portfolio
事業保険 business insurance
事業向け賠償責任保険 commercial liability insurance
事業用資産 assets attached to business
事業用資産の買換え replacement of business property
事業リスク business risk ; commercial risk
事業を廃止した場合の必要経費 necessary expenses in case of closing business
事業を廃止する discontinue an operation
市況回復 market recovery
市況状況 market condition ; running of the market
市況情報センター market information center
市況報告 market report
仕 切 帳 invoice book
仕切売買 one time trading ; transactions on a dealer basis
資金移転 fund transfer
資金移転指示 instructions for funds transfers
資金移動 liquidity transfer ; movement of funds ; transfer of fund
資金移動表 statement of variation of funds
資金運用 fund management ; money management
資金運用収益 income from fund management
資金運用手段 fund management method
資金運用調査官 Special Officer for Research on Foreign Exchange Fund and Money Markets
資金運用表 source and application of funds statement ; statement of sources and uses of funds

資金運用部 Trust Fund Bureau
資金運用部資金 Trust Fund Bureau Fund
資金運用部資金法 Government Trust Fund Law
資金運用部特別会計 Trust Fund Bureau Special Account
資金運用部引受 subscription by the Trust Fund Bureau；underwriting by the Trust Fund Bureau
資金運用部預託金 deposits with the Trust Fund Bureau
資金運用方針 fund investment policy
資金会計 fund accounting
資金回転率 turnover (ratio) of funds
資金化期間 float
資金化資金 good value
資金過不足 financial surplus or deficit
資金監査官 Chief Fiscal Loan Inspector
資金勘定 CMA (cash memorandum account)；fund account
資金管理実務 cash management practice
資金関連スワップ fund swap
資金企画室 Asset-Liability Management Office
資金規制法 financing regulation law
資金吸収 absorption of fund
資金吸収力 fund absorption
資金供給 fund supply；provision of fund
資金供与 cash contribution
資金協力 financial contribution
資金繰り fund procurement(needs)；liquidity management
資金繰計画 funding plans
資金繰りの悪化 liquidity crisis；tightened cash flow；tightened liquidity
資金繰り表 statement of cash receipts and disbursement
資金繰りリスク cash flow risk
資金計算書 statement of funds
資金経理事務 accounting for the government deposits maintained at the Bank
資金決済 fund settlement
資金決済サービス funds transfer service
資金決済指図 money settlement instructions
資金決済の円滑に資するための業務 business contributing to smooth settlement of funds
資　金　源 source of capital；source of financing；source of funds
資金源泉運用表 wheregot and wheregone statement
資金コスト cost of fund
資金サイド payments leg
資金市場からの預金 money market deposit
資金市場への預け金 money market placement
資金実地監査官 Fiscal Loan Inspector
資金使途 fund utilization
資金収支計算書 cash flow statement
資金需要 call on capital；capital requirements；credit demand；financing need
資金循環 money flow
資金循環勘定 flow of funds accounts
資金循環表 money flow tables
資金循環分析 flow of funds analysis
資金償還 capital redemption
資金剰余金 fund surplus
資金生成単位 cash generating unit
資金総合管理勘定 CMA (cash management account)
資金操作 exchange fund operation
資金貸借対照表 fund balance sheet
資金調整取引 exchange fund cover
資金調整法 financing adjustment law
資金調達 corporate financing；fund raising；funding
資金調達額 amount raised
資金調達活動 financing activities
資金調達環境 fund raising environment
資金調達業務 fund raising business
資金調達計画 financing program
資金調達コスト cost of raising funds；funding cost
資金調達サイド funding side
資金調達手段 financing method；

シ

financing tool
資金調達する tap
資金調達の実施 implementation of financing
資金調達費用 financing cost ; fund procurement cost
資金調達方針 financing policy
資金調達リスク funding risk
資金調達利回り yield on funds raised
資金調達力 financing capability ; fund raising capacity
資金調達力低下 reduced access to funds
資金調達を行うための企業 financing conduit
資金手当て financing arrangement
資金提供者 capital provider
資金的収益 cash revenue
資金取引 funding transactions
資金の源泉と使途 source and application of funds
資金の実質価値 real price of money
資金の使途 application of fund ; use of funds
資金の転換 diversion of funds
資金の流れ flow of fund
資金の範囲 scope of funds
資金のみ決済 funds-only settlement
資金の呼び戻し capital inflow back
資金引出し draw down
資金引出可能期間 availability period ; drawdown period
資金プール pool of funds
資金プール法 pool-of-fund approach
資金不足 financial deficit ; funding shortfall ; liquidity shortage ; shortage of funds
資金負担 financial exposure
資金振替サービス fund transfer service
資金フロー計算書 fund flow statement
資金分析 fund analysis
資金ポジション fund position
資金見込額 cash forecast
資金持ち分 fund equity ; fund equity
資金融通 financial accommodation
資金予算 fund budget
資金余剰 financial surplus
資金預託リスク cash deposit risk
資金流入の再開 resumption of capital inflow
仕 組 み mechanism
仕組金融 structured finance
仕組金融市場 structured finance market
仕 組 債 structured bond ; structured note
仕組裁定取引 SAT (structured arbitration transaction)
仕組資産クラス complicated asset class
仕組証券 structured securities
仕組取引 structured transaction
司 計 課 Fiscal Division
時系列データ time series data
時系列分析 time series analysis
時系列変動 time series behavior
時系列要約 historical summary
刺　　激 impetus
刺 激 策 stimulus package
私　　権 private right
試　　験 testing
資　　源 resources
資源エネルギー庁 Agency for Natural Resources and Energy
資源開発 development of resources ; tapping of resources
資源開発投資損失準備金 reserve for loss from investment in the development of resources
資源の集中 concentration of resources
資源の費消 consumption of resources
資源の分配 allocation of resources
資源の流入 inflow of resources
資源配分 resource allocation ; resource distribution
時　　限 prescribed deadline
次　　元 dimension
試験研究費 experimental and research expense
試験研究費税額控除 experimental and research expense tax credit
試験研究費の特別控除 credit for experimental and research expenses

試験研究用資産 property for experimental and research
試験販売 test marketing
紙券使用 paper credit
事件簿 cause-books
事件目録 cause list
時限立法 law with expiration date
施　　行 enforcement
施行規則 enforcement regulations
施行細則 detailed enforcement regulations
施行日 date of enforcement；enforcement day
時　　効 prescription；statute of limitation
時効取得 adverse possession
時効の消滅 prescription extinction
時効の中断 interruption of prescription
時効の停止 suspension of prescription；suspension of statute of limitations
自行引受 own bill
自行ユーザンス own usance
自己宛小切手 self-addressed check
自己回帰 AR (autoregressive)
自己回帰移動平均モデル ARMA (autoregressive moving average) model
自己回帰条件付不均一分散モデル autoregressive conditional heteroskedaticity model
自己回帰モデル auto-regressive model
自己貸株 shares lent by members
自己株券買付 issuer's own stock repurchase
自己株券買付状況報告書 report on state of purchase of treasury stocks
自己株式 company's own shares；treasury stock
自己株式再発行積立利益剰余金 retained earnings appropriated for the re-issuance of treasury stock
自己株式消却 cancellation of treasury stocks
自己株式の取得原価 cost of treasury stock
自己株式の償却 cancellation of company's own share；retirement of treasury stock
自己勘定 own account；proprietary account
自己勘定売買益 investment profit
自己管理型 self-administered
自己金融 internal financing；self-finance
自己金融比率 self-finance ratio
自己口 proprietary ledger
自己計算による取引の制限 limitation of trading on proprietary account
自己査定基準 self-assessment criteria
自己資金 own capital
自己資金投資 equity exposure
自己資金平残 average equity
自己資本 net worth；net worth equity capital；own capital；owner's equity；tangible net worth
自己資本回転率 turnover (ratio) of net worth
自己資本額 shareholders' interests
自己資本基準 capital adequacy standards
自己資本基準の緩和 reduced capital adequacy requirements
自己資本規制 capital requirement
自己資本規制比率 equity capital ratio；net capital regulation ratio
自己資本合計 total net worth
自己資本サイクル equity capital cycle
自己資本時価 equity at market value
自己資本成長率 equity growth rate
自己資本対負債比率 ratio of net worth to total debt
自己資本長期資産率 long-term asset ratio to equity capital
自己資本での売買 trading on equity
自己資本内部収益率 EIRR (equity internal rate of return)
自己資本の充実 sound capitalization
自己資本の補完的項目 Tier II capital
自己資本比率 capital adequacy ratio；equity ratio；ratio of net worth to total capital
自己資本比率基準 capital guideline
自己資本比率規制 capital adequacy

シ

requirements ; capital adequacy rule ; regulatory capital adequacy
自己資本比率指令 CAD (Capital Adequacy Directive)
自己資本負債比率 net worth gearing ratio
自己資本への影響額 effect on equity interests
自己資本簿価 equity at book value
自己資本利益率 earnings on equity ; net profit to net worth ; percentage of profits available on net worth
自己資本を有す保険会社 capitalized insurer
自己修正 self-correction
自己使用不動産 owner occupied property
自己申告 self-assessment ; self-reporting ; self-return
自己申告納付制度 self-assessment system
自己生産に係る固定資産 self-produced fixed assets
自己清算の self-liquidating
自己選択 self-selection
自己相関 autocorrelation
自己創設のれん internally generated goodwill
自己都合 one's own convenience
自己積立 self-funding
自己投資 self-investment
自己取引 principal transaction ; transactions for one's proprietary account
自己に関する証拠 self-regarding evidence
自己に不利益な証拠 self-disserving evidence
自己に有利な供述 self-serving declaration
自己の意見 personal opinion
自己の計算による未決済約定 unsettled transactions on one's proprietary account
自己の計算によるもの for its own account
自己の製造にかかる棚卸資産 self-produced inventories
自己の売買ポジション own trading position
自己の持ち分金融商品 own equity instruments
自己売買 dealing ; proprietary trading ; trading on one's own account ; transaction on a dealer basis
自己破産 voluntary bankruptcy
自己否認 voluntary adjustment
自己分の注文 proprietary order
自己分の取引証拠金 clearing margin for one's proprietary account
自己保有限度額 limited retention
自己保有部分 custody assets
自己融資 financing from brokers' own capital ; funds lent by members
自己流動性 self-liquidity
事故カード invalid card
事故証券 securities with irregularities
事故通知 notice of loss and damage
事故保険 accident insurance
事後アルファ値 ex-post alpha value
事後監査 post audit
事後差異 ex-post variance
事後最適分析 ex-post optimum analysis
事後資格審査 post-qualification
事後修正 subsequent adjustment
事後取得財産 after-acquired property
事後取得資産追加担保条項 after-acquired clause
事後測定 subsequent measurements
事後的貯蓄 ex-post saving
事後的投資 ex-post investment
事後的な評価 ex-post assessment
事後テスト on-going test
事後特性線 ex-post characteristic line
事後の支出 subsequent expenditure
事後の承認 ex post approval
事後の変動 subsequent change
事後評価 post-ante evaluation
事後分析 ex-post analysis ; posterior analysis
事後ベータ ex-post beta
自国銀行監督 HCC (home country control)
自国通貨 domestic currency ; domestic fiat money ; home currency
自国通貨建て denominated in home

currency
自国通貨建格付け local currency rating
自国通貨建相場 rate in home currency
自国通貨建負債 domestic liabilities
自国内 on-shore
試査 testing audit
私財提供益 profit from private funds offered
自在年金 flexible annuity
資材評価 valuation of goods
資材部 materials department
自在変動型の保険料 fixed and variable flexible premium
自在保険料 flexible premium
死差益 mortality profit
試作 trial manufacture
試作機 pilot unit
試作費 experimental manufacturing cost ; testing expenses
試作品 trial product
時差説 time difference theory
試算 trial
試算価値 trial value
試算表 trial balance ; working trial balance sheet
試算ベース pro forma figure
資産 assets
資産移管 asset transfer
資産移替 asset reshuffling
資産運用 asset management
資産運用外収入 non-investment income
資産運用者 money manager
資産化 capitalization
資産会計 asset accounting
資産解体 asset stripping
資産回転率 asset turnover ratio
資産買取 asset acquisition
資産価格 asset price
資産価格の乱高下 volatility of asset prices
資産価格評価モデル asset pricing model
資産化基準 capitalization criteria
資産格差 asset differentials ; asset gap
資産課税課 Property Taxation Division
資産化単位 capitalization unit
資産価値 asset value
資産価値を利用した借換え cash-out refinancing
資産活用 asset utilization
資産活用率 asset-utilization ratio
資産化の終了 cessation of capitalization
資産化の停止 suspension of capitalization
資産化費用 capitalized expense
資産株 income stock
資産貨幣 assets money
資産化利息 capitalized interest
資産化率 capitalization rate
資産勘定 asset account
資産鑑定 appraisal of assets
資産管理 asset-management
資産管理総合口座 asset management account ; central asset accounts
資産管理方針 asset management policy
資産基準 asset basis
資産区分の厳格化 tightening of asset classification
資産クラス asset class
資産グループ group of assets
資産計画 estate planning
資産計上 asset capitalization
資産計上期間 capitalization period
資産形成 wealth accumulation
資産形成退職貯蓄保険 capitalized retirement savings policy
資産決済 asset settlement
資産減価償却範囲 ADR (asset depreciation range)
資産限度 asset limit
資産効果 asset effect
資産交換の税法上の特典 tax benefit for exchange of property
資産構成 asset mix ; asset portfolio ; asset structure
資産構成比率 percentage of each class of assets to total assets
資産構成部分 asset component
資産購入原価 cost of assets purchased
資産項目 asset item
資産効率 asset efficiency
資産再評価 asset revaluation

シ

資産再評価税 asset revaluation tax；tax on the write-up
資産再評価法 asset revaluation law
資産査定 asset assessment；review of the quality of assets
資産自己査定基準 asset self-assessment criteria
資産シフト asset shift
資産収益率 asset return (ratio)
資産取得後の支出 subsequent expenditure on asset purchased
資産証券化 asset securitization
資産状態 asset position
資産譲渡 transfer of assets；transfer of property
資産譲渡制限 limitations on disposal
資産所得 asset income；income from assets
資産所得の合算 aggregation of income from assets
資産所得の世帯合算課税 family taxation of assets income
資産処分 asset disposition
資産所有費用 cost of carry
資 産 税 tax on property
資産セグメント asset pool segment
資産選好 asset preference
資産選好理論 theory of asset preference
資産選択 portfolio selection
資産選択理論 theory of portfolio selection
資産増加 spike in wealth
資産喪失費 loss on property destroyed
資産損失 loss of property；loss on assets
資産代替効果 substitution asset effect
資産台帳 asset register；property records
資産耐用年数 asset life
資産耐用年数指針 asset period guidelines
資産担保型証券 assets-backed securities
資産担保コマーシャル・ペーパー ABCP (asset-backed commercial paper)
資産担保債券 asset-backed bond
資産担保証券 asset-backed securities
資産担保率 asset coverage
資産調査 means test
資産賃貸借契約 asset rental agreement
資産積立 asset accumulation
資産デフレ asset deflation
資産凍結 asset freeze
資産と負債 assets and liabilities
資産と負債の期間構成 term structure of assets and liabilities
資産と負債のミスマッチ mismatch between assets and liabilities
資産と持ち分 assets and equities
資産取引 transaction in assets
資産取引から生ずる利得 gains derived from asset transaction；gains derived from dealings in property
資産内容 asset quality
資産に関する補助金 grant related to assets
資産の悪化 asset deterioration
資産の一時的貸付 temporary loan on property
資産の運用 placement of assets
資産の買換え replacement of assets
資産の改善 improvement to assets
資産の改良 improvement of the property
資産の価値増進 enhancement to assets
資産の価値に対する権利 equitable interest in asset
資産の期日 maturities of assets
資産の強制譲渡 compulsory transfer of assets；compulsory transfer of property
資産の減価償却 depreciation on assets；depreciation on property
資産の減損 impairment of assets
資産の減耗 depletion of assets
資産の交換 exchange of assets；exchange of property
資産の控除項目 deduction against assets
資産の更新率 ratio of replacement of assets
資産の査定 accuracy of counting
資産の質 asset quality
資産の集合 aggregation of assets
資産の集中 concentration of assets
資産の取得 acquisition of asset
資産の取得価額 acquisition cost of assets

資産の取得原価 acquisition cost of property；historical cost of assets
資産の譲渡益 gains from the transfer of assets；gains from the transfer of property
資産の除去 retirement of asset
資産の処分 disposition of assets
資産の処分による手取金 proceeds from disposition of asset
資産の所有 possession of property
資産の清算による損失 loss from liquidation of properties
資産の整理 divesture of assts
資産の専属的利用 exclusive use of assets；exclusive use of property
資産の選択 asset selection
資産の増価 enhancement of asset
資産の相互交換 reciprocal transfer of assets；reciprocal transfer of property
資産の帳簿価額 book value of assets
資産の賃貸 lease of property
資産の特定利率 asset specific rate
資産の廃棄 retirement of the asset
資産の売却 divestiture of assets
資産の売却損 loss on sale of assets
資産売却損 loss on sale of property
資産の破棄 destruction of asset
資産のバブル asset bubble
資産の評価益 profit from valuation of assets
資産評価換え revaluation of assets
資産の評価損 loss from valuation of assets
資産の評価損益 profit or loss resulting from valuation of assets
資産の非流動部分 non-current portion of asset
資産の分配 asset allocation
資産の分類 classification of assets
資産の変動 asset change
資産のポートフォリオ portfolio of assets
資産の保有 holding of assets
資産の滅失 extinguishment of assets；extinguishment of property
資産の流出 asset outflow
資産の流動部分 current portion of asset
資産廃棄損 loss on asset abandoned；loss on property abandoned
資産売却 asset sales；liquidation of assets
資産売却益 portfolio gains；profit from asset sales
資産売却手取金 proceeds from asset sold
資産配分 asset allocation
資産引当金 asset reserves
資産評価 valuation of assets
資産評価企画官 Director (Property Valuation)
資産評価切下げ asset devaluation
資産評価減 asset write down
資産評価準備金 AVR (asset valuation reserve)
資産評価損 loss incurred by revaluation of assets；loss on property revaluation
資産評価論 theory of asset valuation
資産プール asset pool
資産・負債管理 ALM (asset liability management)
資産・負債計算書 statement of assets and liabilities
資産・負債サープラス管理 ALSM (asset-liability surplus management)
資産負債増減法 net worth method
資産負債総合管理 ALM (asset and liability management)
資産分散 asset diversification
資産分配型ミューチュアル・ファンド asset allocation mutual fund
資産分配法 asset allocation technique
資産分布 asset distribution
資産ベースの手数料 asset based commission
資産別アプローチ asset-by-asset approach
資産簿価 asset book value
資産利益率 ROA (return on assets)
資産リスク asset risk
持 参 人 bearer
持参人払い payable to bearer

シ

持参人払小切手 check to bearer
持参人払式証券 bearer instrument ; instrument payable to bearer
持参人払手形 bill payable to bearer
指示信託 directory trust
指示的法律 directory statute
次事業年度 subsequent taxable year
支 持 線 support level
事実記載書 case stated
事実指摘 findings
事実上交換可能通貨 currency convertible in fact
事実上の推定 presumption of fact
事実上の標準 de facto standard
事実認定 fact finding
事実の確認 affirmation of fact
事実の錯誤 mistake of fact
自社カード own named cards ; proper card ; self-issue cards
自 社 株 company's own stock ; corporation's own stock
自社株買い share repurchase
自社株買戻し self-tender ; share repurchase plan
自社株低価格購入権 incentive stock option
自社株の評価 valuation of company's own stock
自社使用 internal use
自社清算参加者 principal clearing participant
自社清算資格 principal clearing qualification
自社製品 in-house product
支社制度 branch system
四捨五入 rounding off in calculation
自主運用型個人退職勘定 self-directed individual retirement account
自主関税 autonomous tariff
自主規制 self-regulation ; self-restraint
自主規制機関 SRO (self regulatory organization)
自主規制金利 self-restraint interest
自主規制計画 voluntary restraint program
自主占有 hostile possession
自主的報告 voluntary reporting
自主納付 voluntary tax payment
支　　出 cash disbursed ; expenditure ; outgo ; spending
支出可能資金 expendable fund
支出原価 outlay cost
支出削減 expenditure curtailment
支 出 税 expenditure tax
支出総額 gross cash payments
支出増大 spending increases
支出費消し outlay expiration
支出負担準備金 reserve for encumbrance
支 出 率 expenditure ratio
次順位保険金受取人 contingent beneficiary
自　　署 autography ; sign manual
地　　所 landed estate
市　　場 marketplace
市場安定操作 market stabilization operation
市場エコノミスト street economist
市 場 課 Financial Markets Division
市場改革 market reform
市場概況 market overview
市場外在荷 invisible supply
市場外取引 off-board transactions
市場介入 market intervention
市場介入金利 market rate of intervention
市場介入の再開 resumption of intervention operations
市場介入の手控え lack of intervention
市場開放 market opening
市場価格 market price
市場価格調整 market value adjustment
市場価格調整済年金 market value adjusted annuity
市場価格の変動 market price movement
市場拡張効果 market expansion effect
市場価値 marketable value
市場価値加重平均指数 market value weighted index
市場価値の下落 decline in market value
市場価値の代替 proxy for market value
市場活動 market conduct
市 場 間 inter-market

市場間監視情報システム ISIS (Intermarket Surveillance Information System)
市場環境 market environment
市場間競争 competition among markets
市場関係者 practitioners in the financial markets
市場慣行 market conventions；market practice
市場間スプレッド cross-market spread；inter-market spread
市場間取引システム ITS (inter-market trading system)
市場感応度 market sensitivity
市場間の均衡関係 equilibrium relationship between markets
市場関連価値 market-related value
市場機会 market opportunity
市場機構の評価 evaluation of market mechanism
市場規制局(SEC) Division of Market Regulation(SEC)
市場機能の活用 use of market mechanism
市場強弱測定値 trin
市場均衡 market equilibrium
市場均衡曲線 market equilibrium curve
市場金利 commercial rate of interest；prevailing rate
市場金利以下の below-market interest rate
市場金利連動型貸出 MML(money market loan)
市場金利連動型定期預金 money market certificate
市場経済 market economy
市場経済モデル market economy model
市場原理 market discipline；market mechanism
市場構造 market structure
市場細分化 market segmentation
市場参加者 market participant；market player
市場時価総額 market capitalization
市場指数 market index
市場施設 market facilities
市場実勢に基づいた情報 market based information
市場支配 market control
市場周期 market cycle
市場需要 market demand
市場需要曲線 market demand curve
市場消滅 market extinction
市場心理 market psychology
市場心理の悪化 hurting sentiment
市場スプレッド market spread
市 場 性 marketability
市場性債券 marketable debt securities
市場性証券 marketable debt；marketable securities
市場性のある注文 marketable order
市場性のある有価証券 marketable securities
市場性のない non-marketable
市場セクター market sector
市場全般 general market
市場占有率 market share
市場創造効果 market creating effect
市場相場 market rate
市場第一部 First Section
市場第二部 Second Section
市場タイミングの評価 market timing assessment
市場地域別 by geographical market
市場秩序維持協定 orderly marketing agreement
市場調査 market research；market survey
市場撤退 market exiting
市場統合 single market
市場動向委員会 MPC (Market Performance Committee)
市場統制 market control
市場と参加者間決済 external settlement
市場取引価格 market transaction price
市 場 内 intramarket
市場内部要因 internal factor of market
市場における価値 market-based value
市場に対する造詣 insight in markets
市場に目を向けた market-driven
市場年金価格 market annuity price

市場の厚み depth of market
市場の勢い market momentum
市場の運営 operation of the market
市場の活発さ depth of the market
市場の考え market view
市場の完全性 market integrity
市場の規制緩和 market liberalization
市場の基調 market rhythm
市場の規程 market regulations
市場の競争 market competition
市場の気配 market tone
市場の現実 reality of market
市場の考察 market insight
市場の効率性 market efficiency
市場のコンセンサス market consensus
市場の地合い market mood；market sentiment
市場の実勢 market state
市場の実勢利回り prevailing interest rate
市場の失敗 market failure
市場の主導株 market leaders
市場の需要見込み expected market demand
市場の情報源 market information source
市場の深度 breadth of the market
市場の成果 market performance
市場のタイミング market timing
市場の調整 market's adjustment
市場の認識度 market awareness
市場の発展 development of the market
市場の反対派の勢い negative market reaction
市場の反応 response of market
市場の不安 market jitters
市場の方向性リスク market directional risk
市場のボラティリティ market volatility
市場の見方 market perception
市場の流動性 liquidity of the market
市場販売権 marketing right
市場評価 market assessment；market valuation
市場付加価値 MVA (market value added)
市場分析 market analysis
市場分断仮説 market segmentation hypothesis
市場分断理論 segmentation theory
市場ベータ market beta
市場別売上 sales by market segment
市場への影響 impact on market
市場への進出 market penetration
市場妨害 forestalling the market
市場ポートフォリオ market portfolio
市場メカニズム market mechanism
市場モデル market model
市場用語 market parlance
市場予測 market consensus；market forecast；market prediction
市場利子率 market rate of interest
市場リスク market risk
市場リスク検査室 Market Risk Inspection Office
市場リスクに敏感な market risk sensitive
市場利回り market yield
市場理論 market theory
市場連動型優遇金利 floating prime rate
市場割引率 market discount rate
市場を失うこと missing the market
事　　象 event
史上最安値 all-time low
市 条 例 municipal ordinance
自署押印の義務 obligation of signature and seal
指　　針 guidance
地震保険 earthquake insurance
地震保険計理官 Actuary for Earthquake Insurance
指　　数 index；quotient
指数オプション市場 IOM (index and option market)
指 数 化 indexation
指数加重移動平均 EWMA (exponentially weighted moving average)
指数化ファクター indexation factor
指数曲線 exponential curve
指数効用関数 exponential utility function
指数裁定取引 index arbitrage trading
指数裁定取引者 index arbitrager
指数採用商品 underlying commodities used for consumer price indices

指数調整後の額面 indexed par
指数調整された原価 indexed cost
指数取引 index transaction
指数の exponential
指数比率 index ratio
指数分布 exponential distribution
指数平滑法 exponential smoothing
指数ポートフォリオ index portfolio
指数保険 index linked insurance
指数保険商品 indexed insurance product
指数保有 index holding
指数マーチンゲール exponential martingale
指数用上場株式 listed stocks used in the computation of indices
指数リスク index risk
指数リンク債 index linked products；index-linked bond
指数連動債務 index-linked obligation
指数連動証券 index-linked securities
指数連動年金 indexed annuity
指数連動ラグ indexation lag
指数ワラント index warrant
システィマティック・リスク systematic risk
システム・アプローチ system approach
システム価格 system value
システム工学 system engineering
システム障害 system failure
システム障害取引参加者 trading participant in system trouble
システム情報局 Information System Services Department
システム銘柄 system issue
システム呼値 system bid and offer
システム・リスク system risk
システム・レポ system repos
次世代 next generation
施設管理運営 facility management
自然営業年度 natural business year
自然権 natural rights
自然減 natural attrition
自然失業率 natural rate of unemployment
自然資本 natural capital
自然人 natural person
自然増 natural increase
自然増収 unearned increment
自然対数 natural logarithm
自然的境界 natural boundary
自然的支持 natural support
自然的自由 natural liberty
自然的推定 natural presumption
自然発火 spontaneous combustion
自然法 law of nature；natural law
自然保険料 natural insurance premium
自然利子率 natural rate of interest
事前価格確認制度 advance pricing agreement
事前加工 prefabrication
事前借換え prerefunding
事前監査 preaudit
事前資格審査 pre-qualification
事前準備期間 pre-preparatory period
事前承認支払い preauthorized payment
事前調査 preparatory audit
事前調整 prior agreement
事前通知 preliminary notice
事前積立 pre-funding
事前積立年金 advance funded pension
事前積立年金制度 advanced funded pension plan
事前積立方式 advance funding method
事前テスト ex-ante test
事前届出制 pre-merger registration system
事前取決取引 prearranged trading
事前認可 prior approval
事前の届出 prior notice
事前販売 presale order
事前評価 ex-ante evaluation
事前分析 ex-ante analysis；prior analysis
事前要件 initial requirements
事前預託 prior deposit
慈善寄付 charitable donation
慈善寄付金 charitable contribution；charities and donations
慈善信託 charitable trust
四川省 Sichuan
試送品 goods on approval
持続 persistence

シ

持続委任状 durable power of attorney
持続可能な開発 sustainable development
持続可能な経済成長率 sustainable economic growth rate
持続可能な成長 sustainable growth
自損事故保険 self-sustained personal accident insurance
仕 損 費 loss due to spoiled work
仕 損 品 defective goods ; spoiled goods
仕損品費 spoilage expenses
時代の要請 demand of times
地代奉仕 rent service
下　　請 subcontract
下請業者 subcontractor
下請工場 subcontract factory
下請前払金 advance to subcontractor
下 口 銭 mark-downs
下 ざ や down spread ; lower in quotation
下 取 り trade-in
下取商品の過大評価 overestimation of goods traded in
下取り品 trade-in articles
下 抜 け break out
下　　値 lower price ; lower quotation
下値支持線 support level ; support line
下値抵抗線を割込む breach the resistance line
下値不安 downside risk
下 放 れ falling off
下引受会社 sub-underwriter
下引受業者 sub-underwriter
下振れのリスク downside risk
下 回 る fall short of ; run below
示　　談 composition ; private settlement ; settlement out of court
示談解決 out-of-court settlement
シ団幹事 syndicate manager
シ団参加資格 eligibility for syndicate membership
シ団の構成 syndicate composition
シ団引受 syndicate underwriting
シ団不成立 under-banked
自　　治 autonomy ; home rule
質　　入 impignoration
質入契約 impignorative contract
質入有価証券 pledged security
質　　権 pledge ; right of pledge
質権口座 pledge account
質 権 者 mortgage creditor ; pledgee
質権設定 establishment of the right of pledge
質権設定者 pledgor
質権登録 registration of the right of pledge
質権の目的 object of pledge
質物受戻し redemption of pledge
質　　屋 pawn-shop
市中貸出 commercial bank discount and loan
市中銀行 high street bank
市中銀行マネー commercial bank money
市中金利 market interest rate ; money market rate ; open market rate
市中消化国債 subscription of government bonds in market
市中相場 free market price ; open market quotation
市中発行 offering for the market
市町村固定資産税 municipal property tax
市町村税 municipal tax
市町村たばこ税 municipal tobacco excise tax
市町村民税 municipal inhabitants tax
実　　価 actual value
実価資産 actual value assets
実 価 法 actual value method
実業操業度 actual volume
失　　業 unemployment
失業給付 unemployment benefit
失 業 者 unemployed
失業手当 dole ; unemployment compensation
失業保険 unemployment insurance
失業保険支出 expenditure on unemployment insurance
失業保険税 unemployment tax
失 業 率 unemployment rate
失業率低減 reducing unemployment rate
失 権 株 forfeited share ; unclaimed

stock
実現価値 realized value
実現可能価額 realizable value
実現可能性の低い偶発事象 remote contingency
実現金額 amount realized
実現減価償却 realized depreciation
実現収益 realized return；realized revenue
実現主義 realization basis；realization principle
実現主義の原則 principle of realization
実現増価額 realized appreciation
実現損益 realized gain and loss；realized profit and loss
実現損失 realized loss
実現ボラティリティー realized volatility
実現利得 realized gain；realization gain；realized income；realized profit
失　　効 lapse
失 効 益 gain from lapsed policies
失効オプション lapsed option
失 効 株 lapsed share
失効契約 lapsed contract
失効小切手 out-of-date check
失 効 率 lapse rate
執行委員会 executive committee
執行期間 term of execution
執行機関 execution organ
執行期日 date of execution
執 行 権 executive power
執行債権者 execution creditor
執行債務者 execution debtor
執行処分 executive measure
執行通知 NOE (notice of execution)
執行停止 suspension of execution
執行手続 executive proceedings
執行ブローカー executing broker
執行命令 executive order
執 行 役 executive officer
執行役員 executive officer
執行役取締役 executive director
執行猶予 probation
執行リスク execution risk
実効価格 effective price
実効為替相場 effective exchange rate
実効金利 actual interest rate；effective interest rate
実効金利法 effective interest method
実効債務 effective debt
実効スプレッド efficient spread
実効税引後 after effective tax
実効税率 effective income tax rate；effective tariff
実効保護率 effective rate of protection
実効ボラティリティー effective volatility
実効利回り effective yield；realized yield
実行可能な feasible
実行機関 executing organization；implementing institution
実行支配 working control
実行段階 implementation phase；implementation stage
実 行 日 start date
実行予算 working budget
実　　査 physical inspection
実在勘定 real account
実際価格 actual price
実際掛金 actual contribution
実際給付 actual benefit
実際原価 actual cost
実際原価計算 actual costing
実際原価計算制度 actual cost accounting system
実際権限 actual authority
実際購入価額 actual purchase price
実際資本維持 maintenance of physical capital
実際収益 actual return
実際主義会計 actual basis accounting
実際取得原価主義 actual acquisition cost basis
実際使用 actual use
実際償却額 actual depreciation
実際譲渡価額 actual transfer price
実際生産高 physical output
実際全部原価計算 actual absorption costing
実際耐用年数 actual useful life

実際的な例外 pragmatic exception
実際の支払い physical payment
実際の支払日 true payment date
実際の使用 active use
実際の使用が不可能となった retired from active use
実際の取引手口 actual trading behavior
実際の判断 pragmatic judgment
実際の反応 real-life response
実際配賦率 actual burden rate
失　策 blunder；policy misstep
実　施 implementation
実施権 enforcement right
実施作業 work performed
実質価格 real price
実質価格の上昇率 real rate of appreciation
実質可処分所得 real disposable income
実質価値 real value；real worth
実質価値の世界 real world
実質株主 beneficial shareholder
実質株主名簿 list of beneficial shareholders
実質貨幣 real money
実質貨幣残高効果 real balance effect
実質借入コスト real cost of borrowing
実質為替レート real exchange rate
実質金利 real interest rate；real yield
実質金利格差 real yield differential
実質経過利子 real accrued interest
実質原価 real cost
実質債務 real liabilities
実質ＧＮＰ成長率 real GNP growth rate
実質GDP real GDP
実質資産 real wealth
実質資本 capital in real terms
実質収益 real return
実質受益者課税の原則 principle of taxation on actual beneficiary
実質出費 real outgoing
実質純資産 effective net worth
実質純投資 real net investment
実質証拠 substantive evidence
実質乗数 real multiplier
実質所得 effective income；real earnings；real income
実質所得者 real income earner
実質所得者課税の原則 principle of taxation on a substantial income earner
実質所有 beneficiary ownership
実質所有者 beneficial holder；beneficial owner
実質成長 real growth
実質成長率 real growth rate
実質総投資 real gross investment
実質単位 real term
実質単位労働コスト real unit labor cost
実質賃金 real compensation
実質的効果 substantive effect
実質的実体 physical substance
実質的証拠 substantial evidence
実質的相違 material variance
実質的ディフィーザンス in-substance defeasance
実質的ディフィーザンス・トラスト in-substance defeasance trust
実質的な存続会社 de facto existing company
実質的な当事者 substantial party
実質的なフロー real flow
実質的履行 substantial performance
実質投資収益率 real investment return
実質投資主 beneficial holders of beneficiary ownership certificates；beneficial investors
実質年金債務 real annuity obligation
実質年利 actual annual percentage rate
実質の世界 real space
実質破綻先 essentially bankrupt borrower；virtually bankrupt borrower
実質は負債 liabilities in substance
実質引当 actual reserves
実質ベースで in real terms
実質ベースに修正した純利益 constant dollar net income
実質優先 substance over form
実質優先出資社員 beneficial holders of preferred equity securities
実質預金 real deposits

実質リターンの収益 real return pay-off
実質利回り real rate of return；real yield
実質利回り計算 real yield calculation
実質利率 real rate
実　需 actual demand
実需原則 actual demand rule
実証経済学 positive economics
実証研究 empirical study；experimentation
実証性テスト substantive test
実証的経験 empirical experience
実証的分析 empirical analysis
実勢為替相場 current exchange rate；real rate of exchange
実勢市場金利 prevailing market interest rate
実勢市場利回りスプレッド current market yield spread
実勢実質利回り quoted real yield
実勢モーゲージ・レート prevailing mortgage rate
実勢預金 deposit minus checks and bills on hand；deposit on a net basis
実勢利回り quoted yield
実勢レート effective rate
実　績 results
実績基準PER trailing PER (price earnings ratio)
実績情報 historical information
実績と見込み results and projections
実績による修正 experience-based adjustment
実績分析 historical analysis
実績利回り historical yield
実　線 solid line
実　践 practice
実践経済 practical economy
実践セミナー practical seminar
実践的な方法 pragmatic means
実践の hands-on
失踪債務者 absconding debtor
実損填補 first-loss insurance
実損填補保険 indemnity insurance
実　体 entity
実体会計 entity accounting
実体経済 real economy
実体経済活動 real economic activity
実体資本 physical capital
実体法 substantive law
実地監査 field audit
実地棚卸 inventory count；physical counts；physical inventory；stock taking
実地棚卸数量 physical counting of inventory
実地調査 site survey
室　長 Director, Office of
失　墜 downfall
実定法 positive law
質的経済政策 qualitative economic policy
質的実質性の原則 qualitative substantiality test
質的信用規制 qualitative credit control
質的特徴 qualitative characteristics
質的要因 qualitative parameters
実働人員 effectives
質の調整 quality adjustment
シッパーズ・ユーザンス shipper's usance
実払プロジェクトコスト as spent project cost
実　費 actual expenses
実費精算契約 cost plus contract
実物資産 real assets
実物資本 real capital
実物商品 physical commodity；real commodities
実物的トランスファー real transfer
実物投資 real investment
疾病休業 sick leave
疾病給付 sickness benefit
疾病手当 sick pay
疾病保険 sickness insurance
質への逃避 flight to quality
実務家 practitioner
実務規定 practice requirement
実務規範 code of practice
実務指針 practical guideline
実務修習生 articled clerk
実務上の疑い practical reservation
実務上の困難 practical difficulty

実務上の問題 practical issue
実務上の理由 practical reason
実務的帰結 practical consequence
質問検査権 authority to inquire and inspect
実用化実験 pilot projects；pilot tests
実用新案 industrial new design；utility model
シ
実用新案権 utility model patent
実 用 性 practicality
シ テ ィ City
指定替え reassignment of sections
指定基金 designated fund
指定寄付金 donation to designated organization
指定金銭信託 designated money in trust；directed money trust
指定金融機関 designated financial institution
指定権者 appointor
指定口座 designated account
指定参加者 designated direct participant
指定下請業者 nominated subcontractor
指定商品 appointed goods
指定清算参加者 designated clearing participant
指定相続分 specified portion of inheritance
指定代理店 appointed representative
指定代理人 authorized agent
指定地域勘定 scheduled territories account
指定通貨 designated currency
指定統計 designated statistics
指定都市 designated city
指定取引 designated trading
指定取引所 designated exchange
指定入札 approved tender
指定入札者 approved bidder
指定の取消 cancellation of designation
指定銘柄 designated stock
指定名義人 designated nominee
指定預金 designated deposit
仕 手 株 speculative stock
仕 手 戦 deal between speculators；speculative dealing
仕手戦での損 taking a bath
仕手銘柄 speculative name
私的会計士 private accountant
私的使用 private use
私的独占の禁止 prohibition of private monopoly
視　　点 perspective
支　　店 branch
支店会計 accounting for branch office；branch accounting
支店勘定 branch account
支店銀行制度 branch banking system
支店相互勘定 inter-branch account
支店相互間損失 inter-branch loss
支店相互間利益 inter-branch profit
支店長会議 General Managers' Meetings
支店元帳 branch ledger
時点決済 designated-time settlement
時点における価値 value prevailing at the time of
自動安定装置 built-in stabilizer
自動延長 automatic extension
自動貸出プール automatic lender pool
自動借入 automatic borrower
自動鑑査機 banknote examination machines
自動給付増額 automatic benefit increase
自動クリアリング・ハウス ACH (automated clearing house)
自動継続定期預金 automatic renewal time deposit
自動決済 automatic settlement
自動口座振替 automatic account transfer
自動更新 automatic renewal
自動債券取引システム automated bond system
自動再投資 automatic reinvestment
自動車検査独立行政法人 National Agency of Vehicle Inspection
自動車事故 car accident
自動車事故対策機構 National Agency for Automotive Safety and Victims' Aid
自動車重量税 automotive tonnage tax
自動車取得税 automotive acquisition tax

自動車傷害保険 automobile accident insurance
自動車税 automobile tax；car tax
自動車総合保険 package automobile policy
自動車損害賠償責任保険 automobile liability insurance
自動車販売金融 automotive sales finance
自動車販売台数 auto sales
自動車保険 automobile insurance；car insurance；motor insurance
自動車保険料率算定会 Automobile Insurance Rating Association of Japan
自動車ローン債権 automobile receivables
自動車ローン証券 auto-backed deal
自動車ローン担保証券 CARS (certificate for automobile receivables)
自動集金サービス automatic collection service
自動証券貸借 automatic securities lending and borrowing
自動注文入力システム automated order entry system
自動調整 automatic adjustment
自動ディーリング取引システム computer assisted execution system
自動停止 automatic stay
自動手形交換 automated clearing
自動的な条項 automatic provision
自動投資プログラム automatic investment program
自動認可方式 automatic approval system
自動引受け automated underwriting
自動引落依頼 standing order
自動引落指図 standing instruction
自動引出 automatic withdrawal
自動復元 automatic reinstatement
自動物価指数連動 automatic indexing
自動振替 automatic fund transfer
自動振替貸付 automatic premium loan
自動振替サービス automatic transfer service
自動預金受払機 ATM (automated teller machine)
自動流動性移動機構 ALT (automatic liquidity transfer) mechanism
自動レポ automatic repo
児童手当 children allowance
指導的判例 leading case
指 導 力 leadership personality
使途限定資金 restricted fund
使途自由助成金 general revenue sharing
使途秘匿金 beneficiary concealed disbursement
使途不明金 expenditure unaccounted for
シドニー先物取引所 SFE (Sydney Futures Exchange)
品 受 け actual receipt of stock purchased
品 薄 株 narrow market securities；rare stock；scarce stock
品薄相場 sold-out market
品 貸 料 stock lending fee
品 不 足 shortage in deliverable securities
品 渡 し actual delivery of stock sold
シナリオ分析 scenario analysis
シニア市場 senior market
シニア・トレーダー senior trader
ジニー・メイ Ginnie Mae (Government National Mortgage Association)；GNMA
ジニー・メイ債 Government National Mortgage Association debenture
ジニー・メイ・パス・スルー証券 GNMA pass-through securities
次入先出法 next-in first-out method
次年度以降の non-first year
地　　場 local dealers
支　　配 control；dominance
支配会社 controlling company
支 配 株 control stock
支配株主持ち分 controlling equity
支配関係 controlling relationship
支配関係の不存在 absence of control
支配機関 governing body
支 配 玉 securities inventory
支配権の移転 transfer of control
支配市場 control market

支配従属 control and subordination
支配集中度 degree of concentration of control
支配できない outside the control
支配の指標 indicators of control
支配持ち分 controlling stake
支配力基準 control criterion
地場筋ディーラー local dealers
自発的項目 autonomous item
自発的失業 voluntary unemployment
自発的組織 voluntary association
自発的貯蓄 voluntary saving
自発的な当事者 willing party
自発的な取引 voluntary transactions
支 払 い disbursement
支払一回飛ばし skip payment
支払い・受取り payment and receipt
支払確認 payment confirmation
支払為替手数料 domestic and foreign exchange commissions
支払勘定 accounts payable
支払完了性 settlement finality
支払期間 payment period；payout period
支払期間延長 dating
支払期限 due date for payment；term of payment
支払期限の到来した債務 mature liabilities
支払期日 repayment due date
支払期日延期書面 letter of license
支払期日の到来した payable
支払記入帳 payment book
支払義務 obligation to pay
支払協定 payment agreement
支払拒絶 under protest
支払拒絶小切手 rejected check
支払拒絶宣言 declaration of non-payment
支払銀行 payer bank；paying bank
支払決済 payment clearing and settlement
支払い・決済委員会 CPSS (Committee on Payment and Settlement Systems)
支払い・決済サービス・システム CPSS (clearing and payment services system)
支払項目 items of payment
支払債務 notes and accounts payable；payment obligation；trade payables
支払債務額上限 net debt cap
支払指図 payment instruction；payment message；payment order
支払差止命令 stop payment order
支払資金の一時的不足 temporary shortage of funds for payment
支払手段 means of payment；payment instrument
支払循環 disbursement cycle
支払準備勘定契約 payment account agreement
支払準備金 reserve for outstanding claims
支払準備制度 reserve requirements system
支払準備率 reserve ratio
支払準備率操作 reserve ratio operation；reserve requirement policy
支払条件 conditions for payment；payment terms and conditions
支払条項 payment provisions
支払承諾 acceptances and guarantees
支払承諾平均残高 average balance of acceptances and guarantees
支払承諾見返金 customer's liabilities for acceptances and guarantees
支払仕訳帳 cash-disbursement journal
支払信用状 payment credit
支払済勘定 account paid
支払済小切手 cancelled check；paid check
支払請求 claim of payment
支払請求額査定 claims adjustment
支払請求者 claimant
支払請求率 claim rate
支払送金 remittance payable
支払代理人 paying agent
支 払 高 amount paid
支 払 地 place of payment
支払地指定手形 domiciled bill
支 払 帳 cash disbursement book
支払超過 disbursement exceeding receipts (net payments)；

unfavorable balance
支払調書 payment record
支払通知書 note of payment
支払停止 payment stop；suspension of payment
支払呈示 presentation for payment
支払呈示期間 presentation period for payment
支払停止通知 stop-payment order
支払手形 acceptance payable；BP (bill payable)；notes and bills payable
支払手形記入帳 note payable register；notes payable book
支払手形割引 discount on notes payable
支払手形割引料 discounts paid on bills
支払手数料 commission paid；del credere commission
支払伝票 debit slip
支払伝票記入帳 voucher payable register
支払伝票制度 voucher system
支 払 人 payer
支払年金 payout annuity
支払能力 ability to pay；solvency
支払能力のある solvent
支払能力課税説 faculty theory of taxation
支払能力基準 ability to pay basis
支払能力評価 evaluation of solvency
支払いの遅滞 delinquency in payment
支払配当金 dividend paid
支払不能 failure to pay；insolvency
支払不能会社 insolvent corporation
支払不能行為 act of insolvency
支払不能条項 insolvency clause
支払不能による貸倒れ bad debt caused by insolvency
支払不能判決 decree of insolvency
支払不能保障制度 insolvency protection system
支払法人税 income taxes paid
支払方法選択権 optional settlement
支払保険金総額 capital sum benefit
支払保証 certification of payment；guarantee of payment
支払保証銀行 payment certifying bank
支払保証小切手 certified check
支払保証地方債 insured bonds
支払明細 payment statement
支払命令 order to pay
支払約束手形 note payable
支払猶予 grace of payment；payment moratorium；postponement of payment
支払猶予期間 days of grace；moratorium period
支払猶予条項 deferment clause
支払猶予日数 dating
支払余力 solvency margin
支払利子の課税控除 tax deduction of interest payment
支払利息 interest paid
支払利息・税金・減価償却控除前利益 EBITDA (earnings before interest, taxes, depreciation and amortization)
支払利息・税金·減価償却前利益 EBITD (earnings before interest, tax and depreciation)
支払利息税引前利益 EBIT (earnings before interest and taxes)
支 払 率 payment rate
支払レッグ payment legs
支払渡し delivery against payment；DP (document against payment)
支払ワラント代理人契約書 paying & warrant agency agreement
支払うべき owing
支払うべき掛金 contribution payable
四 半 期 quarter
四半期国民所得統計速報 QE (Quick Estimation)
四半期ごとに on a quarterly basis
四半期ごとの資金調達 quarterly funding
四半期ごとの支払い payments made quarterly
四半期財務諸表 quarterly financial statements
四半期損益計算書 quarterly income statement
四半期入札 quarterly auctions
四半期払年金 quarterly annuity

シ

四半期ベースの実質成長率 quarterly real growth rate
四半期報告書 quarterly report
四半期利益 quarterly earnings
指　　標 indicator
指標金利 reference rate
指標指数 reference index
指標銘柄 bellwether bond；bellwether issue；benchmark
指標銘柄の流動性 liquidity in benchmark bonds
指標銘柄利回り benchmark yield
CIF CIF (cost, insurance and freight)
ジブチ・フラン DJF (Djibouti franc)
ジブラルタル・ポンド GIP (Gibraltar pound)
紙　　幣 paper currency
紙幣金額 denomination of banknotes
紙幣両替機 bill exchange machine
紙幣類似証券取締法 Law Concerning the Regulation of Securities Resembling Paper Currency
私　　募 direct placement；private offering
私 募 債 private note；private offering bond；private placement bond；privately placed note
私募債シンジケート private placement syndicate
私募債の発行 placement of unlisted notes
私募証券 private placement securities
私募地方債 private placement local government bond
私募転換社債 private convertible bond；private convertible note
私募投資信託 private investment trust
私募特別債 private placement special bond
私募発行 private placement
私募普通社債 private placement straight bond
私募要領 placing memorandum
死　　亡 demise
死亡一時金 lump sum death benefit
死亡給付金 death benefit
死亡給付条項 death benefit clause
死亡記録 bill of mortality
死亡原因 death by cause
死亡時払戻金付年金 refund annuity
死亡者の相続人 successor of the deceased
死亡保険 insurance against death；insurance payable at death
死亡保険金 sum payable at death
死亡保険金繰上給付支払い a.p.o.d.b.(accelerated payment of death benefit)
死亡保険金支払い death payment
死亡保険金の前払い accelerated benefits
死亡保障 death protection
死 亡 率 death rate；mortality rate
司 法 権 judicial power
司 法 省 Department of Justice
司法処分による売却 judicial sale
司法審査 judicial judgment
資　　本 capital；capital fund
資本委員会 capital committee
資本維持 capital maintenance
資本移転 capital transfer
資本移転手段 medium of capital transfer
資本及び負債 equity and liabilities
資本及び負債合計 total equity and liabilities
資 本 家 capitalist
資本下位会社 capital-subordinate company
資本会計 accounting for ownership equity
資本回収 capital recovery
資本回収引当金 capital recovery allowance
資本回転率 turnover rate of capital
資本家階級 capitalist bracket
資 本 額 capital sum
資本課税 capital levy
資本価値 capitalized value
資本稼働率 capital working rate
資本化比率 capitalization ratio
資本株式 capital shares
資本関係のない unaffiliated
資本勘定 capital account；capital stock

account
資本勘定支出 expenditure on capital accounts
資本勘定調整 equity account reconciliation
資本勘定に貸方計上される credited to equity account
資本勘定に計上される recognized in equity account
資本勘定報告書 statement of changes in stockholders' equity
資本基盤 capital base
資本供給国 capital supplier nation
資 本 金 capital stock ; stock capitalization
資本金階層別証券会社 securities companies by size of capital
資本金勘定 capital stock account
資本金組入額 amount credited to capital stock
資本金組入剰余金 capitalized surplus ; surplus credited to equity
資本金計算書 statement of capital
資本金現在高 outstanding capital stock
資本金合計 total capital
資本金5億円の会社 corporation capitalized at 500 million yen
資本金明細表 schedule of capital
資本組入れ capitalization of reserves
資本組入額 amount credited to equity
資本係数 capital coefficient
資本形成 capital formation
資本形成勘定 capital formation account
資本限界効率 marginal efficiency of capital
資本限界効率表 schedule of the marginal efficiency of capital
資本減少 reduction of capital stocks
資本減耗引当て capital consumption allowance
資本合計 total shareholders' equity
資本構成 capital composition ; capital structure ; equity structure
資本構成比率 percentage of capital structure
資本構造リスク capital structure risk
資本項目からの控除項目 deduction from one's equity
資本コスト capital cost ; composite cost of capital
資本固定資産比率 worth and fixed assets ratio
資本固定比率 ratio of net worth to fixed capital
資本固定負債比率 worth to fixed debt ratio
資 本 財 capital goods
資本再構成 recapitalization
資本最低限度 minimum surplus
資本最低水準 capital floor
資本再編 capital reorganization
資本財輸出 capital goods export
資本参加 capital participation ; equity participation
資本・産出高比率 capital-output ratio
資本資産 capital assets
資本資産価格モデル capital asset pricing model
資本資産評価モデル CAPM (capital asset pricing model)
資本支出 capital disposition ; capital expenditure ; capital outlay
資本支出契約 capital commitment
資本市場 capital market
資本市場管理庁（インドネシア） BAPEPAM (Capital Markets Supervisory Board)
資本市場線 capital market line
資本自由化 capital liberalization
資本収支 capital account balance
資本集約 capital intensity
資本集約性の低い産業 low capital intensive industry
資本集約的商品 capital-intensive merchandise
資本集約的な capital intensive
資本主義 capitalism
資本主義市場経済 capitalism market economy
資本所得 capital income

シ

シ

資本需要 demand for capital
資本需要曲線 capital demand curve
資本準備金 capital in excess of par or stated value；capital reserve
資本準備金組入額 excess over par
資本償還 capital redemption
資本証券 capital securities
資本消費 capital consumption
資本消費の調整 capital consumption adjustment
資本剰余金 additional paid-in capital；capital surplus
資本剰余金計算書 statement of capital surplus
資本信用 capital credit
資本ストック調整 capital stock adjustment
資本ストック調整原理 capital stock adjustment principle
資 本 税 capital duty；capital stock tax；capital tax
資本生産性 capital productivity
資本節約産業 capital saving industry
資本節約的技術進歩 capital saving technical progress
資本節約的な capital saving
資本損失 capital loss
資本注入 capital injection
資本調整表 capital-reconciliation statement
資本調達 capital raising
資本的経費 Capex (capital expenditure)
資本的収入 capital receipt
資本的設備 capital equipment
資本的追加 capital addition
資本投資 capital spending
資本等式 capital formula
資本統制 capital control
資本逃避 capital flight
資本と経営の分離 separation between capital and administration
資本取引 capital transaction
資本取引自由化 liberalization of capital transaction
資本取引のコスト cost of equity transaction
資本に計上された recognized in equity
資本の回収 recovery of capital
資本の改善 capital improvement
資本の回転率 turnover (ratio) of capital
資本の額 amount of capital
資本の価値 capital value
資本の拠出 capital contribution
資本の欠損 impaired capital
資本の源泉 capital resources
資本の充実 capital adequacy
資本の充実度 adequacy of capital
資本の修正 capital adjustment
資本の集中 centralization of capital
資本の出動 capital mobilization
資本の生産性 productivity of capital
資本の増加 accrual in equity；contribution to equity
資本の増減 movement of equity
資本の測定 measurement of equity
資本の蓄積 capital accumulation
資本の注入 capital infusion
資本の逃避 flight of capital
資本の年齢 vintage of capital
資本の払戻し repayment of capital
資本の部 shareholders' equity section
資本の部合計 total capital accounts
資本の変動 capital change；movement in equity
資本の有機的構成 organic composition of capital
資本の輸出 export of capital
資本の流通 circulation of capital
資本配当 dividend from capital
資本配分 capital distribution
資本負債 capital liabilities
資本負債比率 capital and liabilities ratio；ratio of net worth to debts
資本部分 equity component
資本部分に借方計上される charged to the equity component
資本への計上 recognition in equity
資本ポジション capital position
資本保全 capital preservation
資本持ち分 equity interest

資本持ち分の個別構成要素 separate component of equity
資本輸出国 country having deficit in capital transaction
資本輸入 capital import
資本予算 capital budget
資本利益率 net earnings ratio to capital；profit ratio of capital；profit ratio of net worth；return on capital
資本利子 capital interest
資本利子税 capital interest tax
資本利潤 capital profit
資本利得率 capital gain yield
資本流出 capital outflow
資本流動負債比率 worth to current debt ratio
資本流入 capital inflow
資本流入の要因 driver of capital inflow
資本理論 capital theory
資本連結 capital consolidation
姉妹会社 sister company
シミュレーション simulation
市民債 citizen bond
事務幹事会社 book runner
事務管理 administration
事務管理課 Information System Management Division
事務管理サービス clerical and administrative service
事務管理室 Information Management Office
事務規程 office manual
事務局次長 Deputy Secretary-General of Executive Bureau
事務局長室(SEC) Office of Executive Director(SEC)
事務次官 administrative vice minister
事務所機器 office equipment
事務所諸経費 office overhead
事務総長室 OSG(Office of the Secretary-General)
事務代理 acting
事務的権能 ministerial power
事務の遵法性と正確性 compliance with relevant rules and accuracy in their operational procedures
事務費 office expenses
事務負担 administrative burden
事務部門 wire room
仕向銀行 payer bank；remitting bank
仕向送金 outward remittance
仕向送金為替 bill sent
仕向地 destination
仕向地持込渡し(関税込) delivered duty paid
仕向地持込渡し(関税抜) delivered duty unpaid
仕向超過限度額 sender net debit cap
締め上げ squeeze
使命 mission
指名委員会 nomination committee
指名買い nomination buying
指名競争入札 selective bid；selective tendering
指名権 power of appointment
指名権者 appointer
指名債権 claim payable to a specific person
指名受託者 named fiduciary
指名入札 designated bid；private tender
指名被保険者 named insured
氏名誤記 misnomer
氏名詐欺 false personation
締切後記入 post-closing entry
締切後試算表 post-closing trial balance
締切試算表 closing trial balance
締切済勘定 closed account
締切日 closing date；cutoff date
締後勘定 post close account
占める account for
下期 second half
下期決算 settlement of accounts for the latter half
地元企業 local company
地元への再投資 community reinvestment
下半期 latter half；second half of the year
諮問委員会 advisory committee
ジャージー・ポンド GBP (Jersey pound)
シャープ・レシオ sharpe ratio

シャーマン反トラスト法 Sherman Anti-trust Act
社員預り金 deposit received from employee
社 員 権 rights and liabilities of members
社員採用 recruitment
社員総会 policyholders' meeting
社員総代会 general meeting of members
シャウプ勧告 Shoup's recommendation
シャウプ税制報告書 report on Japanese taxation by the Shoup Mission
社会意識 social consciousness
社会一般情勢 normal practices in Japan
社 会 化 socialization
社会会計 social accounting
社会会計マトリックス SAM (social accounting matrix)
社会開発 social development
社会還元 social return
社会監査 social audit
社会給付 social benefit
社会経済的要請 socioeconomic requirements
社会契約 social contract
社会原価 social cost
社会貢献 philanthropy
社会貢献ミューチュアル・ファンド socially conscious mutual fund
社会厚生関数 social welfare function
社会指標 social indicator
社会資本 SOC (social overhead capital)
社会資本整備 social capital development
社会総資本 aggregate social capital
社会的影響 social consequence
社会的基盤 social infrastructure
社会的基盤の整備 provision of social infrastructure
社会的限界費用 social marginal cost
社会的責任投資 SRI (socially responsible investment)
社会的責任のある投資 socially responsible investment
社会的な仮定 social assumption
社会的無差別曲線 social indifference curve
社会的要因 social force
社会福祉関連施設 social welfare related facilities
社会扶助 social assistance
社会保険 social insurance
社会保険給付の差押禁止 prohibition of foreclosure on social insurance payment
社会保険税 social insurance tax
社会保険庁 SIA (Social Insurance Agency)
社会保険分担金 contribution for social insurance
社会保険料 social insurance premium；social security premiums
社会保険料控除 social insurance premiums deduction
社会保障 social protection；social security
社会保障掛金 social security contribution
社会保障関係費 social security related expenditure
社会保障給付 social security benefit
社会保障受給者 social security recipient
社会保障障害所得補償保険 social security disability income insurance
社会保障税 social security tax
社会保障制度 social security arrangement；social security system
社会保障税率 FICA (Federal Insurance Contributions Act) tax rate；social security tax rate
社会保障退職給付 social security retirement benefit
社会保障年金 social security pension
社会保障年金信託基金 social security trust fund
社会保障範囲 social security coverage
社会保障番号 social security number
社会保障負担 social contribution burden；social security burden
社会有用性 social good
社外取締役 non-management director；outside director

社外流通株式数 number of shares outstanding
社外利用者 external user
借換政策 funding policy
借記通知書 debit advice
弱 公 準 weak axiom
借地契約の更新または変更 renewal or change of the lease
借 地 権 land leasehold；lease tenant right；tenant right
借地権者 leaseholder
借地権設定 settlement of leasehold
借地権の価格 fair leasehold value
借地権の期間経過 lapse of the leasehold
借地権の取得価額 acquisition cost of leasehold
借地権の設定 establishment of leasehold
借地権の評価 valuation of leasehold
借地権割合 ratio of leasehold to land value
借 地 人 lease-holder；tenant
尺度分析 scale analysis
借　　家 rented house
借 家 権 rented house right
借用概念 adopted concept
借用金状況 status of borrowed money
借用金返済予定 repayment schedule for borrowed money
借用証書 IOU (I owe you)
社交クラブ social club
社　　債 corporate bond；corporate debenture；corporate securities
社債応募 application for subscription of corporate bonds
社債価格 price of corporate bond
社債勘定 bond payable account
社債管理 debt management
社債管理委託契約 agreement for bondholder services
社 債 券 bond certificate；corporate bond certificate；debenture bond
社債券印刷費用 engraving and printing cost of bond certificates
社債減債基金 bond sinking fund
社債権者 corporate bond holder
社債権者集会 meeting of bond holders
社債券譲渡 debenture assignment
社債券信託 debenture trust
社債原簿 bond register
社債最高発行限度 corporate bond authorized
社債取得 acquisition of debenture
社債消化状況 sales of corporate bonds
社債償還 debenture redemption；payment of corporate bonds
社債償還差金 gains on bond redemption
社債償還差損 loss from redemption of bond
社債償却 retirement of bond
社債セクター credit sector
社債相当利回り corporate equivalent yield
社債担保証券 CBO (collateralized bond obligation)
社 債 等 corporate bonds and other non-JGB bonds
社債等担保手形借入オペ outright purchases of bills collateralized by corporate debt obligations
社債等DVP DVP (delivery versus payment) for corporate bonds
社債等登録制度 registration system for corporate bonds and other non-JGB bonds
社債等登録法（社登法） Law for Registration of Corporate Bonds
社債等の振替に関する法律 Law concerning Book-entry Transfer of Corporate and Other Debt Securities
社債投資 investment in bonds
社債登録法 registration act for corporate bond
社債と持ち分への投資 debt and equity investments
社債の格付け bond quality rating
社債の財務制限条項 bond covenant
社債の取得 acquisition of corporate bonds
社債の償還 redemption of corporate bonds

シ

社債の販売 placement of bond
社債配当 bond dividend
社債発行企業 corporate borrowers
社債発行限度 bond authorized
社債発行差益 unamortized premium on bonds
社債発行差金 debt discount and expenses ; discount on bonds issued ; discount on bonds payable
社債発行差金償却 amortization of bond premium
社債発行残高 amount outstanding of corporate bonds
社債発行市場 corporate bond issuance market
社債発行の受託者 trustee for bond issuance
社債発行費 bond issuance cost ; debenture issuing expenses
社債発行費用 debt expense ; expense for issuing corporate bond
社債発行プレミアム corporate bond issuance premium
社債評価 corporate bond valuation
社債ファンド corporate bond fund
社債プレミアム bond premium
社債プレミアム発行 bond issued at a premium
社債未発行高 bond unissued
社債明細表 schedule of bonds payable
社債利子 debenture interest ; interest on corporate bonds
社債利子払資金 cash deposited for payment of interest on corporate bonds
社債利息に課せられた所得税 income tax on interest on corporate bonds
社債割引発行差金 discounts on bonds payable
社債割増発行差金 premium on bonds payable
奢 侈 税 luxury tax
ジャスダック Jasdaq
社団法人 corporate juridical person
社長からのメッセージ message from president
借款享受 loan received
借款供与 loan extension
借款返済 repayment of loan
借記授権書 debit authorization
社内規程 internal rule ; office regulation
社 内 報 house organ
社内預金 company saving
社内留保率 retained earnings ratio
ジャパン・ファンド Japan fund
ジャパン・プレミアム Japan premium
ジャパン・マネー Japan money
ジャマイカ・ドル JMD (Jamaican dollar)
斜陽産業 declining industry
車両保険 automobile physical damage insurance
謝 礼 金 honorarium
ジャンク債 junk issue
ジャンク・ボンド junk bond
上 海 市 Shanghai
上海証券取引所 SHSE (Shanghai Securities Exchange)
ジャンプ拡散 jump diffusion
ジャンプ過程 jump process
趣 意 書 foreword ; statement of intent
主　　因 efficient cause
自　　由 liberty
自由意志 free will
自由円勘定 free yen account
自由円預金 free yen deposit
自由オファー free offer
自由価格 free price
自由株式 free stock
自由貨幣 free money
自由化率 liberalization rate
自由企業体制 free enterprise
自由競争売買手数料 soft commission
自由金利 deregulated interest rate
自由金利商品 deregulated interest rate product
自由経済 free economy
自 由 港 free port
自由交易圏 FTZ (free trade zone)
自 由 財 free goods
自由裁量 discretion

自由裁量的財政政策 discretionary fiscal policy
自由市場 free market
自由市場経済 free market economy
自由資本 free capital
自由準備 free reserves
自由使用権 disposition
自由剰余金 free surplus
自由処分権 right of free disposal
自由世界 free world
自由設計定期保険 flexible term policy
自由地帯 free zone
自由返済システム free payment system
自由変動相場制 free floating exchange rate system
自由貿易 free trade
自由貿易協定 FTA (free trade agreement)
自由保有財産 freehold property
自由料率 free rate
収　　益 earnings
収益カーブ pay-off curve
収益拡大 profit picture
収益活動 revenue earning activity；revenue producing activity
収益稼得活動 revenue generating activity
収益カバレッジ earnings coverage
収益還元価格 earnings discount value
収益関連指標 profit ratio indices
収益曲線 revenue curve
収益計上時期 time of recognizing gain
収益計上の時期 timing of revenue recognition
収益向上 profit pickup
収益構造 payoff structure；profit profile
収益項目 items of income
収益サイクル profit cycle
収益残高勘定 balance of revenue account
収益資産 earning assets
収益支出 revenue expenditure
収益指標 earnings ratio
収益社債 profit debenture；revenue corporate bonds
収益状況 business results
収益スタビライザー earnings stabilizer
収 益 性 profitability
収 益 税 earning tax；profit tax
収益性資産 earnings assets；income-producing asset
収益性指数 profitability index
収益成長率 earnings growth rate
収益性のある営業活動 profitable operation
収益性分析 profitability analysis
収 益 増 earnings growth
収益逓減の法則 law of diminishing return
収益と費用の対応 matching of revenue and expense
収益に関する補助金 grant related to income
収益の安定性 earnings stability
収益の回復 recovery of earnings
収益の元本組入型投資信託 accumulation trust
収益の傾向 trend of earnings
収益の実現 realization of gains；revenue realization
収益の認識 revenue recognition
収益の認識基準 revenue recognition criteria
収益配当 income dividend
収益配当型ミューチュアル・ファンド income mutual fund
収益配当型リミティッド・パートナーシップ income limited partnership
収益費用対応 matching revenue with cost
収益費用対応の原則 principle of matching costs with revenues
収益比率 ratio of expenses to revenues
収益不動産 income property
収益分配 income distribution
収益分布 revenue distribution
収益平均値 mean return
収益報告書 earnings report
収益補償金 compensation for lost revenue
収益満期払い lump-sum payment of dividends at maturity
収益見通し earnings forecast；earnings outlook；profit forecast
収益面で in terms of revenue

シ

収益モデル earnings model ; revenue model
収益ユニット income unit
収益予測 revenue projection
収益予測のコンセンサス consensus on earnings estimate
収益リスク earnings risk
収 益 率 earned rate ; rate of return
収益率格差 differential of return
収益率測定 rate of return measurement
収益率測度 measure of return
収益率の相関関係 correlation between returns
収益留保率 earnings retention rate
収 益 力 earning capacity ; earning power
収益力カバレッジ earning coverage
収益を得ること derivation of revenue
収益を得るための経済活動 profit making business activities
終　　価 accumulated value ; final value ; terminal value
従　　価 ad valorem
従 価 税 ad valorem duty ; ad valorem tax
従価税率 ad valorem tariff
従価保管料 ad valorem storage
州 外 の out-of-state
収穫基準 crop basis
収穫逓減 decreasing return ; diminishing return
重加算金 heavy additional charge imposed
重加算税 additional tax due to fraud ; heavy penalty tax
重 過 失 gross negligence
習 慣 病 behavioral disease
周　　期 cycle
衆 議 院 House of Representatives
周期的な cyclical
住　　居 dwelling house
従 業 員 employee ; work force
従業員預り金 deposit from employees
従業員医療給付 employee health care benefit
従業員掛金 employee contribution
従業員株式購入制度 employee share purchase plan
従業員給付 employee benefit
従業員給付基金 employee benefit fund
従業員給付コスト employee benefit cost
従業員給付債務 employee benefit obligations
従業員給付制度 employee benefit plan
従業員給付の取決め employee benefit arrangement
従業員給与手当 employees salary and allowance
従業員拠出 employee contribution
従業員組合 employees union ; workers union
従業員グループ group of employees
従業員自社株購入権 qualifying employee stock option
従業員死亡率 employee mortality
従業員ストック・オプション employee stock option
従業員選択 employee choice
従業員退職給付 employee retirement benefit
従業員退職給与金 employees retirement allowance
従業員退職給与引当金 reserve for employees retirement allowance
従業員退職所得保障法（エリサ） ERISA (Employee Retirement Income Security Act)
従業員退職率 employee turnover (ratio)
従業員代表 representative of employees
従業員貯蓄プラン employee savings plan
従業員に対する債務 account owed to employees
従業員年金基金積立金 employees pension fund
従業員年金制度 employee pension benefit plan
従業員の自己都合 employees' own conveniences
従業員の報奨 employees' remuneration
従業員配置転換費用 employee relocation

expense
従業員一人当り貸出金残高 loans outstanding per employee
従業員福祉給付制度 employee welfare benefit plan
従業員保険 employee insurance
従業員保障 employee coverage
従業員保障制度 employee security plan
従業員持株制度 ESOP (employee stock ownership plan)
従業員利益分配制度 employee profit sharing plan
就業規則 working rules
就業不能給付 incapacity benefit
就業不能所得補償保険 disability income insurance
就業不能退職年金 disability retirement benefit
就業不能率 disability rate
宗教法人 religious corporation
住居エネルギー税控除 residential energy credit
住居手当 housing allowance
住 居 費 housing expenses
終局差止命令 permanent injunction
終局判決 definitive sentence
集　　計 aggregation
集計勘定 summary account
集計結果 combined results
集計の問題 aggregation problem
集 計 表 summary sheet
重 慶 市 Chongqing
集権経済 centralized economy
州 検 事 state attorney
州限定地方債ファンド single state municipal bond fund
州　　債 state bond
州際協定 interstate compact
州際通商 Interstate Commerce
州際通商委員会 ICC (Interstate Commerce Commission)
州所得税 state income tax
州政府債券 state government bond；state government debenture
州政府証券 state government securities
州内売出し intrastate offering
州内支店設置 state branching
州　　法 state law
州法銀行 state bank
州法銀行の連邦準備制度加盟 Federal Reserve membership of state banks
州法人税 state franchise tax
州保険局 state insurance department
州免許の組織 state-chartered association
集合法人 corporation aggregate
集合理論 aggregate theory
私有財産 private property
収支一覧表 statement of income and expense
収支計算書 statement of receipts and disbursement
収支決算書 statement of settlement of accounts
収支相償 revenue generation covering expenditure
収支相等の原則 principle of equivalence
収支分岐点 cash break-even point；cash flow break-even point
収支分析 cash flow analysis
収支方程式 income and expenditure equation
収支簿記 receipt and payment bookkeeping
収支予測 cash flow forecasts；cash forecasts
収支を合わせる make ends meet
収支を伴わない財務活動 noncash financing activities
収支を伴わない投資活動 non-cash investing activities
収支を伴わない取引 non-fund transactions
週次決算 weekly accounting
充　　実 enrichment
充実確保 enhanced security
収　　集 capture
収　　縮 contraction
住　　所 place of abode
住所裏書 indorsement of address
就職促進手当 allowance for promotion of

シ

employment
終　　身 whole life
終身健康保険 permanent health insurance
終身雇用 guaranteed life-time employment；lifetime employment commitment
終身生命保険 ordinary life, permanent life, straight life insurance
終身年金 annuity for life；lifetime annuity；perpetual annuity；straight life annuity；whole life annuity
終身年金保険 life annuity insurance；life income policy
終身払込保険料 continuous premium
終身保険 lifetime insurance；whole life insurance
終身保険月額給付 lifetime monthly benefit
終身リバース・モーゲージ lifetime reverse mortgage
修　　正 amendment；correction；modification
修正受渡日基準 modified delivery-date basis
修正回帰分析 adjusted regression analysis
修 正 額 amount of adjustment
修正加速償却法 MACRS (modified accelerated cost recovery system)
修正可能信託 revisable trust
修正株主資本 adjusted stockholders' equity
修正監査報告書 modified auditor's report
修正基礎額 adjusted base
修正記入 adjusting entry
修正原価主義 adjusted cost basis
修 正 後 restated
修正後試算表 adjusted trial balance
修正後純利益 adjusted net profit
修正後帳簿価額 adjusted carrying amount
修正後の売上原価 adjusted cost of sales
修正後の減価償却費 adjusted depreciation cost
修正再表示 restatement
修正再表示残高 restated balance
修正再表示を要しない後発事象 subsequent event which does not require restatement
修正財務諸表 modified accounts
修正残高方式 adjusted balance method
修正事項の決定 determination of the necessary adjustments
修正資本主義 modified capitalism
修正取得原価 adjusted historical cost；modified historical cost
修正純ミニマム税 adjusted net minimum tax
修正償還年金 modified cash refund annuity
修正仕訳 adjusting journal entry；AJE (adjusted journal entry)
修正申告 amended tax return；revised return
修正済開示準備金 disclosed reserves as adjusted
修正済行使価格 adjusted exercise price
修正する amend
修正総所得 adjusted gross income
修正積立 modified funding
修正発行届出書 amended shelf registration statement
修正発生主義 modified accrual basis
修正平均株価 revised average stock price
修正ベータ値 adjusted beta value
修正包括主義 modified all-inclusive theory
修正法律 revised statutes
修正養老保険 modified endowment
修正養老保険契約 modified endowment
修正予算 amended budget；revised budget
修正リスク revision risk
修正リストラクチャリング modified restructuring
重　　税 heavy taxation
収　　税 tax collection
収 税 課 taxation division
収 税 官 revenue officer
集 積 圏 accumulation area
修　　繕 overhauling；repair

修繕維持費 repair and maintenance expense
修繕工場 repair shop
修繕コスト repair cost
修 繕 中 under repair
修 繕 費 cost of repairs；maintenance and repairs；repairing expenses
修繕引当金 allowance for repairs；reserve for repairs
修繕引当金繰入れ provision for repairs；provision of reserve for repairs
修繕費予算 repairing budget
修繕平均積立金 repair equalization reserve
修繕保証引当金 liabilities for guarantee against repairs
住専口座 jusen account
従前所得置換率 earnings replacement rate
従前の帳簿価額 previous carrying amount
充　　足 sufficiency
従　　属 subordination
従属変数 dependent variables
週足移動平均 WMA (week moving average)
週足チャート weekly chart
収束分析 convergence analysis
重大な影響 material effect；material impact；significant effect
重大な会計方針 significant accounting policies
重大な疑問 significant doubt
重大な減少 material decrease
重大な誤謬 material error
重大なる不実表示 material misrepresentation
重大な例外 material exception
住　　宅 housing
住宅価格上昇 housing inflation
住宅火災保険 fire insurance on dwelling houses
住宅貸付債権 monetary claims for housing loans
住宅関連株 housing stocks
住宅金融 housing loan
住宅金融会社 housing loan corporation
住宅金融公庫 Government Housing Loan Corporation
住宅建築着工数 housing starts
住宅購入 house purchase
住宅購買力指数 housing affordability index
住宅債券 housing bond
住宅産業統計 housing industry statistics
住宅資産価値を基にした融資口座 homeowner equity account
住宅市場 housing market
住宅取得等特別控除 special credit for acquisition of dwelling house
住宅所有 home ownership
住宅所有者保険 homeowner insurance policy
住宅信用 housing credit
住宅総合保険 house insurance；householders' comprehensive insurance
住宅担保年金 home reversion arrangement
住宅担保ローン home equity loan
住宅着工許可件数 housing permits
住宅貯蓄控除 deduction from tax for housing savings；housing savings tax credit
住宅手当 housing benefit
住宅抵当証券 home mortgage；house mortgage；residential mortgage
住宅投資 housing investment；residential investment
住宅・都市整備公団 Housing and Urban Development Corporation
住宅の資産価値 equity in the house
住宅販売量 home sales volume
住宅保険 home assurance
住宅モーゲージ home mortgage
住宅持ち分 home equity
住宅持ち分転換モーゲージ home equity conversion mortgage
住宅用賃貸物件 residential rent property
住宅用土地 land for residence
住宅用不動産市場 residential property market

シ

住宅用不動産担保証券 RMBS (residential mortgage backed securities)
住宅用モーゲージ証券 home mortgage backed securities
住宅ローン housing loan；residential mortgage
住宅ローン金利 mortgage interest payment；mortgage rate
住宅ローン金利控除 mortgage interest deduction
住宅ローン債権 housing loan claim
住宅ローン事業 mortgage business
住宅ローン保証 housing loan guarantee
従たる給与 salary from secondary source
集団扱更新可能 collectively renewable
集団扱保険 collective insurance；franchise insurance；wholesale insurance
集団管理制度 group administration plan
集団危険 collective hazard
集団競争売買 group auction
集団訴訟 class action
集団代表訴訟 class action lawsuit
集団適用免除 block exemption
私有地通行料 toll traverse
集　　中 concentration
集中決済制度 clearing system
集中効果 concentration effect
集中指値注文控帳 CLOB (centralized limit order book)
集 中 度 degree of concentration
集中投資 concentrated investment；intensive investment
重点分野 priority area
重電銘柄 heavy electrical stocks
充　　当 appropriation
充 当 金 money appropriated；money earmarked
充当順位 priority order of application
収入印紙 revenue stamp
収入印紙税法 stamp duty law
収入階層別 by income layer
収入勘定 revenue account
収入支出 receipts and payments
収入仕訳帳 cash-receipts journal
収入審査 income test
収入増加 augmentation of receipts
収入総額 gross cash receipts
収入に付随して発生する費用 expenses incidental to the receipts of income
収入の先送り postponed income
収入の時期 time of receipts
収入平準化オプション level income option
収入保険料 premium income
10年間の比較財務諸表 ten years comparative financial summary
10年振りの低水準 10-year low
10年物から新発債に乗り換える roll from 10 yrs to WI (when-issued)
10年利付国債 10-year coupon-bearing government bonds
収納機関 agency to receive tax
週払保険料 weekly premium
重病給付 dread disease benefit
重病給付特約 dread disease rider
重　　複 duplication
重複医療保険保障 dual health insurance coverage
重複給付 overlapping benefit
重複保険 overlapping insurance
重複保障 duplicate coverage
十分な市場 deep market
十分な保護 adequate protection
十分な補償 full compensation
十分な流動性 ample liquidity；sufficient liquidity
周辺銘柄 off-the-run issue
週末効果 weekend effect
住 民 税 community charge；inhabitant tax；resident tax
住民税の特別徴収 special collection of inhabitant tax
住民登録 resident registration
住 民 票 resident card
集約尺度 summary measure
週有効注文 GTW (good-this-week) order
収用換地 non-taxable exchanges of properties
収用する condemn

収用補償金 compensation for expropriation
重要事項 important matters
重要事実 material fact
重 要 性 materiality
重要性基準値 threshold of materiality
重要性の原則 principle of materiality
重要性のない項目 immaterial item
重要でない証拠 immaterial evidence
重要でない争点 immaterial issue
重要な影響力 significant influence
重要な活動 significant activities
重要な関係 significant relationship
重要な業務 important part of business
重要な金額 significant amount
重要な子会社 significant subsidiaries
重要な事業体 significant entity
重要な指標 important variable
重要な主張 material allegation
重要な条件 critical terms
重要な成功要因 critical success factor
重要な制度 material plan
重要なテーマ key theme
重要な取引 material transaction
重要な変更 material change
重要な変造 material alternation
重要なポイント basing consideration
重要な役職者 key management personnel
重要な要素 important factor
重要補完情報 material supplementary information
従来型団体年金 conventional group annuity
従来の理論 traditional theory
集落抽出 cluster sampling
修理用材料 material for repair
終了事由 termination trigger
従 量 税 specific duty；specific tax
従量税率 specific tariff
従量保管料 specific storage
重量容積証明書 certificate of weight and measurement
収　　斂 convergence
収斂性の変動 convergent fluctuation
重 労 働 hard labor
10を挟むレンジ range either side of 10.0
受益企業 beneficiary company
受 益 権 beneficiary interest；beneficiary right；right of beneficiary
受 益 者 beneficiary
受益者の権利 rights of beneficiaries
受益者の審査 beneficiary screening
受益者負担金 payment by beneficiary
受益者負担の原則 beneficiary principle
受益証券 beneficiary certificate；beneficiary interest certificate；beneficiary securities
主 幹 事 lead manager
主幹事会社 lead managing underwriter
主幹事の指名獲得 mandate
主観的確率 subjective probability
主観的基準 subjective basis
主観的判断 subjective judgment
主 管 部 competent department
受寄機関 book-entry agency
需　　給 demand and supply
需給価格弾力性 price elasticity of supply and demand
需給ギャップ gap between supply and demand
需給の弾力性 elasticity of demand and supply
需給バランス demand-and-supply balance
受給権確定済みの確定拠出制度 vested defined contribution plan
受給権繰延付与 deferred vesting
受給権付与 vesting
受給権付与済給付 vested benefit
受給資格 benefit eligibility
受給資格のある eligible for benefits
受給資格日 eligibility date
受給資格付与 benefit entitlement
受 給 者 grantee
主金融商品 main financial instruments
宿舎技術専門官 Special Officer for Official Housing Construction and Maintenance
縮　　小 moderation

縮小再生産 reproduction on a diminishing scale
縮小による損失 loss on curtailments
縮小または決済 curtailment or settlement
熟練マネージャー seasoned manager
主　　計 paymaster
主 計 官 Budget Examiner
主計監査官 Chief Budget Inspector
主計官補佐 Deputy Budget Examiner
主計企画官（財政分析、政策評価、予算執行調査） Director for Fiscal Affairs, Policy Evaluation and Expenditure Review
主計企画官(調整) Director for Inter-Division Affairs
主計企画官(法規) Director for Legal Affairs
主 計 局 Budget Bureau；National Accounting Office
主計局局長 Director-General of the Budget Bureau
主計事務管理室 Budget Information Systems Office
主 契 約 main contract
主　　権 sovereign power；sovereignty
主 権 国 sovereign
主権免除 sovereign immunity
主権免除の放棄 waiver of sovereign immunity
主権リスク sovereign risk
主 原 因 proximate cause
授権株式 authorized shares
授権株式数 number of shares authorized
授権資本 authorized capital；stock authorized
授権社債 authorized bond
趣　　旨 gist
主支払い principal paying
主支払代理人 principal paying agent
手術費保険 surgical expense insurance
主 循 環 major cycles
首相官邸 Prime Minister of Japan and His Cabinet
酒 税 課 Liquor Tax and Industry Division
酒税企画官 Director (Liquor Tax and Industry)
主税企画官 Director for International Issues on Taxation；Director for Property Tax Policy；Director for Public Relations on Taxation
主 税 局 Tax Bureau
主税局局長 Director-General of the Tax Bureau
主税調査官 Special Officer for Research on Tax
主 製 品 main product；major product；prime product
主 成 分 principal component
主　　席 chief；head
首席観察官 Chief Personnel Inspector
首席国税庁監察官 Chief Internal Inspector
受 贈 者 donee
主体会社 principal company
主対角線 diagonal
受　　託 acceptance of order
受託商い transactions effected by member for the accounts of others
受託会社 trustee company
受託買付前渡金 advance received on indents
受託業務 fiduciary duties
受託銀行 trustee bank
受託契約準則 Brokerage Agreement Standards
受託契約準則の特例 Special Rule for Brokerage Agreement Standards
受託資本 capital committed
受 託 者 assignee；fiduciary；trustee
受託者責任 fiduciary requirement；fiduciary responsibility；prudent person rule
受託者団体保険 trustee group insurance
受託者としての資格 fiduciary capacity
受託者に対する事務委託 entrustment to trustee
受託者の更迭 replacement of trustee
受託者の報告 trustee's report
受託者賠償責任保険 bailee's liability

insurance
受託者保証証書 fiduciary bond
受託商品 entrusted asset
受託制限 restriction of order acceptance
受託取扱場所 place of fiduciary
受託取引 transactions for customers' accounts
受託に関する契約書 agreements pertaining to acceptance of orders
受託販売 sales on consignment
受託販売立替金 advance on consignment-in
受 託 品 goods on consignment-in
受　　諾 assent
主たる債務者 primary obligor
主たる事務所 main office
主たる所得者 main income earner
主たる利用者 primary user
主たる論点 principal issue
受　　注 acceptance of an order；receipt of orders
受 注 額 order amount
受 注 残 order backlog
受注残高 orders in hand
受注の増加 order increase
主　　張 assertion
主張の要点 points
出荷指図書 ship order
出荷指数 shipments index
出 願 権 application right
出願権の取得 acquisition of the application right
出金伝票 disbursement slip；payment slip
出　　現 emergence
出向社員 detached employees
出港手数料 clearance fee
出再会社 ceding company；transferring company
出 再 者 cedant
出再保険 outwards reinsurance；reinsurance ceded
出再保険会社 ceding insurer
出再保険料 ceded premium
出産育児休暇 maternity and paternity leave
出　　資 capital contribution；capital subscription；equity contribution
出資維持保証 non-abandonment undertaking
出 資 額 amount invested；amount of investment
出資型リート equity REIT (real estate investment trust)
出資義務者 contributory
出資・拠出国債 subscription/contribution bonds
出 資 金 equity capital；investment in capital
出資金手形勘定 share draft account
出資金の払込み payment of capital contribution
出 資 者 equity participant；equity partner；financier
出資証券 equity securities；subscription certificate
出資する subscribe
出資対象 targets for investment
出資の受入れ、預り金及び金利等の取締りに関する法律（出資法） law concerning restrictions on the acceptance of subscription, deposit and interest rate, etc.
出資比率 equity position；investment ratio
出 資 法 law concerning restrictions on the acceptance of subscription, deposit and interest rate, etc.
出資預金 share deposits
出　　所 source
出席した株主の議決権の過半数 majority vote of the shareholders present
出訴期限 limitation of actions；statute of limitation
出 損 金 contributions
出張旅費 traveling expenses for business
出　　廷 jury service
出 版 権 publishing right
出 版 費 publishing cost
出 版 法 press law

出　　費 outlay
受動的事業 passive business
受動的受託者 bare trustee
受動的所得源 PIG (passive income generator)
受動的損失 passive loss
受動的投資家 passive investor
受動的利益 passive income
主 登 録 main registration
取　　得 acquisition；purchase
取得価格 acquisition price
取得価額の算定 determination of acquisition cost
取得企業(結合企業) acquiring entity
取得銀行 acquiring bank
取得原価 acquisition cost；historical cost；original cost
取得原価基準 historical cost basis
取得原価残高比例法 cost depletion method
取得原価主義 historical cost system
取得原価主義安定価値会計 historical cost/constant-dollar accounting
取得原価主義会計 HCA (historical cost accounting)；historical cost basis of accounting
取得原価主義財務諸表 historical financial statements
取得原価主義財務データ historical financial data
取得原価主義名目価値会計 historical cost/nominal dollar accounting
取得原価調整 acquisition cost adjustment
取得原価で計上される carried at cost
取得原価の慣行 historical cost convention
取得原価の構成要素 components of acquisition cost
取得原価の配分 allocation of cost
取得原価法 method of historical cost；original cost method
取得原価モデル historical cost model
取得後の変動 post acquisition change
取得差額 acquisition difference
取得時為替レート historical exchange rate
取得時換算法 translation method at historical rate
取得時効 acquisitive prescription；positive prescription
取得資産 acquired asset；property acquired
取得した資産及び引受けた負債 assets acquired and liabilities assumed
取得時の変動 change at the time of acquisition
取得剰余金 acquired surplus
取得と売却 acquisition and divesture
取 得 日 acquisition date
取得日以前の留保利益 pre-acquisition retained earnings
取 得 前 pre-acquisition
ジュニア・トランシェ junior tranche
主任アナリスト lead analyst
主任会計士 accountant in charge
主任会計士室(SEC) Office of Chief Accountant(SEC)
主任為替実査官 Senior Foreign Exchange Examiner
主任主計事務専門官 Chief Officer for Budget Information Systems
主任調査官室 Office of Chief Account
主任弁護人 leading counsel
ジュネーブ条約 Geneva Convention
守秘義務 confidentiality of information
守秘義務契約 NDA (non-disclosure agreement)；secrecy agreement
守秘義務特権 confidentiality privilege
種苗管理センター National Center for Seeds and Seedings Independent Administrative Institution
主　　部 stating part
手　　法 approach；method
主保険契約 primary vehicle
主務官庁 competent authority
主務省令 ordinance of competent minister
主務大臣 competent minister
主持ち分金融商品 main equity instrument
受 約 者 promisee
授　　与 conferment
需　　要 demand

需要圧力　demand pressure
需要関数　demand function
需要管理　DSM (demand side management)
需要曲線　demand curve
需 要 減　decline in demand
需要サイド経済学　demand side economics
需要指数　demand index
需 要 増　surge in demand
需要弾性値　elasticity of demand
需要弾力性　demand elasticity
需要独占　monopsony
需要の落込み　slowing demand
需要の回復　pickup in demand；recovering demand
需要不足　demand deficiency
需要分析　demand analysis
需要変化　shift in demand
需要見通し　demand prospect
需要予測　demand forecast
主 要 因　key factor；prime factor
主要会計方針の要約　summary of significant accounting policies
主要株主　principal shareholders
主要勘定　main account；principal account
主要企業短期経済観測　short-term economic survey of principal enterprises
主要銀行貸出動向アンケート調査　Senior Loan Officer Opinion Survey on Bank Lending Practices at Large Japanese Banks
主要原材料　main materials
主 要 国　major nations
主要産業　major industry
主要産品　major commodity
主要支持線が試される　expose the primary support
主要事実　fact in issue
主要条項　principal provisions
主要製造指図書　principal production order
主要セグメント　significant segment
主要帳簿　main books；principal books
主要通貨に対して安くなる　extending losses against major currencies
主要ディーラー　responsible and recognized dealer
主要抵抗線の突破　key range breakout
主要データが発表されていない　bereft of key data release
主要取引　main customer
主要な内訳　major component
主要な活動　principal activity
主要な株主　major stockholders
主要な基礎　primary basis
主要な原材料　major raw materials
主要な源泉　predominant source
主要な指標　key indicator
主要な条件　primary conditions
主要な前提　key assumptions
主要な抵抗線　key resistance
主要なテーマ　dominant theme
主要な論点　primary issue
主要部門　crown jewel
受容領域　tolerance territory
受理撤回　withdrawal of receipt
主　　流　mainstream
受 領 証　accountable receipt；receipt
受領対価　consideration received
狩猟免許税　hunter's license tax
主力銀行　major relationship bank
主力市場　core market
主力商品　staple product
主力部門　core business division
種 類 株　class stock
酒類審議会　council on alcoholic beverages
酒類総合研究所　National Research Institute of Brewing
準　quasi
準インフレーション　semi-inflation
準 大 手　second tier
準確定申告　quasi-final return
準 株 式　quasi-share；quasi-stock
準 貨 幣　quasi money
準借入れ　quasi-loan
準　　拠　compliance with

シ

準共有者 quasi co-owner
準拠性テスト compliance test
準 拠 法 applicable law ; governing law
準拠法条項 governing clause
準禁治産者 quasi incompetent person
準禁反言 quasi estoppel
準 契 約 implied contract ; quasi-contract
準現金資産 near cash asset
準 更 生 quasi-reorganization
準固定費 semi-fixed cost
準 債 務 quasi-debt obligations
準じた方法 manner similar to
準司法的権力 quasi-judicial power
準上級会計士 semi-senior accountant
準消費貸借 quasi-loan for consumption
準信認関係 quasi-fiduciary relationship
準政府機関 quasi-government agency
準地役権 quasi easement
準仲裁人 quasi-arbitrator
準 通 貨 near money ; quasi-currency
準備預り金勘定 special reserve accounts
準 備 金 allowance ; reserve ; reserve fund
準備金勘定 reserve account
準備金計算基礎 reserve basis
準備銀行 reserve bank
準備金積立額 provision for general reserves
準備金取崩額 drawings from general reserves ; reserve drawn down
準備金に計上される部分 component accounted for reserve
準備金の妥当性 reserve adequacy
準備資産 reserve asset
準備資本 reserve capital
準備書面 brief ; case
準備制度 reserve system
準備通貨 reserve currency
準備ポジション reserve position
準備預金制度 reserve deposit requirement system
準備預金制度に関する法律 Law Concerning Reserve Deposit Requirement System
準 備 率 reserve requirement ratio
準備率操作 reserve requirement operation
準変動原価 semi-variable cost
準変動費 semi-variable charge
準変動費項目 semi-variable expenses
準　　用 mutatis mutandis
準用規定 provisions applied mutatis mutandis
準用する apply mutatis mutandis
準預対象金融商品 financial instruments for which banks are required to maintain reserves
順イールド normal yield curve ; positive curve ; positive yield
順位相関指数 RCI (Rank Correlation Index)
順月確定日相場 outright forward fixed date rate
順月確定日渡し outright forward fixed date delivery
順 ざ や positive spread
順ざや市場 normal market
順 送 金 credit transfer
順　　調 favorable
順調な売上 steady sales
順調な売上の伸び healthy revenue growth
順調な回復 brisk recovery
順調な消費 smooth consumption
順貿易偏向的成長 pro-trade biased growth
純受取利息 NII (net interest income)
純売上高総計 aggregate net sales
純売りつなぎ net short hedging
純営業損失 net operating loss
純営業利益 net operating profit
純　　益 absolute profit ; net income ; net profit
純益処分 disposition of net income
純 益 率 net profit ratio
純　　額 net amount
純額アプローチ net approach
純額基準 net basis
純額決済 net payment ; net settlement
純額主義 net amount principle
純額表示 net amount presentation

純額ベース net base
純額法 net method
純課税財産 net taxable assets
純貨幣ポジション net monetary position
純借入準備 net borrowed reserves
純換算差額 net translation difference
純金融収入 net financial income
純原価 net cost
純現金収支 net cash balance
純現在価値 net present value
純減少額 net decrease
純交易条件指数 index of net terms of trade
純債権 net receivables
純債権国 net creditor country
純産出 net output
純資産 net assets；net worth equity
純資産価値 net asset value
純資産計算書 statement of net assets
純資産の買入れ purchase of net assets
純資産の引受額 acceptance price of net assets
純資産利益率 profit ratio of net assets
純資本要件 net capital requirement
純収益 NOI (net operating income)
純自由準備 net free reserves
純商品交易条件 net commodity terms of trade
純剰余金 net surplus
純粋インフレ期待 pure inflation expectation
純粋期待仮説 pure expectation hypothesis
純粋金利 pure rate of interest
純粋クレジット・リスク pure credit risk
純粋交換 pure exchange
純粋資産負債ポジション pure asset liability position
純粋証券 pure securities
純粋据置終身年金 pure deferred life annuity
純粋スワップ pure swap
純粋独占 pure monopoly
純粋保険料 pure premium
純粋リスク pure risk
純粋利回り pure yield
純粋割引証券 pure discount securities
純戦略 pure strategy
純増 net increase
純増減 net change；net increase and decrease
純相続財産 net succession
純損益 net profit or loss；net results
純損益区分 net profit or loss section
純損益計算 net profit or loss account
純損失 net loss
純損失の繰越 carryforward of net operating loss；carryover of net loss
純損失の繰戻し carry back of net loss
純貯蓄 net saving
純投資 net investment
純取引 net transaction
純取引高 net trading volume
純農地の評価 valuation of farmland
純負債 net debt；net liabilities
純負債比率 net gearing
純分検定所 assay office
純保険料 net premium
純持越費用 net carryover cost
純有利子負債 net debt
純輸出 net export
純利益 net earnings
純利益・純資産比率 net income to net worth ratio
純利益対総収益比率 ratio of net profit to gross revenues
純利益に対する持ち分 equity in earnings；equity interest in net profit
純利益持ち分 share of net profit
純利益率 net income ratio
純利処分 appropriation of net income
純利息 net interest
純利息費用 net interest cost
純利得 net gain
純流動性収支 net liquidity balance
純割引債 pure discount bond
巡回監査 traveling audit
巡回裁判官 circuit judge
巡回裁判所 circuit court
巡回販売人 travelling salesman
瞬間スポット・レート instantaneous spot

シ

rate
循環資産 circulating assets
循 環 株 cyclical stock ; cyclicals
循環現象 cyclical phenomenon
循環資金 circulating fund
循環的成長 cyclical growth
循環的変動 cyclical fluctuation
循環的要因 cyclical component
循環的要因と趨勢的要因 cyclical and secular reasons
循環不況 cyclical depression
循環要因による回復 recovering cyclically
瞬時通信 real time communication
遵守状況 state of observance
潤沢な流動性供給 provision of ample liquidity
ジョイント・ブックランナー joint bookrunner
ジョイント・ベンチャーの持ち分 interests in joint ventures
ジョイント・リード joint lead
上　　位 top
上 位 債 senior debt
上位債市場 senior sector
上位社債 senior bond
上位集団 major bracket
上位証券 senior issue
上位請求権 senior claim
上位トランシェ senior tranche
上位保険加入者 senior policyholder
上位劣後社債 senior subordinated note
省 エ ネ energy conservation
照　　会 inquiry ; reference
傷　　害 accidental injury
傷害及び健康保険 accident and health insurance
傷害保険 personal accident insurance
障　　害 hurdle ; impediment
障害給付 disability benefit
障害者控除 credit for handicapped person ; exemption for handicapped person ; physically handicapped person allowance
障害手当金 disability allowance
障害認定 disability determination
障害年金 disability annuity ; disability pension
障害年金給付支払い disability benefit payment
障害補償 disablement benefit
生涯教育 life-long education
生涯教育控除 lifetime learning credit
生涯賃金 lifetime wages
生涯不動産権 life estate
照会先銀行 reference bank
照会適合率 matching ratio
紹介手数料 referral fees
紹介ブローカー introducing broker
場外先物取引 off-exchange futures transaction
場外市場 curb market ; off-board market
場外証券 unlisted securities
場外取引 off-board trading ; outside dealing
場外取引店 bucket shop
場外仲買人 street broker
小 海 損 petty average
消化期間 period of digestion
奨学金融資金庫 SLMA (Student Loan Marketing Association)
少　　額 small denomination
少額繰延資産 small sum deferred assets
少額減価償却資産 petty sum depreciable assets
少額現金支払い petty cash payment
少額減耗資産 petty sum wasting property
少額公債別枠非課税制度 tax free small-sum public bond investment system
少額債券 baby bond
少額資産 small sum properties
少額重要資産 small sum and important asset ; small sum and important property
少額償却資産 petty sum depreciable property
少額貯蓄等利用者カード green card
少額貯蓄非課税制度 small-savings tax exemption system ; tax free small-sum savings system

少額通貨 fractional currency
少額通貨整理 voiding of small-denomination currency including banknotes
少額配当所得 small sums of dividend income
少額預金 small sum deposit；small sums of savings
少額預貯金 small sums of deposits and savings
少額老齢年金 small sums of pension paid to old-age persons
少額ローン small loan
使用価値 value in use
使用可能期間 estimated usable period
償　　還 calling；cash in；redemption ；repayment
償 還 益 redemption profit
償還延長 extension of the maturity
償還価格 redemption price
償還価額 redemption value
償還確実性 certainty of redemption
償還可能株式 callable preferred stock
償還可能ワラント redeemable warrant
償還株式 callable shares；callable stock ；redeemable stock
償還基金 redemption fund
償還期限 maturity；repayment terms
償還期限まで保有 held to maturity
償還期日 redemption date
償還金額 redemption amount
償還決定債券 called bond
償 還 権 equity of redemption
償還債券 redeemable bond
償還財源 fiscal resources for redemption
償還財源繰入れ appropriation of fiscal resources for redemption
償還差益 capital accrual；profit from redemption；redemption gain
償還差益課税 tax on redemption profit
償還式年金 annuity refund
償還時の元本保証 minimum redemption floor
償還据置期間 call protection
償還据置終身年金 refund deferred life annuity
償還する amortize；redeem
償還請求 claim for reimbursement
償還請求可能な puttable
償還請求権 claim of redemption；redemption right；right of recourse
償還請求権のない融資 non-recourse finance
償還選択権 cash in option
償還総利回り gross redemption yield
償還通知 notice of redemption
償還に伴う末梢 obliteration accompanied by redemption
償還の仕組み amortization structure
償還の定義 meaning of redemption
償還プレミアム premium on redemption
償還方法 method of redemption
償還保険 redemption insurance
償還免除 discharge of repayment；forgiveness of repayment
償還優先株式 redeemable preference share
償還優先株の償還 retirement of redeemed preferred stock
償還予定額 aggregate redemption amount ；scheduled redemption amount
償還リスク redemption risk
償還利回り redemption yield
商慣習法 customs of merchant
商　　機 business opportunity
使用期間 usable years
試用期間 trial employment period；trial period
小 企 業 small enterprise
小企業課税 taxation on a small business
小企業の事業主 owner of a small sized business；owner of small business
小規模企業共済 small enterprise mutual aid plan
小規模企業共済掛金控除 deduction for the contribution to small enterprise mutual aid plan
小規模企業者 small sized business proprietor
小規模事業者 small scale enterprises

シ

償　却 depreciation and amortization ; write-off
償却額 depreciable amount
償却可能限度額 final depreciable limit
償却可能資産 depreciable and amortizable assets
償却可能年数 depreciable life
償却勘定 depreciation account
償却期間 period of depreciation
償却基金 amortization fund
償却基金法 sinking fund method
償却原価 amortized cost
償却原価法 amortized cost method
償却限度額 allowable limit for depreciation amount ; allowed amortizable limit ; depreciable limit
償却後原価 depleted cost
償却後純利益 net profit after depreciation
償却債権 loan written off
償却債権取立 collection of written-off claims ; recovery of claims written-off
償却債権取立益 gain on the collection of claims written-off
償却債権の回収 recoveries on loans written off
償却資産 depreciable property
償却準備金 reserve for depreciation and amortization
償却済貸倒金の回収 collection of bad debts written off
償却済債権 written-off accounts receivable
償却済債権回収 bad debt recovery
償却対象額 amount to be amortized
償却超過 over-depreciation
償却年数 years of amortization
償却範囲 allowed depreciation
償却費の配賦 appropriation of depreciation
償却費配賦 appointment of depreciation
償却費用 amortization cost
償却不足額の繰越 underdepreciation carried forward
償却方法 amortization method ; manner of depreciation
償却方法の選定 selection of depreciation method
償却方法の届出 registration of depreciation method
償却方法の変更 change in depreciation method
償却方法変更 change of depreciation method
償却前繰延資産 deferred charge before amortization
償却前純利益 net profit before depreciation
償却率 amortization rate ; depreciation rate
償却累計 cumulative depreciation
償却累計額 accumulated amortization
消　却 cancellation ; retirement
消却可能株式 callable shares
消却義務 bearing duty
消却仕訳 eliminating entry
乗客賠償責任保険 passenger liability insurance
昇　給 salary increase
昇給率 rate of salary increase
上級会計学 advanced accounting
上級会計士 senior accountant
上級裁判所 superior courts
上級副幹事 senior co-manager
消　去 elimination
商業送り状 commercial invoice
商業会議所 Association Cambiste Internationale ; chamber of commerce
商業会計 commercial accounting
商業格付け commercial rating
商業貸出 commercial loan
商業貸付 commercial lending
商業銀行 commercial bank
商業銀行家 commercial banker
商業金融 commercial finance
商業組合 mercantile partnership
商業裁判所 commercial court
商業信用 commercial credit
商業信用状 commercial L/C (letter of

credit)
商業信用保険 commercial credit insurance
商業生産 commercial production
商業手形 commercial bill；mercantile paper
商業手形主義 real-bills doctrine
商業的効果 commercial effect
商業的成功 commercial success
商業登記 commercial registration
商業登記簿謄本 certified copy of commercial registration
商業統計 commercial statistics
商業トレーダー commercial trader
商業不動産ローン commercial mortgage loan；commercial real estate loan
商業フライト commercial flight
商 業 法 mercantile law；merchant law
商業簿記 commercial bookkeeping；merchandise bookkeeping
商業モーゲージ担保証券 CMBS (commercial mortgage-backed securities)
商業用不動産 commercial property；CRE (commercial real estate)
商業用モーゲージ commercial mortgage
商業用モーゲージ担保証券 commercial mortgage backed securities
商業用モーゲージ・プール commercial mortgage pool
商業割引 commercial discount
情況証拠 circumstantial evidence
消極財産 negative property
消極資産 negative assets
消極信託 passive trust
消極的確認 negative confirmation
消極的抗弁 negative plea
消極的主張 negative averments
消極的証言 negative testimony
消極的証拠 negative evidence
消極的投資管理 negative investment management；passive investment management
消極的評価勘定 negative valuation accounts
消極的保証 negative assurance
消極のれん negative goodwill
使用許諾者 licensor
使用許諾料 license fee
上記を約因として in consideration of the foregoing
常勤監査役 standing statutory auditor
常 勤 の full time
小グループ subgroup
小 計 sub-total
承 継 succession
承継会社 successor company
承継金融機関 assuming financial institutions
承継担保 linear warranty
承継保険受取人 reversionary beneficiary
上下10% ten percent greater or lower than
上下幅内 at the bounds
使 用 権 right to use
商 圏 trading area
証 言 testimony
条 件 conditions；terms and conditions
条件概要書 term sheet
条件緩和 easing of conditions
条件交渉 negotiation on terms and conditions
条件設定遅延方式 DRS (deferred rate setting)
条件体特約 impairment rider
条 件 付 with a proviso
条件付回帰分析 conditional regression analysis
条件付監査報告書 qualified opinion report
条件付期待値 conditional expectation
条件付給付 contingent benefit
条件付繰上償還 conditional call
条件付契約 conditional contract
条件付決済条項 contingent settlement provisions
条件付国庫補助金 conditional subsidy from the national treasury
条件付支払い contingent payment
条件付使用 contingent use

条件付譲渡 conditional assignment
条件付承認 conditional approval
条件付生命保険信託 contingent life insurance trust
条件付対価 contingent consideration
条件付注文 contingent order
条件付で subject to condition
条件付手数料 contingent fee
条件付取引 conditional transaction
条件付捺印証書 escrow
条件付成行注文 MIT (market if touched) order
条件付年金 contingent annuity
条件付売買 conditional sale
条件付引受 conditional acceptance
条件付不動産権 estate upon condition
条件付船荷証券 claused bill of lading
条件付要求払預金 conditional demand deposit
条件付流動性 conditional liquidity
条件と契約書 terms and documentation
条件引受 qualified acceptance
条件変更負債 restructured debt
上　限 cap；ceiling；top end；upper end；upper limit
上限金利 cap interest rate；ceiling rate
証券アナリスト financial analyst；securities analyst
証券委託納付 request payment by securities
証券受渡済契約 delivered business
証券営業マン customer's man
証券化 securitization
証券課 Securities Business Division
証券会社 brokerage firm；securities company；securities firm
証券会社扱CD brokered CD
証券会社間 street side
証券会社社内規則 house rules
証券会社証拠金基準 house maintenance requirement
証券会社ディーラー securities house dealer
証券買取停止 marketout
証券買取停止条項 marketout clause
証券外務員 customers' broker；registered representative
証券価格 security price
証券価格変動引当金 securities valuation reserve
証券格付け security rating
証券化資産 securitized assets
証券化市場 securitization market
証券化した資産 secirtised asset
証券貸付 security lending
証券化商品 securitization products
証券化法 securitization law
証券化モーゲージ securitized mortgage
証券からの登録 registration of physical securities
証券監督院 Securities Supervisory Board
証券監督官 securities regulators
証券監督者国際機構 IOSCO (International Organization of Securities Commissions)
証券管理 securities management
証券偽造 forgery of securities
証券規定 securities regulations
証券業 securities business
証券業界 securities industry
証券業協会 securities dealers association
証券業協会包括誓約書 blanket certification form
証券行政 securities administration
証券業仲裁委員会 SICA (Securities Industry Committee of Arbitration)
証券業務 securities activities
証券金融 securities financing；security credit
証券金融会社 securities finance company
証券クリアリング業務 securities clearing operation
証券経済日誌 diary on securities market
証券決済 securities settlement
証券決済機関 CSD (central securities depository)
証券決済システム SSS (securities settlement system)
証券決済制度改革 reform of securities settlement systems

証券決済未了 failure to deliver securities
証券口座 stock account
証券固有のリスク security-specific risk
証券先物取引 securities futures transactions
証券残存期間 remaining life of security
証券市場安定化法案 Securities Market Stabilization Act
証券市場改革法案 Securities Market Reform Act
証券市場線 securities market line
証券システム securities system
証券指標銘柄 benchmark securities
証券資本 securities capital
証券清算機関 securities clearing agency
証券貸借 stock lending
証券担保貸付 security loan
証券担保貸付金利 broker loan rate
証券担保信託社債 collateral trust bond
証券担保ローン securities loan
証券ディーラー securities dealer
証券統計年報 annual securities statistics
証券投資 portfolio investment；securities investment
証券投資委員会 SIB (Securities and Investments Board)
証券投資家保護会社 securities investor protection corporation
証券投資家保護公社 SIPC (Securities Investor Protection Corporation)
証券投資家保護法 Securities Investor Protection Act of 1970
証券投資信託 investment trust on securities；securities investment trust
証券投資信託及び証券投資法人に関する法律 Law Concerning Securities Investment Trust and Securities Investment Companies
証券投資信託協会 Investment Trust Association of Japan
証券投資信託の部分解約 partial cancellation of securities investment trust
証券投資信託販売会社 securities investment trust sales company
証券投資相談 securities investment advisory service
証券投資優遇税制 preferential tax treatment for securities investment
証券特別勘定 special account for inward portfolio investment
証券取引 securities trading；securities transaction
証券取引業者協会 securities trade associations
証券取引検査官室 Compliance Inspection Office
証券取引所 bolsa；securities exchange
証券取引所運営評議会 SESC (Stock Exchange Executive Council)
証券取引所準会員 allied members
証券取引所に上場されている有価証券 marketable securities listed on a securities exchange
証券取引所の市場 market of a stock exchange
証券取引審議会 securities exchange commission
証券取引清算機関 registered securities clearing organization；securities exchange clearing house
証券取引税法 securities business tax law
証券取引責任準備金 legal reserve for security transactions
証券取引損失準備金 reserve for loss from securities transactions
証券取引等監視委員会 SESC (Securities and Exchange Surveillance Commission)
証券取引等監視委員会委員 Commissioner of SESC (Securities and Exchange Surveillance Commission)
証券取引等監視委員会委員長 Chairperson of SESC
証券取引の低迷 poor securities trading
証券取引法 Securities and Exchange Law
証券取引法政省令 Cabinet Order and Ordinances of the Securities and Exchange Law

シ

シ

証券納付 tax payment by securities
証券の運用成績 performance of securities
証券の自動貸出 automatic securities lending
証券の種類 class of security
証券の発行と上場 securities offering and listing
証券の分別保管 segregation of securities
証券の保管 custody of securities
証券の銘柄 security issue
証券売買益 trading profit
証券発行 flotation of securities；securities issuance
証券発行市場 primary securities market
証券発行手数料 fee for issuance of securities
証券引受会社 house of issue
証券引受業者の手数料 fee for underwriters
証券引替払い payment against document
証券評価準備金 MSVR (mandatory securities valuation reserve)
証券含み益 unrealized gains in securities
証券振替決済サービス book-entry securities transfer service
証券ブローカー commission house；securities broker
証券分析 securities analysis
証券返却指図 SLR (stock loan return)
証 券 法 Securities Act of 1933
証券法の真実 truth in securities act
証券保管振替機関 depositary trust company
証券保管振替機構 JASDEC (Japan Securities Depository Center)
証券保管振替機構取扱内国株券 JASDEC eligible domestic stock
証券保管振替機構非取扱転換社債型新株予約権付社債券 JASDEC non-eligible convertible-bond type corporate bonds with new share reservation rights
証券保管振替機構非取扱内国株券 JASDEC non-eligible domestic stock
証券保有の需要 demand to hold securities
証券マリー marrying transaction of securities company
証券用収入印紙 documentary stamp
証券リスク線 security risk curve
証券利回り securities yield
証券利回り線 security yield curve
証券レッグ securities leg
証言記録 deposition
証　　拠 evidence；proof
証 拠 金 forward margin；margin
証拠金維持率 retention requirement
証拠金勘定 margin account
証拠金基準額 standard price for margin calculation
証拠金規則 Margin Rules
証拠金コスト margin cost
証拠金システム margin system
証拠金所要額 required margin
証拠金制度 margin money system
証拠金督促 house call
証拠金特例 special rule relating to margin
証拠金取引 margin transaction
証拠金内部規則 house margin rule
証拠金に対する権利の行使 exercise of claim on clearing margin
証拠金の区分 division of margin
証拠金の充当 appropriation of margin
証拠金の引出し withdrawal of deposited margin
証拠金の分離 segregation of margin
証拠金の預託 deposit of margin
証拠金負債 margin debt
証拠金不足 margin debit；margin deficiency
証拠金不足勘定 under-margined account
証拠金余剰 margin credit
証拠金率 margin rate
証拠事実 evidentiary facts
証拠書類 documentary evidence
証拠の重さ weight of evidence
証拠の要約 summing-up
証拠物件 material evidence
商　　号 business name；corporate name；trade name

照　　合 checking；collation；tally
照合会員 comparison-only member
照合確認 reconciliation
照合勘定 adjustment account
照合済記号 check mark
照合済取引 locked-in trade；matched trade
照合棚卸 checking inventory
照 合 票 comparison slip
照合目的 verification purpose
条　　項 article；clause；provision；stipulation
商 行 為 commercial transaction
商工会議所 chamber of commerce and industry
商 工 業 commerce and industry
商工業金融会社 commerce and industry finance company
商工組合中央金庫 Central Co-operative Bank for Commerce and Industry；Shoko Chukin Bank
商工ローン commercial and industrial loan
正午条項 noon clause
使用後届出制 use and file
使用後届出制度 use and file system
照　　査 examination by reference
詳　　細 detail
詳細情報 capsule information
詳細な規定 detailed requirement
詳細な分析 anatomy；detailed analysis
詳細な分類 detailed classification
小　　罪 petty offense
使用時間 used hours
使用時間比例法 hours-of-service method
商事代理 mercantile agency
商事仲裁 commercial arbitration
常時棚卸 running inventory
証紙徴収 tax collection by stamp
焼失兌換券の整理 special conversion of currency to replace banknotes lost after the Great Kanto earthquake
使 用 者 employer
使用者原価 user cost
使用者賠償責任保険 employer's liability insurance
商社金融 trading firm finance
召　　集 convocation
召集権者 convener
召集手続 procedures for the convocation
召集の手続 convening procedure
商 習 慣 business practice；commercial customs
小 集 団 subset
詳　　述 elaboration on
昇　　順 ascending order
小 循 環 minor cycle
仕 様 書 specification
仕様書原価 specification cost
仕様書売買 sale by specification
上　　昇 advance；ascending；rally；upswing
上昇圧力 upward pressure
上昇カーブ ascending curve
上 昇 角 climbing angle
上昇基調 upward trend
上昇局面では in a rally
上昇傾向にある in up trend
上昇順位 ranking of advances
上昇トライアングル ascending pattern triangle
上昇トレンド appreciation trend
上昇トレンドライン rising bottom
上 昇 率 rate of increase
上 昇 力 climbing power；up-pressure
上　　場 listing
上場維持に必要な年間手数料 annual listing fee
上場オプション listed options
上場外国株式 listed foreign stocks
上場会社 listed company；quoted company
上場会社資金調達額 security financing by listed companies
上場会社配当状況 dividends of listed companies
上場会社発行済株式数増減状況 sources in increase in outstanding shares
上 場 株 listed stock
上場株価指数 listed stock price index

シ

上場株券の所属部の指定 assignment of listed stocks to sections
上場株券の所属部の指定替え reassignment of listed stocks to sections
上場株式照合システム Listed Comparison System
上場株式の評価 valuation of listed stock
上場株式平均利回り average yield of listed stocks
上場企業 listed firm
上場基準 criteria for listing
上場規程 listing regulations
上場契約 listing agreement
上場契約違反 contravention of listing agreement
上場契約書 stock listing agreement
上場後の費用 fees after listing
上場債券 listed bonds
上場債券市場 listed bond market
上場債券市場外売買高 off-board transactions of listed bonds
上場先物 listed futures
上場市場の変更 relocation of listed securities to other market
上場市場の変更審査料 examination fee for relocation to other market
上場市場の変更申請者 applicant for relocation to other market
上場証券 listed securities
上場商品 listed product
上場新株引受権証券 listed warrants
上場審査 listing examination
上場審査基準 listing examination criteria
上場審査費 listing examination fees
上場申請 listing application
上場申請書 application form for listing
上場申請に係る株式 stock for which listing application is made
上場申請のための有価証券報告書 securities report for listing application
上場申請日以後における株式分布状況に関する予定書 Expected Shareownership Distribution on or after Listing Application Date
上場申請日以後における預託証券の分布状況に関する予定書 Expected Ownership Distribution of Depositary Securities on or after Listing Application Date
上場生命保険証書 traded policy
上場代理人 listing agent
上場のための有価証券報告書 securities report for listing
上場廃止 delisting
上場廃止基準 criteria for delisting
上場廃止申請 application for delisting
上場日が属する年 year to which listing day pertains
上場費用 listing fee
上場普通債券の種類別上場総額 amount listed by types of straight bonds
上場普通債券の種類別発行額 amount issued by types of straight bonds
上場銘柄 exchange-traded issues ; listed brand ; listed issue
上場有価証券原簿 ledger of listed securities
上場有価証券指数 price index of listed securities
上場有価証券の変更上場申請手続 application procedure for alteration in listed securities
上場要件 listing requirements
証書貸付 loan on deeds ; loan on policy
証書事項 matter in deed
証書証券 certificated securities
証書の交付 withdrawal of certificate
証書の説明部 recital
証書の文面 face of instrument
証書配当 scrip dividend
証書発行のある証券 materialized securities
証書発行を行わないこと dematerialization
証書発行を伴わない証券 dematerialized securities
証書番号 certificate number
証書保有者 certificate holder
昇　進 promotion
乗　数 multiplier
乗数効果 multiplier effect

乗数分析 multiplier analysis
乗数理論 multiplier theory
少数株主 minority interest holder ; minority shareholders
少数株主権 minority shareholders' right
少数株主持ち分 minority interest
少数株主持ち分金額 minority interest amount
少数株主持ち分の買取り minority buy-out
少数支配 minority control
少数精鋭 lean staff
少数代表法 minority representation
少数特定者持株数 number of shares owned by the special few
少 数 派 minority
少数表示取引 decimal trading
小数第3位で表された truncated to three decimal points
小数点以下切り捨て disregard of decimal places
小数点第2位 second decimal place
使 用 税 use tax
使用制限のある with usage restriction
使用総資本利益率 return (ratio) on capital employed
常設委員会 standing committee
常設機関 standing body
上訴裁判所 appellate court
小損害免責 franchise
小損害免責歩合 franchise
状態価格密度 state price density
象徴的引渡し symbolic delivery
焦　　点 focus
商 店 法 shop act
譲　　渡 alienation ; assignment ; cession ; transfer
譲渡裏書 endorsement to transfer
譲渡及び移転 assignment and transfer
譲渡価格 transfer price
譲渡可能 negotiable
譲渡可能貸出 transferable loan
譲渡可能貸付 transferable loan facility
譲渡可能貸付証書 TLC (transferable loan certificate)
譲渡可能信用状 transferable L/C (letter of credit)
譲渡可能定期預金証書 negotiable CD (certificate of deposit) ; negotiable time certificates of deposits
譲渡可能な資産 negotiable asset
譲渡可能払戻指図預金勘定 negotiable order of withdrawal account
譲渡可能RUF TRUF (transferable revolving underwriting facility)
譲渡可能ローン TLF (transferable loan facility)
譲渡銀行 transferor bank
譲渡禁止契約 no assignable contract
譲渡契約 transfer contract
譲渡資産 property for transfer ; transfer property
譲渡資産の取得費 cost of transferred properties
譲 渡 者 assignor
譲渡条項 assignment clause
譲渡証書 deed of conveyance ; written assignment
譲渡所得 capital gain on transfer
譲渡所得の基因とされない資産 property not qualifying for capital gain
譲渡所得の特別控除 special deduction for capital gains
譲 渡 性 alienability
譲 渡 税 transfer tax
譲渡性金融商品 transferable financial instrument
譲渡制限 restriction on transferability
譲渡性証券 transferable securities
譲渡性証書 negotiated paper ; TLI (transferable loan instrument)
譲渡税総合控除 unified credit
譲渡性定期預金証書 certificate of deposit
譲渡性預金 CD (certificate of deposit)
譲渡代金 assignment proceeds
譲渡担保 mortgage by transfer
譲渡担保証書 bill of sale
譲渡通知 assignment notice
譲渡抵当 mortgage of goods
譲渡手数料 assignment charge ; assignment fee ; transfer fee

譲 渡 人 transferor
譲渡の禁止 prohibition of transfer
譲渡の態様 condition of the transfer of the property
譲渡費用 transfer cost ; transfer expenses
譲渡不能保護預り証 nonnegotiable safekeeping receipts
衝動買い impulse buying
焦土作戦 scorched earth defense
衝　突 collision
商 取 引 trading transaction
小トレンド small trend
場　内 inside the room
承　認 acknowledgment ; approval
承認証券取引所 RIE (recognized investment exchange)
承認申請 application for approval
承認済コンファメーション affirmed confirmation
承認適格資産 admitted assets
承 認 日 date of authorization
承認リスト approved list
承認を得る義務 obligation to acquire the approval
常任監査役 full-time statutory auditor ; permanent auditor ; standing auditor
常任代理人 standing proxy
常任理事 standing governor
使用人兼務役員 employee-director
証人尋問 examination of witness
商売上の圧力 commercial pressure
試用販売 sales on approval ; trial sale
試用販売未収金 account due from sales on approval
消費関数 consumption function
消費計画 consumption plan
消 費 財 consumer goods
消費支出関連銘柄 retail and consumer spending sector stock
消 費 者 consumer
消費者関連株 consumer sector stock
消費者業務・情報サービス室(SEC) Office of Consumer Affairs and Information Service(SEC)
消費者銀行 consumer bank
消費者金融 consumer finance ; consumer loan
消費者金融会社 consumer finance company
消費者金利 consumer credit rate
消費者行動 consumer's behavior
消費者支出 consumer expenditure ; consumer spending
消費者需要 consumer demand
消費者信用 consumer credit
消費者信用均等法 ECOA (equal credit opportunity act)
消費者信用残高 consumer installment credit
消費者信用情報 consumer credit report
消費者信用生命保険 consumer credit life insurance
消費者信用保護 consumer credit protection
消費者信用保護法 Consumer Credit Protection Act
消費者信頼度 level of consumer confidence
消費者団体 consumer advocate ; consumer group ; consumer's union
消費者団体信用生命保険 consumer group credit life insurance
消費者調査 consumer research
消費者の信頼 consumer confidence
消費者物価指数 CPI (consumer price index)
消費者保護 consumer protection
消費者保護信託 spendthrift trust
消費者向け保険 consumer lines insurance
消費者リース consumer leasing
消費者ローン金利 consumer interest rate
消費需要 consumption demand
消費乗数 consumption multiplier
消費譲与税 consumption transfer tax
消費水準 consumption level
消 費 税 consumption tax
消費生活協同組合 consumer's cooperative society
消費性向 propensity to consume
消費税室 Consumption Tax Office

消費税申告 consumption entry
消費税法 Consumption Tax Law
消 費 高 amount of consumption
消費単位 consumption unit
消費動向 consumption trend
消費に対する税 tax on consumption
消費の回復 rebound in spending
消費の先送り deferred consumption
消費の伸び consumption growth
消費パターン consumption pattern
消費見通し outlook for consumer spending
消費ラグ consumption lag
消費ローン loan for consumption
消費割当 consumption quota
商　　標 brand name ; trade mark
商 標 権 right of trademark
商標権侵害 trade mark infringement
商標登録法 trade-mark registration law
証憑一覧 schedule of vouchers
証憑書類 evidenced document
商　　品 article ; commodity ; instrument ; merchandise (goods)
商品有り高 amount of stock
商品在高対受取勘定比率 ratio of merchandise to receivables
商品売上帳 book for sold goods
商品オプション commodity option
商 品 化 commercialization
商品回転数 turnover of commodity ; turnover ratio of commodity
商品回転率 merchandise turnover ratio ; rate of stock-turn
商品開発 product development
商品価格指数 commodity price index
商品価格変動準備金 reserve for inventory fluctuation
商品革新の時代 product innovation era
商品貨幣 commodity money
商品勘定 goods account ; merchandise account
商品勘定資産 trading account assets
商品間スプレッド inter-commodity spread
商品管理 merchandise management
商品危険 mercantile risk
商 品 券 gift certificate
商品原価 merchandise cost
商品券勘定 gift tickets account
商品交易条件 commodity terms of trade
商品構成 assortment of goods ; merchandise mix
商品顧客契約 commodity customers agreement
商品在庫 merchandise inventory
商品先物 commodity futures
商品先物契約 commodity futures contract
商品先物指数 commodity futures index
商品先物取引委員会 CFTC (Commodity Futures Trading Commission)
商品先物取引価格 commodity futures price
商品先物取クリアリング・ハウス clearinghouse for commodity futures
商品先物取引値幅制限 price limit on commodity futures
商品先物取引の証拠金 margin on commodity futures
商品先物取引のヘッジング hedging on commodity futures
商品仕入帳 invoice-book inward
商品仕送帳 invoice-book outward
商品市場 commodity market
商品指数 commodity index
商品需要 commodity demand
商品証券 commodity paper ; commodity security
商 品 性 commoditization
商品代金取立手形 commodity draft
商品担保 collateral commodity
商品担保債券 commodity backed bond
商品調達原価 merchandise procurement cost
商品帳簿の法則 shopbook rule
商品デリバティブ commodity derivatives
商品統計 commodity statistics
商品投資信託 commodities investment trust
商品取引 commodity transaction
商品取引企業 commodity firms

商品取引口座 commodity account
商品取引顧問 commodity trading adviser
商品取引受託債務補償基金協会 Association of Compensation Fund for Consigned Liabilities in Commodity Futures, Inc.
商品取引所 commodity exchange
商品取引所委員会 commodities exchange commission
商品取引責任準備金 commodity exchange responsibility reserve
商品取引法 commodity exchange act
商品の運用実績 product performance
商品の記述 trade description
商品の種類 types of product
商品売買帳 merchandise book
商品販売による収益 revenue from merchandise sale
商品引揚げ repossession of goods
商品ファンド commodity fund
商品ファンド・オペレーター commodity pool operator
商品分析 product analysis
商品又は製品 goods or products
商品見本 sample；sample products
商品元帳 merchandise ledger
商品有価証券 securities owned
商品連動債 commodity-linked note
使用不能資金 non-expendable fund
使用便益 use benefit
小 分 類 sub-classification
障　　壁 barrier
商　　法 Commercial Code
商法等の一部を改正する法律 Law Amending Part of the Commercial Code
商法の特例 exception to the Commercial Code
情報会計 information accounting
情報開示 information disclosure
情報開示表明保証 information disclosure statement guarantee
情報価値 information value
情報監査 information audit
情報管理室 Network Systems Management Office
情報技術 information technology
情報経済学 information economics
情報係数 information coefficient
情 報 源 information source
情報検索 information retrieval
情報公害 information pollution
情報公開室 Information Disclosure Office
情報公開法 sunshine law
情報公開前の証券取引 gun jumping
情報交換規定 provision for exchange of information
情報産業 information industry
情報サービス information service；value line
情報サービス局 Public Relations Department
情報システム information system
情報システム管理室(SEC) Office of Information System Management(SEC)
情報システム事業 information system business
情報社会 information society
情報処理 information processing
情報通信技術 information communications technology
情報通信研究機構 National Institute of Information and Communications Technology
情報提供者 common informer
情報動機による取引 information-motivated transaction
情報動機による取引者 information-motivated trader
情報取扱責任者 person in charge of handling information
情報に基づく判断 informed judgment
情報の非対称性 asymmetry of information
情報の付加 data enrichment
情報の要請 RFI (request for information)
情報ハイウェー information highway
情報発信 information supply

情報ベンダー information vendors
情報リスク information risk
情報量基準 information criteria
情報漏洩 information leakage
消防研究所 National Research Institute of Fire and Disaster
消 防 庁 Fire and Disaster Management Agency
上方修正 upward revision
抄　　本 certified abstract
正味受取額 net receipts
正味受取代金 net proceeds
正味売上高 net sales
正味運転時間 net cycle time
正味運転資本 net working capital
正味営業循環日数 net operating cycle
正味営業損失 NOL (net operating loss)
正味営業保険料 gross net premium
正味回収可能額 net collectible amounts
正味回収予定額 net amount expected to be collected
正味価額 net value
正味貸倒償却 net write-off
正味貨幣項目 net monetary item
正味貨幣資産 net monetary asset
正味貨幣負債 net monetary liability
正味危険金額 net amount at risk
正味危険負担額 amount subject
正味金銭項目 net monetary items
正味金利支払い net interest payment
正味現金流入 net cash inflow
正味固定資産 net fixed assets
正味財産 net assets
正味仕入高 net purchase
正味資産 net worth
正味資産価額 net assets value
正味実現可能価格 net realizable value
正味実現可能価額 NRV (net realizable value)
正味実現キャピタル・ゲイン net realized capital gain
正味資本ストック net capital stock
正味剰余金 actual surplus
正味処分受取金 net disposal proceeds
正味生産高 net production value
正味相続財産 net estate
正味帳簿価額 net book value
正味手取額 net avails ; net proceeds
正味当座資産 net quick assets
正味投資額の期首残高 opening net investment
正味投資未回収額 net investment outstanding
正味日数 clear days
正味の現金流入 net cash inflows
正味売却価格 net selling price
正味払込保険料指数 net payment cost index
正味非流動資産 net non-carrent assets
正味保険料比率 retention quotient
正味補償 actual insurance coverage
正味保有 net retention
正味保有額 net line
正味持ち分資産 net equity assets ; net equity interest assets
正味リース投資未回収額 net investment in lease
正味流動資産 net current assets
商 務 省 Commerce Department
常務取締役 managing director
常務理事 managing governor
証　　明 certification ; verification
証 明 者 certifier
証 明 書 certificate
証 明 人 attested witness
消　　滅 extinction ; extinguishment
消滅会社 entity ceasing to exist
消滅原価 expired cost
消滅時効 extinctive prescription ; negative prescription
消滅時点 vanishing point
消滅時配当 settlement dividend ; terminal dividend
消滅する cease to exist
消滅保険料 vanishing premium
消　　耗 exhaustion
消耗的経費 exhaustive expenditure
消 耗 品 consumables ; expendable supplies ; sundry supplies
消耗品勘定 supplies account

シ

消耗品費 supplies expenses
私用元帳 private ledger
条　　約 treaty
条約あさり treaty shopping
賞　　与 bonus
剰余インシュランス surplus insurance
剰余益金 surplus profit
剰余価値 surplus value
剰 余 金 accumulated profit
剰余金勘定 surplus account
剰余金区分 surplus section
剰余金区分の原則 principle of surplus section
剰余金繰入れ transfer of a budgetary surplus
剰余金計算書 statement of surplus
剰余金結合計算書 statement of income and retained earnings
剰余金修正 surplus adjustment
剰余金処分 appropriation of surplus
剰余金処分計算書 surplus appropriation statement
剰余金全体 entire surplus
剰余金調整 adjustment of surplus
剰余金調整書 reconciliation of surplus
剰余金取引 surplus transaction
剰余金の処分 disposal of surplus
剰余金賦課 surplus charge
剰余金分析 surplus analysis
剰余資金 surplus funds
剰余資産 surplus assets
剰余積立金 surplus reserves
譲 与 者 grantor
譲与者収入留保信託 GRIT (grantor retained income trust)
常用対数 common logarithm
賞与支給額の計算期間 term for which the bonus payment is computed
賞与準備金 provision for employee bonus
賞与制度 bonus plan
賞与引当金 reserve for bonus payment
賞与引当金繰入限度額 allowed limit of the bonus payment reserve
賞与前所得 income before employee bonus
将来加算一時差異 taxable temporary difference；taxable timing difference
将来課税対象金額 future taxable amount
将来価値 future value
将来給付 future benefit
将来勤務給付 future service benefit
将来勤務債務 future service liability
将来勤務費用 future service cost
将 来 権 executory interest
将来原価 future cost
将来減算一時差異 deductible temporary difference；deductible timing difference
将来控除対象金額 future deductible amount
将来債務 future obligation
将来準備金 prospective reserve
将来情報 forward looking information
将 来 性 future prospect
将来的な適用 prospective application
将来の回収 future recovery
将来の掛金 future contribution
将来の期間 future period
将来の期間について on a prospective basis
将来の期にわたって over future periods
将来のキャッシュフロー future cash flow
将来のキャッシュフローの現在価値 present value of future cash flow
将来の給与の上昇 future salary increase
将来の勤務 future service
将来の購買力 future buying power
将来の固有リスク future specific risk
将来の資金の流れ future cash flows
将来の市場 future marketplace
将来の事象 future event
将来の事象を条件にした contingent on future events
将来の転換日 future conversion date
将来の動向 future path
将来の特定の日 day certain
将来の変化 future change
将来のリスク future risk
将来配当 future dividend

将来利子率 forward interest rate
上流製品 upstream product
使 用 量 amount of use
奨　　励 encouragement ; incentive
省　　令 ministerial ordinance
条　　例 municipal bylaws ; ordinance by local government
奨 励 金 bounty ; premium
奨励効果 incentive effect
奨励制度 incentive plan
ショーグン債 shogun bond
ショーグンＣＢ shogun convertible bond
ショート short
ショート・クーポン short coupon
ショート・コール short call
ショート・スクイーズ short squeeze
ショート・ストラップ short strap
ショート・ストラドル short straddle
ショート・ストラングル short strangle
ショート・ストリップ short strip
ショート・ドローイング short drawing
ショート・バタフライ short butterfly
ショート・ブック short book
ショート・プット short put
ショート・ポジションを取る building short positions
ショート・リスト short list
除　　外 exclusion ; ruling out
除外期間 elimination period
除外危険 excepted risks
除外事項を記した限定意見 qualified opinion for exclusion
除外条項 exclusion clause ; exemption clause
除外する rule out
初 回 金 amount of the first payment
初回準備金 initial reserve
所　　轄 competent authority
所轄税務署 competent tax office
初　　鑑 first check
初期行動計画 initial action plan
初期償却 initial depreciation
初期段階 early stage
初期直接費用 initial direct cost
初期投資額 initial net investment
初期投入資金 seed money
初期の議論 early argument
初期の購入者 initial buyer
初期発生債務 initial accrued liability
初期費用 upfront cost
初期フランチャイズ料 initial franchise fee
除却会計 retirement accounting
除却価格 retirement price
除却資産 scrapped property
除却損益 profit or loss from retirement of fixed assets
除却単位 retirement unit
除 却 費 retirement cost
除却費用 removal expenses
除 却 法 relief method
職域給付 occupational benefit
職域年金 occupational superannuation ; sponsored pension
職　　業 profession
職業安定所 employment office
職業会計士 professional accountant
職業監査人 professional auditor
職業訓練 vocational training
職業上の規範 professional discipline
職 業 病 occupational disease ; work disease
職業倫理 professional ethics
職種分類 job classification
職　　能 job function
職 能 給 wages on job evaluation
職能組織 functional organization
食品安全担当大臣 Minister of State for Food Safety Commission and Related Matters
食品総合研究所 National Food Research Institute
職別業者 trade contractor
職　　務 duty
職 務 給 functional pay ; pay according to function
職務執行過程 course of employment
職務の執行 discharge of duties
職務評価 job evaluation
職務分析 job analysis
食糧管理特別会計 Food Management

Special Account；Foodstuff Control Special Account
食糧証券 food financing bill
食料切符 food stamp
食料品業界 foods industry
職歴総合評価制度 career sum point plan
助 言 的 advisory
助言的意見 advisory opinion
所 在 地 location；site
諸 雑 費 sundry expenses
所 持 人 holder
所持人払い payable to holder
徐々の切下 gradual devaluation
助 成 金 grant in aid；subvention
処　　置 regulatory disposition
処置に対する異議 objection to disposition
処置の解除 lifting of regulatory disposition
ショック・アブゾーバー shock absorber
職　　権 competence；official power
職権濫用 abuse of one's authority
職権濫用罪 oppression
所定外労働時間 overtime hours
所得移転 income transfer
所得インフレーション income inflation
所 得 額 amount of income
所得格差 income divergence
所得確認 income verification
所得額を申告する file income tax return
所得課税の期間相互配分 interperiod income tax allocation
所得課税の期間内配分 intraperiod income tax allocation
所得課税の配分 income tax allocation
所得金額の合算 aggregation of income amount
所 得 源 income resource
所得源泉 source of income
所得源泉説 limited income method
所得交易条件 income terms of trade
所得効果 income effect
所得控除 deductions from income；exemption and deduction from income
所得再配分 reallocation of income
所得再分配 income redistribution
所得再分配効果 income redistribution effect
所得上限 earnings cap
所得消費曲線 income consumption curve
所得申告 declaration of income；income return
所得申告用紙 income return blank
所得水準 income level
所 得 税 income tax
所得税延納 deferred payment of income tax
所得税額の控除 credit for income tax；withholding tax credit
所得税基本通達 fundamental directives of income tax
所得税減額承認 approval of decrease of income tax
所得税控除 income tax credit
所得税控除額の損金不算入 non-inclusion of income tax credit in deductible expenses
所得政策 income policy
所得税申告 income tax return
所得税申告書 income tax return form
所得税の延納に伴う利子税 interest tax on authorized deferred payment of income tax
所得税の課税 imposition of income tax
所得税の還付 refund of income tax
所得税の減額 decrease of income tax
所得税の更正決定 reassessment of income tax
所得税の税率表 income tax rates table
所得税の速算表 income tax rapid calculation table
所得税の脱税 evasion of income tax
所得税の累進度 progressiveness of income tax
所得税法 Income Tax Law
所得税率 income tax rate
所得接近法 income approach
所 得 層 income bracket
所得操作 income manipulation
所得創出効果 income generating effect

所得弾力性 income elasticity
所得調査 earnings test
所得に対する税 tax on income
所得の帰属 attribution of income
所得の帰属の推定 presumption of a real obtainer of income
所得の使途 disposition of income
所得の種類 kind of income
所得の伸び income growth
所得の平均課税 income averaging
所得比例給付 income related benefit
所得比例年金 earnings related pension；graduated pension
所得分割法 income splitting method
所得分析 income analysis
所得分布 income distribution
所得ベース income basis
所得保障 income security
所得補償給付 disability benefit
所得補償制度 income protection plan
所得補償保険 disability insurance；income compensation insurance
所得要因 income factor
所得預金 income deposit
所得割課税 taxation of income basis
初度適用 first application
初年度手数料 first year commission
初年度特別償却 initial special depreciation
ジョバー jobber
処　分 disposal；disposition；regulatory sanction
処分受取額 proceeds from disposals
処分売り selling out
処分益 gain on disposal
処分買い buy-in
処分価格 disposal price
処分価値 disposal value；salvage value
処分可能見込額 estimated disposal value
処分時の減算 deduction on disposal
処分済利益剰余金 appropriated earned surplus
処分済留保金 appropriated retained earnings
処分・清算計算書 statement of disposal and liquidation
処分損益 profit or loss from disposal
処分代金 proceeds from disposal
処分に対する異議 objection to discipline
処分による損 loss on disposal
処分日 disposal date；disposition date
処分費用 cost of disposal；disposition cost
処分見込額 estimated disposal amount
処分目的保有資産 assets held for disposition
序　文 foreword；preamble
諸未収金 miscellaneous accounts receivable
諸未払金 miscellaneous accounts payable
除　名 expulsion from membership
除名会員 lame duck
署名確認書 signature guarantee
署名証明 guarantee of signature
署名捺印 signed and sealed
署名を付す affix
書面監査 paper audit
書面契約 written agreement；written contract
書面申請 written application
書面による異議 objection in writing
書面引合 written inquiry
所　有 ownership
所有株式数の多い順 order of the size of shareholdings
所有期間 investment horizon
所有期間明細書 statement of holding period
所有期間利回り horizon return；HPR (holding period return)
所有権 ownership right；proprietary right
所有権移転 transfer of title
所有権証 ownership certificate
所有権侵害 infringement of ownership
所有権調査 title search
所有権の移転 passage of title；transfer of ownership
所有権の分割 demerger
所有権の分配 spin-off of ownership

シ

所有権保険会社 title insurance company
所有権利権 royalty interest
所有権留保 reservation of ownership
所有権留保条項 overreaching clause
所有資産運用 owned asset management
所 有 者 owner；proprietor
所有者支配 owner control
所有者不明の unclaimed
所有主勘定 proprietorship account
所有主持ち分 owner's equity；owner's equity interest；proprietorship
所有の付帯権利 incidents of ownership
所有不動産 estate in possession
所有持ち分 ownership interest
所有持ち分の割合 share of ownership interest
所有リターン return on ownership
所 要 額 required amount
所要時間 turnaround time
所要事項 necessary matters
所与のセクター given sector
処　　理 treatment
処理指示 processing indicator
処理能力 processing capabilities
助　　力 aid and comfort
書　　類 document
書類処理 document processing
書類作り paperwork
白地裏書 blank endorsement
白地株式 blank stock
白地式裏書 endorsement in blank
白 地 で in blank
白地手形 blank bill
白地引受 blank acceptance
白地譲渡 assignment in blank
シリア・ポンド SYP (Syrian pound)
シリーズEE債券 Series EE Bond
シリーズE債券 Series E Bond
シリーズHH債券 Series HH Bond
シリーズ別 each series
自力執行権 self-enforcement
じり高傾向にある creep back upwards
自立回復 autonomous recovery
知りつつ knowingly
自律的な回復 self-sustaining recovery
自律反騰 autonomously strong；technical rebound
じ り 安 continuous decline；sliding cheap
資料提出請求権 authority to require submission of report and materials
シリンダー cylinder
知れ渡る trickle through
ジレンマ dilemma
白色申告 white return
素 人 の lay
白地小切手 blank check
仕　　訳 journalizing
仕訳記入 journal entry
仕訳証憑 journal voucher
仕 訳 帳 journal book
仕訳元帳 journal ledger
新　　案 new design；novelty
新案登録 registration of a new design
人為的通貨 artificial currency
人員削減 personnel reduction
人員データ demographic data
新エネルギー・産業技術総合開発機構 New Energy and Industrial Technology Development Organization
新円切替 conversion to the "new yen" immediately after World War II
新外国為替管理法 new foreign exchange law
新会社設立 hive off
新 顔 債 new face bond
新貨条例 New Currency Act of 1871
新型の金本位制 new type of gold standard
進　　化 evolution
侵　　害 transgression
侵害行為 injury
侵害する infringe
人　　格 legal entity
人格代表者 personal representatives
進化している実務 evolving practices
新　　株 new share；new stock
新株落ち ex-new；new share off
新株落ちに係る増加新株 new shares issued through rights-offering

新株価指数 new stock price index
新株券の上場 listing of new stocks
新株付き cum new
新株の発行 issuance of new stocks
新株の申込期限 time limit of the subscription for new stock
新株発行費 new share issuing expense
新株払込金 paid-in advances
新株引受権 pre-emptive right to common shares；stock purchase right；subscription right to new shares
新株引受権証券 warrant
新株引受権証書 certificates of subscription rights；stock purchase warrant；subscription rights to new shares
新株引受権付き cum right；with warrants
新株引受権付債券 bond with subscription warrant
新株引受権付社債 bond with common stock warrant；bond with subscription warrant；bond with warrant attached
新株引受権付社債券 bonds with warrants to new shares；bonds-cum-warrants
新株引受権付優先株式 preferred stock with common stock warrant
新株引受権の行使 exercise of subscription rights
新株引受権の評価 valuation of preemptive right
新株引受権比率 subscription ratio
新株引受権理論価値 theoretical value of a subscription right
新株引受特権 subscription privilege
新株一株当りの払込価額 amount paid per new share
新株一株当り払込価額 amount paid per new stock
新株予約権付社債 corporate bonds with new share reservation rights
新株予約権付融資 financing with new share reservation right
新株ワラント share warrant
新貨幣数量説 neo-quantity theory of money
シンガポール銀行間出し手金利 Singapore inter-bank offered rate
シンガポール金取引所 Gold Exchange of Singapore
シンガポール国際金融取引所 SIMEX (Singapore International Monetary Exchange)
シンガポール証券取引所 SES (Stock Exchange of Singapore)
シンガポール通貨監督庁 Monetary Agency of Singapore
シンガポール通貨庁 MAS (Monetary Agency of Singapore)
シンガポール・ドル SGD (Singapore dollar)
シンガポール預託証書 Depository Receipts of Singapore
新価保険 depreciation insurance；replacement value insurance
真　　贋 authenticity
新規案件 new issue
審議委員 deliberative members
審 議 会 deliberative council
審 議 官 Deputy Director-General of the Planning and Coordination Bureau
審議官(官房担当) Councilor of the Minister's Secretariat
審議官(関税局担当) Deputy Director-General of the Customs and Tariff Bureau
審議官(国際担当) Deputy Commissioner (International Affairs)
審議官(国際局担当) Deputy Director-General of the International Bureau
審議官(主税局担当) Deputy Director-General of the Tax Bureau
審議官(酒税等担当) Assistant Commissioner (Planning, Information System Management, Liquor Tax and Industry)
審議官(理財局担当) Deputy Director-General of the Financial Bureau

シ

信義違反 breach of trust
新規売り open selling
新規オプション付与 new option grant
新規買い open buying
新規貸出 new lending；new loan
新規株式公開 IPO (initial public offering)
新規株式公募 IPO (initial public offering)
新規勘定 new account
新規記載 new description
新規記載又は記録 new description or record
新規求人 new job offer
新規求人数 new job offers
新規記録 new record
新規公開後の売買 aftermarket
新規財源債 new financial resource bonds
新規債券発行通知 official notice of sale
新規参入事業 green field business
新規事業 new business
新規事業育成 fostering of new business
新規事業開発 new business development
新規資金 new money
新規資本 fresh capital
新規住宅販売 new home sales
新規受注 new order
新規上場 initial listing；new listing
新規上場会社 newly listed company
新規上場企業 newly listed corporation
新規上場申請者 applicant for initial listing
新規上場手数料 fees for original listing
新規上場手続 application procedure for initial listing
新規上場料 listing fee
新 規 性 innovation
新規ディスカウント物 new discounts
新規投資金利 new money interest rate
新規のポジション new position
新規のモーゲージ new mortgage
新規発行 new issuance；outright auction
新規発行社債 newly-issued corporate bond
新規発行証券の引受 underwriting of new issue securities
新規プレミアム new premium
新規分野 new field
新規保険料 new policy premium
新規モーゲージ・プール pool of new mortgages
新規ローンに含めた rolled into a new loan
新基軸を開く blazing a trail
真偽鑑定 verification of authenticity
信義・信用債務 full-faith-and-credit debt
信 義 則 just and equitable principles
信義則違反 violation of just and equitable principles
新疆ウイグル自治区 Xinjiang
新協会貨物約款 New Institute Cargo Clauses
新銀行法 new banking law
しんきん信託銀行 Shinkin Trust Bank
信金中央金庫 Shinkin Central Bank
新金融安定化基金 New Financial Stabilization Fund
新金融安定化基金拠出金 provision of funds to the New Financial Stabilization Fund
新金融調節 new monetary adjustment system
新金融調節方式 new scheme for monetary control
信組為替 credit union exchange
シングル・オプション single option
新経済学 new economics
神経質な市場 sensitive market
神経質な市場環境 nervous market
新契約保険料 new business premium
新契約率 new business ratio
新　　券 clean notes
人 件 費 employment cost；personnel cost；personnel expenses
人件費率 ratio of personnel expenses
進行監査 progressive audit
振興企業 start-up companies
振興企業市場 ECM (emerging company marketplace)
振興経済国 emerging economy
振興市場 market for start-ups
新興企業 emerging corporations

新興工業国 NICS (newly industrialized countries)
新興産業 sunrise industry
新興市場の他国 emerging market counterparts
新興都市 boom town
新興マーケット emerging markets
新工業国群 newly industrialized countries
新厚生経済学 new welfare economics
新国際経済秩序 NIEO (New International Economic Order)
人口減 depopulation
人口構成 demographic mix
人口構成の変化 demographic change
人口推移 demographic shift；demographic transition
人口調査標準地域 census tract
人工的な構成概念 artificial construct
人口統計 demographic statistics；demographics；population statistics
人口統計上の変数 demographic variables
人口統計的比率 demographic ratio
人口動態統計 vital statistics
人口の推移 changes in population
人口分布 population mix
人口密度 population density
進行中の工事契約 construction contract in progress
申告 declaration；return
申告及び納付 return and payment
申告価格 value declared
申告期限 due date of filing tax return；due date of the tax return
申告義務 obligation to file return
申告義務のある法人 corporation subject to filing a return
申告区分 filing status
申告時間延長承認 approval of extension of time to file
申告所得 declared income
申告所得税 assessment of income tax；self-assessed income tax
申告所得税（確定納付） self-assessed income tax (final declaration)
申告書の共同提出 joint submission of return
申告書の公示 public notification of returns
申告書の提出 filing of return
申告書の提出期限内 within the due date of filing the return
申告税 taxes assessed by taxpayers
申告調整 adjustment in filing a final tax return
申告に対する経理責任者 accountant responsible for the return
申告納税 tax payment by self-assessment
申告納税額 income tax self-assessed
申告納税制度 self-assessment of taxation system
申告分離課税 separate self-assessment taxation
申告漏れ金額 unreported amount
申告用紙 declaration form；return blank
診査 medical examination
審査 examination；review；screening；scrutiny
審査課 Evaluation Division
審査基準 criteria for examination
審査検査質 Office of Monitoring and Inspection
審査裁決 examination and decision
審査室 Examination Office
審査請求 claim for examination；request for reconsideration
審査請求期間 period of request for reconsideration
審査料 examination fee
人材開発 human resources development
新先物 new futures
人事院 National Personnel Authority
人事課 Personnel Division
人事監査 personnel audit
人事管理 personnel management
人事局 Human Resources Management Department
シンジケート団 syndication
シンジケート方式 syndicated deal
シンジケート・ローン syndicated credit；

syndicated loan
新資源の開発 exploitation of new resources
新市場の開拓 development of a new market
人事室(SEC) Office of Personnel(SEC)
人事調査官 Special Officer for Research on Personnel Management
人事方針 personnel policy
真実貸付法 truth in lending
真実かつ公正の意見 true and fair view
真実性の原則 principle of truth
真実にて公正 true and fair
真実の権利者 really rightful person
伸縮税率 flexible tariff
新種商品 breed of product
新種保険 casualty and surety insurance
信　条 creed
人身の自由 personal liberty
新　税 new tax
申　請 application
申請会員 applicant member
申請による上場 listing by application
申 請 人 applicant
申請の不受理 refusal to accept application
申請報告サービス室 Office of Applications & Report Service
真性貸付法 truth in lending law
新生産方式の独占使用 exclusive use of a new production method
真正価値 intrinsic value
真正準備金 true reserve
真正譲渡 true assignment
真 正 な authentic
真正の原価 bona fide cost
真正の証明 attestation
真正売却 true sale
新製品の企業化 commercialization of a new product
新世代GIC AGIC (alternative guaranteed interest contract)
新設合併 merger for the creation of a new company
新 設 備 new capacity
新設分割 split-up of a company with separated assets transferable to a new entity
新設法人 newly established corporation with assets and liabilities transferred
シンセティック・アービトラージ synthetic arbitrage
シンセティック・キャッシュ synthetic cash instrument
シンセティックCDO synthetic CDO
シンセティック・ショート synthetic short
シンセティック・セキュリティゼーション synthetic securitization
シンセティック・プット synthetic put
シンセティック・ボンド synthetic bond
シンセティック・ロング synthetic long
深圳 Shenzhen
深圳証券取引所 SZSE (Shenzhen Stock Exchange)
迅速な裁判 speedy trial
身体傷害 bodily injury
身体障害者 physically handicapped person
身体傷害賠償責任 bodily injury liability
新 高 値 all-time high；new high
信　託 trust
信託会計 fiduciary accounting；trust accounting
信託会社 trust company
信託型退職年金 bank trusted retirement plan
信託型年金 trust fund plan
信託勘定 trust account
信託元本 trust principal
信託管理勘定 custodial account
信託管理人 trust administrator
信託基金 fiduciary fund；trust fund
信託義務違反 breach of fiduciary duty
信 託 業 trust business
信託業務 fiduciary business；trust operation
信託銀行 trust bank
信 託 口 trust account
信託契約 fiduciary contract；trust agreement

信託権限 fiduciary power
信託公社債 Treuhand bond
信託財産 fiduciary estate；trust estate；trust fund assets；trust property
信託財産の受入 acceptance of trust assets
信託財産の処分により生じた売却利益 profit resulting from the sale of trust estate
信託財産の売却利益 gain on the sale of the trust estate
信託財産表示 indication of trust property
信託収入 trust income
信託証券 trust securities
信託・証券等データ交換システム FIRST (Fund's Information Relay SysTem)
信託証書 trust deed；trust indenture；trust instrument
信託証書受託者 trustee under indenture
信託証書法 Trust Indenture Act of 1939
信託説 trust theory
信託設定 trust execution
信託設定者 settlor；trustor
信託貯蓄 trust saving
信託登録 trust registration
信託年金制度 trusted pension plan
信託法 fiduciary law；Trust Act
信託報酬 trust fee
信託約款 trust contract
信託預金 deposit in trust
信託利益 profit from trust
新築賃貸住宅 new house for rent
新築積立金 reserve for construction
慎重主義 prudent basis
進捗度 stage of completion
人的役務の対価 remuneration for personal services
人的課税 personal taxation
人的課税除外 personal exclusion from taxation
人的管轄権 jurisdiction of the person
人的財産 personalty
人的資源 human resources
人的資源会計 HRA (human resources accounting)
人的資本 human capital
人的相続財産 personal hereditament
人的訴訟 litigation on personnel；personal action
人的担保 personal security
人的判決 personal judgment
人的分割 split-up of a company with shares of a new entity transferable to shareholders of the original entity
人的約款 personal covenant
親等 degree of consanguinity
浸透価格 penetration price
人頭税 capitation tax；head tax；poll tax
人道問題調整部 OCHA(Office for the Coordination of Humanitarian Affairs)
振動理論 oscillation theory
信任義務 fiduciary duty
信認金 participant bond
信任状 credentials
真の値 true measure
真のインフレ率 true inflation
真のDVP true DVP (delivery versus payment)
新発債 fresh issue；new bond；primary paper
新発債市場 primary bond market
新発債の発行 issuance of new debt
新BIS規制案 New Basel Capital Accord
新安値 new low；record low
新安値を試す展開 testing new lows
ジンバブエ・ドル ZWD (Zimbabwe dollar)
消費者信用会社 consumer credit company
審判機関 tribunal
審判人 umpire
人名勘定 personal account
人名簿 name list；roll
人名元帳 personal ledger
シンメトリカル・トライアングル symmetrical triangle
審問 hearing
信用 credit
信用医療保険 credit health insurance
信用売り shares sold short

シ

シ

信用及び保証保険 credit and suretyship insurance
信 用 課 Credit System Division
信用買い margin buying；margin purchase；buying on margin
信用買い方の平均単価 average margin buying price
信用格付け credit rating；credit ratings
信用格付見直し credit watch
信用貸し credit loan
信用貨幣 credit money
信用監査 credit audit
信用緩和 credit ease
信用機会均等法 equal credit opportunity act
信用期間 credit term
信用期間延長 credit extension
信用機構室 Credit System Stabilization Office
信用供給 supply of credit
信用恐慌 credit crisis
信用享受の機会均等 equal credit opportunity
信用協同組合 credit cooperative
信用供与 credit accommodation；extension of credit；grant of credit
信用供与代替 credit substitute
信用供与の鈍化 sluggish credit
信用供与枠 committed line of credit；liquidity facility
信用漁業協同組合連合会 Credit Federations of Fishery Cooperatives
信用金庫 shinkin bank
信用組合 cooperative bank；credit association；credit union
信用決済 payment clearance
信用懸念 credit concern
信用限度 credit ceiling；credit limit
信 用 残 outstanding balance of margin trading
信用残高 outstanding balances of credit
信用指数 credit indices
信用収縮 credit contraction
信 用 状 L/C (letter of credit)
信用照会 credit inquiry；credit reference
信用傷害 credit accident
信用状開設者 accrediting party
信用状開設保証金 L/C guarantee money
信用照会端末 credit authorization terminal
信用状確認銀行 L/C (letter of credit) confirming bank
信用状確認手数料 confirming charge
信用状期限 expiry date of the credit
信用状況 credit standing；credit status
信用証券 bill of credit；credit instruments
信用証拠金 credit margin
信用状受益者 L/C (letter of credit) beneficiary
信用状態 credit standing condition
信用状通知銀行 letter of credit advising bank
信用状付一覧払手形買相場 at sight buying rate with credit
信用状なし一覧払手形買相場 without-credit-at-sight buying rate
信用状なし手形買相場 buying rate without credit
信用状の買い主 accredited buyer
信用状の譲渡 transfer of letter of credit
信用状の名宛人 beneficiary of letter of credit
信用状発行依頼人 opener of letter of credit；requesting party for the issue of letter of credit
信用状発行銀行 letter or credit issuing bank
信用状発行手数料 opening charge for letter of credit
信用状発行人 addressor of letter of credit
信用情報 credit records
信用情報センター credit bureau
信用スプレッド credit spread
信用制限 credit rationing
信用生命保険 credit life insurance
信用創造 credit creation
信用創造論 theory of credit creation
信用秩序の維持 maintenance of an orderly financial system

信用調査 credit investigation
信用調査機関 inquiry agency
信用手形 credit bill
信用度 credibility；creditworthiness
信用度中 medium rating
信用度の高い good credit status
信用取引 margin trading
信用取引委託保証金 margin collateral
信用取引貸証券受入金 margin for stocks lent
信用取引貸付金 loans in margin transactions
信用取引勘定 accounts of margin transactions
信用取引規程 margin loan trading regulations
信用取引契約 margin agreement
信用取引口座 margin trading account
信用取引口座設定約諾書 agreement for establishment of margin transactions account
信用取引残高 open interest in margin transactions
信用取引証券 marginable securities
信用取引で on margin
信用取引特別口座 SMA (special miscellaneous account)
信用取引銘柄 margin securities；stock for margin trading
信用取引融資残高 adjusted debit balance of margin transactions
信用農業協同組合連合会 Credit Federations of Agricultural Cooperatives
信用のおけない fly-by-night
信用の低下 credit decline
信用派生商品 credit derivatives
信用判断 credit decision
信用逼迫 liquidity crunch；tight credit
信用評価 credit assessment
信用評価モデル credit scoring model
信用比率 credit ratio
信用部分に対する引当率 reserve ratio for credit
信用分析 analysis of credit
信用補完 credit enhancement；credit support
信用補強 credit support
信用保険 credit insurance；fidelity bond
信用保証 credit guarantee
信用保証会社 credit guarantee company；financial guarantor
信用保証保険 financial guaranty insurance
信用リスク credit exposure；credit risk
信用リスク・アセット credit risk assets
信用リスク・ウエート credit risk weight
信用リスクがない risk free
信用リスク管理体制 credit risk management system
信用リスクの集中 concentration of credit risk
信用リスク分析 credit risk analysis
信用リスクへのエクスポージャ exposure to credit risk
信用リスク変換の機能 function to change the degree of credit risk
信用リスク方針 credit risk policy
信用力 credit capability；credit strength；credit worthiness
信用力チェック credit check
信用力のある creditworthy
信用力の向上 upgrade in credit
信用力の低い企業 firms with high credit risks
信用履歴の改善 improved credit
信用枠上限 debit cap
信用を表すアルファベット letters denoting credit
信用を失墜させる ruin the reputation
信頼 confidence
信頼維持 maintenance of confidence
信頼関係 confidential relations
信頼区間 confidence interval
信頼係数 confidence coefficient
信頼構築 confidence building
信頼性 reliability
信頼性の欠如 reliability exception
信頼性の揺らぎ erosion of confidence
信頼できる証拠 reliable evidence

シ

信 頼 度 confidence level
信頼度指数 confidence index
信頼を裏切った者 traitor
審　　理 bar
審 理 室 Office of Rulings and Legal Affairs
心理効果 psychological effect
心理的効果 psychological effect
真 利 率 true interest rate
森林火災保険 forest fire insurance
森林総合研究所 Forestry and Forest Products Research Institute

ス

推移確率 transition probability
推移行列 transition matrix
随意契約 negotiated contract ; private contract
スィートナー sweetener
スィープ・アカウント sweep account
推計課税 taxation by estimate
推計による更正 correction by estimate
遂行能力 ability to carry out
水産総合研究センター Fisheries Research Agency
水産大学校 National Fisheries University
水 産 庁 Fisheries Agency
水　　準 level
水準維持 level unchanged
水準掛金 contribution corresponding to the target level of benefits
推 奨 株 recommended stock
推奨再販価格 suggested resale price
推進要因 driving force
スイス・オプション金融先物取引所 SOFFEX (Swiss Options and Financial Futures Exchange)
スイス銀行監督委員会 Swiss Federal Banking Commission
スイス国立銀行 SNB (Swiss National Bank)
スイス・フラン CHF (Swiss franc)
スイス・フラン建債 Swiss franc note
推 薦 書 letter of recommendation
推　　断 implication
垂直スプレッド perpendicular spread
垂直的M&A vertical M&A
垂直的合併 vertical merger
垂直的構造 vertical system
垂直的公平 vertical equity
垂直的顧客制限 vertical territorial customer restrictions
垂直的国際分業 vertical international specialization
垂直的統合 vertical integration
垂直的貿易 vertical trade
垂直統合 vertical integration
垂直分割 vertical divesture
垂直分析 vertical analysis
スイッチ金融 switch finance
スイッチ・バック・オプション switch-back option
推　　定 presumption
推定誤差 estimation error
推定債務 constructive obligation
推定詐欺 constructive fraud
推定サンプリング estimation sampling
推定時価評価額 EFV (estimated full value)
推定市場価値評価額 DIV (derived investment value)
推定証拠 presumptive evidence
推定全損 constructive total loss
推定総収益率 ETR (estimated total return)
推定相続人 heir presumptive
推定値の標準誤差 standard error of estimate
推定的条件 constructive terms
推定的配当 constructive dividend
出　　納 cage
出納事務 collection and disbursement of funds
出 納 簿 account book ; cash-book
SWIFT SWIFT (Society for Worldwide Inter-Bank Financial Telecommunication)
水平型アプローチ horizontal approach
水平合併 horizontal merger
水平乗数 horizontal multiplier
水 平 的 horizontal
水平的M&A horizontal M&A
水平的監査 horizontal audit
水平的公平 horizontal equity

ス

水平的国際分業 horizontal international specialization
水平的統合 horizontal integration
水平的分業 horizontal specialization
水平的貿易 horizontal trade
水平統合 horizontal consolidation
水平分割 horizontal divestiture
水平分析 horizontal analysis
水平分断 horizontal split
水曜日要因 Wednesday-factor
推　　理 inference
水 利 権 water acquisition right
スウィング swing
スウィング・ローン swing loan
スウェーデン・クローナ SEK (Swedish Krona)
スウェーデンJ&P総合指数 Jacobson & Ponsbach General Index
スウェーデン中央銀行 Riksbank
スウェーデン保管振替機関 VPC
数学的解説 mathematical description
数字的調整 numerical reconciliation
数次の支払い series of payments
趨　　勢 trend
スーダン・ディナール SDD (Sudanese dinar)
数値情報 numerical information
数値積分法 numerical integration
数値データ quantified data
数値表示 presentation of figures
数値目標 numeric target
スーパー・ゴールド・トランシェ super gold tranche
スーパー301条 super 301 Article
スーパー・シンカー債 super sinker bond
スーパーNOW勘定 super NOW account
スーパーバイザー supervisor
スーパー・プライム・レート super prime rate
スーパー・フローター・スワップ super floater swap
スーパー・マジョリティー条項 super majority provision
数理経済学 mathematical economics
数理計算 actuarial calculation
数理計算差異 actuarial difference
数理上の不足金 actuarial deficiency
数理上の料率設定 actuarial rating
数理的損益 actuarial gains or losses
数理統計 actuarial statistics；mathematical statistics
数理ファイナンス mathematical finance
数 量 化 quantification
数量化手段 quantitative tool
数量化する quantify
数量過不足容認条件 more or less terms
数量差異 quantity variance
数量制限付分売 limited distribution
数量調整 quantity adjustment
数量的実質性の原則 quantitative substantiality test
数 量 表 bill of quantities
数量表現 quantified description
数量標準 quantity standard
数量リベート volume rebate
数量割引 quantity discount；volume discount
据 置 き deferred；unchanged
据置型年金 deferred annuity
据置期間 period of deferment
据置更新手数料 vested renewal commission
据置債券 deferred bond
据置終身年金 deferred life annuity
据置生命保険 deferred life insurance
据置担保 collateral deposited in advance
据置貯金 deferred savings
据置年金 deferred perpetuity
据置年金保険 deferred payment annuity
据置保険 deferred assurance
据置利益分配 deferred profit sharing
据　　付 installation；mounting
据付工事 installation work
据付台数 number of machines installed
据付費用 installation cost
す か し watermark
すき入紙製造取締法 Law Concerning the Regulation of Manufacturing of Watermarked Paper
す き 間 niche

スキャルパー scalper
スクエア square
スクエアの状態にある squared
スクエア・ポジション square position
スクリップ配当 scrip dividend
優れた近似値 good proxy
優れた収益 superior return
スケジューリング技法 scheduling technique
スケジュール・ペイメント schedule payment
スコットランド（イギリス・ポンド） Scotland (sterling pound)
スシ・ボンド sushi bond
スター・システム star system
スタイル管理 style management
スタイル分析 style analysis
スタグフレーション stagflation
スタンダード・アンド・プアーズ Standard & Poor's
スタンダード・アンド・プアーズ株価指数 Standard & Poor's Stock Price Index
スタンダード・アンド・プアーズ500種 Standard & Poor's 500
スタンダード・アンド・プアーズ500種株価指数 Standard & Poor's '500' index
スタンダード・アンド・プアーズ総合指数 Standard & Poor's Composite Index
スタンダード・アンド・プアーズ400種工業株価指数 Standard & Poor's 400 Industrial
スタンダード・セクション Standard Section
スタンドスティル standstill
スタンドスティル条項 standstill provision
スタンドバイ信用状 standby credit；standby letters of credit
スタンドバイ取決め standby arrangement
スタンドバイ・ファシリティーズ standby facilities
スタンバイ・ファシリティ standby facility
スタンバイ信用状 SBLC (standby letter of credit)
スティープニング steepening
捨て印 marginal seal
ステークホルダー stakeholder
ステップ・アップ・クーポン step-up coupon
ステップ・アップ債 step-up bond
ステップ・アップ・スワップ step-up swap
ステップ償還 step ladder payment method
ステップ・ダウン債 step-down bond
ストキャスティック指数 stochastic index
ストック・インフレーション stock inflation
ストック・オプション share option
ストック・オプション会計 accounting for stock option
ストック・オプション型ワラント stock option type warrant
ストック・オプション制度 share option plan；stock option plan
ストック・オプションの行使 exercise of stock option
ストック・シンボル stock symbol
ストック調整 stock adjustment
ストック・フロー stock flow
ストック・ボーナス・プラン stock bonus plan
ストックホルム証券取引所 Stockholm Stock Exchange
ストック・マインド stock mind
ストック・ワラント stock warrants
ストップ・アンド・ゴー政策 stop-and-go policy
ストップ高 limit high；limit up；stop high；stop-high
ストップ値 maximum limit of fluctuation
ストップ安 limit down；limit low
ストップ・ロス注文 stop-loss order
ストップ・ロス・トレーディング stop-loss trading
ストップ・ロス保険 stop loss insurance
ストライキ騒じょう暴動不担保条項 free from strikes, riots and civil commotion clause
ストラクチャード・クレジット商品

structured credit product
ストラップ strap
ストラドル straddle
ストラドル取引 straddle trading
ストラドル・ポジション取引 straddle position transaction
ストラングル strangle
ストラングル・ポジション取引 strangle position transaction
ストリップ strip
ストリップ・カーブ strip curve
ストリップ・キャップ stripped cap
ストリップ金利キャップ stripped interest rate cap
ストリップ証券 stripped securities
ストリップ・スプレッド strip spread
ストリップ・ゼロ・クーポン stripped zero-coupon
ストリップ適格の strippable
ストリップ・プレイヤー strip player
ストリップ保証 strip guarantee
ストリップ銘柄 stripped issue
ストリップ利回り strip yield
ストレイツ・タイムズ工業株指数 Straits Times Industrial Index
ストレイツ・タイムズ指数 STI (Straits Times Index)
ストレート・カレンシー・スワップ straight currency swap
ストレート・クレジット straight credit
ストレス・テスト stress test
ストロング型効率性 strong form efficiency
ストロング・フォーム strong form
スパイク spike
スピード・レジスタンス・ライン speed resistance line
スプリット split
スプレッド spread
スプレッド売呼値 spread offer
スプレッド運用 spread management
スプレッド買呼値 spread bid
スプレッド勘定 spread account
スプレッド曲線 spread curves
スプレッド・シート spread sheet
スプレッド収入 spread income
スプレッド注文 spread order
スプレッド取引 spread transaction
スプレッド・トレーディング spread trading
スプレッド値段 spread price
スプレッドの拡大 spread back up ; spread widening
スプレッドの獲得 picking up spread
スプレッドの縮小 spread rally ; spread tightening
スプレッド・バンキング spread banking
スプレッド・ポジション spread position
スプレッド・マーケット spread market
スプレッド・リスク spread risk
スプレッド・ローン spread loan
スプレッド・ロック契約 spread lock agreement
スペイン銀行通達 Bank of Spain Circulars
スペイン・ペセタ ESP (Spanish peseta)
スペイン保管振替機関 CADE ; SCLV
スペース裁定 space arbitrage
スペクトル spectrum
スペクトル分析 spectral analysis
スペシャリスト specialist
スペシャリスト大口売買 specialist block purchase and sale
スペシャリスト・ブック specialist book
スペシャル・クレジット special credit
スペシャル・ブラケット・グループ special bracket group
スペシャル・リーエン special lien
スポーツ賭ばく sports gambling
スポット期間 spot period
スポット金利 spot interest rate
スポット・ネクスト spot next
スポット・ファンド spot fund
スポット・フォワード spot forward
スポット・レート spot rate
スポンサー sponsor
スポンサーの選択力 sponsor selectivity
スポンサーの役割 sponsor's role
スポンサーのリスク許容度 sponsor's tolerance to risk

住 替 え housing turnover ; relocation
住替え要因 housing turnover component
スミソニアン合意 Smithsonian Agreements
スミソニアン体制 Smithsonian system
スミソニアン・レート Smithsonian rate
速やかな調整 resiliency
スムージング・アウト・オペレーション smoothing out operation
スムージング介入 smoothing intervention
スモール(100万ドル単位の取引) small
スライド関税 sliding tariff
スライド方式 index adjustment
スランプフレーション slumpflation
スリナム・ギルダー SRG (Suriname guilder)
スリランカ・ルピー LKR (Sri Lanka rupee)
スループット throughput
スルー・プット条項 through-put contract
スローバック原則 throw-back rule
スロバキア・コルナ SKK (Slovak koruna)
スロバニア・トーラル SIT (Slovenian tolar)
スワジランド・リランゲニ SZL (Swaziland lilangeni)
スワップ swap
スワップ・オファー・レート swap offer rate
スワップ・カウンターパーティ swap counterparty
スワップ価格 swap price
スワップ協定 swap agreement ; swap arrangement
スワップ・クーポン swap coupon
スワップ契約 swap contract
スワップ契約書 swap documentation
スワップ決済システム swaps clearing system
スワップ・コスト swap cost
スワップ債 swap bond
スワップション swaption
スワップ・ストライク swap strike
スワップ・スプレッド swap spread
スワップ・スプレッド・カーブ swap spread curve
スワップ取引 swap deal ; swap trading ; swap transaction
スワップの変動金利 variable rate on a swap
スワップ・ビッド・レート swap bid rate
スワップ・ブローカー swap broker
スワップ・プロフィット swap profit
スワップ・ポートフォリオ swap portfolio
スワップ・マージン swap margin
スワップ・レート swap rate
スワップ・レートの底値圏 swap rate basement
スワップを買う long the swap
スワップをショートにする short the swap

セ

SEAQ Stock Exchange Automatic Quotation
SEAQインターナショナル SEAQ (stock exchange automated quotation) for international equities
税　印 tax seal
税外収入 nontax receipts
税外負担 non-tax payment
税　額 amount of tax
税額計算基準 tax computation basis
税額計算基準変更 change of tax computation basis
税額控除 credit against tax；tax credit；tax deduction
税額控除後の純額で net of tax
税額控除の順序 sequence of tax credits
税額直接控除 direct tax credit
税額の確定 settlement of tax amount
税額の計算 computation of tax amount
税額の納付、徴収及び還付 paying, collecting and refunding tax
税 額 表 tax table
税　関 Custom-Houses
税関送り状 custom's invoice
税関研修所 Customs Training Institute
税関考査官 Inspector of the Custom-Houses
税関考査管理室 Office of Inspection of the Custom-Houses
税関調査室 Customs Administration Research Office
税関手数料 customs fee
税管轄地 tax jurisdiction
税 基 盤 tax base
税　金 taxes
税金預り金 tax collected
税金及び異常損益項目控除前利益 net profit before tax and extraordinary item
税金還付 tax refund
税金控除限度額の繰越 carryover of tax credit limit
税金裁定 tax arbitrage
税金債務の転嫁 deflection of tax liability
税金残高 tax balance
税金資産 tax assets
税金条項 tax clause
税金上の損金算入となる deductible for the tax purpose
税金滞納処分 process for the recovery of taxes in arrears
税金調整前純利益 net profit before the adjustment of tax
税金でとられる金額 tax take
税金に関する意見書 tax opinion
税金納付 payment of tax
税金の延納 postponement of tax payment
税金の還付請求 claim of the refund of taxes
税金の還付請求する claim a tax refund
税金のキャッシュフロー tax cash flow
税金の繰延べ deferral of tax
税金の滞納 tax delinquency
税金の払戻し tax rebate
税金配布会計 accounting for income tax allocation
税金配分会計 accounting for tax allocation
税金引当金 tax reserve
税金費用 tax expense
税金補償 tax indemnification
税　源 source of tax
税 効 果 tax consequence；tax effect
税効果会計 deferred tax accounting；tax effect accounting
税効果規則 deferred tax rule；tax benefit rule
税効果リース tax lease
税 効 率 tax efficiency
税 込 み including tax

税込価格 price including tax
税込みで tax inclusive
成　　果 fruit；performance result
成果期間 performance period
成果主義 performance basis
成果主義の performance based
成果配分 payment by the results
成果報酬 performance based fee
正　　貨 specie money
正 会 員 regular member
青 海 省 Qinghai
静学乗数 static multiplier
静学モデル static model
正 確 性 accuracy
正確性の検証 checking of accuracy
正確な価値 precise value
正貨準備 specie reserve
正貨準備義務 standard money reserve requirement
生活基盤 lifestyle infrastructure
生活水準 level of living；living standard
生活に通常必要な動産 ordinary and necessary movable property for living
生 活 費 living expenses
生活費指数 cost-of-living index
生活費スライド条項 cost of living clause
生活必需品 necessaries for living
生活保護 public assistance；public protection
生活保護法 Daily Life Security Law
生活保障商品 life protection product
請　　願 petition
請 願 権 right of petition
正 規 化 normalization
正規確率分布 normal probability distribution
正 規 権 regular interest
正規の監査手続 normal auditing procedures
正規の手続 normal procedure
正規の簿記の原則 principle of orderly system of bookkeeping
正規分布 normal distribution
正規方程式 normal equation
請　　求 demand；request
請 求 額 amount billed；amount claimed
請求業務 billing practices
請求懈怠 non-claim
請 求 権 right of claim
請求原因分割 splitting a cause of action
請求サイクル billing cycle
請求次第 on call
請 求 書 bill；invoice
請求済未出荷販売 bill and hold shipment
請求払い PA (pay on application)
請求明細書 bill of particulars
生　　計 living；sustenance
生 計 費 living cost
生計費指数 cost of living index
生計費指数特約 cost of living rider
生計費調整 COLA (cost-of-living adjustment)
制　　限 limitation
制限因子 limited factor
制限裏書 restrictive endorsement
制限外発行税 tax on excess issue
制 限 株 restricted stock
制限株式 restricted share
制限期間 restricted period
制限償還請求権付ローン limited recourse loan
制限条項 covenant package；restrictive covenant；restrictive provision
制限税率 limited tax rate
制限付勘定 restricted account
制限付償還請求権 limited recourse
制限付剰余金 restricted surplus
制限付転換性 limited convertibility
制限付不動産権 estate upon limitation
制限的慣行 restrictive practice
制限的財産権 qualified property
制限的差止命令 restrictive injunction
制限的な例外 limited exceptions
制限的保証 limited guarantee
制限的要因 limitation factor
制限値幅 limit of the range of price fluctuation
制限納税義務 limited tax liability

セ

セ

制限納税義務者 taxpayer with limited tax liability
制限の影響 effect of the limit
制限法貨 limited legal tender
整合性 conformity
成功の代償 price of success
成功報酬 incentive fee；merit increase；success fee
正誤表 corrigendum
精査 detailed check；due diligence
制裁関税 punitive tariffs
制裁措置 sanction
政策 government policy
政策委員 Policy Board member
政策委員会 Policy Board
政策委員会室 Secretariat of the Policy Board
政策意義 policy significance
政策課 Communications and Policy Division
政策課題 policy issues
政策協調 policy coordination
政策金融 policy-based finance
政策金融課 Government Financial Institutions Division
政策金融機関 policy-based financial institution
政策金融評価 policy-based finance assessment
政策金利 benchmark rate；key rate；official interest rate；policy rate；policy-based interest rate
政策金利引上げ hike in official rate
政策減税 policy-based tax reduction
政策効果 policy effectiveness
政策手段 policy tools
政策手段の割当 policy assignment
政策措置 policy measures
政策的減価償却 policy depreciation
政策当局 policy maker
政策評価 policy evaluation
政策評価官 Councilor for Policy Evaluation
政策評価室 Policy Evaluation Office
政策方針 policy principle
政策ポジション policy state
製作中の資産 progress expenditure property
清算 clearing；winding-up
清算委託契約 Clearing Entrustment Agreement
清算会員 clearing agent member；clearing member
清算確定申告 liquidation final return
清算確定申告書 final return of liquidation
清算価値 break-up value；liquidation value
清算勘定 liquidation account；settled account
清算機関 clearing agency；clearing corporation；clearing house；clearing organization
清算基金 clearing fund
清算基金の返還請求権 right to claim the return of the clearing fund
清算機能 clearing function
清算協定 clearing agreement
清算・決済規程 regulations for clearing and settlement
清算決済制度 clearance and settlement system
清算参加者 clearing participant
清算資格 clearing qualification
清算資格の喪失 waiver of clearing qualification
清算資格の取消 revocation of clearing qualification
清算資格を有する取引参加者 trading participants having a qualification for the settlement
清算指数 settlement index
清算した法人 liquidated corporation
清算事務 liquidation affairs
清算事務所 liquidation office
清算事由 liquidation event
清算受託買(売)建玉 clearing-entrusted long (short) position
清算受託取引 clearing-entrusted transactions
清算受託の停止 suspension of acceptance

of entrustment of clearing
清 算 書 statement of liquidation
清算条項 trigger mechanism
清算剰余金 surplus at liquidation
清算所得 income on liquidation
清算所得税 liquidation income tax
清算所得に対する法人税の予納 prepayment of tax on liquidation income
清算済会社 liquidated company
清算損益 liquidation profit and loss
清算貸借対照表 liquidation balance sheet
清算中の法人 corporation in the course of liquidation
清算手続 clearing procedure；liquidation proceedings
清算手続中の法人 corporation under liquidation
清算取引 clearing contract；clearing transaction
清算による損失 loss on settlements
清 算 人 liquidating partner；liquidator
清 算 値 liquidation price
清算値段 clearing price；settlement price
清算配当 liquidation dividend
精 算 表 statement paper；work sheet
精算表方式 worksheet method
清算ブローカー clearing broker
清算命令 winding-up order
清算優先権 liquidation preference
生産過剰 overproduction
生産勘定 production account
生産関数 production function
生産管理 production control
生産技術 manufacturing technology
生産基準 completion of production method
生産協定 production accord
生産拠点 manufacturing bases；production base
生産工学 industrial engineering
生産工程 production process
生産合理化 rationalization of production
生産合理化用機械設備 machinery for rationalization of production
生産国カルテル producer's cartel
生 産 財 production goods
生産市場 product market
生産指数 index number of production；production indexes
生産実績 actual production
生産資本 production capital
生 産 者 producer
生産者価額 producer's value
生産者出荷指数 index of producers' shipments
生産者製品在庫 producer's inventory of finished goods
生産者製品在庫指数 index of producers' inventory of finished goods
生産者物価指数 PPI (producer price index)
生産者余剰 producer's surplus
生産水準 level of production
生 産 性 productivity
生産性会計 productivity accounting
生産性向上 productivity gain；productivity improvement
生産性指数 index of productivity
生産性指標 productivity ratio
生産性喪失クレーム loss of productivity claims
生産性の向上 productivity gain
生産性の伸び productivity growth
生産性分析 productivity analysis
生産設備 production facility
生産設備の試運転 trial running of manufacturing equipment
生産全量購入 bulk buying
生 産 高 output；production
生産高比例法 service-yield basis；sum-of-the-units method；unit of production method
生産高報告書 production report
生産高保証契約 throughput contract
生産単位 production unit
生産年数 productive life
生産年齢 working age
生産能力 production capacity；productive ability

生産比例法 production based activity method
生産物賠償責任保険 products and completed operation liability insurance
生産分配 production sharing
生産要素 factors of production
生産余力 surplus capacity
生 産 量 quantity of production ; volume of production
生産力の逓減 diminishing marginal productivity
生産労務費 production labor cost
政治安定指数 political system stability index
政治危機 political crisis
政 治 局 DPA(Department of Political Affairs)
政治団体 political corporation
政治的環境 political environment
政治的混乱 political turmoil
政治的責任 political accountability
政治的要因 political force
政治リスク political risk
セイシェル・ルピー SCR (Seychelles rupee)
正式な計画 formal plan
正式な契約 formal agreement
正式な条件 formal term
正式な同意 compact
正式なマンデート official mandate
正式発行日 official original issue date
正式本券 definitive bond
生死混合保険 mixed insurance
誠　　実 good faith
誠 実 性 integrity
誠実保険 fidelity insurance
脆　　弱 vulnerability
脆 弱 性 sign of fragility
税　　収 tax income ; tax proceeds ; tax revenue ; tax yield
税 収 期 tax gathering season
税収歳入見込み tax and revenue anticipation
税収歳入見込証券 TRAN (tax and revenue anticipation note)
税収自然増 automatic increase in tax revenue
税収弾性値 elasticity of tax revenue
税収見返手形 tax anticipation note
税収見返ワラント tax anticipation warrant
税　　政 tax administration
税　　制 taxation system
税制改革 tax reform
税制上の懲罰 tax penalty
税制上の優遇措置 tax advantages ; tax benefits ; tax incentive
税制整理 readjustment of taxation system
税制措置 tax measures
税制第一課 Income Tax and Property Tax Policy Division
税制第三課 Excise Taxes and General National Tax Rules Policy Division
税制第二課 Corporation Tax and Consumption Tax Policy Division
税制調査会 Tax Commission
税制適格確定給付年金制度 tax approved defined benefit scheme
税制適格退職年金信託 tax qualified pension trust
税制適格年金 tax qualified pension plan
税制適格保険契約 tax qualifying policy
税制のグリーン化 greening of the tax system
税制変更リスク risk arising from changes in tax law
税制面で優遇されている tax advantaged
税制優遇項目 preference item
税制優遇措置 tax concession ; tax preferred status
税 体 系 tax structure
税滞納者 tax delinquent
税の還元 amortization of taxes
税の減免 tax relief
税の消転 transformation of tax transit
税の分類 classification of tax
税負担能力 taxable capacity
税負担の平準化 equalization of tax burden
成熟企業 mature company

成熟経済 mature economy
成熟資産 mature assets
成熟したプラン mature plans
成熟段階 mature phase
正常価格 normal price
正常為替相場 normal rate of exchange
正常原価 normal cost
正 常 財 normal goods
正常在庫 normal stock ; ordinary inventory
正常在庫高 normal stock level
正 常 先 normal borrowers
正常資産 normal assets
正常仕損 normal spoilage
正常収益率 normal return (ratio)
正常償却 normal depreciation
正常生産能力 normal capacity
正常な営業循環 normal operating cycle
正常な残高 normal balances
正常配賦率 normal burden rate
正常標準原価 normal standard cost
正常利益 normal return ; NP (normal profit)
正常利潤 normal profit
政 省 令 cabinet order and ordinances
精神的衝撃 nervous shock
盛　衰 ups and downs
整　数 integer
整 数 倍 integral multiple
整数倍の integral times
生成作用素 generator
生前給付 ADB (accelerated death benefit) ; living benefit
生前給付会社 living benefit company
生前給付金 living proceeds
生前給付保険 living benefit policy
生前公益信託 charitable lead trust
生前信託 inter vivos trust ; living trust
生前贈与分 advancement
製造課税 manufacturing taxation
製造間接費 factory expenses ; factory overhead costs
製造間接費配賦 manufacturing overhead allocation
製造間接費配賦額 applied factory burden
製造間接費配賦勘定 applied manufacturing overhead costs account
製造間接費配賦不足額 unapplied burden ; under-absorbed burden
製造間接費元帳 manufacturing overhead costs ledger
製造間接費予算 factory overhead budget ; manufacturing overhead costs budget
製造業雇用者数 manufacturing headcount ; manufacturing payroll
製造業者 manufacturer
製造業者の保証 manufacturer's warranty
製造業生産指数 manufacturing output
製造業部門別投入・産出物価指数 Input-Output Price Indexes of Manufacturing Industry by Sector
製造許可 manufacturing license
製造経費 manufacturing expenses ; production expenses
製造原価 cost of manufactured goods ; cost of production ; fabricating cost
製造原価計算 manufacturing costing
製造原価差額 manufacturing cost variance
製造原価報告書 factory cost report ; statement of production cost
製造原価明細書 schedule of the cost of goods manufactured
製造工程 manufacturing process
製造差異 production variance
製造指図書 manufacture order ; production order ; work order
製造産業 manufacturing industry
製造資産 production asset
製造者リスク manufacturer's risks
製造受注残 factory backlog
製造上の欠陥 manufacturing defect
製造設備 production equipment
製造高予算 production volume budget
製造能率差異 production efficiency variance
製 造 費 on cost
製造費用 production cost

セ

製造費予算 cost of production budget
製造物責任 product liability
製造物責任保険 product liability insurance
製造部門 manufacturing department；production department
製造部門費 producing departments cost
製造報告書 production statement
製造予算 production budget
生存者購入年金 survivorship rider
生存者の取得権 right of survivorship
生存者への権利の帰属 survivorship
生存保険 pure endowment insurance
生 存 率 chance of living
生損保契約 life and general coverage
生損保兼営 all lines
生損保併売外務員 multiple line agent
静態的リスク static risk
静態統計 static statistics
静態比率 static ratio
静態分析 static analysis
静態利回り static return
整　　地 site preparation
成 長 株 growth stock
成長株式 performance share
成長企業 growth company
成長曲線 growth curve
成長経済 growing economy
成長産業 growth industry
成長しうる viable
成長収益ファンド growth and income fund
成 長 性 growth potential；opportunity for growth
成長戦略 growth strategy
成長段階 growth phase
成長通貨 growing currency
成長の起爆剤 trigger for growth
成長見通し growth prospect
成 長 率 growth rate
成長率について弱気姿勢 bearish bet on the growth
成長率の収斂 growth converging
成長率の変化 change in growth rate
成長理論 growth theory
制　　定 enactment
制 定 法 statute law
制定法上の譲渡 statutory assignment
静的均衡 static equilibrium
精　　度 precision
青銅貨幣（10円） bronze coins (10 yen)
正 当 化 justification
正当行為 justifiable act
正当事由 due reason
正 当 性 validity
正当な権限を有する機関 legal organ；organization with valid authority
正当な地代 rent reasonably fixed
正当な注意 due care
正当な補償 just compensation
正当な保有者 holder in due course
正当防衛 self-defense
制度会計 institutional accounting
制度概要 summary plan
制度学派 institutional economics；institutional school
制度加入 plan participation
制度加入者 plan member；plan participant
制度からの脱退 opting out of scheme
制度監査 system audit
制度管理 plan management
制度管理コスト plan administration cost
制度規約 plan document
制度給付 plan benefit
制度給付算定式 plan benefit formula
制度金融 financing by public institutions for implementing policies；organized finance
制度金融市場 organized financial market
制度研究 institutional approach
制度資産運用益 return on plan assets
制度資産として認められる qualify as plan asset
制度資産の期待収益率 expected rate of return on plan assets
制度資産の公正価値 fair value of plan assets
制度修正 plan amendment
制度終了 plan winding up

制度受託者 plan trustee
制度証券市場 organized exchange market
制度証券取引所 organized securities exchange
制度上の要因 institutional factor
制度上のリスク institutional risk
制度信用取引 organized margin transactions
制度設計 plan design
制度提供者 plan sponsor
制度的公準 institutional postulate
制度の打切り plan termination
制度の給付算定式 plan's benefit formula
制度の終了 termination of a plan
制度の種類 type of plan
制度の条件 terms of plan
精度の水準 level of precision
制度の停止 suspension of a plan
制度の廃止 abolishment of system
制度費用 plan cost
精　読 perusal
成　年 full age；lawful age
成年被後見人 person adjudged incompetent
性能発注 performance-based order
性能発注仕様書 output specification
正の共分散 positive covariance
正の金額 positive amount
正の増益効果 favorable leverage effect
正の相関 positive correlation
正の利回り曲線 positive yield curve
正のレバレッジ効果 positive leverage effect
税引き after tax
税引給与 after-tax wage；pay after tax；take-home pay
税引後 post-tax
税引後基準 after tax basis
税引後金額 after-tax amount
税引後実質利回り after tax real rate of return
税引後正味キャピタル・ゲイン net aftertax gain
税引後の手取り額 after-tax gain
税引後法 net-of-tax method
税引後利益 after-tax income；EAT (earnings after tax)；post-tax profit
税引後利益率 after-tax return (ratio)
税引後利回り after-tax yield
税引後割引率 post-tax discount rate
税引値段 prices minus tax
税引費用前の before income tax expense
税引前 before tax；pre-tax
税引前会計利益 pretax accounting income
税引前当期剰余金 net income before taxes
税引前利益 earnings before tax；income before income taxes；pre-tax earnings；pre-tax income；pre-tax profit
税引前利益率 pretax rate of return
税引前割引率 pre-tax discount rate
税引利益率 after-tax profit rate
税引利回り net yield
製　品 manufactured goods；product
製品依存の product driven
製品価格 product price
製品勘定 finished products account
製品基準 product standards
製品機能強化 product enhancement
製品群 product group
製品原価 cost of finished goods；product cost
製品サイクル product life-cycle
製品棚卸額 finished products inventory
製品手持額 finished products on hand
製品投資 product investment
製品のライフ・サイクル product life cycle
製品評価技術基盤機構 National Institute of Technology and Evaluation
製品別原価計算 cost accounting by product
製品ポートフォリオ管理 PPM (product portfolio management)
製品ポートフォリオ・マネージメント product portfolio management
製品保証 product warranties
製品保証等引当金 reserve for guarantee for completed work
製品保証引当金 reserve for after-care of

products
製品元帳　finished goods ledger；finished product ledger
政府アクチュアリー　government actuary
政府移転収支　government transfers
政府援助　government assistance
政府会計　government accounting
政府会計基準審議会　GASB (Government Accounting Standards Board)
政府介護保険　government-run care insurance
政府介入　government intervention
政府開発援助　Official Development Assistance
政府関係預り金　government related deposit
政府関係者　government experts
政府監査　government audit
政府勘定　government account
政府管掌生命保険　government life insurance
政府管掌年金　government managed annuity
政府勘定保管金　withdrawn cash to be returned to the government
政府間の　inter-government
政府間貿易　government to government trade
政府管理下企業　state controlled enterprise
政府関連制度　government contractual arrangements
政府機関証券　government agency securities
政府企業　government enterprise
政府系機関　GSE (government sponsored enterprises)
政府系機関債券　bond issued by government related agency；government agency bond
政府系機関証券　securities issued by government agency
政府系機関プール　agency pool
政府系機関劣後債　agency subordinated debt
政府系金融機関　government-related financial institutions
政府系金融機関モーゲージ・プール　agency mortgage pool
政府経常余剰　government current surplus
政府後援企業　GSE (government sponsored enterprise)
政府購入　government purchases
政府債換算直接利回り　current bond yield equivalent
政府財政　public finance
政府債務　government debt portfolio
政府資金　government fund
政府資金調達計画　government funding plan
政府紙幣　government note
政府借款　government credit
政府出資金　government subscriptions
政府証券　government securities
政府証券償還　redemption of government securities
政府証券の引受　underwriting of government securities
政府証券利息　interest on government securities
政府消費　government consumption
政府所管の　government sponsored
政府所有有価証券　securities owned by the government
政府短期証券　FBs (financing bills)
政府短期証券売現先オペ　sales of FBs (financing bills) under repurchase agreements
政府短期証券買現先オペ　purchases of FBs (financing bills) under repurchase agreements
政府短期証券の発行　issuance of FBs
政府地方交付税特別勘定　Government's Special Account for the Allotment of Local Allocation Tax and Local Transfer Tax
政府調達　government procurement；public procurement
政府貯蓄　government saving
政府貯蓄証券　government saving certificate

政府通貨 currency note
政府抵当金庫 Government National Mortgage Association
政府統計 official statistics
政府当座預金 government current deposit
政府取引 government transaction
政府による収用 expropriation by government
政府の銀行 bank of the government
政府の財貨・サービス購入 purchase of goods and services by government
政府の信用力 government creditworthiness
政府の調達政策 government procurement policy
政府引受債 government-underwritten bonds
政府ブローカー government broker
政府貿易 government trade
政府保管有価証券 securities held by the government
政府保証 government guarantee
政府保証外債 government guaranteed foreign bond
政府保証借入金 government guaranteed borrowing
政府保証公営企業債券 government-guaranteed public corporation bond
政府保証債 government guaranteed bond ; government obligation ; state guaranteed debt
政府保証債務 government guaranteed debts
政府保証モーゲージ government backed mortgage
政府補助金 government grant ; government subsidy ; RSG (Revenue Support Grant)
政府預金 government deposits
政府預金への入金 credits to the government's deposit account
生物資産 biological assets
成分分析 component analysis
成 文 法 written law
税　　法 tax law ; tax legislation ; tax regulations
税 法 学 tax jurisprudence
税 法 規 tax rule
税方式公的年金 tax based state pension
税 法 上 for the purpose of tax law
税法上の特典 various kinds of tax benefits
税法上の優遇措置 preferential treatment for the tax law purpose
税法の無視 disregard of tax rule
税前価格 price before tax
税務アドバイス tax advice
税務会計 tax accounting
税務会計論 theory of tax accounting
税 務 官 tax collector
税務監査 tax audit
税務行政組織 tax administration system
税務顧問 tax advisor
税務諮問委員会 advisory tax board
税 務 署 tax office
税務上許容される allowable for tax purpose
税務上控除の繰越 tax credit carryforward
税務上控除の繰戻し tax credit carryback
税務上損金算入される deductible for tax purposes
税務上の会計年度 tax year
税務上の欠損金 tax loss
税務上の損金 tax deductible expenses
税務上の手続 tax procedures
税務上の例外 exceptional tax treatment
税務署長 chief of the tax office
税務処理 tax treatment
税務書類 tax documents
税務申告書 tax return
税務争訟 tax dispute
税務相談 tax consultation
税務相談官 Tax Counselor
税務訴訟 tax suit
税務大学校 National Tax College
税務代理 tax agency ; tax proxy
税務調査 tax examination
税務調査後所得 income after tax audit
税務調査手続 procedures of tax

adjustments
税務調査の結果 results of the tax examination
税務調整 adjustment for taxable income
税務当局 tax authorities
税務分担 tax sharing
税　　目 tax items
税優遇措置 favorable tax treatment
税 理 士 certified tax accountant ; licensed tax accountant ; tax practitioner
税理士会 certified tax accountant association
税理士試験 tax accountant examination
税理士法 Certified Tax Accountant Law
税理士報酬 tax accountant fee
税理士連合会 Federation of Tax Accountants
税　　率 tax rate
税率委員会 tariff commission
税率区分 tax bracket
税率低減 reduction in tax rate
税率等級 tax bracket
税 率 表 tax rate schedule
税率を軽減する derate
正方行列 square matrix
生保買い life insurance company purchase
生保外務員 ordinary agent
生 保 株 life stock
生保契約査定 life underwriting
生保部門の税引前利益 pretax life earnings
精密機械 precision machinery
精密機器業界 precision instruments industry
精密技術 precision technology
生命・健康保険保証基金 Life and Health Insurance Guaranty Fund
生命・健康保険保証協会 Life and Health Insurance Guaranty Association
生命・健康保険保証協会モデル法 Life and Health Insurance Guaranty Association Model Act
生 命 表 life table
生命保険 life assurance ; life insurance
生命保険受取人 life beneficiary
生命保険及び養老保険契約からの所得 income from life insurance and endowment contract
生命保険会社 life insurance company
生命保険会社課税 life insurance company taxation
生命保険会社所得税法 Life Income Tax Act of 1959
生命保険協会 Life Insurance Association of Japan
生命保険金 proceeds of life insurance
生命保険契約 life insurance contract
生命保険契約保有高 life insurance in force
生命保険原契約者 viator
生命保険コスト life insurance cost
生命保険資金 life fund
生命保険資産 life insurance assets
生命保険市場 life insurance market
生命保険支払額 life insurance payout
生命保険証券 life insurance policy
生命保険証券の譲渡 viatical assignment
生命保険証券売却 viatical settlement
生命保険信託 life insurance trust
生命保険信託付契約 trust policy
生命保険相互会社 mutual life insurance company
生命保険担保債券 death backed bonds
生命保険販売 life underwriting
生命保険募集人 life underwriter
生命保険保障 life cover
生命保険保障基金 life insurance insolvency fund
生命保険料 life insurance premium
生命保険料控除 deduction for life insurance premiums ; LAPR (life assurance premium relief)
生命保険及び年金 life and annuity
制　　約 constraint
制約条件 restrictive condition
整　　理 liquidation
整理回収機構 RCC (Resolution and Collection Corporation)
整理記入 adjustment entry

整理合理化 liquidation and rationalization
整理後試算表 adjusted trial balance
整理資金調達公社 REFCORP (Resolution Funding Corporation)
整理社債 consolidated bond
整理信託公社 RTC (Resolution Trust Corporation)
整理ポスト post for delisting
制　令 fiat
政　令 cabinet order
セーフガード条項 safeguard clause ; safeguard provision
セーフティ・ネット safety net
セーフ・ハーバー safe harbor
セーフ・ハーバー協定 safe harbor accord
セーフ・ハーバー・リース safe harbor lease
セール・アンド・リースバック取引 sale and leaseback transaction
セールス・ミックス sales mix
セール・リースバック sale leaseback
セール・リースバック取引 sale leaseback transaction
世界貨幣 world money
世界企業 world enterprise
世界気象機関 WMO (World Meteorological Organization)
世界恐慌 world crisis
世界銀行 World Bank
世界銀行債 bonds of the International Bank for Reconstruction and Development
世界クラスの投資家 global investor ; world class investor
世界経済 global economy
世界経済の見通し global economic outlook
世界経済見通し world economic outlook
世界市場 world market
世界市場ポートフォリオ world market portfolio
世界食糧計画 WFP (World Food Programme)
世界知的所有権機関 WIPO (World Intellectual Property Organization)
世界通貨 universal currency
世界的な景気回復 global recovery
世界的な景気循環 global economic cycle
世界的な市場 global market
世界的な統合 global integration
世界的な認知度 global awareness
世界貿易機関 WTO (World Trade Organization)
世界保健機関 WHO (World Health Organization)
世界マーケティング world marketing
積載船名未詳 vessel unknown
赤十字国際委員会 ICRC(International Committee of the Red Cross)
積　数 cumulative total of required reserves
積 送 人 consignor ; sender ; shipper
積 送 品 shipment
赤道ギニア（CFAフラン） Equatorial Guinea (CFA (Communauté Financière Africaine) franc)
責　任 responsibility
責任会計 responsibility accounting
責任回避条項 responsibility hedge clause
責任軽減 diminished responsibility
責任原価計算 responsibility costing
責任限度額 total maximum liability
責 任 者 accountable person
責任準備金 actuarial reserve ; liability reserve ; loss reserves ; policy reserve
責任準備金増加額 inside build-up
責任準備金評価 liability reserve valuation
責任準備金評価法 valuation method
責任単位 accountability unit
責任の所在 liability for damage
責任の序列 hierarchy of responsibilities
責任の遂行 discharge of responsibility
責任分担 burden sharing
責任保険 liability insurance
責務遂行 stewardship
石油及びエネルギー需給構造高度化対策特別会計 Special Account for Petroleum and the More Sophisticated

Structure of Demand and Supply of Energy Policies
石油化学コンビナート petrochemical complex
石油化学産業 petrochemical industry
石油ガス税 liquefied petroleum and gas tax
石 油 株 oil stock
石油業法 petroleum act
石油採掘権 oil concession
石油債券承継国債 government bonds converted from Japan National Oil Bonds
石油収入税 petroleum revenue tax
石油証券 petroleum financing bills
石 油 税 petroleum tax
石油精製業 oil refinery
石油税法 petroleum tax law
石油・石炭製品業界 oil and coal product industry
石油輸出国機構 OPEC (Organization of Petroleum Exporting Countries)
石油臨時特別税 special provisional petroleum surtax
石油連動債券 oil-linked bond
セキュリティ管理 security management
積率母関数 moment generating function
世銀グループ World Bank group
世 銀 債 World Bank bond
世銀特措法 IBRD special law
セクター sector；seqs
セクター・アナリスト sector analyst
セクター間の cross sector
セクター固有リスク sector specific risk
セクターの基準値 sector benchmarks
セクター配分 sector allocation
セクター分散 sector diversification
セクター方式 sectoral approach
セグメンテーション segmentation
セグメント会計 segment accounting
セグメント間売上 intersegment sales
セグメント間振替 inter-segment transfer
セグメント間振替価格決定 inter-segment pricing
セグメント情報 segment information
セグメント定義 segment definition
セグメント別会計方針 segment accounting policy
セグメント別開示 segment disclosure
セグメント別資産 asset by segment
セグメント別収益 revenue by segment
セグメント別損益 profit and loss by segment；segment result
セグメント別費用 expense by segment
セグメント別負債 liability by segment
世帯課税 household taxation
世代間会計 generational accounting
世代間公平 intergeneration equity
世代間再配分 intergenerational redistribution
世代間信託 generation skipping trust
世代間振替 inter-generational transfer
世代間利他主義 intergenerational altruism
積極財産 positive property
積極財政 positive financial policy
積極条件 positive condition
積極信託 active trust
積極成長ファンド aggressive growth fund
積極的運用 active management；aggressive portfolio
積極的確認 positive confirmation
積極的調整政策 positive adjustment policies
積極的ディーラー active dealer
積極的投資理論 active investment management theory
積極予算 expansionary budget
設計・建設・ファイナンス・運営 DBFO (design-build-finance-operate)
浙 江 省 Zhejiang
絶好の買い場 attractive trading opportunity
接収による損失 expropriation loss
節　　税 tax saving
節税手段 tax advantaged vehicle
節税生命保険 tax efficient life policy
節税対策 tax planning
節税取引 tax oriented transaction
節税のための売り tax selling
節税レバレッジッド・リース tax saving

leverage lease
節税レバレッジ・リース tax leverage lease
節制要件 abstention requirement
絶対拡散モデル absolute diffusion model
絶対確率 absolute probability
絶対過半数 supermajority
絶対原価 absolute cost
絶対誤差 absolute error
絶対差額 absolute difference
絶対主義 absolutism
絶対所得仮説 absolute income hypothesis
絶対水準 absolute level
絶対全損 absolute total loss
絶 対 値 absolute value
絶対値で in absolute terms
絶対的期間 absolute terms
絶対的固定資本 absolute fixed capital
絶対的譲渡 absolute conveyance
絶対的な absolute
絶対的な率 absolute rate
絶対的パーフォーマンス absolute performance
絶対的不動産保有権 fee simple absolute
絶対的リスク回避度 absolute risk aversion measure
絶対的リターン absolute return
絶対百分率 absolute percentage
絶対命令 rule absolute
絶対優位 absolute advantage
絶対リターン absolute return
切断乗数 truncated multiplier
折衷方式 compromise method
設 定 setting
設定主体 setting body
設定メカニズム setting mechanism
節 点 node
窃盗犯人 thief
説得力のある証拠 persuasive evidence
説得力のある比較 persuasive comparison
Z債券 Z bond
セット保険 commercial package policy
折半方式 match plan
設 備 appliance；equipment；facilities
設備拡張積立金 reserve for expansion
設備過剰 over-capacity
設備稼動率 capacity utilization rate；utilization rate
設備稼動率が低いこと low capacity utilization
設備資金 equipment fund；facility capital；plant fund
設備新規購入額 additions to plant and equipment
設備信託 equipment trust
設備信託証書 ETC (equipment trust certificate)
設備適正価額 equipment fair value
設備投資意欲 capital investment intention
設備投資 capital expenditure；capital investment
設備投資額 amount of capital investment
設備投資キャッシュフロー率 cash flow ratio to capital expenditures
設備投資計画 capital budgeting；capital investment plan
設備投資計画調査 survey on planned capital spending
設備投資の追加 additional capex
設備投資の利益率 return on the capital investment
設備能力 plant capacity
設備売却損益 gain or loss on sale of assets
設備リース・パートナーシップ equipment leasing partnership
説 明 clarification
説 明 会 briefing；road show
説明情報 descriptive information
説明責任 accountability
説明付財務諸表 descriptive financial statement
説明できる意味 describable meaning
説明文書 explanatory material
説明変数 explanatory variables
節約の原則 principle of parsimony
節 約 率 percentage savings
設 立 国 country of incorporation
設立後経過年数 number of years since

incorporation；years elapsed after foundation
設立趣意書 prospectus for foundation
設立償却費 organization expenses amortized
設立手続 formalities of incorporation
設 立 届 notification of incorporation
設立の登記 registration of establishment
設 立 費 organization cost
設 立 法 act of incorporation
セ デ ル CEDEL (Centrale de Livraison de Baluers Mobilieres)；cedel
セトルメント・バリエーション settlement variation
セネガル（CFAフラン） Senegal (CFA (Communauté Financière Africaine) franc)
ゼネラル・クレジット general credit
ゼネラル・パートナーシップ general partnership
ゼネラル・モーゲージ general mortgage
ゼネラル・モーゲージ付社債 general mortgage bond
狭いボックス圏 narrow range
狭いレンジで within a tight band
セラーズ・オプション取引 seller's option trading
セリ上げ bidding up
セリング・クライマックス selling climax
セル・サイド sell side
セル・ダウン（幹事団以外への販売） sell down
セル・プラス注文 sell plus order
セルラー・アプローチ cellular approach
ゼロ課税範囲 zero bracket amount
ゼロ・クーポン永久債 zero coupon perpetual
ゼロ・クーポン・カーブ zero-coupon curve
ゼロ・クーポン構造 zero coupon structure
ゼロ・クーポン債 zero-coupon bond；zero-coupon issue
ゼロ・クーポン債からの乗換え switch from zero coupon bonds
ゼロ・クーポン証券 zero-coupon securities
ゼロ・クーポンTノート zero-coupon T-note
ゼロ・クーポン転換証券 zero-coupon convertible securities
ゼロ・コスト・オプション ZECRO (zero cost rate option)；zero cost option
ゼロ・コスト・オプション取引 zero-cost option trading
ゼロ・コスト・カラー zero-cost collar
ゼロ・サム・ゲーム zero-sum game
ゼロ・プラス・ティック zero-plus tick
ゼロ・ベース予算 ZBB (zero base budgeting)
ゼロ・ベータ・ポートフォリオ zero-beta portfolio
繊維製品業界 textile and apparel industry
善意の解釈 benefit of the doubt
善意の買主 innocent purchaser
善意の契約 bona fide contract
善意の債権者 bona fide creditor
善意の所持人 bona fide holder；holder in good faith
善意の第三者 holder in due course
善意の不実表示 innocent misrepresentation
船　　員 seaman
船員雇入契約書 shipping articles
船員労働委員会 Labour Relations Commission for Seafarers
全員一致で unanimous
全営業の譲渡 transfer of the entire business；transfer of the whole business
前回規則 front-foot rule
全額再保険 whole reinsurance
全額支払い full payment
全額出資の子会社 fully owned subsidiary
全額正貨準備制度 total reserve system
全額担保により保全されている fully secured
全額払込み fully paid-up；payment in full
全額払込済株式 fully paid-in capital stock
全額引受 firm commitment

全額引受方式 underwriting method
全額負担給付 all-pay benefit
全額領収書 receipt in full
船価償却 depreciation of ship costs
全株同一価格買付 any-and-all bid
善管注意義務 prudent man rule
前　　期 preceding period；previous term
前 期 間 prior period
前期繰越 balance brought forward from the previous term
前期繰越欠損金 deficit at the beginning of a period
前期繰越損失 loss brought forward from the previous term
前期繰越利益金 retained earnings at the beginning of a period；surplus brought forward from the previous term
前期繰越利益余剰金 surplus at the beginning of the period
前期修正 correction of prior periods
前期修正項目 adjustments of prior period
前期損益金 profit or loss brought forward from the previous period
前期損益修正 prior period profit and loss adjustment
前 期 比 QoQ (quarter-on-quarter)
全危険担保 against all risks；all risks coverage
全危険担保約款 all risks coverage clause
選挙供託 election deposits
全銀システム Zengin System
全勤務期間平均給与 average earnings throughout service
先 駆 株 forerunner stock
線型回帰 linear regression
線型加速度係数 linear accelerator
線型計画法 linear programming
線形相関 linear correlation
線形補間 linear interpolation
線形補間法 straight-line interpolation
線形モデル linear model
全経費込み all in
先 契 約 precontract
前　　月 preceding month；previous month
前月残高ベースの金利計算方法 previous balance method
先月半ば middle of last month
前 月 比 MoM (month-on-month)
前月比で sequential terms
全　　権 plenipotentiary
先 権 原 elder title
宣言された配当 dividend declared
先 見 性 foresight
全権利落ち ex-all
選　　好 preference
善　　行 good behavior
先行裏書の真正証明 previous indorsements guaranteed
先行系列 leading series
選好順位 order of preference
選好順序 preference ordering
選好の変化 shift in preference
全国企業短期経済観測 short-term economic survey of all businesses
全国企業短期経済観測調査及び主要企業短期経済観測調査（短観） All Enterprises Tankan and Principal Enterprises Tankan (Tankan: Short-Term Economic Survey of Enterprises in Japan)
全国共済農業協同組合連合会 National Mutual Insurance Federation of Agricultural Cooperatives
全国銀行貸出約定平均金利 average contracted interest rates on loans and discounts of all banks
全国銀行協会 Japanese Bankers Association
全国銀行協会連合会 Federation of Bankers Associations of Japan
全国銀行銀行勘定 banking accounts of all banks
全国銀行信託勘定 trust accounts of all banks
全国市街地価格指数 index of urban land prices
全国準備基金 national reserve fund

セ

全国証券取引所協議会 National Conference of Stock Exchanges
全国信用協同組合連合会 Shinkumi Federation Bank
全国信用組合連合会 National Credit Union Administration
全国信用保証協会連合会 National Federation of Credit Guarantee Corporations
全国地方銀行協会 Regional Banks Association of Japan
全国中央値 national median
全国平均 national averages
全国ベースで on a nationwide basis
前後で推移している moving at around
潜在価格 shadow price
潜在株式 residual equity
潜在為替リスク underlying currency risk
潜在失業 latent unemployment
潜在需要 latent demand；potential demand
潜在成長率 potential growth
潜在的意味不明 latent ambiguity
潜在的株式 dilutive common stock
潜在的コール・オプション latent call option
潜在的債務 potential obligation
潜在的収益力 earnings potential
潜在的需要 pent up demand
潜在的存在 potential existence
潜在的損失 possible loss
潜在的な上昇余地 upside potential
潜在的な投資対象 potential investment
潜在的な便益 potential benefit
潜在的費用 implicit cost
潜在的普通株式 potential ordinary shares
潜在的利益 profit potential
潜在ワラント latent warrant
前事業年度 preceding business year
全資産合同方式 portfolio method
前日終値 last close price；previous close price
前日に繰下げる revert to the previous day
前日比変動幅 net change
前四半期比 quarter-on-quarter
全社レベル enterprise level
専従者控除 deduction for family employees
船主責任相互保険組合 ship owner protection and indemnity association
戦術的アセット・アロケーション tactical asset allocation
戦術的資産配分 TAA (tactical asset allocation)
先順位債権者 senior creditor
先順位担保付社債 senior mortgage bond
先順位の貸手 senior lender
先順位保険 underlying insurance
先順位モーゲージ senior mortgage
先順位留置権 prior lien
前　条 preceding article
前所有者 previous holder
前　進 way forward
先進工業国 major leagues
先進国 advanced countries；developed countries；major industrial nations
先進国首脳会議 Economic Summit
先進諸国 developed economies
全信連 Zenshinren Bank
宣　誓 oath
宣誓管理官 commissioners for oaths
宣誓供述書 affidavit
宣誓書 statement of declaration
陝西省 Shanxi
宣誓付供述 sworn statement
船籍港 home port
戦争危険 war perils；war risk
戦争危険免責条項 war risk exclusion clause
戦争年金 war pension
戦争約款 war clause
専属委任契約 exclusive listing
専属外務員制度 career agency system
専属管轄権 exclusive jurisdiction
専属管轄に服する submit to the exclusive jurisdiction
専属代理人 captive agent
専属仲介者 tied-agent
全　損 total loss
全損のみ担保 TLO (total loss only)

全体的影響 overall effect
全体的な水準 overall level
全体の企業収益 aggregate corporate profits
全体の財務情報 aggregate financial information
全体の貿易統計 overall trade picture
選　択 selection
選択型価格決定 alternative pricing
選択関税 alternative duties
選択基準 selection criteria
選択契約 alternative contract
選択権付為替予約 exchange contract with option
選択権保有者 optionee
選択効果 effect of selection
選択債務 alternative obligation
選択肢 option
選択式特約 optional rider
選択性 optionality
選択的機能 selective function
選択的救済 alternative remedy
選択的経過規定 transitional option
選択的償還条項 optional repayment provision
選択的消費 optional consumption
選択的信用規制 selective credit regulation
選択的な再評価 selective revaluation
選択的な方法 acceptable alternative
選択と集中 choice and concentration
選択配当 optional dividend
千単位 thousands of units
専断的 arbitrary；peremptory
センチメント指標 sentiment index
センチメントの改善 boost to the sentiment
船長用船荷証券 ship's bill
選定基本要領 criteria for selecting operation
選定方法 selection method
選定銘柄 selected issue
尖　点 cusp
先導銘柄 leading stock
先導役 path finder
セントキッツ＆ネイビス（ECドル） St. Kitts & Nevis (EC (East Caribbean) dollar)
セントヘレナ・ポンド SHP (St. Helena pound)
セントラル・カウンターパーティ CCP (central counterparty)
セントルシア（ECドル） St. Lucia (EC (East Caribbean) dollar)
前任監査人 predecessor auditor
前任者の残任期間 remaining term of the predecessor
専　念 devotion
前　年 preceding year；previous year
前年度 preceding fiscal year
前年同期 corresponding period of the last year
前年同月比 YoY (year-on-year)
前年比変化率 year-to-year percentage change
前納法人 advance corporation tax
前納保険料 advance premium；premium paid in advance
前　場 morning session
専　売 public monopoly
専売課税 monopoly assessment；taxation on government monopoly
専売納付金 state monopoly payment
専売利益 monopoly profit
先買権の申請 preemption entry
船　舶 ships and vessels
船舶管理人 ship's husband
船舶検査官 water-bailiff
船舶建造保険 ship builders' risks insurance
船舶修繕保険 ship repairing risks insurance
船舶証明書 certificate of registry of a ship
船舶税 shipping tax
船舶備付書類 ship's paper
船舶抵当権 mortgage of ship
船舶保険 hull insurance
船舶モーゲージ ship mortgage
船舶旅客運送費 haulage
船費保険 ship related disbursements

insurance
全 範 囲 gamut
全般資産 general corporate assets
全般の損益計算書 extensive income statement
前 日 付 pre-date
全費用込み FOC (free of charge)
全部原価 absorption cost；full cost；total cost
全部原価計算 absorption costing；full costing；total costing
全部原価原則 full cost principle
全部差押 grand distress
全部参加型の fully participating
全部資本直入 all included directly in capital
全部保険 full insurance
全部持ち分法 full equity method
前　　文 preamble
全米アナリスト協会連合会 Financial Analysts Federation
全米ACH協会 NACHA (National Automated Clearing House Association)
全米購買部協会 NAPM (National Association of Purchasing Management)
全米先物協会 National Futures Association
全米市場システム NMS (National Market System)
全米市場取引所 national market exchanges
全米証券業協会 National Association of Securities Dealers
全米証券業協会統一慣習規則 Uniform Practice Code
全米証券業協会紛争処理規則 Code of Procedure for Handling Trade Practice Complain
全米証券業者協会 Securities Industry Association
全米証券決済機構 NSCC (National Securities Clearing Corporation)
全米消費者金融財団 National Foundation for Consumer Credit
全米退職者協会 AARP (American Association of Retired Persons)
全米投資家協会 National Association of Investors Corporation
全米不動産業協会 NAR (National Association of Realtors)
全米保険監督官協会 NAIC (National Association of Insurance Commissioners)
選別開示 selective disclosure
選別融資 selective financing；selective lending
先方勘定 their account；Vostro account
先方統合 forward integration
前方差分 forward difference
戦没者遺族 war bereaved
専務取締役 senior managing director
専務理事 senior managing governor
全銘柄の across-the-board
全 面 高 rise across the board
全面的な禁止 outright prohibition
全面的な景気後退 widespread downturn
全 面 安 fall across the board
専門家証人 expert witness
専門家の意見書 professional pronouncements
専門家の共同託宣 jury of executive opinion
専門家報酬 professional fee
専門機関 specialized institution；specialized organization
専 門 語 jargon；technical term
専 門 誌 professional journal
専門証券会社 boutique
専門商品取扱業者 special product firm
専 門 職 profession
専門職業人賠償責任保険 professional liability insurance
専門調査官 Special Officer for Research, Minister's Secretariat
専 門 品 specialty goods
専門保険会社 monoline insurance company
専門用語 technical terms

占　　有 possession
占有継続債務者 DIP (debtor in possession)
占 有 権 monopoly
占有合同 unity of possession
占有債務者 debtor in possession
占有した seized
占 有 者 occupant
占有的リーエン possessory lien
占有引渡し livery
専　　用 exclusive use
専用住宅 exclusive-occupation house
占用権の評価 valuation of occupancy right
前　　葉 preceding page
戦　　略 strategy
戦略産業 strategic industries
戦略的意思決定 strategic decision making
戦略的提携 strategic alliance
戦略的パートナー strategic partner
戦略的買収 strategic buyout
戦略投資 strategic investment
戦略分野 strategic field
戦略リスク strategic risk
善良約因 good consideration
先　　例 precedent
前例のない unprecedented

ソ

粗 悪 化 adulteration
総アクティブ・リスク aggregate active risk
草　案 draft statement；proposal
総 遺 産 gross estate
総売上原価 gross cost of merchandise sold
総売上高 gross revenue；gross sales；total sales
総売り建玉 total selling contract
総運転資本 gross working capital
総運転資本及び純運転資本回転率 turnover of gross and net working capital
総運用ポートフォリオ aggregate managed portfolio
総営業利益 TOP (total operating profit)
総営業利幅 gross operating spread
相 違 点 dissimilarity
増　益 increased earnings；profit increase
増 益 率 earning growth rate
総益テスト gross profit test
総 益 法 gross profit method
総 益 率 gross profit ratio
層　化 stratification
増　価 value appreciation
増 価 税 appreciation duty；increment value duty
増価土地 accommodation lands
増価共有モーゲージ SAM (shared appreciation mortgage)
増　加 increase
増加運転資本 increasing working capital
増加株式 incremental shares
増加キャッシュフロー incremental cash flow
増加金額 accreted amount
増加資本 additional capital
増加資本コスト incremental cost of capital
増加収益 incremental return
増加償却 additional depreciation
増加所得税 increased income tax
総　会 general assembly；general meeting
総会・会議管理局 DGACM (Department of General Assembly and Conference Management)
総会の決定 decision of the general meeting
総会の召集 convocation of general meetings
総会の定足数 quorum for a general meeting
総買い建玉 total buying contract
増改築積立金 additions and betterments reserve
増改築ローン home improvement loan
総　額 aggregate amount；aggregate value；gross amount；total amount
総額アプローチ gross approach
総額規制 aggregate limits
総額主義 gross amount principle
総額の不足額 deficit in aggregate amount
総額表示 gross presentation
総額ベース gross base
総 額 法 gross method
総額補償 extra coverage
総額予算会計 principle of gross budget accounting
総貸出貸倒率 ratio of actual loan losses to the total loans
層化抽出法 stratified sampling
総括運賃 lump sum freight
総括勘定 summary account
総括審議官 Deputy Vice Minister for Policy Planning and Co-ordination
総括引当金 grouping allowance method
総括引受再保険 assumption reinsurance；en bloc reinsurance

総 括 表 summary of statistics
総括評価 overall evaluation
総括文句 general words
総括予算 summary budget
総カッパ値 total kappa
相　　関 correlation
相関係数 correlation coefficient
相 関 図 correlation diagram
相 関 表 correlation table
相関比率 correlation ratio
相関分析 correlation analysis
総幹事受託者 master trustee
総勘定元帳 general ledger
総勘定元帳勘定 general ledger account
総ガンマ値 total gamma
早期完済 full repayment before maturity
早期完了 early completion
早期警告 early warning
早期決済オプション early settlement option
早期行使 early exercise
早期償還予想 prepayment projection
早期償還リスク prepayment risk
早期消滅 early extinguishment
早期是正措置 prompt corrective action
早期償還条項 early settlement provision
早期退職 early retirement
早期退職給付 early retirement benefit
早期退職者 early leaver
早期退職年金 early retirement pension
早期退職優遇制度 window plan
早期適用 early application
操　　業 operation
操業損益 profit or loss from operations
操業短縮 curtailed operation；output reduction；reduction of operation
操業停止 plant outages
操 業 度 operation capacity；production level；rate of output
操業度差異 operation variance；production volume variance
操業度指数 volume indicator
操業日数 operated days
操 業 率 operation ratio
創業者利益 founder's profit；promoter's profits
創 業 費 formation expenses；initial expenses；organization expenses；start-up expenses
創業費償却 amortization of initial expenses；amortization of start-up expenses
総供給関数 aggregate supply function
総供給量 aggregate supply
送金為替 mail transfer payable；money order
送金為替手形 bank remittance bill；DD (demand draft)
送金小切手 remittance check
送金通知書 remittance advice
送金付け替票 credit note
送金伝票 remittance slip
総　　計 aggregate；grand total；total sum
総 計 の combined
総 原 価 aggregate cost；gross cost
増減対照式 self-balancing type
増 減 法 increase and decrease method
相互アクセス cross access
相互遺言 mutual wills
相互依存する interdependent
相互委託販売 reciprocal consignment
相互運用性 interoperability
相互会員 cross membership
相互会社 mutual company
相互掛金 mutual premium payment
相互関係 interrelationship
相互勘定 two way account
相互関連する interrelate
相互協議 mutual agreement procedure
相互協議室 Office of Mutual Agreement Procedures
相互協定 reciprocal arrangement
相互共有 mutual sharing
相互組合 mutual association
相互計算 mutual account
相互決済 parallel clearing
相互決済制度 mutual offset system
相互作用 interaction
相互参照 cross reference

相互主義 reciprocity
相互需要曲線 reciprocal demand curve
相互需要均等の法則 law of equation of reciprocal demand
相互条件 mutual condition
相互生命保険契約 mutual life insurance policy
相互接続性 interconnectivity
相互貸借 mutual credits
相互貯蓄銀行 mutual savings bank
相互統制勘定 reciprocal control account
相互独立的出来事 mutually exclusive event
相互捺印契約 mutual covenant
相互の利益 mutual interest
相互賠償 cross indemnification
相互配賦法 reciprocal distribution method
相互販売 cross sell；tie-in sale
相互販売禁止 anti-tie-in
相互福利社団 mutual benefit society
相互扶助団体 beneficial association
相互貿易協定 bilateral trade agreement
相互保険 mutual insurance
相互補償組合 mutual protection association
相互免除理論 mutual exclusion doctrine
相互持株会社 mutual holding company
相互約束 mutual promise
総合意見 comprehensive opinion
総合医療費保険 comprehensive medical expense insurance
総合医療保障 comprehensive medical coverage
総合掛金 aggregate cost
総合掛金率 aggregate cost ratio
総合課税 comprehensive income taxation；taxation on aggregate income
総合合算比率 aggregate combined ratio
総合株価指数 broad based stock index；composite stock price index
総合株式ティッカー consolidated stock ticker
総合金融機関 full service financial institution
総合金融機関化 allfinanz
総合金融サービス会社 bancassurer
総合気配表示システム consolidated quotation service
総合原価計算 process cost system
総合減価償却 composite depreciation
総合効果税率 effective aggregate tax rate
総合口座 multiple purpose bank account
総行使価格 aggregate exercise price
総合指数 composite index；general index
総合収支 overall balance of payment
総合収支の黒字 favorable balance of overall
総合償却資産 composite depreciation assets
総合証券会社 full line securities firm
総合仕訳帳 summary journal
総合政策課 Policy Planning and Research Division
総合清算会員 GCM (general clearing member)
総合税率 synthesis tax rate
総合相場表 composite stock price tables
総合耐用年数 composite useful life；synthetic useful life
総合取引参加者 general trading participant
総合取引情報システム CQS (consolidated quotation system)
総合賠償責任保険 comprehensive general liability insurance
総合品質管理 TQC (total quality control)
総合保険 all lines insurance；comprehensive insurance；packaged insurance
総合保税地域 comprehensive bonded area
総合持ち高 overall position
総合利回り total return
倉庫・運輸関連業 warehousing and harbor transportation service industry
倉庫証券 warehouse receipt
倉 庫 料 warehouse fee
操　　作 manipulation

総　　裁 governor
相　　殺 set-off；offset
相 殺 額 amount of the offset
相殺勘定 off-setting account
相殺関税 compensation duties；countervailing duty
相殺基準 offsetting criteria
相殺効果 offsetting effect
相殺項目 offset item
相殺誤差 compensating error
相殺誤謬 offset error
相殺される netted against
相殺信用状 reciprocal credit
相殺することなしに without netting
相殺する法的権利 legal right of set-off
相殺表示 disclosure by netting；offsetting presentation
相殺ポジション offsetting position
相 殺 前 before netting
相殺利子 compensating interest
総再生産率 gross reproduction rate
総 債 務 gross debt
総債務額 gross obligation
造作勘定 leasehold improvement account
捜　　索 search
操作変数 operating variable
操作目標 operating target
総 産 出 gross output
増　　資 additional equity；amount added to capital；capital increase；increase in capital stock；increase in the capital subscription
増資圧迫 potential over-supply produced by new issues
増資権利落ち ex-rights of capital increase
増資権利付株式 stock cum rights
増資新株買取権 purchase right to new shares for capital increase；stock right
増資により取得した株式 stock acquired by capital increase
総シータ値 total theta
総 資 産 combined assets；gross assets；total assets
総資産売上率 ratio of sales to total assets
総資産回転率 total asset turnover (ratio)
総資産償却率 rate of depreciation to total assets
総資産の帳簿価額 total book value of assets
総資産利益率 net earnings ratio to total assets；ratio of return on total assets
総 支 出 gross expenditure
総市場価額 total market value
総市場デルタ値 total market delta
相次相続 successive inheritance
総支払減額法 revenue abatement method
総 資 本 gross capital；total liabilities and net worth
総資本回転率 turnover (ratio) of total liabilities and net worth
総資本経常利益率 ratio of ordinary profit to total capital
総資本自己資本比率 equity capital ratio to total assets
総資本収益率 ratio of return on total capital；total capital profit ratio
総資本純利益率 ratio of earnings on total capital
増　　収 increase of revenue
増収増益 increased revenue and profit
総 収 益 gross revenue；total earnings
総収益乗数 gross income multiplier
総収益率 total ratio of return
総 収 入 total receipts
贈 収 賄 bribery
創　　出 origination
総出資金額 all amounts invested in capital
総 需 要 aggregate demand
総需要関数 aggregate demand function
総 準 備 total reserves
相　　乗 synergy
相乗効果 synergy effect
総商品売買差益 gross merchandise margin
総 所 得 gross income
総所得金額 total net income
増　　税 tax increase
増設積立金 reserve for additions

ソ

総 生 産 gross product ; total production
総 選 挙 general election
総　　則 general provisions
総 損 失 gross loss
相　　続 heredity ; inheritance
相 続 権 right of inheritance
相続権を奪う disinherit
相続財産 hereditaments ; inherited property
相 続 税 death tax ; estate duty ; estate tax ; inheritance tax
相続税控除 inheritance tax credit
相続税準備保険 inheritance tax insurance
相続税申告 inheritance tax return
相続税の物納 inheritance tax paid in kind
相続税法 Inheritance Tax Law
相続税免除 exemption of inheritance tax
相 続 人 heir/heiress
相 続 法 law of succession
相　　対 relative
相対価格 price relatives ; relative price
相対価値 relative value
相対価値アノマリー relative value anomaly
相対価値分析 relative value analysis
相対誤差 relative error
相対市場価額 relative market value
相対収益 relative revenue
相対所得 relative income
相対所得仮説 relative income hypothesis
相対的格差 relative differential
相対的価値 relative value
相対的強弱度 relative strength
相対的重要度 relative importance
相対的所有持ち分 relative ownership interest
相対的信用リスク relative credit risk
相対的測度 relative measures
相対的な確率 relative probability
相対的なクーポン効果 relative coupon effect
相対的な独立性 relative autonomy
相対的パフォーマンス relative performance
相対的変動 relative change
相対約免責危険 relative excepted risk
相対評価 relative valuation
相対力指数 relative index ; relative power index ; RSI (relative strength index)
送 達 簿 chit book
相 談 役 counselor
総体的利益 overall profit
総代理店 general agent
総代理店制度 general agency system
総代理人 universal agent
総長期資金 total capitalization ; total long-term fund
総帳簿価格 gross book value
総 貯 蓄 gross savings
総賃料乗数 GRN (gross rent multiplier)
総出来高 total turnover
総デルタ値 total delta
総 投 資 gross investment
総投資率 gross investment rate
総 取 引 gross transaction
総取引高 gross trading volume
総認識利得損失計算書 statement of aggregate recognized gains and losses
総ノーマル・ポートフォリオ aggregate normal portfolio
総 配 当 gross dividend
総発行額 gross issuance
総発行済株式数 total shares outstanding ; total stocks issued
総費用曲線 total cost curve
総 費 用 gross cost
総負債自己資本比率 equity capital ratio to total liabilities
総負債自己資本率 equity capital ratio to total debt
総 平 均 aggregate average
総平均法 periodic average method ; progressive average inventory method
総保険料 gross insurance premium
総補填限度額 aggregate limit of liability
総 務 省 Ministry of Public Management, Home Affairs, Posts

and Telecommunications
総務大臣 Minister for Public Management, Home Affairs, Posts and Telecommunications
総持ち分 total equity
総 預 金 total deposit
総 利 益 gross profit
総利益分析 gross profit analysis
総利益率 gross profit percentage
総利回り gross yield
総 流 入 gross inflow
総ロー値 total roh
総和法指数 index number by aggregative method
早朝レポート morning report
想定インフレ率 inflation assumption
想定元本 notional principal
想定キャッシュフロー pro forma
想定取引費用 hypothetical transaction cost
争点事項 matter in issue
争点たる事実 question of fact
争点に達した at issue
相 当 額 amount equivalent to
相当する要件 comparable requirement
相当な理由 probable cause
相当の改善 significant improvement
相当の償却 reasonable depreciation
相当の地代 equivalent rent
蔵匿する harbor
相　　場 quoted price
相 場 観 forecast for market tendency
相場掲示板 quotation board
相場気配 market quotation
相場上昇 higher quotation
相場情報 market information
相場情報システム market information system
相場操縦 daisy chain；market manipulation；rigged market
相場の動き market behavior
相場の大幅下落 market crash
相場の公表 publication of market information
相場の上昇 market rally
相場の大転換日 key reversal day
相場の反転 reversal
相場の変動 price volatility
相 場 表 list quotation
相場表要約 run-down
相場報道システム Market Information System
増　　配 increase in dividend
増 配 率 dividend growth rate
増分価値 incremental value
増分原価 incremental cost
増分収益率 incremental rate of return
増分分析 incremental analysis
増 分 法 incremental method
増分利益 incremental profit
造 幣 局 Japan Mint
層 別 の stratified
層別標本抽出 stratified sampling
双方向市場 two-sided market
双方建値 two way price
双務契約 bilateral contract；reciprocal contract
双務主義 bilateralism
贈　　与 gift
贈 与 株 donated stock
贈与財産 donated property
贈与資本 donated capital
贈与剰余金 donated surplus
贈 与 税 CTT (capital transfer tax)；donation tax；gift tax
贈与税控除 gift tax credit
贈与税の課税価格 taxable value of gift tax
贈与税の税率 tax rate of gift tax
贈与税の配偶者控除 spouse exemption on gift tax
贈与税免除 exemption of gift tax
贈与見込証券 GAN (grant anticipation note)
創　　立 creation
創立委員 organization committee
創立委員会 foundation committee
創立事務所 organization office
創 立 者 founder；organizer
創立準備費 preopening expenses
創立総会 general meeting for

establishment；inaugural meeting
創 立 費 organization cost
ソーサー saucer
素　価 prime cost
素価配賦法 prime cost method
阻害クレーム disruption claims
遡及義務 recourse obligations
遡及義務あり with recourse
遡及義務ありで売却 sold with recourse
遡及義務なしで売却 sold without recourse
遡及義務のない金融負債 non-recourse financial liabilities
遡及義務免除裏書 endorsement without recourse
遡 及 権 recourse right
遡及債務 recourse obligation
遡及修正 catch-up adjustment；retroactive adjustments
遡及修正再表示 retrospective restatement
遡及修正報告書 retroactive restatement
遡及償還義務不免除信用状 with recourse credit
遡及償還義務免除信用状 without recourse credit
遡及償還請求権 recourse
遡及条項 lost-or-not-lost clause
遡及徴収 retroactive levy
遡及的給与 back pay
遡及適用 retrospective application
遡及転換 retroactive conversion
遡及払配当金 back dividend
遡 及 法 retrospective law
遡及保険 retrospective policy
遡及料率 retrospective rate
遡及割引率 retroactive discount
遡求計算 retrogressive accounting
速 算 表 calculating table
即時開始年金 immediate annuity
即時加入 immediate participation
即時完売 blowout
即時グロス決済 RTGS (real time gross settlement)
即時決済 RTS (real-time settlement)
即時執行 fill or kill
即時執行注文 immediate or cancel order
即時受給権付与 immediate vesting
即時償却 immediate write-off
即時追及 fresh pursuit
即時転売債券 going away
即時年金 immediate annuity
即時の修正 immediate adjustment
即時払い prompt payment
即時ファイナリティ instantaneous finality
即時保障 immediate protection
即時または取消注文 fill-or-kill order；immediate-or-cancel order
即日受渡し cash delivery
即日資金 same day funds
即日利用可能な資金 immediately available fund
促進クレーム acceleration claims
促進税制 special incentive tax system
属　性 attribute
属性標本抽出 attribute sampling
測　定 measurement
測定基準 measurement basis；measurement principles
測定基礎 measurement base
測定契約 measurement contract
測定原則 measurement principle
測定単位 measuring unit
測 定 値 measure
測定通貨 measurement currency
測 定 日 measurement date
測定方法 measurement method
測定要件 measurement requirement
即　売 spot sale
速　報 preliminary report
続　落 consecutive declines
測　量 surveying
訴　権 cause of action
底 bottom
底 入 れ bottoming out；touching the bottom
底入れする bottom out
底 堅 い staying resilient
底 固 い firm
底固い動きをする form a base against
底　値 bottom price
底値買い bottom fishing

底 離 れ turning upward
そこで約因として now, therefore, in consideration of
損ねることなく without any prejudice to
素材産業 basic industry
組織運営 organization management
組織改革 organizational changes
組織化された市場 organized market
組織監査 organization audit
組織計画 organization planning
組織形態 organization form
組織構成 organizational structure
組織単位 organizational unit
組織的区分 organizational grouping
組織的構成要素 organizational component
組織変更 reorganization
粗資本ストック gross capital stock
訴　　訟 lawsuits；legal action；litigation
訴訟原因 cause of action
訴訟原因の発生 accrual of cause of action
訴訟事件 contentious case；court case
訴訟事件の解決 resolution of court case
訟務専門官 Special Officer for Lawsuits
訴訟続行 further maintenance of the action
訴訟中止 stay of proceedings
訴訟手続 judicial proceedings；service of process
訴訟手続費用 cost for judicial proceedings
訴訟当事者 parties to lawsuit
訴訟による損失 loss from litigation
訴 訟 人 suitor
訴訟の解決 litigation settlements
訴訟の債務 liability under litigation
訴訟の重複 multiplicity of action
訴訟の分離 severance of actions
訴訟費用の担保 security for costs
訴訟費用保険 legal expense insurance
訴訟放棄 abandonment of action
訴訟方式 form of action
訴訟法典 code of procedure
租　　税 tax
租税及び印紙収入 tax and stamp revenues
租税改革法 Tax Reform Act of 1984
租税回避 tax avoidance
租税勘定 tax account
租税関数 tax function
租税還付請求権 claim for tax refunds
租税区域全体 across jurisdictions
租税原則 tax principle
租税公課 taxes and public charges
租税公債勘定 treasury tax and loan account
租税控除項目 tax preference item
租税構造 tax structure
租税国家 tax state
租税債権 tax claims
租税裁判所 tax court
租税債務 tax liabilities
租税債務関係説 theory of liabilities taxation
租税査定 tax assessment
租税準備証券 tax anticipation bill
租税条約 tax convention；tax treaty
租税政策 tax policy
租税先取特権 tax lien
租税選択 tax selection
租税体系 tax system；taxation regime
租税徴収 collection of rates；collection of taxes
租税特別措置 special taxation measures
租税特別措置法 Special Taxation Measures Law
租税特別措置法施行令 Cabinet Order of the Special Taxation Measures Law
租税取立請負 farming of taxes
租税取引 tax transaction
租税の帰着 tax incidence
租税の減免 reduction or exemption of tax
租税の受益者負担原則 compensation principle of taxation
租税の中立性 neutrality of taxation
租税の転嫁 shifting of tax burden
租税の予納 prepayment of tax
租 税 犯 tax criminal
租税負担 burden of tax；tax burden
租税負担者 ratepayer

租税負担の軽減 tax relief
租税負担率 tax burden ratio
租税法律関係 legal relationship in tax
租税免除 exemption of taxes
租税優遇 tax privilege
租税優先権 priority of taxes
組成手数料 origination fee
措　置 countermeasure
卒業条項 graduation clause
卒業銘柄 graduated security
即金で cash down
続　行 further directions
外・内外債 out-in external bonds
外税方式 tax exclusive price
「外－外」外債 bond issued and purchased by offshore parties
祖父条項 grandfather clause
ソフト・ドル soft dollar
ソフト・ランディング soft landing
ソフト・ローン soft loan
ソブリン・アナリスト sovereign analyst
ソブリン格付け sovereign rating
ソブリン銀行 sovereign bank
ソブリン債 sovereign bond
ソブリン・シーリング sovereign ceiling
ソブリン発行体 sovereign issuer
ソブリン発行体回収率 sovereign recovery value
ソブリン銘柄 sovereign name
ソブリン・リスク sovereign risk
ソブリン・ローン sovereign loan
ソマリア・シリング SOS (Somali shilling)
ソルベンシー基準 solvency standards
ソルベンシー評価 solvency valuation
ソルベンシー・マージン solvency margin
ソルベンシー・マージン比率 solvency margin ratio
ソロモン諸島・ドル SBD (Solomon Islands dollar)
損　益 gain and loss ; income and expenses ; profit and loss
損益勘定 income account ; profit and loss account
損益計算書 earning statement ; income statement ; profit and loss statement ; statement of earnings
損益計算書(純損失の場合) statement of loss
損益計算書監査 income statement audit
損益計算書勘定 income statement account
損益計算書原則 income statement principles
損益計算書項目 items on income statement
損益計算書等式 profit and loss equation
損益計算書に計上された recognized in income statement
損益計算書に収益計上される credited in income statement
損益計算書に費用計上される charged in income statement
損益計算書の補足資料 supplementary income statement information
損益計算書表示項目 line items of income statement
損益計算書比率 income statement ratio
損益計算書分析 analysis of income statement
損益状況 profit and loss situation
損益通算 aggregation of profit and loss
損益取引 profit and loss transaction
損益認識 recognition of gain and loss
損益の計上基準 recognition criteria for profit and loss
損益の実現 realization of profit and loss
損益の潜在的可能性 potential for gain or loss
損益の発生額 profit and loss accruals
損益の持ち分 share of profit and loss
損益分岐為替相場 exchange rate at break-even point
損益分岐期間 break-even time
損益分岐債券価格 break-even bond price
損益分岐図表 break-even chart
損益分岐点 BEP (break even point) ; profit and loss break-even point
損益分岐点分析 break-even point analysis
損益分岐等式 break even equation

損益分岐値段 break-even price
損益分岐分析 break-even analysis
損益分岐利回り break-even yield
損 益 法 profit and loss method
損益報告 profit and loss report
損　　壊 destruction
損　　害 damage
損 害 額 amount of damage
損害査定人 loss adjuster
損害査定費 loss adjustment expense
損害担保契約 guaranty insurance
損害通知条項 claim notice clause
損害填補額 insured loss
損害の証明 proof of loss
損害の分担 apportionment of a loss
損害の弁済 compensation of the damage
損害賠償 compensation for damages
損害賠償額 damages payment；liquidated damages
損害賠償額の査定 assessment of damages
損害賠償金 restitution costs
損害賠償請求 claim for damage
損害賠償請求訴訟 action in damage
損害賠償責任保険 public liability insurance
損害賠償利子 moratory interest
損害発生頻度 loss frequency
損害発生率 chance of loss
損害防止義務 duty to sue and labor
損害防止条項 sue and labor clause
損害防止費用 sue and labor charges
損害保険 damage insurance；general insurance；non-life insurance；property casualty insurance
損害保険会社 non-life insurance company
損害保険控除 deduction for damage insurance；fire and other casualty insurance premiums deduction
損害保険事業研究所 Non-Life Insurance Institute of Japan
損害保険代理店 non-life insurance agent
損害保険料 casualty insurance premium
損害保険料控除 taxation allowance for non-life insurance premium
損害保険料率算定会 Fire and Marine Insurance Rating Association of Japan
損害補償金 indemnity allowance
損害補償条項 indemnity clause
損害・保証保険 casualty and surety insurance
損害補填契約書 letter of indemnity
損害保有額 underlying retention
損 害 率 loss ratio
損害を与える inflict a loss
損害を回復する recoup
損 切 り loss cut；stop loss
損切り注文 stop loss order
損　　金 charge against revenues；deductible expenses
損金経理 recognizing as expense
損金算入 inclusion in expenses
損金算入外国税 foreign tax deductible as expenses
損金算入限度額 amount allowable
損金算入される deducted in determining taxable income
損金算入賞与 bonus payment entered into expenses
損金算入できる引当金 deductible reserve；tax deductible reserve
損金不算入 exclusion from non-taxable expenses；not deductible for tax purpose
損金不算入の交際費 entertainment expenses not qualifying for deduction
損金不算入の租税課金 nondeductible taxes
損　　失 loss
損失回収率 loss recovery ratio
損失勘定 loss account
損失関数 loss function
損失計上時期 time of recognizing loss
損失除外 exclusion of loss
損失処理計算書 loss disposal statement
損失申告書 final return in case of loss
損失認識 loss recognition
損失の繰戻し carry back of loss
損失の資産化 capitalization of loss

損失の認識 recognition of losses
損失の配分 loss allocation
損失の分担 loss share
損失の補填 making up for loss
損失発生地 location of loss or damage
損失引当金 loss provision
損失分担ルール loss-sharing rule
損失防止 loss prevention
損失補償証書 back bond
損失補填 compensation for loss
損失を埋める cover the loss
損　　傷 detriment；mutilation
損傷銀行券 damaged or worn banknotes
存続会社 surviving company
存続企業 continuing company
存続事業 existing business
存続実体 surviving entity
存続バイアス survivorship bias
損保会社 general insurer；property and casualty underwriter
損保資金 general insurance fund
損　　耗 wear and tear
損 耗 料 dilapidations

タ

タークス・カイコス（米ドル） Turks & Caicos (US dollar)
ターゲット発行 target issue
ターゲット・ポートフォリオ target portfolio
ターゲット・リターン target return
ダーティ・フロート dirty float
ダービン・ワトソン比 Durbin-Watson ratio
ターミネーション・デート termination date
ターム債権 term receivable
ターム・スワップ term swap
ターム・フェッド term fed
ターム・フェデラル・ファンド term federal fund
ターム・フェド・ファンド・レート term fed fund rate
ターム物 term instruments
ターム・レポ term RP
ターム・ローン term loan
ターンキー turnkey
ターンキー契約 turnkey contract
ターン・キー・システム turn key system
ダイアグラム diagram
ダイアゴナル・スプレッド diagonal spread
ダイアログ dialogue
代　　位 subrogation
代 位 権 subrogation right
代位債権 subrogated right
代位通知書 advice of subrogation
代位納付 subrogation payment
代位弁済 payment in subrogation；subrogated performance
代位領収書 subrogation receipt
大域的最小分散 global minimum variance
第一拒否権 first refusal
第 一 券 first exchange
第一原価 primary cost
第一次受取人 primary beneficiary
第一次オイル・ショック first oil crisis
第一次オンライン first generation on-line system
第一次貨幣 primary currency
第一次勘定 primary account
第一次債務者 primary obligor
第一次産業 primary industry
第一次産品輸出 primary industry product export
第一次資本 primary capital
第一次準備資産 primary reserve asset
第一次書類 first papers
第一次超過額特約 first surplus treaty
第1四半期 Q1 (first quarter)
第一次負債 primary liability
第一次分売 primary distributions
第一次平価 initial par value
第一次募集 primary offering
第一受益者の原則 primary benefit rule
第一順位抵当権付社債 first mortgage bond
第一順位モーゲージ first lien mortgage
第一順位モーゲージ・ローン first mortgage loan
第一抵当 first mortgage
第一定理 first theorem
第一当事者 primary party
第一優先株 prior preferred stock
第一優先株式 first preferred stock
第一回繰上償還日 first call date
第一種郵便 first class mail
第 一 審 first instance
第一審管轄権 original jurisdiction
退役軍人住宅ローン VA (Veterans Administration) mortgage
対 応 額 corresponding amount
対応関係 reciprocal relationship
対応勘定 reciprocal account
対応原則 matching principle

対応していない状態 unmatched position
対応する減少 corresponding reduction
対応する修正 equivalent adjustment
対応する数値 corresponding figure
対応するプール equivalent pool
対応的調整 correlative adjustment
対応の概念 matching concept
対応の原則 principle of matching
対 応 表 cross reference
対　　価 consideration
滞　　貨 backlog
滞貨金融 financing for carrying inventories；stockpile financing
滞貨融資 loan for carrying inventories
対外援助 foreign aid
対外株式投資 foreign equity investment
対外借入れ international borrowing
対外関係 international affairs
対外均衡 external equilibrium
対外債権債務 foreign claims and debts
対外債務 external debt；external liabilities；foreign debt；foreign liabilities；international debt
対外債務返済 foreign debt servicing
対外債務利払い interest payments on foreign debt
対外資産 external assets
対外資産残高統計 international investment position
対外支払手段 means of foreign payment
対外支払いのための為替 exchange for foreign payment；exchange for means of foreign payment
対外収支 external account；external balance
対外収支の赤字 current account deficit
対外収支の黒字 current account surplus
対外純貸出 net foreign credit
対外純資産 net external assets
対外純負債 net external liabilities
対外証券投資 Japanese investment in foreign securities
対外政策 international policy
対外投資 outward investment；overseas investment
大学建設融資保険協会 Connie Lee (College Construction Loan Insurance Association)
大学入試センター National Center for University Entrance Examinations
耐火建築物の割増償却 additional depreciation on fire-proof buildings
対価受領 value received
待機期間 waiting period
大 企 業 large company
大規模市場介入 heavy currency intervention
大規模償却資産 large depreciable property
大規模な投資 major investments
耐久材受注 durable goods orders
耐久消費財 consumer durables；durable consumer goods
大 恐 慌 great depression
対　　極 other end of the spectrum
代金先払販売 CBD (cash before delivery)
代金取立手形 BC (bills for collection)
代金引換販売 cash on delivery sales
代金引替渡し cash on delivery
代金平均 average value
体系的構成 systematic structure
体系的財務表現 structured financial representation
体系的標本抽出 systematic sampling
代行カード credit cards issued by the agent
代行給付 substitution benefit
代行部分の返上 return of substitution part
対抗要件 requirements against
対抗要件を具備した担保権 perfected security interest
対 抗 力 countervailing power
対抗力の具備 perfection of the interest
対顧客為替相場 exchange quotation
対顧客取引 customer transaction
大 黒 札 Daikoku satsu
対　　策 countermeasure
第三限月取引 farthest contract month
第 三 国 third countries
第三債務者 garnishee

第 三 次 third generation
第三次オンライン third generation on - line system
第三次産業 tertiary industry
第三市場 third market
第3四半期 Q3 (third quarter)
第 三 者 third party
第三者貸付 TFA (tripartite financing agreement)
第三者小切手 third party check
第三者信用補填 third-party credit support
第三者信用リスク third party credit risk
第三者対抗要件 protection conditions against third parties
第三者によって発行された手形 note issued by a third party
第三者に割当てられた株式 stock allotted to third party
第三者納付及び代位 tax payment and subrogation by a third party
第三者の介入 intervention by a third party
第三者の権原 outstanding title
第三者賠償個別保険 comprehensive general liability insurance
第三者賠償特約保険 third party liability cover
第三者払約款 loss payable clause
第三者保険 third party insurance
第三者預託証書 escrow receipt
第三者リスク third-party risk
第三者割当 allocation of new shares to a third party；third party allocation
第三者割当株 stock allotted to third persons
第三世界 Third World
第三世界各国 third world countries
第三セクター quasi-public corporation；third sector corporation
退　社 retirement from a corporation
貸借勘定 debtor and creditor accounts
貸借対照表 BS (balance sheet)；financial position statement；statement of financial condition
貸借対照表監査の覚書 memorandum of balance sheet audit
貸借対照表項目 balance sheet items
貸借対照表上の区分 balance sheet classification
貸借対照表等式 balance sheet formula
貸借対照表の修正再表示 restatement of balance sheet
貸借対照表の取扱い balance sheet treatment
貸借対照表日 balance sheet date
貸借対照表日後の発生事項 event subsequent to balance sheet date
貸借対照表負債法 balance sheet liability method
貸借対照表分析 balance sheet analysis
貸借取引 borrowed transactions；debt-credit transaction
貸借平均の原理 principle of loan equilibrium
貸借銘柄 loanable issue
対社債プレミアム premium over bond value
大衆課税 taxation upon the general-public
大衆消費社会 mass consumption society
大衆投資家 investing public
大衆リスク mass risks
大　証 OSE
大証株価指数 Osaka Stock Price Index
対象会社 target company
対象株券 underlying stock
対象株券の売買単位 trading unit of the underlying stocks
対象株式 target stock
対象債務 target liability
対象事業 projects covered
対象資産 reference asset
対象資産価額 target assets value
対象指標 underlying index
対象証券 target securities；underlying securities
対象スワップ underlying swap
対象となる資源 underlying resources
対象になる債務者 underlying debtor
対象分野 area coverage

対照勘定 contra account；per contra account
対照した謄本 examined copy
対 照 表 list of differences between
対照変数 antithetic variable
対称トライアングル・パターン symmetrical triangle pattern
対称分布 symmetrical distribution
タイ証券取引所 SET (Securities Exchange of Thailand)
退職一時金 retirement lump-sum grants
退職一時金制度の年金化 transformation of lump sum payment of retirement allowance to pension plan
退職延期 delayed retirement
退職勘定 retirement account
退職関連給付 retirement related benefits
退職給付 retirement benefit
退職給付会計 accounting for retirement benefit
退職給付会計の適用 introduction of the retirement benefit accounting
退職給付債務 retirement benefit obligation
退職給付債務積立額不足 shortfall in funding for retirement benefit liabilities
退職給付信託 retirement benefit trust
退職給付スキーム retirement benefit scheme
退職給付制度 retirement benefit plan
退職給付制度間の移行 switch from one retirement benefit plan to another
退職給付積立 retirement benefit accumulation
退職給付引当金 allowance for retirement benefit；reserve for retirement and severance
退職給付見込額 expected retirement benefit
退職給与 retirement allowance
退職給与規程 retirement allowance regulations
退職給与積立金 reserve for pension fund
退職給与引当金 reserve for employee retirement allowance
退職給与引当金繰入限度額 allowed limit of retirement allowance reserve
退職共済年金 retirement mutual aid pension
退 職 金 retirement pay
退職金規程 regulations for retirement allowance
退職金共済契約 mutual aid contract for retirement allowance
退職金制度 retirement allowance plan；severance payment system
退職金積立 retirement accumulation
退職金積立金 accumulation for retirement allowance；superannuation reserve
退職金積立不足 deficiency in retirement allowance fund
退職金の一括支給 lump sum payment of retirement allowance；retirement allowance in a lump sum
退職金の打切支給 payment of retirement allowance for termination
退職後医療給付 post-retirement medical care
退職後医療制度 post-employment medical plan
退職後給付 post-employment benefit
退職後給付コスト postretirement benefit cost
退職後給付債務 post-employment benefit obligation
退職後給付費用 post-employment benefit cost
退職後死亡給付 post retirement death benefit
退職後生命保険 post-retirement life insurance
退職後年金 post retirement pension
退職時給与による制度 final salary plan
退職時給与による年金制度 final salary pension scheme
退職時給与年金制度 final salary pension plan
退職した従業員 retired employee
退 職 者 retiree

退職者医療給付 health care benefits to retirees
退職所得 retirement income
退職所得控除 allowed retirement income deduction；deduction for retirement income
退職所得申告書 return form for retirement income
退職所得付保険 retirement income policy
退職所得保険 retirement income insurance
退職手当 employment termination indemnities；terminal pay allowance
退職手当とみなす一時金 lump sum payment regarded as retirement allowance
退職年金 retirement annuity；retirement pension；retirement vehicle
退職年金掛金 premium payment for a retirement annuity
退職年金加算 delayed retirement credit
退職年金課税 taxation on retirement annuity；taxation on retirement pension
退職年金基金 retirement fund
退職年金業務 retirement annuity business
退職年金計算 pension calculation
退職年金制度 superannuation scheme
退職年金積立金 reserve for retirement annuity；retirement annuity reserve
退職年金の受取人 beneficiary of the retirement annuity
退職年金保険 pension annuity；retirement policy
退職年齢 age of retirement
退職保障 retirement coverage
対所得負債比率 debt-to-income ratio
大臣官房 Minister's Secretariat
大臣政務官 parliamentary secretary
大臣秘書官 Personal Secretary to the Minister
対 人 税 personal tax
対人賠償責任保険 personal liability insurance
対人賠償保険 automobile bodily injury liability insurance
対数渦巻線 logarithmic spiral
対数グラフ logarithmic chart
対数効用関数 logarithmic utility function
対数正規分布 lognormal distribution
対数線形 log linear
大数の法則 law of large numbers
大　　勢 major trend
大 勢 観 macro view
体制の構築 adjustment of organization
対政府取引に関する基本要領 principal terms and conditions for the Bank's transactions with the government
対前月比変化 month-to-month change
対前日変動率分布 distribution of single day advances and declines
代　　替 substitution；surrogate
代 替 案 alternatives
代替エネルギー alternative energy
代替オプション replacement option
代替会計原則 alternative accounting principles
代替会計処理 alternative accounting treatment
代替介護 alternate care
代替可能性 fungibility
代替可能物 fungible goods
代替契約 alternate policy
代替効果 substitution effect
代替固定資産 substitute fixed assets
代替資金 alternative funds
代替資金調達手段 alternative financing choice
代替資産 property for substitution；substitute assets；substitute property
代替証券 fungible securities
代替商品 product alternatives
代替所得 replacement income
代替処理 alternative treatment
代替スワップ replacement swap；substitution swap
代替製造工程 alternative production process

代替製品 alternative product
代替測定値 surrogate measure
代替担保債務 substitute collateral obligation
代替通貨 currency substitute
代替的方法 alternative approach
代替の弾力性 elasticity of substitution
代替費用 alternative costs；substituted expenses
代替表示 alternative presentation
代替法律 law of substitution
代替見積値 alternative estimate
代替ミニマム税 AMT (alternative minimum tax)
代替流動性 alternative liquidity
態　度 attitude
対　当 matching
対当数量 matching positions
対当取引 crossing trading
対等合併 merger for establishing a new entity on an equal basis
大投資銀行 large investment bank
対ドル versus dollar
対ドル円貨額 yen value per one U.S. dollar
対ドル為替相場 exchange rate against dollar
対ドルで頭の痛い展開 struggle against the dollar
対ドルで強い strong relative to the dollar
対ドルでの円 yen vs dollar
対ドルでの円高 yen rising against the dollar
対ドルでの上昇 strengthening against the dollar
対内間接投資 indirect inward investment
対内証券投資 foreign investment in Japanese securities
対内直接投資 direct inward investment
対内投資 inward investment
対内投資促進 promotion of foreign investment in Japan
ダイナミック・クレジット・スワップ dynamic credit swap
ダイナミック戦略 dynamic strategies
ダイナミック・プログラム dynamic programming
ダイナミック・ヘッジ dynamic hedge
ダイナミック・ヘッジ戦略 dynamic hedge strategy
ダイナミック・ポートフォリオ dynamic portfolio
第二限月取引 second nearest contract month
第二差押 second-distress
第二次オンライン second generation on-line system
第二次産業 secondary industry
第二次証券 secondary securities
第二次超過額特約 second surplus treaty
第二次的不動産移転行為 secondary conveyance
第二次納税義務 secondary tax liability
第2四半期 Q2 (second quarter)
第二次負債 secondary liability
第二次ボイコット secondary boycott
第二順位モーゲージ second lien mortgage
第二順位モーゲージ・ローン second-lien mortgage loan
第二次流動資産 secondary liquidities
第二地銀加盟行 member bank of the Second Association of Regional Banks
第二地銀協会 Second Association of Regional Banks
第二当事者 secondary party
対日アクセス access to Japan
滞　納 delinquency
滞納者 delinquent taxpayer
滞納処分 attachment for delinquent tax
滞納税 back tax；tax on delinquency
滞納督促手数料 charge for demand for payment of tax in arrears
滞納家賃 back rent
代　納 payment for another
大納会 closing session of the year；final session of a year
タイ・バーツ THB (Thai baht)
大発会 first session of a year；opening session of the year

代表貨幣 representative money
代表者代理人 substitute representative
代表者又は管理人 representatives or administrators
代表受託者 representative trustee
代表清算人 representative liquidator
代表訴訟 representative suit
代表的消費者 representative consumer
代表的標本 representative sample
代表取締役 representative director
代表民主制 representative democracy
代表銘柄 representing issue
代　物 substitute
代物弁済 accord and satisfaction；payment in kind；payment in substitution
代物弁済担保物件取得 strict foreclosure
対物管轄権 jurisdiction of the res
対物契約 real contract
対物信用 real credit
対物訴訟 real action
対物担保 impersonal security
対物賠償保険 automobile property damage liability insurance
太平洋経済文化圏 Pacific Economic and Cultural Enclave
太平洋地域経済協力機構 Organization of Pacific Economic Cooperation
太平洋保険会議 Pacific Insurance Conference
大名債 daimyo bond
タイミング・オプション timing option
タイミング・スワップ timing swap
タイミングのずれ timing mismatch
タイム・オプション time option
タイム・カード time card
タイム・スパン time span
タイム・ディケイ time decay
タイム・バイアス time bias
タイム・フィルター time filter
タイム・ラグ time lag
タイム・ラグのない指数連動 contemporaneous indexation
タイムリー・ディスクロージャー timely disclosure
対面交付 in person delivery
ダイヤモンド・フォーメーション diamond formation
代用差入れ deposit of the security in lieu of cash
代用証券掛目率 collateral value of substitute security
代用証書 substitute certificates
代用通貨 proxy currency
代用納付証券 negotiable securities submitted in payment of treasury funds
代用有価証券 securities in lieu of cash；substitute securities
耐用年数 durable years；service life；useful life
耐用年数の計算 computation of useful life
耐用年数の短縮 shortening of useful life
耐用年数の長い long lived
耐用年数表 useful life table
第4四半期 Q4 (final quarter)
代　理 deputy；proxy
代理受取人 substitute payee
代理貸付 agency loan
代理関係 agency relationship
大陸式元帳締切手続 continental form of closing the ledger
大陸法 continental law
代理権 power of representation
代理権を証する書類 written proxy
代理交換 clearing for nonmember
対　立 confrontation
対立する利害 competing interests
代理手数料 agent commission
代理店 agency
代理店貸し agency account receivable；current credit accounts with agencies
代理店勘定 agency account
代理店経費 agency cost
代理店契約 agency contract
代理店契約書 agency agreement
代理店検査 agent inspection
代理店出資会社 agent owned company

代理店制度 agent system
代理店手数料 agency commission；agency fee
代理店元帳 agency ledger
代理人 agent；attorney in fact；procurator
代理人資金 agency fund
代理人簿記 agency bookkeeping
代理人理論 agency theory
代理販売 sale by agent
大量売り unloading
大量玉取引 block transaction
大量受注 major order
大量推奨販売 mass sales
大量生産 mass production
大量生産技術 mass production techniques
大量退職 large retirement
大量注文 significant order
大量取引 block trading
大量売買取引 block sales
大量保有報告書 large holding report；substantial shareholding report
ダイレクト・バンキング direct banking
ダイレクト・ペーパー direct paper
台湾 Taiwan
台湾証券取引所 Taiwan Stock Exchange
台湾ドル TWD (Taiwan dollar)
多因子 multi factor
ダウ工業株 Dow Jones Industrial
ダウ工業株30種平均 Dow Jones 30 Industrial Average
ダウ公共株15種平均 Dow Jones 15 Public Utility Average
ダウ工業平均 DJIA (Dow Jones Industrial Average)
ダウ式商品指数 Dow Jones Commodity Index
ダウ20種債券指数 Dow Jones 20 Bond Index
ダウ平均 Dow Jones Average；Dow Jones Industrial Average；NY Dow
ダウ輸送株20種平均 Dow Jones 20 Transportation Average
ダウ理論 Dow Theory
TAURUS TAURUS (Transfer and Automated Registration of Uncertificated Stock)
ダウン・アンド・アウト・コール・オプション down and out call option
ダウンサイジング downsizing
他益信託 third party benefit trust
他会計 other accounting
高い公算 high possibility
高い値段の売呼値 higher offer
高い値段の買呼値 higher bid
高い伸び strong growth
高いマージン wide margin
高いリスクの資産 riskier assets
高い流動性 high liquidity
高い利率のクーポン generous coupon
多角化戦略 diversification strategy
多角化の経済性 economies of scope
多角経営企業 diversified business enterprise
多角決済 multilateral settlement
多角的清算協定 multilateral clearing agreement
多角的貿易交渉 multilateral trade negotiations
多額債務者 over-indebted person
多額納税者 high income brackets；high taxpayers
多額の変動 significant movement
多額の保証状 significant guarantee paper
高唱え quoting high
高止まり topping out
高止まりで looking toppy
高値 high price；record price
高値の突破 topside breakout
高値引け closing high
高値銘柄 highs
高目誘導 aggressively held up
高保合い holding high
宝くじの賞金 prize of raffle
兌換券発行税 tax on bank note system
兌換紙幣 convertible note
兌換準備 convertible reserve
兌換通貨 convertible currency
兌換できない inconvertible
抱合せ株式 combined equity interests

抱合せ信用状 reciprocal credit
抱合せ販売 combination sale；tie-in sale
多期間モデル multiperiod model
他企業比較 cross sectional analysis
妥　　協 compromise
妥協契約 accommodation line
多業種企業 diversified enterprise
択一注文 alternative order；selective order
択一的申立 disjunctive allegation
タクシー免許 taxi license
諾成契約 consensual contract；contract entered into by mutual consent
宅地開発税 land development tax
宅地造成費 development cost of residential site
宅地の評価 valuation of residential site
蓄　　え nest egg
多桁式計算書 artificial statement
多桁式現金出納帳 tabular cash book
多元相関 multiple correlation
多元的証拠 multiple evidence
他行預け placement with other banks
他行預け金 deposit with other bank
他行からの預金 deposits from other banks
他行引受 bill of others
多国間開発銀行 MDB (multilateral development bank)
多国間協定 multilateral agreement
多国間交渉 multilateral initiative
多国間投資保証機関 MIGA (Multilateral Investment Guarantee Agency)
多国間保険共同受託 multi-national insurance pooling
多国籍企業 MNE (multinational enterprise)
多国籍銀行 multinational bank
多国籍グループ multi-national group
タ コ 配 bogus dividend
タコ配当 fictitious dividend
タジギスタン・ルーブル TJR (Tajiku ruble)
多事業主制度 multi-employer plan
多事業主福祉制度 multi-employer welfare agreement
出し手レート offered rate
他社株償還条項付社債 exchangeable bond
他社株転換社債 EB (exchangeable bond)
他社清算参加者 Agency Clearing Participant
他社清算資格 Agency Clearing Qualification
多重回帰 multiple regression
多重回帰分析 multiple regression analysis
多重回帰モデル multiple regression model
多重債務 card-holic
多種目販売会社 multi-line company
太政官札 Dajokan satsu
他所払小切手 out town check
他所払手形 out town bill
他所渡り out town delivery
多 数 決 majority decision
多数国間投資保証機関 Multilateral Investment Guarantee Agency
多数国同時開示システム MJDS (multi-jurisdictional disclosure system)
多世帯住宅 multi-family house
多大なコミットメント significant commitment
但　　書 proviso
但書条項 provisory clause
多段階式 multiple-step form
立　　会 attendance；trading session
立 会 外 off-trading session
立会外対当取引 off-auction cross transaction
立会外取引 after hour trading；off-auction trading；trading outside the floor
立会外売買取引 off-hours trading
立会外分売 off-auction distribution；off-floor distribution
立会外分売取扱正会員 regular member handling off-floor distribution
立会外分売取扱料 fees for off-floor distribution
立会外分売引受料 fee for undertaking

タ

off-auction distribution
立会外ベーシス取引 off-auction basis transaction
立 会 時 trading hour
立会時間 market hours；session period
立会終了時の約定値段 closing contract price
立会場会員 floor member
立会場事務合理化システム Floor Order Routing and Execution System
立会場伝票 floor ticket
立会場取引 floor trading
立会場銘柄 floor issue
立会代表者 floor representative
立会停止 suspension of transactions
立会内売買取引 on-hours trading
立会日数 trading days
立会場従業員 floor middleman
立会場で取引できる会員 physical access member
立会場ブローカー FB (floor broker)
立入検査権 authority to conduct on-site inspections
立退費用の補償 compensation for moving expenses
立退命令 eviction order
多通貨会計 multiple currency accounting
多通貨条項 multi-currency clause
脱銀行化 debanking
タックス・アブソープション tax absorption
タックス・シェルター tax shelter
タックス・スワップ tax swap
タックス・パラダイス tax paradise
タックス・フレーション taxflation
タックス・ヘブン tax haven
タックス・ホリディ tax holiday
タックス・リース tax lease
タックス・リゾート tax resort
脱工業化 deindustrialization
脱工業化社会 post industrial society
達成時期 milestone date
達成目標 bogey
脱　　税 tax dodging；tax evasion
脱 税 者 tax dodger；tax evader
脱税取引 sham
脱税の従犯 accessory to tax evasion
脱 税 犯 criminal of tax evasion
脱　　退 contracting out；transferring out；withdrawal of membership
脱退会員 withdrawing member
脱退給付金 withdrawal credit
脱退申請 application for withdrawal
脱退リベート contracting out rebate
ダッチ・オークション Dutch auction
ダッチ・オークション・レート優先株 DARPS (dutch auction rate preferred stock)
ダッチ・ギルダー債 Dutch guilder bond
ダッチ方式 Dutch auction method；single price auction
タップ債 bond on tap；tap stock
タップス taps
タップ発行 tap issue
タップ・ビル tap bills
脱　　漏 omission
立 替 金 advance money；receivables from customers
立替経費 reimbursed expenses
立替払い charges forward
建替需要 rebuilding demand
建　　玉 open contract；open position
建玉残高 open interest
建玉の移管 transfer of positions
建玉の調整 adjustment of open positions
縦　　軸 x-axis
建　　値 price quotation
建　　物 plants and buildings
建物減価償却 depreciation of building
建物再評価 revaluation of building
建物の生産的使用への変更 conversion of a building for productive use
建物用敷地 building lot
堕 天 使 fallen angel
妥当な基礎 adequate basis
妥当な取引レンジ acceptable trading range
棚　　卸 inventory control；inventory taking；physical verification
棚卸資産 inventory；inventory assets

棚卸資産売上率 sales to inventories
棚卸資産会計 accounting for inventories
棚卸資産回転期間 average age of inventory
棚卸資産回転日数 number of days' sales in inventories
棚卸資産回転率 inventory turnover
棚卸資産価格変動勘定 inventory fluctuation account
棚卸資産監査 inventory audit
棚卸資産勘定 inventory accounts
棚卸資産計算法 inventory method
棚卸資産正味運転資本比率 ratio of inventory to net working capital
棚卸資産税額控除 inventory relief
棚卸資産増減 inventory variation
棚卸資産担保貸付 inventory lending
棚卸資産陳腐化 obsolescence of inventory
棚卸資産陳腐化引当金 allowance for obsolete inventory
棚卸資産に適用する資産基準 property basis applicable to inventories
棚卸資産の価格の低落 decline in prices of inventories
棚卸資産の減損 impairment of inventories
棚卸資産の構成 composition of inventory
棚卸資産の時価 market value of inventory
棚卸資産の取得価額 acquisition cost of inventory
棚卸資産の取得原価 cost of inventory
棚卸資産の測定 measurement of inventories
棚卸資産の陳腐化 inventory obsolescence
棚卸資産の取崩し liquidation of inventory
棚卸資産の評価 valuation of inventory
棚卸資産の評価減 inventory write-down
棚卸資産の評価方法 cost flow assumption ; inventory valuation method
棚卸資産の保管 storage of inventories
棚卸資産評価引当金 inventory valuation-reserves
棚卸資産プール inventory pool
棚卸資産保有日数 days to sell inventory
棚卸資産利益 inventory profit
棚卸商品 merchandise inventory
棚卸証明書 inventory certificate
棚卸数量 inventory quantities
棚 卸 損 inventory loss
棚卸単位 inventory unit
棚卸日現在の使用価格 purchase price prevailing at the date of (pyshical) inventory taking
棚 卸 票 inventory tag
棚 卸 表 inventory sheet
棚卸評価額 inventory value
棚 卸 品 clearance goods ; stock in the inventory
棚ぼた利益 windfall profit
他人資本 borrowed capital ; debt capital
他人資本回転率 turnover ratio of total liabilities
他人資本への影響額 effect of borrowing
他の口座への振替 transfer to other account
他ファンド連動型の linked to the performance of other funds
たばこ消費税 tobacco consumption tax
だぶつき overhang
タフト・ハートレー法 Taft-Hartley Act
多部門分析 multi-sectoral analysis
WTI WTI (West Texas Intermediate)
ダブル・アップ double-up
ダブル・オプション double option
ダブル・クロスオーバー double crossover
ダブル・トップ double top
ダブル・レバレッジ double leverage
多変量解析 multivariate analysis
他保険条項 other insurance clause
ダミー会社 dummy company
ダミー勘定 dummy account
為決時点（17時） designated settlement time of 17:00
為　　券 tame ken
試す展開 testing times
多目的財務諸表 all-purpose financial statements
保合い相場 quiet market

タ

保合いパターン continuation pattern
多様化した銀行業務モデル diversified banking business models
多様性と複雑性 diversity and complexity
多様な資産 diverse assets
たらい廻し（売掛金の） lapping
多欄形式 columnar format
ダ　ン done
単　位 unit
単位価額 unit value
単 位 型 unit type
単位型債券投資信託 bond unit trust
単位型地方債投資信託 municipal bond unit investment trust
単位型投資信託 UIT (unit investment trust)
単位型投信 unit type investment trust
単 位 株 even lot；shares making up one trading unit；unit shares
単位株式 round lot
単位原価 unit cost
単位購入方式 unit purchase plan
単位算出経過利子 accrued interest computed on a unit-of-trading basis
単位積増し unit credit
単位積増費用 unit credit cost
単位出来高 unit of output
単位年金 unit annuity
単位年金購入方式 unit benefit plan
単位年金積増方式 unit credit method
単位補助金 unit grant
単位未満株 fractional share
単一欧州議定書 Single European Act
単一価格 uniform price
単一価格入札 common price auction
単一加重平均割引率 single weighted average discount rate
単一株式 share of one kind
単一為替市場制 monorate of exchange system
単一為替相場制 unitary exchange rate system
単一為替レート single exchange rate
単一銀行制度 unit banking system
単一銀行免許 single banking license
単一銀行持株会社 one bank holding company
単一区分計算書 single-step statement
単一区分損益計算書 single step income statement
単一計算方式 single statement approach
単一系統の方式 single group of methods
単一顧客分離勘定 single customer separate account
単一財務報告 single financial report
単一事業主型給付建年金制度 single employer defined benefit pension plan
単一事業主制度 single employer plan
単一資産会社 SAPCO (single asset property company)
単一指標モデル single index model
単 一 税 single tax
単一税率 single tariff
単一税率制 simple tariff system
単一通貨 single currency
単一手形 sola bill
単一取引 single transaction
単一の処理 single treatment
単一の貸借対照表 single balance sheet
単一の投資 single investment
単一評価 single valuation
単一表示項目 single line item
単一満期債 term bonds
単一満期預金 single maturity deposit
単一銘柄 single name
単一銘柄オプション single name option
単一目的カード monopurpose credit card
単一要因 one factor
単一要因モデル one factor model
単一利回り uniform yield
単 因 子 one factor
単　価 unit price
単価契約 unit-price contract
単価積算法 unit pricing
単会計制度 single accounting system
段階給付 graded benefit
段階式原価 stepped cost
段階的な建設 phased construction
段階的売却 piecemeal sale

段階的廃止期間 phase-out period
段階的平価変動制 crawling peg system
段階的利付債 stepped coupon bond
段階的料率 tiered rating
段階方式 step-up method
段階料率 step rate
短　　観 Tankan
短　　期 short period；short-term
短期運用 investment in short-term products
短期格付け short-term debt rating
短期貸付 short-term lending
短期貸付金 short-term loans
短期借り borrowing short
短期借入金 money borrowed for short-term；short-term borrowing
短期借入有価証券 short-term securities borrowed
短期供給曲線 short run supply curve
短期均衡 short run equilibrium
短期金融 short-term finance
短期金融勘定 money market account
短期金融市場 money market；short-term credit market
短期金融市場指数 money market index
短期金融市場操作 money market operations
短期金融市場預金勘定 money market deposit account
短期金融商品 money market instrument
短期金融商品ファンド money market fund
短期金利 money market rate；short-term interest rate
短期金利引上げ tightening of short rate
短期国債売現先オペ sales of TBs (treasury bills) /FBs (financing bills) under repurchase agreements
短期国債買入オペ outright purchases of TBs (treasury bills)/FBs (financing bills)
短期国債買現先オペ purchases of TBs (treasury bills) /FBs (financing bills) under repurchase agreements
短期国債市場 short-term government bond market
短期国債売却オペ outright sales of TBs (treasury bills) /FBs (financing bills)
短 期 債 short end；short-dated bonds；short-term bond
短期債ファンド short-term bond fund
短期債務 unfunded debt
短期差入保証金 short-term margin
短期事業活動 short-term operation
短期資金 short-term fund
短期資金繰りの調整 short-term funding requirements
短期資金調達費用 cost of short-term funds
短期資金レート short-term facility rate
短期志向 short-term oriented
短期資産 short term asset
短期市場金利連動債 exchangeable variable note
短期支払能力 short-term solvency
短期資本 short-term capital
短期資本収支 short-term capital balance
短期資本取引 short-term capital transaction
短期従業員給付 short-term employee benefit
短期償還期日 short maturity
短期証券 short-term instrument；short-term securities
短期証券投資信託 money market mutual funds
短期譲渡所得 short-term capital gain
短期スワップ short-term swap
短期的傾向 short-term trending
短期的な相場反転 near-term reversal
短期的な利食い short-term profit taking
短期的リンク short-term link
短期投資 current asset investment；short-term investment
短期投資勘定 short-term investment account
短期投資利益 return on short-term investment
短期取引 short-term transaction
短期NIF SNIF (short-term note issuance facility)

タ

短期の通知 short notice
短期の投資収益 short-term returns
短期の変動 short-term fluctuations
短期売買益 short swing profits
短期売買の short-term trading
短期売買目的金融資産 financial asset held for trading
短期払い payment in a short time
短期費用 short-period cost
短期負債 quick liabilities；short-term debt；short-term liabilities
短期プライムレート short-term prime rate
短期保有資産売却損益 short-term gain or loss
短期保有目的 short tenure horizon
短期見通し near-term outlook；short-term outlook
短 期 物 front end of market bonds；shorter on the curve
短期利益投資家 stag
短期利回り short-term yield
短期流動性要因 short-term liquidity factor
単　　元 basic lot
単項演算 monadic operation
談合競買 knock out
堪航能力欠如 unseaworthy
堪航能力のある seaworthy
タンザニア・シリング TZS (Tanzanian shilling)
第三者賠償責任保険 third party liability insurance
短資会社 call loan dealer；money market dealer；tanshi company
単　　式 single expression
単式記入 single entry
単式簿記 simple accounting；single entry bookkeeping
短資協会 Association of Call Loan and Discount Companies
短資業者 money market broker；short-term money house
短資市場 call loan market；call money market
短資取引担保センター Collateral Center for Short-Term Money Market Transactions
短　　縮 cutback
短縮可能満期 retractable maturity
単純移動平均 simple moving average
単純回帰モデル simple regression model
単純海損 simple average
単純仮説 simple hypothesis
単純契約 simple contract；unconditional contract
単純個人退職勘定 simple IRA (individual retirement account)
単純再生産 simple reproduction
単純裁定 simple arbitrage
単純債務 simple obligation
単純作業 routine tasks
単純算術平均指数 simple arithmetic average index
単純指数 simple index
単純自白 simple confession
単純ジャンプ・モデル simple jump model
単純準備法 simple reserve method
単純乗数 simple multiplier
単純仕訳帳 simple journal
単純信託 simple trust
単純総合原価計算 simple cost accounting
単純総和 simple aggregate
単純な方式 vanilla structure
単純売買 outright buying and selling
単純破産 straight bankruptcy
単純不動産 fee simple
単純平均 arithmetic average；simple average
単純平均株価 arithmetic stock price average；simple average stock price
単純平均値 simple mean value
単純平均法 simple average cost method；straight average cost method
単純平均利回り arithmetic dividend yield average；simple average yield
単純暴行 simple assault
単純保証 simple guarantee
単純保証人 simple guarantor；simple suretyship
単純モーゲージ条項 open mortgage

clause
単純予測 simple prediction
単純利益率 simple rate of return
男女共同参画担当大臣 Minister of State for Gender Equality
男女同一原則 unisex principle
淡水濡れ fresh water damage
単数保険者 specialist insurer
担 税 者 tax bearer
担税能力説 ability theory of taxation
担 税 力 tax bearing capacity ; tax paying capacity
単生年金 single life annuity
弾性のない inelastic
断続労働 intermittent work
団体扱契約 wholesale group insurance
団体医療保険 corporate health insurance
団体介護保険 group care insurance
団体協約 collective bargaining agreement
団体健康保険 group health insurance
団体交渉 collective bargaining
団体交渉権 right of collective bargaining
団体個人年金 group personal pension
団体傷害保険 group accident insurance
団体職員 corporation personnel
団体信用生命保険 group credit life insurance ; group life insurance for credit
団体信用生命保険組合 group credit insurance association
団体据置年金 deferred group annuity
団体据置年金契約 group deferred annuity contract
団体生命保険 group life insurance
団体長期保険契約 group permanent insurance contract
団体定期保険 group term insurance
団体提供保険 association insurance
団体年金 collective pension ; group annuity ; group pension
団体年金投資契約 group annuity pension investment contract
団体年金保険 group annuity insurance
団体変額保険 group variable annuity
団体保険 group insurance
団体保険型年金 group insurance annuity
団体保険査定 group underwriting
団体保険証券 group policy
団体保険料 group premium
団体保障 group coverage
団体モーゲージ補償生命保険 group mortgage insurance
団体ユニバーサル保険 GULP (group universal life policy)
団体養老保険 group endowment insurance
団体預託管理契約 group deposit administration contract
団体割引保険料 group discounted premium
単体自己資本比率 non-consolidated capital adequacy ratio
団地保険 apartment dwellers' comprehensive insurance
タンデム通貨 tandem currencies
担当審議官 Deputy Director-General
単独海損 PA (particular average)
単独海損担保 WA (with average)
単独財務諸表 separate financial statements
単独ベース parent base
単独ベースの売上 parent sales
単独ベースの収益見通し parent-basis earning outlook
単独保険商品 independent policy
単独保有 entire tenancy
段取原価 pre-production cost
段取時間 make-ready time ; setup time
単なるショート outright short
単なる投資対象 stand alone investment
単なる名義人 merely nominal persons
単なるロング outright long
単 年 度 single business year
ダンピング dumping
ダンピング提訴 dumping petition
短文式監査報告書 short form audit report
ダンベル・ポートフォリオ dumbbell portfolio
担　　保 collateral ; security
担保預り金 security deposits

担保解除 release of security
担保掛目 assessment rate of collateral
担保貸し loan on security ; secured loan
担保貸付 collateral loan
担保価値 collateral value
担保可能証券 potential collateral
担 保 株 collateral shares
担保勘定 assigned account ; security account
担保管理 collateral management
担保管理システム collateral monitoring system
担保危険 insured risk ; risk covered
担保給付 insured benefit
担保金利率 interest rate on cash collateral
担 保 権 security interest ; security right
担保権行使資産 foreclosed assets
担保権行使による売却 foreclosure sale
担保権行使不動産 property in possession
担保権執行 foreclosure
担保権者 secured party
担保権の行使 exercise of security right
担保権の設定 establishing security interest
担保権のつかない資産 unencumbered assets
担保権を行使する foreclose
担保債権 pledged accounts
担保再設定 repledging
担保差入れ hypothecation ; pledging
担保差入株式総額 omnium
担保差入資産 assets pledged as security ; assets subject to lien
担保差入証 letter of confirmation of collateral
担保差入証券 securities given as collateral
担保差入同意書 hypothecation agreement
担保差入部分 loaned securities liabilities
担保差入有価証券 pledged securities as collateral ; securities deposited as collateral
担保資産 backing assets ; hypothecated assets ; pledged assets
担保資産の予想購入額 collateral accumulation projection
担保証券 collateral security
担保譲渡 collateral assignment
担保制限条項 negative pledge clause
担保付貸出 secured credit
担保付貸付 secured advance
担保付貸付金 mortgages receivable
担保付借入 borrowing with collateral
担保付金利 collateral rate
担保付固定資産の譲渡 transfer of fixed assets given in pledge
担保付債券 secured debenture
担保付債務 secured debt
担保付社債券 mortgage debentures
担保付社債信託 mortgage debentures in trust
担保付社債信託法 mortgage debentures trust law
担保付証券 secured securities
担保付信託債券 collateral trust bond
担保付投資信託 mortgage investment trust
担保付取引 secured transactions
担保付引受け acceptance on security
担保付負債 secured liabilities
担保付約束手形 collateral note ; secured note
担保付リース債権債 SLOB (secured lease obligation bond)
担保付ローン collateralized loan
担保提供額 assigned amount
担保適格融資 conforming loan
担保として提供されている資産 assets pledged as a security
担保と保証 collateral and guarantee
担保による銀行借入 bank loan secured by mortgage
担保の最適化 collateral optimization
担保の処分可能見込額 amounts expected to by settled by means of collateral
担保の処分見込額 anticipated proceeds from the collateral
担保の提出 submission of collateral
担保の適切性 adequacy of collateral
担保の取決め collateral arrangement

担保の評価額 appraised value of collateral
担保範囲 coverage by security
担保物件 underlying collateral
担保補償商品 collateral protection product
担保保留条項 negative clause
担保マネージャー collateral manager
担保目録 inventory of items pledged as security
担保有価証券 securities received as collateral
担保優先順位 security priority ranking
担保預金 deposit as collateral
担保余力 net worth of collateral
単本位制度 monometallic standard
単　　名 single name
単名手形 one name paper ; single name paper
単　　利 simple interest
単利ベース on a simple interest basis
単 利 法 method of simple interest
単利マージン simple margin
単利利回り yield by simple interest
単利割引 simple discount
弾力関税 elastic tariff
弾力条項 elasticity clause
弾力性アプローチ elasticity approach
弾力性オプティミズム elasticity optimism
弾力性ペシミズム elasticity pessimism
弾力的需要 elastic demand
弾力費用 flexible expense
弾力予算 flexible budget

チ

地域開発 regional development
地域格差の是正 reduction of regional disparities
地域活性化 simulation of regional vitality
地域カルテル regional cartel
地域間振替 transfers between geographic areas
地域協力課 Regional Financial Cooperation Division
地域金融市場 regional financial markets
地域経済 local economies；regional economy
地域経済学 regional economics
地域国際化 regional internationalization
地域社会基盤 regional social infrastructure
地域社会資本 regional social capital
地域主義 regionalism
地域政策 regional policy
地域調整 public involvement
地域内貿易 intraregional trade
地域フランチャイズ area franchise
地域別管理 geographic control
地域別検査 zone examination
地域別セグメント geographical segment
地 域 法 local law
地域連関分析 interregional analysis
地域連携 regional tie-up
小さな欠陥 glitch
小さな利益 modest profit
地位濫用の abusive
チェーン・バンキング chain banking
地 役 権 easement；servitude
地役権者 easement holder；servitude holder
地役権の設定 settlement of easement
チェコ・コルナ CZK (Czech Republic koruna)
チェスティテイ債 chastity bond
チェック・ギャランティ・カード check guarantee card
チェック・ライター check writer
遅延クレーム delay claims
遅延損害金 delinquent charge；late charge；late fee；late payment charge；penalty charge
遅延認識 deferred recognition
遅延利息 delayed interest；interest for arrears
地 価 land price
地価公示制度 government appraisal of land price
地 価 税 land value tax
地価税法 Land Value Tax Law
治外法権 extraterritoriality
地下経済 underground economy
地下条件クレーム adverse physical conditions claims
力強い回復 strong rebound
力強い内需 robust domestic demand
力強い変化 vigorous change
地球環境問題 global environmental problems
地 金 銀 gold and silver bullion
地銀バンクカード regional bank card
チキン・マーケット chicken market
地区外務員 home service agent
地区連銀報告書 beige book
逐次処理 sequential processing
逐次取引 sequential trading
蓄積資本 accumulated capital
蓄積利率 accumulative rate
チケット販売金融 ticket sale finance
遅行系列 lagging series
遅行指数 lag indicator
知識工学 knowledge engineering
知識産業 knowledge industry
知識集約産業 knowledge intensive industry
知識の開発 development of knowledge

地上権 domain of use；superficies；surface right
地上権者 superficiary
地上権設定 settlement of superficies
地政学的リスク geopolitical risk；geopolitical uncertainty
地積 acreage
地租 land tax
地租委譲 transfer of land tax
地租付加税 surtax on land tax
地代表 rent roll
地代負担 rent charge
秩序ある金融システム orderly financial system
秩序ある輸出 orderly export marketing
CHIPS Clearing House Inter-Bank Payment System
知的財産専門官 Director for Intellectual Property Rights
知的所有権 intellectual property right
知的所有権担保融資 loan secured by intellectual property rights
知的所有権担保ローン intellectual property backed loan
チベット自治区 Xizang
地方課 Division Controlling Local Finance Bureaus
地方業者 regionals
地方銀行 local bank；regional bank
地方銀行協会加盟行 member banks of the Regional Banks Association of Japan (regional banks)
地方公共財 local public goods
地方公共事業体 MUD (municipal utility district)
地方公共団体 municipal corporation
地方公共団体債券ファンド municipal bond fund
地方公共団体の債務の調整 adjustment of the debts of a municipality
地方交付金 central government transfers to local governments
地方交付税 local allocation taxes；local grant tax
地方交付税交付金 distribution of local allocation tax
地方債 LAB (local authority bond)；local government bond；municipal bond；prefectural bond
地方債公募 public offering municipal bond
地方債先物 municipal futures
地方債証券 municipal securities
地方債信用保険 municipal bond insurance
地方債投資信託 MIT (municipal investment trust)
地方債とTBの利回り格差 MOB (municipal over bond) spread
地方債利息 municipal bond interest
地方財政 local public finance
地方財政計画 local public finance plan
地方財政法 Local Public Finance Law
地方自治 local autonomy
地方自治体 local authorities；local government；local public entity
地方支分部局 Local Branch Offices
地方事務所 regional office
地方証券取引所 local stock exchange；regional stock exchange
地方消費税 local consumption tax
地方譲与税 local transfer tax
地方条例 municipal ordinances
地方税 local tax
地方税納付 local tax payment
地方税の延滞金 arrears of local tax
地方政府機関発行債 project bond；project note
地方税法 Local Tax Law
地方税率 local tax rate
地方道路税 local road tax
地方特定財源債 municipal revenue bond
地方取引所 regional exchange
地方配布税 local distribution tax
地方費 local expenditure
地方分権 decentralization of power
地方分与税 partial tax transfer to local government
知名度 rate of awareness
地目 class of land；land category
地目変換届 registration of change of land

category
チャージ・アカウント charge account
チャージ・バック charge back
チャーター・パーティB/L charter party B/L
チャーター料 charter fee
チャーティスト chartist
チャート chart
チャート・パターン chart pattern
チャイニーズ・ウォール Chinese wall
着実な伸び steady rise
着船渡し EXS (ex ship)
着地取引 Chakuchi transactions ; transaction with delayed settlement
着　荷 arrival of shipment
着払い運送費 freight collect
着工戸数全体 total starts
CHAPS CHAPS (Clearing House Automated Payment System)
チャド（CFAフラン） Chad (CFA (Communauté Financière Africaine) franc)
チャンネル・ライン channel line
注　意 care ; diligence ; prudence
注意喚起 nudge
注意義務 duty of care
中位数 median
中位の額の契約 medium policy
中央アフリカ共和国（CFAフラン） Central African Republic (CFA (Communauté Financière Africaine) franc)
中央銀行 central bank
中央銀行券 central bank note
中央銀行再割引 rediscounting with the central bank
中央銀行による政府与信の禁止 prohibition against the Bank extending loans to the government
中央銀行の市場介入 central bank intervention
中央銀行の中立姿勢 neutral central bank activities
中央銀行のドル買い central bank buying of USDs
中央銀行への預け金 deposit with the central bank
中央銀行マネー central bank money
中央銀行割引歩合 central bank discount rate
中央決済口座 central payment account
中央市場 central market
中央照合システム central comparison system
中央省庁 central ministries
中央政府 central government
中央値 median
中央積立基金 CPF (Central Provident Fund)
中央の清算機関 central counterparty
仲　介 mediation
仲介機関 intermediary agents
仲介規程 mediation regulations
仲介業者 finder
仲介業務 broking business
仲介銀行 intermediary bank
仲介者 intermediary
仲介代理人 middleman
仲介手数料 intermediation fee
仲介料 finder's fee
中価格品 mid-range product
中　核 core
中核事業 core business
中核資本 core capital
中核的保有 core holding
中型株 medium-sized stock ; mid cap ; middle capitalization stock
中間売上 interim sales
中間営業活動 interim operations
中間監査 semi-annual audit
中間監査概要書 semiannual summary audit report
中間監査日 interim examination date
中間監査報告書 semi-annual audit report
中間勘定 interim account
中間管理職 middle management
中間期間 interim period
中間期決算 six month closing of accounts
中間技術 middle range technology
中間業者 intermediate party

中間計算書 interim statement
中間決算 interim closing ; interim results ; semi-annual closing of accounts ; semi-annual results ; six months closing of accounts
中 間 財 intermediate goods
中間財務情報 interim financial information
中間財務諸表 interim financial statements
中間財務報告 interim financial reporting
中間財務報告書 interim financial report
中間支払額 progress payments and advances
中間申告 interim tax return
中間申告書 interim return form
中間数値 interim figure
中間請求 progress bidding
中間税引前利益 interim period pre-tax income
中間製品 intermediate product
中間税率 intermediate tariff
中間段階 intermediate stage
中 間 値 intermediate value
中間的金融商品 intermediate vehicles
中 間 点 mid-point
中間配当 interim dividend
中間発行 issue at an intermediate price
中間払利息 interim interest payment
中 間 日 interim date
中間報告 interim report
中間戻し secondary rally
中間ラグ intermediate lag
中期ギルト債 medium gilt
中期金融資産 medium-term financial assets
中期国債 5-year Japanese government bond
中期国債先物取引 5-year government bond futures
中期国債標準物 standardized mid-term government bonds
中期国債ファンド medium-term government securities funds
中 期 債 medium-term bond
中期債入札 medium note auctions
中期資金の調達 medium-term funding
中期証券 medium-term securities ; note
中期政策方針 medium-term policy principle
中期的な安定期 interim plateau
中期的な下落 medium-term decline
中期展望 medium-term outlook
中期トランシェ medium-term tranche
中期目標 medium-term target
中 期 物 mid-maturities
中期ユーロ債 Euronote
中期予想 intermediate market outlook
中期ローン medium-term loan ; intermediate loan
註 記 explanatory note
注記事項 note description
注記文書 notes material
中級会計学 intermediate accounting
中銀当預 current accounts at the central bank
中継センター central hub
中 堅 株 middle-sized stock
中堅企業 middle-size company
中國銀行 BOC (Bank of China)
中 国 元 CNY (Chinese yuan)
中国人民銀行 People's Bank of China
中国人民保険公司 People's Insurance Company of China
中古資産 used property
中古資産の使用可能期間 usable period of used property
中古資産の見積耐用年数 estimated useful life of used property
中古住宅販売 sales of existing homes
仲 裁 arbitration
仲裁委員会 arbitration panel
仲裁裁定 arbitration award
仲裁条項 arbitration clause
仲裁手続 arbitration proceedings
仲 裁 人 arbitrator
仲裁人選定機関 appointing authority
駐 在 員 liaison
駐在員事務所 liaison office ; representative office
駐在監査人 resident auditor

中産階級 bourgeoisie
註　　釈 annotation
中小企業 small- and medium-sized enterprises
中小企業貸出信託 loan trust for small enterprises
中小企業近代化施策 small- and medium-sized enterprise modernization activities
中小企業金融機関 financial institutions for small business
中小企業金融機関勘定 principal accounts of financial institution for small-business
中小企業金融公庫 Japan Finance Corporation for Small and Medium Enterprise
中小企業構造改善準備金 reserve for improvement of structure of small- and medium-sized enterprise
中小企業庁 SME (Small and Medium Enterprise Agency)
中小企業動向調査 trend survey of small businesses
中小企業投資会社 SBIC (small business investment companies)
中小企業の近代化 modernization of smaller enterprise
中小企業用の機械 machinery acquired by small sized entrepreneur
中心傾向 central tendency
中心相場 central rate
中心レート central parity；central rate
抽　　選 drawing of number；lottery
抽選償還 redemption by drawing；redemption by lottery
抽選償還証券 securities called by lot
抽選償還当選債券 bonds called by lot
抽選償還特約 rider of redemption by the drawing of lots
抽選付き cum-drawing
鋳造価格 mint price
鋳造貨幣 mintage
中　　断 disruption
中断クレーム suspension of work claims
中長期協調融資 syndicated term loan
中長期債券 term bond
中長期ファイナンス term financing
中途解約 cancellation before maturity
中途切替契約 convertible contract
中途清算配当金 interim liquidating dividend
中途退職 severance of employment
中米機構 Organization of Central American States
中米共同市場 Central American Common Market
注 目 株 high flyer
注目銘柄 hot issue
注　　文 order
注文受付時間 order-taking hours
注文エントリー order entry
注文執行確認書 exchange ticket
注文伝票 order ticket
注文取次業者 introducing firm
注文の相対 order negotiation
注文の殺到 rush order
注文の執行 execution of order；filling of orders
注文の不均衡 order imbalance
注文の有効期間 effective period of order
注文控え order book
注文簿取引 order book trading
注文履行費 order-filling cost
中　　立 neutral reading
中立貨幣政策 neutral money principle
中立国船証明書 sea brief；sea letter
中 立 性 neutrality
中立的均衡 neutral equilibrium
中立的なエンジニア IE (independent engineer)
中立的な基準 neutral basis
チューリッヒの小鬼 gnomes of Zurich
駐留軍等労働者労務管理機構 Labor Management Organization for USFJ Employees, Incorporated Administrative Agency
治癒効果 curing effect
チュニジア・ディナール TND (Tunisian dinar)

弔 慰 金 condolence money
超一流銀行 prime name bank
超インフレ hyperinflation
超インフレ経済 hyperinflationary economy
懲戒処分 disciplinary action
懲戒免職 dishonorable discharge
超 過 額 excess amount
超過額再保険 excess reinsurance；surplus relief reinsurance
超過額特約再保険 surplus treaty reinsurance
超過額保険 excess insurance
超過掛金 excess contribution
超過給付 excess benefit
超過供給 excess supply
超過経費 excess expense
超過限度額 excess limit
超過差押え excessive seizure
超過資金 excess fund
超過支出 deficit spending
超過支払い excess payment；extra payment
超過収益力 excess earnings power；excess revenue generating power
超過需要 excess demand
超過償却 depreciation in excess of the limit
超過証拠金 excess margin
超過使用時間 over-used hours
超過所得 excess income
超過スプレッド excess spread
超過税率 tax rate higher than standard
超過損害額 excess of loss
超過損害額特約再保険 excess of loss treaty reinsurance
超過損害再保険 excess of loss reinsurance
超過損害保険 stop loss coverage
超過損失 extra loss
超過担保比率 TOL (total overcollateralization level)
超過積立税 excess accumulation tax
超過年金資産の回収 pension plan reversion
超過配賦 over-absorption
超過負担 excess burden
超過方式 excess method
超過保険 over insurance
超過利益 above-normal earnings
超過利潤 excess profit
超過利潤控除 excess profit credit
超過利潤性 excess profitability
超過利息 excess interest
超過リターン excess return
超過利得税 excess gain tax
超過利回り excess yield
超過累進制 progressive reserve ratios
長 官 commissioner
長官官房 Commissioner's Secretariat
長 期 long-run；long-term
長期請負 long-term contract work
長期請負工事 long-term contract
長期買い long-term buying
長期外貨建債権 long-term accounts receivable in foreign currency
長期外貨建債務 long-term accounts payable in foreign currency
長期介護保険 long-care coverage
長期貸付金 long-term loan；long-term loan receivable
長期化するデフレ continuing deflation
長期株式期待証券 LEAPS (long-term equity anticipation securities)
長期借入からの資金増 proceeds from long-term debt
長期借入金 long-term borrowing；long-term loan payable
長期借入返済額 reductions in long-term debt
長期為替 LTFX (long-term foreign exchange)
長期為替予約 long-term forward exchange agreement
長期供給曲線 long-run supply curve
長期均衡 long-run equilibrium
長期勤続休暇給付 long-service leave benefit
長期金融 long-term finance
長期金融市場 long-term credit market；

long-term money market
長期金融商品への投資 investment in long-term financial instruments
長期金利 long-term interest rate
長期金利の急上昇 upsurge in long-term interest rates
長期計画 long-term planning
長期下落トレンド long-term downward trend
長期現物期間 long cash period
長期工事引渡し delivery of long-term contract work
長期国債 long-term government bond
長期国債先物取引 10 year government bond futures
長期国債標準物 standardized long-term government bonds
長期国債流通利回り yields on long-term bonds
長　期　債 long-dated issue；long-term bond；long-term securities；longer dated bonds
長期債借換予定証券 BAN (bond anticipation note)
長期債への借換え senior refunding
長期債務 funded debt；long-term debt；long-term liabilities；non-current liabilities
長期債務増加 long-term debt assumed
長期債務の増加 increase in long-term debt
長期債務比率 long-term debt ratio
長期債利息 interest on funded debt
長期先渡取引 long-dated forwards
長期事業 long-term business
長期事業活動 long-term operation
長期資金 long-term fund
長期資金調達 long-term financing
長期資産 long-lived assets；long-term assets
長期資産運用 term asset management
長期実質金利 long-dated real rate
長期実質利回り long-term real yield
長期支払能力 long-term solvency
長期資本 long-term capital
長期資本収支 long-term capital balance
長期資本取引 long-term capital transaction
長期資本利益率 rate of return on long-term liabilities plus equity capital
長期社債 bond with a long maturity；loan stock
長期従業員給付 long-term employee benefit
長期従業員給付債務 long-term employee benefit obligation
長期障害給付 long-term disability benefit
長期譲渡所得 long-term capital gains
長期所得 long-term income
長期信用 long-term credit
長期信用銀行 long-term credit bank
長期信用金融機関 financial institutions for long-term credit
長期戦略 long-term direction
長期総合保険 long-term comprehensive insurance
長期損失 long-term loss
長期棚上債権 long-term suspended claims
長期賃貸契約預り金 deposits on long-term leases
長期賃貸借契約 long-term lease
長期低下 secular decline
長期手形 long-dated bill；long-term bill
長期的経済成長率 long-term economic growth rate
長期的財務業績 long-term financial performance
長期的貯蓄ニーズ long-term savings needs
長期的な強気 longer bullish stance
長期的リンク long-term link
長期デュレーション証券 long duration securities
長期投資 long-term investment
長期投資の処分 disposal of long-term investment
長期トレンド long-run trend
長期トレンド水準 long-run trend rate

長期の運用成績 long-term performance
長期波動 long waves
長期不況下 undergoing prolonged recession
長期負債キャッシュフロー率 cash flow ratio to long-term liabilities
長期負債自己資本比率 equity capital ratio to long-term liabilities
長期負債自己資本率 equity capital ratio to long-term capital
長期負債正味固定資産 net tangible asset ratio to long-term debt
長期負債の今期返済額 current maturities of long-term debt
長期負債の当期返済額 current maturity of long-term debt
長期プライムレート long-term prime rate
長期平均 long run average
長期米国財務省証券 long treasury bond
長期変動要因 secular
長期報奨制度 LTIP (long-term incentive plan)
長期保有 buy and hold
長期保有戦略 long-term buy and hold strategy
長期保有の資産 long-term investment property
長期前払税金 accumulated income tax prepayment
長期前払家賃 long-term prepaid rent
長期目標 long-term goal
長期利得 long-term gain
長期利回り long-term yield
長短利回格差平坦化 flattening of yield curve
長期利率 long-term rate
兆　　候 indication；signs
超国籍企業 transnational corporation
調 査 課 Examination Division；Research Division
調査企画官 Director for Research and Planning
調査研究 research study
調査研究室 Research and Development Office
調査査察部 Examination and Criminal Investigation Department
調査査察部部長 Assistant Commissioner (Examination and Criminal Investigation)
調 査 室 Research Office
調査資料 materials for investigation
調査段階 research phase
調査データ survey data
調査統計官 Special Officer for Research and Statistics
調査統計局 Research and Statistics Department
調 査 費 research expenditure
調査保税課 Post-Entry Examination and Customs Area Division
調査を重ねた分析 informed analysis
徴 収 課 Collection Division
徴 収 額 collected amount
徴収額計算書 accounting sheet of collected amount
徴 収 権 power of collection
徴収権の消滅時効 statute of limitations on collection
徴収順位 precedence rule on tax collection
徴収措置 collection measure
徴収の嘱託 entrustment of collection
徴収の猶予 postponement of tax collection
徴収標準率 standard rate of charge
徴 収 部 Revenue Management and Collection Department
徴収部管理課 Revenue Management Division
徴収部部長 Assistant Commissioner (Revenue Management and Collection)
徴 収 率 rate of charge
徴 収 料 collection fee
帳尻決済 settlement of balance
調　　整 adjustment
調整圧力 adjustment pressure；downward pressure
調整インフレ adjustment inflation

調整可能固定相場 adjustable peg system
調整可能利付手形 adjustable rate notes
調整勘定 reconciliation account
調整基準 adjusted basis
調整局面 ongoing correction
調整金利抵当ローン adjustable rate mortgage loan
調整係数 adjustment factor
調整後ＥＰＳ増加率 adjusted EPS increase
調整項目 adjustment item；reconciliation item
調整後純利益 adjusted net income
調整後譲渡所得 adjusted capital gain
調整後総所得 AGI (adjusted gross income)
調整後中央銀行通貨ストック adjusted central bank money stock
調整後当期利益 ACE (adjusted current earnings)
調整後配当増加率 adjusted dividend increase
調整作業 rectification work
調 整 室 Co-ordination Office
調整証券 adjustment securities
調整剰余金 adjusted surplus
調整所得金額 adjusted income
調整済み adjusted
調整済インフレ adjusted inflation
調整済計画 coordinated plan
調整済項目 adjusted item
調整済一株当り利益 adjusted earnings per share
調整パターン consolidation pattern
調整保険料 adjusted premium
調整利率 adjustable rate
調整レンジ consolidation range
調　　製 compilation
徴　　税 tax collection
徴税機構 tax collection system
徴 税 権 taxing power
徴税コスト cost of tax collection
徴税上の便宜 convenience of tax collection
徴税の公平 equalization of tax collection
調達価格 acquisition cost price
調達金利 borrowing rate
調達コスト funding cost
調達コストの削減 reduced borrowing costs
調達資金 funds procured
調 達 費 procurement cost
調達費用 cost of borrowing
超短期債券ファンド ultra-short-term bond fund
超短期ファイナンス制度 VSTE (very short-term financing) facility
長短利回格差縮小 curve flattening
長中期金利 long- and medium-term interest rate
超 長 期 super long-run；super long-term
超長期国債 super-long-term government bond；ultra long-term national bond
超長期国債先物 20 year government bond futures
超長期国債標準物 standardized super long-term government bonds
調　　停 reconciliation
調停の申立 petition filed for arbitration
調定税額 tax amount settled
挑　　発 provocation
懲　　罰 discipline
懲罰委員会 disciplinary committee
懲罰的損害賠償 punitive damages
帳票管理 forms control
重複勘定 overlapping account
重複債務 overlapping debt
重複上場 dual listing
重複上場企業 multi-market listed company
重複保険 double insurance
長 プ ラ LTPR (long-term prime rate)
長文式監査報告書 detailed audit report；long-form audit report
長文式報告書 long-form report
帳　　簿 account book；shopkeepers' books
帳簿価格 book value
帳簿価額純額 net carrying amount

帳簿価額総額 total carrying amount
帳簿価額の回収 recovery of carrying amount
帳簿価額の調整 reconciliation of the carrying amount
帳簿価格の減少 decrease in book value
帳 簿 係 book-keeper
帳簿貨幣 book money
帳簿監査 book audit
帳簿記入 book entry；booking
帳簿原価 recorded cost
帳簿残高 book balance
帳簿準備金 book reserve
帳簿上の口座振替 transfer on books
帳簿書類の整理保存 maintenance of books and records
帳簿整理 adjustment of accounts
帳簿棚卸資産 book inventory
帳簿方式 account method
貯金金利 interest on savings deposit
直・先スプレッド spot-forward spread
直近の2限月取引 two nearest contract months
直接売りペーパー direct issue paper
直接援助 direct aid
直接介入 direct intervention
直接借方記入 direct debiting
直接為替裁定 direct exchange arbitrage
直接為替取引 direct currency transaction
直接金融 direct finance
直接金融型リース direct financing lease
直接経費 direct expense；direct overhead
直接原因 direct cause
直接減額 direct reduction
直接減額による取崩し dispositioning by direct write-down
直接原価計算 direct costing
直接攻撃 direct attack
直接行使 direct exercise
直接購入 direct purchase
直接国税 direct national tax
直接材料費 direct material cost
直接参加者 direct participant
直接参加方式 direct participation program
直接支払い direct payment
直接資本 direct capital
直接収益還元法 direct capitalization
直接償却 direct method of depreciation；direct write-off
直接証券 primary securities
直接証拠 direct evidence
直接処理 direct disposal
直 接 税 direct tax
直接清算会員 DCM (direct clearing member)
直接積算法 direct pricing
直接賃金 productive wages
直接的影響 direct consequence
直接的関連 direct association
直接テスト direct test
直接投資 direct investment；direct or equity investment
直接投資規制 foreign direct investment regulation
直接投資総額 aggregate amount of direct investment
直接登録システム DRS (direct registration system)
直接取引介入 DD (direct dealing) intervention
直接の控除 direct deduction
直接の認識 personal knowledge
直接の利害関係 direct interest
直接発行 direct issuance
直 接 費 direct cost
直接評価 direct valuation
直接表示 direct presentation
直接部門 direct department
直 接 法 direct method
直接貿易 direct trade
直接保険料 direct premium
直接募集契約 direct writing policy
直接預託 direct deposit
直接利回り current yield；direct yield；income yield
直接リンク direct link
直接労働 direct labor
直接労務費 direct labor cost

直前事業年度 immediately preceding business year
直前の約定値段 last sale price
直　　販 direct selling
著 作 権 copyright
著作権のある情報 proprietary information
著作権の使用料 royalty of the copyright
著作権の評価 valuation of copyright
貯蔵経費 storage costs
貯蔵原材料 materials in storage
貯 蔵 品 inventories of merchandise and supplies；stored goods
貯蔵品管理 storage management
貯蓄貸付組合 S&L (savings and loan association)
貯蓄型商品 savings plan
貯蓄型年金 cash value pension
貯蓄型保険 cash value insurance
貯 蓄 株 savings share
貯蓄勘定 savings account
貯蓄関数 saving function
貯蓄銀行 savings bank
貯蓄銀行生命保険 savings bank life insurance
貯蓄金融機関 thrift institution；thrifts
貯蓄金融機関監督局 Office of Thrift Supervision
貯蓄金融機関保険基金 SAIF (Savings Association Insurance Fund)
貯蓄金融業界 thrift industry
貯蓄債券 savings bond；savings debenture；savings note
貯蓄債券給与天引貯蓄プラン savings bond payroll savings plan
貯蓄収入 savings income
貯蓄手段 savings vehicle
貯蓄商品 savings product
貯蓄性向 propensity to save
貯蓄制度 thrift and savings plans
貯蓄動向調査 family saving survey
貯蓄・投資の所得決定論 savings-investment theory of income determination
貯蓄・投資の利子率決定論 savings-investment theory of interest-rate determination
貯蓄取扱機関 institution handling savings
貯蓄年金 savings annuity
貯蓄払戻し savings withdrawal
貯蓄プール savings pool
貯蓄部分 savings element
貯蓄保険 savings policy
貯蓄預金 savings deposit
貯 蓄 率 ratio of saving to disposable income；savings rate
直間比率 ratio of direct and indirect taxes
勅許会計士 chartered public accountant
勅許会計士協会 ICA (Institute of Chartered Accountants)
勅許会社 chartered company
勅 許 状 charter
直近売り last sale
直近原因 immediate cause
地理的立地 geographical location
チリ・ペソ CLP (Chilean peso)
治療費保険 physician's expense insurance
チルメル控除 Zillmer deduction
賃 上 げ wage increase
賃上交渉 wage negotiation
賃上要求 request for wage increase
賃 上 率 rate of wage increase
賃　　金 pay；salaries and wages
賃金インフレーション wage-push inflation
賃金外給付 non-wage benefit
賃金勘定 labor account
賃金給料 wage and salary
賃金給料支払簿 payroll register
賃金協定 wage contract
賃金控除 payroll deduction
賃金差異 wage variance
賃金指数 wage index
賃金下請代金支払保証証券 labor & material payment bond
賃金所得 wage income
賃金水準 wage level
賃 金 税 payroll tax
賃金生活者 wage-earner
賃金勢力説 power theory of wages

賃金体系 wage structure；wage system
賃金台帳 payroll book
賃金単位 wage unit
賃金統計 wage statistics
賃金凍結 pay-freeze；wage freeze
賃金のシーリング設定 wage ceiling
賃金物価ガイドライン wage-price guideline
賃金・物価統制 wage-price control
賃金元帳 wages ledger
賃借契約 sell-and-lease agreement
賃 借 権 right of lease
賃借権の評価 valuation of right of lease
賃借権利権 working interest
賃 借 地 leased land
賃借手数料 rental agents' commissions
賃 借 人 lessee；renter；tenant
賃借不動産 leasehold estate
賃借保険 leasehold insurance
陳 述 書 representation letter
賃　　貸 let
賃貸価額 rental value
賃 貸 業 rental service
賃貸契約 lease contract
賃貸契約の残存期間 remaining period of the lease
賃貸借保証 lease bond
賃貸収益 rental revenue
賃貸住宅の着工戸数 rental starts
賃 貸 人 lessor
賃貸の保証金 security deposit for rent
賃貸物件の改良 leasehold improvement
賃 貸 料 rental income
賃貸料及び使用料収入 rents and royalties
賃貸料収入 rent income；rents received
賃貸料なしの rent-free
陳 腐 化 obsolescence
陳腐化資産 obsolete assets；obsolete property
陳腐化資産の償却 depreciation of obsolete assets
陳腐化した obsolete
陳腐化償却資産 obsolescent depreciable property
陳腐化引当金 obsolescence reserve
沈　　没 sinking
沈　　黙 silence
沈黙による by silence
賃　　率 wage rate
賃率差異 labor rate variance
賃率標準 labor rate standard
賃　　料 ancient rent
賃料減額請求権 claim for reduced rent
賃料収益 rent revenue
賃料負担 rent coverage

ツ

追加開示 additional disclosure
追 加 型 open-end type
追加型証券投資信託 open-ended securities investment trusts
追加型投資信託 open investment trust
追加借入 additional debt
追加借入利子率 incremental borrowing rate of interest
追加記入 post entry
追加購入特典付株式 carrot equity
追加債券発行限度額基準 additional bond test
追加債務負担 incurrence of additional indebtedness
追加差入れ additional deposit
追加支払 pay-up
追加謝金 refresher
追加出資 additional capital increase ; additional investment
追加条件 kicker
追加証拠金 maintenance call ; margin call
追加上場 additional listing
追加情報 additional information
追加所得補償 supplemental security income
追加設定 additional establishment
追加設定型の open-end type
追加設定不可の closed end
追加的給付 additional benefits
追加的所得補償 SSI (supplemental security income)
追加的な開示 supplementary disclosure
追加手数料 additional commission
追加特別預金制度 supplementary special deposit scheme
追加任意拠出 additional voluntary contribution
追加年金費用 additional pension cost
追加年金負債 additional pension liability
追加の規定 additional requirement
追加発行 added float
追加発行を考える consider using taps
追加払込資本金 additional paid-in capital
追加費用 additional charge ; additional expenses ; extra cost
追加フィールド additional field
追加負担金 additional contribution
追加プレミアム extra premium
追加文書 addenda
追加報告書 additional report
追加保障 additional coverage
追加リース additional lease
追加利下げ further interest rate cut
追加割当オプション over-allotment option
追撃売り follow-up selling
追随投資 coat tail investment
追跡可能原価 traceable cost
追徴可能保険 assessable insurance
追徴処分 punishment on penalty tax
追 徴 税 penal tax
追補書類 supplementary document
追補目論見書 supplementary prospectus
ツイン・カード twin-card
通院患者 ambulatory patient
ツー・ウェイ・マーケット two way market
通　　貨 currency
通貨安定 monetary stability
通貨インフレ currency inflation
通貨オプション取引 currency options trading
通貨及び金融の調節 currency and monetary control
通貨及び金融の調節に関する報告書 Semiannual Report on Currency and Monetary Control
通貨及証券模造取締法 Law Concerning the Regulation of Counterfeit

Currency and Securities
通貨買い currency purchases
通貨改革 monetary reform
通貨価値 currency value
通貨価値下落 currency depreciation
通貨価値の低下 depreciation of currency value
通貨換算 currency translation
通貨監督官事務所 Office of the Comptroller of the Currency
通貨間取引 cross-currency trade
通貨管理 currency control；monetary control；monetary management
通貨管理目的 monetary control purpose
通貨危機 currency crisis；monetary crisis
通貨協定 monetary agreement
通貨切上げ currency upvaluation
通貨切下げ currency devaluation
通貨・金融政策 monetary and financial policy
通 貨 圏 currency area
通貨交換制限 currency exchange restriction
通貨先物 currency futures
通貨先物価格動向 currency futures price movement
通貨先物取引 currency futures trading
通貨主義 currency principle
通貨準備 monetary reserve
通貨条項 currency clause
通貨乗数 money multiplier
通貨商品 currency commodity
通貨浸透説の trickle down
通貨ストック money stock
通貨スワップ cross-currency swap
通貨スワップ債 currency swap bond
通貨制預金 transferable deposits
通貨性預金 currency deposit
通貨総供給高 total money supply
通貨体系 currency system
通貨代用国債 promissory notes issued by the Japanese government in lieu of subscription fees to international organizations
通 貨 高 currency strength
通貨単位 currency unit；monetary unit
通貨調整 currency adjustment；currency alignment
通貨デフレ currency deflation
通貨騰貴 currency appreciation
通貨当局 currency authority；monetary authority
通貨同盟 monetary union
通貨の機能 function of currency
通貨の総じての下落 general weakness of currency
通貨の単位及び貨幣の発行等に関する法律 Law Concerning the Unit of Currency and the Issuance of Coins
通貨バスケット currency basket；exchange rate basket
通貨発行益 seigniorage
通貨不安 monetary instability
通貨ブロック currency bloc；monetary bloc
通貨変動 currency fluctuation
通貨防衛 protecting the currency
通貨膨張 expansion of currency
通貨補償 currency indemnity
通貨流通高 currency in circulation
通　　過 passage
通過貿易 transit trade
通　　関 customs clearance
通関情報処理センター NACCS (Nippon Automated Cargo Clearance System) Operations Organization
通関手続 customs procedures
通関ベース customs clearance basis
通関用送り状 customs invoice
通期課税口 taxable-through-period account
通 行 権 way
通 行 税 passengers tax；toll charges
通 行 料 toll
通告処分 notification procedure
通　　査 walk-through test
通　　商 trade and commerce
通商拡大法 trade expansion act
通商協定 agreement on commerce

通商条項 commerce clause
通商条約 treaty of commerce
通常受渡し regular delivery；regular way of delivery
通常英国国債 nominal gilts
通常外国税額控除 ordinary foreign tax credit
通常解散 common liquidation
通常業務 regular business
通常決済 ordinary payment
通常決算 general closing of accounts
通常国債 nominal government debt
通常債券 conventional bonds；nominals
通常債券の名目利回り yield on nominal bond
通常私会社 ordinary private company
通常市場規模 NMS (normal market size)
通常使用時間 normal and average use hours
通常譲渡証書 ordinary conveyance
通常総会 ordinary general meeting；periodic general meeting
通常相続人 heir general
通常定款 articles of association
通常取引 nominal trading
通常の運営 ordinary and normal recurring operations；ordinary operations
通常のオプション standard option
通常の支払条件 usual payment term
通常の第三者間取引 arm's length transaction
通常の注意 ordinary care
通常の通貨以外の通貨で表示する quantize
通常の投資慣行 normal investment practice
通常の費用 ordinary charges；regular fee
通常の物価 regular price
通常の利子率 ordinary interest rate
通常必要な経費 ordinary and necessary expenses
通常保険料 ordinary premium
通常約款 usual covenants
通常利付債券 nominal instruments
通信業界 communications industry
通信制御装置 communications control units
通信販売 mail order
通信費 communication charges
通信法 Telecommunications Act of 1996
通達 directive
通知 notice
通知銀行 advising bank；notifying bank
通知支払い advise and pay
通知書類 information statement
通知伝票 advice slip
通知払い advice payment
通知保険 declaration policy
通知預金 deposit at notice；deposit requiring advance notice for withdrawal
通知を送達する serve a notice on
通帳 passbook
通帳貯蓄預金口座 passbook savings account
通年 full year
通年の指標 annual measure
使込み misapplication
次入先出 NIFO (next-in, first-out)
次入先出法 next-in next-first method
月掛投資計画 monthly investment plan
月払年金 monthly annuity
月平均売買高 average monthly trading volume
月割計算 accounting by month
作り相場 forced quotation
つなぎ為替 bridging exchange
つなぎ資金 interim financing
つなぎ信用枠 swing line
つなぎ年金 bridging pension
つなぎ融資 bridge finance；interim loan
つなぎ融資枠 swing facilities
ツバル（豪ドル） Tuvalu (Australian dollar)
積上げ予算 bottom-up budget
積換え transshipment
積換船荷証券 transshipment bill of lading
積み期間 reserve maintenance period
積込費用 loading charges

積　　立 accumulation
積立型商品 accumulation product
積立期間 accumulation period；reserve period
積立基準 funding requirements
積立給付 funded benefit
積立金 accumulated fund；reserve fund
積立金会計 reserve accounting
積立金勘定 reserve account
積立金繰入 additions to reserves；provision for surplus
積立金不足の under funded
積立金戻入れ reversal of surplus
積立金利率 interest reserve rate
積立限度額 allowed limit of accumulation
積立式社会保障 funded social security
積立式年金 funded pension
積立手段 accumulation device
積立状況 funding position
積立上の考慮 funding consideration
積立定期預金 installment time deposit
積立ファンド accumulation fund
積立プラン accumulation plan
積立方式 funded approach
積立保険 savings type insurance
積立率 funding ratio
積取比率 trade sharing
積荷価格申告書 valuation form
積荷目録 manifest
積増し buildup
積増し予算 incremental budget
強いチャンネル bullish channel
強い抵抗線 strong resistance
強　　気 bullish sentiment；bullish tone；strong feeling
強気買い bull buying
強気コンソリデーション・パターン bullish consolidation patterns
強気材料 bullish factor
強気市況 strong market
強気支持線 bullish support line
強気筋 bull clique；bull interests
強気相場 bull market
強気抵抗線 bullish resistance line
強気見通し bullish view
強気モメンタム bullish momentum
強気・弱気 bull and bear
強気リバーサル・パターン bullish reversal patterns
強張る strengthen
強含み firmer tone
強持ち合い unchanged to slightly higher
釣り合う symmetry with
ツリー構造 tree structure
ツリーモデル tree model
つり保険 anglers' insurance
つれ安 weaker in tandem

テ

出 合 い come to terms
出合相場 exchange cover rate
出合注文 good till canceled order
手　　当 allowance
提案依頼 RFP (request for proposal)
TRORスワップ TROR (total return of rate) swap
TIIS TIIS (Treasury Inflation-Indexed Securities)
DES暗号 DES (Data Encryption Standard)
TOPIX指数オプション TOPIX index option
低 位 株 lower-priced stock
T勘定法 T-account method
T規則超過証拠金 Regulation T excess
DK取引 DK (Don't Know)
ティーザー物ARM teaser ARM
T+3決済 T+3 settlement
T字型勘定 T account；skeleton form account；T form account
T字型勘定様式 skeleton form
TTレート telegraphic transfer rate
TBオペ TB operation
TB金利 TB rate
ディープ・アウト・オブ・ザ・マネー deep out of the money
ディープ・イン・ザ・マネー deep in the money；deep in-the-money
ディープ・ディスカウント deep discount
ディープ・ディスカウント債 DDB (deep discount bond)
ディープ・ロック主義 deep rock doctrine
DVP delivery versus payment
DVP決済 DVP (delivery versus payment) settlement
DVP清算値段 DVP Settlement Price
T-ボンド先物オプション T-bond futures option
T-ボンド先物取引 T-Bond Futures trading
T-ボンド入札最安値 stop-out price of T-bond
ディーラー dealer
ディーラー間市場 inter-dealer market
ディーラー市場 dealer market
ディーラーズ・オプション dealer's option
ディーラー手数料 dealer commission；dealer's fee
ディーラーの参加 dealer participation
ディーラー・ペーパー dealer paper
ディーラー・ポジション dealer's position
ディーラー・ローン dealer loan
T料率 T rate
ディーリング相場 dealing market
ディーリング・リスク dealing risk
T+1検討委員会 T+1 Steering Committee
低インフレ low inflation
低価格市場 lower end of the market
低価格商品 low price product
低価格輸入品 low-priced imports
低価主義 lower-of-cost-or-market value basis
低 価 法 LCM (lower of cost or market)
低価法による評価 valuation by lower of cost or market method
定　　額 fixed amount；fixed fee
定額請負契約 lump sum contract
定額会費 fixed amount membership fee
定額課税 fixed amount taxation
定額給付 level benefit
定額給付特約 income benefit rider
定額拠出年金 money purchase plan
定額減価償却法 straight-line depreciation
定額控除 flat deductible
定額支払変動利付債 level pay floating rate note
定額償却法 straight line amortization
定額生命保険 fixed life insurance
定額即時年金 fixed immediate annuity
定額貯金 teigaku deposit

定額貯蓄商品 savings certificate
定額定期保険 level term insurance
定額年金 conventional annuity ; fixed annuity ; fixed-rate annuity ; flat pension ; level annuity
定額払保険 fixed term policy
定額引出プラン systematic withdrawal plan
定額部分 fixed amount component
定 額 法 constant dollar plan ; fixed amount method ; fixed installment method ; straight line method
定額報酬実費支払契約 cost plus fixed fee contract ; fixed fee plus out-of-pocket expense contract
定額法で on a straight-line basis
定額法に準じた方法 manner similar to straight line depreciation method
定額保険 fixed sum policy ; fixed return insurance
定額保険料 fixed premium
定額保険料終身保険 fixed premium whole life insurance
定額保証定期生命保険 straight term insurance policy
定額前渡資金 imprest fund
定額前渡制 imprest system
低額譲渡 transfer at low price
低格付け below-investment grade
低格付クラス lower rated class
低額面株式 low par issue
低 下 率 decreasing rate
定　　款 articles of association ; articles of incorporation ; by-laws ; constitution
定款細則 by-laws
定款の変更 amendments to the by-laws
定款変更 amendments to the articles of incorporation
定　　義 definition
定義された用語 defined terms
定義する define
定期貸付 time loan
定期刊行物 periodicals
定期監査 periodic audit
定期現先 term repo
定期コール市場 period call market
定期市場 terminal market
定期実地棚卸 periodic actual inventory ; periodic physical inventory
定期支払い periodic payment ; term payment ; time payment
定期生命保険 term life insurance
定期棚卸 periodic inventory
定期積金 installment savings
定期的収益 periodical return
定期的修繕 periodic maintenance
定期的取引 periodical transaction
定期的な periodic
定期的な助言 periodic advice
定期的なリターン periodic return
定期取引 time bargains ; time transaction
定期払込据置年金保険 periodic purchase deferred contract
定期不動産権 estate for years
定期部分買増特約 term options rider
定期保険 term insurance
定期保険買増し term addition
定期保険転換 term insurance conversion
定期保険特約 term insurance rider
定期保険を買う buy term
定期預金 fixed deposit ; term deposit ; time deposit ; time savings
定期預金勘定 time deposit account
定期預金金利 interest rate on time deposit
定期預金証書 certificate of time deposit ; term certificate
定期預金担保貸出金利 interest rate on loans secured by time deposit
提議する propound
低金利資金 cheap money
低金利通貨 low yielding currency
低金利ローン low interest loan
テイク・アンド・ペイ契約 take-and-pay contract
テイク・オア・ペイ契約 take-or-pay contract
提　　携 collaboration
提携カード affiliated credit card
提携販売 tied sales

提携ローン affiliated loan；tie-up loan
提携ローンによるモーゲージ条件 introduced mortgage business
定型貿易条件 trade terms
逓減課税 degressive tax
逓減原価 degressive cost
逓減原価法 diminishing balance method
逓減残高法 reducing balance method
逓減成長率 declining growth rate
逓減定期保険 decreasing term insurance；reducing term policy
逓減定期保険特約 decreasing term rider
逓減的費用 decreasing charge
逓減年金 decreasing annuity
低減する erode
抵 抗 線 resistance level
低コスト low cost
停　　止 cessation；suspension
停止解除 withdrawal of suspension
停止期間 blackout period
停止条件 condition precedent；suspensive condition
呈　　示 presentment
呈示期間 time of presentation
呈示銀行 presenting bank
呈示の遅延 late presentation
定時株主総会 regular general meeting of shareholders
定時監査 regular audit
定時減債 scheduled amortization
定時償還 redemption at fixed date；scheduled redemption；scheduled repayment
定時総会 regular general meeting
定時払い payment at regular fixed times
定時払使用料 royalty to be paid every fixed time
定式繰入額 formula additions
低 次 財 lower order goods
低 収 益 low earnings
定収入のある個人 individual with regular income
提出締切日 deadline for filing
提出する file；submit
提出の延期 extension of time to file
提 出 日 filing date
定常状態 stationary state
低所得国 low income countries
低所得者層 low income group
低信用力 impaired credit
低 水 準 low level
低水準で安定した steady at low levels
ディスインターメディエーション dis-intermediation；disintermediation
ディスインフレ disinflation
定　　数 constant
定数付加保険料 expense constant
ディスカウント・キャッシュフロー DCF (discounted cash flow)
ディスカウント債 discounts
ディスカウント・ブローカー discount broker
ディスカウント・レート discount rate
ディスクレイマー disclaimer
ディスクロージャー制度 disclosure system
ディスクロージャーの充実 enhanced disclosure
訂正売り corrective selling
訂正相場 corrective market
訂正有価証券届出書 amended registration statement of a security
定性情報 qualitative information
定性分析 qualitative analysis
低 成 長 growth to remain subdued；low growth；slower growth
低成長産業 low growth industries
低 税 率 lower tax rate
ディセンディング・カーブ descending curve
ディセンディング・トップス descending tops
ディセンディング・トライアングル descending triangle
停 船 料 demurrage
低操業度原価 idle capacity cost
逓増年金 increasing annuity
逓 増 費 progressive cost
逓増保険 escalating annuity

逓増保険金 increasing benefit
逓増保険料 graded premium；increasing premium
定 足 数 quorum
停滞産業 stagnant industry
定弾性分散モデル constant elasticity of variance model
定置行列 definite matrix
低中所得 low- and moderate-income
ティック tick
ティック・テスト・ルール tick-test rule
DIP DIP (debtor in possession)
TIPS TIPS (Treasury's inflation-protection security)
低手数料ファンド low load fund
抵当借入金 mortgage payable
抵当機関 mortgage agency
抵当銀行 mortgage bank
抵当金融会社 mortgage finance company
抵 当 権 hypothec；mortgage rights
抵当権者 lien holder
抵当権設定 attachment of lien；settlement of mortgage
抵当権設定者 mortgage debtor；mortgagor
抵当権設定登記 register of settlement of mortgage；registration of lien
抵当権設定約款 mortgage clause
抵当権付借入 mortgages
抵当権付社債 secured bond
抵当権の消滅 extinction of hypothec；extinguishment of hypothec
抵当権の設定 establishment of hypothec
抵当権のついている encumbered
抵当権を抹消する expunge the mortgage
抵当順位第2位の second secured
抵当証券 mortgage backed securities；mortgage note；mortgage securities
抵当証券流通市場 secondary mortgage market
抵当証書類 mortgage documents
抵当信用組合 Mortgage Credit Association
抵当信用債 mortgage credit bond
抵当となりうる動産 mortgageable chattels
抵当に入っていない free and clean
抵当の優先権 priority of mortgage
抵当保険 mortgage insurance
抵当ローン mortgage loan
抵当ローン担保証券 securities backed by mortgage loan
定 年 retirement age
定年延長 deferred retirement
定年退職一時金給付 lump-sum retirement benefit
定年退職日 retirement date
低 配 株 low dividend stock
停 泊 料 groundage
ディファード・スワップ deferred swap
ディフィーザンス defeasance
ディフィーザンス条項 defeasance clause
ディフェンシブ運用 defensive management
ディフェンシブ銘柄 defensive stock
低保険料保険 low cost insurance
低ボラティリティ資産 lower volatility asset
ディマンドプル・インフレ demand-pull inflation；demand pull inflation
低 迷 stagnation
低迷価格 depressed price
低迷した業績 subdued performance
低迷する languish
低迷相場 stagnant market
定 理 theorem
廷 吏 usher
出入禁止 off limit
ディリクレ境界条件 Dirichlet boundary condition
低リスク・ポートフォリオ lower risk portfolio
定 率 fixed-rate
定率会費 fixed-rate membership fee
定率期限前償還率 CPR (constant prepayment rate)
定率組入れ fixed-rate transfer
定率減価償却法 declining balance depreciation method；fixed percentage depreciation method

テ

定率減税 fixed-rate tax reduction
定率公募・日銀残額引受け public offering of FBs at a fixed discount rate and underwriting of FBs by the Bank when bids from financial institutions fall short of the amount offered
定率償却 diminishing balance depreciation
定率償却法 percentage on diminishing value plan
定率成長配当割引モデル constant growth dividend discount model
定率成長評価モデル constant growth rate valuation model
定率手数料 level load
定率投資法 constant ratio plan
定 率 法 constant percentage method ; declining balance method ; fixed percentage method
定率補助金 percentage grant
定率利回り法 constant yield method
低率株式配当 small stock dividend
低利のティーザー物 low coupon teasers
低利回り資産 low return asset
低利融資 reduced rate loan
定量アセット・アロケーション quantitative asset allocation
定量分析 quantitative analysis
ティルティッド・バスケット tilted basket
定例理事会 regular meeting of the Board of Governors
低廉譲渡 assignment at lower-than-proper price
テークアウト・ローン takeout loan
テーク・オア・ペイ契約 take-or-pay contract
データ改ざん防止 fraud prevention
データ収集 data capture
データ処理業務 data processing business
データ通信 data communications
データ入力 data entry
データの暗号化 data encryption
データの集計 aggregation of data
データ・バンク data bank
データ・ベース data base
デー・トレーダー day trader
デー・トレード day trade
デェフォルト確率 probability of default
デェフォルト相関 default correlation
デェフォルト・バスケット default basket
テーリング tailing
テ ー ル tail
テール期間 tail period
テール・ヘッジ tail hedge
出遅れ株 lagging stock ; soft spot
出遅れている lagging
手　　形 bills and notes
手形売出オペ outright sales of bills drawn by the Bank of Japan
手形買入れ bill purchasing
手形買入オペ bill purchasing operation ; outright purchases of bills
手形買入制度 bill buying system
手形回収 bill collection ; note collection
手形買取銀行 negotiating bank
手形買取授権書 authority to purchase
手形買取手数料 negotiation charge
手形書換え renewal of bills and notes
手形貸付 advance on a promissory note ; loan on bill
手形貸付延滞利息 overdue interest on loan on bills
手形貸付担保 collateral on loans on bills
手形貸付利息 interest on loans on bills
手形勘定帳簿 bill book
手形記入帳 note register
手形金額 amount of bill
手形交換 bill clearance ; bill clearing ; check and bill clearing
手形交換勘定 clearing account
手形交換決済 bank clearing of bill
手形交換決算表 clearinghouse proof
手形交換所 bill clearing house ; clearinghouse
手形交換所加盟銀行 member banks of the clearing house
手形交換所取引停止処分 suspension of transactions in a bill clearing house
手形交換尻 bill clearing balance
手形交換制度 Bill and Check Clearing

System；clearing system
手形交換高 amount of clearing bill
手形交換のため for bill clearing house purposes only
手形・国債その他の有価証券を担保とする貸付 loans collateralized by bills, JGSs, or other marketable securities
手形サイト sight of a bill
手形市場 bill market
手形売買市場平均残高 bills market average outstanding
手形授権書 authority to pay
手形所持人 bill bearer
手形取立手数料 charge for collection of bill
手形の経過日数 days prior to discount on notes payable
手形の再割引 rediscounting of bills
手形の支払場所 domicile for payment of bills and notes
手形の日数 days of note
手形の振出し drawing of a bill
手形の満期 due date of bills
手形の割引 discounting of bills
手形売買レート bill buying and selling rate
手形発行枠 note issuance facility
手形払い payment by bill
手形引受 acceptance of bill
手形引受銀行 accepting bank；bill accepting bank
手形引受商社 bill accepting house
手形引渡 surrender of bill
手形振出 drawing of bill
手形振出通知 letter of advice on the drawing of bills
手形振出人 drawer of bill
手形ブローカー bill broker
手 形 法 law on bills
手形保証 assurance of bill
手形満期日 due date of bill
手形割引 bill discounting；discount on bill；discount on note receivable
手形割引料 discount on note
手堅い経営 conservative management
適格受渡し good delivery
適格海外機関投資家 QFII (Qualified Foreign Institutional Investors)
適格外国仲介業者 qualified foreign intermediary
適格機関投資家 qualified institutional investor
適格給付 relevant benefit
適格公益企業 qualifying utility
適格債券 qualified bond
適格資産 qualifying asset
適格社債 qualifying corporate bond
適格従業員 eligible employee；qualified employee
適格住宅ローン qualifying residential mortgage
適格証券 qualified securities
適格審査 process of qualification
適 格 性 eligibility；qualification
適格退職年金 approved retirement annuity；approved superannuation fund；qualified pension plan；qualified retirement annuity
適格退職年金基金 approved pension funds
適格退職年金契約 approved retirement annuity contract；qualifying retirement pension contract
適格退職年金制度 approved retirement annuity plan；qualifying retirement annuity plan
適格退職年金積立金 reserve for qualifying retirement pension
適格団体 eligible group
適格担保 eligible collateral；eligible security
適格担保取扱基本要領 guidelines on eligible collateral
適格投資 eligible investment
適格投資家 accredited investor
適格投資額 qualified investment
適格な税務専門家 qualified tax expert
適格年金 qualifying annuity
適格年金信託 qualified trust
適格年金信託基金 qualified pension trust

テ

fund
適格年金制度 approved pension scheme ; qualified plan
適格年金積立金 qualifying pension funds
適 格 の qualified
適格費用 eligible expense
適格法人 eligible business
適格保険証券 qualifying insurance policy
適格補償制度 defined compensation plan
適格モーゲージ qualified mortgage
適格有価証券 eligible securities
適格融資者 qualifying lender
適合性規則 suitability rule
適合範囲 relevant range
適債基準 issuance criteria ; issuance guidelines ; requirements for issuing bonds
適時開示 timely disclosure
適時開示に関する規則 rules on timely disclosure
適時開示情報伝達システム Timely Disclosure Network
適 時 性 timeliness
適正外貨準備高 optimum foreign exchange reserves
適正価格 adequate cash value
適正上下限界収益率 optimal threshold return ; optimal threshold return ratio
適正成長率 warranted rate of growth
適正賃金 fair wage
適正表示 fair presentation
適正ベーシス equilibrium basis
適正流動性 adequate liquidity
適正利率 appropriate interest rate
適 切 性 appropriateness
適切な機能を確保する secure proper functioning
適切な情報 relevant information
適切な測定 relevant measurement
適切な測定値 relevant measure
適切な代替 adequate substitute for
適切な配慮 due consideration
適切なポートフォリオ appropriate portfolio
適切な利益 adequate profit
敵対的買収 hostile acquisition ; hostile takeover ; unwanted takeover
敵対的買収を考える株式取得者 raider
出 来 高 crop ; total volume ; trading volume ; turnover
出来高加重平均株価 VWAP (volume weighted average price)
出来高給制度 piece rate plan
出来高原価 cost of work performed
出来高集中銘柄 highly traded stock
出来高払い progress payment
出来高払制 reimbursement method
適当な時 apt time
適度に伸びている growing at a moderate speed
出 来 値 actual price
適法契約 legal contract
適法証明書 compliance certificate
適法手続 due process of law
適法投資 legal investment ; statutory investment
適法投資リスト legal list
適法な通知 legal notice
適 法 の lawful ; legal
摘 要 abridgment
適用金利 interest rate applied
適用原価 applied cost
適用しうる耐用年数 applicable useful life
適用しうる法定耐用年数 applicable statutory useful life
適用事業所 covered establishment
適用指針 implementation guidance
適用除外 contracted out ; exemption from the application
適用除外給付 contracted-out benefit
適用除外個人年金 contracted-out personal pension
適用除外証券 exempted securities
適用除外範囲 exemption regime
適用除外法人 exempt corporation
適用すべき applicable
適用する基準 applicable standard
適用する正当な理由 justifiable reason to apply

適用税率 applicable tax rate
適用の順序 order of application
適用範囲 application coverage
適用免除証券 exempt securities
適 用 例 illustrative example
手口ファイル teguchi file
テクニカル指標 technical index
テクニカル・トレーディング technical trading
テクニカル分析 technical analysis
テクニカル分析指標 technical analysis indicator
テクニカル分析用グラフ technical graph
テクニカル要因 technical
テクニカル予測 technical forecast
テクニカル理論 technical theory
手じまい closed out；closing out；evening up
手じまいコスト closing-out cost
手じまいする close one's position
手　順 routing
手 数 料 charge；commission；concession；fee；fee and commission；mark-up
手数料後取りの back loaded
手数料開示 commission disclosure
手数料各自払い each way
手数料勘定 commission account
手数料構造 commission structure
手数料込み PC (plus commission)
手数料先取りの front loaded
手数料差引後 less fees；net of commission
手数料差引前 before fees
手数料収入 commission income；fee income
手数料のみの保険 commission only policy
手数料売買 sales and purchases on commission
手数料配分オプション load spread option
手数料払戻し passing on commission
手数料販売 commission sale
手数料不要生命保険 no load life policy
手数料不要投資商品 no load investments
手数料不要ミューチュアル・ファンド no load mutual fund
手数料分割 commission splitting
手数料分配 split commission
手数料前払い commission advance
手数料明細書 commission schedule
手数料料率 commission rate
手数料割引 commission rebate
手数料割引業者 discounter
手数料割戻し refund of fees
手数料割戻し前 before refund of fees
撤　回 revocation；withdrawal
撤回しえない irrevocable
撤去資産 removed assets
手　付 good faith deposit
手 付 金 earnest money；God's penny；hand money
鉄鋼業界 iron and steel industry
撤　退 phasing out
撤退する withdraw from
手　続 procedure
手続監査 procedural audit
手続差止予告 caveat
手続の履行 fulfillment of procedures
手 続 法 adjective law
TED TED (Treasury bill/Eurodollar)
鉄道建設・運輸施設整備支援機構 Japan Railway Construction, Transport and Technology Agency
鉄 道 債 railroad bonds
鉄道渡し FOR (free on rail)
デット・エクイティ・スワップ DES (debt equity swap)
デット・クロス debt cross
デット・サービス・カバレッジ・レシオ DSCR (debt service coverage ratio)
デット・サービス・レシオ DSR (debt service ratio)
TEDスプレッド TED (Treasury Eurodollar) spread
TEDスプレッド取引 TED spread trading
デット・ワラント fixed income warrant
デット・ワラント債 bond with debt warrant；debt warrant
デディケーティッド・ポートフォリオ

テ

dedicated portfolio
テナントの維持 tenant retention
デ ノ ミ denomination reduction ; downward redenomination
デノミ関連株 denomination related stocks
手 張 り trade on one's own account
デビット・カード debit card
デビット・スプレッド debit spread
デビット・ノート debit note
デビット保険 debit insurance ; debit policy
デフォルト基金 default fund
デフォルト曲線 default curve
デフォルト債権 default receivables
デフォルト宣言 declaration of default
デフォルト損失 default loss
デフォルトリスクのない default free
デフォルト率 default rate
デ フ レ deflation
デフレ圧力 deflationary pressure
デフレーション・ギャップ deflation gap
デフレーター deflator
デフレ期間 deflationary period
デフレ期待 deflation expectation
デフレ・ギャップ deflationary gap
デフレ効果 deflationary effect
デフレ時の元本保証 principal deflation floor
デフレ・スパイラル deflationary spiral
デフレ政策 deflation policy
デフレの悪循環 debt deflation
デフレのさらなる進行 renewed bout of deflation
デフレ・フロアー deflation floor
デポジトリー・コルレス depository correspondent
デポジトリー・バンク depository bank
デマーレッジ demurrage
手待時間 idle time
デモグラフィック・スコアリング demographic scoring
デモグラフィック分析 demographic analysis
手 持 株 stock on hand
手持債券 bond in portfolio
手持在庫水準 inventory level ; stock level
手持資材 materials on hand
手持証券 securities in portfolio
手持製品 finished goods on hand
手持注文 backlog of orders ; order stock ; unfilled orders
手持ちの金 cold cash
手許キャッシュフロー RCF (retained cash flow)
手許現金 cash on hand ; ready money ; vault cash
手許現金有高 cash in hand
手許在庫品 goods on hands
手許残高 balance in hand
手許流動性 liquidity in hand
デモンストレーション効果 demonstration effect
デュアル・カレンシー債 dual currency bonds
デュアル・キャパシティ dual capacity
デュアル・クローズド・エンド型ファンド dual closed-end fund
デュアル転換社債 dual convertible bonds
デュアル・トランシェ dual tranche
デュアル・ファンド dual-purpose fund
デュエット債 duet bond
デュレーション duration
デュレーション加重利回り duration-weighted yield
デュレーション・ギャップ duration gap
デュレーション計算 duration statistics
デュレーション法 duration method
デュレーション・マッチ duration-matching
テ ラ ー teller
デリバティブ derivatives
デリバティブ型契約 derivative type contract
デリバティブ金融商品 derivative financial instrument
デリバティブ資産 derivative assets
デリバティブ取引に関する定例市場報告（吉国委統計）の日本分集計結果 Results

of Regular Derivatives Market Statistics in Japan (Yoshikuni Statistics)
デリバティブの管理 management of derivatives
デリバティブの期限満了 expiry of derivatives
デリバティブの執行 implementation of derivatives
デリバティブの目的 purposes for using derivatives
デリバティブ負債 derivative liabilities
テルアビブ証券取引所 Tel Aviv Stock Exchange
デル・クレデール・エージェント del credere agent
デ ル タ delta
デルタ値 delta value
デルタ・ニュートラル・ヘッジ delta neutral hedge
デルタ・ヘッジ delta hedge
デルファイ予測 Delphi forecast
テレフォン・バンキング telephone banking
テレフォン・マーケット telephone market
テレフォン・ローン telephone loan
展　開 deployment
展開待ち waiting for further development
転 貸 し sublet
転貸契約 sub-letting agreement
転嫁する pass on
転嫁性理論 shiftability theory
転　換 conversion
転換オプション conversion option
転換価格 conversion price
転換価格方式 conversion price formula
転換価格を超える額 premium over conversion value
転換加算条項 conversion credit provision
転換価値 conversion value
転換仮定法 if-converted method
転換可能金融商品 convertible instruments
転換株式 convertible stock
転 換 権 conversion privilege ; conversion right
転換交換可能優先株 CEPS (convertible exchangeable preferred stock)
転換資産 convertible assets
転換社債 CB (convertible bond) ; convertible debt ; equity convertible ; mezzanine money
転換社債型新株予約権付社債券 convertible-bond type corporate bonds with new share reservation rights
転換社債利回り convertible bond index
転換証券 convertible securities
転換条件 conversion conditions ; conversion terms
転換条項 conversion clause ; conversion feature
転換請求 demand for conversion
転換請求期間 conversion period
転換代理人 conversion agent
転換停止 suspension of convertibility
転換ディスカウント conversion discount
転 換 点 turning point
転換特典 conversion privilege
転換特典付定期保険 convertible term insurance
転換特典付保険 convertible insurance
転換取引 conversion transaction
転換パリティ conversion parity
転 換 日 conversion date
転換比率 conversion ratio
転換プレミアム conversion premium
転換モーゲージ convertible mortgage
転換優先株 convertible preferred stock
転換優先株式 convertible preference shares
転　記 posting
電気・ガス業 utility and gas industry
電気・ガス税 electricity and gas tax
電気機器業界 electric appliances industry
電気機器先物 electric appliances futures
電気業界 electric industry
電 気 税 electricity tax
電気通信事業 telecommunications business
電気通信事業者 telecommunications

carriers
電気通信市場 telecommunications market
転記上の誤り errors in posting
10 Qレポート 10-Q report
10 Kレポート 10-K report
電源開発株式会社 Electric Power Development Co., Ltd.
電光情報板 broad tape
天候デリバティブ weather derivatives
天候保険 weather insurance
天災資金 natural disaster relief loans
天災地変 natural disaster
電算システム管理官 Special Officer for Information System
電算システム専門官 Special Officer for Information Technology
電算センター computer center
電子貸付 electronic loan
電子決済 electronic fund transfer ; electronic payment
電子工学 electronic engineering
電子航法研究所 Electronic Navigation Research Institute
電子国庫 digitized treasury fund
電子資金決済システム EFTS (electronic fund transfer system)
電子証券取引システム ECN (electronic communication network)
電子商取引 electronic commerce
電子情報処理組織 electronic information processing facility
電子署名 electronic signature
電子申告 electronic filing
電子政府 digital government
電子注文伝達システム electronic order transfer system
電子帳簿保存 keeping of electronic account books
電子データ交換 EDI (electronic data interchange)
電子的市場 electronic market
電子的データ収集・検索システム EDGAR (electronic data gathering analysis and retrieval)
電子的な形式 electronic form
電子取引 electronic transaction
電子取引市場 electronic trading market
電子取引照合 ETC (electronic trade confirmation)
電子認証機能 electronic certification function
電子認証業務 electronic certification service
電子納税 electronic payment of taxes
電子納付 electronic payment
電子販売 electronic distribution
電子マネー electronic money (e-money)
電磁的記録 electromagnetic record
電磁的方法 electromagnetic means
天 井 圏 vicinity of the upper limit
天井しらずの相場 skyrocketing price
天井相場 ceiling price
天井掴み buying at top price
天井を打つ reaching the top price
電信売相場 telegraphic transfer selling rate
電信買相場 telegraphic transfer buying rate
電信為替 telegraphic transfer
電信送金 cable transfer ; wire transfer
電信送金為替 telegraphic transfer payable
電信取立為替 reverse telegraphic transfer ; telegraphic transfer receivable
天 津 市 Tianjin
転　　籍 change in employment
テンダー・オプション tender option
テンダー価格 tender price
テンダー・パネル tender panel
テンダー・ビル tender bill
転 貸 借 under lease
点弾力性 point elasticity
転置行列 transposed matrix
店　　頭 OTC (over-the-counter)
店頭オプション OTC (over-the-counter) option
店 頭 株 over-the-counter stock
店頭管理銘柄 over-the-counter managed issues
店頭金利オプション OTC interest rate option

テ

店頭気配 quotation of over-the-counter issue
店頭市場 over-the-counter market
店頭証拠金株式 OTC margin stock
店頭通貨オプション over-the-counter currency option
店頭登録企業 OTC company
店頭登録銘柄 issues listed on the over-the-counter market
店頭取引 OTC (over-the-counter) transaction；trading on the OTC (over-the-counter) market
店頭取引掲示板 OTC bulletin board
店頭取引市場 third market
店頭取引銘柄 OTC firm
店頭売買高 volume of over-the-counter transaction
店頭売買利回り over-the-counter sales yield
店頭表示 indication at a store counter
店頭銘柄気配自動通報 National Association of Securities Dealers' Automated Quotation
店頭銘柄気配自動通報システム National Association of Securities Dealers Automated Quotations
店頭渡しで ex store
伝統市場 traditional market
伝統的小売棚卸法 conventional retail inventory system
伝統的商品市場 conventional commodity market
天然果実 natural fruits
天然資源 natural resources
天然資源減耗償却費 depletion of natural resources
天然資源の探鉱 exploration for natural resources
転　　売 offsetting sale transaction；resale
天 引 き withholding
天引貯金 deposit through deduction from monthly pay；savings deducted at source
伝　　票 chit；slip；ticket；voucher
伝票式会計法 slip system of accounting
伝票式簿記 slip bookkeeping
伝票制度 slip system
伝票突き合わせ vouching
伝票払制度 chit system
点描する map
転　　覆 capsized
添付書類 accompanying document；appendix；attached document；exhibit
添付明細書通り as per specifications attached
転付命令 assignment order
店舗休業保険 store business interruption insurance
店舗総合保険 storekeepers' comprehensive insurance
填補限度額 liability limits
填補責任限度額 limit of liability
テンポラリー・ボンド temporary bond
テンポラル法 temporal method
デンマーク・クローネ DKK (Danish krone)
デンマーク保管振替機関 VP
10ライン特約 10 line treaty
電力・ガス株 utilities stock
電力供給契約 PPA (power purchase agreement)
電 力 債 electric power bonds；utility bonds
電 力 費 electric power expense；power expense
電話確認 verification by telephone
電話加入権 telephone subscription right
電話注文 order by telephone
電話による取引勧誘 cold call
電話の普及率 penetration of phones
電話ブース telephone booth
電話料金 telephone rates
電話料金支払い telephone bill payment

テ

ト

ドイツ国債 German Bunds
ドイツ証券取引所 Deutche Borse AG
ドイツ証券保管機構 DKV (Deutscher Kassenverein AG)
ドイツFAZ 指数 Frankfurter Allgemeine Zeitung Index
ドイツ保管振替機関 Clearstream
ドイツ・マルク DEM (German mark)；Deutch mark
ドイツ・マルク先物オプション Deutsche Mark futures option
ドイツ・マルク通貨先物 Deutsche Mark currency futures
ドイツ無記名証書 GBC (German bearer certificate)
ドイツ連銀 Bundesbank
ドイツ連銀金利 Buba
ドイツ連邦中期債 Bundeskassenobligationen
ドイツ連邦中期特別債 Bundesobligationen
ドイモイ Doi Moi
同一オプション series of option
同一期間 identical term
同一危険群保険料率 class rate
同一金額 identical amount
同一証明付コピー conformed copy
同 一 性 identity
同 一 の identical with
統一会計基準 uniform accounting standards
統一会計規則 uniform accounting regulations
統一会計制度 uniform accounting system
統一慣習規則 uniform practice code
統一基金債 unity bond
統一基準 uniform standards
統一規制 single regulation
統一原価計算 uniform cost accounting
統一原価計算制度 uniform cost accounting system
統一証券法 Uniform Securities Act
統一商事法典 Uniform Commercial Code
統一商標 unified brand
統一清算機関 unified clearing organization
統一的な運用 unified operation
統一的な会計方針 uniform accounting policies
統一保険法 Uniform Life Insurance Act
統一約款 uniform provisions
統一様式 prescribed format
同意判決 consent decree
動　　員 mobilization
動員解除 demobilization
等　　価 equivalence
等価課税利回り equivalent tax yield
等価係数 equivalent coefficient
等価交換 exchange of equivalents
等価資産 assets of equal value
等価利回り equivalent yield
同　　化 assimilation
当該企業 enterprise concerned
当 該 の concerned
動学乗数 dynamic multiplier
動学的産業連関分析 dynamic input-output analysis
投下資本 invested capital
投下資本利益率 rate of return on investment；return on invested capital
統括勘定 control account
統括国税査察官 chief investigator
統括国税調査官 chief examiner
統括国税徴収官 chief revenue officer
導 関 数 derived function
導管理論 conduit theory
当　　期 current period；current term；current year；reported period
当期売上高 sales for this term

当期営業利益 current operating profit
当期業績主義 current operating performance basis
当期業績主義による損益計算書 current operating performance income statement
当期勤務 current service
当期勤務年金保険料 current service cost
当期決算 current term settlement of accounts
当期減少額 decrease amount in current term
当期支出原価 current-outlay cost
当期純損益 current term net profit or loss
当期純損失 current term net loss
当期純利益 current term net income；net income for the year；net profit for the period
当期償却額 write-offs in current term
当期処分利益余剰金 unappropriated surplus for the current taxable
当期税金 current tax
当期税金資産 current tax asset
当期税金費用 current tax expense
当期税金負債 current tax liability
当期税引前利益 pretax profit of the current term
当期増加額 increase amount in current term
当期損失金 deficit for the current term；loss for the current term；loss for the current year
当 期 の reported term
当期の金額 current period amount
当期の年金費用 current pension expense
当期費用 current expenses
当 期 分 current portion
当期末残高 term-end outstanding balance
当期満期部分 current maturity
当期未処分利益剰余金 unappropriated earned surplus for current term
当期未処理損失 unappropriated losses at the end of the year
当期利益 current income
当期利益金 profit for the current term
当期利益調整 ACE (adjustment for current earnings)
投　　機 speculation
投機買い bull speculation；speculator buying
投機市場 speculative market
投 機 筋 speculators
投機的格付け speculative grade
投機的債券 speculative grade bond
投機的資金 speculative money
投機的動機 speculative motive
投機的取引 speculative transaction
投機的リスク speculative risk
投機取引 speculation transaction
投 機 熱 craze for speculation；speculative enthusiasm
投機目的 speculative purpose
投機利潤 speculative gain
投機を行うこと taking a flier
登 記 所 registry office
登記済み registered
登記手続 registration formalities
登記番号 registered number
登 記 簿 commercial register
登記抹消 cancellation of register
登記未済 non-registered
登 記 料 registration fee
騰　　貴 appreciation；flier
討議資料 discussion paper
討議報告書 issues paper
動　　機 cause inducement；motivation
動機調査 motivation research
動　　議 motion
道義的危険 moral hazard
道義的支払保証債券 moral obligation bond
道義的説得 moral suasion
等　　級 degree
等級別原価 class cost
等級別原価計算 class cost system；group costing system
等級別手数料 graded commission
東京オフショア市場 Japan Offshore Market；Tokyo offshore market
東京オフショア・センター Tokyo

offshore center
東京外国株式市場 Tokyo foreign stock market
東京外国為替市場 Tokyo foreign exchange market
東京銀行間取引金利 TIBOR (Tokyo Inter-Bank Offered Rate)
東京銀行協会 Tokyo Bankers Association
東京金市場 Tokyo gold market
東京工業品取引所 Tokyo Commodity Exchange
ト
東京金融先物取引所 Tokyo International Financial Futures Exchange
東京市場 Tokyo market
東京証券清算株式会社 Tokyo Securities Settlement Corporation
東京証券取引所 Tokyo Stock Exchange
東京証券取引所外国部 Foreign Section of the Tokyo Stock Exchange
東京手形交換所 Tokyo Clearing House
東京ドル・コール市場 Tokyo dollar call market
東京ドル債 Tokyo dollar bond
同業組合 craft union ; guild
同業他社 peer companies
当　　局 authorities
当局の許可 ministerial clearance
当　　限 current month delivery
等金額ポートフォリオ equal weighted portfolio
統　　計 statistics
統 計 学 statistics
統計誤差 statistical error
統計センター National Statistics Center
統計総括表 key statistics
統計的決定理論 statistical decision theory
統計的処理 statistical procedure
統計的推測 statistical inference
統計的な測度 statistical measure
統計的品質管理 SQC (statistical quality control)
統計的分析 statistical analysis
統計的見積り statistical estimation
統 計 法 Statistics Law
統計モデル statistical model
統計用語 statistical terminology
統計理論 statistical theory
当月限り有効な注文 good for this month order
凍結勘定 frozen account
凍結資産 frozen assets
統合経済 integrated economy
統合気配値情報システム consolidated quotation system
統合された事業 integrated operations
統合市場構造 consolidated market structure
統合する consolidate
統合担保管理 ICM (integrated collateral management)
統合抵当証券 consolidated mortgage bond
統合テープ consolidated tape
統合費用 integration cost
統合比率 integration ratio
統合物価指数 HIPC (harmonized index of consumer prices)
統合リスク管理 integrated risk management
当 座 貸 cash credit
当座貸越し O/D (overdraft) ; TOF (technical overdraft facility)
当座貸越極度額 maximum amount of the overdraft
当座貸越約定書 agreement for overdraft
当座貸越枠 overdraft line
当座貸付 demand loan
当座借越勘定 overdraft account
当座借越契約 overdraft facilities
当座勘定 book account ; current account ; current deposit account ; running account
当座勘定付替え transfer of current account
当座勘定取引契約 contract for current account services
当座勘定入金票 account deposit slips
当座小切手 current account check
当座資金 current fund
当座資産 quick assets

当座照合表 reconciliation statement for current account
当座性預金 checkable deposit
当座比率 acid ratio ; quick assets ratio
当座預金 cash at bank ; checking deposit ; current deposit ; deposit in current account ; quick deposit
当座預金サービス current account service
当座預金残高 outstanding balance of current accounts
当座預金取引 current account transaction
動　　産 chattel ; effects ; movables ; personal assets ; personal estate
動産遺贈 bequest
動産回復訴訟 claim and delivery
動産貸付 chattel loan
動産契約 personal contract
動産差押 personal distress
動 産 質 pawn ; pledge
動産質権者の留置権 pledgee's lien
動産信託 movable property in trust
動 産 税 personal property tax
動産総合保険 movables comprehensive insurance
動産抵当 chattel mortgage
動産抵当証券 chattel paper
動産・不動産 premises and movable property
動産不動産勘定 movable and immovable asset account
動産不動産処分 disposal of premises and equipment
動産包括保険証券 personal property floater
動産モーゲージ chattel mortgage ; mortgage of goods
倒産隔離 bankruptcy remote
投　　資 investment
投資アナリスト investment analyst
投資安全確保の範囲 margin of safety
投資委員会 investment committee
投資運用 investment management
投資延期 postponement of investment
投 資 家 investor ; trading accounts
投資買い investment buying
投資会社 investment company
投資会社法 Investment Company Act of 1940
投資回収 fund recovery ; investment recovery
投資解除 disinvestment
投資回転率 investment turnover
投資カウンセラー investment counselor
投資価値 investment value
投資活動 investing activities
投資活動からのキャッシュフロー cash flow from investing activities
投資活動で使用された資金純額 net cash used in investing activities
投資家の買い investor buying
投資家の関心 investor interest
投資家の信頼 investors' confidence
投資家の税務上の会計年度 investor tax year
投資家の見方 investor perceptions
投資家の持ち分 investor's share
投 資 株 investment stock
投資家別公社債売買状況 bond transaction by investor types
投資家保護 protection of investors
投資家保護室 Office of Consumer Affairs & Information Service
投資家保護信託 IPT (investor protection trust)
投資家向けセミナー investor briefings
投資環境 investment climate ; investment environment
投資勘定部門 investment account
投資関数 investment function
投資管理会社 IMI (investment management institution)
投資管理規制機関 IMRO (Investment Management Regulatory Organization)
投資管理局(SEC) Division of Investment Management(SEC)
投資管理コスト investment administration cost
投資管理者と顧客の関係 manager-client relations

投資管理費用 investment management cost
投資機会 investment opportunity
投資期間 investment holding period ; investment horizon ; investment period
投 資 業 investment business
投資許可リスト authorized investment list
投資曲線 investment curve
投資金額（取得額、投資持分） stake
投資銀行 investment bank
投資銀行家 merchant banker
投資銀行金融機関 Investment Banking Financing Company
投資銀行事業 investment banking business
投 資 口 beneficiary ownership ; unit of investment securities
投資クラブ investment club
投資繰延べ deferment of investment
投資計画 investment program
投資計画期間分析 horizon analysis of investment plan
投資決定 investment decision
投資限界効率 marginal efficiency of investment
投資減税 tax reduction for investment
投資控除 investment credit
投資子会社 investment vehicle
投資顧問 investment advisor ; investment counsel
投資顧問会社 investment management company
投資顧問規制機関 IMRO (Investment Managers Regulatory Organization)
投資顧問業 advisory service ; investment advisory service
投資顧問業界 investment advisory industry
投資顧問法 Investment Advisor Act of 1940
投 資 財 investment goods
投資債券 investment bond
投資採算 investment profitability
投資再評価損 deficit on revaluation of investments
投資再評価積立金 investment revaluation reserve
投 資 先 investment choice
投資事業組合 investment business association
投資資金 investment capital ; portfolio capital ; speculative fund
投資資金の流れ portfolio flows
投資資産 investment assets
投資支出 investment expenditure
投資支出分評価法 capital value method
投資市場 investment market
投資実績 investment experience ; investment history
投資資本 investment capital
投資尺度 investment criteria ; measure of investment
投資者保護 protection of investor
投資収益 return on investment
投資収益の予測 projection of investment return
投資収益率 rate of return on investment ; ROI (return on investment)
投資柔軟性 investment flexibility
投資需要 investment demand
投資証券 beneficiary ownership certificate ; investment security
投資証書 investment certificate
投資乗数 investment multiplier
投資承認額 investment approvals
投資承認リスト approved list of investment
投資商品 investment products
投資情報源 investment information sources
投資所得 investment income
投資信託 investment fund ; investment trust
投資信託委託会社 investment trust management company
投資信託委託業務 management business of investment trust
投資信託受益証券 investment trust beneficiary certificate

投資信託設定 sales of investment trusts
投資信託の運用状況 distribution of net assets of investment trusts
投資信託の受益証券 beneficiary certificate of investment trust
投資信託の有価証券保有 securities ownership by investment trusts
投資信託有価証券 securities held for investment trust
投 資 税 investment tax
投資成果 investment result
投資税額控除 ITC (investment tax credit)
投資性向 investment propensity；propensity to invest
投資政策 investment policy
投資選択資産 assets of choice
投資選択の概括 investment selection summary
投資戦略 investment strategy
投資戦略委員会 investment strategy committee
投資総額 aggregate investments
投資ソフト investment software
投資損失準備金 investment reserve
投資損失引当金 reserve for investment loss
投資損失引当金繰入額 provision for investment loss reserve
投資対象 investment outlet
投資対象企業 investment grade corporate
投資対象選択権付年金 wraparound annuity
投資単位 investment unit
投資通貨 investment currency
投資適格 investment grade
投資適格格付け investment grade rate
投資適格債 investment grade securities
投資適格債券 investment grade bond
投資適格対象 legal investment
投資適格ローン investment grade loan
投資哲学 investment philosophy
投資ドル investment dollar
投資主総会 general meeting of investors
投資年度別方式 investment year method
投資の回収 recovery of investment
投資のための資金需要 demand for investing funds
投資の二重性 dual character of investment
投資の伸び growth of investment
投資の売却 liquidation of investments；sale of investment
投資パフォーマンス規準 IPS (investment performance standards)
投資判断 investment decision；investment judgment
投資ブーム investment boom
投資物件 investment tools
投資不動産 investment property；investment real estate
投資不動産所有者 investment property owner
投資分析 investment analysis
投資紛争解決国際センター International Centre for Settlement of Investment Disputes
投資変動準備金 investment fluctuation fund
投資ポートフォリオ investment portfolio
投資摩擦 investment friction
投資マネージャー investment manager
投資マネージャーの構成 investment manager structure
投資未回収額 investment outstanding
投資メリット investment merit
投資目的確認書 investment letter
投資目的資産 asset for investment purposes
投資目標 investment objectives
投資誘因 inducement to invest
投資有価証券 investment securities
投資有価証券市場 investment securities markets
投資有価証券収益 investment securities gains
投資有価証券取引 investment securities transaction
投資有価証券ポートフォリオ investment securities portfolio
投資予算 investment budget

投資利益率 rate of return on invested capital ; return on investment
投資リスク investment risk
投 資 率 investment rate
投資を引き上げる disinvest
等式の左側 left side of the equation
同時火災保険 concurrent fire insurance
同時災害条項 common disaster clause
同時修正 concurrent adjustment
同時上場 multiple listing
同時処理 simultaneous processing
同時担保 self-collateralization
同時調査 simultaneous tax audit
同時積立方式 contemporaneous reserve accounting
同時振替決済 simultaneous book-entry transfer
同時募集 concurrent subscription offering
同時履行条件 condition concurrent
当 事 者 party
同　　質 homogeneity
同質原価 homogeneous cost
同質的市場 homogeneous market
同日決済 SDS (same-day settlement)
同日代替 same-day substitution
当日決済取引 cash transaction ; same-day value transaction
当日資金 good money
当日中の変動幅 intraday fluctuation margin
当日中の変動率 intraday fluctuation rate
当日取引 cash transaction
当日のみ有効な注文 good for day order
当日返済貸付 day loan
当日変動状況 intraday deviations
当日有効注文 same day effective order
当日渡し value today
同種商品 like goods
同 種 の in kind
同順位先取特権 concurrent liens
同順位で pari passu
当初受入額 amount initially received
搭乗者傷害保険 automobile passengers' personal accident insurance
東　　証 TSE
東証株価指数 Tokyo Stock Exchange stock price index ; Tokyo Stock Price Index
東証株価平均 TSE Stock Price Average
東証監事 auditor of TSE
東証正会員 regular members of the Tokyo Stock Exchange
東証第二部総合指数 Tokyo Stock Exchange Second Section Index
東証定款 Constitution of the Tokyo Stock Exchange
東証平均株価 Tokyo Stock Exchange Price Average
当 所 株 stock exchange share
当初金額の償却後の金額 amortized original amount
当初購入者 original purchaser
当初資本 initial capital
当初証拠金 original margin
当初証拠金率 initial margin requirement
当初設定 initial establishment
当初測定 initial measurements
当初登録 initial registration
当初認識 initial recognition
当初の営業損失 initial operating loss
当初の期限 original term
当初の取得原価 original cost of asset
当初の手数料 initial fee
当初のポートフォリオ initial portfolio
当初の保険料 initial premium ; original premium
当初発行価格 original issue price
当初負担原価 starting-load cost
当初満期 original maturity
当初渡り initial delivery
投信会社 unit investment trust company
投信組入株式 shares held by investment trusts
投信銘柄 portfolio of investment trust
統制会計 control accounting
統制経済 controlled economy ; directed economy
統制商品 regulated commodities
統制範囲 span of control

統制貿易 controlled trade
統制予算 control budget
統制リスク control risk
同族会社 closed corporation ; personal holding company ; family company ; private holding company
同族株主の同族会社 personal family corporation
同族関係会社 affiliated family corporations
同族組合 family partnership
動態経済学 economic dynamics
動態的リスク dynamic risks
動態統計 dynamic statistics
動態分析 dynamic analysis
到達時刻 first hitting time
到達年齢 attained age
統治行為 sovereign act
到着原価 laid-down cost
到着後一覧払手形 arrival draft
頭　　注 headnote
動的計画法 dynamic programming
同等同質の of like grade and quality
道徳上の義務 moral obligation
道徳的約因 moral consideration
東南アジア諸国連合 Association of South-East Asian Nations
東南アジア諸国連合会 ASEAN (Association of South East Asian Nations)
盗難小切手 stolen check
盗難手形 stolen bill
盗難保険 burglary insurance
投　　入 infusion
投入係数 input coefficient
投入算出表 input-output table
投入産出分析 input-output analysis
投入費用 input cost
導入預金 deposit to be lent to a third party
投 入 量 input
当年中に支払うべき due for the year
当年度の概況 year in brief
同　　輩 peer
逃避資金 flight money
投　　票 ballot ; voting
等費用曲線 equal cost curve
道府県債 prefectural government bonds
道府県税 prefectural tax
動物保険 animal insurance ; livestock insurance
等 分 散 constant variance
当　　方 our side
当方勘定 nostro account ; our account
当 方 国 nostro
当方負担 on our risk
謄　　本 duplicate tenor ; transcript
同　　盟 alliance
同盟会社 allied company
透明性のある transparent
当面の流動性 immediate liquidity
投 融 資 investment and loan ; loans and investments
投融資指針 investment and loan guideline
当用買い hand-to-mouth buying
当預取引先 financial institutions that hold current accounts with the Bank
当預振替 funds transfer
騰落順位 biggest single day advances and declines
騰 落 線 advance-decline line
騰 落 率 percentage change
騰落レシオ advance decline ratio ; increase and decrease ratio ; up-down ratio
同類証券のグループ homogeneous security group
道路関係四公団民営化推進委員会 Promotion Committee for the Privatization of the Four Highway-related Public Corporations
登　　録 enrollment
登録売出し registered secondary offering
登録会社 registered company
登 録 株 registered share
登録株主 shareholders of record
登録機関 registrar ; registration agency
登録ギルト債 registered gilts

登録金融機関 registered financial institution
登録組合 registered society
登録繰上げ acceleration of registration
登録小切手 registered check
登録国債 registered government bonds ; registered JGSs
登録コンペティティブ・トレーダー registered competitive trader
登録コンペティティブ・マーケット・メーカー registered competitive market maker
登 録 債 registered bond
登録債決済確約書 Note for Delivery in Registered Bonds
登録質権者 registered pledgee
登録証券外務員 registered representative
登録商標 registered trade-mark
登録除却 deletion of registration
登 録 税 registration tax
登録請求 registration request
登録請求承諾書 Consent to Instruction for Registration
登録退職金貯蓄制度 RRSP (registered retirement savings plan)
登録代理人 enrolled agent
登録投資会社 RIC (registered investment company)
登録投資顧問 RIA (registered investment adviser)
登録トレーダー registered trader
登録年金商品 registered annuity product
登録の取消 withdrawal of registration
登録番号票 charge plate
登 録 日 date of record
登録銘柄 registered issues
登録名義人 name of the JGS holder ; registered owner
登録免許 registration license
登録免許税 registration and license tax
登録免許税法 Registration and License Tax Law
登録免除取引所 exempt stock exchange
道路料金所 toll gate
トーゴ（CFAフラン） Togo (CFA (Communauté Financière Africaine) franc)
通し船荷証券 through B/L (bill of lading)
トータル・リターン・スワップ total return swap
トータル・リターンの分布 distribution of total returns
トービンのq Tobin's q
トーレンス式登記法 Torrens System
ドキュメント・ディスカウント・ノート documented discount note
得 意 先 client
得意先受入保証金 customer's deposits
得意先前受金 advance by customers
得意先元帳 customer's ledger
特 金 tokkin
独自商品 proprietary product
独自取引システム PTS (Proprietary Trading System)
独自の属性 distinct attribute
独自平均 self-balancing
特殊会社 special corporation
特殊関係者 party with particular interest
特殊関係人 special associated person
特殊関税専門官 Director for Trade Remedy Affairs
特殊均衡 special equilibrium
特殊原価調査 special cost studies
特殊構造のスワップ tailored swap transactions
特 殊 債 specific bonds
特殊受益 peculiar benefits
特殊仕訳帳 special journal
特殊的生産要素理論 specific productive factors
特殊な事業 specialized business
特殊な税務処理 unique tax treatment
特殊引受け special acceptance
特殊比率 salient ratio
特殊法人 special public institution of the government
特殊法人の整理合理化 reorganization and rationalization of special public corporations
特殊保険 specific insurance

特殊元帳 special ledger
特殊用途免税 non-taxable goods for special use
特　　性 parameters
特 性 線 characteristic line
特性線の定義 definition of characteristic line
独占価格 monopoly price
独 占 権 exclusive privilege；exclusive right；sole right
独占資本 monopoly capital
独占代理店 exclusive agent
独占地位 monopoly position
独占的競争 monopolistic competition
独 占 度 degree of monopoly
独占販売業者 exclusive distributor
独占販売権 exclusive right to sell listing；franchise
督　　促 reminder
督 促 状 collection letter；reminder
督促手続 summary procedure
督 促 料 charge for call
特　　損 special loss
特 注 の tailor made
特　　徴 characteristics；features
特定医療法人 specified medical corporation
特定医療法人の特別税率 reduced tax rate on specified medical corporation
特定合併 special merger
特定合併をした直後の資本 capital immediately after the specified merger
特定可能資産 identifiable assets
特定期間渡し broken term
特定危険 named peril
特定危険担保保険 named perils insurance
特定期日受渡し odd date or broken date delivery
特定寄付金 specified donation
特定共済 specific mutual aid
特定業種 specific industry
特定金銭信託 specified money in trust
特定金融情報室 Financial Intelligence Office
特定グループ crowd
特定契約 particular contract
特定現物出資 specified investment in kind
特定国外営業所 specified foreign branch
特定国有財産整備室 Office for Consolidation of Specific National Property
特定財源債 limited obligation bond；self-supporting debt
特定債権法 law concerning the regulations on business related to specified receivables
特定債務等の調整の促進のための特定調停に関する法律 Law Concerning Specified Arbitration for Promotion of Reconciliation of Specified Liabilities, etc.
特定再割当金 specified reallocated amount
特定産業ファンド industry specialized fund
特定事業 specified business
特定事業の用地買収 land purchase for specified business
特定資産 specified assets
特定資産の流動化に関する法律 Law on Securitization of Specified Assets
特定市場選好理論 preferred habitat theory
特定疾病保険 specified disease policy
特定疾病保障保険 specified disease insurance
特定時点の価格 time specific price
特定社員 holders of specified equity securities
特定社債 specified corporate bond
特定収入高 restricted receipts
特定出資 specified contribution
特定準備金 reserve for special purpose
特定情報 specific information
特定済株式 identified shares
特定税源債 limited tax bond
特定製造指図書 special production order
特定設備廃棄税額控除 scrapping of equipment tax credit

特定線引小切手 special crossed check
特定退職金共済団体 mutual aid organization for specific retirement allowance
特定担保 fixed charge；fixed lien；specific charge；specific lien
特定地域支店設置 limited branching
特定地域ポートフォリオ specific regional portfolio
特定当座預金 specified current deposit
特定投資法人 specified investment corporation
特定取引勘定 special trading accounts；specified transaction accounts
特定取引損益 special trading income or loss
特定の期間 specified period
特定の現物出資によって取得された資産 property acquired by the specified investment in kind
特定の現物出資によって取得された証券 securities acquired by the specified investment in kind
特定の順序 particular order
特定の動向 specified path
特定のリーエン particular lien
特定のリスク identified risk
特定範疇 specific category
特定プール specified pool
特定保険 limited policy
特定民間都市開発 specified private-sector urban development
特定銘柄 specified stock
特定銘柄投資信託 specialized investment fund
特定銘柄ミューチュアル・ファンド specialized mutual fund
特定目的 special purpose
特定目的財務諸表 special purpose financial statements
特定持ち分信託 specified equity trust
特定用途免除 tax exemption for specific use
特定履行 specific performance
特定利子 specified interest

ト

特別扱い special treatment
特別委員会 ad hoc committee；special committee
特別売出し special offering
特 別 円 special yen
特別会員 special member
特別会計 special accounts
特別会計貸付 loans to Special Account
特別会計借入金 special account borrowing
特別会計による民間借入 special account private borrowing
特別買付け special bid
特別会費 special membership fee
特別解約返戻金 special surrender value
特別掛金 special contribution
特別加算 special addition
特別貸出金利 special advances rate
特別貸付勘定金利 special loan account interest rate
特別課税基金 special assessment fund
特別課徴金 special assessment
特別加入金 special admission fee
特別関係人 affiliated person
特別監査 special audit
特別勘定 special account
特別勘定残高 balance of the amount charged to special account
特別勘定に算入された補助金 subsidy charged to the special account
特別基金 special fund
特別危険 special risks
特別給付 special benefit
特別教書 Special Message
特別行政区 special administrative region
特別銀行勘定業者 special bank account firm
特 別 区 special ward
特別区民税 special ward inhabitants tax
特別決議 special resolution
特別決済 special payment
特別決済配当 special settlement dividend
特別気配 special quotation
特別現金勘定 special cash account
特別検査 special inspection

特別減税国債 special tax reduction bond
特別交換 special exchange
特別控除 special deduction
特別項目 special item
特別国際金融取引勘定 special international transaction accounts
特別国税調査官 special examiner
特別国税徴収官 special revenue officer
特 別 債 special bond
特別債券勘定 special bond account
特別裁定取引勘定 special arbitrage account
特別参加権 special participation right
特別参加者 special participant
特別参加者参加金 special participant participation fee
特別参加者預託金 special participant deposit
特 別 市 county borough
特別支出条件付売上割引 sales rebate with special payment terms
特別修繕費 special repair expenses
特別準備金 special reserve
特別償却 extraordinary depreciation；special depreciation
特別償却限度額 maximum special depreciation allowance
特別償却準備金 special depreciation reserve
特別償却不足額 shortage of special depreciation
特別償却率 rate of special depreciation deduction
特別条件危険 substandard risk
特別条件書 special conditions of the contract
特別条件付きの substandard
特別条件付保険料 substandard premium
特別証拠金要件 special margin requirement
特別剰余積立金 special surplus fund
特別所得税 special income tax
特別信用取引 special margin transaction
特別清算 special clearance；special liquidation
特別清算指数 special quotation；special settlement index price
特別清算承認 approval of special liquidation
特別清算の同意 agreement of special liquidation
特別清算料 Special Clearing Charge
特別税収債 special assessment bond
特別早期退職 special early retirement
特別損益 extraordinary gain or loss；extraordinary profit and loss；unusual profit and loss
特別損益項目 extraordinary item；extraordinary profit and loss item
特別損益前利益 earnings before extraordinary items
特別損害 special damage
特別損失 extraordinary loss
特別対価 special consideration
特別地方交付税 special local grant tax
特別地方消費税 special local consumption tax
特別調査課 Investigation Division
特別徴収 special collection
特別徴収義務者 special collecting agent
特別調整 ad hoc adjustment
特別積立金 special reserve
特別積立剰余金 assigned surplus；special surplus fund
特別当初償却 special initial depreciation
特別土地保有税 special landholding tax
特別トン税 special tonnage due
特別な業種 specialized industry
特別な経済的利益 special economic benefit
特別な減価償却方法 special methods of computing depreciation
特別な償却の方法 special depreciation method
特別な評価法 special valuation method
特別な目的に限る ad hoc
特別の機関 Attached Organizations
特別媒介機関 special intermediary institution
特別配当 bonus dividend；extra

dividend ; plum ; special dividend
特 別 費 special expenses
特別引当金 special reserve
特別引出権 Special Drawing Rights
特別引出権保有額 holdings of Special Drawing Rights
特別引出権利息 interest on Special Drawing Rights
特別費用 special charges
特別負担金 Special Dues
特別便益説 special benefit theory of taxation
特 別 法 special law
特別法人税 special corporate tax
特別マル優 special non-taxable treatment on small government bond
特別マル優制度 Special Maruyu program
特別目的会社 special purpose company ; special purpose vehicle
特別目的事業体 special purpose entity
特別目的税債券 special tax bond
特別目的トラスト special purpose trust
特別目的媒体 SPV (special purpose vehicle)
特別約款 special clause
特別融資 special loan
特別融資の実行 extension of special loan
特別養護老人ホーム special nursing home for the aged
特別預金制度 special deposit scheme
特別利益 extraordinary gain
特別利害関係者 persons having a special interest ; special interest party
特別料率 special rate
匿名組合 anonymous association ; secret partnership
匿名組合員 dormant partner
匿 名 性 anonymity
匿 名 の anonymous
匿名パートナー secret partner
特　約 special condition
特約医療機構 Preferred Providers Organization
特約再保険 treaty reinsurance
特約支払条件付仕入割戻 purchase rebate with special payment terms
特約条項 additional provision
特約取引 specified day transaction ; transaction with special condition
特約販売 selective selling
特約日受渡し delayed delivery
特約日決済取引 transaction with seller's option
特約日取引 transaction with specified date
特約リベート loyalty rebate
毒薬条項防衛 poison pill defense
特有財産 separate property
特融等に関する4原則 four principles of conducting business necessary to maintain financial system stability
独立会計士 independent accountant
独立会計制 self-accounting system
独立価格比較法 comparable uncontrolled price method
独立監査 independent audit
独立機関 autonomous agency
独立企業間価格 arm's length price
独立企業間の原則 arm's length principle
独立行政法人 independent administrative institution
独立行政法人評価委員会 Independent Administrative Institution Evaluation Committee
独立系発電事業者 IPP (independent power producer)
独立契約 independent contract
独立採算 self-support accounting
独立採算制 self-supporting accounting system
独立した鑑定人 independent appraiser
独立した事象 isolated event
独立した専門家の査定 independent professional assessment
独立した第三者 independent third party
独立指名権 power in gross
独 立 税 independent tax
独立性基準審議会 Independence Standards Board
独立生計 self-support subsistence

独立性の原則 independence rule
独立責任額比例主義 independent liability method
独立第三者間取引条件で arm's length
独立仲介者 independent intermediary
独立投資 autonomous investment
独立の構成部分 separate component
独立販売組織 independent marketing organization
独立変数 independent variables
特　例 special exception；special regulations；special rule
特例公債 Special Deficit-Financing Bonds
特例公債法 Special Deficit-Financing Bond Law
特例国債 special deficit financing bond；special JGSs
特例参加者 exceptional participant
特例条項 exception clause
特例取扱い interpretation of special rule
都市化 urbanization
都市開発 urban development
都市開発税 urban development tax
都市改良事業 urban remodeling enterprise
都市基盤 urban infrastructure
都市基盤整備公団 Urban Development Corporation
都市銀行 city bank
都市計画 town planning scheme
都市計画税 city planning tax
都市財政 municipal finance
都市周辺地帯 urban fringe
度数分布 frequency distribution
ToSTNet特例 Special Regulations on ToSTNeT
ToSTNet取引 ToSTNeT (Tokyo Stock exchange Trading Network system) trading
ToSTNet取引に関する業務規程、信用取引・貸借取引規程及び受託契約準則の特例 Special Regulations of Business Regulations, Margin/Loan Trading Regulations and Brokerage Agreement Standards Concerning ToSTNet Trading
土　地 land；land lot
土地改良 land improvement；land reform
土地改良事業 land improvement enterprise
土地改良費 land improvement expenses
土地課税台帳 land tax register book
土地勘定 land account
土地供与 land grant
土地収用 eminent domain；expropriation of land
土地収用権 land expropriation right；right of eminent domain
土地収用法 land expropriation law
土地所有 land ownership
土地所有者 land proprietor；landowner
土地信託 land trust
土地税制 land taxation
土地税制改革 land taxes reform
土地占有 possession of land
土地造成費 ground-making expenses；land grading cost
土地代金モーゲージ purchase money mortgage
土地台帳 land ledger；terrier
土地建物 land and building
土地建物に抵当権を設定する setting up mortgages for the real estate
土地賃貸権 lease of land
土地登記 land registration
土地登記所 land registry office
土地に対する後順位の権利 junior encumbrance
土地の収用 condemnation of land
土地の賃貸借契約 ground lease
土地売買契約 land contract
土地配分制度 allotment system
土地負担 land charges
土地分配法 agrarian laws
土地法 land law
土地保有 land tenure
土地保有者 land tenant
土着資本 indigenous capital

ト

どちらでも in one's own right
特　　化 specialization
特化係数 location quotient
凸 関 数 convex function
凸 集 合 convex set
凸版印刷 relief printing
特　　許 patent
特 許 局 Patent Bureau
特 許 権 patent right
特許権勘定 patent account
特許権使用料 royalty of patent right
特許権侵害 infringement of patent right
特許権の評価 valuation of patent right
特許出願中 patent applied for ; patent pending
特 許 証 letters patent
特許所有権者 patentee
特 許 庁 Japan Patent Office
特 許 品 patented article
特許紛争 patent dispute
特許弁理士 patent attorney
特 許 法 patent law
特許保有地 charter-land
特許有効期間 patent period
特 許 料 patent fee
独 禁 法 anti-monopoly law
ドック使用料 dockage
特恵関税 preferential duty ; preferential tariff
特 恵 的 preferential
特　　権 special concession
特権及び免除 privileges and immunities
特権的財 positional goods
特権濫用 breach of privilege
特 権 料 option money
ドッジ・ライン Dodge Line
トッピング・アウト topping out
トップス trust obligation participating securities
トップ・ストラドル top straddle
トップ・ダウン型投資 top-down investment
トップ・ダウン型予測 top-down forecasting
トップ・バーティカル・コンビネーション top vertical combination
トップ・リバーサル・デー top-reversal day
独 歩 安 falling into a weaker range across the board
都道府県分布 prefectural location
届　　出 registration
届出後使用制 file and use
届出事項 matters to be notified
届 出 書 registration statement
届出統計 registered statistics
届出目論見書 prospectus for securities registration
賭博保険（証書） wager policy
TOPIX TOPIX
トピックス TOPIX
TOPIXオプション TOPIX option
TOPIX先物取引 TOPIX futures
TOPIXニュー・インデックス・シリーズ TOPIX New Index Series
TOPIXの推移 TOPIX trends
土木研究所 Public Works Research Institute
富 affluence ; wealth
ドミニカ・ペソ DOP (Dominican peso)
ドミノ効果 domino effect
都 民 税 metropolitan inhabitant tax ; Tokyo inhabitants tax
トム・ネクスト tomorrow-next
トライアングル・リバーサル・パターン triangle reversal patterns
ドライバー保険 automobile drivers' liability insurance
ドラゴン債 dragon bond
トラスト・レシート trust receipt
トラベラーズ・チェック TC (traveler's check)
トランシェ tranche
トランシェ取引 tranche trading
トランシェ評価 tranche valuation
トランシェ分けされた tranched
トランス・ドニエストル（ルーブル） Transdniester (ruble)
トランスファー・メカニズム transfer mechanism

トランスファー問題 transfer problem
トランスファー・リスク transfer risk
トランプ税 playing cards tax
取扱経費 handling expenses
取扱注意 use with care
取 扱 費 handling cost
トリガー trigger
トリガー価格 trigger price
取 替 え replacement
取替価格 replacement price
取替原価会計 replacement cost accounting
取替原価保険 replacement cost insurance
取替資産 replaced asset；replacement assets
取替単位 replacement unit
取替費用 renewal expenses；replacement expenses
取 替 法 replacement method
取 崩 額 dispositioned amount
取 崩 す withdraw
取消さざる許可 irrevocable license
取消されうる権原 defeasible title
取　　消 revocation；withdrawal
取消可能 voidable
取消可能信託 revocable trust
取消可能信用状 revocable L/C (letter of credit)
取 消 権 annulment right
取消訴訟 revocation suit
取消注文 cancel order
取消不能信託 irrevocable trust
取消不能信用状 irrevocable L/C (letter of credit)
取消不能生前信託 irrevocable living trust
取消不能な選択 irrevocable choice
取消不能のコミットメント irrevocable commitment
取消不能保証 non-cancelable guarantee
取消まで有効注文 GTC (good-till-cancelled) order
取消まで有効な注文 good-till-canceled orders
取 消 す annul；countermand；revoke
取りこわし費 demolition expenses
取下届出書 statement of withdrawal
取下げる abandon；withdraw
取締役会決議 decision of the Board of Directors
取 締 役 director
取締役会 board of directors
取締役会議事録 minutes of meeting of the board of directors
取締役会規則 rules on the board of directors
取締役会決議 corporate resolution
取締役会召集通知 notice of board of directors' meeting
取締役会の承認 clearance from the board
取締役限定株式 shares qualified for directors
取締役任期の分散 staggered board of directors
取締役の員数 number of directors
取締役の選任 election of directors
取締役の任期 terms of office of directors
取立為替 bill receivable；exchange for collection
取立業者 collecting agent
取立銀行 collection bank
取立債務 debt for collection
取立手形 collection bill
取立手形管理サービス management service for bill for collection
取立手数料 charge for collection
取立費用 collection expenses
取立不能見込額 estimated uncollectable amount
取立命令 order for collection
取　　次 introducing
取次銀行 transmitting bank
取 次 者 agent
取次者差換預託 agent replacement deposit
取次証拠金 agency margin
取 付 け run upon a bank
取り手レート bid rate
トリニダード・トバゴ・ドル TTD (Trinidad & Tobago dollar)
取　　引 bargain；market transaction；

trade；transaction
取引相手探し seeking a market
取引赤字 trading deficit
取引一件ごと基準 trade-by-trade basis
取引一件ごとの決済 trade-for-trade settlement
取引オプション traded option
取引価格 sale price
取引価額 value of the transaction
取引確認 trade validation
取引勘定 dealing account
取引機会 trading opportunity
取引期間 time horizon
取引規則 trading regulations
取引規模 lot size
取引基本要領 principal terms and conditions for money market operations
取引拒否 refusal to deal
取引銀行 relationship bank
取引金融機関 correspondent financial institution
取引後から決済前 post-trade and pre-settlement
取引後処理 post-trade processing
取引コスト transaction cost
取引再開 resumption of suspended trading
取引再構築コスト transaction restructuring cost
取引最終日 last trading day
取 引 先 correspondent in a business；trade party
取引先総合管理 relationship management system
取引先の倒産 counter party failure
取引サマリー表 compared trade summary
取引参加権 trading right
取引参加者 trading participant
取引参加者規程 trading participant regulations
取引参加者契約 trading participant agreement
取引参加者代表者 trading participant representative
取引参加者の自己の計算に基づく取引 transaction for the trading participant's own account (or principal transaction)
取引参加者負担金 trading participant fee
取引参加者保証金の預託 trading participant security deposit
取引参照番号 TRN (transaction reference number)
取引資格 qualification for trading
取引資格停止 suspension of qualification for trade
取引資格の喪失 waiver of trading qualification
取引資格の取消 revocation of trading qualification
取引資格の付与 grant of trading qualification
取引シフト transaction shift
取引種類別 by types of trading
取 引 所 bourse；stock exchange
取引条件 business terms；trade term；trading conditions
取引条件書 schedule of terms and conditions
取引照合 trade comparison；trade matching
取引証拠金 clearing margin
取引証拠金基準額 standard amount of clearing margin
取引証拠金額算定基準日 base date for clearing margin calculation
取引証拠金の換金 liquidation of clearing margin
取引証拠金の管理 management of clearing margin
取引証拠金の区分 classification of clearing margin
取引証拠金の返戻 refund of clearing margin
取引証拠金返還請求権 right to claim the return of clearing margin
取引証拠金率算定基準値 standard value for clearing margin rate calculation
取引上の圧迫 trading constraints

取引所会員 exchange member；member of stock exchange；trading member
取引所買付け exchange acquisition
取引所外取引 ex-pit transaction；off-exchange transactions
取引所外取引市場 third market
取引所会費 member's fee
取引所市場 exchange market
取引所準会員 allied member
取引所税 bourse tax；exchange tax
取引所特別税 securities exchange special tax
取引所取引 exchange traded transaction；exchange transactions；stock exchange transaction；transaction on exchange
取引所取引オプション exchange traded options
取引所取引基金 exchange fund
取引所取引税 bourse transaction tax
取引所の開設 provision of an exchange market
取引所の清算機関 stock exchange clearing house
取引所分配 exchange distribution
取引所法 exchange law
取引所有価証券市場 market of the exchange
取引事例 trade example
取引事例比較法 comparison of business transactions
取 引 税 trading tax；transaction tax
取引制限契約 restraint of trade agreement
取引相場のない株式の評価 valuation of stock without quotation
取引総費用 total cost of transaction
取引代金 contract value；transaction value
取引代行取引参加者 acting trading participant
取 引 高 trading volume
取引高削除 volume deleted
取引高税 turnover tax
取引単位 normal trading unit；underlying size；unit of trading
取引単位制度 trading unit system
取引担保金 trading collateral
取引中断 trading halt
取引停止 suspension from transactions
取引停止処分 disposition by suspension of business
取引手数料 brokerage commission；transaction fee
取引動機 transaction motive
取引内容 particulars of transaction
取引に係るリスク risks on transactions
取引に対する税 tax on transaction
取引日計表 blotting book
取引の一時停止 trading halt
取引の一方を解消 lifting of a leg
取引ノウハウ trading know-how
取引の影響 effect of transaction
取引の確認 confirmation of transaction
取引の貸方側 credit side of the transaction
取引の借方側 debit side of the transaction
取引の再開 resumption of trading
取引の執行 trade execution
取引の失敗 missing of the market
取引の種類 kinds of transactions
取引の信義則 just and equitable principles of transactions
取引の制限 restrictions on trading
取引の性質 nature of transaction
取引の締結 closing of transaction
取引の内容 content of transactions
取引の流れ transaction chain
取引の媒介 intermediation of trading
取引の与信条件 trade credit terms
取 引 日 T+0；trading day
取引日基準会計 trade date accounting
取引ピット trading pit
取引日の契約 T contracts
取引費用 dealing cost
取引フロー・マネージャー TFM (transaction flow manager)
取引ポスト trading post
取引マージン dealer's margin
取 引 前 pre-trade
取引明細 schedule of transactions

ト

取引約定書 agency arrangement
取引約諾書 customer's agreement and consent
取 引 量 volume of transaction
取引レンジ trading range
取引を手じまう unwind a trade
取引を白紙にする busting a trade
トリプル・クロスオーバー法 triple crossover method
トリプルDES暗号 triple-DES (Data Encryption Standard) algorithm
トリプル・トップ triple top
トリプル・ボトム triple bottom
取 戻 し recapture
取 戻 権 right of resumption
度量標準 standard of price
トリレンマ trilemma
ド ル buck ; dollar
ドル売り介入 intervention by selling dollars
ドル・円市場 yen-dollar foreign exchange market
ドル・円相場 price auction in USDJPY
ドル・円相場を支える supporting USDJPY
ドル買い円売り buying USDJPY
ドル外交 dollar diplomacy
ドル価格 dollar price
ドル加重収益率 dollar-weighted rate of return
ドル過剰 overhung dollar
ドル為替本位 dollar exchange standard
ドル換算レート exchange rate per dollar
ドル勘定 dollar account
ドル危機 dollar crisis
トルクメニスタン・マナト TMM (Turkmenistan manta)
ドル口座開設書類 documents for opening a U.S. dollar account
ドル・コール・オプション dollar call option
ドル・コスト平均法 dollar cost averaging
トルコ・リラ TRL (Turkish lira)
ド ル 債 dollar bond
ドル先物安 forward discount of U.S. dollar
ドル資産 US portfolio assets
ドル・シフト dollar shift
ドル選好 dollar preference
ドル相場への圧迫 negative implication for the dollar
ド ル 高 strong dollar
ドル高基調 firm tone of the U.S. dollar
ドル建て in dollar terms
ドル建債務 debt in U.S. dollar
ドル建転換社債 dollar convertible bond
ドル建ての dollar denominated
ドルとの連動 maintaining the dollar peg
ドルに換算して dollar wise
ドルに対し安値 low against the dollar
ドルの下落 dollar decline
ドルの下落圧力 pressure the dollar
ドルの購買力 purchasing power of dollar
ドルの対円での下落 USDJPY down
ドルの低キャリー low carry on the dollar
ドル・プール dollar pool
ドル不足 dollar gap ; dollar shortage
ドル・プット・オプション dollar put option
ドル・ブロック dollar bloc
ドル平価 dollar parity
ドル平均 dollar averaging
ドル平均法 dollar average method
ドル防衛 dollar defense
ド ル 安 adding to USD downside ; depreciation of dollar ; USD fall ; weakening dollar
ドルを買い支える supporting USD
トレーダー trader
トレーディング・スタンプ trading stamp
トレーディング対象（アカウント） trading accounts
トレーディング・プール trading pool
トレーディング目的有価証券 trading securities
トレード・オフ trade-off
トレード・チケット trade ticket
トレジャリー・ダイレクト Treasury Direct
トレンドGDP成長率 trend GDP growth

トレンド・チャンネル trend channel
トレンドの転換 reversal in the trend
トレンド・フォロアー trend follower
ドロップアウト・オプション dropout option
ドロップ・ロック債 drop-lock bond
トロント工業株指数 Toronto Industrial Index
トロント先物取引所 Toronto Futures Exchange
トロント証券取引所 Toronto Stock Exchange
鈍　　化 deceleration ; slowdown
トンガ・パアンガ TOP (Tonga pa'anga)
ト ン 税 tonnage due
トン税納付書 note for payment of tonnage dues
トンチン年金 tontine annuity
トンチン配当 tontine dividend
トンネルの中のへび snake in the tunnel
問　　屋 wholesale merchant

ナ

名 宛 人 addressee ; drawee
内外価格差 price differentials between domestic and overseas markets
内外金利差 international interest-spread
内閣官房 Cabinet Secretariat
内閣官房長官 Chief Cabinet Secretary
内閣官房副長官 Deputy Chief Cabinet Secretary
内閣設置法 Law Establishing the Cabinet Office
内閣総理大臣 Prime Minister
内 閣 府 Cabinet Office
内閣府令 cabinet office ordinance
内閣法制局 Cabinet Legislation Bureau
内規の改正 revision of office regulation
内航貨物海上保険 coastwise cargo insurance
内 国 株 domestic stock
内国為替 inland exchange
内国為替運営機構 Organization for Management of Domestic Fund Transfers
内国為替制度 Domestic Fund Transfer System
内国為替手形 inland bill of exchange
内国為替取引 domestic exchange
内 国 債 internal bond
内国歳入委員会 IRC (Inland Revenue Commissioners)
内国歳入局 Bureau of Internal Revenue
内国新株引受権証書 domestic warrants
内 国 税 internal tax
内国貿易 internal trade
内国法人 domestic corporation
内国法人の合併 merger of a domestic corporation
内国民待遇 national treatment
内　　債 internal debt
内 在 化 internalization
内在価値 implied value
内在的コール価格 implicit call price
ナイジェリア・ナイラ NGN (Nigerian naira)
内　　需 domestic demand
内需拡大 domestic demand expansion ; increasing domestic demand
内需関連株 domestic demand related stock
内需減速 slower growth of domestic demand
内需産業 domestic demand oriented industry
内需振興 domestic demand stimulation
内需を引っ張って leading domestic demand
内生部門 endogenous sector
内生変化 endogenous change
内生変数 endogenous variable
内　　諾 informal acceptance
内地勤務 home service
内部売上 internal sales
内部運用 in house management
内部会計統制 internal accounting control
内部開発 internal development
内部格付け internal rating
内部格付制度 internal credit rating system
内部化注文 internalized order
内部監査 internal audit
内部監査基準 internal audit standard
内部監査制度 internal audit system
内部監査人 internal auditor
内部監査人協会 Institute of Internal Auditors
内部監査部 OIOS(Office of Internal Oversight Services)
内部監査報告書 internal audit report
内部管理システム check and balance system
内部規程 internal regulations

内部キャッシュフロー internal cash flow
内部金融 internal financing
内部経営情報 internal management information
内部経営分析 internal business analysis
内部牽制 internal check
内部牽制システム internal check and balance
内部牽制制度 internal check system
内部構造 internal structure
内部告発者 whistle blower
内部財務報告制度 internal financial reporting system
内部財務予算 internal financial budgeting
内部資金 internal fund
内部資本 internal capital
内部者取引・証券詐欺取締法 Insider Trading and Securities Fraud Enforcement Act of 1988
内部収益率 internal rate of return
内部証拠 internal evidence
内部情報 inside information
内部情報源 internal source of information
内部資料 internal document
内部信用補完 internal credit enhancement
内部整合性 internal consistency
内部セグメント internal segment
内部創出資金 internally generated fund
内部統制 internal control
内部統制組織 internal controlling organization
内部統制のテスト test of internal controls
内部取引 internal transaction
内部評価 internal evaluation
内部部局 Internal Subdivisions
内部負債 internal liability
内部振替 intra-company transfer
内部振替価格 intra-company transfer price
内部振替差額 intra-company transfer variance
内部振替利益 interdepartmental profit；internal transfer profit
内部分析 internal analysis
内部報告 internal reporting
内部報告会計 accounting for internal reporting
内部報告制度 internal reporting system
内部報告セグメント internally reported segment
内部報告目的 internal reporting purpose
内部利益 internal profit
内部利子率 internal rate of interest rate
内部留保 retained profit
内部留保金 internal reserve
内部労働市場 internal labor market
内包金利 implicit interest
内容証明郵便 content-certified mail
内容表示文言 words of limitation
NOW negotiable order of withdrawal
NOW勘定 NOW account
NOW預金 NOW deposit
ナウル（豪ドル） Nauru (Australian dollar)
仲 買 人 commission merchant
仲 立 人 go-between
仲継加工貿易 intermediate improvement trade
中　　値 mid-market level
仲　　値 mid-market value；TTM (telegraphic transfer middle rate)
長年の先例 historical precedent
長引く景気の低迷 prolonged weakness in the economy
流抵当約款 insecurity clause
投 売 り distress selling；fire sale；forced sale；sacrifice sale；shaking-out；slaughter sale
投げ売る offload
ナショナル・トラスト national trust
ナショナル・ミニマム national minimum
ナスダック NASDAQ (National Association of Securities Dealers Automated Quotation)；Nasdaq
ナスダック・ジャパン Nasdaq Japan
ナスダック総合株価指数 NASDAQ Composite Index
NASD様式FR-1 NASD Form FR-1
捺印証書 title deed
捺印証書契約の違反 breach of covenant

捺印の印章照査 collation of seals
70%の戻り 70% retracement
ナノ秒 nano-second
波が大きい fluctuating
並為替 exchange bill payable；ordinary remittance
並手形 ordinary bill
並替え permutation
ナミビア・ドル NAD (Namibia dollar)
成行き at the market
成行注文 market order；order without limit
成行呼値相互間の順位 precedence among market orders
なれあい売買 accommodation trades；matched order
ナレッジ活動 knowledge activities
縄張り争い turf war
軟化 weakening
軟貨 soft currency
軟貨国 soft currency country
難色 reservation
軟調 sag；weak tone
ナンピン averaging
ナンピン売り average down
ナンピン買い average up
ナンピン売買 scale trading

ニ

ニア・ザ・マネー near the money
荷受け人 consignee
二営業日渡し one day skipped
荷落信用状 documentary clean credit
2カ月に1回の bimonthly
ニカラグア・コルドバ NIO (Nicaraguan Cordoba)
荷為替信用状 documentary letter of credit
荷為替手形 documentary bill ; documentary draft
荷為替手形の買取 negotiation of endorsed documentary drafts
二極化する undergoing polarization
二極化プレミアム schizophrenic premium
二計算書 two statements
二元的所得税制 dual income tax system
二項過程 binominal process
二項格子 binomial lattice
二項分布 binomial distribution
二項分布モデル binomial model
二国間協定 bilateral agreement
二国間貿易 bilateral trade
西アジア経済社会委員会 ESCWA(Economic and Social Commission for Western Asia)
ニジェール（CFAフラン） Niger (CFA (Communauté Financière Africaine) franc)
二次関数 quadratic function
二次計画法 quadratic programming
二次的証拠 secondary evidence
二次的責任 secondary obligation
二次的特性 secondary qualities
二次的トレンド secondary trend
二次的要因 secondary effect
二次分売 secondary distribution
二次変分 quadratic variation
二者択一 forced choice
二者択一注文 either or order
二重裏書小切手 double endorsed check
二重運賃制 dual rate system
二重価格 double price
二重価格買付 two-tier bid
二重課税 double taxation
二重課税防止条約 convention for the avoidance of double taxation ; DTA (double taxation agreement)
二重為替相場制 dual exchange market
二重勘定取引 dual trading
二重関税 double tariff
二重競売制度 double auction system
二重銀行制度 dual banking system
二重金利政策 dual interest policy
二重経済 dual economy
二重経済構造 economic dualism
二重計算 double counting
二重契約主義 duplex system
二重構造 dual structure
二重構造市場 two tier market
二重公民権 dual citizenship
二重差押 double attachment ; double seizure
二 重 性 duality
二 重 損 chatter
二重担保公債 combination bond
二重通貨建債 dual currency bond
二重の危険 double jeopardy
二重の効果 dual effect
二重の費用 double charge
二重負債 double liability
二重分配 double distribution
二重満期 double dated
24時間市場 round-the-clock market
24時間取引 24 hours trading
荷　　印 shipping marks
二 親 等 consanguinity in the second degree
偽 ド ル green goods
2000年問題 year 2000 glitches
2000年を100とした normalized to 100

in 2000
2層の two layer
二段階オファー two tier offer
二段階最小自乗法 TSLS (two-stage least squares) method
日額給付 daily benefit ; per diem benefit
日銀預け金 deposits with the Bank of Japan
日銀応募 subscription by Bank of Japan
日銀会計規程 Accounting Rules of the Bank
日銀貸出 BOJ lending
日銀が振り出した drawn by the Bank of Japan
日銀監事 Executive Auditor of the Bank of Japan
日銀小切手 BOJ check
日銀再割適格手形 commercial bill eligible for rediscounting with the Bank of Japan
日銀信用 Bank of Japan credit
日銀政策委員会 Policy Board of the Bank of Japan
日銀総裁 Governor of the Bank of Japan
日銀短観 BOJ (Bank of Japan) Short-Term Observation ; BOJ (Bank of Japan) Tankan
日銀当座預金 deposits in the Bank of Japan current accounts
日銀当座預金残高 outstanding balance of current accounts at the Bank of Japan
日銀当座預金増減要因と金融調節 Sources of Changes in Current Account Balances at the Bank of Japan and Market Operations
日銀当預 BOJ current accounts
日銀当預から引落される debited from the BOJ accounts
日銀当預残高 outstanding balance of BOJ accounts
日銀当預増減の銀行券要因 banknotes factor affecting current account balances
日銀当預増減の財政等要因 treasury funds factor affecting current account balances
日銀当預増減要因 sources of changes in CABS (current account balances)
日銀当預取引先 BOJ account holders
日銀当預に貸方計上される credited to the BOJ accounts
日銀当預の資金不足要因・資金余剰要因 funds shortage factor and a funds surplus factor
日銀当預の入金・引落 credit and debit to BOJ accounts
日銀特融 special loan by the Bank of Japan
日銀ネット BOJ net
日銀ネット（当座預金系） BOJ-NET funds transfer system
日銀ネット（国債系） BOJ-NET JGB services
日銀引受 underwriting by the Bank of Japan
日銀副総裁 Deputy Governor of the Bank of Japan
日銀法施行規則 Enforcement Regulations of the Bank of Japan Law
日銀法施行令 Bank of Japan Law Enforcement Order
日銀理事 Executive Director of the Bank of Japan
日常業務 day-to-day operation ; routine business
NICS NICS (newly industrialized countries)
荷造費 baling charges ; packing and wrapping expenses
日経225指数オプション Nikkei 225 Index option
日経300オプション Nikkei 300 Options
日経300株価指数 Nikkei 300 Stock Price Index
日経300株価指数連動型上場投資信託 Nikkei 300 Index fund
日経300先物取引 Nikkei 300 Futures
日経300投資信託 Nikkei 300 Investment Trust

日経ダウ Nikkei Dow-Jones Average
日経225オプション Nikkei 225 Options
日経225先物取引 Nikkei 225 Futures
日経の動き behavior of the Nikkei
日 計 表 blotter ; daily trial balance
日経平均 Nikkei 225 ; Nikkei Average ; Nikkei index
日経平均株価 Nikkei Stock Average
日経平均株価先物 Nikkei 225 index futures
日経平均の急落 sharp sell off in the Nikkei
ニッケル黄銅貨幣（新500円） nickel-brass coins (500 yen)
日証決済状況 settlement at the Japan Securities Clearing Corporation
日足移動平均線 DMA (Days Moving Average)
日足チャート daily chart
日中高低値 intraday high and low
日中証拠金請求 intra-day margin call
日中当座貸越 intraday overdraft
日中ブリッジ daytime bridge
日 当 daily allowance ; per diem allowance
日本経団連(日本経済団体連合会) Japan Business Federation ; Nippon Keidanren
2ドルブローカー 2 dollar broker
荷主危険持ち owner's risk
2年に1度の biennial
二番譲渡抵当 wraparound
二 番 底 double dip recession
二番抵当 second mortgage
二番抵当付社債 second mortgage bond
二番天井 double peak
2ファンド現金分離 two fund monetary separation
二部上場 listing on the Second Section
2分2乗法 split taxation
2分の1所有会社 50 percent owned company
2分の1償却法 50% depreciation
二 分 法 dichotomy
日本育英会 Japan Scholarship Foundation
日本インベスターズ・サービス Japan Investors Service
日 本 円 JPY (Japanese yen)
日本円先物オプション Japanese yen futures option
日本円短期金利先物 Japanese yen short-term interest futures
日本円通貨先物 yen futures
日本学術振興会 Japan Society for the Promotion of Science
日本格付研究所 JCR (Japan Credit Rating Agency)
日本型レバレッジド・リース JLL (Japanese leveraged lease)
日本株投信 Japanese equity fund
日本機械保険連盟 Union of Machinery Insurers of Japan
日本銀行 Bank of Japan
日本銀行が保有する国債の銘柄別残高 Japanese Government Bonds held by the Bank of Japan
日本銀行勘定 accounts of the Bank of Japan
日本銀行金融研究所 Institute for Monetary and Economic Studies
日本銀行金融ネットワークシステム（日銀ネット） BOJ-NET (Bank of Japan Financial Network System)
日本銀行券 Bank of Japan note
日本銀行券及び当座預金 Bank of Japan notes and deposits
日本銀行券の発行 issuance of Bank of Japan notes
日本銀行券の引換え exchange of Bank of Japan notes
日本銀行券発行税 Bank of Japan note issue tax
日本銀行代理店 Bank of Japan's agent bank
日本銀行定款 By-laws of the Bank of Japan
日本銀行の会計 Bank's accounts
日本銀行の財務の健全性 financial soundness of the Bank of Japan

日本銀行の自主性 autonomy of the Bank of Japan
日本銀行の消却義務 performance of bearing duty by Bank of Japan
日本銀行振替決済規程 Bank of Japan Book-Entry Regulations
日本銀行振替決済制度 Bank of Japan Book-Entry System
日本銀行法 Bank of Japan Law
日本クレジット産業協会 Japan Credit Industry Association
日本経営者団体連盟(日経連) Japan Federation of Employers' Associations
日本経済団体連合会(日本経団連) Japan Business Federation ; Nippon Keidanren
日本芸術文化振興会 Japan Arts Council
日本工業規格 JIS (Japanese Industrial Standards)
日本工業標準調査会 JISC (Japanese Industrial Standards Committee)
日本航空保険プール Japanese Aviation Insurance Pool
日本公社債研究所 Japan Bond Research Institute
日本公認会計士協会 Japan Institute of Certified Public Accountants
日本国債 JGB (Japanese government bond)
日本国債清算機関 clearing corporation for JGBs (Japanese Government Bonds)
日本国有鉄道清算事業団 Japan National Railways Liquidation Corporation
日本国有鉄道清算事業団債券等承継国債 government bonds converted from Japanese National Railways Settlement Corporation bonds and the like
日本CP協議会 JCPA (Japan Commercial Paper Association)
日本証券アナリスト協会 SAAJ (Security Analysts Association of Japan)
日本証券業協会 Japan Securities Dealers Association
日本証券金融 Japan Securities Finance Company
日本証券クリアリング機構 JSCC (Japan Securities Clearing Corporation)
日本証券経済研究所 Japan Securities Research Institute
日本商工会議所 Japan Chamber of Commerce and Industry
日本消費者金融協会 JCFA (Japan Consumer Finance Association)
日本商品先物協会 Commodity Futures Association of Japan
日本商品投資販売業協会 Japan Commodities Fund Association
日本信託証券 Japanese trust certificate
日本スポーツ振興センター National Agency for the Advancement of Sports and Health
日本政策投資銀行 Development Bank of Japan
日本政策投資銀行法 Development Bank of Japan Law
日本政府保証債 Japanese government-guaranteed debt
日本税法学会 Japan Tax Jurisprudence Association
日本税務協会 Japan Tax Association
日本税理士会連合会 Japan Federation of Certified Tax Accountants' Associations
日本船主責任相互保険組合 Japan Ship Owners Mutual Protection & Indemnity Association
日本船舶保険連盟 Japanese Hull Insurer's Union
日本損害保険協会 Marine and Fire Insurance Association of Japan
日本損害保険代理業協会 Independent Insurance Agents of Japan
日本的経営 Japanese management
日本道路公団 Japan Highway Public Corporation
日本農林規格 JAS (Japan Agricultural Standard)
日本万国博覧会記念機構 Commemorative

Organization for the Japan World Exposition '70
日本版ビッグバン Japanese big bang
日本版401kプラン Japanese 401k Plan
日本標準時間 JST (Japan standard time)
日本フィナンシャル・プランナーズ協会 Japan Association for Financial Planners
日本貿易振興機構 JETRO (Japan External Trade Organization)
日本貿易保険 Nippon Export and Investment Insurance
日本保険医学会 Association of Life Insurance Medicine of Japan
日本保険学会 Japanese Society of Insurance Science
日本マルチペイメント・ネットワーク運営機構 JAMMO (Japan Multi-Payment Network Management Organization
日本郵政公社 Japan Post
日本預託証書 Japanese Depositary Receipts
荷もたれ感相場 heavy market
入院給付 hospital benefit
入院給付特約 hospital confinement benefit
入院日額給付保険 hospital cash cover
入院賠償責任保険 hospital liability policy
入院費保険 hospital expense insurance
入院保険 hospitalization insurance
入院補償 hospital indemnity
入院補償保険 hospital indemnity insurance
ニュー・エコノミー new economy
入会金 admission fee；entrance fee；initiation fee
入会金の負担 burden of payment of entrance fees
入会権 common
入会審査 examination of entrance qualification
ニューカレドニア（CFPフラン） New Caledonia (CFP (Comptoirs Francais du Pacifique) franc)
入居状況 occupancy
入金 money received；receipts of money
入金総額 aggregate proceeds
入金通知 advice of credit
入金伝票 paying in slip；receipt slip；receipt voucher
入金表 credit slip
入金予測額 prospective cash receipts
入港税 harbor dues；port dues
入港費用 expenses of entering port
入国税 landing tax
入札 bidding
入札オペ tender operation
入札価格 bidding price
入札が未達になる go undersubscribed
入札期間 auction period；tender period
入札公告 advertisement for bid
入札者 bidder
入札者への指示書 instruction to bidders
入札書 form of bid
入札総額 offering size
入札の受理 acceptance of bids
入札の通知 announcement of auction
入札のプロセス procedures of auction
入札発行 issue by tender
入札日 auction date
入札引受 tender
入札方式優先株 AMPS (auction market preferred stock)
入札保証書 tender bond
入札保証証券 bid bond
入札保証保険 bid guarantee insurance
入札前取引 JGB transactions prior to auction
入札累積優先株式 CAMPS (cumulative auction market preferred stock)
ニュージーランド準備銀行 RBNZ (Reserve Bank of New Zealand)
ニュージーランド証券取引所 New Zealand Stock Exchange
ニュージーランド・ドル NZD (New Zealand dollar)
入手可能性 availability
入手可能な証拠 available evidence
入手可能な情報 available information

入 場 税 tax on admission
ニュー・ディール New Deal
ニュートラル・ヘッジ neutral hedge
ニューマネー優先株 new money preferred
ニューメレール numeraire
ニューヨーク・オフショア市場 New York Offshore Center
ニューヨーク銀行 BONY (Bank of New York)
ニューヨーク銀行間出し手金利 New York inter-bank offered rate
ニューヨーク金融市場 New York money market
ニューヨーク先物取引所 NYFE (New York Futures Exchange)
ニューヨーク場外取引所 New York Curb Exchange
ニューヨーク証券取引所 Big Board ; NYSE (New York Stock Exchange)
ニューヨーク証券取引所株価指数 NYSE (New York Stock Exchange) Index
ニューヨーク証券取引所総合指数 NYSE (New York Stock Exchange) composite index
ニューヨーク商品取引所 New York Commodity Exchange
ニューヨーク総合指数 NYSE Composite
ニューヨーク引受信用状 New York acceptance credit
ニューヨーク・マーカンタイル取引所 New York Mercantile Exchange
ニューヨーク綿花取引所 NYCE (New York Cotton Exchange)
ニューヨーク・リファイナンス New York refinance
ニューヨーク連邦準備銀行 Federal Reserve Bank of New York
入力データ data input
二 流 株 secondary stock
にわか景気の booming
荷渡指図書 delivery order ; release order
任意医療保険 voluntary health insurance
任意受渡し free payment
任意解散 voluntary dissolution ; voluntary winding up
任意解約 voluntary cancellation
任意型継続投資プラン voluntary accumulation plan
任意加入 voluntary participation
任意加入年金制度 voluntary pension plan
任意監査 voluntary audit
任意規定 adoptive provisions
任意拠出 voluntary contribution
任意組合 voluntary association ; voluntary partnership
任意繰入額 voluntary additions
任意再保険 facultative reinsurance
任意再保険協定 facultative reinsurance agreement
任意従業員給付組合 VEBA (Voluntary Employee Beneficiary Association)
任意準備金 optional reserve ; voluntary reserve
任意償還 optional redemption ; voluntary redemption
任意償還可能証券 callable securities
任意償還債券 callable bond
任意償還債務 callable obligation
任意償還条項 call provision
任意償還プレミアム call premium
任意償還利回り yield to call
任意償却 voluntary depreciation
任意償却法 voluntary depreciation method
任意整理 voluntary liquidation
任意仲裁 voluntary arbitration
任意的給付 voluntary benefit
任意デフォルト・シナリオ random default scenario
任意納税地 voluntary place of tax payment
任意の適用 voluntary adoption
任意の配分 arbitrary allocation
任意の日 given date
任意の費用 discretionary expenses
任意付加拠出 AVC (additional voluntary contribution)
任意不動産貸借権 tenancy at will
任意不動産物件 estate at will
任意プラン voluntary plan

任 意 法 adoptive act
任意保険 voluntary insurance
認　　可 authorization
認可会社 admitted company
任　　期 tenure of office；term of office
人 気 株 active stock；favored stock；popular stock
人気50銘柄 favorite fifty；nifty fifty
人気の落ちた銘柄 wall flower
人間関係 HR (human relations)
人間工学 human engineering
人間の生命価値 human life value
認　　識 recognition
認識基準 recognition criteria
認識された損失 recognized loss
認識された利益 recognized profit
認識時点 timing of recognition
認識上の制限 limit on recognition
認識トリガー recognition trigger
認識の延期 delayed recognition
認識の識閾 threshold for recognition
認識の消滅 derecognition
認識の消滅要件 requirements for derecognition
認識の中止基準 derecognition criteria
認識要件 recognition requirement
認　　証 authentication
認証基準 authorization criteria
認証制度 Accreditation Program
認証謄本 attested copy；certified copy
認証番号 authorization number
認　　知 cognizance；public acknowledgment
認 知 法 recognition method
認知ラグ recognition lag
認定期間 qualification period
認定勤務年数 credited service
認定収入 constructive receipt
認定賞与 constructive bonus
認定生命保険士 chartered life underwriter
任　　務 mission
任　　命 appointment
認容資産 admissible assets

ネ

値上り　price appreciation
値上り益　capital appreciation；capital appreciation gain
値上り期待　upside potential
値上り局面で　at an increase in price
値上げ　price hike；price rise
値洗い　marking to market
値洗い価値　mark-to-market value
値洗い勘定　mark-to-market account
値洗い基準　mark-to-market basis
値洗い日　mark-to-market date
寧夏回族自治区　Ningxia
値入　marking
値動き　movement of market price；price action；price change
ネーキッド・オプション　naked option
ネーキッド・コール　naked call
ネーキッドの売り　writing naked
ネーキッド・ポジション　naked position
ネーキッド・ワラント　naked warrant
値がさ株　fancy stocks；heavy share；high-priced stock
ネガティブ・アモチゼーション　negative amortization
ネガティブ・オプション　negative option
ネガティブ・キャリー　negative carry
ネガティブ・コベナント　negative covenant；negative covenants
ネガティブ・プレッジ条項　negative pledge clause
ネガティブ・プレッジ・パリパス条項　negative pledge pari passu clause
ネガティブ・リスト　negative list
ネガティブ領域　negative territory
値切った価格　knock-down price
値決め　price fixing
値頃　reasonable price
値下り　pullback
値下り局面で　at a decrease in price
値下り余地　downside potential
値下げ　price cut
値下げ圧力　pressure on pricing
値ざや稼ぎ　speculation for difference
Necigef（オランダ保管振替機関）　Necigef
値段の限度　limit of price
根担保　blanket collateral；pooled collateral；revolving collateral
根強い　persistent
根抵当　blanket lien；blanket security；fixed collateral；maximal collateral
根抵当権　blanket security interest；fixed mortgage
根保証　blanket guarantee；revolving guarantee
熱狂相場　feverish market
ネックライン　neck line
値付け　making of a price
値付け機能　market making function
値付け状況　market making condition
捏造　fabrication
ネッティング　netting
ネッティング会員　netting system member
ネッティング契約　netting arrangement
ネッティング決済率　netting ratio
ネット売手　net seller
ネット・オープン・ポジション　net open position
ネット買手　net buyer
ネット・キャッシュ　net cash
ネット・キャッシュフロー　net cash flow
ネット・キャピタル・ルール　net capital rule
ネット決済情報　net settlement information
ネット・プライス・インデックス　net price index
ネット・ブロック・フロー　net block flow
ネット・リース　net lease

ネパール・ルピー NPR (Nepalese rupee)
値　　幅 price difference；range of price fluctuation
値幅制限 daily price limit；daily trading limit；fluctuation limit；price movement limit
値幅注文 stop limit order
値　　引 mark down；reduction in price
値 増 金 excess receipt over contract price
年1回後払い annual payment
年1回の計算 annual calculation
年1回払いの取決め annual yield convention
年央準備金 mean reserve
年 会 員 annual member
年 会 費 annual dues；annual membership fee
年 価 法 annual value method
年間期限前償還率 conditional repayment rate
年間雇用率 annual employment
年 換 算 annual basis
年間支出当座比率 quick assets to year's cash expenses
年間純益 yearly net earnings
年間所得 annual earnings
年間生産能力 annual capacity
年間定額払法 equal annual payment method
年間年金給付額 annual pension benefit
年間の回転回数 times per year
年間の利益総額 total annual earnings
年間非課税項目 annual exclusion
年間保険料 annual premium
年間保証所得 guaranteed annual income
年間保証賃金 guaranteed annual wage
年間利益処分額 annual profit disposition amount
年間リターン annual return
年　　金 pension
年金移管 pension mobility
年金運用口 pensions accounts
年 金 化 annuitization
年金改革 pension reform
年金会計 pension plan accounting
年金価格 annuity price
年金掛金 annuity premium
年金掛金調整 pension adjustment
年金型ローン annuity loan
年金加入 pension participation
年金管理 pension administration
年金期間 annuity period
年金基金 pension fund
年金基金運用収益率 rate of return on pension funds
年金基金管理 pension fund management
年金基金資産 pension fund assets
年金基金剰余金 pension plan surplus
年金基金積立機関 funding agency
年金基金積立契約 funding instrument
年金基金の資産運用 pension fund investment
年金基金の使命 pension fund's mission
年金基金の受益者 pension fund beneficiary
年金基金の剰余 pension fund surplus
年金規約 rules on pension plan
年金給付 pension benefits
年金給付額 pension credit
年金給付額算定方式 benefit formula
年金給付専用ファンド PCMF (pension cash management fund)
年金給付発生分 pension accrual
年金給付保証公社 PBGC (Pension Benefit Guaranty Corporation)
年金給付保証保険 pension plan insurance
年金給付率 annuity rate
年金給付累積額 accumulated plan benefits
年金業務 pension business
年金協約 annuity agreement
年金契約 pension contract
年金契約者 annuity policyholder
年 金 権 pension right
年金現価 present value of annuity
年金現価係数 uniform series worth factor
年金現価充足方式 terminal funding method
年金現価積立方式 terminal funding

ネ

年金購入基金 annuity purchase fund
年金購入方式 annuity purchase plan
年金購入料率 annuity purchase rates
年金コスト pension cost
年金財政 pension financing
年金財政方式 pension financing method
年金再保険 annuity reinsurance
年金式支払生命保険 income policy
年金式分割受取り annuity settlement
年金支給 pension award；pension payout
年金支給開始年齢 age when pension is granted；pensionable age
年金支給額 annuity distribution；annuity payout
年金資金 pension money
年金資金預り金 annuity fund deposit
年金資金運用基金 Government Pension Investment Fund
年金資産 pension assets；plan assets
年金資産預り金 fund deposit
年金資産実際運用収益 actual return on plan assets
年金資産の実際収益 actual return on pension assets
年金支払オプション annuity payout option
年 金 者 pensioner
年金終価 future value of an annuity
年金収入 pension income
年金受益者 plan beneficiaries
年金受給額上限 pension cap
年金受給権 pension entitlements；right to benefit
年金受給権付与率 pension vesting rate
年金受給資格 pension eligibility
年金受給者 annuitant
年金受給者に対する債務 pensions-in-payment liabilities
年金受給対象額 pensionable earnings
年金受給率 pension recipiency
年金受託者 pension plan trustee
年金受領者の生存 survival of annuitant
年金証書 pension certificate
年金商品 annuity product；pension business lines
年金消滅保険 pension termination insurance
年金剰余の金利感応度 interest sensitivity of the pension surplus
年金信託 pension trust
年金水準 pension level
年金数理人 pension actuary
年金数理費用計算方式 actuarial cost method
年金生活者 pensioner
年金制度 pension plan；pension program；pension scheme
年金制度資産 pension plan assets
年金制度終了保険 plan termination insurance
年金制度上の年金会計 accounting for the cost of pension plans
年金制度スポンサー plan sponsor
年金制度責任準備金 pension plan liability reserve
年金制度の移管 pension transfer
年金生命保険 life insurance annuity
年金担保住宅ローン pension mortgage
年金貯蓄 pension savings
年金付生命保険 income endowment policy
年金付き保険 endowment annuity；income endowment；insurance with annuity；insurance with annuity
年金積立 pension buildup
年金積立金 pension reserve
年金積立金算定方式 pension fund method
年金提供者 pension provider
年金点数 pension point
年金投資基金信託 pension investment fund trust
年金特約 annuity rider
年金の期間原価 periodic pension cost
年金のコスト cost of pension
年金の消滅 pension termination
年金の政治的側面 politics of pensions
年金払い annuity payment
年金パラシュート pension parachute
年金費用 benefit plan expense；pension

expense
年金評価 pension valuation
年金費用積立 pension pan funding
年金費用積立年金保険 pension plan annuity
年金プール pension pool
年金賦課方式 unfunded pension plan
年金負債 pension liability
年金プラン規定書 pension plan documents
年金プラン純資産 net pension plan assets
年金プランのスプレッド pension fund spread
年金返還 pension reversion
年金ポイント制 pension point system
年 金 法 pensions legislation
年金保険 annuity；annuity insurance
年金保険受給開始日 annuity starting date
年金保険信託併用退職年金 combination funding plan
年金保険領域 annuity territory
年金保証 pension guarantee
年金未加入者 non-pensioner
年金持ち分 pension equity
年金約定 pension commitments
年金ユニット annuity unit
年金利回り法 actuarial method
年功序列賃金制度 seniority order wage system
年 功 制 seniority system
年次株主総会 annual meeting of shareholders
年次監査 annual audit
年次計算書 annual statement
年次決算 annual accounting
年次決算書（NAIC） convention report (NAIC)
年次財務諸表 annual financial statements
年始準備金 initial reserve
年次上昇率 annual increase
年次総会 annual meeting
年次の決算書 annual accounts
年次報告書 annual report
年次報告書期間 annual reporting period
年　　収 annual income
年収益率 annual rate of returns
年次有給休暇 paid annual leave
念　　書 comfort letter；letter of undertaking
年初からの累積で on a year-to-date basis
年初来の YTD (year-to-date)
年数依存 age dependent
年税主義 yearly taxation
年 増 法 advance-in-age plan
年 代 順 chronology
年　　度 FY (fiscal year)
年度間税配分 inter-period tax allocation
年度区分 classification of fiscal years
年度決算 accounts for fiscal year
年度締切 annual closing
年度初め beginning of the fiscal year
年 度 別 by fiscal year
年 度 末 end of the fiscal year
年2回決算の会社 corporation settling accounts twice a year
年2回払いの市場 semi-annual market
年の中間までに by mid-year
年払いクーポン annual coupon
年払保険料 yearly premium
年　　賦 annual installment；yearly installment
年賦課金 annual fees
年 賦 金 annuity
年賦償還 redemption by yearly installment
年複利収益率 ratio of compound annual return
年平均成長率 CAGR (compound average growth rate)
年俸制度 annual compensation package
年　　末 year-end
年末残高 outstanding at the year-end
年末相場 year-end market
年末調整 year-end adjustment；year-end settlement
年末の資金需要 year-end demand for fund
年末ラリー year end rally
年　　利 annual interest rate；APR (annual percentage rate)；interest

per annum；per annum rate
年　　率 annualized rate
年率換算 annualized basis
年率換算したボラティリティ annualized volatility
年率のパーセンテージ annual percentage rate
年利回り annual yield；annualized yield
燃料勘定 fuel account
燃 料 費 fuel cost
年齢構成 age distribution
年齢制限 age limit
年 齢 層 age group
年齢別保険料 age-based premium
年齢料率制 age-rated system

ネ

ノ

納　　会 final session of a month
納　　期 delivery schedule
納期限 due date for tax payment ; time for tax payment
納期限の延長 extension of due date
農業会計 farm accounting
農業環境技術研究所 National Institute for Agro-Environmental Sciences
農業協同組合 Japan Agricultural Cooperatives
農業銀行 agricultural bank
農業金融 agricultural credit
農業組合 agricultural society
農業経営費 agricultural expenditure
農業経済学 agricultural economics
農業工学研究所 National Institute for Rural Engineering
農業先取特権 agricultural lien
農業者大学校 National Farmers Academy
農業住宅局 FmHA (Farmers Home Administration)
農業所得 agricultural income
農業所得の免税 tax exemption for agricultural income
農業生産法人 agricultural production corporation
農業・生物系特定産業技術研究機構 National Agriculture and Bio-oriented Research Organization
農業生物資源研究所 National Institute of Agrobiological Sciences
農業簿記 agricultural bookkeeping
農業保険 agricultural insurance
農業補助金 farm subsidy
農産物価格政策 price policy of agricultural products
農産物関税 agricultural tariff
農場抵当貸付 farm mortgage loan
農水産業協同組合貯金保険機構 Agricultural and Fishery Co-Operative Savings Insurance Corporation
納　　税 tax payment
納税委託 consignment of tax liability
納税額 amount of tax payment ; tax due
納税管理人 administrator of tax payment ; tax agent ; tax manager
納税管理人の届出 notification of tax agent
納税期日 tax due date
納税義務 tax liability ; tax obligation
納税義務者の区分 classification of a taxpayer
納税義務のある法人 corporation liable to taxation ; corporation subject to taxation
納税義務の確定 establishment of tax liability
納税義務の継承 succession of tax liability
納税義務の成立 realization of tax liability
納税義務の負担 burden of tax liability
納税協会 Tax Payment Association
納税組合 taxpayer's association
納税告知書 notification of tax payment ; rate papers ; tax papers
納税者 taxpayer
納税者訴訟 taxpayers' suit
納税者の選択 taxpayer's option
納税者番号 taxpayer identification number
納税者番号制度 taxpayer identification number system ; taxpayer numbering system
納税準備金 deposit for tax payment
納税準備証券 anticipation tax bill
納税準備預金 deposits for tax payment
納税証明書 certificate of tax payment
納税申告区分選択 tax status selection
納税申告書 tax return form

納税申告明細書 tax schedules
納税申告用紙 tax forms
納 税 済 duty-paid
納税済証書 certificate of completion of tax payment
納税専用口座 exclusive account for tax payment
納税担保 security for tax payment
納 税 地 place for tax payment
納税地異動の届出 notification of transfer of place of tax payment
納税地指定 designation of place for tax payment
納税地の異動 transfer of the place of tax payment
納税地の変更 change of the place of tax payment
納税調整 tax preparation
納税貯金 savings in preparation for tax payment
納税貯蓄組合 savings-for-tax association
納税通知書上の納税期間 tax period appearing on tax bill
納税の公平 equalization of tax payment
納税引当額 tax provision
納税引当金 accrued income taxes；provision for income tax；reserve for tax liability
納税負担 burden of paying tax
納税弁護士 tax lawyer
納税保証 guarantee of tax payment
納税未済 tax unpaid
農畜産業振興機構 Agriculture and Livestock Industries Corporation
納入告知 notice of payment
ノウハウ使用料 royalty as to know-how
ノウハウ漏洩 leak of know-how
納 品 書 delivery note
納品不足 short delivery
納　　付 paying tax
納付委託 consignment of tax payment
納付義務の承継 succession of tax obligation
納付催告書 notice of demand to guarantor
納 付 書 tax payment slip
納付すべき税金に対する税額控除 tax credit against the tax payable
納付の督促 demand for tax payment
農薬検査所 Agricultural Chemicals Inspection Station
能率監査 efficiency audit
能率差異 efficiency variance
能率専門官 Special Officer for Efficiency
能　　力 ability；competency
能 力 給 incentive wage；pay according to ability
能力原価 capacity cost
能 力 者 legal ability person
能力のある当事者 competent parties
能力の低下 deterioration of capacity
農林漁業金融機関 financial institution for agriculture forestry and fisheries
農林漁業金融公庫 Agriculture Forestry and Fisheries Finance Corporation
農林漁業信用基金 Agriculture, Forestry and Fisheries Credit Foundations
農林水産業 fishery, agriculture and forestry industry
農林水産省 Ministry of Agriculture, Forestry and Fisheries
農林水産消費技術センター Center for Food Quality Labeling and Consumer Services
農林水産大臣 Minister of Agriculture, Forestry and Fisheries
農林中央金庫 Central Cooperative Bank for Agriculture and Forestry；Norinchukin Bank
農林中金 Norinchukin Bank
ノー・アクション・レター no action letter
ノート・イシュアンス・ファシリティ note issuance facility
ノード方式 node method
ノーフォルト自動車保険 no fault automobile insurance
ノーブランド商品 generics
ノーマル・アセット・ミックス normal asset mix
ノーマル・ターゲット・アロケーション

normal target allocation
ノーロード・ストック no load stock
ノーロード・ファンド no load fund
ノーロス・ノープロフィット no loss no profit
残りの資産 remaining asset
望ましい現金の流れ favorable cash flows
望ましい資金の流れを産み出す能力 ability to generate favorable cash flows
望ましくない引締め unwelcome tightening
ノック・アウト・オプション knock-out option
ノック・アウト・オプション取引 knock-out option trading
ノック・オン効果 knock-on effect
ノック・ダウン製品 knock-down product
乗取り屋 corporate raider
伸び止まる slow
伸び悩みの lackluster
NOBスプレッド NOB (notes over bonds) spread
延払基準 deferred payment basis
延払条件 delayed payment terms
延払条件付請負 contract works with the condition of deferred payment attached
延払条件付販売 deferred payment sales
延払信用 supplier's credit
延払輸出 deferred export
延払輸入 maker's credit
延 渡 し deferred delivery
乗合勘定 omnibus account
乗 換 え switch
乗換オークション switch auction
乗換特権 exchange privilege
乗換保険契約 replacement policy
乗換募集 twisting
ノルウェー・クローネ NOK (Norwegian krone)
ノルウェー中央銀行 Norges Bank
の れ ん goodwill
のれんに帰属する金額 amount attributable to goodwill
のれんの補完 enhancement of goodwill
ノンコーラブル・ボンド non-callable bond
ノンデポジトリー・コルレス non-depository correspondent
ノン・フリート契約者 non-fleet insured
ノン・マリン代理店制度 non-marine agency system
ノン・リコース non-recourse
ノン・リコース形式 non-recourse form
ノン・リコース・ローン non-recourse loan

ハ

パー・イールド par yield
バーコード bar code
パーシェ方式 Paasche formula
バーゼル委員会 Basel Committee
バーゼル銀行監督委員会 BCBS (Basel Committee on Bank Supervision)
バーゼル合意 Basel agreement
パーセンテージ注文 percentage order
パーセンテージ・リース percentage lease
パーソナル・チェック personal check
パーソナル・ファイナンス personal finance
バーター貿易 barter trade
パーチェス契約 purchase contract
パーチェス法 purchase method
バ ー ツ baht
バーティカル・スプレッド vertical spread
バーティカル・スプレッド取引 vertical spread transaction
パーティシペーション契約 participation agreement
ハードウエア市場 hardware market
ハード・ドル hard dollar
パートナーシップ partnership
パートナーシップ契約 partnership agreement
パートナーシップ財産 partnership property
パートナーシップ保険 partnership insurance
パートナーシップ持ち分 partnership interest
ハード・マネー hard money
ハード・ランディング hard landing
ハードル・レート hurdle rate
ハード・ローン hard loan
パー発行 issue at par
パーフォーマンス特性 performance attribution
パーフォーマンスの測定 performance measurement
パー・フォワード par forward
バーベル型運用 barbell portfolio management
バーベル戦略 barbell strategy
バーベル・ポートフォリオ barbell portfolio
ハームレス・ワラント債 harmless warrant
パールハーバー・ファイル pearl harbor file
バイアス bias
バイ・アンド・ライト戦略 buy and write strategy
ハイ・イールド債への移行 move into high yield
ハイ・イールド銘柄組入枠 high yield bucket
廃　　貨 demonetarization
売　　価 labeled price
売価按分法 relative sales value method
バイカイ crossed trade
バイカイ手数料 each way
媒　　介 intermediary
媒介機関 conduit
売価還元法 retail method
倍額減債約款 option to double
倍額支払い double indemnity
倍額支払災害給付 double accident benefit
倍額支払災害年金 double indemnity annuity
倍額支払養老保険 double endowment assurance
倍額定率法 double declining balance method
倍額保障保険 double protection insurance
売価棚卸法 selling price inventory method
廃　　棄 abandonment
廃棄価値 abandonment value
廃 棄 物 waste

廃棄物処理委託料 tipping fee
廃 棄 法 retirement method
売　　却 divestiture
売 却 益 gain on sale；profit on sale
売却価格 exit price
売却価額 exit value；sale value
売却可能 available-for-sale
売却可能金融資産 financial assets available-for-sale
売却可能資産 assets available-for-sale
売却可能証券 securities for sale
売 却 権 power of sale
売却原価 cost of products sold
売却時価 current exit value
売却時返済条項 due on sale clause
売却制限株式 letter stock
売却戦略 exit strategy
売 却 損 loss on sale
売却手取額 net sale proceeds
売却による全額返済 due on sale
売 却 年 sales year
売却の対価 sale consideration
ハイ・キャリー high carry
配給制度 rationing
廃　　業 discontinuance of business
廃 棄 率 abolition rate
配 偶 者 spouse
配偶者控除 deduction for spouse；marital deduction；spouse tax credit
配偶者特別控除 special exemption for spouse
ハイ・クーポン債 high-coupon bond
背　　景 backdrop
背景説明資料 background material
背景的事項 background information
バイ・サイド buy side
廃残設備 discarded equipment；retired equipment；scrap equipment
廃　　止 abolition；abrogation
廃止された税金 repealed taxes
廃止事業 discontinued operation
廃止セグメント discontinued segment
廃疾条項 disability clause
廃止に伴う損益 gain or loss on discontinuance
廃止部門 discontinued operations
廃止部門からの利益 income from discontinued operations
敗者のゲーム losers game
買　　収 acquisition
買収額面金額 purchase face amount
買収価値 takeover value
買収・合併・撤退 M&A&D (merger, acquisition and divesture)
買収関連株 deal stock
買収関連銘柄 issues in play
買収契約書 purchase agreement
買収原価 cost of acquisition
買収条件 terms of acquisition
買収事例方式 acquisition multiple method
買収する buy out
買収戦略 acquisition strategy
買収による裁定取引 takeover arbitrage
買収の会計 acquisition accounting
買収の任意調査 purchase investigation
買収ブーム takeover boom
賠 償 金 indemnity；reparations
賠償責任保険 general liability insurance
賠償責任免除契約 hold harmless agreement
排除可能リスク avoidable risk
排除の原則 exclusionary rule
媒　　体 media
媒体広告 media advertising
媒体手数料 media commission
配達証明郵便 delivery-certified mail
ハイチ・グルデ HTG (Haiti gourde)
ハイテク株 technology shares
ハイテク株式 high-tech stock
ハイテク株ファンド technology fund
ハイテク商品開発者 rocket scientist
配　　当 dividend
配当受取選択権 dividend option
配当落ち dividend off；XD (ex dividend)
配当落期間 ex-dividend period
配当落ち日 day of ex-right for the dividend
配当落日 ex-dividend date

配当会社 dividend paying company
配当額とみなす金額 amount regarded as dividend
配当可能剰余金 divisible surplus
配当可能利益 profit available for dividend；surplus available for dividend
配 当 株 dividend stock
配当還元 dividend capitalization
配当還元価額 capitalized value of stock
配当還元株式評価 stock valuation based on dividend
配当還元方式 dividend discount method
配当還元モデル dividend discount model
配当期間 distribution period
配当期待権 expectancy right of dividend
配当金異動会社 companies changing the amount of dividend
配当金勘定 dividend account
配当金控除 dividend credit
配当金再投資 dividend reinvestment plan
配当金支払事務委任契約 dividend payment business commission agreement
配当金支払取扱銀行 dividend payment bank
配当金総額 amount of dividends paid
配当金同等物 dividend equivalents
配当金の支払いをする法人 company paying dividend
配当金の除斥期間 limitation for claiming payment of dividends
配当金引出 dividend withdrawal
配当金割引再投資 discount dividend reinvestment
配当軽課 reduced tax rate on dividend paid
配当決議 declaration of dividend
配当決議日 dividend declaration date
配当源泉選択課税 alternative withholding tax on dividends
配当控除 credit for dividend；deduction for dividends；tax credit for dividend
配当込株価指数 dividend-included stock price indices
配当込みTOPIX dividend-included TOPIX
配当算入率 dividend compounding rate
配当算入利率 compounding rate
配当支払い delivery of dividends；dividend distribution；dividend payment；dividend payout
配当支払機関 dividend paying agent
配当支払銀行 dividend paying bank
配当支払必要額 dividend requirements
配当社債 income bond
配当重視投資会社 income investment company
配当収入 receipts of dividends
配当証書 scrip certificate
配当所得 dividend income
配当所得損失 loss from dividend income
配当所得の損失 loss of dividend income
配当所得の帰属者 real obtainer of dividend income
配当水準 dividend scale
配当据置支給 deferred distribution
配当請求権 dividend right
配当制限 limitation on dividend；restriction on dividend payment
配当性向 dividend payout ratio；dividend propensity
配当政策 dividend policy
配当宣言 dividend declaration
配当宣言日 declaration date
配当損金法 dividend-paid deduction method
配当付き cum dividend；dividend on
配当付終身保険 participating whole life insurance
配当付生命保険証券 participating life insurance policy
配当付年金 with-profit annuity
配当付保険 dividend paying insurance；with-profit insurance
配当付保険剰余金 participating policy surplus
配当付保険保険料 participating premium
配当積立 dividend accumulation；

ハ

dividend deposit
配当積立金 dividend reserve；reserve for dividend
配当積立ユニット accumulation unit
配当取り dividend capture；dividend rollover plan
配当に対する課税 taxation on dividend
配当による買増し dividend addition
配当年度 dividend year
配当能力 ability to pay dividend
配当の決定 determination of dividend
配当倍率 equity dividend cover
配当パズル dividend puzzle
配当含み cum-dividend
配当不算入 dividend exclusion
配当フロー dividend flow
配当分離課税 separated taxation on dividend income
配当平均準備金 reserve for equalization of dividend
配当平均積立金 dividend equalization reserve
配当平準化積立金 dividend equalization reserve
配当への配慮の欠如 failure to consider dividend policy
配当変動準備金 dividend fluctuation reserve
配当保証利率 dividend crediting rate
配当優先株式 dividend preferred stock
配当予定 dividend schedule
配 当 率 dividend rate
配当率調整優先株 ARP (adjusted rate preferred stock)
配当利回り dividend yield
配当割引 dividend discount
配当割引モデル DDM (dividend discount model)
配当割引率 dividend discount rate
配当を受ける carry dividend
配当を目玉にした販売 selling dividend
配当率入札方式優先株 auction rate preferred stock
バイナリー・オプション binary option
背　　任 misappropriation
ハイパー・インフレーション hyper inflation
売　　買 buying and selling；purchases and sales
売買一任勘定 discretionary account
売買一任勘定取引 discretionary account trading
売買委任 trading authorization
売買回転率 turnover ratio
売買価格帯 closing range
売買確認書 contract slip
売買額面金額 face value of the position
売買可能権原 marketable title
売買勘定 trading account
売買監理 market supervision
売買計算書 purchase and sale statement
売買契約 sales contract
売買契約上の債務 purchase commitment
売買契約締結 contract formation
売買契約の譲渡 assignment of sales contract
売買契約の締結 conclusion of a transaction contract
売買契約前受金 advanced collection on sale contracts
売買システム trading system
売買照合 transaction collation
売買証拠金 margin for transactions
売買数量 transaction volume
売買損益勘定 trading profit and loss account
売買代金 trading value
売 買 高 trading volume
売買高の少ない市場 narrow market
売買立会時 trading hours
売買立会による売買 trading in trading session
売買立会の区分 division of trading sessions
売買立会の臨時挙行 temporary holding of trading session
売買単位 unit of trading
売買単位未満数量 number of shares less than the unit of trading
売買停止 suspended trading

売買等損益 trading income or loss
売買に適する権利 marketable title
売買の安全をはかる securing completion of transactions
売買の一時中断 temporary trading halt
売買の回数 number of trading
売買の仕組み trading mechanism
売買の受託 acceptance of orders for trading
売買の精度 trading precision
売買の態様 form of transactions
売買のための施設 trading facilities
売買報告書 purchase and sale statement
売買目的 trading purpose
売買目的以外の有価証券 non-dealing securities
売買目的金融資産 financial assets held for trading
売買目的で保有する負債 liability held for trading
売買目的有価証券 securities held for trading；trading account securities
バイパス bypass
バイパス信託 bypass trust
ハイパワードマネー（マネタリーベース） high-powered money (monetary base)
配賦勘定 absorption account
配賦基準 apportionment base
配賦済製造間接費 absorbed burden
配付税 apportioned tax；distribution tax
配賦超過原価 over-absorbed cost
配賦不足 under absorbed
配賦率 absorption rate；burden rate
ハイブリッド確率 hybrid probability
ハイブリッド市場 hybrid market
ハイブリッド商品 hybrid instrument
ハイブリッド信託 hybrid trust
ハイブリッド選定 hybrid selection
ハイブリッド・トレーディング・システム hybrid trading system
ハイブリッド変額商品 hybrid variable product
配分 allocation
配分可能利益 distributable income
配分効率 allocation efficiency
配分地管理人 allotment warden
配分判決 decree of distribution
配分方法 attribution method
配分モデル allocation model
配分率 allocation ratio
HIBOR HIBOR (Hong Kong inter-bank offered rate)
PIBOR PIBOR (Paris interbank offered rate)
バイ・マイナス注文 buy minus
バイヤーズ・クレジット buyer's credit
ハイヤ・パーチェス hire purchase
バイ・ライト戦略 buy-write strategy
ハイリスク・ハイリターン high-risk high-return
倍率方式による評価 valuation by multiplier
パイロット・プラント pilot plant
ハウス・エージェンシー house agency
ハウス・ビル house bill
破壊処分 destructive disposition
墓場市場 graveyard market
端株 fractional lot；odd lot；odd lot shares
端株株券 scrip
端株空売比率 odd-lot short sale ratio
端株業者 odd lot dealer
端株原簿 list of holders of fractional shares
端株整理 odd lot consolidation
端株注文 fractional order
端株取引 odd-lot transaction
端株取引基準株価 effective sale
端株の買取り purchase of fractional shares from holders
端株売買手数料 odd lot differential
端株分を含まない based on round lots
端株理論 odd-lot theory
破棄差戻し reversed and remanded
パキスタン・ルピー PKR (Pakistan rupee)
波及経路 transmission mechanism
波及効果 knock-on effect；multiplied

effect；repercussion effect
波及効果クレーム impact claims
白紙委任 carte blanche
白紙委任公募 blank check offering
白紙委任信託 blind trust
剥　奪 deprivation
白銅貨幣（旧500円、100円、50円） copper-nickel coins (500 yen, 100yen, and 50 yen)
爆発的な伸び explosive growth
激しいインフレ rampant inflation；volatile inflation
覇　権 hegemony
派遣する dispatch
ハザード関数 hazard function
ハザード・モデル hazard model
破　産 bankruptcy
破産管財 administration in bankruptcy
破産管財人 administrator in bankruptcy；receiver in bankruptcy；trustee in bankruptcy
破産監査官 comptroller in bankruptcy
破産企業 bankrupt entity
破産規則 bankruptcy rules
破産原因 cause of bankruptcy
破産行為 act of bankruptcy
破産更生債権及びこれらに準ずる債権 bankrupt or quasi-bankrupt assets
破産告知 bankruptcy notice
破産債権 claim in bankruptcy
破産財団 bankruptcy estate
破産財団持ち分 bankruptcy estate equity
破産裁判所 bankruptcy court
破産債務者 bankruptcy debtor
破 産 者 bankrupt；insolvent debtor
破産者財産差押令状 warrant in bankruptcy
破産者債務免除 discharge of bankruptcy
破産申請 bankruptcy filing
破産審理人 referee in bankruptcy
破産清算人 accountant in bankruptcy；liquidator in bankruptcy
破産宣告 adjudication of bankruptcy；declaration of bankruptcy
破産宣告された adjudicated bankrupt
破産手続 insolvency proceedings
破産手続開始決定 determination of commencement of bankruptcy procedure
破産の管理 bankruptcy administration；case administration
破産の整理品 distress goods
破 産 法 bankruptcy law；insolvency law
破産命令 adjudication order
破産申立 bankruptcy petition
破産優先支払い preferential payment in bankruptcy
破産予期 contemplation of bankruptcy
パシフィック証券取引所 Pacific Stock Exchange
パシフィック取引所 PCX (Pacific Exchange)
始　値 opening rate
始値・引値 opening rate and closing rate
始めの約定値段 opening contract price
端　数 fractional figure
端数期間支払年金 apportionable annuity
端数金額 fractional sum
端数桁処理方法 rounding convention
端数保険料 fractional premium
端数利息 fractional interest
バスケット basket
バスケット対当取引 basket cross trading
バスケット通貨 basket currency
バスケット取引 basket trading；basket transaction
バスケット方式 basket system
バスケット・ワラント basket warrant
パス・スルー pass-through
パス・スルー証券 pass-through securities
パス・スルー証書 PTC (pass-through certificate)
パス・スルー比率 pass-through rate
は ず み momentum
派生需要 derivative demand
派生証券 derivative securities
派生商品 contingent claim；derivative instrument；derivative product；derivatives

派生商品会社 DPC (derivative product company)
派生商品市場 derivative market
派生商品ポートフォリオ derivative portfolio
派生訴訟 derivative suit
派生的な contingent
派生的収入 derived income
派生的需要 derived demand
派生的所得 derivative income
派生的預金 derivative deposit
派生取引 derivative transaction
派生パス・スルー証券市場 derivative pass-through securities market
破　損 breakage
破損銀行券 soiled and damaged banknotes
パターン情報処理 pattern information processing
パターン認識 pattern recognition
裸信託 bare trust
裸　値 ex-coupon
裸値段 net price
裸値取引 net price trading
裸本文 bare body
場立ち floor clerk
バタフライ・スプレッド butterfly spread
バタフライ・スプレッド取引 butterfly spread trading
破綻企業 blow-up entity；failing company
破綻金融機関 failed financial institution
破綻金融機関債務 obligations of the failed financial institution
破綻金融機関の整理 resolution of the failed financial institution
破綻懸念先 deemed bankrupt borrower
破綻更生債権 loans in bankruptcy and regeneration
破綻先 legally bankrupt borrower
破綻先債権 loans to borrowers in legal bankruptcy
破綻メンバー以外による損失負担 survivor's pay
8営業日決済 T+7
場違い筋 outsider
バチカン（イタリア・リラ） Vatican City (Italian lira)
8桁精算表 eight column work sheet
発　会 first session of a month
罰科金 fine and penalty
罰　金 amercement
パッキング・クレジット packing credit
バックアップ・ファシリティ back-up facility
バックアップ・ライン back-up line
バック・オフィス back office
PAC債 PAC (planned amortization class) bond
パックス・アメリカーナ pax Americana
バック・ツー・バック信用状 back to back credit
バック・ツー・バック取引 back to back transaction
バック・ツー・バック・ローン back to back loan；back-to-back loan
パックマン・ディフェンス Pac-man defense
パッケージ・ディール契約 package deal contract
パッケージ保険 package policy
パッケージ・リース package lease
発見危険の原則 doctrine of discovered peril
発券局 Currency Issue Department
発券銀行 bank issuing banknotes
発券制度 system of note issue
発見リスク detection risk
発行開始日 launch date
発行会社 issuer；issuing corporation
発行会社の信用状態 creditworthiness of the issuers
発行価格 issuance price；offer price
発行価額 issuance value；issue value
発行額 issuance volume
発行環境 issuing environment
発行規模 volume of issuance
発行銀行 issuing bank
発行銀行券 banknotes
発行国債の当初登録・当初寄託請求

requests for initial registration or initial deposit of issued JGSs
発行根拠法 legal status of issuance
発行差額 issue difference
発行差金 agio
発行残高 outstanding balance of issue amount
発行時額面超過額 OIP (original issue premium)
発行市場 issue market ; primary market
発行時満期 original maturity
発 行 者 issuer
発行者支払コスト NIC (net interest cost)
発行者費用 issuer's cost
発行条件 conditions of issuance ; issue terms ; terms and conditions of issuance
発行条件書 pricing supplement
発行商社 issuing house
発行時割引 original issue discount
発行時割引額 OID (original issue discount)
発行済み issued and outstanding
発行済株式 capital stock issued ; old shares ; shares issued ; shares outstanding
発行済株式資本金 issued capital stock
発行済株式数 number of stocks issued
発行済株式総数 all-issued stocks
発行済債券 bond issued
発行済資本 outstanding capital
発行済資本金 issued capital
発行済証券 securities outstanding
発行済のワラント warrant outstanding
発行済普通株式 ordinary shares outstanding
発行済累積優先株 outstanding cumulative preferred shares
発 行 税 issue tax
発行体の債務不履行 issuer defaults
発 行 高 amount issued
発行手数料 opening commission
発行登録 shelf registration
発行登録効力発生通知書 Notice of Shelf Registration Having Taken Effect
発行登録制度 shelf registration system
発行登録追補書類 Supplementary Documents to the Shelf Registration Statement
発行登録取下届出書 statement of withdrawal of shelf registration
発行登録目論見書 prospectus prepared in connection with shelf registration
発行届出書 shelf-registration statement
発行年限 years to maturity
発行パターン issuance pattern
発 効 日 effective date
発 行 日 date of issuance
発行日基準 when-issued basis
発行日決済取引に係る委託証拠金 margin for when-issued transactions
発行日決済取引の委託 entrustment on when-issued transactions
発行日取引 WI (when-issued transaction)
発行日取引の解消 cancellation of when-issued transaction
発行保証制度 reserve for banknote issuance system
発行目的 issuance purpose
発行目的別分類 classification by issuance purpose
発行予定 visible supply
発行予定債券 bond in a pipeline
発行利回り issuing yields
発 行 量 volume on offer
パッシブ運用 passive management
パッシブ運用のポートフォリオ passive portfolio
パッシブ損失 passive loss
パッシブ・パートナー passive partner
パッシブ・マーケット・メーキング passive market making
抜粋計算書 abstract of accounts
抜粋財務データ selected financial data
発　　生 accrual
発生確率 probability of occurrence
発生期間 accrual period
発生給付費用 accrued benefit cost
発生給付評価 accrued benefit valuation
発生給付評価方式 accrued benefit

valuation method
発生給付方式 accrued benefit method
発生金額 amount already accrued
発生経費 expense incurred
発生原価 incurred cost
発生源となる事業 underlying business
発生項目 accrual accounts
発生債務負担 obligations incurred
発生した日 date of origin
発生主義 accrual basis
発生主義会計 accrual accounting；accrual basis accounting
発生主義会計の前提 accrual accounting assumptions
発生主義で on an accrual basis
発生時レート current rate；historical rate
発生損益 accrued gains and losses
発生年金権移管金 accrued right premium
発生年度基準 earned basis
発生年度方式 incurred to earned basis
発送運賃 freight and cartage outward
発送通知書 advice note
発 送 費 delivery expenses；shipping expense
罰　　則 penal provision
罰則条項 penalty clause
バッチ取引システム batch trading system
発注者免責条項 disclaimer clause
発 注 量 order quantity
発展段階 developmental stage
発展途上国 developing countries；LDC (less developed country)
発表税率 announced tax rate
波動関数 wave function
波動ストラクチャー wave-count structure
波動調整 rolling readjustment
歯止め効果 ratchet effect
花 形 株 leading share
花形銘柄 leaders
パナマ・バルボア PAB (Panamanian balboa)
バニラ・オプション vanilla option
バニラ・スワップ vanilla swaps
バヌアツ・バツ VUV (Vanuatu vatu)
派　　閥 clique
バハマ・ドル BSD (Bahamian dollar)
バハレーン・ディナール BHD (Bahraini dinar)
パプアニューギニア・キナ PGK (Papua New Guinea kina)
パフォーマンス証拠金 performance margin
パフォーマンス評価 performance evaluation
パフォーマンス・ファンド performance fund
バブル経済 bubble economy
バミューダ・オプション Bermudian option
バミューダ・ドル BMD (Bermuda dollar)
早受渡制度 premature delivery futures system
早 出 料 dispatch money
早 め る lead
払 い 超 excess disbursement
払込期日 last payment date；payment date
払込期日現在の新株の価格 price of new stocks on the day to be paid in
払込金額 paid amount
払込時期 time of payment
払込資本 paid-in capital；paid-up capital
払込資本金 capital stock paid in
払込資本収益率 profit rate of paid-up capital
払 込 者 paying person
払込出資金 contribution to equity capital
払込剰余金 capital contributed in excess of par (value)；paid-in surplus
払込済価額 paid-up value
払込済株式 paid-up stock
払込済証券保管庫 free box
払込済年金 paid-up annuity
払込済保険 paid-up insurance；paid-up policy
払込中断保険料 skip premium
払 込 付 cum call
払込取扱銀行 payment handling bank
払 込 日 due date of payment；payment day

払込融資貸付 loan of subscription payment funds
払済保険 paid-up insurance
払済保険購入式生命保険 paid-up life insurance
払出証票 voucher for disbursement
払 戻 し refunding
払戻方針 refund policy
パラオ（米国ドル） Palau (US dollar)
ハラキリ・スワップ harakiri swap
パラグアイ・グァラニ PYG (Paraguay guarani)
パラメーター parameter
パラメトリック法 parametric method
パラレル・マーケット parallel market
パラレル・ローン parallel loan
バランス型マネジャー balanced manager
バランスシート・アプローチ balance sheet approach
バランス・ファンド balanced fund
バランス・ファンド・ポートフォリオ balanced fund portfolio
パリ・クラブ Paris Club
パリ証券取引所 Paris Bourse
パリ宣言 Declaration of Paris
パリ総合株価指数 French Institute Index
パリティ価値 parity value
パリティ直線 parity line
パリティ価格 parity price
パリティ・グリッド parity grid
パリティ計算 parity account
パリティ指数 parity index
バリデーション validation
パリパス条項 pari passu clause
バリュー・アット・リスク value at-risk；VaR (value at risk)
バリュー・アプローチ value approach
バリュー株 value stock
バリュー・ダイヤグラム value diagram
バリュー・ファンド value fund
バリュー・フォー・マネー VFM (value for money)
バリューライン・インデックス value line index
バリューライン・オプション value line option
バリューライン株価指数 value line stock index
バリューライン総合指数 value line composite index
バリューライン投資調査 value line investment survey
バリューライン平均 value line average
バリューライン・ランキング value line ranking
バルーン金利 balloon interest
バルーン償還 balloon maturity
バルーン・ペイメント balloon payment
バルーン・モーゲージ balloon mortgage
バルク・カーゴ bulk cargo
バルバドス・ドル BBD (Barbados dollar)
パルプ・紙業界 pulp and paper industry
パレート最適 Pareto optimal
パレート定数 Pareto's constant
破　　裂 burst
パワー全開 full steam
範囲の限定 scope limitation
汎 欧 州 pan-European
半額養老保険 semi-endowment assurance
ハンガリー・フォリント HFU (Hungarian forint)
半　　期 semi-annual
半期毎の half-yearly
反希薄化 anti-dilution
半期賦払い semi-annual installment
半期報告書 half-year report；semi-annual report
半 休 日 half day holiday
反響原理 echo principle
反響効果 echo effect
バンキング・フランクフルト Banking Frankfurt
バンクーバー証券取引所 VSE (Vancouver Stock Exchange)
バンク・ベーシス bank basis
バンク・ライン bank line
バングラデッシュ・タカ BDT (Bangladesh taka)
バンクラプシー・リモート bankruptcy remote

バンクワイヤー bankwire
判　　決 adjudication ; decree
判決債権者 judgment creditor
判決債権の相殺 judgment set-off
判決債務者 judgment debtor
判決登録 entry of judgment
判決の破棄 reversal of judgment
判決の復活 revival of judgment
版権侵害 infringement of copyright
版権登録 registration of copyright
番号口座 numbered accounts
バン・コール ban call
バンコク・オフショア市場 BIBF (Bangkok International Banking Facility)
万国郵便連合 UPU (Universal Postal Union)
犯　　罪 offense
反社会勢力 anti-social element ; anti-social power
反循環政策 countercyclical policy
反循環的 counter cyclical
反　　証 rebutting evidence
反証可能な rebuttable
反証可能な前提 rebuttable presumption
半成工事 uncompleted works
半 製 品 half-finished goods
半製品元帳 partially finished goods ledger ; semi-finished goods ledger
ハンセン中国レッドチップス指数 Hang Seng China-Affiliated Corporations Index
反　　訴 demand in reconvention
搬送・保管のコスト costs of delivery and safekeeping
ハンター保険 hunters' insurance
反対意見 contrary opinion ; dissenting opinion
反対株主 dissenters' shares
反対勘定 opposite accounts
反対記入 reversing entry
半耐久材 semi-durables
反対給付 counter-benefit
反対権原 outstanding title
反対証書 counterdeed
反対仕訳 reversal entry
反対スワップ mirror swap
反対請求 cross-demand
反対訴訟 cross action
反対注文 offsetting order
反対投票 con
反対取引 closing purchase or sale ; mirrored trade
反 対 人 dissenter
反対の結果 opposite effect
反対売買 closing transaction ; reversing trading
判断の行使 exercise of judgment
反ダンピング法 anti-dumping code
範　　疇 category
判定基準 judgmental criteria
判定の基礎となる株主 basic stockholder for judgment
判定用数値 control number
反　　転 turn around
反転パターン reversal pattern
バンド・アンド・クロール band and crawl
反　　騰 hard rally ; rebound ; sharp rally
半年ごとに semi-annually
半年ごとの複利計算 semi-annual compounding calculation
半年払いのクーポン semi-annual coupon payment
半年払保険料 half yearly premium
反トラスト法 antitrust law
バンドワゴン効果 band wagon effect
半トンチン semi-tontine
半 日 物 half-day call transactions
搬 入 費 carrying-in expenses
反応曲線 reaction curve
万能貸借対照表 all-purpose balance sheet
販　　売 sale
販売員前渡金 advance made to salesmen
販売運賃 freight out
販売会計 sales accounting
販売価格差異 sales price variance
販売型リース sales type lease
販売価値 sales value
販売活動 distribution activities

販売可能性 market feasibility
販売間接費 selling overhead
販売管理費 administrative and selling expense；sales and general administrative expenses
販売金額 sales amount
販売金融 sales finance
販売金融会社 sales finance company
販売契約 selling agreement
販売経路 marketing channel
販 売 権 franchise right
販売原価 cost of sales
販売子会社 sales subsidiary
販売時点情報管理 point of sales
販売時費用 point-of-sale cost
販売循環 selling cycle
販売条件 conditions of sale
販売諸掛り selling charges
販売資料 sales literature
販売数量 quantity sold
販売促進 sales promotion
販売促進費 sales promotion expense
販売代金回収額 cash received from customers
販 売 団 selling group
販売団契約 selected dealer agreement
販売団契約書 selling group agreement
販売帳票 sales record
販売通知 notice of sale
販売適性品質 good merchantable quality
販売手数料 commission on sale；front end load；placement commission；sales charge；sales commission；sales load；selling concession
販 売 費 selling expense
販売費差異 selling expense variance
販売費用 selling cost
販売比率 placement ratio
販売方法 sales method
販売目的資産 asset for sale
販売目的保有 held for sale
販売用商品 goods for sale
販売用土地 land for sale；real estate held for sale
販売予算 sales budget
販 売 力 sales force
販売割当 sales quota
反復監査 repeating audit
反復計算 repeated calculation
ハンプト・カーブ humped curve
判別分析 discriminant analysis
汎用カード all-purpose card；general purpose card
汎 用 性 general usability
反　　落 reactionary fall
反落する ease；fall back
判　　例 judicial definition；judicial precedent
凡　　例 legend
判 例 集 law book
判例法の先例 case law precedent
販　　路 sales network
販路の開拓 development of distribution channel

ヒ

ピア・レビュー peer review
BIS国際与信統計の日本分集計結果 Results of Locational International Banking Statistics in Japan
PIK証券 PIK (payment-in-kind) securities
P&I保険 protection and indemnity risk insurance；protection and indemnity risks
PERの上昇 increase in PER
BAレート BA rate
PO証券 principal-only securities
BOT build operation transfer
ピーク・ロード peak load
非一時金支給 non-lump payment
BD報告書 BD form
PBR分布 distribution of PBR
BB格全銘柄 all BB rated
BBB格 BBB；triple B
BB/BBの買い buy 4B
BBレシオ BB (booking to billing) ratio
被裏書人 endorsee
非運用資産 non-operating assets
非営業債務 non-trade payable
非営業用資産 non-business property
非営業用償却資産 depreciable property for non-business
非永住者 non-permanent resident
非営利会計 non-profit accounting
非営利会社 non-profit corporation；non-profit-making company；noncommercial enterprise
非営利機関 nonprofit institution
非営利企業 non-profit enterprise
非営利事業 nonprofit making business
非営利組織 non-business organization
非営利団体 non-profit entity
非営利法人 not-for-profit
冷え込む at low ebb
非会員会社 non-member securities company
非会員証券会社 non-member firm
非 開 示 non-disclosure
被害資産 damaged property
被害資産の帳簿価額 book value of properties suffering damage
被 害 者 aggrieved party
非会社型合弁事業 unincorporated joint venture
被害者直接請求 direct claim of claimant
比　　較 comparison
比較可能性 comparability
比較可能な市場 comparable market
比較可能な情報 comparable information
比較可能な利益率 comparable returns
比較計算書 comparative statement
比較原価 comparative cost
比較原価調査 comparative cost studies
比較財務諸表 comparative financial statements
比較収支計算書 comparative statement of cash flows
比較情報 comparative information
比較情報の金額 comparative amount
比較生産費説 theory of comparative cost
比較性の原則 principle of comparability
比較損益計算書 comparative income statement；comparative profit and loss statement
比較貸借対照表 comparative balance sheet
比較対象年度 comparative year
比較対象物 comparator
比較統計学 comparative statistics
比 較 表 comparison table
比較分析 comparative analysis
比較分析法 method of comparative analysis
比較目的 comparative purpose
比較優位 comparative advantage；

relative advantage
比較優位説 theory of comparative advantage
比較優位の原理 principle of comparative advantage
比較優位理論 comparative advantage theory
非確率モデル non-stochastic model
東アジア保険会議 East Asian Insurance Congress
東アフリカ共同体 East African Community
東カリブ・ドル XCD (East Caribbean dollar)
非 課 税 exclusion from taxation；exemption for taxation；free of tax
非課税扱い withholding tax exempt
非課税扱いの経過利子 accrued interest subject to non-taxable treatment
非課税益金 non-taxable gross income
非課税機関 tax exempt organization
非課税口 nontaxable account
非課税区分額 zero-bracket amount
非課税交換 tax free exchange
非課税財産 exempt property；non-taxable property
非課税仕入れ tax free purchase
非課税証券 tax exempt security
非課税所得 exempt income；non-taxable income
非課税贈与 exempt gift
非課税地方債 municipal tax free bond
非課税貯蓄 non-taxable savings；tax exempt saving
非課税貯蓄口 non-taxable saving account
非課税登録免許 non-taxable registration license
非課税となる有価証券 nontaxable securities
非課税取引 non-taxable transaction
非課税の tax exempt；tax free
非課税の譲渡所得 capital gain free of taxation
非課税引当金 tax free reserve
非課税品 tax free article
非課税文書 non-taxable document
非課税法人 corporation free from taxation；non-taxable corporation；tax exempt corporation；tax free corporation
非課税マネー・マーケット・ファンド tax exempt money market fund
非課税有価証券 non-taxable securities
非課税利子所得 non-taxable interest income
非 割 賦 non-installment
被合併会社 merged company；transferor corporation
被合併会社から引き継いだ欠損金 net operating loss assumed from a transfer of corporation
被合併法人 corporation amalgamated
非株式オプション NEO (non-equity options)
非株式指数先物 non-equity index futures
非貨幣運転資本 non-monetary working capital
非貨幣性 non-monetary
非貨幣性給付 non-monetary benefit
非貨幣性資産 non-monetary asset
非貨幣性取引収支 balance of nonmonetary transactions
非貨幣性の補助金 non-monetary grant
非貨幣性負債 non-monetary liability
非貨幣的間接証券 non-monetary indirect security
非借入準備 non-borrowed reserves
非管財人型 non-trustee
非管財人型倒産企業 non-trustee bankrupt company
非関税障壁 NTB (non-tariff barrier)
非関税措置 non-tariff measures
悲観的シナリオ pessimistic scenario
被管理金融機関 financial institutions placed under the hands of financial reorganization administrator
非関連会社株 unaffiliated stock
非関連事業利益 unrelated business income
非関連当事者 unrelated party

引当金 reserve
引当金勘定 allowance account；provision account；reserve account
引当金繰入れ addition to reserve
引当金計算書 statement of reserves
引当金計上額 charge to provision
引当金計上基準 accounting standards for reserves for possible loan losses
引当金控除後の net of allowance and provision
引当金債務 reserve liability
引当金設定法 allowance method
引当金に賦課される charged to a provision
引当金の税効果 deferred tax effect of the provision
引当金の増加 increase in reserve
引当金の戻入 reversal of provision
引当剰余金 reserved surplus
引当済財産 property reserved
引受け acceptance；honor
引受売出し sale on an underwriting basis
引受会社 underwriting company；underwriting firm
引受額 underwriting commitment
引受幹事団 management group
引受業者 underwriter
引受業者間契約 agreement among underwriters
引受行の割当額 underwriters' allocations
引受業務 underwriting business
引受拒絶 dishonor
引受金 assumed amount
引受契約 underwriting contract
引受契約書 underwriting agreement
引受限度 acceptance line
引受限度額 underwriting limit
引受再保険 assumed reinsurance
引受市場 underwriting market
引受条件付信用状 acceptance credit
引受シンジケート団 underwriting syndicate
引受スプレッド underwriting spread
引受済為替手形 bill accepted
引受済資本金 capital stock subscribed
引受済荷為替手形 trade acceptance
引受損益 underwriting profit and loss
引き受けた負債 liabilities incurred
引受団 syndicate；underwriting group
引受団契約 purchase group agreement
引受通知 acceptance notice
引受通知書 acceptance advice
引受手形 trade acceptances payable
引受手数料 acceptance commission；underwriting commission；underwriting fee
引受人 acceptor
引受けのための呈示 presentation for acceptance
引受払い payment against acceptance
引受不調 under-subscribed
引受普通株式 common shares subscribed
引受募集手数料 gross spread
引受リスク underwriting risk
引受ける underwrite
引受渡し DA (documents against acceptance)
引落承認 debit authorization
引落通知 advice of debit
引落す debit
非危険資産 non-risk assets
非危険利子率 non-risk interest rate
引締め restraint；tightening
引締色の強い金融政策 tighter monetary policy
引締政策 restraint measures；stringent policy
引締バイアス tightening bias
非期待運用収益 unexpected return on pension assets
引出 takedown
引出金勘定 drawing account
引出権 drawing right
引出プラン withdrawal plan
引継ぎ subrogation
引継資産の過大評価 overestimation of inherited assets
引継負債 assumed liability
引継ぐ assume
引取課税 taxation at time of receipt from

bonded area
引き取り手 off-taker
非求償債務 non-recourse debt
非競争入札 non-competitive bid ; non-competitive tender
非競争枠 non-competitive facility
非居住者 non-resident
非居住者円預金 non-resident yen deposit
非居住者円預金勘定 non-resident yen account
非居住者及び外国法人 non-residents and foreign corporations
非居住者及び外国法人への支払い payment to nonresidents and foreign corporations
非居住者外貨預金 non-resident foreign currency deposits
非居住者外貨預金勘定 non-resident foreign currency account
非居住者等口 nonresident etc. account
非居住者に対する減免 tax relief for non-resident
非居住者の課税所得 taxable income earned by nonresident
非居住者の給与所得 payment to nonresidents
非居住者発行円建債 bond in yen issued by nonresidents
非居住者非課税 FOTRA (free of tax residents abroad)
非拠出制度 non-contributory plan
非拠出年金制度 non-contributory pension plan
引渡価格 delivered price
引渡基準 delivery basis
引渡後の post delivery
引渡指図 delivery instruction
引渡資産 asset given up
引渡済み delivered
引渡場所 place of delivery
引渡す bring over ; deliver
非銀行金融機関 non-bank financial institution
非銀行系の private label
非金銭項目 non-monetary items
非金融勘定 non-financial accounts
非金融資産 non-financial assets
非金融市場 non-financial market
非金融取引 nonfinancial transactions
非金利資産 non-rate earnings assets
非金利負債 non-interest-paying liability
低い頭金 lower up-front cost
低い実質利回り lower quoted real yield
低い障害 lower hurdle
低い信用状態 poor credit
低い成長率 weak growth
低い短期金利 low short rate
低い手数料の保険 low-load policy
低い値段の売呼値 lower offer
低い値段の買呼値 lower bid
低く売る sell low
引け close of the market ; close of the session
引け味 closing tone
引け跡気配 after-session undertone
非経営執行者 non-executive
非景気循環株 counter cyclicals
非経常的な non-recurring
非継続規準 discontinued standards
非継続事業 discontinued business
被契約者 covenantee
引け際 at the close of the market
引け後相場 street price
引け高 higher quotation at the close
引け注文 MOC (market on close) order
被結合企業 acquired entity
引け値 last quotation
引値買い buy on close
引値指値注文 limit on close order
引け値段 closing price
引値注文 on-the-close order
引け安 lower closing quotation
非原価項目 non-cost items
非現金給付 non-cash benefit
非現金項目 non-cash items
非現金資産 non-cash assets
非現金性金融資産 non-cash financial assets
非現金対価 non-cash consideration
非公益電気事業者 NUG (non-utility

generator)
非公開会社 closely-held company
非公開会社事業保険 close company insurance
非公開企業 going private；non-public company；private company
非公開準備金 undisclosed reserve
非公開情報 non-public information
非公開での開廷 sit in camera
非公共目的債 private purpose bond
非公式慣行 informal practice
非公式業績予測 whisper number
非公式資本の流出 unofficial capital flight
非公式組織 informal organization
被控訴人 appellee
非公的年金 non-state pension
非公認資産 unadmitted assets
非公募債 non-public issues；privately placed bond
非 効 率 inefficiency
非国営化 denationalization
被告側弁護士 defense attorney
被 告 人 accused
被告人席 dock
非コミットメント・ファシリティ uncommitted facilities
被雇用者年金プラン employee pension plan
被災事業用資産 business assets suffering from disaster
被災事業用資産の損失 loss from damaged business assets
非債弁済 money paid under mistake
非債務者預金 deposit of non-debtor
非財務的開示 non-financial disclosure
被査定者 assessee
非参加優先株式 nonparticipating preferred stock
非事業活動 non-business activity
非資金的項目 non-cash item
非資金的収益 non-cash revenue
非資金的取引 non-cash transaction
非資金的費用 non-cash expense
非市場経済 non-market economy
非市場性証券 non-marketable issue；non-marketable securities
非市場性リスク non-market risk
非市場性リスクの源泉 non-market risk sources
非システマティック・リスク unsystematic risk
非自然的損益 involuntary loss or gain
ビジネス・リスク business risk
被支配会社 controlled company
非自発的失業 involuntary unemployment
日次平残 average daily balance
被仕向為替 inward exchange
被仕向銀行 payee bank；receiving bank
被仕向送金 inward remittance
非住宅用資産 non-residential assets
非出資組合 non-investment cooperative association
被取得企業 acquiree
批　　准 ratification
非 準 拠 non-compliance
非常海損 extraordinary average
非償還の non-redeemable
非償却資産 non-depreciable assets；non-depreciable property
非商業トレーダー noncommercial trader
非常勤の part time
費消原価 consumed cost
非訟事件手続法 Law of Procedure in Non-Contentious Cases
非上場外国株 foreign stocks unlisted
非上場会社 unlisted company
非上場株 unlisted stock
非上場債 unlisted note
非証書証券 un-certificated securities
非常措置 emergency measures；extraordinary measures
非譲渡性 non-transferability
非譲渡性金融商品 non-transferable financial instrument
秘 書 課 Secretarial Division
肥飼料検査所 Fertilizer and Feed Inspection Services
非仕訳記入 blind entry
BIS基準 BIS standards
BIS国際資金取引統計の日本分集計結果

ヒ

Results of Consolidated International Banking Statistics in Japan
ヒストグラム法 histogram method
ヒストリカル・データ historical data
ヒストリカル・ベータ historical beta
ヒストリカル・ボラティリティー historical volatility
BISマーケット・リスク規制 capital adequacy requirements against market risk
非制限資産 unrestricted assets
非清算会員 non-clearing member
非清算参加者 non-clearing participant
非生産的融資 non-productive loan
非製造間接費 non-production indirect cost
非制定法 unwritten law
非政府債市場 non-government market
非切断乗数 untruncated multiplier
被説明変数 explained variables
非 線 形 non-linearity
非線形回帰 non-linear regression
非線形相関 non-linear correlation
非線形モデル non-linear model
非戦略部門 non-strategic division
微　　増 marginal rise
非相互化 demutualizing
非相互的 non-reciprocal
被相続人 ancestor
被相続人にかかる所得 income in respect of a decedents
非対称の asymmetric
非対称バスケット方式 adjustable basket technique
非担保危険 uninsured peril
非弾力的需給 inelastic demand and supply
非弾力費用 inflexible expense
微 調 整 fine tuning
微調整する true up
非直線的トレンド・ライン curving trend line
ピックアップ債 pick up bond
ビッグバン Big Bang
必需家具 necessary household furniture
必須条件 essential condition；mandatory clause；pre-requisite
必須フィールド mandatory field
ピ ッ ト pit
ヒット商品 hot seller
ピット・ブローカー pit broker
ピット・レポーター pit reporter
逼　　迫 crunch；tension
必要経費 necessary expense
必要経費になる損失 loss qualifying for necessary expenses
必要資本金 net capital
必要資本係数 required capital coefficient
必要条件 cause sine qua non；necessary condition
必要証拠金 margin requirement
必要証拠金法 margin required method
必要性原則 principle of need
必要成功率 required success rate
必要性の否定 obviation of need
必要当事者 necessary party
必要な証拠書類 necessary documentary evidence
必要な税務手続 necessary tax procedure
必要な評価方法の選択 selection of a necessary appraisal method
必 要 物 estovers
必要要件 requisite
非DVP決済 FOP (free of payment)；Non-DVP Settlement
非提携ローン non-tie-up loan
否定的意見 adverse opinion
否定的誓約 negative covenant
非適格ストック・オプション NSO (non-qualifying stock options)
非適格投資家 non-accredited investor
非適格年金 non-tax qualified pension
非適格年金制度 non-qualifying pension plan
非適格年金保険 non-qualifying annuity
非鉄金属業界 nonferrous metals industry
非デリバティブ貨幣性資産 non-derivative monetary assets
非デリバティブ貨幣性負債 non-derivative

monetary liabilities
非デリバティブ商品 non-derivative instruments
非伝統的なアセット・クラス nontraditional asset class
被統括勘定 controlled account
非統計的サンプル non-statistical sampling
被投資会社 investee
被投資企業 investee company
非同時決済 asynchronous settlement
非同質性 non-homogeneity
非投資適格 non-investment grade
非同時取引 non-synchronous trading
非同族会社 non-family corporation
非同族株主 shareholder of non-family corporation
非同族の同族会社 non-personal family corporation
非登録債 letter bond
非登録私募債 letter securities
一株当り運用益 net investment income per share
一株当り額面金額 par value per share
一株当り株主資本 stockholders' equity per share
一株当り行使価格 exercise price per share
一株当り収益成長率 earnings growth rate per share
一株当り純資産 book value per share；net asset per share；net assets per share
一株当り正味有形資産 net tangible assets per share
一株当り損失 loss per share
一株当りの価額あるいは資産額 money and/or property distributed per stock
一株当りの数値 per share data
一株当りの利益の変動 changes in earnings per share
一株当り配当 DPS (dividend per share)
一株当り配当金 dividend per share
一株当り簿価 BPS (book-value per share)
一株当り利益 EPS (earnings per share)
一株当り利益の希薄 dilution of earnings per share
一株一議決権ルール one share one vote rule
一株株主 one share shareholder
非独占的 nonexclusive
人 保 険 personal insurance
一人当り per capita
一人当り公債発行残高 per capita debt
一人当り国民総生産 per capita gross national product
一人当り税率 per capita rate
一人当りのGNP per capita incomes
一人当りの賞与 bonus paid per employee
一人当りの所得 per capita income
一人当りの生産 per capita product
一人会社 one man company
避　　難 parking
否　　認 denial
否 認 権 right of avoidance
被任命者 appointee
非年換算の non-annualized
非 農 業 non-farm
被買収会社 acquired company
日計り商い day trading；in-and-out trading
批　　判 criticism
批判的機能 critical function
日々残高 daily balance
日々の活動 day-to-day activity
非標本誤差 non-sampling error
非比例割合再保険 non-proportional reinsurance
日　　歩 contango；daily rate；interest per diem
BIF BIF (Bank Insurance Fund)
非不定値行列 non-negative definite matrix
被扶養者 dependant
微分係数 differential coefficient
非分散投資型投資会社 non-diversified investment company
微分方程式 differential equation
非分離型 non-detachable
非 分 類 non-classification
ビヘイビア behavior

日別株価指数 daily stock price index
備忘価格 memorandum price ; reminder price
備忘価額 memorandum value
備忘勘定 memorandum account
非保険型年金 non-insurance annuity
非保険型年金制度 uninsured pension plan
被保険危険 insured peril ; perils insured against
被保険者 assured ; insured person ; insuree
被保険者証 individual certificate
被保険者の裁量 discretion of the insured person
被保険物 insured property
被保険利益 insurable interest
被保佐人 quasi-incompetent person
被保証メンバー口座 sponsored membership account
非保証要素 non-guaranteed element
秘密勘定 secret account
秘密準備金 hidden reserves
秘密信託 secret trust
秘密積立金 hidden reserve ; secret reserve
秘密の利益処分 hidden profit distributions
秘密負債 secret liability
秘密保持契約 confidentiality agreement
秘密漏洩 breach of confidence
非明示的要件 implicit requirement
非免税債 non-tax exempt bond
罷免責債権 undischargeable claim
費　　目 expense item
ひも付援助 aid with attachment ; tied aid
ひも付表示 linked presentation
ひも付融資 conditional loan ; tied loan
非約定トランシェ uncommitted tranche
100パーセント子会社 totally-held subsidiary
100倍台の株価収益率 three digit PER
100分の1 one hundredth
百 分 率 percentage
百分率財務諸表 common-size financial statement ; percentage financial statements
百分率損益計算書 common-size income statement ; one hundred percent income statement ; percentage income statement
百分率貸借対照表 common-size balance sheet ; percentage balance sheet
百分率表 percentage table
百分率法 percentage method
百万単位 millions of units
百貨店売上高 department store sales
ヒヤリング hearing
ピュア・キャップ pure cap
ピュア・ディーラー pure dealer
費　　用 charge
病院歳入債 hospital revenue bond
病院料金 hospital rate
評　　価 appraisal ; assessment ; evaluation ; valuation
評価アクチュアリー valuation actuary
評 価 益 valuation gain
評価益の益金不算入 exclusion of profit accrued from valuation profit
評価替え reappraisal ; reassessment
評価替資本 appraised capital
評 価 額 amount appraised ; amount assessed ; appraisal value
評価額の減少 reduction in valued amount
評価価値 assessed valuation
評価科目 valuation item
評価勘定 valuation account
評価基準 valuation basis
評 価 減 write-down
評価減後価格 written down value
評価原則 valuation principle
評価コスト valuation cost
評価差額 variance of the estimate
評価差額の会計処理 accounting for valuation differences
評価査定 appraisement
評価手法 valuation technique
評価水準 assessed level
評価済保険 valued policy
評価済保険契約 valued policy
評価性引当金 valuation allowance ;

valuation reserve
評 価 損 appraisal loss；valuation loss
評価損益 valuation gain or loss
評価手続 valuation procedures
評価特性 valuation characteristics
評 価 人 appraiser
評価の時期 timing of valuation
評価の視点 evaluation perspectives
評価の枠組み evaluation framework
評 価 日 valuation date
評 価 法 appraisal method
評価方式 assessment plan
評価方法の選択 selection of appraisal method
評価方法の変更 change in valuation method
評価増し write-up
評価モデル valuation modeling
評価利率 technical interest rate；valuation rate of interest
費用関数 cost function
評 議 会 board of trustees；council
費用機能法 function of expense method
費用曲線 cost curve
表 形 式 tabular form
評　決 verdict
表見上の権利 color
表見代理 apparent agency
表見代理権 apparent authority
表見的所有 order and disposition
表見的所有者 reputed owner
費用効果 cost utility
費用込み gross of charge
費用削減 cost cutting
表札だけの店 brass-plate office
氷山理論 iceberg theory
表示価額 stated value
表式元帳 tabular ledger
表示原価 scheduled cost
表示項目 line item
表示項目ごとに on a line-by-line basis
表示作業 representation work
表示した手数料 quoted fee
表示資本金 stated capital
表示単位 precision in presentation
表 示 値 stated terms
表示通貨 presentation currency
表紙手形 master bill
表示による売買 sale by description
表示の目的上 for the presentation purpose
表示負債 stated liabilities
被用者負担給付 employee paid benefit
費用収益対応 matching cost with revenue
費用収益対応の原則 cost matching income principle
費用収益の対応 matching costs and revenues
標　準 benchmark
標準案件 plain deal
標準EPS base EPS；normalized EPS
標準意見 standard opinion
標 準 化 standardization
標準価格 standard price
標準化された測定方法 standardized measurement
標準化収益 normalized earnings
標 準 株 barometer stock；standard stocks
標準化ボラティリティー standardized volatility
標準簡易生命保険表 standard industrial mortality table
標準機械時間 standard machine time
標準銀ドル standard silver dollar
標準金利 standard interest rate；standard rate
標準クロス・デフォルト条項 standard cross default provision
標準下体保険契約 insurance of substandard lives
標準原価 standard cost
標準原価計算 standard cost accounting
標準原価計算制度 standard-cost system
標準原価法 standard cost method
標準控除 standard deduction
標準誤差 standard error
標準財務諸表 standardized financial statements
標準材料仕様書 standard bill of materials

標準材料費 standard materials cost
標準産業分類 standard industrial classification
標準傷害保険 level accident insurance
標準書式 standard documentation
標準所得補償約款 standard disability provisions
標準処理 standard treatment
標準生産量 standard-run quantity
標準製造間接費 standard manufacturing expense
標準税率 standard tax rate
標準責任準備金評価法 Standard Valuation Law
標準相関係数 standard correlation
標準損料 standard depletion expenses
標準体階層 standard class
標 準 値 standard value
標準抵当権者払約款 union mortgage clause
標準的な政府系機関 standard agency
標準的なデュレーション standard duration
標準的な取決め standard arrangement
標準的保険 standard policy
標準手数料 standard commission
標準デフォルト・モデル・カーブ standard default assumption curve
標準年金死亡表 standard annuity mortality table
標準の性能 standard of performance
標準配賦率 standard burden rate
標準バスケット方式 standard currency basket system
標 準 日 standard date
標 準 物 standardized bonds ; standardized instrument
標準物と受渡適格銘柄との交換比率の算定 computation of factors for conversion of deliverable grades into standardized instrument
標準物売買 sale on standard
標準偏差 standard deviation
標準ポートフォリオ・リスク分析 SPAN (standard portfolio analysis of risk)
標準保険 usual policy
標準保険料 standard premium
標準銘柄 standard issue
標準約款 standard clause
標準有効フロンティア standard efficient frontier
標準利益 standard profit
標準料率 standard rate
標準労務費 standard labor cost
表示要件 presentation requirement
表彰制度 commendation system
費用性質法 nature of expense method
費用節減 cost consideration
費用総額 overall charge
費用・操業度・利益分析 cost-volume-profit analysis
表　　題 headline
費用対効果分析 cost effectiveness analysis
表定コスト tabular cost
表定保険料 book premium ; tabular premium
費用データ cost data
費用動向 cost behavior
費用認識 recognition as expense
費用の性質 nature of expense
費用配賦 expense distribution
費用配分の原則 principle of cost allocation
費用配分方法 cost allocation formula
評　　判 reputation
費用分担 cost sharing
費用分担法 distribution plan
費用分類 cost classification
費用便益の cost benefit
費用便益分析 cost benefit analysis
費用保証契約 guaranteed cost contract
標本誤差 sampling error
標本サンプル mean sample
標本抽出 sampling
標本調査 sampling survey
標本分布 sampling distribution
標本平均 sample mean
費用見積り cost estimate
表　　明 representation
表明されている要望 expressed need

表明と保証 representations &warranties
表面金利 nominal interest rate ; stated rate of interest
表面所得 nominal income
表面税率 nominal tax rate
表面預金 nominal deposit ; nominal gross deposit
表面利率 apparent rate of interest ; coupon rate ; nominal coupon
表面利率の引上げ coupon hike
表面利率の低い銘柄 low coupon securities
漂 流 物 flotsam
漂流ミックス drifting mix
ピラミッディング過程 pyramiding process
ピラミッド型管理方式 pyramid management method
非利付債 non-interest-bearing bond
比率分析 ratio analysis
比率分担 percentage participation
比 率 法 ratio method
比率法減耗償却 percentage depletion
非流通証券 nonnegotiable instrument
非 流 動 non-current
非流動資産 illiquid assets ; non-current assets
非流動性 illiquidity
非流動性資産 non-liquid assets
非流動的 illiquid
非流動負債 non-current liability
非流動部分 non-current portion
非良心的契約 unconscionable bargain
非累積型配当 non-cumulative dividend
非累積型優先株式 non-cumulative preferred stock
非累積的 non-cumulative
非累積の non-accumulating
非累積優先株 noncumulative preference stock
ビル・セール bill sale
ビルディング・ソサイエティ委員会 BSC (Building Society Commission)
ビルトイン・フレキシビリティ built-in flexibility
ビル・パス bill pass
比例課税法 proportional taxation
比例原価計算 proportional calculation
比例再保険 share reinsurance
比例準備制度 proportional reserve system
比例準備法 proportional reserve method
比 例 税 proportional tax
比例代表 proportional representation
比例的可変費用 proportionally variable cost
比例的な取り分 pro rata share
比例的平等条件 proportionally equal terms
比例的変化 proportionate change
比例的持ち分 proportionate share
比例特約再保険 quota share treaty reinsurance
比例配当 ratable distribution
比例配分 pro rata allocation ; proportional allocation
比例配分した pro rata
比例配分による pro-rated on
比 例 費 proportional cost ; proportional expenses
比例連結 proportionate consolidation
比例割合再保険 proportional reinsurance
比例割当制度 PQS (percentage quota system)
非 劣 後 unsubordinated
非劣後無担保社債 unsubordinated debenture
非連結子会社 unconsolidated subsidiary
非連帯保証 severally but not jointly
疲労因子 fatigue factor
ビロウ・ザ・ライン below the line
ビロウ・マーケット below market
広 さ breadth
非割当積立方式 unallocated funding instrument
日割り計算 computation on a per diem basis
日割りベース day count basis
ビン(BIN) BIN (bank identification number)
貧困指数 misery index

貧 困 線 poverty line
貧困のわな poverty trap
貧 困 率 poverty rate
品質管理 quality control
品質基準 quality standards
品質費用 quality cost
便　　乗 piggy backing
頻　　度 frequency
PIN番号 PIN number

フ

FTD FTD (fast-to-default)
ファースト・ディマンド・ボンド first demand bond
ファースト・ロス信用補完 first loss subordination
ファーム・オファー firm offer
ファーム・バンキング firm banking
ファーム・ビッド firm bid
歩　　合 override
歩 合 制 commission system
ファイナンスの仲介 financial arrangement
ファイナンス・リース finance lease
ファイナンス・リース債務 finance lease liability
ファイナンス・リースの目的 purpose of finance lease
ファイヤー・ウォール fire wall
ファイリング filing
ファインダー finder
ファウルB/L foul B/L
ファクター感応度 factor sensitivity
ファクター・ベータ factor beta
ファクター・リスク factor risk
ファクタリング factoring
ファクタリング手数料 factorage
ファジー理論 fuzzy theory
FASB解釈指針 FIN (FASB Interpretation)
ファシリティ・フィー facility fee
ファニー・メイ Fannie Mae
ファブレス fabless
ファミリー・ファンド family fund
ファンダメンタル均衡為替レート FEER (fundamental equilibrium exchange rate)
ファンダメンタルズ fundamentals
ファンダメンタルズの悪化 fundamentals deterioration
ファンダメンタルの脆弱さ underlying weakness
ファンダメンタル分析 fundamental analysis
ファンダメンタル要因 fundamental factor
不安定指数 instability index
不安定性 variability
不安定な変動 volatile fluctuation
不安定の権利 precarious right
不安定要因 cause of instability
ファンド運用成果 fund performance
ファンド・オブ・ファンズ fund of funds
ファンド・ステートメント funds statement
ファンド損失 fund loss
ファンド・トラスト fund trust
ファンドの乗換え fund switching
ファンド・ベータ値の比較 comparison of beta values of funds
ファンド・マネージャー fund manager
ファントラ fund and trust
ファンライン fan line
ファン理論 fan theory
VRN VRN (variable rate note)
フィージビリティ・スタディ feasibility study
フィードバック feedback
フィードバック価値 feedback value
フィー・ビジネス fee business
V字 V formation
フィジー・ドル FJD (Fiji dollar)
フィスカル・エージェント fiscal agent
フィッシャー効果 Fisher effect
フィッシャー方程式 Fisher equation
不 一 致 disparity
フィッチ・インベスター・サービス Fitch Investors Service, Inc.
フィナンシャル・アドバイザー FA (financial adviser)
フィナンシャル・タイムズ株価指数 FT Industrial Ordinary Stock Index

フィナンシャル・タイムズ工業株価指数 Financial Times Index of Industrial Ordinary Shares
フィナンシャル・タイムズ商品相場指数 Financial Times Index of Sensitive World Commodity Prices
フィナンシャル・ニューズ指数オプション Financial News index option
フィナンシャル・プランナー financial planner
フィナンシャル・レバレッジ financial leverage
フィボナッチ数列 Fibonacci sequence
フィラデルフィア証券取引所 PHLX (Philadelphia Stock Exchange)
フィラデルフィア商品取引所 PBOT (Philadelphia Board of Trade)
フィラデルフィア・プラン Philadelphia plan
フィラデルフィア連銀 Philadelphia Fed
フィリップス曲線 Phillips curve
フィリップ・フロップ債 fillip flop bond
フィリピン証券取引所 Philippine Stock Exchange
フィリピン・ペソ PHP (Philippine peso)
フィンランド・マルカ FIM (Finland markka)
封　鎖 blockade
封鎖経済 closed economy
ブ ー ス booth
風水害保険 windstorm and flood insurance
ブータン・ニュルタム BTN (Bhutan ngultrum)
ブーメラン効果 boomerang effect
プーリング会計 pooling accounting
プーリングによる証券化 securitization by pooling
プール・オブ・ファイナンシング pool of financing
プール協定 pool agreement
プール協約 pooling arrangement
プール契約 pooling contracts
プール構成 pool composition
プール残高 pool balance
プール操作 pool operation
プール特定取引 specified pool trade
プール内のローン loans in the pool
プール・ファンド pooled fund
フェアー・アイザック社 Fair, Isaac & Co.
フェイド・アウト方式 fade-out formula
フェール failed transaction
フェッドワイヤ Fed wire (Federal Reserve's wire transfer system)
フェデラル・ファンド FF (federal fund)
フェデラル・ファンド金利 FF interest
フェデラル・ファンド市場 federal fund market
フェデラル・ファンド・レート federal fund rate
フェド・ウォッチャー Fed watcher
フォークランド諸島ポンド FKP (Falkland Islands pound)
フォーミュラ・タイミング formula timing
フォーミュラ投資 formula investing
フオーミュラ・ファンド formula fund
フォーミュラ・プラン formula plan
フォレックス・クラブ forex club
フォワード・イールド forward yield
フォワード価格 forward pricing
フォワード・カレンダー forward calendar
フォワード・キャッシュ額 forward cash amount
フォワード経過利子 forward real accrued
フォワード実質利回り forward real yield
フォワード・スプレッド forward spread
フォワード・スワップ forward swap
フォワード中立測度 forward neutral measure
フォワード中立評価法 forward neutral valuation
フォワード・マーケット forward market
付　加 addition
付 加 益 loading surplus
付加価値 value added
付加価値計算書 added value statement
付加価値税 VAT (value added tax)
付加価値通信網 value added network
付加価値分析 value added analysis
付加価値報告書 value added statement

フ

付加勘定 adjunct account
付加危険 extraneous risk
付加給付 fringe benefit
付加拠出 additional contribution
付加条項 rider
付 加 税 supertax；tax surcharge
付加年金 top-up pension
付加保険料 expense loading；loading
賦　　課 imposition
賦 課 額 amount imposed
賦課課税制度 official assessment
賦課期日 base date for assessment
賦課決定 assessment and decision
賦課徴収 assessment and collection
賦課方式 current disbursement approach；pay-as-you-go system
賦課保険 assessment insurance
深 押 し big push in the downward move
不確定債権 unliquidated claim
不確定財産権 contingent estate
不確定事象 principal uncertainty
不確定年金受給権付与 contingent vesting
不確認信用状 unconfirmed credit
不可欠部分 integral part
不可抗力 act of God；force majeure；vis major
不可抗力条項 force majeure clause
不可譲の権利 inalienable rights
不 可 争 indisputability
不可争条項 incontestability clause
不活動勘定 inactive account
不活発債券取扱業者 cabinet crowd
不活発資産 inactive asset
不活発証券 cabinet security
不稼動債権 non-performing claim
不稼動資産 non-performing assets
不可避的危険 unavoidable dangers
不可避的事故 inevitable accident；unavoidable accident
不可分権 undivided interest
不可分債権 indivisible credit
不可分な integral
負 荷 率 load factor
不換銀行券 inconvertible bank note
不換紙幣 inconvertible banknote
不完全受渡し bad delivery
不完全確率変数 defective random variables
不完全義務 imperfect obligation
不完全競争 imperfect competition
不完全競争市場 imperfect competition market
不完全雇用 underemployment
不完全雇用乗数 underemployment multiplier
不完全市場 imperfect market
不完全信託 imperfect trust
不完全性 imperfection
不完全な defective
不完全ヘッジ imperfect hedge
不完全法貨 partial legal tender
不規則性 irregularity
不規則な価格変動 random price changes
付記電文付振替 third-party transfer
付記登録 supplementary registration
吹 き 値 revived quotation
吹き値売り selling on spurt
普 及 率 diffusion rate
不　　況 depression；doldrums
不況カルテル depression cartel
不 均 衡 asymmetry；disequilibrium；imbalance
不均衡成長 disequilibrium growth
不均等払い irregular installment payment
復員軍人局 Veterans Administration
福岡財務支局 Fukuoka Local Finance Branch Bureau
複会計制度 double-account system
副 幹 事 co-manager
複 関 税 dual tariff
複関税制 multiple tariff system
副 議 長 vice chairman
復元保険料 restoration premium
複合運送書類 combined transport document
複合オプション compound option
複合危険保険 multiple peril insurance
複合記入 compound entry
複合金融商品 compound financial

instruments；hybrid instruments
複合資本 hybrid capital
複合証券 hybrid securities
複合乗数 compound multiplier
複合商品 synthetic instrument
複合仕訳 compound journal entry
複 合 性 complex nature
複合取引 compound transaction
複合年金保険 combination annuity
複合連生死亡保険 compound survivorship assurance
複 雑 な complex
複雑な規定 complex provisions
複雑な記録 complex records
複雑な資本構造 complex capital structure
複雑な取引 sophisticated arrangements
副 作 用 side effect
副 産 物 accessory product
福祉医療機構 Welfare and Medical Service
福祉改革 welfare reform
複式会計 double accounting
複式記帳法 bookkeeping by double entry
複式簿記 double-entry bookkeeping
複式簿記の原則 principle of double-entry bookkeeping
福祉給付 welfare benefit
福祉国家 welfare state
福祉社会制度 welfare social program
副次的結果 by product
副次的効果 side benefit
副署する countersign
複数機関 multiple institutions
複数均衡 multiple equilibriums
複数銀行制度 multiple banking system
複数銀行持株会社 multibank holding company
複数区分計算書 multiple-step statement
複数市場間トレード cross market trade
複数所得 multiple income
複数生存者連生保険 multiple life plan
複数税率 multiple tax rate
複数通貨介入 multi-currency intervention
複数保険者 composite insurer
複数満期預金 multiple maturity deposit
複数要因モデル multi-factor model
複　　製 replication
複製ポートフォリオ replicating portfolio
副 総 裁 deputy governor；vice president
副 大 臣 senior vice minister
副　　の duplicate
復　　配 resumption of dividend
複本位制 bimetallism
含 み 益 embedded profit；unrealized gain
含み資産 hidden assets；latent assets；off-the-book assets
含み資産株 asset play；asset-backed stock
含み収益 latent return
含 み 損 book loss；embedded loss；latent loss；paper loss；unrealized loss
含み損益 unrealized profits and losses
服　　務 ethical discipline
複名手形 double name paper
覆面介入 covert intervention
複　　利 compound interest
複利型保険金増額配当 compound bonus
複利計算 calculation of compound interest
複利現価 present value discounted at compound interest
福利厚生基金 welfare benefit fund
福利厚生施設 welfare facilities
福利厚生制度 welfare plan
福利厚生費 welfare expense
福利施設負担額 contribution to welfare facilities
副理事長 executive vice president
複利成長率 compound growth rate
複利年率 compound annual rate
複利方式 compound interest method
複利利回り compound interest yield
複 割 引 compound discount
不 景 気 depression of business
不 経 済 diseconomy
不計上基準 non-accrual basis
附合契約 contract of adhesion

不 行 使 nonuser
不公正な競争方法 unfair method of competition
不 抗 争 no contest
不 公 平 inequity
不 効 用 disutility
不 合 理 absurdity
負　　債 debt；liability；negative capital
負債及び資本 liabilities and capital
負債及び資本合計 total liabilities and capital accounts
負債及び資本の部 liabilities and shareholders' equity；liabilities and stockholders' equity
負債会計 liability accounting
負 債 側 liability side
負債勘定 debt account；liabilities account
負債管理 liability management
負債期間 debt maturity
負債減少額 reduction in liability
負債限度 debt limit
負債合計 total liabilities
負債構造 debt mix；liability structure
負債項目 liability item
負債コスト cost of liability
負債残高 outstanding liability
負債残高の返済部分 reduction of the outstanding liability
負債・資産比率 debt asset ratio
負債資本勘定 liabilities and capital accounts
負債資本合計 total liabilities and shareholders' equity
負債・資本比率 debt-equity ratio
負債純額 net liability
負債純資産比率 debt to equity ratio
負債償却準備金 debt amortization fund
負債条項 debt covenant
負債性引当金 liabilities reserve
負債増加額 increase in liability
負債総額 gross debt
負債ダイナミクス debt dynamics
負債と株式の関係 debt/equity relationship
負債の回収率 percentage of debt collection
負債の期限 term of debt
負債の金利 liability rate
負債の決済 settlement of liability
負債の資本への転換 conversion of debt to equity
負債の純額の変動 movements in net liability
負債の消滅 extinguishment of the debt
負債のディスカウント debt discount
負債の引受け assumption of liability
負債のプレミアム debt premium
負債爆弾 debt bomb
負債引当金 reserve for liability
負債比率 debt equity ratio；debt ratio；leverage ratio；ratio of total liabilities to net worth
負債比率上昇 upturn in gearing
負債比率の大きい企業への貸付 HLT (highly leveraged transaction)
負債部分 liability component
負債平均期間 average maturity of debts
負債ヘッジ liability hedge
負債返済 debt repayment
負 債 法 liability method
負債利子 interest on borrowed fund
負債利子控除 deduction of interest on borrowed fund
負債利率 liability ratio
不採算部門 loss making division
不　　在 absence
不 在 者 absentee
不在所有権 absentee ownership
不在所有者 absentee owner
不作為約款 restrictive covenant
不実記載 misstatement
不実表示 mispresentation
不十分な証拠 insufficient evidence
不 受 理 refusal to receive
扶　　助 alimony
不償還債 irredeemable bond
負傷死亡補償金 compensation for injuries and deaths
不承認資産 inadmissible assets

扶助基金 employees' relief fund
扶助信託 support trust
扶助料課税 benefit taxation
不振事業 declining business
不 信 任 distrust
付随給付 ancillary benefit
付随業務 secondary activities
付随権限 mediate powers
付随サービス ancillary services
付随条件 incident
付随的救済 ancillary relief
付随的事実 collateral fact
付随的収入 incidental gains
付随的取引 incidental transaction
付随費用 incidental cost
不　　正 fraud
不正競業 unfair competition
不正契約 fraudulent contract
不正行為 fraudulent act；irregular practices；turpitude；wrong doing
不正行為に対する警告 warning against fraud
不正小切手 defective check
不正使用 unauthorized use
不正申告 false declaration
不正な金 dirty money
不正な手段 foul means
不正な乗替勧誘（保険） twisting
不正乗換勧誘 churning
不正防止条項 anti-fraud provision
不正利益 unfair advantage
不正利得 fraudulent gains
不 誠 実 bad faith
不　　足 dearth；shortfall
不 足 額 balance due；shortage
不足額保証 deficiency guarantee
不足金処理計算書 deficit reconciliation statement
不足金の処理 reconciliation of deficit
不足資金負担 cash deficiency undertaking
不足資金補填保証 guarantee for cost over-run
不足資本の猶予 capital forbearance
不足責任準備金 deficiency reserve；unfunded actuarial reserve
付　　則 supplementary provision
付属書類 annex；attachment；supporting documents
付属設備 accessory equipment；annexed structure
付属建物 outbuilding
付属地役権 easement appurtenant
付属明細書 supplementary statement；supporting schedule
付属明細表 supplementary schedule
不測の債務 unforeseen liabilities
付帯価値 extrinsic value
付帯契約 accessory contract
付帯収用 excess condemnation
付帯条件 collateral condition；condition collateral；incidental conditions
付帯証書 collateral bond
付 帯 税 additions to tax
付帯設備 fixtures
付帯訴訟 incidental appeal；incidental suit
付帯費用 extra charges；incidental expenses
二桁増益基調 double-digit recurring profit growth
二 桁 の double-digit
双子の赤字 twin deficits
負　　担 burden
負 担 金 burden charge
負担軽減 curtailment of burden；reduction of incidence
負担時間 burden hour
負担資産 onerous property
負担付贈与 onerous gift
負 担 費 obligation fees
負担利益倍率 earnings coverage ratio
不単純引受 qualified acceptance of bill
不知約款 unknown clause
不注意な事務処理 careless business practices
普通買為替 MTP (money transfer payable)
普通会計決算公告 public announcement of settlement of accounts under

ordinary accounting
普　通　株　common equity；ordinary share；straight equity
普通株式　common share；common stock
普通株式購入権　warrant to purchase common shares
普通株式資本　equity share capital
普通株式相当証券　common stock equivalents
普通株式に転換可能社債　bond convertible into common shares
普通株式の端数　fraction of an ordinary share
普通株式一株当り純利益　earnings per share of common stock；net income per share of common stock
普通株式一株当り利益　earnings per common stock
普通株取引　ordinary share transaction
普通株主　ordinary shareholder
普通株主資本利益率　return on common equity
普通株主に帰属する純利益　net profit attributable to common shareholders
普通株主持ち分　ordinary shareholders' equity
普通株の帳簿価格　common stock book value
普通株の評価　valuation of common stock
普通株配当金　dividend on common stock
普通株倍率　common stock coverage
普通株比率　common stock ratio
普通株ファンド　common stock fund
普通株保有に関する統計　common stock ownership statistics
普通借入債務　straight debt
普通為替　mail transfer
普通銀行　ordinary bank
普通組合　ordinary partnership
普通契約　regular way contract
普　通　語　plain language
普通交付税　ordinary local grant tax
普通小切手　open check；uncrossed check
普通国債　straight government bond
普通個人保険　ordinary individual life insurance
普通差止命令　common injunction
普通社債　SB (straight bond)；straight corporate bond
普通社債公募　public offering of straight bond
普通終身保険　straight life policy
普通出資者　ordinary equity contributors
普通出資者総会　meeting of ordinary equity contributors
普通出資の口数　number of units of ordinary equity contribution
普通償却　ordinary depreciation and amortization
普通所得　ordinary corporate income
普通仕訳帳　general journal
普　通　税　general tax；normal tax
普通生命保険　ordinary life insurance；regular life insurance
普通生命保険年金信託　ordinary life pension trust
普通送金　ordinary remittance
普通徴収　ordinary collection
普通取引　ordinary transaction；regular way transaction
普通年金　ordinary annuity
普通の金融商品　common financial instruments
普通の購入　regular purchase
普通配当　common dividend；ordinary dividend；regular dividend
普　通　法　common law
普通法株式会社　common law corporation
普通法上の所有権　legal title
普通法上のモーゲージ　legal mortgage
普通法人　ordinary corporation
普通法信託　common law trust
普通保険　ordinary insurance
普通保険約款　general insurance clause
普通モーゲージ・ローン　conventional mortgage loan
普通預金　ordinary deposit
物　　価　commodity price
物価・正貨流出入機構　price-specie-flow

mechanism
物価安定政策 price stabilization policy
物価指数 price index
物価指数連動 price index linked
物価水準 level of price
物価スライド給付 indexed benefit
物価スライド制廃止 inflation de-indexation
物価動向 price development
物価に関する研究会 Bank of Japan Workshop on Price
物価に連動した indexed to prices
物価変動 price variation
物価変動による price induced
物価連動 inflation indexation ; inflation linking
物価連動英国国債 index-linked gilt
物価連動債 index linked bond ; inflation indexed bond ; linkers
物価連動債券 inflation-linked debt instrument
復活折衝 second-round budgetary negotiation
復帰財産権 reversion
復帰信託 resulting trust
復帰年金 reversionary annuity
ブック・ビルディング book building
ブック・ビルディング方式 BB (book-building) formula
復　　権 restoration
物　　権 real right ; right in rem
復権財産 escheat
福 建 省 Fujian
物 件 費 non-personnel expenses
物 権 法 laws of realty
復　　興 restoration
復興金融会社 RFC (reconstruction finance company)
復興ローン rehabilitation loan
物質・材料研究機構 National Institute for Materials Science
プッシュ・ダウン会計 push down accounting
プッシュ・プル push pull
物上担保付社債 mortgage bond
物上保証 real guarantee
物色買い selective buying
物　　税 impersonal tax ; tax on goods and possessions
プッタブル・スワップ puttable swap
プッタブル・スワップション puttable swaption
プッタブル・ボンド puttable bond
プッタブル・ワラント puttable warrant
仏中央銀行国債決済システム SATURNE System
FTSE全世界指数 FTSE All-World Index
物的課税除外 impersonal exclusion from taxation
物的勘定 impersonal account
物的控除 impersonal deduction
物的資本利益 return on physical capital
物的証券 securities on property
物的証拠 physical evidence ; real evidence
物的担保 collateral on property ; real security
物的動産 real chattels
物的分割 split-up of a company with shares of a new entity transferable to the original entity
物的流通 physical distribution
プット・アンド・コール put and call
プット・オプション put option
プット価格線 put-value line
プット・コール比率 put-call ratio
プット・コールを組合せたオプション option combination
プット・スワップション put swaption
プット・ダイヤグラム put diagram
プット保持者 put holder
プット保証書 put guarantee letter
プット・ボンド put bond
プット利回り YTP (yield to put)
プット・レシオ・バック・スプレッド取引 put ratio back spread trading
プット・ワラント put warrant
物　　納 payment in kind
物 納 税 levy in kind ; tax in kind
物品横領 misappropriation of goods

物品貨幣 commodity money
物 品 税 commodity excise；commodity tax；excise duty
物品税法 commodity tax law
物品納付 delivery of articles
物々交換 barter
歩積預金 compensating deposit
歩積両建預金 compulsory deposit as a condition for loans
不釣合い imparity
物理的完成割合 completion of physical proportion
物理的減価 physical depreciation
物理的減耗 physical wear and tear
物理的耐用年数 physical age；physical useful life
物理的な限度 physical limit
物理的な劣化 physical deterioration
物理的変化 physical change
物理的変数 physical variables
物理的予備費 physical contingency
物流ネットワーク distribution networks
不定期船 tramper
不定期な勤務 service on a casual basis
不呈示特約小切手 memorandum-check
不定置行列 negative definite matrix
不定利子 contingent interest
不適格債 ineligible bill
不適格な disqualified；ineligible
不適格銘柄 dirty stock
不適切な内容 disqualified substance
不適切な不安定性 irrelevant volatility
不適当な合併 inappropriate merger
不適当な内容 inappropriate substance
不 同 意 disagreement
不当威圧 undue influence
不当営業行為 unfair trade practice
不当解雇 unfair dismissal；wrongful dismissal
不当課税 unreasonable taxation
不当行為 malpractice
不当支出 misappropriation of funds
不当手数料 commission kickback
不 当 な unjustified
不当な取引 unfair trade
不当な履行請求 unfair call
不当評決 false verdict
不当利得 excessive gain；unjust enrichment
不当利得者 profiteer
不当労働行為 unfair labor practice
不 動 化 immobilization
浮 動 株 floating shares
浮動株式数 number of floating shares
浮動株主 floating shareholder
浮 動 玉 floating supply
浮動債務 floating debt
不 動 産 fixed property；immovable property；immovables；real estate；real estate property；things real
不動産一覧 property inventory
不動産価格 property prices
不動産貸付 loan on real estate；loan on real property
不動産貸付業 loan business on real estate
不動産株 real estate stock
不動産株投資の利回り real estate yield
不動産勘定 immovables account
不動産鑑定 real estate appraisal
不動産業 real estate industry；realty business
不動産業者 estate agent；real estate agent
不動産金融 mortgage credit
不動産契約 estate contract
不動産権 legal estate；tenancy
不動産減価償却準備金 reserve for depreciation of real estate
不動産権利書 title deeds
不動産差押え real distress
不動産市場 property market；real estate market
不動産収入 income from real estate
不動産取得税 real estate acquisition tax；real property acquisition tax
不動産取得税の非課税 exemption of real estate acquisition tax
不動産上の権利 rights existing on real estate
不動産情報ネットワークシステム REINS

(Real Estate Information System)
不動産所得 real estate income
不動産信託 real estate in trust
不動産信託受益権 beneficiary right to real estate
不動産占有回復 re-entry of real estate
不動産相場 real estate price
不動産担保 real estate security
不動産担保貸付 mortgage lending
不動産担保貸付業 loan business on real property
不動産仲介委託契約 listing
不動産仲介業 real estate agency
不動産仲介業者 listing broker
不動産賃貸料 rent on real estate
不動産抵当貸付 loan on mortgage
不動産抵当貸付金 loan secured by real estate
不動産抵当長期貸付金 real estate long-term loan receivable
不動産的動産 chattel real
不動産登記簿謄本 certified copy of real estate register
不動産投資信託 REIT (real estate investment trust)
不動産に伴う負担 encumbrance
不動産の共同保有 cotenancy
不動産の証券化 securitization of real estate
不動産の譲渡 transfer of real property
不動産の賃貸 rental of real property
不動産売却益 gain on sale of real estate
不動産売却損 loss on sale of real estate
不動産売買益 profit from immovables transactions
不動産販売 real estate sale
不動産評価損益勘定 profit and loss on valuation of real estate
不動産ブローカー real estate broker
不動産ポートフォリオ property portfolio
不動産モーゲージ real estate mortgage
不動産モーゲージ投資コンディット REMIC (real estate mortgage investment conduit)
浮動資産 floating assets
浮動資本 floating capital
浮動証券 floating securities
浮動担保 floating charge
浮動担保の結晶 crystallization of floating charge
不道徳行為 moral turpitude
不動能力差異 idle capacity variance
不 働 費 idle cost
浮 動 票 floating vote
浮動負債 floating liability
浮動保険証券 floating insurance policy
不 透 明 uncertainty
不透明要因 uncertain factor
埠頭持込渡し delivered ex quay
埠頭渡し EXQ (ex quay)
不特定の他人のためにする保険 insurance for account to whom it may concern
不 突 合 unmatched
歩 留 り yield rate
歩留り差異 yield rate variance
船底浸水 bilge
船積完了証 on board notation
船積指図書 S/O (shipping order)
船積諸掛り shipping charges
船積書類 shipping document
船積遅延 late shipment
船積払い cash on shipment
船積品質条件 shipped quality terms
船荷証券 bill of lading
不人気株式 big uglies
不人気債券 inactive bond
不人気産業 out-of-favor industry
船側渡し free alongside ship
不能な契約 impossible contract
不納付加算税 additional tax on nonpayment
負の運転資本 negative working capital
負の過去勤務費用 negative past service cost
負のキャッシュフロー negative cash flow
負の金額 negative amount
負の効果 negative effect
負の純資産 deficit net worth
負の所得税 negative income tax
負の増益効果 unfavorable leverage effect

負の相関 negative correlation
負のデュレーション negative duration
負ののれん negative goodwill
負の返済 negative amortization
負のレバレッジ効果 negative leverage effect
腐敗行為防止法 Corrupt Practices Acts
賦 払 い installment plan
賦払購買 installment purchase
付番機関 NNA (national numbering agency)
不備指摘書 deficiency letter
付　　表 attached schedule
部品勘定 parts account
不服審査 administrative review
不服の申立 administrative protest；statement of disagreement
部分開放 partial opening
部分解約 partial withdrawal
部分監査 partial audit
部分給付 partial benefit
部分給付権付与 partial vesting
部分業務利益 POP (partial operating profit)
部分拒否権 item veto
部分均衡 partial equilibrium
部分繰上返済 curtailments；partial prepayment
部分原価計算 partial costing
部分資本直入法 partial fair value method
部分退職 partial retirement
部分的一任注文 fractional discretion order
部分的競争入札 partial competitive auction bidding
部分的直接償却 partial direct write-off
部分的なカバード・オプション partially covered option
部分的な検討 limited review
部分撤退 partial withdrawal
部分年金 partial pension
部分保証 partial guarantee
部分持ち分法 partial equity method
不 併 合 non-joinder
不偏検定 unbiased test
不変資本 constant capital
不偏推定量 unbiased estimator
不偏分布 unbiased distribution
不変リスク許容度 constant risk tolerance
不　　法 illegality；unlawfulness
不法行為 misfeasance；unlawful act
不法行為責任保険 tort insurance
不法行為賠償債務 tort liabilities
不法集会 unlawful assembly
不法就労 illegal employment
不法占有 dispossession；unlawful entry
不法立入 breach of close
不法妨害 nuisance
不没収給付 non-forfeiture benefit
不没収法 non-forfeiture act
踏　　み short covering at a loss
踏 上 げ short squeeze
踏上げ相場 bear squeeze market
不 明 瞭 ambiguity
部　　門 division
部門売上 divisional sales
部門間勘定 interdepartmental account
部門監査 department audit
部門間接費 departmental overhead
部門間接費差異 department variance on overhead
部門間振替 interunit transfer
部門間振替価格の決定 interunit pricing
部門計算 sectional calculation
部門原価 departmental cost
部門個別費 direct department cost
部 門 費 departmental charge；departmental expenses
部門費計算表 overhead distribution sheet
部門費予算 departmental expenses budget
部門負担費 departmental burden
部門別内訳 segmental breakdown
部門別売上 segmental sales
部門別売上内訳 divisional sales breakdown；segmental sales breakdown
部門別原価計算 cost accounting by department；departmental cost accounting；departmental costing

部門別損益 division results ; divisional breakdown of profit and loss
部門別貸借対照表 sector balance sheet
部門別利益 departmental profit
富 裕 税 wealth tax
付　　与 grant
扶養家族 dependent family member
扶養義務 duty of support
扶養控除 allowance for dependent ; child tax credit ; deduction for dependents ; tax exemption for dependents
扶 養 者 supporter
扶養約款 maintenance clause
付与加算率 credited rate
付 与 日 grant date
付与日価値 grant date value
付与日測定 grant date measurement
プライス・フィルター price filter
プライス・メーカー price maker
プライス・リーダー price leader
プライバシーの侵害 invasion of privacy
プライベート・エクイティ・ファンド private equity fund
プライベート・セール private sale
プライベート・パス・スルー private pass-through
プライベート・バンク事業 private banking
プライベート・ブランド・カード private label card
プライベート・リスク private risk
プライマリー・ディーラー primary dealer
プライマリー・バランス primary balance
プライム・ネームCD prime name CD
プライム・レート prime interest rate
ブラウン運動 Brownian motion
プラザ合意 Plaza Accord
ブラジル・リアル BRL (Brazilian real)
プラス・ティック plus-tick
フラッグ flag
ブラック・ショールズ・オプション価格決定モデル Black-Scholes option pricing model
ブラック・ショールズのオプション評価式 Black-Scholes formula on option valuation
ブラック・ショールズ方式 Black-Scholes method
ブラック・ショールズ・マートン・モデル Black-Scholes-Merton model
ブラック・ショールズ・モデル Black-Scholes model
ブラック・ボックス・オークション black box auction
ブラック・マンデー Black Monday
ブラックリスト blacklist
フラット flat
フラット・カーブ flat curve
フラット・マーケット flat market
フラット・ローン flat loan
フラワー・ボンド flower bond
フランクフルト証券取引所 Frankfurt Stock Exchange
フランスAGEF指数 AGEF Index
フランス財務省 Trésor
フランスCAC 工業株指数 CAC General Index
フランス証券決済機関 Sicovam (Société Interprofessionelle pour la Compensation des Valeurs Mobilières)
フランス・フラン FRF (French franc)
フランス保管振替機関 Euroclear France
フランチャイズ運営者 franchiser
フランチャイズ加盟者 franchisee
フランチャイズ契約 franchise agreement
フランチャイズ店 franchise outlet
フランチャイズ料 franchise fee
ブランド品 brand item
フリー期間 free period
フリー・キャッシュフロー free cash flow
フリー・キャッシュフロー・バリュエーション FCFV (Free cashflow valuation)
フリート保険契約者 fleet insured
フリー・フィナンシャル・ファンド free financial fund
フリー・ライダー free rider
フリー・ライディング free riding
フリー・ローン free loan

振　　替　transfer
振替依頼　payment instruction
振替可能勘定　transferable account
振替勘定　transfer account
振替記入　transfer entry
振替業の営業譲渡　transfer of book-entry business
振替決済　book-entry transfer
振替決済機関　book entry transfer institution
振替決済システム　book-entry system
振替決済証券　book-entry securities
振替決済制度　book-entry transfer system
振替決済手数料　fee for book-entry transfer
振替決済のみ　BEO (Book-Entry-Only)
振替口座　postal transfer account
振替口座簿　transfer account book
振替口座簿の閲覧　inspection of transfer account book
振替口座簿の備付け　location of transfer account book
振替貯金口座　transfer savings account
振替手数料　book-entry transfer fee；transferring charge
振替伝票　journal slip；transfer slip；transfer voucher
振替取引　transfer transactions
振替納税　tax payment by transfer account
振替番号　transfer number
振替元帳　transfer ledger
振替利益　profit transferred；transfer profit
振替利益引当金　reserve for intercompany profit
振決国債　Book-entry JGSs
振決国債の金額の単位　unit of amount of book-entry JGSs
振決国債の範囲　scope of book-entry JGSs
不 履 行　failure；non-fulfillment；non-performance
不履行債券　sour bond
不履行者　defaulter
不履行事由　event of default
不履行ポジション　fail position
不履行モーゲージ　non-performing mortgage
振込指定　designation for transfer
付利最高限度　maximum limit for interest rate
振 出 し　drawing
振出銀行　drawing bank
振 出 地　place of issue
振出手形　drawn bill
振 出 人　drawer
振出人回し　R/D (refer to drawer)
振 出 す　draw
付利単位　minimum denomination on which interest is calculated
ブリッジ決済　bridge settlement
ブリッジ・ローン　bridge loan
フリップ・フロップ債　flip flop FRN (floating rate note)
フリップ・フロップ証券　flip flop securities
プリペイド・カード　prepaid card
不良会員　bad member
不良貸出　doubtful loan
不良債権　bad debt；doubtful account；impaired loan；underperforming loans
不良債権隠し　hidden bad loans
不良債権区分　classification of bad debts
不良債権償却　bad debt written-off
不良債権処理　NPL (non-performing loan) disposal；write-off of bad loan
不良債権の最終処理　final disposition of bad loans
不良債権の証券化　securitization of bad loans
不良債権の処理　troubled-loan cleanup
不良債権問題　NPL (non-performing loan) problem
不良債権問題の解決　resolution of NPL problem
不良債権率　bad debt ratio
不良在庫　dead stock
不良資産　problem assets
不良モーゲージ　underperforming mortgages

フ

富力審査 wealth test
プリンシパル会員 principal member
フリンジ・バンキング fringe banking
ブルー・スカイ法 blue sky law
ブルー・チップ blue chip
プルーデント・マン・ルール prudent man rule
ブルームバーグ Bloomberg
ブル型原油リンク債 BOLTS (bull oil-linked transactions)
ブルガリア・レフ BGL (Bulgarian lev)
ブルキナ・ファソ（CFAフラン） Burkina Faso (CFA (Communauté Financière Africaine) franc)
フル・クーポン債 full coupon bond
ブル・スプレッド取引 bull spread transaction
プル戦略 pull strategy
ブルッセル証券取引所 BSE (Brussels Stock Exchange)
ブルドッグ債 bulldog bond
ブルネイ・ドル BND (Brunei dollar)
フル・バンキング・サービス full banking service
ブル・ベア債 bull bear bond
フル・ヘッジ full hedge
ブルンジー・フラン BIF (Burundi franc)
プレ・アド preliminary advice
ブレイディ構想 Brady plan
ブレーク・イーブン・レポ・レート break-even repo rate
ブレークスルー breakthrough
プレーン・バニラ plain vanilla
プレーン・バニラ・オプション plain vanilla option
プレーン・バニラ・スワップ plain vanilla swap
プレーン・バニラの変動利付債 plain vanilla floater
フレッシュ・スタート法 fresh-start method
フレッディ・マック Freddie Mac
ブレット・スワップ bullet swap
ブレトンウッズ Bretton Woods
ブレトンウッズ協定 Bretton Woods Agreement
プレビッド契約 prebid agreement
プレミアム premium
プレミアム貸付 lending at a premium
プレミアム還元 return of premium
プレミアム債 premium bond
プレミアム証券 premium securities
プレミアム状態 premium condition
プレミアム建値方式 premium quotation system
プレミアムの償却 amortization of premium
プレミアム発行 premium issue
不連続な急騰 discontinuous jumps
ブレンド型保険 blended insurance
PRO PRO (planned redemption obligation)
フロア付償還額 floored redemption amount
フロア付スワップ floored swap
フロア・トレーダー floor trader
フロア・ブローカー floor broker
不労所得 unearned income
不労所得者層 rentier class
ブローカー broker
ブローカー及びディーラーによる証券金融 security credit by brokers and dealers
ブローカー会社 brokerage agency
ブローカー業務 broker's business； brokerage
ブローカー経由介入 intervention through brokers
ブローカー市場 broker market
ブローカーズ・ブローカー broker's broker
ブローカーズ・ローン broker's loan
ブローカーズ・ローン金利 broker's loan interest
ブローカー・ディーラー broker dealer
ブローカー仲間 crowd
ブローカーのコール・ローン broker's call loan
ブローカーへの貸付 broker loan
フロー・スルー法 flow through method

フ

フロー・ダイアグラム flow diagram
フロー・チャート flow chart
フローティング・ベーシス floating basis
ブロード・マネー broad money
フロート預金 deposit float
プログラム・トレード program trade
プログラム売買 program trading
プログラム評価 program evaluation
プログラム予算 program budgeting
プロジェクト管理 PM (project management)
プロジェクトの可能性 project potential
プロジェクト評価 project evaluation
プロジェクト・ファイナンス project finance
プロジェクト・リスク project risk
プロジェクト・ローン project loan
プロセス・イノベーション process innovation
プロダクション・ローン production loan
プロダクト・サイクル論 product cycle theory
プロダクト・ミックス product mix
ブロック・オファー block offer
ブロック経済 bloc economy
ブロック資金 blocked fund
ブロック・トレーダー block trader
ブロック・フロー block flow
ブロック・ポジショナー block positioner
プロテクション protection
プロテクションの買い buying protection
プロテクティブ・プット protective put
プロテクティブ・プット取引 protective put trading
プロビジョナル・サム provisional sum
プロフィット・シェアリング profit sharing
プロフィット・センター profit center
プロフォーマ・インボイス pro-forma invoice
プロフォルマ pro forma
プロポーザル方式 proposal method
プロポーザル・レター proposal letter
プロラタ条項 pro-rata clause
フロンティング fronting
フロント・エンド・フィー front-end fee
フロント・ランニング front running
不渡小切手 dishonored check ; returned non-sufficient-fund check
不渡事由 reason for dishonor
不渡通知 dishonor notice ; non-payment protest
不渡手形 dishonored bill ; note dishonored ; past due bill
不渡返却 bounce
分解分析 decomposition
文化財研究所 National Research Institute for Cultural Properties
文 化 庁 Agency for Cultural Affairs
分　　割 apportion
分割売り split sale
分割可能性 divisibility
分割基準 basis to prorate local tax
分割共同 split joint acceptance
分割拠出 split-funding
分割拠出年数 installment contribution years
分割契約 several contract
分割契約書 agreement for demerger
分割個人年金 split annuity
分割受託 split acceptance
分割償還 installment redemption ; installment repayment
分割所有権 several ownership
分割仕訳帳 sectional journal
分割相続制 division of succession
分割贈与 gift splitting
分割注文 order splitting
分割納付 installment payment of tax ; payment in installments
分割発行 split offering
分割発行方式 tranche issue
分割払い easy payment ; installment payment ; installment settlement
分割払現金 cash installments
分割販売保険 installment sales floater insurance
分割引出し partial draw down
分割船積み partial shipment
分割付保 divided coverage

分割返済 loan amortization；repayment installment
分割返済型貸付 amortization loan
分割返済型タームローン amortizing term loan
分割法人 corporation which has transferred its assets and liabilities through split-up
分割保険料 installment premium
分割元帳勘定 split ledger account
分　　権 decentralization
分　　散 dispersion
分 散 化 diversification
分散型投資会社 diversified type investment company
分散型普通株ファンド diversified type common stock fund
分散型ポートフォリオ diversified type portfolio
分散化投資 diversification investment
分散可能リスク diversifiable risk
分散株式投資ポートフォリオ diversified portfolio on stock investment
分散したポートフォリオ diversified portfolio
分散スコア diversity score
分散投資 diversified investment
分散投資効果 diversification benefit
分散投資で排除できないリスク unavoidable risk by diversified investment
分散投資の有効性 effectiveness of diversified investment
分散の分解分析 variance decomposition
分 散 比 variance ratio
分散不能リスク undiversifiable risk
分散分析 analysis of variance
分　　子 numerator
紛失カード lost card
紛失・盗難のリスク risks of loss and theft
紛失保険証券 lost policy
分　　社 spin-off
分　　譲 lotting out
分 譲 地 building lots for sale
文 書 課 Overall Co-ordination Division
文書為替 mail exchange bill
文書偽造 forgery of documents
文書毀損 mutilation of documents
文 書 局 Budget and Management Office
粉　　飾 embellishment；manipulation of account；window dressing
粉飾決算 account rigging；window dressing settlement of accounts
粉飾決算による法人税の過大納付 overpayment of corporation tax due to window dressing
粉飾財務諸表 window dressing financial statements
粉飾預金 window dressing deposit
文書による通知 notification in writing
文書の閲覧 inspection of documents
文書の本文 body of an instrument
分　　析 analysis；analytics
分析手法 tools of analysis
分析証明書 certificate of analysis
分析ツール analytical tool
分析データ analytical data
分析的アプローチ analytic approach
分析的会計 analytical accounting
分析的手続 analytical procedure
分析的報告書 analytical reports
紛　　争 dispute
紛争解決 dispute settlement
分　　損 partial loss；particular loss
分損担保 with average
分損担保約款 average clause
分損不担保 FPA (free from particular average)
分担式生命保険 split dollar life insurance
ブンデスバンク Bundesbank
ブ ン ド Bund；Bundesanleihen
分納の合意 installment agreement
分　　配 distribution
分配型ミューチュアル・ファンド flexible mutual fund
分 配 金 profit distribution
分配国民所得 national income distributed
分売執行日 distribution date
分売要領 details of distribution

フ

分 配 率 relative share
分布関数 distribution function
分別管理 segregated accounts
分別管理口 separate management account
分別年齢 age of discretion
分別保管口座 non-fungible account
分　　母 denominator
分　　与 distribution
分　　離 severance
分離課税 separate taxation from other income ; separated taxation
分離型の detachable
分離型ワラント detachable warrant
分離型ワラント債 bonds with detachable warrant
分離可能原価 separable cost
分離勘定 segregated account ; separate account ; separate investment account
分離勘定基金積立 separate account funding
分離勘定資産 separate account assets
分離勘定生命保険 separate account policy
分離元本振決国債 separated principal component
分離銀行制度 separate banking system
分離計算方式 two statements approach
分離適格振決国債 book-entry JGSs eligible for STRIPS
分離投資勘定 separate investment account
分離不能ワラント non-detachable warrant
分離利息振決国債 separated coupon component
分　　類 classification
分類過程 classification process
分類された株式 classified stock
分類所得税 classified income tax ; scheduler income taxation
分類の変更 transfer among categories

へ

ベア・コール・スプレッド bear call spread
ベア・ボンド bear bond
ベア・インデックス債 bear index bond
ベア・スプレッド取引 bear spread trading
ベア・ハッグ bear hug
ベア・ブル・ボンド bear bull bond
ペイオフ limitation on deposit payoff
ペイオフ行列 pay-off matrix
ペイオフ・ダイヤグラム pay-off diagram
ペイオフ・パターン pay-off pattern
平　価 parity
平価以上 above par
平価切上げ revaluation
平価調整 parity adjustment
平価発行 par issuance
平 滑 法 smoothing method
平均回帰 mean reversion
平均回帰過程 mean reverting process
平均回収期間 average collection
平均価格加重 price weighted
平均価格加重指数 price weighted index
平均課税 average taxation
平均株価採用銘柄 issue used in the average ; stock used in the average
平均期間 average period
平均給与方式 average salary plan
平均金利 average interest rate
平均金利キャップ average interest rate cap
平均原価 average cost
平均原価法 average cost method
平均行使価格オプション average strike price option
平均個人税率 personal average tax rate
平 均 差 mean difference
平均差異 mean difference
平均在庫 average inventory ; average stock
平均債務コスト average cost of debt
平均残存期間 average life
平均残存期間利回り YTAL (yield to average life)
平均残存勤務年数 average remaining service years
平均残存年数 average life
平均残高 average balance ; average of daily figures ; average outstanding
平均時価法 average current cost method
平均自乗誤差 MSE (mean square error)
平均実働時間 actuarial hours ; average actual working hours
平均支払期日 equaled date of payment
平均資本コスト average cost of capital
平均収益 average earnings
平均寿命 expectation of life
平均償還年限 average term to maturity
平均消費者物価指数 average consumer price index
平均消費性向 average propensity to consume
平均所得 average income
平均スポット・レート・オプション average spot rate option
平均生産期間 average period of production
平均税率 average tax rate
平均絶対偏差 average absolute deviation ; mean absolute deviation
平均総額 average aggregate amount
平 均 値 mean value
平均投資収益 average return on investment
平均と分散 mean-variance
平均2乗誤差 mean squared error
平均2乗収束 mean squared convergence
平均伸び率 average growth rate
平均配当金 average dividend paid
平均配当率 average rate of dividend
平均売買代金 average trading value
平均発行残高 average balance

outstanding
平均発行高 average issued
平均引当率 average provision rate
平均標準月額報酬 average monthly earnings
平均標準報酬月額 average index monthly earnings
平均品質 fair average quality
平均・分散ポートフォリオ選択 mean-variance portfolio selection
平均偏差 mean deviation
平均変動率 average volatility
平 均 法 average method
平均法人税率 corporate average tax rate
平均保険金額 average policy amount
平均保険料 average premium
平均余命 life expectancy
平均余命保険 expectancy policy
平均利益 average profit
平均利益率 average return
平均利回り average yield
平均ローン年数 average loan age
併 合 annexation
平行移動 parallel shift
平衡介入 central bank intervention
平衡勘定 equalization account
平行起債 parallel issue
平衡控除 balancing adjustment
平衡裁判所 court of equity
併行市場 parallel money market
平行取引 parallel transaction
平衡簿記 position bookkeeping
並行本位制度 parallel standard
平行輸入 parallel import
平 衡 力 counterpoise
米国一般会計局 U.S. Government General Accounting Office
米国会計学会 American Accounting Association
米国会計検査院 U.S. General Accounting Office
米国会計士協会 AIA (American Institutes of Accountants)
米国会計人協会 National Association of Accountants
米国株式 US equities
米国株式の売り selling US equities
米国企業改革法 Sarbanes-Oxley Act
米国教職員保険・退職年金組合 Teachers' Insurance Annuity Association of America
米国銀行協会 American Bankers Association
米国経営者協会 American Management Association
米国憲法修正第1条 First Amendment
米国憲法修正第5条 Fifth Amendment
米国公認会計士協会 American Institute of Certified Public Accountants
米国公認証券アナリスト協会 Institute of Chartered Financial Analysts
米国国務省 Department of State
米国個人投資家協会 AAII (American Association of Individual Investors)
米国コマーシャル・ペーパー USCP (US commercial paper)
米国債市場 Treasury market
米国債指標利回り US treasury benchmark yield
米国財政赤字 federal deficit
米国債の買い切りオペ coupon pass
米国財務省 Department of Treasury；US Treasury
米国財務省証券 treasuries；Treasury issue
米国債利回り Treasury yield
米国債理論利回り CMT (constant maturity treasury yield)
米国先物業者協会 Futures Industry Association
米国奨学金融資金庫 Sallie Mae (Student Loan Marketing Association)
米国奨学資金金庫 Sallie Mae
米国証券業協会 SIA (Securities Industry Association)
米国証券市場認知の統計的格付機関 NRSRO (nationally recognized statistical rating organization)
米国証券収益ファンド US government income fund

米国証券取引委員会 Securities and Exchange Commission
米国証券取引所決済機関 National Securities Clearing Corporation
米国商品先物取引委員会 Commodity Futures Trading Commission
米国商務省 Department of Commerce
米国政府抵当金庫証券 GNMA (Government National Mortgage Association) certificate
米国政府保証付き USGG (US government guaranteed)
米国大学教職員退職変額年金基金 College Retirement Equities Fund
米国貯蓄債 U.S. savings bond
米国通商代表部 USTR (United States Trade Representative)
米国ドル USD (United States of America dollar)
米国ドル債市場 Yankee bond market
米国ドル資金決済 US dollar funds settlement
米国内国歳入庁 Internal Revenue Service
米国内国歳入法 Internal Revenue Code
米国法曹協会 American Bar Association
米国法律協会 American Law Institute
米国輸出入銀行 Export-Import Bank of USA
米国預託株式 ADS (American Depositary Shares); American depository share
米国預託証券 ADR (American Depository Receipt)
閉　　鎖 closure
閉鎖市場 closed market
米州開発銀行 Inter-American Development Bank
米州機構 Organization of American States
平準化準備金 equalization reserve
平準化積立金 equalization reserve
平準化配当 equalization dividend
平準拠出 level contribution
平準相場 parity quotation
平準積立コスト level funding cost
平準積立方式 level annual premium method
平準保険料 level premium
平準保険料式積立金 level premium reserve
平準保険料準備金 net level premium reserve
ペイ・スルー債券 pay-through bond
併設プラン tandem plan
併存原因 concurrent causes
併存賃借権 concurrent lease
米ドル紙幣 greenback
米ドル短期金利先物 U.S. dollar short-term interest futures
平 年 度 full year
並　　売 cross selling
ペイメント・イン・カインド 優先株 payment-in-kind preferred stock
ペイヤー・スワップション payer's swaption
ベーシス・ギャップ basis gap
ベーシス条件付取引 transaction with basis condition
ベーシス・スワップ basis swap
ベーシス取引 basis trading; basis transaction
ベーシス・ポイント bp (basis point)
ベーシス・マーケット basis market
ベーシス・リスク basis risk
ベース・マネー base money
ベ ー タ beta
ベータ係数 beta coefficient
ベータ・サービス beta service
ベータ値 beta value
ベータ値が低いポートフォリオ low beta portfolio
ベータ値の情報源 information sources on beta value
ベータ調整値 beta adjusted
ベータの標準誤差 standard error of beta
ベータの予測方程式 beta value prediction equation
ペーパー・カンパニー paper company; shell corporation
ペーパーレス地方債 certificateless municipals

ペーパーレス・トレーディング　paperless trading
ベ　ガ　vega
ベガ・ニュートラル　vega-neutral
北京市　Beijing
ペセタ　peseta
ペ　ソ　peso
別扱い危険　classified risk
別勘定　separate account；separate bill
別居手当　separate maintenance
別口預金　special deposit account
ヘッジ　hedge
ヘッジ売り　hedge selling
ヘッジ買い　hedge buying
ヘッジ会計　hedge accounting
ヘッジ会計基準　hedge accounting standards
ヘッジ会計処理　hedge accounting treatment
ヘッジ関係　hedging relationship
ヘッジ勘定代行書　hedge account representation letter
ヘッジ期間　hedge period
ヘッジ機能　hedging function
ヘッジ・コスト　hedging cost
ヘッジ債　hedged bond
ヘッジされていないリスク　unhedged risk
ヘッジ指定　designation of hedges
ヘッジ手段　hedging instrument；hedging vehicle；means for hedging
ヘッジ手段の更新　rollover of a hedging instrument
ヘッジ手法　hedging technique
ヘッジ条項　hedge clause
ヘッジ証拠金　hedge margin
ヘッジ商品　hedge instrument
ヘッジ・スキーム　hedging scheme
ヘッジ操作　hedge operation
ヘッジ損失　hedging loss
ヘッジ対象項目　hedged item
ヘッジ対象の識別　identification of hedged items
ヘッジ対象リスク　hedged risk
ヘッジド・ポートフォリオ　hedged portfolio
ヘッジ取引　hedge trading；hedge transaction；hedging
ヘッジなしの債券　unhedged bond
ヘッジの期間　life of hedge
ヘッジの有効性　hedge effectiveness
ヘッジ非有効部分　ineffective portion of hedging
ヘッジ比率　hedge ratio
ヘッジ・ファンド　hedge fund；hedged fund
ヘッジ方針　hedging policy
ヘッジ・ポジション　hedged position
ヘッジ・ボンド　hedge bond
ヘッジャー　hedger
ヘッジ利益　hedge gains
ヘッジ・リスク　hedged risk
ヘッジ利得　hedging gain
ヘッジ割合　hedging proportion
別人格勘定　separate customer account
ヘッセ行列　Hessian matrix
別段勘定　separate and restricted account
別段の定めがない限り　not otherwise provided；unless otherwise specified
別段預金　special deposits
ヘッド・アンド・ショルダー　head and shoulder
別途支出　special outlay
別途収益基金　special revenue fund
別途積立金　other reserve；special reserve fund；unconditional reserve
別封で　under separate cover
別　名　alias
ベトナム・ドン　VND (Vietnamese dong)
ペナルティ・ビッド　penalty bid
ペナント　pennant
ベニン(CFAフラン)　Benin (CFA (Communauté Financière Africaine) franc)
ベネズエラ・ボリバール　VEB (Venezuelan Bolivar)
ベビー・ファンド　baby fund
ヘムライン理論　hemline theory
ベラルーシ・ルーブル　BYR (Belarus ruble)

ベリーズ・ドル BZD (Belize dollar)
ペルー・ヌエボソル PEN (Peruvian nuebo sol)
ヘル・オア・ハイ・ウォーター条項 hell or high water clause
ベルギー先物オプション取引所 BELFOX (Belgian Futures and Options Exchange)
ベルギー長期国債 OLO (Obligation Lineaire Obligaties)
ベルギー・フラン BEE (Belgium franc)
ベルギー保管振替機関 CIK
ヘルスケア health care
便益関税 beneficial duty
便益工作物 accommodation works
便益費用分析 benefit cost analysis
便益分析 benefit analysis
変額給付方式 variable benefit formula
変額契約 variable contract
変額市場 variable marketplace
変額支払い variable payout
変額終身年金 variable life income
変額商品 equity product ; variable product
変額生命保険 variable life insurance
変額即時年金 variable immediate annuity
変額投資勘定 equity account
変額年金 equity annuity ; variable annuity
変額年金単位 variable annuity unit
変額保険 interest sensitive policy ; variable insurance
変額保険料 variable premium
変額ユニバーサル保険 variable universal life insurance
変額生命保険 flexible-premium variable life insurance
変 化 率 rate of change
変換係数 CF (conversion factor) ; price factor
返還権付売買 sale or return
返還請求権 right to claim refund
返還不能な保証金 non-refundable guarantee deposit
返還保証証券 refund bond
返還を請求する claim the refund
便　　宜 convenience
返却小切手 returned check
偏　　見 prejudice
偏向した biased
変　　更 alteration ; change
変更型パス・スルー modified pass-through
変更クレーム change claims
変更工事 alteration work
変更後の条件 changed terms
変更された貸付 modified loan
変更時差異費用 transitional cost
変更時差異未処理額 remaining transitional amount
変更請求 alteration demand
変更登記 registration of alteration
変更の影響 effect of change
変 更 日 change date
変更報告書 change report
変更又は訂正 changes or correction
弁 護 士 advocate ; attorney ; lawyer
弁護士顧問料 retaining fee
弁護士責任 lawyer's liability
弁護士賠償責任保険 lawyer's liability insurance
弁護士報酬 legal fee
弁護士リーエン attorney's lien ; retaining lien
弁護士料 lawyer's fee
偏　　在 maldistribution
返　　済 repayment
返済意志 willingness to pay
返済回数 number of scheduled payments
返済期間 payment periods
返済期限 repayment period
返済期日 repayment date
返済原資 pledged revenue
返済条件 repayment conditions
返済免除条件 terms of forgiveness
返済免除条件付融資 forgivable loan
返済猶予 grace of repayment
返済リスク repayment risk
返済利息 paid interest
返 済 率 repayment rate

弁　済 reimbursement
弁済期限 deadline for repayment ; settlement period
弁済期日 due date
弁済条件 payment conditions
弁済の順序 order of repayment
弁済の猶予 respite for repayment ; standstill agreement
弁済補償金 repayment compensation
弁　償 indemnification
変　数 variable
変数サンプリング variables sampling
変数の関数 function of quantities
変　造 alteration
変造カード forged card
変造紙幣 alteration of banknotes
変　則 anomaly
変則決算会社 company having changed its fiscal year
ベンダー連合 vendor alliance
偏弾力性 partial elasticity
ベンチマーク・ポートフォリオ benchmark portfolio
ベンチャー育成 development of venture business
ベンチャー育成ファンド funds for development of venture business
ベンチャー・キャピタル venture capital
ベンチャー・ビジネス venture business
偏導関数 partial derivative
変動オプション variable option
変動価格圏 variable price zone
変動額の受取 receipt of floating payments
変動から固定への金利スワップ floating to fixed interest rate swap
変動為替相場 floating exchange rate
変動為替相場制 floating exchange rate system
変動間接費 variable indirect cost ; variable overhead cost
変動管理費 variable overhead
変動金利 floating interest rate ; variable-rate interest
変動金利貸出 floating rate lending
変動金利型不動産ローン variable rate mortgage loan
変動金利借入 borrowing at a floating rate
変動金利債 FRN (floating rate notes)
変動金利債務 variable-rate debt
変動金利CD variable rate CD ; floating rate certificate of deposit
変動金利支払人 floating-rate payer
変動金利指標 floating rate index
変動金利スワップ floating swap
変動金利モーゲージ adjustable rate mortgage ; VRM (variable rate mortgage)
変動金利要求払債 VRDO (variable rate demand obligation)
変動金利要求払証書 variable rate demand note
変動金利ローン variable-rate loan
変動計算書 statement of changes
変動係数 CV (coefficient of variation) ; variability factor
変動原価率 variable cost ratio
変動実績 historical change
変動上限金利付勘定 floating interest rate account with ceiling
変動条項 fluctuation clause
変動証拠金 variation margin
変動証拠金支払 variation margin call
変動所得 fluctuating income ; transitory income
変動所得及び臨時所得 fluctuating and extraordinary income
変動所得計算 variable income computation
変動所得の平均課税 average taxation on fluctuating income
変動する fluctuate
変動性の減少 reduction of volatility
変動相場 floating system
変動相場制 floating exchange rate regime
変動年金契約 variable annuity contract
変動の激しい公正価値 volatile movement in fair value
変動配当優先株 variable rate preferred stock

変 動 幅 band；range
変動幅の上限 stronger half of the band
変 動 費 variable charge；variable costs and expenses；variable expenses
変動費率 rate of variable expenses
変動分析 fluctuation analysis
変動持ち分 variable interest entity
変動予算 variable budget
変動予算差異 flexible budget variance
変動リース料 contingent lease payments
変動利益 variable profit
変動利付クーポン floating rate coupon
変動利付国債 floating rate JGB
変動利付債 floater；floating rate instrument；floating rate note
変動利付債券 floating rate bond
変動利付債市場 floating rate market
変動利付転換優先株 CAPS (convertible adjustable preferred stock)
変動利付きの variable interest bearing
変動利付モーゲージ floating rate mortgage
変動率の標準偏差 standard deviation of volatility
変動利率 variable interest rate
変動利率保険料 variable rate premium
変動利率優先株 adjustable rate preferred stock
偏頗リスク preference risk
偏微分方程式 partial differential equation
返　　品 returned goods unsold
返品期間 try-out period
返品差損費 loss on sales returns
返品調整引当金 reserve for adjustment of sales returns；reserve for loss on goods unsold
返 品 率 rate of returned goods unsold；rate of sales returns
片務契約 unilateral contract
返 戻 金 refundment

ホ

ポイズン・ピル poison pills
ボイラー・ルーム boiler room
ポイント・アンド・フィギュア point and figure
ポイント・アンド・フィギュア・チャート point and figure chart
ポイント・アンド・フィギュア法 point and figure method
棒上げ straight climb
防衛買い defensive purchase
防衛施設庁 Defense Facilities Administration Agency
防衛庁 Japan Defense Agency
防衛庁長官 Minister of State for Defense
防衛費 defense expenditure
貿易相手国 trading partner
貿易赤字 foreign trade deficit
貿易赤字・黒字 trade deficit or surplus
貿易依存 dependence on foreign trade
貿易外収支 invisible account；invisible trade balance；service balance
貿易外取引 invisible trade
貿易加重指数 trade weighted index
貿易加重ベース・バスケット trade weighted basket
貿易関連投資措置 TRIM (Trade Related Investment Measures)
貿易協定 trade agreement
貿易金融 foreign trade finance；trade credit
貿易クレーム trade claim
貿易決済通貨 currency invoicing
貿易交渉委員会 Trade Negotiations Committee
貿易産業省 Department of Trade and Industry
貿易指数 index of trade
貿易自由化 liberalization of trade
貿易収支 trade balance；trade position
貿易収支黒字 favorable trade balance
貿易収支黒字幅 trade surplus amount
貿易収支実績 trade figure
貿易収支の黒字 favorable balance of trade
貿易信用 foreign trade credit
貿易政策 foreign trade policy
貿易創出効果 trade creation effect
貿易統計 foreign trade data；foreign trade statistics；trade statistics
貿易統制 trade control
貿易摩擦 trade friction
貿易連関分析 trade matrix analysis
邦貨 Japanese currency
崩壊 breakdown
法外な利益 exorbitant profit
邦貨買入外国為替 home currency bill bought
邦貨国債 government bonds in domestic currency
包括遺贈 universal legacy
包括受遺者 universal legatee
包括基準 all-inclusive basis
包括給付 unallocated benefit
包括個人責任保険 umbrella personal liability policy
包括財産 floating property
包括主義 all-inclusive principle
包括主義的利益概念 all-inclusive income concept
包括主義の原則 principle of all-inclusiveness
包括損益計算書 all-inclusive income statement
包括担保設定方式 blanket system
包括通商法案 comprehensive trade bill
包括抵当 package mortgage
包括抵当権付債券 blanket bond
包括的権限 general authority
包括的調査 exhaustive study
包括的な exhaustive

包括的な基準 comprehensive standards
包括的な情報 comprehensive information
包括的モーゲージ blanket mortgage
包括年次財務報告書 CAFR (comprehensive annual financial report)
包括標準契約書 umbrella master agreement
包括ヘッジ blanket hedges
包括保険 blanket insurance；open cover；umbrella cover
包括保険契約 blanket policy
包括保険証書 open policy
包括融資担保契約 general loan and collateral agreement
包括輸出信用方式 umbrella export credit facility
包括預金保険 blanket deposit insurance
包括予算 comprehensive budget
包括予定保険 open insurance
包括利益 comprehensive income
包括利益計算書 statement of comprehensive income
包括利益累計額 accumulated comprehensive income
邦貨手形 bill in domestic currency
傍 観 者 bystander
法 規 課 Legal Division
法規顧問室 Office of the General Counsel
法規裁量 controlled discretion
法規上の環境 regulatory environment
法規調査官 Special Officer for Research on Legal Matters
放棄利息 waived interest
邦銀ユーザンス Japanese banks usance
棒グラフ bar chart
傍系血族 collateral consanguinity
方 向 性 directional movement
方向性指数 directional index
報告会社 reporting company
報告期間 reporting period
報告企業 reporting enterprise
報告義務 duties of report；reporting requirement
報告形式 reporting form
報告された利益 reported earnings
報 告 式 narrative form；report form；schedule form
報告式貸借対照表 report form balance sheet
報告事項 matters to be reported
報告主体の変更 change in reporting entity
報 告 書 report
報告所得税 reported income tax
報告制度 reporting system
報告セグメント reporting segment
報告単位 reporting unit
報告通貨 reporting currency
報告内容 content report
報告の方針 reporting policy
報告目的 reporting objective
報告様式 reporting format
防災科学技術研究所 National Research Institute for Science and Disaster Prevention
防災担当大臣 Minister of State for Disaster Management
棒 下 げ straight fall
法施行地 law enforced territory
放射線医学総合研究所 National Institute of Radiological Sciences
報 酬 compensation；fee；remuneration；reward
報酬委員会 compensation committee
報酬額上限 upper earnings limit
報酬ストック・オプション compensatory stock option
報酬体系 compensation structure
報酬費用 remuneration expense
報 酬 表 fee schedule
報奨給付 compensation benefit
報 償 金 incentive payment
報奨費用 compensation expense
法 人 corporation；incorporated body；juridical person；legal person
法 人 化 incorporation
法人カード corporate card
法人会員 corporate member

ホ

法人買付け institution buying
法 人 格 juridical personality ; legal identity ; legal status
法人格のない会社 unincorporated company
法人格のない社団 non-juridical organization
法人課税 company taxation
法人課税課 Corporation Taxation Division
法人株主 corporate shareholder
法人企業 corporate businesses
法人擬制説 fictional theory of corporation
法 人 権 corporate right
法人顧客 corporate customer
法人事業税 enterprise tax on corporation
法人事業税の課税標準 tax base of enterprise tax on corporation
法人実在説 real entity theory of corporation
法人資本 corporate capital
法人住民税 corporate inhabitant tax
法人所得 corporate income
法人所得税控除後 after income taxes
法人所得税控除前 before income taxes
法人所得税費用 corporate income taxes expenses
法人所得税法 corporate income tax law
法人所得税率 corporate income tax rate
法人信託 corporate trust
法人信用組合 CCU (corporate credit unions)
法 人 税 corporate income tax ; corporation tax
法人税額損金不算入 exclusion from expenses of corporation tax
法人税確定申告書の提出 filing of final return on corporation tax
法人税額の損金不算入 exclusion from corporate tax expenses
法人税額の特別控除 special credit of corporation tax
法人税繰越欠損金 corporate tax loss carryforward
法人税控除 corporation tax credit
法人税控除前純利益 net profit before corporation tax
法人税の脱税 evasion of corporation tax
法人税引当金 reserve for corporate tax
法人税引前純利益 net profit before corporate tax
法人税負担 tax charge
法人税への税効果 tax effect on corporate tax
法人税法 Corporation Tax Law
法人税率 corporation tax rate
法人税割り corporation levy
法人税割課税 taxation on corporation tax basis
法人設立 incorporation of enterprise
法人団体 corporate body
法人貯蓄 corporate savings
法人登記簿 corporate registration
法人登記簿謄本 certified copy of company registration
法人投資家 corporate investor
法人特別税 special corporate surtax
法人の益金 gross income of corporation
法人の解散 dissolution of corporation
法人の設立 establishment of corporation
法人の代表者 representative of corporation
法人預金 corporate deposit
法人利得税 tax on corporate gain
法人理論 entity theory
放 送 債 N.H.K bond
包 装 費 packing charge
包装明細書 packing list
膨張経済 expansion economy
法定会計原則 statutory accounting principle
法定外普通税 general tax not stipulated in Local Tax Law
法定貸出限度枠 legal lending limit
法定果実 legal fruits
法定監査 statutory audit
法定議決権 statutory voting
法定期限 legal term
法定給付 legal benefit

ホ

法定金利 legal rate of interest
法定減耗償却法 statutory depletion method
法定後見人 legal guardian
法定詐欺 legal fraud
法定資本 legal capital
法定準備 required reserve
法定準備金 legal reserve；statutory reserve；statutory surplus
法定準備金資本組入れ recapitalization of legal reserve
法定準備金積立額 transfer to legal reserve
法定準備金積立保険 legal reserve insurance
法定準備率 required reserve ratio
法定償還日 stated maturity date
法定償却 statutory depreciation
法定償却方法 statutory depreciation method
法定剰余金 statutory surplus
法定申告期限 statutory due date of tax return
法定信託 constructive trust；implied trust；trust by act of law
法定信用枠 mandatory line of credit
法定推定相続人 presumptive heir
法定税率 statutory tariff
法定責任 legal liability
法定相続 per stripes
法定相続動産 heir-looms
法定相続人 heir apparent；heir at law
法定相続分 legal portion of legacy
法定相続分課税 taxation according to legal portion of legacy
法定代位 legal subrogation
法定耐用年数 legal durable years；statutory useful life
法定代理人 legal representative
法定棚卸評価法 legal valuation method of inventory
法定通貨 lawful currency；lawful money；legal tender
法定年齢 legal age
法定納期限 statutory due date of tax payment
法定の占有 possession in law
法定賠償責任保険 legal liability insurance
法定発行限度額 statutory debt limit
法定評価 legal valuation
法定評価方法 statutory valuation method
法定福利費 legal welfare expense
法定普通税 general tax stipulated in Local Tax Law
法定平価 mint par of exchange
法定返戻金 mandated surrender value
法定保険価額 insurable value
法定目論見書 statutory prospectus
法定有価証券評価準備金 mandatory securities valuation reserve
法定利益準備金 legal earned surplus reserve
法定利息 legal rate of interest
法定利率 legal interest rate；statutory rate of interest
法的合併 legal merger
法的関係 legal relationship
法的規制 mandatory control
法的形式 legal form
法的見解 legal opinion
法的権利 legal right
法的効力 legal effect
法的根拠 legal basis
法的債務 legal obligation
法的実体 legal entity
法的手段 legal proceedings
法的譲渡 legal transfer
法的書類 legal documentation
法的請求権 legal claim
法的制約 legal limit
法的整理 legal liquidation
法的責任 legal responsibility
法的措置 legislative action
法的対抗策 legal resistance
法的手続 process of law
法的独占 legal monopoly
法的な承認 legal approvals
法的に保全されている legally protected from
法的要因 legal factor
法的リーエン legal lien

法的リスク legal risk ; legislative risk
法的枠組み legal framework
法 典 化 codification
報道教育サービス室 Office of Communication and Education Service
冒 頭 部 introduction
法の行為 act of law
法の裁量 discretion of law
法の作用 operation of law
法の支配 rule of law
法の枠組み legal boundary
報復関税 retaliatory duties
方 法 論 methodology
法 務 省 Ministry of Justice
法務処理 management of juristic act
法務大臣 Minister of Justice
法 務 部 legal department ; legal section ; OLA(Office of Legal Affairs)
訪問販売業者 call-sales merchant
暴　　落 collapse ; shakeout
暴　　利 excessive profit
法律意見書 statement of legal opinion
法律違反 breach of law
法 律 学 jurisprudence
法律格言 maxims
法律関係 legal relations
法律業務 legal services
法律行為 judicial act ; juristic act
法律顧問 counselor ; legal adviser
法律顧問室(SEC) Office of General Counsel(SEC)
法律施行局(SEC) Division of Enforcement(SEC)
法律事務所 law office ; legal office
法律上の義務 legal duty
法律上の最終期限 legal final maturity
法律上の証拠 legal evidence
法律上の職員 officer de jure
法律上の所有 legal ownership
法律上の推定 legal presumption
法律上の制限 legal restrictions
法律上の占有 legal possession
法律上の先例 legal precedent
法律上の争点 issue of law
法律上の身分 legal status
法律上の要件 statutory requirements
法律書類 legal document
法律専門家 legal expert
法律相談 legal aid services
法律相談料 fee for legal advice
法律代理人 legal representation
法律的推定 artificial presumptions
法律的な消滅になる貸倒れ bad debt which runs into the statute of limitation
法律的な消滅による貸倒れ bad debt caused by the legal effect
法律と事実との混合問題 mixed question of law and fact
法律になっていない基準 non-legal standards
法律による譲渡 cession by law
法律による非効率 legal inefficiency
法律の委任 authorization by law ; delegation by law
法律の定める相手方 legal counterparty
法律の変更 legal changes
法律の要求する形式 form required by law
法律費用 legal cost
法律変更 change in law
暴力不正腐敗防止法 Racketeer Influenced and Corrupt Organization Act
法　　令 laws and regulations
法令違反操業 non-compliant operation
法令遵守 legal compliance
法令上の制限 statutory restriction
法令による statutory
法令による変更 legislative change
ポアソン分布 Poisson distribution
ボーダーレス cross border
ボード取引 board trading
ポートフォリオ・インカム portfolio income
ポートフォリオ・インシュアランス portfolio insurance
ポートフォリオ・インシュランス portfolio insurance
ポートフォリオ・エンジニア portfolio engineers
ポートフォリオ・オプティマイザー

portfolio optimizer
ポートフォリオ価格決定法 portfolio pricing methodology
ポートフォリオ管理 portfolio management
ポートフォリオ基準 portfolio basis
ポートフォリオ・クレジット portfolio credit
ポートフォリオ構成 portfolio composition
ポートフォリオ最適化 portfolio optimization
ポートフォリオ手法 portfolio approach
ポートフォリオ・セレクション portfolio selection
ポートフォリオ選択 portfolio selection
ポートフォリオ取引 portfolio trade
ポートフォリオの価値 portfolio value
ポートフォリオの関連付け portfolio linkage
ポートフォリオの見地 portfolio view
ポートフォリオの再編 portfolio restructuring
ポートフォリオの収益パターン pattern of portfolio return
ポートフォリオの修正 portfolio revision
ポートフォリオの特性線 portfolio characteristic line
ポートフォリオの分散 broader portfolio
ポートフォリオの分散投資 portfolio diversification investment
ポートフォリオの利回り portfolio's yield
ポートフォリオ・バランス・アプローチ portfolio balance approach
ポートフォリオ分析 portfolio analysis
ポートフォリオ・ヘッジ portfolio hedging
ポートフォリオ・マネージャー portfolio manager
ポートフォリオ・ミックス portfolio mix
ポートフォリオ・モニタリング portfolio monitoring
ポートフォリオ・リスク portfolio risk
ポートフォリオ・リスク・モデル portfolio risk model
ポートフォリオ理論 portfolio theory
ボード・ブローカー board broker
ボーナス支払い bonus payment
ボーナス方式 bonus method
ホーム・エクイティ・ローン HEL (home equity loan)
ホームオフィス控除 home office deduction
ホーム・バンキング home banking
ホーム・メード・インフレ home made inflation
ポーランド・ズロチ PLN (Polish zloty)
ホールセール証券会社 wholesale securities firm
ホールセール・バンク wholesale bank
ホール・ローン WL (whole loan)
簿　　価 book-value；carrying amount
簿価株式購入制度 book value stock purchase plan
簿価合計額 aggregate book value
簿価修正 adjustment of the carrying amount
簿価修正額 adjustment in the book value
簿価方式 book value method
簿価利回り book yield
簿外債務 off-balance sheet debt；unlisted liability
簿外債務保証 hidden guarantee of obligation
簿外資金調達 off-balance-sheet financing
簿外資産 assets off the book；off-balance sheet assets；unlisted assets
簿外借金 debt off the book
簿外の事象 off-balance-sheet event
簿外負債 off-balance-sheet liability
捕獲だ捕不担保条項 free from capture and seizure clause
保　　管 custody；safe keeping
保管及び振替 central custody and book-entry transfer
保管勘定 custodial account
保管機構 central depository
保管銀行 custodian bank；depository bank
保管国債 government securities in

custody
保管手数料 custodian fee
保 管 箱 box
保 管 費 inventory carrying cost；warehousing and carrying charges
保管費用 storage cost
保管比率 custody ratio
保 管 品 articles in custody
保管振替機関 central securities depository；custody and book-entry transfer institution
保管振替機関への預託 deposit with depository
保管振替機関名義株式 shares registered in the name of depository
保管振替事業 central custody and book-entry transfer services
保管振替制度 central depository system
保管有価証券 customers' securities；securities deposited from others
保 管 料 custodian charge；custody fee
補完契約 supplemental agreement
補 完 財 complementary goods
補完的貸付制度 complementary lending facility
補完的自己資本 secondary capital；Tier 2
補完的資本項目 supplementary capital
補完的手段 complementary means
補完的な業績報告書 secondary performance report
補完年金 supplementary plan
補完年金制度 complementary pension plan
補完ファンド supplementary fund
補完保険 supplemental policies
補完ローン complementary loan
簿　　記 bookkeeping
簿 記 係 book keeper
補強証拠 corroborating evidence
北欧閣僚会議 Nordic Council of Ministers
北欧理事会 Nordic Council
北米自由貿易協定 NAFTA (North America Free Trade Agreement)
保　　健 health service
保健医療 health and medical care
保　　険 assurance；insurance
保険受取金 policy proceeds
保険運用信託 funded insurance trust；investment insurance trust
保険オプション insurance option
保 険 課 Insurance Business Division
保 険 界 insurance world
保険会計 insurance accounting
保険会社 insurance carrier；insurance company；insurance enterprise
保険会社負債 insurance liabilities
保険買取り policy buyback
保険買取業界 viatical industry
保険買取証券提供者 viatical provider
保険解約 policy cancellation
保険価額 insurance value；policy value
保険格付機関 insurance rating agency
保険型契約 insurance type contract
保険型年金 insurance scheme；insured pension plan
保険加入者への債務 policyholder obligations
保険加入者保険料率 subscriber rate
保険加入者ローン policyholder loan
保険加入年数 insurance years
保険加入歴 insurance history
保険可能リスク insurable risk
保険が付された制度 insured plan
保険監督機関 insurance regulator
保険監督法 insurance law
保険管理 insurance management
保険期間 policy period；policy term
保険期間条項 duration of risk clause
保険危機 crisis in insurance
保険基金 insurance fund
保険規制責任者 chief insurance regulators
保険機能 insurance function
保険給付 insurance benefit；policy benefit
保険給付の生前利用 early access to insurance benefit
保 険 業 insurance business
保険業界 insurance industry；insurance

sector
保険業参入 entry into insurance business
保険業参入銀行 bank in insurance
保険業法 insurance business law
保険業法令 Insurance Business Law and Regulations
保険局長 commissioner of insurance
保険拠出金 insurance contributions
保険記録簿 insurance register
保 険 金 claim paid or payable；insurance money
保険金一括受取選択権 cash settlement option
保険金受取人 assured
保険金受取方法 settlement options
保険金額 amount covered；insurance amount；insured amount
保険金額帯別等級付け band grading
保険金額比例主義 sums insured method
保険金繰上げ accelerated cash benefit
保険金繰上オプション accelerated cash benefit option
保険金控除 deduction for insurance proceeds
保険金削減支払制度 lien plan
保険金差損 loss on insurance claims
保険金支払い claim payment；insurance settlement
保険金支払額 incurred claim
保険金支払業務 claim processing
保険金支払準備金 reserve for outstanding claims
保険金支払請求 policy claim
保険金支払代理店 claim agent
保険金支払不能 insurance insolvency
保険金支払平準化準備金 claims equalization reserve
保険金収入 insurance proceed
保険金増額配当 reversionary bonus
保険金増額保険 increasing insurance
保険金定額受取オプション amount option
保険金逓増保険 progressive policy
保険金の現価への割引 discounting claims
保険金の支払禁止 exception of proceeds
保険金負担可能性 affordability of payment of insurance amount
保険・金融総合化 assurfinance
保険経過期間 policy duration
保険契約 insurance contract
保険契約覚書 cover note
保険契約加算金 policy charge
保険契約経過年数 age of policy
保険契約交換 policy exchange
保険契約査定 policy underwriting
保険契約者 party insuring；policyholder
保険契約者貸付担保債券 policyholder loan bond
保険契約者債務 policy holder liabilities
保険契約者剰余金 policyholder's surplus
保険契約者配当 dividend to policyholders；insurance dividend
保険契約者配当金 policy-holders' dividend
保険契約者保護機構 Insurance Policy-holders Protection Corporation
保険契約者保護法 Policyholders' Protection Act
保険契約収益率 return on policy
保険契約準備金 technical provision
保険契約照会 policy inquiry
保険契約信託 policy trust
保険契約による求償 claim under an insurance policy
保険契約年齢 age of insured
保険契約の失効 lapse of insurance policy
保険契約の復活 reinstatement
保険契約の変更 change of policy contract
保険契約乗換え policy switch
保険契約日 date of policy
保険契約評価 policy valuation
保険契約申込書 insurance proposal form
保険計理人 actuary；valuation actuary
保険原価 cost of policy
保険原理 insurance principle
保険購入 insurance purchase；policy purchase
保険購入者 insurance buyer
保険債務 policy obligation
保険・財務アナリスト協会 Association of

Insurance and Financial Analysts
保険差益 gains on insurance claim
保険差益特別勘定 special account of gains on insurance claim
保険詐欺 insurance scam
保険先物 insurance futures
保険査定基準 underwriting criteria
保険事故 insured event
保険市場 insurance market
保険支払保証基金 insurance guaranty fund
保 険 者 insurer
保険受給失業 insured unemployment
保険種類 category of insurance
保険種類変更 change of policy
保 険 証 insurance certificate
保険証券 IP (insurance policy)
保険証券買取契約 viatical contract
保険証券貸付 policy loan
保険証券交付 policy delivery
保険証券書式 policy form
保険証券所有者 policy owner
保険証券の期間 life of policy
保険証券の競売 auctioning of policies
保険証券の拘束力に関する条項 clause as to the binding effect of policy
保険証券の交付 delivery of policy
保険証券の保険金 proceed of insurance policy
保険証券発行 policy issuance
保険消費者 insurance consumer
保険商品取扱業者 insurance product firm
保険商品ポートフォリオ insurance product portfolio
保険証明書 certificate of insurance
保険審議会 insurance council
保険人口 insurance population
保険審査 insurance examination
保険信託 insurance trust
保険数理額 actuarial science
保険数理計算要素 actuarial calculation factor
保険数理差益 actuarial gain
保険数理上の仮定 actuarial assumption
保険数理上の技法 actuarial technique
保険数理上の現在価値 actuarial present value
保険数理上の実績 actuarial experience
保険数理上の損益 actuarial gains and losses
保険数理上の評価 actuarial appraisal
保険数理上の評価方法 actuarial valuation method
保険数理上のリスク actuarial risk
保険数理専門家の報告 actuary's report
保険数理損 actuarial loss
保険数理による資産価値 actuarial asset value
保険数理利回り actuarial yield
保 険 税 insurance tax
保険請求 insurance claim
保険制度 insurance plan
保険設計 policy design
保険総引受額 gross line
保険代位 insurance subrogation
保険対象となるリスク insurable risk
保険退職商品 insured retirement product
保険代理店 insurance agency
保険代理店手数料 insurance agency commission
保険仲介人 insurance intermediary
保険貯蓄 insurance saving
保険通達 insurance directive
保険付給付 insured benefit
保険付給付制度 plan with insured benefit
保険付口座 insured account
保険提携会社 insurance affiliate
保険デリバティブ insurance derivatives
保険特性 policy characteristics
保険特約 policy rider
保険取引所 insurance exchange
保険年度 insurance year
保険年度末準備金 terminal policy reserve
保険年齢 age at entry；insurance age
保険の移転 policy transfer
保険の種類 class of insurance
保険の包括移転 portfolio transfer
保険の目的 subject-matter of insurance
保険の利益配当 participating policy dividend

保険乗換特約 insurance exchange rider
保険乗換率 replacement rate
保険販売 insurance distribution
保険引受け insurance underwriting
保険引受証 insurance cover note
保険引受損失 underwriting loss
保険引受団 underwriting syndicate
保険引受年度別計算 policy year basis
保険引受能力 insurability
保険引受不可危険 uninsurable risk
保険引受利益 insurance profit；underwriting profit
保険非補填損失 uninsured loss
保険費用 claim cost；cost of insurance；policy cost
保険評価額条項 valuation clause
保険プール insurance pool
保険不能保険 non-insurable risk
保険付保可能金額 insurable value
保険付保範囲 coverage limit
保険ブローカー insurance broker
保険ブローカー登録評議会 Insurance Brokers Registration Council
保険ブローカー法 insurance brokers act
保 険 法 general insurance law
保険法定会計 insurance statutory accounting
保険保障 insurance cover；insurance protection
保険ボンド insurance bond
保険明細書 policy exhibit
保険免許 insurance license
保険申込み policy application
保険持株会社 insurance holding company
保険約款 insurance clause；terms and conditions of insurance policy
保 険 料 insurance charge；insurance expense；insurance premium
保険料及び運賃込み値段 CIF price
保険料課税所得控除 insurance premium tax relief
保険料基準 insurance premium base
保険料計算 insurance premium calculation
保険料控除 insurance premium deduction
保険料控除申告書 return form for insurance premium deduction
保険料構造 insurance premium structure
保険料コスト insurance premium cost
保険料支出 insurance premium outlay
保険料税 insurance premium tax；premium tax
保険料設定 pricing of policies
保険料全期払込み continuous payment
保険料相殺 insurance premium offset
保険料相殺配当 dividend deduction from insurance premium
保険料積立金 insurance premium fund；insurance premium reserve；premium reserve
保険料手形 insurance premium note
保険料転換制度 insurance premium conversion plan
保険料等分解 unbundling of insurance premium
保険料の欠損 deficiency in insurance premium
保険料の上限 premium cap
保険料の免除 waiver of insurance premium
保険料払込期日 insurance premium due date
保険料払込免除 waiver of premium
保険料払戻し insurance premium credit
保険料負担 insurance premium contribution
保険料振替貸付 premium loan
保険料返還 insurance premium refund；return of insurance premium
保険料返還特約 return-of-premium rider
保険料返還保証 money back guarantee
保険料免除の free of insurance premium
保険料有限払込保険 insurance with limited premium
保険料融資保険 financed insurance
保険料預託 insurance premium deposit
保険料率 insurance policy rate；insurance premium rate
保険料割引 insurance premium discount；insurance premium rebate

保険レバレッジ insurance leverage
保護預り safe custody；safekeeping deposit
保護預り制度 safe custody system
保護関税 protective duty；protective tariff
母国市場 home market
保護主義政策 protectionist policies
保護主義的な経済圏 protectionist economic regionalism
保護条項 protective covenant
保護信託 protective trust
保護付エクイティ・ノート PEN (protected equity note)
保 護 領 protectorate
ポジティブ・キャリー positive carry
ポジション拡大 bigger positions
ポジション・ガンマ position gamma
ポジション指導 position instruction
ポジション・セータ position theta
ポジション調整 position adjustment
ポジション積上げ position building
ポジション・デルタ position delta
ポジション・トレーダー position trader
ポジション売買 position trading
ポジション・リスク position risk
ポジション・リスク所要額 PRR (position risk requirement)
ポジティブ情報 positive credit file；positive information
保釈金喪失 forfeiture of bail
保釈契約書 bail-piece
保釈保証人 safe-pledge
補　　充 replenishment
募　　集 offering；soliciting
募集案内書 offering circular
募集価格 offer price
募集型CLO primary CLO (collateralized loan obligation)
募集型CBO primary CBO (collateralized bond obligation)
募集期間 subscription period
募集機関 soliciting agent
募集契約 subscription agreement
募集代理人 subscription agent
母 集 団 population
母集団の項目 population of items
補充注文 fill-in
補充手続 supplementary proceedings
募集人販売 agent distribution
募 集 費 recruiting expense
募集引受契約 underwriting agreement
募集方法 method of offering for subscription；subscription details
募集要項 memorandum for offering
補 充 率 supplementary rate
保守主義 conservatism
保守主義の原則 principle of conservatism
保守的な会計 conservative accounting
保守的な見方 conservative view
補　　償 indemnification
補償給付 indemnity benefit
補 償 金 compensation
補償銀行 reimbursing bank
補償契約 indemnification arrangement；indemnity agreement；indemnity contract
補償限度額 limit of indemnity
補償債務 reimbursement obligation
補償支払授権書 reimbursement authorization
補償授権書 RA (reimbursement authorization)
補償融資 compensatory financing facility
補償預金残高 compensating balance of deposit
保　　証 guarantee；surety；suretyship
保証違反 breach of warranty
保証解約返戻金 guaranteed cash value
保証価格 guaranteed value
保 証 額 guaranteed amount
保証額上限 debit cap
保証貸し loan on personal guarantee
保 証 株 guaranteed stock；stock for guarantee
保証株価指数連動商品 guaranteed equity product
保証期間付終身年金 life annuity certain
保証期間付年金 years certain annuity
保証給付 guaranteed benefit

保証協会 Credit Guarantee Corporation
保証協会連合会 Federation of Credit Guarantee Corporations
保証業務 guarantee business
保 証 金 caution money；guarantee deposits；guarantee money
保証銀行 guarantor bank
保証銀行団 syndicate of guarantor
保証契約 contract of guaranty
保証契約の混同による消滅 merger of guaranty
保証決済債務 assured payment obligation
保証決済方式 assured payment mechanism
保証債務 cautionary obligation；liabilities for guarantee；liability for endorsement；surety money
保証債務の履行 performance of obligations of guarantee
保証債務見返り customers' liabilities on guaranties
保証作業 guarantee work
保証差入有価証券 deposit of securities on contracts
保証残存価値 guaranteed residual value
保証残高 guarantees outstanding
保証資産配分 IAA (insured asset allocation)
保証社債 assumed bond；guaranteed bond
保証準備 securities for fiduciary issue
保 証 状 guarantee letter
保証証券 guaranteed securities；surety bond
保証証券様式 bond form
保証条項 warranty provision
保証請求 warranty claims
保証生存保険 guaranteed endowment
保証付委任 commission del credere
保証付貸付 loan with third party's guarantee
保証付勘定 secured account
保証付ワラント guaranteed warrant
保証投資契約 GIC (guaranteed investment contract)
保証による回収見込額 anticipated recovery from the financial guarantee
保 証 人 guarantor；security suretyship
保証年金 guaranteed annuity
保証の供与 provision of guarantee
保証の引受け assumption of guarantee
保証配当 guaranteed dividend
保証発行 fiduciary issue
保証費用 warranty cost
保証報酬 covered compensation
保証保険 bond insurance；guarantee insurance
保証モーゲージ証書 GMC (guaranteed mortgage certificate)
保証文言 guarantee clause
保 証 料 guarantee charge；guarantee commission
保証利率 guaranteed interest
保証類似行為 acts similar to guarantees
保証ローン guarantee loan
保　　障 coverage
保障継続 continuation of coverage
補　　助 accessory
補助貨幣 subsidiary money
補助規則 auxiliary rules
補助記入帳 subsidiary journal
補 助 金 grant；subsidy
補助金交付 delivery of subsidies
補助金付輸出 subsidized export
補助金によって得た資産 property acquired by subsidy
補助金による取得 acquisition by subsidies
補助金の返済 settlement of subsidy
補助金返還免除 exemption from return of subsidy
補助金見込債 GRN (grant anticipation note)
補助原価 service cost
補助公債 aid bond
補助材料費 subsidiary material cost
補助帳簿 auxiliary journal
補助付物品 subsidized good
補助的基金 auxiliary fund

補助部門 subsidiary department
補助部門費 subsidiary department charge
補 助 簿 auxiliary book ; subsidiary book
補助元帳 auxiliary ledger ; subordinate ledger ; subsidiary ledger
補助元帳勘定 subsidiary accounts
POSシステム point of sales system
ポスト・ケイジアン post Keynesian
ボストン証券取引所 Boston Stock Exchange
ボスニア・ヘルツェゴビナ・マルカ BAD (Bosnia-Herzegovina marka)
保　　税 in bond
保税運送 transportation in bond
保税倉庫 bonded warehouse
保税地域 bonded area
保税調査官 Special Officer for Research on Customs Area
補 整 後 graduated
補整効果 compensatory effect
補整的項目 compensatory item
補整的財政政策 compensatory fiscal policy
補整的予算政策 compensatory budget policy
補整的余剰 compensatory surplus
補正予算 additional budget ; extra budget ; supplementary budget
墓石広告 tombstone ad
保全差押え preservative seizure
保全担保 preservative security
保全手数料 conservation commission
保 全 率 collateral coverage ratio
補足給付 supplementary benefit
補足財務情報 supplemental financial information
補足財務諸表 supplementary financial statements
補足従業員退職給付 supplement employee retirement
補足情報 supplementary information
補足的開示要求事項 required secondary disclosure
補足的業績報告書 second performance statement
補足的情報 secondary information
補足的な条件 subsidiary conditions
補足的な保険 supplementary insurance
補足的に on a supplementary basis
補足的費用 supplementary cost
補足的様式 secondary format ; supplementary format
補足融資 supplementary financial measure
北海道開発土木研究所 Civil Engineering Research Institute of Hokkaido
北海ブレント North Brent
発 起 人 originator ; promoter
発起人会 meeting of promoters
発起人株 promoter's share
ボックス圏の動き range-bound market
ボックス・ジェンキンス法 Box-Jenkins method
ボックス・スプレッド box spread
没　　収 confiscation ; forfeiture
没収不許可条件 non-forfeiture condition
没収保全 preservation
ホット・マネー市場 hot money market
ボツワナ・プラ BWP (Botswana pula)
補　　填 compensation
補填義務 obligations to compensate
補填の開示 presentation of reimbursements
補填の権利 reimbursement right
ボトム・アップ型 bottom-up process
ボトム・アップ型予測 bottom-up forecasting
ボトム・ストラドル bottom straddle
ボトム・バーティカル・コンビネーション bottom vertical combination
ボトム・リバーサル・デー bottom reversal day
ボトルネック・インフレーション bottle-neck inflation
募入決定の通知 notification of auction results
募入の決定 determine auction results
募入平均価格 average price of competitive auction bidding

ホフマンの法則 Hoffmann's law
母 分 散 population variance
母 平 均 population mean
保有株式 portfolio stocks
保有株の含み latent equity holdings
保有期間収益率 holding period return
保有期間相対価値 holding period value-relative
保有形態 type of holding
保有形態別 classification by the form of JGSs
保有契約 total amount of insurance in force
保 有 権 tenure
保有債券 bond held；portfolio bonds
保有財産 tenement
保有需要曲線 demand-to-hold schedule
保有証券 securities holdings
保有損益 holding gain or loss
保有損失 holding loss
保有超過額 surplus
保有費用 holding cost
保有保険契約 insurance in force
保有目的区分 holding-purpose category
保有目的に応じた区分 classification according to holding purpose
保有目的変更の有価証券 securities for which the holding-purpose category has changed
保有有価証券平均残高 average balance of securities held
保有利得 holding gain
ボラティリティ volatility
ボラティリティ価値 volatility value
ボラティリティ・スプレッド volatility spread
ボラティリティ標準化 volatility-normalized
ボラティリティ予測 volatility forecast
ボラティリティ・レシオ volatility ratio
ポリシー・アセット・アロケーション policy asset allocation
ポリシー・アセット・ミックス policy asset mix
ポリシー・ミックス policy mix
ホリゾンタル・スプレッド horizontal spread
ボリビア・ボリビアーノ BOB (Bolivian boliviano)
ボリューム・アキュミュレーター volume accumulator
ボリューム・レシオ volume ratio
保留論点 points reserved
ポルトガル・エスクード PTE (Portuguese esucudo)
ポルトガル保管振替機関 Interbolsa
ボ ロ 株 cats and dogs stock
ホワイト・ナイト white knight
ホワイト非課税債格付サービス White's Tax-Exempt Bond Rating Service
ポワソン過程 Poisson process
本位貨幣 standard coin；standard money
本位貨幣制度 standard money system
本位政策 monetary standard policy
本位制度 monetary standard；standard system
本格的流通市場 full-fledged secondary market
ポンカス債 ex-warrant bond
本　　業 main business
本 拠 州 home state
本 拠 地 domicile
本クレーム final claim
本契約に基づく義務 obligations hereunder
本 決 算 full year business result
本源的価値 intrinsic value
本源的価値基準法 intrinsic value based method
本源的貨幣 original money
本源的証券 primary securities
本源的預金 primary deposit
本　　国 home country
香港銀行間出し手金利 HIBOR (Hong Kong inter-bank offered rate)
香港銀行間出し手レート Hong Kong inter-bank offered rate
香港ドル HKD (Hong Kong dollar)
香港ドルのペッグ制 HKG peg
香港ハンセン指数 Hang Seng Index

香港預託証書 Hong Kong depositary receipts
本支店勘定 inter-office account
本支店レート inter-office rate
本社勘定 head office account
本社事務所 registered office
本社費用 head office expenses
本州四国連絡橋債券承継国債 government bonds converted from Honshu-Shikoku Bridge Authority bonds
ホンジュラス・レンピラ HNL (Honduras lempira)
本　省 Main Organs
本　税 principal tax
本　籍 permanent domicile
本船持込渡し delivered ex ship
本船渡し FOB (free on board)
本　訴 formal lawsuits
本　体 face
本　店 head office；parent store
本店扱い口座 house account
本店勘定 home office account
本店所在地 registered head office
ポンド為替本位制 sterling exchange standard
ポンド危機 British Pound crisis
ポンド残高 sterling balance
ポンド・スワップ・レート sterling swap rate
ポンド対米ドル相場 cable
ポンド建て債券 sterling bonds
ポンド建てCP SCP (sterling commercial paper)
ポンド建て変動利付債 sterling floaters
ポンド通貨先物 sterling currency futures
ボンド・トレーダー bond trader
ポンド・ブロック pound bloc
本人確認書類 identification document
本　文 body；purview
ボンベイ証券取引所 Bombay Stock Exchange
本邦ローン Tokyo loan
本邦ローン方式 domestic loan system
本予算 main budget
本来的預金 intrinsic deposit
本来の価格を下回って売却される証券 bargain counter

マ

マーク・アップ率 mark-up ratio
マーケット・アウト条項 market out clause
マーケット・イフ・タッチド・オーダー market-if-touched order
マーケット・オン・クローズ・オーダー market-on-close order
マーケット・タイマー market timer
マーケット・デュレーション・トレード market duration trade
マーケット・ニュートラル運用 market neutral investment management
マーケット・バスケット指数 market basket index
マーケット・バスケット方式 market basket contract
マーケット・メーカー MM (market maker)
マーケット・リスク market risk
マーケット・リターン market return
マーケティング機能 marketing function
マーケティング経費 marketing expense
マーケティング・プッシュ marketing push
マーケティング・プル marketing pull
マーケティング・ミックス marketing mix
マーケティング予算 marketing budget
マーシャル曲線 Marshall curve
マーシャル諸島（米国ドル） USD (Marshall Islands US dollar)
マーシャル的需要曲線 Marshallian demand curve
マーシャルのK Marshallian K
マーシャル・プラン Marshall Plan
マーチャント・バンク merchant bank
マーチンゲール過程 martingale process
マートン・モデル Merton model
マーコビッツ理論 Markowitz theory
埋葬保険 burial insurance
毎月支払保険 monthly income policy
毎月の返済額 amount of monthly payment
毎月払い monthly payment
毎年更新 yearly renewal
マイナス影響 negative effect；negative impact
マイナス・シーリング minus-ceiling
マイナス成長 minus growth；negative growth；subzero growth
マイナス・ティック minus tick
マイナスのインフレ率 negative inflation
マイナスの影響 negative influence
マイナスの資産価値 negative equity
マイナス要因 adverse element；minus factor；negative factor
マイルド・リセッション mild recession
マ イ ン mine
前受益金 unearned revenue
前 受 金 advance received；customer advance
前受金支払利息 interest incurred on advance received
前受収益 advance received profit；income in advance；revenue received in advance
前受保証料 guarantee fee received in advance
前受家賃 prepaid rents on buildings
前受利息 accrued interest (income)
前受利息勘定 deferred interest account
前 売 り advance sale
前貸信用状 red clause credit
前貸制度 putting-out system
前 借 り borrowing in advance
前　　金 advance payment
前 金 で cash before delivery；payment in advance
前 倒 し front loaded；rolling forward
前倒金利削減債 FLIRB (front loaded interest reduction bond)

前の日付にする predate
前 払 い up-front payment
前払運賃 advance freight ; prepaid freight
前払給付 front end benefit
前払給与 advance salary
前払金返還保証 refundment guarantee
前払金返還保証証券 advance payment bond
前払式割賦販売金融 finance for prepaid installment sales
前払資産 prepaid asset
前払地代 forehand rent
前払賃金 advance wages
前払手数料 prepaid commission ; up-front commission
前払年金費用 prepaid pension expense
前払費用 prepaid expense
前払プレミアム up-front premium
前払法人税 prepaid income taxes
前払保険料 prepaid insurance
前払利益 prepaid income
前払利息 interest advance ; prepaid interest
前払旅費 travel advances
前 引 け closing of the morning session
前日付小切手 antedated check
前渡給料賃金 prepaid salaries and wages
前 渡 金 advanced money ; imprest cash
マ カ オ Macao
マカオ・パタカ MOP (Macau pataca)
マカロニ防衛 macaroni defense
巻 戻 し unwinding
マクファデン法 MacFadden Act of 1927
マクロ会計 macro accounting
マクロ経済 macro picture ; macro-economy
マクロ経済政策 macroeconomic policy
マクロ経済的 macroeconomic
マクロ経済の需給バランス supply-demand balance in macroeconomy
マクロ経済分析 macroeconomic analysis
マクロ経済モデル macroeconomic model
マクロ経済要因 macroeconomic factor
マクロ的な観点 macro-perspective
マクロ分析 macro analysis
マクロ・ヘッジ macro hedge ; macro hedges
マクロ・モデル macro model
マケドニア・デナール MKD (Macedonian denar)
孫 会 社 sub-subsidiary
マザーズ Mothers
マザーズへの上場 listing on Mothers
マザー・ファンド mother fund
摩擦的失業 frictional unemployment
増し担保 additional collateral
増値保険 increased value insurance
マスター契約 master agreement
マスター・トラスト master trust
マスター・ネッティング契約 master-netting contract
マスター・リース master lease
マダガスカル・フラン MGF (Malagasy franc)
待ち行列 queuing
マチュリティ・ストリッピング maturity stripping
マチュリティ・スワップ maturity swap
末期症状給付 terminal illness benefit
抹　　消 obliteration
抹消会社 defunct company
抹消の申請 application for obliteration
マッチング matching
マッチング・スワップ matching swap
マッチング取引 matching transaction
窓　　口 window
窓口指導 window guidance
窓口販売 over-the-counter sale
マトリックス matrix
マトリックス価格決定モデル matrix pricing model
マトリックス・トレーディング matrix trading
マトリックス表示 matrix presentation
マドリッド証券取引所 Madrid Stock Exchange
マネー・ゲーム money game
マネー・サプライ monetary aggregate ; money stocks ; money supply

マネー・サプライ（速報） Money Stock (preliminary)
マネー・サプライ管理 money supply control
マネー・サプライ統計 statistics on money supply
マネー・サプライ分析統計 statistics on money supply analysis
マネージド・アカウント・レポート MAR (managed account report)
マネージド・ファンド契約 managed fund contract
マネージメント・サイエンス management science
マネージメント・システム規格 MSS (Management System Standard)
マネージメント・バイアウト management buyout
マネージャーの寄与度 manager's contribution
マネー・スプレッド money spread
マネー・センター・バンク money center bank
マネー・フロー表 money flow table
マネー・フロー分析 money flow analysis
マネー・ポジション money position
マネー・マーケット・アカウント money market account
マネー・マーケット・ノート money market note
マネー・マーケット・ファンド money market fund
マネー・マーケット優先株 money market preferred stock
マネー・マーケット・ユニット・トラスト money market unit trust
マネー・マーケット利回り money market yield
マネー・ロンダリング money laundering
マネタリー・アプローチ monetary approach
マネタリー・サーベイ monetary survey
マネタリー・ターゲット monetary target
マネタリー・ベースと日本銀行の取引 Monetary Base and the Bank of Japan's Transactions
マネタリー・ベースの伸び率 growth rate of the monetary base
マネタリスト monetarist
マネタリズム monetarism
真　　水 real water
マラウィ・クワチャ MWK (Malawi kwacha)
マリ（CFAフラン） XOF (Mali CFA (Communauté Financière Africaine) franc)
マ リ ー marry
マルク債 mark bond
マルコフ性 Markov property
マルコフ連鎖 Markov chain
マル専手形 special bills for installment sales credit
丸　　損 dead loss
マルタ・リラ MTL (Maltese lira)
マルチカレンシー・ローン multi-currency loan
マルチ商法 multilevel marketing
マルティプル・オプション・ファンディング・ファシリティ multiple option funding facilities
マ ル 優 Maruyu tax-exempt savings system
マル優制度 Maruyu program
マレーシア商品取引所 Malaysia Commodity Exchange
マレーシア・リンギット MYR (Malaysian ringgit)
マロニー法 Maloney Act of 1938
回 し 玉 wash order
回し手形 endorsed bills exchanged between two related parties
回り手形 note endorsed
満額給付 full benefit
満額年金 full pension
満　　期 maturity
満期一括償還 bullet maturity；bullet redemption at maturity
満期一括償還債 bullet bond；bullet deal
満期一括償還銘柄 bullet issue
満期一括払い payment by a lump sum at

maturity
満期受取金 maturity proceeds
満期がある有価証券 securities with maturity dates
満期書替え roll over
満期価値 maturity value
満期が近づいた債券 seasoned bond
満期元本増加支払い balloon payment
満期金額 amount at maturity
満期繰上選択権 endowment option
満期5年のゼロ・クーポン債 5-year zero coupon bond
満期後の裏書 after maturity endorsement
満期債券 matured bond
満期債務 matured liability
満期時償還額 maturity payment
満期日構成 maturity structure
満期日表 maturity list
満期支払高 amount due
満期10年の利付債 10-year coupon bond
満期償還 redemption at maturity
満期償還財務省証券 non-callable treasury
満期スケジュール maturity schedule
満期請求額 termination claim
満期前償還 prior redemption
満期対当 maturity matching
満期短縮プラン accelerated endowment plan
満期手形 matured bill；matured notes
満期到来債 maturing bonds
満期年齢 age at exit
満期の近い銘柄 shorter dated maturities
満期の分散 staggering maturities
満期バスケット maturity basket
満期日 expiration date；maturity date
満期分散 staggering maturity
満期分布の差 maturity distribution range
満期返戻金 maturity repayment
満期保証 maturity guarantee
満期保有債券 bonds held to maturity
満期保有投資 held-to-maturity investment
満期保有目的の債券 held-to-maturity securities
満期前の裏書 before due endorsement
満期前引受 anticipated acceptance
満期間近の債務 maturing liability
満期までの期間 tenor
満期までの収益の一定率 constant rate of return to maturity
満期までのベータ値 full-life beta
満期までの保有 hold-to-maturity
満期利回り yield to maturity
マンスリー・リバーサル monthly reversal
慢性的 chronic
慢性的インフレ deep-rooted inflation
慢性的インフレーション chronic inflation
慢性的怠業 chronic absenteeism
慢性的デフレーション chronic deflation
満足基準 satisfying principle
マンデート mandate
マンデートの入札 mandate bid
マンデート・レター mandate letter
満年齢 age last birthday
満日計算 entire day basis computation
満了 termination
満了日 expiry date

ミ

見 合 い match making
見合勘定 corresponding account
見合基金 matching funds
見合預金 corresponding deposit
見えざる手 invisible hand
見えざる輸出 invisible export
見えざる輸入 invisible import
未解決の行為 pending action
未解決の紛争 unresolved dispute
未回収原価 unrecovered cost
未開拓市場 untapped market
見返勘定 offsetting account
見返購入 counterpurchase
見返再保険 counter cession
見返資金 counterpart fund
見返りとして in return
見返輸出 collateral export
見返輸入 collateral import；counter-purchase
見返預金 collateral deposit
未確定給付 non-vested benefit
未確定条項 intermediate provision
未確定の契約 executory contract
見かけの所得 phantom income
見　　方 perception
未稼動資本 non-performing capital；unproductive capital
未稼得金融収益 unearned finance income
未 監 査 unaudited
未監査財務諸表 unqualified financial statements
未完了取引 incomplete transaction
右下がり利回曲線 negative yield curve
未記入帳簿 blank book
ミクロ会計 micro accounting
ミクロ経済 microeconomy
ミクロ経済学 microeconomics
ミクロ経済的 microeconomic
ミクロ経済の改善 microeconomic improvement
ミクロ分析 microanalysis
ミクロヘッジ micro hedge
未 経 過 unexpired
未経過再保険料 portfolio premium
未経過費用 expenses paid in advance；unexpired expenses
未経過保険料 prepaid insurance premiums；unearned insurance premium；unexpired premium
未経過利子 unearned interest；unexpired interest
未経過割引料 unearned discount
未 決 済 non-settled
未決済勘定 outstanding account；unsettled account
未決済月次残高 remaining monthly balance
未決済残高 amount outstanding of unsettled transactions
未決済総額 aggregate amount outstanding
未決済取引 unsettled contracts；unsettled transactions
未決済取引の整理 completion of unsettled transactions；settlement of unsettled transactions
未決済の unsettled
未決済約定 unsettled transactions
未決済約定の引継ぎ transfer of unsettled contracts；transfer of unsettled transactions
未 決 算 unsettlement of accounts
未決算勘定 accounts yet to be settled；open account；unbalanced account
未決算帳簿 unbalanced book
未決算の open；unbalanced
未決算保険金 unsettled insurance claims
未決算元帳 open ledger
未公開株 non-introduced stock
見越勘定 accrual account；accrual item

見越債務 accrued liabilities
見越資産 accrued assets
見込客リスト lead
見込原価 anticipated cost
見込顧客 potential customer
見込みのない喪失 irretrievable deprivation
見込利益 anticipated profit
見込料率算定 prospective rating
未済借金 outstanding debt
短い説明 thumbnail description
未実現為替差損益 unrealized foreign currency gain and loss
未実現収益 unrealized revenue
未実現損 unrealised loss
未実現損益 unrealized gain and loss
未実現損失 unrealized loss
未実現利益 unrealized income；unrealized profit
未実現利得 unrealized gain
未実行貸出 undisbursed loans
未　収 unearned
未収受取勘定合計 total receivables
未収受取利息 accrued interest receivable
未収還付税金 tax refund receivable
未 収 金 accounts due；uncollected balance
未収銀行預金利息 interest receivable on bank deposits
未収金の経過期間 accounts-receivable aging
未収最低リース料総額 minimum lease payments receivable
未収支勘定 accruals
未収資金 uncollected funds
未収地代 uncollected rent
未収収益 accrued revenue；uncollected income；uncollected revenue
未 収 税 tax receivable
未修正残高試算表 unadjusted trial balance
未収賃貸料 rent receivable
未収手形・小切手 bills and checks in process of collection
未収手数料 commission receivable；uncollected commission
未収配当 dividend receivable
未収配当金 accrued dividend receivable
未収保管料 storage accounts receivable
未収保険金 insurance claims receivable
未収保険料 due and deferred premiums；outstanding insurance premiums；premium in arrears；uncollected premium
未収保証金 guarantee money receivable
未収保証料 accrued guarantee fee
未収有価証券利息 accrued interest on securities
未収利益 accrued income
未収利益処分禁止 restraint on anticipation
未収利息 interest receivable；uncollected interest
未収利息不計上貸出金 loans for which accrued interest is not shown
未収利息・割引料 unearned interest and discount
未消化証券 undigested securities
未使用借入限度枠 unused line of credit
未償還債券 bond outstanding
未償却過去勤務費用 non-amortized past service cost
未償却原価 unamortized cost
未償却建設利息 unamortized interest during construction
未償却減耗資産 undepreciated wasting property
未償却債務 unamortized obligation
未償却残高 unamortized and undepreciated balance
未償却社債割引 unamortized bond discount
未償却投資差金 unamortized premium on investments
未償却発行差金 unamortized discount
未上場証券 unlisted security
未上場証券市場 USM (unlisted securities market)
未上場取引 unlisted trading
未上場取引権 UTP (unlisted trading privilege)
未使用の繰越税額控除 unused

carryforward of tax credit
未使用の税務上の繰越欠損金 unused tax loss carryforward
未使用不動産 unused real estate
未使用付与権利 unused entitlement
未使用有給休暇 unused compensated absence
未 処 分 undisposed
未処分欠損 undisposed deficit
未処分剰余金 unappropriated retained earnings
未処分利益 unappropriated income；unappropriated profit
未処分利益剰余金 unappropriated earned surplus
未処分留保利益 unappropriated retained surplus
未処理欠損金 unappropriated deficit
水資源機構 Japan Water Agency
ミスプライス mispricing
水増株式 watered stock
水増雇用要求 featherbedding
水増資産 watered assets
水増資本 watered stock
ミスマッチ mismatching
ミスマッチ変動利付債 mismatched FRN
ミスマッチ・リスク mismatch risk
未請求小切手 unclaimed check
未請求の unbilled
未請求配当金 unclaimed dividend
未成工事 construction in progress
未成工事支出金 cost for contract work in progress
未成熟資産 immature assets
未成年者 minor
未成年者口座 custodial account
未成年者控除 minor tax credit
未成年者の取引口座 minor account
未成立契約 outstanding business
みせかけの店 shell branch
未宣言者 non-declarant
見 出 し heading
未達預け入れ deposit in transit
未達勘定 account in transit；transit account
未達現金 cash in transit
未達項目 item in transit
未達商品 merchandise in transit
未達取引 dealing in transit
未 達 の in transit
未 着 品 goods in transit
未着品販売 sale to arrive
ミックス・トラスト mixed trust
ミッド・アメリカ商品取引所 Mid-America Commodity Exchange
ミッドウエスト証券取引所 Midwest Stock Exchange
未積立生命保険信託 unfunded insurance trust
未積立年金債務 unfunded pension liability
未積立保証給付 unfunded guaranteed benefit
未積立予想給付債務 unfunded projected benefit obligation
見 積 り estimation
見積売上勘定書 pro forma account sales
見積価額 estimated value
見積過程 estimation process
見積為替手形 pro forma bill；pro forma draft
見積金額変更 changes in estimates
見積原価 estimate cost
見積原価計算 estimated cost accounting
見積原価計算制度 estimated cost accounting system
見積減価償却 observed depreciation
見積原価制度 estimating-cost system
見積工事原価 estimated cost of construction work
見積誤差 error in making the estimate
見積債務 estimated liabilities
見積財務諸表 pro forma financial statements；projected financial statements
見積時期 estimated timing
見積資金運用表 pro forma cash flow statement；pro forma statement of application of funds
見積修正 pro forma adjustment

見積税額 estimated tax
見積操業度 estimated volume
見積損益計算書 estimated profit and loss statement；pro forma profit and loss statement
見積貸借対照表 estimated balance sheet；pro forma balance sheet
見積耐用年数 estimated useful life；expected life
見積耐用年数表 estimated useful life table
見積りによる債務 liability of estimated amount
見積年次実効税率 estimated annual effective income tax rate
見積売却価額 estimated exit value
見積比較可能情報 pro forma comparative information
見積費用 estimated expenses
見積変更 change in estimate
見積利益 estimated profit
見 積 る assess；estimate
密　　輸 smuggling
密輸情報専門官 Director for Intelligence
ミディアム・ターム・ノート medium-term note
未 登 記 unregistered
未登録社債 unregistered debenture
見 通 し outlook
認められる代替処理 allowed alternative treatment
緑資源機構 Japan Green Resources Agency
未取付小切手 outstanding check
見 直 し rebalance
みなし会員 quasi member；quasi-member
みなし掛金建て notional defined contribution
みなし課税対象ローン tax spared loan
みなし課税負担 deemed tax assessment
みなし加入 deemed participation
みなし株価 deemed stock price
みなし寄付金 deemed donations
みなし交付金 deemed bounty
みなし賛成 deemed approval
みなし事業年度 constructive taxable year；deemed accounting period
みなし取得価格 deemed acquisition price
みなし取得日 deemed acquisition date
みなし譲渡 deemed transfer
みなし所有 constructive ownership
みなし審査請求 deemed request for reconsideration
みなし税額控除 tax sparing
みなし税額控除ローン tax sparing loan facility
みなし相続財産 deemed inherited property
みなし配当 constructive dividends；deemed dividend；payment deemed as dividends
みなし配当税制 taxation on consent dividend
みなし法人 deemed corporation
みなし法人課税 taxation on deemed corporation
みなし預託 deemed deposit
みなし利息 fictitious coupon
みなし利息計算 imputation of interest
みなし利率 imputed rate of interest
港　　税 port toll
南アフリカ先物取引所 SAFEX (South African Futures Exchange)
南アフリカ・ランド ZAR (South African rand)
ミニ株式市場 mini stock
ミニ・タップ mini tap
ミニ投資 mini investment
ミニ・マックス原理 mini max. principle
ミニ・マックス債 mini. max. bond
ミニ・リファンディング mini-refunding
未認識過去勤務費用 unrecognized prior service cost
未認識金融商品 unrecognized financial instruments
未認識残高 unrecognized balance
未認識純損益 unrecognized net gain/loss
未認識損失 loss not yet recognized
未認識年金債務 unrecognized pension liability

未認識年金資産 unrecognized pension assets
未認識変更時差異債務 unrecognized transitional obligation
ミネアポリス穀物取引所 Minneapolis Grain Exchange
未　納 non-payments
未納税引取り non-taxable receiving
身代金保険 ransom insurance
未配賦の unallocated
未配分剰余金 unassigned surplus
未配分利益 undistributed profit
未発行株式 unissued stock
未発行銀行券 unissued banknotes
未発行資本 unissued capital stock
未払い unpaid
未払勘定 accrued account
未払寄付金 accrued donation；unpaid donation
未払給与 accrued payroll
未払給料 accrued salaries
未払給料賃金 accrued payrolls
未払金 accounts payable；amount in arrears；claims payable
未払工賃 accrued wages
未払込資本 subscribed capital stock
未払込資本額 capital stock unpaid
未払最低リース料総額 minimum lease payments payable
未払債務 accrued liability
未払資本金 unpaid capital
未払税金 tax payable；unpaid tax
未払税金勘定 tax payable account
未払賃金 unclaimed wages；wages payable
未払賃貸料 rent payable
未払手数料 accrued commission；commission payable
未払年金費用 unfunded accrued pension cost
未払配当 dividends in arrears
未払配当額 accrued dividend
未払配当金 dividend payable；unpaid dividend
未払費用 accrued charge；accrued expenses payable
未払負債 outstanding liabilities
未払返戻金 unpaid returns
未払法人税 income taxes payable
未払保険金 accrued premium；outstanding claim；unpaid claim
未払保険料 premium due
未払家賃 accrued rent
未払利子 interest payable
未払利息 accrued interest payable
未費消原価 unexpired cost
未必利益保険 contingency insurance
未評価保険 unvalued policy
未分割遺産 undivided bequest
未分割遺産の相続税 inheritance tax on undivided bequest
身分証明書 identification card
未分配実現利益計算書 statement of undistributed realized earnings
未分配剰余積立金 unassigned surplus
未分配利益 undistributed earnings
未返済元本 unpaid principal
未報告保険事故 unreported claim
見本積送品 sample shipment
見本費 samples expense
見舞金 money in token of sympathy；solatium
身元信用保険 fidelity guarantee insurance
ミャンマー・キャット MMK (Myanmar kyat)
ミューチュアル・ファンド mutual fund
ミューチュアル・ファンド再投資プログラム mutual fund reinvestment program
ミューチュアル・ファンド自動積立プログラム mutual fund debit program
ミューチュアル・ファンド引受業者 mutual fund underwriters
未来原価計算 accounting for future cost
ミラノ証券取引所 Milan Stock Exchange
未履行契約 unexecuted contracts
未流通硬貨 coins reserved for circulation
未利用地税 tax on unutilized land
魅力株 glamour stock
民営化 privatization
民営化計画 privatization scheme

民 活 法 Private-Sector Participation Promotion Law
民間会社 private company ; private corporation
民間貸付 private loan
民間機械受注高 private machinery order
民間企業 private business ; private enterprise
民間企業年金制度 private employer pension plan
民間銀行 private bank
民間銀行貸出 commercial bank credit
民間金融会社 private funding corporation
民間金融機関 private financial institution
民間金融機関貸出 loans by private financial institutions
民間金融奨励 encouragement of private financing
民 間 債 non-government bond ; private bond
民間債務 private debt
民間事業 civilian enterprise ; private undertaking
民間事業費 private activity bond
民間資金等活用事業 PFI (private finance initiative)
民間支出 private spending
民間市場 private market
民間資本 private capital
民間就労人口 civilian employed population
民間需要 private demand
民間消費 private consumption
民間貯蓄 private saving
民間投資家 private investor
民間トランシェ commercial tranche
民間取引 private transaction
民間年金基金 private pension fund
民間年金資産 private pension assets
民間部門 private sector
民間保険 private insurance
民間保険会社 commercial insurer
民間モーゲージ保険 private mortgage insurance
民間労働者 civilian worker
民業圧迫 suppression of private businesses
民事再生手続 civil rehabilitation proceedings
民事再生法 Civil Rehabilitation Law
民事裁判所 civil court
民事執行 civil execution
民事上の救済措置 civil remedy
民事上の罰金 civil fine
民事責任 civil liability
民事訴訟 civil action ; civil litigation ; civil suit ; common law action
民　　需 civilian demand
民生用エレクトロニクス consumer electronics
民　　法 civil code

ミ

ム

ムーディーズ Moody's
ムーディーズ投資適格 Moody's investment grade
ムーバブル・バンド movable band
向かい風介入 intervention against market
無害の誤謬 harmless error
無格付け not rated
無格付債券 non-rated
無格付けの法人 unrated entity
無確認信用状 unconfirmed L/C
無 額 面 no par value
無額面株 non-par-value stock；stock without par value
無額面株式 no value stock
無額面普通株式 common stock without par value
無 過 失 no fault
無過失責任 absolute liability；liability without fault
無為替輸出 non-draft export
無為替輸入 non-draft import
無基金の年金 unfunded pension
無議決権株 non-voting stock
無期限差押 distress infinite
無期限保証 continuing guaranty
無記名株 bearer stock
無記名株券 stock certificate to bearer
無記名株式 bearer share；uninscribed stock
無記名債券 bearer bond
無記名参加証券 BPC (bearer participation certificate)
無記名式 bearer form
無記名式小切手 bearer check
無記名社債 bearer debenture
無記名証券 bearer securities
無記名投票 unsigned vote
無記名の bearer
無記名普通株式 bearer common stock
無記名預託証券 BDR (bearer depository receipt)
無給介護 unpaid care
無給付期間 blackout period
無拠出給付 non-contributory benefit
無区分式 single step
無形価値 intangible value
無形減価償却資産 intangible depreciable assets
無形固定資産 intangible fixed assets；intangibles
無形財産 intangible property
無形資産 intangible assets
無形資産減価償却 amortization of intangible assets；amortization of intangibles
無形資産とのれんの償却 amortization of intangible assets and goodwill
無形資本 intangible capital
無形償却資産 intangible depreciable property
無形の効果 intangible effects
無形費用 intangible cost
無権カード unauthorized card
無限責任 unlimited liability
無限責任会社 unlimited liability company
無限責任組合 general partnership；unlimited partnership
無限責任社員 general partner
無権代理 nominal proxy
無限定意見 clean opinion；unqualified opinion
無限定監査報告書 non-opinion report；unqualified audit report
無限定適正意見の監査証明書 unqualified audit certificate
無限の経済的耐用年数 indefinite economic life
無限の耐用年数 indefinite life；unlimited useful life
無券面化 dematerialization

無券面化決済　scrip-less settlement
無券面の　paperless
無　　効　no effect；nullity
無効会員　unauthorized member
無控除保障　first dollar coverage
無効取引　void transaction
無効な契約　void contract
無効な合意　void agreement
無効判決　decree of nullity
向こうみずの相場師　plunger
無　　罪　innocence
無差別曲線　indifference curve
無作法抽出　random sample
無事故払戻し　return for no claim
無事故割引　no claim discount
無視しうる価額　negligible amount
無失効保証　no lapse guarantee
矛　　盾　contradiction
無　　償　gratis
無 償 株　bonus stock；free share
無償株式　bonus issues
無償株発行　capitalization issue
無償還債券　defaulted bond
無償還社債　debenture stock
無償還の　irredeemable
無償寄託　gratuitous bailment
無償継承的不動産処分　voluntary settlement
無償契約　gratuitous contract
無償減資　reduction of capital without compensation
無償交付　bonus issue
無償取得者　volunteer
無償譲渡　voluntary conveyance
無償の技術援助　free technical advice
無償の財産使用　gratuitous use of property
無償の信用供与　extension of free credit
無償の提供　free provision
無償発行　free issue
無償ローン　grant loan
無条件オペレーション　unconditional operation
無条件監査報告書　unqualified opinion report
無条件債権　unconditional receivables
無条件債務　unconditional debt；unconditional payables
無条件受給権付与　unconditional vesting
無条件の推定　unconditional estimate
無条件売買　absolute sales
無条件引出権　unconditional drawing right
無条件引渡し　absolute delivery
無条件補助金　unconditional grant
無条件流動性　unconditional liquidity
無資力者　straw man
無 申 告　failure to file a return
無申告加算税　additional tax due to failure to file a return
無診断保険付保　guaranteed insurability
無　　税　free of taxation
無制限債務　open end liability
無制限税源債　unlimited tax bond
無制限適正意見　unqualified report
無制限配偶者控除　unlimited marital deduction
無制限ファシリティ　unlimited facility
無制限法貨　unlimited legal tender
無税品表　free list
無制約の不動産　real estate without encumbrance
無相関の収益率　uncorrelated return
無 体 権　intangible right
無体財産　incorporeal property
無体動産　chose in action；incorporeal chattel
無段階式　single step form
無担保裏書　qualified endorsement
無担保オーバーナイト物金利　uncollateralized overnight call rate
無担保貸付　signature loan
無担保勘定　unsecured account
無担保コール　uncollateralized call；unsecured call loan
無担保債　unsecured debt
無担保債権者　unsecured creditors
無担保債務　unsecured obligations
無担保社債　non-collateralized bond；unsecured bond
無担保上位債務　senior unsecured debt
無担保信用　unsecured credit

無担保信用状 clean credit
無担保抵当証券 unsecured mortgage
無担保手形 open note
無担保取引 unsecured trading
無担保の unsecured
無担保負債 unsecured liability
無担保ローン unsecured loan
無等級（無格付け）債券 unrated bond
無等級債券 z rated bond
無投票当選 return without voting
無登録株 unregistered stock
無　　配 no dividend；non-dividend；omitted dividend
無配会社 no dividend company
無配継続 continued non-dividend
無配転落企業 companies previously paying dividend
無 配 当 passed dividend
無配当生命保険証書 non-participating life insurance policy
無配当保険 non-par insurance；non-participating insurance；without-profit insurance
無配にする pass dividend
無日付手形 undated bill
無 負 担 freedom from encumbrance
無弁護士意見地方債 ex legal
無　　謀 recklessness
無防御の undefended
無保険者保険 uninsured insurance
無保証残存価格 unguaranteed residual value
無保証残存額 unguaranteed residual value
無保証残存価値 unsecured residual value
無保証の unguaranteed
無約因契約 bare contract；naked contract
無約因抗弁 no consideration
無遺言死 intestacy
無遺言資産分配 intestate distribution
無利子社債 passive bond
無利子の金銭貸与 loan without interest
無利子負債 non-interest bearing liability
無リスク金利 risk-free interest rate
無リスク裁定 riskless arbitrage
無リスク資産 risk-free assets
無リスク実質金利 risk-free real rate of interest
無リスク証券 risk-free securities
無リスク投資 risk-free investment
無リスク・リターン risk-free return
無リスク利率 risk-free rate
無利息貸付 loaned flat
無利息債務 passive debt
無利息信用 interest free credit
無利息融資 loan at nil
無料譲渡権 free right of exchange

メ

メイカーズ(修正加速償却法) MACRS
明確な禁止 explicit prohibition
明確な権原 just title
明確な変動 definite change
銘　　柄 name of issue
銘柄入替勘定 substitution account
銘柄間格差 difference among issues
銘柄選別 name selection
銘 柄 品 brand-named item
銘柄併合 consolidation for trading
名　　義 street name
名義書換え name transfer；stock transfer
名義書換事務受託者 transfer service delegatee
名義書換請求 demand for name registration
名義書換代理人 transfer agent
名義書換停止 shut for dividend
名義書換手数料 fees for stock name transfers
名義書換費 stock name transfer expenses
名義貸し lending a street name
名 義 株 dummy stock
名義株配当 dividend on dummy stock
名義借り name borrowing
名義上の株主 owner of record
名義だけの地代 peppercorn rent
名 義 人 nominee
明　　細 schedule
明細勘定 itemized account
明 細 書 specification
明 細 表 exhibit
明示契約 express contract
明示信託 express trust
明治通宝札 Meiji Tsuho satsu
明 示 的 explicit
明示的条項 explicit clause
明示的費用 explicit cost
明示の契約 explicit contract
明示保証 express warranty
明示モデル explicit model
明示要件 explicit requirement
名　　称 title
名証株価指数 Nagoya Stock Price Index
メイプルリーフ・コイン mapleleaf coin
名簿登録株主 holders of the record
名目イールド・カーブの傾斜 slope of the nominal yield curve
名目額面 nominal par
名目株式資本 nominal share capital
名目勘定 nominal account
名目金利の理論値 implied nominal rate
名目行使価格 nominal exercise price
名目国民所得 nominal national income
名目固定金利債券 nominal fixed rate debt
名目債務 nominal liabilities
名目ＧＮＰ nominal GNP
名目GNP成長率 nominal GNP growth
名目GDP成長率 nominal GDP growth
名目資産 nominal assets
名目資本 nominal capital
名目収益率 nominal rate of return
名目収入 nominal income
名目主義 nominalism
名目乗数 nominal multiplier
名目相場 nominal quotation
名目対価 nominal consideration
名目賃金 nominal compensation；nominal wage
名目的財産税 nominal wealth tax
名目的取決め nominal arrangement
名目的パートナー nominal partner
名目取引 nominal transaction
名目ドル nominal dollars
名目の世界 nominal space
名目負債 nominal liabilities
名目ベース nominal terms
名目ベースの世界 nominal world
名目保護率 nominal rate of protection
名目呼値 nominal quote

名目利益 nominal profit
名目利回り nominal return；nominal yield
名目利率 nominal rate of interest
名目割引率 nominal rate of discount
名誉会長 chairman emeritus
名誉毀損 slander
明瞭性の原理 principle of clarity
命令的差止命令 mandatory injunction
命令的法律 imperative statute
命 令 日 rule day
メールオーダー・ローン mail-order loan
メール・クレジット mail credit
メール・クレジット・ファシリティ mail credit facility
メール・コンファメーション mail confirmation
メキシコ証券取引所 Mexican Stock Exchange
メキシコ中央銀行 Mexican central bank
メキシコ・ペソ MXN (Mexican peso)
目　　先 immediate future；near future
目 先 観 near time prospect
目 先 筋 day-to-day trader；in-and-put dealer
メザニン債 mezzanine bond；mezzanine debt
メザニン債務 mezzanine debt
メザニン・トランシェ mezzanine tranche
メザニン・ファイナンス mezzanine finance
メザニン・ブラケット mezzanine bracket
メジャー・マーケット指数 major market index
メジャー・ムーブ major move
メジャリング・ギャップ measuring gap
メッセージ認証コード MAC (Message Authentication Code)
メディア効果 media effect
メディア戦略 media strategy
メディア・ミックス media mix
メディアム・ターム・ノート MTN (medium term note)
メディケア Medicare
メディケア経済指標 Medicare Economic Index
メディケイド Medicaid
目に見えない費用 hidden cost
メニュー・アプローチ menu approach
目 減 り decrement；reduction
免 疫 化 immunization
免許更新 license renewal
免許種類 type of licenses
免 許 制 licensing system
免 許 税 license tax
免許制・登録制 granting of licenses or registering of entities
免 許 別 by types of licenses
免 許 料 fees and permits；license expense
免　　除 exemption；immunity
免除私会社 exempt private company
免除比率 exclusion ratio
免　　税 duty exemption；tax exemption
免 税 債 tax-exempt paper
免税証券 non-taxable securities；tax-exempt securities
免税所得 tax free income
免 税 点 tax exemption limit
免税投資 tax free investment
免税特別貯蓄 TESSA (tax exempt special savings account)
免税特権 extraterritoriality on tax laws
免 税 の duty free
免 税 品 free article；free goods；non-taxable goods；nontaxable goods
免税輸入品 duty free imports
免　　責 discharge；exoneration
免責期間 excepted period
免責危険 excepted perils；excluded risk
免責事項 disclaimer
免責事項の削除 deletion of exclusion
免責条項 escape clause；exclusion clause；negligence clause
免責歩合条項 franchise clause
免 責 法 act of indemnity
免責文言 disclaimer
免責約款 exemption agreement

メ

免訴を言渡す acquit

メンテナンス・リース maintenance lease

モ

モーゲージ担保証書 CMO (collateralized mortgaged obligation)
申 込 金 application money ; subscription money
申込時間 application hour
申込証拠金 advance on subscription
申込代理店 application agent
申込日基準 application date base
申　　立 instance ; petition
申立審理日 motion day
申 立 人 petitioner
モーゲージ mortgage
モーゲージ開放証書 satisfaction of mortgage
モーゲージ貸付 mortgage lending
モーゲージ借換え mortgage refinancing
モーゲージ期間 mortgage term
モーゲージ権者 mortgage creditor
モーゲージ・サービシング権 mortgage servicing rights
モーゲージ債 mortgages
モーゲージ債務 mortgage debt ; mortgage indebtedness
モーゲージ債務不履行 default on mortgage obligation ; mortgage delinquency
モーゲージ参加証券 mortgage participation certificates
モーゲージ市場 mortgage market
モーゲージ社債金利 mortgage bond coupon
モーゲージ償還 mortgage cancellation
モーゲージ償還保険 home protection policy
モーゲージ証券 mortgage backed securities
モーゲージ証券市場 mortgage market
モーゲージ承認件数 mortgage commitments
モーゲージ・ストリップ証券 mortgage strips
モーゲージ・スワップ mortgage swap
モーゲージ生命保険 mortgage life insurance
モーゲージ設定手続 mortgage process
モーゲージ担保型 mortgage collateral type
モーゲージ担保債券 mortgage backed bond
モーゲージ担保債務証書 collateralized mortgage obligations
モーゲージ担保証券 mortgage backed certificate
モーゲージ付社債券 mortgage debentures
モーゲージ取次業者 mortgage correspondent
モーゲージ年金 mortgage annuity
モーゲージの価格弾力性 mortgage elasticity
モーゲージの新規発行市場 primary mortgage market
モーゲージの清算 liquidation of mortgage
モーゲージの部分繰上返済 curtailment of mortgage
モーゲージの併合 consolidation of mortgages
モーゲージ・パス・スルー証券 mortgage pas-through securities
モーゲージ・パス・スルー証書 mortgage pass-through certificate
モーゲージ派生商品 mortgage derivatives
モーゲージ発行銀行 mortgage writing bank
モーゲージ・ファンド mortgage fund
モーゲージ・プール mortgage pool ; pool of mortgages
モーゲージ不動産投資信託 mortgage REIT (real estate investment trust)
モーゲージ返済額 mortgage payment
モーゲージ返済保障 mortgage payment

protection
モーゲージ・ポートフォリオ mortgage portfolio
モーゲージ保証保険 mortgage guarantee insurance
モーゲージ補償保険 mortgage indemnity policy
モーゲージ申込み mortgage application
モーゲージ流通市場 secondary mortgage market
モーゲージ利用者 mortgage holder
モーゲージ・レート mortgage rate
モーメンタム・オシレータ momentum oscillator
モーメンタム指標 momentum indicators
モーメンタム戦略 momentum strategy
モーメント moment
モーメント法 method of moments
モーリシャス・ルピー MUR (Mauritius rupee)
モーリタニア・オーギヤ MRO (Mauritanian ougiya)
木材取引税 timber delivery tax
黙示許容 implied license
黙示権限 implied authority
黙示信託 implied trust
黙示担保 implied warranty
黙示保証 implied warranty
目的関数 objective function
目的自由ローン non-purpose loan
目的申告書 purpose statement
目 的 税 earmarked tax；object tax；special purpose tax
目的積立金 appropriation surplus；reserve for specific purpose
目的適合性 relevance
目的融資 purpose loan
目的ローン purpose loan
黙　　認 acquiescence；connivance
目　　標 goal
目標売上 target sales
目標価格 target price
目標格付け target rating
目標為替相場 target zone of exchange rate
目標管理 management by objective
目標原価 target cost
目標相場圏 target zone
目標突破 overshoot
目標配当性向 target payout ratio
目標変動幅 target range
目標保険料 target premium
目標母集団 target population
目標利益 target income；target profit
目標利回り target yield
黙　　約 tacit contract
目論見書 prospectus
モザンビーク・メティカル MZM (Mozambique metical)
モジリアーニ・ミラーの命題 Modigliani-Miller theory
モスクワ銀行間通貨取引所 MICEX (Moscow Interbank Currency Exchange)
持 合 い cross-holding
持合い株式 cross held shares
持家制度 house ownership plan
持株会社 holding company
持株買取協定 buy-out arrangement
持株奨励 share incentive
持 株 数 number of stocks held
持株制度実施会社 companies with employee stock ownership plan
持株比率 percentage of shareholding；ratio of shareholding
持 越 費 over-carrying cost
持越費用 carryover cost
持 越 品 goods carried over
持込資本 brought-in capital
持込渡し条件 DDP (delivered duty paid)
持 ち 高 position
持高限度 position limit
持高ゼロ flat
持 ち 分 equity；interest
持ち分会計 accounting for equities；equity accounting
持ち分株式 equity share
持ち分勘定 equity account
持ち分金融商品 equity financial instrument

持ち分証券 equity instrument
持ち分所有者 equity owner
持ち分逓増モーゲージ growing equity mortgage
持ち分転換 equity conversion
持ち分の継続 mutual sharing of interests
持ち分の結合 combination of equity interests
持ち分の譲渡 transfer of ownership of capital
持ち分の払戻し refunding of equity
持ち分の変動 changes in equity interest
持ち分の法的形式 legal form of equity interest
持ち分評価替 equity revaluation
持ち分プーリング pooling of interests
持ち分プーリング法 pooling of interests method
持ち分プーリング方式 pooling of interest method
持ち分変動計算書 statement of changes in equity
持ち分法 equity accounting method；equity method
持ち分報奨 equity compensation
持ち分報奨給付 equity compensation benefit
持ち分報奨制度 equity compensation plan
持ち分法で会計処理された accounted for using equity method
持ち分法適用会社 equity method investee
持ち分法適用関連会社 equity method affiliates
持ち分法適用関連会社投資 investment in equity method affiliates
持分法投資 equity method investment
持ち分法による損益 equity income of subsidiary
持ち分利益 equity benefit；equity income；equity theory
モディファイド・デュレーション modified duration
モ デ ル model
モデル価格 model price
モデル誤差 model error
モデル分析 model analysis
モデル理論 model theory
元受会社 writing company
元受市場 direct market
元受保険 direct insurance；original insurance；primary insurance
元受保険会社 direct insurer
元受保険者 primary carrier
元受保険料 direct writing premium
元 契 約 prime contract
戻入基準 reversal criteria
戻し売り selling on temporary
戻し運賃 return freight
戻し為替 re-exchange
戻し口銭 return commission
戻 し 税 tax rebate
戻し税給付 drawback allowance
戻し税証明書 customs debenture
戻 し 品 goods returned to vendor
戻し品明細書 PRB (purchase return book)
元　　帳 ledger
元 帳 係 ledger clerk
元帳勘定 ledger account
元帳残高 balance on ledger
元帳資産 ledger assets
元帳締切 closing of the ledger
元帳に転記する post to the ledger
元帳の各勘定を締切ること closing all accounts in the ledger
元帳振替 ledger transfer
元帳ページ数 ledger folio
戻り売り selling on rally
戻り高値 recover high
戻 り 品 return inward
モナコ（仏フラン） Monaco (French franc)
もみあい range trading
モメンタムの和らぎ waning momentum
模様ながめ wait and see；watch and wait
モラル・ハザード moral hazard
モラル・リスク moral risks
モルディブ・ルフィア MVR (Maldives rufiyaa)
モルドバ・レウ MDL (Moldovan leu)

モロッコ・ディルハム MAD (Moroccan dirham)
モンゴル・トゥグリク MNT (Mongolian tugrik)
問題債権 problem credit；problem loan
問題債権処理損失 loss on the disposal of problem loans
問題処理 workout
問題の少ない制度 lesser evil
モンテカルロ・シュミレーション Monte Carlo simulation
モンテセラト（東カリブ・ドル） Montserrat (EC (East Caribbean) dollar)
モンテネグロ（ユーゴ・ディナール） Montenegro (Yugoslav dinar)
モントリオール証券取引所 Montreal Exchange
文部科学省 Ministry of Education, Culture, Sports, Science and Technology
文部科学大臣 Minister of Education, Culture, Sports, Science and Technology
モンロー主義 Monroe Doctrine

ヤ

夜間金庫 night deposit safe
夜間交換 exchange at night
夜間裁判所 night court
夜間処理 overnight processing
夜間取引 night session
夜間バッチ決済 overnight batch settlement
夜間ブリッジ overnight bridge
役　　員 officer
役員貸付金 loan to director
役員給料 directors' salary；officer's salary
役員賞与 directors' bonus；officer's bonus
役員選挙の細則 bylaws for the election of officers
役員退職給与 directors' retirement benefit
役員退職金 director's retirement allowance
役員の解任 discharge of officers
役員の債務免除 cancellation of debts of directors
役員の職務及び権限 duties and powers of executives
役員の身分の保証 guarantee of the executives' status
役員報酬 compensation paid to directors；director's salaries and remuneration；executive salaries
役員報酬の損金不算入 exclusion of remuneration of director from non-taxable expenses
役員報奨のためのオプション executive compensation option
約　　因 consideration；covenants
約因条項 consideration clause
約因の滅失 failure of consideration
約　　定 agreement；matching
約定価額 contract value
約定期日 contractual maturity date
約定給付金 contracted benefit
約定金利 agreed-upon interest rate；contracted interest rate
約定後処理費用 post trade processing cost
約定された取引 committed transaction
約定指数 contract index price
約定書の差入れ submission of agreement
約定損害賠償額 stipulated damages
約定担保権 stipulated security
約定通知 contract notice
約定値段 agreed-upon price；contract price；contracted price
約定値段の公表 dissemination of transaction price；posting of contract price
約定の制限数量 maximum limit of contracts
約 定 日 trade date
約定返済 scheduled payment
約定返済付きスワップ amortizing swap
約定満期利回り agreed yield to maturity
約定利子率 contract interest rate
約定利息 agreed interest
約 定 料 commitment fee
約定利率 agreed rate of interest；contracted rate；stated interest rate
約定レート contracted rate
役 職 者 management personnel
約　　束 commitment；promise
約束手形 promissory note
約 諾 者 promisor
役　　得 spoils of office
安 気 配 bearish tone
安　　値 low price
安値株式 penny stock
安値にシフトする trade in a weaker range
安値引け closing lower
安値待ち anticipation of falling market
安 寄 り open down

家賃相場 rental market value
家賃手当 rental allowance
家賃統制 rent control
約款上の保証 contractual guarantee
約款の交付 delivery of agreement
や　ま adventure
ヤマアラシ条項 porcupine provision
闇価格協定 price-fixing agreement
闇ディーリング black market dealing
ヤリ気配 asked quotation
や り 手 rainmaker
ヤンキー・ドル市場 Yankee-dollar market
ヤンキー・ボンド Yankee bond

ユ

ユアーズ(売った時) yours
遺　　言 testament
遺 言 者 testator
遺言信託 testamentary trust
遺言の撤回 revocation of will
遺言の復活 revival of will
友愛組合 friendly society
優　　位 precedence
有意水準 significance level
誘　　因 inducement
誘　　引 invitation
有益な報告 informative reporting
優越する権原 title paramount
優越する権利 paramount right
有価証券 securities ; valuable instrument ; valuable papers
有価証券移転税 tax for transfer of securities
有価証券オプション securities option
有価証券オプション取引 securities option trading
有価証券買集め collection of securities by purchase
有価証券買入れ securities purchase
有価証券買入記入帳 investment purchased register
有価証券借入能力 borrowing power of securities
有価証券借入料 charge on securities borrowed
有価証券勘定 securities account
有価証券管理信託 securities administration trust
有価証券記入帳 securities register
有価証券債務引受け assumption of liabilities of securities
有価証券債務引受業 central counterparty services to equities and fixed income products
有価証券市場 securities market
有価証券指数先物取引 futures trading of securities price index
有価証券取得価額 acquisition cost of securities
有価証券取得による支出 payments on purchase of securities
有価証券準備 securities reserve
有価証券上場規程 security listing regulations
有価証券上場申請書 application for listing of a security
有価証券上場予備申請書 preliminary application for listing of a security
有価証券信託 securities in trust
有価証券損益 securities income and expense
有価証券担保貸付 lending of funds against securities collateral
有価証券担保貸付金 loan secured by securities
有価証券担保借入 borrowing of funds against securities collateral
有価証券通知書 Notice of a Security
有価証券届出効力発生通知書 notice to inform of taking effect of securities registration statement
有価証券届出書 registration statement of securities
有価証券取扱者 securities handling clerk
有価証券取扱責任者 person responsible for handling securities
有価証券取引税 securities transaction tax ; securities transfer tax
有価証券取引税法 securities transaction tax law
有価証券取引損引当金 reserve for possible losses on securities transactions
有価証券取引前利益 IBST (income before securities transactions)
有価証券の売出しに関する届出

ユ

registration of a public selling of a security
有価証券の貸付 lending of securities
有価証券の区分 classification of securities；division of securities
有価証券の組合せ combination of securities
有価証券の減損処理 treatment for an impairment of securities
有価証券の種類 class of securities
有価証券の償還による収入 proceeds from redemption of securities
有価証券の譲渡 transfer of securities
有価証券の譲渡所得 gain on transfer of securities；income from transfer of securities
有価証券の消費寄託契約 deposit contracts for securities
有価証券の消費貸借契約 lending and borrowing contracts for securities
有価証券の新規上場 initial listing of securities
有価証券の信託 security trusts
有価証券の清算取次 transactions pertaining to agency-based clearing of securities
有価証券の貸借 lending or borrowing of securities
有価証券の売買 transactions in securities
有価証券の範囲 scope of securities
有価証券の評価 valuation of securities
有価証券の評価方法 appraisal method of securities
有価証券の返還 withdrawal of securities
有価証券の変更上場 alteration in listed securities
有価証券の法定評価方法 statutory valuation method of securities
有価証券の募集に関する届出 registration of a public offering of a security
有価証券の見本 specimens of certificates of the security
有価証券の銘柄 designation of security
有価証券売却益 capital gains from sales of securities；gain on sale of securities
有価証券売却記入帳 securities sold register
有価証券売却損 loss on sale of securities
有価証券売買 buying and selling of securities
有価証券引受業法 securities underwriting business law
有価証券引渡票 due bill；promise-to-deliver ticket
有価証券引渡票の交付 delivery of due bill
有価証券評価 appraisal of securities
有価証券評価益 gain on appreciation of securities
有価証券評価基準 valuation standards for securities
有価証券評価差益 valuation gains on securities
有価証券評価損 loss from revaluation of securities
有価証券評価方法 appraisement method of securities
有価証券報告書 periodic securities report
有価証券報告書届出書 registration statement of securities report
有価証券保有 securities investment
有価証券明細表 schedule of securities
有価証券元帳 investment ledger；securities ledger
有価証券利息 interest on securities
有価証券利息配当金 interest and dividends on securities
有価約因 valuable consideration
有期限年金 limited annuity
有期年金 temporary annuity；terminable annuity
有期有限パートナーシップ finite-life limited partnership
有誼的訴訟 friendly action
有給休暇 compensated absence；vacation with pay
有給休暇会計 accounting for compensated absences
有給疾病休暇 paid sick leave
遊休資産 idle assets

ユ

遊休施設 idle facilities
遊休資本 idle capital
遊休生産能力 idle capacity
遊休設備 idle equipment；spare plant capacity；surplus equipment
遊休建物 unused buildings
遊休土地 unused land
遊休工場 idle plant
優遇貸出金利 prime rate
優遇税制 special tax preferences
優遇税制給付 tax favored benefit
優遇税制措置 preferential tax treatment
優遇税制の tax privileged
優遇措置 favorable treatment
優遇措置期間 free ride period
優遇手形 preferential bill
優遇料率 preferential rate
有形固定資産 property, plant and equipment；tangible fixed assets
有形固定資産からの控除 deduction from property, plant and equipment
有形固定資産の会計処理 accounting for property, plan and equipment
有形固定資産明細表 schedule of tangible fixed assets
有形資産 physical assets；tangible assets
有形資産価値 tangible value
有形資産に潜在している implicit for tangible assets
有形償却資産 tangible depreciable property
有形費用 tangible cost
有限会社 private limited company
有限差分 finite difference
有限責任 limited liability
有限責任会社 limited liability company
有限責任組合 limited partnership
有限責任保証会社 company limited by guarantee
有限耐用年数資産 limited life assets
有限の耐用年数 limited useful life
有限払込保険 limited payment insurance
有限払込保険料 discontinued premium
有効活用 effective utilization
有効期間 effective period
有効期限 term of validity
有効求職者数 job applications
有効競争 effective competition；workable competition
有効金利 effective rate of interest
有効需要 effective demand
有効需要の原理 principle of effective demand
有効性の評価 assessment of the effectiveness
有効的な支配 effective control
有効統計 efficient statistics
有効な抗弁 available plea
有効な参照点 valid reference point
有効な保険証券 policy in force
有効に関する先行条件 conditions precedent to the validity
有効フロンティア efficient frontier
有効フロンティア分析 efficient frontier analysis
友好的買収 friendly takeover
ユーゴスラビア・ディナール YUM (Yugoslav dinar)
ユーザー所有の公益企業 user-owned utility
ユーザンス usance
融 資 額 loan amount
融資慣行 lending practice
融資期間 loan period
融資期間の短縮 shortening of loan term
融資規制 loan restrictions；regulation of lending
融資拒否 redlining
融資限度 loan limit
融資合意 finance close
融 資 残 balance of loans
融資残高 outstanding loan balance
融資残高全額支払い full payment of outstanding balance of the loan
融資資産運用 loan asset management
融資実行残高 outstanding balance of loans extended
融資実行日 draw down date
融資準則 financing regulation
融資条件 loan conditions

融資承諾 loan consent
融資審査 loan application examination
融資組成手数料 loan origination fee
融資年限 loan term
融資の実行 execution of loan ; extension of loan
融資の約束 loan commitment
融資比率 loan-to-value ratio
融資比率引下げ reduction of lending ratio
融資保険 loan insurance
融資未実行残高 balance of the unused credit
融資申込み loan application
融資リスク loan risk
有資格者 good and lawful men
有識者 academics
有償契約 compensatory contract ; onerous contract
有償取得 acquisition for value
有償所持人 holder for value
有償信託 trust for value
有償増資 paid-in capital increase
有償増資権利落ち rights offering
有償発行済株式 paid-in outstanding shares
有償保有者 holder for value
融通 accommodation
融通裏書 accommodation endorsement
融通小切手 kiting check
融通債 bonds issued for daily fund raising of the national treasury
融通証券 bills issued for stopgap financing
融通手形 accommodation bill ; accommodation note ; kite bill
融通手形の振出人 accommodation maker
郵政官署 postal agencies
郵政事業庁 Postal Services Agency
郵政民営化 privatization of postal services
郵税先払い postage to be paid on delivery
郵税支払済み postage paid
有税償却 taxable depreciation
有税品 dutiable goods

優勢である nudge ahead of
優先受取人 preference beneficiary
優先買取権 preemption
優先貸付 senior loan
優先株 preferred equity ; preferred share ; preferred stock ; prefs
優先株株主 preferred stockholder
優先株式 preference shares
優先株式資本 preferred stock capital
優先株資本金 capital stock preferred
優先株償還準備金 reserve for retirement of preferred stock
優先株主 preference shareholder
優先株配当金 dividend on preferred stock
優先株倍率 preferred stock coverage
優先株比率 preferred stock ratio
優先権 preferential right
優先権付社債 prior bond
優先交渉権 first refusal right
優先項目 prior items
優先コード priority code
優先債権 preferred claims
優先債権者 preferential creditor ; preferred creditor ; priority creditor
優先債務 preferred liability
優先差押権 priority of attachment
優先させる overriding
優先支払い preferential payment
優先支払債務 privileged debts
優先出資口 preferred equity contribution unit
優先出資者 holder of preferred capital contribution certificates ; preferred equity contributors
優先出資社員 holders of preferred equity securities
優先出資者総会 meeting of preferred equity contributors
優先出資証券 preferred capital contribution certificate ; preferred equity contribution securities
優先出資引受権証書 subscription warrant to preferred equity contributions
優先出資法 Preferred Equity Contribution Law

ユ

優先証券 senior securities
優先処理 preferred treatment ; priority processing
優 先 性 priority
優先担保権付社債 prior lien bond
優先的買戻権 first refusal right to repurchase
優先的普通株 preferred ordinary share
優先取引株式 stock ahead
優先入札者 preferred bidder
優先配当 preferred dividend
優先配当負担倍率 preferred dividend coverage ratio
優先劣後構造 senior-sub structure
郵 送 料 mailing cost ; postage
有体動産 chose in possession
有担保コール collateralized call transactions ; secured call loan
有担保社債 secured corporate bond
有担保の collateralized
有担保翌日物 collateralized overnight
ユーティリティ消費 utility consumption
尤　　度 likelihood
尤度比検定 likelihood ratio test
誘 導 形 reduced form
誘導目標 target level
誘導モデル reduced-form method
有配会社平均配当金 average dividend of paying companies
有 配 株 dividend-paying stock
誘発投資 induced investment
郵便為替 postal money order
郵便小切手 postal check
郵便貯金 postal savings deposit
郵便貯金の利子 interest on postal savings
郵便貯金法 Postal Savings Law
郵便日数 mail days
郵便料金後納担保 collateral for post-dated payment of postal charges
猶　　予 grace
猶予期間 grace period
有 用 性 utility
有用な情報 useful information
有利差異 favorable variance
有利子借入金 interest bearing borrowing
有利子負債 interest bearing liability
有利子負債の1年内返済分 current portion of interest bearing liability
有利な価格 better price
有利なキャリー favorable carry
有利な条件 lucrative terms
有利な立場 ground floor
有利な投資 high grade investment
有利な変化 favorable change
有利発行 advantageous placement ; interest bearing issuance
優 良 株 blue chip stock ; quality stock
優良危険 good risk
優良社債 high quality corporate bond
優良社債利回り yield on high quality corporate bond
優良証券 gilt-edged securities
優良である in good standing
優良手形 prime bill ; prime paper
優 良 な premier
優良発行体 prime issuer
優良銘柄 blue chips
優良銘柄株式市場 blue chip equity market
有料自動車道 toll motorway
有力銀行 prime bank
幽 霊 株 bogus stock
ユ ー ロ EUR (Euro)
ユーロ/英ポンド EURGBP
ユーロ円 Euroyen
ユーロ円金利 Euroyen interest rate
ユーロ円債 Euroyen bond
ユーロ円債発行 Euroyen bond issue
ユーロ円市場 Euroyen market
ユーロ円変動利付債 Euroyen floater
ユーロ貸付市場 Eurocredit market
ユーロ加盟 euro entry
ユーロ加盟賛成派 pro-euro member
ユーロカレンシー市場 Eurocurrency market
ユーロカレンシー・シンジケート・ローン市場 Eurocurrency syndicated loan market
ユーロ銀行間出し手レート EURIBOR (Euro Inter-Bank Offered Rate)

ユーロ金融市場 Eurocurrency banking market
ユーロ金利 interest rate on the Eurocurrency market
ユーロ金利差先物 diff (Eurorate differential)
ユーロクリア Euroclear
ユーロ圏 Euro area；Euro-zone；Euroland
ユーロ圏の経済 Euro zone economy
ユーロ・コマーシャルペーパー ECP (Euro commercial paper)
ユーロ債 euro denominated bond；Eurobond
ユーロ債市場 Eurobond market
ユーロ債利回り Euro yield
ユーロCD ECD (Euro certificate of deposit)
ユーロ資金 Eurocurrency
ユーロ資金市場 Eurocurrencies market
ユーロ市場 Euromarket
ユーロ証券 Eurosecurity
ユーロシンジケート・ローン Eurosyndicate loan
ユーロ/スイスフランのショート short EURCHF
ユーロ中期債 EMTN (Euro medium-term note)
ユーロトップ100指数 Eurotop 100 Index
ユーロトラック Eurotrack
ユーロドル Eurodollar
ユーロドル債 eurodollar bond
ユーロドル先物オプション Eurodollar futures option
ユーロドルCD eurodollar CD (certificate of deposit)
ユーロドル市場 Eurodollar market
ユーロドル定期預金 Eurodollar time deposit
ユーロドル預金 Eurodollar deposit
ユーロドル預金金利先物 Eurodollar depositary interest futures
ユーロノート・ファシリティ Euronote facility
ユーロピアン・オプション取引所 EOE (European Options Exchange)
ユーロ/米ドル EURUSD
ユーロポンド債 Europound bond
ユーロボンド市場 European bond market
ユーロマネー Euro-money；Euromoney
ユーロマルク先物 Euromark futures
行 過 ぎ overshoot
雪だるま式の snowballing
行 詰 り impasse
行詰り相場 locked market
行き場の定まらない資金 idle money
輸出依存 export dependence
輸出依存度 degree of dependence upon exports
輸出依存の export-dependent
輸出カルテル export cartel
輸出関数 export function
輸出管理規定 export compliance program
輸出関連株 export stocks
輸出規制 export restriction
輸出業者信用 export supplier credit
輸出競争 export competition
輸出競争力への低下圧力 pressure on competitive exports
輸出許可 export permission
輸出禁制品 contraband of export
輸出金融 export financing
輸出構成 export mix
輸出産業 export industry
輸出自主規制 voluntary restriction of export
輸出自主規制協定 VRA (voluntary restraint agreement)
輸 出 者 exporter
輸出承認 approval of export license
輸出承認証 export license
輸出奨励金 export bounty
輸出所得安定化制度 STABEX (stabilization of export earnings)
輸出申告 export declaration
輸出信用 export credit；shipper's usance
輸出信用状 export letter of credit
輸出信用保証 export credit guarantee
輸 出 税 export duties；export tax
輸出セクター export sector

輸出代金 export proceeds
輸 出 高 export volume
輸出手形 export bill
輸出ドライブ export drive
輸 出 入 EXIM (Export-Import)
輸出入銀行 eximbank；export-import bank
輸出入物価指数 export and import price index
輸出入ローン export import loan
輸出の収益性 export profitability
輸出の伸び export growth
輸出の不調 disappointing export；sluggish level of export
輸出物価指数 export price index
輸出変動補償融資制度 cooperative financing facility
輸 出 法 export law
輸出補助金 export subsidy
輸出前貸し export advance
輸出前貸勘定 export advanced account
輸出前貸金融 export advance loan
輸出免許 EL (export license)
輸出免税 export exemption
輸出ユーザンス export usance
輸出利益 export earnings
譲受会社 transferee company
譲 受 人 assignee；transferee
輸 送 transport
輸 送 費 transportation cost
輸送方法 mode of transportation
輸送保険 transportation insurance
輸送用機器業界 transportation equipment industry
輸送用機器先物 transportation equipment futures
油濁賠償責任保険 oil pollution liability insurance
ユニーク・セリング・プロポジション unique selling proposition
ユニタリー・タックス unitary tax
ユニット・オブ・アカウント債 unit of account bond
ユニット型投資信託 unit type investment trust
ユニット投資信託 equity investment trust
ユニット投信単独運用ファンド single exempt fund
ユニット・トラスト unit trust
ユニット・リンク・ファンド unit linked fund
ユニット・リンク保険 unit linked insurance
ユニット・リンク保険ボンド unit linked bond
ユニット・シェア投資信託 USIT (unit share investment trust)
ユニバーサル生命保険 universal life insurance
ユニバーサル・バンキング universal banking
ユニバーサル保険 universal life insurance
輸入依存度 degree of dependence upon imports
輸入インフレ import-driven inflation
輸入課徴金 import surcharge
輸入カルテル import cartel
輸入関数 import function
輸入管理 import control
輸入規制 import restriction
輸入許可 import permit
輸入許可証 IL (import license)
輸入禁制品 contraband of import
輸入金融 import finance
輸入決済手形制度 import settlement bill system
輸 入 国 import country
輸入資金貸付制度 import financing system
輸入承認証 import license
輸入申告 declaration of import
輸入信用 import credit
輸 入 税 import duty；import tax；impost
輸入性向 propensity to import
輸入税表 import duties tariff
輸入セクター import sector
輸入代替 import substitute
輸入担保荷物保管証 TR (trust receipt)
輸入通関 import clearance

輸入手形 import bill
輸入手形決済相場 acceptance rate
輸入比率 import ratio
輸入物価 import price
輸入物価指数 import price index
輸入保証金 import guarantee money
輸入ユーザンス import usance
輸 入 量 import volume
輸入割当 import quota
緩やかな回復 moderate recovery

ヨ

要　　因 factor
要因分析 factor analysis
用役生産高法 services output method
用役潜在力 service potential
用役単位 service unit
用役提供 service provision
要 役 地 dominant estate
要確認先 referable name
要管理先債権 loans to substandard borrowers
要求払い payable on demand
要求払勘定 demand account
要求払債務 demand debt；repayable on demand
要求払手形 demand note
要求払負債 demand liability
要求払預金 demand deposit
要求利益率 required rate of return
要　　件 requirements
様　　式 format
様式の例示 illustrative format
要式契約 formal contract
養生期間 cure period
用水地役権 servitude for use of water
様 子 見 on the sideline
様子見スタンス wait-and-see stance
容積貨物 measurement cargo
用船契約 charter contract；charterparty
要素価格 factor price
要素技術 factor technology
要素原価 factor cost
要素収益率 factor return
要素所得 factor income
要素所得の支払い payment of factor income
要素の合計 aggregation of elements
要素別計算書 objective statement
要素別原価 object cost
要素別原価計算 elementary cost accounting
用　　地 land required for
用地修復引当金 provision for site restoration cost
用 地 費 land cost
用地品質条件 land quality terms
要注意先 tagged borrowers
要注意先債権 loans requiring attention
要注意銘柄 watch list
容認される投資 permissible investment
容認賃借物件 tenancy at sufferance
容認できる水準 acceptable level
容認不動産物件 estate at sufferance
要物契約 contract in kind
要　　約 abstract；summary
要約勘定式 condensed account form
要約財務情報 condensed financial information
要約財務諸表 summarized financial statements
要約財務データ selected financial data
要約された情報 summarized information
要約式キャッシュフロー計算書 condensed cash flow statement
要約式財務諸表 condensed financial statements
要約損益計算書 condensed income statement
要約貸借対照表 condensed balance sheet
要約中間財務情報 condensed interim financial information
要約分類された condensed and classified
要約報告式 condensed report form
要　　覧 fact book
要　　領 gist
養老年金満期までの期間 endowment period
養老保険 endowment insurance
養老保険証書 endowment policy
養老モーゲージ endowment mortgage
ヨーヨー株式 yo-yo stock

ヨーロッパ経済委員会 ECE (Economic Commission for Europe)
ヨーロピアン・オプション European option
予期しないインフレ unanticipated inflation
予期しないディスインフレ unanticipated disinflation
預　　金 money in bank
預金（政府預金除く） deposits (excluding those of the government)
預金集め deposit taking business
預金受入機関の所要準備 reserve requirements of depositary institutions
預金受入金融機関 depository institution
預金貸付 deposit loan
預金勘定年金 deposit account pension
預金記入帳 deposit diary
預金金利 deposit rate；interest on deposit
預金現金 cash in banks and hand
預金小切手 bank cashier's check
預金債務 deposit liability
預金シェア deposit share
預金市場 deposit market
預金支払準備率 cash reserve ratio
預金者保護 depositor protection
預金準備 reserve requirements
預金準備率 deposit reserve ratio；reserve requirement
預金承継方式 purchase and assumption
預金証書 deposit certificate
預金乗数 deposit multiplier
預金精算払方式 deposit payoff
預金制度 deposit system
預金全額支払い deposit payoff
預金戦争 deposit war
預金担保貸付 loan secured by deposit
預金通貨 deposit currency；deposit money
預金通帳 deposit book
預金伝票 deposit slip
預金等受入金融機関に係る検査マニュアル Inspection Manual for Depository Financial Institutions
預金の預け入れ placement of deposit
預金の譲渡禁止 prohibition of deposit transfer
預金の全額保護 protection of the full deposited amount
預金の引出 deposit withdrawal
預金ファシリティ合意 DFA (deposit facility agreement)
預金ファシリティ融資合意 DFLA (deposit facility loan agreement)
預金歩留り deposit-to-loan ratio
預金振替方式 deposit transfer
預金保険 deposit insurance
預金保険機構 DIC (Deposit Insurance Corporation)
預金保険機構住専勘定拠出金 provision of funds to the Deposit Insurance Corporation's "Jusen account"
預金保険機構特例業務基金等国債 government bonds issued to Deposit Insurance Corporation
預金保険機構の改革 reform of the deposit insurance system
預金保険救済 deposit insurance bailout
預金保険制度 deposit insurance system
預金保険法 Deposit Insurance Law
預金窓口 deposit window
預金目減り depreciation of deposit by inflation
預金元帳 deposit ledger
預金利子税 tax on deposit
預金利率 rate of interest on deposit
翌営業日渡し regular settlement
翌月受渡し over-the-month delivery
翌　月　物 over-month loan
翌月渡し value next month
翌日受渡し overnight delivery
翌日決済 T(trade day)+1 settlement
翌日資金化資金 next day fund
翌日に繰り下げる revert to the following day
翌日物レポ overnight repo
翌日返済 overnight payment
翌　日　物 overnight money

翌日物コール overnight call
翌日物コール・レート overnight call rate
翌日渡し value tomorrow
抑止力 deterrent
抑制効果 damping effect
抑制措置 control measure
翌月物 over-month repurchase
翌々日決済 skip-day settlement ; T(trade date)+2 settlement
横軸 y-axis
横ばいになる level off
予算 budget
予算案 proposed budget
予算委員会 Budget Committee
予算移替え rearrangement of budget item
予算・会計管理局 Office of Budget and Fiscal Operations
予算化されている損失 budgeted loss
予算監査 budget audit
予算勘定 budgetary account
予算繰入れ direct budget transfer
予算原価 budgeted cost
予算原則 budget principle
予算合意 budget agreement
予算差異 budget variance ; spending variance
予算差異分析 analysis of budget variance
予算削減 spending cut
予算策定 budgeting
予算支出 budget outlay ; budgetary expenditure
予算実地監査官 Budget Inspector
予算循環 budget cycle
予算純計 net budget
予算制度 budget system
予算総則 general provisions of the budget
予算単一主義 principle of single budget
予算単年度主義 one year budget principle
予算超過 cost overrun
予算手続 budgetary procedure
予算統制 budgetary control
予算の計上 budgetary appropriation
予算の配賦と執行 allocation and execution of budget
予算配分 budget allotment
予算編成 budgetary process ; compilation of the budget
余資 surplus funds
予実管理 actual expenses versus budget control
余剰金 surplus
余剰材料 surplus material
余剰資金 excess cash
余剰人員解雇計画 redundancy plan
余剰スプレッド excess spread
余剰の現金 idle cash
余剰保険料 dump in premium
与信監査 credit reviews
与信管理 credit control ; credit exposure management
与信管理目的で for credit management purposes
与信基準 lending standards ; underwriting standards
与信業務 credit business
与信限度額 credit limit
与信残高 existing exposure
与信承認 credit approval
与信の質 credit quality
与信の提供 extending credit
与信分析 credit analysis
与信リスク credit exposure
与信リスクの自己査定 self-assessment of credit exposure
予想以上の金利引下げ larger-than-expected rate cut
予想売上高 forecast of sales ; projected sales
予想外の動き surprise move
予想外の事象 unexpected event
予想給付評価方式 projected benefit method
予想原価 predicted cost
予想最大損害額 probable maximum loss
予想最大損失率 PML (probable maximum loss)
予想支払額 expected future payment
予想収益水準 prospective pay-off
予想収益率 prospective return

予想増益率 earnings growth expectations
予想損失 anticipated loss；expected loss；prospective loss
予想耐用年数 probable life
予想超過額 expected excess
予想超過リターン anticipated excess return
予想能力 expected output
予想PER prospective PER
予想売価 estimated selling price
予想配当 expected dividend；projected dividend
予想配当率 prospective dividend rate
予想平均利回り prospective yield average
予想変動率 expected volatility
予想保有期間収益率 estimated holding period return
予想利益 prospective earnings
予想リスク・プレミアム prospective risk premium
予想リターン prospective return
予想利回り prospective yield
予想レンジ forecast broad range
予想を上回る業績 better-than-expected results
予　　測 forecast；projection
予測売上 expected sales；forecasted sales
予測価値 predictive value
予測可能性 predictability
予測可能な期間 foreseeable future
予測給付 projected benefit
予測給付債務 PBO (projected benefit obligation)
予測原価 projected cost
予測誤差 prediction error
予測収益率 projected rate of return
予測需要量 forecasted demand；projected demand
予測成長率 expected growth rate
予測耐用年数 projected useful life
予測単位積増方式 projected unit credit method
予測の修正 forecast change
予測配当率 projected dividend rate
予測パターン expected pattern
予測平均利回り projected yield average
予測保有期間収益率 projected holding-period rate of return
予測モデル forecasting model
予 測 率 projected rate
預貸金調査結果 Deposits, Loans, and Discounts Outstanding (Amount Outstanding of Deposits by Depositor, Loans and Discounts Outstanding by Industry, and Others)
預 貸 率 bank loan-deposit ratio
預　　託 deposit
預託株券 deposited stock certificate
預託株式 depository shares
預託勘定 deposit account
預託管理 deposit administration
預託管理基金 deposit administration fund
預託管理契約 deposit administration contract
預託機関 depositary organization
預託基金 deposit fund
預託期限 depository period
預 託 金 cash on deposit；deposited money
預託銀行 depositary bank；depository bank
預託金への繰入れ appropriation for the deposit
預託契約 depositary agreement
預託資産 depository assets
預託証券 DR (depository receipt)
預託証券の分布状況 distribution of depository shares
預託信託会社 DTC (depository trust company)
預託する offer the deposit
預託手数料 deposit fee
預託前株券 pre-deposited stock certificates
預託有価証券 deposited securities
預 貯 金 deposits and savings
予定給付支払額 expected benefit payment
予定原価 predetermined cost

ヨ

予定原価計算 predetermined cost system
予定購入 forecasted purchase
予定財源債 RAN (revenue anticipation bond)
予定された責務 envisaged obligation
予定されているキャッシュフロー scheduled cash flow
予定死亡率 expected mortality rate
予定収入 expected income
予定申告 provisional return
予定投資収益率 required return
予定取引 anticipated transactions
予定納税 estimated tax prepayment
予定納税額滞納処分 disposition of failure to pay income tax in advance
予定納税額の通知 notification of estimated tax prepayment
予定納税額の督促 claim of prepayment of income tax
予定納税制度 income tax prepayment system；provisional tax payment system based on the previous year's tax amount
予定配賦率 predetermined burden rate
予定ヘッジ anticipatory hedge
予定保険 provisional insurance
予定保険金支払額 expected claims
予定保険証券 provisional policy
予定保有期間 anticipated holding period
予定利率 crediting rate；expected rate of return on insurance premium invested；projected interest rate
ヨハネスブルク証券取引所 JSE (Johannesburg Stock Exchange)
予備格付け preliminary rating；prospective rating
予備株券 unissued certificate
予備監査 preliminary audit
予備クレーム preliminary claim
予備源泉徴収 backup withholding
予備支払人 referee in case of need
予備情報 preliminary information
予備審査 preliminary review
予備申請 preliminary application
予備貸借対照表 preliminary balance sheet
呼出状 summons
呼出板 annunciator board
呼　値 bid and asked price；bid and offer；nominal price quotation
呼値主導型 quote driven
呼値スプレッド bid ask spread；bid-offer spread
呼値単位 tick size
呼値の周知 announcement of bids and offers
呼値の順位 precedence of bids and offers
呼値の状況 bid and offer situation
呼値の単位 minimum variation of bids and offers
呼値の付合せ matching of bids and offers
予備報告書 preliminary statement
呼び水 pump-priming role
呼び水効果 pump-priming effect
余分工事クレーム extra work claims
余分な開示 redundant disclosure
読替え rewording
読み易さ legibility
予約公募 offer by subscription
予約販売 sale by subscription
予約販売収益 subscription income
余裕資金 fun money
余裕度 affordability
寄付き opening session
寄付買い buy on opening
寄付気配 opening tone
寄付値段 opening price；opening quotation
寄付値段注文 on-the-opening order
寄付値注文 at the opening order
寄付きばな just after the opening
ヨルダン・ディナール JOD (Jordanian dinar)
弱い市場 weak market
弱いチャンネル bearish channel
弱いドル weak dollar
弱　気 bearish
弱気コンソリデーション・パターン bearish consolidation patterns
弱気支持線 bearish support line
弱気市場 bearish market

弱 気 筋 bear interests
弱気相場 bear market；soft market
弱気抵抗線 bearish resistance line
弱気の地合 bearish mood；bearish sentiment
弱気見通し bearish view
弱気リバーサル・パターン bearish reversal patterns
弱 含 み negative
弱含みな需要 weaker demand
弱含みになっている stalling
弱もちあい unchanged tc slightly lower
4営業日決済 T+3
4営業日目決済 T(trade day)+3 settlement
4営業日渡し triple settlement
4限月取引 four contract months
400を試す展開 attempt of the 400 mark
401k cash or deferred arrangement
401k年金制度 401 (k) plan
403b年金制度 403 (b) plan

ラ

ライセンス契約 license agreement
ライフ・コンサルタント life consultant
ライフ・サイクル life cycle
LIBOR London Inter-Bank Offered Rate
LIBOR以下 sub-LIBOR
ライン部門 line department
ラウンディング・リバーサル・パターン rounding reversal pattern
ラオス・キップ LAK (Lao kip)
ラグ効果 lag effect
落　札 successful bid
落札決定書 letter of acceptance；letter of award
落札者 successful bidder
落札利回り auction clearing yield
ラグ分析 lag analysis
ラスト・リゾート last resort
ラスパイレス方程式 Laspeyres formula
ラダー型運用 ladder portfolio management
ラッセル指数 Russel Index
ラッファー曲線 Laffer curve
ラップ口座 wrap account
ラップ商品 wrapper
ラテンアメリカ・カリブ経済委員会 ECLAC(Economic Commission for Latin America and the Caribbean)
ラトビア・ラット LVL (Latvian lat)
RUF revolving underwriting facility
欄外約款 marginal clauses
ランキング制度 ranking system
乱高下 erratic fluctuation；violent fluctuation
乱高下相場 wide fluctuation of market
乱　数 random number
乱数表 table of random numbers
ランダム・ウォーク理論 random walk theory
ランナウェイ・ギャップ runaway gap
乱　用 abuse

ラ

リ

利上げ interest rate raise；rate hike
リアルタイム real time
リアルタイム決済 real time settlement
リアルタイム処理 real time processing
リーエン lien
リーエンの解除 discharge of lien
リーエンの放棄 release of lien
リーエンの保有者 holder of lien
リーガル・ディフィーザンス legal defeasance
リース lease
リースアップ lease-up
リーズ・アンド・ラグズ leads and lags
リース会計 lease accounting
リース会計基準 lease accounting standards
リース会社 leasing company
リース買取契約 lease purchase agreement
リース解約 canceled lease
リース期間 lease period；lease term
リース業務 leasing business
リース金融 lease financing
リース契約 lease agreement；leasing contract
リース契約条件 leasing arrangement
リース契約条項 lease provision
リース行為 leasing activity
リース債権 lease receivable
リース債権債 LOB (lease obligation bond)
リース財源債 lease obligation bond
リース債権担保証券 lease backed note
リース債権の流動化 securitization of leases
リース債務 lease liability
リース産業 leasing industry
リース資産 assets under the lease；leased asset；leased property
リース資産からの控除 deduction from the leased asset
リース支払額の指数 lease payment index
リース収益 lease income；revenue from leases
リース取得費用 lease acquisition cost
リース条項の確約 commitment to the provisions of the lease
リース上の計算利子率 interest rate implicit in the lease
リース設備資産の債務 leased equipment liability
リース投資未回収額 investment in lease
リース投資未回収総額 gross investment in lease
リース取引 lease transactions
リースの開始 inception of lease
リースの継続 continuation of lease
リースバック leaseback
リースバック取引 leaseback transaction
リース物件 lease property
リース物件の所有権 ownership of the leases
リース分類 lease classification
リース預託金 lease deposits
リース料 lease payment；rent expense
リース料受取額 lease payment receivable
リード・タイム lead time
利益 income；profit
利益確定を目的とした売却 selling at a profit
利益稼得能力 earnings-generating capacity
利益稼得過程 earnings process
利益が変動する事業 business with fluctuating profit
利益からの控除項目 deductions from income；deductions from profit
利益勘定 profit account
利益管理 profit control；profit management
利益共有契約 profit sharing arrangement

リ

利益曲線 profit curve
利益金対配当比率 ratio of dividends to earnings
利 益 減 profit slide
利益減額 reduced profit
利益貢献度 profit contribution
利益控除項目 income deduction
利益差異 profit variance
利益参加型金利契約 PIRA (participating interest rate agreement)
利益参加型投資 participating investment
利益参加金利契約 PRA (participating rate agreement)
利益参加社債 participating bond
利益実現 income realization
利益集団 special interests group
利益取得者 pernor of profits
利益準備金 earned reserve；earned surplus reserve；retained surplus
利益剰余金 accumulated earnings；earned surplus；retained earnings
利益剰余金計算書 statement of earned surplus；retained earnings statement
利益剰余金積立の取崩し return of the appropriation to the retained earnings
利益剰余金の処分 appropriation of retained earnings
利益剰余金への振替 addition to retained earnings
利益処分 appropriation of profit；distribution of net profit
利益処分勘定 net profit appropriation account
利益処分による株式消却 cancellation of stock by distribution of net profit
利益処分による社外流出額 amount to the outside by distribution of net profit
利益処分の部 profit appropriation section
利益図表 profit control chart
利益成長率 profit growth rate
利益積立金 revenue reserves
利益積立金額 revenue reserve amount
利益積立金の資本組入 capitalization of accumulated earnings
利益手数料 contingent commission
利益に反する供述 declaration against interest
利益の足かせ lagging profit
利益の安定化 income stability
利益の回復 rebound in profit
利益の額 amount of profit
利益の確定 lock in gain
利益の再投資 plowing-back
利益の時系列変動 time series behavior of earnings
利益の質 quality of earnings
利益の増減 changes in profit
利益の共変動 co-movement of earnings
利益の伸び profit growth
利益の発表 profit announcement
利益の平準化 income leveling；income smoothing
利益の変動性 volatility of the return
利益の予想外の変動 surprises in earnings
利益配当 distribution of profits；interest dividend
利益配当株 participating stock
利益配当税 tax on dividend
利益配当ファンド with-profit fund
利益発表 earnings announcement
利益分配 profit share
利益分配金含み cum-profit distribution
利益分配債 income share note
利益分配社債 profit-sharing bond
利益分配制度 profit-sharing plan
利益分配プラン profit-sharing plan
利益への寄与 earnings contribution
利益保険 loss of profit insurance；profit insurance
利益保険証券 policy proof of interest
利益モーメンタム earnings momentum
利益目標 earnings target
利益戻し profit commission
利益余剰金計算書 statement of retained earnings
利 益 率 margin of profit；profit rate
利益率の低下 decrease in profit rate；slimmer profit margins

利益留保 retention of earnings
利益累積型投信 contractual accumulation plan
利益連動型給与 PRP (profit related pay)
利益割当 profit quota
利益を乗せる mark up
リオープン re-opening
利 落 ち ex-interest；XC (ex coupon)
利落期間 ex-interest period
利落債券 ex-interest bond
リカード効果 Ricardo effect
理解可能性 understandability
利害関係 particular interest
利害関係者 interested party
利害対立 conflict of risk
利害の一致 community of interests
利害の衝突 conflict of interest
陸揚期間 lay-days
利 食 い profit taking
利食い売り profit taking pullback
陸 運 業 land transportation industry
陸上運送費 overland freight
利 権 right and interest
利権獲得 acquisition of concessions
利権譲渡 transfer of rights
利 権 屋 concession hunter
利 源 source of profit
履 行 fulfillment
履行期日到来後3カ月以上経過した債権 loans past due three months or more
履行計算書 discharge statement
履行証拠金 performance guarantee deposit
履行費用 executory cost
履行不能 impossibility of performance
履行保証 performance guarantee
履行保証証券 performance bond
履行保証保険 performance bond insurance
リコース形式 recourse form
リコース契約 recourse agreement
リコース・ローン recourse loan
リザーブ・トランシェ reserve tranche
理 財 局 Financial Bureau
理財局管理課 Fiscal Investment and Loan Management Division
理財局局長 Director-General of the Financial Bureau
理財局次長 Deputy Director-General of the Financial Bureau
理財調査官 Special Officer for Research on Finance
利 下 げ rate cut
利下圧力 pressure to cut interest rates
利下げの実施 easing decision
利 ざ や interest rate spread；profit margin of interest rate；rate spread
利ざや設定 interest margin charges
利ざやの拡大 margin improvement
離散時間型 discrete time
離散分布 discrete distribution
離散変数型 discrete variable
理 事 executive director
理 事 会 board of governors
理事会構成員 board member
理事会声明 board statement
理 事 長 president
利子一括払利付金融債 debenture with lump-sum interest payment at maturity
利子及び割引料 payment on interest and discount rate
利子計算期間 interest accrual period
利子計算期間に対応する利子 accrued interest corresponding to the interest accrual period
利子源泉税 withholding tax on interest
利子支払額 coupon amount
利子支払期間 coupon period
利子支払日 interest due date
利子所得 interest income
利子所得の帰属者 real obtainer of interest income
利 子 税 interest tax
利子税金控除前利益 PBIT (profit before interest and taxes)
利子積立 accumulations of interest
利子の元金組入 inclusion of interest into principal
利子の現金支払額 cash value of coupon

利子の日割計算 computation of interest on a per diem basis
利子払いのみ融資 interest only loan
利子費用 interest charge ; interest cost
利子含み cum-interest
利子負担 interest burden ; interest cover
利子平価理論 interest-rate parity theory
利子平衡税 IET (interest equalization tax)
利子補給金 interest subsidy
利子率体系 system of interest rates
利子率に関するリスク interest-rate risk
利子率変化 interest rate change
利子理論 theory of interest
利潤インフレーション profit inflation
利潤原理型投資関数 investment function of profit principle type
利潤証券 profit-sharing securities
利潤分配信託 profit sharing trust
利殖部分 inside buildup of cash value
離職補償 termination indemnity
離 職 率 labor turnover
リスク・アービトラージ risk arbitrage
リスク愛好者 risk lover
リスク・アタッチ attachment of the risk
リスク・アセット比率 risk asset ratio
リスク移転 risk transfer
リスク・ウエート risk weight
リスク・エクスポージャー risk exposure
リスク開示書 risk disclosure statement
リスク回避 risk aversion
リスク回避志向の強まり spike in risk aversion
リスク回避姿勢の軟化 easing risk aversion
リスク回避者 risk averter
リスク回避的態度 risk averse attitude
リスク回避の risk averse
リスク格差 risk differentials
リスク・カテゴリー risk category
リスク・カバー率 adequacy of coverage
リスク・カントリー・コントロール risk country control
リスク感応度指標 risk sensitive index
リスク管理 risk control
リスク管理債権 risk management loan ; risk-managed claims
リスク管理戦略 risk management strategy
リスク管理体制 risk management system
リスク管理の厳格化 tightening of risk management
リスク管理方針 risk management policy
リスク管理方針文書 written risk management policy
リスク関連資本 risk bearing capital
リスク・キャピタル risk capital
リスク許容度 risk tolerance
リスク軽減手段 risk reduction measure
リスク軽減戦略 risk reduction strategy
リスク源 source of risk
リスク減殺 risk reduction or elimination
リスク限度額 risk threshold
リスク構造 risk structure
リスク債権 risk-monitored loans
リスク削減 risk reduction
リスク査定 risk underwriting
リスク資産 risky assets
リスク資産ミックス risky assets mix
リスク・収益グループ risk-return group
リスク証券 risk securities
リスク情報 risk information
リスク制御 risk-controlled
リスク・セクター risk sector
リスク選好 risk appetite ; risk preference
リスク選好態度 risk seeking attitude
リスク選好度 risk preference
リスク選択 risk selection
リスク測度 measure of risk
リスク対応資本 RBC (risk based capital)
リスク仲介機能 risk intermediary function
リスク中立者 risk neutral
リスク調整 risk adjustment
リスク調整後の割引率 risk-adjusted discount rate
リスク調整済資産 risk-adjusted assets
リスク調整済資本 risk-adjusted capital
リスク調整済収益 risk-adjusted return
リスク調整分析 risk-adjusted analysis
リスク調整法 risk-adjusted approach

リスク特性 risk characteristics；risk profile
リスクと収益の関係 risk-return relationship
リスクと収益率のトレードオフ risk-return trade-off
リスクと報酬 risk and reward
リスクとリターンの選好 risk return preference
リスク・ニュートラル確率 risk neutral probability
リスク・ニュートラル姿勢 risk neutral attitude
リスク・ニュートラル測度 risk neutral measure
リスク・ニュートラル評価法 risk-neutral valuation
リスク認識プロファイル risk perception profile
リスクの大きい risky
リスクの市場価格 market price of risk
リスクの種類 risk class
リスクの定量化 quantification of risk
リスクのない取引 riskless transaction
リスクの負担 exposure to risk
リスク評価 risk appraisal；risk assessment；risk evaluation
リスク・ファクター risk factor
リスク負担 risk seeking；risk taking
リスク・プレミアム risk premium
リスク・プロファイル exposure profile
リスク分散 risk distribution；risk diversification；risk sharing；spread of risk
リスク分類 risk category
リスク・ベース自己資本比率 risk-based capital ratio
リスク・ベース資本金 risk-based capital
リスク・ベースの自己資本基準 risk based capital standards
リスク・ベースの自己資本比率 RBC (risk based capital)
リスク・ベースの保険料 risk based premium
リスク・ヘッジ risk hedge
リスク・ペナルティ risk penalty
リスク保険 risk insurance
リスク保険商品 risk insurance product
リスク・マネジメント risk management
リスク見積り risk estimation
リスク見通し risk picture
リスク無取引 risk free transaction
リスク要因 risk parameter
リスク要素分解 risk decomposition
リスケジューリング rescheduling
リストラ関連株 restructuring related stock
リストラ経費 restructuring charge
リストラ資金 restructuring capital
リストラ費用 cost of restructuring
リスボン証券取引所 LSE (Lisbon Stock Exchange)
リセット債 reset bond
理想標準原価 ideal standard cost
利　　息 interest rate
利息受取方法選択権 deposit option
利息カバレッジ比率 times interest earned ratio
利息起算日 dated date
利息繰延債券 deferred interest bond
利息クレーム interest claims
利息計算 interest computation
利息計上停止 non-accrual of interest
利息控除 interest deduction
利息収益 interest revenue
利息制限法 law concerning restrictions on the maximum interest rate
利息付債券 active bond
利息の資産化 capitalization of interest
利息の支払猶予 interest payment moratorium
利息の調整額 yield adjustments
利息のみストリップ債 interest only strips
利息の未払い accrual of interest
利息配当 dividend on interest
利息費用 interest expense
利息負担倍率 times interest earned
利息部分 interest element
利息付与 interest credit
利 息 法 interest method

リ

リターン極大者 return maximizer
リターン分布 return distribution
リターン変動幅 return volatility
リターン・ライン return line
リターンをもたらす pay off
利他主義 altruism
利付き interest bearing
利付金融債 coupon bank debenture；interest-bearing bank debenture
利付国債 coupon-bearing government bond
利付債 coupon bearing bond；coupon bond；coupon paying issues；interest-bearing bond
利付債券の裸値 ex-interest for interest-bearing bond
利付債利回り曲線 coupon curve
利付資金 coupon fund
利付証券 interest-bearing security
利付手形 interest-bearing note
利付転換社債型新株予約権付社債券 coupon-bearing-convertible-bond type corporate bonds with new share reservation rights
利付投資 interest-bearing investment
利付負債 interest-bearing debt
立証 demonstration
立証可能な想定 supportable assumption
立証責任 burden of proof
立証できる債権 provable debt
立法措置 legislation
リテール金融機関 retail institutions
リテール・バンキング retail banking
リトアニア・リタス LTL (Lithuanian litas)
利得 gain
利得関数 payoff function
利得上限 maximum gain
リニア債 linear bond
リバーサル・デー reversal day
リバース・スワップ reverse swap
リバース・ゼロ・クーポン・スワップ reverse zero coupon swap
リバース・デュアル・カレンシー債 reverse dual currency bond
リバース・デュアル債 reverse dual bond
リバース・モーゲージ reverse mortgage
リバース・レポ reverse repo；reverse repurchase agreement
リパッケージ債 repackage bond
利幅 profit margin
利幅率 margin ratio
リハビリ・リース譲渡 RLT (rehabilitate-lease-transfer)
利払い coupon payment；interest outlay；interest payment
利払回数 coupon frequency；number of coupon payments
利払期日 coupon payment date
利払繰延モーゲージ deferred interest mortgage
利払税引前利益 EBIT (earnings before interest and tax
利払いのミスマッチ payment mismatches
利払日 coupon date
利払費 interest payment expense
利払方式別分類 classification by the method of interest payment
利払方法 interest payment method
利払いを残している債券 bonds with remaining cash flows
リバランス戦略 rebalancing strategies
リビア・ディナール LYD (Libyan dinar)
リヒテンシュタイン・フラン CHF (Liechtenstein franc)
リファイナンス方式 refinance system
リフォーマット版 reformatted version
利札 coupon；cuttings；interest coupon
利札落ち coupon off；ex-coupon
利札付き coupon on；cum coupon
利札付債権 coupon bond
利札付保険 coupon policy
利札面に記載される利子 interest indicated on the coupon
リフレーション reflation
リフレーション政策 reflation policy
リベリア・ドル LRD (Liberian dollar)
リボルビング・アンダーライティング・ファシリティ revolving underwriting

facility
リボルビング・カード revolving card
リボルビング・クレジット revolving credit
リボルビング引受保証枠 revolving underwriting facilities
リボルビング・ローン revolving loan
利 回 り yield
利回買い buying on a yield basis
利回改善スイッチ yield improvement switch
利回格差 difference in yield ; yield curve differential ; yield divergence ; yield spread
利回期間構造 term structure of yield
利回基準 yield measure
利回曲線 yield curve
利回曲線の平坦化 yield curve flattening
利回曲線の平板化 flattening of the yield curve
利回曲線リスク yield curve risk
利回計算 yield formula
利回向上 yield enhancement
利回構造 yield structure
利回りコンベンショナル方式 conventional method of competitive yield auction
利回上昇 rise in yields
利回水準 yield standard
利回追求 quest for yield
利回低下 easing of yield
利回等価 yield equivalence
利回入札 yield auction
利回りの圧縮 spread compression
利回りの改善 pick-up of yield
利回りの逆乖離 reverse yield gap
利回りの下落局面 falling yield environment
利回りの上昇局面 rising yield environment
利回りの魅力 yield appeal
利 回 表 yield book
利回物色 reach for yield
利回りベース yield base
利回りへの上昇圧力 upward pressure on yield
利回保証契約 guaranteed return contract
利回問題 yield bogeys
利回優位 yield advantage
利回要因 yield factor
利回りを生む投資 yielding investment
リミティッド・リコース債務 limited recourse obligation
略式手続 summary proceedings
略　　称 short title
流　　出 exodus ; outflow
流　　通 circulation
流通革命 distribution revolution
流通貨幣 current money
流通機構 distribution structure
流通業界 distribution industry
流通系カード retail credit card
流通経路 distribution channel
流通権原証券 negotiable document
流通合理化 streamlining of distribution channels
流通市場 after market ; secondary market ; trading market
流通市場CDO secondary CDO
流通市場操作 operation in the secondary market
流通市場の形成 formation of secondary market
流通市場の流動性 secondary market liquidity
流通資本 circulating capital
流通証券 negotiable instrument ; traded securities
流通証券法 Negotiable Instruments Act
流 通 税 circulation tax
流通速度 velocity of circulation
流通手形 negotiable bill
流通銘柄 liquid stock
流　　動 current
流動資産 current assets ; liquid assets
流動資産回転期間 current-asset cycle
流動資産回転率 current assets turnover (ratio)
流動資産仮説 liquid-asset hypothesis
流動資産比率 current asset ratio
流動指数 liquidity index

流動資本 liquid capital
流 動 性 liquidity
流動性格差 liquidity differential
流動性管理 liquidity management
流動性危機 liquidity crisis
流動性効果 liquidity effect
流動性指向相場 liquidity-driven market
流動性需要 liquidity demand
流動性準備金 liquid reserve
流動性ジレンマ liquidity dilemma
流動性スキーム liquidity scheme
流動性選好 liquidity preference
流動性選好仮説 liquidity preference hypothesis
流動性選好理論 liquidity preference theory
流動性創出 liquidity creation
流動性相場株 liquidity-driven issue
流動性調整済みの liquidity adjusted
流動性動機による売買 liquidity-motivated transactions
流動性のある市場 liquid market
流動性のある投資 liquid investment
流動性の管理 liquidity management
流動性の供給 provision of liquidity
流動性の順序 order of one's liquidity
流動性の乏しさ reduced liquidity
流動性のニーズ liquidity needs
流動性の低い資産 illiquid assets
流動性の低い銘柄 illiquid issues
流動性の逼迫 tightening of liquidity
流動性の不足 liquidity scarcity
流動性のワナ liquidity trap
流動性配列 current-first order
流動性配列法 current arrangement；order of liquidity
流動性比率 liquidity ratio；solvency ratio
流動性不足 illiquidity
流動性プレミアム liquidity premium
流動性分散 liquidity diversification
流動性分析 liquidity analysis
流動性変換の機能 function to change the degree of liquidity of funds
流動性ポジション liquidity position
流動性預金 liquid deposit
流動性リスク liquidity risk
流動性リスクへのエクスポージャ exposure to liquidity risk
流動比率 current ratio；working capital ratio
流動負債 current liability
流動負債比率 ratio of current liabilities to net worth
流動部分 liquid part；current portion
流　　入 inflow；influx
留　　保 retention
留保株式 shares reserved for issuance
留 保 金 retention money
留保金額 undistributed profits
留保控除額 allowance for undistributed profits
留保事項 reservation
留保資産 reserved property
留保収益税 accumulated earning tax
留保条件 under reserve
留保剰余金 accumulated surplus
留保所得に対する税 tax on undistributed profits
留保持ち分 retained interests
留保利益 accumulated profit；reserved profit；retained earnings
留保利益合計 cumulative retained profit
留保利益控除額 accumulated earnings credit
留保利益税 accumulated profit tax
留 保 率 retention rate
流　　用 diversion
領　　域 spectrum
領　　海 maritime belt；territorial waters
両　　替 exchange of money
両 替 商 money changer
利用価値 usefulness
利用可能債券 available bond
利用可能資産 available assets
利用可能資本 available capital
利用可能な純資産 net assets available
利 用 権 leasehold interest
利用原価 utilized cost

利用者グループ user group
利用上限額 net debit cap
料　金 dues
料金財源債 toll revenue bond
料金条項 rate covenant
糧　券 ryo ken
量産原価 volume cost
量産効果 volume efficiency
領事送り状 consular invoice
領収日 date of receipt
領収未済で received in arrears
両建て straddling
両建注文 cross order
両建預金 compensatory deposit
領　置 official retain
量的緩和 monetary easing
量的基準値 quantitative threshold
量的金融指標 quantitative monetary indicator
量的経済政策 quantitative economic policy
量的情報 quantitative information
量的信用規制 quantitative credit control
量的な指針 quantified guidance
量的要因 quantitative factor
遼寧省 Liaoning
両端入れ both days included
両罰規定 penalty against employer and employee
両方向の値付け making two-sided markets
療養費用 confinement cost
料率規制 rate regulation
料率協定 tariff agreement
料率構造 rate structure
料率設定リスク pricing risk
料率段階の変更 bracket creep
料率の基礎 rate base
料率の適用差別 rate discrimination
料率変動リース graduated lease
旅客収入 passenger traffic receipts
旅行者税 tourist tax
旅行信用状 traveller's letter of credit
旅費交通費 traveling expenses
旅費手当 traveling benefits
LYON LYON (liquid yield option note)
利率格差 interest differential
利率交渉型モーゲージ negotiable rate mortgage
利率特進年金 jump rate annuity
利率保証インデックス・ファンド guaranteed index fund
利率保証勘定 guaranteed account
利率保証契約 guaranteed interest contract
利率要因 interest factor
リレーショナル銀行 relational bank
リレーショナル・データベース relational database
リレーションシップ貸付 relationship lending
リロード reload
リロード・オプション reload option
リロード特性 reload feature
理論価格 theoretical price
理論価格算出 calculation of theoretical price
理論価値 theoretical value
理論金利 theoretical rates
理論先物価格 theoretical futures price
理論上の変化 hypothetical change
理論値 theoretical value
理論値モデル theoretical value model
理論的為替相場 theoretical rate of exchange
理論的生産能力 theoretical capacity
臨界値 critical value
リンク債 link note；linked bond
臨　検 official inspection
臨時会員代表 substitute member representative
臨時株主総会 special meeting of security holders
臨時挙行 temporary holding
臨時金利調整法 Temporary Money Rates Adjustment Law
臨時繰上償還 extraordinary call
臨時経費支出 extraordinary expenditure
臨時決議 extraordinary resolution
臨時雇用 non-regular employment
臨時資産損失 unexpected property loss

臨時支出 casual expenses
臨時修繕費 extraordinary repairs
臨時収入 perquisite
臨時所得 extraordinary income ; temporary income
臨時税理士 temporary tax accountant
臨時総会 extraordinary general meeting ; special general meeting
臨時損益項目 nonrecurring item
臨時賃貸料 extraordinary rent
臨時停止 extraordinary suspension ; temporary suspension
臨時的損益 unusual gains or losses
臨時の徴収 urgent collection
臨 時 費 contingent outlay ; emergency funds ; extra expenditure
臨時変更 temporary change
臨時報告書 current report
臨時利益 nonrecurring profit
臨時利得 nonrecurring gain
臨店検査 field examination
輪番オペ operations conducted in rotation
輪 番 制 rotational system
倫　　理 ethics
倫理規程 code of ethics
倫理ファンド ethical fund

ル

累 加 法 cumulative method
累計発生労働時間 percentage of labor hours
類　　似 resemblance
類似金融機関 similar financial statements
類似資産 similar asset
類似証券 comparable securities
類似する取引 like transaction
類 似 性 similarity
類似の投資媒体 similar investment media
類 似 品 similar goods
類以物の作製 imitation
類似乱数 pseudo-random numbers
累進課税 graduated taxation；progressive taxation
累進所得税 progressive income tax
累 進 制 progressive nature
累 進 税 progressive tax
累進税率 progressive tax rate
累　　積 accumulation
累積赤字 accumulated deficit；cumulative deficit
累 積 額 accumulated amount
累積課税 cumulative taxation
累積型取引高税 cascade-type turnover tax
累積為替換算調整 cumulative translation adjustment
累積為替差額 cumulative exchange difference
累積給付債務 accumulated benefit obligation
累積黒字 cumulative surplus
累積限度額 cumulative maximum amount
累積限度額基準 cumulative limit
累積誤差 cumulative error
累積最低保険 cumulative minimum premium
累積債務 accumulated debt
累積債務国 heavily indebted country
累積修正額 cumulative adjustment
累 積 税 cascade tax
累 積 的 accumulative
累積的遺贈 cumulative legacy
累積的影響額 cumulative effect
累積的制限 cumulative limitation
累積的遡及修正額 cumulative retrospective adjustment
累積出来高 volume accumulation
累積的優先株 cumulative preferred shares
累積的優先権 cumulative preference right
累積投資 accumulated investment；cumulative investment
累積投資期間 accumulative investment period
累積投資プラン accumulative investment plan
累積投資ユニット accumulative investment unit
累積投票 cumulative voting
累積配当 accumulated dividend；cumulative dividend
累積配当型株式 accumulative stock
累積配当優先株式 accumulated preferred stock
累積発生原価 cost incurred to date
累積判決 accumulative judgment
累積引当額 accumulated allowance
累積部分 accumulation value
累積変化 cumulative change
累積優先 cumulative preference
累積優先株 cumulative preferred stock
累積優先配当 cumulative preference dividends
累積ユニット accumulation unit
累積利益 accumulated income
累積利息 accumulated interest
累　　損 cumulative loss
ルーズリーフ式帳簿 loose leaf book
ルーティッド・オーダー routed order
ルーブル合意 Louvre Accord

ルーマニア・レウ ROL (Romanian leu)
ルクセンブルグ金融協会 Luxembourg Monetary Institute
ルクセンブルグ・フラン LUF (Luxembourg franc)
ルック・バック・オプション look-back option
ルワンダ・フラン RWF (Rwanda franc)

レ

例外規定 exceptions
例外事項 exceptional items
例外的税率 exceptional rates of tax
例外的な性質 exceptional nature
例外の原則 exception principle
冷却期間 cooling time
例示の付録 illustrative appendix
例示目的 illustrative purpose
レオンチェフ逆説 Leontief's paradox
暦　月 calendar month
暦月制先物相場 calendar month delivery rate
暦月渡し calendar month delivery
暦月渡制 delivery system by calendar month
歴史的要因 historical factor
暦　年 CY (calendar year); natural year
暦年基準による方法 method based on the calendar year
暦　日 calendar day
レシオ ratio
レシオ・コール・スプレッド取引 ratio call spread transaction
レスキュー債 rescue bond
劣化資産 deteriorated assets
列　挙 enumeration
劣後案件 B-piece deal
劣後株 junior stock; subordinated stock
劣後株式 deferred share
劣後債 capital debenture; subordinated debenture
劣後債権 subordinated debt; subordinated receivables
劣後債権者 subordinated creditor
劣後債市場 subordinated debt market
劣後債務 junior debt
劣後資金の調達 subordinated funding
劣後資本 subordinated capital
劣後社債 subordinated bond
劣後受益権 subordinated beneficial rights
劣後証券 junior securities; subordinated securities
劣後条項 subordination clause
劣後条項付社債 subordinate debenture
劣後請求権 junior claim; subordinated claim
劣後性無担保社債 subordinated unsecured debenture
劣後トランシェ subordinated tranche
劣後の subordinated
劣後ペイメント・イン・カインド債 subordinated payment-in-kind bond
劣後持ち分 subordinated interest
劣後優先株 second-preferred stock
劣後預託金 subordinated deposit
劣後ローン subordinated loan
劣後割引債 subordinated discount bond
レッセフェール laissez-faire
劣等財 inferior goods
劣等資産 inferior assets
レッドヘリング目論見書 red-herring prospectus
劣マーチンゲール sub-martingale
レバノン・ポンド LBP (Lebanese pound)
レバレッジ leverage
レバレッジ型先物オプション・ファンド GFOF (geared futures and options fund)
レバレッジ係数 leverage factor
レバレッジ効果 leverage effect
レバレッジド・オプション leveraged option
レバレッジド資本再構成 leveraged recap
レバレッジド従業員持株制度 LESOP (leveraged employee stock ownership plan)
レバレッジド・ストック leveraged stock
レバレッジド・ストラテジック・アクイジシ

ョン leveraged strategic acquisition
レバレッジド・スワップ leveraged swap
レバレッジド投資会社 leveraged investment company
レバレッジド・バイアウト leveraged buyout
レバレッジド・ファイナンス証券 leveraged finance securities
レバレッジド・ホールディング leveraged holding
レバレッジド・ポジション leveraged position
レバレッジド・リース leveraged lease
レバレッジド・リキャピタライゼーション leveraged recapitalization
レバレッジ取引マーチャント LTM (leverage transaction merchant)
レバレッジド・ローン leveraged loan
レバレッジの高い high-leveraged
レバレッジ比率 leverage factor ratio
レバレッジ変化 leverage change
レビュー範囲 scope of review
レファレンス・ゾーン reference zone
レポ会員 repo member
レポ金利 repo rate；repurchase interest rate
レポ市場 repo market；RP market
レポ取引 repurchase transaction
レポ・レート repurchase rate
REMIC REMIC (real estate mortgage investment conduit)
連銀公開市場委員会 Federal Reserve Open Market Committee
連　結 consolidation
連結売上 consolidated sales
連結運転資金 consolidated working capital
連結営業利益 consolidated operating income
連結会計 consolidated accounting
連結勘定 consolidated account
連結キャッシュフロー計算書 consolidated statement of cash flow
連結グループ consolidated group
連結経常利益 consolidated current profit；consolidated ordinary income；consolidated recurring profit
連結決算 consolidated accounts
連結子会社 consolidated subsidiary
連結財務諸表 consolidated financial statements
連結財務諸表原則 accounting standards for consolidated financial statements
連結財務統計 consolidated financial statistics
連結差益 profit from consolidation
連結自己資本比率 consolidated capital adequacy ratio；consolidated net capital ratio
連結資産 consolidated assets
連結資本 consolidated capital
連結純損失 consolidated net loss
連結消去仕訳 consolidated journal entry by elimination
連結情報 consolidated information
連結剰余金 consolidated retained earnings；consolidated surplus
連結剰余金計算書 consolidated statement of retained earnings
連結所得税 consolidated income tax
連結精算表 consolidated statement paper
連結税務申告書 consolidated tax return
連結総資産 consolidated total assets
連結総負債 consolidated total liabilities
連結損益計算書 consolidated income statement；consolidated profit and loss statement
連結貸借対照表 consolidated balance sheet
連結対象外関連会社 unconsolidated affiliates
連結超過額 consolidation excess
連結手続 consolidation process
連結納税申告 consolidated return
連結納税制度 consolidated tax payment system
連結のれん consolidated good will
連 結 日 consolidation date
連結負債比率 group gearing
連結付属明細票 consolidated schedule

連結ベース consolidated base
連結方針 consolidation policy
連結前利益 profit prior to consolidation
連結元帳 consolidation ledger
連結利益 consolidated income
廉 潔 性 integrity
連合規約 articles of confederation
連合協約 joint agreement
連 産 品 joint product
レンジ内で推移 established in ranges
レンジ・フォワード取引 flexible forward contract；range forward contract
連　　署 countersignature
連生生存者年金 joint survivor annuity
連生年金 joint annuity
連生被保険者 joint insured
連生保険 joint life insurance
連生保険契約 joint policy
連生養老保険 joint endowment assurance
連続確率分布 continuous probability distribution
連続監査 recurring audit
連続決済処理 continuous settlement processing
連続時間 continuous time
連続四半期 consecutive quarters
連続償還債 installment bond
連続償還債券 serial bonds
連続償還債償還 serial redemption
連続償還証券 serial securities
連続する借り手の変化 continuous spectrum of borrower types
連 続 性 continuity
連続ゼロ・クーポン債 serial zero-coupon bond
連続増配 consecutive dividend increase
連続データ・サンプル consecutive data sample
連続取引市場 continuous market
連続年金 continuous annuity
連続配当 continuous dividend
連続売買 continuous trading
連続発行 serial issue
連続複利 continuous compound interest rate
連続複利計算 continuous compounding calculation
連続分布 continuous distribution
連続変数 continuous variables
連続元帳 progressive ledger
連続割引 continuous discounting
連　　帯 joint and several
連帯債務 joint and several obligation
連帯証書 joint and several bond
連帯責任 joint and several liability
連帯納税義務 joint and several obligation for tax liability
連帯納付責任 joint and several liability for tax payment
連帯保証 joint and several guarantee
連帯保証債務 joint-and-several liability
連帯保証人 joint and several guarantor；joint surety
レンタル費用 rental expense
連　　騰 consecutive advances
連　　動 interlocking
連動期間 indexation period
連動契約 linked contract
連動誤差 tracking error
連動指数 linking index
連動した社債 bond indexed to
連動物価指数 linking price index
連邦エネルギー規制委員会 FERC (Federal Energy Regulatory Committee)
連邦管財 United States trustee
連邦機関 federal agency
連邦機関証券 federal agency securities
連邦銀行委員会 Federal Banking Commission
連邦金融機関検査委員会 FFIEC (Federal Financial Institution Examination Council)
連邦金融銀行 FFB (Federal Financing Bank)
連邦公開市場委員会 FOMC (Federal Open Market Committee)
連邦公開市場操作 Federal Reserve open market operation
連邦裁判所 federal court
連邦失業保険税法 FUTA (Federal

Unemployment Tax Act)
連邦諮問委員会 Federal Advisory Committee
連邦社会保障法 Social Security Act
連邦住宅貸付銀行 FHLB (Federal Home Loan Bank)
連邦住宅貸付銀行制度 Federal Home Loan Bank System
連邦住宅貸付銀行理事会 Federal Home Loan Bank Board
連邦住宅局 FHA (Federal Housing Administration)
連邦住宅金融抵当金庫 FHLMC (Federal Home Loan Mortgage Corporation)
連邦住宅金融理事会 FHFB (Federal Housing Financing Board)
連邦準備改革法 Federal Reserve Reform Act
連邦準備銀行 Federal Reserve Bank
連邦準備証書 Federal Reserve Notes
連邦準備制度 FRS (Federal Reserve System)
連邦準備制度加盟銀行 member banks of the Federal Reserve System
連邦準備制度規則 Federal Reserve Regulation
連邦準備制度理事会 Board of Governors of the Federal Reserve System；Fed
連邦準備地区 Federal Reserve District
連邦準備法 Federal Reserve Act
連邦職員退職年金制度 federal employee retirement system
連邦所得税 federal income tax
連邦信用組合法 Federal Credit Union Act of 1934
連 邦 税 federal tax
連邦政府 federal government
連邦政府支出 federal spending
連邦政府年金資産 federal fund assets
連邦政府のローン保証 federal loan guarantee
連邦贈与税 federal gift tax
連邦地方裁判所 federal district court
連邦中期信用銀行 federal intermediate credit banks
連邦調達公社 FICO (Financing Corporation)
連邦調達法 federal procurement law
連邦貯蓄貸付保険会社 Federal Savings and Loan Insurance Corporation
連邦貯蓄貸付保険公社 FSLIC (Federal Savings and Loan Insurance Corporation)
連邦通信委員会 FCC (Federal Communications Commission)
連邦抵当金庫 Federal National Mortgage Association
連邦土地銀行 Federal Land Bank
連邦取引委員会 Federal Trade Commission
連邦農業金融抵当金庫 Farmer MAC (Federal Agricultural Mortgage Corporation)
連邦農業信用銀行 Federal Farm Credit Bank
連邦農業信用制度 Federal Farm Credit System
連邦破産法 Federal Bankruptcy Act
連邦物品税 FET (federal excise tax)
連邦法人税費用 federal income tax expense
連邦保険拠出金法 FICA (Federal Insurance Contributions Act)
連邦預金保険 federal deposit insurance
連邦預金保険公社 FDIC (Federal Deposit Insurance Corporation)
連邦預金保険公社改革法 FDICIA (Federal Deposit Insurance Corporation Improvement Act)
連邦預金保険法 FDIA (Federal Deposit Insurance Act)
連邦政府介入 federal involvement
連絡事務所 liaison office

ロ

ロイズ証券 Lloyd's policy
ロイヤルティ royalty
ロイヤルティ信託 royalty trust
労災保険 workmen's compensation insurance
労使関係 labor relations；management labor relation
労使交渉 labor negotiation
労使紛争 labor trouble
老人扶養親族 aged dependent
ろうそく足 candlestick chart
漏　　損 leakage
労　　賃 labor cost
労働協約 labor agreement
労働協約による規定 regulations according to the labor agreement
労働金庫 labor credit association
労働金庫連合会 National Federation of Labor Credit Associations
労働組合 labor union；trade union
労働経済学 labor economics
労働係数 labor coefficient
労働権法 right to work law
労働災害 industrial injury；work accident
労働災害総合保険 workers'accident comprehensive insurance
労働市場 labor market
労働者災害補償再保険 workers compensation catastrophe cover
労働者災害補償法 workmen's compensation acts
労働者災害補償保険 workmen's compensation insurance
労働者年金 workers pension
労働者賠償法 workmen's compensation law
労働集約 labor intensive
労働集約的産業 labor-intensive industry
労働需給の緩和 looser labor markets
労働所得 labor income
労働政策研究・研修機構 Japan Institute for Labour Policy and Training
労働生産 industrial output
労働争議 industrial dispute；labor dispute
労働統計局 BLS (Bureau of Labor Statistics)
労働投入量 labor input
労働日数 working days
労働分配率 labor share
労 働 法 industrial law；labor law
労働法規 labor regulations
労働保険料 labor insurance premium
労働補償 workers' compensation
労 働 力 labor force
老 年 者 aged person
老年者控除 deduction for old-age person ；exemption for aged person
ろうばい売り panic selling
浪 費 家 spendthrift
浪費者信託 spendthrift trust
労務監査 labor audit
労務費差異 labor variance
労務費用部分 labor content
老齢遺族障害者年金 old-aged, survivor and disability insurance
老齢遺族傷害年金 OASDI (Old Age, Survivors and Disability Insurance)
老齢遺族年金 OASI (Old Age and Survivors Insurance)
老齢基礎年金 old-age basic pension
老齢年金 old age pension
老齢年金付生命保険 old age income life insurance
ローカル・クレジット local credit
ローカル・コンテント local content
ローカルズ locals
ローザ効果 Roosa effect
ローザ構想 Roosa plan

ローザ・ボンド Roosa bond
ローラーコースター・スワップ roller coaster swap
ローリー・ポーリーCD roly poly CD
ローリング・イールド rolling yield
ローリング決済 rolling settlement
ロールオーバー・ローン rollover loan
ロール・ダウン roll down
ロール・ダウン効果 rolling down effect
ロールバック rollback
ロール・フォワード roll forward
ローレンツ曲線 Lorenz curve
ローン開始時期 loan origination
ローン債権 loan claims
ローン債権売買 loan sales
ローン残高 loan balance
ローン支払済年数 age of loan payments
ローン審査 screening of loan application
ローン・スプレッド loan spread
ローン・スワップ loan swap
ローン設定時 at loan origination
ローン担保証券 CLO (collateralized loan obligation)
ローンの書換え balance renewal
ローンの額 loan size
ローンの既払い年数 loan age
ローンの残存部分 residue of the loan
ローンの実行部分 disbursed loan
ローンの組成 origination of loan
ローン・パーティシペーション loan participation
ローン・ポートフォリオ loan portfolio
ローン・ポジション loan position
ローンダード・マネー laundered money
ローンチ launch
ローンチ・スプレッド launch spread
ローンチ日 launch date
60年償還ルール 60-year redemption rule
ロシア・ルーブル RUB (Russian ruble)
ロジスティック回帰 logistic regression
ロス・リーダー loss leader
路線価方式による評価 valuation by road rating
6カ月複利 compounded every six months
6カ月前の応答日の指数 index from six months prior
6桁仕訳帳 six column journal
ロックアップ lock-up
ロックアップ・オプション lock-up option
ロックアップ期間 lock-up period
ロックイン効果 lock-in effect
ロックド・マーケット locked market
ロックボックス lockbox
ロット債 lot bond
ロボット・テラー robot teller
ロング・カレンダー・スプレッド取引 long calendar spread transaction
ロング・クーポン long coupon
ロング・コール long call
ロング・コンドル long condor
ロング・ストラドル long straddle
ロング・ストリップ long strip
ロングにする go long
ロングの状態にある remaining long
ロング・バタフライ・スプレッド取引 long butterfly spread transaction
ロング・プット long put
ロング・ポジション long position
ロング・ポジションの手じまい clearout of longs
ロング・リスト long list
論　証 reasoning
論　点 issue
論点整理 issues summary
ロンドン・アクセプタンス London acceptance
ロンドン銀行間出し手金利 LIBOR (London Inter-Bank Offered Rate)
ロンドン銀行間取り手金利 LIBID (London inter-bank bid rate)
ロンドン銀行間仲値金利 LIMEAN (London interbank mean rate)
ロンドン金市場 London gold market
ロンドン金属取引所 LME (London Metal Exchange)
ロンドン・クラブ London Club
ロンドン・クリアリング・ハウス LCH (London Clearing House)
ロンドン国際金融先物オプション取引所

LIFFE (London International Financial Futures and Options Exchange)
ロンドン国際金融先物取引所 London International Financial Futures Exchange
ロンドン国際石油取引所 IPE (International Petroleum Exchange)
ロンドン商品取引所 LCE (London Commodity Exchange)
ロンドン手形交換所加盟銀行 London clearing banks
ロンドン保険業者協会 Institute of London Underwriters
ロンドン預託証書 London depositary receipts
ロンドン・リファイナンス London refinance
ロンドン割引市場協会 London Discount Market Association
ロンバード街 Lombard Street
ロンバード貸出 Lombard lending
ロンバード貸付 Lombard credit
ロンバード型貸付 Lombard-type lending
ロンバード借入れ Lombard borrowing
ロンバード・レート Lombard rate

ワ

ワールド・インデックス world index
歪　　曲 distort
ワイダー・バンド wider band
ワイルド・カード・オプション wild card option
ワイルド・カード期間 wild card period
和　　解 concord
和解提案 offer in compromise
分かち計算 calculation for division
若手頭脳集団 whiz kids
和　　議 bankruptcy and composition
和議の決定 determination of composition
ワシントン州公共電力供給システム Whoops (Washington Public Power Supply System)
僅かな低下 small drop
僅かな変動 insignificant movement
僅かなリスク negligible risk
渡切り交際費 social and entertainment expenses provided in lump sum
ワラント warrant
ワラント契約書 warrant agreement
ワラント購入価格 warrant purchase price
ワラント債 debenture with warrant；warrant bond
ワラント債償還 warrant bond redemption
ワラント市場 warrant market
ワラント指数 warrant index
ワラント代理人 warrant agent
ワラント付転換社債 convertible bond with warrant
ワラントの行使 exercise of warrant
ワラント・パリティ warrant parity
ワラント・バリュー warrant value
割　　当 allotment；apportionment
割当型予算 appropriation budget
割当危険分担制度 assigned risk plan；joint underwriting facilities
割当契約 allocated contract
割当債権 assigned accounts receivable
割 当 証 allotment letter
割 当 状 letter of allotment
割当済配当 dividend allocated
割当積立方式 allocated funding instrument
割当費用 assignment expense
割当予算元帳 allotment ledger
割 当 量 quota
割り当てる appropriate
割込んで上昇する thrive below
割　　高 over-priced；overvalued
割高・割安証券 mispriced security
割 高 株 over-valued stock
割高な先物 overvalued futures
割高なセクター rich sector
割 引 き discounting
割引受取勘定 account receivable discounted
割引売上債権 accounts receivable discounted
割引価格 discounted value
割引額期間対応割付 accrual of discount
割引額の償却 amortization of discount
割引価値 discount value
割引関数 discount function
割引基準 discounted basis
割引キャッシュフロー分析 discount cash flow analysis
割引銀行 discount bank
割引禁止 anti-rebating
割引金融債 discount bank debenture
割引係数 discount factor
割引現在価値 discounted present value
割引限度 line of discount
割 引 後 discounted at
割引効果 effect of discount
割引国債 discount government bond
割 引 債 discount bond
割引債償還益 gain on redemption of discount bond

割引債の償還益 profit on redemption of discount bond
割引市場 discount market
割引収益 discounted cash flow
割引準備金 reserve for discount
割引証券 discount paper；discount securities
割引商社 discount house
割引政策 discount policy
割引専門ブローカー discount broker
割引短期国債 treasury bills
割引短期国債売現先オペ sales of TBs (treasury bills) under repurchase agreements
割引短期国債買現先オペ purchases of TBs (treasury bills) under repurchase agreements
割引手形 bills discounted；note discounted；note receivable discounted；sold bill
割引手形勘定 bill discounted account
割引手形記入帳 discount register
割引手形見返勘定 per contra noted discounted account
割引手形元帳 discount ledger
割引適格手形 eligible bill
割引手数料 discount commission
割引と割増 discount and premium
割引日数 discount days to run
割引の影響 effect of discounting
割引の巻戻 rewinding of the discount
割引発行 discount issuance；original issue discount
割引ベース discount basis
割引保険料 discounted premium rate
割引前基準 undiscounted basis
割引前の金額 undiscounted amount
割引窓口 discount window
割 引 率 discount rate
割引率の大きい deep discount
割引率のリスク構造 risk structure of discount rate
割引利回り discount yield
割 引 料 discount expenses
割引料率 reduced rate
割増運賃 additional freight
割 増 金 extra money
割増償却 additional depreciation deduction；extra depreciation
割増償却率 additional depreciation ratio
割増退職金 increased retirement payments
割増貯蓄債券 premium savings bond
割増賃金 extra wage
割増手当 additional allowance
割増保険料 AP (additional premium)；extra premium；premium surcharge
割 戻 し rebate
割 戻 す gross up
割　　安 cheap；undervalued
割 安 株 bargain stock
割安株ファンド bargain stock fund
割安更新オプション bargain renewal option
割安購入権 bargain purchase option
割 安 な modestly-priced
割安な購入 bargain purchase
割安なセクター cheap sector
割安の資産 undervalued asset
割安・割高 out of line
ワルシャワ条約機構 Warsaw Treaty Organization
湾岸協力会議 Gulf Cooperation Council
ワン・ストップ・ファイリング one stop filing
ワン・デー・リバーサル one day reversal
腕力相場 forced market

編者
株式会社アイ・エス・エス（ISS）
1965年日本で最初の同時通訳養成所を設立。以後、国際会議の運営、通訳、翻訳等の分野で活躍。特にビジネス専門分野の翻訳業務では高い評価を得ている。編著に『英和・和英 金融用語辞典』『英和・和英 法律・会計・税務用語辞典』『英和・和英 国際ビジネス用語辞典』（共に小社刊）。
東京都千代田区一番町23-3　日本生命一番町ビル4階
TEL　03-3230-3553　mail to: dic@issnet.co.jp

監修者
安達　精司（あだち　せいじ）
1949年11月27日生まれ。1971年3月中央大学商学部会計学科卒業、同年4月東京証券取引所入所。以後、ロンドン駐在員事務所長、上場部上場審査室主任上場審査役、シンガポール駐在員事務所長、派生商品部派生商品総務室長などを経て、2002年より経営企画部審議役。共著に『コーポレート・ガバナンス～英国の企業改革～』（商事法務刊）等がある。

編集協力
安徳　久仁理（あんとく　くにまさ）日本銀行業務局。
原　俊太郎（はら　しゅんたろう）日本銀行国際局。

〈第3版〉英和・和英 金融・証券・保険用語辞典
THE DICTIONARY OF SECURITIES INSURANCE & FINANCIAL TERMS

1995年4月1日第1版第1刷発行　　定価（本体8,900円＋税）
2007年4月25日第3版第2刷発行

編　者　　株式会社アイ・エス・エス
監修者　　安　達　精　司
発行者　　玉　越　直　人
発行所　　WAVE出版
〒102-0074 東京都千代田区九段南4-7-10
TEL 03-3261-3713　FAX 03-3261-3823
振替 00100-7-366376
DTP　　ワイズ
印刷所　　萩原印刷
製本所　　島田製本

©ISS 2004 Printed in Japan
落丁・乱丁本は送料弊社負担にてお取り替えいたします。
本書の無断複写・複製・転載を禁じます。
ISBN 978-4-87290-203-7